No Peace
with
Hitler

WHY CHURCHILL CHOSE TO FIGHT WWII ALONE
RATHER THAN NEGOTIATE WITH GERMANY

ALAN I. SALTMAN

For information about this title or to order other books and/or electronic media, contact the publisher:
WG Hobart Publishers
www.wghobartpublishers.com
support@wghobartpublishers.com

ISBN: 979-8-9854794-2-3 (hardcover)
          979-8-9854794-0-9 (softcover)
          979-8-9854794-1-6 (eBook)

Printed in the United States of America
Cover and Interior design: 1106 Design

For Beryl
without whose support and help this book
could not have been written.

CONTENTS

Thank You vii

Foreword ix

Chronology. xiii

Introduction xxix

1: From Birth to Age 24 (1874–1898) 3

2: November 1899–June 1900 The Boer War. 23

3: Early Years in Parliament and Government 1900 through
April 1908 27

4: Early Years in the Cabinet April 1908 through September 1911 35

5: September 1911–December 1918 The Admiralty, WWI, Gallipoli,
and Its Aftermath 45

6: January 1919–November 1922 A Return to the Cabinet 71

7: January 1923–October 1924 Out in the Cold, Churchill Morphs.
Meanwhile, in Germany. 87

8: October 1924–April 1929 Churchill Elected as Conservative—
Returns to Cabinet 95

9: May 1929–December 1936 The Early Wilderness Years 107

10: May 1937–March 1938 Chamberlain, Appeasement, and the
Road to the Anschluss 155

11: March–December 1938—The March to Munich and
its Aftermath 175

12: January–August 1939 Czechoslovakia,
The Polish Guarantee, etc. 245

13: September 1, 1939–May 9, 1940 Poland, The Phoney War,
and Norway 323

14: May 9–May 24, 1940 Churchill's first two weeks as
Prime Minister 377

15: Saturday, May 25, 1940 425

16: Sunday May 26, 1940. 435

17: Monday May 27, 1940 451

18: Tuesday, May 28, 1940. 463

19: What Could Churchill Have Possibly Been Thinking? 477

20: Using Personal History and Psychodynamics to Examine and
Understand Churchill's Decision to Commit to War. 517

21: May 29, 1940 to June 22, 1941 The Evacuation from Dunkirk,
The Battle of Britain, The Blitz, and the Invasion of the Soviet Union . . 553

22: Churchill Thereafter. 599

Endnotes. 665

Bibliography 703

Index. 727

Thanks To

Lori R. F. Monroe

Tom Troxel

Allan Goodman

Richard Bernstein, M.D.

Ragon Willmuth, M.D.

Howard Schultz

Gregory Ambrose

Neil Richman

Ben Ligas

Allyn Ford

Russ Molari

Jim Longo

Jared Saltman

*for their advice and their incisive review of
various drafts of this book, and to*

Matthew Foy

Julia O'Malley

Kevin Greene

Tomas Moreno

Michaila Peters

Sam Billings

Elizabeth Crocco

Gerardo Fernandez Herrero

for all of their research assistance and other help.

Special Thank You

To

Dr. Mark S. Schultz, psychiatrist, and University of Vermont professor, for his valuable assistance with every chapter in this book. Without his help, this book would not be all that it is.

FOREWORD

BY

ANDREW ROBERTS, BEST-SELLING AUTHOR OF CHURCHILL: WALKING WITH DESTINY; NAPOLEON: A LIFE; THE LAST KING OF AMERICA

'I felt as if I were walking with destiny,' Winston Churchill wrote of the moment he became prime minister on 10 May 1940, 'and that all my past life had been but a preparation for this hour and for this trial.' In this well-researched, well-written and above all wise book, Alan I. Saltman, with insight from a psychiatrist, conclusively proves that all of Churchill's past life had also been a preparation for his refusal to negotiate peace with Hitler later that same month.

Through a profound mastery of all the most important sources, and several unexpected ones too, Mr. Saltman establishes how the decision to fight on after defeat on the Continent rested largely on character traits that Churchill had been consciously and unconsciously evolving over the previous sixty-five years. While I am no psychologist and thus unqualified to judge from a medical perspective, it strikes me that remarks about what are called Churchill's 'psychodynamics' are substantially correct, and that the decision to fight on in May 1940 can indeed essentially be traced back to his personality traits.

What certainly cannot be questioned is the importance of Churchill's decision for the continued survival of Western Civilization. If in the wake of the evacuation of the British Expeditionary Force from Dunkirk in May 1940 and the catastrophic Fall of France the following month, Britain had cobbled together some kind of ignoble compromise peace with the Nazis, then the fate of the world would have been very different, and the whole of Europe would have fallen into what Churchill called 'the abyss of a new Dark Age.' With no two-front war to fight, Adolf Hitler could have timed his invasion of the Soviet Union, Operation Barbarossa, differently, and moreover undertaken it with 100% of his forces. Victory over Russia would have left him master of everywhere from Brest to the Urals or even beyond. Britain would have lost all credibility with the United States, which could not have used the United Kingdom as its unsinkable aircraft carrier from which to launch any eventual liberation of Europe.

Everything therefore hinged on the War Cabinet's decision over those fateful five days in May 1940, and Mr. Saltman's coverage of each hour of its deliberations, with the psychology and motivations of its members minutely analyzed, is a fine work of psychohistory. Contained within these crucial chapters are observations about human nature that go beyond the historical and have relevance both in ordinary life and in modern politics and foreign affairs. The statement that 'Bullies do not cease being bullies once they get their way', for example, applies equally to Vladmir Putin in the 2020s as it did to Adolf Hitler in the 1930s, and we would do well to remember that when we consider the various outcomes posited for the present war in Ukraine.

This book also provides an opportunity for readers, perhaps particularly in the United States, to consider anew the policy of Appeasement of the 1930s. The Munich Agreement that dismembered Czechoslovakia in the fall of 1938 came as the result of a policy that is too often seen in terms of black and white, but which was in fact far more nuanced, and Mr. Saltman is right to accentuate that. For however disastrous, indeed sinister, Appeasement turned out to be, there were perfectly sound strategic reasons for the British Governments to try to pursue it, at least in the early years.

The British Chiefs of Staff consistently warned British decision-makers that Britain could not fight against Germany, Italy, and Japan simultaneously. The harshness of the Versailles Treaty had created a good deal of sympathy for Germany—the word 'appeasement' was originally a Christian one with no pejorative overtones. There was an assumption that the aerial bombing of London would lead to six hundred thousand deaths. The British imperial colonies and the United States supported Appeasement; President Roosevelt even cabled Neville Chamberlain the words 'Good man' about the Munich Agreement.

Churchill was seen as a warmonger by millions of Britons who signed the League of Nations' Peace Pledge Ballot, as few could believe Germany wanted to start another war so soon after the devastation of World War One. As Mr. Saltman also rightly points out, Churchill had made plenty of blunders in his career, and many people thought his stalwart opposition to Hitler was merely the latest in a long list of them.

In fact, as we now know, Churchill had been completely correct and the Appeasers entirely wrong in their analyses, but the aim of well-written history such as Mr. Saltman's must be to not cloud our view of the past by our knowledge of the present. Moreover, it is only when one considers quite how universally popular the Appeasement policy was in the mid-1930s that one can fully grasp the moral courage that Churchill displayed in opposing it.

The differing rules by which totalitarian countries conduct their foreign policies from democratic ones explains why in August 1939 Nazi Germany were always capable of outbidding Britain and France when it came to allying with the Soviet Union. No democratic country could offer Stalin half of Poland and all three Baltic states in exchange for a non-aggression deal, in the way that Joachim von Ribbentrop was able to do to V.I. Molotov in the Nazi-Soviet Pact, which set Europe on the path to war.

Churchill is today beset by revisionists who seek to detract from his reputation. As recently as February 2020 a conference took place—in Churchill College, Cambridge, of all places!—where four revisionist academics even concluded that Churchill 'was as bad as Hitler.' His statue in Parliament Square was vandalized three months later. What calm, sane, evidence-based books such as this one achieve is to redress the balance, by placing the unwavering spotlight of history on what actually happened and by putting the momentous events of May 1940 into their proper context.

Once that is done, objective readers will I believe emerge from the process with their appreciation of Winston Churchill's qualities and legacy even possibly enhanced, for, as Mr. Saltman successfully delineates, Churchill's moral and physical courage were truly remarkable, and his foresight was also exceptional, something he showed both before World War One and after World War Two, as well as in his struggle against Appeasement during the Wilderness Years.

Prof Andrew Roberts
London
June 2022

CHRONOLOGY

June 20, 1837	Victoria becomes Queen
February 17, 1874	Benjamin Disraeli (Conservative) becomes P.M.
November 30, 1874	*Winston Churchill born at Blenheim Palace in Oxfordshire, approximately 60 miles west of London. Winston's father, Lord Randolph Churchill elected to Parliament as a Conservative nine months later*
January 1877	*Having earned the wrath of the Prince of Wales. Lord Randolph resigns from Parliament and is "self-exiled" to Ireland*
April, 1880	*Churchill family returns from "exile" in Ireland. Lord Randolph Churchill soon re-elected to Parliament*
December 18, 1885	Liberals form a coalition Government with the Irish Nationalists; William Gladstone becomes P.M. again
July 27, 1886	Conservatives & Liberal Unionists win a majority, Lord Salisbury becomes P.M.
July 26, 1892	Conservatives win the largest number of seats in the election but do not have a majority; Gladstone forms a minority Government dependent on support from the Irish Nationalists
December 1894	*Winston graduates from the Royal Military College at Sandhurst*
January 24, 1895	*Winston's father, Lord Randolph Churchill, dies at age 45*
1895	*Churchill goes to Cuba as a military observer joining a fighting column of the Spanish Army*
August 7, 1895	Conservatives and Liberal Unionists win a majority; Lord Salisbury becomes P.M. again

1896–1897	*Churchill serves in India*
1898	*Churchill serves in Sudan*
July 6, 1899	*Churchill unsuccessfully runs for Parliament as a Unionist from Oldham (a town in Greater Manchester)*
October 11, 1899	Boer War declared
October 14, 1899	*Churchill heads to South Africa as London's highest-paid war correspondent*
	There he is captured by the Boers and imprisoned in Pretoria
	After a month Churchill makes his escape
	Churchill makes it to Portuguese East Africa (located 300 miles from Pretoria)
December 23, 1899	*Churchill returns to the British controlled portion of South Africa and immediately seeks and obtains a commission in the Army*
July 20, 1900	*Churchill returns to Britain as a national hero; is asked to run for Parliament from numerous Conservative constituencies*
October 24, 1900	**Conservative/Liberal Unionists win a landslide victory; Lord Salisbury remains P.M.**
	Churchill elected to Parliament as a Conservative from Oldham
January 22, 1901	Queen Victoria dies; Edward VII becomes King
May 31, 1902	Boer War ends
July 12, 1902	**Lord Salisbury relinquishes the Premiership to his nephew Arthur Balfour (Conservative)**
May 31, 1904	*After publicly disagreeing with his party's leadership over their plans to impose high tariffs on imports from outside the Empire, Churchill* **"crosses the floor"** *of the House of Commons leaving the Conservative Party to sit with the Liberals. (He*

would return to the Conservative Party twenty years later)

December 4, 1905	Balfour resigns as P.M.
December 5, 1905	At The King's request, Henry Campbell-Bannerman (Liberal) forms a caretaker Government and calls for a national election
	Churchill appointed to the non-Cabinet position of Under-Secretary of State for the Colonies
January 12, 1906	The Liberals win in a land slide; Campbell-Bannerman remains as P.M.
	In the election, Churchill is elected to Parliament as a Liberal from Manchester
May 1, 1907	*Churchill is named a Privy Counselor*
April 5, 1908	Campbell-Bannerman resigns for health reasons; H. H. Asquith (Liberal) becomes P.M.
April 12, 1908	*Churchill is appointed to the Cabinet post of President of the Board of Trade. Under the law, he is required to resign from Parliament and seek re-election*
April 23, 1908	*Churchill loses the by-election in Manchester by 529 votes*
May 9, 1908	*Churchill wins another by-election in Dundee Scotland and finally assumes the office of President of the Board of Trade*
September 12, 1908	*Winston marries Clementine Hozier*
January 14, 1910	General election. Liberals win the largest number of seats and form coalition Government with Irish Nationalist Party. Asquith continues as Prime Minister.
February 19, 1910	*Churchill becomes Home Secretary*
May 6, 1910	Edward VII dies; George V becomes King

December 2–19, 1910	General election. Liberals and Conservative/Unionists each win 272 seats. Liberals again form coalition Government with Irish Nationalists. Asquith continues as Prime Minister
	Churchill continues as Home Secretary
September 30, 1911	*Churchill accepts the position of First Lord of the Admiralty*
July 28, 1914	World War I begins
August 14, 1914	Britain declares war against Germany
February 1915–January 1916	Dardanelles/Gallipoli campaign
May 1915	P.M. Asquith's Liberal Government is brought down. Asquith forms a new coalition Government with the majority of the new cabinet coming from his own Liberal Party and the Conservative/Unionists
May 17, 1915	*Asquith removes Churchill as First Lord of the Admiralty; Churchill is given cabinet post (without any authority) as Chancellor of the Duchy of Lancaster and a place in the War Council*
November 11, 1915	*Churchill resigns from the Government*
January 1916	*While still an MP, Churchill serves as a battalion commander on the front line*
May 1916	*Churchill's unit is absorbed by another. With no command spots available, Churchill returns to civilian life*
August 1916	Full scale Commission of Inquiry into the Dardanelles/Gallipoli campaign is convened
December 6, 1916	After mass resignations from the Cabinet, P.M. Asquith resigns as well. David Lloyd George (Liberal) becomes P.M. of a coalition Government formed with the Conservatives
	*Churchill is **not** given a position in the new Lloyd George Government*
February 1917	Interim report of the Dardanelles Commission is issued

April 2, 1917	The United States enters the war
July 17, 1917	*Churchill is appointed to the non-Cabinet position of Minister of Munitions*
December 1917	The Dardanelles Commission issues its final report largely exonerating Churchill
November 11, 1918	World War I ends
December 14, 1918	**The existing Liberal/Conservative coalition Government led by Lloyd George wins the general election in a landslide**
January 10, 1919	*Churchill accepts P.M. Lloyd George's offer to become Secretary for War and Air*
April 28, 1919	Covenant of the League of Nations is adopted
June 28, 1919	Treaty of Versailles is signed by Germany
December 1919	Parliament enacts the Government of the India Act—a first step toward representative government
February 1921	*Churchill is named Secretary of State for the Colonies*
April 1921	*Lloyd George passes over Churchill for the senior position of Chancellor of the Exchequer*
July 29, 1921	Hitler becomes the leader of the Nazi party
December 5, 1921	The Irish Treaty is agreed to
October 23, 1922	**In the wake of the collapse of the Liberal/Conservative coalition, Andrew Bonar Law (Conservative) becomes P.M.**
November 18, 1922	**In the general election, the Conservatives obtain a majority; Bonner Law continues as P.M.**
	Churchill is defeated for re-election to Parliament
March 7, 1923	Neville Chamberlain (Conservative) is appointed Minister of Health
May 22, 1923	**Due to Bonar Law's illness, King George turns to Stanley Baldwin (Conservative) to become Prime Minister**

	Baldwin calls for another general election set for December 6, 1923
August 7, 1923	Neville Chamberlain (Conservative) is appointed Chancellor of the Exchequer
November 8–9, 1923	Beer Hall Putsch in Munich: Hitler is jailed
December 6, 1923	In the general election, the Conservatives lose 87 seats. They now hold 258 seats; Labour holds 191 and the Liberals hold 158. Unwilling to continue the coalition with the Liberals or form one with Labour, the Conservatives are in trouble
	Asquith Liberals agree to form a coalition with Labour
	Churchill runs as a Liberal seeking to represent West Leicester and is crushed
January 22, 1924	Labour/Liberals form a coalition Government; Ramsay MacDonald (Labour) becomes P.M.
March 19, 1924	*Churchill runs as an "Independent Anti-Socialist" in the by-election in Westminster and loses by 43 votes*
September 1924	Labour/Liberal coalition collapses; new elections called for October
October 29, 1924	Landslide victory for the Conservative Party. Baldwin is P.M. again
	Churchill is elected to Parliament as a Conservative from Epping (a seat he would hold continuously for the next forty years)
October 31, 1924	*Churchill accepts P.M. Baldwin's offer to become Chancellor of the Exchequer (a post that his father had held)*
April 1925	Decision is made to restore pre-WWI sterling–gold parity
July 18, 1925	*Mein Kampf* is published

December 1, 1925	Locarno treaties for European security are signed by Britain, Italy, France, and Germany
September 8, 1926	Germany is admitted to the League of Nations
June 5, 1929	General election—MacDonald (Labour Party) became P.M. again. Minority Government formed—coalition of Labour and Liberals
	Although he remains as an MP, Churchill will not hold a cabinet position again until September 1939)
June 30, 1930	French evacuate the Rhineland
September 14, 1930	In German election, Nazi party garners the second largest number of votes
January 27, 1931	*Churchill resigns from the Conservative Business Committee (and thus the Conservative front bench) over the party's support of dominion status for India*
August 1931	Labour Government collapses
August 21, 1931	At the King's urging a National Government is formed with the Conservatives; Ramsay MacDonald (Labour) remains P.M.
September 19, 1931	Japanese invade Manchuria
October 27, 1931	General election—landslide for the National Government. The Conservatives are the majority party, holding 471 seats; Ramsay MacDonald (Labour) remains as titular P.M.
November 5, 1931	Chamberlain is appointed Chancellor of the Exchequer
Feb 1, 1932	Conference for the Reduction and Limitation of Armaments opens in Geneva
January 30, 1933	Hitler is appointed Chancellor of Germany
February 27, 1933	German Reichstag is destroyed by arsonists
March 12, 1933	First concentration camp is opened at Oranienburg outside Berlin
March 22, 1933	Nazis open Dachau concentration camp

March 23, 1933	Enabling Act gives Hitler dictatorial power
July 14, 1933	Nazi Party is declared Germany's only political party
October 14, 1933	Germany quits the League of Nations
June 30, 1934	The Nazi "Night of the Long Knives"
July 25, 1934	Nazis murder Austrian Chancellor Dolfuss; but attempted coup fails
August 2, 1934	German President Hindenburg dies
August 19, 1934	Hitler becomes Fuhrer of Germany
November 1934	Geneva Disarmament conference ends in failure
January 13, 1935	The Saar is returned to Germany by plebiscite
March 9, 1935	In violation of the Versailles Treaty, Germany announces the formation of an Air Force
March 16, 1935	Germany violates Treaty of Versailles by introducing military conscription
April 11, 1935	Britain, Italy, and France meet in Stresa, Italy to renew their pledges under the Locarno Treaty of 1925
June 7, 1935	**Baldwin (Conservative) replaces MacDonald as P.M. of the National Government**
	Halifax becomes Secretary of State for War
June 18, 1935	Anglo-German Naval Treaty is signed
October 2, 1935	Italy invades Abyssinia (Ethiopia)
November 14, 1935	**The National Government wins the 1935 general election. The Conservatives remain the majority party albeit with a reduced majority holding 387 seats. Baldwin continues as P.M.**
	Halifax becomes Lord Privy Seal
January 20, 1936	King George V dies; Edward VIII becomes King
March 7, 1936	German military forces enter the Rhineland in violation of the Versailles Treaty
May 9, 1936	Italian forces take Abyssinia

July 18, 1936   Civil war erupts in Spain

December 11, 1936   King Edward VIII abdicates; George VI becomes
                     King

May 28, 1937   **Baldwin retires as P.M.; Neville Chamberlain
                     (Conservative) becomes P.M.**

November 19, 1937   Halifax goes on hunting trip to Germany, visits Hitler

February 1938   Anthony Eden resigns as Foreign Secretary and is
                     replaced by Halifax

March 12, 1938   Austria is annexed by Hitler (the event is commonly
                     known as the Anschluss)

March 14, 1938   Churchill proposes Grand Alliance against Hitler

April 1938   Britain recognizes Italy's conquest of Abyssinia

August–September   German Generals plot to arrest/assassinate Hitler if
1938   he orders the invasion of Czechoslovakia

September 15, 1938   Chamberlain's first trip to Germany (Bertschgaden)
                     about the Sudetenland

September 22, 1938   Chamberlain's second trip to Germany (Godesberg)
                     about the Sudetenland

September 29, 1938   In Munich, Chamberlain and French Premier Edouard
                     Daladier agree to Hitler's annexing the Sudeten Area
                     of Czechoslovakia; (Chamberlain is cheered wildly
                     upon his return to London and declares "Peace for
                     our time")

October 5, 1938   The Czech Government resigns

October 15, 1938   German troops occupy all of the Sudetenland

November 9–10, 1938 Kristallnacht—the Night of Broken Glass—in Germany

March 15, 1939   Hitler takes over Czechoslovakia

March 30, 1939   Britain and France guarantee the independence of
                     Poland—they enter temporary mutual assistance
                     agreement (The Polish war guarantee)

April 1, 1939   Spanish Civil War ends

April 18, 1939   Russia proposes an alliance with Britain and France

May 22, 1939	Nazis sign "Pact of Steel" with Italy
August 23, 1939	Hitler and Stalin sign a non-aggression pact (known as the Molotov-Ribbentrop Pact)
August 25, 1939	Britain and Poland finally sign an official Mutual Assistance Treaty (formalizing the Polish war guarantee)
September 1, 1939	**Hitler invades Poland**
September 2, 1939	*Churchill accepts Chamberlain's offer to join the six-man War Cabinet as Minister Without Portfolio*
September 3, 1939	Chamberlain gives Hitler a two-hour ultimatum to stop all hostilities in Poland. When deadline passes, Chamberlain broadcasts that Britain was at war
	Churchill accepts Chamberlain's offer to serve as First Lord of the Admiralty (a position he'd held from 1911 to 1915)
September 17, 1939	Soviets invade Eastern Poland
October 6, 1939	Hitler makes peace offer to England and France
October 12, 1939	This peace overture is rejected
April 8, 1940	Britain commences mining Norway's coastal waters to prevent the Germans from transporting Swedish iron ore to Germany. Plan to take over Narvik, where ore is transferred to German ships
April 9, 1940	Hitler invades Norway and Denmark
April 13, 1940	Over Churchill's objection, Britain's primary objective in Norway campaign is changed from Narvik to Trondheim
May 2, 1940	Britain evacuates troops from Norway
May 7–8, 1940	House of Commons' debate over the Norway debacle turns into a vote of confidence on the Chamberlain Government
	Despite a more than 200 vote Conservative majority, the vote is only 281 to 200 in favor of Chamberlain's Government

May 9, 1940   Conservatives attempt to form a coalition Government, but Labour is unlikely to do so under Chamberlain. Halifax declines to become P.M.

May 10, 1940   Hitler invades Luxembourg, the Netherlands, and Belgium

Chamberlain considers staying on as P.M. but Labour makes it clear they will not participate in a Government led by him

Chamberlain advises the King that he wishes to resign. Both the King and Chamberlain want Lord Halifax to become the P.M., but with Halifax unwilling to serve, the King and Chamberlain agree that Churchill is the man to form a new Government. Churchill agrees to do so. At 9 PM Chamberlain announces his resignation in a broadcast to the nation

The Allied Military Coordination Committee orders the French and British armies to begin their march into Belgium

May 13, 1940   *Churchill gives his first speech to Parliament as P.M., says: "You ask, what is our aim? I can answer in one word:* **It is victory,** *victory at all costs ..."*

May 14, 1940   Dutch forces surrender to Germany

May 25, 1940   Halifax indicates to the Italian Ambassador that Britain might be interested in Mussolini's brokering peace negotiations between Britain and Hitler

Some 225,000+ British soldiers (and approximately 175,000 French, Belgians) are stranded in northwest France

May 26, 1940   French Premier Reynaud essentially tells Churchill that France has little choice but to capitulate. *Halifax asks Churchill if he would consider entering into a peace treaty if it would preserve Britain's independence.* Churchill sarcastically says that he'd love it if a lasting overall peace could be achieved by doing something as simple as agreeing to give away some territory, "[B]ut the only safe way [to get out of our

	present difficulties] was to convince Hitler he couldn't beat us."
May 27, 1940	At 4:30 meeting of the War Cabinet, Churchill states his objection to Halifax's suggested approach
	Halifax threatens to resign if he cannot pursue peace negotiations
	The evacuation of BEF from Dunkirk begins
May 28, 1940	Belgian Army surrenders
	Churchill calls meeting of the twenty-five-man "outer" cabinet at 6:15 PM. At that meeting Churchill says that he will not consider a negotiated peace. They overwhelmingly support him. The War Cabinet does not attempt to override
May 29, 1940	By the end of the day the total number of troops evacuated from Dunkirk so far totals 73,000; but not many more are expected to be saved
May 30, 1940	Total number evacuated so far rises to 126,000 (15,000 of which are French)
May 31, 1940	Number of evacuees to date—193,000
June 4, 1940	*Churchill gives his "we shall fight on the beaches …" speech in the House of Commons*
	Total number evacuated from Dunkirk—an amazing 338,000 British, French and Belgians. Between 30,000 and 40,000 more (mostly French) were left behind and captured by the Germans
June 10, 1940	Mussolini declares war on Britain and France
June 14, 1940	Germans enter Paris
June 16, 1940	French replace P.M. Reynaud with Marshal Petain who immediately orders the French Army to surrender
June 18, 1940	*Churchill gives his "This was their finest hour" speech in the House of Commons and to the country*
June 22, 1940	France signs an armistice with Germany

July 3, 1940	British seize the part of the French fleet tied up in English harbors and attack another part anchored in Algeria
July 5, 1940	French (Vichy) Government breaks diplomatic relations with Britain
July 10, 1940	Battle of Britain begins. The Luftwaffe attacks English Channel convoys and ports, RAF airfields and supporting industries
July 16, 1940	Hitler issues Directive No. 16 ordering the start of preparations for an invasion of Britain
July 19, 1940	In a speech before the Reichstag, Hitler makes another peace proposal to Britain
July 23, 1940	Soviets take Lithuania, Latvia, and Estonia
July 26, 1940	Halifax gives the radio address officially rejecting the German peace proposal
July 31, 1940	German High Command commences planning the attack on Russia (then called Operation Otto)
August 12, 1940	Goering gives orders to launch *der Alderangriff* (the Eagle Attack); the objective—attain air superiority over Britain
August 20, 1940	*Churchill gives his "never have so many owed so much to so few" speech in the House of Commons and to the country*
September 7, 1940	Germans change tactics. The Blitz—nighttime bombing of British cities (principally London) commences. Ends May 11, 1941
November 12, 1940	In a meeting with Soviet Foreign Minister Molotov about the spheres of influence of the Axis powers and Russia, Hitler proposes that the Soviets look toward taking over India
March 11, 1941	Roosevelt signs the Lend-Lease Act
April 2, 1941	Churchill's forwards a message to Stalin supposedly from "a trusted agent" in the German high command that in late March, three German armored divisions had been ordered to move from the Balkans

to Krakow in Poland but that the order had been countermanded in late March, immediately after a successful British- back coup d'état in Yugoslavia. Unlike Stalin, the Chiefs of Staff and most of the intelligent services, Churchill suspects that this means that Hitler is planning to invade Russia as soon as his southern flank has been secured in Yugoslavia and Greece

April 6, 1941	Hitler invades both Yugoslavia (opposition collapses on April 18) and Greece (which capitulates on April 20)
May 10, 1941	Rudolph Hess makes a solo flight to Scotland where he hopes to arrange peace talks with the Duke of Hamilton, who he believes to be a prominent opponent of the British Government's war policy
May 11, 1941	The Blitz ends
June 21, 1941	Germans defeat the Allies at Tobruk in Libya. One of the low points in the war
June 22, 1941	Hitler invades the Soviet Union
June 22, 1941– July 9, 1941	Battle of Bialystok-Minsk (Germans kill 341,000 Soviets)
August 7, 1941– September 26, 1941	First Battle of Kiev (number of Soviets killed, captured, or missing—616,000)
September 8, 1941– January 27, 1944	Siege of Leningrad; estimated Soviet deaths (military and civilian—1.5 million)
October 2, 1941– January 7, 1942	Battle of Moscow (number of Soviets killed, captured, or missing—581,000)
August 23, 1942	Battle of Stalingrad* commences
Late October 1942	British retake El Alamein in Egypt
November 9, 1942	Allies land in Morocco and Algeria. Operation Torch begins. The next day Churchill announces that this is "perhaps the end of the beginning"
January 14, 1943	Casablanca Conference between Churchill and Roosevelt commences

---

Stalingrad is located 1,475 miles southeast of Moscow

February 2, 1943	After five months of fighting, Soviets win the Battle of Stalingrad (479,000 Soviet troops killed or missing)
May 12, 1943	Start of meetings in Washington DC between Churchill and Roosevelt. They finally set date for cross-channel invasion of Europe—May 1944
May 13, 1943	Allies control Tunisia; all Axis forces expelled from North Africa
July 5– August 23, 1943	Germans and Russians fight the Battle of Kursk*
July 10, 1943	Allied invasion of Sicily commences
July 25, 1943	Mussolini is overthrown
August 17, 1943	Allies are in full control of Sicily
August 19, 1943	First Quebec Conference between Churchill and Roosevelt commences. They agree to deindustrialization or "pastoralization" of Germany. Churchill later reneges**
September 2, 1943	Allies invade southern Italy; small force lands at Calabria
September 8, 1943	Italy surrenders; joins the Allies
September 9, 1943	Allies make larger landing at Salerno, south of Naples
November 4, 1943	The Soviets retake Kiev, the capital of the Ukraine***
November 22, 1943	Cairo Conference among Churchill, Roosevelt and Chang Kai Shek (the leader of China) commences
November 28, 1943	Tehran Conference among Stalin, Roosevelt, and Churchill
June 6, 1944	D-Day; Western Allies invade Normandy
September 11, 1944	Second Quebec Conference between Churchill and Roosevelt commences
February 4, 1945	Yalta Conference among Stalin, Roosevelt, and Churchill

*Kursk is located 325 miles south of Moscow
**Addison, Churchill: The Unexpected Hero p. 205
***Kiev is located 260 miles west of Kursk

April 12, 1945	Roosevelt dies
May 8, 1945	**War in Europe ends**
July 17, 1945	Potsdam Conference among Stalin, Truman, and Churchill* commences
July 26, 1945	**Conservatives are voted out of office; Clement Attlee (Labour) becomes P.M. Churchill becomes Leader of the Opposition**
July 27, 1945	Potsdam Conference reconvenes with Attlee having replaced Churchill
1948	*Churchill publishes first portion of epic six-volume history of WWII*
August 1949	The Soviet Union detonates an atomic bomb
October 26, 1951	**Conservatives are voted back in; Churchill becomes P.M. again**
February 6, 1952	King George VI dies; succeeded by Elizabeth II
1953	*Churchill receives the Nobel Prize for literature*
April 5, 1955	*Churchill retires*
January 24, 1965	*Churchill dies at age 90, exactly 70 years to the day after the death of his father, having lived twice as long*

---

*Given the election in Britain, Churchill brings leader of the opposition, Clement Atlee, to the conference

Introduction

What would become World War II began on September 1, 1939, when Germany invaded Poland. On September 3, 1940, both Britain and France responded by declaring war on Germany. Over the next 8+ months, Hitler not only conquered Poland but Norway, Denmark, Holland, Belgium, Luxembourg, and France as well. With the United States firmly neutral. By late May 1940, Britain had no allies and stood alone against the substantial threat of an imminent German invasion.

In those dark times, under the leadership of Winston Churchill, who had only become Prime Minister on May 10, Britain had to decide whether to continue the war against Germany alone or to enter into peace negotiations with Hitler.

When this book was being conceived, my plan was to first lay a foundation of facts about Churchill and the events that got Britain into the predicament described. This would be followed by a discussion in some detail of the innerworkings of the War Cabinet in the days preceding the final announcement on May 28, 1940 that there would be no peace negotiations. Then, once that was accomplished, the book would attempt to show what things Churchill could have been thinking about as he chose continuing the war over peace negotiations and how the makeup of the man may have psychologically affected his decision.

That plan has largely been followed. But, in addition to examining Churchill's decision from many perspectives, the book also sheds light on a number of lesser known things in Churchill's life and career as well as key events preceding (or resulting from) the decision not to negotiate. These include:

- *How Churchill survived his upbringing and how it affected him in making his decision,*

- *The role that Neville Chamberlain played in Britain's choosing not to negotiate a peace agreement with Hitler and how that role came about,*

- *What things could have been done to avoid WWII and the Holocaust,*

- *The poor judgments that Churchill made throughout the course of his career,*

- *Hitler's reluctance to invade Britain,*

- *How the greatly undermanned Royal Air Force defeated the Luftwaffe in the Battle of Britain,*

- *How Churchill tried to guilt and scare Franklin Roosevelt into helping Britain stave off Germany,*

- *Whether Britain misled Poland about the level of assistance she would provide if Germany attacked,*

- *Britain's efforts to assure that the French fleet did not fall into the hands of the Nazis,*

- *The numerous efforts to depose or assassinate Hitler,*

- *The disastrous Dardanelles/Gallipoli Campaign of 1915 and its lasting effects on Churchill,*

- *Churchill's fascinating role in settling the crisis over Ireland in 1921,*

- *How Chamberlain sold out Czechoslovakia at Munich,*

- *Why the Nazis halted their drive just outside Dunkirk (something which allowed the British Army to be rescued), and*

- *Churchill's efforts as a major social reformer.*

Any examination of Churchill as Prime Minister, particularly in 1940, must begin with a thorough discussion of his early life and proceed through an analysis of his career to that point. It is also important to understand the things that took place in the world particularly after the armistice was signed ending WWI—most specifically, the Treaty of Versailles and appeasement—and how they were the ostensible bases for most of the assertive actions Hitler took in the years leading up to WWII and Britain's reaction to them.

In writing this book, among these things, I came to realize that an examination on the scale noted—the 65½ years before Churchill became Prime Minister—potentially involves trillions of facts, most of which have already been given multiple interpretations by various historians. Indeed, it has been said that "... more ink has been expended on Churchill than on any other figure in history." As such, no book, or even multi-volume treatise, can begin to cover everything.* This book, even as long as it is, is no different.

Recognizing this, my principal purpose was to set out clearly (and to the extent possible somewhat concisely) and analyze

- Those events that put Britain in the position of having to make that peace/war decision in May 1940. (This took many more pages than I originally anticipated.)

- Selected events that provide a glimpse into the Churchill that existed beneath the public figure (about so much is already known) which could have impacted his thinking in May 1940.

- The factors that could have, and did, play into his decision to reject the idea of negotiating a way for Britain to exit the war (including, most importantly, the psychological makeup of the man himself and its potential to affect his decision).

- The inter-personal dynamics between Churchill and Chamberlain, particularly between the start of WWII and May 28, 1940, that was so crucial to Britain's decision to continue to fight WWII alone rather than enter into peace talks with Germany.

In addition the final two chapters represent an epilogue of sorts generally discussing events after May 28, 1940, which Churchill affected or had an effect on Churchill.

I hope that you will find that the book has been at least somewhat successful in achieving these goals.

Alan I. Saltman

---

*A number of works have, however, done an excellent job of trying. Particularly notable among them are Roberts, Churchill: Walking with Destiny, Shirer, The Rise and Fall of the Third Reich, and the multi-volume official biography written by Churchill's son Randolph and Sir Martin Gilbert.

PART I

Churchill as a Second Lieutenant in the 4th Hussars (1896)

1

From Birth to Age 24 (1874–1898)

From Birth to Age 7
Boarding School
  • St. George School (1882–1884)
  • The Brunswick School (1884–1887)
  • Harrow (April 1888–June 1892)
The Road to Sandhurst
Sandhurst
Lord Randolph's Death; The Death of Woomy Everest
Winston's Military Career
  • Cuba
  • India
  • The Sudan
Churchill Resigns His Commission and Runs for Parliament

From Birth to Age 7

Winston Leonard Spencer Churchill was born November 30, 1874, at Blenheim Palace in Oxfordshire, England. He was the elder of two sons of Randolph Churchill and his wife, the former Jennie Jerome. (Winston's brother, Jack, was born February 4, 1880.) At the time of Winston's birth, Randolph was twenty-five; Jennie was twenty. The birth had been intended to take place at the couple's home in London, but a few days earlier while at Blenheim, Jennie had fallen—thus her confinement at Blenheim, the home of Randolph's parents—Lord Randolph Churchill, the 7th Duke of Marlborough and Frances Vane, a daughter of the 3rd Marquess of Londonderry.

The Churchills' aristocratic lineage traced to John Churchill, whom Queen Anne had made the first Duke of Marlborough in 1702, recognizing his distinguished career as statesman and soldier. An even older and equally potent strain in Winston's bloodline was that of the Spencers.*

The late Princess Diana (nee Diana Spencer) was a distant relative of Churchill's.

3

Fifteen generations earlier John Spencer had been knighted by Henry VIII.[1] As Churchill later wrote, "he had been born into one of the three or four hundred families which had for three or four hundred years guided the fortunes of the nation."[2]

Winston's mother, Jennie, was born in Brooklyn, New York, in 1854. Her mother, Clarissa Wilcox, was believed to have had Native American roots from the Iroquois confederacy.[3] Jennie's father, Leonard, from whom Winston got his middle name, was a flamboyant and successful financier. Before the wedding, Randolph's parents had Jerome investigated and determined that he was "a vulgar kind of man," "a bad character," and "from the class of speculators."[4] (As a result, they did not attend the wedding.) That said, Jerome did found the American Jockey Club, built a racetrack in the Bronx, for a time was a part owner of the *New York Times,* and was a patron of the arts, particularly the opera. He had been enormously rich until he suffered massive reversals in the stock market crash of 1873. As a result, Jerome could only afford to give the newlyweds a stipend of £2,000 per year ($315,000 in today's money) plus pay the rent on their house in London. This, along with the £1,200 per year that Randolph's father contributed, should have been more than sufficient. However, Randolph and Jennie were notorious spendthrifts. As Winston would later recall, "We were not rich ... I suppose we had about three thousand pounds per year and spent six thousand."[5] (In this regard, the acorn doesn't fall far from the tree. For most of his life Winston, too, lived on the financial edge. He may not always have had the money to do so, but he always lived like an aristocrat.)

Jennie and Randolph had been introduced at a British regatta in 1873 by the man who would become King Edward VII. Three days later, the couple agreed to marry. Lady Randolph, as she was known after the marriage, was an iconic figure among the English social elite; she was feted for her beauty, wit, and intelligence, and made little secret of her multiple love affairs. She did not play an active role as her sons' mother, both because those duties were expected to be handled by the nanny and because she much preferred the high life to the constraints of domestic responsibility.

In Victorian England, upper-class parents rarely interacted with their children except when Mother appeared for goodnight kisses. "Like popes granting audiences, they received the children at appointed times when the small ones, scrubbed and suitably dressed, presented themselves. The Churchills appeared to have omitted even those token meetings."[6] For all her beauty, charm, and social prowess, Jennie was no more cut out to be a parent than her promiscuity showed she was cut out to be a wife.

As was the custom, when Winston was a month old the Churchills hired a nurse/nannie—forty-three-year-old Elizabeth Anne Everest.[7] "Mrs." Everest (along the way, Winston nicknamed her "Woomy" and "Womany") would, during his youth, be the dearest figure in his life.* Indeed, her picture hung in his bedroom until he died.[8]

Nine months before Winston was born, his father had been elected to Parliament. Within six years he had become a leader of the Conservative Party. He championed "Tory Democracy," a concept originated by Disraeli, in which the traditionally patrician Conservative Party was urged to embrace positions designed to deal directly with the public welfare. He was also known for his eloquent and inspiring rhetorical ability, something Winston both witnessed and inherited. Eminent Churchill biographer Andrew Roberts describes Randolph as "controversial, mercurial, opportunistic, politically ruthless, a brilliant speaker ... and [someone who was] marked out as a future prime minister—as long as his inherent tendency to recklessness did not get the better of him."[9] As the next chapters will reveal, almost all of the above would also apply to Winston, who would also show a tremendous interest in social welfare.

In the time after Winston's birth, Jennie and Randolph were achieving great success in fashionable society. They had become members of a clique made up of the Prince of Wales and his friends.[10] But in 1876, Randolph earned the ire of the Prince when he appeared to be attempting to blackmail him as part of an ill-conceived effort to help his brother George out of a delicate situation.[11] Randolph asked Disraeli for advice as to how to untangle the mess. The Prime Minister said that the time had come for Randolph to leave London for a bit. To facilitate this, in January 1877, Disraeli appointed Randolph's father to be the Viceroy and Lord Lieutenant of Ireland and urged Randolph to leave Parliament and serve as his father's unpaid secretary in Dublin.[12]

As a result of Randolph's "exile," from age two to five-and-a-half, Churchill lived in Ireland. During that time, he would have the first of the many serious incidents that marked his life. While he was riding a donkey in the park his nanny saw what she feared was an Irish Republican demonstration and screamed. The donkey bolted. Four-year-old Winston was thrown off and suffered a concussion.[13]

The years in Ireland did little to improve Jennie and Randolph's parenting. As in England, there were "balls, theaters, dinner parties every evening, amusing friends to be made, and splendid steeple chasing, point-to-points and foxhunting."[14] Jennie became the darling of society and was the epitome of style—often wearing a diamond star in her hair. But things were different when it came to her child. Mrs. Everest, Winston's nanny, had to pester Jennie about getting Winston new clothes, saying that it was quite a disgrace how few things he had and how shabby they were. But shabby clothing was

---

*Whether or not married, nannies, cooks, and housekeepers were called "Mrs."

not the thing that troubled young Winston most. As he wrote years later, his mother and father "hunted continually on their large horses; and sometimes there were great scares because one or the other might not come back for many hours after they were expected."[15] Fearing abandonment, young Churchill cherished his relationship with Woomy.[16] As Winston's son would later observe, "the neglect and lack of interest in him shown by his parents were remarkable, even judged by the standards of the late Victorian and Edwardian days."[17] Apropos of this, Manchester makes several interesting observations about young Churchill:

- Even Woomy's unconditional devotion was not enough—after all she was just a hired servant.

- Affection was something that had to be earned.

- While one might expect that he would be hostile toward his parents—he wasn't. Not wanting to lose the little attention they showed him, he revered them.

- Instead, his parents' aloofness bred resentment of authority (particularly during his school years).[18]

A lesser person could not have withstood the emotional cruelty that Winston's parents showed him. His desire to succeed was huge.

Randolph's banishment ended in April 1880. Thus, the Churchills returned to London. They came back just in time to see the opposition Liberal Party regain control of the House and reinstall William Gladstone as British Prime Minister. A life-long member of the Conservative Party, Randolph soon ran for and was elected to the House, where he fought against Gladstone's bill to give Ireland Home Rule.[19]

As for Winston, after returning to London, he had no playmates. He was a child who was either contemplative or constantly running and jumping with no concern at all about getting hurt.[20]

Churchill's oldest surviving letter was written when he was seven, most likely with help from Woomy. He had spent the holidays at his grandparents' home while his parents enjoyed Christmas elsewhere.[21] On January 4, 1882, he sent the following heartfelt letter to his heartless mother: "My dear Mamma, I hope you are well I thank you very much for the beautiful presents those Soldiers and Flags and Castle they are so nice it was so kind of you and dear Papa. I send you my love and a great many kisses. your loving Winston."[22]

The gift was appropriate. Winston was exceedingly proud of his aristocratic heritage, and perhaps most notably of its military resume. His ancestor, the Duke of Marlborough, was an accomplished and admired warrior. As the leader of his own two-inch-high army of toy soldiers, Winston's imagination ran wild. One of Churchill's cousins later recalled that:

> His playroom contained from one end to the other a plank table on trestles, upon which were thousands of lead soldiers arranged for battle. He organized wars. The lead battalions were manoeuvered into action, peas and pebbles committed great casualties, forts were stormed, cavalry charged, bridges were destroyed.[23]

These battles were "played with an interest that was no ordinary child game."[24]

The gift of toy soldiers for which young Winston thanked his parents implies that his parents were being generous. But remember, his parents had spent Christmas away from him. In today's society, the persistent physical as well as emotional distance Randolph and Jennie demonstrated would most likely be considered child abuse. In this regard, in diary entries spanning many months of 1882, Winston's mother documented having tea with one particular friend twice as often as she saw her seven-year-old son.[25]

Boarding School

St. George School (1882–1884)

In 1882, Jennie and Randolph decided to send Winston to boarding school. Indicative of the Churchills' lack of attentiveness, it was five weeks into the fall term when Winston was enrolled at the St. George School near Ascot (about 25 miles west of London). St. George was a wretched place which young Churchill hated, although that was something he would never tell his parents.[26] One thread that runs through his heartbreaking correspondence home was that he desperately wanted visitors and constantly begged his parents to come visit.[27] But in the two years that he was at St. George, they never came to see him once. Woomy and his five-and-a-half years younger brother Jack were his only visitors.

Worse yet, the school was led by a sadistic Headmaster who wouldn't hesitate to lay up to "twenty strokes of birch on a boy's bare rump" for any infraction of the rules.[28] Because Churchill was rebellious, he was often beaten. A contemporary recalled that "[Churchill's] sojourn at the school [was] one long feud with authority."[29] As Winston's son, Randolph would write in Volume 1 of Churchill's official biography: "His pugnacious and rebellious nature never adapted itself to discipline."[30] (This could be said not just about his conduct as a child.) Examples of his naughtiness at St. George included taking sugar from the pantry and removing the Headmaster's straw hat from the hat rack and kicking it to pieces. Moreover, his classmates did not seem to sympathize with him.[31] The two years of abuse that he suffered not only inflicted pain but also damaged his health.[32] When Winston could no longer take it, he fled home to Woomy Everest. When she saw the welts on his back and bottom, she advised Jennie, who took him out of the school immediately.[33]

The Brunswick School (1884–1887)

In the fall if 1884, the ten-year old Winston was enrolled in the Brunswick School, an institution run by two maiden sisters named Thomson in the seaside town of Brighton (located 47 miles due south of London). The new school was a marked improvement over St. George. But Churchill continued to be a discipline problem. In each of his first two terms he ranked near or at the bottom of his class in conduct. Much of this naughtiness seems to have stemmed from a yearning to "draw attention," something not common in children of the era.[34] Yet owing to some kind treatment and understanding from the Thomson sisters, after a time Winston began to respond and even started to enjoy school.[35] It was also about this time that he began reading every newspaper he could find.[36] With his father's career on the upswing, Lord Randolph was in the news all the time. Winston clipped stories and cartoons of his father and memorized his speeches.[37]*

Winston also started collecting stamps, autographs, and goldfish, and began to share the interests of the other boys.[38] While his parents never visited, teachers and relatives would take him on trips to see plays, and so forth.[39] As Manchester puts it, "Jennie had her priorities to consider," and, while Winston "was not at the bottom of the list, he scarcely led it."[40] Jennie and Randolph did come to Brighton in the early spring of 1886 when Winston came down with a life-threatening case of double pneumonia (temperature 104 degrees) and propriety gave them no choice.[41]** "[She] had been scared and was doubtlessly relieved when Winston recovered, but if gratitude meant changing her lifestyle, she wouldn't have it."[42] Put differently, "behind Lady Randolph's vivid beauty there lay an essentially selfish and frivolous character."[43]

During his years at the Brunswick School, young Churchill constantly begged his mother to visit—sometimes promising her "billions of kisses" if she would. But "[s]he never found the time."[44] When he had the lead role in a class production, he asked her to come and see him perform, adding that

---

*Notwithstanding, what can charitably be called Lord Randolph's disinterest in his son, Winston idolized his father and would do so forever.

**Of course, Woomy was there, although Winston's doctor placed such a priority on quiet and sleep that he feared the effect of Winston's excitement at seeing her. That said, she was barred from his sickroom for a time. Randolph Churchill, Youth p. 71.

"I shall be miserable if you don't." She didn't. Later, when he asked her to come down and see a production of the *Mikado* in which he was appearing, he wrote, "Please come, I've been disappointed so many times."[45] She still did not come, and this was not the last time that she would disappoint him.

Sadly, Winston's relationship with his father was not as good as the one he had with his mother. Randolph disliked him.[46] Indeed, one Sunday, Randolph had an appointment in Brighton. Though it was only a short walk from Winston's school, he didn't stop in to see his oldest child. When Winston found out, he wrote to his father saying, "I cannot think why you did not come to see me on Sunday while you were in Brighton, I was very disappointed. ..." He added, "but I suppose you were too busy to come."[47]

The years 1885 and 1886 were busy ones in Randolph's career. In June 1885, Liberal P.M. Gladstone resigned, and a new minority Government was formed by Lord Salisbury, the leader of the Conservatives. Lord Randolph was appointed Secretary of State for India. This was done because of his political talents (and his ability to cause trouble) not for any party loyalty he showed.* After a general election in December 1885, the Liberals achieved a plurality and Gladstone was reinstalled as the P.M. Another general election was held in July 1886. In it, the Conservatives, who had entered an electoral pact with the breakaway Unionist wing of the Liberal party, won a majority of seats in the House. Lord Randolph's eloquence was a key factor in the coalition's victory.[48]

In recognition, in August 1886, Randolph was promoted to Chancellor of the Exchequer,[49] a position from which many prime ministers had ascended. Unfortunately, his term in office lasted only five months.

Used to being a critic of the opposition party, Randolph found the job at Treasury to be dreary, and he started to take interest in the affairs of the other ministers.** In October 1886, without consulting Salisbury, Randolph delivered a speech to fourteen thousand people at Oakfield Park, demanding more sovereignty for local governments in England; closer ties with Germany and Austria-Hungary; and stiff protests against Russian influence in the Balkans. Unfortunately, each of these positions clashed with the views of the Prime Minister.[50] Soon after, Randolph continued his insolent ways. He prepared an astonishing budget, one which proposed to reduce taxes and military spending (two ideas on which Gladstone and the opposition Liberals had run in the recent elections).[51] Lord Randolph was staging a coup to take power from Prime Minister Salisbury. When Salisbury rejected the

---

*As described in ensuing chapters, Winston's capacity to be loyal, particularly to the party of which he was a member, would likewise be frequently found wanting.

**This was a trait that Winston would not only inherit but greatly expand on. Whenever he was in Government, Winston was simply incapable of keeping his nose out of the business of other Cabinet ministers.

budget, Randolph, thinking himself indispensable, submitted his resignation. Salisbury accepted it.[52]* Moreover, not one cabinet minister raised any objection. During the remaining eight years of his life, Lord Randolph never served in Government again. Despite Randolph's public humiliation, Winston still idolized him.[53]

During the summer of 1887, Randolph spoke with his sister's husband, Edward Marjoribanks, about a suitable public school for twelve-year-old Winston. The Marjoribanks had just sent their son, who was slightly older than Winston, to Harrow, one of the greatest public schools in England. As an indication of the distance between young Winston and his family, he was unaware that Churchill boys (including his father) had, since 1722, all attended Eton (Harrow's archrival).[54] Winston would break tradition. The decision to send Winston to Harrow was because it sits high on a hill near Wembley, while Eton is near Windsor in the misty Thames valley. Doctors believed that Winston, with his propensity for lung problems, would not fare well in the climate at Eton.[55]** Although Winston studied for weeks before the Harrow entrance examination, when it was administered, he froze. Even so, he was accepted—after all, his father was the former Chancellor of the Exchequer.[56]

At Christmas in 1886, during his last year at the Brunswick School, Winston wrote his mother about coming home to celebrate the holidays with her and his father rather than staying at school. But before he could have known it, his parents were off on a seven-week holiday to Russia.[57] (The trip likely was a response to P.M. Salisbury's having accepted Randolph's resignation just before Christmas.) Winston would spend Christmas at his parents' house with his younger brother Jack, looked after by Woomy.[58] Unfortunately, during the holidays Woomy contracted diphtheria, a disease often fatal back then. His grandmother whisked the boys off to Blenhiem for the rest of their school vacation. On January 12, 1887, Winston wrote this to his mother that "[Woomany] is much better. ... My holidays have chopped about a good deal but ... I do not wish to complain. It might have been so much worse if Woomany had died."[59]

Harrow (April 1888–June 1892)

Winston entered Harrow in April, 1888.[60] He was thirteen. In time he would say that Harrow was the place where he "spent the unhappiest

---

Young Winston learned never to resign from Government unless he was prepared to go into the wilderness or did so along with several other people capable of bringing down the Government.

**Churchill was prone to bronchial infections his entire life.*

days of his life."[61] During his time at Harrow, Winston's conduct remained problematic:

- he often talked back to the Headmaster;

- he wasn't generous;

- he was not liked by his schoolmates; and

- he was bullied.[62]

Moreover, his parents still visited only rarely even though he continued to beg them to do so.[63] He was miserable most of the time. This no doubt affected Winston's academics. As his housemaster put it, "As far as ability goes, he ought to be at the top of this form whereas he is at the bottom."[64]

One of Winston's contemporaries at Harrow later recalled that Churchill was often beaten because he broke almost every rule and constantly talked back to his teachers.[65]* Roberts writes that nevertheless, "Churchill was somewhat of a success at Harrow."[66] Churchill became accomplished in fencing, admired Napoleon, and relished learning about famous battles. He also took great interest in and derived great pleasure from the School Rifle Corps. Among other things, it was at Harrow that Churchill developed courage. He was willing to stand up to his teachers (and even correct them if they misquoted Shakespeare).[67] He also ignored the snobbish jeers of his schoolmates such as when he escorted Woomy around the campus. Churchill would not let anything or anyone hurt the only person that ever really showed him love.[68]

During his time at Harrow written communication from his parents, which was poor to start with, seemed to get worse. Not only did he write four letters for every one he received from them, but their letters were almost always filled with remonstrations. For example, his mother wrote: "Father is very angry with you for not acknowledging the gift of 5£ for a whole week, and then writing an offhand careless letter."[69] About school work: "Your father and I are both more disappointed than we can say. ... Your work is an insult to your intelligence. ... I must say that you repay [your father's] kindness to you badly."[70]

In September 1889, fourteen-year-old Winston joined the Army Class at Harrow. There, the boys took special lessons aimed at helping them get admitted to one of England's military academies. This involved extra work in the evenings and half holidays, which made it difficult for them to achieve a high class ranking.

---

*Worse yet, while at Harrow, Winston suffered several illnesses and injuries—toothaches, a concussion from a bike accident, severe fever, measles, and an incipient hernia. Golland, Not Winston p. 31.

Winston was not all that good in mathematics. Thus, it was decided that he would not seek admission to Woolwich, the military academy for artillery and engineering officers. Rather, it was thought best for him to apply to The Royal Military Academy at Sandhurst, which was for infantry and cavalry officers.[71]

In his last year at Harrow (1891–92), when Winston was asked what he planned to do upon graduation he said, "The Army, of course, so long as there's fighting to be had. When that's over, I shall have a shot at politics."[72] He was elated that his father supported his desire for a military career. He believed that Lord Randolph "with his experience and flair had discerned in [him] the qualities of military genius."[73] (Sadly, several years later Winston learned that his father's support of an army career stemmed from his belief that Winston lacked the cleverness to succeed in anything else.)

Later in that final year at Harrow, Winston's relationship with his parents went from bad to worse. Jennie was getting exasperated with the now seventeen-year-old Winston, who continued to do poorly, particularly in French. As Christmas approached, Jennie told him that he would spend the holiday in France working on the language at the house of one of Harrow's French masters, rather than at home.[74] Winston begged his mother not to do this, but she was unmoved and responded quite sternly. In his response, Winston upbraided her for being "so sarcastic to me since it is I not you will have to make the sacrifice. ... I am required to give up my holidays— not you. ... You were asked to give up a short part of the year to take me abroad—you promised—refused & I did not press the point. ... Please do have a little regard for my happiness."[75] She returned his next note without comment. When he wrote again and asked why, she wrote back: "I have only read one page of your letter and I send it back to you—as its style does not please me. ... My dear you won't gain anything by taking this line."[76] In his reply, though still castigating his mother while seeking to secure her pity, Winston wrote:

> Never would I have believed that you would have been so unkind. I am utterly miserable. That you should refuse to read my letter is most painful to me. There is nothing in it to give due grounds for rejecting it. ... Oh my Mummy! Next: I am more unhappy than I can possibly say ... Darling, if you want me to do anything for you, especially so great a sacrifice don't be so cruel to Your loving son Winny.[77]

In a follow-up two days later, he added an apology:

> Don't let my silly letters make you angry. Let me at least think that you love me ... Please write something kind to me. I'm very

sorry if I have "riled" you before, I did only want to explain things from my point of view.[78]

Even so, none of this availed Winston in the least. Jennie was unmoved.

From France, he wrote his mother every day. Even though she'd promised to write three times a week, in his time in Versailles he received one letter and it was from Woomy.[79] Jennie was at the remote ancestral home of Lord and Lady Howe, and could not receive or send mail easily.[80] To add insult to injury, before Winston had left for France, Jennie had promised him that upon his return from Versailles he could take a week off from school so that he would at least have some sort of a Christmas vacation. Lord Randolph would, however, have none of it. He believed that every moment that Winston spent in school was important, particularly with the entrance examination to Sandhurst looming in June.[81]

The incidents described above notwithstanding, young Winston still idolized his father and adored his mother. In the first volume of the autobiography he wrote in 1930, Churchill explains that his mother Jennie "shone for me like the Evening Star. I loved her dearly"—but, he added, "at a distance."[82] Neither of his parents, was, however, equipped temperamentally to impart to their son a true sense of being loved and valued. Moreover, owing to Randolph's political career and Jennie's active social life they had no time for him. Some of this distancing may have been inherent in an aristocratic life, where child-rearing often was delegated to hired help. His father was uniformly harsh in his assessment of his son's early capabilities and pessimistic about how successful his son might become as an adult; and he did not shield his sensitive son from these disdainful emotions. Winston's childhood friend F.E. Smith* wrote later in life that Winston's father "discerned nothing remarkable, nothing of singular promise in a very remarkable and original boy."[83]

The Road to Sandhurst

Sixteen-year-old Winston was one of twelve (out of twenty-nine) Harrow candidates who passed all subjects on the November 1890 preliminary exam for Sandhurst.[84] To no one's surprise, Lord Randolph did not even congratulate his son on the achievement. Owing to this snub, Winston "temporarily lost interest in the military and even thought briefly about joining the clergy."[85] While he had breezed through the preliminary exam, he would not pass the main exam for admission to Sandhurst in June 1892. Nor did his second attempt in November 1892 go well. Winston was by now tense, distraught, and admittedly depressed.[86] So, when Jennie's sister Lily offered

---

Later in life, Smith became Lord Birkenhead.

the Churchills the run of her large estate near Bournemouth for the winter (of '92–'93), they accepted. Winston, Jack, and Woomy spent the Christmas holidays there. During that stay, while playing a game with Jack and a fourteen-year-old cousin, to avoid being "captured" Winston would once again risk death when he jumped off a thirty-foot-high footbridge hoping that the branches of the trees below him would slow his descent. They did not. When he hit the ground he suffered another concussion, a ruptured kidney, and a broken bone in his back. The doctors ordered him to stay in bed for three months. Problem: Winston's last chance to take the entrance exam for Sandhurst was looming in June 1893 and he had hired a tutor (a "crammer") who specialized in the Sandhurst exam. But the doctors said that Winston should not return to hard study during his period of bed rest.[87] That was out of the question, though. The cramming thus proceeded, but Winston's casual manner and inattentiveness persisted.[88] This was due mainly to the fact that at this same time Lord Randolph was making what would be his final attempt at a political comeback.

Nonetheless, as the June exam date grew closer, Winston, knowing what was at stake, buckled down a bit. He still resisted doing all the lessons laid out by the crammer. Instead, he would spend much time, much to the crammer's dismay, reading English history for pleasure. (Of course, Churchill outscored all other candidates on the history portion of the exam.[89])

After the exam, Winston immediately set out on a hiking trip to Switzerland with his brother Jack, and J.D.G. Little, a young master at Eton. In Lucerne he learned that he passed the exam—but not by much. Moreover, he had not scored high enough to become an infantry cadet as his father had wanted. Young Churchill had been admitted to the cavalry. Winston received congratulatory telegrams from his grandparents, aunts, uncles, cousins, and the Headmaster at Harrow but did not get one from his parents. Randolph had gotten his friend, the Commander-in-Chief of the Army, the Duke of Cambridge, to agree to find a place for Winston in the crack Sixtieth Rifles once Winston had been commissioned as an infantry officer. Now, not only would Randolph have to bear the costs of horses, but one day he would also have to go through the humiliation of telling the Duke that his son was too stupid to get into the infantry. Jennie sent a warning to Winston in which she said that "I'm glad of course that you have got into Sandhurst but Papa is not pleased at your getting in by the skin of your teeth and missing the infantry. ... He is not as pleased by your exploits as you seem to be!"[90]

A week later, a blistering letter from Lord Randolph arrived. Winston was stunned and depressed by his father's words.[91] In a reply letter, young Churchill said that he was very sorry that he had displeased his father and that he would try to change the elder Churchill's opinion by his work and conduct at Sandhurst. Winston ended the letter saying, "Thank you very much for writing to me. I'm very sorry indeed that I have done so badly."[92]

Winston almost didn't get the chance to prove himself at Sandhurst because of a boating incident later that summer at Lake Geneva. Winston and his brother had rented a boat and rowed it out about a mile. After they stopped to take a swim, a light breeze came up and started to blow the boat away from them. As Churchill wrote in *My Early Life,* "the rising wind ... continued to carry the boat away from us at about the same speed we could swim. ... [and] [u]naided, we could never reach the shore." Swimming for his life, Winston finally caught up with the boat and rowed it back to pick up Jack.[93] Once again, Winston had escaped a close brush with death.

When Winston arrived back in London, there was a letter waiting for him from the military secretary. Several boys who had achieved higher scores than he had on the entry exam had dropped out and Winston could become an infantry cadet if he chose. He declined.

Sandhurst

Winston Churchill became a cavalry cadet at Sandhurst on September 1, 1893. At Sandhurst he was considered a junior[94] and would graduate after three terms spread over sixteen months. (Upon entering Sandhurst he ranked 92nd in a class of 102.) After a few weeks, he began to love military life. He enjoyed studying tactics, topography, military law, military administration, and fortifications. He took to horsemanship with relish and became accomplished.[95] He also became Sandhurst's second-best writer. No longer having to deal with subjects that he hated, such as Latin, French, and mathematics, Winston was finally enjoying school. After the long dreadful years of being bullied and taunted, he was accepted at Sandhurst as a comrade and he rejoiced.[96] Only seven weeks into his son's tenure at Sandhurst, Lord Randolph wrote that "[Winston] has smartened up. He holds himself quite upright and he has got steadier. ... Sandhurst has done wonders for him. ..."[97] His father's view of him even improved to the point that he gave Winston a fancy gold pocket watch.[98] But several months later, when Randolph learned that the gold watch had fallen out of Winston's tunic pocket and had been severely damaged, he reverted to form calling Winston stupid and telling him that his brother Jack was vastly his superior.[99] Ten days later Lord Randolph had calmed down and in a letter to Winston said, "You need not trouble any more about the watch. It is quite clear that the rough work of Sandhurst is not suitable for [such a fancy watch]."[100]

Throughout 1893 Randolph was having serious money problems. He and Jennie sold their house in London and moved in with his mother, Duchess Fanny, in her London mansion. With Winston at Sandhurst and Jack at

Harrow, Woomy became a housekeeper for the Duchess. Unfortunately, in short order the Duchess was forced to economize and fired Woomy Everest.[101] (Woomy was sixty-two and had been with the Churchills for almost twenty years, during which time she was able to save little.) Winston did not learn of her departure until three months after she was gone. When he wrote to his mother about the firing, she said it was none of his business. He would not, however, let go of the matter, writing in response that "... if I allowed Everest to be cut adrift without protest in the manner which is proposed I should be extremely ungrateful.... She is an old woman—who has been your devoted servant.... At her age she is invited to find a new place and practically begin all over again.... I am very sorry but I cannot bear to think of Everest not coming back much less being got rid of in such a manner. If you can arrange with the Duchess and persuade her to let Everest stay till after Christmas—I should feel extremely relieved."[102] Lord Randolph sent Woomy £17. After that, she received other "presents" from time to time. But otherwise, she had been "discarded like a shabby cradle."[103] She would continue to write to Winston and Jack, and despite her meager finances, she would also remember them with little gifts on their birthdays and Christmas.[104]

As Winston neared graduation from Sandhurst he was selected as one of fifteen seniors to compete for the school's annual riding prize. He would finish second. He wrote to tell his father, who by that time was so ill that he was in no condition to express pleasure or displeasure. Winston knew two things: first, anything to do with riding would reopen the subject of whether he would join the Sixtieth Rifles or enter the cavalry and second, he did not want to join the infantry.[105] Winston graduated from Sandhurst in December 1894. He was 20th in his class. His father died a month later.

Lord Randolph's Death; The Death of Woomy Everest

Just after Winston's birth, Lord Randolph started visiting doctors about an illness which, over a twenty-year period, would grow increasingly debilitating. Theories abound that Randolph had syphilis, although that view has been questioned.[106]

In any event, by 1892 Randolph's condition had worsened—paralysis had started to set in, and his speech had become slurred. Jennie, who was nursing her husband, wondered what to tell seventeen-year-old Winston and twelve-year-old Jack. Because they rarely saw him, neither boy knew that Lord Randolph was seriously ill.[107] By 1894, Randolph had entered the final stages of his disease. Still, in June, Jennie and Randolph left on a round-the-world tour, which she told her sons was being taken on the doctors' recommendation that their father go on a long sea cruise. Jennie and Randolph were accompanied on the trip by a young doctor, Dr. George Keith.

Unsurprisingly, the trip turned into a six-month ordeal. Winston managed to get the doctors to tell him the true facts about his father's condition. He had never known how bad things were and he feared the toll that the trip might be having on his mother.[108] In India in late November, Dr. Keith ended the trip. Lord Randolph's condition had deteriorated greatly. The Churchills would return to London.[109] At that point, the doctors advised twenty-year-old Winston that his father would soon be dead.[110]

After a month's journey, the Churchills reached London on Christmas Eve. Lord Randolph died thirty days later, on January 24, 1895. He was forty-five.* Three days later a memorial service was held for him at Westminster Abbey. Churchill would say afterward that his father's passing left him prostrate with grief for a whole day and night. So began Winston's life-long efforts to vindicate his father's memory and prove that his father's opinion of him was wrong.

The year 1895 was one of funerals for Winston. After his father's death, Jennie's mother passed away a few months later. Then he learned that his beloved Woomy, Elizabeth Everest, had been stricken with peritonitis, which can be serious even with today's antibiotics. When her condition deteriorated, he hurried to her bedside and held her hand until she passed. He then organized the funeral and paid for both the headstone and upkeep of the grave. He wrote his mother: "I feel very low … and find that I never realized how much that poor old Woom was to me."[111]

Winston's Military Career

Shortly after Randolph's death, Jennie, still young and beautiful, successfully negotiated Winston's release from any commitment to join the Sixtieth Rifles.[112] In mid-February he joined the 4th Queen's Own Hussars, a regiment that in 1854 had participated in the infamous Charge of the Light Brigade during the Crimean War. Churchill loved every aspect of being an officer in the cavalry, including the horses, the distinctive uniforms, and even the drilling. But what he consciously sought was a war he could join.

Over the next four years he would serve in Cuba, India, the Sudan, and South Africa, with a brief interlude to run unsuccessfully for a seat in the House of Commons in June 1899.

Cuba

With his well-connected mother pulling strings, in 1895 Winston got his wish to be assigned to a region of conflict: the Cuban war of independence.

---

*Winston Churchill died seventy years later to the day. He was ninety and had lived twice as long as his father. Given that his father died young, Churchill had always believed that his life would be short and relied on that fact to explain "his own thrusting nature." Roberts, p. 31.

In November 1895, financed in part by his mother and in part by becoming a war correspondent for *The Daily Telegraph,* he landed in Cuba, where rebels were waging a guerilla war against Spain. Winston did come under fire, likely inadvertently, and in *My Early Life* he described the incident breathlessly:

> ... (S)uddenly, close at hand, almost in our faces it seemed, a ragged volley rang out from the edge of the forest. The horse immediately behind me—not my horse—gave a bound. There was excitement and commotion. The bullet had struck the horse; ... blood dripped on the ground, and there was a circle of dark red on his bright chestnut coat about a foot wide. He hung his head, but did not fall. Evidently however he was going to die.... I could not help reflecting that the bullet which had struck the chestnut had certainly passed within foot of my head. So at any rate I had been 'under fire.' That was something.[113]

"Something" good, it seems. Churchill's experiences in Cuba did not dissuade him from seeking to immerse himself in even more conflict-laden situations.

India

After Cuba, in the fall of 1896, he persuaded a senior commander to make sure he would be in a position to see action and he was sent to India. Churchill's social standing and political connections could have ensured that he would NOT be assigned any post that would have put him in harm's way, especially since Britain at that time was not actively engaged in warfare imperiling the Empire, let alone the Homeland. But he would have none of that. An added inducement for Churchill to seek out battle was his growing notoriety as a war correspondent, something which proved to be an entirely separate means for him to link war with personal recognition.

While in India, Winston started writing dispatches for *The Daily Telegraph,* and he soon developed into a prolific and admired writer; he would go on to win the Nobel Prize for Literature in 1953. Throughout his time in politics, this side career gave him the money he sorely needed and provided him the exposure he craved with the British people.

Indicative of his continuing willingness to gain attention by risking his life, in 1897 he wrote his mother about a battle in which he'd participated in the northwest of India. Churchill said he "rode on my grey pony all along the skirmish line where everyone else was lying down in cover. Foolish perhaps, but I play for high stakes and given an audience there is nothing too daring or too noble. Without the gallery," he summed up, "things are different."[114] Almost immediately afterward, Churchill began to turn exploits from the subcontinent into the first of his forty-three book-length works (seventy-two volumes), published over the next six decades of his life and, posthumously, another two decades later. The first six books, which included his only novel, were about war.

The Sudan

In the summer of 1898 Churchill again furiously pulled strings to be assigned to the Cairo headquarters of soon-to-be-famous Lord Kitchener. In the final days of August and the initial days of September, Kitchener's army, greatly outnumbered, engaged tens of thousands of Dervish warriors in furious fighting in the Sudan.

Churchill's feelings about confronting such a fearsome army? He was relieved his efforts were not fruitless. A little more than a year later, Churchill finished a two-volume memorialization, nearly a thousand pages long, on the Sudan conflict, in which he recounted the grim details of the campaign in riveting detail.

Churchill Resigns His Commission and Runs for Parliament

At the end of April 1899, Churchill resigned from the army to pursue a political career. The Conservative Party was, and for some time had been, firmly allied with the Liberal Unionists led by Joseph Chamberlain.* (The group that had left the Liberal Party in 1886 to oppose Gladstone's proposed legislation to give the Irish Home Rule.) There was hardly a more divisive issue in Parliament than Home Rule. In fact, the Conservatives' opposition to Home Rule is what kept Tory Democrats like Lord Randolph and his son Winston members of the Party. In a letter to his mother in 1897, young Churchill revealed that: "Were it not for Home Rule—to which I will never consent [**]—I would enter Parliament as a Liberal."[115]

In June, Churchill accepted the invitation of the Oldham Conservative Association in Lancashire to run for Parliament from that district for the Conservatives/Unionists. Oldham had been represented by two Conservative MPs; one had retired, and the other had passed away. Thus, the need for the by-election to fill the empty seats. Churchill lost, finishing a close third in the election which was won by two Radical Liberals.

The loss, however, proves the point that things happen for a reason (even if one doesn't know what it is at the time). Had Churchill won a seat

---

*Joseph Chamberlain was the father of future Prime Minister Neville Chamberlain and his older half-brother Austen, who would also become powerful Conservative members of Parliament (MPs).

**In future years, Churchill would, however, agree to a form of Home Rule for Ireland.

in Parliament he would not have been able to go to South Africa to cover the Boer War a few months later. There, he would become a British hero.

Winston as a youth

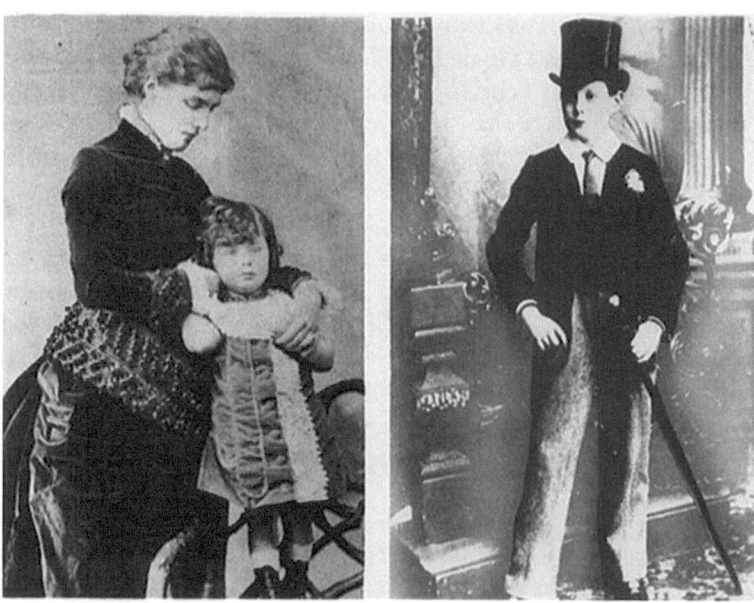

Winston with his mother Jennie/As a young man

Winston's father Lord Randolph Churchill

*As war correspondent during
the Boer War, 1899*

Churchill on the lecture tour in 1900

2

November 1899–June 1900 The Boer War

After the Sudan conflict, Churchill resigned his army commission.[1] Even so, Churchill's penchant for burnishing his personal reputation by inserting himself into others' conflicts would continue, reaching its zenith in November 1899, during the Boer War in South Africa. Hired and paid handsomely by *The Morning Post,* Churchill traveled to South Africa with his valet in tow to report on the war between Britain and Afrikaner independence factions. There had been strong competition among the London newspapers for Churchill's services. Only twenty-five years old, he was the highest-paid journalist covering the war, a fact made even more impressive by the names of others—Rudyard Kipling, Edgar Wallace, and Arthur Conan Doyle, to name three—hired to do the same thing.[2] Churchill's previous writings had been hailed as "exceedingly brilliant." Indeed, his reporting had been seen not just as being relentless but fearless, "even to the point of recklessness."[3] His recounting of the Boer War would exceed even these descriptions.

Once in South Africa, desperate to be a part of the war, Churchill tried to make his way to Ladysmith, a city deep in Boer-held territory, but it was under siege and thus inaccessible. He was therefore stuck at the front in the town of Estcourt, 42 miles south of Ladysmith.[4] At Estcourt, all the small British force stationed there could do was try to monitor the Boers' movements until a supplemental force arrived. The reconnaissance was accomplished using both cavalry and a rather makeshift armored train. The train's engine was placed in the middle of its carriages, which consisted of flat cars to which steel boiler plates (each measuring six-and-a-half-feet high and pierced with holes at shoulder height for rifles) had been affixed. The cars had no roofs, and access and egress required climbing into and out of the carriage.[5] Moreover, the boiler plates offered little protection against the Boers' high velocity shells. One carriage contained an old navy gun.

Because this slow-moving, jerry-rigged train, which departed every day at the same time, was an easy target for Boer ambushes, riding on it was a dangerous and unpopular assignment among the troops. Yet on November 15, Churchill asked to ride along on the train's patrol, because, as he told fellow journalist John Atkins, he was "eager for trouble" and had "a feeling, a sort of intuition, that if I go, something will come of it."[6] This was the same sort of glory-seeking "something" he had searched for in Cuba four years earlier.

On the train's journey up to the town of Chieveley, Boer soldiers had been spotted along the way. Still, Churchill, with his burning desire to see a battle, persuaded the officer commanding the train not to turn back.[7] Sure enough, after the train reached Chieveley and was backing its way home to Estcourt, the Boers opened fire after the train stopped at the crest of a hill to do some reconnaissance.[8] The train then started down the hill, picking up speed along the way as it tried to get away from the shooting. Near the bottom of the hill, around a curve, the Boers had blocked the track with a pile of large rocks.[9] When the train hit the pile at speed, the first car catapulted into the air, flipped, and landed at the bottom of the hill. All onboard that car were killed or severely injured. The second car went down the tracks another twenty yards before it derailed and threw its riders out too. The third, just in front of the engine, remained upright; but half of it derailed, thus blocking the tracks.[10]

A firefight ensued during which Churchill assumed command and sought volunteers to free the engine. The plan was to use the engine as a ram to push the third car off the tracks and run what was left of the train into the town of Frere just a half mile down the line.[11] Easier said than done. It took nine men nearly an hour to get the crippled third car off the tracks.[12] Finally, with the engine and its coal tender loaded with fifty wounded men, the train chugged its way to Frere. As that effort was taking place, the Boers intensified their fire.[13] Despite Churchill's valorous actions, once the engine was gone, there was nothing for him and the remaining men to do but surrender.*

Over the next four days the Boers forced the captured survivors of the attack to march nearly 150 miles northward to a railway station at Saps Elandslaage.[14] There they boarded a train for the remaining 200-mile trip to Pretoria. Although the trek was long, the prisoners were treated humanely. They were given food and water and were allowed to sleep. When they finally made it to Pretoria, they were all imprisoned in a former school. The incident and Churchill's bravery were quickly front-page news in London. As Candice Millard writes in *Hero of the Empire*, "Talk about Churchill's political career was also revived, with predictions for his soaring success—should he make it out of South Africa alive."[15]

It didn't take long for Churchill to start planning an escape. The scheme that he and two compatriots came up with was for Churchill and one of

---

That Churchill took command even though he was merely a civilian says much about how war would separate him from other men. See broader discussion in Chapter 20.

the others to make a dash to an unlit corner of the prison yard behind the latrine and climb the fence when the sentry was distracted. The third would follow upon an agreed signal. That said, when Churchill saw an opportunity—the sentry having turned to light a pipe—he took it and got over the fence.[16] He waited an hour for his comrades, but they couldn't make it past the now-suspicious sentry.[17] Churchill's comrades wanted him to climb back in, but he declined.

Even though he had only £75, little food (four small pieces of chocolate and a biscuit), no water, no weapons, no compass, no map, and no knowledge of Pretoria or South Africa, he was prepared make the 300-mile journey to safety in Portuguese East Africa (now Mozambique) alone.[18] The Boers were equally intent on not letting Churchill get away. This was particularly true after they uncovered a snarky letter he had deliberately left, chastising them for not having released him because he was a war correspondent not a soldier. (Churchill himself admitted that as a civilian who took an active and prominent part in the fight after the train derailment, he could have been shot on sight.) The Boers quickly printed wanted posters offering a reward for his capture "dead or alive"[19] and undertook a sprawling manhunt.

Delighted by the thrill of adventure, Churchill walked through the dark streets of Pretoria, followed railroad tracks for hours, and hopped on a moving train not knowing exactly where it was heading. Hours later, he jumped from the train in what turned out to be the northeastern part of the country, seventy miles east of Pretoria.[20] He spent the next day hiding in a grove of trees. That night he planned to hop another train as it slowly chugged up a nearby hill.[21] However no trains came by.[22] Because of his escape, the Boers had suspended night train traffic.[23] After waiting for hours for the train that never came, he began walking across the veld toward the bright light of furnaces in the distance. Churchill had stumbled upon a coal mining operation.[24] Desperate, he knocked on the door of the mine's manager, John Howard, who turned out to be one of the few Englishmen who had been allowed to remain during the war. Howard agreed to help him even though he could have been shot for doing so. In fact, Boer soldiers had visited Howard's house just hours earlier as part of their massive manhunt for Churchill,[25] and the house and mine were filled with non-Britons who would not have hesitated to turn Churchill in.

For three days Howard hid Churchill deep inside a pitch-black mine shaft infested with hordes of savage albino rats with poor eyesight. After three more days, during which Churchill was hidden behind packing cases in Howard's office, the mine manager finally came up with a way to get him out of the country.[26] The man who ran the company store, Charles Burnham, also had a small business on the side—buying wool for a German company and shipping it to Portuguese East Africa where it was forwarded on to Germany. Burnham had enough bales of wool to fill seven boxcars. He would leave a hole between two bales big enough for Churchill to crawl into for what would turn out to be a nearly three-day journey. Burnham not only agreed to hide Churchill in the wool but rode in one of the train's passenger cars all the way to Portuguese East Africa, bribing guards and inspectors at every stop, until one prevented the wool from traveling with him any farther.[27] The wool would be part of the next goods train to the capital, Lourenco Marques.[28] When Burnham got to the capital, he waited in the shadows for the box cars to arrive. When they did, Churchill, covered with coal dust, jumped out of his hiding place, and with Burnham, headed to the British Consulate.[29] After a chance to have a hot bath, burn his filthy clothes, and have some dinner, Churchill boarded a steamer headed to the British-controlled South African city of Durban.

The armored train incident was the ultimate confirmation of Churchill's quest for recognition through heroic—or perhaps hare-brained—exploits. By the time he arrived in Durban, his escape had become widely known, and a mob of well-wishers was there to greet him at the dock.

Almost immediately, Winston asked for and received an army commission and special permission to remain a war correspondent, a job that paid twelve times what he would have earned as a soldier. (As part of the deal, Churchill would receive no payment for his military service.[30]) Upon rejoining the army, Churchill continued to display gallantry and a desire to find fame. He participated in the renewed campaign to break the siege of Ladysmith and was there when the siege broke on the 168th day (February 28, 1900).[31] Later, he entered Pretoria and liberated the prison in which he had been held captive. On May 16 he published a book about his time in South Africa titled *London to Ladysmith via Pretoria*. It quickly became a bestseller.

Churchill would return to Britain in June 1900. But the war would continue until the Boers surrendered in 1902. The cost to Britain: thirty thousand dead and £250 million (some $111 billon in today's money).

3

Early Years in Parliament and Government 1900 through April 1908

The First Few Years
The Attack on Free Trade Begins
Churchill's Attack on P.M. Balfour and Its Consequences
Crossing the Floor—1904
Election of January 1906 and a New Job
Under-Secretary of State for the Colonies

The First Few Years

When Churchill returned to Britain in July 1900, he was a national hero. Conservative constituency associations from all over the country besieged him with offers to run for Parliament from their district in the general election scheduled for the fall. Owing to Britain's success in the Boer War, it was expected that the Conservative Party would do well in the election. Churchill decided to avenge his loss at Oldham just a year earlier. Churchill and his running mate believed they would easily unseat the two Radical Liberals who had finished ahead of them in Oldham's 1899 by-election.[1] They were wrong. In the election, held in October, Churchill finished a close second and was therefore elected, but his running mate finished fourth. Churchill's narrow victory notwithstanding, the nationwide vote was a landslide victory for Prime Minister Salisbury's Conservative/Unionist coalition.

Before 1911, members of Parliament received no pay as such. After election to the House of Commons in 1900, Churchill had to look for ways to make money. He quickly found one. He spent much of his time after being elected and before taking his seat on February 14, 1901, lecturing about his adventures while in South Africa throughout Britain and North America. He boasted about having earned £10,000 for these lectures. (About $1.4 million in today's dollars.) On this he believed he could live for four or five years,[2] and even help his forty-seven-year-old mother who, as usual, had money problems.[3]

Churchill's initial time in Parliament bore substantial similarity to the first years his father was in the House of Commons. That is, when his father, touted as one of the four or five greatest parliamentarians of the previous century,[4] was first elected in 1874, he joined a group of rebels known as the Fourth Party. Winston Churchill, during his first years in Parliament, was a member of a small group of aristocratic rebels nicknamed the "Hughligans"—"bright young men who were being rebellious in order to draw attention to themselves in the hopes of gaining office."[5] Soon, Winston would be their undisputed leader.

What Churchill may have lacked in formal education, he more than made up for in ambition.[6] Churchill did not wait long for a chance to rebel. In March 1901, William Broderick, the Secretary for War, announced that the Government intended to increase the size of the Army by 50 percent. Taking an opportunity to vindicate his father's memory, rather than supporting the Conservatives' position, Churchill proposed seriously *cutting* rather than increasing military spending and reducing income taxes.* By doing so he was able to stick it to both Lord Salisbury, the Prime Minister, who, in Churchill's view, had destroyed his father's career[7] and Secretary Broderick, who had also been a foe of his father's in 1886.[8] Churchill described himself as "a Conservative by tradition, whose fortunes are linked indissolubly to the Tory party." But he added that he still would argue for cuts in military spending "... for this is a cause I have inherited, and a cause for which [my father] made the greatest sacrifice of any minister in modern times."[9]

In 1902 he began research for a biography of his father—doing so reminded him yet again of the supposed ill-treatment his father suffered at the hands of the Conservative party hierarchy. Unsurprisingly, at best, Churchill had mixed feelings about the Tories.

Churchill would in no time establish himself as a speaker who was fast on his feet in Parliamentary debate—a rising political star.[10] He was making a name for himself "attacking the [Government's] mismanagement, or what he regarded as the misapplication of funds" appropriated by Parliament.[11] Liberal leader David Lloyd George wrote that "the applause of the House is the breath of his nostrils ..." However, famed biographer William Manchester disagrees with this assessment and points out that "Churchill wanted not approval, but attention. He didn't mind the boos. He expected them, for he was preparing to hoist the banner of rebellion."[12]

Churchill was more than willing to strengthen the Navy—but not the Army. See, e.g., HC Deb 13 May 1901 vol 93 cc1562–1579.

The Attack on Free Trade Begins

In mid-April 1902, Chancellor of the Exchequer Sir Michael Hicks-Beach proposed, as part of the budget for FY 1902, a small duty on imported corn, grain, flour, and meal.[13] The Liberals immediately saw this as a tax on food. But protectionist Tories applauded the new duties.[14]* In a speech to the House, Churchill stated his belief that this so-called Corn Tax would raise the whole question of free trade.[15] He was correct. Shortly after, the Hughligans had a dinner meeting with Joseph Chamberlain, the powerful leader of the Unionists, who, along with the Conservatives, made up the current Government. Chamberlain told the young MPs that tariffs were "the politics of the ... near future."[16] He could have added that adopting protectionist tariffs would be a matter of great contention. As promised, Churchill soon began to advocate against tariff reforms.

At the Colonial Conference, which started at the end of June, 1902, the Corn Tax was used as a lever to advance a case for the imposition of tariffs on imports from outside the British Empire—a so-called Imperial Preference. That said, right in the middle of the conference, Lord Salisbury, who had been in office for thirteen and a half of the preceding seventeen years, stepped down as Prime Minister.[17] Free Trade had been a fundamental tenant of British economic policy for a half-century. The issue of tariffs brought about a deep split in the ruling coalition. Besides the P.M., Chancellor of the Exchequer Hicks-Beach and two other cabinet members also resigned.[18] Salisbury's nephew, Arthur Balfour, succeeded him. Joseph Chamberlain, to whom Balfour had given the task of formulating tariff policy,[19] believed that he could bring the party around; and largely succeeded. There were, however, a few important holdouts—one of whom was the obstreperous young Winston Churchill.[20] As Churchill had told Balfour, "I am utterly opposed to anything that will alter the free-trade character of this country."[21] This was a position in which Churchill was substantially invested both "intellectually and emotionally."[22] Balfour, however, wanted to walk a middle course; Churchill was exasperated.[23] As Churchill's son writes in *Young Statesman*: "Throughout the summer [of 1902] Balfour took the sophisticated, urbane line that his colleagues should be permitted to differ, expound their views, and discover how the party reacted. The result was inevitable: lesions in the party grew."[24] In July, Churchill was one of the leaders of the approximately sixty rebel Conservative MPs that formed the Free Food League.[25]

Despite his general abhorrence of tariffs, Churchill voted for the budget. His son Randolph suggests that Churchill did so "because he knew that his father's old friend Hicks-Beach [who had sponsored the bill] was at heart a staunch Free Trader." Quoted in Randolph Churchill, Young Statesman p. 49.

In mid-May 1903, Joseph Chamberlain renewed his campaign for the "Imperial preference." Two weeks later, Churchill responded with a speech to the House arguing that Chamberlain's policy meant a "change ... in the conditions of our public life"[26] Just after that, he wrote an incredible letter to Prime Minister Balfour in which he promised "absolute loyalty" to the party if Balfour would pledge his support for free-trade.[27] Churchill also said that if Balfour had made up his mind to support tariff reform that he (Churchill) "must reconsider [his] position in politics."[28] Balfour's response missed the mark. He said only that he did not understand Joseph Chamberlain to be advocating protectionism.[29] Manchester reports that "[d]issent within Conservative ranks alarmed [Balfour] and he had been offended by Winston's tactics"[30] The fighting within the party over tariff reform would go on for years. Joseph Chamberlain even quit as Secretary of State for the Colonies in September 1903 to devote himself to the cause of Tariff reform.[31]

Churchill's Attack on P.M. Balfour and Its Consequences

On July 16, 1903, Churchill attacked Prime Minister Balfour, asserting that the P.M. was trying to silence Conservative/Unionist MPs who supported free trade.[32] When Balfour publicly came out in favor of tariffs in October 1903, Churchill accused him of turning his back on the principles of free trade, which he had endorsed when he became P.M. in 1902.[33] Balfour could have easily silenced Churchill months earlier. All he had to do was bring Churchill into the government—given him a position from which it would have been nearly impossible for him to criticize the Government's efforts at tariff reform and its budget requests for the Army.*

This is not to say that Churchill's attack on the leader of his own party was without consequences. In December, after Churchill endorsed a Liberal free trader in an adjacent by-election, the members of the Oldham Conservative Association passed a resolution saying that they had no longer had confidence in Churchill.[34] While he offered to resign, the Association told him he could finish out his term, even though by that point Churchill was

---

Such a tactic would be used or contemplated several times in Churchill's long career as a chief critic of his own party. One such instance occurred in December 1916 when Lloyd George thought about bringing Churchill into his Government but was overruled by his Conservative coalition-mates. Another was in 1939 when Neville Chamberlain did bring Churchill into his Cabinet as WWII commenced.

Had Balfour brought Churchill into the Government and thus tied his tongue about tariff reform, it would not have been possible for Churchill to have crossed the floor and become a Liberal in 1904. Randolph Churchill, Young Statesman p 50. Moreover, Churchill would more than likely have "gone down to defeat with the Tories in 1906 [and h]is whole career would have assumed a different path." Ibid. Once again, an event happened (or in this case, didn't happen) in Churchill's life for a reason that couldn't have possibly been understood then.

a Conservative in name only. He sat on the Conservative side of the House, but day after day continued to savage its leaders.[35] He was often called "a most infernal nuisance."[36] Churchill had come to embrace the Liberals' point of view on many issues including "wider suffrage, [the] eight-hour day, a graduated income tax, less expenditure on foreign and imperial affairs, [and most significantly] ... Irish Home Rule."[37]* In early April 1904, Churchill announced that in the next election he would run as a Free-Trade candidate (with Liberal support) in another district—Manchester North West.[38] He sensed that in the next election the Conservative Government would be swept out in a Liberal landslide.[39]

Crossing the Floor—1904

Churchill's official break with the Conservative/Unionists came on May 31, 1904. On that day, the twenty-nine-year-old Churchill, who had been in Parliament for sightly over three years, "crossed the floor." That is, he entered the House chamber as he always did and strode up the aisle. After bowing to the speaker, rather than turning left to the Government benches, he turned to his right and sat with the opposition—the Liberals.[40]* He seated himself next to Liberal leader Lloyd George, in the very same seat that his father had occupied when the Conservatives were the opposition. He "denied that ambition had played any role in his decision."[41] But most people did not believe him. Other rebel Conservatives would also soon take Churchill's path.

Churchill did not feel that he had any chance of ever returning to the party in which he had been raised since childhood—the party to which nearly all his family and friends belonged. Roberts says that "Churchill had paid a high price for his Free-Trade principles."[42] One of his closest friends would later maintain that had Churchill not crossed the floor in 1904, by 1914 "he would ... unquestionably have been the leader of the Conservative/Unionist party."[43]

While both Churchill and his father were rebellious MPs, there was one great distinction between the two—Lord Randolph never left the Conservative Party. Winston's loyalty was not nearly as great.** As we will see, throughout his career, loyalty to his party and the men who led it was not Winston's strong suit. For example, he could viciously attack a Government official

---

*By adopting the Irish Nationalist position, he disagreed with the Conservative/Unionists, the views of his father, and beliefs that he had held earlier in his life. He was now very much charting his own course. Churchill, My Early Life p. 367.

**As noted in Chapter 1, Churchill said that but for their commitment to Home Rule for the Irish, he would have entered Parliament as a Liberal in 1901. Ironically, not only would his opposition to Home Rule mellow over time, but in 1921 he would be one of the principal negotiators of the treaty by which Ireland's twenty-six southern counties were finally given freedom from Britain.

from his own party in the afternoon and think nothing of having dinner or a drink with him that evening. To him, there was nothing unusual that the two were from the same party. (Principle was more important than party.) Likewise, there was also nothing personal in such attacks, and he held few grudges. As he would say many years later about Neville Chamberlain, "I have not always agreed with [him], but we have always been personal friends."[44] That didn't mean that his victims (including Chamberlain) felt the same way. But ultimately, his loyalty to party leadership and what it engendered in return would prove critical when he had to face the biggest decision in his life thirty-six years later.

During the rest of 1904 and into 1905, Churchill continued to be an annoying critic of the Balfour Government. Among other things, he criticized the fact that the Viceroy of India, Lord Curzon, was being forced to leave India after he got into a disagreement over military reorganization with Lord Kitchener, the Commander-in-Chief who Churchill called a "military dictator."[45] Churchill's use of such biting invective even caused him to incur King Edward's wrath. Despite having been one of Jennie Churchill's lovers, Edward considered her older son to be a "born cad."[46]

Elections of January 1906 and a New Job

Balfour resigned on December 4, 1905. King Edward immediately called for Liberal leader Sir Henry Campbell-Bannerman, to establish a caretaker government for one purpose—to call a new election. Churchill was offered and accepted the non-cabinet position of Under-Secretary of State for the Colonies. Because the actual Secretary was a member of the House of Lords, his ability to deal with the Commons was limited. Churchill was ready, willing, and able to take on the responsibility. Although he had no administrative experience, he practically ran the Colonial office.

The new election began on January 12, 1906. Churchill set the tone of the election (and his efforts over the next few years) when he announced at a campaign gathering in Glasgow that it was the "duty of the Liberal Party to embrace the cause of 'the left-out millions'"[47] When the final results came in, the Liberals had won in a landslide, garnering 400 of the 670 seats in the House of Commons. Even former P.M. Balfour was caught in the Conservative debacle and lost his seat in Parliament. Churchill on the other hand, was elected from Manchester North West by a substantial margin.

Under-Secretary of State for the Colonies

When Churchill returned to the Colonial Office after the election, he was assigned the task of dealing with the two defeated Boer republics—Transvaal and the Orange Free State—that had surrendered in 1902, become British colonies, and were now seeking self-government. Self-government as soon as circumstances would permit was provided for in the Treaty of Vereeniging which ended the Boer War. As Churchill put it, the Liberals hoped for reconciliation; they did not want to build "upon the rivalry of races."[48]

Churchill managed to work out a basis for internal self-government: equal treatment for both Britons and Boers with voting based on universal adult white male suffrage. But the Boers were unwilling to do anything with regard to the treatment of the native population. Indeed, the treaty had specifically provided that there would be no discussion of allowing blacks the right to vote until after some self-government had been granted by the British. Thus, even though there was limited black voting in the British colony at the tip of Africa known as the Cape Colony, there was little that Churchill could do to bring it about in Transvaal and the Orange River colonies.

Several years later, in the South Africa Act of 1909, Parliament created the Union of South Africa (joining Transvaal, Orange River, Cape Colony, and Natal) and gave it self-governing Dominion status equivalent to that already achieved by other white-led former colonies—Canada (in 1867) Australia (in 1901) and New Zealand (in 1907). Under the Act, limited black voting could continue in the former Cape Colony. But over time, even that limited franchise was eliminated by the white citizens of the country.

Another problem that Churchill had to deal with was the mistreatment of some fifty thousand Chinese brought into South Africa to work the mines. The previous High Commissioner of South Africa, Lord Milner, held in high esteem by many Conservative/Unionist MPs, had permitted the corporal punishment of Chinese workers. Such floggings were, however, illegal and violated assurances given by the Government to China and the Parliament.[49] Churchill denounced the practice but refused to condemn the since-retired Milner.

The year 1906 was also one in which a larger problem began to emerge. The Liberals, now with a huge majority in the House of Commons, began to enact progressive, social welfare legislation. The Tory-controlled House of Lords strongly opposed change and started doing something that it had never done before—use its veto power to curtail such Liberal legislation. This would become much more serious in future years.

4

Early Years in the Cabinet
April 1908 through September 1911

Churchill's Appointment as President of the Board of Trade (1908) and
  the Ensuing By-elections
Churchill on Woman's Suffrage
Churchill as a Crusader for Social Welfare
Churchill on Defense Spending
Class Warfare
  • The Election of January 1910
  • The Parliament Bill
The Home Office—February 1910
  • Prison reform
  • Eugenics
  • Strikes, the Use of Troops, and the Tonypandy Riots
The General Election of December 2, 1910
Sidney Street
The Parliament Bill Is Enacted—August 1911
Britain Turns to Matters of Foreign Affairs

Churchill's Appointment as President of the Board of Trade (1908) and the Ensuing By-elections

In the summer of 1907, Churchill went on a five-month tour of the
African colonies. As was typical of Churchill, he agreed and was paid to
write five articles and a book about the trip.[1] Also nearly as typical, on the
trip he had at least two death-defying incidents—he was nearly killed by a
charging rhinoceros[2] and had a tsetse fly, possibly carrying incurable sleep-
ing sickness, brushed off his shoulder before it had a chance to bite him.[3]
While he was away, Prime Minister Campbell-Bannerman's health declined
substantially. Campbell-Bannerman would resign in early April 1908 and
pass away a few weeks later. His successor was Chancellor of the Exchequer
Henry Asquith. One of Asquith's first acts as Prime Minister was to ask the

thirty-three-year-old Churchill to serve in the Cabinet as President of the Board of Trade. Churchill accepted.

There was, however, a rule that required MPs who were newly appointed to a Cabinet post to resign from Parliament and stand for re-election before they could join the Cabinet. Although the rule was usually waived by the opposition, in Churchill's case, the Conservatives had no intention of doing so.* Much to Churchill's chagrin, he lost the by-election in Manchester by 529 votes.[4] His popularity in the party, however, quickly led to eight or nine other "safe" and quick opportunities for election back to the House. He chose the one in the working-class district of Dundee, Scotland. The Liberal MP from Dundee had just been given a peerage, elevating him to the House of Lords. There was a by-election to fill the vacancy.[5] Churchill ran in it, and just two weeks after his defeat in Manchester, was elected by a substantial margin. Once back as an elected member of the House he could and did fulfill his appointment as a Cabinet member—the youngest one in over four decades.[6]

Churchill on Woman's Suffrage

Churchill, like many Liberal candidates, first encountered the suffragettes during the run-up to the 1906 general election. The women believed that they could turn somewhat ambivalent Liberal MPs like Churchill to their side. Their approach was to interrupt campaign rallies, get arrested, and, upon refusing to pay the fine for disturbing the peace, spend time in jail where some even went on hunger strikes. Churchill's campaign in the 1908 by-election in Manchester was targeted. Women often resorted to interrupting his speeches by hissing, throwing tomatoes and eggs, and shouting out: "When are you going to give women the vote?"[7] So, too, during the campaigning in Dundee, he was again dogged by suffragettes who attempted to drown out his speeches by ringing bells and shouting.[8] Just before the election in January 1910, he was even assaulted in Bristol by a woman with a dog-whip.[9]

Shortly after, Churchill was approached about supporting a new non-party suffrage committee. He agreed. Although he refused to commit to any specifics, he wrote that he was "anxious to see women relieved in principle from a disability which is injurious to them. ..."[10] Still, when the committee wrote a bill that was introduced in the House, he opposed it. His problems with the bill stemmed from its granting the vote to only certain women—those who either earned a living or owned property. These were prerequisites that he felt were not only unfair and undemocratic but easily subject to abuse, such as permitting a woman to vote simply because she was given a token salary by her husband or father and allowing property-class women multiple votes if

---

This rule was abolished in 1926. Randolph Churchill, Young Statesman *p. 245.*

they had property in multiple districts.[11] Churchill's views notwithstanding, the bill made it through a second reading, but was doomed when Asquith dissolved Parliament in November 1910 and called for an election.

After the election, a second conciliation bill was introduced in May 1911. It contained none of the attributes of the first bill that Churchill had found objectionable. Although it received a favorable vote, no front-bench Liberal spoke during the debate and it was sent back to committee, where it languished.[12] On the matter of woman's suffrage, Churchill still had three significant questions:

1. Do women really want it?
2. Would it be for the good of the country to give it now?
3. Have the [voters] ever expressed any concise opinion?[13]

Although Asquith had always secretly opposed women's suffrage,[14] the suffragettes were temporarily appeased by a letter from him stating that the Government would meet the women's demands.[15] In November 1911, Asquith announced that he would introduce a bill in the next session of the House to extend the franchise to the many men who were excluded but would leave it to the members of the House whether that extension would include women. The suffragettes saw this as a huge step backward and were enraged. The war for woman's suffrage was back on—both figuratively and literally. But the suffragettes' return to violence did not help their cause. That is, when the Second Conciliation Bill finally emerged from committee in March 1912, it was defeated by a small margin even though Churchill voted for the bill.

Suffragettes did not campaign for the vote during World War I. Women would not get the vote in England until early 1918, when passage of the Representation of the People Act granted the franchise to women over thirty years old who met property qualifications. Interestingly, that legislation, as originally drafted, would have only removed property and other restrictions on the 40 percent of British men over twenty-one who were ineligible to vote.[16] But many members of Parliament, including Churchill, advocated for the inclusion of women in the bill.[17] It was, however, not until 1928 that the voting age for women was reduced to twenty-one and property ownership prerequisites were lifted.

Churchill as a Crusader for Social Welfare

Churchill became a Cabinet member during a time of economic decline, which led to reduced wages and to inevitable strikes. With this as a backdrop, he came to accept more Liberal positions on social welfare issues as he read and learned more about the plight of the downtrodden. The "intuitive rebel" was becoming more "humane."[18] And as a Liberal he was taking "Tory Democracy" to places Disraeli and his father never dreamed. With no inhibition about government having a role in solving social and economic problems, Churchill introduced legislation to do away with sweatshops in the clothing industry.[19] He, who was accused by many of being an alcoholic, even became a temperance advocate. Believing it would reduce the incidence of alcoholism, he supported legislation that would limit the number of pubs in Britain. Among other things, he and Lloyd George, who had become Chancellor of the Exchequer, worked to establish labor exchanges (places where the unemployed could meet potential employers), provide for old age pensions, expand national health care, and establish compulsory unemployment insurance.[20]* The Liberals' purview was expanding in response to growing industrialization and the problems that it brought about, as well as the effect of the depression of 1907–8. Given his strong anti-socialist views, Churchill nonetheless had little problem committing to at least "a form of Liberal collectivism."[21] These social reforms, as progressive as they were, were only some of the radical positions Churchill, Lloyd George, and the Liberals had in mind.

Churchill on Defense Spending

As Manchester writes, "If it is difficult to accept Churchill as a grandfather of the welfare state, it is even harder to picture him fighting plans to arm England against saber-rattling Germans."[22] But he did. That is, even though back in 1904, Britain had entered into an informal alliance with France to rebuff any possible German aggression, Churchill, along with others in the Cabinet, were of the unpopular belief that defense spending should be kept low. Among other things, they fought unsuccessfully against building six new dreadnoughts.[23]** As we will see, over the next thirty years when the subject was defense spending, Churchill's position was subject to great swings—he would shift from being parsimonious to being a spendthrift and back again several times. The first of these swings toward increased defense

---

Before this, Parliament had enacted relatively little, if any, social reform legislation. Manchester, Visions p. 371.

In 1908, Churchill and Lloyd George were called the "terrible twins of Social Reform" Randolph Churchill, Young Statesman p. 238. Throughout Churchill's time as President of the Board of Trade he was enthralled by Lloyd George. Roberts, p. 131. Over time, Churchill's relationship with Lloyd George would, however, blow hot and cold.

**Battleships similar to the Royal Navy's HMS Dreadnaught launched in 1906.*

spending would occur in 1911 when he became convinced that the Kaiser was a menace.[24]*

Class Warfare

The more he tried to help the wage-earning class, the more Churchill also began attacking the upper class and the Conservatives. In early 1909, he described the Conservatives as "the party of the rich against the poor. ... of the lucky, the wealthy, the happy, and the strong against the left-out and the shut-out millions of the weak and poor."[25] Soon after that, Lloyd George "unleash[ed a] naked class war" by introducing a revolutionary bill, dubbed the People's Budget, that would, among other things, increase income taxes generally, but impose also a special tax on high-income earners, and increase taxes on luxury items like autos.[26] To say that the bill was disfavored by the upper class would be an understatement.

The social reforms and plans to effectively reallocate some of the wealth of society's highest echelon were still merely a prelude to something larger. Churchill and the Liberals wanted to strip the unelected House of Lords of its power to veto legislation passed by the elected members of the House of Commons. Historically, the Lords did this rarely. There was a reason why. Until this point, regardless of party, the members of both houses had similar backgrounds (elite boarding school education, degrees from prestigious universities, upper class) and similar ideas and values, particular about treatment of the working class. The Asquith Government was changing that. It and the Liberal majority that supported it wanted change—something at odds with the position of the appropriately named Conservative members of the House of Lords. Indeed, the House of Lords had started to block or seriously dismember Liberal social legislation. Because of Churchill's aristocratic background and his having turned his back on the Conservatives, his association with the Liberals' ideas (not to mention his sharp attacks on the wealthy) made him a prime target for denunciation by the Tories.[27] Even Liberal Prime Minister Asquith felt that Churchill's remarks about the uncaring rich had crossed the line.[28] The rest of the Tories not only considered him a traitor to the Conservative Party, but they also believed him to be a "traitor to his class" and "utterly contemptible."[29] King Edward VII even had his secretary write *The Times* complaining about Churchill's invectives against the well-to-do, even though doing so was unconstitutional.[30] For Churchill, all this was tough to take. Fearing he might wilt in response,

---

While he may have oscillated on spending for war, he never lost his fascination with it. From 1907 through 1910, he attended many great military maneuvers held in England, France, and Germany.

more than once, his wife, Clementine, urged him not to let the epithets of the Tories cause him to change his course.[31]

The People's Budget, slightly moderated, was approved by the House on November 4, 1909. But would the House of Lords veto it? During the debate in the House, the Government, in the person of Mr. Churchill, had made it clear that if the Budget were to be rejected by the Lords, that Asquith would immediately call for a general election.[32] Churchill should have saved his breath. On November 30, the Lords overwhelmingly rejected the Budget. This was the first time they had ever supplanted the spending prerogatives of the Commons.[33] As promised, Asquith immediately dissolved Parliament and called for an election starting on January 14, 1910. Whether the House of Lords should be stripped of this power, would now be put before the voters.

During the election campaign, some believed the King had promised Asquith that, if necessary, he would pack the House of Lords with hundreds of new Liberal peers. But a review of communications between the secretaries for the King and Asquith's staff has revealed that the King would not do so until after a second election had taken place.

The Election of January 1910

When the votes of the January election were counted, the Liberals had lost 104 seats, and no longer held a majority. They did, however, still have more seats than any other party (274 to the Conservatives' 272) and managed to form a coalition government with help from the Irish Nationalist Party. Indeed, but for the help of the Irish Nationalists, who controlled seventy-one seats, the Liberals would likely have been out. Such critical assistance did not come cheap—the Liberals had to pledge support for Irish Home Rule, something for which abolition of the House of Lords' veto power would also likely be needed. As for Churchill, running from what was said to be a "safe" Liberal seat in Dundee,[34] he was re-elected, but by fewer than four hundred votes. Several days later, Asquith offered Churchill the non-cabinet position of Chief Secretary of Ireland.[35] Churchill responded that the office did not attract him. In fact, "many circumstances connected with it ... repell[ed him]." Churchill also made it known that he would prefer the Admiralty or the Home Office.[36] His argument was that "ministers should occupy a position in the Government which corresponds to some extent with their influence in the country."[37] Asquith capitulated and made him Home Secretary. But he would only serve in that position for nineteen months.

The Parliament Bill

In the middle of March 1910, Asquith declared that "the House of Lords must be rebuilt on a democratic basis."[38] Soon after, Lloyd George introduced the "Parliament Bill," which would take away the House of Lords' ability to veto any bill dealing with money that the Commons had appropriated. Fearing these changes, within hours of the House's adoption of the People's Budget, the House of Lords did the same.[39] Even so, the Liberals continued to press the Parliament Bill. Churchill felt that a consensus could be reached with the Conservatives, not only about reforming the House of Lords, but also on other difficult matters such as Home Rule for Ireland, compulsory state-assisted National Insurance, and a military draft.[40] He was wrong. Asquith, on the other hand, believed that if the Lords rejected the Parliament Bill, King Edward would use his prerogative and create hundreds of new members of the House of Lords. But King Edward died on May 6, 1910 and thus was never put to the test.

The Home Office—February 1910

The scope of Churchill's duties as Home Secretary were equal—if not greater—than those he had as President of the Board of Trade, yet Churchill could not refrain from trying to run more ministries than just the one he officially administered. Broadly stated, his actual duties as Home Secretary were to maintain law and order and oversee the police, the courts, the prisons, immigration, mine safety, and social services (such as they were).

Prison Reform

As Home Secretary, he was required to review every criminal case in which the defendant had been sentenced to death and determine whether the sentence should be commuted to life imprisonment. Churchill, who supported the death penalty, considered this to be the hardest part of his job.[41] Interestingly, in the decade before Churchill became Home Secretary, his predecessors had commuted the sentence in 40 percent of the death penalty cases reviewed.[42] But during his term, Churchill commuted nearly 50 percent.[43] Churchill also championed prison reform. He ended the practice of flogging and created prison libraries.[44] He also wanted to reduce Britain's prison population by releasing prisoners whose real "crime" was being poor and thus not paying a fine, especially one for drunkenness, on time.[45] Reducing the penalty for minor offenses, particularly if committed by children, was also part of his plan. Churchill's reforms proved successful. In the end, the number of Britons incarcerated plummeted.

Eugenics

The humanity shown in such actions to help the working class was harder to find in other aspects of Churchill's thinking. For example, he was briefly enamored with eugenics and even helping draft legislation calling for the permanent incarceration of "the feeble minded" and "moral defectives."[46] Churchill's views were not controversial at the time. They were also held by people such as science fiction writer H.G. Wells and the great economist John Maynard Keynes. Moreover, the Mental Deficiency Act of 1913 passed overwhelmingly.[47] Under it, approximately sixty-five thousand people were institutionalized. Within a couple of decades, these repulsive ideas would be championed by men like Hitler, Goering, and Goebbels, Churchill's archest enemies.

Strikes, the Use of Troops, and the Tonypandy Riots

Another aspect of Churchill's duties as Home Secretary was to maintain order during several hard-fought and violent strikes during his term. Such labor unrest was unlike anything ever seen in Britain.[48] The combination of a continuingly weak economy, high unemployment, and the substantial growth of trade unionism made a volatile mix. The question in the Home Office was often whether to call in the military—something Churchill did not want to do.[49] The most famous incident during Churchill's tenure was Tonypandy—a November 1910 strike in Wales involving thirty thousand coal miners, some of whom had rioted.

Local authorities asked London to send in troops. Churchill instead dispatched police constables and demanded that the rioting cease. He withheld troops, saying that the use of soldiers was inappropriate in a civil disorder. But the rioting did not stop, and one man was killed. The rioters looted and destroyed many shops in Tonypandy. At that point, without Churchill's permission, the officer in charge of the regional command dispatched four hundred soldiers to the tiny mining town. But Churchill did not recall them. Even though he ordered that the soldiers not come in direct contact with rioters unless the police had taken action, he was still viewed by many as having breached his word about not sending in troops against the striking miners. This view would still exist thirty years later when Churchill was being considered for Prime Minster.

Churchill did order in troops to help quell riots on several other occasions. In August 1911, when he felt he had no alternative,[50] Churchill even placed armed troops at the disposal of local commanders to help end a nationwide rail strike that halted much of the country's food deliveries. As he told Parliament: if the strike were not ended, Britain would be "hurled ... into an abyss of horror which no man can dare to contemplate. ..."[51] Because Churchill permitted the use of troops to break the strike, the public forgot about all his work on social reform and labor supporters soundly criticized him.[52] That said, Churchill was not a foe of organized labor. Among other things, in 1913 he helped in getting a bill passed that allowed trade unions to lobby and make political contributions.[53] He also publicly advocated that "every workmen ... join a trade union,"[54] calling unions "the bulwarks of our industrial system."[55]

The General Election of December 2, 1910

With the question of the Lords' veto power of legislation passed by the House still unresolved, in November 1910 Asquith once again dissolved Parliament and called for a new election (the second in 1910). This one was to be held between December 2–29, 1910. The results: both the Liberals and Conservatives/Unionists each won 272 seats. The Liberals again formed a coalition government with the Irish Nationalist Party and Asquith continued as Prime Minister.

Sidney Street

In the middle of the voting, a group of Latvian anarchists perpetrated a string of bank messenger ambushes and tried to tunnel into a jewelry store. In the process they had killed three police officers and wounded several more. Churchill wanted the anarchists captured, not only to bring them to the justice they deserved but also to exonerate the Liberal Party, whose refusal to restrict immigration was thought by many to have abetted the violence.[56] The group was spotted again on January 3, 1911. Heavily armed, they were trapped in a house on Sidney Street in London's East End. A shooting-filled armed siege was taking place between the anarchists and the police. Churchill could not resist—he headed to Sidney Street to see the action. He did not take command of the situation but recommended that the police use some nearby steel plates as portable cover.[57]* (This resembled the armored train back in South Africa. Moreover, the anarchists were using high quality German rifles made by Mauser, just as the Boers had used a decade earlier.)

When the Sidney Street house caught fire unexpectedly, firefighters wanted to put out the fire, but Churchill approved the police's decision to do nothing.[58] He did not want to "spend good British lives in rescuing these ferocious rascals."[59] Two charred bodies were found in the ruins. The whole thing was incredibly exciting to Churchill. But the unnecessary presence of the Home Secretary on Sidney Street once again raised questions about Churchill's judgment.[60] People were sure that he simply could not resist any chance to appear heroic.[61] He recognized that he had been wrong to go to the scene[62]—to succumb to his natural instinct—one that would rear its head many times in future years. But the damage had been done. Sidney Street was just one more black mark, among many, against his judgment. The photographs and films of Churchill at the scene likewise proved harmful

---

*From this, Churchill's idea for a tank was conceived. Daily News *January 4, 1911.*

both to him personally and to the Liberals. When the newsreels were shown of "Mr. Churchill directing the operations," they were met with boos, cat-calls, and shouts blaming him for letting the terrorists into the country in the first place.[63]

The Parliament Bill Is Enacted—August 1911

The Parliament Bill was debated in the House in early April 1911 and was finally passed on August 10. Churchill had been greatly involved in working out language in the final bill tolerable to most Liberals and Conservatives. But to hardline Tories and members of the upper class, his efforts did nothing except increase the animus they felt toward him.[64]

Britain Turns to Matters of Foreign Affairs

With that fight over, Asquith's interest quickly turned from domestic matters to foreign affairs. In late August 1911, he met with the Committee of Imperial Defence to discuss Britain's plans in the event of German aggression against France. Asquith was not pleased with the existing situation, which he felt was chaotic. He believed that he had to move Churchill to the Admiralty to sort things out. At the end of September 1911, he officially asked Churchill to do so.

Churchill with the Royal Scots Fusiliers
in Ploegstreet, Flanders 1916

5

September 1911–December 1918 The Admiralty, WWI, Gallipoli, and Its Aftermath

Churchill Becomes First Lord of the Admiralty
WWI
Antwerp (1914)
The Dardanelles/Gallipoli Campaign (1915)
- Phase 1
- Phase 2a
Churchill Is Removed from the Admiralty/Asquith Government Is
  Brought Down/Asquith Forms Coalition with the Conservatives
Phase 2b of the Dardanelles/Gallipoli Campaign
Churchill Quits the Government to Command an Infantry Battalion
  in France
- Another Display of Bad Judgment
Churchill Returns to England
The Dardanelles Commission
The Collapse of the Asquith Government/The Start of the Lloyd George
  Government
No Place for Churchill
Minister of Munitions

Churchill Becomes First Lord of the Admiralty

On September 30, 1911, Churchill took office as the First Lord of the Admiralty. What he faced and what he accomplished in that position would play an important part in how Britons would view him over the next twenty years and beyond. On the positive side, he would be thought of as the man who got the Royal Navy ready for the Great War. On the negative side, he would be also remembered as the foolhardy minister who ran off to Belgium to personally lead troops in the defense of Antwerp. More permanently, he would, unfairly, also always be thought of as the man behind the debacle known as Gallipoli.

As late as mid-May 1911, Churchill believed that war between Britain and Germany was "unthinkable."[1] However, during the summer of 1911 a seemingly unprovocative event—the appearance of a small German warship in a Moroccan harbor—quickly embroiled France, Italy, the Ottoman Empire, and discontented nationalities in the Balkans and Russia in a series of actions that moved the world closer to war, and caused Churchill to do an about-face.[2] His years in the Cabinet had well-positioned him to examine Britain's strategic plans in the event of German aggression. As Anthony McCarten* writes, Churchill was promoted to First Lord of the Admiralty as the man that "Asquith wanted to shake up the Navy."[3] Traditionally, the role of the First Lord was to take the advice of the Board of Admiralty on almost all matters and protect the Navy when it came to appropriations.[4] Churchill would be different. Yes, he would be a strong advocate for the Royal Navy, but not one to accept its positions without inquiry. A first impression of Churchill in his new position was "[a] bit impetuous, but extraordinarily hard working."[5]

He also started giving pointed speeches about the dangers posed by German naval expansion. To most, any such threat still seemed "far off."[6] Even Lloyd George, the newly appointed Chancellor of the Exchequer and Churchill's friend, talked about Germany's being a peace-loving nation. As McCarten writes, Churchill "found himself a lone sabre-rattler on the beach as the tide washed up a sudden sea of pacifists."[7] Nevertheless, advocating a policy of building 60 percent more warships than Germany, he got annual spending on the Royal Navy increased by 28 percent (from £39 million to £50 million).[8] Churchill had come a long way from the parsimonious view of defense spending he had when he was President of the Board of Trade, just three years earlier.

WWI

In June 1914, Archduke Franz Ferdinand, the heir to the Austro-Hungarian throne, was assassinated in Sarajevo, the capital of Bosnia, by a group of Serbian nationals. In retaliation, Austria-Hungary decided to destroy Serbia once and for all for stirring up trouble among ethnic Slavs. Russia, led by Czar Nicholas II, intervened to protect Serbia, despite there being no treaty requiring Russia to do so. The Czar had the support of the President of France. Russia mobilized its army against Austria-Hungary. France did

---

*Author of Darkest Hour *and the screenplay for the movie of the same name.*

likewise. In early August, Germany declared war on Russia and France, and invaded France through Belgium. Seventy-five years earlier, Britain, France, and Prussia (the predecessor of the German Empire) had signed the Treaty of London guaranteeing Belgium's sovereignty. Based on that agreement, Britain issued an ultimatum to the Germans for it to remove troops from neutral Belgium by midnight on August 3. When the ultimatum expired, Britain declared war on Germany. But the underlying reason for Britain's entry into the war was to prevent a French defeat that would have left Germany in control of Western Europe.

Antwerp (1914)

In early September 1914, German forces in Belgium had begun to advance on Antwerp. The Belgians asked for help in staving off the advance. France promised support, but in the end sent only half the number of troops it had promised. British forces would take time to mobilize. Antwerp was a critical fortress—one necessary to prevent the Germans from gaining access to the Channel. Lord Herbert Kitchener, Secretary of State for War, feared that if the enemy reached the Channel at Calais in northwest France an invasion of England would be feasible.

Churchill knew that the Royal Navy had twenty to thirty thousand reservists yet to be assigned to ships. With Kitchener's approval, Churchill molded this force into a new Royal Naval Division (RND)—an infantry force strangely under the control of the Admiralty, not the Army.[9] Churchill proposed sending the RND to defend Antwerp "until it could be relieved by a new regular corps ... that was not yet quite ready to deploy."[10] As the news from Antwerp got worse, although highly irregular, it was agreed that Churchill should take the RND there and help hold the city until reinforcements arrived. Churchill told the Belgians that he was bringing over eight thousand members of the RND. But the men were raw recruits.[11] The RND arrived in Antwerp on October 5. Churchill soon sent a letter from Antwerp to the Cabinet in which he said that "... because [he was] sure this arrangement will afford the best prospects of a victorious result," he was willing to resign his position in the Cabinet and take full command of the forces at Antwerp.[12] The thought of the First Lord of the Admiralty rushing off to Antwerp to personally save the besieged city was bewildering to the Cabinet and every other Briton.[13] Accordingly, Churchill's offer was declined and he returned to England. Despite the efforts of the RND, Antwerp fell on October 10, 1914. It was, however, surprising that, with only the green RND troops defending it, the city endured that long.[14]

Shortly after Churchill's return to London, criticism of his actions in Antwerp started. The *Morning Post* on October 19 caustically reminded him that he was not "a Napoleon, but a Minister of the Crown with no time to organize or lead armies in the field. ..."[15]* The leader of the Conservative Party, Andrew Bonar Law, said that Churchill "seems to have an entirely unbalanced mind which is a real danger at a time like this."[16] His supposed friend Lloyd George even commented that "Churchill went to the front waiving his sword, but the net result was [only] that the evacuation was delayed a few days, that the Belgians lost twenty thousand men interned and that Antwerp was half ruined."[17]

Well before the dust had settled over his antics in Antwerp, Churchill had turned his attention to what became the misadventure of his life—the Dardanelles/Gallipoli campaign.

The Dardanelles/Gallipoli Campaign (1915)

The Dardanelles/Gallipoli campaign was a millstone that Churchill would undeservedly wear around his neck from 1915 until the day he died. Even today, many decades after his death, a recounting of the many accomplishments in his life is frequently accompanied by "but, of course, there was also Gallipoli." This is said to question Churchill's judgment by some people who may not even know where Gallipoli is, what happened there in 1915, and most importantly, why it happened.

Turkey is a country that lies mostly in Asia, but it does have a portion in Europe. The two parts are divided by connecting waterways that run from the Mediterranean northeasterly to the Black Sea—the famous Dardanelle straits (41 miles long and between one and four miles wide), the Sea of Marmara and the Bosporus (a 19-mile strait that is straddled by Istanbul, which in 1915 was still called Constantinople). The Bosporus opens to the Black Sea. The portion of the country on the European (western) shore of the Dardanelles is the Gallipoli Peninsula. A military force holding the peninsula would dominate the Dardanelles.

Because the Dardanelles is the only shipping route between Britain, France, and Russia, as well as Romania and Bulgaria, it was, as it always has been, a waterway having substantial military and commercial significance.

In an essay he would write seventeen years later, Churchill agreed that "I ought to have remained in London." Churchill, Thoughts and Adventures pp. 11–12.

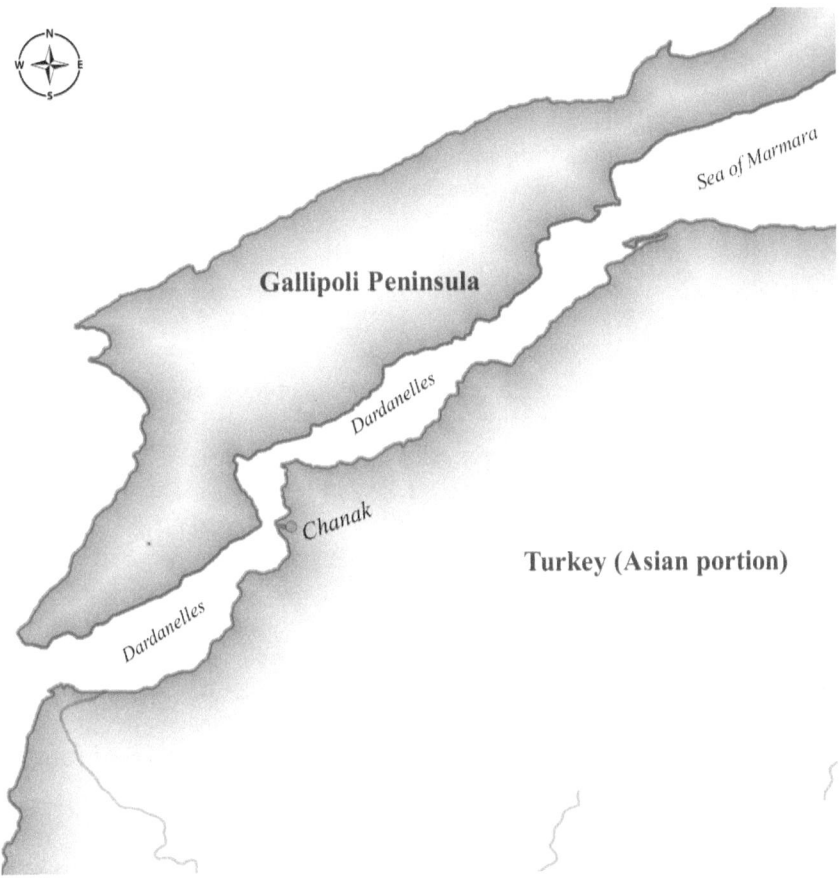

When World War I broke out in August 1914, Turkey was part of the Ottoman Empire and neutral, at least for the moment. Nevertheless, given the importance of the Dardanelles, Churchill sought to form a group of Generals and Admirals to work out a plan for a Greek army of adequate size to seize the lightly defended Gallipoli Peninsula, ensure that the Dardanelles remained open to Allied shipping,[18] and thus allow Britain to take Constantinople.[19]

But before any of this could happen, with German assistance, the Dardanelles was mined and declared closed. The Ottoman Empire then entered the war on Germany's side. As a result, the Dardanelles was off limits to all Allied shipping. This cut lines of communication between Britain, France, and Russia and significantly hampered getting goods, including food stuffs and military equipment, to and from Russia.[20] Tons of grain needed to feed the Allies were piled up in Russian ports along the Black Sea. In normal times, almost all of Russia's grain export and a good portion of its other exports passed through the Dardanelles.[21]

In the months before the Dardanelles/Gallipoli campaign, the British and French were engaged in intense trench warfare with the Germans in France. While neither side was gaining an advantage, the fighting was producing huge casualties—"[b]y the end of November 1914 Britain and France had suffered nearly one million casualties."[22] The Allies needed every man they could lay their hands on; none could be spared from the fighting in France. As such, an attack on the Dardanelles was at first viewed as peripheral, although it ultimately gained War Council approval in January 1915.

The Dardanelles/Gallipoli campaign had two phases. The key players in each were not the same. The reasons why each phase failed also differed. If there was anything consistent in the phases, it was that each was run by committee and almost every committee member vacillated about almost every detail. Particularly with Phase 1, key elements of the plan remained in flux almost to the end. While Churchill was the original proponent of the Dardanelles/Gallipoli campaign and its "most visible advocate, and its most eloquent spokesman"[23]; he ultimately had little control over the campaign and certainly was not the cause of its demise. If any criticism of him is warranted it is that, when his superiors withdrew the bulk of the troops scheduled for the operation in Phase 1, Churchill ignored his trepidations about proceeding without them. That he was a man with no physical fear of dying,[24] was constantly willing to risk his life, and had a remarkable record of coming out unscathed, may have prevented him from appreciating the true perils of the Royal Navy's trying to force the Dardanelles without adequate troop support.* Engaging in activities where there was a substantial risk of injury or even death was something Churchill had done even as a child.[25] That said, his innate equanimity about death was likely heightened by the recognition, common among soldiers like himself, of the absolute randomness of death in wartime—something that, as he said, "makes one suspect a bigger plan" is at work.[26] Churchill could walk in the Valley of the Shadow of Death without fear. But did he realize or care how fearful those walking with him were, especially when he was the one who ordered the walk in the first place?

Phase 1

After the Ottoman Empire entered the war, worried about the security of Egypt, Churchill asked First Sea Lord Jackie Fisher to investigate the

---

Discussed further in Chapter 20.

Gallipoli is hardly the only time Churchill may have failed to appreciate the true danger of a situation. His adventure with the armored train during the Boer War is another.

possibilities of using the Royal Navy to bombard Turkish sea forts along the Dardanelles and open the straits.[27] Fisher was a retired Admiral of the Fleet who, like Churchill, was a favorite among average Britons.[28] Over the objection of the King, Churchill had just brought Fisher out of retirement to serve as an adviser. In time, Churchill would come to regret having done so.

Per Churchill's request, Fisher immediately went to the Dardanelles and was onboard a British warship when she shelled one of the Turkish forts. During the ten-minute engagement, a shell hit the fort's magazine. "The fort and most of its guns" were destroyed in the ensuing explosions.[29] As a result, Fisher believed the prospects of success via a naval bombardment to be excellent.

Back in 1807, the British had forced open the Dardanelles using only naval power.[30] More recently, however, both Churchill and Fisher had written negatively about replicating that feat. In 1904 Fisher had described any plan to attack the Dardanelles using only naval forces as "mightily hazardous,"[31] while in 1911, Churchill had written the Cabinet that "it is no longer possible to force the Dardanelles [with only the Navy]. Nobody would expose a modern fleet to such perils."[32] In 1914, Churchill believed that "the price to be paid in taking Gallipoli would no doubt be heavy but there would be no more war with Turkey. *A good army of 50,000 & sea-power*—that is the end of the Turkish menace."[33] [emphasis added]

It was based on a combined army-navy operation that, at the War Council meeting on November 25, 1914, Churchill had first floated the idea of forcing the Dardanelles, sailing all the way up to Constantinople and taking the city either by naval bombardment, occupation, or both. Such an operation would not only have opened the Dardanelles from the Mediterranean to the Black Sea, but it would also have cut off Turkey's head and gotten her out of the war. As noted, Churchill's original intention was to have the Greeks provide ground troops to support the operation, but continued Greek neutrality rendered that impossible.[34] Without ground troops, Prime Minister Asquith was "altogether opposed" to proceeding.[35] Churchill's desire for a campaign in the Dardanelles notwithstanding, in a letter to Admiral Fisher on December 22, 1914, he said that he agreed with Asquith.[36] Fisher replied that he favored an attack on the Dardanelles but only if it could be done immediately with seventy-five thousand British troops.[37] But there were no troops available for the proposed operation.

World events would soon intervene in the debate. Russia, which had suffered major defeats at the hands of the Germans in East Prussia and lost a million men, was, in November 1914, being threatened by the Turks in the Caucasus. The Russians advised that if the Turkish drive there continued, its Army would have to turn away from fighting the Germans, and deal with the Turks. Unfortunately for Britain and France, were that to occur, some of the German troops that had been fighting the Russians could then be shifted to the fighting in France.[38] Such being the case, it became important for the Allies to prevent this by knocking Turkey out of the war. Lord Kitchener immediately talked to Churchill about a naval operation against the Dardanelles.

Churchill, who still thought that troops would need to accompany the Royal Navy on any such mission, discussed Kitchener's suggestion with his senior admirals, each of whom agreed that troops were necessary to carry it out.[39] Before breaking this bad news to Kitchener, on January 3, 1915, Churchill asked Vice Admiral Sir Sackville Carden, the recently installed commander of British naval forces in the Mediterranean, whether he believed that the Dardanelles could be forced open with a fleet of older battleships.[40] Admiral Carden responded on January 5, saying that he believed the Dardanelles "might be forced by extended operations with large number of ships."[41] Churchill and the Sea Lords were "startled"; Admiral Fisher even "enthusiastically volunteered to send Carden the Royal Navy's newest superdreadnought, the *Queen Elizabeth,* whose huge 15-inch guns had not even been fired yet."[42] Because of Carden's telegram, Churchill's reservations about a naval-only operation temporarily dissipated.

On January 8, 1915, Kitchener read a report to the War Council from the War Department. It said that "The Dardanelles appeared to be the most suitable objective, as an attack here could be made *in coordination with the Fleet.*"[43] [emphasis added] Kitchener agreed. He believed that the operation could be done with one hundred and fifty thousand men. Lloyd George, then Minister of Munitions, thought it would require more.[44] What did it matter though? There were no men available—they were all need for the fighting in France.

All this changed three days later. On January 11, Vice Admiral Carden came up with the details of his all-naval plan for the Dardanelles. Under it, battleships would shell Turkish forts on the peninsula from ten thousand yards out, after which a passage would be swept through the minefield laid to block the straits.[45] To accomplish all this, Carden wanted a flotilla of thirty-five surface ships, six submarines, twelve minesweepers, and lots of ammunition.[46]

After discussing Carden's plan with Asquith and Kitchener, Churchill presented it to the War Council on January 13. Not only did Asquith and Kitchener embrace the plan, but so did all other members of the Council. (In fact, on hearing of the plan, France even agreed to send four battleships).[47] The War Council unanimously issued a directive:

> That the Admiralty should prepare for a naval expedition in February to bombard and take the Gallipoli peninsula with

Constantinople as its objective. *Companion Volumes* III /1
p. 411

Unfortunately, the wording of the Council's directive did not make sense; only the Army (not the Navy) could take an objective like the Gallipoli or Constantinople.

Even though he had participated in every step culminating in the War Council's decision, just a few days later, Admiral Fisher urged the recall of the flotilla sent to the Dardanelles. He asserted that those ships were needed in the Home waters.[48] Fisher also wrote to the Admiral of the Fleet, objecting to the Dardanelles operation, unless the operation included 200,000 troops.[49] These and similar actions that Fisher would take in the ensuing few weeks, such as his frequent threats to resign, were taken as "signs of mental aberration."[50] Fisher's protestations notwithstanding, Churchill proceeded with Admiral Carden's plan as approved by the War Council.

While all this was happening in London, one of the reasons for continuing the Dardanelles operation, which was to prevent Russia from being diverted from fighting Germany by a Turkish drive against her in the Caucasus, disappeared.[51] That is, from late December 1914 until January 17, 1915, the Russians and the Turks had been engaged in the Battle of Sarikamish in the Caucasus. Ill-prepared for winter conditions, the Turks suffered a major defeat. Accordingly, the Turks no longer constituted a threat to Russia. Nevertheless, now with a seeming life of its own, the proposed all-naval Dardanelles/Gallipoli campaign remained on track.

Some thought Churchill was "ignorant" to believe that he could capture the Dardanelles without troops.[52] If for no other reason, troops would be needed to occupy any forts that the Navy had razed and did not want the Turks to retake.[53] While Churchill was musing about the fact that the Royal Navy had forced open the Dardanelles with a minimal loss of life back in 1807 and Carden's all-naval plan, his concerns about the all-navy scheme returned. Moreover, Carden was also not the man that Churchill had wanted for the job. He was approaching sixty and lacked the temperament of a fighter. Churchill wanted a younger admiral who was both extremely knowledgeable about the Dardanelles and assertive.[54]

Although the expedition had yet to be formally authorized by the War Council, the remnants of the Royal Naval Division that Churchill had led in Antwerp were sent to the campaign's staging area on the Greek Island of Lemnos (located near the mouth of the Dardanelles). As chance would have it, the 29th Division, whose availability for the Dardanelles/Gallipoli campaign had been bandied about for some time, was not going to be used in a planned expedition with the Greeks. Hearing this, Prime Minister Asquith called an emergency meeting of the War Council. At the meeting, Kitchener agreed that the 29th should participate in the Gallipoli campaign. It set sail for Lemnos immediately. Also headed there would be a Marine brigade as well as troops from Australia and New Zealand who were stationed in Egypt. Kitchener advised Churchill, "You get through! I will find the men."[55]

But just a few days later, on February 19, Kitchener told the War Council that he had decided against sending both "the nineteen thousand trained men of the Twenty-ninth Division and the thirty thousand Australians and New Zealanders in Egypt."[56] Efforts to change his mind made by Asquith, Churchill, and Lloyd George were of no avail. Greatly concerned at this turn of events, Churchill had an extraordinary memo entered into the Council's minutes:

> "[Mr. Churchill] wished it to be placed on record that ... [i]f a disaster occurred in Turkey owing to the insufficiency of troops, he must disclaim all responsibility."[57]

Prime Minister Asquith also became rather anxious about the campaign and the fact that it would not be supported by the Army, but he was not willing to overrule Kitchener on a military question.[58] Critically, on February 25, despite Kitchener's having denied the campaign some 50,000 troops, Churchill embraced the naval-only approach wholeheartedly and informed the War Council that "With proper military and naval cooperation, and *with forces which are available,* we can make certain of taking Constantinople by the end of March, and capturing or destroying all Turkish forces in Europe."[59] [emphasis added]

Churchill was wrong. Years later he would write:

> It seems clear now that when Lord Kitchener went back upon his undertaking to send the 29th Division to reinforce the army gathering in Egypt for the Dardanelles expedition ... *I should have been prudent then to have broken off the naval attack.* It would have been quite easy to do ... I did not do it, and from that moment I became accountable for their operation the vital control of which had passed to other hands.[60] [emphasis added]

He also indicated had he known that ultimately eighty to one hundred thousand troops would be made available (as they were in May) there never would have been any navy-only effort.[61]

On February 13, the warships detailed to the flotilla assembled off Cape Helles, a rocky headland at the southwest tip of the Gallipoli Peninsula. Admiral Carden commenced the shelling of forts on the peninsula on February 19 and had good success. Based on this encouraging news, in

London, spirits, including Churchill's, were high.[62] The bombardment of Turkish forts would continue sporadically for the next month with the grand assault scheduled for March 17. But as that date approached, things began to unravel. On March 12, British minesweepers reached Kephez Point, the first of three places where the Dardanelles narrows substantially. There, Turkish artillery turned them back. After that, Admiral Carden had "something akin to a mental breakdown."[63] Command then fell to the next most senior officer, Admiral John de Robeck, someone who had his doubts about the operation.[64] Still, de Robeck ordered the flotilla to force the straits on March 18.

At the start of the battle, the British ships fared well. Keeping beyond the range of the Turkish guns, they destroyed Turkish forts on both the Gallipoli and the Asian sides of the Dardanelles without sustaining any damage.[65] In the early afternoon, Admiral de Robeck planned to sweep a path through the remaining mines in the Dardanelles and steam northeast into the Sea of Marmara.[66] Then trouble started—the French battleship *Bouvet* hit a mine and sank in minutes with a loss of almost all of its 674-man crew. Shortly thereafter, three other battleships, HMS *Inflexible, Irresistible*, and *Ocean* encountered floating mines drifting with the current. These ships ultimately sank as well. Other British ships were damaged. When this occurred, Admiral de Robeck ordered the flotilla to withdraw from the straits. Over the strong objection of three senior admirals (including Jackie Fisher), Churchill drafted a telegram for Admiral de Robeck urging him to press the attack.[67] But Churchill never sent it.

In the wake of the failed attempt to force the Dardanelles, the War Council decided that Allied infantry had to take the Gallipoli Peninsula to give the navy another chance to open the Dardanelles. With the straits opened, "it was hoped that [de Robeck's] powerful fleet could get to Constantinople where, if the Turkish Government had not evacuated and moved inland, they might be forced to renounce their alliance with the Central Powers."[68] With the Army now given a primary role in opening the Dardanelles, Churchill "knew he was beaten."[69]

Phase 2a

One of the first steps in Phase 2 of the campaign was Lord Kitchener's appointing his protégé, General Sir Ian Hamilton, to command the Mediterranean Expeditionary Force in Gallipoli. Hamilton was also a good friend of Churchill's. For Phase 2, the overall command structure changed. Every decision was made by either Kitchener or General Hamilton while Admiral de Robeck became Hamilton's subordinate.[70] Indeed, the Royal Navy provided support only when and where requested.[71] Churchill and the

Admiralty became mere spectators. In Phase 2 the Royal Navy never tried to force the straits.[72]

In the weeks following the failed attempt to force the Dardanelles in March, the number of Turkish troops in Gallipoli grew to sixty thousand. Under the field leadership of Mustafa Kemal Atatürk, they dug entrenchments, strung barbed wire, set machine gun emplacements, and brought in heavy artillery. The Allies, in turn, built up a force of some seventy-eight thousand men made up of troops from Australia and New Zealand (ANZAC), the 29th Division, the Royal Navy Division, and two brigades of French troops. General Hamilton decided to make an amphibious landing on the southern part of the Gallipoli peninsula. He did not anticipate any opposition to the landing because the Allies discounted the fighting ability of the Ottoman soldiers. The Allies planned to land at five beaches and capture Turkish forts and artillery batteries so that a naval force could advance through the narrows of the Dardanelles without harassment. Because of bad weather the landings were postponed until April 25. The invasion force was supported by the Royal Navy's shelling the beaches before the landings and a small force of sea planes and other aircraft. Still, Allied casualties were heavy. Just off the landing beach, the Aegean had a strip fifty yards wide that was "absolutely red with blood."[73]

ANZAC forces landed at Gaba Tepe, several kilometers north of where intended. There they found ground that rose steeply from the beaches rather than the open ground they had anticipated. From those ridges the Turks delivered withering fire.[74] By evening Hamilton decided to remove these troops from the peninsula. But the Navy advised that doing so was impossible and the troops were ordered to dig in. Other landings went about as poorly as the one at Gaba Tepe. Of the nine thousand men of the 29th who landed on the beaches, three thousand were killed or wounded. The force commander, even with twenty thousand men, was reluctant to advance.[75]

When Turkish reinforcements arrived, the possibility of a swift Allied victory on the peninsula disappeared and the fighting became a battle of attrition. Over time, the fighting devolved into trench warfare much like what was occurring in France.[76] In the first month, the British suffered forty-five thousand casualties without making any strategic advances. At the end of April 1915, Churchill is recorded as having said about the Gallipoli campaign that "I am not responsible for the Expedition. ... I do not shirk responsibility, but it is untrue to say that I have done this off my own bat."[77] The British public disagreed (many of them, in fact, still believe he was responsible for Gallipoli).[78]

In London, Churchill's reputation was spiraling downward. The word around town was that "[a]fter Antwerp, and now the Dardanelles, the

Government really ought to get rid of [Churchill]."[79] There were sharks in the water and the hope was to serve Churchill to them for lunch.

Churchill Is Removed from the Admiralty/Asquith's Government Is Brought Down/Asquith Forms Coalition with the Conservatives

Because of the carnage both in Gallipoli and in France, by May 1915, ten-month-old WWI already seemed interminable to Britons, and the Asquith Government grew increasingly unsteady. Not only was the news coming from both the Western Front and Gallipoli discouraging, but Asquith's "emotional stability ... had just been dealt a cruel blow." Venetia Stanley, the young mistress with whom he was in love, told him that she was marrying someone else.[80] With the Liberals likely to face defeat if Asquith called for a new election, many in power, including Churchill, had been suggesting that Asquith form a new coalition government with the increasingly powerful Conservatives.[81] In mid-May, Conservative leader Bonar Law proposed just such an arrangement. After several days of negotiations, agreement was reached on a new coalition.* At that time, Churchill did not realize that his dismissal as First Lord of the Admiralty was "Bonar Law's price for Conservative participation in the Government" or that Lloyd George, Churchill's ostensible friend and supporter, had gone along with Law's demand to do Churchill in.[82]

Roberts writes that "Lloyd George needed no persuasion to throw over his old friend and ally."[83] At the time, George would also make the following cutting but insightful comment about Churchill: "When the war came [Churchill] saw in it the chance of the glory for himself, and has accordingly entered on a risky campaign without caring a straw for the misery and hardship it would bring to thousands, in the hope that he would prove to be the outstanding man in this war."[84] Whether true or not, substantially similar words would be used by some to describe Churchill's steadfast position in May 1940 that Britain should not enter into peace negotiations with Hitler but should fight the Nazi juggernaut all by herself.

Hoping to save his job, Churchill wrote letters to Asquith and Bonar Law. In his letter to Law, Churchill asked that the new Cabinet review the Dardanelles operation independently rather than allow "a newspaper campaign necessarily conducted in ignorance ... to force his resignation."[85] All he asked for was to be judged fairly. Law responded that Churchill's removal was "inevitable," while Asquith called it "settled."[86] Churchill also drafted a

---

In the new Government, Asquith would continue as Prime Minister, Kitchener would stay as Secretary for War, Lloyd George would become Minister of Munitions, and Bonar Law would be the Secretary for the Colonies.

letter, which he hoped to publish, justifying his conduct during the Gallipoli campaign. He showed it to Lloyd George, who was appalled.[87] Churchill's justification depended on many facts that were still top secret. Churchill lost his temper and told Lloyd George: "You don't care if I am trampled underfoot by my enemies."[88] Churchill's old ally responded, "No, I don't. ... The only thing I care about now is that we win this war."[89] Afterward, Lloyd George did, however, call Churchill's dismissal, "a cruel and unjust degradation."[90] Both the public and most members of Parliament knew of Churchill's actions during the Gallipoli campaign only from the newspapers. And he could not reveal the truth and vindicate himself because doing so would "put ... England's security at hazard."[91]

While the position that he loved, First Lord of the Admiralty, was gone—now held by former P.M. Arthur Balfour, and Kitchener had said he could no longer work with Churchill, Asquith offered Churchill the lowest post in the Cabinet Chancellor of the Dutchy of Lancaster.[92] In that position, Churchill's only duty was to appoint county magistrates.*

As they would have been to almost anyone, Churchill found the events of May 1915 dispiriting. In the wake of his leaving the Admiralty, his depression deepened.[93] About a month later, while weekending at a farmhouse in Surrey that he had rented for the summer with his brother, Churchill watched his sister-in-law, Goonie, painting, and decided to try it for himself. It turned into a lifelong passion and a stress-relieving lifesaver. Over time, he became very good.[94] During his life, he produced more than five hundred and forty paintings.

Churchill stayed as the Chancellor of the Dutchy until November 1915. In that position, he continued to attend meetings of the War Council (which now called itself the Dardanelles Committee) and made substantive recommendations such as for the expansion of Hamilton's army in Gallipoli. However, his opinion wasn't wanted or even trusted.[95] For example, in mid-July Kitchener asked Churchill to make an official trip to the Dardanelles and Gallipoli. Maurice Hankey, Secretary to the Committee of Imperial Defence was asked to accompany him. The purpose of the trip was to find out why the campaign had degenerated into a trench-warfare deadlock.[96] At the eleventh hour, Bonar Law and other Conservatives learned of and vetoed the trip. Churchill was disappointed by the cancellation but genuinely hurt when he heard the reason Kitchener wanted Hankey to go along: to watch Churchill.[97] As if that were not bad enough, it became time to resign when on November 5, the Dardanelles Committee was reorganized and officially renamed the War Cabinet, but Churchill was excluded from it.[98] Churchill

---

As Chancellor of the Dutchy he was also paid only £2,000 per year rather than the £4,500 he received to head the Admiralty.

would later write that when he was leaving the Admiralty only two of his colleagues came by to wish him well. And the first of these was Kitchener.[99]

In *Their Finest Hour,* Churchill admitted that "I was ruined for the time being in 1915 over the Dardanelles."[100] Clementine would go further, telling famed Churchill biographer Martin Gilbert that "The Dardanelles haunted [Churchill] for the rest of his life. He always believed in it. When he left the Admiralty he thought he was finished. ... I thought he would never get over the Dardanelles: I thought he would die of grief."[101] She also feared that he might commit suicide.[102] In early 1916, she even told her husband, who, as noted, was notorious for his risk-taking, that if he were killed in action because he had overexposed himself "the world might think that [he] had sought death out of grief for [his] share in the Dardanelles."[103]

Despair in the wake of Gallipoli and the political toll it took on Churchill was not surprising. Some historians, including Manchester, believe that Churchill suffered from severe depression, and that after his dismissal from the Admiralty "[h]is Black Dog had never been so bad; he was in the pit of the worst depression of his life."[104]* Neither Gilbert nor Roberts believes that Churchill suffered from severe depression.[105]

Phase 2b of the Dardanelles/Gallipoli Campaign

After the unsuccessful landings on Gallipoli at the end of April, with the Asquith Government in disarray, the formation of a new coalition Government, and the ouster of Churchill from the Admiralty, there was little focus on the next phase of the campaign until early June. At that time, the Dardanelles Committee decided to send six more divisions to Gallipoli.

On May 19, some forty-two thousand Turkish troops launched an attack intended to push seventeen thousand ANZAC troops back into the sea. The attack failed and the Turks suffered thirteen thousand casualties, while the Allies suffered only six hundred. A subsequent attack by the Allies at Krithia was repulsed, with each side suffering a casualty rate of about 25 percent. In August, a well-designed plan to break out from the ANZAC-controlled area involved another landing by Australian and New Zealand forces. Unfortunately, it failed. Despite Hamilton's army having been increased to one hundred and twenty thousand, battles fought afterward generally led to negligible physical gains for either side.

After the failure of the Allies' "August Offensive," the Gallipoli campaign began to drift. Turkish successes began to affect public opinion in Britain; criticism of Commanding General Hamilton's performance was increasing. Hamilton told the War Office that he needed another ninety-five

---

"Black dog" was a term used by Victorian and Edwardian nannies to describe their charges as being out of sorts or ill tempered.

thousand men.[106] Kitchener was disinclined to reinforce a failing operation. To Churchill's alarm, in early October 1915, the possibility of evacuation was raised for the first time. Gen. Hamilton resisted, fearing the damage to the British prestige that such a withdrawal would have. However, he was replaced soon after. As fall turned into winter, the weather turned bad—the Gallipoli Peninsula was besieged by gales, blizzards, and flooding. This resulted in men drowning and freezing to death while thousands of others suffered frostbite. On November 23, Kitchener recommended withdrawal from Gallipoli. Throughout December, Allied troops were removed from the peninsula. The last troops left on January 9, 1916.

During the eight-month-long Dardanelles/Gallipoli campaign, Britain and the Commonwealth countries suffered 56,700 dead (approximately the same number that the United States would lose during the twelve-year-long war in Vietnam during the 1960s and '70s). In addition, the French suffered total casualties of twenty-seven thousand. The Allies established thirty-two cemeteries on the peninsula. Over fifty-six thousand Turks were killed.

Hindsight being 20/20, Roberts writes that the "Council should have abandoned its strategy after the first disastrous day." But that was impossible, it was felt, both by the Council generally and Churchill in particular, that admitting defeat to a Muslim power, "would weaken the British Empire, which ruled over tens of millions of Muslims."[107] The British had readily assumed that the Turks were not good soldiers.[108] As to Churchill, Roberts points out that "The reverse side of [his] unquestioning belief in the greatness of the British race ... was his dangerous assumption of the inferiority of other races. ..."[109] That assumption did not serve him well at Gallipoli.[110]

Churchill Quits the Government to Command an Infantry Battalion in France

Churchill did not have to fight in the war; as a married man of forty-one he was exempt from service. Choosing to fight was another example of him unnecessarily taking an action in which he was risking his life. In the months immediately preceding his resignation from the Cabinet in November 1915, he had asked both Asquith and Kitchener for a field command, but nothing came of it. Still in possession of his commission in the Queen's Own Oxfordshire Hussars, Churchill decided to join them in France. He felt that "if he could not serve [his country] in politics he should do so by fighting."[111] Indeed, sharing the dangers of being at the front with his troops was something that would also give him "a powerful sense of personal redemption."[112] Moreover, in France, he would at least be "among friends."[113] After reporting to his regiment, he had dinner with the head of the British Expeditionary Force, General Sir John French. French offered Churchill the choice of serving as an aide-de-camp to him or commanding a brigade. Winston chose the latter. As such, it was decided that Churchill would spend some time training with the 2nd battalion of the Grenadier Guards (who were headed to the front the next day), be appointed a brigadier general, and then given a command.

One of the Grenadiers' officers would later write that "there was great opposition to 'the damned politician' but in two days [Churchill] had won them all over."[114] This was the story throughout Churchill's time in the army—initial opposition was followed by "quick acceptance as a result of his charm, bravery and willingness to learn."[115] So, too, he won over the enlisted men. In early letters from France back to his wife Clementine, he wrote about how happy he was and what a release from care being in the army was compared to his last few months in civilian life.[116] He added, "How I could ever have wasted so many months in impotent misery which I might have spent in war, I cannot tell."[117] He also promised her that he would not "run any foolish risks" or do anything "not obviously required."[118]

That said, his time in the army was nonetheless marked by several fortuitous events, and foolish risks taken. These include:

- Five minutes after he left for a meeting, a German shell came through the roof of his dugout and blew a soldier's head off.[119]

- He and his second in command were lunching with several other officers at battalion headquarters when a shell struck the roof and burst in the very next room—but it did not burst properly.[120] As a result, Churchill and many others who could have been seriously injured or killed did not suffer even a scratch.[121]

- One night, he decided to climb over the top of the parapet and walk the entire thousand-yard length of the battalion line. As he did, a German flare went up, making him visible to the enemy. German machine guns opened up, but Churchill was never hit.[122]

- He abandoned his battalion headquarters as his wife had asked him to do only to establish himself in what he called his "advance headquarters"—a hundred yards closer to the wire.*

- He made nearly thirty night-time tours of no-man's-land. During these tours he could sometimes hear the enemy talking, but he refused to speak extremely softly himself.[123]

---

*Manchester writes that "Here, as in India nearly 20 years earlier, he hoped to win recognition, be mentioned in dispatches, possibly awarded a medal or two—some distinction which would attract attention in London." Manchester, Visions p. 594.

• Nearing the end of his command, the Germans fired thirty shells at his battalion headquarters, hitting it four times. No one was hurt.[124]

His time at the front was also marked by at least one act of compassion. When he was assigned to the Grenadiers, he found a sentry asleep at his post in the middle of the night (a crime for which the penalty could be death). Saying that he was not an officer in the regiment, Churchill did not, however, bring the young fellow up on charges.[125]

In December 1915, as his training time with the Grenadiers passed its midpoint, Churchill's proposed appointment to the rank of brigadier general was rescinded by Prime Minister Asquith.[126] In a letter to Clementine, he said that Asquith's "conduct reached the limit of meanness and ungenerousness...."[127] Still, in another stunning display of his humanity, Churchill nevertheless visited Asquith's son, who was serving in the trenches, and, on a three-day Christmas pass, took time to meet with Asquith to tell him of that visit.[128]

Despite Asquith's and General French's early promises to let Churchill command a brigade (about 2,800 men), on January 1, 1916, Churchill was given the command of an infantry battalion—the seven hundred men of the 6th Battalion of the Royal Scots Fusiliers—and was only given the rank of lieutenant colonel.[129] The battalion was on the front line near the village of Ploegsteert in Flanders (48 miles southwest of Ghent, Belgium and 39 miles southeast of Dunkirk, France). Churchill was a commander to whom the morale of his men was very important. Among other things, during his command he organized concerts and games. To brighten their lives, he had commanding officers give daily lectures to the troops, and he allowed his officers to use alcohol in moderation.[130] He also ordered them to teach the enlisted men in their charge to have good humor—even under fire.[131]

Another Display of Bad Judgment

During his command, Churchill would sometimes take short leaves to attend sessions of the House. One such occasion was March 7, 1916. Concerned about the prosecution of the war, in a speech to the House, he attacked, in no uncertain terms, the way his successor, Arthur Balfour, was running the Admiralty.[132] Manchester describes Churchill's speech as "exceptionally impressive"—having garnered "the complete attention of every man there."[133] Unfortunately, it was only impressive until Churchill "dealt a savage blow to his credibility in a single sentence."[134] He did so when he urged Balfour "to fortify himself, to vitalise and animate his Board of Admiralty by recalling Lord Fisher to his post as First Sea Lord."[135] This was the very same "old man who had ruined [Churchill's] Dardanelles strategy and evicted him from the Admiralty."[136] Churchill believed his suggestion to be a great gesture of magnanimity toward Fisher. In this regard, he was an ilk of one.

There was much truth to assertions that Churchill put forward about Balfour's running of the Admiralty. But when Balfour spoke in response, he made Winston's suggestion on how to fix the "problem"—by bringing back Fisher—seem as ridiculous as it actually was. Calling it "the most amazing proposition that has ever been laid before the House of Commons," Balfour reminded the members that Churchill had said, when Lord Fisher served under him at the Admiralty at the time of Gallipoli, Fisher had failed to provide him with "either the clear guidance before the event or the firm support after it which he was entitled to expect."[137] "Nevertheless" Balfour continued, "this is the man" that Churchill feels "ought to be given as a supporter and guide to anybody who happens to hold ... the responsible position of first Lord of the Admiralty."[138]

On top of all the criticism of Churchill's judgment about Gallipoli and Antwerp, his suggesting that Lord Fisher, who was well into his seventies, return to the Admiralty to provide his "wisdom," generated yet more concern and vitriol. A good example of this was contained in a letter to Balfour from Margot Asquith, wife of the P.M., in which she wrote that "[Churchill] is ... a fool of the lowest judgment. ..."[139]

Churchill Returns to England

In May 1916, following heavy losses within Churchill's division, several battalions were merged. Churchill's 6th was one of them. Officers with higher rank than Churchill filled all the slots in the newly combined battalions. That being the case, even though he had only served for six months, Churchill was free to leave the service and go back to civilian life.[140]

While several newspapers rejoiced at his return, and one even wanted to see him appointed to the Government, he came back as somewhat of an outcast. As Manchester posits, "he would never be forgotten; he was unforgettable. But he could be ignored, mortified, and taunted, and all these would be his miserable lot throughout the year ahead."[141] Among other things, Churchill was told that leaving the Army after only six months proved that he was just "a cheap opportunist."[142] Yet, this was nothing compared to the statement that Lord Derby, (soon to be the new Secretary for War) wrote in a letter to Lloyd George: "... Nothing would induce me to support any Government of which [Winston Churchill] was a member. ... He is absolutely untrustworthy as was his father before him, and he has got to learn that, just as his father had to disappear from politics, so must he, or at all events, from official life."[143]

Shortly after Churchill returned to England, Lord Kitchener was killed. He was on board the cruiser HMS *Hampshire* enroute to Russia for a meeting with the Czar when she hit a mine off Scotland and sank, with a loss of 737 lives. While Kitchener's vacillations had contributed substantially to the debacle at Gallipoli, particularly in Phase 1 of the campaign, it was unseemly to criticize a dead hero—something extremely relevant, since a commission to investigate the Gallipoli campaign had been announced and was getting ready to start its investigation.

Once the commission proceedings began in August 1916, Churchill became busy with its work.[144] Of course, he still found time to be critical of the Government—its makeshift policies on almost everything, as well as its seeming inertia in prosecuting the war. Churchill thought that Asquith must go. A majority of Conservative MPs agreed.[145] This view increased as a result of the Battle of the Somme, which was fought in northern France between July and November 1916. Allied casualties in just the first three weeks of that battle exceeded the casualties suffered in the whole eight-month Gallipoli campaign.[146] By the time the Battle of the Somme ended (in a stalemate) in November 1916, it had become one of the deadliest battles in history with more than three hundred thousand men killed and over a million wounded.

The Dardanelles Commission

On June 1, 1916, just as Churchill had been advocating for months, the Government announced that a commission of inquiry was being formed to investigate the Dardanelles/Gallipoli defeat. All relevant official papers were to be made public. But, like so many decisions involving Gallipoli, someone (in this case Prime Minister Asquith), changed his mind about that level of disclosure.[147]

The Dardanelles Commission began the first of twenty-two hearings in August 1916 and published an interim report in February 1917. As for Churchill, the commission's only criticism was that he had been "carried away by his sanguine temperment and his firm belief in the success of the operation which he had advocated."[148] The commission found that Asquith had failed to keep his colleagues informed and had established an "atmosphere of vagueness and want of precision which seem to have characterized the proceedings of the War Council."[149] Although the interim report did not treat Churchill harshly, he was still angry because many of the charges leveled against him were not fully dealt with.[150]

The commission's final report, issued in December 1917, was much harder on General Hamilton and Lord Kitchener than the interim report had been. It also concluded that Churchill's plans had been fine but that others had failed to properly execute them.[151] The general conclusion of the commission was that sufficient thought had not been given both on strategic and tactical levels to measures needed to carry out the expedition successfully.[152] While Churchill had been cleared by the official inquiry, acquittal by the public was another matter altogether.[153] A number of people were responsible for the decision to proceed with the Gallipoli campaign "but [Churchill] was the politician most closely associated with the catastrophe. ..."[154]

The Collapse of the Asquith Government/The Start of the Lloyd George Government

In December 1916, five Cabinet ministers, led by Liberal Lloyd George and the Conservative leader, Bonar Law, resigned from the Government over Asquith's poor management of the war.[155] These departures caused Asquith to resign as Prime Minister and split the Liberal Party in two. King George called on Bonar Law to form a new government. But, pursuant to an agreement with Lloyd George, Bonar Law declined the King's offer.[156] As a result, the King gave the opportunity to Lloyd George, who immediately accepted. With the strong support of the Conservatives, he created an all-party coalition that was committed to vigorously prosecuting the war.[157] In the new Government, Lloyd George would be the P.M., Bonar Law the Chancellor of the Exchequer, and Balfour (another Conservative who presently was the First Lord of the Admiralty), would become Foreign Secretary. Most of the other cabinet posts went to Conservatives as well.

As Asquith departed Downing Street, he felt that Lloyd George had betrayed him. Though he still controlled the Liberal Party machinery, he had no interest in reuniting the party. Nor did he pressure Liberals not to join the coalition Government, though a few Liberals did. Nevertheless, there was much hostility toward Lloyd George, who had fomented the Liberal Party split.

In Parliament, Asquith pursued a course of quiet support for the new Government, retaining a heavy, continuing responsibility for the decision to declare war in 1914. In a "gracious" reply to Lloyd George's first speech to the House as Prime Minister, Asquith made clear that he did not see his role "in any sense to be the leader of what is called an opposition."[158] From the spring of 1917 on, Asquith's reluctance to criticize the Government began to exasperate some of his supporters and the press.

No Place for Churchill

Lloyd George knew that the Conservatives in his Cabinet did not want Churchill to join the Government. Nonetheless, he flirted with the idea of naming Churchill to the Cabinet.[159] He specifically asked Bonar Law if Churchill were "more dangerous for you than when he is against you?"

To which Law replied, "I would rather have him against us every time."[160] Four other members of the new cabinet told Lloyd George that they would serve in the new Government only if Churchill were excluded.[161] In the end, Churchill was not offered any post. In Lloyd George's defense, it should be noted that the Dardanelles investigation was still ongoing. Churchill had, however, counted on Lloyd George's accession to office for his own return to the Cabinet and was distraught about not being asked to join the new Government. Years later he recalled that his exclusion from the new Government in December 1916 was the "toughest moment of his life."[162]

While Churchill fared well in the interim report of the Dardanelles Commission issued in February 1917, he still spent much of 1917 trying to get the Commission to deal with issues that were important to him but not included in the interim report. This activity did not, however, preclude him from also continuing the role for which he, like his father, would become infamous—criticizing any Government from which he was excluded. During 1917, among other things, he spoke before the House about the Government's misuse of wounded men, and its need to use mechanical inventions to replace men—what he had in mind were tanks and airplanes.*

Although the United States entered the war in April 1917, Churchill, asserting that the Allies lacked numerical superiority, superiority in the air, or more tanks than the Germans, ardently urged the Allies to defer any offensive action until 1918.[163] As Gilbert writes, Lloyd George knew that Churchill wanted to return to a position of authority and that "if no place were found for him, he would continue to attack the Government's war policy."[164] Thus, in early spring he discussed the possibility of employing Churchill within the Ministry of Munitions. The P.M. suggested that Churchill might join the Ministry as the chairman of a committee or board to examine the development of mechanical aides to warfare.[165] In *The World Crisis*, Churchill later recalled that in mid-May, Lloyd George "assured me of the determination to have me at his side. From that day, although holding no office, I became to a large extent his colleague."[166] But this merely collegial status did not prevent Churchill from continuing to be critical of the Government's war

---

Churchill was known as the father of the tank. While science fiction writer H.G. Wells had written about such a vehicle in 1903, it was Churchill's efforts several years later that brought such an armored vehicle into existence. See, Manchester, Visions pp. 510–11.He believed that the tank was the surest way to "beat the trench" and "augment the power of the human." See, Ibid. p. 620. In contrast, one short-sighted general called the tank "Winston's folly." Birkenhead, Contemporary Personalities p. 121. Among other things, Churchill was also involved in the invention or advancement of air-to-air communications, hydrophones, plastic surgery, the mobile use of x-rays, blood transfusion, and daylight saving time.

policy. At the time, Lord Esher, a permanent member of the Committee of Imperial Defence, wrote what many people were feeling, that:

> The power of Winston for good and evil is, I should say very considerable. ... To me he appears not as the statesman but as a politician of keen intelligence lacking in those puissant qualities that are essential in a man who is to conduct the business of our country for the coming year. I hope therefore that he may remain outside the government.[167]

Minister of Munitions

The *Sunday Times* echoed that thought, declaring that Churchill's appointment to any Cabinet position would be "a grave danger to the Administration and to the Empire as a whole."[168] Nonetheless, after Churchill's being out of office for twenty months, in July 1917, Lloyd George appointed him to the non-Cabinet position of Minister of Munitions. In a cutting editorial, *The Morning Post* declared that Churchill's appointment "proves that although we have not yet invented an unsinkable ship, we have discovered the unthinkable politician. ... [Churchill had] 'committed at least two capital blunders ... The attempt to save Antwerp and the attack on the Dardanelles. ...'"[169] Blaming Churchill for Gallipoli once again became a popular pastime.[170] Despite all this, on July 29, 1917, he was successfully reelected in the by-election necessitated by his appointment.

Upon becoming Minister of Munitions, although he was wrongly perceived as anti-labor (and would be again in future years), he immediately tried to resolve a serious labor dispute that had festered for eighteen months at munitions factories in Glasgow. Trade union leaders, who had organized several strikes and brought all work to a halt, had been arrested, fired, and forbidden to reside in Glasgow.[171] Churchill met and had tea and cake with the leader of the deportees, David Kirkwood. During the meeting, Kirkwood told Churchill that the Government had deported him without cause, but now he was just an unemployed engineer who had forgiven all that was done to him. What he wanted was only to get his job back.[172] Churchill then met with the plant's owner. Three days later Kirkwood received an offer to manage the factory. Moreover, within six weeks, as a result of the bonus scheme devised by Kirkwood, shell production at the factory was the highest in Britain.[173] Soon after, Churchill even introduced a bill in the House enabling special wage awards to be made to skilled workers. That did not, however, resolve the dispute throughout munition factories involving wage discrepancies between skilled and piece workers (who were earning much more). He appointed a representative committee to examine the discrepancy. Although it required several machinations, the result was a 12½ percent increase for engineering workers, foundry workers, as well as tool room, supervising, and maintenance classes. The cost to the Government was £5,700,000.[174]

During his time as the Minister of Munitions, among other things, Churchill also reorganized the Ministry—reducing the management structure from fifty department heads to a council of eleven (each being in charge of the several departments).[175] He also oversaw enormous increases in the production of tanks, machine guns, aircraft, and mustard gas.[176] In the latter regard, he also advocated for the immediate construction of a new plant to increase production of poison gas shells.[177] In fact, he was irate upon learning that the Red Cross had proposed to outlaw poison gas.[178] As he would later put it in a letter to Clementine, "I'm trying ... to give the Germans a good first dose of the Mustard gas."[179] Before the war ended, Britain, like Germany, had used both mustard gas and the far more lethal chlorine gas. In fact, "by 1918, one out of every three [artillery] shells" being fired by the British contained poison gas.[180]

When in December 1917, the Dardanelles Commission issued its final report and exonerated Churchill, he hoped that "the current of public opinion and the weight of the popular displeasure" which had been "directed upon [him]," would now fade.[181] The exoneration did not, however, result in an immediate improvement in his station. He remained Minister of Munitions for the remainder of the war (actually, until January 1919). His duties at the Ministry did not, however, prevent him from being a gadfly who was simply incapable of not interfering with other ministers' departments—an offense of which he would be guilty countless times in his long career.

WWI would take a significant turn on November 7, 1917, the day that the Bolsheviks seized power in Russia. The Russians had lost nine million soldiers in the war, and its new leaders wanted peace at any price. Thus, they accepted the brutal terms laid down by the Kaiser and withdrew from the war.[182] Germany was now free to move a million men no longer needed to fight Russia to the Western Front, something that had long scared the Allies. The Germans' great offensive in the West started in March 1918 and continued well into the spring. The German leadership hoped that the influx of what amounted to fifty new divisions into France would overwhelm the Allied forces and end the war before the Americans could cross the Atlantic and reinforce the French and British. Although Churchill was not in the War Cabinet, during the offensive, Lloyd George often asked him to visit the fighting in France and report back.

At the start of the 1918 campaign the Germans did well. But the German offensive was stemmed by an American counterattack in early June. Using tactics that went against French military doctrine—a rolling artillery barrage to soften enemy positions and create a clear path for infantry units to follow, the Americans drove five German divisions back through a forest called Belleau Woods. The Americans ultimately deployed a million men on the Western front.

The actual fighting in WWI ended upon the signing of an armistice on November 11, 1918. Just days before this in Germany, the Kaiser was forced to abdicate and the Weimar Republic was proclaimed.[183] In Britain, a general election was called for December 14, 1918. Churchill campaigned in Dundee as a "Coalition Liberal" as distinct from an Asquith Liberal.* Not only did he receive an endorsement from Lloyd George, surprisingly, he also got one from leader of the Conservative, Chancellor of the Exchequer Bonar Law.[184] Churchill campaigned on a pledge to "Rebuild the ruins. Heal the wounds,"[185] and oppose Bolshevism.

---

*This was a first step in his metamorphosis back to being a Conservative. Over the next few elections he would use varying adjectives to describe his party affiliation at the time.

Clementine Churchill

6

January 1919–November 1922
A Return to the Cabinet

Churchill Returns to the Cabinet as Secretary for War and Secretary
  for Air
The Continued British Blockade of Germany, Even After the Armistice
Wilson's Fourteen Points
The Paris Peace Conference
The Treaty of Versailles
The League of Nations
The Government of India Act
Disarmament
Meanwhile, in Germany
Churchill Becomes Colonial Secretary
Ireland
Chanak, Its Impact, and the Election of 1922

Churchill Returns to the Cabinet as Secretary for War and Secretary for Air

The election that started on December 14, 1918, was an overwhelming pat on the back for Lloyd George and his Liberal/Conservative coalition. Churchill himself was again reelected from Dundee by a large majority. Although the position was not one within the inner Cabinet, on January 10, 1919, Churchill accepted Lloyd George's offer to become Secretary for War and for Air. The press was displeased with Churchill's appointment. For example, *The Morning Post* pointed out that "there is some tragic flaw in Mr. Churchill which determines him on every occasion in the wrong course."[1]

At that time, Britain had a small contingent of troops and ships in Russia that had been sent there in 1918 to help the White Russians (Russians loyal to the Czar) fight the Bolsheviks. Churchill's strong anti-Bolshevik views led, among other things, to plans for an offensive in northern Russia and to his responding to Lloyd George's suggestion to invite the Russians to discussions about Turkey by saying, "One might as well legalize sodomy as recognize the Bolsheviks."[2] During the 1920s he also referred to the Bolsheviks and Russia as "That foul combination of criminality and animalism"[3] ... "the avowed enemies of civilization" ... "the blood-dyed tyrants of Moscow" ... "filthy butchers of Moscow," and in many other colorful ways.[4] In June of 1919, he urged that permission be granted to have thirteen thousand British troops join the White Russians in an attack on the Bolsheviks in North Russia.[5] The plan was never implemented.[6] At a War Cabinet meeting in July 1919, Lloyd George made it clear that all British forces were to be evacuated from Russia with the least possible delay.[7] Ultimately, the Bolsheviks, led by Leon Trotsky, prevailed over the White Russians. Britain's cost for assisting them was £100 million (nearly $5.5 billion in today's money).[8] "[The] withdrawal and total defeat ... solidified the ... view that [Churchill] was a rash military adventurer not to be trusted."[9] Of course, this view had been well established long before Churchill advocated helping the White Russians.

The Continued British Blockade of Germany, Even After the Armistice

The actual fighting in WWI ended upon the signing of an armistice on November 11, 1918. However, it took nearly six months of Allied negotiations at the Paris Peace Conference (which began on January 18, 1919) to conclude the peace treaty signed on June 28, 1919. Britain maintained its blockade of shipments to Germany, including the shipment of much needed food, until after the treaty was executed.

Perhaps based on his longtime support for a zealous prosecution of the war, Churchill has been accused of being responsible for maintaining the blockade.[10] The fact is that on the first night the armistice was in effect, Churchill had desired to send shiploads of food to Hamburg,[11] only to be overruled by Lloyd George.[12] The Prime Minister was thinking about a new election and a campaign in which he would promise to "make Germany pay 'til the pips squeak."[13] Thereafter, Germany refused to agree to the demand by the Allies that Germany surrender its merchant ships so the Allies could use them to transport food supplies. Germans considered the armistice a temporary cessation of the war. They feared that if fighting broke out again, the ships would be confiscated outright. In fact, upon hearing the harsh terms of the Treaty of Versailles, Germany would have continued the war had there been any chance of successfully opposing the Allies.[14]

In a speech to the Commons on March 3, 1919, Churchill said:

There is another matter which calls for very prompt settlement. It is the last to which I shall refer before I sit down. I mean the speedy enforcing of the Peace Terms upon Germany. At the present moment we are bringing everything to a head with Germany. We are holding all our means of coercion in full operation, or in immediate readiness for use. We are enforcing the blockade with rigour. We have strong Armies ready to advance at the shortest notice. Germany is very near starvation. ...

Now is, therefore, the moment to settle. To delay indefinitely would be to run a grave risk of having nobody with whom to settle, and of having another great area of the world sink into Bolshevik anarchy.[15]

Well-known political commentator and author Pat Buchanan asserts that in this speech Churchill was exulting the success of the blockade. Historian Scott Manning responds by pointing out Churchill's expressly stated abhorrence of the use of starvation after hostilities had ceased and that Churchill wanted to see the blockade ended as soon as possible by getting the treaty signed immediately.[16] All of this is true. Moreover, as previously noted, it is also true that Churchill was a proponent of shipping food into Germany immediately after the armistice.[17] However, an objective reading of his March 3 speech to the House does indicate a willingness on Churchill's part to put his principles aside and stand with those who would use the denial of food to the civilian population of a defeated enemy to expedite its agreement to peace terms. Accordingly, this would not appear to have been Churchill's finest hour.*

Wilson's Fourteen Points

Ten days prior to the official opening of the Paris Peace Conference, on January 8, 1918, U.S. President Woodrow Wilson issued his country's postwar goals, known as the Fourteen Points.[18] It outlined a policy of free

---

Despite his hatred of the Soviet Union, when needed to countermand Hitler, he had little problem with Britain's aligning herself with Russia. This is not the only time that Churchill would forsake his principles to achieve a goal. See discussion in Chapters 9 and 16.

In 1943, Churchill would again be accused of denying food to a hungry population. This time it was to the people of Bengal in eastern India whose crops had been destroyed by a cyclone. Although he refused to move wheat from Canada to Bengal on grounds of limited shipping capacity during wartime, Roberts p. 786, and did say the "Indians are not the only people who are starving in this war," he was ultimately able to get grain delivered from Australia. Ibid. [The Bengal famine is discussed in detail in chapter 22.]

trade, open agreements, and democracy. While the term was not used, popular self-determination was assumed. It also called for disarmament "to the lowest point consistent with domestic safety," the withdrawal of the Central Powers from occupied territories, the creation of a Polish state, the redrawing of Europe's borders along ethnic lines, and the formation of a League of Nations to guarantee the political independence and territorial integrity of all states. It called for a just and democratic peace uncompromised by territorial annexation.

The Paris Peace Conference

The conference began on January 12, 1919. The principal players were the United States, Britain, France, and Italy. Procedurally, the conference was a nightmare—there was no plan on how to proceed, nor could the participants decide on two very fundamental things:

- Would the treaty be preliminary or final?

- Would it be imposed on Germany or be negotiated with the former adversary?

According to Harold Nicholson, a member of the British delegation, this indecision "was the cause of much subsequent muddle, misunderstanding, and injustice."[19] The confusion resulted in delay—which in turn resulted in the diminution of the Allied armies (as a result of the popular clamor for demobilization), further starvation in Germany (owing to Britain's continued blockade), and the continuing danger of Bolshevism taking hold in Central Europe.

The British contingent was led by Lloyd George, who was hamstrung by the desire and expectation of the House of Commons and the British people for retribution. After all, the war had cost Britain more than £25 billion ($125 billion) to wage, and resulted in the death of some 750,000 British servicemen—about 11.5 percent of all men of military age. Clemenceau headed the French delegation. Having lost more than 1.3 million men in the war, France's priority was simple: security. France was "passionately determined" to use the short time she had leverage "to create a zone of protection against the day when the German menace would again loom threateningly in the east."[20] Orlando, the Prime Minister of Italy, strove to provide Italy with as many spoils of war as he could.

Then there was a delegation from the United States headed by President Woodrow Wilson himself. Wilson saw himself as "the man chosen by God to give the whole world a new message and a more righteous order."[21] But he knew a settlement of true moderation was not possible at that time. Instead, he hoped the Covenant of the League of Nations would provide an instrument by which the treaty could be modified in the future to be less retaliatory.[22] Wilson disagreed with almost everything his European colleagues suggested. And he did not realize that the fourteen points (later expanded to twenty-three) he had proposed did not represent the current position of either the Senate or the American people.[23] After all, the United States had just lost over 116,000 men in only eighteen months of fighting.*

The Treaty of Versailles

Of the many provisions in the treaty, one of the most important and controversial required "Germany [to] accept the responsibility ... for causing all the loss and damage" during the war. The treaty required Germany to disarm, make territorial concessions, and pay reparations to certain countries. In 1921 the total cost of these reparations was assessed at 132 billion gold marks (then worth $31.4 billion or £8.6 billion, roughly equivalent to $442 billion or £284 billion today). At the time, economists, notably John Maynard Keynes (a British delegate to the Paris Peace Conference), concluded that the treaty was too harsh—a "Carthaginian peace"—and said the reparations figure was excessive and counter-productive. Churchill agreed.[24] Churchill thought that the reparations provisions were "malignant and silly to an extent that made them obviously futile."[25] On the other hand, prominent figures on the Allied side, such as French Marshal Ferdinand Foch, criticized the treaty for treating Germany too leniently.

The treaty stripped Germany of 25,000 square miles of territory and seven million people.** Among other things, under the treaty Germany was required to:

- restore the provinces of Alsace-Lorraine to France;

- renounce "all rights and title over the territory" making up Poland;

- transfer Pomerelia (Eastern Pomerania) to Poland so that the new state could have access to the sea (this would become known as the Polish Corridor);

---

*Much like Lincoln at the end of the American Civil War, Churchill did not favor imposing a harsh peace on the vanquished enemy. Ironically, among those that took the opposite position was a young MP who later would become Lord Halifax, the chief proponent for negotiating a peace agreement rather than fighting Hitler in May 1940. Buchanan p.71. McCarten writes that after Halifax served as Viceroy of India in the late 1920s, he mellowed and "expressed a certain sympathy for Germany over the penalties" that were imposed. McCarten pp. 90–91.

**This was approximately 10 percent of her people and 12.5 percent of her territory.

- cede the city of Danzig for the League of Nations to establish as a Free City;

- cede parts of the province of Silesia to the newly created independent country of Czechoslovakia (which had largely been controlled by Austria);

- cede the Saar Basin to the protection of the League of Nations (where it would remain until a plebiscite in 1935 returned it to Germany);

- cede the city of Memel in Lithuania to the Allies for disposal according to their wishes; and

- renounce sovereignty over its former colonies.

The treaty also imposed many restrictions upon the post-war German military. These provisions, some of which are listed below, were intended to make Germany incapable of undertaking offensive action and to encourage international disarmament.

- Germany was to have an army of no more than one hundred thousand men.

- She was prohibited from having an air force.

- Conscription was abolished.

- The number of civilian staff supporting the army was reduced.

- The police force was reduced to its pre-war size, with increases limited to population increases.

- Paramilitary forces were forbidden.

- The Rhineland was to be demilitarized:
  - All fortifications in the Rhineland and 50 kilometers east of the river were to be demolished
  - New construction was forbidden

- Limits were imposed on the type and quantity of weapons that Germany could possess.

- Germany was prohibited from manufacturing or stockpiling chemical weapons, armored cars, tanks, and military aircraft.

- The number, by type, of ships that Germany could have in her navy was limited.

- The navy was not to exceed fifteen thousand men.

The non-negotiable terms of the Versailles treaty were presented to the Germans in early May 1919. Only four of the twenty-three points that President Wilson had espoused were included in the treaty.[26] Germans of all political shades denounced the treaty—particularly the provision that blamed Germany for starting the war. Germany had anticipated, based on Wilson's original fourteen points, that she would receive something much less punitive.[27] The Germans thus never felt bound by the treaty.[28]

In a passionate speech before the National Assembly on May 12, 1919, Germany's first post-war chancellor, Philipp Scheidemann, called the treaty a "murderous plan" and ultimately resigned rather than sign it. Nearly all members of the Weimar Republic's provisional government opposed the treaty. This is all the more understandable given that as of the date of the armistice, November 11, 1918, the Germans had not seen themselves as having been defeated.[29]

In mid-June, the Allies gave Germany an ultimatum: accept the treaty by June 24 or the armistice would be rescinded and the Allies would continue the war.[30] German President Friedrich Ebert told the Army leadership that if there were "the slightest possibility of successful military resistance to the Allies" he would have the Assembly vote to reject the treaty.[31] Leader of the Army, Field Marshal Paul von Hindenburg, responded that resistance was impossible. As a result, the Assembly voted overwhelmingly to accept the treaty.

WWI certainly left Germany weak. But as English history Professor A.J.P. Taylor points out, she nevertheless remained the "greatest power on the continent" (having a strong industrial capability and a population of sixty-five million vs. France's forty million).[32] Moreover, as a result of the Bolshevik revolution (followed by a loss in the Russian-Polish war of 1920), Russia, which formerly acted to restrain Germany, practically vanished from the scene.

The League of Nations

The proposal to create a League of Nations, was, after a fair amount of negotiation and compromise, approved one week into the Paris Peace Conference. Part I of the Treaty of Versailles was in fact the Covenant of the League of Nations, which provided for the creation of the League as an organization for the arbitration of international disputes. Key elements of the Covenant were Articles 8 and 10, pursuant to which members "recognize[d] that the maintenance of peace requires the reduction of national armaments to the lowest point consistent with national safety and the enforcement by common action of international obligations. [The means to fulfill its portion of the collective obligation to preserve the territorial integrity and political independence of all other members."[33]]

The Government of India Act

India, with its population of two hundred and fifty million, had been a colony of Britain's since 1858, after having been ruled for a century by the British East India Company. In December 1919, Parliament passed the Government of the India Act of 1919. The act represented the end of what the British viewed as benevolent despotism there. It was a first step toward representative government. The next step was accomplished with great upheavals both in India and in the House of Commons a decade and a half later.

Under the act, in each of the major provinces, control of some administrative functions was given to a native government made up of Indian ministers answerable to a provincial council. All other areas of government remained under the control of the British Viceroy. Also established was a bicameral legislature for all India. The Viceroy also maintained veto authority over the enactment of any bill.

The act also provided that a commission would be set up at the end of ten years, the purpose of which was to assess how well the changes were working and make appropriate recommendations.

Disarmament

For many years in post-WWI Britain, there was "a firm and widely held conviction that armaments were one of the primary causes of war"[34] and that "any increase in armaments was a blow to the League of Nations."[35] Likewise, it was the concomitant assumption that, as nations acted collectively against aggression pursuant to the League's Covenant, their combined strength would ipso facto be so great, that there would be no need for any country to rearm fully.[36] The preamble to Part V of the Treaty of Versailles talks about German disarmament, as required by the treaty, making "possible the initiation of a general limitation of the armaments of all nations. ..."[37]

Additionally, the notes to the League's Covenant provide "... The Allies recognized that 'the acceptance by Germany of the terms laid down for her disarmament will facilitate and hasten the accomplishment of a general reduction of armaments and they intended to open negotiations immediately with the review to the eventual adoption of a scheme of such general reduction.'"[38] The Germans read this as a contractual commitment by the Allies to disarm, while the British felt that it was at least a moral obligation for the Allies to do so.[39] They believed that German disarmament would and should be followed by the disarmament of Britain and the rest of the world.[40] During the 1920s, because security was supposedly guaranteed by the collective action of the League, it was believed that the Allies would in fact agree to disarm. They did not. A prime reason for this was the tremendous blow that collective security suffered when the United States refused to join the League.[41]

Meanwhile, in Germany

When it became clear in August 1918 that Germany was going to lose the war, her leading generals, Paul von Hindenburg and Erich Ludendorff, rushed to hand their power over to the moderate Chancellor, Max von Baden and several Social Democrats. However, before the new government could get its feet on the ground, the German Navy, in the interest of defending German pride, ordered a last-ditch attack against the British. Seeing such an attack as wholly unnecessary and suicidal, ordinary German sailors led a mutiny on November 3. Sailors dispersed throughout the country, fomenting revolution and making the attack impossible. The Kaiser was forced to renounce his power and flee the country six days later.[42] Despite his ousting, revolutionary political tensions continued, leading to a total upheaval of the previous regime. The military offered the Social Democrats, particularly Chancellor Friedrich Ebert, support for instituting a new democratic regime, the Weimar Republic, so long as they did not decrease military power.

This new government would be responsible for working out peace terms with the Allies, signing the Versailles Treaty, and managing the economic catastrophe that had been created by the war.[43] Elections to the National Assembly were held in January 1919. Amid violent demonstrations from February to July 1919, a new constitution was crafted and signed on August 11. It created a republic with the legislature (the Reichstag) elected by proportional representation, Ebert was named President.

With the signing of the Versailles Treaty in June 1919, Germany faced huge obstacles: debilitating debt in the form of reparations payments to the Allies, and the loss of 13 percent of its territory, including major shares of its coal and iron resources.[44] From 1919 until 1922 inflation in Germany was also a huge problem. In January 1920, one dollar equated to 64.8 German marks. By January 1923, the exchange rate was eighteen thousand marks to the dollar. Unemployment skyrocketed from 1.5 percent in 1922 to 9.6 percent in 1923.[45] From 1914 to 1922, the cost of living multiplied twelve-fold. As a result, worker strikes multiplied, and violent confrontations emerged between parliamentary movements on the right and the left.

Amid this economic and political crisis, Germans became increasingly dissatisfied with the Weimar administration.[46] Early on, the German Workers' Party (which in 1920 would become the National Socialist German Worker's Party—i.e., the Nazi Party) tapped into this resentment in order to gain power.

Adolph Hitler had initially encountered this party while working as an education officer for the German Army. The Army was concerned that the group was a left-wing revolutionary organization and sent Hitler to spy on it.[47] Hitler, who shared much of the party's ideology, was drawn into a debate with one of the members, and upon showing oratorical promise, was invited to become a member.*

Churchill Becomes Colonial Secretary

In late 1920, Churchill told Prime Minister Lloyd George that he wanted to move from Secretary of War to another cabinet post. Not wanting to lose the brightest member of his Cabinet,[48] on February 14, 1921, Lloyd George appointed Churchill to be Colonial Secretary, where his most immediate concern remained the seemingly insoluble problem of Ireland.[49]** In April, Edward Wood (later Lord Irwin, then Lord Halifax) was appointed Under Secretary at the Colonial Office.[50] As the future Lord Halifax recognized, shortly thereafter Churchill became angry with Lloyd George for passing him over for Chancellor of the Exchequer in favor of Austen Chamberlain (Neville's older half-brother).[51] and in having been given Halifax as Under Secretary when he would have preferred someone else.[52] As Halifax writes in his 1954 autobiography, after a discussion with Churchill on the latter point "... no one could have been kinder than Churchill was to me." And his time as Churchill's deputy was the beginning of a "much valued friendship."[53]***

Ireland

"The Irish question had been a primordial Parliamentary issue for generations."[54] In April 1916, Irish Republicans launched the Easter Rising against British rule and proclaimed an Irish Republic. Although it was crushed after a week of fighting, "the Rising" and the British response led to greater

---

One of only fifty-four members at the time, through his leadership in the party's executive committee and propaganda management, Hitler worked to gain recognition by consolidating far right nationalist parties and conservatives who were unhappy with the economic and political upheaval. In September 1919, Hitler issued a road map for the Nazis in the form of a public comment on Karl Marx's 1843 work "On the Jewish Question." Available at: https://www.jewishvirtuallibrary.org/ adolf-hitler-s-first-anti-semitic-writing. In it, Hitler argued that the Weimar leaders and Jews had been responsible for the loss of the war and the resulting desperate conditions in Germany. He asserted that only a dictatorship and complete removal of the Jews could offer legitimate leadership and return Germany to prominence. By 1923, Hitler had declared himself the leader of the Nazi Party. Available at: https://encyclopedia.ushmm.org/content/en/article/adolf-hitler-1919-1924.

**Churchill had experience in this ministry, having served two years as Under Secretary of State for the Colonies in 1906–07.*

***An interesting comment, given the battle that Churchill and Halifax would have in May 1940.*

popular support in Ireland for independence. In the UK's December 1918 election, seventy-three members of the Irish Sinn Féin Party were elected to Parliament. However, they refused to take their seats.[55] In January 1919, they formed a break away assembly in Dublin (the Dáil Éireann) and insisted on Irish independence.[56]

Throughout 1919, the Irish Republican Army (IRA), led by its commander, Michael Collins, made sixty-seven attacks on British soldiers and officials, killing eighteen.[57] This led to the introduction of legislation (The Government of Ireland Bill) in the House on December 22, 1919, to partition Ireland. Under the bill, the twenty-six mainly Catholic counties in the south would get Home Rule, for which they had fought for years. Those twenty-six counties would be ruled from Dublin while the six predominantly Protestant counties in the north would be ruled from Belfast and would remain part of the UK.[58]

Notwithstanding the introduction of this historic legislation, in 1920 the violence increased.[59] The reason: The bill did not grant Home Rule to all of Ireland. There was even an IRA plan to kidnap Prime Minister Lloyd George and several Cabinet officials, including Churchill.[60] In response, in May 1920, the Cabinet approved creating a force to deal with the violence, stipulating that the force be raised, paid for, and administered by Churchill's War Office.[61] Eight thousand men were to be recruited chiefly among former soldiers. These troops would become known as the "Black and Tans."[62]

During the discussion of The Government of Ireland Bill, Churchill employed the Black and Tans to crush the IRA.[63] "Once it was clear that his attempt ... had resoundingly failed, Churchill was the first to champion a wide and generous offer to the south, despite opposition from both the Tory right, who thought it went too far, and Sinn Féin, who did not think it went far enough."[64]

On July 8, 1921, a truce was reached, which for the first time allowed direct negotiations between the leaders of the IRA and the British Government.[65] Nonetheless, it took three months before pre-negotiations even commenced.[66] When face-to-face negotiations started, included in the Irish delegation was IRA leader Michael Collins. Some Cabinet members refused to shake hands with Collins et al.—men they regarded as murderers.[67]*

Churchill was not part of that group. According to Manchester, Churchill and Collins were "alike in many ways: fearless, charismatic, fiercely patriotic. ... ready to sacrifice everything for principle ... and they shared a ready

---

*Fifteen years later, shaking hands with murderers, both literally and figuratively, would start to become de rigeur for senior British ministers; first as part of the appeasement process and then in Britain's various dealings with Stalin.

wit."[68] In fact, during the negotiations, their friendship grew. After a day of exhausting deliberations, "Winston would take his recent enemy home and sit up late, talking, arguing, drinking, even singing."[69] At one point, Collins reminded Churchill that he had put a price on the IRA leader's head. Churchill responded that "At any rate it was a good price—£5000." Grabbing a framed copy of the reward offered by the Boers for Churchill's recapture in 1899, he added, "Look at me—£25 dead or alive. How would you like that?"[70]

Peace negotiations dragged on until Lloyd George gave the Irish an ultimatum on the night of December 5, 1921. The treaty was signed at 2:20 the next morning.[71] Under the agreed terms, the twenty-six southern counties would be known as the Irish Free State, have complete domestic independence, but would be a part of the British Commonwealth where it would have Dominion status, as did Canada, South Africa, Australia, and New Zealand.[72] The six northern counties would remain part of the UK.

The pact was immediately repudiated by hardline Irish Republicans and diehard Tories, especially the Orangemen of Northern Ireland to whom the Free State was anathema.[73] Nonetheless, the agreement was ratified overwhelmingly by both houses of Parliament. On January 9, 1922, it was approved by a slim margin in the Dáil. Collins was elected chairman of the provisional Irish Government, which was to serve until a general election could be held there. All this represented great change, but at the same time very little had changed. The very existence of the pact led to a murderous civil war that would last nearly a year.[74]

During that time, anti-treaty factions engaged in numerous attacks and assassinations. In June 1922, Sir Henry Wilson, one of the most senior British Army staff officers during WWI, was killed by anti-treaty IRA gunmen just outside his home in London. And on August 22, 1922, anti-treaty IRA also killed Collins in an ambush in County Cork. He was just thirty years old. As he lay dying, Collins told a friend to "tell Winston that we could never have done anything without him."[75] In October, the Dáil adopted the constitution which had been written in substantial part by Collins and Churchill.[76]

All of this also took its political toll on Lloyd George's coalition Government with the Tories. Conservative MPs were angry. Among other things, the Irish treaty seemed to have favored the IRA; Sir Henry Wilson had been assassinated;[77] unemployment was higher than it had been in decades and there was a scandal: an agent of the Prime Minister had effectively been giving out peerages, in exchange for political contributions to the P.M.[78] The Liberal/Conservative coalition that had governed Britain since 1916 was cracking. To make matters more interesting, in the fall, a serious international crisis would take place in Turkey.

Chanak, Its Impact, and the Election of 1922

During WWI, Turkey had fought on the side of the Germans. After the war it was partially occupied by the Allies. In September 1922, in an effort to restore Turkish rule to Allied-occupied portions of the country, nationalist Turkish forces led by Mustafa Kemal Atatürk were advancing on Chanak, a city on the Asiatic (eastern) side of the Dardanelles. Chanak was located in a neutral zone established by the 1920 Treaty of Sèvres. The city was populated by Greeks and protected by British troops.[79] The entry of the Turkish Army (aka the Kemalists) into Chanak would constitute a treaty violation. Lloyd George was determined to keep the Kemalists out of the European side of the Dardanelles—the Gallipoli peninsula—and was prepared to use force to do so if necessary.[80] The P.M. told the Cabinet on September 7 that under no circumstances could Britain allow the Gallipoli peninsula to be held by the Turks.[81] Controlling the peninsula would allow the Turks to close the Dardanelles to commercial shipping once again, something Churchill believed would make a war in the Balkans inevitable.[82] The only Allied troops on the peninsular were French and Italian, and it was feared they might just surrender the peninsula to the Turks.[83] (France and Italy had, in fact, been providing the Kemalists with military equipment.[84]) It was also feared that a successful military action by the Kemalists could stir up nationalist feelings elsewhere in the Empire, most particularly in Iraq and India.[85]

On September 15, 1922, the Cabinet agreed that Chanak should be defended.[86] As requested by the Cabinet, Colonial Secretary Churchill drafted a telegram for the P.M. to send the Dominions asking them for military reinforcements to help stop the Kemalists from taking Chanak and the Gallipoli peninsula.[87] (Thereafter, local French commanders sent a contingent to Chanak, but the French Government promptly insisted on their withdrawal.[88]) After a discussion with the Prime Minister, Churchill also prepared a press communiqué, the aim of which was to have the Turks withdraw from the Chanak area. The draft also indicated that Britain was prepared to take military action.[89] The tone of the draft was, however, widely felt to be too bellicose and led to substantial castigation of Lloyd George and Churchill, both in Conservative circles and in the British press.[90] Nonetheless, on September 29, the Cabinet approved the British commander in Turkey's sending an ultimatum to the Turks at Chanak, saying that if they did not withdraw within a time period specified by him, all British forces in the region would attack.[91] (British intelligence believed that the Soviet Government was pressing Kemal to attack Chanak.[92]) "Churchill believed that the ultimatum would result in negotiations with the Turks, not war."

So did Lloyd George.[93] In contrast, even though the Turks were violating a treaty, Foreign Secretary Lord Curzon and Stanley Baldwin (then President of the Board of Trade), believed that Lloyd George's Government was engaging in irresponsible brinkmanship—taking Britain close to a new war just to stop the Turks from "reclaiming their own territory."[94]* As Gilbert writes, "it was widely believed that the Cabinet were being pushed forward by a small group of irresponsible Ministers."[95]

The ultimatum was, however, never sent because Gen. Harington, the British commander, received news of Kemal's willingness to negotiate.[96] In an October 1 telegram to the Dominion prime ministers, Churchill said that in his opinion it was doubtful that anything would come out of these negotiations.[97]

While negotiations between the British and the Turks were proceeding, on October 7, retired Prime Minister Bonar Law wrote a letter to *The Times* criticizing Lloyd George's and Churchill's "brinksmanship and an encouragement to Tory MPs to destabilize the [existing Liberal/Conservative] Coalition."[98] According to Gilbert, "Bonar Law's letter reflected the public distress at the possibility of a war with Turkey in which Britain would have no allies."[99]

An agreement was reached between the British and the Kemalists on October 11, 1922. At Chanak, the Turks were to withdraw 16 km from the Dardanelles and not increase the number of their troops.[100] News of the agreement brought great relief in London.[101] But it did nothing to ease the growing tensions between the Conservatives and the Liberals whose coalition government ruled the country.

On October 19, the Conservatives met at the Carlton Club in London to discuss whether to continue the Coalition with the Liberals in the next election. The vote was two to one against doing so.[102]** Upon learning of this, Prime Minister Lloyd George promptly resigned and advised the King

---

Baldwin would take a similar view in 1936, when, also in violation of treaty, Hitler marched into the demilitarized Rhineland and the Allies took no action. Roberts p. 291.

**Manchester writes that Churchill was "widely blamed for the coalition's fall and not only because of its controversial policies. His loyalty to Lloyd George was suspect"—the P.M. had received letters indicating that Churchill "was conspiring against him." Manchester, Visions, p. 738. While Churchill and Lloyd George often worked well together, Churchill thought that "George's attitude toward him revealed 'a certain vein of amiable malice,'"—Winston's belief that George had betrayed him after his eviction from the Admiralty in 1915; George's having found no place for Winston in the Coalition's Cabinet in 1916; and George's having bypassed him for Chancellor of the Exchequer in 1921. Ibid.*

to send for the retired leader of the Conservatives, Bonar Law, to form a new government, which the King did. Bonar Law promptly dissolved Parliament and called a general election for November 15, 1922.

Unfortunately for Churchill, on October 17, 1922, he had an emergency appendectomy.[103] While the operation was successful, he was not able to move for weeks. Indeed, he was not able to campaign for reelection to his seat in Dundee until four days before the election.[104]

The fact that Britons, including Churchill's working-class constituency in Dundee, did not look favorably on the Chanak crisis or the honors scandal, and were also greatly troubled by continued high unemployment, did not bode well for the Liberals, especially Churchill. On November 15, the Conservatives won a clear majority in the House (345 of the 603 seats in Parliament), while Lloyd George's National Liberals garnered only sixty-two seats. Churchill was also soundly defeated; finishing behind the Prohibitionist candidate who was running for the seat for the fifth time.[105] Churchill received less than 14 percent of the total vote.

Loyalty had been an issue surrounding Churchill even as a young Liberal Cabinet Member in 1905–1915. As English-American journalist and historian George Dangerfield writes:

> *By nature flamboyant, insolent in his bearing, impatient in his mind, and Tory in his deepest convictions, [Churchill] was a curious person to be found holding a responsible position in the Liberal party, and few men could have been more distrusted, or have taken a more curious pleasure in being* distrusted. *Dangerfield,* The Strange Death of Liberal England *p. 89.*

Loyalty, and what it engendered, would be critical in the ultimate determination of whether Britain would enter into peace negotiations with Hitler in May 1940.

7

January 1923–October 1924 Out in the Cold, Churchill Morphs. Meanwhile, in Germany

1923
- December—Churchill's Campaign for the West Leicester Seat

1924
- March—Churchill's Campaign for the Westminster Seat as an "Independent Anti-Socialist"
- October—Epping—The Return to the Conservatives and the Cabinet

Meanwhile, in Germany
- The Beer Hall Putsch—November 1923
- The "Trial"—February 1924

In the wake of Churchill's defeat in 1922, he recuperated by renting a villa on the Riviera for the winter, where he painted.[1] He also published the first volume of his memoirs on WWI.

1923

December—Churchill's Campaign for the West Leicester Seat

Andrew Bonar Law would serve, ineptly, as Prime Minister for six months. In May 1923, he was forced to resign for health reasons. King George then turned to the Conservative Chancellor of the Exchequer, Stanley Baldwin, to become Prime Minister (even though Baldwin had been in the Cabinet only fifteen months and a senior minister for only seven). Baldwin believed that the solution to the country's continuing high unemployment rate was the institution of high tariffs, something that Bonar Law and the Conservatives had campaigned against in the election of November 1922.[2] Because of that change in position on a major issue, Baldwin felt obliged to dissolve Parliament and have another general election on December 6, 1923.[3]

Maintaining free trade was an issue near and dear to Churchill's heart. It had caused him to "cross the floor" and join the Liberals back in 1904. Now, it would bring him back into public life. It also drew the two wings of the Liberal Party together.[4] Although he was offered the opportunity to run for several seats in Manchester that were more winnable,[5] for the 1923 election, he accepted the offer to run as the Liberal candidate from West Leicester. He was a candidate who was "more anti-Labour than anti-Tory."[6] Like his old district (Dundee), West Leicester was blue-collar.[7] There he also faced a hostile press and was followed around by a gang of hecklers. The insults hurled at him included many cracks about Gallipoli and Antwerp.[8]

Those were not the Churchill's only problems in the election. His candidacy was based on opposing the imposition of tariffs. But the Labour Party took the same position—and it controlled West Leicester.[9] As a result, Churchill was crushed by the Labour candidate—receiving only 30 percent of the vote. Nationally, the Conservatives lost 87 seats. They now held 258 seats (42 percent); Labour held 191, and the Liberals, who gained 43 seats in the election, now held 158.

1924

The Conservatives were in trouble. They lacked a majority and were unwilling to continue their coalition with the Liberals or enter one with Labour. Thus, they left the door open for the Asquith Liberals to form a coalition with Labour,[10] which in late January made Ramsey MacDonald Labour's first Prime Minister.[11] (MacDonald would, however, stay in office for only ten months.) Although Labour shared Churchill's view on free trade, Churchill began a tirade in which he argued that Labour represented Socialist rule.[12]

March—Churchill's Campaign for the Westminster Seat as an "Independent Anti-Socialist"

Less than five weeks after MacDonald became Prime Minister, Churchill had dinner with two of his most influential friends, press barons Lord Beaverbrook and Lord Rothermere. The two owned most of the newspapers in the UK.[13] They advised him of an imminent by-election to fill the seat of a retiring MP in the Abbey division of Westminster, a district in which Buckingham Palace and the homes of scores of MPs were located.[14] It was "the Conservatives' choicest preserve."[15] More importantly, Beaverbrook and Rothermere offered Churchill their support if he would run. They revealed that there was even a chance of an endorsement from the Conservative Association of Westminster.[16] As Churchill would tell his wife, based on a subsequent long, friendly talk with Prime Minister Baldwin, also it was clear that the P.M. "wants very much to secure my return and cooperation."[17]

On March 4, 1924, Churchill announced his candidacy for the Westminster seat.[18] He would run as an Independent Anti-Socialist.[19] In a press release, Churchill stated that "My candidature is in no way hostile to the Conservative Party and its leaders."[20] This represented a first step in the metamorphosis of Churchill, the erstwhile Liberal, back to being a full-fledged Conservative. Prime Minister Baldwin even considered supporting Churchill, until the editor of The Morning Post rushed in to stop it.[21]

Although there was a Conservative in the race, the Labour candidate, Fenner Brockway, focused almost exclusively on Churchill.[22] Brockway called Churchill "the chief exponent of class war" and added that Churchill's "forte is to be a disturber of the peace, whether at home or abroad. He is a political adventurer with a genius for acts of mischievous irresponsibility."[23] Nevertheless, thirty Conservative MPs supported Churchill.[24]

The votes were counted on March 19, 1924. As renowned Churchill biographer Martin Gilbert tells it, as the last packet of votes was being carried up to the counting table someone told Churchill that he was "in by 100." The "news" quickly spread around the room and Winston's supporters burst into cheers. The sound was heard by the crowd waiting outside and soon the "news" of Churchill's victory was telegraphed all over the world. But it was wrong. When the official figures were announced, Churchill had lost by 33 votes. After a recount, the margin increased to 43 out of more than 22,000 cast.[25] Winston Churchill, the man who would be selected in future years as the greatest Briton of the 20th century, had just lost his third election in sixteen months.*

October—Epping—The Return to the Conservatives and the Cabinet

In the ensuing months, the coalition Government formed by Labour and the Asquith Liberals mucked along until the Liberals withdrew their support. Manchester calls the coalition "a prickly marriage of convenience" and adds that "[i]n the suit for divorce, Bolshevism was named as a correspondent."[26] (Not only had Labour P.M. MacDonald formally recognized the Soviet Union, but he had lent it money. The final straw for the Asquith Liberals was MacDonald's dropping charges against a "Communist editor who had incited mutiny among British troops,"[27] after which the Government would lose a confidence vote.[28]) MacDonald had little choice but to call for another general election. This one to be held on October 29, 1924.

Churchill's participation in the Westminster by-election was "generally regarded as a blunder, another example of his impetuosity."[29] But on the

---

*Of the twelve elections in which Churchill participated up to 1924, he won only six.

other hand, "[h]ad he routed the Tories' candidate, [the Conservatives] would have found it hard to forgive him."[30]

As Gilbert reports, in early April 1924, Churchill told Baldwin that "there were more than 30 Liberal MPs who would be willing to act with the Conservatives in Parliament. ..."[31] The notion of the Conservatives working in concert with a group of Liberal MPs was received approvingly by Baldwin's Shadow Cabinet.[32] A month later, for the first time in twenty years, Churchill made a major speech to a Conservative group, and told them that there was no longer any place for an independent Liberal Party; only the Conservatives offered a strong enough base "for the successful defeat of Socialism."[33]

Throughout the spring and summer of 1924, Conservative surrogates explored potential constituencies from which Churchill could run.[34] They found him an opportunity at Epping (17 miles northeast of London) and on September 11, 1924, he accepted the offer to run there and "officially stood as a Constitutionalist and Anti-Socialist candidate."[35] He was back in the Conservative fold. Churchill's famous quote on this auspicious occasion was "Anyone can rat, but it takes a certain ingenuity to re-rat."[36] On September 25, Churchill spoke before the Scottish Conservatives in Edinburgh. In his speech, not only did he attack Labour as the party of Socialists and fellow travelers with the Soviet Union, but he described the Soviet Union as "one of the worst tyrannies that has ever existed in the world."[37]

One day earlier, Churchill had written that the danger for another war still existed in Europe, and that the causes had in some ways been aggravated by the Treaty of Versailles. He said:

> The enormous contingents of German youth growing to military manhood year by year are inspired by the fiercest sentiments, and the soul of Germany smoulders with dreams of a War of Liberation or Revenge. These ideas are restrained at the present moment only by physical impotence." [Germany is disarmed while] France is armed to the teeth ... for the present at any rate overwhelming force is on their side. But physical force alone, unsustained by world opinion, affords no durable foundation for security. *Germany is a far stronger entity than France, and cannot be kept in permanent subjugation.*"[38] [emphasis added]

Churchill, who had never been regarded as a fan of the League of Nations, nonetheless appealed to the world to embrace it, calling it "the sole organization capable of averting catastrophe."[39] Farsighted and perceptive as the article was, writing about the Versailles treaty and its satellite treaties in this way in 1924 (just six years after WWI) was "shocking to readers."[40]

Meanwhile, in Germany

The Beer Hall Putsch—November 1923

In 1923 the German economy was still in ruin and the value of the mark plunged to nearly zero. In January, it took eighteen thousand marks to buy one dollar; by the end of the year, it took trillions. With the mark worthless, the life savings of middle-class Germans were wiped out. Shockingly, the Weimar Government not only let it happen, they encouraged it. Why? To wipe out public debt, escape having to pay reparations, and allow German heavy industry to repay its existing debts with valueless marks.[41]

Hitler called the state a "swindler" and shouted, "we want a dictatorship."[42] He felt that the conditions were right to overthrow the Government. But the Nazis were still an obscure party, virtually unknown outside the state of Bavaria. Could Hitler do what Mussolini had done in 1922—lead a march to the capital and bring down the national government? As tensions between Bavaria and the national government in Berlin grew, and Berlin warned the Bavarian leaders (Gustav von Kahr, General Otto von Lossow, and Col. Hans Ritter von Seisser) and Hitler that any rebellion would be put down by force. Hitler pleaded for a march on Berlin.[43] The Bavarian leaders were not interested. They were thinking of having Bavaria secede from the Republic; Hitler wanted to supplant the leaders in Berlin with strong national governance. Nor did they want to be hurried into any action. Hitler could not wait for Kahr et al., even though he still needed their support if his revolution were to have any chance of success. His plan: kidnap the three leaders and force them to do as he demanded.

On the evening of November 8, 1923, all three were scheduled to attend a meeting at a large beer hall in Munich where Kahr would speak. About half an hour into Kahr's speech, the *Sturmabteilung* (SA) (the Nazi storm troopers) surrounded the beerhall. Hitler then pushed his way into the crowded building, jumped on a table and fired his gun into the air. As Kahr paused, Hitler walked to the stage and grabbed the mike. He told the crowd of three thousand that "The National Revolution has begun!" He added that the hall was surrounded and, falsely, that the army and police had joined the revolution.[44] With the help of a few storm troopers, Hitler hustled Kahr, Lossow, and Seisser off stage into an anteroom. There, Hitler threatened them with death if they did not agree to join the new government he was forming with WWI hero General Erich Ludendorff. (Ludendorff was a leading proponent of the theory that Germany's defeat in the war had resulted from its army's betrayal by Marxists, Freemasons, and Jews, who were likewise responsible for the emasculating settlement reached in the Treaty of Versailles.) The

Nazis were in the process of bringing Ludendorff to the beer hall, but he knew nothing about Hitler's planned coup.[45]

While Hitler was making no progress with Kahr, Lossow, and Seisser, the crowd was growing uneasy. Hermann Goering (Hitler's loyal lieutenant in the Nazi Party) assured them that "there was nothing to fear"—they should just continue to drink beer while a new government was being created just off stage.[46] Shortly, Hitler appeared and masterfully told the following lies: The three Bavarian leaders were joining him in forming a new national government, a new German National Army was being formed under the leadership of General Ludendorff, and the new government was organizing a march on Berlin to unseat the current national leaders.[47] The crowd cheered.

After Ludendorff arrived at the beer hall and got over his anger at not being told of Hitler's scheme in advance or that Hitler planned to become dictator, not him, he seemingly got Kahr, Lossow, and Seisser to cooperate.[48] Before the meeting broke up, the three were led back on stage where each made a brief speech in which they falsely swore loyalty to the new regime.[49] But at the first opportunity, rather than working on tasks for the new regime (most importantly, the march to Berlin), Kahr, Lossow and Seisser left.

Ludendorff proposed a new plan. In the morning, he and Hitler would march their followers to the War Ministry located in the center of Munich and seize the city. The General reasoned that neither German soldiers nor the police (many of whom were war veterans) would open fire upon him.[50] He was only partially correct. The next morning, heading a column of some three thousand armed storm troopers, Ludendorff was able pass through several police roadblocks with little trouble. But such would not be the case when they approached the War Ministry. There, on a narrow street, one hundred armed police refused to yield.[51] Soon, a shot rang out and shooting by both sides commenced in earnest. The skirmish only lasted one minute, but that was time enough for nineteen men to be killed—sixteen Nazis and three police—with many more, including Goering, wounded.

Ignoring the shooting, Ludendorff calmly continued to walk toward the War Ministry. No one, including Hitler, walked with him. In fact, the future German chancellor was among the first to fall back and flee. He was rushed into a waiting car and taken to a house outside the city.[52] Two days later he was arrested. With the exception of Goering and Rudolf Hess (another pillar of the Nazi Party), who had fled to Austria, all the Nazi leaders were taken into custody.[53] For all intents and purposes, Hitler and National Socialism seemed dead.

The "Trial"—February 1924

The prospects for Nazism and Hitler looked quite dismal when he and Ludendorff went on trial together for high treason on February 26, 1924.

The "trial," however, was much more of a four-week-long platform for Hitler to put on a show before a cadre of newspapermen from near and far, than it was a prosecution for trying to overthrow the Government.[54] First and foremost, the fix was in—the pro-Nazi Bavarian Minister of Justice had seen to that. Hitler was not going to be convicted of anything serious. Second, under the "rules" of the proceeding, Hitler could cross-examine witnesses at will and speak at any time for as long as he liked. Indeed, in addition to his four-hour-long opening statement, he made numerous other lengthy speeches. On the subject of guilt, he said quite succinctly: "I alone bear the responsibility. But I am not a criminal because of that. ... There is no such thing as high treason against the traitors of 1918."[55]

That said, Ludendorff was acquitted but Hitler was found guilty. However, rather than receiving the life sentence prescribed by law, he was sentenced to only five years in prison (of which he would only serve nine months). Even though the putsch itself was a fiasco, the trial greatly increased Hitler's national visibility. He had gone from the undistinguished head of a fringe party headquartered in Munich to a veritable hero in many quarters. He had also not gone unnoticed by Churchill, who even raised the failed Beer Hall Putsch during his successful reelection campaign in Epping in the fall of 1924.[56]

In the nine months Hitler spent in Landsberg prison, he was afforded considerable privileges, including a private cell, frequent visitors, and even a personal secretary (Rudolf Hess)—and he wrote *Mein Kampf*.[57]

*Churchill as Chancellor of
the Exchequer in 1929*

*Austin Chamberlain, Prime Minister
Stanley Baldwin, and Churchill*

8

October 1924–April 1929. Churchill Elected as Conservative—Returns to Cabinet

Winston Elected to Parliament as a Conservative and Joins the Cabinet as
 Chancellor of the Exchequer
Defense Spending and Spending on Social Programs
War Debt
Churchill's View of Mussolini
Decision to Go Back to the Gold Standard
General Strike of 1926
Britain Can "Stand Alone"
Pact of Locarno
Disarmament in Britain
Meanwhile, in Germany

Winston Elected to Parliament as a Conservative and Joins the Cabinet as Chancellor of the Exchequer

On October 29, 1924, Churchill won the election in Epping handily. At the national level, the Conservatives gained 161 seats (and now held 419—a huge majority); Labour lost forty seats (and now held 151); while the Liberals lost 118 seats (and now held only forty*). These results showed two things: (1) in the 10 months that the Labour/Liberal coalition was in office, Labour had lost a lot of popularity; and (2) the public believed Churchill was right when he said that it was the Conservatives, not the Liberals, who were well suited to counteract Labour.

Despite Churchill's return to the Conservative ranks, and the party's impressive showing in the election of November 4, Churchill did not believe that he would be invited to join the Government, because "owing to the size of its majority it will probably be composed only of impeccable Conservatives."[1] Churchill was wrong. At that very moment Baldwin was

---

Even former Prime Minister Henry Asquith, the leader of the Asquith Liberals during WWI, was defeated.

contemplating what cabinet post he should give Churchill.[2] As it turns out, Neville Chamberlain played an important role in Baldwin's decision. The P.M. wanted to return Chamberlain to the post he had held in the first Baldwin Government—Chancellor of the Exchequer—and thought about the Ministry of Health for Churchill.[3] But Chamberlain had different ideas. He wanted to go back to Health,[4] told Baldwin so, and suggested Churchill for the Chancellorship.[5]*

Chamberlain's eminent biographer, Robert Self, writes that, beneath his harsh exterior, Chamberlain was "a reformer motivated by genuine humanitarian impulses," and that rejecting the most important cabinet post for the far less important position at the Ministry of Health, "never caused Chamberlain a moment's regret."[6] A few minutes after Chamberlain turned down the Chancellorship, Baldwin offered it to an astonished Churchill, who told the P.M. that "This fulfills my ambition. I still have my father's robes as Chancellor. I shall be proud to serve you in this splendid Office."[7] Indeed, "Churchill had long wanted to vindicate his father's brief tenure at the Exchequer in 1886."[8] The robes, carefully packed in tissue paper and camphor since 1886, were aired. Winston wore them at his first official function.

When Austen Chamberlain (who would become Churchill's great ally a decade later) heard what Baldwin had done, he was greatly disturbed and felt that it would be a shock to the party. Others told Baldwin that the appointment was genius because it would hamstring Churchill.[9] Baldwin said that now "It would be up to [Winston] to be loyal, *if he is capable of loyalty.*"[10]** [emphasis added] The *Guardian* discussed Churchill's fealty more sarcastically, referring to his having switched parties once before, then said that Churchill had "shall we say—quitted [a] sinking ship for the second time and for the second time the reward of this fine instinct has been ... high promotion."[11] Several of the other London papers also attacked Baldwin's decision.[12]

So ended Churchill's two years out of government—two years without his salary as an MP. or, more importantly, without the additional compensation for being a member of the Cabinet.*** "Just as in July 1917, Churchill's

---

*According to Manchester, "Tory indifference to tariff reform had soured" Chamberlain on any return to the Treasury. Manchester, Visions p. 784.

**Churchill's good friend, F.E. Smith, 1st Earl of Birkenhead, said that Churchill "... has never in all his life failed a friend, however embarrassing the obligations." Birkenhead, Contemporary Personalities p. 115.

***For these two years Churchill supported his family by editing collections of his speeches and writing books and newspaper and magazine articles (for which he earned about $200,000 in today's money). Manchester, Visions p. 765.

political career had been saved by a prime minister whose primary motivation was the fear of his powerful voice being raised in opposition on the back benches."[13] As Neville Chamberlain would also conclude in September 1939, Baldwin believed that Churchill "would be more under control inside [the Cabinet] than out."[14]

When Churchill became Chancellor, the British economy had still not recovered from WWI. Both inflation and unemployment were high, income taxes were at historically high levels, and the coal industry, Britain's largest employer, was exporting only about one-third of the tonnage shipped before the war.[15] On top of this, Britain had problems with its war debt (both the amount it owed to America and collecting the amounts others owed her). There was pressure for the country to return to the Gold Standard, and the Royal Navy wanted to modernize the fleet. Churchill himself wanted to expand social welfare, revive trade, and cut taxes to stimulate growth. And just to make accomplishing all of this even harder, a majority in the House believed that the budget had to be balanced at all costs.[16]

Defense Spending and Spending on Social Programs

One of the vexing political issues facing Churchill and the Government during this period was how to balance a national desire for disarmament with the military's wish for replenished resources. As Baldwin would explain to the House years later, "from 1924 to 1929, when we did cut down the Services, we all did it, including [Mr. Churchill,] the Chancellor of the Exchequer, after due and full consideration, and we did it because we still had hopes of disarmament, because we believed that there was no danger of a major war within a decade and because we were very anxious to conserve the finance of the country."[17] Of course, in the mid-1920s there was no country that seemed to be a potential enemy. At that time Hitler was certainly not seen as a significant threat—until the depression, the Nazis had simply been thought of as part of the lunatic fringe.[18] Regarding another future combatant, Churchill was of the view that there was not "the slightest chance of [a war with Japan] in [his] lifetime,[19] a position with which the Foreign Office agreed.[20]

Churchill felt that funneling money into rearmament would work against the wish for balanced budgets and impede accomplishing the other things he wanted to do. As a result, he slashed spending for both a new naval base in Singapore and a new cruiser program the Royal Navy wanted. Churchill was "oppose[d] to rearmament as late as 1929."[21] His own parliamentary private secretary, Robert Boothby, said that "Churchill disarmed the country as nobody has ever disarmed this country before."[22] Despite the fact that during Churchill's Chancellorship the Royal Navy's annual budget actually increased from £105 million to £113 million,[23] Churchill was viewed by some during the ominous years of the 1930s as "much to blame for Britain's [military] weakness...."[24*]

Manchester describes Churchill's 1925 budget as "an abrupt departure from the traditional Tory approach."[25] Along with limitations on defense spending for all services except the RAF,[26**] Churchill proposed to lower taxes on the poor and raise them on unearned income, have the Treasury assume responsibility for the victims of industrial distress, provide benefits to more than two hundred thousand widows and three hundred and fifty thousand orphans, reduce the age for retirement pensions from seventy to sixty-five, and provide health insurance (partially paid for by employers) to thirty million individuals.[27***] The social reformer from the first decade of the century had been resurrected.

War Debt

In 1924 Britain still owed the United States about £1 billion for loans taken out to fight the war,[****] while countries including France, Japan, Belgium, and Italy owed Britain £2 billion. (This did not include the reparations Germany owed.) The United States was a demanding creditor that mandated scheduled payments.[28] Unfortunately, the countries that owed money to Britain were much more lackadaisical in their approach to repayment. In early January 1925, Churchill attended a conference in Paris, the goal of which was to negotiate and restructure war debts and reparations. After a week of negotiations, at the Cabinet meeting of January 15, 1925, Churchill reported that he had been able to get the Americans to agree to his proposal to accept payments that were directly linked to the payments that Britain received.[29] This was a major achievement and a testament to Churchill's negotiating skills.

Churchill's View of Mussolini

Late in 1925, Italy settled her war debts with Britain and Churchill would make the first of many glowing statements about Mussolini (all of which he would come to regret). Churchill did not, however, agree when

---

*In Robert's view, if either Neville or Austen Chamberlain had been Chancellor at the time, they would have been then even tougher on the Royal Navy. Roberts p. 312.

**Prime Minister Baldwin managed to negotiate the restoration of some of the Royal Navy's appropriation. Manchester, Visions p. 790.

***According to Manchester, with these proposals Churchill had "stolen ... Chamberlain's thunder and Chamberlain resented it." Manchester, Visions p. 789.

****Interest cost on this amount exceeded £35 million per year. After WWI, British debt was fourteen times greater than it had been before the war. Buchanan p. 101.

it was suggested in response that perhaps Britain should have a Fascist government.[30] In 1927 Churchill, the arch anti-Communist, would again praise Mussolini by saying that he had "provided the necessary antidote to the Russian poison" and that Fascism had "rendered a service to the whole world."[31] These and similar statements caused the *New Leader* to say that "We have always suspected that Mr. Winston Churchill was a fascist at heart. ..."[32] After Mussolini saddled up to Hitler, Churchill would change his tune and call him a swine and a jackal.[33]

Decision to Go Back to the Gold Standard

Before WWI, the value of the British pound was tied to the price of gold. The so-called "Gold Standard" was abandoned in 1914 to halt the rapid fall in value of the pound. After the war, a government commission as well as the current head of the Bank of England, several economists, and politicians of all parties urged a return to Gold.[34] Both the United States and Germany had already done so.

Even so, famous Cambridge economist John Maynard Keynes, among others, opposed the idea. In his efforts to make a proper decision, Churchill set up a symposium dinner with Keynes, another opposer (Reginald McKenna, a former Chancellor of the Exchequer) and two leading proponents of the return to Gold (economic advisor Lord John Bradbury and Otto Niemeyer, a British banker).[35] While impressed with Keynes' arguments,[36] ultimately, the pro-gold position prevailed, overcoming even Churchill's own doubts. The return to the Gold Standard was announced in the budget presented on April 28, 1925. As Churchill told the House that day, "No responsible authority has advocated any other policy."[37]

In July 1925, Keynes republished a paper he had written in 1919, now renamed "The Economic Consequences of Mr. Churchill." In it he argued that because the Gold Standard overvalued sterling, wages would fall. He also attacked Churchill's decision to return to Gold because: Churchill had "no instinctive judgment to prevent him from making mistakes" and because he had been "gravely misled by experts."[38]

Churchill later regretted returning to the Gold Standard without "adjust[ing] wage and taxation policy."[39]* As a result of this failure, the cost of producing British coal greatly increased at a time when the end of

---

*Robert Boothby, Churchill's parliamentary secretary, writes that, in retrospect, "with the exception of the unilateral guarantee to Poland without Russian support,[(see Chapter 12) returning to the Gold Standard] was the most fatal step taken by the country." Boothby, Rebel p. 39.

In 1945, Churchill would call listening to the experts about returning to the Gold Standard "The biggest blunder of my life. Moran, Struggle p. 326.

the French occupation of the Ruhr (the industrial heart of Germany) brought enormous quantities of cheap German coal onto the world market.[40] British mine owners, who had over the previous seven years reduced wages by 35 percent, threatened to cut wages even further.[41] Churchill was thus required to fund a temporary nine-month supplement of wages to avoid a massive strike.

General Strike of 1926

By the spring of 1926 Britain's temporary subsidy of coal miners' wages was ending, but the National Union of Mine Workers (NUM) continued to reject the mine owners' demand for wage reductions, and for an eight- rather than seven-hour, workday, and setting wages on a local, rather than national, basis. In April, the situation escalated when the union's position was supported by the Trade Union Congress (TUC), a group made up of representatives from every union in Britain. The TUC threatened to call a nationwide general strike to support the miners.[42] In the absence of a settlement, on May 1, the owners locked out the miners.[43] The TUC immediately declared a general strike that began on May 3, 1926.

Because of his involvement in both a clash with miners at Tonypandy in 1910, and railway workers at Llanelli in 1911, Churchill was easily portrayed as anti-Labor, when, in fact, he was more sympathetic to the miners' position than anyone else in the Cabinet. Even so, Churchill knew that a general strike would be devastating to Britain.[44]

Intent on getting its position about the strike out to the public, and radio being in its infancy, the Government was perturbed that none of the London newspapers would be printed during the General Strike. As a result, they asked London's leading newspapers to help them print their own paper. Baldwin put Churchill, an experienced newspaperman, in charge.[45] With Churchill writing many of the unsigned articles, despite a somewhat chaotic production process, on the morning of May 5, 1926, two hundred and thirty thousand copies of the *British Gazette* were printed at *The Morning Post* and were sold throughout the country for a penny.[46] By its final edition on May 13, circulation had risen to an astounding 2.2 million a day.[47] (To do this, Churchill had to commandeer large amounts of newsprint from other papers as well as ink from sources that included the *British Worker*—a paper the unions were trying to publish.[48])

As to content, Churchill attempted to keep all details of rowdyism and intimidation by the strikers out of the *Gazette*.[49] Instead, it included articles

---

Still, he learned something from the experience. In Roberts' view, Churchill's willingness to attack appeasement in the mid-1930s, when it was accepted by almost everyone else (see Chapters 10–11) "might not have been so complete had he not seen ... experts proved wrong time and time again, and had he not, in the case of the Gold Standard, been forced to take ultimate responsibility." Roberts p. 315.

that stressed the fact that the general strike was inflicting substantial loss and inconvenience but that the country was muddling along. It also included stern messages from Baldwin in which, among other things, he called the strike "the road to anarchy" and something that "will break the country."[50] "...[R]eaders of the *Gazette* were led to believe that the country was in the grip, not of an industrial dispute, but of incipient revolution."[51] Churchill's refusal to yield to the strikers demands, coupled with Baldwin's tough response, caused the general strike to crack on May 11.[52] The news was reported in the final edition of the *Gazette*. The strike lasted only eight days, but still Churchill was once again wrongly viewed as being anti-labor. ...[53] Noting Churchill's long standing as a progressive, Manchester, calls the enmity between organized labor and Churchill "inexpiable" and "tragic."[54]

While the national strike ended, the coal strike continued. Churchill advised the Cabinet that the financial position of the Government was likely to be aggravated by any continuance of the coal strike. He was also one of the few Cabinet members who urged the Government to take further action—which it did. In July, the Coal Mines (Eight Hours) Act was passed which increased the cap on hours a miner could work from seven to eight. Churchill would later defend the Act as "permissive" rather than "obligatory" and "a necessary feature in any economic settlement."[55]

In August, Baldwin was forced to take an extended holiday in France to recover from a severe attack of lumbago[56] and left things in Churchill's hands.[57] Despite the unabashed hostility of many Tory ministers toward the coal strikers, Churchill:

- saved the miners' right to picket peaceably;

- sidetracked efforts to outlaw strikes;

- built homes and established "training schemes and other forms of assistance for displaced miners" and

- preserved the miners' right to a secret ballot.[58]

Even so, the strike continued. During the fall, knowing that winter was approaching and that the strikers were getting desperate and growing hungrier every day, the mine owners refused to make any concessions.[59] Churchill warned the owners that "if they continued to be 'unreasonable' the Government would appoint arbitrators and fix a national minimum wage."[60] The owners remained unmoved. Nonetheless, the strike ended on November 20, 1926. The owners had won out. They got the workday lengthened from seven to eight hours, lower wages, and wage scales set on a district-by-district basis.[61] Adding insult to injury, in the wake of the coal strike, the Conservatives passed much anti-union labor legislation which, among other things, eliminated all the gains Churchill had achieved for unions, and even outlawed picketing.[62]

In early December 1926, the Labour Party brought an unsuccessful motion to censure the Government for its conduct of the coal negotiations.* In his response, Churchill noted that "Time after time terms [had] been offered and turned down," first by the owners and then by the miners.[63]

Churchill also raised an intriguing point about the influence of Russia in the strike: that £1.2 million had been given to the miners' cause, ostensibly by Russian miners (through their trade unions).[64] Of course, the real wages of these Russian miners were less than one-third those of the striking British miners.[65] He also noted that the amount putatively contributed through Russian "unions" was two and a half times greater than the amount contributed to the coal miners by British unions.[66] The Soviets had meddled in the strike. Some months earlier, the Cabinet had even considered cutting off diplomatic relations with the USSR over its involvement in British labor matters.[67] None of this did anything to reduce Churchill's continuing suspicion of the Soviets.

Britain Can "Stand Alone"

In February 1925, Churchill wrote a series of notes about the age-old antagonism between Germany and France. He sent a copy to the former P.M.—and later Foreign Secretary—Arthur Balfour. In them Churchill pointed out that Germany was now prostrate, but sooner or later Germany would be rearmed. One of the notes discussed a hypothetical war between France and Germany and what Britain would do if Germany controlled all the Channel ports in Europe. Churchill said, "The answer depends on who has the best and most powerful weapons. If in addition to sea superiority we had air supremacy, we might maintain ourselves as we did in the days of Napoleon for indefinite periods, even when all the Channel ports and all the low countries were in the hands of a vast hostile military power." Churchill added: *"It should never be admitted in this argument that England cannot, if the worst comes to the worst, stand alone."*[68] [emphasis added]

As discussed in future chapters, this exact situation would come about in the spring of 1940 when at Churchill's urging, Britain did chose to "stand alone."

More specifically, Labour argued that the Government deserved to be censured "… for its partiality toward the mine owners, for its failure to control the price of coal, and for the passing of the Coal Mines (Eight Hours) Act, which prolonged and embittered the dispute and resulted in the imposition of harsh terms upon men no longer able to resist." HC Deb 08 December 1926 vol 200 cc2131.

Pact of Locarno

Under the Treaty of Versailles, France was scheduled to end her occupation of the Ruhr Valley in January 1925. Well before that, German Foreign Minister Gustav Stresemann sensed that the French were getting nervous about pulling out of the Ruhr and that, fearing for her security, France might even cancel the withdrawal. The French wanted Britain to guarantee her postwar borders, but the British Government were not willing to do so. Such being the case, with Germany eager to get the French out of the Ruhr, Stresemann came up with a plan pursuant to which all sides could get what they wanted.

The foreign ministers of most Western European countries met in the Swiss town of Locarno in October 1925. What came to be known as the Pact of Locarno was several agreements by which Germany, France, Belgium, Great Britain, and Italy mutually guaranteed peace in Western Europe. The treaties were initialed at Locarno, and signed in London.

The agreements consisted of (1) a treaty guaranteeing assistance in the event of aggression signed by Germany, Belgium, France, Great Britain, and Italy; (2) arbitration treaties between Germany and Belgium and between Germany and France; (3) a note from the former WWI Allies to Germany explaining the use of sanctions against a covenant-breaking state as outlined in Article 16 of the League of Nations Covenant; (4) arbitration treaties between Germany and Czechoslovakia and between Germany and Poland; and (5) specific treaties of guarantee between France and Poland and between France and Czechoslovakia.

Locarno was significant in that Germany renounced the use of force to change its western frontier while Britain promised to defend Belgium and France in the event of aggression—something that was a great relief to the French. As Roberts writes, Locarno, along with Germany's admission as a permanent member of the League of Nations in September 1926, "brought Germany back into the international diplomatic mainstream."[69] Notably at Locarno, Britain did not guarantee to come to the assistance of either Poland or Czechoslovakia if they were attacked.

The Locarno Treaties marked a dramatic improvement in the political climate of western Europe in 1925–1930. They promoted expectations for continued peaceful settlements, often noted as being in the "spirit of Locarno." This spirit was made concrete when (1) Germany joined the League, and (2) Allied troops were withdrawn from the Rhineland in 1930.

During the mid to late '30s, the Locarno Treaties would be center stage as they were renounced, reaffirmed, undermined, or ignored as Europe slid toward another war.

Disarmament in Britain

Another thing that would have its origins in the '20s and a significant impact in the '30s was disarmament. Throughout the early to mid-1920s, some effort to disarm was made in just about every country that had participated in WWI.[70] Unsurprisingly, no country had disarmed more than Germany.[71] As noted, the Versailles treaty, allowed her only a meager military. As a result, when she joined the League of Nations in 1926 she immediately started pressing other members to disarm to the lowest point consistent with national safety and ability to contribute proportionally to common action pursuant to international obligations as the League's covenant provided.

In no country other than Germany was the feeling for international disarmament stronger than in Britain.[72] Britons were strong supporters of the League of Nations. Given that the League was supposed to provide collectively the security that each nation had formerly tried to obtain by arming itself to the teeth, it was only natural that those who favored the League also saw no need for any country, including their own, to have a substantial stockpile of weapons. Ardent supporters of the League would be wary of British rearmament well into the 1930s.

Meanwhile, in Germany

Following the major economic and political turmoil that ensued after the founding of the Weimar Republic, Germany underwent a period of stabilization.[73] The U.S. took over control of German reparations payments after being established as the world's leading economic power following the war.[74] American interest in economic expansion throughout Europe led to its support of financially reasonable reparation payments from Germany. The plan for new reparations payments was put forward by a Reparations Commission headed by an American banker, Charles Dawes, in April 1924.[75] Making reparations, which had debilitated the German economy, more manageable allowed the Germans to move beyond its political isolationist policy.[76]

The broader reformation of German foreign policy was led by former Chancellor and later Foreign Minister (1923–29), Ernst Stresemann, who supported a national revisionist foreign policy to "restore Germany to its former greatness."[77] He believed that nationalism wouldn't be successful if it challenged the victors of the war directly, so it instead framed European "reconciliation" as its key policy. He believed, for example, that by supporting the Dawes Plan, and finding a way to pay reparations to France, which needed them most (having been most heavily impacted by the war), Germany could rebuild and form an alliance with France, which sought protection from the other European powers—particularly the growing Soviet Union.[78]

At the same time, Germany surreptitiously launched a rearmament plan, repeatedly violating the Treaty of Versailles, while at the same time making efforts to get other countries to disarm.

Meanwhile, following his release from prison in 1923, Hitler worked for several years to legalize the Nazi Party and maintain his control of it.[79] He actively organized parliamentary units under the leadership of the Nazi Party. In 1925 the "SS" (Schutzstaffel), or "Protection Squadron" was established to protect Hitler and the other party leaders. The structure of power within the party was revamped to ensure loyalty to Hitler by all regional leadership. By the end of 1925, the Nazi Party comprised over 27,100 members. The Party restructured to allow for its engagement in elections, control over parliament, and ability to conduct extensive recruiting programs to attract voters to the Nazi ideology. Recruitment propaganda continued to focus on anti-establishment grievances. Religious, social, and economic class conflicts were unified under the Nazi populist message. As would always be one of its hallmarks, the Party engineered artificial emergencies and exacerbated fears of inadequate national defense, communism, the "unfair" and "debilitating" terms of the Treaty of Versailles, and societal moral depravity which it attributed to Jewish and international influences that gained power as a result of weak, democratic post-war government.[80] The Nazis argued that under its leadership Germany would be restored as a strong economic and cultural power with no asocial behaviors or "immoral, criminal" activities. All citizens would be brought into one homogenous community under totalitarian control. Of course, this meant that "foreign and Jewish influences" had to be removed from German society—politically, economically, culturally, intellectually, and genetically. Hitler framed human history as an instinctual struggle between races trying to survive through imperialism and domination of resources, such that one "pure" race should be able to perpetuate itself above inferior races.

In 1928, the Nazi Party introduced this ideology during national parliamentary elections through violent intimidation of voters. While doing so did not have a favorable electoral outcome, forming alliances with other conservative parties in Germany did give the Nazis more political legitimacy than they had had in the past.

9

May 1929–December 1936
The Early Wilderness Years

Disarmament

Disarmament had been a worldwide topic of interest since Versailles and would remain so through a good portion of the '30s. The Treaty of Versailles had required Germany to disarm and urged other countries to follow suit.[1] In the 1920s and the early 1930s, substantial international nongovernmental campaigns developed to promote disarmament.

A commission on disarmament was established by the League in 1925. But from 1926 to 1931, with the sole exception of Britain (whose annual defense spending during the period *decreased* by 3.3 percent*), annual defense spending across the globe had increased, sometimes significantly: France (+116.6 percent), Italy (+24.6 percent), Russia (+59.95 percent), Japan (+10.5 percent), United States (+123 percent).[2]

The British viewed the reduction in defense spending as "taking [a] risk ... for peace."[3] Professor A.J.P. Taylor, on the other hand takes the cynical view that "there was British disarmament from economy; there was disarmament from negligence and mistaken judgment; there was no disarmament from principle."[4] (Other cynics and other countries saw British disarmament as merely the results of the desire to increase spending on social programs[5] or just a function of the great economic problems facing Britain and the rest of the world.) British spending on defense in the '20s and early '30s was also limited by application of the so-called "Ten Year Rule" drawn up by Churchill in 1919 when he was the Secretary for Air and War.[6] Under the Rule, the amount of defense spending in a given year was based on whether war was anticipated within ten years. The Rule was modified in July 1928 when Churchill persuaded the Committee of Imperial Defence to adopt a standing assumption in establishing the amount to be spent on defense in any given year that there would be no major war for ten years.[7]

For much of the period, England was going through a tremendous austerity program.

The Rule, which was discarded in 1932, did its job. As noted, defense spending in Britain was kept at a very low level.

As the '20s turned into the '30s, the desire for disarmament had gained strength in almost every country. By 1931, there was sufficient support worldwide to hold the long-awaited League sponsored conference on the subject—the Conference for the Reduction and Limitation of Armaments, which would open in Geneva in February 1932. Speaking to the House in June 1931, Prime Minister MacDonald admitted that the example of disarmament that Britain was trying to display had more or less gone to its limit. Nevertheless, he told the conference attendees that not only did he intended to seek more arms reductions in Europe, but upon his return he would make "still further reductions" in Britain.[8] Churchill, now two years out of the Cabinet, warned that Britain had already disarmed too much and had made herself extremely vulnerable.[9] He:

- also sensed a threat from the Soviet Union, which he called "aloof, malignant, and actively preparing for war"; and

- feared that France would be forced to disarm unduly which would have a terrible effect on the Eastern European states that looked to her "for guidance and leadership."[10]

While the conference was in session, Churchill expressed a view that he'd had for some years, which he felt was "continually confirmed by events ..." He said, "I am very doubtful whether there is any use in pressing national disarmament to a point where nations think their safety is compromised while the quarrels which divide them and which lead to armaments and lead to their fears are still unadjusted."[11] In the case of the French, he felt that forcing disarmament on her would also increase Britain's risks and liabilities to go to the aid of France under the Treaty of Locarno.[12] He added, "I have always tried to urge upon the House that to redress the grievances of the vanquished should precede the disarmament of the victors."[13]

1929
- Defense Spending for 1929–1930
- General Elections Held–May 30, 1929
- Minority Government Formed by Labour Party Leader Ramsey MacDonald

Defense Spending for 1929–1930
Overall defense spending in fiscal year 1929–1930 was 0.6 percent less than it had been in 1928–29. In contrast, spending on air defense increased by 4 percent.[14]

By 1929, many described the incumbent Conservative Government as old and tired. In the year before, the Conservatives had not fared well in by-elections. Even so, Prime Minister Baldwin had called for a general election at the end of May. Churchill was not optimistic about the Tories' chances, feeling that Conservatives were assailable on unemployment and many other issues.[15] Still, the campaign was enthusiastic. For example, in Churchill's first major speech he told the crowd that if a Labour government "came to power" they would "bring back the Russian Bolsheviks, who will immediately get busy ... planning another general strike" like the one experienced in 1926.[16]

In the 1929 general election, for the first time, the Labour Party, headed by Ramsay MacDonald, won more seats in the House than any other party, although it still failed to get an overall majority. Liberals regained some of the ground they had lost in the 1924 election. More importantly, they held the balance of power. Labour and the Liberals thus formed a Government headed by MacDonald. While the Conservatives lost their majority in the House and thus control of the Government, Churchill, although no longer a Minister, at least retained his seat in the House.* But "for the first time since 1917 (when he was still a Liberal)," Churchill was on the front bench for the opposition party.[17]**

Even before the election, there had been dissension within the Cabinet and a split over who would be Baldwin's successor as head of the Conservative Party—Churchill or Chamberlain.[18] Some members of the Cabinet agreed with Lord Derby's statement that "I believe in Winston's capability if only he were a bit more steady."[19] Churchill was also becoming estranged from his party. He did not agree with the Conservatives on the imposition of protective tariffs. As a result, Chamberlain suggested that if the Conservatives prevailed in the election, Churchill should leave the key position of Chancellor of the

---

*While Churchill would continue to receive his stipend as an MP, the loss of his salary as a Cabinet minister, coupled with the downturn in the stock market, created a financial crisis in the Churchill household. See, McCarten p. 55. Book deals, such as the one for a four-volume history about his famous ancestor, John Churchill, the Duke of Marlborough, See, Gilbert, Prophet pp. 319, 337, an agreement to write articles for The Daily Telegraph, a lecture tour of North America, Ibid. p. 334, as well as two directorships, Ibid. p.337, helped fill the gap. Within weeks of the election, Churchill started on the Marlborough project.

Research for Marlborough: His Life and Times would cause him to visit Munich, where he got to see what was happening in Germany firsthand.

**The election of 1929 is often called the "Flapper Election" because it was the first election in which women aged 21 to 29 voted. It also took place against a background of rising unemployment, with the memory of the general strike of 1926 still fresh in voters' minds.

Exchequer.[20]* Ideas bandied about included making Churchill Secretary of State for India, Foreign Secretary,** Lord President of the Council or Leader of the House.[21] "... by Spring it was obvious that Chamberlain had become Baldwin's favored minister."[22] Churchill told his old friend Leo Amery that if the Tory party persisted with the idea of imposing tariffs he would quit politics.[23]***

The Viceroy of India, Lord Irwin (who would later assume the title Lord Halifax****) was similarly against Churchill's being offered the position of Secretary of State for India.[24] As interesting as where to put Churchill might have been, it all became moot when Baldwin decided not to reshuffle the Cabinet and then the Conservatives lost the general election. At that time, Baldwin remarked that Churchill was a major reason for the Conservatives' defeat.[25]

Churchill would not serve as a minister in government again for ten years—1929–1939. This period is commonly called Churchill's "wilderness years," but are probably better described as his "impotent years" or perhaps "the years he spent crying out from the wilderness." Although not a member of the Cabinet, during this period, Churchill was as active and as well-known as ever. Besides remaining a member of Parliament, he was a syndicated columnist reaching millions as his columns were published all over the world.[26] Except for the Prime Minister, Churchill remained "the most famous political figure in Britain"—not unlike "the leader of an opposition party."[27]***** Still, the Government came to view him as a "meddler and

---

Ironically, as noted, it had been Chamberlain, who, five years earlier, suggested that Churchill be appointed Chancellor. Manchester, Visions p. 821.

**When Chamberlain was asked about the possibility of Churchill's serving as Foreign Secretary, he said that "the P.M. would not run such a risk and would dread to find himself waking up at night with the cold sweats at the thought of Winston's indiscretions." Gilbert, Prophet p. 314.*

***As also noted, it was the Conservatives' intention to impose tariffs that had caused Churchill to "cross the floor" in 1904 and join the Liberal Party.*

****He would become Viscount Halifax in 1934. Lord Halifax is the title by which he is best remembered. Under this title he served as Foreign Secretary to Churchill in 1940. (Upon his succeeding to the title of Viscount Halifax, the Churchill family nicknamed him "the Holy Fox" for his political dexterity, love of fox hunting, and High Church predilections.*

As discussed in future chapters, Halifax and Churchill would cross paths and sometimes swords in the late 1930s and in 1940. Most significantly, in May 1940 they would clash about whether Britain should negotiate a peace agreement with Hitler.

*****Famous as he was, during that period he often remained just a few steps ahead of his creditors. Shirer, 20th Century Journey: The Nightmare Years 1930–1940. A Memoir of the Life and Times p. 311.*

a Cassandra."[28]* They also believed that any "criticism of the Third Reich" (something Churchill would come to do regularly) "blackened a man's name."[29] While in the 1920s his speeches in the House always drew large crowds, for much of the '30s no one cared to listen to what he was saying or take any action based on it. Most of his speeches to the House were to empty seats.[30]

One of Churchill's first cries from the wilderness came in a speech in July 1929 when, according to his esteemed biographer Martin Gilbert, he "reasserted his complete devotion to free trade."[31] Churchill's support of free trade was challenged the very next day by Chamberlain, who showed his strong support for higher tariffs in a speech before the Empire Industries Association.[32] As it was becoming clearer that Neville Chamberlain would be Baldwin's successor as leader of the Conservatives, Churchill recognized that the Conservative Party no longer needed him. At the beginning of August 1929, Churchill left on a three-month tour of North America, during which he would promote his books, line up publishers for future projects, and give speeches. Three weeks into the trip, he wrote a letter to his wife in which he said that if Neville Chamberlain or anyone else of that kind became the leader of the Conservatives, he would leave politics.[33] The gulf between him and the Conservative Party was widening. And it would continue to do so for some time.

Near the end of the tour, Winston and his entourage found themselves in New York City. The date was October 24, 1929—better known as "Black Thursday."[34] The stock market crashed that day, causing Churchill to lose some £10,000 ($500,000 in today's money).[35] It was a huge sum for the inveterate stock-speculating spendthrift.

While Churchill was on his North American tour, the Royal Commission on India, appointed in 1927 and headed by Liberal MP Sir John Simon, was moving nearer to finishing its long-awaited report on granting India some measure of self-government (most likely at the provincial level.)[36]** But MacDonald's new Labour Government was interested in putting something far more comprehensive on the table: Indian self-government at the national as well as provincial levels (with limited British control) and eventual Dominion status.[37]*** Lord Irwin, the Viceroy of India whom Baldwin had appointed in 1926, approved the idea. As a result, MacDonald hoped that he could get Baldwin and the rest of the Conservatives to support it as well.[38] At a meeting held just before Churchill returned from North America, Baldwin

---

*In Greek mythology Cassandra was given the gift of prophecy but was also cursed by Apollo so that her prophecies, while true, would not be believed.

**This would have been acceptable to Churchill. Manchester, Visions p. 844.

***Granting India Dominion status would have been historic; to that point all former colonies which had achieved that position had had at least a substantial white population.

did urged his former Cabinet ministers to adopt Labour's goal—eventual Dominion status for India as Australia, New Zealand, Canada, and South Africa had.* In late October, over some objection, Baldwin suggested that the Viceroy issue a formal declaration saying that the natural progression for India was "the attainment of Dominion status."[39] The resulting document became known as the Irwin Declaration. On the same day it was issued, at the request of the Viceroy, Labour placed word in the *Indian Gazette* of a conference to which not only British, but Indian leaders would be invited, to discuss the matter.[40] Baldwin would also announce to the House that granting India Dominion status was his party's "'one duty' should they return to power in the future."[41]

Churchill returned from America on November 5, 1929. Two days later, the House debated the Labour Government's proposed India policy. At that session, Baldwin revealed that the Conservatives supported MacDonald's approach. This was, however, an exaggeration. Many Tories were prepared to vote against the proposal.[42] Some questioned "not only [Baldwin's] wisdom, but also his integrity."[43] Lloyd George, speaking for the Liberals (as well as for Churchill and a great many Tories who feared reprisals for speaking against Baldwin[44]) also did not approve of the Viceroy's declaration or any plan which created the impression that full Dominion status would be granted to India without delay, particularly before the soon-to-be-completed Report of the Simon Commission was issued.[45] Churchill, Austen Chamberlain, and a few other MPs were apoplectic.[46]** In a letter from one of Baldwin's senior colleagues, Sir Samuel Hoare, to Viceroy Irwin (Halifax), Hoare wrote that "Throughout the debate Winston was almost demented with fury. ..."[47]

Manchester explains that demented as Churchill might have been, "a clear majority of the Tory MPs thought [he] was right, but most of them had too much to lose to say so." In private, even Neville Chamberlain had shown a preference to go slow on Indian self-government, however, in public, he was an avid supporter of Baldwin's position.[48]

Churchill would lay out his case against giving India Dominion status in the *Daily Mail* on November 16, 1929. There he first discussed some of

---

Under the Balfour Declaration of 1926, later codified in the Statute of Westminster (1931), the British parliament no longer had the power to legislate for the Dominions. Jan Smuts, the former and future Prime Minister of South Africa, believed that "the statute was in fact a blueprint for the dismantling of the Empire." Manchester, Visions p. 833. Ireland could and did quote the statute as justification for its complete secession from the Commonwealth and converting itself into a "sovereign independent and democratic state." Morris, Trumpets p. 337.

**One of Churchill's few allies at the time was Austen Chamberlain, Neville's older half-brother, who had, among other things, in 1916 refused to serve in any government that included Churchill and in 1922 objected to Baldwin's appointing Churchill Chancellor of the Exchequer.*

the things that Britain had brought to India during the colonial period—the banishment of war, the elimination of famine, a fair and equal justice system, and the principles of Western science. He then gave two reasons why, in his view, India was far from being ready for Dominion status:

- Under the caste system, the Hindus treated sixty million of their people as "Untouchables, whose approach is an affront and whose very presence is pollution"* and

- India was prey to fierce racial and religious dissensions and thus when British protection was withdrawn there would be an "immediate resumption of medieval wars."[49]

In Churchill's view, the immediate grant of Dominion status to India would have been a "crime against civilisation."[50] According to Gilbert, Churchill's "unease about the possible effects of the promise of Dominion status was reinforced on December 23, when an attempt was made to kill [Viceroy] Irwin as his train entered Delhi."[51] Irwin was to meet that afternoon with leading members of the Indian Congress Party, including Mahatma Gandhi and his lieutenant Jawaharlal Nehru, who, in 1947, would be the first prime minister of an independent India.** Despite the attempted assassination, the meeting took place.[52] There Gandhi told Irwin "that the promise of eventual Dominion status" for India "must become one of immediate Dominion Status" and that he doubted the Labour Government's sincerity on the question.[53]

Churchill's opposition to Dominion status for India had a far deeper source than just concern for the Indian populace. He fervently believed in the British Empire. Indeed, Roberts says that Churchill made the Empire into his "secular religion."[54] He was labeled as someone "steeped in the politics of his father's period, and unable ever to get the modern view."[55] Unsurprisingly, he was guilty of racial insensitivity that bordered on racial intolerance—something that, although unpardonable, was then "not only acceptable in polite society, [but] fashionable, even assumed."[56]***

As Manchester writes, Churchill believed that:

Abolition of the caste system was not something that even Mahatma Gandhi (the leader of the nonviolent resistance movement which eventually achieved independence for India) was advocating.

**Like Churchill, Nehru went to Harrow. Nehru later attended Cambridge.*

***As discussed in Chapter 22, like most of his peers, Churchill held the racist view that "white people were superior." Yet Churchill did not believe that it was acceptable to treat people inhumanely based on their race or religion. While certainly no crusader for civil rights, unlike most of his peers, he generally believed that it was not acceptable to treat people unfairly based on race, religion, or class status.*

The Empire gave Britain its prestige; it made Britain the world's most powerful nation. Without its Imperial possessions the country would be merely an obscure island lying off the European continent. England deprived of its Imperial possessions would ... be like Sampson shorn of his hair. ...[57]

In his own words, Churchill said that to yield India would be "a hideous act of self-mutilation."[58] Roberts writes that it is only with an understanding of these deeply ingrained beliefs about the Empire, can one comprehend how and why, by his stance on India, which was completely at odds with the position of his party, he "consciously threw away what appeared to be his last chance of winning the premiership."[59]

1930
- Defense spending for 1930–1931
- The Continuing Struggle Over What to Do About Indian Self-Government
- Heinrich Bruening Becomes the Twelfth Chancellor of the Weimar Republic
- The French Evacuate the Rhineland

Defense Spending for 1930–1931

Overall defense spending for fiscal year 1930–1931 continued the decreasing trend from the year before. Here, the decrease was some £3.9 million (from £113.9 to £110 million) while spending on air defense increased from £16.9 to £17.8 million.[60]

The Continuing Struggle Over What to Do About Indian Self-Government

The struggle over what to do about Indian self-government continued into 1930. In India, large-scale rioting resumed, there were hit-and-run attacks on British garrisons, and Gandhi protested the Crown's monopoly on the production of salt and a tax on its sale by what came to be known as the Salt March (a scheduled 240-mile trek to the coast of the Arabian Sea). The march led to brutal repression and the arrest of Gandhi, Nehru, and one hundred thousand followers. Though MacDonald and Baldwin kept pushing their support for India's movement toward Dominion status, the tide was "running pretty strong against [it]."[61]

In June 1930, the Simon Commission published its two-volume report. It recommended significant measures toward the establishment of representative self-government in the provinces.[62] While the original plan had been to submit the report to a joint parliamentary committee and then proceed with legislation,[63] this did not happen. Rather, at the end of September, Labour, with Baldwin's concurrence, announced that a Round Table Conference of British and Indian leaders would start in London in November to discuss India's future.[64] Churchill warned that the promise of Dominion status had begun to undermine British authority in India. He also criticized the Government's exclusion of Sir John Simon from the conference as an effort "to placate Gandhi—'this malevolent fanatic.'"[65]

The Round Table conference, which turned out to be the first of three such gatherings held before 1933, commenced on November 12, 1930.[66] The Congress Party boycotted the meeting. Its leaders, Gandhi and Nehru, remained in prison after the Salt March. In any event, the Indian attendees pressed for the fullest degree of self-government as soon as possible.[67] Churchill's proposed solution: "Each province should move forward toward 'more real, more intimate, more representative organs of self-government,' leaving the central power firmly in British hands and giving as much autonomy as possible to provincial home rule"[68]—just as the Simon Commission had suggested.

India would not, however, be the only divisive issue facing the Conservative Party as the 1930s started. As economic times got harder, the classic debate between free trade and protective tariffs reared its ugly head in the ranks of both the Conservative and Liberal parties. Baldwin formally announced the Conservatives' support for new tariffs in October. Shortly after, Baldwin wrote a letter to Viceroy Irwin in India in which he said, "I think it probable Winston will resign on it."[69] It has even been suggested that Baldwin hoped Churchill would step aside and clear the way for Neville Chamberlain.

In any event, as 1930 moved to an end, the gulf between Churchill and Baldwin had widened considerably.

Heinrich Bruening Becomes the Twelfth Chancellor of the Weimar Republic

In Germany, after the collapse of the grand coalition under Social Democrat Hermann Müller at the end of March 1930, President Hindenburg appointed Heinrich Bruening as Chancellor. With Germany in another economic crisis, this time because of the Depression, Bruening's principal objective was to have the burden of war reparations and repayment of foreign debt lifted. This he believed also required tight credit as well as rolling back wage increases. Both policies were unpopular and promptly rejected by the Reichstag. When Hindenburg invoked his emergency powers to adopt Bruening's financial policies, the Reichstag passed a resolution demanding rescission of the decree.[70] Hindenburg, who already believed the Reichstag had too much power, with Bruening's consent, called for new parliamentary elections.

The elections occurred on September 14, 1930. They produced a highly fragmented Reichstag. This made the formation of a stable government just about impossible. The elections saw the Nazi Party rise to national prominence—taking 107 of 395 seats (and garnering the second largest number of votes). Unable to form a coalition government, Chancellor Bruening's fiscal policies, implemented via presidential decree, not only failed to solve the economic crisis but weakened the parliamentary system.

Churchill was closely following the unfolding developments in Germany. A classified German memorandum prepared in October 1930, which was seized by the Allies after the war, contained the report of a German counselor who encountered Churchill at a weekend house party. The memorandum stated that Churchill believed Hitler "to be a congenital liar" and that "although Hitler had 'declared that he has no intention of waging a war of aggression, he, Churchill is convinced that Hitler or his followers would seize the first available opportunity to resort to armed force.'"[71] Of course, they had already done so once, in the Beer Hall Putsch of 1923.

The French Evacuate the Rhineland

Among other things, the Treaty of Versailles allowed Allied troops to occupy portions of the right and left banks of the Rhine for as long as fifteen years. The left- and right-bank strips—30 miles wide on either side of the Rhine—were also to remain permanently off limits to the German military. The Germanophobic French resisted U.S. and British efforts toward conciliating Germany, and the last French troops did not leave the Rhineland until June 30, 1930.

1931
- Defense Spending 1931–1932
- India
- Churchill's First Public Warning about Hitler
- The Labour Government Collapses/A National Government Is Formed under Ramsey MacDonald (Labour)
- The National Government Wins the 1931 General Election in a Landslide
- Japan Invades Manchuria
- Meanwhile, in Germany

Defense Spending 1931–1932

For fiscal year 1931–1932 there was a minuscule decrease of £66,200 (0.6 percent) in Britain's defense appropriations as compared to spending in 1930. The attitude of the Labour Government was one of apology that they had not reduced defense spending further.[72]

India

Because the Congress Party had boycotted the first Round Table conference, Viceroy Irwin wanted to have another such meeting that party officials would attend. To facilitate this, Gandhi was freed from prison in January 1931.[73] Manchester describes most British officials in India and Conservatives in Britain (but not Churchill) as being "speechless."[74] In the House the very next evening, in his first Parliamentary speech against his party's India policy, Churchill unleashed a stinging attack against Dominion status for India, as well as the Government's decisions to ignore the Simon Report and bar its authors from participating in the Round Table.[75] The next day Churchill resigned from the Conservative Business Committee (Baldwin's Shadow Cabinet) "in furious opposition to his party's support for self-government for India"[76] and "whole hog" protectionism.[77] Now, without a leadership role in the Conservative Party, he felt even less constrained.

In India, the great civil disobedience struggle that started in 1930 was finally ended by conversations between Lord Irwin and Gandhi in February 1931; this led to an agreement in March.[78] As Lord Irwin (later Lord Halifax) states in his autobiography: "… these conversations gave me an opportunity such as I could never otherwise have had, and for which I shall always be thankful, of knowing Mr. Gandhi …"[79]

In stark contrast, in a speech on February 23 to a Conservative group in Essex, Churchill said, "It is alarming and also nauseating to see Mr. Gandhi, an Inner Temple lawyer, now become a seditious fakir of a type well known in the East, striding half-naked up the steps of the Vice-regal palace while he is still organising and conducting a defiant campaign of civil disobedience, to parley on equal terms with the representative of the King-Emperor."[80] As WWII historian Lynne Olson writes, "Churchill's resignation and his invective-filled campaigning against the government over India were major factors in his future exclusion from any high posts in the Baldwin and Chamberlain administrations."[81]

The second Round Table conference was held at St. James palace in London in September 1931. Gandhi was India's sole representative. When he arrived in London, he was greeted by no less than Prime Minister MacDonald.[82] The conference ended two months later in a deadlock over how to safeguard Muslims and other minorities.[83]

During the House debate on His Majesty's Government's (HMG's) India policy, Churchill, in a ninety-minute speech, attacked the Conservatives for having accepted the Labour Party's policy. He also offered an amendment, one which said that nothing in the Government's proposed policy would commit the House to give India Dominion status or "impair the ultimate responsibility of Parliament for the peace, order, and good government of the

Indian Empire."[84] Once the amendment was defeated, MacDonald "proceeded to set up three Commissions of Inquiry to make detailed proposals."[85]*

After the India debate, fed up with "Irwinism," Churchill, and his wife immediately embarked on another long tour of America. The main purpose of the trip was to regain some of the money he had lost in the stock market crash of '29. He would do so by giving forty lectures and writing several articles for the *Daily Mail*.[86]

Fate nearly ended the tour shortly after he arrived in New York. On the evening of December 13, 1931, he was invited to the house of his friend Bernard Baruch (one of America's richest and most powerful men). He took a cab from his hotel uptown to Baruch's house on Fifth Avenue across from Central Park. The cab let him out on the park (west) side of Fifth Avenue (which then accommodated two-way traffic). When he crossed the street halfway, he forgot that he was no longer in London and looked left instead of right and was hit by a car proceeding north at about 35 mph before slamming on the brakes.[87] A passerby screamed that "a man has been killed."[88] Not true. Once again, Churchill had cheated death. He did suffer a concussion and contusions all over his body, and he was in the hospital for over a week.[89] But apropos of his ability to turn lemons into lemonade, he would write an article about the accident for which he received £500 ($34,000 in today's money) from the *Daily Mail*.

Churchill's First Public Warning about Hitler

On March 23, 1931, the day Germany and Austria proposed to form a customs union, in a syndicated column for the Hearst newspapers, Churchill issued his first public warning of an approaching war. He wrote that he feared a more formal union between Germany and Austria would flow out of their proposed customs pact. He further speculated that Germany would end up producing twice as many males of military age as France could produce (given France's dwindling population) and that Czechoslovakia would soon find herself surrounded on three sides by Germans.[90]

Former colleagues believed that Churchill was mistaken about the Nazis just as he had been about India. After Hitler became Chancellor in early 1933, Churchill's old friend, Lord Beaverbrook, even suggested that Churchill retire from Parliament.[91]

The three Commissions were: the Federal Finance Committee, the Indian State Enquiry, and the Finance Committee. Gilbert, Prophet p. 419.

The Labour Government Collapses/A National Government Is Formed under Ramsey MacDonald (Labour)

In August 1931 the Labour Government collapsed. Unconvinced by either their own record in office or their ability to steer Britain out of an accelerating economic decline, Labour's two leading ministers—Prime Minister Ramsay MacDonald and Chancellor of the Exchequer Philip Snowden—agreed to join a Conservative-led all-party coalition known as the National Government. MacDonald would, at least titularly, continue to serve as P.M. Baldwin would serve as Lord President of the Council. Churchill was not invited to become a member of the new administration. Interestingly, Lord Irwin, having recently completed his tenure as Viceroy of India, was asked to serve in the Foreign Office of the new National Government.*[92] He declined, believing that the Conservative right would have strenuously objected.[93]

Thereafter, the economic situation in Britain went from bad to worse. The Government managed to avoid national bankruptcy only by reducing welfare payments and obtaining additional loans from the United States.[94] This was followed by raising income taxes as well as taxes on gasoline, tobacco, and beer. Normally, the Conservatives would have opposed such efforts, but in this crisis, even they supported the new measures.[95] The economic crisis was, in fact, so great that Churchill would relent on his lifelong opposition to the imposition of protective tariffs. As he told the House on September 15, "a tariff ought to be an integral part of" the Government's plan "to deal with the present emergency."[96] Other lifelong free traders agreed.[97]

The National Government Wins the 1931 General Election in a Landslide

In October 1931 Britain held a general election. The campaign was a bitter one. The fledgling National Government ran on two key planks—a rigid economy with spending only for essential items and a balanced budget. It won a landslide victory. Collectively, the parties forming the National Government received 67 percent of the votes and won 554 of the 615 seats available. The bulk of this came from the Conservative Party, which won 470 seats. (Labour won only thirteen.) Baldwin could have ousted MacDonald but chose not to.[98] He would instead be the power behind the throne and again serve as Lord President of the Council. MacDonald would continue as the ostensible P.M. Over time, Baldwin would take over many duties of Prime Minister because of MacDonald's failing health—until he officially replaced

---

*As noted previously, in 1918, Lord Irwin had strongly supported imposing severe penalties on Germany at Versailles. After India, McCarten writes, Irwin had mellowed and "expressed a certain sympathy for Germany over the penalties" that had been imposed on her. McCarten p. 91.

MacDonald as Prime Minister in 1935. At that time, Neville Chamberlain succeeded Snowden as Chancellor of the Exchequer. He would serve in that office until he became Prime Minister in the spring of 1937.

In 1931, Churchill was not called on to join the new Government. Many disparaging comments were hurled his way. Their general nature is summed up in the one asking, "What sensible man is going to place confidence in Mr. Churchill in any situation which needs cool headedness, moderation, or tact?"[99]

Japan Invades Manchuria

On September 19, 1931, the Japanese invaded Manchuria. While this was an act of war in violation of the Covenant of the League of Nations, to Europeans it also appeared to be a localized action on the other side of the world. Although in 1931 no one could predict it, the invasion of Manchuria would deal the first of several blows to the League from which it was never able to recover. It would ultimately show that collective security, on which Britain and other powers had built their security, "was worthless"—and would reshape defense spending around the world.[100]

Manchuria was the first major test of the Covenant system. Many of the smaller members of the League, and its supporters everywhere, called for the strict application of the Covenant and an economic boycott of Japan. The League would, however, take no action until it had investigated what had occurred in Manchuria. This would take more than a year to accomplish.

Meanwhile, in Germany

By late summer 1931, Chancellor Bruening realized that his govern-ment was in serious trouble. To cope with the Depression, he had, among other things, decreed lower wages and, in secret, had started a fairly small program to rearm.[101]

Emerging from the chaos that was the Weimar Republic was General Kurt von Schleicher, a name that would come to mean "sneak" in German.[102] Schleicher would play a significant, largely back-room role in ending the Republic and in Hitler's becoming Chancellor of Germany. General von Schleicher rose to power as head of the army's Armed Forces Department and a close advisor to President Hindenburg from 1926 onward. Schleicher became head of the Defense Ministry's Office of Ministerial Affairs in 1929. In 1930 he was instrumental in toppling Hermann Müller's government and getting Hindenburg to appoint Bruening as Chancellor.

1932
- Defense Spending 1932–1933
- Perceptions of Churchill

- Manchuria and the League of Nations
- Hitler and the Presidential Election of 1932
- The Lausanne Conference
- Parliamentary Elections in Germany
- Meanwhile, Back in Britain

Defense Spending 1932–1933

1932 saw another substantial decrease of £5,270,700 (4.8 percent) in Britain's annual defense appropriations compared to spending in 1931. This resulted from a continuing drive for economy coupled with the opening of the Geneva Disarmament Conference.[103] Unsurprisingly, given Britain's limited spending in preceding years, the RAF found itself ten squadrons short of the minimum established under the 1923 defense scheme.[104] This did not, however, appear to be problematic because the Government hoped that the Disarmament Conference would lead to the internationalization of air forces and a general reduction in arms.[105]

The Conference for the Reduction and Limitation of Armaments began in February. It was the culmination of a decade's effort and opened with high expectations. Indeed, it would significantly influence defense spending in Britain during the years it was in session (1932–1934).[106] During that period there was also a very strong pacifist movement in Britain, one which had a particularly strong hold on the Labour Party.[107] Because of this and a basic psychology of island immunity, in his prescient book *Why England Slept,* future president John F. Kennedy argues that the British saw less need for rearmament than other countries.[108]* Kennedy also asserts that the conference was doomed almost from the outset because France and England failed to make sufficient concessions to German Chancellor Bruening to enable him to satisfy his people that countries other than Germany were disarming.

Perceptions of Churchill

As Manchester writes, Churchill, "[a]t the very least ... the greatest Englishman since Disraeli ... [was now] a back bencher—an elected member of Parliament excluded from the cabinet. [By 1932, i]n his fifty-eighth year, he is already regarded as an anachronism."[109] "The British left, led by Clement Attlee and pledged to passivism and disarmament, deeply distrusted

---

*Kennedy was the son of the United States Ambassador to Britain and a senior at Harvard. Why England Slept was the published version of his senior thesis.

him."[110]* The press saw him "as wine which passed its point. Still vigorous, still brilliant, he was nevertheless to out of tune with the times."[111]

During the 1930s Churchill would clash with, as Manchester puts it, "three political mediocrities" (Prime Ministers Ramsay MacDonald, Stanley Baldwin, and Neville Chamberlain), each of whom was convinced that "Hitler would never make war if his demands were met with diplomatic finesse."[112]

Manchuria and the League of Nations

After five months of negotiations, on February 24, 1932, a commission of inquiry, known as the Lytton Commission, was appointed by the League of Nations to investigate what had occurred in Manchuria. The commission went there in April 1932 and found the new Japanese puppet state of Manchukuo already established. Japan claimed that this removed the matter from the League's jurisdiction. Even so, in October 1932, the commission drew up a full report in which it found Japanese aggression and concluded that Manchuria should be returned to Chinese sovereignty, with various safeguards for the rights and needs of Japan. When the findings of the report were announced before the Assembly in late February 1933 and a motion was made to condemn Japan as the aggressor, the Japanese delegation walked out of the session. The report's conclusions were adopted unanimously by the Assembly. But Japan rejected them. On March 27, 1933, Japan announced her withdrawal from the League.[113] Thus, in its first attempt to protect a member country from aggression, the League had failed miserably.**

Hitler and the Presidential Election of 1932

On March 23, 1932, Germany held a presidential election, but no candidate received the required 50 percent. Independent incumbent Paul von Hindenburg, who was eighty-five and senile, finished first with 49.6 percent of the vote. Hitler, the Nazi candidate, got 30.1 percent. In a runoff held on April 10 Hindenburg won a second seven-year term garnering 53 percent of the vote while Hitler got 37 percent. (The remaining 10 percent went to the Communist candidate.) Interestingly at the start of the campaign, Hitler was not even eligible to run for president since he was a citizen of Austria, not Germany. This problem was solved by what William Shirer, the author of the encyclopedic *The Rise and Fall of the Third Reich,* calls "a comic opera

---

*Ironically, in 1940, Attlee would serve as close confederate of Churchill's in the latter's five-man War Cabinet.

**Professor A.J.P. Taylor takes a different view, arguing that the League had done exactly "what the British thought it was designed to do"—"limited ... a conflict and brought it, however unsatisfactorily, to an end." Taylor, Origins p. 64.

Manchuria also led to the League's setting up machinery to impose economic sanctions on offending countries. Ibid.

maneuver": The Nazi minister in the State of Brunswick named Hitler an attaché to the legation of Brunswick in Berlin, something which made him a citizen of Brunswick and therefore of Germany.[114]

The Lausanne Conference

In June 1932, a crucial conference opened in Lausanne, Switzerland, among Britain, Germany, and France to discuss the suspension of Germany's obligation to pay reparations under the Versailles Treaty. (This was in keeping with Article 19 of the Treaty, which said that provisions which, over time have raised problems that may lead to most undesirable conflicts, ought to be subject to revision.) Because of the Depression, a moratorium had already been placed on the reparations payments in 1931. At Lausanne, Germany argued that as the Depression continued it was nearly impossible for her to resume making payments.* But Britain, France, and other Allies had borrowed heavily from the United States to fight the war and she was an unforgiving lender. Therefore, they in turn counted on reparation payments from Germany to cover their obligations to the United States.

Reparations had been a heated topic, which helped keep the anger of the war alive.[115] Yet by the time the Lausanne conference ended on July 9, the participants had come to an informal understanding that the permanent elimination of Germany's debt and war reparations would be subject to the European Allies' reaching an agreement with the United States over their outstanding war debts. As a result, as Prof. Taylor says, paying reparations no longer constituted Germany's principal grievance: "the one-sided disarmament of Germany had taken its place."[116] Churchill wanted further revisions of the Versailles Treaty but strongly opposed the concept of equalizing armaments.[117] He feared that Germany would go beyond any such figure as she saw fit.[118]

In December 1932, the U.S. Congress rejected the Allies' latest war debt reduction plan. As a result, reparations and debt reverted to the debt reduction level previously granted Germany in 1929. But Germany would make no more payments. By 1933, Germany had made World War I reparations of only one-eighth of the sum required under the Treaty of Versailles.

Parliamentary Elections in Germany

At the end of May 1932, Hindenburg dismissed Bruening as Chancellor of Germany. The kingmaker, General Schleicher, then foisted Franz von Papen on the president. Papen had no political support and had never been

---

*Prof. Taylor contends that "the Germans could have paid reparations.... if they had regarded them as an obligation of honour... In actual fact ... Germany was a net gainer by the financial transactions of the 1920s: she borrowed far more from private American investors (and failed to pay back) than she paid in reparations." Taylor, Origins p. 44.

elected to the Reichstag.[119] Schleicher and Hitler had worked out a deal: in exchange for Nazi support of Papen to be the new chancellor, Papen would lift the recent ban on the SA (the paramilitary wing of the Nazi Party, aka, the Brownshirts) and dissolve the Reichstag (thus triggering a new parliamentary election).[120]

Following the dissolution of the Reichstag at the beginning of June, and with over 15 million Germans on the dole,[121] Germany held a parliamentary election on July 31, 1932. The election campaign took place under violent circumstances, as Papen had lifted the token ban on the SA, which Chancellor Bruening had put in place during the last days of his administration. Emancipating the Nazi brownshirts inevitably led to clashes with the Communists, anyone with "leftist sympathies, Jews of every age and sex, and anyone who failed" to give the heil Hitler salute.[122] In the election, the Nazis made significant gains, winning 230 of 608 seats. Although this was less than a majority, the Nazis held more seats in the Reichstag than any other party.

Hitler then withdrew support for Papen and in negotiations with kingmaker Schleicher demanded both the chancellorship and the passage of an enabling act that would allow him to rule by decree for a specified period.[123] Schleicher would not agree and insisted that Hitler rule with the consent of a Reichstag majority (something that Hitler could not obtain) otherwise he would support Papen (in which case Hitler would become Vice Chancellor.)[124] The matter was ultimately settled by Hindenburg, who "could not in good conscience" transfer power to the Nazis.[125]

As a result, Papen's minority government continued in office, the Reichstag was again dissolved, and another parliamentary election was called for November.

In the German parliamentary elections held on November 6, 1932, Hitler's popularity seemed to have waned because the Nazis lost thirty-four seats, while there were slight increases for the Communists and others. Although still the largest party in the Reichstag, once again the Nazis were unable to form a coalition government on acceptable terms. The stalemate persisted despite the publication, on November 19, 1932, of the *Industrielleneingabe*, a letter signed by twenty-two important representatives of industry, finance, and agriculture, asking Hindenburg to appoint Hitler as chancellor. Papen, on the other hand, proposed to keep ruling by decree while drafting a new electoral system. Schleicher proposed instead that Hindenburg sack Papen and appoint him Chancellor. He promised to form a workable coalition. Hindenburg agreed and Schleicher became Chancellor on December 2, 1932. Schleicher planned to form a viable coalition government by bypassing Hitler, contacting the number two man in the Nazi Party, Gregor Strasser, and suggesting that Strasser bring as many of the Nazis members of the Reichstag as possible and join him in forming a government.[126] Strasser, who appealed to the left-wing of the party, was willing to do so because he felt that Hitler had taken the now-bankrupt Nazi Party as far as he could.[127]

As expected, Hitler accused Strasser of stabbing him in the back while Strasser derided Hitler's leadership of the party. In the end, Strasser wrote a letter resigning from the party. It laid out several grievances he had been harboring since at least 1925, and he gave a copy to the press. As Goebbels wrote in his diary, Hitler was "embittered and deeply wounded by this treachery" and said that "if the party falls to pieces I'll put an end to it all in 3 minutes with a pistol shot."[128] (From the depths of this despair, within seven weeks Hitler would be Chancellor of Germany.)

Strasser, worn out by the quarrel with Hitler, immediately departed for a vacation in Italy. With Strasser out of the country, Hitler quickly took over the political organization that Strasser had built up inside the party and purged Strasser's friends. Next, Hitler had all remaining party leaders sign a new declaration of loyalty to him. Lastly, just after Papen left office, he told Hitler that he still held considerable sway with President Hindenburg and he would use his influence with the president to make Hitler Chancellor—provided that Hitler agreed to let him be the Vice Chancellor. (Papen believed that he could "tame" Hitler.) Hitler agreed.

Meanwhile, Back in Britain

Finally back from his extended tour of America, Churchill was urging revision of Versailles while the victors still had ample superiority[129] and the disarmament debate continued unabated. In a famous speech to the House on November 10, 1932, Baldwin asserted that disarmament was the only way to peace because of what he called "the terror of the air"—the bombing of civilian populations.[130] "... [I]t is well ... for the man in the street to realise that there is no power on earth that can protect him from being bombed. Whatever people may tell him, the bomber will always get through ..."[131] On November 17, 1932, Churchill wrote a forceful response in the *Daily Mail* saying that if the Geneva Disarmament Conference failed it was incumbent on Parliament "to place our air force in such a condition of power and efficiency that it will not be worth anyone's while to come here and kill our women and children in the hope that they may blackmail us into surrender."[132] In a speech to the House a few days later, he noted that "none of the nations concerned in the Disarmament Conference except Great Britain has been prepared, willingly, to alter to its own disadvantage its ratio of armed strength."[133] He also addressed Germany's request for rearmament and urged House members not to delude themselves that "all ... Germany is asking for is equal status."[134]

1933
- Hitler Named Chancellor of Germany
- The Start of Rearmament in Britain
- Arsonists Destroy the Reichstag/Hitler Issued Decree Suspending Civil Liberties Sections of the German Constitution
- Parliamentary Elections again in Germany/Enabling Act Passed, Establishing a Dictatorship in Germany
- Formal Persecution of German Jews
- Disarmament/Failure to Allow Germany to Reach Arms Parity/Pro-German Feelings in Britain
- Hitler Violates the Treaty of Versailles
- Germany Withdraws from the League of Nations and the Geneva Disarmament Conference
- The New Defense Requirements Committee in Britain

Hitler Named Chancellor of Germany

In large part because of Hitler's maneuverings, General Schleicher was ultimately unable to obtain the support of a Reichstag majority, could not form a Reichstag majority government, and resigned on January 28, 1933.[135] Given that the parliamentary elections of July and November 1932 had not led to the formation of a majority government, President Hindenburg asked Papen to try to form one under Hitler "within the terms of the constitution."[136] He did—a coalition of the Nazis and the conservative German National People's Party (DNVP). On January 30, 1933, a new cabinet was sworn in. Hitler was named Chancellor, and Hermann Goering became Minister without Portfolio (and Minister of the Interior for Prussia).[137] Hitler also appointed Goering to be the President of the Reichstag.[138] The SA and the SS (the Schutzstaffel, another major paramilitary organization under Hitler and the Nazi Party) led torchlit parades throughout Berlin. The Nazis were a decided minority in the new Government, holding only three of the eleven cabinet posts. (All the important ministries went to conservatives who, as William Shirer writes, "were sure they [had] lassoed the Nazis for their own ends ..."[139] but had committed "[t]he cardinal error of the Germans who opposed Nazism with their failure to unite against it."[140])

Holding only three cabinet posts was not a great situation for the Nazis. Moreover, they and the DNVP together did not command a majority of the seats in the Reichstag. As a result, upon taking office, Hitler immediately talked to leaders of the Center Party, which held seventy seats, about joining the coalition.[141] But the Centrist leaders demanded concessions which the Nazis were unwilling to give. Hitler therefore got President Hindenburg to again dissolve the Reichstag and call for new parliamentary elections which were set for March 5. With the resources of the state now behind them, the Nazis felt that they would win an absolute majority, in which case they could dispose of all the non-Nazis in the Cabinet.

The Start of Rearmament in Britain

At the British Cabinet meeting of February 15, 1933, several ministers pointed out deficiencies in their departments in terms of defense preparation and asked that an investigation be done to correct them in the upcoming 1934–1935 budget.[142] Both Chancellor of the Exchequer Neville Chamberlain and Prime Minister MacDonald argued that Britain's financial condition would not support such an inquiry and that the Cabinet would simply have to take the responsibility for the deficiencies of the Defence Departments.[143] The Cabinet agreed and no investigation was made.[144]

During the debate in the House on March 14 over the air appropriations for fiscal year 1933–1934, Under-Secretary of State for Air Sir Philip Sassoon continued the Government's line, stressing the need for economy. The air appropriations for 1933 showed a decrease from the year before of approximately £340,000.[145]

Arsonists Destroy the Reichstag/Hitler Issued Decree Suspending Civil Liberties Sections of the German Constitution

On the night of February 27, a fire destroyed the Reichstag building in Berlin. The evidence suggests that a small detachment of Nazi storm troopers using gasoline and other accelerants started the fire. The Nazis blamed Marinus van der Lubbe (described as "a half-witted Dutch Communist with a passion for arson") for the fire, even though the idea almost surely came from Goering and Propaganda Minister Joseph Goebbels.[146] On February 28, 1933, Hitler, who had been in office for all of four weeks, used the Reichstag fire to get President Hindenburg to issue a decree suspending the sections of the German Constitution guaranteeing freedom of speech, freedom of the press, freedom of assembly, and the requirement for a warrant to conduct a search.[147] Under the decree, the Government could even impose the death sentence for crimes including "serious disturbances of the peace" by armed persons.[148] Thousands of Communist officials as well as leaders of the Liberals and Social Democrats were arrested.

Parliamentary Elections again in Germany/Enabling Act Passed, Establishing a Dictatorship in Germany

As the March 5, 1933 Parliamentary elections approached, with all the resources of the Government available to them, the Nazis carried on an unprecedented campaign—one which included broadcasts over state-run radio, mass rallies, torchlight parades, and billboards emblazoned with

Nazi slogans.[149] The SA also did everything it could to disrupt the election, including beating and torturing Nazi opponents. "Only the Nazis and their Nationalist party allies were allowed to campaign unmolested."[150] Amazingly, despite all the violence, the Nazis received only 44 percent of the vote.[151] But with the seats won by Papen's Nationalist Party, the two parties could and did form a coalition government with a Reichstag majority.[152] They did not, however, have the two-thirds majority needed to pass the act allowing Hitler to establish his dictatorship. This seemingly substantial barrier would be easily solved. First, the eighty-one Communist members of the Reichstag would conveniently be "absent" when the vote on the Enabling Act occurred. Second, the balance of the problem would, if necessary, be resolved by temporarily refusing a few Social Democrats admittance to the Reichstag during the vote.[153] When the Enabling Act came to the floor on March 23, 1933, only the eighty-four Social Democrats in the Reichstag stood up for the principles of humanity, justice, and freedom. The vote was 441 to 84.[154]

The Reichstag had just voted German democracy out of existence. "Except for the arrests of the Communists and some of the Social Democratic deputies, it was all done quite legally, though accompanied by terror [largely from the SA]."[155]

In a speech before the House of Commons that day, Churchill said Britain and France had just passed through a very anxious month watching what was taking place in "one of the most gifted, learned, scientific and formidable nations in the world."[156] They had seen "with surprise and distress, the tumultuous insurgence of ferocity and war spirit, the pitiless ill-treatment of minorities, the denial of the normal protections of civilised society to large numbers of individuals solely on the ground of race."[157]*

"The French must be greatly concerned at what is taking place in Germany"[158] he added, because "France is the guarantor and protector" of many small countries including Belgium, Yugoslavia, and Romania.[159] He said, "Thank God for the French Army," which he believed to be the best in the world.[160]** As such, he urged Britain not to advance a proposal at the Geneva Disarmament Conference (the so-called "MacDonald Plan") that would ask France to halve her army while Germany doubled hers. He said the French Government considered that proposal to be unreasonable.[161] The MacDonald plan, however, had widespread support in the House.[162] Notably, the first Cabinet minister to chastise Churchill for attacking MacDonald's attempt to appease Hitler was none other than Neville Chamberlain.[163]

Manchester writes disdainfully of the fact that Churchill's eloquent appeal to the British virtue of decency fell on deaf ears in the House. Manchester, Alone pp. 91–92.
**In years to come, Churchill would have a very different view of the French army.*

Formal Persecution of German Jews

Just a week later, on April 1, 1933, the German government's oppression of its Jewish citizens began with a boycott of Jewish-owned businesses enforced by the SA.[164] On April 13, Churchill told the House that when he read about what was occurring in Germany, he rejoiced that Germany did not have the canons, airplanes, and tanks for which she had been pressing in Geneva to achieve equality with other countries.[165]

Kennedy writes that Britons denounced Hitler's treatment of the Jews and his "regimentation" of German life.[166] But Kennedy also appears to excuse the British for not viewing Hitler as critically as did Churchill when he adds:

- "Since many in Germany had been fooled by Hitler in the early years, it's unsurprising that many in England also failed to see his true colors.

- "…[D]uring this period, the fear of Communism, not of Nazism, was the great British bogey. Germany under Hitler with its early program of vigorous opposition to Communism, was looked on as a bulwark against the spread of the doctrine through Europe,"[167] and that

- "Many Britons believed that Nazism was a nationalistic movement, that would eventually die a natural death."[168]

Disarmament/Failure to Allow Germany to Reach Arms Parity/Pro-German Feelings in Britain

On the question of disarmament, Churchill continued to believe that HMG was being unfair and inconsistent with France. It wanted France to disarm to achieve parity but would not commit to giving France the security guarantees she believed she had to have if she were to disarm.[169] At the time, Manchester reports, frustrated members of the British delegation to the Geneva disarmament talks were telling Churchill that "to talk disarmament while Hitler secretly armed was absurd."[170] But talk they did. British leaders realized that they "had failed to give former Chancellor Bruening … support" to reach arms parity with the other nations of Europe; "they did not wish to make the same mistake again. All of these reasons plus the natural rightist feelings of a good many of the British aristocracy, combined to make entirely dissimilar groups friendly to [Hitler's] Germany."[171] This included groups having trade connections with Germany, those with an abiding hatred of Communism, as well as Germanophiles and anti-Semites.[172]

Through most of the 1930s, portions of the British press aided and abetted the pro-Germany feelings among the English elite. Newspaper magnates Lord Beaverbrook (who owned the *Daily Express,* with the largest circulation in the world, the *Sunday Express*, and the *Glasgow Evening Citizen*) and Lord Rothermere (who owned the *Daily Mirror*, the *Sunday Pictorial*, the *Evening News*, the *Sunday Mail*, and the *Glasgow Daily Record*) each had extensive connections with the Third Reich.[173] While other newspapers condemned Nazi excesses, papers owned by Beaverbrook and Rothermere slanted stories to be favorable to Germany or to show that Hitler's intentions were peaceable.[174]* Even correspondents at the *London Times* believed that their paper excluded anything that the Nazis might regard as unreasonable.[175]

Hitler Violates the Treaty of Versailles

Just after taking office in January 1933, Hitler, despite the limitation set out in the Treaty of Versailles, secretly ordered the German Army to triple in size by October 1934.[176] In May 1933, Germany, which under the treaty was also prohibited from having an air force, secretly established the Luftwaffe and soon started the production of war planes.[177]

Germany Withdraws from the League of Nations and the Geneva Disarmament Conference

On October 14, 1933, Germany withdrew from the League of Nations and the Geneva Disarmament Conference. The ostensible reason was the refusal of the Western powers to acquiesce in Germany's demands for military parity. British politicians condemned Germany's action. For various reasons, including internal economic ones, nearly all of them still wanted to achieve disarmament.[178]

The New Defence Requirements Committee in Britain

Soon after, in Britain, a newly created Defence Requirements Committee concluded that significant rearmament was needed over the rest of the decade if the UK were to be ready for war by decade's end.[179] As Chancellor of the Exchequer, Neville Chamberlain, however, opposed spending the money needed to meet the recommendations of the committee. He feared that such spending would "threaten precarious post-Depression growth."[180]

1934
- The Situation in Britain in the First Part of 1934
- Night of the Long Knives in Germany
- Meddling in Austria
- Rearmament in Britain

Despite Beaverbrook's anti-Semitism and strong preference for isolation, he and Churchill were friends. In 1940, Churchill would even appoint him to be Minister of Aircraft Production—a position in which he would do a stupendous job.

The Situation in Britain in the First Part of 1934

The year 1934 was fateful. In June, the Geneva Disarmament Conference ended without resolution, ending Britain's hope of achieving disarmament. While the financial crisis, which had kept defense spending low for several years, had eased a bit, Britain still made no major push to rearm. Britain, in fact, did not start her rearmament drive in earnest until 1936. In Kennedy's view, this amounted to a two-year delay—something which came home to roost at the time of the Munich crisis four years later.* The delay largely resulted from the fact that 1935 was an election year and a strongly pro-rearmament platform in 1934 would have been a sure recipe for the Conservatives to go down to defeat.[181]

In a speech to the House on February 7, 1934, Churchill addressed Britain's failure to rearm. First he noted that the unsolved grievances and injustices perceived by the nations of Europe and the Far East had caused countries all over the world, except Britain, to rearm.[182] He added that Britain's paralysis was happening at a time when the development of aerial warfare was revolutionizing the whole concept of war.[183] Britain, he said was "vulnerable as we have never been before."[184] She needed "an Air Force at least as strong as that of any power that can get at us."[185] Unfortunately, few others agreed with him.[186] The air appropriations for 1934–1935 (£17.5 million) showed an increase of only seven-tenths of one percent over 1933–1934.[187] Under-Secretary of State for Air Sir Philip Sassoon told the House on March 8, 1934, that there was to be an increase of four new squadrons: two for home defense, one for the Navy and one flying boat squadron.[188] He added that the appropriations:

> ...[were] the outcome of our desire to pursue disarmament and to study economy on the one hand, and, on the other, of our reluctant conviction that the policy of postponement cannot be continued. ... But we do not want to put forward a programme of construction which might prove to be the starting gun for a race in air armaments. In the interests of world peace, the initial measure of advance which is indicated in these Appropriations is designedly placed within the most modest bounds.[189]

Gilbert writes that even this small expansion of the RAF provoked an "immediate and widespread protest" from the disarmament faction led by Labour and the Liberals.[190]

Discussed in Chapter 12.

In his speech to the House on March 8, 1934, Baldwin made the following significant addition to what the Air Secretary had said that if the disarmament efforts in Geneva failed, then HMG "...will see to it that in air strength and air power this country shall no longer be in a position inferior to any country within striking distance of our shores."[191] Churchill accepted the statement, believing it to have been made in good faith[192] but warned against delaying a review of Britain's defenses.[193] On March 19, 1934, the Cabinet agreed that it must without delay consider partnering with other countries to bolster mutual security against any breach of the peace, and discuss greatly increasing expenditures on armaments.[194]

Night of the Long Knives in Germany

The Night of the Long Knives was a purge that took place from June 30 to July 2, 1934, when, urged on by Goering and Assistant Gestapo head Heinrich Himmler, Hitler ordered a series of political executions. The executions had two purposes: to consolidate Hitler's hold on power in Germany and to eliminate Ernst Roehm, the power-hungry leader of the *Sturmabteilung* (SA)—and thereby rein in the SA.

Roehm, despite being a known homosexual,* was a long-term close friend of Hitler, since well before having played a prominent role in the Beer Hall Putsch of 1923. Roehm was also one of only a few people allowed to address Hitler by his first name, "Adolf," or even his nickname, "Adi," rather than *"mein Führer."* He had been hugely successful in building up the SA, which in 1933 had about two million members.[195] SA intimidation had contributed to the rise of the Nazis and the violent suppression of right-wing parties during electoral campaigns. After becoming Chancellor, Hitler named Roehm to the Cabinet as a Minister Without Portfolio[196] and gave the SA the task of sweeping aside all enemies of the state. But over time, the SA's plans—as well as its reputation for street violence and heavy drinking, plus the open homosexuality of Roehm and other SA leaders—became a hindrance to Hitler's desire for permanent power over Germany.

Roehm had grandiose plans for the SA, which by early 1934 had grown to three million strong. They included having the smaller existing German army (the Reichswehr) merged into the SA to form a true "people's army" under his leadership. SA officers would replace the elite Prussians who had long filled the officer ranks of the Reichswehr.[197] Unsurprisingly, Roehm's plan caused significant consternation within the Reichswehr hierarchy, who believed the SA was an undisciplined mob of street thugs. The Nazi Party leadership also did not approve of Roehm's idea, due, in substantial part, to the fact that Hitler needed the support of the Reichswehr.[198] Accordingly,

---

*A group that would ultimately be severely persecuted by the Nazis.

in exchange for the Reichswehr's agreeing to support Hitler's efforts to succeed the dying Hindenburg (who, as President, had the power to remove the Chancellor), Hitler agreed to reduce the size of the SA, suppress Roehm's ambitions, and guarantee that the Reichswehr would be Germany's only military force. Under this pact, the until-this-point-honorable Reichswehr assured its continued existence but had agreed to provide a megalomaniacal dictator with the help he needed to gain unconditional control over everything in Germany, including it.

Roehm and the SA were also strongly anti-capitalist. And the rank-and-file, working-class SA storm troopers thought that the National Socialist revolution in which they were key participants would lead to the destruction of capitalism and "bring them loot and good jobs, either in business or the government."[199] Their ideas were not all that dissimilar from what the Communists advocated and were threatening to Hitler's corporate financial backers—including many German industrial leaders on whom Hitler would rely for arms production. Those leaders even complained about Roehm to Hindenburg, who then told Hitler to get Roehm and the SA under control or he would declare martial law and remove Hitler as Chancellor. Hitler swiftly assured Hindenburg that he would do so and that there would be no revolution as espoused by Roehm and his gang of party radicals.

Hitler already had plans in the works to deal with Roehm and the SA. Even before what has come to be known as "The Night of the Long Knives," Himmler (the head of the SS) had assembled a dossier of manufactured evidence suggesting that France had paid Roehm and kingmaker Kurt von Schleicher handsomely to overthrow Hitler.[200] Furthermore, at Hitler's direction, Goering, Himmler, and others had drawn up lists of people in and outside the SA that needed to be eliminated for various reasons.

Hitler and SA leadership were to meet in the town of Wiesse, just outside Munich, on June 30. Very early that morning, Hitler, along with a large group of SS and regular police flew to Munich and arrived at the hotel where Roehm and many SA leaders were staying. Before 8:00 AM the SS men stormed the hotel and arrested the SA leadership, still in bed. Hitler personally placed Roehm under arrest.

Back at party headquarters in Munich, Hitler addressed an assembled crowd. Consumed with faux-rage, Hitler denounced "the worst treachery in world history," and said that "undisciplined and disobedient characters and asocial or diseased elements" of the SA had to be annihilated. Goering then let loose the execution squads on the rest of their unsuspecting victims.

Hitler subsequently ordered the SS to form a special execution squad and go to Stadelheim prison in Munich where Roehm and other top SA leaders were being held. In the prison courtyard, the SS executed many high-ranking SA officers. Some received one-minute "trials" before being shot. Roehm himself remained a prisoner. Hitler was hesitant about authorizing Roehm's execution, perhaps because of loyalty or just embarrassment about having to execute such an important confederate.

Even so, he eventually did, but in what, according to Shirer, Hitler thought was an act of grace, said that Roehm should first be given the chance to commit suicide.[201] On July 1, two SS officers visited Roehm's cell, handed him a loaded pistol, and told him he had ten minutes to kill himself or they would do it for him. Roehm responded, "If I am to be killed, let Adolf do it himself."[202] Having heard nothing in the allotted time, the officers returned to Roehm's cell. There they found him standing, with his bare chest puffed out in a gesture of defiance. Upon seeing this, the SS men shot Roehm.[203]

Some Germans were shocked by the killings, the exact number of which remains unknown. Those killed included kingmaker General Kurt Schleicher, Gregor Strasser (formerly the second- in-command of the Nazi Party), and three SA men who were believed to have started the Reichstag fire.[204] Many in Germany saw Hitler as having restored "order" to the country. Although the German Army had not directly participated in the murders, it had prodded Hitler to deal with the SA problem. Thus, Shirer writes, the Reichswehr "incurred responsibility for the barbarity" that ensued.[205] The purge of the SA was legalized on July 3 with a one-paragraph decree which said: "The measures taken on 30 June, 1 and 2 July to suppress treasonous assaults are legal as acts of self-defense by the State."[206] In a nationally broadcast speech to the Reichstag on July 13, 1934, Hitler justified the purge as a defense against treason.

One thing that stands out about the purge is how willingly Hitler endorsed mass murder as a political strategy, even including the execution of one of his closest friends. Loyalty and friendship be damned: Hitler would do anything necessary to achieve his political and megalomaniacal ends. A week later, Churchill told his constituents how difficult it was to believe that the highly educated country of Germany had devolved into "a tyranny maintained by press and broadcast propaganda and the ruthless murder of political opponents."[207] He also called for an immediate 100 percent increase in the size of the RAF and a further expansion beyond that.[208]

In stark contrast, Chancellor Chamberlain wanted to reduce defense spending substantially by (1) entering into a treaty with Germany that would confine the German Navy to one-third of the size of the Royal Navy and (2) scaling down Britain's commitment to furnish troops to France in case of war.[209] The plan was kept low profile. Chamberlain feared that Britons would not look upon it favorably and that the French would likely not be keen about it either.

In July 1934, as an alternative to appeasing Hitler, Churchill and Austen Chamberlain announced themselves in favor of having the Soviet Union admitted into the League of Nations.[210] For someone who was a staunch anti-Communist as Churchill, this proposal was, to say the least, shocking. But as Roberts correctly says, "it was [just] a measure of how necessary [Churchill] considered the building of collective security against Hitler to be."[211] Here, too, pragmatism would prevail over principle.

On August 2, 1934, German President Hindenburg died. In a plebiscite held two weeks later, the German electorate (by a vote of 38.4 million to 4.3 million) approved the unification of the positions of President and Chancellor and made Hitler Fuhrer of the Reich—a position from which he could not legally be removed. Churchill said that he was at least glad that four million Germans had voted against "making that gangster autocrat for life."[212]

Hitler now required officers in the armed forces to swear an oath of "unconditional obedience" not to Germany, but to him.[213]

Meddling in Austria

As Hitler had described in *Mein Kampf,* he desired to bring all Teutonic races into the Reich—to bring back to the fatherland both those areas expressly split off from Germany by the Treaty of Versailles and others populated with citizens of German descent.[214] Areas in which he was interested included Austria.

In July 1934, Austrian and German Nazis had tried to overthrow the existing government of Austria. The Austrian Chancellor, Englebert Dollfuss, was assassinated, but the coup failed. Thereafter, Austrian Nazis continued to do everything possible to subvert the government of his successor, Kurt Von Schuschnigg.[215] Despite all this, in a May 21, 1935, speech to the Reichstag, Hitler professed that "Germany neither intends nor wishes to interfere in the internal affairs of Austria, to annex Austria, or to conclude an Anschluss [—political union]."[216]

Persuaded by Mussolini to reach some sort of a negotiated settlement with Hitler, Chancellor Schuschnigg entered into an agreement with Germany. Schuschnigg and Hitler issued a joint communiqué on July 11, 1936. In it, Austria acknowledged herself to be a German state, and Germany recognized "the full sovereignty of the Federal State of Austria."[217] (Secret stipulations required Austria to muzzle the press and grant amnesty to Nazi "political prisoners," including storm troopers convicted of murdering Jews, and critics of the Fuhrer).[218] Schuschnigg thought the agreement would end Austria's trouble with the Nazis; it didn't.[219]

Rearmament in Britain

The Geneva Disarmament Conference concluded unsuccessfully in the early summer of 1934. Baldwin, who had temporarily taken over as Prime Minister because of MacDonald's ill health, then introduced the first in a long series of defense programs caused by the menace of Nazi Germany. He announced a program covering the present and the four ensuing years calling for an increase of 492 planes (forty-one squadrons of twelve).[220] It was small, both compared with later programs, and compared to what Churchill felt was required. Although done grudgingly, according to Roberts and Kennedy, "it mark[ed] the beginnings of the change from a disarmament psychology to one of rearmament."[221] In a speech to the House in July 1934, Baldwin admitted that in pursuing a policy of international disarmament, successive British Governments, including the present one, had reduced British armaments "to a dangerously low level in the hopes that others would follow our lead."[222]* He then said,

> ... in view of [Britain's]commitments under the Covenant of the League and the Locarno Treaty, the many symptoms of unrest in Europe and elsewhere, and the failure of other countries to follow Britain's example by comparable arms reductions. ... [w]e have come to the conclusion that we cannot delay any longer measures which will in the course of the next few years bring our air forces to a level more closely approaching that of our nearest neighbours."[223]

Baldwin's program was immediately attacked by Churchill as insufficient.[224] On the other hand, Labour denounced it as unilateral *rearmament*.[225] Labour asked: if the League of Nations was worth anything, why was there a need for this rearmament?[226] The argument put the Government in a difficult position. It knew additional planes were needed, but with an election coming up in a year or so, it could not say or do anything to show a lack of faith in the League on which it had built its defense policy.[227] Baldwin thus retreated to the position that the new aircraft were needed so that Britain remained "capable of effective co-operation in any system of collective security under the League of Nations."[228] He also defended against Churchill's assertion

---

Manchester writes that "No one who held high office in the 1920s, Churchill included..." can avoid "responsibility for the shocking deterioration of England's defenses." Manchester, Alone p. 12.

that the increase was insufficient by saying that the proposed increase was, in "the judgement of our experts, and ... the Government as a whole," "in light of all indications at present available," sufficient to meet Britain's "future defensive needs in the air."[229]

On November 26, 1934, the Cabinet held a special meeting about German rearmament, more particularly to discuss the contents of a specially appointed Cabinet committee's report on the subject. Among other things, the report said,

- "That the evidence of German rearmament is now so formidable that we feel it can no longer be officially ignored, and that, if the situation in Germany is allowed to develop without let or hindrance on present lines, the German forces may ultimately become a menace to the peace of Europe."

- "That particular importance is attached to making as specific and comprehensive a statement as possible on the Government's air expansion programme, particularly as to the greatest number of squadrons that it may be possible to form ... during the next two years ..."[230]

During the Cabinet debate, some urged that the additional squadrons by which the Government's proposed to increase the RAF in the ensuing four years, be made available in two years.[231] Chamberlain pointed out that "there was nothing in our information in regard to the German preparations to justify the proposed acceleration" as well as the huge impact that doing so would have on future budgets.[232]* Chamberlain's arguments notwithstanding, on November 26 the Cabinet voted to accelerate the provision of the additional squadrons.[233]

On November 28, Churchill proposed a motion in the House to advise the King that Britain's national defenses, especially her air defenses, were no longer adequate to secure the peace, safety, and freedom of the British public.[234] During the debate on the motion, Churchill, who, as noted, had amazing access to secret military information both in Germany[235] and Britain,[236] said, "Germany already ... has a military air force ... and that this illegal air force is rapidly approaching equality with our own."[237] He predicted that, given the respective programs of Germany and Britain, by

---

*Kennedy is quite critical of Chamberlain's parsimoniousness "as a member of the Baldwin Cabinet, which had done so little to wake up the country." Kennedy p. 193.

the end of 1935 "the German military Air Force ... will ... be ... at least as strong as ours and may be even stronger," while "by the end of 1936 ... [it] will be nearly 50% stronger ..."[238]*

Until this time, except for Austen Chamberlain, virtually no one in the House supported Churchill's calls for rearmament and for Britain to have binding military alliances with other European countries.[239] In the vote on Churchill's motion, thirty-five MPs voted in favor.

In his response to Churchill's speech, Baldwin admitted that Germany was creating an air force,[240] and had between six hundred and one thousand airplanes[241] but that

- Germany's strength was less than 50 percent of Britain's current strength in Europe;

- By the end of 1935 "we shall still have in Europe a margin ... of nearly 50 per cent," and

- "... His Majesty's Government are determined in no conditions to accept any position of inferiority with regard to what air force may be raised in Germany in the future."[242]

Baldwin then revealed that on top of the four squadrons already forming in 1934, the Government proposed to form twenty-five more by the end of 1936—and thus add some three hundred aircraft to Britain's first-line strength.[243] He also advised that the Government had selected the sites for eleven new aerodromes and that plans were advancing for increasing or altering some forty existing stations.[244]

In 1934, tangible evidence of a rearmament effort was hard to come by, although some small progress (far less than Churchill believed necessary) toward increasing the number of aircraft in future years had been made.

---

*The question naturally arises as to how Germany, which, just a few years earlier, had been in dire economic circumstances, could afford to rearm. The answer: Prior to WWI, Germany had great industrial capability. After the war, it was only a matter of time until her industry was revitalized. This revitalization was sped up by the deficit spending of a totalitarian state which only had one aim. As Hitler said:

> "The future of Germany depends exclusively and only on the reconstruction of the Wehrmacht [the new name for the German Army]. All other tasks must cede precedence to the task of rearmament" and "[i]n ... case of conflict between the demands of the Wehrmacht and demands for other purposes, the interests of the Wehrmacht must in every case have priority." See, Tooze, The Wages of Destruction p. 38.

Like the U.S., the Nazis also sold bonds, and, to hide some of its borrowing for rearmament, used MEFO bills—a corporate bond-like instrument paying four percent interest issued by a fictitious company set up by the State.

Years later, in the spring of 1940—before Churchill would demonstrate the mastery of warfare that helped Britain defeat the Nazis in World War II—Kennedy looked back at Churchill's efforts in the 1930s to warn his country of the German threat. His observations are enlightening:

> In light of the present-day war, we are amazed at the blindness of British leaders, in the country as a whole, that they could fail to see the correctness of Churchill's arguments ...
>
> In studying Churchill's warnings, which have proved to be so accurate, it is necessary to realize the somewhat peculiar position he has always occupied in British politics. No one has ever questioned his ability or his dynamic energy. But these very qualities, which now cause Britain to consider him the only man who can carry through a successful war policy, have in times of peace caused him to be considered "dangerous" and a little uncomfortable to have around. Then, too, Churchill has always represented the extreme viewpoint. He has never stood on middle ground—he went "all out" for anything he advocated, with the result that his opinions have always been taken advisedly by most British leaders.[245]

Manchester makes the following similarly incisive and succinct observation, that in 1934, Britain was "just not ready for Churchill."[246]

1935

- Rearmament
- Whispers of an Anglo-German Coalition
- Self-Government for India's Provincial Governments
- Anglo-German Naval Agreement
- Abyssinia
- The General Election of 1935

The year 1935 witnessed Germany's reemergence as a first-class military power. As the year progressed and Hitler announced his continuing breaches of the terms of the Versailles Treaty relating to German conscription, the size of its army and its having an air force, Europe began to tremble[247] and public opinion in England began an almost imperceptible shift toward rearming.[248]

Rearmament

Starting in late 1934 and carrying on into '35, the League of Nations, acting through the National Declaration Committee, went door-to-door in Britain to get the view of Britons on five questions about the League and collective security. The questions became known as the "Peace Ballot." The results showed that Britons were not only overwhelmingly still in favor of the League and the notion of collective security, but they also strongly supported arms reduction and the abolition of military aircraft.[249] Pacifism remained intense in Britain. Furthermore, as Kennedy writes, for most of 1935, Britons still "looked on the League as the means by which they would avoid [war]. This belief would not change appreciably until after the Abyssinia experience,* when it appeared that League sanctions might drag Britain into a conflict with Italy."[250]

The first movement toward a change in the public's attitude occurred after Goering officially announced the creation of a German Air Force on March 9, 1935, and on March 16, 1935, Hitler proclaimed new laws providing for an army of 500,000 men and universal military service. Each of these actions clearly violated the Versailles Treaty, "but Hitler knew that no one either in France or England was ready to go to war about it."[251] Instead, on April 11, 1935, representatives of Britain, France, and Italy met in Stresa, Italy, to condemn Germany's actions and to reiterate their support for Austria's independence under the Locarno treaty of 1925. (Thereafter, the three countries would frequently be called the Stresa Front.**)

At the Stresa conference, MacDonald could have but did not warn Mussolini against aggression in Abyssinia (now Ethiopia).[252] Mussolini took the Prime Minister's lack of response to an amendment calling out the Stresa partners' intention to maintain "peace in Europe" as a sign of British acquiescence to his plan to attack Abyssinia.[253]

On March 19, 1935, Under-Secretary of State for Air Phillip Sassoon made a presentation to the House of air appropriations for the upcoming fiscal year (April 6, 1935 to April 5, 1936), and a supplementary estimate of £200,000—"almost entirely moneys required to get the expansion scheme under way."[254] The proposed air appropriations for 1935–1936 showed a 17.5 percent increase.[255] This increase in defense spending angered Germany.[256]

In the House debate, Churchill specifically attacked the figures that Baldwin had put forward back on November 28, 1934, showing that German aircraft strength was between six hundred and eleven hundred planes—figures on which the new air appropriations were premised.[257] Churchill argued that Baldwin "should have said that Germany had 600 first-line air strength [planes]"—planes "with pilots, mechanics and establishments all as part of

---

Discussed later in this chapter.

**The three countries agreed to back the independence of Austria. But P.M. MacDonald had assured Parliament that he would enter into no agreement requiring Britain to take any action against Germany. Buchanan p. 143.*

the air force" and total (military) aircraft (first-line plus those planes without all of the necessary backup) of eleven hundred.[258] Noting that official figures on Britain's air strength had only just become known because they had appeared in preceding day's *Daily Telegraph,* Churchill asserted that, as of the end of November 1934, a correct comparison between the British and German Air Forces would have been:[259]

	Britain	Germany
First Line planes	560	600
Total	1020	1100

These figures he said, "show[ed] the two countries virtually ... neck and neck," and disproved Baldwin's statement in November that Germany's strength was less than 50 percent of Britain's current strength in Europe. They "therefore, require and further elucidation from the Government. ..."[260] Churchill then said that 600 was the lowest number of first-line aircraft that Germany would admit to, but that her true first-line strength "may easily be double ... or more than double ..." that number.[261] He then pointed out that while the Government says that Britain will have added an additional 150 planes to the fleet (not all first-line) by April 4, 1936 (the end of the next fiscal year),[262] over the same period Germany would have added some 1,775 planes (less those being replaced.)* Using these calculations, by the end of fiscal year 1935–1936, in comparison to Britain's total aircraft (1,170) Germany could have up to 2,875. This was certainly not the margin of superiority in Europe "of nearly 50 per cent" that Baldwin had promised.

His Majesty's Government (HMG) came to realize that its earlier numbers, including its projection of aircraft production during the next few years, were seriously off. In fact, at the April 30, 1935, meeting of the Ministerial Committee on Defence Requirements, MacDonald said that by April 1937 "Germany will have 1,512 [first-line] aircraft and we shall have 740."[263]**

---

*Based on (a) figures from The Daily Telegraph, which showed that Germany had added between two hundred and fifty and three hundred planes to its fleet since November 1934, and (b) an estimated production rate of 125 planes per month.

**The April 15, 1935, report prepared by the Chief of the Air Staff on which MacDonald relied said only that "Germany hopes" to achieve 1,512 aircraft "early in 1937. CAB 24/254 CP (35) 85 p.3 394. However, the air staff believed that it would be "virtually impossible" for Germany to achieve that level until 1939. Ibid. pp. 4, 5 394, 395.

Chamberlain and other committee members said that information about this anticipated shortfall could not (and should not) kept from the House.[264]*

Accordingly, on May 22, 1935, Baldwin backhandedly admitted that much of the information he had provided the House in November 1934, was erroneous. He told the House that "with regard to the figure I ... gave of German aeroplanes, nothing has come to my knowledge since that makes me think that that figure was wrong. I believed *at that time* it was right.[265] [emphasis added] In a statement that did not respond to Churchill's criticism, Baldwin went on to say that "Where I was wrong was in my estimate of the future. There I was completely wrong." In the realm of actions speaking louder than words, the Government quickly sought new appropriations levels that were much greater than those proposed in March. They were resolved to keep even with Germany and confident that the increased appropriations, which would nearly triple the RAF's home forces within two years, would do so.[266] In a conversation between Hitler and the British Foreign Secretary, Sir John Simon, on March 25, 1935, the Fuhrer had revealed that his goal was parity with France, which had approximately 1,500 first-line aircraft.[267] On May 22, 1935, Baldwin told the House, "that is the figure at which we are aiming, and to which we intend to proceed with all the speed that we can."[268]

On June 7, 1935, Prime Minister MacDonald resigned due to ill health. Baldwin immediately assumed the office the Prime Minister and almost immediately brought Lord Halifax into the Government as Secretary of State for War. Since the National Government had been in office for over four years, Baldwin felt obliged to call for a general election—and ultimately did.

During the ensuing election campaign, the Labour Party agreed with the Liberals to rearm to the extent required to fulfill Britain's obligations for collective action but made it clear that they were against "competitive armaments."[269] The significant efforts toward British rearmament taken in 1935 notwithstanding, in a speech just three weeks before the general election Churchill warned that "800 million pounds of Sterling [was] being spent ... in the present year on direct and indirect military preparations by Germany."[270] Without chastising the Baldwin Government or its predecessor, he also said that HMG "will [not], I imagine, disagree ... that Germany is already well on her way to becom[ing] ... the most heavily armed nation in the world and the nation most completely ready for war," while "we have no speedy prospect of equaling the German Air Force ... whatever we may do in the near future."[271] While HMG likely did not disagree with Churchill's dire forecast, for purposes of the election, even the Conservatives, who had

---

It was also agreed that airpower would no longer be judged by the number of aircraft but by the amorphous new term "air strength." Manchester, Alone p. 138.

promised to keep even with Germany,* disavowed provoking a new arms race, and declared only that "gaps" and "deficiencies" in Britain's defenses must be taken care of.[272] According to Churchill, just two weeks before the election, the P.M. himself had also said there would be no huge expenditure on armaments.[273] A year later, Baldwin would speak to the House with "appalling frankness," and say that, if, during the 1935 campaign, had he been honest with Britons about how much the country had to rearm, the Conservatives would have lost the election.[274]

These election contortions notwithstanding, a few weeks after the election, newly appointed Foreign Secretary Anthony Eden warned the Cabinet of the tremendous strides that Germany was making in its rearmament efforts and that "there was no time to lose in the preparation and completion of our own defensive arrangements …"[275] (German air production had even reached a point where Germany was trying to sell aircraft abroad.[276])

Whispers of an Anglo-German Coalition

Roberts reveals that in May 1935, Hitler wrote to British newspaper magnate Lord Rothermere suggesting an Anglo-German alliance, asserting that it "would protect 'the interests of the white race.'"[277] (This would not be the last time that Hitler would speak of some sort of Anglo-German collaboration.) Churchill's telling response was twofold. First, he reminded Rothermere of the parable about the jackal and the tiger who went out hunting together, after which the tiger ate the jackal.[278] Second, he explained that throughout history Britain had never yielded to the strongest power in Europe and said that "I see no reason myself to change from the traditional view."[279]**

Self-Government for India's Provincial Governments

On June 5, 1935, after years of debate, Parliament passed a bill giving India's provincial governments a wide measure of self-government and a path to Dominion status. India was a matter over which Churchill was so adamant as to split with the Conservative leadership, go into a form of

---

This pledge notwithstanding, with the 1935 general elections looming, the Baldwin Government did not even appoint Thomas Inskip as Minister for the Coordination of Defence to oversee this effort until March 1936. See, HC Deb 12 November 1936 vol 317 cc1104.

Churchill viewed "Inskip's appointment as another missed opportunity to warn the Nazis of British resolve." Roberts p. 398. In contrast, Chamberlain saw Baldwin's appointment of Inskip, rather than Churchill, quite favorably, writing to his sister Ida that he was thankful "we have not got Winston as a colleague." ed Self, Diary Letters Vol 4 p. 179.

**As discussed in upcoming chapters, Churchill would maintain these views in May 1940 during the War Cabinet discussion on whether to enter into a peace agreement with Hitler.*

self-exile in 1931, and fight with his fellow Conservatives. Still, when the dust had settled a bit, Churchill asked one of Gandhi's friends to "tell Mr. Gandhi to use the powers that are offered to make the thing a success."[280] Churchill added, "I am generally sympathetic towards India. I have got real fears about the future ... But you have got the things now; make it a success and if you do I will advocate you're getting much more."[281]* As Gilbert relates, "Gandhi [had] gone very high in [Churchill's] esteem since he stood up for the untouchables."[282] It is hard to believe that Churchill was the same man who was described as being "almost demented with fury" during the 1931 debate over India,[283] or the one who would hold a grudge against his former friend and colleague Stanley Baldwin. Churchill's considerable softening on positions about which he could have hardly been more entrenched belies any general perception that he was totally intractable. Still, stubbornness (often called doggedness by others) was a trait he had exhibited since his boyhood,[284] and he would display it throughout his career.

Gandhi's response was equally surprising. He told the go-between that he had a good recollection of Mr. Churchill from when Winston was Under Secretary of State for the Colonies and they had met (for the one and only time) in 1908. And that he had held the opinion since then that he could always rely on Churchill's "sympathy and goodwill."[285]

The Anglo-German Naval Agreement

On June 7, 1935, right after passage of the India bill and Ramsey MacDonald's resignation, the new Prime Minister, Stanley Baldwin, showed that like MacDonald, he was an appeaser. That is, on June 18, 1935, Britain and Germany executed the Anglo-German Naval Agreement. The Agreement fixed a ratio by which (except for submarines) the total tonnage of the German Navy was to be 35 percent of the total tonnage of the Royal Navy. Within that general limitation, as for submarines, Germany was, except for necessity, to limit itself to a tonnage equal to 45 percent of the total tonnage of submarines possessed by the members of the British Commonwealth. At the June 19 Cabinet meeting, Baldwin told members that the arrangement over submarines would most likely be criticized but "the Admiralty were rather less apprehensive of the submarines today than they had been during

---

Churchill no doubt would have been less gracious to Gandhi had he foreseen that during WWII Gandhi would write Hitler praising his "bravery [and] devotion to the Fatherland" and telling him he was not "the monster described by your opponents." Hermann, Gandhi and Churchill p. 446. Of course, Gandhi may have not been inclined to praise Hitler had he known that the Fuhrer's advice to Halifax during a meeting in 1937 had been to "shoot Gandhi." Roberts, Holy Fox p. 97.

[WWI]"[286]* He added that the agreement would enable Britain "to control German programmes of naval armaments, instead of the probable alternative of an Anglo-German competition ..."[287]

The Agreement was an ambitious attempt on the part of both the British and the German governments to achieve better relations. Hitler saw the agreement as an indication that his dreamt-of alliance between the two countries was possible.[288] But Britain "had nothing to gain from the ... pact" and it "shatter[ed] what remained of Versailles's claim to the legitimacy," since it allowed Germany to build a navy beyond the limits set by the treaty.[289] Churchill attacked the agreement, calling it the "the acme of gullibility."[290] More broadly, he condemned it as having condoned the violation of Versailles and having been made without Britain's even conferring with either of the other members of the Stresa Front—France and Italy.[291] Still, Churchill, all principles aside, voted to approve the agreement, hoping somehow that his vote might help him be invited to into the Cabinet should the National Government win the upcoming election.[292]

Abyssinia

Mussolini threatened to invade Abyssinia (Ethiopia) in August 1935. HMG told Italy that, if she did, Britain would fulfill her duties under the Covenant of the League of Nations.[293] This threat notwithstanding, on October 2, 1935, Mussolini invaded Abyssinia as he had been planning to do for months. In an unpublished note that Churchill would write some twelve years later he said, "Mussolini, like Hitler, regarded Britannia as a frightened, flabby old woman, who at worst would only bluster, and was anyhow incapable of making war."[294] That said, the invasion of Abyssinia put Britain on the horns of a dilemma: whether "to make a futile protest, which would irritate Mussolini and perhaps drive him out of the Stresa Front, out of the League, and into the arms of Germany" or "to make no protest and give the appearance of pusillanimity."[295] The Cabinet was also fully aware that ignoring or evading the collective security obligations under the League of Nations' Covenant "would amount to an admission that the attempt to give the League coercive powers was a mistake—an admission that would have serious effects in increasing the existing confusion abroad as well as on public opinion at home."[296] The Cabinet felt that the key to collective action was France: if she were prepared to honor her League obligations, other nations would probably follow.[297]

Like Churchill, the Admiralty was wrong about the effectiveness of submarines in any future war. Contrary to their belief, the submarine proved to be a devastatingly effective weapon.

As for the League's imposing economic sanctions on Italy, although Italy had, in violation of treaty, used poison gas and bombed Red Cross hospitals, Chamberlain was concerned that "[e]ven the mildest economic sanction might in the end lead to a war."[298] Nevertheless, on October 9, 1935, the Cabinet agreed that if oil producing or supplying League members, such as Romania, were prepared to impose an embargo on exporting oil to Italy, HMG would be prepared to join.[299]

The League did impose interim economic sanctions—prohibiting member countries from supplying Italy with many items. But the list did not include items essential for waging war—most notably oil.[300] Discussions continued both inside and outside the League about imposing an oil embargo to halt Italy's ongoing aggression in Abyssinia. At the Cabinet meeting held on December 2, 1935, Foreign Secretary Eden revealed that (1) the oil-producing members of the League had almost unanimously agreed to participate in an oil embargo of Italy,[301] but that (2) he had received several reports tending to show that Mussolini would regard an oil embargo as rendering defeat inevitable and use it as a pretext for attacking Britain, even though doing so would be suicidal.[302] Additionally, the United States, the world's largest exporter of oil at the time, had brought pressure to bear on its oil companies to reduce exports to Italy,[303] but those companies were politically powerful and had resisted. In fact, after the invasion of Abyssinia, the United States had quietly increased its oil shipments to Italy.[304] Eden explained that all members of the League (this did not include America, which never joined) were now willing to impose the oil sanction.[305]

In the ensuing Cabinet discussion, some members thought the risk of Italian retaliation was remote and that the success of the embargo would depend on the level of oil exports from America.[306] (In the latter regard, if the United States had supplied Italy with only the average monthly amount of oil it had provided from January 1932 to October 1935, "Italian industrial production would have come to a complete stop in March 1936 ..."[307]) That said, Eden urged that Britain proceed with the imposition of an oil embargo, but seek to delay implementation. After all, an embargo might not be necessary—because peace talks between the Italians and Abyssinians were showing a reasonable prospect of success.[308]

A week later, France abruptly changed her mind and said that if the negotiations between Italy and Abyssinia failed, the oil sanction should not be imposed.[309] The French were frightened of potential retaliation by Mussolini if they voted for the oil sanction; they intended that the brunt of any such hostilities fall on Britain, and that no reliance be placed, upon them.[310]*

In 1935, France may have had the largest army in Europe. However, these actions showed that when the chips were down, France would be an extremely unreliable

At the Cabinet meeting held on December 11, 1935, a pragmatic view met with much support—that Britain should aim at maintaining the existing sanctions and do her best to avoid an oil sanction.[311] Surprisingly, Churchill had not been among those calling for HMG to support imposition of the oil sanction. Despite what Mussolini had done to the Abyssinians, he, too, did not want to upset Italy and cause her to withdraw from participating in the fragile Stresa Front to protect Austria.[312]* The Labour Party correctly accused Churchill of trying to curry favor with Baldwin, hoping to be appointed to the Cabinet if the Conservatives prevailed in the upcoming national elections.[313] During the House debate about HMG's actions, Churchill also said that "[t]he League of Nations is alive ... [but it] is fighting for its life."[314] As it turned out, the League's ultimate failure to prevent Italy's conquest of Abyssinia greatly discredited it and the notion of collective security.

In January 1936, the League adopted a resolution creating a Committee of Experts, to consider the effectiveness of an oil sanction against Italy. The experts met from February 3 to 12 and issued a report which stated that "if an embargo on oil were *universally* applied" and the United States did not increase its exports above pre-1935 levels, the embargo "would be effective."[315] [emphasis in original] At the Cabinet meeting held on February 26, 1936, after a full analysis of each factor favoring or disfavoring the oil sanction, the Cabinet authorized the Foreign Secretary to advise the League that Britain favored imposing the oil sanction.[316] As weighty as that decision was, it came too late. Mussolini had already overrun most of Abyssinia and American oil companies had already increased their sales to Italy. To make matters worse, Mussolini took offense at Britain's belated support of sanctions. As feared, Britain had driven him out of the Stresa Front and into the arms of Germany.

The General Election of 1935

In the election held in November 1935, the Conservatives lost eighty-four seats but still held 387 out of a possible 615. (The National Government held 429—a loss of 125 seats.) In the new National Government, Stanley Baldwin continued as Prime Minister with Neville Chamberlain also continuing as Chancellor of the Exchequer. Halifax moved up from Secretary of State for War to Lord Privy Seal, and Anthony Eden, at thirty-eight, a rising star in the Conservative ranks, moved into the Cabinet as Foreign Secretary. But Churchill, who erroneously believed that his old friend Baldwin "thought well of him,"[317] received no invitation to join the new Government. While he

---

ally, as she proved to be in 1940. Little provision for this undependability would be made by either the Baldwin or the Chamberlain Governments.

This is an early example of Churchill's willingness to put practicality ahead of principle when it came to lining up countries who would join Britain in opposing Hitler. Question: Was this appeasement?

had served in the Cabinets of both Baldwin governments in the '20s and, in the months before the election had greatly reduced his attacks on Baldwin, the fact is, that ever since 1931, he had been Baldwin's strongest critic. In turn, the Baldwin Government had largely discredited him and labeled him a war monger.[318] According to the late American historian Ernest R. May and others, Baldwin had also joked to friends that "No one person has a right to so many gifts" as Churchill has. That's why "he was denied judgment and wisdom. And that is why, while we delight to listen to him in the House, we do not take his advice."[319] Others shared Baldwin's belief.*

Churchill never forgave Baldwin for not inviting him into the Cabinet in 1935. Moreover, "he saw Baldwin as responsible for the 'locust years' when Britain, if differently led, could have easily rearmed, and kept well ahead of the German military and air expansion."[320] When asked in 1947 to write a tribute to Baldwin in honor of his eightieth birthday, Churchill wrote: "It would have been better for our country if he had never lived.[321] This rancor differed from his general willingness to forgive people who had wronged him and at least be cordial toward people with whom he disagreed.[322]**

1936

- The Abdication Crisis
- Rearmament and Related Events
- German Troops Enter the Rhineland
- Abyssinia
- The Effect

In 1936, the number of planes planned for the defense of the UK was raised from the 1,500 proposed in 1935 to 1,750. The air appropriations for 1936–1937 (£39 million) were nearly twice what they were the year before. England was engaged in a building program "revised to keep abreast a change in circumstances."[323] At the Cabinet meeting of February 17, 1936, Prime Minister Baldwin reminded the members that six months earlier no one had taken much interest in defense spending and the present dire defense situation resulted from "17 years of neglect."[324] In 1936, rearmament was, however, affected by many events both at home and abroad.

For example, May writes that Chamberlain had a similar view. Moreover, Chamberlain feared that if Churchill were allowed back into the Government he would demand excessive spending for defense and make jingoistic speeches offending foreign governments." May, Strange Victory p. 173.

**Although some have criticized Chamberlain, when he was Baldwin's Chancellor of the Exchequer, for helping to delay Britain's rearming, see, Kennedy p. 193, Churchill neither attacked Chamberlain nor held any animus toward him about this.*

The Abdication Crisis

On January 20, 1936, King George V died at age seventy. Succeeding him was his eldest son, forty-two-year-old Edward VIII. Even before the King's death, the public knew that Edward was in a relationship with Mrs. Wallis Simpson, an American socialite who was at the time still married to her second husband. She had, in fact, been Edward's mistress for some time. Soon after Edward became King, she instituted divorce proceedings, and in February 1936, Edward sent word to Baldwin that he desired to marry Mrs. Simpson when her divorce became final.[325] The crisis, which would not end until Edward abdicated in mid-December, was on.

Cutting comments abounded about Mrs. Simpson such as "If the man existed with whom Wallis had enjoyed a platonic friendship, his name is lost to history."[326] However, we now know that many Britons were fine with the marriage, and it was supported by the Beaverbrook and Rothermere press, the Communist Party, the British Union of Fascists, and, to some extent, Churchill. On the other hand, it was vehemently opposed by the powerful forces of both the Church of England and the Baldwin Government[327]—both of which believed that the King as head of the Church of England had to support its position against divorce.[328] Churchill's support, such as it was, for Edward's cause, stemmed from his being a long-standing monarchist.* His efforts would, however, in the end call his judgment into question once again and represented "one of the sorriest episodes in Churchill's career."[329]

While historians debate whether Churchill favored the marriage, it is clear that he was not willing to accept Mrs. Simpson as Queen.[330] That said, he proposed an imaginative solution to resolve the situation—a morganatic marriage under which Mrs. Simpson would have become Duchess of Cornwall, but not Queen, and her children would not be in line for the throne.[331] But neither the Cabinet nor the public approved of Churchill's idea.

On Friday, December 4, after Mrs. Simpson's divorce decree had been granted preliminarily (it would not become final until late April 1937), Baldwin made it clear to Edward that he would have to choose between Mrs. Simpson and the throne. He could not have both.[332]** Baldwin also

---

*The frequent assertion that Churchill supported Edward out of friendship is dispelled by David Freeman, who presents evidence that Churchill never knew the former Prince of Wales all that well. Freeman, "The Uncrowned King: Edward VIII" Finest Hour no. 184 (2nd quarter 2019) p. 21.

**The evidence shows that Edward did not want both. Two years earlier he had said that he liked the job of being Prince of Wales and he did not believe that he could tolerate all the restrictions and so forth that would be placed upon him were he to become King. Manchester, Alone p. 229. Moreover, just before George V died,

told the King that the Cabinet wanted a decision by Monday, if not sooner, and the King agreed to provide it.[333]

Churchill wrongly believed that Edward's relationship with Mrs. Simpson was merely a royal infatuation and would pass in a few months.[334] Churchill's friend Leo Amery told him that "the country as a whole was getting progressively more shocked at the idea that the King could hesitate between his duty to the Throne and his affection for a woman."[335] Still, on December 7, Churchill pleaded for the House to give the King more time. The members shouted him down. Lord Winterton, who served in the House for forty-seven years, wrote that this was "one of the angriest manifestations I have ever heard directed against any man in the House of Commons,"[336] while *The London Times* called it "the most striking rebuff in modern parliamentary history."[337]

Professor David Freeman, editor of "Finest Hour," published by the International Churchill Society, explains why Churchill had so misjudged the situation:

- Unlike Baldwin, who had been in close touch with the new King during his time on the throne, Churchill did not see that Edward would never give up marrying Mrs. Simpson no matter how much time he was afforded and would willingly accept abdication as the price;

- Churchill was therefore pressing the House of Commons for time that the King did not want or need; and

- Churchill did not realize that the public spectacle of a sovereign pondering his duty was far more damaging to the monarchy than abdication.[338]

All that is true. But given Churchill's minor role in the abdication crisis, Manchester's thesis that the explosion in the House against Churchill and his poor judgement about the abdication crisis was disproportionate and actually represented a release of tensions arising from "frustration over rearmament and the growing likelihood of another European war" ... "Churchill's recitation of alarming facts" ... and "the growing danger"[339] is also likely correct.

Edward announced his abdication in a radio broadcast on December 11, 1936. He said, "I have found it impossible to carry the heavy burden of responsibility and to discharge my duties as King as I would wish to do without the help and support of the woman I love."[340] His younger brother George VI succeeded him. Edward and Mrs. Simpson married on June 3,

---

the then Prince had a fight with the King during which he "screamed that he didn't want the throne." Ibid. p. 222.

1937.* George forbade members of the Royal family from attending the wedding; Edward would be an outcast for the rest of his life.

Rearmament and Related Events

The initial defense appropriations for 1936–1937 were prepared in late 1935/early 1936 and were presented to Parliament in March. They did not, of course, foresee the events that would take place over the ensuing months.

German Troops Enter the Rhineland

On Saturday, March 7, German troops entered the Rhineland. This part of western Germany is bounded on the east by the Rhine, on the west by France and Belgium, and includes the industrial Ruhr Valley and the cities of Bonn, Cologne, and Düsseldorf. The use of the Rhineland as a military base had been permanently banned as part of the Treaty of Versailles to protect the eastern borders of France and Belgium. Under the treaty, if Germany violated this provision, the Allies could reoccupy the Rhineland.[341] Germany's actions were quickly accompanied by the kind of disingenuous declaration from Hitler that would become all too familiar. He declared that, with the Rhineland in hand, "We have no territorial claims to make in Europe."[342] At a meeting of the House of Commons' Foreign Affairs Committee, Churchill urged a "coordinated plan" under the League of Nations to help France challenge the German action.[343] But nothing was done; everyone just hoped Hitler was being truthful.[344]

In a speech before the House on March 26, 1936, Churchill suggested that Hitler had marched into the Rhineland even though he had been advised against doing so by his military experts.[345] Churchill did not appear to know that the German General, Blomberg, who was in charge of the operation, was inclined to retreat back to Germany if France put up a fight.[346]** But he nevertheless believed that Hitler would have retreated if pressed.[347]*** As it turns out, Lord Halifax felt the same way, although he believed that the British public would have opposed any offensive action.[348] The general view in Britain at the time was that Germany should be free "to liberate" her own territory.[349]

That said, in his March 26 address to the House, Foreign Secretary Eden laid out several approaches acceptable to the Baldwin Government, aimed

---

*Giving up the throne to marry the woman he loved sounds like a fairy tale. However, information revealed in recent years suggests that the marriage was anything but that, largely because Edward was quite suffocating, wanting to be with Wallis 24/7.

**Interestingly, during the last months that MacDonald served as Prime Minister, the Cabinet had concluded that the demilitarization of the Rhineland was not a vital British interest. CAB 23/2 3 (35) p.8 28.

***General Jodl testified at Nuremberg that the French Army could easily have repelled the German forces. Trial of Military War Criminals XV p. 352.

at assuring peace in Europe; the most significant of which was premised on a suggestion by Hitler. It involved the creation of multiple pacts of mutual assistance between the powers of Western Europe, including Germany. Under a pact, each participant would be guaranteed the help of all other signatories should it be attacked, and all would have to provide assistance should another signatory be attacked.[350*] Participants need not be a signatory to every pact. Britain's only pre-condition was that Germany not fortify the Rhineland while negotiations over the approach were ongoing—something to which Eden was told Germany would not agree.[351] The reaction: the Liberals said, "we will enter into no military alliance against anyone." In contrast, Churchill urged all nations alarmed at the growth of German armaments to combine in pacts of mutual assistance, approved by the League of Nations, just as Eden had advocated.[352**] (For now, he even proposed that Britain agree to guarantee Germany against aggression by others.[353]) He said that his aim was not to encircle Germany but rather engulf any power that sought to impose its will by aggression.[354] (While the French wanted Hitler to be part of the collective security arrangement in Eastern Europe, they viewed the encirclement of Germany as a very acceptable alternative.[355])

In a speech to the House on April 6, 1936, Churchill warned that in six months or less Germany would erect fortifications in the Rhineland that would enable her to seize Belgium and Holland enroute to attacking France.[356] He said that these two countries being controlled by Germany, and having German air bases established there, would represent grave danger to Britain. He added that the construction of fortifications in the Rhineland would also not only immediately affect central European countries such as Austria, but also threaten Poland, Czechoslovakia, and the Baltic states, among others.[357]

Noted author Richard M. Langworth points out that in 1936, Churchill was growing ever more disillusioned with the League of Nations. The Rhineland had caused him to think in terms of a collective security pact made up of countries that could surround and contain Germany—one which, by definition, must include the Soviet Union.[358] (In 1936, the Soviet's Red Army was more than six million men strong.) The need for Soviet participation was reinforced after Churchill attended a June 1936 luncheon honoring anti-Nazi Albrecht von Bernstorff, a longtime member of the diplomatic staff at the German Embassy in London. Churchill asked Bernstorff if and how Britain could avert another war. Bernstorff responded with two words: "Overwhelming Encirclement."[359] Even so, Churchill's view as to the proper

---

*This idea was originally proposed by Churchill in 1925. See, Gilbert, Prophet p. 121.
**In doing so, Churchill reiterated something he had last spoke about in the House in 1933—something that would become a recurring message until just before the start of WWII—form an alliance to resist aggression.

role for Russia in a collective security scheme vacillated.[360] Roberts writes that it was not until Czechoslovakia fell in March 1939 that Churchill "openly embraced the need for a Russian alliance."[361] Churchill's skittishness may have come from his having read a book in 1936 titled *Uncle Give Us Bread* by Strom Arne, which left him with the impression that Russia might not be nearly as strong as he believed.[362] Churchill also feared that public opinion was also not ready to accept an all-out alliance with the Soviets.[363]

Abyssinia

Meanwhile, in Abyssinia, after Italian troops finally made their way into the capital city of Addis Ababa, Italy annexed the country on May 9. The failure to prevent Italy's conquest of Abyssinia was another substantial blow to the League and collective security, on which Britain had relied for many years. On July 4, 1936, the League lifted the ineffective sanctions it had imposed.

The Effect

As noted, the events of 1936 affected defense spending. The appropriations first submitted in March called for a total expenditure of £158 million. By the end of the year they had increased by nearly 19 percent, to over £188 million.[364]* Not only were the air appropriations nearly doubled (and the number of planes for home defense increased from 1,500 to 1,750[365]), but the naval appropriations were increased by one-third, from £60 to £80 million.[366]

As noted, in April 1935, Britain had about six hundred first-line planes (and a total of 1,434) while France had 1,500 (and a total of 2,286). Germany had between six hundred and one thousand first-line planes and a total of approximately 1,300.[367] But Britain and France together had a clear advantage in both categories. Through 1935 into 1937, much of this advantage would, however, dissipate. While Britain's airplane production was increasing, the level of production it desired to achieve was set with the expectation that the French Air Force could be counted on to supplement the RAF. But over time, the French Air Force could be counted on less and less.

Two things occurred which, despite increased production in Britain, seriously impacted maintaining combined British–French aircraft superiority. First, political unrest in France, most particularly the installation of a new Socialist government in early 1936, caused airplane production there to come to a virtual halt.[368] Second, during that period, great developments were being made in aircraft design. Without the introduction of new models into its fleet, by September 1938 France's Air Force was simply outmoded.[369]

This was nearly twice the amount spent in 1932 and represented a 42 percent increase over spending in 1935. See, chart on defense spending Kennedy p. 113.

The year 1936 was an inflection point. Because of the Italian sanctions fiasco and the weaknesses they demonstrated, Britain's foreign policy would no longer focus on the failed idea of collective security through the League of Nations. Germany's entering the Rhineland also eviscerated another foundation of British foreign policy—the Locarno Pact, under which Germany, France, Belgium, Britain, and Italy mutually guaranteed peace in Western Europe.[370]

Former Edward VIII and wife visit Hitler in 1937

Halifax on hunting trip with Goering in 1937

10

MAY 1937–MARCH 1938 CHAMBERLAIN, APPEASEMENT, AND THE ROAD TO THE ANSCHLUSS

1937

- Chamberlain Becomes Prime Minister
- Appeasement
- Germany's Revelation of Its Goal
- Halifax's Trip to Germany—Fall 1937

The combined defense estimate for fiscal year 1937–1938 was £277 million.[1] This was another huge increase in defense spending (47 percent) compared to the previous year's spending of £188 million and was nearly three times the size of the defense budget in 1932.[2] Churchill was glad to hear the amount that had been allocated.

Chamberlain Becomes Prime Minister

On May 31, 1937, Neville Chamberlain succeeded Stanley Baldwin, who, at seventy, retired at the height of a great popularity brought about by the way he had handled the abdication crisis.[3]* In contrast, Churchill had declined in both popularity and influence.[4] Even so, Churchill got to second Chamberlain's nomination to be leader of the Conservative Party and talk about Chamberlain's accomplishments as Chancellor of the Exchequer.[5] (In the speech, he did, however, put the party on notice that he intended to continue in his role as chief gadfly.[6]) Churchill continued to be seen as a scaremonger, not only by Chamberlain and the rest of the Conservatives, but by the public as well. For this reason, as well as the fact that he and Chamberlain had clashed constantly over the course of their political careers (most recently over relations with Germany and the abdication crisis) Churchill was not invited to join the new National Government.

Chamberlain was sixty-eight.

Key members of Chamberlain's Cabinet included Anthony Eden as Foreign Secretary (he was held over from the Baldwin Administration), and Lord Halifax (previously Baldwin's Lord Privy Seal) as President of the Council.

Appeasement

After Hitler took power in 1933 there was a gradual recognition by forward thinking British politicians and the British people that Germany had been "treated unfairly by the Treaty of Versailles."[7] Chamberlain "believed that the key to peace was rectifying the wrongs of Versailles [peacefully], and he wanted to be the British statesman" that did so.[8] He felt that "if some compromises were made, [Hitler] would not be forced to go to war to save [his] popularity at home and Europe might have peace."[9] Moreover, the British people had no desire to get into another war.[10] Nor could Britain afford one.

While Chamberlain abhorred war[11] and sincerely believed that appeasing Hitler was the way to maintain the peace, he also believed that because of the very poor state of its armed forces, Britain had no alternative but to rearm. Her belated rearmament program, which he had come to support, would, however, not be concluded until 1939 or 1940. Thus, war had to be avoided at least until after that time.[12] While appeasement is always associated with Chamberlain, the strategy had already been reflected in the Allies' "decisions" not to act when Hitler breached the Versailles Treaty by increasing the size of the German Army to more than 100,000, reinstituting conscription, establishing an Air Force and when he reentered the Rhineland.

Germany's Revelation of Its Goal

In May 1937, Churchill was invited to a meeting at the German Embassy in London with the ambassador at the time, Joachim von Ribbentrop. Ribbentrop said that Hitler proposed to guarantee the integrity of the entire British Empire in exchange for a "free hand" in Eastern Europe—to secure Lebensraum*—in the form of Poland, the Ukraine, and the Soviet Republic of Byelorussia (Belarus).[13] (This proposal would be reiterated several times over the next few years.) Churchill responded that in his opinion no British Government would ever agree to that. Ribbentrop replied "[i]n that case, war is inevitable ..."[14] Churchill replied that if war were the result, Britain would again bring the whole world against Germany.[15] Ribbentrop fired back that she would not be able to.[16] When Churchill reported this to the Foreign Office, they were not surprised.[17]

The ideological principle of Nazism that Germany must have more "living space." The Nazis aimed to replace the indigenous population of Central and Eastern Europe with Germanic colonists.

At the Nuremberg rally in September 1937, Goering publicly laid out what Ribbentrop had discussed with Churchill. In his speech to the crowd of one hundred thousand, Goering spoke hopefully of an understanding between the British sea empire and Germany with an empire in Central Europe. He said that should London fail to participate in such a scheme, Germany would be forced to prepare for the destruction of Britain.[18]

In October, Churchill would write his Hitler-praising cousin, Lord Londonderry, on the subject of giving Germany a free hand. He reiterated that this was something Britain could not agree to and pointed out that under such an agreement Germany "would devour Austria and Czechoslovakia as a preliminary to making a gigantic middle-Europe bloc."[19]

Halifax's Trip to Germany—Fall 1937

In the fall of 1937 Goering invited Halifax on a hunting trip in Germany. Along with the trip also came an invitation to meet Hitler. Chamberlain, wanting to create an atmosphere in which a European settlement could be discussed, persuaded Halifax to go.* Foreign Minister Anthony Eden did not favor the meeting.[20] When it was clear that Halifax would attend, Eden gave Halifax strict instructions to stand firm on matters involving Hitler's intentions with regard to a unification with Austria, transferring the Sudetenland in Czechoslovakia, and securing the return of the Polish city of Danzig.[21]

During his meeting with Hitler, Halifax praised Nazi Germany "[a]s a bulwark of the West against Bolshevism"[22] and "sympathized with past German grievances."[23]** Among other things, he also spoke about the "great services the Führer had rendered in the rebuilding of Germany."[24] Anthony McCarten, the author of *The Darkest Hour,* describes Halifax as having been "sycophantic."[25] Buchanan also reports that notwithstanding Eden's instructions, Halifax let it be known to the Fuhrer that Britain would not go to war over Germany's intention to bring Austria, the Sudetenland, or Danzig into the Reich.[26] Needless to say, Hitler was encouraged by what Halifax had to say.[27]

Halifax returned from his trip singing the praises of the Fuhrer. He also admitted that he found Goering "frankly attractive" and Propaganda Minister Joseph Goebbels "very likable."[28] On November 24, he advised the Cabinet that Hitler had said that the question of returning the African colonies that Germany had before WWI was the only outstanding issue between Britain and Germany.[29] Halifax thought therefore that the basis of an understanding

---

*Halifax's visit came just a few weeks after former King Edward VIII and his wife spent twelve days in Nazi Germany as Hitler's guest.
**This was ironic because, as noted, Halifax had been a strong proponent of imposing harsh terms on Germany back in 1919.

about Central and Eastern Europe might not be too difficult to achieve.[30] He also reported that "the Germans had no policy of immediate adventure. They were too busy building up their country ..."[31] and that Goering had told him that war was "inconceivable."[32] Halifax's belief that Hitler had no intention of starting a war held no weight with Foreign Secretary Eden and marked the beginning of the end of Eden's time in Chamberlain's Cabinet.[33]

In his diary of November 26, 1937, Chamberlain wrote that Halifax's visit had achieved its objective of creating an atmosphere in which to discuss a European settlement. He then described, quite correctly, that besides recovering colonies lost after WWI, "[o]f course [the Germans] want to dominate Eastern Europe ... they want as close a union with Austria as they could get without incorporating her into the Reich, and they want much the same thing for the Sudeten Germans [in Czechoslovakia]." In conclusion he wrote "... I don't see why we shouldn't say to Germany, 'give us satisfactory assurances that you won't use force to deal with the Austrians and Czechoslovakians and we will give you similar assurances that we won't use force to prevent the changes you want if you can get them by peaceful means.'"[34] In this one-sentence diary entry he summed up how Britain would proceed over the next year.

In the afterglow of Halifax's trip to Germany (and Hitler's misleading statement that the colonial question was the only outstanding issue between Britain and Germany), Chamberlain and Halifax lost focus. They paid no attention to the critical message that the Nazis had sent in the preceding few months—that absent Britain's agreeing to give Germany a free hand in the East, Germany would be forced to destroy her.

When the House of Commons voted to learn the details of Halifax's trip, Chamberlain was taken aback. The Prime Minister felt that any criticism of the trip might offend Hitler at a time when the P.M. wanted to build friendship and trust with Germany.[35] Fear of offending Hitler would become a significant consideration in almost every action contemplated by Chamberlain's Government until the spring of 1939 and even occasionally thereafter.

1938
- Moving Toward Anschluss
- Schuschnigg Announces a Plebiscite and Hitler Reacts
- What Was Britain and France's Response to All This?
- Russia's Request for a Conference to Discuss Joint Action to Protect Czechoslovakia

---

The air appropriations for 1938–1939 were £93.5 million—an increase of 13.3 percent over the year before. The appropriations for all services increased by nearly £65 million (23 percent) to £342.5 million. In his speech to the

House on March 24, 1938, Chamberlain advised that the present circumstances required yet further increases in spending on the Royal Air Force and Britain's antiaircraft defenses.[36] This amounted to an additional 22 percent increase in spending on armaments—an added appropriation of nearly £23 million, which brought the total supplementary appropriations for the year up to £126.4 million.[37] Among other things the money was used to buy—

- four hundred airplanes from the United States; and

- to place an order for one thousand Spitfire fighters

In January 1938 Chamberlain officially announced his policy of colonial appeasement, under which Germany would get back colonies she lost after WWI in exchange for Hitler's agreement not to seize neighboring countries on the continent and some form of arms agreement.[38] Foreign Secretary Eden was less than enthusiastic about the plan and Chamberlain knew it.[39] When Hitler rejected this approach, Chamberlain sweetened the pot by offering the Fuhrer territories in Africa that were never German colonies and which were never covered by the Versailles Treaty.[40]

As 1938 progressed, Hitler made demands for the incorporation into Germany of various German-inhabited lands such as Austria and the portion of Czechoslovakia known as the Sudetenland. The Chamberlain Government's willingness to accede to these demands as a partial redress of justified grievances took on the moniker—"appeasement." Besides wanting to right the wrongs of Versailles, Chamberlain subscribed to the general, seemingly logical, belief that once a country's legitimate claims were met, it would become content and pacific.[41] That may have been true before Hitler took power in 1933, but now, aside from making "legitimate claims," Germany was also seeking to take over all of Central and Eastern Europe—a fact with which Chamberlain never fully came to grips.

As young Jack Kennedy correctly described it, the essence of Chamberlain's "double-barreled" policy was first to remove the causes for war, and second to make Britain so strong that no one would dare attack her.[42]* This would go beyond the traditional British theory of war—that Britain merely had "to build up [her] defenses to prevent a knockout blow and then keep 'business going as usual.'"[43] It is interesting that Chamberlain, the main apostle of appeasement, someone who detested war, and an opponent of increased spending when he was Chancellor of the Exchequer under Baldwin, would

---

*As of March 1938, the Under-Secretary for Air estimated that Britain had a first-line strength of about 1,600 planes and was producing, on average, thirty-seven new planes per month (including replacement, reserve, and training planes). Kennedy p. 180. This was an increase of 450 planes over the 1937 figure.

advocate increased spending on armaments to such a degree (although he did resent the waste of money involved).[44]

While today appeasement is generally looked upon with disdain, once upon a time it was seen as an enlightened policy, the noble aim of doing away with shameful strictures on Germany that should have never been imposed.[45]* (According to Manchester, "[a]ppeasement became evangelical; indeed, for some, the line between foreign policy and religion became blurred."[46]) Chamberlain called the Treaty of Versailles "a problem that ought to have been solved long ago if only the statesmen of the last twenty years had taken broader and more enlightened views of their duty. It had become like a disease which had been long neglected, a surgical operation was necessary to save the life of the patient."[47] Of course, had that problem been addressed in a timely fashion, Hitler may have never come to power.

However, here he was. And appeasement went only so far in keeping him at bay. Manchester writes that "Chamberlain was ... tempted by Churchill's soaring proposal" to create a broad coalition of countries threatened by Hitler.[48]** But, in the end, the P.M. could never get sufficiently enthusiastic about doing the only thing likely to stop Hitler—adopt Churchill's idea of forming an alliance of countries strong enough to stand up to Hitler; an alliance that would, by necessity, have to include the Soviet Union.

In Churchill's view:

> ... grave and largely irreparable injury to world security took place in the years 1932 to 1935 ... In those days I ventured repeatedly to submit to the House the maxim that the grievances of the vanquished should be redressed before the disarmament of the victors was begun. But the reverse was done. *Then was the time to make concessions to the German people and to the*

Churchill had from the outset disapproved of the Versailles Treaty, particularly its punitive clauses. Manchester, Alone p 56. Surprisingly, as far back as 1925, Churchill had argued that the treaty was substantially flawed by deliberately keeping some regions with large German populations separate from Germany itself. Manchester, Alone pp. 288–89. He would have torn up the treaty and redrawn the frontiers of the German state. Ibid. p. 289. For example, in 1933 he said, recognizing that it was inhabited entirely by Poles, that he would like to see the Polish corridor adjusted. HC Deb 13 April 1933 vol 276 cc2791. He also spoke of "a pyramid of peace, which might be triangular or quadrangular, three or four great Powers shaking hands together and endeavouring to procure a rectification of some of the evils arising from the treaties made in vile passion of war, which if left unredressed will bring upon us consequences we cannot name." Ibid. cc549.

**As noted in Chapter 9, in 1934 the Cabinet agreed that it must without delay consider partnering with other countries to bolster mutual security. CAB 23/ 3 10 (34) p. 15 292.*

German ruler. Then was the time when they would have had
their real value. But no attempt was made.[49] [emphasis added]

But during the mid- to late-30s, many members of the British upper class were sympathetic toward Hitler and endorsed acts of appeasement.[50] Such pro-German leanings could even be found in members of the Royal family.[51] Because Hitler was the arch anti-Communist, he was not seen as someone who was dangerous or antithetic to British interests.[52] That the British upper class (including Chamberlain and Halifax), was to varying degrees anti-Semitic, also made Hitler a bit easier for them to swallow. As for Churchill, because he did not share their prejudice and was "a man who wouldn't laugh at anti-Semitic jokes,"[53] some British aristocrats simply felt awkward around him. As Manchester adds, "Winston's criticism of the new Germany was also considered bad form—even disloyal to His Majesty's Government."[54]

The general view today is that Chamberlain, other appeasers (like Halifax) and before that Prime Ministers Macdonald and Baldwin, were either both weak-kneed individuals who were intimidated or simply taken in by Hitler. As Professor A.J.P. Taylor writes, appeasement came to be equated with capitulation—"a surrender to fear."[55] Appeasers just kept feeding the tiger to keep it from attacking and hoped he'd be satiated. They gave little thought about what would happen when the food ran out and the tiger was still hungry.

Taylor is likely correct, but there is at least one other way to look at it. John Stuart Mill, the most influential English language philosopher of the nineteenth century, once famously observed that "Bad men need nothing more to compass their ends than that good men should look on and do nothing."[56] Accepting the truth of that statement, one can say without fear of contradiction that Chamberlain, unlike Churchill, was simply slow to recognize that Hitler was evil. He would not do so until after Germany invaded Czechoslovakia in March 1939. In contrast, Churchill was someone who early on recognized Hitler as a duplicitous, demon–genius. Churchill was also a vociferous opponent of allowing dictators to do whatever they wanted with no fear of repercussion. As noted, in the '30s, Churchill supported both rearmament and strong collective action by members of the League of Nations. In time he felt that this approach had unfortunately been replaced by just "bowing to the dictators."[57]

In 1938 and 1939, the clash between appeasement and standing up to Hitler—between Chamberlain (and his disciples) on the one hand and Churchill (and his) on the other, would be center stage. Although Britain had not raised an eyebrow when Hitler reinstituted conscription, formed an air force, marched into the Rhineland, or intervened in the Spanish Civil War, 1938 would provide several opportunities for it to do so and more. The first instance involved Hitler's designs on Austria. But since the Austrian

Nazis' unsuccessful coup/assassination of Dollfuss in July 1934, the Western democracies had shown that they would overlook Fascist violence "so long as they were not themselves directly assailed[58];—the treatment of the Jews and others in Germany and Italy's invasion of Abyssinia being two more good examples.

Moving Toward Anschluss

As discussed in Chapter 9, Hitler, desired to bring all areas populated by Teutonic races into the Reich. One such area was Austria, another was the Sudetenland, a mountainous region in Czechoslovakia populated by Germans. Absorbing the Austrian Republic would, however, open the door to the conquest of all of Czechoslovakia and southeastern Europe.[59]

When WWI started, Austria was a part of the Austro-Hungarian Empire which fought on the side of the Germans in the war. Defeat led to the dissolution of the Empire; the German-speaking part of Austria proclaimed itself the Republic of German-Austria and had the specific intent of a union with Germany. Article 2 of its provisional Constitution said that Germany–Austria was "an integral part of the German Reich."[60] Still, the 1919 Treaties of St. Germaine and Versailles explicitly forbade any union between Austria and Germany[61] and forced "Germany-Austria" to rename itself "the Republic of Austria," which subsequently became the "First Austrian Republic."[62] In 1921, several plebiscites were held in Austria about a union with Germany. The votes for union were overwhelming. Still, permission was again denied.[63]

After WWI, not only did the Allies want Austria and Germany to be two separate countries, but they also restricted economic relations between the two. The Allies feared that a union would make Germany too strong. When, at the 1919 Paris Peace Conference, Austria requested permission to enter into a free-trade zone agreement with Germany, even permission for that was denied.[64] Similarly, under the resulting treaties, even a customs union between Austria and Germany was forbidden without approval of the League of Nations. Thus, Britain, France, and Italy had a veto power over trade between the two countries.[65]

When, at the beginning of the Depression, German Chancellor Heinrich Bruening again asked for permission to form a customs union with Austria, the Allies again refused. British historian Richard Lamb views that refusal as a huge mistake that would have "dire consequences for both the German and Austrian economies." Moreover he concludes that "the resulting economic distress contributed to the rapid rise of the Nazis to power in Germany," and Chancellor Bruening's resignation.[66] Because of Germany's escalating economic crisis, Bruening's successor, Franz von Papen, begged the Allies to cancel Germany's war reparations. But Britain's new Chancellor of the

Exchequer, Neville Chamberlain, refused. He even demanded another four billion marks (but settled for three).[67]

As 1938 started, Roosevelt proposed a meeting in Washington of representatives mainly from smaller European counties to discuss growing differences on the continent.[68] Even though reparations had been waived, he recognized that other adjustments to the Treaty of Versailles were appropriate: "... it is possible that before the foundations of a lasting peace can be secured, international adjustments of various kinds must be found for the pacification of the universe in order to remove such inequities as may exist by reason of the nature of certain settlements reached during termination of the Great War."[69] His hope was that the initiation of discussions in Washington would give impulse to negotiations between Britain and France with Germany and Italy.[70] As Roosevelt told Chamberlain in a secret memo, he would only proceed with this scheme if he received assurance from the Prime Minister that it met with the approval of the British Government.[71] Chamberlain promptly rejected the offer without even consulting Foreign Secretary Eden, and asked Roosevelt to postpone his efforts indefinitely. His "reason": Britain was in the midst of its "own efforts to reach a general appeasement by improving relations with the Italian and German governments."[72] Viewing the willingness of the United States to involve herself as an event more important than any other "to stave off or even prevent war," Churchill writes that "[w]e must regard [Chamberlain's] rejection—for such it was—as the loss of the last frail chance to save the world from tyranny otherwise than by war."[73]

Chamberlain, eager to build upon Halifax's visit to Germany the previous fall, came up with a proposal under which Germany would get back her colonial possessions in central Africa in exchange for a reduction of the Luftwaffe and some satisfactory resolution of the Czech problem.[74] The proposal was submitted to Hitler on March 3, 1938.[75] The Fuhrer quickly rejected it[76] and rebuked Britain, saying that "Germany would not allow third parties to interfere in the settlement of her relationship with the countries of the same nationality or countries with large German populations" and that "if in Austria or in Czechoslovakia internal explosions took place, Germany would ... act like lightning."[77] As Halifax told the Cabinet, "the German Government appeared to be set head-on to achieve their desiderata in Central Europe and did not want to tie their hands by talks, and still less by undertakings to ourselves."[78] This of course was 180 degrees opposite what Hitler had told Halifax the previous fall when he said that the colonial question was the only direct issue outstanding between the UK and Germany.[79]

Hitler was anxious to get on with bringing Austria into the Reich, something he had demanded ever since he came to power in 1933. As discussed in Chapter 9, in 1934 Germany had been involved in a failed coup and the assassination of Austrian Chancellor Dollfuss. Dolfuss's successor, Dr. Kurt von Schuschnigg, tried to negotiate a way to keep Austria independent. But that did not mesh with Hitler's plans. Indeed, in July 1936, at the same time Hitler signed an agreement recognizing the full sovereignty of Austria, he also instructed the German General Staff to draw up military plans for the occupation of Austria. He crystallized those plans by special directive and in early November 1937 unfolded his future designs to the Chiefs of his armed forces.[80]*

While Hitler wanted to bring the Germanic peoples of Austria into the Reich, he also had another reason for wanting to annex Austria—Lebensraum.[81] Annexing Austria was a prelude to grabbing Czechoslovakia and then all of southeastern Europe[82]—a significant and necessary first step toward obtaining the Lebensraum that was such a central goal of Nazism. While the appeasers were busy righting the wrongs of Versailles and "solving" the sequential crises that Hitler created by his land grabs, they appeared to have forgotten that this fundamental precept of Nazism inspired Hitler's actions. Until Hitler abandoned the concept of Lebensraum, which he showed no intention of doing, he could never be appeased. Such being the case, Hitler likely knew that at some point he would probably have to reckon with British and French leaders like Churchill and Eden—non-appeasers who believed that his control of central Europe would be "intolerable."[83]

As Hitler applied increasing pressure on Austria, the question became: could peace be maintained by appeasement as Chamberlain and his colleague, Lord Halifax, believed, or was permanent peace to be achieved by taking a firm stand (and necessary actions through the League of Nations, if needed), as Foreign Secretary Eden and Churchill urged? In *Why England Slept*, Kennedy writes that there was considerable feeling in Britain that Hitler was just bluffing.[84] America was also sympathetic to the Churchill/Eden "stand firm" approach.[85] The problem was that in 1938, Britain was generally thought to be weak militarily[86] and it would therefore be taking "a terrific risk" trying to bluff anyone, let alone someone as mercurial as Hitler.[87]

The first step toward a showdown about the annexation of Austria took place on February 12, 1938. Hitler had summoned Austrian Chancellor Schuschnigg to a meeting at the Eagles Nest, Hitler's retreat in the Bavarian Alps near Berchtesgaden.[88] Schuschnigg looked forward to the meeting. He intended to lay out his complaints about Nazi-fomented unrest in Austria and intended to offer concessions, but only in exchange for a German repudiation of the Nazi extremists.[89] As summarized by Foreign Secretary Eden

---

Professor Taylor contends that despite these plans, Hitler did not intend to carry out the annexation of Austria by military means. Taylor, Origins pp. 142, 143. Rather, according to Taylor, Hitler intended that the absorption of Austria occur by evolution. Ibid. p. 144.

on February 16, during the meeting, which, to the surprise of the Austrian Chancellor, was also attended by three top Nazi generals,[90] "Hitler brought great pressure to bear on Schuschnigg with the object of accelerating the absorption of Austria by Germany. ..."[91] The Fuhrer also misleadingly informed Schuschnigg that "Lord Halifax completely approved of Germany's actions toward Austria and Czechoslovakia."[92] As Dr. Schuschnigg recounts, at the morning session:

> Hitler said: "I have only to give an order, and in one single night all your ridiculous defense mechanism are blown to bits. You don't seriously believe that you can stop me or even delay me for half an hour? ... Do you want to make another Spain of Austria?"

> To this, Schuschnigg responded: "... I am fully aware that you can invade Austria, but Herr Reichskanzler, whether we like it or not, that would mean bloodshed. We are not alone in this world, and such a step would probably mean war."

> Hitler's retort: "... Don't think for one moment that anybody on earth is going to thwart my decisions. Italy? I see eye-to-eye with Mussolini. ... England? *England will not move one finger for Austria.* ... And France? Well, three [sic] years ago when we marched into the Rhineland with a handful of battalions, I risked everything. If France had stopped us, then we would have had to retreat ... But for France it is now too late!"[93] [emphasis added]

After lunch, newly appointed Foreign Minister Ribbentrop and the Ambassador to Austria, former Chancellor von Papen, presented Schuschnigg with a written ultimatum, acceptance of which would pave the way for Austria to become a mere puppet state.[94] Its terms were:

- appoint the Austrian Nazi leader, Arthur Seyss-Inquart, as Minister of Security;

- give amnesty to all Austrian Nazis who were in jail; and

- incorporate the Austrian Nazi party into the government-sponsored Fatherland Front (the ruling political organization in Austria).[95]

Later that day, Hitler told the Austrian Chancellor that he expected the ultimatum to be agreed to within three days.[96] At 11:00 PM, Schuschnigg gave in and, to save whatever remnant of Austrian independence might still exist, signed the protocol (although it still needed to be ratified by the Austrian

Government).[97] He did gain one concession—Germany would repudiate the illegal activity of Austrian Nazis, but in exchange, Hitler required that all Austrian Nazi fugitives be repatriated to Germany.[98]

To keep the pressure on Schuschnigg, almost immediately after the meeting Hitler began feigning military action against Austria.[99] Given the threat of an invasion, on February 15, Austrian President Wilhelm Miklas agreed to the ultimatum. Notwithstanding the content of the ultimatum or the way it came about, in a March 2 speech to the House, Prime Minister Chamberlain described the process as "... two statesmen hav[ing] agreed to certain measures being taken with a view to improving relations between their two countries." Shirer writes that based on what had been provided to Chamberlain about the ultimatum and the actual content of it, the Prime Minister's characterization of Hitler's agreement with Austria to Parliament was "astounding" and a free pass from Britain for Hitler to march into Austria.[100]

In a speech before the Reichstag on February 20, Hitler said, "I am happy to be able to tell you, gentlemen, that during the past few days a further understanding has been reached with the country that is particularly close to us for many reasons."[101] Hitler then talked about how he and the Austrian Chancellor had corresponding views as to the benefits of the Anschluss—the political union of Austria and Germany. He then expressed his "sincere gratitude to the Austrian Chancellor for the great consideration and warm-hearted readiness with which he accepted my invitation and endeavored, with me, to find a solution doing equal justice to the interests of both countries ..."[102] The speech set off many celebrations by Austrian Nazis.[103] The next day, the leader of the Austrian Nazi underground was brought before Hitler. He and his associates were ordered to leave Austria.[104]

Just after the first disquieting reports of the Hitler-Schuschnigg confrontation became known, the simmering differences of opinion between Foreign Secretary Eden and Chamberlain as to the direction of Britain's foreign policy boiled over. Ever since Chamberlain had become Prime Minister in May 1937, Eden, who had been Foreign Secretary since 1935, had taken issue with Chamberlain's desire to get on good terms with Hitler and Mussolini and his belief that conciliation and the avoidance of anything likely to offend either dictator was the best method to do so.[105] Eden also strongly disagreed (as did President Roosevelt) with Chamberlain's idea of recognizing Italy's right to retain Abyssinia (which it had conquered in 1936) as a prelude to a general settlement of differences.[106] Accordingly, on February 20, 1938, Eden resigned.[107] Chamberlain was not upset—"he considered Eden too difficult to manage."[108] Despite Halifax's disobedient, sycophantic performance in front of Hitler the previous fall, or perhaps because of it, Chamberlain quickly appointed him to replace Eden. The change was received well in Berlin.[109]

Eden's resignation caused a stir.[110] To show support for Eden's "firm stand" policy, the Labour Party even moved to censure Chamberlain for dismissing him.[111] While Labour was not ready to endorse a "stand up and *fight*" policy, it did support returning to a policy of collective security through the League of Nations,[112] a position previously espoused by Chamberlain but now was one in which he had little faith.[113] When asked by the press about his apparent change of position, Chamberlain said that conditions had changed so much that a policy of collective security through the League was now impracticable.[114]

When Eden spoke before the House on February 21, 1938 he said that he did not believe Britain could make progress in European appeasement if it allowed the impression to gain currency abroad that it constantly yields to pressure.[115] Then, Churchill, commenting on Britain's having failed, just as when Hitler reoccupied the Rhineland in 1936, to take action under the authority of the League of Nations to prevent the looming annexation of Austria, added, "Austria has been laid in thrall and we do not know whether Czechoslovakia will not suffer a similar attack."[116] Presciently, he added, "I predict that the day will come when at some point or another on some issue or other you will have to make a stand, and I pray God that when that day comes we may not find that through an unwise policy we are left to make that stand alone."[117]

Owing to the Conservatives' substantial majority in the Commons, the debate on Labour's censure motion turned out to be an impressive demonstration of support for Chamberlain's policies. Only one Conservative MP voted for censure.[118] The motion was defeated by 330 to 186. Twenty MPs, including Churchill, abstained.

On February 23, Mussolini, no fan of having a Nazi puppet state as a neighbor, sent a message to Schuschnigg saying that he considered the Austrian attitude taken at Berchtesgaden to have been appropriate.[119] Mussolini also reassured Schuschnigg of his personal friendship and Italy's continuing support for Austria.[120] The day after receiving this, Schuschnigg gave a courageous speech to the Austrian Parliament, declaring that Austria would never surrender her independence.[121]* It appeared that Schuschnigg had something up his sleeve; but what? The answer was revealed on March 7 when Schuschnigg sent a confidential message to Mussolini revealing that he intended to hold a plebiscite.[122] Mussolini responded that the plebiscite was a definite mistake; but Schuschnigg had made up his mind.[123]

Schuschnigg's speech caused mobs of angry Austrian Nazis to march through the streets hauling down Austrian flags and replacing them with Nazi ones. As they proceeded, they shouted, "Heil Hitler" and demanded that Chancellor Schuschnigg be lynched. Manchester, Alone p. 273.

Schuschnigg Announces a Plebiscite and Hitler Reacts

On March 9, 1938, Schuschnigg announced that a plebiscite on the Anschluss would be held in Austria four days later, on Sunday, March 13.[124] While some predicted that the results of the plebiscite would be at least 80 percent in favor of the Nazis,[125] Georg Franckenstein, the Austrian Ambassador to Britain, advised Churchill that the well-informed people with whom he had consulted agreed that the majority of Austrians favored maintaining the country's independence.[126] In Shirer's opinion, in a free election, the results of the plebiscite would have been close.[127]

Seemingly there was no reaction from Hitler about the proposed plebiscite. However, on March 10 he decided to occupy Austria.[128] Early on the morning of Friday March 11, 1938, Schuschnigg learned that the German–Austrian frontier had been closed[129] and that the German Army had been mobilized with the idea of invading.[130] Later that morning, Austrian Nazi leader Seyss-Inquart called Schuschnigg to say that he had just received a phone call from Goering—the plebiscite must be called off immediately *or else*.[131] Manchester points out that until the announcement of the plebiscite Hitler had not planned a full Anschluss; all he wanted was to make Austria a vassal state with a puppet government.[132]* Moreover, until he was sure that he would get no objection from Italy, France, and Britain, Hitler did not know for certain if he could successfully do that.[133]

Believing that the police and the Austrian army could not be counted on,[134] Schuschnigg agreed to postpone the plebiscite.[135] This capitulation notwithstanding, Goering then demanded that Schuschnigg resign immediately and nominate Seyss-Inquart to succeed him as Chancellor. Goering said that unless both things were done within two hours, Germany would invade.[136] Among the people that Schuschnigg called immediately was Lord Halifax, Britain's newly appointed Foreign Secretary. Looking for British support, Schuschnigg asked Halifax what he should do in response to Goering's demand.[137] After consulting with Chamberlain, Halifax coldly replied that "His Majesty's Government could not take the responsibility of advising the Chancellor to take any course of action which might expose his country to dangers against which HMG are unable to guarantee protection."[138] Hearing that the British Government would be of no help, Schuschnigg resigned. Because nominating a new chancellor was part of Schuschnigg's job, that task now fell to the president of Austria. But President Miklas refused to nominate any Nazi to be Chancellor.[139] Accordingly, at 8:00 PM Seyss-Inquart appointed himself Chancellor.[140] Chamberlain directed the British ambassador in Berlin to write a note to Germany's acting Foreign Minister,

---

Hitler would do likewise with other countries that he subjugated, e.g., Czechoslovakia and France.

Konstantin von Neurath, saying that if the reports about Germany's having given Austria an ultimatum were in fact true, British Government felt "bound to register a protest in the strongest terms."[141] (Von Neurath responded on March 12, saying that this was a matter of concern to the German people and not the British Government.[142])

At 9:10 PM, the new Austrian Chancellor sent an agreed-upon telegram to the Fuhrer requesting German help to stem non-existent Communist-inspired unrest in Austria.[143] But the telegram proved unnecessary—Hitler had ordered the invasion twenty-five minutes earlier.[144]

Concerned about Italy's reaction to his aggression,[145] before invading Austria, Hitler had a phone call with his special envoy to Mussolini, Prince Philip of Hesse, who had just met with El Duce on the subject.* Prince Philip told Hitler that Mussolini "[had] accepted the whole thing in a very friendly manner and sends you his regards. He had been informed from Austria; Schuschnigg gave him the news. To which Mussolini had responded that any Italian intervention [to help Austria] would be a complete impossibility." Hitler's reaction to this good news was: "then please tell Mussolini I will never forget him for this. ... Never, never, never, whatever happens."[146] Manchester is likely correct when he says that Mussolini responded as he did because the British and French had tried to chastise him for his adventure in Abyssinia.[147] It should be noted that Hitler had also told Mussolini that if he did not object to Germany's absorption of Austria, Italy could retain the province of South Tyrol,[148] which, under the Versailles Treaty, had been taken from Germany and annexed by Italy in 1919.**

At dawn on March 12, 1938, German troops rolled over the Austrian border.*** They met with no resistance from the Austrian Army. In fact, they were largely greeted as heroes.[149] Later in the day, Hitler himself drove

---

*There was also concern about Czechoslovakia's reaction; after all, she did have thirty-five divisions of well-equipped troops—at least seven times more than the British Army had. Such being the case, at the gala performance of the State Opera in Berlin that evening, Goering pulled Czech diplomat Dr. Vojtech Mastny aside and told him, on his word of honor, that Czechoslovakia had nothing to fear from Germany. See, Shirer p. 346. Mastny conferred with his foreign minister in Prague, then advised Goering that the Czechs did not intend to interfere in Austria. See, Shirer p. 346. As Shirer points out, "There were some in Europe ... who thought the Czech government was shortsighted ... [and that] the Czechs should have acted on the night of March 11." Ibid.

**Hitler was willing to cede South Tyrol, even though it had a majority German population of 200,000.

***After the invasion, Schuschnigg was arrested, kept in solitary confinement, and eventually interned in various concentration camps until he was liberated by the United States Army in 1945. Leixner, A German War Correspondent's Account p. 377.

across the border to Linz, the town of his boyhood.[150]* There he made the sudden decision not just to make Austria a vassal state but rather to dissolve the Austrian Republic and absorb it into the Reich.[151] (After that, Austria was known as the German province of Ostmark.[152]) In a plebiscite supervised by the Gestapo and the SS, the people of Austria and Germany were asked to ratify the full Anschluss. In Germany 99.08 percent voted in favor; in Austria the figure was 99.75 percent.[153] That said, outside Germany, the methods by which Hitler had accomplished the Anschluss were generally condemned.[154]

What Was Britain and France's Response to All This?

After meeting with Halifax, on March 10, Joachim Ribbentrop, the Nazis' newly appointed Minister of Foreign Affairs, reported that the answer was: nothing.[155] After German troops marched into Austria, Chamberlain told the Cabinet that "there was probably not very much that could be done."[156] and that "Nothing short of an overwhelming display of force would have stopped it."[157]** He added that "the manner in which the German action in Austria has been brought about was most distressing and shocking to the world and was a typical illustration of power politics. ... [It would also make] International appeasement much more difficult."[158]***

The British failed to do anything to help Austria, despite having pledged in the Final Declaration of the 1935 Stresa Conference to support Austrian independence and resist any future attempt by Germany to change the Treaty of Versailles.[159] The Chamberlain Government believed that it was too weak to challenge Germany militarily.[160] (At the Cabinet meeting of February 16, 1938, it concluded that the maximum force which Britain could have contributed to any action to aid Austria would have been two regular divisions and three mobile divisions within three weeks followed by two more regular divisions.[161]) A suggestion was even made that the Germans should be told that Britain would not interfere in Austria because of Britain's limited capability to do so.[162] As Labour Party leader Clement Attlee pointed out, this passive approach was unsurprising because at the time of the Anschluss, the British Government were pursuing friendly conversations with the German Government.[163] Embellishing slightly on what he had said to the Cabinet on the 12th, on March 14 Chamberlain told the House that "The hard fact

---

*Hitler would make his triumphant entry into Vienna on March 14.

**The latter statement was prescient. Unfortunately, the failure to form an alliance of countries opposed to Hitler that could collectively display such overwhelming force ultimately resulted in WWII.

***The absorption of Austria into the Reich had been laid out in Mein Kampf. See, Buchanan p. 199.

is ... that nothing could have arrested this action by Germany unless we and others with us had been prepared to use force to prevent it."[164]

The position that there was nothing that could have been done to save Austria is not universally accepted. Perhaps chief among the naysayers is William Shirer, who writes that "Without firing a shot and without interference from Great Britain, France and Russia, whose military forces could have overwhelmed him,[*] Hitler had added seven million subjects to the Reich and gained a strategic position of immense value to his future plans."[165] As Manchester puts it, by allowing Hitler to absorb Austria, "the governments of Europe ... betrayed tens of thousands of anti-Nazis ..."[166]

The discussion about what had occurred in Austria aside, on March 12, 1938, Halifax asked the Cabinet to ponder the following question: How do we prevent similar action being taken in *Czechoslovakia?*[167]** [emphasis added] Chamberlain responded by directing Halifax to consider this question with the French, who had a treaty with Czechoslovakia and had announced their intention to fulfill it.[168] (Permanent Under-Secretary for Foreign Affairs Alexander Cadogan wrote in his diary that "We are helpless as regards Austria—that is finished. We *may* be helpless with regard to Czechoslovakia ..."[169]) [emphasis in original]

In a speech to the House on Monday, March 14, 1938, Churchill said that what had taken place in Austria should be brought before the League of Nations.[170]*** And he once again expressed his concerns about appeasing Hitler rather than taking a stand:

> The gravity of the events of March 11 cannot be exaggerated.
> Europe is confronted with a program of aggression, nicely

---

*It's worth noting that in early 1938 Churchill, long a fan of the French Army, told the House that the "[French] army at the present time is the finest in Europe, but with every month that passes its strength is being outmatched by the ceaseless development of the new forms into which the vastly superior manhood of Germany is being formed." HC Deb 22 February 1938 cc246.

**At the Cabinet meeting, the ministers were advised that Churchill intended to attack the Government for the inadequacy of its rearmament program. CAB 23/1 12 (38) pp. 8 352. This was viewed as inappropriate at a time when "the only hope of saving Czechoslovakia from the German menace was by creating an impression of force." Ibid. pp. 8–9 352–53. Of course, this overlooked the fact that in the fall of 1937, at Chamberlain's invitation, a Luftwaffe mission spent a week in England inspecting the RAF's latest models (and verifying Germany's belief that the RAF was inadequate). Manchester, Alone p. 267.

***Churchill had previously spoken with Halifax about bringing the Austrian matter before the League. But the Foreign Secretary rejected the idea. Manchester, Alone p. 283. The British Foreign Office felt that bringing the Austrian situation before the League would have led to a military coup toppling Hitler's regime. DBFP Series 3, Vol I, no. 57.

calculated and timed, unfolding stage by stage, and there is only one choice open, not only to us but other countries, either to submit like Austria or else take effective measures while time remains to ward off the danger. ...[171]

In his speech, Churchill also laid out the precarious position in which Czechoslovakia, with all of its substantial manufacturing capabilities, now found itself.[172] (At that time, the Cabinet was receiving information that the Germans intended to deal with Czechoslovakia just like Austria—the Sudeten Deutsch were to rise and that was to be an excuse for an invasion.[173]) As a solution, Churchill again suggested forming a "Grand Alliance": "... a number of States [would be] assembled around Great Britain and France in a solemn Treaty for mutual defence against aggression."[174] (The Third Reich would virtually be encircled.)

As Chamberlain wrote in his diary on Sunday, March 20:

> The plan of the "Grand Alliance" as Winston calls it, had occurred to me long before he mentioned it ... I talked about it to Halifax, and we submitted it to the chiefs of the Staff and Foreign Office experts. It is a very attractive idea; indeed, there is almost everything to be said for it until you come to examine its practicability. ...[175]

In his diary entry, he also responded to Halifax's rhetorical question of "How do we prevent [what took place in Austria from happening] in Czechoslovakia?" with this chilling entry:

> You have only to look at the map to see that nothing that France or we could do could possibly save Czechoslovakia from being overrun by the Germans if they wanted to do it ... I therefore have abandoned any idea of giving guarantees to Czechoslovakia, or to the French in connection with her obligations to that country.[176]

Chamberlain's bleak, immutable assessment of Czechoslovakia's fate would not be buoyed by a subsequent report from the Chiefs of Staff Subcommittee on the Military Implications of German Aggression against Czechoslovakia,[177] which was circulated before the Cabinet met on Tuesday, March 22, 1938. The dominant conclusion of the report was that no pressure which Britain and its possible Allies could apply would suffice to prevent the defeat of Czechoslovakia.[178] The report found both the French Air Force and Britain's anti-aircraft defenses to be in deplorable shape. It also found that an alliance with Yugoslavia, Romania, Hungary, Turkey, and Greece would be of limited assistance in any attempt to save Czechoslovakia.[179] (The Chiefs of Staff had, however, been *specifically instructed* to leave Russia out of the calculation.[180]*)

The report also stated that Germany was ill-prepared for a long war.[181] But, the Cabinet was intent on reaching the conclusion that nothing could be done for the Czechs as soon as they heard anything that supported their pre-disposition. Thus, they came to the consensus that, even if Britain and France were stronger militarily than they had been in previous years, because Czechoslovakia was so far away, they would be unable to protect it. Moreover, they also concluded that neither could the Russians, who were separated from Czechoslovakia by both Poland and Romania.[182] Thus, if Germany invaded Czechoslovakia:

- France, which was treaty-bound to come to the Czechs' defense, would enter the fray; and

- Britain, out of self-interest, would be compelled to join in the struggle because it could not afford to see France go under; and

- For these reasons, each would go down to defeat.[183]

Under the circumstances, it appeared that the best solution was to induce the Government of Czechoslovakia to make every effort to reach a settlement with the Sudeten Germans.[184] In his speech to the House on March 24, Chamberlain iterated this point, adding that his Government "will at all times be ready to render any help in their power, by whatever means might seem most appropriate, towards the solution of questions likely to cause difficulty between the German and Czechoslovak Governments."[185] Of course, he quickly eschewed any military intervention, saying that "there is no need to assume the use of force, or, indeed, to talk about it. Such talk is to be strongly deprecated."[186]

Russia's Request for a Conference to Discuss Joint Action to Protect Czechoslovakia

On March 18, 1938, the Russians said they wanted a conference to discuss how, in the event of a major threat to peace by Germany, mutual assistance furnished Czechoslovakia under the Franco-Soviet pact of 1936 could be encompassed within any collective security action that the League of Nations would be taking.[187] This was all in keeping with Churchill's idea of a Franco—British—Russian alliance, the aim of which was to check the Nazi aggression toward other states in Central and Eastern Europe. The Soviet Foreign Commissar, Maxim Litvinov, condemned the Anschluss, praised the

---

This is not the last time that the Chamberlain Government would fail to view Soviet participation as essential to holding back Hitler's plans to conquer Central Europe.

idea of a Grand Alliance, and said that Russia was "prepared immediately to take up, in the League of Nations or outside of it, the discussion with other powers of the practical measures which the circumstances demand."[188] But the Soviets' idea met with little enthusiasm in Paris, where the French Government was distracted by other things—strikes at aircraft factories and the success that Franco's armies were having against the Spanish Loyalists.[189] Although the Russian idea was viewed favorably by many Britons,[190] the reaction to it in official London was similarly cool.

Churchill believed that such an alliance could and should work through the League of Nations,[191] although by 1938 many believed that the League was a walking corpse.[192] In a speech to the House on March 24, Chamberlain for one made it clear that he no longer believed in the League[193] and that confederations like the Grand Alliance, even if sanctioned by the League, "[did] not differ from the old alliances of pre-war date which we thought we had abandoned in favour of something better."[194] Citing, among other things, Britain's existing, nonbinding obligation under the League's Covenant to assist victims of aggression, he added that the British Government could not accept being required (under a confederation such as the Grand Alliance) to provide military force in aid of Czechoslovakia, a country where Britain's vital interests were not involved to anywhere near the same extent they were in France and Belgium.[195] Chamberlain also made it clear that he believed such confederations would lead to counter-coalitions and thus were "inimical to the prospects of European peace."[196]

As Churchill points out in *The Gathering Storm*, a year later, Chamberlain would take a different position about participating in the defense of another Eastern European country where Britain's vital interests were not concerned.

*Chamberlain Returning from
Munich with Hitler's signature*

11

MARCH–DECEMBER 1938—THE MARCH TO MUNICH AND ITS AFTERMATH

Czechoslovakia and the Sudetenland
Plan Z and the Trip to Berchtesgaden on September 15
Anglo-French Pressure on the Czechs
The Trip to Godesberg—September 22
Continuing the Pressure on Czechoslovakia?
The Halifax Communiqué
Unrest Within the German Military
Meanwhile, on Matters Other Than Those Directly Involving the
  German General Staff
The Trip to Munich—September 29
Should Chamberlain Have Pushed for the Munich Agreement? What
  Realistic Options Existed? Was Hitler Just Bluffing? Could Hitler Have
  Been Toppled and World War II Averted in September 1938?
The Immediate Aftermath of Munich
  • Kristallnacht
  • The Final Months of 1938

Czechoslovakia and the Sudetenland

In March 1931, two years before Hitler came to power and some seven years before the Anschluss, Churchill wrote that if Germany ever annexed Austria, "Czechoslovakia would lie in dire peril."[1] As Kennedy wrote, in 1938, with Austria in Hitler's pocket, the international situation was worsening and if that continued, Britain could be drawn into a war she didn't want.[2]

Hitler had long had a covetous eye on Czechoslovakia. It was an important piece to the Nazi's achieving their ultimate ambition—*Lebensraum*—the Nazi ideological goal of replacing the indigenous population of Central and Eastern Europe with Germanic colonists. Initial plans for a surprise attack on Czechoslovakia had, in fact, been drawn up in June 1937.[3]

Within weeks of the Anschluss, Konrad Henlein, the leader of the Czech Nazi party, which was secretly subsidized by Germany, was demanding the transformation of Czechoslovak foreign policy so that Czechoslovakia would become a German satellite.[4]

Because of concern with world opinion, Hitler believed there needed to be some "provocation" before Germany could invade Czechoslovakia.[5] Czechoslovakia also had mutual assistance treaties with both the Soviet Union and France (although the French seemed reluctant to live up to their obligation). Even so, Hitler was determined to destroy Czechoslovakia.[6]

The principal area encompassed by Czechoslovakia had been a part of the Austro-Hungarian Empire until the empire collapsed at the end of World War I. Czechoslovakia was founded as one of the successor states of the Austro-Hungarian Empire under the Treaty of St. Germain (an offshoot of Versailles). The newly created country was made up of the territories of Bohemia, Moravia, Slovakia, and Carpathian Ruthenia. The founding fathers of Czechoslovakia were Tomáš Masaryk and his close ally Edvard Beneš. Masaryk served as its first president from 1918 to 1935, at which time he was succeeded by Beneš.

Czechoslovakia was a multi-ethnic state, with Czechs and Slovaks constituting the bulk of the population. But the population also contained many Germans as well as some Hungarians and Poles. (Because it lacked "ethnic integrity," Hitler considered Czechoslovakia's mere existence to be abhorrent.[7]) The country's official ideology was that there were no separate Czech and Slovak nations, only one nation—Czechoslovakia. This policy led to unrest among the non-Czech population, particularly in German-speaking Sudetenland. This was a region bordering Germany. Just after WWI it had proclaimed itself part of the Republic of German-Austria, which, as noted, shortly evolved into the Austrian Republic. The Sudeten's proclamation notwithstanding, in 1919, the Treaty of St. Germain made the Sudetenland, with its three million German inhabitants, part of Czechoslovakia. Hitler intended to exploit this fact to obtain all of Czechoslovakia.

The Sudetenland was a mountainous region that ran along the border with Germany on three sides of the western end of the country. Czechoslovakia, which came into existence in 1919, had feared Germany ever since; as a result, it had built many fortifications in the Sudetenland.

After Hitler came to power in 1933, Sudeten Germans became enchanted with National Socialism and formed the Sudeten German Party (the SGP) which, in the end, was a local version of the Nazi Party. A majority of the Sudeten Germans belonged to the SGP. Even though their lives in Czechoslovakia compared favorably to those of minorities in other countries, by 1938, the Sudeten-Germans, as well as other ethnic groups, desired more autonomy from the central government in Prague.[8] German citizens of

the Sudetenland had had enough of Czech rule and wanted to join the new Reich. "In a fair plebiscite perhaps 80 percent" of the Sudeten-Germans may have "voted to secede."[9]

If the principle of self-determination had been applied across the board to all areas arbitrarily shifted by the Versailles treaty,* it was likely that all such areas would have chosen to join the Reich, in which case Germany would have quickly become larger and potentially stronger than it was in World War I. This was something that, for security reasons, the Allies were unwilling to allow in 1919[10] and still feared, even in the 1930s. Moreover, as Foreign Secretary Halifax put it, "the idea of a plebiscite [is] infectious."[11]

---

*These areas included the Sudetenland, the predominately German city of Danzig in Poland (which was internationalized at Versailles to be supervised by the League of Nations), South Tyrol (taken from Germany and annexed by Italy), and the city of Memel (in East Prussia but given to Lithuania at Versailles).

Just after the Anschluss, in the spring of 1938, ostensibly to achieve his goal of bringing all German people back into the Reich, Hitler used an approach against Czechoslovakia that he would come to use several times. With German propaganda chief Joseph Goebbels in charge, the Nazis would find incidents of Czech mistreatment of Sudeten-Germans and magnify them, allowing Hitler to complain vociferously about the "widespread maltreatment" of the German minority. He would use such "incidents" to undermine the Czech Government, and then, based on the alleged need to protect the German minority, threaten military action.

While Britain had no alliance with Czechoslovakia, and thus was not obliged directly to come to her assistance if she were invaded, France did and was. But that is not the end of the story. Yes, if the Czechs were attacked, the French ostensibly had to come to their defense; but Britain as an ally of France was also thus duty-bound to join the fray.[12] Czechoslovakia also had an agreement with the Soviet Union under which the Russians had to come to the Czechs' aid should she be invaded.[13] That obligation was, however, conditioned on France's coming to the aid of Czechoslovakia.[14]

By 1938, enlightened European statesmen had concluded that separating the ethnic Germans in the Sudetenland from those in Austria, as the Versailles treaty had done, had been a mistake, which, much like keeping Germany and Austria apart, should be corrected.[15] Many Britons believed that "under Woodrow Wilson's principle of self-determination," the Sudeten-Germans should have been permitted to meld into Austria[16] and not arbitrarily made to stay a minority in Slav-majority Czechoslovakia. Although giving the Sudetenland back to Germany would take away Hitler's excuse for invading Czechoslovakia, it would have substantial implications for the country. Czechoslovakia would no longer have access to huge portions of its reserves of coal, iron, and timber, as well as most of its production capability in chemicals, cement, textiles, steel, and electric power.[17] Czechoslovakia would also lose the mountain fortifications it had built over the preceding decade and a half along its border with Germany—"Prague's Maginot line"—which were built to protect it against any future German invasion.[18]

When Hitler started talking about the Sudetenland, Britain, fully believing that all he wanted was to protect the Sudeten-Germans and that by acceding to Hitler's demands, it would be making partial amends for the injustices imposed by Versailles, was willing to see the return of the Sudetenland to Germany. In 1961, British historian, Professor A.J.P. Taylor wrote that in 1938, idealists could have argued that a British policy intent on returning the Sudetenland to Germany was long overdue.[19] Moreover, as discussed above, one doesn't have to be an idealist to realize that if the mistakes of Versailles had been undone much earlier, Hitler would not have had the unfairness of the treaty as a rallying cry around which to incite the masses—and may have never come to power.

Chamberlain certainly did not want to go to war to *prevent* the Sudeten-Germans from exercising their right to self-determination.[20] The complication—as noted, Czechoslovakia was an ally of France (and by implication an ally of Britain). Because of this entanglement, Chamberlain believed that Britain had to become involved diplomatically to address German grievances and prevent a war between Germany and Czechoslovakia.[21] Any failure to do so would likely have dragged Britain into a war she didn't want.

Based on interviews with Chamberlain, in the spring of 1938, the *New York Times* reported that the British did not expect to fight for Czechoslovakia, and the Czechs therefore needed to accede to reasonable German demands with respect to the Sudetenland.[22] Similar stories appeared in the *Montréal Daily Star* and the *New York Herald Tribune*. Chamberlain never denied the veracity of these stories,[23] and the German military did not fail to note them.[24]

At one point, Britain's Ambassador to Germany, Nevile Henderson, an unabashed Germanophile,[25] told German Foreign Minister Ribbentrop that "the Sudeten-Germans and the Czechs are a matter of complete indifference to Great Britain."[26] In a similar vein, the German Embassy in London had passed on information to Berlin, believed reliable –which it was—that Britain had no problem with the separation of the Sudetenland from Czechoslovakia, provided it was done without force.[27] As Chamberlain later admitted, he "didn't care two hoots whether the Sudetens were in the Reich or out of it, according to their own wishes."[28] Conversely, in a letter to a German confidant, Churchill wrote: "I am sure that the crossing of the frontier of Czechoslovakia by German armies or aviation in force will bring about a renewal of the World War."[29]

What also made the prospect of going to war on the Czechoslovakian side distasteful to Chamberlain was his belief that as a people the Czechs were "not out of the top drawer."[30] He had more important issues to deal with than the concerns of the Czechoslovaks.[31] While he sympathized with a small nation being confronted by a powerful neighbor, he eschewed going to war, as he put it, "because of a quarrel in a faraway country between people of whom we know nothing ... If we have to fight it must be on larger issues than that."[32]

As noted, Chamberlain also believed that Britain lacked the military power and strategic reach to save Czechoslovakia. As he said, "[y]ou would have only to look at the map to see that nothing we or France could do could possibly save Czechoslovakia from being overrun by the Germans if they wanted to do it.[33] His view was based at least in part on a very pessimistic report prepared by the Chiefs of Staff regarding the military implications of a German attack on Czechoslovakia which was provided to the committee on Foreign Policy on March 28, 1938 (just two weeks after the Anschluss). Its principal conclusion was that "no pressure which [Britain] could exercise would suffice to prevent the defeat of Czech-Slovakia."[34] In addition, early on, Chamberlain had also concluded that France was in a "hopeless position."[35] France had a treaty with Czechoslovakia to come to her defense if attacked but would have loved to find a way to relieve itself of that obligation.[36] At the Cabinet meeting of March 22, 1938, Chamberlain said that "he was not in a position to recommend a policy involving a risk of war."[37] (Notably, at the time, only one-third of British voters were in favor of any kind of commitment to Czechoslovakia.[38]) Importantly, he added that "we should speed up our existing plans for rearmament,"[39] which the Cabinet ultimately did. Unsurprisingly, at Cabinet meetings up to the one held on September 25, 1938, the clearly dominant conclusion about Czechoslovakia was that there was nothing the Allies could do to prevent her military defeat and that appeasing Hitler by forcing the Czechs to give up the Sudetenland was the only course available to avoid war.[40] This was a view Chamberlain had held for some time. He and others also resented constantly having to knuckle under to dictators, owing to Britain's presumed lack of sufficient military strength.[41] Chamberlain said that it "made his blood boil to see Germany getting away with it time after time and increasing her domination over free peoples."[42]

Nevertheless Chamberlain's intention was to coordinate with France in applying concerted pressure on Czech President Edvard Beneš to do whatever was needed to satisfy the Sudeten-Germans by implying—and then threatening that, should Beneš fail to do so, Britain and France would not come to Czechoslovakia's assistance in the event of a German invasion.[43] With this end in mind, Chamberlain invited the new French Premier, Èdouard Daladier, to London for talks on April 28 and 29, 1938.[44] The French agreed that putting pressure on the Czech government was the way to go—and that a diplomatic appeal would be made to Beneš in Prague by both the French and British Governments to secure the maximum concessions from him.[45]

Thus, in May 1938, Britain asked the Czech Government to save the country by going as far as possible to meet Sudeten-Germans' demands. (French Foreign Minister Georges Bonnet, who was both pro-appeasement and someone who did not see France faring well in this crisis, made it clear that he wanted the British Government to put as much pressure as possible on Dr. Beneš to reach a settlement with the Sudeten-Germans to save France from having to choose between dishonoring her agreements or becoming involved in a war.[46]) Aside from the long and short term negative effect that allowing the Sudetenland to become a portion of the Reich would have on Czechoslovakia (which was no small thing), such an approach did reflect British principles (supporting the right of self-determination) and British policy (building a permanent peace by remedying the injustices of Versailles). It also reflected the opinion of the British public, who were not sufficiently aroused by problems involving Czechoslovakia. Most Britons felt "[i]t's not worth a war to prevent Sudeten-Germans from going back to Germany."[47] It just wasn't very fair to Czechoslovakia, and the millions of non-German Czechs in the Sudetenland (and ultimately in all of Czechoslovakia) who would come under Nazi rule as a result.

Because the British saw the German demands for the return of the Sudetenland as being reasonable, they also came to see the Czech Government as merely being stubborn when it refused to simply give away a resource-rich portion of their country, which also happened to be vital to the country's defense.[48]

As noted, in the spring of 1938, Germany started putting out false information about the vicious way that the Czech government was treating Sudeten-Germans. Likewise, rumors also began to circulate that Germany was planning to invade Czechoslovakia.[49] There were also many reports indicating the presence of a heavy concentration of German troops in Saxony, one of the German states that bordered the Sudetenland.

The Czech Government did not believe the German explanation that the troops in Saxony were simply conducting training exercises.[50] On the night of May 20–21, to deal with the perceived crisis, President Beneš mobilized some 180,000 troops (largely reservists) to man garrisons in the Sudetenland.[51] Britain and France believed that a German invasion of Czechoslovakia was imminent[52] and were in a panic.[53]

Halifax called in the German Ambassador to Britain, Eduard von Dirksen, to show how grave Britain believed the situation was.[54] According to von Dirksen, the furthest that Halifax would go, however, was to say that "[i]n the event of a European conflict it was impossible to foresee whether Britain would not be drawn into it."[55] Others say that Britain, although politely, had threatened to retaliate if Germany invaded Czechoslovakia.[56] At the same time, the Russians and the French, at least ostensibly, reaffirmed that they would come to help the Czechs if an invasion occurred.[57] This was followed by another warning from Halifax in which he said, "I would beg [Herr Hitler] not to count on this country being able to stand aside if from any precipitate action there should start a European conflagration."[58]

All of this constituted a rare show of at least some backbone by a seemingly united Europe. The feelings of those opposed to appeasement are captured in a note written by Robert Vansittart, Britain's permanent Undersecretary of State for Foreign Affairs, which read, "the best way to deal with Germany is firmness. The last days have shown that it pays and that no other method does." To some, Chamberlain even appeared as a "strong man."[59] Perhaps Hitler was shocked by Britain's stance. More than likely, he simply resented the pushback (the first he ever received). In any event, he felt that he had to announce that Germany had no intention of invading Czechoslovakia.[60]

Germany's "backing down" would prove temporary. Nonetheless, as Chamberlain biographer Robert Self reveals, because of Chamberlain's "ostensibly successful intervention in the 'May crisis,'" the Prime Minister felt "less pessimistic about Czechoslovakia."[61]

Interestingly, Shirer contends that if in the spring of 1938, Chamberlain had said that Britain (and France) would do whatever was needed to defend the territorial integrity of Czechoslovakia, "the Fuehrer would never have embarked on the adventure which brought on the Second War."[62] WWII would have been unnecessary.* Shirer asserts that the failure to do this was Chamberlain's "fatal mistake."[63] But doing so was antithetical to who Chamberlain was. And in the spring of 1938, he certainly was not yet ready to take any action that bold.

Shirer's thesis about standing up to Hitler in May 1938 (like Vansittart's note on the efficacy of firmness) must also be tempered because in May 1938, while Hitler backed down, there was no imminent German invasion of Czechoslovakia in the works. That is, there was no intensely desired then-present action from which Hitler had to back away. Thus, while firmness likely was the best way to deal with Hitler, upon all the facts becoming known, what happened in May 1938 is not strong evidence that firmness worked then or that it would work in a real crisis.

In any event, the Czech Government took the opportunity to tell the world how it had confronted Hitler and he backed down.[64] Hitler believed that President Beneš, in his mind a lowly Czech, had done all this to humiliate Germany[65] and make Hitler out to be a coward. In ordering his foreign office to advise the Czechs and the world that Germany had no aggressive intentions, Hitler had to swallow his pride. His manhood thus questioned, Hitler became consumed with exacting revenge on the Czechs.[66]

At the end of May, in an angry tirade, he told the Army that the matter of Czechoslovakia needed to be solved and that "[p]reparations for military action must be completed by October 2."[67] He wanted Czechoslovakia to be "wipe[d] off the map.[68] He planned to do this through a "lightning march into Czechoslovakia"[69]—one so fast that Britain and France would have no time to intercede.[70]

Many considered the "crisis" of May 1938 to have been a grave blunder and blamed Beneš for it.[71] Churchill thought that how it was handled was "a triumph for England."[72] But the Chamberlain Government vowed

---

The contention seems a bit strained since it presumes that Hitler would have permanently scrapped his ambitions based solely on these verbal threats from Britain and France.

never to run so grave a risk of war again.[73] In his book, *Churchill, Hitler, and "The Unnecessary War,"* conservative American journalist, politician, commentator, and author Pat Buchanan writes that the "crisis" created by Prague in May 1938 "... must be seen in the same light as Schuschnigg's hurried attempt to hold a plebiscite in Austria. Both were desperate cries of imperiled prey who sensed the predator was close at hand."[74]

It didn't take long after the May "crisis" for Hitler to get back on plan, if in fact he ever really got off his longer-term strategy. The Nazi propaganda attacks on President Beneš, the Czechs, and the Czech Government were substantial throughout the summer of 1938. In August, Germany stationed 750,000 soldiers along its border with Czechoslovakia—"officially as part of army maneuvers,"[75] although London knew this was not the case.[76] These military maneuvers prompted Chamberlain's calling his Cabinet back from holiday for an emergency meeting on August 30.

The minutes of that meeting provide a fantastic insight into what the British Government was thinking on the eve of negotiations (if one can call them that) with Hitler over the Sudetenland. At the session, Foreign Secretary Halifax laid out these points:

1. There was a great deal of evidence—much of it from good sources—that, against the advice of the Army and of the moderates in the party, Hitler was determined to intervene in Czechoslovakia by force.

2. Three reasons had been advanced for his determination:

    a. first, he believed that a solution over the Sudetenland could be obtained only by force;

    b. second, he wished to wipe out the bad taste left by the events of May 21 when the Czechs mobilized and seemed to force him to back down; and

    c. third, he wanted a spectacular success for internal reasons.

3. Alternatively, Hitler's attitude was perhaps just a mixture of bluff and reliance on force. But Halifax said that it was impossible to say which.

4. Halifax would feel extremely uneasy at making the threat that Britain was prepared to retaliate with force unless he were sure that the country would carry it out. In this regard, he also pointed out that

    a. If Hitler invaded Czechoslovakia, there was nothing Britain, France, or Russia could do to prevent Czechoslovakia from being overrun (this generally tracked the report from the Chiefs of Staff dated March 28).

b.   Referring to the defiant statements made in May, Britain's previous efforts at deterrent intimidation had, in the end, failed.

c.   Such threats also did not cause the Czechs to be more conciliatory in their negotiations with the Sudetens, and

d.   Potentially disastrous consequences could ensue if Hitler called Britain's bluff.[77]

Halifax also told the group that a few days earlier he had asked the French chargé d'affaires the following question—if Germany invaded Czechoslovakia, would France be likely to declare war on Germany? The Frenchman responded that he thought, in such an event, "the position in France would be 'confused,' but that, if war started, opinion would come round to the view that [France] must take some action."[78] Given the tepidness of France's anticipated response to an invasion of Czechoslovakia, Halifax had concluded that Britain should keep Germany guessing about whether it would or would not come to the defense of Czechoslovakia while doing all that it could to forward the success of the mission sent to mediate the dispute between the Czech Government and Henlein's Sudeten German Party.[79]* (However, neither Halifax nor the Czechs knew that Henlein had been instructed months earlier by Hitler to make demands that were clearly unacceptable to the Czech Government.[80]**)

    After hearing all of the above, the Cabinet unanimously agreed that (1) no statement should be made to the effect that if Germany invaded Czechoslovakia Britain would declare a war, (2) Britain should try to keep the Germans guessing as to its ultimate position on this matter, and (3) every effort should be made to encourage the ongoing negotiations for a settlement of the Sudeten-German question.[81]

    Chamberlain later sent over a short note to Halifax. In it, he reminded the Foreign Secretary to downplay the gravity of the Cabinet meeting. He was concerned that it could exacerbate existing anxiety in the British stock market.[82] Any attempt to minimize the importance of the Cabinet meeting notwithstanding, the next morning the following banner headline appeared

---

With the agreement of both parties, in July 1938, the Cabinet had authorized sending Lord Walter Runciman to Prague as a mediator. CAB 23/2 35 (38) p. 2 220, July 27, 1938.

**While Halifax told the Cabinet that Hitler's plan to invade Czechoslovakia was, based on solid information against the advice of the Army, he did not reveal that the British Government had also received credible evidence that an actual order from Hitler to commence the invasion would cause the generals to stage a coup and arrest or assassinate Hitler.*

in the London *Daily Express*: *"THERE WILL BE NO WAR."* Lord Beaverbrook, the owner of the *Express*, and as noted previously, a fan of Hitler's, put his own signature on the following front-page lede:

> There will be no European war. Why? Because the decision of peace and war depends on one man, the German Fuehrer. And he will not be responsible for making war at present. Hitler had shown himself throughout his career to be a man of exceptional astuteness.[83]

Chamberlain did not agree. As he asked his sister Ida rhetorically: "Is it not positively horrible to think that the fate of hundreds of millions depends on one man and he is half mad?"[84]

On September 3, 1938, the Foreign Office strongly urged Czech President Beneš to make concessions large enough to deter Hitler from starting a war.[85] As a result of this pressure, on September 7, the Czech Government officially proposed regional autonomy to the Sudeten leaders.[86] The proposal, known as the "Fourth Plan," exceeded Sudeten-German demands.[87] Privately, Beneš did not believe that Hitler would allow the Sudetens to accept the proposal,[88] but he still wanted to put it on the table so as "to convince the French and British governments that not even the biggest concessions could satisfy either Berlin or the Sudeten Pan-Germans ... [This was] the only and last way ... to bring the Western Powers on to our side should armed conflict break out between us and Germany."[89]

As for trying to keep the Germans guessing as to Britain's ultimate position, the September 7 edition of the *London Times*, a paper known to have had a close relationship with the Chamberlain Government, included an editorial in which it suggested an idea—one which it claimed "had found favour in some quarters"—that the Czech Government should simply cede the Sudetenland to Germany.[90] This was even more than Hitler had said he wanted.

In the wake of the editorial, the Labour Party issued a formal demand: "the British Government must leave no doubt that they will unite with the French and Soviet governments to resist any attack on Czechoslovakia."[91] Shockingly, even Halifax, who was an old, close friend of *Times'* editor Geoffrey Dawson,[92] agreed. The Foreign Office also issued a formal denial that *The Times* editorial had been government-inspired.[93]

No one, including the German Government bought the Foreign Office's denial.[94] Theodor Kordt, Germany's chargé d'affaires in London, told Foreign Minister von Ribbentrop it was likely that the thoughts in the editorial had been "derive[d] from a suggestion which reached *The Times* editorial staff from the Prime Minister's entourage."[95] Dawson, rather than being in any way repentant, revealed that he had had dinner with Halifax two nights before the editorial came out and that Halifax did "not dissent privately from the suggestion that any solution, even the secession of the German minorities, should be brought into free negotiation at Prague."[96]

In a September 10, 1938, speech at the huge annual Nazi Party rally in Nuremberg, Hermann Goering called the Czechs a "miserable pygmy race" that is "harassing the human race." He then said that "Moscow and the external grimacing Jewish—Bolshevist rabble are behind "the machinations of the Czech government."[97]

On the morning of September 11, 1938, Chamberlain told a group of journalists that—(1) Britain "could not stand aside if a general conflict were to take place in which the security of France might be menaced" and (2) Germany should not be under the illusion that a "successful campaign against Czechoslovakia could be safely embarked upon without the danger of subsequent intervention first by France and later this country."[98]

On the third day of the party rally, Hitler spoke about the Sudeten crisis. In his speech he denounced Czechoslovakia as a fraudulent state that violated international law concerning national self-determination, and he claimed the Germans, the Slovaks, the Hungarians, the Ukrainians, and the Poles all rejected Czech hegemony.[99] Hitler accused Czechoslovakia's president, Beneš, of seeking to exterminate the Sudeten-Germans, asserting that since Czechoslovakia's creation, over six hundred thousand Germans had been intentionally forced out of their homes.[100] He alleged that the Beneš' Government was persecuting Germans as well as Hungarians, Poles, and Slovaks, and accused Beneš himself of threatening these nationalities with being branded traitors.[101] Hitler did not speak of war directly but stated that he, as the head of Germany, would support the right of self-determination for fellow Germans in the Sudetenland—he had an obligation to protect the Sudeten-Germans.[102] He condemned Beneš for his government's recent execution of several German protesters.[103] He also accused Beneš of being belligerent and threatening toward Germany, which, if war broke out, would lead to Beneš forcing Sudeten-Germans to fight, against their will, in opposition to their German brothers.[104] Lastly, Hitler accused the government of Czechoslovakia of being a client regime of France.

On September 12, 1938, among other things, Halifax told the Cabinet that he thought Hitler was possibly or probably mad.[105] He also reported seeing Churchill the day before, at which time Churchill suggested Britain tell Germany that if she set foot in Czechoslovakia, we should be at war with her.[106] No such message was sent. Chamberlain did remind the Cabinet that if Germany tried to use force after the negotiations proceeded, he believed "the French would probably be involved, and, if so, our opinion was that we could not stand aside."[107] That said, Halifax suggested that in any speeches given by Cabinet ministers they take the line used by Chamberlain with the press: "that negotiations had reached a stage in which no reason was seen why a settlement should not be arrived at without recourse to force, and in our view, no justification was seen for recourse to force."[108]

Worried about what looked like an imminent invasion of Czechoslovakia, on the evening of September 13–14, French Premier Daladier told Chamberlain that "at all costs Germany must be prevented from invading Czechoslovakia because in that case France would be faced with her obligation" to come to the assistance of the Czechs.[109] Daladier believed a joint approach to Hitler on a personal basis by French and British leaders might be of value.

After hearing Daladier out, just before midnight, Chamberlain sent a telegram to Hitler proposing that *he* fly to Germany for a one-on-one meeting "with a view to trying to find a peaceful solution."[110] The Prime Minister consulted neither the French nor the full Cabinet before sending the wire.[111] Chamberlain biographer Robert Self suggests that Chamberlain's actions were driven by "his fears about the consequences of the French panic at having to honor their treaty obligations to the Czechs."[112]

At the Cabinet meeting held at 11:00 AM on September 14, 1938, the ministers felt that Hitler's speech at the party rally had contained some ominous phrases. Although Hitler did not commit himself to a plebiscite, he used words that pointed in that direction. But the practical difficulties of a plebiscite were enormous. Chamberlain said that rejecting the plebiscite out of hand was not his view or Halifax's.[113] Of course, it would be difficult for the democratic countries to go to war in order to prevent Sudeten-Germans from saying what form of government they wanted to have.[114]

Plan Z and the Trip to Berchtesgaden on September 15

During the September 14 Cabinet meeting, Chamberlain revealed Plan Z (with Z standing for zero hour)—something he had conceived in late August. Under Plan Z, on the eve of a German invasion of Czechoslovakia, Chamberlain would fly to Germany, meet with Hitler, and work out an agreement that would end the crisis. Almost a week before revealing Plan Z to the Cabinet, Chamberlain had advised Halifax, Simon (Chancellor of the Exchequer) and Hoare (Home Secretary)—the members of the prime minister's "Inner Circle"—of his intention to go to Germany. At that meeting, permanent Under-Secretary of State for Foreign Affairs Robert Vansittart strongly argued against the proposal; he opposed what he thought was likely to be a humiliating submission to Hitler.[115] Chamberlain told the Cabinet that up until the preceding afternoon (Tuesday September 13) he was thinking of putting Plan Z into effect at the end of the week. It was then that the P.M. told the group of his call with Daladier and that later he and Foreign

Secretary Halifax, with the advice of the Chancellor of the Exchequer and the Home Secretary, had decided to put Plan Z into operation at once and sent a telegram to Hitler.[116]

Chamberlain hoped that the members of Cabinet would not feel that he had gone beyond his proper duty in taking this action without first consulting them.[117] Chamberlain had been criticized from time to time in the past by Lord Swinton, the Secretary of State for Air (and one of Chamberlain's oldest friends) for assuming "the pretensions of the Presidential system of one-man government."[118] Some Cabinet members were in fact quite upset about "being told, not being consulted" about the telegram that had been sent.[119]

Chamberlain told the Cabinet he believed the fact that a British Prime Minister would take so unprecedented a step would appeal to Hitler's vanity. Wanting to give the Cabinet some idea of the lines on which he planned to talk to Hitler, Chamberlain said that:

- The right course was to appeal to Hitler on the grounds that he had a great chance of obtaining fame for himself by making peace and thereby establishing good relations with Britain, which was something that he had said was always his aim.

- This could be achieved only if the dispute over the Sudetenland were not settled by force.

- Britain was neither pro-Czech nor pro-Sudeten-German.

- Britain had put substantial pressure on President Beneš, who had prepared a proposal that went much further than had been expected.

- Neither he nor Halifax believed that the demand for a plebiscite should be rejected out of hand.

- He doubted whether Czechoslovakia would ever have peace so long as the Sudeten-Germans were part of the country, and

- He was most unwilling to have Britain join in guaranteeing the integrity of the rest of Czechoslovakia.[120]

The Cabinet members loved Plan Z, calling it "magnificent" and "inspired by courage and vision." The Chancellor of the Exchequer called it "brilliant" and added that if Chamberlain came back with the seeds of peace with honor he would be universally acclaimed as having carried out the greatest achievement of the last twenty years.[121] Another member wanted to remind the group that Hitler was carrying out the plan he had set forth in *Mein Kampf.*[122] That said, Plan Z was still unanimously endorsed by the

Cabinet.[123] Chamberlain told the group that he was "much touched by the confidence placed in him by his colleagues."[124]

The Cabinet had some concern that Hitler might not agree to receive the P.M., but that concern was dispelled shortly after the Cabinet session ended when Hitler replied and invited Chamberlain to Berchtesgaden, a city in Bavaria, near the border with Austria. Chamberlain accepted. Of course, by deliberately not including the French in his meeting with Hitler, Chamberlain was not doing much to preserve Britain's longtime friendship with France. Unsurprisingly, the French were incensed upon learning that they had not been immediately brought into the consultation.[125]

In polls taken then, 70 percent of the British public viewed the trip favorably.[126] In Germany the news "was greeted by the public with an enormous relief and satisfaction."[127] Churchill, on the other hand, said that Plan Z "was the stupidest thing that has ever been done."[128]

The diplomatic historian John Charmley aptly describes Plan Z as "the conception of the brave man" with "a deep humane desire to leave no stone unturned to avoid war." Chamberlain biographer Robert Self appropriately adds that, in doing so Chamberlain "was prepared to risk his personal reputation." Self and Charmley are 100 percent correct, but there is also some truth to what Churchill said as well. Plan Z would, in the end, cost Chamberlain virtually everything.

Hitler was astounded and extremely flattered that the sixty-nine-year-old Prime Minister of Great Britain—the leader of the entire British Empire— who had only made one brief flight in his entire life,[129] would make the seven-hour trip to Berchtesgaden to meet with him—a man twenty years his junior! Hitler did not just glory in Chamberlain's decision—he could scarcely believe his luck.[130] The Fuhrer also took this as further indication that, just as with Austria at the time of the Anschluss, Britain (and France) would not intervene on the side of the Czechs.[131]

Because France had a mutual assistance treaty with Czechoslovakia, Foreign Minister Bonnet had made it known that France would accept virtually any solution that would avoid war. As a last resort, the French would even agree to a plebiscite.[132] At that time, the British Ambassador to Germany, Nevile Henderson, was also reporting "that only *immediate* action by Czechoslovak Government can avert recourse to force by Germany … If the Czechoslovak Government cannot or will not give satisfaction, war will ensue whatever the consequences."[133] [emphasis in original] Henderson urged giving the Czechs an ultimatum.[134]

To make things worse, on the evening of September 14, the Chiefs of Staff issued an update of their March report on the state of military preparedness in Britain. As described by the Minister for Co-ordination of Defence Sir Thomas Inskip, the updated report "reaffirmed" [the Chiefs'] view [expressed

on March 28] that no pressure Britain and France could bring to bear—by
sea, land, or air—could stop Germany overrunning [Prague], and inflicting
a decisive defeat on Czechoslovakia.[135] Inskip also advised that "The war
would be an unlimited war, in which, while we should initiate no air bombardment, sooner or later we must experience to the tune of possibly 500
or 600 tons of bombs a day for 2 months."[136] The latter was a thought that
terrified Chamberlain and most Britons.

Chamberlain flew to Germany at dawn on the morning of September
15 accompanied by Sir Horace Wilson, his trusted advisor and confidant
(who also had "sympathies for the Third Reich" and was strongly pro-
appeasement)[137] and William Strang, head of the Foreign Office Central
Department.[138] Chamberlain landed in Munich at noon. Despite the rain,
there was a sizeable crowd at the airport. They accorded him an enthusiastic
welcome, even giving him the Nazi salute and shouting "Heil" all the way
to the train station.[139] There he boarded a special six-car train provided by
Hitler and arrived in Berchtesgaden around 3:00 PM. At 5:30, after tea, the
actual meeting with Hitler commenced.

Because Chamberlain believed that keeping the Sudeten-Germans under
Czech rule was not worth war and that, in any event, Britain could not prevent
the annexation, he went to Germany merely to effect a peaceful transfer. While
there he hoped to convince Hitler that "he had an unequaled opportunity
of raising his own prestige in fulfilling what he so often declared to be his
aim, namely the establishment of an Anglo-German understanding ..."[140]
He also wanted to remind Hitler that Germany's general desire to repatriate
peoples who wanted to belong to the Reich could be achieved—but only if
Hitler disavowed using force to do so.[141] In this regard, if it met that criteria,
Chamberlain was prepared to accept almost any plan proposed by Hitler
about the Sudetenland.[142]

When the members of the Czech government learned of Chamberlain's
trip, they were astonished. Beneš believed that having yielded to pressure
from the British Government, and having just made an extremely generous proposal to the Sudeten-Germans, the Czechs had both reversed the
public's opinion that the Sudetens had valid grievances about the political
posture of their region[143] and thought, though wishfully, that they finally
might have the internal situation in the Sudetenland under control. (Of
course, as soon as *The Times* editorial hit the street a week earlier saying that there were those in the British Government who favored simply
ceding the Sudetenland to Germany there was no need for the Sudeten-
German negotiators to accept Beneš's proposal, no matter how generous.)
The Czechs felt the British Prime Minister's visit with Hitler could only
"weaken their position."[144] If only that had been the case. Chamberlain's

mission to Berchtesgaden was much worse for the Czechs—it was the first step to their being sold out by him.

Interestingly, when Mussolini learned that Chamberlain had flown to Berchtesgaden, he is reported to have made the following insightful remark: "There will be no war. But this is the liquidation of English prestige."[145]

The last thing Hitler wanted was a satisfactory bargain between the Sudeten leaders and the Czech Government. Even though the Sudeten leaders could find no fault with the Czechs' proposal,[146] Hitler ordered it to be rejected.[147] Acceptance of the proposal would deny him the revenge he wanted to take out on President Beneš and the rest of the Czech Government, which had so offended him in May. To do this, he felt that "at least a *military occupation* was necessary. It could be bloodless, as was the military occupation of Austria, but it must take place."[148] [emphasis in original] Chamberlain's journey also gave Hitler an opening to raise his demands, and he did.[149]

When Chamberlain landed in Germany, the first thing he heard were German broadcasts by the leader of the Sudeten-Germans, Konrad Henlein, "demanding the annexation" of the Sudetenland into the Reich.[150] There was to be no plebiscite—just an immediate cession of all regions that had a population at least 50 percent German.[151] This surprised Chamberlain because "annexation had never been raised either by the German Government or by Henlein" and a few days earlier, the British Foreign Office had said that annexation was "not the accepted position" of His Majesty's Government.[152]

The meeting consisted largely of rants and long rambling speeches by Hitler. When Chamberlain finally got a chance to talk about the difficulties in determining which Sudeten communities could/should be ceded to Germany and the fact that under almost any arrangement there would still be many Germans left in Czechoslovakia, Hitler, uninterested in such minutia, exploded.[153] He shouted that he would not "put up with this any longer" and would settle the Sudeten question by taking matters into his own hands.[154] Chamberlain angrily responded by asking "if … you're determined in any event to proceed against Czechoslovakia why have you had me coming to Berchtesgaden at all? Under these circumstances its best if I leave straightaway."[155] Surprisingly, Hitler calmed down and said, "If you recognize the principle of self-determination for the treatment of the Sudeten question then we can discuss how to put the principle into practice."[156] Chamberlain told Hitler that he personally "recognized the principle of the detachment of the Sudeten areas."[157] This was, of course, hardly a statement that complied with the Cabinet's desire to keep the Germans guessing as to Britain's position. Still, Chamberlain added he had to return to London to consult with the Cabinet but would return for further discussions.

At the end of the meeting, Chamberlain asked the Fuhrer "how the situation was to be held in the meantime, and Hitler promised not to give the order to march unless some outrageous incident forced his hand."[158]

With his meeting with Hitler having been much shorter than expected, Chamberlain flew back to Britain on the 16th to meet with the Cabinet. Hitler, believing that he had induced Chamberlain "to work for the cession of the Sudetenland" proceeded with his plans to invade Czechoslovakia.[159] He felt that he couldn't lose—if, as he suspected, Chamberlain could not get the requisite Cabinet approval,[160] or the Czech Government proved obstinate and forced an invasion, he would grab all of Czechoslovakia now; and he would get "the little war" he wanted.[161] On the other hand, if the Czechs yielded on the Sudeten question, he'd get the Sudetenland now and the rest of the country would be annexed by the following spring.[162]

Chamberlain had gone to Germany expecting to spend a fair amount of time in back-and-forth negotiations with a fellow world leader, with each making concessions where necessary and finally reaching an agreement. The meeting at Berchtesgaden had been nothing like that. Rather than return with an agreement, all he came back with was a demand from Hitler coupled with a threat of war should that demand not be met.[163]

Reports circulated that Hitler had been impressed by Chamberlain. Among other things, Foreign Minister Ribbentrop's personal secretary told Horace Wilson that Hitler had said that when he talked with Chamberlain "he felt he was speaking to a *man*."[164] As Self reveals, "[s]uch flattery was cynically calculated to exploit Chamberlain's vanity and it more than succeeded."[165] Chamberlain was delighted by these reports and often repeated them with obvious satisfaction.[166] In reality, Hitler thought so little of Chamberlain that he ordered his translator not to give Chamberlain a transcript of the meeting.[167]

Chamberlain "had gone to Germany hoping not only to solve the Czech crisis, but also to establish a personal relationship with Hitler and build a lasting Anglo-German settlement. Incredibly, he returned to London convinced that he had …"[168] He would also tell Parliament a few weeks later that "I have no doubt whatever now, looking back, that my visit alone prevented an invasion [of Czechoslovakia], for which everything was ready."[169] As Faber puts it, all he needed now was to "persuade his own, [as well as] the French and the Czechoslovak Governments to agree to the annexation…"[170]

At the 11:00 AM Cabinet meeting of Saturday, September 17, 1938, Chamberlain reported on his meeting with Hitler:

- He saw no signs of insanity in Hitler but many signs of excitement. At times, Hitler would lose the thread of what he was saying and would go off into a tirade.

- Hitler was the commonest little dog he had ever seen but still it was impossible not to be impressed by the power of the man.

- He had formed the opinion that Hitler's objectives were strictly limited.

- Hitler had said that the Sudeten-Germans wanted to come into the Reich, and if they were not allowed to do so he would have to see that they did; if necessary, he would run the risk of a world war to bring them in.

- He had asked Hitler if the Sudeten-Germans were in the Reich, was that all that he wanted or did he have some other aims. Hitler responded that what he was concerned with was the German race. He did not wish to include Czechs in the Reich. The only other place that he mentioned was the city of Memel, which he was prepared to leave alone, provided the Lithuanians stood by the Statute of Memel (which provided that Memel would be an autonomous region within Lithuania rather than in East Prussia).

- Chamberlain viewed Hitler as truthful and a man who meant what he said.

- Hitler said that if the British Government could not accept the principle of self-determination there was no use in pursuing negotiations, but if they could, he thought that he and Chamberlain could get to work and discuss the details.

- At the end of the conversation, Hitler said that when the Czechoslovakian question was settled, he wanted to discuss improving Anglo-German relations and especially the question of colonies—Germany would not give up her demand for the return of her African colonies, but that was not a matter of sufficient gravity to go to war.[171]

At that point the Cabinet agreed to conduct discussions with the French and try to reach a joint decision but also give the Cabinet time to discuss things before involving a French representative.[172]

The Cabinet met again at 3:00 PM. Chamberlain told the group about a telegram received from the French, who, as noted, were irate at not being involved in the Berchtesgaden meeting. The P.M. thought their pique could be put right at the agreed-upon upcoming discussions with them.[173] The members of the Cabinet then expressed views that covered the spectrum of possible opinions, although there was little discussion about giving Czechoslovakia any form of guarantee. The Cabinet adjourned after directing Halifax to invite representatives of the French Government to come to London for discussions intended to reach a joint decision on how to proceed further.

French Premier Daladier and Foreign Minister Bonnet came to London early on Sunday morning, September 18. (Neither the British nor the French thought to include the Czechs.[174]) The British contingent at this meeting with the French included Chamberlain, Halifax, Sir Samuel Hoare (Secretary of the State For Home Affairs) and Sir John Simon (the Chancellor of the Exchequer).[175] The French were still torn between their treaty obligations and wanting to avoid war at all costs. They were also strongly opposed to the idea of a plebiscite.[176] They feared that if one were given to the Sudeten-Germans, other minorities in Czechoslovakia would want one as well.[177]

Anglo-French Pressure on the Czechs

The French felt that they could get the Czechs to agree to a cession of territory in the particular case of the Sudeten-Germans. The British and French thus agreed that the proposal to be given Hitler would be for all areas of Czechoslovakia containing over 50 percent German inhabitants to be handed over to Germany immediately, without a plebiscite.[178] It didn't matter that those areas also contained many non-Germans.

Daladier believed (as did some members of the British Cabinet) that Hitler's real aim was the domination of Central and Southeast Europe, and for this purpose the Fuhrer was eager to see the total dissolution of Czechoslovakia.[179] To avoid this, the French Government felt it was imperative to get the approval of the proposal by the Czech Government, and for Britain to join in giving an international guarantee to safeguard the portion of Czechoslovakia that would remain after the Sudetenland was ceded back to Germany.[180] The French said that they were not prepared to urge the acceptance of the proposal by Beneš unless the Czechs were given that security.[181]

Chamberlain told the French that while Britain would not exclude consideration of a guarantee, there were several problems with doing so. Nonetheless, the French representatives continued to press the British on this point.[182]

The British contingent believed that it was essential to reach an agreement with France at once. Until that was done no steps could be taken to get the all-important agreement of the Czech Government.[183] They therefore felt that they had to make an immediate decision with regard to Britain's joining in the guarantee.[184] After requesting a break in the meeting to give themselves time to consider the matter, the British delegation came back and agreed that, with a few adjustments, Britain would be part of an international guarantee of the independence of the portion of Czechoslovakia that remained after the Sudetenland was reunited with Germany.[185] The British and French also agreed that "it should be made quite clear to Dr. Beneš that, unless he gave a prompt acceptance of the present proposal, the French and British governments would not be responsible for the consequences."[186] Faber writes that when Daladier OK'd the draft of the telegram to be sent to Beneš, he realized that he was selling out an ally but believed that France had no other choice.[187]

The next day, the French Cabinet forced Daladier to say that the Czech Government would not be pressured into accepting the proposal and that even if the proposal were rejected, France would still honor its treaty obligations to Czechoslovakia. His assurance that the Czechs would not be pressured would be eviscerated just a few hours later.[188]

At the Cabinet meeting on Monday, September 19, Chamberlain laid out everything that had been agreed to with the French. Halifax then added that he had had considerable misgivings about the guarantee but had come down in favor of it, largely because he felt that it would have been disastrous if there had been any delay in reaching an agreement with the French.[189] After all, Hitler was waiting to see Britain's next proposal about the Sudetenland.

Despite Daladier's recent renewal of France's solemn pledge to go to war in the defense of Czechoslovakia, the French had given the clear impression that they still wished to avoid having to fulfill that obligation.[190] Because that guarantee was conditioned on Czechoslovakia's revoking all existing military treaties (such as those with France and with Russia)[191] the guarantee would provide France with an easy way out.[192]

Chamberlain and Daladier also agreed that there should be no negotiation with the Czechs as to the content of the proposal. The Czechs should simply be given a "take it or leave it" ultimatum.[193] Chamberlain told the Cabinet that if President Beneš did not accept "the advice" set out in the proposal "the Cabinet would be called together at short notice."[194]

The Anglo-French ultimatum was included in a Joint Message to Czech President Beneš sent at noon on September 19.[195] As Halifax later revealed, the Joint Message had been sent even before Cabinet approval had been given.[196] In the message, with what has been called "appalling insincerity," both the British and the French indicated their recognition of how great a sacrifice was being required of Czechoslovakia in the cause of peace.[197] (As Self says, Chamberlain knew that he would be charged with the rape of Czechoslovakia but believed it was the only alternative to being drawn into a war that was probably unwinnable.) Because Chamberlain had to resume conversations with Hitler no later than Wednesday, September 21, the Czechs were asked to respond at the earliest possible moment.[198]

Beneš had for some time believed that he could not rely on British support if it required Chamberlain to stand up to Hitler. The proposal confirmed that, but it also reflected desertion by France, Czechoslovakia's closest ally. The British and French ambassadors to Prague who had presented the message to Beneš were visibly embarrassed. Beneš exhibited self-control but was bitter and told the two diplomats the obvious—that he and his Government "were being abandoned."[199]

On Tuesday, September 20, the Czechs rejected the proposal. In the rejection, the Czechs reminded the French of their treaty obligations and even proposed to submit the entire Sudeten question to arbitration under the German-Czechoslovak treaty of 1925.[200]

When Chamberlain received the rejection that evening, he was "furious."[201] Not willing to let a little thing like the desires of the Czech Government get in Britain's and France's way, upon receipt of the rejection, at 11:00 PM Chamberlain had Halifax come back to Downing Street. There he, Halifax, and Sir Horace Wilson "drafted [a] reply driving the screw home on [the] poor Czechs."[202] Following instructions from the Foreign Office on what no doubt was an extremely embarrassing mission, at 2:15 in the morning on September 21, the British and French ambassadors in Prague got President Beneš out of bed to inform him that ceding the Sudetenland to Germany was the only way to avoid war.[203] There would be no arbitration under the German-Czechoslovak treaty and the Czechs should accept the Anglo-French proposal before creating a situation in which Czechoslovakia would have to fight the Nazis on its own[204]—a fight in which the French would take no part[205] (which meant that neither would the British). Chamberlain would later describe this to his colleagues in the House (although without the detail) as "urg [ing the Czechs] to accept the Anglo-French proposals immediately."[206]

Beneš thought that both the ambassadors "were ashamed to the bottom of their hearts of the mission they had to discharge.[207]

Under this pressure, and recognizing that its treaty with Russia called for the Soviets to come to Czechoslovakia's assistance *only* if France did the same,[208] later that day the Czechoslovak Government capitulated and agreed to the Anglo-French proposal.[209] The British Ambassador later was instructed to inform Dr. Beneš that London was profoundly conscious of the immense sacrifices to which the Czech Government had agreed, and was grateful for the great public spirit they had shown. Humiliated, and shamelessly betrayed, almost all of the top members of the Czech Government resigned.[210]

In a letter to his sister Hilda, Chamberlain had once called the Germans "bullies by nature." That said, there is a certain degree of disappointment and disgust seeing Chamberlain, a man whose aim was to do right by those harmed by Versailles, turn into an unfeeling, self-serving bully when it appeared that little Czechoslovakia would get in the way of his steadfast, but erroneous, belief that appeasement was the path to world peace. But then again, being a bully was part of Chamberlain's makeup. For example, journalists who wrote stories critical of the Chamberlain Government were bullied by him into supporting the Government's policies.[211] For example, when reporters asked questions about certain legitimate subjects such as the persecution of the Jews or Hitler's broken promises, Chamberlain would often express feigned surprise "that such an experienced journalist as you was susceptible to Jewish-Communist propaganda."[212] *Viewed in this light, it is not shocking to learn that "Chamberlain saw nothing shameful in buying peace by coercing a pretentious little state on the far side of Germany."[213]

Chamberlain's unseemly behavior toward Czechoslovakia was, if possible, even more reprehensible, as Self writes, because of "the alacrity with which the Western Powers forced the Czechs to comply with the German demands:" something that encouraged Hitler to be even more intractable and bellicose.[214]

On September 21, Churchill issued the following press statement:

> The partition of Czechoslovakia under pressure from England and France amounts to the complete surrender of the Western democracies to the Nazi threat of force. Such a collapse will bring peace or security neither to England nor to France. On the contrary it will place these two nations in an ever weaker and more dangerous situation. The mere neutralization of Czechoslovakia means the liberation of 25 German divisions which will threaten the Western front; ... It is not Czechoslovakia alone which is menaced, but also the freedom and the democracy of all nations. *The belief that security can be obtained by throwing a small state to the wolves is a fatal delusion.* The war potential of Germany will increase in a short time more rapidly than it will be possible for France and Great Britain to complete the measures necessary for their defense.[215] [emphasis added]

At the 3:00 PM Cabinet meeting that day (September 21), Chamberlain spoke to the question of minorities in Czechoslovakia other than the Sudeten-Germans and advised that the subject had come up at his meeting with Hitler. Hitler said he had no interest in them. The Prime Minister noted, however, that representatives of both Hungary and Poland had visited Berchtesgaden in the last few days.[216] He believed that each country was there to outline its claim to the portion(s) of Czechoslovakia in which many of its kinsman lived. Chamberlain did not feel that Hitler was likely to say that he must have a settlement of Hungarian and Polish claims at the same time as the

---

*In his book, published in 1962 on Chamberlain,Conservative Party politician, Iain Macleod, writes that "To Chamberlain ... antisemitism was alien and repugnant ..." Macleod, Neville Chamberlain p. 287. The evidence suggests that this is an overstatement, although as discussed earlier, in comparison to many of his contemporaries, Chamberlain was only moderately anti-Semitic.

question related to the Sudeten-Germans; nonetheless the Prime Minister told the group how he intended to react if it came up at their next meeting. He would say that such a demand conflicted with what Hitler had told him at Berchtesgaden. If that proved insufficient, he would then say that he was unable to proceed further on the matter and needed to return home to again consult with his colleagues.[217]

Halifax and others agreed that Chamberlain should not yield to pressure from Hitler about an immediate settlement of these other minority questions.[218] This position was adopted by the Cabinet.

Chamberlain later read the telegram from Prague, which reported full acceptance of the joint British and French proposal on the supposition that Britain and France would not tolerate a German invasion of Czechoslovak territory. As for the guarantee of Czechoslovakia, the Cabinet wanted Russia to be one of the guarantors and that if Hitler objected, the matter should be referred back to the Cabinet.[219]

The Trip to Godesberg—September 22

On September 22, Chamberlain flew to Germany for further talks, this time at Bad Godesberg located on the Rhine just outside Bonn. A small group of citizens booed him at the London airport as he boarded the plane. Chamberlain was not pleased.[220]

The ostensible purpose of the meeting in Godesberg was to negotiate the geographic extent of Germany's absorption of the Sudetenland.[221] Chamberlain carried the details of the Anglo-French proposal to which the Czech Government had reluctantly agreed[222] and brought with him a small team, including a lawyer and two secretaries to deal with the details of the agreement.[223] Chamberlain was confident: having strong-armed the Czech Government into agreeing to the German annexation of all of the Sudetenland, he thought a deal with Hitler would be imminent.[224] The P.M. also thought that Hitler would be surprised, and even grateful, that he had managed to convince the Cabinet, France, and the Czech Government to cede the Sudetenland (something Hitler thought impossible[225]). Gratitude, however, was not in the cards.[226]

When William Shirer, who covered the Godesberg meeting for CBS radio, saw Hitler before the meeting, he reported that Hitler seemed shaky, perhaps on the edge of a nervous breakdown.[227] At the meeting, Chamberlain almost immediately faced an unexpected snag. Expressing appreciation for the efforts made to reach a settlement, Hitler then asked whether the joint British-French proposal had been submitted to the Czechs. When he was informed that it had, Hitler said he was sorry since the proposal was not acceptable to him.[228]

Ranting and raving that the Czech Government had been harassing and even killing some of its German citizens, Hitler raised his demands.[229] He also said that there could be no agreement until the territorial demands of Hungary and Poland had also been met.[230] He would settle for nothing less than the Sudetenland being turned over to Germany, which was to be followed immediately by self-determination plebiscites in *other* areas of the country. Hitler also demanded that the timetable for turning over the Sudetenland be sped up: the Sudeten problem must be resolved by October 1 at the latest.[231] The Czechs would have to start evacuating the area on September 26—in just two days—and complete it by September 28.[232] Evacuees could not take any possessions with them,[233] and the area would be occupied by Germany immediately.[234] Hitler would also not compensate the Czechs for the property they had to leave behind.[235]

Chamberlain was taken aback by Hitler's position and said he was both "disappointed and puzzled."[236] He told the German Chancellor that to get his Cabinet's approval of the principles agreed to at Berchtesgaden he "had risked his whole political career."[237] Hitler could not have cared less.[238] After three hours, the session was adjourned until 11:30 the next morning.

As Chamberlain described the meeting to the Commons upon his return:

> ... I expected that when I got to Godesberg I had only to discuss quietly within the proposals that I had brought with me; and it was a profound shock to me when I was told at the beginning of the conversations that these proposals were not acceptable, and that they were to be replaced by other proposals of a kind which I had not contemplated at all. ..."[239]

Even after Hitler had, without warning, switched gears at Godesberg about a Sudeten settlement, in a speech to the House a few days later Chamberlain would tell his colleagues that "I do not want the House to think that he was deliberately deceiving me—I do not think so for one moment."[240] That Chamberlain did not see Hitler as duplicitous defies credulity.

While the meeting was taking place in Godesberg, there had been reports that troops had crossed into Czechoslovakia from Germany and were occupying several Sudeten towns.[241] Czechoslovakia wanted to mobilize, and the French saw no reason why it should not. In London, the members of the Cabinet's Inner Circle felt the same way. Thus, at 8:00 PM, instructions were sent to the British Ambassador in Prague, telling him to inform the Czech Government that the British and French Governments "cannot continue to take responsibility of advising them not to mobilize."[242] Chamberlain, however, strongly opposed allowing the Czechs to mobilize. He wanted nothing to be done to adversely affect the meeting at Godesberg.[243] Accordingly, the

Inner Circle met again and told Britain's Ambassador in Prague to delay the delivery of the message.

Later that evening, Chamberlain called Halifax to talk about the disastrous Godesberg meeting and said that "Hitler's demand would not do."[244] Halifax told the P.M. that public opinion was changing; Britons were starting to feel that His Majesty's Government had made enough concessions and now it was up to Hitler to reciprocate.[245]

After breakfast the next morning, September 23, Chamberlain wrote Hitler saying that he could not approve the dictator's plan and that the world would denounce Hitler's demand for an immediate military occupation as "an unnecessary display of force."[246] Hitler promptly canceled the session scheduled for that morning.[247]

While the Godesberg meeting was in "recess," back in London, Halifax contemplated approaching the Russians. He directed R.A. Butler of the Foreign Office to talk with Soviet Foreign Commissar Maxim Litvinov about Russia's intentions with respect to Czechoslovakia.[248] Litvinov replied with his usual answer: if the French Government responded to the Czechs' need for assistance, the Soviet Union would do so as well.[249] Distinguished historian Professor A.J.P. Taylor suggests that given the rumors circulating that Poland would side with Germany in the event of a war,[250] Russia may have been even more keen to aid Czechoslovakia, because in those circumstances it would not be barred from cutting across Poland to do so.[251]

Meanwhile, Czechoslovakia continued to wait impatiently for the OK to mobilize.[252] Back in London, Halifax called another meeting of the Inner Circle for 3:00 PM. There, he told his colleagues that he had decided to ignore the strong opinions expressed by Chamberlain and would advise the Czech Government that it could mobilize if it saw fit.[253] Halifax noted that he was also going to tell the Czechs that publicity about the mobilization was not in their interest.[254] When Chamberlain learned of Halifax's moves, he offered "a rather feeble protest."[255] A mini anti-appeasement rebellion was brewing in the Cabinet, and, surprisingly, Halifax was one of its leaders.

Godesberg was the first time Halifax, whose attitude toward Hitler would vacillate over the next few years, showed a strongly negative bent toward the German strongman.

Hitler's reply to Chamberlain's letter of that morning finally arrived in mid-afternoon. Hitler showed no sign of yielding[256]—it largely repeated what he had said in the meeting the previous night. Chamberlain would later describe the tone of the reply as not being as courteous or considerate as one would have wished; but, he added, it was worth remembering that the Germans are apt to express themselves curtly.[257]

Upon digesting the reply, Chamberlain drafted a response for the purposes of (1) getting details of Hitler's proposal in writing (which he could then forward to Prague); (2) obtaining an extension of the assurance that he had obtained at Berchtesgaden that Hitler would not invade Czechoslovakia while negotiations continued; and (3) proposing a return to London.[258]

The threat of departure seemed to work. The Germans then invited Chamberlain and his advisors to come to Hitler's hotel that night where they would have a chance to look through the German memorandum in private.[259]

At 10:00 PM, Halifax, with the approval of the Cabinet, sent Chamberlain a strongly worded cable suggesting that no other concessions should be made. The cable stated:

> [The] great mass of public opinion seems to be hardening in sense of feeling that we have gone to the limit of concession and that it is up to the Chancellor to make some contribution. ... [F]rom the point of view of your own position, that of Government, and of the country, it seems to your colleagues of vital importance that you should not leave without making it plain to the Chancellor if possible by special interview that, after great concessions made by Czechoslovak Government, for him to reject opportunity for peaceful solution ... would be an unpardonable crime against humanity.[260]

Chamberlain's meeting with Hitler and his Foreign Secretary, Ribbentrop started just before 11:00 PM. Accompanying Chamberlain were Britain's Ambassador to Berlin, Sir Nevile Henderson; Sir Horace Wilson, and Sir Ivone Kirkpatrick, permanent Under-Secretary of State for Foreign Affairs.[261]

At this session, Hitler was far more cordial than he had been earlier. He said that he had not appreciated the tremendous efforts that Chamberlain had made to reach a peaceful settlement and expressed his gratitude to the Prime Minister.[262] Chamberlain thanked the Chancellor and asked to see the memorandum, which contained precisely the same proposals as had been put forward earlier. The memorandum included an ultimatum that the Czechs were to evacuate from the ceded area by September 28 (which was only five days away).[263] Hitler, in a quiet voice, then gave a detailed explanation of the scheme and the reasons for it.[264]

As Hitler spoke, Ambassador Henderson and Sir Horace Wilson read through the memorandum. It was not long before Henderson and Sir Horace informed Chamberlain that it was an outrageous document expressed in the most peremptory of terms. Among other things, it demanded that the evacuation of Czechoslovak troops and police from the Sudetenland start on Monday, September 26, and be completed a day or two later.[265] Areas shaded in red on the accompanying map were to be turned over to Germany almost immediately (the Czechs had four days to clear out). Any Czech found in the area after that "would be arrested or shot as a trespasser."[266] The appendix to the memorandum added that "no foodstuffs, goods, cattle, raw materials, etc. were to be removed" from those areas.[267] Other areas, where plebiscites were to be held, were shown in green.[268]

Chamberlain said, given the tone and substance of the memorandum, there was nothing more for him to do. As he half rose from his chair to leave, he told Hitler of the risks that Germany was running by insisting on these terms and of the appalling loss of life and suffering that would ensue—suffering that would affect not merely the Sudeten-Germans but all Germans. Chamberlain also reproached Hitler for having made no concessions, despite all that the P.M. had done.[269]

Hitler replied that he had held off implementing his original plans to invade Czechoslovakia—which would have encompassed a frontier much larger than the one in the present proposal.[270] (Notably, Hitler never used as direct a word as "invade."[271]) Chamberlain told Hitler that when the German memorandum was communicated to the Czechoslovak Government, its publication would produce an outcry throughout the world.[272]

At that point in the conversation, a message was brought in saying that the Czechoslovak Government had ordered its army to mobilize. Hitler's immediate response was, "that settled matters," but Chamberlain pointed out that the Czechs were only acting out of self-protection.[273] A fierce argument ensued.[274]

Hitler, not wanting Chamberlain to walk out of the meeting, then made a minuscule concession: he agreed that the Czechs could have two more days, until October 1, to complete their evacuation.[275]* Hitler told Chamberlain that this concession was a "gift" out of respect for the fact that Chamberlain had been willing to back down somewhat on his earlier position,[276] and he remarked that Chamberlain was "one of the few men for whom [Hitler had] ever done such a thing."[277] Faber writes that "Chamberlain appeared delighted by this bogus flattery."[278] As Chamberlain would later advise the Cabinet, Hitler then reiterated that Germany would have no further territorial ambitions in Europe after completing the annexation of the Sudetenland.[279]

The meeting broke up at 1:30 AM. In the early hours of September 24, Hitler issued the Godesberg Memorandum, which demanded that Czechoslovakia cede the Sudetenland to Germany and that plebiscites be held in other unspecified areas under the supervision of German and Czechoslovak forces. The memorandum also stated that if Czechoslovakia did not agree to

---

*The fact is that the German Army could not move until October 1. Manchester, Alone p. 343. So by telling Chamberlain Germany would hold off an invasion until then, Hitler was conceding nothing.

the German demands by 2:00 PM on September 28, Germany would take the Sudetenland by force.

Pathetically, Hitler's meager two-day concession impressed Chamberlain, who thanked Hitler for it.[280] In this respect Chamberlain acted like a young child who was thrilled upon receiving a small shiny bauble. Perhaps more understandably, Hitler repeating his repudiation of future territorial demands, although untrue, also impressed Chamberlain.[281]

In a speech to the House a few days after his return to London, Chamberlain described the Godesberg meeting like this:

> [F]or the first time, I found in the memorandum a time limit. Accordingly, on this occasion I spoke very frankly. I dwelt with all the emphasis at my command on the risks which would be incurred by insisting on such terms, and on the terrible conse-quences of a war, if war ensued. I declared that the language and the manner of the document, which I described as an ulti-matum rather than a memorandum, would profoundly shock public opinion in neutral countries, and I bitterly reproached the Chancellor for his failure to respond in any way to the efforts which I had made to secure peace. I should add that before saying farewell to Herr Hitler I had a few words with him in private, which I do not think are without importance. In the first place he repeated to me with *great earnestness* what he had said already at Berchtesgaden, namely, that *this was the last of his territorial ambitions in Europe* and that he had no wish to include in the Reich people of other races than Germans. In the second place *he said, again very earnestly, that he wanted to be friends with England and that if only this Sudeten question could be got out of the way in peace he would gladly resume conversations*. It is true he said, "There is one awkward question, the Colonies, but that is not a matter for war."[282] [emphasis added]

What Chamberlain didn't say, and didn't know, was that Godesberg was just one more in a series of great performances by Hitler. Once again, Hitler had gone to great lengths to show the side of him that did not fear going to war, suppressing any misgivings he may have had about the adequacy of his military and largely hiding his desire to gain the Sudetenland without having to fire a shot. As for the Allies, Godesberg was another shameful performance by Chamberlain. The Prime Minister continued to show that he was totally averse to, and unprepared for, military conflict, and that he would do virtually anything (including sacrificing Czechoslovakia) to stave off a war. As a result, he was a horrible choice to negotiate with Hitler over the Sudetenland. "Hitler's insight into the weakness of his potential opponents was the greatest source of his actual strength."[283] Although he often didn't understand the British, Hitler had taken "Chamberlain's measure at a glance."[284] Of course, it wasn't all that hard to do.

The Godesberg Memorandum enraged those in Britain and France who wanted to confront Hitler once and for all, even if it meant war.[285] After reading it, even Alexander Cadogan, Halifax's assistant and an ardent supporter of appeasement and a Chamberlain loyalist, wrote that the proposal was "awful" and that within a week a goal of autonomy for the Sudetenland had morphed into complete cession of the region to Germany. "Thank God [Chamberlain] hasn't yet recommended it for acceptance."[286]

Neither could the Czechs believe what Chamberlain had done.[287]

The situation in Britain was tense. As described by Jock Colville, Chamberlain's private secretary, "In those last days of September 1938, trenches were dug in Hyde Park, plans were made to evacuate schoolchildren, gas masks were prepared for distribution and every young man I knew, not already a soldier or sailor, joined a 'Supplementary Reserve.'"[288]

Chamberlain returned to London later on September 24. At 5:30 PM Chamberlain outlined what had happened at Godesberg to the Cabinet. As he explained, on the first day he felt indignant that, even though the self-determination of the Sudeten-Germans had been agreed to, Hitler was now pressing new demands. After further conversation with Hitler, though, he said the tone of the meeting softened. He then described Hitler as someone who had a narrow mind and was violently prejudiced on certain subjects, but that he would not deliberately deceive a man whom he respected and with whom he had been in negotiations. Nor did Chamberlain believe that Hitler thought he was departing in any way from the spirit of what he had agreed to at Berchtesgaden.[289]

Chamberlain added he was sure that Hitler was eager to secure the friendship of Great Britain and that the demand for the Sudetenland was merely part of Hitler's desire to bring all the Germans within the Reich and was not part of a plan to dominate Eastern Europe.[290]

Chamberlain was also sure that Hitler now felt some respect for him.[291] He wrongfully continued to place great importance on the personal dynamics between himself and the German Chancellor. Whether out of self-delusion or naïvety, or both, Chamberlain even told the Cabinet that he also thought "he had established an influence over Herr Hitler," and that the German leader trusted him and was willing to work with him.[292]* He believed it would be a great tragedy if Britain lost this chance to reach agreement with Germany on all points of difference between the two countries.[293] As Self puts it, Chamberlain's

---

Faber attributes "breathtaking conceit and naïveté" to Chamberlain. Faber, p. 346.

"tragic misapprehension stemmed directly from [his] faith in the value of the 'personal touch.'..."[294] "His mistake was ... that of the little boy who played with a wolf under the impression that it was a—sheep—a pardonable zoological error, but apt to prove fatal to the player who makes it."[295]

Despite Chamberlain's self-perceived "influence over Hitler" and the harsh words he had used in Godesberg just the night before to describe the German proposal, Chamberlain advised the Cabinet that he saw no chance of getting a peaceful solution on a basis other than the terms proposed by Hitler in the Godesberg Memorandum.[296] He then craftily set out the tasks that lay before the Cabinet: (1) to review the differences between the proposals that Britain had made to Hitler the preceding Sunday and the present proposals from Hitler; and (2) to decide whether those differences justified Britain going to war.[297]

British-French proposal	Hitler's proposal (The Godesberg Memorandum)
	Proposal must be accepted by 2:00 PM September 28
Areas where the population was more than 50% German would be ceded to the Reich	The Sudetenland was to be ceded to Germany by September 28; German forces were to enter by October 1; Czech troops were to be out by October 1
	No plebiscite in any transferred area until then
No plebiscite	Plebiscites in certain undefined areas
	German and Czech troops to occupy these areas until just prior to the plebiscite
	Persons who were not in these areas in 1918 would not be entitled to vote
	Germany would not abandon war as an option until all claims by Poland and Hungary had been satisfied
	No goods or cattle could be removed prior to occupation by German troops
The new Czechoslovakia would be given an international guarantee of its integrity in the case of unprovoked aggression	

Based on the task laid out by Chamberlain, there appeared to be only one answer—accept the Godesberg Memorandum—the differences between the proposals did warrant going to war. Nonetheless, the Cabinet, where the anti-appeasement rebellion was still brewing and the rebels were vocal, decided nothing and adjourned until the next morning (September 25).

Commenting on the cabinet meeting of September 24, 1938, Halifax's assistant, Alexander Cadogan, wrote that when the "P.M. made his report to us. I was completely horrified—he was quite calmly for total surrender. More horrified still to find out that Hitler had evidently hypnotized him to a point. Still more horrified to find that P.M. has hypnotized [Foreign Secretary Halifax] who capitulates totally. ..."[298]

Driving Halifax home that evening, Cadogan "gave [the Foreign Secretary] a bit of [his] mind." As Cadogan put it, "but [that] didn't shake him."[299] But it had. Halifax woke up in the middle of the night with Cadogan's words on his mind and could not go back to sleep.[300] In the morning he said to Cadogan, "Alec, I am very angry with you. You gave me a sleepless night. ... But I came to the conclusion you were right."[301]

On September 25 the Cabinet met in the morning and afternoon and, after conferring with the French, met yet again late that evening.

Continuing the Pressure on Czechoslovakia?

Halifax led off the morning session and spoke about his vacillation over the last week about how to approach the Czechoslovakia problem. He said that when the Anglo-French proposal had been drawn up a week earlier, he had strongly felt the immorality of yielding to force, but since then he had to some extent overcome that objection. Indeed, just the day before he felt that the difference between acceptance of last Sunday's proposal and the scheme now put forward did not involve an acceptance of new principle. However, today he was not quite sure that he still held that view.[302] He noted that Hitler was dictating terms just as though he had won a war but without having had to fight.[303]

Continuing, he said that his reflections through the night had led to the tentative conclusion that it would be hard to put any pressure on Czechoslovakia to accept Hitler's proposal.[304] Halifax then made it clear that he wished to see the destruction of Nazism, because as long as Nazism existed, peace would be uncertain. For this reason, too, he did not feel that it would be right to put pressure on Czechoslovakia to accept.[305] Many Cabinet members agreed.[306]

In conclusion, Halifax, who had supported Chamberlain's position to transfer the Sudetenland rather than provoke a war because of it, said that although he had worked closely with the Prime Minister throughout this long crisis, he was "not quite sure that their minds were still altogether as one. Accordingly, he thought it right to expose his own hesitations to the Cabinet with complete frankness."[307]

Halifax's change of position was a terrible blow to Chamberlain, and he said so in a note he passed to the Foreign Minister across the Cabinet table.[308] Chamberlain then addressed this talk of "pressure." First, he set up the following strawman argument: "we are not saying that if the Czechs rejected the terms of Hitler's proposal that we should go to war against them." Continuing his fallacious argument, he said, "thus there is no pressure which we could assert in the literal sense." Nonetheless, he felt sure that "those who talked about pressure did not suggest that we were debarred from putting before Czechoslovakia all the considerations which should properly be borne in mind in its reaching a decision." He added, "[w]e owe it to them to do no less."[309]

He then noted that "[t]he only pressure which we could exercise on Czechoslovakia was negative," that is, "by saying that if it rejected the proposal we should not come to their assistance." Then, premised on hyper-technicalities, he told the Cabinet that Britain could not make any such statement, because only France was treaty-bound to defend Czechoslovakia.[310] He also pointed out that he could not pledge British assistance to the Czechs because, as the current discussion revealed, the Cabinet was not united in support of doing so.[311]

After this dissimulation, the Cabinet ministers, more and more who were loath to consider more concessions to Hitler, agreed not to make a final decision with regard to the German proposal until determining the attitude of the French, who were scheduled to arrive in London that evening.

Before the arrival of the French, an interim reply was received from the Czech Government. It was an unqualified rejection of Hitler's Godesberg Memorandum.[312]

Premier Daladier and Foreign Secretary Bonnet arrived at about 9:30 PM and spent two hours in conversation with the Prime Minister and members of the Inner Circle. At the 11:30 PM Cabinet session, Chamberlain first reported that the French Council of Ministers, at a meeting held earlier that day in Paris, had unanimously rejected many points in Hitler's proposal:

1. an international guarantee of the integrity of the remaining portions of Czechoslovakia in the case of unprovoked aggression;
2. Hitler taking possession of the Sudeten-German areas by force; and
3. a plebiscite in areas where Hitler knew that there was a Czech majority.

Chamberlain then said that the French believed reaching a fair arrangement with Hitler was now moot, because his object was to destroy Czechoslovakia and dominate Europe.[313] Chamberlain also told the Cabinet that after pointing out several misunderstandings which the French had of Hitler's proposal, he directly asked the French what they proposed to do. Daladier responded, "I propose that it should be suggested to Herr Hitler that he should return to the [Anglo-French] plan" to which the Czechs had agreed before Godesberg.

Upon cross-examining Daladier to clarify the French position, Chamberlain said it was clear that if Hitler refused to negotiate further and resorted to the use of force, in the words of Premier Daladier, "Germany would be guilty of an unprovoked aggression," and "France would fulfill her obligations of assistance to Czechoslovakia ... within 5 days."[314]

Given the somewhat surprising French position, and his fear that the Cabinet would also reject Hitler's proposal, Chamberlain announced that "he was unwilling to leave unexplored any possible chance of avoiding war."[315] He thus made the following suggestion to the Cabinet: Chamberlain would write a personal letter to Hitler saying he was making one last appeal because, based on an intimation he received, the Prague Government was likely to reject the Fuhrer's current proposal. He would then ask Hitler to agree to the appointment of a joint commission made up of Czech, German, and British representatives who would try to resolve the problem. The letter would be delivered to Hitler by Sir Horace Wilson and Ambassador Henderson. If the letter failed to secure a response from Hitler, Wilson would be authorized to give Hitler a personal message from the Prime Minister to the effect that if this appeal were refused, France would go to war and, if that happened, it seems certain that Britain would be drawn in as well.[316] This complete reversal of Chamberlain's past position agreed with most of what his Cabinet was currently supporting.

The Prime Minister said that because it was just possible that there was some element of bluff in Hitler's attitude, this proposed plan would afford Hitler a possible way out.[317] In the end, the Cabinet directed Chamberlain to send a letter to Hitler along the lines he suggested.

On September 26, Chamberlain had Horace Wilson and Ambassador Henderson deliver the letter to Hitler. In it, he advised that the Czechs had found the Godesberg Memorandum to be "wholly unacceptable," and he proposed a meeting of Czech and German officials to work out how the territory would be transferred. He reiterated that the Allies wanted a peaceful resolution to the Sudeten crisis but added that if Germany invaded, the Czechs resisted, and France honored her agreements with Prague, Britain would fight at France's side.[318] As Self explains, the purpose of the Henderson/Wilson mission "was not to threaten Hitler but rather to request a friendly gesture" from him, something that would "strengthen [Chamberlain's]... ability to resist" Cabinet members who opposed making any more concessions.[319]

When Daladier heard of Chamberlain's letter and its contents, he was in absolute accord.[320]

Already in an ugly mood, Hitler was outraged by the letter and shouted to Wilson and Henderson that "[t]here is no sense at all in negotiating further!" and marched out of the room.[321] He returned to yell out, "Now I will really smash the Czechs."[322] "That old shit-hound [Chamberlain] must be crazy if he thinks he can influence me in this way."[323] Wilson decided not to pass on the verbal warning that he had been instructed to give Hitler.[324] When Wilson later telegraphed the Foreign Office to debrief about the meeting, he described it as a "[v]ery violent hour."[325]

Later that evening, Hitler responded publicly to Chamberlain's letter in a speech at the Sportpalast in Berlin which has been described as a "mad outburst," where Hitler lost control. He spent hours shrieking vicious personal insults at Beneš, and he put all responsibility for war on the Czechs.[326] Hitler screamed that he had no faith the Czechs would fulfill any promises they made.[327] In the speech he did manage to thank Chamberlain for his efforts to maintain the peace and reiterated what he had said privately that the Sudetenland was "the last territorial demand I have to make in Europe," adding that "it is a claim for which I will not recede, and God willing, I will make good."[328] This was a refrain that had, of course, been heard several times before.

Leo Amery, a Conservative MP who was fluent in German, described the speech as —

> ... the most horrible thing ... more like the snarling of a wild animal than the utterance of a human being, and the venom and vulgarity of his personal vilifications of "Beneš the liar" almost made me feel sick. There was something terrifying and obscenely sinister in this outpouring of sheer hatred.[329]

In response to Hitler's speech, shortly after midnight, Chamberlain issued a special statement promising that the British Government "would be morally responsible ... for seeing that Czech promises were carried out. ..."[330]

The Halifax Communiqué

Either by invitation or on his own initiative, Churchill met with Chamberlain at 3:30 PM on September 26, on what he recognized was a "critical day."[331] Meeting with the P.M. and Halifax in the Cabinet room, Churchill pressed them to adopt an idea he had previously presented to Halifax—to issue a declaration showing "the unity of sentiment and purpose between Britain, France, and Russia against Hitlerite aggression."[332] After a

long discussion, he continued that "we seemed to be in complete agreement."[333]
A telegram from Halifax to Henderson sent at 4:10 advised that:

> Lord Halifax [this afternoon] authorized the issuance of the
> following communiqué to the press [which stated in pertinent
> part that]:

> ... If, in spite of the efforts made by the British Prime Minister,
> a German attack is made upon Czechoslovakia the immedi-
> ate result must be that France will be bound to come to her
> assistance and Great Britain *and Russia* will certainly stand
> by France. ...[334] [emphasis added]*

The final draft of the communiqué had been approved by Halifax but
was not sent to Chamberlain for his OK.

At 8:00 PM the Foreign Office issued the communiqué.[335] The substance
of it was then broadcast. It was also reported in the morning newspapers.[336]

Although difficult to believe, Halifax later claimed that he had approved
the communiqué believing that it reflected what Chamberlain had wanted.[337]
Of course, except for the reference to Russia (which was no small thing),
the communiqué was not substantially different from what was in the letter
Chamberlain had had delivered to Hitler earlier that very day.

To Churchill "[i]t seemed that the moment of clash had arrived and the
opposing forces were aligned. The Czechs had a million and a half men
armed behind the strongest fortress line in Europe and equipped by a highly
organized and powerful industrial machine. The French army was partially
mobilized, and albeit reluctantly, the French ministers were prepared to
honour their obligations to Czechoslovakia."[338]

When Churchill returned home from his meeting with Halifax and
Chamberlain, there were about fifteen Conservative MPs there.[339] According
to Churchill everyone focused on one point: "We must get Russia in."[340] He
wrote that "I was impressed and indeed surprised by this intensity of view
in Tory circles, showing how completely they had cast away all thoughts
of class, party, or ideological interests, and to what a pitch their mood had
come. I reported to them what happened at Downing Street and described
the character of the communiqué."[341]

The Halifax communiqué was, however, ineffective.[342] The right-wing
press in France treated it with suspicion and disdain. French Foreign Minister
Bonnet "told several Deputies that he had no confirmation of it."[343] It was

---

*Churchill commended Halifax for sending out the communiqué.

even suggested in the French newspapers ("inspired by the French Foreign Office") that the communiqué was "a forgery."[344]*

Much more significant, however, was the fact that, after it was issued, Chamberlain released another statement saying that Britain intended to meet Hitler's demands.[345] The statement, issued on behalf of the Prime Minister at 1:50 AM, said:

> I have read the speech of the German Chancellor and I appreciate his references to the efforts I have made to save the peace. I cannot abandon those efforts since it seems to be incredible that the peoples of Europe who do not want war with one another should be plunged into a bloody struggle over *a question on which agreement has already been largely obtained*.[346] [emphasis added]

The Halifax communiqué was dead.

On September 27, the statement that Britain would be morally responsible for seeing that Czech promises were carried out was brought to Hitler's attention by Wilson.[347] The Fuhrer showed no interested in it, repeatedly shouting that if Czechoslovakia rejected his demands he would "Smash the Czechs."[348] Wilson responded, "in that case, I am entrusted by the Prime Minister to make the following statement[349]: 'If ... French forces were to become actively engaged in hostilities with Germany ... then Britain would feel obliged to support France.'"[350]

Likely not believing that either country would get involved, Hitler did not flinch. Worked up, he shouted, "if France and England strike, let them do so! ... Today is Tuesday; by next Monday we shall be at war."[351] Wilson said he would "still try to make those Czechs sensible."[352] Hitler replied, he "would welcome that."[353]

Back from Germany, that night Wilson told the Cabinet that Hitler had taken the actual message very quietly and said while Germany was prepared for any eventuality it had no intention of attacking France. The German leader then switched gears and said Britain must understand that Czechoslovakia was responsible for the present situation, after which he broke into his usual tirade against Czechoslovakia. Hitler said he believed Czech President Benes would refuse his terms because Benes thought that France and Great Britain would support him.[354] Hitler continued that he could not understand why Britain was under Benes' influence[355]; he repeated that at this hour there were only two alternatives and asked Britain to do whatever it could to find a settlement and avoid war.[356]

Professor Taylor attributes the forgery allegation to Foreign Minister Bonnet himself. See, Taylor, Origins p. 182.

Interestingly, Chamberlain told the Cabinet that the latest intelligence suggested that if there were a war, Poland would side with Germany (after all Hitler had promised Poland unconditional support if it joined the conflict[357]).[358] This disclosure, he said, reflected the fact that Poland had rejected the Czechs' proposal to cede the disputed Teschen region of Czechoslovakia (its population was heavily Polish) to Poland if it would provide Czechoslovakia with a guarantee of assistance should Germany invade.[359]

That evening, still hoping that Britain could make the Czechs "sensible" and having Chamberlain's "utter fear of war" in the forefront of his mind, Hitler prepared another letter to the Prime Minister.[360] In it he urged Chamberlain, who really needed very little urging, to try and bring the Czech government "to reason."[361]

While Hitler wanted to invade Czechoslovakia, an equal, if not stronger, desire was to secure the Sudetenland (a key step to the eventual takeover of all of Czechoslovakia) without firing a shot. Despite his passionate desire to crush Czechoslovakia, he still expended substantial effort trying to "negotiate" a solution before resorting to force. As historian John Lukacs succinctly puts it, "[Hitler] did not want war with England, though he did not fear it."[362]

Unrest Within the German Military

About the same time in Germany, "behind the brazen front which Hitler presented to the British and French Governments,"[363] Churchill writes in his 1948 book *The Gathering Storm*, there was growing concern within the military that Germany did not have the strength to get involved in a war of any length. "General [Ludwig] Beck, the Chief of the Army General Staff, had become profoundly alarmed about Hitler's schemes."[364] Churchill notes that "Beck was universally trusted and respected by the Army Staff, who were united not only in professional opinion but in resentment of civilian and party dictation."[365] After the invasion of Austria, and Hitler's speech of May 28, General Beck presented several memoranda for his boss, Supreme Commander of the German Army General Walther von Brauchitsch, to pass along to Hitler. The memoranda showed that catastrophe would follow if Germany continued with a program of conquest. Although General Beck agreed with Hitler that Czechoslovakia was critical for the Nazis to obtain Lebensraum,[366] he felt that any conflict there would grow into a world war and did not believe that Germany was strong enough to take on the world powers.[367] Unfortunately, von Brauchitsch, described by noted American historian Gerhard Weinberg as a "man without a backbone,"[368] did not pass on the memoranda to Hitler.

When an attack on Czechoslovakia appeared imminent, General Beck wrote a third memorandum advocating that Hitler "avoid a general catastrophe for Germany,"[369] and personally delivered it to von Brauchitsch.[370] The memorandum said that if the Army's senior commanders could not persuade Hitler to abandon his reckless plans for the invasion of Czechoslovakia, then they should all tender their resignations.[371] Hitler is reported to have responded that "the Army was the instrument of the State, that he was the Head of the State, and that the Army and other forces owed unquestioning obedience to him and his will."[372] Upon hearing this, General Beck resigned.[373]

The disagreement between the General Beck and Hitler evidenced the increasing struggle between the Fuhrer and his expert advisers. An interesting contemporaneous observation about the German generals is in the diary of General Alfred Jodl, assistant to Field Marshal Wilhelm Keitel, Chief of the General Staff. Jodl wrote:

> There is only one undisciplined element in the army—the generals, and in the last analysis this comes from the fact that they are arrogant. They have neither confidence nor discipline because they could not recognize the Fuehrer's genius.[374]

The day before Sir Horace Wilson stood before Hitler and said that France would fulfill her treaty obligations and that Britain would stand with her, a group of generals deputized by the General Staff called at the Chancery of the Reich intent on meeting with Hitler. Wanting to discuss the impending invasion, they were turned away; but a few days later they left a memorandum at the Chancery. The document would ultimately be published in France in November 1938.[375] Included among the items in the eighteen-page document were areas of divergences between the political and military leadership of the Reich; a description of the low morale of the German population (rendering it incapable of supporting a large European war); a mention of various deficiencies in German armaments, (e.g., the hastily constructed Siegfried Line of defense along the French border); and a warning about the shortage of officers.[376] The memo also presented reasons why defeat should be anticipated in anything but a strictly local war and the fact that only 20 percent of Army officers believed that Germany could win a wider war. It also pointed out that, even without aid from the Allies, "the Czech army could hold out for three months," and that the General Staff did not believed hostilities would remain localized.[377]

At the Nuremberg trials following the end of World War II, Field Marshal Keitel was asked, "Would the Reich have attacked Czechoslovakia in 1938 if the western powers had stood by Prague?" His answer: "Certainly not, we were not strong enough militarily. The object of [our agreement at Munich] was to get Russia out of Europe, to gain time, and to complete the German armament."[378]

The generals' warnings were finally conveyed to Hitler on the evening of September 27 when Admiral Erich Raeder, the Commander of the German Navy, got to meet with him.[379]

Many historians believe that the extent of Hitler's supposedly vast military buildup before the war was a myth. While he did rearm, "[Hitler] greatly exaggerated the extent of rearmament to his contemporaries and was careful not to curtail civilian consumption. As a result, in 1938 Germany was surprisingly unready for a long war,"[380] just as both Churchill and Chamberlain believed. In 1938–1939 Germany spent virtually no more of its Gross National Product on armaments—about 15 percent—than did the British.[381]

Bringing the limitations of the German armed forces to Hitler's attention as he contemplated invading Czechoslovakia was not the only activity in which German generals were involved in August and September 1938. In *The Gathering Storm*, Churchill writes about a plot by German generals.[382]* Churchill's brief discussion of the conspiracy stemmed from his actual involvement and testimony later given at Nuremberg.[383]

The scheme, which came to be known as both the "Halder Plot" and the "Oster Conspiracy," was organized and developed by Lieutenant Colonel Hans Oster, the Chief Assistant to Admiral Wilhelm Canaris at the Abwehr—the intelligence bureau of the High Command of the German Armed Forces. The conspiracy, which received a substantial impetus from the resignation of General Beck, also included many important German figures: Beck himself; his successor General Franz Halder; Admiral Canaris; General Walther von Brauchitsch; Generals Wilhelm Adam and Erwin von Witzleben; Fritz Dietlof von der Schulenburg, Chief of the Berlin Criminal Police; and Hitler's interpreter, Paul Schmidt.[384]

According to Halder, who testified about the plot during his trial for war crimes at Nuremberg, as soon as Hitler ordered the invasion of Czechoslovakia, a small group of soldiers were to storm the surprisingly lightly guarded Reich Chancellery and either arrest or kill Hitler.[385] The Chief of the Berlin police would then arrest Goering, Goebbels, and Himmler.[386] The Nazi Party

---

*In Churchill's Shadow, *British author Geoffrey Wheatcroft asserts that Churchill* "grossly exaggerated the strength of the opposition to Hitler" and that in captivity, German generals embellished the story. Wheatcroft, Churchill's Shadow p. 372. In support, he cites Sir Orme Sargent, Deputy Under-Secretary at the Foreign Office, having told Churchill about the danger "of overrating the possibility of an army revolt in September 1938. eds. Cannadine, and Quinault, *Winston Churchill in the Twenty-first Century pp. 127–28. Wheatcroft also points to the fact that many of the generals that Churchill asserted would restore "sane and civilized conditions" to Germany in 1938, in captivity had revealed themselves to be diehard Nazis who boasted about the number of Jews they had killed. Wheatcroft, *Churchill's Shadow p. 373.*

apparatus would be neutralized and the invasion of Czechoslovakia, which the plotters believed would have led to a war that would ruin Germany, would be halted.

Critical to the conspirators' scheme was knowing that Britain and France intended to stand up to Hitler—that France would honor her obligation to the Czechs and Britain would stand by France. However, parsing France's (and Britain's) military intentions was difficult, and it was similarly unclear whether Chamberlain would shrink from the risk of conflict and choose instead to capitulate to Hitler on the Sudeten question. As a result, the plotters decided to send an emissary to Britain to determine the British Government's intention and, if necessary, influence its decision. Oster, Canaris, and Beck selected Ewald von Kleist, a conservative anti-Nazi lawyer, to go to London.[387] On August 14, 1938, over the objection of the British Ambassador Henderson, Sir Robert Vansittart, chief diplomatic advisor to Halifax, met with Kleist. Kleist also met with Winston Churchill. To each he unveiled details of the plot. He said that if Britain would publicly issue a stern warning to Germany to the effect that any aggression would be met with force, the German generals would carry out the plot if Hitler ordered an invasion.[388] Kleist also said that further appeasement of Hitler on the issue of the Sudeten-Germans would prevent the generals from carrying out the plot.[389]

Vansittart thought Kleist credible enough to submit a report on his meeting both to Halifax and to Chamberlain. Chamberlain discounted much of what Kleist said—after all, he was a traitor, so how seriously could he be taken?[390] But the Prime Minister nonetheless decided that something should be done.[391] Chamberlain called Ambassador Henderson back from Berlin for consultations that led nowhere, even though Henderson himself had received a substantially similar message from the conspirators.[392]

The plotters also used Theodor Kordt, chargé d'affaires at the German Embassy in London, to convey details of the plot to Halifax.[393] Kordt was not some "little-known emissary" but the "second-in-command at the German Embassy" and "a respected figure in diplomatic circles" in London.[394] When Kordt spoke with the Foreign Office, he, too, hoped for a public statement that Britain would support France in the event of an attack on Czechoslovakia.[395] What Kordt said matched the other information that the Foreign Office had received.[396] However, before Halifax could make any statement, *The Times* of London came out with its infamous editorial saying that the Czechs should simply cede the Sudetenland to Germany, and Chamberlain told the Foreign Secretary about Plan Z.

The public statement that the plotters had requested was never made. More importantly, as a result of the Munich Agreement signed on September 29, Hitler never had to order an invasion of Czechoslovakia, and the plot thus was never triggered.

Meanwhile, on Matters Other Than Those Directly Involving the German General Staff

As Britain's Ambassador to Germany, Sir Nevile Henderson, explains in his book, *Failure of a Mission,* another event occurred on September 27 that purportedly caused Hitler to change his mind about starting a war at that time.

> In the afternoon of that Tuesday, a mechanized division had rumbled through the streets of Berlin up the Wilhelmstrasse past the Chancellor's window. For 3 hours Hitler stood at his window, and watched it pass. Germans love military displays, but not a single individual in the streets applauded its passage. The picture which it represented was of a hostile army's passing through a conquered city. Hitler was deeply impressed. At that moment he realized for the first time that the cheers of his sycophants in the Sportpalast the previous evening were far from representing the true spirit and feelings of the German people.[397]

The people evidently opposed another war.[398]

Hitler muttered to himself, "I can't wage war with this nation yet" and wrote Chamberlain urging him not to give up his efforts to find a peaceful resolution.[399]

September 27 was eventful for other reasons as well:

- The German military attaché in Paris wired the Foreign Ministry and the General Staff that France was mobilizing.

- The President of the United States was getting involved in the Sudetenland crisis. On September 26, Roosevelt had wired Hitler asking him to help keep the peace. Hitler promptly responded that whether there would be war depended on the Czechs, not him. Roosevelt sent another message the next day suggesting an immediate conference of all the nations involved.[400]

- The High Commissioners of the Dominions visited Downing Street that afternoon, and all said that further pressure should be put on the Czechoslovak Government to accept Hitler's terms.[401]

- Chamberlain used this visit as an excuse to wire the Czechs as part of Britain's "clear duty to lay before the Czechoslovak government the information which we have received as to Germany's intentions if Herr Hitler's proposals were not accepted."[402] The wire said the Germans would invade just after 2:00 PM the next afternoon unless

Czechoslovakia accepted the Germans' proposal. This would cause Prague to be overrun and there was nothing that any other country could do about it.[403]

- Before the Czechs could respond, Chamberlain sent them another telegram. This one contained a plan in which the German takeover of the Sudetenland would occur over a ten-day period, from October 1 through October 10. The telegram said the only alternative to this plan would be the "dismemberment" of Czechoslovakia "by forcible means," something that could lead to an "incalculable loss of life."[404] (So much for the Cabinet's direction not to pressure the Czechs.*) Chamberlain advised the Cabinet of the content of the two telegrams only after they were sent.[405]

- At 8:00 PM the British fleet was ordered to mobilize.[406]

On the evening of September 27, 1938, Chamberlain made a radio broadcast to the nation. In it he tried to explain why standing up to Hitler over Czechoslovakia, and as a result likely ending up in a war, made little sense. "How horrible, fantastic, incredible it is that we should be digging trenches and trying on gas masks here because of a quarrel in a faraway country between people of whom we know nothing."[407] Of course, this disingenuous comment ignored the fact that, at least ostensibly, Britain knew a fair amount about Czechoslovakia because it had been heavily involved in bringing that country into existence at Versailles.[408]

After the broadcast, Chamberlain received Hitler's reply to the letter he had sent through Horace Wilson the day before. The reply was conciliatory in tone. But in it, Hitler did not offer much. He denied that he had any intent to cripple Czechoslovakia or occupy the entire country, and he said that Czechs left behind in the Sudetenland would not be mistreated. He added that he was willing to negotiate details with the Czechs if they agreed to (1) accept the Godesberg Memorandum (which they had just rejected), and (2) affirm, by 2:00 PM on September 28, agreement to German occupation of the Sudetenland by October 1.[409] He also urged Chamberlain to continue his efforts to "bring the government in Prague to reason at the very last hour."[410]

Besides these two telegrams, a third wire, with even stronger language of capitulation, was drafted, stating that rejecting the proposal would mean Germany would overrun the entire country. CAB 23/1 46 (38) p. 11 271. This third telegram never received Cabinet approval and was not sent. Faber pp. 377–78.

At the hastily called Cabinet meeting on the night of September 27, Halifax revealed that for his part he would have great difficulty sending the third telegram, because it amounted to complete capitulation. CAB 23/ 1 46 (38) p. 13 273. His colleagues generally agreed.

In the middle of the night the British sent a telegram to the French Foreign Minister Bonnet, revealing the revised plan to have a phased-in occupation of the Sudetenland.[411] The French took the revised plan, expanded on it, and passed it on to German Foreign Minister Ribbentrop. The Czech Government was not informed of this revised plan. Nonetheless, if Hitler liked the idea, France would "demand acceptance from the Czech Government."[412]

Early the next morning, September 28, Chamberlain also drafted the following personal message to Hitler:

> After reading your letter I feel certain that you can get all essentials without war, and without delay. I am ready to come to Berlin myself at once to discuss arrangements for transfer with you and representatives of the Czech government together with representatives of France and Italy if you desire. I feel convinced that we could reach an agreement in a week.[413]

At 10:00 AM, only four hours before the deadline and with no agreement to Hitler's demand having been received from Czechoslovakia, Chamberlain sent a telegram to Mussolini. He asked the Italian leader to intercede with Hitler to try and get a twenty-four-hour extension of the deadline, and to ask for an emergency conference with Hitler that evening to settle the matter.[414]

That morning, in anticipation of Chamberlin's speech to the House later in the day, a white paper was produced for the benefit of the members.[415] Excised from the document were references to the strong and continuous pressure that had been put upon the Czechoslovak Government by the British and French.[416] It was hoped that this omission would forestall demands from MPs for a copy of the actual telegrams sent to the Czechs, telegrams in which "brutally unpleasant language" had been used to apply pressure.[417]

At 3:00 PM, as Chamberlain was addressing the House of Commons, he was handed a note. Hitler had sent messages to him and French Premier Daladier proposing a conference that would also include Mussolini. The meeting was to be held in at Munich the next day.[418] After reading the note to himself, Chamberlain, who Harold Nicholson of the Foreign Office said immediately looked ten years younger,[419] announced to the House: "I have now been informed by Herr Hitler that he invites me to meet him at Munich tomorrow morning. He has also invited Signor Mussolini and M. Daladier. Signor Mussolini has accepted, and I have no doubt M. Daladier will also accept. I need not say what my answer will be."[420] After a period of stunned silence, the House "broke into ecstatic cheering and sobbing."[421]

Hitler's biographer reveals that Mussolini's intervention was decisive in getting Hitler to agree to meet.[422]

No invitation to the conference was extended to Russia. Chamberlain knew that Hitler would not permit the Russians to be there, and frankly, Chamberlain didn't want them there either,[423] because he feared they might object to ceding the Sudetenland to Germany and thus scuttle his plan to prevent a war. Likewise, Hitler did not want the Czechs at the conference, so they too were not invited.

On the evening of September 27, Chamberlain sent Czech President Beneš a telegram stating that he was going to Munich with "the interests of Czechoslovakia fully in mind" and "with the intention of trying to find accommodation between the positions of the German and Czechoslovak Governments."[424] As acclaimed historian David Faber succinctly puts it, Chamberlain "had no such intention. ..."[425] All he wanted was to avoid a war.

The Trip to Munich—September 29

Chamberlain boarded the plane for Munich early on the morning of September 29, 1938. Surprisingly, all Cabinet members, save one, were there to wish him Godspeed.[426] The meeting in Munich began at 12:45 PM and lasted until well after one o'clock the next morning.[427]

During the meeting Mussolini introduced his supposed compromise plan to resolve the Sudetenland question. Unbeknownst to both Chamberlain and French Premier Daladier, the Italian proposal, which was strikingly like Hitler's Godesberg terms,[428] had in fact been written by the Germans.[429]

The "negotiations" were tough. For example:

- When Chamberlain said that he needed to know the position of the Czech government on a particular point, and suggested that two Czechs listed as "observers" attached to the British delegation be allowed to join the conference, Hitler went into a tirade. He refused to share the room with a Czech.[430] It was agreed, however, that the Czechs could sit in a nearby anteroom in case they were needed.[431]

- When Chamberlain asked who would compensate the Czechs evicted from the Sudetenland for the possessions they would have to leave behind,[432] Hitler shouted, "Our time is too valuable to be wasted on such trivialities."[433]

The session was chaotic and, as a result, moved along at a snail's pace. As the French Ambassador to Germany, François Poncet, described it, "No one was in the chair. There was no agenda. The discussion was uncontrolled, laborious, confused and dragged along handicapped by the burden of a double translation. It shifted from point to point; and came to a stop whenever there was a deadlock."[434]

Nonetheless, at 10:00 PM an agreement was finally reached. Britain and France had accepted all the terms of the Godesberg ultimatum with a few adjustments.[435] Under the agreement:

- The Sudetenland would be evacuated by the Czechs in five stages, beginning on October 1 and completed by October 10, with no installations being destroyed or damaged.

- An international commission would be created to supervise the carrying out of the agreement and would be made up of representatives from Germany, Britain, France, Italy, and Czechoslovakia.

- The commission would lay down conditions governing the evacuation.

- The commission would determine the territories in which a plebiscite was to be held and would determine the final frontiers of Czechoslovakia.

- Britain and France would act as guarantors of Czechoslovakia's new borders.[436]

The adjustments were an improvement over the terms in the Godesberg memorandum. But the five-country international commission quickly devolved into a panel made up of only Germany and Italy. They decided the claims that the Polish and Hungarians had to various portions of Czechoslovakia.[437]

As a result of the agreement, Czechoslovakia lost access to huge portions of its reserves of coal, iron, and timber, as well as much of its production capability in chemicals, cement, textiles, steel, and electrical power.[438] The Munich Agreement was also strategically disastrous for the Czechoslovaks because the Sudetenland contained the country's mountain fortifications along its border with Germany; these fortifications, Prague's Maginot line, could have protected against any future German invasion.[439]

Czechoslovakia, which took no part in the negotiations, was now asked to agree to the results. At 10:00 PM on September 29, Horace Wilson, on behalf of Chamberlain, approached the two Czech diplomats who had waited all day and told them about the major points in the agreement. When they started to voice objections, they were cut off. "Without putting any pressure on them," the head of the Economic Section of the British Foreign Office told the diplomats that if Czechoslovakia didn't agree with what had been worked out, it would have to settle the matter with the Germans on its own.[440]

Getting the agreement finalized and published in four separate languages took more than three hours. Finally, Britain, France, Italy, and Germany all signed the agreement. As the proceedings were ending, Premier Daladier was described as "glum and silent." He knew that the French and the British had just sold out an ally.[441] On the other hand, William Shirer, who covered the meeting for the American radio network CBS, related that when Chamberlain returned to his hotel around 2:00 AM he "looked particularly pleased with himself."[442]

If asked, Chamberlain would likely have said: (1) he had righted one of the mistakes of the Versailles process; (2) more importantly, he had once and for all taught Hitler (and shown both France and Italy) that German grievances can be settled through peaceful negations; and (3) long-term peace with Germany was now virtually assured. (He said as much to the House just a few days later.) Chamberlain no doubt believed that his policy of using negotiation to avert armed conflict was a major success.

At 2:30 AM, the Czech delegation was asked to come to Chamberlain's suite. The Prime Minister and Premier Daladier shared with them the negotiated fate of their country.[443] Although he, like everyone else was exhausted, Chamberlain made a long speech defending the agreement. Hubert Masarik, one of the two Czechs who spent most of the day in the anteroom, felt that while the French were embarrassed, Chamberlain did not seem to be anything but tired.[444]

The Czechs were angry, mostly at the French. They just saw Chamberlain as entirely "contemptible."[445] The Czech Republic as constituted in 1919 would disappear.[446] Having no other choice, Czechoslovakia "accepted" the Munich Agreement the next day but not without protest "against the decisions which were taken unilaterally and without our participation."[447] In a radio speech given by the Czech Prime Minister, General Jan Syrový, on the afternoon of September 30, he said that Czechoslovakia was "under pressure" to accept "terms which are without parallel in history for their ruthlessness. We were deserted. We stood alone."[448]

Hitler had once again displayed his great poker-playing skills: he threatened an invasion even though the German forces might not have been strong enough to succeed. Of course, even a mediocre poker player has an advantage when the opponent shows his cards at the outset and, in any event, is more than happy to fold. The German General Staff was much impressed. As Churchill writes, the Generals' distrust was replaced with admiration for Hitler's abilities and his "miraculous luck."[449] The German people were also elated: the Sudetenland was annexed without the German Army having to fire a shot.[450] And since Hitler never had to order an invasion, the planned coup was never put in motion.

While waiting for the experts to draft the final version of the agreement, Chamberlain, in a side conversation about at 1:00 AM, asked Hitler if the two could have a talk the following morning. At the morning meeting, news of which was kept from the French,[451] Chamberlain produced a document that he had prepared that said:

> We, the German Füehrer and Chancellor, and the British Prime Minister, have had a further meeting today and are agreed in recognizing that the question of Anglo-German relations is of the first importance for our two countries and for Europe.
>
> We regard the agreement signed last night and the Anglo-German Naval Agreement as symbolic of the desire of our two peoples never to go to war with one another again.
>
> We are resolved that the method of consultation shall be the method adopted to deal with any other questions that may concern our two countries, and we are determined to continue our efforts to remove possible sources of difference, and thus to contribute to assure the peace of Europe.[452]

He handed it to Hitler, who read the one-page document and immediately signed it.[453] While Chamberlain thought that Hitler had signed with enthusiasm, two other observers in the room, Hitler's interpreter Paul Schmidt and future British Prime Minister Alec Douglas-Home, each characterized Hitler as being reluctant[454] and uninterested.[455] Later, when von Ribbentrop questioned the wisdom of Hitler signing the document, the Chancellor replied that there was no need for concern because "that the piece of paper is of no further significance whatsoever."[456] After learning about it, French Premier Bonnet was jealous of "Chamberlain's private pact with Hitler."[457]

Manchester writes that the signing of this declaration was the "high point of the conference for Chamberlain."[458] Self suggests that getting the signed document was "the ultimate goal and vindication of all his efforts."[459] Chamberlain told Douglas-Home that "the personal agreement represented far more than the temporary avoidance of a war. At best, it meant permanent peace with a sated Germany. At worst, any future threat to peace would expose Hitler to the entire world as an evil monster bent on global domination."[460]

Chamberlain returned to London later that day, September 30, 1938. As he got off the plane, a beaming Chamberlain proudly waved the sheet of paper containing Hitler's signature and shouted to the jubilant crowd gathered at the airport, "I've got it. Here is a paper which bears his name." He then read his declaration to the crowd.[461] British philosopher Sir Isaiah Berlin observed that Britons were incredibly relieved that the threat of an imminent war had been eliminated, even though that relief was tinged with shame.[462]*

Chamberlain sincerely thought a great step had been taken toward "healing one of Europe's fever sores."[463] Some at the Foreign Office were stunned by Chamberlain's gullibility. How could Chamberlain have believed that getting Hitler's signature on a three-sentence statement would somehow ensure that he would peacefully cooperate to resolve all future disputes? And did Chamberlain really believe that Hitler meant it when he said that the Sudetenland was his last territorial demands in Europe? (Had he given up his designs on Danzig? The Polish Corridor? Memel?) Chamberlain naysayers would have much to point out to deflate the Prime Minister's hopefulness about Hitler, including:

- o Hitler's writings in *Mein Kampf;*
- o the Nazis' central goal of Lebensraum in Eastern Europe;
- o Hitler's association with the Brown Shirts and attempted putsch in Bavaria;
- o his willingness to murder his rivals, including his close friend and leader of the SA, Ernst Rohm;
- o his many violations of the Versailles treaty;
- o his violation of pledges made after both the Rhineland occupation and the Anschluss; and
- o his duplicity in the negotiations over the Sudetenland.

How could Chamberlain have trusted Hitler? The answer is because he believed he could and rejected all evidence to the contrary.

American historian John Lukacs notes that "Neville Chamberlain, looking more and more like an old bird, flew ... over the to the Continent [three times] to talk with Hitler [and solve the problem of the Sudetenland]. The entire world was impressed, [albeit] mistaking the old bird and the Angel of peace."[464]

In *Churchill, Hitler, and the "Unnecessary War,"* Buchanan describes Chamberlain as "a good man who wanted peace [who] deceived himself into believing that he had achieved it" at Munich, and someone who "staked his place in history on his assessment that Hitler was a man he could do business with and trust to keep his word."[465] Chamberlain added that "In spite of the hardness and ruthlessness I thought I saw in his face, I got the impression

---

Of course, things were much more somber in Prague in the wake of its government's capitulation and acceptance of the Munich Agreement.

that he [(Hitler)] was a man who could be relied upon when he had given his word."[466] Shirer calls this Chamberlain's "comforting illusion. ..."[467] Chamberlain believed that Herr Hitler "would not deliberately deceive a man whom he respected and with whom he had been in negotiation." Unfortunately, Chamberlain was not the reader of men that Hitler was. Nor could he perceive that Hitler had nothing but disdain for him.[468] Manchester writes that "Hitler had taken a strong personal dislike to Chamberlain," whom he regarded as an 'insignificant man.'"[469] After Munich it is reported that Hitler said, "if ever that silly old man comes interfering here again with his umbrella, I'll kick him downstairs and jump on his stomach in front of the photographers."[470]

The King requested that Chamberlain come to Buckingham Palace immediately upon landing, and the Prime Minister complied. Although the trip from the airport to the palace was only nine miles, the crowds were so dense that it took an hour and a half for Chamberlain to get there.[471] At the palace, Chamberlain and his wife were invited to join the King on the balcony. This was "the first time a ruling Monarch had allowed a commoner to be acknowledged in this fashion."[472] However, the King's honoring Chamberlain in this fashion was premature. The Munich Agreement was opposed by both opposition parties and still needed to be voted on in Parliament.[473]

Later, from a window at 10 Downing Street, Chamberlain delivered his most famous speech. Addressing a delirious crowd, he said, "My good friends, this is a second time in our history that there has come back from Germany to Downing Street peace with honor.[*] I believe it is peace for our time."[474] Viewing the scene, one British diplomat summed things up succinctly when he said, "You might think that we'd won a major victory, instead of just betraying a minor country."[475]

When French Premier Daladier flew home from Munich he was stunned at the large crowd at Le Bourget Airport, although he was not sure if the crowd were there to cheer him or to hang him.[476] Looking out on the exuberant crowd as he walked down the steps from the plane, Daladier is reported to have turned to a colleague and whispered, "Fools!"[477] Daladier knew that for France "Munich was a disaster"[478] and that France's days of having the most powerful army in Europe were numbered. Germany not only had twice the population of France, but it also had a huge demographic advantage in number of men of military age. Because its ability to produce weapons was far less than that of Germany, France had built up alliances with small countries that could bolster the French Army with both men and equipment.[479]

The first was the return of the infamous British Prime Minister, Benjamin Disraeli, from the Congress of Berlin after the Russo-Turkish War in 1878. Roberts p. 434.

One of those countries, Czechoslovakia, would have been counted on for its thirty-five divisions of well-equipped troops and its substantial capability to manufacture armaments; but Czechoslovakia was now gone. Also gone was France's credibility to honor its alliances, like the one it had with Czechoslovakia.[480] Munich marked the moment when France surrendered her position as the leading European power, a title she had held since 1919.[481]

The joy in the French crowd was shared by statesmen and newspapers throughout the Western democracies.[482] *The Times* of London wrote that "no conqueror in history ever came home from a battlefield with nobler laurels [than Chamberlain]."[483] The New York *Daily News* even said that "[Hitler] has made a significant gesture towards peace. ... Now is the time for haters of Hitler to hold their harsh words."[484] Chamberlain could not have been happier. He had become the savior of Europe.[485]

Overlooked during these times of celebration, though, were several disquieting things:

- Chamberlain had implemented Plan Z without consulting the Cabinet.[486]

- Britain's participation at Berchtesgaden and Godesberg was, as Manchester puts it, "a gross violation of Parliamentary government."[487]

- There had never been a House debate over Chamberlain's and Horace Wilson's dubious exchanges with Hitler.[488]

- Neither the Cabinet (including the Foreign Secretary) nor Parliament had participated in the formation of the policy that led to Munich.

- Chamberlain, without consultation with the Cabinet or Parliament, had volunteered Britain for inclusion in an international guarantee of the integrity of post-Sudetenland Czechoslovakia in the case of unprovoked aggression.

- At Berchtesgaden, by giving his opinion about the cession of the Sudeten areas to Hitler, Chamberlain had likely violated his Cabinet's directive not to disclose Britain's position on the Sudetenland.

The feeling of jubilation over the Munich Agreement was not universal. Fifteen thousand people protested the agreement in Trafalgar Square, three times the crowd that welcomed Chamberlain at 10 Downing Street. *The Daily Telegraph* wrote that "It was Mr. Disraeli who said that England's two greatest assets in the world were her fleet and her good name. Today we must console ourselves that we still have our fleet."[489] And Labour spokesman

Hugh Dalton publicly suggested that the piece of paper which Chamberlain was waving was "torn from the pages of *Mein Kampf.*"[490]

The paean in the *Daily News* notwithstanding, nowhere was the Munich Agreement criticized more strenuously than in America, where it was largely viewed as a victory for Hitler.[491] Chamberlain was seen by some as "a doddering old man who had been completely taken in."[492]

In London, Churchill did not wait long to attack the Munich Agreement. Speaking of Chamberlain, Churchill declared, "You were given the choice between war and dishonour. You chose dishonour and you will have war."[493] Perhaps a more apt characterization might have been—You were given the chance to play your hand but you chose to fold before the game even got started.

A Cabinet meeting at 7:30 PM on Friday, September 30, 1938, had one express purpose: allowing Chamberlain to reveal what went on at Munich. The meeting began in an irregular fashion with Chancellor of the Exchequer Sir John Simon speaking first. He wanted to "express, on behalf of the whole Cabinet, their profound admiration for the unparalleled efforts of the Prime Minister."[494] Chamberlain said that he was deeply grateful for Sir John's remarks and the support of the Cabinet throughout the crisis, which, he felt, "we could now safely regard ... as ended."[495]

When he spoke about Munich, Chamberlain first tried to explain why the Czechs had not been directly included in the negotiations. According to the Prime Minister, he had suggested that the Czech representative be sent for, but it was feared that the matter was too urgent to permit that much delay. (Mussolini, for instance, had to be back in Rome on October 1.[496]) Chamberlain failed to mention to the Cabinet that there were Czech diplomats staying at the same hotel as the British delegation and that two of them spent hours sitting in an anteroom just outside the conference.

He then pointed out the difference between the Godesberg Memorandum and the final Munich Agreement. He said that the Munich Agreement was "a vast improvement" over the Godesberg Memorandum and that it represented "a triumph for diplomacy that representatives of the Four Powers concerned should have met and reached the peaceful settlement of the matter."[497]

Alfred Duff Cooper, the First Lord of the Admiralty and most vocal critic of Chamberlain's efforts, had come to the meeting to resign over Munich. He admitted that the differences between the Godesberg Memorandum and the Munich Agreement were much greater than he had recognized.[498] Wanting more time to reflect on the many important questions raised as a result of Chamberlain's visit to Munich, the Cabinet decided to adjourn for the weekend and to take the matter up again on Monday.

The next morning, Saturday, October 1, the Germans walked into the Sudetenland. Starting on October 3 and continuing for four days, the

House of Commons met about the Munich Agreement. Duff Cooper, who did resigned from the Cabinet over the Munich Agreement the day before, told the House on the 3rd why he did so. His words are an insight into Chamberlain's actions and how little good had really been accomplished at Munich. Duff Cooper said that:

- After the assault on Austria, the Prime Minister made an excellent but guarded speech in the House to the effect that if there were a war it would be "unwise for anybody to count upon the possibility of our staying out." However, "[t]hat is not the language which the dictators understand."

- We Cabinet members were always told that "on no account must we irritate Herr Hitler; it was particularly dangerous to irritate him before he made a public speech, because if he were so irritated he might say some terrible things from which afterwards there would be no retreat."

- "The Prime Minister has believed in addressing Herr Hitler through the language of sweet reasonableness. I have believed that he was more open to the language of the mailed fist. I am glad so many people think that sweet reasonableness has prevailed, but what actually did it accomplish? The Prime Minister went to Berchtesgaden with many excellent and reasonable proposals and alternatives to put before the Führer, prepared to argue and negotiate, as anybody would have gone to such a meeting. He was met by an ultimatum."

- "After long deliberation the Cabinet decided to accept that ultimatum, and I was one of those who agreed in that decision. I felt all the difficulty of it; but I foresaw also the danger of refusal. I saw that if we were obliged to go to war it would be hard to have it said against us that we were fighting against the principle of self-determination, and I hoped that if a postponement could be reached by this compromise there was a possibility that the final disaster might be permanently avoided."

- "It was not a pleasant task to impose upon the Government of Czechoslovakia so grievous a hurt to their country, no pleasant or easy task for those upon whose support the Government of Czechoslovakia had relied on to have to come to her and say 'You have got to give up all for which you were prepared to fight'; but, still, she accepted those terms. The Government of Czechoslovakia, filled with deep misgiving, and with great regret, accepted the harsh terms that were proposed to her."

- At Godesberg, "[s]weet reasonableness ... won nothing except terms which a cruel and revengeful enemy would have dictated to a beaten foe after a long war. Crueler terms could hardly be devised. ..."

- At Munich, the Prime Minister was able to acquire some important improvements from the Godesberg Memorandum, and this is a great triumph for Mr. Chamberlain.

- However, "I spent the greater part of [last] Friday trying to persuade myself that those terms were good enough for me. I tried to swallow them—I did not want to do what I have done—but they stuck in my throat. ... [Czechoslovakia] was to [have been] invaded, and I had thought that after accepting the humiliation of partition she should have been spared the ignominy and the horror of invasion"—but in reality she has not been spared.

- The Prime Minister "brought home also from Munich something more than the terms to which [the Cabinet] had agreed. At the last moment, at the farewell meeting, he signed with the Fuhrer a joint declaration ... but I would suggest that for the Prime Minister of England to sign, without consulting with his colleagues and without, so far as I am aware, any reference to his Allies, obviously without any communication with the Dominions and without the assistance of any expert diplomatic advisers, such a declaration with the dictator of a great State, is not the way in which the foreign affairs of the British Empire should be conducted"

- "The Prime Minister has confidence in the good will and in the word of Herr Hitler" even after he has broken that word many times. "The Prime Minister may be right. ... I hope and pray that he is right, but I cannot believe what he believes. I wish I could. Therefore, I can be of no assistance to him in his Government ... and it is much better that I should go."[499]

Chamberlain rose in the House and briefly responded to Duff Cooper's speech then expressed gratitude and praise to Foreign Secretary Halifax for his efforts during the crisis. Chamberlain's tribute to Halifax was especially interesting because of the times in recent weeks when Halifax had disagreed with or challenged him, e.g., on the mobilization of the Czechoslovak military, pressuring the Czechs to accept the terms the Munich Agreement, and the communiqué saying that when France comes to the defense of Czechoslovakia, Britain, and Russia will certainly stand by her. Chamberlin's praise of Halifax's efforts leading up the Munich Agreement is even more interesting given that in his autobiography, Halifax would later reveal that had he not been in a position of responsibility at the time, he "should very possibly indeed have been among the critics [of the Munich Agreement]."[500]

A few days later, Chamberlain told the House his view of what had happened at Munich and why the agreement was an improvement over the Godesberg Memorandum. He talked about how the agreement had provided Britain with relief from the threat of war, albeit linked with "a profound feeling of sympathy" for Czechoslovakia.

At that point, several members of the House shouted "Shame!" However, unbowed, Chamberlain continued, "I have nothing to be ashamed of. Let those who have, hang their heads. We must feel profound sympathy for a small and gallant nation in the hour of their national grief and loss."[501] He felt this way because he had, at the expense of Czechoslovakia, achieved what he sincerely believed to be a "real triumph." Munich, he continued, showed that "representatives of four great Powers can find it possible to agree on a way of carrying out a difficult and delicate operation by discussion instead of by force of arms, and thereby they have averted a catastrophe which would have ended civilisation as we have known it."[502]

On the other hand, and in contradiction to the pride he expressed in securing peace, Chamberlain pointed out that "[f]or a long period now we have been engaged in this country in a great programme of rearmament, which is daily increasing in pace and in volume,"[503] and that "we must renew our determination to fill up the deficiencies that yet remain in our armaments and in our defensive precautions, so that we may be ready to defend ourselves and make our diplomacy effective."[504]

On October 5, Churchill pulled no punches in a forty-five-minute speech to the House about Munich.[505] He started off saying that "… we have sustained a total and unmitigated defeat and … France has suffered even more than we have. …" Conservative MP Nancy Astor then shouted, "Nonsense!"[506] After a period of raucousness in the House during which he was often interrupted by MPs shouting, "Is peace,"[507] Churchill continued by metaphorically describing the events at Munich as:

> £1 was demanded at the pistol's point. When it was given, £2 were demanded at the pistol's point. Finally, the dictator consented to take £1 17s. 6d. and the rest in promises of good will for the future.[508]

He added that:

- "The terms which the Prime Minister brought back with him could easily have been [negotiated] through ordinary diplomatic channels at any time during the summer."

- "...[L]eft to themselves and told they were to get no help from the Western Powers, [the Czechs] would have been able to make better terms than they have got."

- "... There has been gross neglect and deficiency in our defenses. ..." "I venture to think that *in the future the Czechoslovakian state cannot be maintained as an independent entity. You will find that in a period of time measured only by months, Czechoslovakia will be engulfed in the Nazi régime.*" [emphasis added]

- The power and influence of France, Great Britain, and Russia, "added to the other deterrents which combinations of Powers, great and small, ready to stand firm upon the front of law and for the ordered remedy of grievances, would have formed what might well have been effective [in deterring Hitler]."

- "...[W]e have sustained a defeat without a war, the consequences of which will travel far with us along our road."

- "The whole equilibrium of Europe has been deranged."

Churchill ventured that the Sudetens had "never expressed a desire to go into Nazi rule." Although likely incorrectly, he added the belief that "if their opinion could be asked, they would" answer in the negative.[509] He concluded his speech with a series of stern warnings about Germany:

> "[Nazi Germany] cannot ever be the trusted friend of the British democracy."

> "... [T]here can never be friendship between the British democracy and the Nazi Power, that Power which spurns Christian ethics, which cheers its onward course by a barbarous paganism, which vaunts the spirit of aggression and conquest, which derives strength and perverted pleasure from persecution, and uses, as we have seen, with pitiless brutality the threat of murderous force."

> "What I find unendurable is the sense of our country falling into the power, into the orbit and influence of Nazi Germany, and all our existence becoming dependent upon their goodwill or pleasure."

> "In a very few years, perhaps in a very few months, we shall be confronted with demands with which we shall no doubt be invited to comply. Those demands may affect the surrender of territory or the surrender of the liberty."

"This is only the first sip, the first foretaste of a bitter cup which will be proffered to us year-by-year unless by a supreme recovery of moral health and martial vigor we arise again and take our stand for freedom as in the olden time."[510]

Churchill's words were unfortunately as prescient as they were pointed. He saw the Nazis as a metastasizing malignancy that could not be stopped until Europe created a coalition great enough that Hitler could not ignore it, as he had ignored Britain and France at Munich.* As Churchill put it, "I have always held the view that the maintenance of the peace depends on the actual accumulation of deterrents against the aggressor, coupled with a sincere effort to redress grievances."[511]** He recognized that if you planned to play with Hitler, regardless of the venue or reason, you first had do everything possible to strengthen your hand.

After Munich, there was a press campaign aimed a painting Churchill as a blackguard for his attack on the Munich Agreement and portraying Chamberlain as a hero.[512] Conservative Party leaders in the Epping District that Churchill represented said that they would not nominate him for re-election, and he was nearly censured by the party.[513]

In the end, the House approved Chamberlain's actions at Munich by a vote of 366 to 144. Thirty dissident Conservatives, including Churchill, abstained.[514] Despite having prevailed by over two hundred votes, Chamberlain wrote to his sister Ida a few days later that "All the world seemed to be full of my praises except the House of Commons."[515] He couldn't imagine that something which was so clearly right to him could be perceived otherwise by anyone.

Edvard Beneš, under pressure from Germany, resigned as President of Czechoslovakia.[516] On November 30, he was succeeded by Emil Hácha.[517] Two weeks after his resignation, Beneš took refuge in London. Following the outbreak of World War II, he would form a Czechoslovak government-in-exile.

Buchanan suggests that Chamberlain knew he had not brought home a lasting peace. As support for this speculation, he notes that during the triumphant ride from the airport to Buckingham Palace Chamberlain told Halifax that "[a]ll this will be over in three months."[518] Both historian Professor A.J.P. Taylor and Buchanan take the phrase to mean that in three months all of the optimism surrounding the Munich Agreement will have passed and Britain will be right back in a crisis with Germany over

---

*As noted in Chapter 9, the Cabinet had agreed that it must consider partnering with other countries to bolster mutual security since 1934. CAB 23/3 10 (34) p. 15 292.
**By this time, Churchill had repudiated the idea of redressing German grievances by returning colonies it lost after WWI. Roberts p. 406.

Czechoslovakia or something else. Halifax, to whom the words were spoken, largely agreed with this interpretation. He wrote that when Chamberlain said those words "...he was concerned with the spirit in which he believed Hitler to have signed the declaration and which at that moment he was disposed to trust."[519] This is not an unfair interpretation of Chamberlain's words, but the phrase is latently ambiguous. At first read, the interpretation that the benefits of the Munich Agreement will have evaporated within ninety days does not jump out as being unreasonable. But, equally reasonably, the phrase could also mean that in three months Britain and Germany will have put all of their disagreements behind them, achieved "peace in our time," and all of Britain's anguish over a possible war with Germany will be a thing of the past.

Much of the surrounding detail would signal that the latter of the two interpretations was the one intended by Chamberlain. First, when Chamberlain uttered the phrase, he appears to have been of the belief, captured in the words of Roosevelt's 1932 campaign song, that "Happy Days Are Here Again." Note also what Chamberlain said just after arriving back at 10 Downing Street: "This is the second time in our history that there has come back from Germany to Downing Street peace with honor. I believe it is peace for our time."[520] Chamberlain was optimistic and upbeat. Moreover, as Roberts writes, during the drive from the airport to London, Halifax had also suggested that Chamberlain widen the Government to include members of the Labour and Liberal parties. Chamberlain, however, rejected doing so because "he did not see any advantage to that, as he *had convinced himself that he had genuinely brought peace.*"[521] [emphasis added] As Manchester explains, Chamberlain expected that after Munich there would be a growing rapport with both Germany and Italy, followed by trade agreements and movement toward multinational disarmament.[522] Chamberlain was, in fact, so proud of what he had achieved at Munich that his Christmas card for 1938 featured a picture of the airplane in which he had flown back from Germany.[523] All these facts support the more optimistic interpretation of Chamberlain's remark. He seemed to be saying that by New Year's Day all our worries will be over.

Buchanan also posits that, by reveling in the celebration of the Munich Agreement, Chamberlain could not tell the British people that a war with Germany was still a possibility and that the nation must therefore sacrifice much more than it already was and prepare accordingly.[524] While it is true that Chamberlain did not make somber statements along those lines, the reason was not that he was somehow unable to do so; it was because, as he wrote on October 16, 1939, "we are very little nearer to the time when we can put all thoughts of war out of our minds. ..."[525]*

Should Chamberlain Have Pushed for the Munich Agreement? What Realistic Options Existed? Was Hitler Just Bluffing? Could Hitler Have Been Toppled and World War II Averted in September 1938?

It's fascinating to ponder what might have happened if Chamberlain had never gone to Germany. One outcome, though unlikely, is that the Czech Government and the Sudeten-Germans would have worked things out and eliminated Hitler's excuse to threaten an invasion of Czechoslovakia. In that case, Hitler may have turned his attention to Poland.

If an internal solution failed, then, according to Buchanan, "Hitler would have had to fight for the Sudetenland and Europe might have united against him."[526] This thesis is not dissimilar from one championed by Churchill.

In *The Gathering Storm*, Churchill reflects his belief that:

- Czech President Beneš was wrong to have yielded when Chamberlain bullied the Czechs into sitting quietly while he gave their country away.

- Trusting its fortresses in the Sudetenland, Czechoslovakia should have fought the Germans, and

- Once the fighting had begun, France, Britain, and Russia would have come to the Czechs' assistance.[527]

However, Buchanan and others believed that the Russians would not (or could not) have come to the aid of the Czechs and questioned the Czechs ability to prevail over Germany with help from only Britain and France, each of which was weaker militarily than Germany.[528]

Conversely, Churchill posited that the Czechs could have prevailed against the Nazis as part of a Grand Alliance among itself, Britain, France, and Russia acting under the aegis of the League of Nations. He had espoused such a strategy at least since the Anschluss back in March 1938.[529] That

---

This is not to say that Chamberlain believed there was no chance of a war with Hitler. Surprisingly, despite his belief that at Munich he had in fact brought about "peace for our time," in 1938 and beyond he was also one of the leading advocates for increasing British defense spending. See, CAB 23/1 15 (38) p. 6 37. In doing so, he was not being pessimistic—just cautious.

Churchill envisioned this alliance's including the very same Bolshevists he had been attacking for more than twenty years was eye-opening.[530]* But would Russia have really gotten involved in a war over Czechoslovakia in September 1938? For that matter, how battle-ready were the armed forces of the countries that Churchill imagined in the Grand Alliance?

In a memo issued just weeks before Munich, B.H. Liddell Hart, one of Britain's foremost military experts, laid out what could be expected if a war should break out over Czechoslovakia. He concluded "that the Czechs could not possibly hold out unless Russia could keep them from being dominated from the air."[531] But Russia was six hundred miles away from any possible target[532] and, according to all reports that the British had received, the Russian Air Force was in extremely poor condition. This opinion was confirmed in the famous [Charles] Lindbergh Report.[533]** Lindbergh also provided substantial details about the prodigious strength of the Luftwaffe and Germany's aircraft production capacity.[534] He even said the democracies must not go to war because they would be "crushed absolutely and finally."[535] Similarly, the updated report issued by the British Chiefs of Staff on September 14, 1938, repeated that no pressure that Britain and France could bring to bear—by sea, land, or air—could stop Germany from inflicting a decisive defeat on Czechoslovakia.[536]

Chamberlain agreed: "Nothing that we could have done, nothing that France could have done, or Russia could have done could possibly have saved Czechoslovakia from invasion and destruction.[537] In a letter to his sister Hilda, he later remarked that Germany had "missed the bus" in September 1938, when, given the poor state of the British and French military, Hitler "could have dealt France and ourselves a terrible, perhaps a mortal, blow."[538] He later wrote that "...it was as clear as daylight that if we had to fight in 1938 the result would have been far worse [than it actually was in 1940.]"[539] Chamberlain was convinced that the Munich Agreement was necessary to buy Britain time to rearm.[540]*** This position is challenged by John H. Maurer, Professor at the U.S. Naval War College, who writes that the year's

---

Churchill would later justify his willingness to align with the Soviets, saying, "he had only one single purpose—the destruction of Hitler—and his life was much simplified thereby." Colville p. 404.

**The report was an on-site assessment of Soviet aviation done by Lindbergh in the summer of 1938 at the request of the U.S. Embassy in London. Berg, Lindberg pp. 373–74.*

***When the war intensified in May 1940 Chamberlain still felt that Britain needed more time. In a letter to his sister he wrote, "If only we had another year of preparation we should have been in a far stronger position and so would the French." ed. Self, Vol 4 p. 534 Chamberlain to his sister Ida, May 25, 1940.*

delay in taking on Germany that resulted from the Munich Agreement, did allow Britain time to get stronger in the air but "... instead of improving Britain's relative strategic position ... on balance [the additional year] favored Hitler's ambitions."[541]

In his autobiography, Halifax takes Chamberlain's position about Britain's strength and ability to help Czechoslovakia even further. He writes, "Czechoslovakia was no longer a defensible proposition." He also asserts that critics of the Munich Agreement "either didn't know or greatly care that there was grave doubt whether the Commonwealth would" support a British intervention in 1938 to help Czechoslovakia.[542]

Buchanan, in turn, contends that Churchill's belief in the strength and determination of the Czech Army was misplaced.[543] As support, he cites the fact that at Munich, when Britain and France told the Czechs to let the Sudetenland go, the Czech Army "folded without firing a shot."[544] That may be true, but it doesn't necessarily signify that the Czechs could not have contributed to an Allied war effort. For one thing, the Czechs had at least thirty-five trained and well-equipped divisions, far more than the British Army.[545]

The snapshot of the Czech Army's "folding" was also taken just after the country had been abandoned by the large nations (France, Russia, and Britain) it was counting on to stand shoulder to shoulder with in resisting a German invasion. The Czech Army "folded" because it was deserted by its purported friends, not because of any inherent weakness in that army itself. In fact, as noted previously, some members of the German General Staff believed that if Germany had invaded the Sudetenland, the Czech Army, with no assistance from Britain, France, or Russia could have held the Wermacht at bay for three months. French General Maurice Gamelin also believed that the Czechs, with their thirty-five divisions, could have held out against the Germans' forty divisions.[546]

The apparent willingness of the Czechs to fight should also be noted. When Czechoslovakia mobilized on September 23, 1938, its citizen-soldiers did so "with an incredible enthusiasm." It took only four hours for Czechoslovakia's mountain fortresses in the Sudetenland to be fully manned.[547]

Whether Russia would have honored its obligation to defend Czechoslovakia if she were attacked (and France came to her assistance) has been the subject of much speculation. It has been said that the Soviets signed its treaty to aid Czechoslovakia in bad faith and that Stalin "was even less inclined to honor his military pact with the Czechs than were the French."[548] In any event, aligning with Russia to halt Hitler in his tracks was an idea that appalled Chamberlain, "who despised and distrusted the Bolsheviks more than the Nazis."[549] As Buchanan writes, "[f]orced to choose between Nazi Germany and Stalin's Soviet Union controlling Eastern and Central Europe [Chamberlain, unlike Churchill] would have preferred the former."

"'Better Hitler than Stalin' was a sentiment shared by the leaders of all nations bordering on Stalin's Empire: Finland, Estonia, Lithuania Latvia, Poland, and Romania. ...[*] By the time of the Munich Agreement, when the number of Hitler's victims still numbered in the hundreds, Stalin had already murdered millions...."[550]

"Chamberlain also believed that an alliance between Britain and Russia meant certain war with Germany," with the result being that either Hitler or Stalin would wind up being the master of Eastern and Central Europe.[551] Chamberlain did not feel that winding up with such a result was "worth Britain's fighting another European war."[552] In a perfect world, Chamberlain would have wanted Germany and Russia to exist at equal strength in perpetuity.

Sir Nevile Henderson, Britain's Ambassador to Berlin, also believed that Hitler attached little importance to Russia (except regarding airplanes) and would have had little hesitation in proceeding militarily against the combination of France, Russia, and Britain.[553]

Professor A.J.P. Taylor interestingly observes that the Soviet policy on coming to Czechoslovakia's assistance in 1938 was "a mystery".[554] He also asserts that it is unlikely that we will ever know what the Soviets would have done had they been called on.[555] On paper they were treaty-bound to come to the aid of Czechoslovakia if France did. Russia said as much many times in the months before Munich.[556] And, right up to the end, Soviet Foreign Commissar Maxim Litvinov said that Russia would comply with her treaty obligations to Czechoslovakia.[557] But if a hesitant France didn't step up, Russia would not have to; so promising to help the Czechs was an easy statement for the Soviets to make. In *The Gathering Storm*, Churchill suggests that rather than saying Russia would not have come to the aid of Czechs, a "[m]ore precise look at it is probably that the Soviet offer was effectively ignored."[558] According to Commissar Litvinov, he approached the French right after the Anschluss and again on September 2, 1938, to discuss issuing a joint declaration vowing to come to the assistance of Czechoslovakia. The Soviet Ambassador to Britain had likewise approached London on the subject. But neither France nor Britain showed any interest.[559] Nor were the Soviets invited to participate in the negotiations at Munich. They were

---

*As discussed in the next chapter, this sentiment had not faded by the time the Soviets formally proposed a Grand Alliance in the spring of 1939.

looked upon with "indifference" if not "disdain."[560] One plausible reason: the British and French governments did not want the Russian bear to sneak its communist nose under the edge of the European tent.[561]

Manchester notes that Czechoslovakia and the fortifications that it had in the Sudetenland were strategically important to the Soviet Union. Having them fall into Hitler's hands meant that Russia would lose "the outer bastion of [its] defense system."[562] Career diplomats in the British Foreign Office appreciated this fact and urged their political superiors to use it as leverage in discussions with the Soviets; but "the appeasers kept pretending that the USSR didn't exist."[563]

If the Soviets had been involved, both Churchill and Manchester believe that standing up to Hitler in September 1938 would have averted WWII. Historian John Lukacs takes the opposite view: "Most people, including those who ought to have known better," such as Churchill, "believe even now that, while in 1938 the French and the British betrayed the Czechs, the Soviet Union was ready to enter a European war in order to stand by its Democratic Central European ally. ... Most of this is nonsense. ... In September 1938, a few Soviet diplomats, when hard-pressed, dropped remarks to the effect that the Soviet Union would stand by the Czechs, provided that the French observed *their* alliance commitments; and again, provided that Poland and Romania would let the Red Army pass through their countries to Czechoslovakia, something that was wholly out of the question. In 1938, Stalin was no more prepared for war with Germany than were Chamberlain or Daladier."[564] [emphasis in original]

Shirer acknowledges that Russia's willingness or ability (or both) to join the Western Powers in 1938 to save the Czechs is debatable,[565] noting that even Churchill recognized that Poland and Romania would not accept the Russians crossing through their territory to aid Czechoslovakia.[566] Of course, that problem may have been obviated if the rumors of the day were true and in 1938 Poland would have entered any war over Czechoslovakia on the side of the Nazis. Another possible way that Russia could have obtained permission to cross through other counties to help the Czechs would have been by bringing an appeal to the League of Nations under Article XI of the Covenant (which gave the League broad power to take emergency actions to safeguard the peace.)[567]

All of the above notwithstanding, Shirer suggests that the Anglo-French capitulation at Munich was unnecessary because Hitler was, in fact, bluffing.[568] His support: The German generals who survived the war agreed that, but for the Munich Agreement:

- Hitler would have invaded Czechoslovakia;

- Ultimately Britain, France, and Russia would have come to her defense[569];

- Germany would not have been able to pierce the frontier fortifications of the Sudetenland[570];

- Germany would have lost the war "in short order."[571]

Taylor concurs. He points out in some detail that "[f]ew preparations" had been made in Germany "even for a defensive war against France."[572] There was also a huge disparity in the number of troops between France and Germany along the Siegfried line.[573] Field Marshals Jodl and von Manstien each concurred when they testified at Nuremburg. Each said that stationed at the Siegfried line, which was hardly more than a large construction site, were one hundred French divisions but only twelve German divisions (seven of which were reserves)[574]*

The ultimate evidence supporting Shirer's thesis that Allied capitulation at Munich was unnecessary is that Hitler admitted as much. In a speech to his Commanders in Chief on August 22, 1939, Hitler admitted that he had created a Greater Germany by bluffing about a German military that was "doubtful" and untested.[575]

What does all this amount to? Answer:

> A good case can be made that decisive action at the time of Munich may very well have made WWII unnecessary. This is not to say that other opportunities didn't exist, both before and after Munich, to do the same thing. (The latter is discussed further the next chapter.)

The Allies were aware of their superiority along Germany's western border. Just before the final push to Munich started, French General Gamelin told Premier Daladier that if Germany started a war in Czechoslovakia, because of the strength of the French military (combined with that of the British and the Czechs) "the democratic nations would dictate the peace." The French Army would not only hold onto the Maginot line but could carry out successful offensive drives into Germany. Faber p. 275. Gamelin said that "France would attack Germany" both by air and through weak points in Germany's yet-to-be-completed west wall "within five days of an invasion of Czechoslovakia." Ibid. p. 361. He even provided Daladier and Chamberlain with analyses to support his position. Shirer p. 425.

Simply put, if Hitler had invaded Czechoslovakia (and were not deposed) not only would he have had a tough fight there, but he would have also had to fight the French along Germany's western border. He would have had the two-front war he never wanted.

If Chamberlain saw his interactions with Hitler metaphorically, it most likely would not have been as a poker game. Rather, he was trying to train Hitler, much like one would train a puppy: "Sit" (i.e., don't threaten to use force) and you will be given a treat. (Churchill said that Chamberlain hoped to reform Hitler.[576]) The training would start with the Sudetenland crisis; down the road it could be applied to resolve other grievances. But as history has shown, reward training works with puppies and prime ministers susceptible to flattery but doesn't work well with deranged dictators.

In *Churchill, Hitler, and the "Unnecessary War,"* Buchanan asks the intriguing question: "How [would] bringing the Red Army into Czechoslovakia [have] save[d] Czechoslovakia?" Answer: It may not have. Although if, after a British, French, Russian, and Czech defeat of Germany, the Russians planned to remain in Czechoslovakia, the Czech Army may have been able to force them to leave. (N.B. in the fall of 1939 the Finnish Army, which was not as potent as the Czech Army, was able to substantially resist a Soviet invasion.) But even if the Red Army could not be dislodged and the Czechs fell under Soviet rule, it cannot be emphasized enough that defeating Hitler in 1938 would have saved millions of the lives lost in Europe. There never would have been a Holocaust, the bloody invasion of the Soviet Union, D-Day, and the many other battles that took place in WWII.

The Immediate Aftermath of Munich

A poll in October 1938 revealed that 93 percent of the British *did not* believe that Hitler had made his last territorial demand in Europe.[577]

On September 30, the Polish Government delivered an ultimatum to the Czechs: cede the coal-rich region of Teschen to Poland or it would be taken by force. (Poland had massed troops along its border with Czechoslovakia.[578]) Hungary, in turn, made demands for the southern portion of Slovakia, a large region in central Czechoslovakia that shared its long southern border with Hungary. The Czechs acceded to the Poles' demand, and on November 2, what remained of the international commission formed at Munich (Italy and Germany) awarded Hungary 7,500 square miles of Slovakia inhabited by five hundred thousand Magyars and half that number of Slovaks.[579]

In addition, under the Munich Agreement, Czechoslovakia wound up ceding "11,000 square miles of territory" to Germany "inhabited by 2.8 million Sudeten-Germans and nearly a million Czechs." That territory also contained about 75 percent of the country's industrial capacity.[580] This was a much greater loss of territory than had been anticipated. It occurred largely because the commission that was to determine the "remaining territory of preponderantly German character" which was to become the subject of a plebiscite, decided to forgo the plebiscite and simply awarded that territory to Germany.[581]

Despite the successful plundering of large parts of Czechoslovakia, Hitler was sullen and silent in the wake of Munich. He was disappointed at the results.[582] He despised the Czechs' "mongrel state," hated Czech President Beneš, had wanted to crush Beneš regime in a lightning war, and then ride through Prague as the triumphant victor.[583] Chamberlain's getting the Czechs to accede to all of Germany's demands had deprived Hitler of this show.[584]

The principal thing for Hitler to do now was to work out plans to take over the rest of Czechoslovakia. That planning started with an October 21 directive.[585] He also told the new Czech Government that at the first sign of resistance to Nazi direction, he would destroy the country in "twenty-four, no, in eight hours."[586]

As noted, in the Anglo-French proposal that Chamberlain brought to Munich, the post-Sudetenland "new" Czechoslovakia was to have been given an international guarantee of its integrity in the case of unprovoked aggression. That provision was, however, never incorporated into the agreement. Still, perhaps feeling guilty for having sold out the Czechs, Britain said that it had a moral obligation to guarantee what was left of Czechoslovakia. Dominions Secretary, Sir Thomas Inskip, said that "… His Majesty's Government feel under a moral obligation to Czechoslovakia to keep the guarantee [even though not technically in force]. … In the event therefore of an act of unprovoked aggression against Czechoslovakia His Majesty's Government would certainly be bound to take all steps in their power to see that the integrity of Czechoslovakia is preserved."[587] However, if, as Chamberlain believed, Britain and France couldn't prevent the annexation of the Sudetenland, how could they have prevented Hitler from overrunning the rest of Czechoslovakia after it had been stripped of its mountain defenses?[588]

When questioned by the House as to why, in the face of this moral obligation, Britain looked the other way when Poland demanded that the Czechs cede Teschen to it, Chamberlain explained that the Anglo-French offer of an international guarantee did not affect the existing borders of the new Czechoslovakia "but referred only to the hypothetical question of future unprovoked aggression."[589] He suggested that action related to the Polish ultimatum over Teschen was "merely a readjustment of the frontiers laid down in the Treaty of Versailles."[590]

As for resolving the Hungarian demands, Britain and France simply allowed Germany and Italy to decide the question; and that inaction led to Hungary receiving a portion of Czechoslovakia in early November 1938.

Did these failures of will represent a further betrayal of the Czechs? Probably, but as laid out in the next chapter, they would not be the last time that the British and French avoided their "moral obligation" to help the Czechs.

In a letter Chamberlain wrote to the Archbishop of Canterbury, he sized up the state of the Czech situation with the same inaccuracy as he had sized up Hitler. The Prime Minister predicted that down the road the Czechs would realize that Britain had "save[d] them for a happier future."[591] For roughly four hundred and fifty thousand Czech citizens, their "happier future" would be death: two hundred thousand in concentration camps and two hundred and fifty thousand during the German occupation. For hundreds of thousands of other Czechs, the "future" meant becoming slave laborers.

In his autobiography, Halifax describes Munich and the betrayal of Czechoslovakia as "a horrible and wretched business"[592] and talks about the "misfortune [of him having been the minister] presid[ing] over the Foreign Office at that time. ..."[593] Whether merely convenient, well deserved, or somewhere in between, Halifax places a good portion of the blame for Munich on the Governments that preceded Chamberlain's, saying that the critics of Munich "ought to have criticized the failure of successive Governments, and all of the [political] parties, to foresee the necessity of rearming in the light of what was going on in Germany."[594] He was particularly critical of Baldwin's failure to stand up to Hitler when the Germans reoccupied the Rhineland in March 1936.

Halifax believed that because of Britain's failure to act in 1936, in 1938 Germany had been able to boast about having the superior army and air force. He viewed choosing between defending Czechoslovakia against the Nazi invasion on the one hand and selling out the Czechs on the other to have been a Hobson's choice, with betraying the Czechs "the lesser of two evils."[595] As callous as that sounds, and it is, it should at least be remembered that after Godesberg, Halifax had a change of heart and opposed pressuring Czechoslovakia to accept its death sentence.

Halifax probably deserves a good deal more credit for issuing the communiqué on the eve of Munich saying that Great Britain and Russia would stand by France as she fulfills its obligation to come to Czechoslovakia's assistance. If Chamberlain had not squelched that communiqué almost immediately, and if the Soviets had somehow emerged from the shadows and forcefully said they would fight for the survival of Czechoslovakia, that country might have survived and, more importantly, Hitler might have been stopped then and there even if the Halder Plot were not executed.

As Lukacs writes, "both Hitler and Chamberlain got what they wanted out of Munich."[596] Hitler received the valuable Sudetenland, which provided a firm foothold for taking the rest of Czechoslovakia, and his prize came at no cost. Chamberlain received what he thought was peace and the glory of being the person who saved the world from war.[597]

With the Sudetenland in the fold, Hitler started looking at two other targets: the rest of Czechoslovakia and Poland. Securing the first target would be the subject of a directive from the Chancellor to his military leaders.[598] After Munich, Hitler would try to lure Poland into his sphere of influence without using force. Adding Poland and Czechoslovakia to the German side was important to the German leader since they each provided a means of access to the Ukraine[599] Hitler coveted this portion of the Soviet Union as a place into which the German state could expand as part of its efforts to obtain Lebensraum. Though not well managed under Stalin's collective-farming policies, the Ukraine had the ability to produce substantial quantities of grain.*

_____

*As it turns out, Poland also had a covetous eye on the Ukraine. DGFP Series D, Vol. V, p. 168 "Minutes By Ribbentrop" Feb 1, 1939, No. 126.

On November 1, 1938, Halifax wrote the British Ambassador in Paris that German hegemony in Central and Eastern Europe was "inevitable."[600] Soon after, he also described such expansion as "a normal and natural thing."[601]

Germany proposed that Poland permit the city of Danzig, with its German majority, to rejoin the Reich and allow Germany to build an autobahn and a two-track railway line across the Polish Corridor, the strip of Polish land in which Danzig was located and that lay between the main portion of Germany and East Prussia. In return, Germany would guarantee Poland's frontiers[602] and agree to a Berlin-Warsaw alliance against Russia.[603] Thus began the pressure campaign over the return of Danzig, which would intensify over the next year.[604]

When Foreign Minister Ribbentrop approached Josef Lipski, the Polish Ambassador to Berlin, with the proposal, Lipski reminded Ribbentrop of two recent occasions in which Hitler said he would not support any change in Danzig's status.[605] The Poles had believed these statements; they felt they would not have been made frivolously given how intensely the German people despised the provisions of the Versailles treaty that made Danzig a free city supervised by the League of Nations and established the Corridor cutting off East Prussia from the rest of Germany.[606]

The role Hitler had in mind for Poland was that of a partner in his new anti-Communist order in Europe. Hitler was astonished when Poland turned him down.[607] He had thought that Poland's Foreign Minister, Colonel Józef Beck, was "a man he could do business with."[608] Over the years, Beck had also attempted "to bring Poland closer to the Third Reich. ..."[609] As mentioned earlier, there were even thoughts at the time of Munich that, if war broke out, Poland might side with Germany.

Hitler had said that if Danzig were returned to Germany, it could remain under Polish economic control. He argued that a connection between Germany proper and its isolated province of East Prussia "was as vital a matter to the Reich as a connection with the sea was for Poland."[610] Despite Hitler's persuasiveness, Beck refused. The Polish rejection did not generate any concessions from Hitler.[611] But Danzig and Poland never left Hitler's purview. They would, in fact, prove to be the spark that set off World War II, even though in late 1938, as Taylor writes, men like French Premier Bonnet and German Foreign Minister Ribbentrop both felt that Poland was already "a loyal German satellite" and that the problem of Danzig would be settled "quietly ... without a European crisis."[612]

Kristallnacht

Kristallnacht took place November 9–10, 1938. It was a nationwide rampage in Germany against Jews and their shops and synagogues. Hundreds of Jews were murdered, thousands were beaten up, and tens of thousands were sent to concentration camps.[613] Thousands of synagogues and stores were ransacked, and several hundred were burned down. Although contrived by Goebbels,[614] Kristallnacht was speciously portrayed as a spontaneous retaliation for the murder of a German diplomat in Paris by a German-born Polish Jewish refugee.[615]

One outcome of this gruesome organized pogrom was that "during the winter of 1938–39 the mood in Britain changed to accept war as inevitable."[616] For that reason and others, Kristallnacht, besides being "a shameful crime" was also "a historic blunder."[617] Kristallnacht revolted many Germans, even some Nazis, and did not play well in world opinion, particularly in the United States. It also soured the fantasy world that existed just after Munich. Even Chamberlain was appalled.[618]

The Final Months of 1938

As 1938 moved toward its close, Churchill kept up his stinging rebukes of Chamberlain and his Government. Unlike the kid-glove way he dealt with Hitler, Chamberlain had no problem responding to these statements with sharply critical words of his own.[619] More important, though, than the ongoing war of words between the two British politicians, was whether the Prime Minister would begin to realize who Hitler really was and how profoundly untrustworthy he could be.

As 1938 ended, when and if Chamberlain would come to those realizations remained to be seen. Certainly, no one could have predicted then that Churchill and Chamberlain, two bitter political adversaries, would come together and be of one mind about Hitler seventeen months later, when Britain faced perhaps the biggest crisis in its history.

Chamberlain, Halifax, and Mussolini in Rome January 1939

12

January–August 1939. Czechoslovakia,
The Polish Guarantee, etc.

Hitler Takes Over Czechoslovakia
Initial Efforts Toward a Peace Front Against Germany
The British War Guarantee to Poland
Efforts to Create a Grand Alliance
The Molotov-Ribbentrop Pact and Other Games Hitler Played in a Failed
   Attempt to Get a Limited War over Poland
August 24, 1939 (Eight Days Before the Invasion of Poland)
August 25, 1939 (Seven Days Before the Invasion of Poland)
August 26, 1939 (Six Days Before the Invasion of Poland)
August 27, 1939 (Five Days Before the Invasion of Poland)
The Mysterious Mr. "D"
August 28, 1939 (Four Days Before the Invasion of Poland)
August 29, 1939 (Three Days Before the Invasion of Poland)
August 30, 1939 (Two Days Before the Invasion of Poland)
August 31, 1939 (One Day Before the Invasion of Poland)
Should Britain Have Given Poland a War Guarantee? Would It Have Been
   Better Off Doing Nothing? Or Was War With Germany Inevitable?
Churchill and Others also Believed that WWII Was "Unnecessary"
Hitler's Speech of April 28, 1939—A Reply to Roosevelt and More
- The Polish War Guarantee
- Munich
- Affection for Britain
- How Allied Nations Had Achieved Their Current Prosperous Positions
- Disavowal of the Anglo-German Naval Agreement of 1935
- Response to Roosevelt's Telegram

By New Year's Day 1939, Germany, Poland, and Hungary had all taken bites out of the rest of Czechoslovakia to reclaim lost kinsmen in

Sudeten, Teschen, and Slovakia, respectively. The Czech nation would fall apart in early March. In the afterglow of his imagined triumph at Munich, Chamberlain anticipated there would be a growing friendship and trade agreements with both Germany and Italy followed by a movement toward worldwide disarmament.[1] King George had a very similar view.[2] The real world, however, held a very different future.

In mid-January Chamberlain and Halifax went to Rome to confer with Mussolini. The meeting was "designed as the culmination of Chamberlain's policy" of teaching dictators that grievances can be settled through peaceful negations, thus assuring long-term peace.[3] The two returned home satisfied that Chamberlain "had established a rapport" with the Italian dictator.[4] Mussolini had a different view. Describing his British guests to his son-in-law, Count Ciano, Mussolini said that "these men are not made of the same stuff as Francis Drake and the other magnificent adventurers who created the Empire. [They are merely] the tired sons of a long line of rich men, and they will lose their Empire."[5] Ciano replied that "[t]he British did not want to fight, they try to draw back as slowly as possible but they do not want to fight. ..."[6]

Shortly after the meeting, Mussolini told Hitler that he was ready to sign a formal alliance with Germany. The Chamberlain/Halifax visit had moved the Italian strongman further to the Nazi side.[7]

Hitler Takes Over Czechoslovakia

After Czech President Beneš resigned, Hitler installed a new pro-Nazi government to run what was left of Czechoslovakia. The new regime did the Nazis' bidding, such as dissolving the Communist Party and suspending all Jewish teachers in ethnic-German majority schools, but these moves were not sufficient to please Hitler.[8]

On March 8, 1939, Halifax reported to the Cabinet on the recent visit to Berlin of Frank Ashton–Gwatkin of the Foreign Office. There, Ashton-Gwatkin met with Foreign Minister Ribbentrop and Field Marshal Goering, and from those meetings he came away with the impression that Germany was done for the moment—at least with large-scale adventures. However, Germany could still exert further pressure on Czechoslovakia.[9] In fact, just a week later there were rumors of troop movements in both Germany and Austria.[10] At the same time, the remaining portion of the state of Slovakia, which had already been granted substantial autonomy by the Czech Government,[11] was asked to send its leader, Monsignor Jozef Tiso, to Berlin. Hitler, who had been goading Slovakia for months to secede from Czechoslovakia, knew well that Slovakia's declaring its independence would be the beginning of the end for Czechoslovakia.[12] In Berlin, Tiso "was received with the honours due a Prime Minister."[13] Polish Foreign Minister Józef Beck, who was greatly relieved that Germany's attention was being directed toward Czechoslovakia and not Poland, declared that his government had "full sympathy with the aspirations of the Slovaks."[14]

On March 14, 1939, 167 days after the Munich Agreement was signed, the Slovak State was proclaimed,[15] and the world witnessed the further dissolution of Czechoslovakia. When he heard the news about Slovakia, Czech President Emil Hácha immediately caught a train to Berlin, hoping to persuade Hitler not to gobble up the rest of his country. During the trip, Hácha learned that German troops were lined up along the perimeters of the two remaining Czech states, Bohemia, and Moravia.[16]

When Hácha got to Berlin, Hitler told him that if Czechoslovakia cooperated with Germany, the "entry of German troops would take place in a tolerable manner" and Germany would "permit Czechoslovakia a generous life of her own, autonomy and a degree of national freedom. ..." He added that on the other hand, "resistance would be broken by force of arms, using all means."[17] Hácha, however, refused to sign a prepared document urging his countrymen not to fight the incoming German forces. When Goering threatened to have the Luftwaffe flatten Prague, Hácha collapsed onto the floor.[18] After being resuscitated by Hitler's personal physician, at 4:00 AM, no longer able to withstand the pressure, Hácha signed over his country's fate to the Nazis. Czech radio soon broadcast a call to the people of Czechoslovakia not to resist the invading Wehrmacht.

At 6:00 AM on March 15, 1939, the Wehrmacht crossed into Bohemia and Moravia. They met no opposition.[19] By 9:30 AM German troops had reached the outskirts of Prague.[20] Halifax told Cabinet that the French Government shared his view that there was no possibility of effectively opposing what was taking place or of influencing the situation.[21] He added that French Foreign Minister Bonnet had even remarked that the renewed rift between the Czechs and the Slovaks showed that "we nearly went to war last autumn on behalf of a state which was not viable."[22] Later that day, Hitler traveled the two hundred miles from Berlin to Prague, where he proclaimed all of Czechoslovakia a German protectorate "which was thereby incorporated into the Reich."[23]

That afternoon, Chamberlain spoke to the House and advised that the German forces had begun the occupation of Czechoslovakia and that the Czech Government had ordered its citizens not to offer any resistance.[24] He also said that "Herr Hitler issued an order to the German armed forces this morning to the effect that German military detachments had crossed the frontier of Czech territory in order to assume impartial control of the safety of the lives and property of the inhabitants of the country."[25] (The fact that only two days earlier, Chamberlain had publicly announced that tensions on the continent were easing, once again raised concerns in the House about the Prime Minister's leadership.[26]) In his speech, Chamberlain noted that after Munich, Dominions Secretary Sir Thomas Inskip had once said: "... His Majesty's Government feels under a moral obligation to Czechoslovakia to keep the guarantee [of its borders] as though it were technically in force. ... In the event therefore of an act of unprovoked aggression against Czechoslovakia His Majesty's Government would certainly be bound to take all steps in their power to see that the integrity of Czechoslovakia is preserved."[27] But Chamberlain went on to say:

> *That remained the position until yesterday,* and I may say that recently His Majesty's Government have endeavoured to come to an agreement with the other Governments represented at Munich on the scope and terms of such a guarantee, but up to the present we have been unable to reach any such agreement. In our opinion *the situation has radically altered since the Slovak Diet declared the independence of Slovakia.* The effect of this declaration put an end by internal disruption to the State whose frontiers we had proposed to guarantee and, accordingly, the Halifax condition of affairs described by my right hon. friend the Secretary of State for the Dominions, which was always regarded by us as being only of a transitory nature, has now ceased to exist, and *His Majesty's Government cannot accordingly hold themselves any longer bound by this obligation.*[28] [emphasis added]

The fact is, that even with the declaration of independence by Slovakia and by the region of Ruthenia, Czechoslovakia still comprised Bohemia (in which Prague is located) and Moravia, though both had been occupied by the German army that morning. Chamberlain did note that even if the German occupation of Bohemia and Moravia had taken place with the free assent of the Czech Government, he could not regard the manner and method of the actions taken by the Germans as being "in accord with the spirit of the Munich agreement."[29] Chamberlain also told the House that though he bitterly regretted what had occurred, "remember that the desire of all the peoples of the world still remains concentrated in the hopes of peace."[30] Self writes that during his speech to Parliament, "Chamberlain looked miserable" but nothing suggested that he was moved "either by the Czech tragedy or the Nazi's betrayal."[31]

Chamberlain told the Cabinet that "It might, no doubt, be true that the disruption of Czechoslovakia had been largely engineered by Germany, but our guarantee was *not a guarantee against the exercise of moral pressure. ...*

[T]he German action had all been taken under the guise of an agreement with the Czechoslovak Government. The Germans were, therefore, in a position to give a plausible answer to any representations which were made."[32] [emphasis added] Chamberlain biographer Robert Self calls this "logic which conveniently evaded" Britain's moral obligation to keep the guarantee it and France had made to Czechoslovakia after Munich.[33]

Halifax had just previously told the Cabinet that Britain could also use the argument that its guarantee to Czechoslovakia was only a way to steady the Czechs' position during what could be thought of as a purely transitory situation. "We had, however, never intended permanently to assume responsibility for a monopoly of obligation in this matter."[34] As if the Chamberlain Government's perfidy toward Czechoslovakia at Munich had not been enough, here, by hypertechnical interpretation of its obligations, Britain once again betrayed the Czechs. Hitler had again grabbed territory without being challenged militarily, and without having to shed any blood.

The British did file an official protest of Germany's occupation, with remarkably milquetoast wording:

> His Majesty's Government have no desire to interfere unnecessarily in a matter with which other Governments may be more directly concerned. ... They are, however, as the German Government will surely appreciate, deeply concerned for the success of all efforts to restore confidence in a relaxation of tension in Europe. ... [T]hey would deplore any action in Central Europe which would cause a setback to the growth of this general confidence. ...[35]

As can be seen, the "protest" did not even mention the occupation of Bohemia and Moravia or say that such an occupation violated the Munich Agreement. To his credit, the straight-talking French Ambassador to Germany, Robert Coulondre, made these objections abundantly clear in his March 15 meeting with Ernst von Weizsäecker, the German State Secretary.[36]

The march into Czechoslovakia started Hitler down the path of imposing German rule on non-Germanic peoples. Hitler may have gained new territory and inhabitants, but at the price of losing "the moral advantage" that had made his conquests of the Rhineland, Austria, and the Sudetenland easy.[37] As Taylor puts it, with a few exceptions—the Free City of Danzig and Memel in Lithuania—Hitler could no longer successfully assert he was merely addressing grievances with the Versailles Treaty and appealing to the British and French sense of wanting to remedy past wrongs. Rather, now he would have to "play ... on British and French fears."[38]

In his 1994 book *Diplomacy,* Henry Kissinger, Secretary of State under President Nixon, writes that "... the destruction of Czechoslovakia made no geopolitical sense whatever; it showed that Hitler was beyond rational calculation and bent on war."[39] Hitler detested Czechoslovakia as a "Slav state" and an ally of both France and Bolshevik Russia.[40] For these and other reasons, Pat Buchanan agrees with Kissinger and characterizes Hitler's takeover of Czechoslovakia as another "blunder of historic magnitude" and an action that was "utterly unnecessary":

- Czechoslovakia had already lost the Sudetenland and was facing a hostile breakaway of Slovakia.

- It was already a vassal state to Germany.

- Accordingly, "why send in an army and humiliate a British Prime Minister who had shown himself willing to accommodate Hitler's demand for the return of the German territories and peoples, if Hitler would only proceed peacefully?"

- For little gain, Hitler had burned his bridges with the leaders of a British Empire which he had, at least superficially, sought to befriend and who were prepared to work with him to redress grievances stemming from the Versailles Treaty.[41]

The German takeover of Czechoslovakia also caused Poland, now flanked by the Germans on three sides, to question Hitler's motives and trustworthiness, and thus moved it a bit closer to the British. It must be remembered, however, that Czechoslovakia was critical to Germany achieving the Lebensraum that it so fervently desired. By conquering Czechoslovakia, Hitler gained an important steppingstone and hundreds of thousands of slave laborers. Moreover, by taking over Czechoslovakia, Hitler also gained control over Skoda, one of the largest European industrial conglomerates of the twentieth century—a major arms producer that also produced steam locomotives, freight, and passenger cars, aircraft, ships, machine tools, steam turbines, and power-engineering equipment.

Some historians feel that Hitler's takeover of Czechoslovakia marked the end of appeasement.[42] It didn't: Chamberlain remained willing to negotiate with Hitler for many more months. What the actions of March 15 did show was that Hitler had been lying at Munich. He was not just interested in having ethnic Germans brought back into the Reich.

In a wide-ranging speech to the Reichstag several weeks later, Hitler accomplished the impossible by enhancing his credentials as a prevaricator supreme. Talking about Czechoslovakia, Hitler reminded everyone that he had warned Czech President Beneš not to mistreat the large German minority still living in Czech territory after the annexation of the Sudetenland. He then pointed out that there was a huge military arsenal in Czech territory and that the maintenance of such an arsenal in Central Europe, for no reason or purpose, could only be regarded as a danger to the Reich. On these bases, Hitler tried to justify the German takeover of the rest of Czechoslovakia:

1. because of "A constantly growing stream of underground propaganda and a gradual tendency of Czech newspapers to relapse into their old trends made it obvious even to the veriest simpleton that the old state of affairs would soon be restored"; and

2. to avoid "the possibility that some madman might get control of those vast stores of munitions [that were in the country]."[43]

He added that, since the occupation, Germany had taken over huge numbers of airplanes, anti-aircraft guns, tanks, machine guns, and rifles, along with a billion rounds of ammunition and over three million artillery shells. He said that all these munitions were now in "safe keeping."[44] He also patted himself on the back for solving this heretofore unknown problem of Czech armaments falling fall into the wrong hands (and, in the process, not violating the Munich Agreement).

Soon after Hitler occupied Czechoslovakia, Halifax, who feared that Germany may be seeking world domination,[45] began to take command of British policy toward the Reich.[46] He told Chamberlain that his March 15 speech to the House showed too little outrage at what Hitler had done to Czechoslovakia.[47] Because of this comment, the shock felt by Britons that Hitler had broken a promise only six months old,[48] and the realization that Hitler's actions carried potentially grave consequences,[49] Chamberlain would hereafter be different. Old habits would die hard, but Chamberlain no longer intended to be the sycophant he was at Munich. It has been said that, at this point, Chamberlain saw that it was impossible to deal with Hitler.[50] This is only partially correct. As we will see, Chamberlain's conversion would remain a work in progress for at least several more months.

The "new" Chamberlain made his first appearance at a speaking engagement on March 17, 1939, in Birmingham. Chamberlain had planned to give a speech to the Birmingham Unionist Association on trade, employment, and other domestic matters. On the way up to Birmingham he decided to discard his prepared speech and began jotting down notes about what had occurred in Czechoslovakia. During the speech, which was broadcast nationwide and to many countries, Chamberlain said things that should have been included in his speech before the House two days earlier. He did not admit that appeasement had failed; that policy was too ingrained in him to do so.[51]

But he did call Germany's grab of Czechoslovakia exactly what it was: a clear violation of Hitler's own declaration in Munich that the Sudetenland was "the last territorial claim I have to make in Europe ... I shall not be interested in the Czech state anymore and I can guarantee. We don't want any Czechs anymore."[52] Though he did not state it explicitly, Chamberlain knew and made it known to the world that he could not trust Hitler not to invade other countries. Chamberlain also reiterated something he had said six weeks earlier, that "any demand to dominate the world by force was one which the democracies must resist."[53] He added, "no greater mistake could be made than to suppose that, because [Britain] believes war to be a senseless and cruel thing, this nation has so lost its fibre that it will not take part to the utmost of its power in resisting such a challenge if it ever were made."[54]

The Birmingham speech came at the same time as a shift in British public opinion.[55] The German takeover of Czechoslovakia had burst the bubble of serenity, hope, and optimism in which Britons had been living since Munich.*

Chamberlain's speech in Birmingham, which showed his intent to turn his back on the misjudgments of the past, surprised Churchill.[56] As Churchill writes in *The Gathering Storm*:

> If Chamberlain failed to understand Hitler, Hitler completely underrated the nature of the British Prime Minister ... [Hitler] mistook [Chamberlain's] civilian aspect and passionate desire for peace for a complete explanation of his personality and thought that his umbrella was his symbol. He did not realize

---

*As previously noted, in the speech, Chamberlain, for perhaps the first time, expressed sympathy for the Jews and other non-Nazis who had, as a result of appeasement, become subjected to German rule. Of course, nine weeks later, owing to ongoing pressure from Palestinian Arabs, Chamberlain ended the policy of unlimited Jewish immigration to Palestine, Manchester, Alone p. 397, thus trapping thousands of Jews in Austria and Czechoslovakia. Remember, even in the "new" Chamberlain, at least some of his old ways—his moderate anti-Semitism and being quite meek when it came to saving imperiled Jews—were still visible. Chamberlain announced the Palestine policy change in Parliament on May 22. During the Cabinet debate on the new policy, held on May 1, 1939, the Secretary of State for the Colonies admitted that certain items had been inserted in the new policy "to meet Arab pressure" and that these items "perhaps would have been omitted if the matter were looked at on strict merit." CAB 23/1 25 (39) p. 4 91.

It is worth knowing that before the policy was changed, the Cabinet seriously considered making some British territory in another part of the world available for Jewish immigration. For some time, the Colonial Office believed that the South American colony of British Guiana, where there was a good deal of suitable land, was by far the most likely possibility. CAB 23/6 24 (39) p. 14 68.

There was, however, a belief among Cabinet members that, by handing over part of the colony to the Jews, they would be open to considerable criticism, Ibid. pp. 14–15 69–70; so it never came about.

that *Neville Chamberlain had a very hard-core and that he did not like being cheated.*"[57] [emphasis added]

Malcolm MacDonald, Secretary of State for the Colonies, said after the Birmingham speech that "whereas the prime minister was once a strong advocate of peace he is now definitely swung around to the war point of view."[58] Chamberlain promptly rejected that observation saying, "I am no more a man of war today that I was in September [1938 at Munich]; ... I trust that our actions begun but not concluded, will prove to be the turning point not towards war, which wins nothing, cures nothing, ends nothing, but towards a more wholesome era, when reason will take the place of force."[59]

On March 18, Chamberlain told the Cabinet that his speech in Birmingham had been received warmly by the ambassadors from the United States and France. The Cabinet then signified its approval as well. More importantly, Chamberlain finally said the words that both he and his colleagues needed to hear: "No reliance [can] be placed on any of the assurances given by the Nazi leaders."[60]

Significantly, the Cabinet agreed:

1. to approach Poland, Yugoslavia, Turkey, Greece, Romania, and the Soviet Union to obtain assurances that they would join with Britain in resisting any act of German aggression aimed at dominating southeastern Europe[61]; and
2. to make a public announcement if, in fact, these nations provided satisfactory assurances that they would resist German aggression.[62]

Chamberlain, bitter at having been betrayed by Hitler, added that "the real issue was that if Germany showed signs that she intended to proceed with her march for world domination, we must take steps to stop her by attacking her on two fronts."[63] Though he would later prove reluctant to take such steps, he told the Cabinet that "he was satisfied that nothing less would have any value."[64]

Halifax, in his autobiography, sets out another reason why the events of March 1939 affected Chamberlain.[65] He writes that, in December 1938, a member of the British Embassy staff in Berlin had been invited to a secret meeting with a German staff officer whom he had befriended. The German revealed that Hitler had given orders to prepare plans for an all-out air attack on England and that those plans were to be completed by mid-March.[66] The officer also said that if and when further orders were issued, he would communicate them to his friend at the Embassy via a homemade code, one made from a page torn out of the Berlin phone book. The British Government took the incident seriously and used it to justify accelerated military production.

As Halifax writes, "... the events of March, though not accompanied by the page of the telephone book, left little doubt of what was shaping in Hitler's mind and marked a turning point in Chamberlain's thought."[67]

Initial Efforts Toward a Peace Front Against Germany

On March 18, the Russian Government proposed a six-power conference to be held in Bucharest, Romania. The purpose was for Russia, Romania, Poland, Britain, France, and Turkey to form a peace front in opposition to Germany.[68] Similar proposals had been made a year earlier both by Churchill[69] and Soviet Foreign Commissar Litvinov.[70]* Chamberlain reviewed the proposal but felt that it was "premature."[71] When the Soviet Ambassador to Britain asked Halifax to explain, Halifax responded that the Foreign Office was short-staffed and no one could be spared for the conference.[72] On March 22, Halifax told the Cabinet that Commissar Litvinov was perturbed that Britain had not been more enthusiastic about his proposal for a conference.[73] At an Anglo-French meeting held later that day, Halifax did express concern that Britain was giving the Soviets the idea that they were being pushed to one side.[74]

On March 21, Chamberlain concluded that a declaration by Britain, France, Poland, and Russia that they would act together in response to new German aggressive ambitions was more appropriate than the Soviet idea of a formal conference. The declaration was not intended to advocate encircling Germany (something Hitler greatly feared). Rather, its purpose "was one of self-defense."[75] Chamberlain passed his idea of a joint declaration on to Polish Foreign Minister Colonel Beck.[76] The Poles said emphatically that they would not participate in any declaration, peace front, coalition, or alliance with the Russians. They feared the Soviets and were, to say the least, reluctant to rely on Russia for security.[77] Thus, in one fell swoop, both the idea of issuing a four-power declaration and the Soviet proposal of a six-power conference were dealt a death blow.

Reluctance to embrace the Soviets was hardly unique to Poland. In a private letter, Chamberlain wrote:

> I must confess to the most profound distrust of Russia. I have no belief whatever in her ability to maintain an effective offensive, even if she wanted to. And I distrust her motives, which seem to me to have little connection with our ideas of liberty. ...

As previously noted, according to Litvinov, he had approached the French, both right after the Anschluss and again on September 2, 1938, proposing a joint declaration pledging assistance of Czechoslovakia. The Soviet Ambassador to Britain had done likewise. Neither France nor Britain showed any interest. Manchester, Alone p. 450.

Moreover, she is both hated and suspected by many of the smaller states, notably by Poland, Rumania, and Finland.[78]

French Prime Minister Bonnett, on the other hand, "could not believe that Poland would refuse to collaborate [with Russia]. The question was of life and death to her."[79]

But Britain felt it could not outright reject the Russian proposal for a six-power conference. Doing so "would have been bad manners, bad diplomacy, and bad politics."[80] Besides, Britain "would need every friend [it] could get."[81]

On March 21 Hitler threatened to attack Lithuania if it did not agree to German re-annexation of the city of Memel, which had been seized by Lithuania from a disarmed Germany in 1923 and made autonomous within Lithuania by the League of Nations.[82] Memel was reannexed to the Reich the next day. The British Cabinet accepted Memel's fate matter-of-factly, perhaps because, in Halifax's words, "There was, of course, more justification for this course than for certain [other] recent events."[83]

On that day, in secret talks with Poland, the Germans also made the following proposal: if the Poles agreed to return the city of Danzig to the Reich and granted Germany the right to construct a highway and railroad across the Polish Corridor to provide access to Danzig, then Germany would guarantee the security of the Corridor and agree to a twenty-five-year nonaggression treaty.[84] Proposals about Danzig became public five weeks later, when, on April 28, Hitler addressed the Reichstag.[85] He called his proposal "the greatest imaginable concession in the interest of European peace."[86] Polish Foreign Minister Beck saw it differently. Speaking before the Polish Parliament, he said that the Government of the Reich was demanding unilateral concessions from Poland and that "[A] self-respecting nation does not make unilateral concessions."[87] Beck also saw that his nation would be endangered if the Soviets perceived that a Polish-German treaty threatened Russia.[88]

By March 23, the annexation of Memel was complete. As he had in Prague, Hitler made another triumphant entry, and he addressed the jubilant citizens of the city.[89] Yet another territory had been added to the Reich without bloodshed. On March 26, unbeknownst to the world, the Polish Government rejected the German proposal of March 21; they refused to yield on Danzig, and the ongoing secret Polish-German discussions broke down.[90] As Hitler put it in his speech on April 28, "the Polish Government has rejected my offer and has declared itself prepared only to negotiate concerning the question of a substitute for the Commissioner of the League of Nations, and to consider facilities for the transit of traffic through the Corridor."[91]

Foreign Minister Beck took care that the British did not learn about any of this. In fact, when asked by the British, Beck implied that the Danzig question would soon be resolved.[92] Hearing that, Britain feared Poland might quickly be drawn into the German sphere of influence.[93] Hitler, on the other hand, was concerned about driving Poland into the arms of the British. As a result, on March 25 he issued a secret directive saying that the problem of Danzig would *not* be resolved by force.[94] He did not want war with Poland and certainly did "not want to drive Poland into the arms of Britain"[95]—which is exactly what happened in about a week. The role Hitler had in mind for Poland was that of a partner in his new order in Europe.

The British War Guarantee to Poland

Despite Hitler's secret directive, in the waning days of March 1939 there were German troop movements near Danzig and the Corridor.[96] At an 11:00 AM emergency Cabinet meeting on March 30, 1939, Halifax proposed that Britain make a clear declaration of her intention to support Poland if Poland were attacked by Germany.[97] Among his stated goals was educating the German public that Hitler's strategy would result in Germany becoming engaged in a war on two fronts.[98] Halifax recognized that such a declaration would be very provocative to Germany and would be somewhat reminiscent of the action Britain took in May 1938 when it wrongly chastised the Germans for allegedly amassing troops along the border with Czechoslovakia.[99]

Chamberlain worried that the Germans would precipitate a coup in Poland within the next week, "before we could decide what action we could take."[100] He noted that "it would be a very serious matter if Poland, instead of being a potential ally, became added to the resources of Germany."[101] The Prime Minister was uneasy about two things: the fact that he had no information on the progress of the presumedly still ongoing secret negotiations between Germany and Poland, and the distasteful possibility that the Polish negotiators were in fact giving way to Germany.[102]

As a result, the Cabinet authorized Halifax to dispatch telegrams to the British ambassadors in Warsaw and Paris seeking input in advance of an important question being put to Chamberlain in the House of Commons the following—"[W]hat action [would] His Majesty's Government ... take" if a German attack on Poland was imminent?[103] Chamberlain's response would be that:

> "... His Majesty's Government would at once lend them all the support in their power."[104]

Unfortunately, this answer was disingenuous. Britain had no intention of sending its military to assist Poland in the event of an attack by Germany.

Fearing the possibility of a German attack on Danzig[105] or that Poland might accept a deal with Germany[106]—either voluntarily or through coercion—on March 30 the British hastily quizzed Polish Foreign Minister Beck on how he would feel about a unilateral British/French guarantee of Polish independence in the event of an attack by Germany.[107] (The inclusion of France in the guarantee offer was done without consulting the French,[108] though France and Poland were already bound by the Franco-Polish Alliance of 1921 to assist each other in case of an unprovoked attack.) Beck agreed without hesitation.[109]* According to historian John Lukacs, "for once Halifax and Chamberlain reacted with un-British haste."[110] Manchester characterizes the guarantee as a response to Hitler's betrayal of Chamberlain when Germany took over Prague and the rest of Czechoslovakia.[111] Buchanan similarly attributes Chamberlain's actions at least in part to his "shame and humiliation at having been played for a fool."[112] Of course, Chamberlain was also likely telling himself that "I am not going to let that happen again" and probably believed it to be true. In his autobiography, Halifax provides a simpler explanation for the war guarantee. He writes that "[a]fter March and the final rape of Prague, it was no longer possible to hope that Hitler's purposes and ambitions were limited by any boundaries of race, and the lust of continental or world mastery seem to stand out in stark relief."[113] Halifax's two-sentence justification of the decision to give the guarantees was:

1. to do something Britain had failed to do in 1914—make it unmistakably clear to Germany that particular acts of aggression would result in a general war; and
2. even if that warning did not restrain Hitler, "it was better that the nations under threat should stand and fight together than they should await German attack one by one."[114]

Buchanan adds that "Chamberlain thought that a war guarantee to Poland might block a Polish-German deal, force Hitler "to think about a two-front war" where it would have to engage Poland's fifty divisions, "and enable Britain to avoid an alliance with Stalin" as Churchill, Lloyd George, and others wanted.[115]

On March 31, Chamberlain advised Parliament of the war guarantee. The key portion of the notification consisted of these three sentences:

As the House is aware, certain consultations are now proceeding with other Governments. In order to make perfectly clear the position of His Majesty's Government in the meantime before those consultations are concluded, I now have to inform the House that during that period, *in the event of any action*

The guarantee was given even though Beck had worked hard to remain on the best possible terms with Hitler. Manchester, Alone p. 266. Remember that it was rumored just six months earlier that Poland would enter the war on the side of Germany.

which clearly threatened Polish independence, and which the
Polish Government accordingly considered it vital to resist with
their national forces, His Majesty's Government would feel
themselves bound at once to lend the Polish Government all
support in their power. They have given the Polish Government
an assurance to this effect.[116] [emphasis added]

The guarantee did not say that Britain would fight to keep Danzig from being reannexed by Germany but only that Britain would fight for Poland's independence. Unfortunately, this diplomatic subtlety was lost both on Hitler and the Poles. According to Buchanan, each "read Chamberlain's declaration as a solemn British commitment to stand by [Poland] and [its] resolve never to return Danzig."[117]

The guarantee turned British policy upside down.[118] Britain had seemingly committed itself to fight for Poland.[119] But as Roberts explains, "Britain and France could do nothing militarily to defend Poland's independence ... the promise was intended to serve as a trip wire for Hitler if he made further attempts to dominate Europe."[120]*

The guarantee to Poland was issued even though Poland had joined in the rape of Czechoslovakia[121] and the Beck regime was not one that the British trusted.[122] Moreover, Chamberlain, like every Prime Minister who had preceded him, did not believe that Britain had any vital interest in Eastern Europe.[123] Taylor points out that right after WWI, some Allied statesmen were so disinterested in Eastern Europe that they were willing to let the Kaiser keep his eastern conquests if he would restore Belgium and France to their pre-war state.[124] Buchanan reiterates the point: "British statesmen ... were prepared to offer the Kaiser's Germany the same dominance in Eastern Europe they would go to war to deny Hitler's Germany in 1939."[125]

In a speech to the House, Chamberlain explained how he saw the war guarantees functioning. He pointed out that the guarantees were "not the end of the measures that we had in mind," but were only a "first aid treatment given to avoid any further deterioration of the situation."[126] He said

---

As Taylor puts it, "The British had no practical means with which to fulfill their assurance. It was a declaration of words only." Taylor, Origins p. 212.

Such being the case, with Chamberlain's hope of working with Hitler quashed, and the Cabinet's becoming convinced that Hitler wanted war, the P.M. went beyond the war guarantee offered to Poland and on April 13 proffered war guarantees to Greece and Romania and made an alliance with Turkey. Churchill, The Gathering Storm p. 322. Churchill writes that the guarantees to Poland, Romania, and Greece had no "military value except within the framework of a general agreement with Russia." Ibid. p.325. (Hitler no doubt recognized this as well, and history would prove that position correct.)

that, besides "doing all that we can in this country to back up our [guarantees]" by increased defense spending and the reinstitution of a military draft,[127]* "[i]t still remains [for us] to strengthen [the guarantees] by more permanent arrangements and to try and get more support for them from any other quarters that are able and willing to give that support."[128] [emphasis added] He was ostensibly seeking to get countries like Russia, which were "much nearer to the possible seat of trouble," to also join in underwriting the independence of the counties to which the guarantees had been given.[129]**

Comments about the guarantee included:

- "Englishmen who possessed strategic vision were, with few exceptions, appalled."[130]

- The guarantee linked Britain's "destiny to that of a regime that was every bit as undemocratic and anti-Semitic as that of Germany."[131]

- It was "incomprehensible."[132]

- The French thought that the guarantee was "madness" and went along with it "only because they had no alternative."[133]

Over time, other assessments have gone even further. For example, Pat Buchanan asserts that "had Britain not issued the war guarantee to Poland and declared war over Poland, there might have been no war in Western Europe and no World War II. Hence, as the title of his book indicates, he views WWII as having been "unnecessary"[134]***

Just after the guarantee was announced, on April 3, 1939, the Germans issued a top-secret directive on "Case White." This plan for a limited war over Poland would use sudden heavy blows to gain rapid success. Preparations were to be made so the operation could be carried out at any time after September 1, 1939.[135] This timeline reflected the view that Germany did not have the strength earlier in 1939 to engage in a general war and, as Professor Taylor writes, "probably did not intend war at all."[136] Chamberlain also came to believe that Hitler wanted a short war in Poland followed by a settlement

---

*The draft was restarted in the UK in April 1939. Roberts p. 448

**This was consistent with what he had said to Parliament nearly a year earlier: "The value of any guarantee which we may give ... must in the last resort depend upon our ability to implement ... the guarantees upon which we have entered." HC Deb 24 March 1938 vol 333 cc1403. Chamberlain's ambivalence about aligning with the Soviets, coupled with Halifax's postwar revelations (discussed later in this chapter) that the guarantee was known by Poland to be hollow, suggest that the guarantee may have always been little more than an effort to save face—mere words, and an empty promise never to be acted on. But words that would come to spark WWII.

***Buchanan's thesis and the views of others asserting that WWII could have been averted are discussed later in this chapter.

with the Western Powers.[137] For once he was right: the army that Hitler had built lacked reserves and was designed for "quick strike[s]."[138]

Not all immediate reactions to the Polish guarantee were negative. While Manchester writes that Churchill's response was "ambivalent,"[139] given his belief that WWII need have never happened had no guarantee been issued, Buchanan disparages Churchill as one of the few in Britain who were not appalled by it.[140] In this regard, Buchanan quite correctly identifies Churchill as someone who, at least at first, thought that giving the guarantee to Poland was a splendid idea.[141] On April 3, 1939, just a few days after the news of the guarantee first became known, Churchill told the House of Commons that:

- "I am going to give my full support to the policy which the Prime Minister has now declared."

- "It is indeed wonderful that our country has been led by the Prime Minister to declare, in the clearest terms and with almost unanimity, that 'the defence of European freedom and the reign of law constitute causes in which this country will dare all and do all.'"[142]

Churchill knew that England lacked forces for a continental war[143] and thus could not make good on its own to honor its promise to protect Poland.[144] But, he saw the war guarantee as a first step toward creating "a Grand Alliance against aggression"; and he publicly called for "the maximum cooperation possible with the Soviet Union.[145] On April 3, 1939, Churchill told the House:

> The arrangement is strictly limited at present to three Powers, but others are being consulted, and others have dangers and also have resources, and undoubtedly we must measure each case, so far as we can, because our own resources are not unlimited. But *undoubtedly the process of building up mutual security on the basis of mutual exertion and effort, large, strong armed strength maintained in all quarters—that process must continue.* To stop here with a guarantee to Poland would be to halt in No-man's Land under fire of both trench lines and without the shelter of either. That is why it seems to me that the announcement of the Prime Minister on Friday, which is explained and emphasized by his statement to-day, constitutes a milestone in our history. We must go forward now until a conclusion is reached. *Having begun to create a Grand Alliance against aggression, we cannot afford to fail. We shall be in mortal danger if we fail.* We shall be marked down and isolated if we fail. It has become a matter of life or death. The policy now proclaimed must be carried to success—to lasting success—if war is to be averted, and if British safety is to be secured.[146] [emphasis added]

Among those in the gallery to hear Churchill's speech was the Soviet Ambassador to Britain, Ivan Maisky.[147] Just after the House adjourned that evening, Churchill met with Maisky in the lower smoking room. Also in attendance were former P.M. Lloyd George and MP Harold Nicolson. As Nicolson recorded in his diary that night, Churchill told Maisky:

> "Now look here, Mr. Ambassador, if we are to make a suc-
> cess of this new policy, we require the help of Russia.[*] Now
> I don't care for your system and I never have, but the Poles
> and the Romanians like it even less. Although they might be
> prepared at a pinch to let you in, they would certainly want
> some assurances that you would eventually get out. Can you
> give us such assurances?"[148]

Maisky demurred, and no acceptable assurance was ever provided.

Despite his coolness to Russian Commissar Litvinov's proposal for a Grand Alliance, Chamberlain appeared to share Churchill's view of the guarantee when he told the House that Britain would try to get more support for it from any quarters willing to give it.[149] It seemed both Chamberlain and Churchill had correctly concluded that the efficacy of the Polish war guarantee was inescapably tied to success in forming a coalition that would, of necessity, have to include Russia.** But Chamberlain "was deeply suspicious of Russia's intentions" and could never fully see them as a member of the Alliance.[150] In his book *Burying Caesar*, historian Graham Stewart writes, "Chamberlain profoundly mistrusted the Soviet Union and questioned the altruism of its interest in European affairs."[151] One need look no further that the Soviet's involvement in the British coal miner strike of 1926 (in Chapter 9) than to realize that there was a basis for Chamberlain's mistrust.***

Churchill's speech to the House on April 3, 1939 "approached a blanket endorsement" of the war guarantee.[152] Buchanan agrees but points out that "within a week Winston was raising doubts about the ... guarantee."[153] It

---

*In 1939, the Soviets had a huge army and a large air force, although its airplanes were dated.

**Robert Boothby, Churchill's Parliamentary Secretary when he was Chancellor of the Exchequer in the late 1920s, writes that, in retrospect, the unilateral guarantee to Poland without Russian support was "the most fatal step taken by the country." Boothby, Rebel p. 39.

***Stewart also says, without equivocation, that "Destroying the wealth and man-hood of the British Empire in order to condemn eastern Europe to a Communist police state rather that than a Fascist Police state was of marginal benefit." Stewart p. 357. Thought-provoking as it is, Stewart's pronouncement misses the mark. As explained later in this chapter, it was not at all clear in 1939 that Hitler did not pose an immense present threat to Western civilization.

is perhaps worth noting that shortly after the Polish guarantee was given, it also became evident that Chamberlain's "heart [was] not really in this new policy. ..." The P.M. appeared "unhappy in his new role of the protagonist of diluted collective security."[154] As Taylor explains, Chamberlain had "plunged into an alliance with a country far in Eastern Europe" containing a disputed region—the Polish Corridor—that years before had been described as something for which no British Government would ever risk the bones of a British Grenadier to guarantee.[155]

Taylor also writes that "the British were no sooner committed [to the guarantee] than they realized the flaws in what they had done: [it contained] no condition that the Poles would be reasonable over Danzig ... [and] no prospect that Poland would cooperate with Soviet Russia."[156] These are things which Lloyd George had advocated in his speech before the House about the guarantee.[157] According to Taylor, the British intended to "remedy these flaws" in the guarantee during Beck's visit to London in the first week of April, 1939.[158]* But Beck, who had stood up to Hitler, would not be moved by the far gentler efforts of Chamberlain and Halifax to soften his position that Poland would have nothing to do with the Soviet Union.[159]

On April 6, Britain and Poland signed an accord which converted Britain's unilateral guarantee into "a temporary pact of mutual assistance"—one that would not be made permanent until August 25.[160] In his speech to the Reichstag on April 28, Hitler said the Anglo-Polish agreement was "contrary to the terms of the German-Polish nonaggression pact [of 1934]" and the latter "having been unilaterally infringed by Poland ... [was] therefore voided."[161]

In *The Gathering Storm*, Churchill never explains his initial enthusiastic statements in the House about the guarantee. Unfortunately, he merely writes that "the guarantee to Poland was supported by the leaders of all parties and groups in the House. 'God helping, we can do no other,' was what I said."[162] He also does not reveal where and when he made this statement. It appears to exist only in Churchill's book. Interestingly, though, his words do bear a substantial similarity to the famous utterance of Martin Luther at the Diet of Worms in 1521: "Here I stand; I can do no other, God help me."

That said, Churchill is, however, on record in a May 9, 1939, speech before the Commons as criticizing the war guarantee, ostensibly because the Chamberlain Government had committed Britain to it without analyzing "the technical aspects to the defence of Poland. ..."[163] A more plausible explanation for his displeasure is that, as noted, though he saw the guarantee

---

Britain's intention to remedy flaws in the guarantee belie statements from Halifax and others that the guarantee was always intended only to be a hollow promise, a mere charade intended to fool Hitler into thinking that an invasion of Poland would be resisted by the British, French, and Polish.

as a first step toward forming a coalition able to deter Hitler, he quickly realized that Poland and Chamberlain's concerns about Russia might mean that there would never be a second step.

Manchester opines that the most generous explanation for the chasm between Churchill's original support and subsequent criticism of the guarantee was that he was initially excited to discover that Chamberlain "would fight for *something*."[164] [emphasis in original] A far less generous explanation is that Churchill's recanting in 1948 is just another example of his willingness to engage in revisionist thinking in order to achieve a particular end or cast himself in a more favorable light. Of course, yet a third possibility is that in 1948, Churchill, having lived seventy-three hard years—the five war years as P.M. being the hardest of his life—may simply not have remembered exactly why he did or said certain things nine years earlier.*

In any event, Buchanan's criticism of Churchill's immediate reaction to the war guarantee is fairly taken. Churchill never explained why his first reaction to the Polish war guarantee was so favorable and why he lost enthusiasm for the guarantee thereafter.**

In *The Gathering Storm*, Churchill did write: "… [H]ow could we protect Poland and make good our guarantee? … Here was a decision taken … at the worst possible moment and on the least satisfactory ground, which must surely lead to the slaughter of tens of millions of people."[165] Buchanan assails these postwar words from Churchill as wholly disingenuous.[166] He writes: "By March 1939, [Churchill] had been hounding Chamberlain for a year to draw a line in the sand and go to war if Hitler crossed it. Now Chamberlain had done what Churchill had demanded and threatened Germany with war over Poland. … Yet here is Churchill in 1948 asking in feigned innocence: "[H]ow could we protect Poland and make good our guarantee?"[167]

Churchill's initial enthusiasm for the Polish war guarantee most plausibly resulted from his correctly seeing it as a first step to creating something he had long wanted, a coalition of countries that would stand up against potential German aggression. His disappointment with the guarantee would be understandable when it became apparent that there would be no meaningful next step, but Britain was now stuck with the guarantee.

For example, when writing eight years after the fact about a meeting that took place in May 1940, just before he was selected to succeed Chamberlain, a meeting that he rightfully called the most important interview of his life, in Churchill's account of the interview, he was wrong about the time, date, and attendees. Roberts p. 504.

**Acclaimed military historian Sir Basil Lidell Hart called it "a hotheaded impulse instead of … the cool-headed judgment that was once characteristic of British statesmanship," Liddell Hart, History of The Second World War p. 15. But Churchill never confirmed or denied this.*

Buchanan characterizes the decisions to give the war guarantee and then to honor it as "victories for Churchill."[168] That characterization is inapt. Churchill shared Buchanan's view that the guarantee was itself useless without a willing coalition including Russia to carry out its terms.[169]

When viewed retrospectively, the guarantee is a testament of sorts (and an extremely costly one in terms of lives lost) to Chamberlain's inability or unwillingness to form a coalition that would have made the guarantee a meaningful deterrent to Hitler and thus avert a world war.* It is also a symbol of Chamberlain's refusal, after Czechoslovakia, to ever appear again willing to back away from a pledge made to a small country. Halifax writes that ignoring Polish misgivings would have ignored British public opinion and would have only been seen as justifiable if it were done to secure some important advantage.[170] He then says that, whether or not correct, the British staff felt that the Russian military was not strong and that bringing the Soviet Union into the coalition would therefore not have been all that helpful.[171] Halifax repeatedly made these points in real time. For instance, at the Foreign Policy Committee meeting on March 27, he noted that the fifty-division-strong Polish Army would be a better deterrent against Germany than the Red Army.[172] And at the Cabinet meeting on April 26, he said, "... the general conclusion reached was that the value of Russia as a potential ally was by no means as high as seems to be believed by prominent members of the Labour Party."[173] He also made note of the April 25 report of the Chiefs of Staff that disparaged the Red Army's state of readiness.[174]** But both at these meetings and in his writing, Halifax chose to ignore contrary conclusions in the Chiefs' report, such as the following: "Russian cooperation would be invaluable. ..." The Russian Navy would be an added deterrent to any Japanese military action against Australia, New Zealand, and Singapore; Russia had nine-thousand tanks; and Russian fighter planes might form a valuable supplement to the air defense of Poland.[175] Halifax was, however,

---

*Taylor views it in reverse fashion, stating, "It is pointless to speculate whether an Anglo-Soviet alliance would have prevented the second World War. But failure to achieve this alliance did much to cause it." Taylor, Origins p. 247. [emphasis added] Unsurprisingly, "Churchill regarded the failure to bring Russia into an anti-German alignment as Chamberlain's 'fundamental mistake.'" Harbutt, The Iron Curtain p. 33.

**The report had only been requested six days earlier, on April 19. CAB 24 163 285 (39), (CP (39) 95) p. 1. For what it's worth, Hitler expressed a similar feeling in meeting with the League of Nations' High Commissioner for Danzig on August 13, 1939, where he said, "The Russians ... have no offensive strength and will not pull the chestnuts out of the fire." Referring to Stalin's 1937 purge of thousands of Red Army officers, he added, "A country does not kill off its officers if it intends to fight a war." DBFP (Documents of British Foreign Policy), Series 3, Vol. I, No. 659 p. 692, "Minute by Makins" August 14, 1939.

quick to mention to his Cabinet colleagues the negative effects that close British relations with Russia would have on Poland, Romania, and other countries, including Germany.[176]

Some room for criticism of Churchill vis-a-vis the guarantee does, however, exist in the fact that he feared that despite it, HMG "would recoil from waging war upon Germany if she attacked Poland."[177] This seeming call by Churchill for Britain to fulfill the guarantee even though it couldn't do anything militarily to help Poland must, however, be viewed in the context of Churchill's view of the looming war. First, as Churchill points out, Britain had many opportunities to contain Hitler well short of a war. Churchill, like Buchanan and others, believed that WWII was avoidable. Second, as Churchill said in his speech before the House on September 3, 1939, he did not view a war with Hitler as a fight for Danzig or Poland or for geopolitical domination or material aggrandizement. Rather, he said, "We are fighting to save the whole world from the pestilence of the Nazi tyranny and in the defence of all that is most sacred to man."[178] If the West could no longer live with Hitler as he had evolved by 1939, then there was little alternative to war. Of course, such a clear, concise statement of purpose was never issued by the British Government; Chamberlain may not have been capable of having those thoughts.

Some assert that Foreign Minister Halifax, the decisive force behind the guarantee,[179] "had come to believe that if Hitler continued with his bloodless victories, Germany would dominate Europe economically and no longer be at the mercy of a British blockade."[180] He, like Churchill and Chamberlain, knew that "there was probably no way in which France and [Britain] could prevent Poland ... from being overrun,"[181] something the Poles came to realize. However, as noted, Halifax feared that "Poland might disclaim Danzig," and permit Hitler to "chalk ... up yet another bloodless coup."[182] According to Buchanan, rather than see this occur, London gave the unsuspecting Poles an illusory guarantee to aid in its defense just to forestall another easy Hitler victory. Britain, he asserts, preferred that the Poles fight what, because Britain never intended to come to Poland's defense, would be a war in which the Poles would simply be slaughtered.[183] Thus, Britain's admittedly unfulfillable guarantee to Poland is viewed by some, like Buchanan and Britain's Ambassador to Germany, Nevile Henderson, as having led the Poles "far up the garden path" toward a war it would have to fight alone, against a vastly superior opponent.[184]

Unsurprisingly Halifax challenges the Buchanan/Henderson view. Writing about the guarantee, Halifax states that "the Polish Government was [not] under any illusion as to the measure of concrete help they might expect from Great Britain in the event of Hitler's choosing war. For them, as for us, the guarantees were the best, and indeed the only chance of warning him off that decision."[185] (This is a position with which Taylor largely agrees. According to Taylor, these guarantees were issued not to prepare for war but as "warnings designed to avoid ... a war," while keeping "the door ... open for negotiations."[186*])

If, in the spring of 1939, the Polish Government had seen the guarantee as promising nothing, as Halifax asserts, it seemed to have changed its opinion when Poland was experiencing the Nazi Blitzkrieg in September. When its country was being invaded, the Polish Government pleaded for Britain to fulfill its defense obligations to Poland.[187] Reeling under the Luftwaffe's relentless bombing and strafing, the Polish Government wired Chamberlain on September 2 to say, "the engagement of German aircraft by allied forces is of the greatest urgency."[188**]

Moreover, the topic of the Allies conducting operations in support of Poland was discussed by the War Cabinet on September 4 where "It was generally agreed that a combined plan for an operation against Germany to relieve the pressure on Poland was a vital necessity."[189] (Churchill urged that "every means possible should be employed to relieve the pressure," including operations against the thinly manned Siegfried Line on Germany's border with France and Belgium.[190]) On the other hand, Sir Cyril Newall, the Chief of the Air Staff, argued against doing so. His reasoning: "It was important to conserve the resources of the Air Striking Force, so that it would be ready to meet any great emergency, such as heavy air attack on [the UK], or an attempted break-through in France."[191] The War Cabinet's general agreement on helping the Poles notwithstanding, the Allies undertook no operations against Germany to relieve the pressure on Poland.

Possible British duplicity to the Poles aside, the principal reason why the war guarantee could not be fulfilled, and why Poland was left to fight alone on September 1, was the absence of Russia in a coalition supporting the guarantee.*** Russia's exclusion primarily resulted from Poland's own unyielding refusal to enter any coalition that included the Soviet Union. As tragic as the death, devastation, and horror at the hands of the Nazis were,

---

*Of course, if Hitler, like the Poles, knew that the guarantee was illusory, it would have lost whatever coercive power it might otherwise have held. All Hitler had to do was call the bluff of the English and French, which is what he ultimately did.

**Had the Poles appreciated how little assistance Britain and France would provide, they likely would not have declined to supplement their air defenses with Russian fighters as they did five months earlier.

***At the time, Britain had the strongest navy in the world but a small professional army and a modest-sized air force. France, on the other hand, had a large, defensive-minded but unmotivated army and an obsolete air force. Both countries were located to the west of Germany, while Poland was some 1,000 miles away and on the other side of Germany. Simply put, neither were well positioned to effectively intervene directly in Poland's fight with Germany.

Poland (although perhaps between a rock and a hard place) was not led up the garden path by anyone or anything. The Poles wanted their cake and the ability to eat it, too. First, they demanded the exclusion of Russia from any coalition effectuating the guarantee, even though the Soviets were the key to the guarantee working. Then they wanted Britain and France, which lacked the military means, to supply forces to carry out the guarantee.*

The sad fact is that virtually from the outset Britain did little to make its war guarantee meaningful. Not only would Britain ultimately provide no military support when the Germans invaded Poland—no troops, and no help against the Luftwaffe—but in the five months between announcing the war guarantee and the invasion of Poland, Britain did not sell or otherwise provide Poland with a British tank, an airplane, or a single bullet.[192] While the Grand Alliance was being negotiated, London also did little to obtain adequate assurances from the Soviets that they would leave Poland once any military situation had eased. Furthermore, in response to the Poles' prewar request for a loan of £60 million, Britain offered credits, which had to be spent in Britain, that totaled only £8 million.[193] Halifax explained that Britain simply did not have the means to grant the Poles' loan request. He later added that "in the event of war, one of the strongest weapons in the hands of Great Britain must be that of economic staying power, which, accordingly it was essential not to impair."[194]** As Taylor writes, it "is unlikely that the Poles were mollified by Halifax's explanation. ..."[195] Hitler's overall take was a brutally simple one: "This suggests that England does not really want to support Poland."[196]

Efforts to Create a Grand Alliance

As noted, on March 18, Russia proposed a six-power conference to discuss forming an anti-Nazi coalition. Rather than simply rejecting the idea, a month later Britain grudgingly proposed that the Soviet Union just "affirm the independence of Poland and Romania."[197] Poland found even that mild suggestion objectionable. The French, in turn, proposed a mutual defense agreement among France, Britain, and Russia.[198]

---

*There is no question that Britain did not live up to the express language in its Agreement of Mutual Assistance with Poland signed on August 25, 1939. The Agreement read: "Should one of the Contracting Parties become engaged in hostilities with a European Power in consequence of aggression by the latter against that Contracting Party, the other Contracting Party will at once give the Contracting Party engaged in hostilities all the support and assistance in its power." British War Bluebook No. 19. [emphasis added]

**Chamberlain biographer Robert Self attributes much of Britain's resistance to providing Poland with financial assistance to Chamberlain, who believed "Britain had neither arms nor money to spare." Self p. 370.

Specific efforts to form a Grand Alliance started on April 18, when Soviet Foreign Commissar Maxim Litvinov surprised British Ambassador to Russia Sir William Seeds with a formal proposal to create a united front of mutual assistance among Britain, France, and the Soviet Union.[199]* Poland would be added to the group if possible.[200] Under the proposed agreement, each signatory, in case of aggression would (1) have to render military assistance to the other signatories and other Eastern European states; and (2) commit to maintaining a specified strength of its army, navy, and air force.[201] (The proposed agreement to take concerted action in the face of aggression dovetailed with the Covenant of the League of Nations, but would not fall under it. This stipulation was to avoid any small non-signatory country that was a member of the League from effectively vetoing the concerted action.) According to the proposed agreement, any Nazi offensive toward France, for example, would produce a Polish–Soviet counterattack from the east. Likewise, any German attack to the east would be met not just by forces from Poland but by the Red Army as well, while the French and British would have simultaneously launched an attack on Germany's Western border. Honoring the agreement, therefore, could lead to the encirclement of Germany that Hitler had feared was the unyielding goal of the Western democracies.[202] On its face, except for the possibility of the Nazis annexing the German-majority-free city of Danzig, had a Grand Alliance been formed, Hitler would have been hamstrung.

Shirer says that in 1939 Germany was not, and perhaps "would never be, strong enough to take on France, Britain, *and* Russia in addition to Poland."[203]** [emphasis in original] Manchester basically agrees, writing that, with such an alliance, the encirclement of Germany "would be real, and it would be awesome."[204]

On April 22, the French Cabinet, with due wariness of the Soviet Union and concern about Poland's unwillingness to accept Russia as an ally, nonetheless agreed to the Litvinov proposal.[205] As Taylor writes, the French, like Churchill, "believed that Hitler would be deterred only by an overwhelming show of force; and the Soviet alliance would help to provide it."[206]

The small states of Eastern Europe were justifiably terrified that the Red Army would march through their country to defend them from the Nazis but then never leave.[207] Poland, Romania, Finland, Estonia, Latvia, and Lithuania did not know what they dreaded more—"German aggression or Russian rescue."[208] As Halifax colorfully put it, "[a]n intelligent rabbit would hardly

---

*For an in-depth analysis of the dance among Britain, France, and Russia over this proposal, see Michael Jabara Carley's book, 1939: The Alliance That Never Was and the Coming of World War II.

**At the time, the Soviet Union was the second largest industrial nation in the world. Taylor, Origins p. 219.

be expected to welcome the protection of an animal 10 times its own size, whom it credited with the habits of a boa constrictor."[209] Churchill called the question facing the Poles a "hideous choice that paralyzed British and French policy,[210] although he raises the Pollyannaish notion that if Poland were in the Grand Alliance with Russia, the Poles could take comfort in the fact that it would not be easy "for one ally to enter the territory of another unless invited."[211]

The Soviets stated that they would agree to a pact of mutual assistance only if Poland, Finland, and the Baltic states were also included.[212] They also made it clear that in the event of war they would need to go through Poland to fight the Germans, because it was their intention to counterattack the Nazis with armored columns.[213] On April 26, Halifax told the Cabinet that British policy should stress that, if war broke out, Russia either be neutral or should come in on the Allies' side. He therefore suggested that Britain:

- not act in any way to preclude the chance of Russian help in war; but

- not jeopardize the common front with Poland; and

- not imperil the cause of peace.[214]

Of course, although achieving all these goals would be much easier said than done, the Cabinet expressed general approval of the policy Halifax had outlined.[215]

British historian A.J.P. Taylor believed that, in the spring of 1939, "[t]he need for a Soviet alliance was obvious to every competent British observer."[216] Yet at the Cabinet meeting held on May 3, Halifax told the Cabinet quite bluntly that, among other objections, "a tri-partite pact along the lines proposed would make war inevitable."[217] Though Halifax was not unmindful that rejection of Russia's proposal would also have consequences, he thought the impact would be minimal: "Russia would sulk'" and "there [is] a bare possibility that a refusal of Russia's offer might even throw her into Germany's arms."[218]* An indication of just how valuable an Allied agreement with Russia might be surfaced because of an Anglo-French staff conversation also held on May 3. At that session, British representatives asked the French staff what action France was prepared to take should Germany attack Poland. The response was that France would stand on the defensive behind the Maginot line and would aim to concentrate its forces to take the offensive against Italy. When asked what they would do if Italy remained neutral, the French said they had received no express instructions on how to respond in that situation. The British Chiefs of Staff were disturbed at the

---

*Clearly, this last assessment totally missed the mark: Russia and Germany would enter a mutual non-aggression pact in August 1939.

prospect that, if war were declared, the French would not attack Germany and thus would not immediately create the critical second front. The memo about the May 3 conversation concluded that "If the French were going to do nothing to draw off the weight of the German attack on Poland, the assistance of Russia would be of great value to the latter."[219] Of course, when the Germans attacked Poland four months later, as we will see, "nothing" was exactly what the French did.

In his semi-monthly column in *The Daily Telegraph,* Churchill, on May 4, continued to urge acceptance of the Russian proposal, saying:

> Above all, time must not be lost. Ten or twelve days have already passed since the Russian offer was made. ... Not only must the full cooperation of Russia be accepted but the three Baltic states, Lithuania, Latvia, and Estonia must also be brought into the association. ... *There is no means of maintaining an Eastern front against Nazi aggression without the active aid of Russia.* Russian interests are deeply concerned in preventing Herr Hitler's designs on Eastern Europe.[220] [emphasis added]

Chamberlain understood that without Russia, Poland, and the Polish guarantee were doomed. As he had said about Austria and believed to be true of Hitler's other land grabs: "Nothing short of an overwhelming display of force would have stopped it."[221] But once again, Chamberlain's words did not translate into any action. The result: WWII.* "... [H]istorians often argue that if the British had pursued ... negotiations [with the Russians] more vigorously during the summer of 1939" an alliance with the Soviet Union would have resulted which "would have been the best, even the only hope, of curbing Germany without a war. ..." As biographer Robert Self puts it, "... Chamberlain bears a substantial burden of personal responsibility for ensuring that [the process of forming a Grand Alliance] was consistently obstructed and prejudiced ..."[222]

Churchill recognized that Poland's reluctance to align with Russia was because the Russians had invaded and partitioned Poland many times in its history. Even so, he believed that the Government of Poland needed to realize that Russia "may be decisive in preventing war and will in any case be necessary for ultimate success. ..." Therefore, an association between Poland and Russia was "indispensable."[223] In hoping that Poland understood how deeply concerned the Russians were in seeing that Hitler's designs on Eastern

---

With no Grand Alliance in place, the constraint of a substantial two-front war didn't exist. Hitler was free to attack Poland without fear that the Russians would intervene on her behalf and certainly felt free after the conquest of Poland to attack Western Europe.

Europe did not come to pass,[224] Churchill conveniently glosses over the fact that the Soviets had designs on Poland and many of the same countries that Hitler was threatening.

Despite Churchill's call for alacrity in dealing with Russia's proposal, the process dragged out while half measures and compromises were being formulated in London. The Russian offer perturbed the Chamberlain Government.[225] Chamberlain himself wrote: "I confess I very much agree with [Polish Foreign Minister Beck] for I regard Russia as a very unreliable friend ... with an enormous irritative power on others."[226]

If the delay in responding to the proposal ultimately destroyed any chance to consummate the alliance,[227] then much of the blame must fall on Chamberlain.[228]* After a few weeks passed with no progress on the Russian proposal, Stalin considered Commissar Litvinov's mission a failure.[229] On May 3, Litvinov, "the archapostle of collective security, of strengthening the power of the League of Nations, of seeking Russian security against Nazi Germany by a military alliance with Great Britain and France," was abruptly dismissed.[230]

Litvinov's replacement, Vyacheslav Molotov, signaled a changing Soviet view. In the ensuing months Russia would ultimately abandon the idea of a security pact with the Allies and the possibility of organizing an Eastern front against Germany. Stalin would come to believe that Litvinov's approach could lead the Soviet Union into a war with Germany in which the Western democracies might very well find a way not to participate.[231] Halifax's efforts to convince the Russians otherwise failed.[232]

On May 8, the British quietly replied to the Litvinov proposal. They did so by counter proposing that if Britain and France, in order to fulfill a war guarantee given to Poland or Romania, requested Soviet assistance, Russia would respond quickly and in a "manner and on such terms as might be agreed."[233] But Molotov rejected the British proposal and insisted that the pact had to be one of mutual assistance—the Soviet Union did not want its military to be put on a call-when-needed basis. Britain then advised that it would restudy the Litvinov proposal,[234] although, as Taylor writes, London "nearly gave up in—despair—or on principle."[235]

Apart from the concerns that the nations of Central Europe had about Russia and apart too from Chamberlain's personal doubts about the Soviets, the fact is that the Grand Alliance may have never come into being for other, wholly unrelated reasons. At the time of the discussions in mid-April between British Ambassador to the Soviet Union Sir William Seeds and Commissar Litvinov, there were also discussions underway

---

*Self does not believe that the Grand Alliance would have "permanently deterred Hitler from aggression," but it would have been a constant reminder that he was facing a potential war on two fronts. Self p. 369.

between German Secretary of State Ernst von Weizsäecker and the Russian Ambassador to Berlin, Alexej Merekalov, about the normalization of relations between Russia and Germany.[236] As Shirer puts it, "Stalin had made his first serious move to play the other side of the street."[237] (Interestingly, at the Cabinet meeting held on May 10, Halifax said he found it difficult to attach much credence to reports of a move toward a secret agreement between Russia and Germany.[238]) Had the Western Powers been looking closely, they would have noticed that Hitler's speech to the Reichstag on April 28, 1939, did not include his usual diatribe against the Soviet Union as a festering den of Jewish Bolshevism.

Other reasons why the Grand Alliance may never have come about were the relatively meager military assistance that the Western Powers had to offer in any prospective war and the aforementioned Soviet suspicions that Britain and France might duck out of their obligations if Russia came under attack.[239] On the other hand, British statesmen feared that Russia might stay on the sidelines "while the other European powers tore each other to pieces."[240] As Anglo-Russian negotiations droned on into the summer of 1939, Halifax even suggested that if a formal agreement were reached with the Soviets, it might not be worth anything. Despite what a final agreement might say, Halifax felt that if a war broke out, the Soviets would probably take whatever course best suited them, agreement or no agreement.[241]

On May 19, when it seemed that Chamberlain and Halifax would turn down Litvinov's offer officially, Churchill gave a fiery speech in the House. He was critical of Chamberlain for his handling of Czechoslovakia, for giving war guarantees to Poland and Romania, and for failing to consummate the Grand Alliance:

> If His Majesty's Government, having neglected our defences for a long time, having thrown away Czechoslovakia with all that Czechoslovakia meant in military power, having committed us without examination of the technical aspects to the defence of Poland and Rumania, now reject and cast away the indispensable aid of Russia, and so lead us into the worst of all wars, they will have ill-deserved the confidence and, I will add, the generosity with which they have been treated by their fellow countrymen.[242]

In a speech to the House on October 5, 1938, Churchill had said, "I have always held the view that the maintenance of the peace depends on the actual accumulation of deterrents against the aggressor, coupled with a sincere effort to redress grievances."[243] By the mid-spring of 1939, however, Churchill had come to recognize that the Polish guarantee was not what he had initially hoped: the start of accumulating those crucial deterrents against aggression. and a first step "to creating a Grand Alliance against aggression."[244]

Any talk to the contrary, Soviet assistance would be "indispensable"[245] if there were to be any chance of saving Poland from a German invasion. Even if she were unreliable, Russia had to become a member of the Grand Alliance. The mere presence of Russia's huge army in the alliance would likely have some deterrent effect on Hitler. At the Cabinet meeting on May 10, even Halifax had good things to say about the Soviets: "[I]f Russia were an active and whole-hearted ally, she would be of great assistance, particularly in containing substantial enemy forces and supplying war material to other allies in Eastern Europe."[246]

At the May 19 session of the House, Lloyd George, Clement Attlee (leader of the opposition Labour Party), and Churchill each complained about the secrecy surrounding the negotiations with the Soviet Union over the Grand Alliance. They wanted Chamberlain to explain why the negotiations seemed stalled. Did His Majesty's Government have a basic mistrust of Soviet ideology?[247] In his rambling response, Chamberlain said that negotiating such an agreement was a matter of great difficulty and delicacy, requiring the Government to proceed cautiously. He denied that his Government was concerned with Russia's "internal political doctrine," adding that "[t]he suggestion that we despised the assistance of the Soviet Union is without foundation." He concluded by saying, "if we can revolve a method by which we can enlist the cooperation and assistance of the Soviet Union in building up [what he referred to as a "peace front against aggression" rather than as "an alliance"], we welcome it; we want it; we attach value to it."[248] Churchill characterizes Chamberlain's response to the Soviet's offer as "cool and ... disdainful."[249] The Prime Minister did, however, exhibit a bit of frustration when he discussed the Soviets' unwillingness to indicate their agreement to those matters on which agreement could be/had been reached and said, "I cannot help feeling that there is a sort of veil, a sort of wall, between the two Governments which is extremely difficult to penetrate."[250]

In his speech in reply to the P.M., Churchill cut to the quick, saying that for some weeks he had been unable to understand why making an agreement with Russia was so difficult to achieve given the Prime Minister's supposed wish for it to happen. Churchill then said he had learned nothing from the Prime Minister's speech that day "which [threw] the least light on [the question]."

Although Chamberlain's speech showed a willingness to reach an agreement with Russia, the Prime Minister was still not completely forthcoming regarding his true feelings about the Soviets. Like many Britons, he also could not get out of the habit of seeing Russia as a second-class power, one whose views really did not matter.[251]

Chamberlain had explained that the Government's view of strife on the continent following Hitler's takeover of Czechoslovakia had led to "an enormous departure from the policy" that was being pursued at the time of Munich.[252] Chamberlain was referring specifically to Britain's having given war guarantees. He reiterated that the guarantees were "not the end of the measures that we had in mind" but were only a "first aid treatment given to avoid any further deterioration of the situation."[253]

As noted, he made clear that, besides "doing all that we can in this country to back up our [guarantees]" by increased defense spending and the reinstitution of a military draft,[254] it "... *still remains to strengthen [the guarantees] by more permanent arrangements and to try and get more support for them from any other quarters that are able and willing to give that support.*"[255] [emphasis added] Chamberlain was seeking to get countries like Russia, which were "much nearer to the possible seat of trouble," to join in underwriting the independence of the countries to which the guarantees had been given. As he put it, "[w]e had to ... convince others, as well as ourselves, that we were in a position to make good on our guarantees."[256]

What Chamberlain was describing sounded a lot like the Grand Alliance. The Prime Minister continued:

> I agree that we in this country are not prepared to buy peace at the price of concessions which would only lead to further demands, but surely that does not mean that we would refuse to discuss any method by which we could satisfy reasonable aspirations on the part of other nations even if it meant some adjustment of the existing state of things. ... There are many concessions which might without too great difficulty be made if one could be quite certain that those concessions would be used only for the purposes for which they were given, and not used to bolster up some strategic aim.[257]

In sum, during the May 19 session, Chamberlain laid out his policy: to accumulate deterrents against any potential aggressor; to increase defense spending; to reinstitute the draft; to form something that looked a lot like the proposed Grand Alliance; and to couple all of this with a sincere effort to redress bona fide German grievances if possible. In the latter regard, Chamberlain's post-Czechoslovakia "double policy," of "rearmament and appeasement"[258] certainly "did not exclude the possibility of a peaceful settlement, which he would have preferred, but *required the dictators to make gestures of good faith which Chamberlain had no confidence they would do.*"[259] [emphasis added]

Surprisingly, Chamberlain's ideas were not far from what Churchill had been espousing for years. Throughout the 1930s there had been no bigger proponent of rearmament in Britain than Churchill. Moreover, as noted, back at the time of Munich, Churchill had explained that peace depends on the actual accumulation of deterrents against the aggressor, coupled with a sincere effort to redress grievances. Indeed, this had been part of Churchill's approach to avoiding war since at least 1934. On November 15 of that year, in a broadcast over the BBC, he said, "To remove the causes of war, we must go deeper than armaments. We must remove grievances and injustice."[260]

Given the above, in May 1939 it appeared that, after years of disagreement, Chamberlain might have finally climbed aboard Churchill's policy bandwagon. But the reality was quite different. As already noted, by May 19, Churchill felt that Chamberlain had done nothing to "accumulate any more deterrents"—Chamberlain had failed to nail down support for the guarantee from other quarters (i.e., Russia) and likely never would. As a result, the guarantee to Poland may not even have amounted to the "first aid treatment" that Chamberlain called it.

Criticism was heaped upon Chamberlain during the House session of May 19, and public support was growing for a coalition to stand up to Hitler. At a Foreign Policy Committee meeting of the same day, the P.M. learned that Halifax and Sir John Simon (the Chancellor of the Exchequer and a close friend of Chamberlain) were now of the view that an alliance was preferable to nothing at all.[261] Under the circumstances, Chamberlain was forced to change his position (at least outwardly) and support the alliance. As a result, the Chamberlain Government trudged onward with negotiations with Russia.*

In Berlin, at a May 23 meeting with his military chiefs to talk about the inevitability of a war, Hitler said that if the Soviet Union were to align itself with Britain and France, that development "would lead me to attack England and France with a few devastating blows."[262] Doing so, however, would have come with at least the following problems:

- Germany could not attack the West with its full force. Many divisions would have to remain on its eastern border to defend against a counterattack from Russia and Poland. Thus, defending Western Europe in the spring of 1939 would not have been as difficult for the Allies as it would turn out to be a year later.

---

*Relying on a "sixth sense," Hitler correctly surmised that the negotiations would fail. Taylor, Origins p. 247. Thus, when they did collapse in mid-August, Hitler "seemed to have won another victory." Ibid.

- Likewise, dealing a "devastating blow" to Britain could not have happened immediately. As Hitler himself noted in the May 23 meeting, because of the limited range of its aircraft, Germany would need to gain airfields in Holland, Belgium, and France before any effective air attack could be made against the United Kingdom.

At the meeting with his military chiefs, Hitler also said:

- The reacquisition of Danzig was really not a big deal. What he really wanted were conquests in the East to secure Lebensraum and a long-range, fully self-sufficient food supply for a growing German population.

- Accordingly, Poland, a key gateway to the Ukraine and the rest of eastern Europe, had to be attacked *"at the first suitable opportunity."* [emphasis in original]

- *The conflict with Poland would succeed only if the West stayed out of it.** [emphasis added]

- He did not believe that a peaceful settlement could be reached with Britain, because Britain viewed Germany's development as a hegemony which was not in Britain's best interest. Therefore, despite Hitler's purported desire for Anglo-German friendship and cooperation based on the similar racial origins of their two peoples, England would be Germany's arch enemy, and "[t]he aim will always be to force England to her knees."

- Defeating Britain would be in some respects easier now than it was in the past. That is, back when England could feed herself, merely defeating the Royal Navy was not sufficient. "To conquer England [back then] she had to be invaded." But that is no longer the case "... if the Fleet is annihilated instant capitulation results." "The moment England is cut off from her [imported] supplies she is forced to capitulate."[263]

In the spring and summer of 1939, Chamberlain believed that the German military would not let Hitler "take the fatal plunge into war over so minor a cause as Danzig."[264] The Prime Minister was wrong in two respects. First, reacquiring Danzig was not Hitler's primary goal—conquering Poland

---

**As explained later in this chapter: (1) Hitler would expend substantial effort trying to keep Britain out of the conflict with Poland by trying to entice London to split with the intransigent Poles and not honor its war guarantee; and (2) his threats against England closely followed the effusive language of friendship in his April 28 speech before the Reichstag. He was intent on having his war stay small.*

was. Second, unlike the situation with past planned invasions, the German generals did not oppose Hitler's wish to invade Poland. They did not fear that Germany was too weak to carry out the Chancellor's wishes.[265] On the contrary, they now felt Germany was strong enough for a war with Poland.

At a special session of the British Cabinet held on May 24, Halifax was surprisingly optimistic about the Grand Alliance. He told the ministers that "we should be prepared to enter into a direct mutual guaranty agreement with the Soviet Government," and he did not believe that the suggested arrangement would provoke Hitler into starting a war.[266] More specifically, he advised that (a) "the difference between the proposal which the Russian Government had made to us and the counter proposal which we have put forward ... was not substantial enough to prevent an arrangement with Russia being made use of for propaganda purposes"; (b) the governments of Poland and Romania "did not appear to see any great difficulty in the conclusion of an arrangement between this country and Russia"; and (c) "the position of the Baltic countries might be eased if [the arrangement included] some kind of guarantee of the neutrality of the Baltic states."[267]

Chamberlain, after laying out his personal misgivings as well as the similar misgivings of others (like the Catholic Church) to such an agreement, said he too saw no reason why the arrangement would not be accepted by the Russian Government and that he now favored the conclusion of an agreement with Russia along the lines of her proposals.[268] He did, however, want to make the agreement temporary by tying it to Article XVI of the Covenant of the League of Nations as it then existed.[269]*

The above notwithstanding, it is still doubtful that Chamberlain embraced the idea of an alliance. As Manchester says, by the end of May 1939 "virtually every powerful [politician] in Europe had endorsed the triple alliance except the British Prime Minister."[270] Taylor puts it more colorfully, writing: "With the narrow moralism of a reform drunkard, [the British Government which] had not scrupled to desert [Czechoslovakia] now felt themselves bound to observe [Poland's] every whim."[271] Britain gave Beck a veto over the proposed membership of any country in the Grand Alliance, and "he used it."[272] Shirer is kinder, saying only that by late May Chamberlain was "again mulling over" such an agreement.[273]

The Cabinet authorized Halifax to negotiate with the Russian Government on the mutual guarantee agreement. The arrangement would appear to implement Britain's obligation under Article XVI of the League's Covenant,[274] which required concerted military action by member countries to halt

---

His reasoning: that Article might have to be revised in the future. Tying the agreement to the present version of Article XVI would cause the arrangement to terminate without specifically mentioning a time limit. CAB 23/1 30 (39) p. 10 278.

aggression and preserve the peace. On May 24, Chamberlain updated the House, and on May 27 he directed Britain's Ambassador to the Soviet Union, Sir William Seeds, to resume negotiations with the Soviets.[275] The German Foreign Office took Chamberlain's actions seriously and believed that an Anglo-Russian agreement was imminent unless Germany did something significant to intervene.[276]

So began the real courtship of the Soviets, men whom in 1919 Churchill had called the "foul baboonery of Bolshevism"[277] and "[a] pestilence more destructive of life than the Black Death or the Spotted Typhus."[278] For the next three months Russia would hop from one leg to the other discussing arrangements with Berlin one day and with Paris and London the next.[279]

Churchill did not change his feelings about the Soviet system, though he became less vituperative. He believed that Communism was a lesser evil than Nazism, and his willingness to embrace the Russians as an ally was purely pragmatic: he believed that Britain's survival was at stake.[280]*

According to Lukacs,

> Churchill understood something that not many people under-
> stand even now. The greatest threat to Western civilization was
> not Communism. It was National Socialism. The greatest and
> most dynamic power in the world was not Soviet Russia. It was
> the Third Reich of Germany. The greatest revolutionary leader
> of the 20th Century was not Lenin or Stalin, it was Hitler.[281]

This premise surely is debatable. For example, Buchanan points out that "Hitler never remotely represented the strategic threat to the U.S. homeland that a nuclear-armed Russia did" years later.[282] Buchanan is likely correct, but a comparison between two eras in not a fair or meaningful one. Moreover, that was not the question facing Britain from 1939 to 1940. Then, the question was whether Hitler represented a grave threat to it and to Western civilization. Buchanan ignores the fact that by controlling all of Western Europe, Hitler had already impinged on Western civilization. He asserts that Hitler would have left the West alone had the West left him free to do what he wanted in the East, and that Hitler lacked the ships needed to invade England, let alone the number he would have needed to convey an army, its artillery, tanks, planes, guns, munitions equipment, fuel, and food across the Atlantic to attack America.[283]

As explored later in this book, when Hitler had just about completed his conquest of Western Europe a year later and threatened to invade Britain, Prime Minister Churchill's steadfast refusal to negotiate a peace treaty with Germany was anything but pragmatic. And he was criticized as being irrational or worse.

Even if Britain had let Hitler run free, how long would it have taken the Nazis to recover from a successful war against Russia, build up their war material sufficiently and then turn on Britain and France? Remember that in a war between Germany and Russia, the British "expected the Germans to win," and that, Germany, which at that point would occupy all of Europe east of the Rhine (and have achieved its goal of Lebensraum) would still "turn against the British and French empires."[284]

As part of his argument about why Germany would not turn against the Western democracies after defeating Russia, Buchanan points out that Nazism was an ideology handicapped by the narrowness of its appeal. Not even an ideology of white supremacy, Nazism focused single-mindedly on Aryan supremacy. Almost by definition, "nationalism, especially a virulent strain like Nazism, is difficult to export."[285] Thus, while Nazi ideology was sculpted for Germany, even Hitler did not believe in imposing Nazism on or exporting it to the West.[286] Moreover, unlike in the Soviet Union, there was no one in Hitler's inner circle who could be expected to sustain his ideology after he was gone. Nazism "could not long survive the death of its messiah."[287]

But in the spring of 1939, Hitler was far from dead; and the increasing panic he was provoking in Britain, Western Europe, and America was a rational response to the dictator's increasingly bellicose words and actions throughout the 1930s. Hitler had come for Austria, he had come for Czechoslovakia, and it looked like he would be coming for Poland soon. And, of course, his treatment of his Jewish citizens was appalling. Furthermore, Buchanan's "might have beens" result from seventy years of hindsight. In May 1939, Britain was looking down the barrel of a gun held by a madman whose supreme narcissism told him he was invincible. Buchanan raises some thought provoking points, but overlooks the death and destruction that, in 1939, the world feared Hitler could bring about until he was crushed. He also overlooks the fact that Hitler was mad—a supreme narcissist and didn't believe he could ever lose. Buchanan's point might be logical, but Hitler was not constrained by logic.

Furthermore, evidence indicates that Hitler had no intention of leaving Britain and the British Empire alone—even if they would have left him free to do what he wanted in the East. First, in early November 1940, Hitler met with Soviet Foreign Minister Molotov to talk about how the British Empire would be liquidated and distributed among Russia and the Axis members.[288] At the meeting, Hitler also told Molotov that as soon as the weather improved, Germany would strike "the final blow against England."[289] Second, and again contrary to any idea that Germany would seek to peacefully co-exist with Britain, Hitler made it clear (in Directive 21, issued on December 18, 1940) that after Germany crushed the Soviets in the upcoming land offensive, it would complete its war against England,[290] or, at the very least, "force England to make peace."[291] As Lukacs explains, to Hitler "[t]ime was of the essence."[292] Thus, if Hitler wanted peaceful coexistence with Britain, he could always have issued a unilateral ceasefire while exercising his "freedom in the east." Instead, as discussed in later chapters, Hitler always wanted Britain to become a vassal state (just as France would become).[293] As Lukacs points out, Hitler believed that this subjugation needed to be accomplished before Britain, either on her own or along with "the Fleets and air power of the United States," became strong enough to cause Germany serious trouble.[294] Hitler would not be happy until and unless he had completely neutralized both Britain and France.

———

When, on May 27, 1939, Soviet Foreign Minister Molotov received the British proposal, which included the reference to Article XVI of the League's Covenant, he rejected it because it would have allowed uninvolved members of the League to effectively delay any action planned by the signatories of the agreement.[295] Molotov also made it plain that if the Western democracies were serious about reaching an agreement with the Soviet Union, they had better get moving.[296]

In an article in the June 8 edition of *The Daily Telegraph*, Churchill continued to press for the creation of a Grand Alliance. Churchill wanted the Government to increase its efforts to secure an alliance with Russia. He even wrote that there was reason to doubt that the Chamberlain Government was negotiating in good faith.[297] It appeared that reaching an agreement was not imperative to Chamberlain. One suggestive example is how the Government staffed the team negotiating with the Russians. On June 12, Britain sent a special envoy to Moscow, Mr. William Strang. Strang was an able but low-level official in the Foreign Office. Churchill said it was "another mistake" to send such a subordinate official from the Foreign Office to negotiate with Molotov and Stalin. The Russians were, in fact, offended,[298] and saw the selection of Strang as a sign that Chamberlain really did not want to reach an agreement. This is exactly how the headline in *Pravda* read on June 29.[299] Others have also described Chamberlain's negotiation of the agreement as half-hearted.[300]

In June, news of the British-Russian negotiations started to appear in German newspapers. Halifax told the Cabinet that the Russians were denying the veracity of these reports and he said it would be desirable for the British Government to deny them as well.[301] However, the problem with the negotiations was not a lack of secrecy; rather, the negotiations had reached an impasse because of the continuing refusal of Poland, Romania, and the Baltic states to ally with the Soviets.

As reflected in the minutes of the Cabinet meeting held on June 21, 1939, Foreign Minister Molotov suggested that it might be best for just Britain, France, and the Soviet Union to enter into obligations limited to mutual assistance in the event of a direct attack by an aggressor on the territory of one or more of them[302]; the agreement would not include an attack against Poland.

By early July some members of the Cabinet believed that it would be better for Britain to reach an immediate agreement of some sort with Russia rather than allow the negotiations to drag on indefinitely.[303] The Cabinet was responding to more than just frustration—it didn't want other important matters to go ignored. For instance, the Cabinet asked about the situation relating to Danzig. Chamberlain responded that he had considered giving the outline of a possible solution of the Danzig problem to the Pope, but he had concluded that, in the present atmosphere, the time to settle the issue by negotiation was not opportune.[304]

As a result of the policy he had adopted after the takeover of Czechoslovakia, Chamberlain somehow "believed German assurances that they had no plans to attack Danzig."[305] In his view, the Germans now realized that, even though the return of Danzig to the Reich was justified,[306] they could not get "what they wanted without fighting for it," and any use of force to take Danzig would start a war in which Britain would be involved.[307] There were, however, several flaws in this thinking. First, as Chamberlain himself pointed out more than once, the war guarantee kicked in only if, in the opinion of the British, Poland's independence were threatened.[308] Moreover, as Halifax made quite clear, under the guarantee as given, Britain was not committed to fight for Danzig unless a threat to Polish independence arose from an attack on the city.[309] Furthermore, Hitler still felt that the Western Powers would not assist Poland in the event of war,[310] and Chamberlain knew that Hitler was correct. In a June 27 speech, Chamberlain told the audience that he wished he could convince Hitler that the British nation and the British Empire had reached the limit of their patience.[311] But speeches by Chamberlain (and Halifax) about Britain's putative support for Poland had no effect on Hitler. The German Chancellor had heard what he believed to be meaningless British babble like this before.[312] That the negotiations over the Grand Alliance had taken as long as they had gave Hitler another reason to feel that no one would come to the aid of Poland when it was attacked.[313]

At the July 12 Cabinet meeting, Halifax was asked to assess the Soviets' attitude toward the negotiations. The Foreign Secretary said he was unsure what interpretation should he placed upon the attitude of the Soviet Government. He added that the British Ambassador to Russia's news about Danzig was, however, rather upbeat. Chamberlain said he agreed with Halifax that the present international situation was best left to cool down, but that a reasonable solution of the Danzig problem should not be impossible once that occurred.[314]

At the next weekly Cabinet meeting, Halifax shared several interesting revelations. First, he said that even a total breakdown of the British-Russian negotiations would not distress him much, because, as he had said before, if war broke out the Soviets would likely be guided by their self-interest and not by any formal agreements they may have signed. Second, when asked about the prospects of reaching agreement based on a simple tripartite pact, Halifax said that he was rather disposed to think that the Soviets were not very keen on concluding an agreement of any kind.[315] In reply to other questions, Halifax said that there was some evidence that Germany was trying to make British negotiations with the Soviets as difficult as possible. Britain had also learned that discussions of some kind were proceeding between the German Government and the Soviet Government.[316] He added that though it was impossible to assess the real value of those discussions, it seemed likely that they related only to industrial matters.[317] (He was wrong, of course.) Chamberlain remarked that he could not bring himself to believe that a real alliance between Russia and Germany was possible.[318]*

Because negotiations on the political side of the Grand Alliance were not progressing, on July 24 Molotov suggested that Britain, France, and Russia concentrate on the military side—spelling out their obligations in the event of a German attack.[319] France accepted eagerly; the British agreed as well but were much more reserved.[320] The military talks were to take place in Moscow as soon as arrangements could be made. As August began, Britain and France remained hopeful that the continuing negotiations with the Soviets would deter Hitler. But Danzig had not gone away as a problem. In fact, local Nazis had just increased their provocations.[321] At the August 2 Cabinet meeting, Halifax said it was important to be clear that, when discussing the Danzig position, Britain was not in fact committed to fighting for Danzig. Danzig itself should not be seen as providing a *casus belli*. Still, he stressed that if a threat to Polish independence arose from issues about Danzig, then Britain would clearly become involved.[322] Interestingly, while Danzig would, in less than a month, be the ostensible spark that ignited WWII, on August 2 Halifax stated that the situation in the Far East was causing him more anxiety than any other problem in the world.

Parliament adjourned on August 4, 1939, and, unless there was an emergency, it was not scheduled to meet again for two months.[323] The length of the recess was settled only after an unpleasant debate in the Commons in which Churchill and others "backed a Labour amendment calling for Parliament to

---

He was wrong here, too. The two nations concluded a mutual nonaggression pact on August 23, 1939.

reassemble within three weeks on the implicit ground that the Prime Minister could not be trusted."[324] Labour and Churchill feared that with the House scattered, Chamberlain might try to pull off "another Munich."[325]

————

From August 6 to 8, a conference arranged by a mysterious Mr. "D" had taken place at "D's" house in Germany.* The attendees were Goering and seven British businessmen. At the meeting, the Britons sought to persuade Goering that Britain would in fact stand by its guarantee to Poland and that Germany needed to understand that.[326] "D" believed the message got through to Goering.[327] Taylor writes that these intermediaries had, however, overstated the inclination of each side to compromise.[328]

Since his trip to Germany in the fall of 1937, Halifax had been of the view that "once Hitler showed his readiness for peace," there would be "little problem in meeting" Germany's desires.[329] Doing so would be easy with regard to Danzig, because Germany's claim to the city had considerable merit.

The Anglo-French-Soviet military talks opened in Moscow on August 12. The British and French were apparently in no hurry to get there: rather than taking a plane they took a "slow boat" to Leningrad (an old cargo-passenger ship, *The City of Exeter*, which had a top speed of 13 knots[330]). The trip to Moscow took six days.[331] In Taylor's view, the British Government were not interested in military cooperation with Soviet Russia. They just wanted to "chock a Red bogey on the wall, in the hope that this would keep Hitler quiet."[332] The Russians were represented by officers of the highest rank: Marshal Kliment Voroshilov, Commissar for Defense, and the commanders in chief for both the Navy and the Air Force.[333] The French delegation was led by one of the most brilliant officers in France, General of the Army André Doumenc; he had been the deputy to General Maxime Weygand, former Chief of Staff of the French Army.[334] Having learned nothing from the debacle of sending a low-level official to the negotiations a month earlier, Britain repeated the error by failing to send a high-ranking military delegation to the new session. Rather, in an act that seemed designed to "deliberately offend the Kremlin,"[335] Chamberlain had sent an "obscure and

————

*D's name was Birger Dahlerus, a Swedish businessman and amateur undercover diplomat. His identity was revealed after the war through a book he'd written about his adventures. His contacts with Goering were close, alarmingly close: he was the guardian to Goering's stepson from his first marriage.

As discussed later in this Chapter, during the week before WWII, "D" would play a role in a bizarre Anglo-German scheme that on its face appeared to be an effort to avoid war but was just part of a game by Hitler to entice Britain not to go to war in support of Poland.

undistinguished British party" led by the poorly credentialed and practically retired Admiral Sir Reginald A.R. Plunkett-Ernle-Erle-Drax. Worse yet, in violation of the rules of diplomatic courtesy, Sir Reginald "wasn't even given written authority to negotiate" for Britain.[336] The Soviets were not amused.

On August 14, the Soviets again asked if Britain could obtain permission from Poland and Romania for Russian forces to operate in those countries in case of war. The Soviets said it would be useless to continue the negotiations if such permission were not forthcoming.[337] The British ambassador in Warsaw and his military attaché again approached the Poles. The Poles repeated their objection and reiterated their view that the Russians' objective was to find an excuse to occupy Polish territory permanently.[338] (As it turned out, that view was spot on.) Polish Foreign Minister Beck also continued to assert that an agreement allowing Russia to bring troops through Poland to fight the Nazis would push Germany to declare war.[339] He felt that Poland had a far better chance of negotiating an agreement with Hitler if it remained independent.[340]

Unable to give the Russians an answer on the Polish question, on August 17, the British and French moved to adjourn the negotiations. The group agreed to reassemble on August 21,[341] but the talks never resumed.[342]

As noted earlier, Churchill had, without success, already implored the Poles to recognize that an association between Poland and Russia was "indispensable" and thus to accept Russia as an ally. Chamberlain believed similarly: "[I] would like to have taken a much stronger line with ... [Poland as well as Romania, Finland, and the Baltic states] all through, but I could not have carried my colleagues with me," nor would he have carried the French.[343] He also, however, was "insistent on not accepting any formula 'which would drive the Baltic states and Finland into Germany's arms. ...'"[344] The fact of the matter is that because Chamberlain would not even attempt to force these countries to accept an alliance with Russia, no matter how much he wished them to do so, there simply was no "stronger line" that he would have taken with them. As Feiling writes, "Without Russia, Poland was, in the military sense, doomed, but Chamberlain could not speak out."[345] Unlike Britain, France was so bent on getting Russia on the side of the Western Powers that it didn't care about any consequences to Poland, and so advised the Soviets. Britain, of course, did not agree.[346]

Both Manchester and Taylor raise the interesting point that the British, who had had little problem deserting Czechoslovakia, nonetheless felt themselves "bound to observe [Polish Foreign Minister] Beck's every whim."[347] Put differently, why didn't Britain and France tell Poland that if she refused to enter into an alliance that included the Soviets then they would not be bound by the guarantee? It would have been possible to insist on such a condition because the temporary Anglo-Polish mutual security pact signed back in April was not formalized until August 25.[348] As noted, the idea of cancelling the guarantee if the Poles continued to object to Russian participation in the alliance, had been suggested by former Prime Minister Lloyd George in his speech before the House on the Polish guarantee back on April 3, 1939,[349] and after that also by French Foreign Minister Bonnet.[350] According to Manchester, "Chamberlain frostily replied that he declined to be party to such a 'maneuver.'"[351]*

Could the answer to why London would not back away, even a little, from the Polish guarantee be found in the words of Lord Halifax when he addressed the House of Lords on April 19? At that time, he declared that the Government's policy was "founded on the principle that the rights of smaller States shall not be set aside by the stronger ..."[352] and that entering into an alliance with Russia over the protests from the smaller states would cause a loss of "the moral effect" of the alliance and might even be to Germany's benefit.[353] The full answer is likely more complex. Britain's steadfast adherence to a war guarantee that Poland rendered impotent, was likely also the product of not wanting to revive the guilt and shame of having abandoned the Czechs. Taylor, on the other hand, reveals a belief that the British Government were "striving to preserve the peace of Europe, *not* to win a war," and their policy was governed "by morality, not merely strategical calculations."[354] [emphasis added] But where was that morality when they were pressuring Czechoslovakia to accept terms so clearly not in the Czechs' best interest?

Just as the Anglo-French-Soviet negotiations were collapsing, the German Ambassador to the Soviet Union delivered a message from Foreign Minister Ribbentrop to Commissar Molotov about forming a Soviet-German non-aggression pact.[355] After some back and forth, the next day, August 16, Germany presented Molotov with a first set of details and also proposed a joint guarantee of the Baltic states.[356] Molotov responded that improvement in the Soviet-German relationship, to the degree Ribbentrop was proposing, would take a long time to accomplish.[357]

The argument has been made that Britain should have made an alliance with Russia before making one with Poland and that Chamberlain's distrust of Russia, which led him to choose a Polish alliance over one with Russia, was "the sheerest kind of folly." Lukacs, The Last European War p. 40. Lukacs writes that this "sounds convincing in retrospect; yet there is less substance in it than appears at first sight. It was Poland, not Russia that was threatened by Hitler; and it was Poland not Russia that was willing to conclude an immediate alliance with Britain." Ibid. He goes on to express his belief that Stalin was not ready to conclude an alliance with Britain in 1939, noting that, only four-and-a-half months after a war guarantee was given to Poland, Stalin entered into a nonaggression pact with Hitler. Lukacs, however, ignores the fact that it was Russia that proposed the Grand Alliance, and that had Chamberlain promptly agreed to it, the Alliance would likely have come into being.

Hearing this, the Germans, in sharp contrast to the lackadaisical manner in which the British had negotiated, put on a full-court press to move the nonaggression pact along. Hitler sent a personal message to Stalin on Friday, August 20, agreeing to all Soviet demands and asking that Foreign Minister Ribbentrop be received by the Soviets immediately.[358] A commercial treaty between Russia and Germany was also settled that day, and it was agreed that Ribbentrop would come to Moscow on the following Monday to work out the nonaggression pact.[359] Clearly, Germany was in an extreme hurry to take advantage of the lack of progress in Anglo-French-Soviet discussions. As Manchester aptly puts it, Hitler "had to outbid the Allies ... quickly, and price was no object."[360] Manchester also points out that Britain and France played a sorry role by not acting quickly or decisively. He adds—had, for example, the former British Foreign Secretary, Anthony Eden, been sent to Moscow instead of a group of low-level officials, "Hitler might never have had his chance."[361]

On August 16, Chamberlain went fishing in Scotland. Based on rumors of German-Soviet negotiations, he was recalled in four days,[362] and an emergency meeting of the Cabinet was called for August 22. Halifax reported on what had happened to British negotiations with the Soviets. He said that the military conversations with the Soviet Union had been proceeding amicably until the Soviets began insisting that their demand that Poland and Romania allow Russian forces to operate through them reach a resolution. With no agreement on the issue, the talks had been suspended.

Halifax next spoke about the nonaggression pact, which rumor had it was being negotiated between Russia and Germany. He said that if Russia would pledge to remain neutral in a war in which Germany was involved, then no useful purpose would be served by continuing the British-Russian military conversations.[363] Trying to minimize the import of any German-Soviet accord, Halifax added that such a pact might not, in and of itself, be "of very great importance," even though "the moral effect of such an agreement would be very great."[364]

Later in the Cabinet meeting, Halifax reported that the situation in Danzig had improved somewhat.[365] On August 13, Carl Burckhardt, the League of Nations' High Commissioner for Danzig, had spoken at length with Hitler. Hitler talked little about Danzig itself but said a good deal about the unreasonableness of the Poles and how necessary it was that Germany have grain and timber, which, not incidentally, were products that could flow more easily into Germany if the port of Danzig were returned to the Reich. Hitler also told Burckhardt that he did not want war, but if war came, the responsibility would not be his.[366] He wanted the Poles to agree to the terms he had demanded back in March and said that if those terms were not forthcoming he would "strike like lightning with the full force of a mechanized army, of which the Poles have no conception."[367] Burckhardt was unaware that Hitler had scheduled the invasion of Poland for September 1. It was crucial to German military plans that there be little or no delay, otherwise its forces risked getting caught up in the October rains that would make the Polish dirt roads impassable.[368]

Hitler did not expect the Poles to yield to German demands on their own, but he did expect that the Western Powers would pressure Poland into submission just as they had done with Czechoslovakia a year earlier.[369] He always thought what happened with Czechoslovakia was an instructive lesson about the Allies. Despite a strong Czech army and a formal Franco-Czech alliance, France reneged on its obligations, which forced the Czechs to capitulate. Hitler expected something similar to occur with Poland;[370] but the Poles had also learned from the Czechoslovakia situation: appeasing Hitler when he was growling at your border did not ensure that he would leave your country alone. As a result, the Poles made no concessions and would remain immovable.[371]

In his talk with Burckhardt, Hitler then said that:

> I have no desire to dominate. Above all I want nothing from the West. ... But *I must have a free hand in the East.* Once more it is a question of grain and timber (which I can only find outside of Europe) in sufficient quantity ... *I want to live in peace with England and to conclude a definitive pact; to guarantee all the English possessions in the world and to collaborate.*"[372]* [emphasis added.]

In the weeks before Hitler's meeting with Burckhardt, the German press had become more heated about German minorities supposedly being mis-treated in Poland.[373] This was an old tune with a new verse. As the Cabinet meeting of August 22 progressed, Halifax revealed that, a few days earlier, he had sent a telegram to the British Ambassador in Warsaw urging him to appeal to Polish Foreign Minister Beck to approach Germany to discuss the minority "problem."[374] Halifax said the Poles had taken this suggestion quite well, but it did not appear to have produced any results.[375] As Taylor writes, the Poles did "not respond to Nazi provocations; but equally they ignored the pleas for concession which came to them from the West."[376]

Halifax then said that there was a good deal of information from many sources indicating that Germany planned to attack Poland between August 25 and 28.[377] German troops had been moving toward the Polish border since the 19th[378]; and SS men had been smuggled into Danzig to seize the city

---

*Hitler would present this proposition directly to Chamberlain on August 25.

just after the start of German operations.[379] If Germany intended to attack, Halifax continued, it was probably based on the dual assumption that they would win a speedy victory and that other powers would not interfere.[380] Efforts to disabuse Hitler of the latter assumption remained unsuccessful.

Chamberlain added that Germany also now believed it was impossible for Great Britain to save Poland, and that Britain should therefore make no attempt to fulfill its obligations to the Poles.[381] He said that Hitler continued to feel that the British war guarantee "was a bluff."[382] To Chamberlain it was unthinkable that Britain would not carry out its obligations.[383] The same man who refused to stand by Czechoslovakia at Munich now bristled at the notion that the Allies, in the hopes of still negotiating an agreement with Hitler, might sit on their hands and leave Poland to fight Germany alone.[384] In fact, Chamberlain believed an announcement should be made that evening to reaffirm that, whatever arrangement was made between Germany and Russia, Britain's obligations to Poland and its determination to support Poland would remain unbowed.[385] Upon hearing this, the Cabinet broke out in applause.[386] Of course, Chamberlain's idea of carrying out Britain's obligation to Poland did not mean coming to her defense against attack with Britain's entire military arsenal.*

The Cabinet discussed and approved Chamberlain's dispatching a personal letter to Hitler. The gist of the letter, but not the text, would also be communicated to Mussolini and to the French and Polish governments. Chamberlain's letter started off following his long-standing policy of avoiding provocation even when the most moderate measure of deterrence was being raised,[387] and even though rearmament was proceeding apace. Chamberlain began the letter by assuaging any concern Hitler might have about Britain's mobilization. He wrote that these preparations had become necessary because of military movements reported to be underway in Germany. Then, in an uncharacteristically strong tone, he wrote that the announcement of the Molotov-Ribbentrop agreement apparently "... is [being] taken in ...

Noted historian Richard Overy posits several reasons, besides the deep sense of guilt Chamberlain felt over what he had done to Czechoslovakia, why the Prime Minister was willing to stand up to Hitler in 1939 when he was not willing to do so in 1938. Two among these reasons were: (1) rearmament in Britain, particularly with regard to aircraft, had strengthened the military; and (2) British public opinion had shifted from an attitude of avoiding war at almost any cost to accepting the real possibility that a war could not be avoided. Overy, 1939 p. 27–28. Perhaps a third "reason" is the very cynical notion that because Chamberlain never planned to do anything for Poland, he really wasn't standing up to Hitler—even if he declared war on Germany.

Berlin to indicate that intervention by Great Britain on behalf of Poland is no longer a contingency that [Germany] need[s] to be reckoned with." Chamberlain then wrote:

> No greater mistake could be made. *Whatever may prove to be the nature of the German-Soviet agreement, it cannot alter Great Britain's obligation to Poland.* ...
>
> If the need should arise, [we] are resolved and prepared to employ without delay all the forces at [our] command and it is impossible to foresee the end of hostilities once engaged. *It would be a dangerous delusion to think that, if war once starts, it will come to an early end,* even if a success on any one of the several fronts on which it will be engaged should have been secured. ...
>
> I trust that your Excellency will weigh with the utmost deliberation the considerations which I have put before you."[388] [emphasis added]

On August 23, Ambassador Henderson flew to Berchtesgaden to hand the letter to Hitler,[389] and to tell him face to face that Germany's pact with Moscow would not dissuade Britain from fulfilling her obligations to Poland.[390] Henderson met with Hitler twice that day. During the second meeting, Hitler scared Henderson when he told him that "he was '50 years old' ... and 'preferred war now' to when he 'would be 55 or 60.'"[391]

After the session with Henderson, Hitler prepared a reply to Chamberlain in which he said that:

- Germany was prepared to settle the questions of Danzig and the Corridor based on a proposal of truly unparalleled magnanimity.

- But the allegations broadcast by England about a German mobilization against Poland, as well as the so-called Guarantee, had destroyed Poland's inclination to negotiate an acceptable agreement.

- The war guarantee had also spurred the Poles to unleash a wave of appalling terrorism against the one and a half million German inhabitants living in Poland.

- The Polish Government had been informed that Germany would not tolerate the persecutions of the German minority or the extermination of the Free City of Danzig by economic measures.

- Britain's statement that it is obliged to render assistance to Poland in any case of intervention on the part of Germany would not affect the determination of the Reich to safeguard its interests.

- He shared Chamberlain's belief that should Britain actually render such assistance, the resulting war would be long.*

- The question of the treatment of European problems on a peaceful basis is not a decision which rests on Germany but primarily on those who, since the crime committed by the Versailles dictates, have stubbornly opposed any peaceful revision.[392]

In *The Gathering Storm,* Churchill writes that Hitler's assertion that the war guarantee had emboldened the Poles to commit atrocities against German inhabitants in Poland was a piece of "lying effrontery."[393]** The duplicity in Hitler's "concern" for the million and a half Germans living in Poland would be exposed in mid-September when, as agreed, the Soviets invaded Poland from the East and grabbed nearly half the country, including thousands of Germans. They would now, with Hitler's blessing, fall under the rule of Stalin, one of the most ruthless despots who ever lived.***

The Molotov-Ribbentrop Pact and Other Games Hitler Played in a Failed Attempt to Get a Limited War over Poland

On August 23, 1939, Hitler and Stalin signed the nonaggression pact, known as the Molotov-Ribbentrop Pact. The pact provided a written mutual guarantee of peace toward each other, and a commitment that neither country would ally itself with, or aid an enemy of, the other party.[394]**** The news of the pact was a severe disappointment to the French, who had always been optimistic about achieving an alliance with the Soviets.[395] The pact also

---

It is largely for this reason that Hitler worked tirelessly to entice the British to disavow its obligation to assist Poland and not get into a war. As previously noted, in a speech to his Commanders in Chief on August 22, 1939, Hitler revealed why a limited war was desired. He admitted that he had created a Greater Germany by bluffing about a military that had been "doubtful" and untested, but now it was necessary to test the military. DGFP, Series D, Vol. II. No. 192 p. 202 "Memorandum of the Speech by Hitler to Commanders in Chief" August 22, 1939. And a limited war was just the way to do so.

**Berlin newspapers were also guilty of "lying effrontery" by telling the German people that Poland was threatening an armed invasion of the Reich. Shirer pp. 563–64.*

***The new border between Germany and Russia was confirmed by the supplementary protocol of the German–Soviet Frontier Treaty. The portions of Poland annexed by the Soviet Union after the invasion remained in the USSR at the end of World War II. They currently comprise parts of Ukraine and Belarus.*

****The pact was terminated on June 22, 1941, when Germany launched Operation Barbarossa and invaded the Soviet Union.*

included a secret protocol that defined the borders of Soviet and German spheres of influence; it split Poland between them and assigned Lithuania, Latvia, Estonia, and Finland to the Soviets.[396] This protocol was just a rumor until it was made public at the Nuremberg trials in 1946.

While the pact provided for the obliteration of Poland, both Hitler and Stalin believed it would prevent a wide-scale war.[397]

The pact did not discuss the German goal of obtaining Lebensraum (areas to colonize) in Eastern Europe. In fact, German newspapers at the time indicated that the country did not covet any Russian territory, including the Ukraine.[398]

Interestingly, the pact caused Hitler to lose favor among some Conservatives in the British Parliament who had seen him as an immovable opponent of Communism. The staunchly anti-Fascist Labourites were, in turn, critical of Stalin for entering into such an agreement.[399] Although the British Government tried to downplay the significance of the pact, Manchester reveals that the impact it had on the average Englishman was roughly comparable to how Pearl Harbor affected Americans.[400]

Polish Foreign Minister Beck thought that the pact was good news for Poland—he believed the Soviets were "withdrawing from Europe."[401] He couldn't have been more wrong; of course, he did not know about the pact's secret protocols, Stalin's plan to invade eastern Poland, or the effect that the pact would have on French politics. Churchill, who was in Paris when the pact was announced, didn't know about them either. In fact, upon returning to England the next day, Churchill believed that the French were not concerned by the pact and were still prepared to support Poland.[402] Not so. French politics would prevent making a strike against the Ruhr,[403] Germany's main industrial area. (Manchester calls this planned attack "Poland's only hope."[404]) Because of the pact, the French became concerned that Germany could now shift units from positions in the East, where they had been needed to protect against a Russian attack, to its undermanned western border. As a result, no significant French attack along that frontier would ever occur.[405] In fact, when Germany invaded, Poland received no military support of any consequence from either France or Britain.

On the day that the news of the German-Soviet agreement became public, Hitler certainly believed that Britain and France would not join in the fight.[406] The British Government did take precautionary measures, such as assembling key members of the coast and antiaircraft defenses, bringing the regional organizations to a war footing, and calling up reservists.[407] But these were just preparations to do nothing.

On the evening of August 25, Lord Halifax received a telegram from the British Ambassador to Italy. The Ambassador reported on a conversation he'd had with Italy's Foreign Minister, Count Ciano, who, in turn, relayed the views of his father-in-law, Benito Mussolini. Ciano explained that Mussolini wanted peace and was willing to cooperate with His Majesty's Government in a search for a way to maintain it. The Italian dictator felt the present situation was very grave; and if peace were to be preserved there was not a moment to lose. By the end of the week there would likely be war.

As noted, Mussolini believed that Poland should return Danzig to the Reich and asked London to make that suggestion to the Poles. He said that if London could not do so, there would be little he could do to intervene with Hitler to any good purpose.[408] Mussolini did promise that once peace negotiations got started, he would use all his influence in Berlin to obtain a fair and honorable settlement. He believed that once negotiations were underway they could be expanded into a more generalized conference aimed at establishing a stable and durable peace. This was the outcome that the Paris Peace Conference of 1919, which produced the Versailles Treaty, had failed to achieve.[409]

On August 23, the Poles ordered a general mobilization of army units in the Corridor, Upper Silesia, and western Poland.[410] In France, Premier Daladier asked the heads of his armed forces to report on their readiness for war. He received favorable reports from the Army and Navy; the Air Force replied that while it still lagged behind Germany, its readiness had improved enough to allow it to participate.[411]

August 24, 1939 (Eight Days Before the Invasion of Poland)

A Cabinet meeting took place at 12:45 PM, before sessions of both Houses of Parliament, which Chamberlain had recalled, were to convene. Lord Halifax opened by reminding his colleagues of Hitler's reply to Chamberlain's August 22 letter,[412*] then he said he had recently made several suggestions to Polish Foreign Minister Beck advising that Poland should attempt to deal with minority questions. He thought it would be undesirable to press those suggestions again now, because doing so might cause the Poles to lose confidence in Britain.[413]

Chamberlain then told the Cabinet he planned to inform the House that the Government intended to reserve final judgment on the Russo-German Pact until it had had a chance to consult with the French. He added it appeared to be contrary to good faith that, while Russia was negotiating with Britain, it had also been negotiating with Germany behind Britain's back.[414] Chamberlain also revealed that his recent letter to Hitler, which certainly was not intended for publication, had already been circulated in garbled versions throughout Germany. As such, he said the German people

---

In that reply, among other things, Hitler asserted that the war guarantee had caused the Poles to increase its mistreatment of German inhabitants living in Poland.

were being led to believe that the letter contained only threats, with no constructive proposals.[415] The moral of the story was that Hitler could not be trusted, period.

Halifax said that after speaking to the Prime Minister, he wired instructions to Britain's Ambassador to Italy to inform Mussolini that two conditions were crucial in order for London to suggest that the Polish Government negotiate with Germany about returning Danzig to the Reich. The conditions: (1) the Polish Government must be assured that Poland's independence and vital economic rights in Danzig would be secured; and (2) any arrangement agreed to would be internationally guaranteed. Halifax said he had also asked the Ambassador to express appreciation for Mussolini's helpful attitude, and to say that if the Italian leader could get Hitler to agree to these conditions, there might be a possible basis for an approach to Poland. Halifax believed that if the conditions were not agreed to, it would be useless to approach Poland.[416] Was there to be another Munich-type conference between Britain and Germany to avoid war?

In his speech to the House on that afternoon, Chamberlain reminded the MPs that when Parliament was last in session on July 31 he had said there were no pending international matters that could not be solved by peaceful discussion. In the ensuing four weeks, not only had nothing been formally discussed about Danzig and the Corridor, but the international situation revolving around the issue had steadily deteriorated. Britain now found itself confronted with the imminent peril of war. The P.M. then spoke of the new German-Russian pact as a "bombshell" devastating the ongoing discussions between Britain and the Russians. Distressed by Soviet duplicity, Chamberlain added that because the text of the pact had only just been published that morning, it would be premature to discuss the meaning and consequences of the agreement until after there had been a chance to consult with the French.

Chamberlain spoke of the guarantee given to Poland and reminded the House that it "was given before any agreement with Russia was talked of, and that it was not in any way made dependent upon any such agreement being reached."[417] He said therefore there would be no justification for Britain to go back on its obligation to Poland. In fact, upon the P.M.'s hearing of the Russo-German pact his "first act was to issue a statement that our obligations to Poland and to other countries remained unaffected."[418] Lastly, Chamberlain rejected Hitler's reiterated plea for a free hand in the East (in exchange for leaving Britain and France alone). He said:

> The German Chancellor's reply includes what amounts to a restatement of the German thesis that Eastern Europe is a sphere in which Germany ought to have a free hand. If we—this is the thesis—or any country having less direct interest choose to

interfere, the blame for the ensuing conflict will be ours. This thesis entirely misapprehends the British position. We do not seek to claim a special position for ourselves in Eastern Europe. We do not think of asking Germany to sacrifice her national interests, but we cannot agree that national interests can only be secured by the shedding of blood or the destruction of the independence of other States.[419]

Hitler had hoped that Chamberlain would announce that, with Russia out of the picture, Britain was not going to honor its war guarantee to Poland. When Chamberlain did not oblige, Hitler decided to find other means to split off the British from the Poles before the German invasion began.[420] Hitler would try hard to find Britain an honorable, unassailable excuse to walk away from its guarantee to Poland.[421] If he succeeded, he believed Britain would stay out of the Polish war.

August 24 was also the start of a week-long secret Anglo-German dialogue in which the previously mentioned Swedish businessman known as Mr. "D" shuttled back and forth between London and Berlin in an ostensible effort to avoid war. On that day, Goering asked "D," who was in Stockholm, to come and meet with him in Berlin.[422] The public mood in Germany was calm and somewhat upbeat. William Shirer wrote in his diary that night: "... the Germans are still confident Hitler will pull it off again without war."[423]

August 25 (Seven Days Before the Invasion of Poland)

The informal Polish war guarantee had languished for nearly five months, when, on August 25, just two days after the Molotov-Ribbentrop Pact had been announced, the British Government signed a formal Agreement of Mutual Assistance with Poland. The Agreement stipulated that should one party be the subject of aggression, the other would *"at once* give the ... Party engaged in hostilities *all the support and assistance in its power."*[424] [emphasis added] Richard Overy explains that, although Halifax was aware of the implications, the signing of the agreement just two days after the Molotov-Ribbentrop Pact was simply fortuitous, having resulted from months of discussion and weeks of drafting.[425] Nevertheless, there were those in London who feared announcing the treaty would hinder any negotiations with Hitler.[426]

In what Manchester calls "an act of prodigious diplomatic incompetence," the agreement included a secret clause in which Britain guaranteed to defend the status quo in Danzig, and not just guarantee Polish independence.[427] The Foreign Office even sent the Germans a note warning them not to take any action relative to Danzig.[428] There were other problems surrounding the agreement: some members of the French Government were looking for ways for the Western Powers to get out of their obligation to Poland under the war guarantee;[429] the Poles were still refusing to give an inch on any issue; and there were those in London who still believed Hitler could be bought off.[430]

On the morning of the August 25, Hitler notified Mussolini that the invasion of Poland was imminent and asked British Ambassador Henderson to meet with him at 12:30 that afternoon. Because the German invasion of Poland was scheduled to take place the next morning, the unstated purpose of the meeting with Henderson, like many Anglo-German interactions in the last week of August 1939, was not to settle the Danzig question but to put enough on the table to get Britain to back away from its guarantee if the Poles ultimately refused to budge from their current position.[431]* Britain's walking away from Poland would get Hitler the limited war he wanted. He would also achieve something else he desired: to make Poland "appear culpable."[432]

Hitler had been continuing to turn things over in his mind about Britain, and he decided to make a move. At the meeting with Henderson, Hitler orally communicated a message for the Ambassador to deliver to Chamberlain immediately. The message was that an understanding between Germany and England might yet be possible. On top of reiterating things he'd said earlier, Hitler made these other points:

1. The Prime Minister's speech to the House would not induce any change in the German attitude. At the most, the result of this speech could be a bloody and incalculable war between Germany and England.

2. Unlike the last great war, Germany's agreement with Russia would obviate the need for a two-front war.

3. Hitler's colonial demands, which were limited, could be negotiated by peaceful methods.

---

*In his autobiography, Halifax reveals that in the last weeks and days before the invasion of Poland, his principal fear was "that Hitler would produce specious terms which would appear superficially very reasonable but which the Poles would feel bound to reject." Halifax pp. 215–16. This would have been a situation in which Britain could have only lost. On the one hand, if Britain had supported Poland's rejection, she would have been criticized for having "precipitated war by giving the Poles a blank cheque." Ibid. p. 216. On the other, if Britain had pressured the Poles to accept Hitler's terms it would have been doing what it had done to Czechoslovakia and might well have entered the war without "complete national or Commonwealth unity" or worldwide public support. Ibid.

4. Hitler was ready to conclude an agreement that would guarantee the existence of the British Empire in all circumstances as far as Germany is concerned. (Details would be presented once the matters of Danzig and the Corridor were resolved.)

5. He would then also be ready to accept a reasonable limitation of armaments.

6. If London would consider these ideas, both Germany and British Empire stood to be blessed.

7. If London rejected these ideas, there will be war.*

In his message to Chamberlain, Hitler also said that as long as "the last fragment of the accursed Versailles [Treaty]" remained, "his dream of an Anglo-German friendship could not come true."[433] He begged the British to let him have what he wanted with regard to Poland, and in exchange he promised that he would make the British Empire an historic offer.[434] Hitler called this his "last offer."[435]

Henderson's meeting with Hitler lasted about an hour. At the end, the German leader said he had an airplane ready to fly Henderson to London so he could communicate the offer directly to Chamberlain. Instead, Henderson went to back to the embassy, translated his notes, and sent them on to London. He flew out the next day.

Just after the meeting with Henderson, Hitler gave the order for the invasion of Poland to begin the following morning.[436] Hitler then received the news that Britain and Poland had signed the Anglo-Polish Treaty of Mutual Assistance.[437] Later that day, Hitler received the awaited reply from Mussolini to Hitler's letter of the 25th. It explained that, given the present state of Italy's war preparations, Italy would be unable to take the initiative in any military operations in a war that did not remain localized. Mussolini reminded Hitler that, in earlier meetings, war was anticipated for 1942, by which time Italy would be ready on land, sea, and in the air to participate fully.[438] After the Italian Ambassador to Germany delivered the letter from Mussolini, he was coldly dismissed by Hitler, who was not pleased.[439]

It has been said that the Anglo-Polish treaty, coupled with Mussolini's backing away from the Pact of Steel** troubled Hitler enough to cause

---

Hitler verbally communicated his message to Henderson, who then translated and sent it on to Chamberlain. The British War Bluebook No. 68, telegram from Henderson to Chamberlain, August 25, 1939.

**The Pact of Steel was the agreement to a military and political alliance signed by Germany and Italy on May 22, 1939.*

him to call off the August 26 attack on Poland.[440] At least one other factor also contributed to the postponement. In a diary entry a few weeks later, Chamberlain wrote that communications with Hitler and Goering looked rather promising at one time. "[Goering] gave the impression that it was possible to persuade Hitler to accept a peaceful and reasonable solution of the Polish question in order to get an Anglo-German agreement, which he continually declared to be his greatest ambition." Chamberlain felt that "Hitler apparently got carried away by the prospect of a short war in Poland and then a settlement [with the Western Powers]."[441]

The main reason Hitler delayed the attack was simply to give himself a little more time to obtain the limited war that he so desired. His plan: Germany would make another superficially reasonable proposal about Danzig and the Corridor; the intransigent Poles would reject it; and Britain would thus be enticed to back out of its war guarantee.[442] Such a proposal, Hitler reasoned, would be tempting to Chamberlain, who would at long last receive a seemingly good faith gesture from Hitler that could lead to peace.[443] Moreover, if, as was likely, the Poles remained intransigent and rejected the proposal, then more dominoes would fall: (a) Britain and France would be totally justified in declaring that they would not honor their war guarantees; (b) they thus would not be involved in any fighting; and (c) the Poles would suffer a fate that they had brought upon themselves. That fate—having to face Germany alone—would be similar to the one that Britain and France had said a year earlier would befall Czechoslovakia if it remained stubborn and did not accept the German-dictated terms of the Munich Agreement.

This explanation of Hitler's delay is supported by these observations:

- When Hitler pulled the plug on the August 26th invasion of Poland and Goering asked him whether the attack was cancelled or merely postponed. Hitler said, "No, I will have to see whether we can eliminate England's intervention."[444]

- As Overy opines, "... [N]o sense can be made of [Hitler's] desperate efforts to break the Polish-Western alliance [in the last week of August 1939] unless his preferred solution was the local war he planned for."[445] And,

- According to Churchill, "[Hitler's] real object was not ... to reach an agreement with Poland, but to give His Majesty's Government every opportunity to escape from their guarantee."[446]

At 6:30 PM, shortly after the invasion had been called off, during the scheduled meeting between Goering and Mr. "D", the Field Marshal spelled out what he had in mind: an "understanding" with Britain.* To obtain this "understanding," "D" would shuttle almost constantly between Berlin (where he consulted with Hitler and Goering) and London (meeting with Chamberlain and Halifax) in one of Goering's own planes.[447] More than likely, "D" was an unwitting participant in one facet of Hitler's plan to present Britain with a seemingly bona fide reason to renounce its war guarantee.

August 26 (Six Days Before the Invasion of Poland)

In a plane furnished by the Germans,[448] Ambassador Henderson flew to London from Berlin to discuss his meeting with Hitler and to transmit the message that Hitler had dictated. What was also remarkable about the flight is that it took place even though all German airports had been shut down and German airspace had been restricted.[449] Henderson arrived at Downing Street about 1:00 PM but his oral report added little to what he had already sent the evening before.[450]

The August 26 Cabinet meeting commenced at 6:30 PM. Chamberlain told the members of the Cabinet that, after discussions with Henderson, the conclusion had been reached that it would be undesirable for a reply to be sent to Hitler that evening, because "this might create the impression that we could be rushed. It would be right that we should take time to consider our response."[451]

Before leaving Berlin that morning, Ambassador Henderson had sent a note to Foreign Minister Ribbentrop to the effect that because the British Government might take some time discussing Hitler's message, it was by no means certain he could return to Berlin with an answer that night. After the Cabinet meeting, Henderson sent another message to Ribbentrop saying he hoped to return to Berlin some time the following afternoon.[452]

Halifax remarked that the technique imbedded in Hitler's words was not unfamiliar. The message Hitler transmitted through Henderson was intended to divide Britain from the French and the Poles, and to try to make Britain realize that, given the new reality created by the Russo-German pact, Poland's friends could not help it and should therefore make no attempt to do so.[453] Halifax also thought that two significant but conflicting desires were expressed in the letter. The first was Hitler's keen desire to settle the Polish question. The second, a desire to avoid a quarrel with the British Empire. Hitler had referred more than once to the situation as it would exist when the Polish question was settled, but he was very careful not to say what kind of settlement he had in mind. Halifax thought there was some discrepancy between the written message and what Hitler had said in his conversation

---

Goering was anxious to avoid a general war and was sympathetic to the idea of reaching an agreement with Britain. Overy, 1939 p. 53.

with Henderson. This disparity might be evidence that Hitler had not quite made up his mind what form of settlement he was prepared to accept. The ultimate question, of course, was whether Hitler wanted a settlement with Poland on his own terms more than he wanted to avoid war involving Great Britain.[454]

Halifax said he could not answer that question with any degree of certainty.[455] He then informed the Cabinet ministers that:

- During the day, fairly precise information from sources alleged to be reliable had reached him to the effect that Germany intended to march into Poland that night (August 26) or, according to later reports, the next morning (August 27).

- He thought that for the German Government to arrange for the British Ambassador to fly home from Berlin with a special message, and to do so *in a German airplane,* was not consistent with an intention to start a war within hours.[456] (Of course, Halifax had no way of knowing that by this time Hitler had decided to reschedule the invasion of Poland for September 1.[457*])

- Viewed in the most sinister light, the object of the message transmitted through Ambassador Henderson might have been just for Hitler to get another peace offer on record. But there was no point in making such an offer if London was not afforded time for a reply. It might well be that the objective in causing these reports to be circulated was to influence the substance of Britain's reply, and to dispose Britain to concede to what Hitler wanted.[458]

In Shirer's view, Hitler "would have his war with Poland."[459] And the German Chancellor recognized that there was a good chance that doing so would result in a war with the West, and so continued trying to keep the British out.[460]

These and related thoughts were also spinning in Churchill's head. As he writes in *The Gathering Storm*:

> In these final weeks [before the war] my fear was that His Majesty's Government, in spite of our guarantee, would recoil from waging war upon Germany if she attacked Poland. There is no doubt that at this time Mr. Chamberlain had resolved to take the plunge, bitter though it was to him. But I did not know him so well as I did a year later. I feared that Hitler might try a

---

Likewise, Halifax did not know if Hitler had rescheduled the invasion just to throw the British off the scent.

bluff about some novel agency or secret weapon which would baffle or puzzle the overburdened Cabinet.[461]

The headlines of *The Daily Telegraph* on August 26 read: "Fresh Talks in Berlin" and "German Demands Modified?"[462] Serious people were still hopeful that a peaceful solution might yet be possible.[463]

Halifax had more to reveal at the Cabinet meeting:

> He received a message the previous night from the so-called Mr. "D," an outsider in touch with Field Marshal Goering. The message called Britain's signing of the formal Anglo-Polish Treaty a dreadful action likely to precipitate a crisis.[464] But other information Halifax had received indicated that signing the Polish Treaty had been seen in Berlin as demonstrating Britain's determination to stand with Poland.[465]

> "D" was returning to Germany that day (August 26). Halifax, after consultation with Chamberlain,[466] gave "D" a suitable message to present to Goering.[467] London wanted Goering to know that Britain hoped to see a settlement reached and would give Hitler's offer careful consideration. "D" said he found the response gratifying.[468]

Halifax added that

> ... he had given a good deal of thought about a reply to Hitler. It would be necessary, on the one hand, to acknowledge the spirit in which the appeal was made and to say that Britain, too, was anxious to see a peaceful settlement. But on the other hand, Britain had obligations to Poland it was bound to honor. London's reply should point out that Hitler had not explained how he envisioned a settlement of the Polish question looking; but London hoped it would be reasonable. If the [proposed] solution safeguarded Poland's vital interests and was subject to international guarantees, then the British Government could recommend it to Poland. London might also be prepared to help with the minority question, but addressing other questions would have to wait until more precise information was forthcoming.[469]

Asked by a member of the Cabinet whether he thought the message from Hitler represented an attempt by him to find a way out of the crisis with Poland, Ambassador Henderson said he thought the message had been sent partly for propaganda reasons. The message might enable Hitler to say he had made a magnanimous offer to Britain, which had been rejected.[470] Chamberlain added that he assumed the points made in the message had been in Hitler's mind all along. He believed that Hitler's underlying idea was that if Britain would leave Germany alone in its sphere of interest (namely eastern Europe), then Hitler would leave us alone.[471] But Hitler well knew that such a scenario was unlikely to happen. As he had written in *Mein Kampf*, for centuries, the first rule of British foreign policy had been to prevent any single nation from dominating the Continent.[472]

Asked about allegations regarding the persecution of the German minority in Poland, Ambassador Henderson thought that 80 percent of the reports being published in Germany were exaggerated, but that the remaining 20 percent likely were true. The reports of minority troubles could for a time be kept out of the papers, but he doubted whether, without some drastic change, the question could ever be permanently settled to Germany's satisfaction.[473]

As to the military advice he believed the German General Staff had given Hitler, Henderson said that Hitler's military advisers would no doubt favor war with Poland alone. If, however, Germany was facing an imminent general war, he thought the advice of the German generals would be divided. He agreed with the supposition that the German pact with Russia was due, at least in part, to the influence of the Army, whose historical policy had always favored an alliance between Germany and Russia. Henderson shared his belief that the military probably enjoyed more influence with Hitler than any other group of German opinion leaders.

When asked at what point Hitler would decide to fight if his demands were not met, Ambassador Henderson replied he had thought all along that Hitler had intended to start a war of nerves, to see how much he could get without fighting. At the same time, he said, if we got into a position in which neither side could give way, and dictators were notorious for never backing down, then war would result.[474]

Lastly, Henderson confirmed that both Hitler and Ribbentrop had told him Germany had no interest in making Great Britain break her word to Poland. This revelation was viewed with great favor by the Cabinet.[475] Ambassador Henderson thought that the real value of Britain's guarantee to Poland was to enable Poland to come to a negotiated settlement with Germany.[476]

On August 26, French Premier Daladier sent Hitler a letter stating that France intended to be true to the promise it had made to Poland. In his reply, Hitler said he had no territorial demands against France and saw "no reason for [France] to go to war."[477] (At the Cabinet meeting held on August 28, Chamberlain told the Cabinet members he had been unaware of the letter Premier Daladier had sent to Hitler, or any reply from Hitler.[478])

German General Franz Halder's diary entry for August 28 outlined Hitler's plan to drive a wedge between Britain and Poland, by demanding Danzig, a corridor through Polish territory, and a plebiscite. Hitler thought that while the Poles would probably not agree to these demands, Britain might.[479]

August 27 (Five Days Before the Invasion of Poland)

At the 3:00 PM Cabinet meeting held on Sunday, August 27, the discussion centered on drafting a reply to Hitler. The Cabinet decided to hold off settling on the terms of the response until more comments from within the Cabinet and the Foreign Office could be solicited. Chancellor of the Exchequer Sir John Simon would review the input that evening, and Ambassador Henderson was scheduled to return to Berlin the next day with Britain's reply.[480]

The Mysterious Mr. "D"

At the Cabinet session, Halifax reminded his colleagues that at the Cabinet meeting held the previous day he had informed them of a message he'd received from a so-called Mr. "D" on Friday night (August 25–26) to discuss the Anglo-Polish treaty.[481] Purportedly, the Germans had been shocked by the signing.[482] "D" flew to London early on Saturday morning and informed Halifax that Goering believed the only way to conceivably avoid a war now would be "a conference between representatives of Britain and Germany."[483] After consulting with Chamberlain, "D" was tasked with carrying an important message back to Goering, informing the Field Marshal that Britain would give Hitler's offer careful consideration.

Despite restrictions on German airspace, "D" flew back to Berlin on August 26 and immediately met with Goering. The two men then rushed to the Reich Chancery, arriving around midnight. Though Hitler had gone to sleep, Goering had him awakened.[484]

The meeting with Hitler, which took place in the early hours of August 27, initially consisted of diatribes by Hitler on various subjects, including the strength of the German military and the nature of the British people. When those had run their course, Hitler discussed the proposal he had made through Henderson on August 25 and said his offer would be adjusted somewhat. Hitler was unwilling once again to put the proposal in writing, so "D" had to memorize the points before flying back to London to urge the British to accept the adjusted offer.[485]

Halifax told the Cabinet he then received a telephone call from Germany from Mr. "D," who spoke briefly of his meeting with Hitler and, more importantly, said he was returning to England immediately and was bringing with him a message from Hitler and Goering.[486] After his arrival back in Britain, "D" met with Chamberlain and Halifax.[487] He said he had been left with the impression that Hitler was making a serious peace proposal regarding Danzig and the Corridor[488]—in exchange for ceding Danzig and the Corridor to Germany, Poland would retain a free harbor at Danzig, could keep the port of Gdynia (located 15 miles north of Danzig), and would be granted a corridor to it.[489] Hitler also said he was very eager to meet with British representatives to discuss terms with them.[490]

It was clear that Hitler had sent Britain two proposals. One, sent through Ambassador Henderson, offered to guarantee the entire British Empire once the problem of Danzig was resolved; while the other, through "D," suggested giving something of value to the Poles in exchange for Danzig.

Chamberlain said he told Mr. "D" that if Germany was demanding the Poles give up Danzig and the Corridor, then he could see no prospect of a settlement. The Poles would fight rather than surrender the Corridor. But Chamberlain thought that the most the Poles would concede Danzig, subject to the retention of special Polish rights, and extraterritorial roads for Germany across the Corridor; although such a settlement would require an international guarantee.[491]

"D" responded, "The only way to get Herr Hitler to understand things was that they should be discussed with him by somebody who was accustomed to talking to him, such as Field Marshal Goering."[492] It was agreed therefore that "D" should confine his communications with Goering and Hitler to a few simple points, such as:

- Britain would not deal with Anglo-German relations until the Polish question had been settled;

- it was essential that direct negotiations take place between Germany and Poland;

- any agreement should be guaranteed by the Great Powers; and

- while Britain desired a settlement with Germany, it certainly would not fail to carry out its obligations to Poland.[493]

Thus it was arranged that several rough notes making these essential points, would be prepared by Sir Alexander Cadogan (the permanent Under-Secretary of State for Foreign Affairs). After approval by the Prime Minister and Halifax, the notes would be handed to "D," who would return to Germany with them that night.[494] "D" was to get back to Halifax with Hitler's reaction so that Britain's official response to the German Chancellor's proposal could be adjusted as necessary.[495]

Chamberlain and Halifax said it would be made clear to Mr. "D" that he was not carrying Britain's official response to Hitler's message. The full British reply would be carried to Berlin the next day by Ambassador Henderson.[496] At that point, "D" flew back to Germany.

Halifax then sat down with the other twenty members of Chamberlain's Cabinet to share some details about Mr. "D," whose very existence was unknown to the Poles. Although Halifax appreciated the risk of arousing suspicion if the Polish Government got wind of secret negotiations carried out through an unknown intermediary, he still thought it essential to maintain absolute secrecy. As for "D" himself, he was a Swede who had lived in England for ten years but had previously lived in Germany. He had a close personal friendship with Field Marshal Goering, who often stayed with him in Sweden.*

When "D" met with Goering on August 27 immediately after returning to Germany, the Field Marshal was not particularly impressed with the British reply.[497] Goering called Hitler, who was more favorably inclined, although he said that Britain's official response must reflect that Britain had tried to persuade the Poles to negotiate with Germany.[498] Hitler wanted to strengthen the case that Polish refusal to meet with Germany left him no choice but to invade Poland in response to its provocative actions against Germany and its harassment of Germans living in Poland.

August 28 (Four Days Before the Invasion of Poland)

At the noon Cabinet meeting, Halifax read out a telegram from Berlin setting out the three points "D" had transmitted to Field Marshal Goering. Goering had spoken to Hitler, and Hitler then called "D."[499]

Copies of a revised draft response to Hitler were then handed out to the Cabinet, and discussion got underway. The Prime Minister said the response as then constituted was not only dignified and firm but also quite provocative. He believed it would meet the situation admirably, especially when supplemented by Ambassador Henderson's explanatory remarks.[500] The Cabinet agreed to send the response to the German Chancellor, once clarifying amendments being drafted by the P.M. and the Secretary of State for Foreign Affairs were incorporated. A final check would then be made to ensure that the response reflected any last-minute developments that might arise before Ambassador Henderson left for Berlin that afternoon.[501]

After the Cabinet meeting concluded, Halifax received another telegram from "D" through the British embassy in Berlin. It stressed the need for immediate Polish-German negotiations. After reading the telegram, and without

---

Some weeks earlier, "D" had seen Goering and had persuaded him that it was a great misfortune that the Field Marshal did not understand the British point of view. As a result, it was arranged that six British men of good standing should meet Goering and talk to him frankly. As previously noted, this had been done on the 7th of August. Annex to CAB 23 /1 44 (39) p.3 400 August 27, 1939.

consulting the Cabinet, Halifax immediately wired the British Ambassador in Warsaw, Sir Howard Kennard, and directed him to deliver an urgent message to Foreign Minister Beck that London "earnestly hopes that ... the Polish Government ... is ready to enter at once into direct discussion with Germany."[502] This, Overy writes, "has to be understood ... as a sign that the British Government believed Hitler's willingness to talk might be a measure of his willingness to climb down from war (a view which could scarcely be supported by anything in Hitler's earlier record except Munich)."[503]

Two hours later, Ambassador Kennard replied that Poland had agreed to enter direct discussions with Germany. As Overy puts it, the Polish Government felt it possible that Germany was sincerely prepared to discuss the issues, signaling an important change in atmosphere.[504] Manchester, on the other hand, asserts that the Poles agreed to direct discussions "under pressure and against their better judgment."[505] In either event, Poland's surprising willingness to negotiate was immediately incorporated into Chamberlain's response to Hitler.[506]

Because the British response needed to be translated into German, and because of the time it took Henderson to fly back to Berlin, the Ambassador did not present Chamberlain's response to Hitler until 10:30 PM.[507] The letter civilly postponed any talk about ameliorating a long-term Anglo-German relationship. It went on to say that no offer made to Britain, however historic in scope, would cause it to "acquiesce in a settlement which put in jeopardy the independence of the State to whom [it] had given [its] guarantee." It also insisted that Germany open direct negotiations with Poland and that any settlement be guaranteed by all powers. Most importantly, it informed Hitler that Britain had "already received a definite assurance from the Polish Government that they are prepared to enter into discussions on this basis. ... [Accordingly] His Majesty's Government hope[d] the German Government would for their part also be willing to agree to this course."[508]

At the meeting, Ambassador Henderson asked Hitler point blank if he were willing to negotiate directly with the Poles.[509] Hitler, who almost certainly was surprised (and likely disappointed as well) by Poland's willingness to talk, responded that he would have to give "careful consideration" to Chamberlain's note and consult with Goering.[510]

August 29 (Three Days Before the Invasion of Poland)

"D" received a call from one of Goering's assistants at 1:30 AM telling him that the British reply had been favorably received by Hitler, Ribbentrop, and Goering.[511] The Swede telephoned Halifax from Berlin. In "D's" opinion things were proceeding satisfactorily.[512] This rosy assessment was confirmed when "D" met with Goering a few hours later.[513] Immediately thereafter

"D" headed to the British embassy in Berlin; there he reiterated that the Germans agreed with the main point of the British reply and that they were only asking for Danzig and one train track across the Corridor (not the whole Corridor).[514] Notably, this was the exact proposal that Germany had made back to Poland in March which she had rejected.

August 30 (Two Days Before the Invasion of Poland)

Hitler's formal rejoinder to Chamberlin's letter of August 28, and the answer to the question of direct negotiations with Poland, came in the form of a telegram received in London in the wee hours of August 30. The telegram contained a "concession" for a reason that seemed eerily similar to the reason Hitler had given Chamberlain a minuscule concession at Munich a year earlier. The wire said that, although the Germans were "skeptical as to the prospects of a successful outcome, they [were] still prepared to accept the English proposal and to enter into direct discussions [with the Poles]. [Germany agreed to] do so ... solely as the result of the impression made ... by the written statement received from the British Government that they too desire a pact of friendship in accordance with the general lines indicated to the British Ambassador."[515]

British historian Sir Keith Feiling, like Churchill and others, believed that Hitler's ostensible agreement to discussions with the Poles was merely a continuation of his efforts to seduce Britain into acquiescing to German demands before the invasion of Poland.[516]

At the Cabinet meeting held later in the morning of August 30, Halifax talked about Hitler's early morning telegram. Responding to the German demand that a Polish emissary with full powers be in Berlin *that day*, Halifax advised the group that he had sent a telegram to Berlin at 2:00 AM,[517] saying that though London would give careful and prompt consideration to the position of the German Government, it could not arrange for a Polish representative to arrive in Berlin that day.[518] Britain put no pressure on the Poles to rush a representative to Berlin. Because they themselves had never been directly approached by Germany, the Poles took no action.[519]

Four other messages would be sent from London to Berlin that day, including a personal note from Chamberlain to Hitler saying that a reply to his latest telegram "was being considered 'with all urgency.'"[520]

Though the wording of Hitler's telegram had been somewhat bombastic, Halifax thought that, when stripped of its inflammatory language, it revealed a man who was trying to extricate himself from a difficult position.[521] Aside from the demand that Poland send an authorized negotiator to Berlin that day, Germany also demanded that:

• Poland return Danzig *and* the entire Corridor territory;

- Poland provide safeguards for the German minorities living there; and

- the Soviet Union be involved in any settlement.[522]

As Halifax told the Cabinet members, the telegram also stated that "the German Government never had any intention of touching Poland's vital interests or questioning the existence of an independent Polish State."[523] In its concluding sentence, the telegram said: "The German Government will immediately draw up proposals for a solution acceptable to themselves and will, if possible, place these at the disposal of the British Government before the arrival of the Polish negotiator."[524]

Halifax then told the Cabinet that, earlier that day, he and the Prime Minister had spoken with Mr. "D," who was now back in England. They discussed his meeting with Field Marshal Goering late the night before.[525] "D" talked about the remarkable effect that Britain's formal reply of the 28th had in Berlin. No quarrel was taken with the positions set out in the reply, and those officials who hoped for peace thought it offered a way out.[526] "D" said that, but for Britain's reply, war would have broken out the previous morning. Stories of Germans being shot in Poland had purportedly thrown Goering into a state of almost hysterical anger.

Mr. "D" also said that the Germans felt that in negotiations with the Poles they would encounter unreasonable demands by the Poles. He advised that on the previous Thursday, Hitler had said that he meant to annex all Polish territories which had been within the boundaries of Germany before World War I, but that Goering had persuaded him to limit his demands to Danzig and the Corridor. Goering also suggested that Hitler base negotiation with the Poles on the following points:

- Danzig would be returned to the Reich.

- As for the Corridor, both sides should demobilize. Then, a plebiscite should take place, based on the Saar model. (The reference to the "Saar model" meant, presumably, that the Poles who had been brought into the Corridor area since the end of WWI would not be eligible to vote.)

- If the majority voted for the Corridor to stay with Poland, Germany would be content with a road and railway alley across the Corridor.

- If the majority voted for the Corridor return to Germany, the Poles would be given two corridors, one to Danzig and one to Gdynia, a port city located 15 miles north of Danzig.

- It was also proposed that the plebiscite, if it occurred, should be under the control of Great Britain, Russia, or some neutral state.[527]

Did Goering's mention of a plebiscite for the Corridor, rather than outright annexation, represent a modification of Germany's proposal? If yes, was this change authorized? Did it mean Germany might be uncertain about what it wanted? Or was this just another part of the overall plan to put some proposal—any proposal—on the table to please Britain even if it would be unacceptable to Poland?

The answers probably matter little. As Shirer opines, "If the Poles ... did not rush the emissary to Berlin, or even if they did and the negotiator declined to accept Hitler's terms, then [on the very eve of war] Poland could still be blamed for refusing a 'peaceful settlement' and [there was still a chance that] Britain and France might be induced not to come to its aid when attacked."[528]

"D" found Chamberlain, Halifax, Sir Harold Wilson (Chamberlain's advisor and confidant), and Alexander Cadogan (permanent under-secretary at the Foreign Office) all "highly mistrustful" of both Hitler and Goering[529] and tired of the games spinning out of Berlin. Still, "D" kept trying. Among other suggestions to move the process forward, he called Goering and tried to get him to move any negotiations with Poland to a neutral site. Goering refused.[530]

At midnight, after the long eventful day of August 30, Ambassador Henderson presented Foreign Minister Ribbentrop with Britain's reply to Hitler's telegram.[531] Among other things, the reply noted the German Government's agreement to enter into direct discussions with Poland and appeared to wonder what exactly Germany was proposing. "They understand that the German Government are drawing up proposals for a solution. No doubt these proposals will be fully examined during the discussions."[532]

The meeting between Henderson and Ribbentrop quickly turned confrontational. When emotions had cooled, Ribbentrop produced a list of sixteen German demands of Poland, which he rattled off angrily and at great speed.[533]* Ostensibly, these were the proposals, acceptable to the German Government, that Hitler had indicated would be forthcoming. Henderson could not make notes of all of it. When finished, Ribbentrop refused to give Henderson a copy of the list saying that, because no Polish plenipotentiary had arrived before the deadline established by Germany, the proposals were meaningless.[534]

Later that evening, Halifax wired Ambassador Kennard in Warsaw asking him to urge Polish Foreign Minister Beck to tell Berlin that Poland was prepared to negotiate without delay. Halifax said that "[w]e regard [it] as most important from the point of view of the internal situation in Germany and of world opinion that, so long as the German Government professes themselves ready to negotiate, no opportunity should be given for

---

Just as happened at Godesberg nearly a year earlier, once again the Germans were changing the game.

them placing the blame for conflict on Poland."[535] Kennard did as Halifax requested. Beck told him that he would have to consult with his Government but that a considered reply would be forthcoming by midday on August 31.[536] Kennard informed Halifax of Beck's reply, which, of course, was not at all consistent with what the Poles had told Kennard two days earlier and what Britain had conveyed to Hitler.

August 31 (One Day Before the Invasion of Poland)

Back in Germany, Mr. "D" again met with Goering just after midnight. He was told that Ribbentrop had presented Ambassador Henderson with a "'democratic, fair and workable offer' to Poland."[537] After the meeting, "D" called the British embassy and learned that not only had Ribbentrop spewed out the terms so quickly that Henderson could not fully understand them, but he then refused to provide the Ambassador with a copy of the text.

In the morning, "D" told Goering that this was no way to treat the British Ambassador and asked him for permission to telephone the text of Ribbentrop's sixteen points to the British embassy.[538] Goering approved;[539] in fact at 10:00 AM he dispatched "D" to the British embassy with a typed copy of the list.[540]

During the afternoon, Jozef Lipski, the Polish Ambassador to Germany, attempted unsuccessfully to meet with Hitler or Ribbentrop to advise them that "Poland 'was favorably considering' the British Government's suggestion"[541] of direct negotiations between Poland and Germany; he also wanted to determine whether these discussions would still be possible.[542] Notably, Foreign Minister Beck had told the British that Lipski would be instructed to say that "Poland had accepted the British proposals for direct negotiations."[543] When Ambassador Lipski was finally able to see the Foreign Minister at about 6:00 PM, Ribbentrop immediately asked him if he had the authority to agree to anything. As soon as Lipski said "No," he was promptly dismissed.[544] At that point, all telephone service between Berlin and Warsaw was cut.

To add to the illusion that the Poles were responsible for the impending German invasion, at 8:00 PM a group of SS troops dressed in Polish army uniforms "seized" a German radio station in the Polish city of Gleiwitz. There they broadcast a short anti-German speech in Polish and shot several drugged concentration camp prisoners whom they left at the scene as "casualties" of the "Polish" raid.

At 9:15 PM Ribbentrop sent a message to Ambassador Henderson stating that Hitler had "waited two days in vain for the arrival of a Polish negotiator with plenary powers." As a result, he said Germany would regard its proposals, which, "in the form in which they were made known to the British

Government ... were more than loyal, fair, and practicable," to have "been to all intents and purposes rejected" by Poland.[545] Although the text of the sixteen points had never officially been given to Britain or Poland in writing, Ribbentrop nonetheless said he had given "the British Ambassador on the occasion of the presentation of the last British note [late the previous night] precise information as to the text of the German proposals which would [have been] regarded as a basis of negotiation in the event of the arrival of the Polish plenipotentiary."

Clearly wanting to show the world how magnanimous Germany was being to Poland, Ribbentrop's message also said that "The Reich Government consider it timely to inform the public of the bases for negotiation which were communicated to the British Ambassador by the Minister for Foreign Affairs, Herr von Ribbentrop."[546] At that time, the sixteen-point Polish peace proposal was being read over German radio, along with reports of the gruesome "Polish attack" on the radio station in Gleiwitz.[547]

For what it's worth, which is not much because Hitler likely never intended to comply with any of the proposals he put forward, the sixteen points conveyed by Ribbentrop bore a substantial resemblance to what seemed to be a modified proposal that "D" had conveyed to the Chamberlain and Halifax the previous day.[548]

Later telegrams to Berlin from the Poles and the British tried in vain to keep the prospect of the discussions between Poland and Germany alive. Germany didn't deign to reply. Within hours, at 4:45 AM on September 1, 1939, the invasion of Poland commenced.

——

Much took place in the weeks before the start of what would become World War II. Shirer aptly labels that activity as "but a flailing of the air, completely futile, and, in the case of the Germans, entirely and purposely deceptive."[549]

Mr. "D" had the adventure of a lifetime. Some authorities have labeled his efforts as superfluous to the game playing out in the final weeks before war,[550] but that characterization is a bit unfair. He had an interesting role in what can be seen as one aspect of Hitler's choreographed charade intended to make an obstinate Poland look like the cause of the war and give Britain an excuse for not honoring its war guarantee. As Overy writes, "['D'] represented another iron in the fire in Hitler's brief attempt to split the British-Polish alliance."[551] Lukacs, on the other hand, views "D's" shuttling between London and Berlin with Goering's support, as a sincere effort to obtain peace. Lukacs's thesis is rooted in Goering's belief in an alliance of Nordic peoples—principally Britain, Germany, the United States, and Scandinavia—for the purpose of maintaining western civilization.[552]

Despite his best efforts, Hitler failed to create the split between Britain and Poland that he wanted so badly. While Britain was enthusiastic over the seeming willingness of Germany to negotiate with Poland, Hitler was outflanked when Chamberlain advised him that Poland, had agreed, perhaps reluctantly and contrary to its obstinate ways, to negotiate with Germany over Danzig and the Corridor. This willingness eliminated Britain's ability to base a disavowal of her guarantee to Poland on Polish intransigence. Denying Hitler the satisfaction of splitting Britain and Poland, something he'd put a lot of effort into, was a tiny victory for Poland. Unfortunately it didn't change the fact that Poland was a country for which nothing could be done to avoid obliteration a few weeks later. Hitler's remaining hope for avoiding a generalized war was now based solely on whether Britain and France would, in the end, simply renege on their obligations under the war guarantees given to Poland.

Nonetheless, in the course of invading Poland and gambling that the conflict could stay limited, the genie of world war got out of the bottle and no one could get it back in. Germany's invasion of Poland was a military action that, in the end, engulfed the entire planet and resulted in the death of three percent of the world's population (fifty to eighty million people).[553]

The cards held by each side in late August 1939 were quite different than the hands they held in Munich just a year earlier. Hitler's military was stronger. Feiling writes that Ribbentrop had repeatedly said that the Western democracies "would never fight for Danzig, and certainly not, if Russia were against them."[554] Hitler believed—or hoped—this was true. Thus, he felt that even after the invasion of Poland, Britain might still show an unwillingness to take up arms. Besides, he felt that even if Britain didn't back down, it lacked both the means and desire to effectively engage Germany in a war over Poland. Lastly, Hitler did not believe Britain's announcement that it was preparing for a three-year war.[555]

In sum, Hitler continued to feel, and hope, that even if the Allies did declare war, they would do little to nothing to provide Poland with meaningful military assistance. He still thought the Polish war would likely be a localized one after all, and believed he would soon be able to negotiate a peace agreement with both Britain and France.[556] This would give him the freedom he wanted in the East.

The hand held by the British in September 1939 was also different from the one they held in 1938. Britain's military strength had improved since Munich. While Britain no longer had Czechoslovakia (and the possibility of Russia) on her side, Halifax believed that, unlike the situation in 1938, the entire British Commonwealth would now stand with the Britain if war broke out. Also new since 1938, was a resolve on Britain's part not to fold, even if she believed that Germany might have the better hand.

Accordingly, the game was played. As we will see, the fact is that ultimately Hitler was partially correct—neither Britain nor France did much of anything directly to assist Poland in its fight against the Nazis. Albeit reluctantly, each of the Allies did, however, declare war against Germany. Put differently, while in response to the Nazis' invasion, Britain and France provided no military assistance to Poland, which was quickly crushed under the Nazis' boot heel, because of Poland, the British and French were reluctantly drawn into a war that ultimately cost them each hundreds of thousands of lives. One of the sad ironies of this is that just as Britain and France had believed in 1938 that precluding the Sudetenland from becoming part of the Reich was not worth fighting for, they were equally "convinced that Danzig was not worth going to war over,"[557] but into a war involving Danzig they were dragged.

Should Britain Have Given Poland a War Guarantee? Would It Have Been Better Off Doing Nothing? Or Was War With Germany Inevitable?

Some historians assert that doing nothing would have been better for Britain than giving Poland a war guarantee. They suggest that Britain should just have written off Eastern Europe as geographically indefensible and let Hitler move eastward to fight Russia.[558]

As British diplomat Sir Roy Denman writes:

> If Chamberlain had not committed the two monumental blunders of his personal involvement and then humiliation in the Czechoslovakia affair and then the guarantee to—Poland—if he had backed isolation on these issues but accompanied it with a firm emphasis on rearmament and drawn a realistic line in the sand, Britain, the sea routes, the Empire, France and the Channel ports, then he would have faced a rising tide of doubt and discontent in the press and more eloquent speeches by Churchill, but would have had no serious difficulty in carrying with him a massive House of Commons majority in favor of staying out of a German-Polish war. Churchill would never have become Prime Minister. Germany, after Poland, would have turned on Russia.[559]

This view was reiterated by George Kennon, a famed American diplomat and historian, who wrote that "the British Government could not improve anything by offering to the Poles a support they were quite unable to give. [Britain] would have done better to shut up, to rearm as speedily as possible, and to avoid further formal commitments of any sort, while waiting the future turn of events."[560]

As noted, Buchanan asserts that "had Britain not issued the war guarantee to Poland and declared war over Poland, there might have been no war in Western Europe and no World War II."[561]* His reasoning suggests that a broader war might have also been averted if Britain had renounced its guarantee or had made the guarantee contingent on Poland agreeing to allow the Soviets to participate. In either case, without the guarantee in place, Britain would not have had reason to declare war on Germany.

Linking the guarantee to Poland's acceptance of an active Soviet role, as had been advocated by both Lloyd George and the French, would have put Poland in the crosshairs of her own stubbornness. Had Poland continued to veto Russia's participation in a Grand Alliance, the guarantee would have evaporated; and Britain and France would have been absolved of their responsibilities to aid the Poles.** As Buchanan and others suggest, after the Nazis trampled Poland, Germany would then have moved eastward to fight Russia.

Would Britain have been better off had it never issued the guarantee, or had renounced it before it declared war on Germany for invading Poland? The answer lies in what would have happened after Hitler had turned against Russia and prevailed. Would Hitler have then turned against Western Europe?

The British believed Germany would prevail in a war with Russia and would "at once turn against the West."[562] The idea that if the West had let Hitler be free to do what he wanted in the East he would have abided by an agreement to leave the West alone, presumes that Hitler could be trusted. As discussed, the evidence on this point resoundingly supports the negative. Even Chamberlain finally admitted that: "No reliance [can] be placed on any of the assurances given by the Nazi leaders."[563]

Moreover, as discussed earlier in this chapter, there is evidence (Directive 21 dated December 18, 1940) that once Germany had defeated Russia, even if it remained tied up in the East, Hitler's plan was to go back and "conclude the war against England," either to subjugate or neutralize it. [564] He needed to defeat Russia and then complete the war with England or "force her to make peace" and turn Britain into a vassal state before she could grow strong enough on her own or along with the fleets and air power of the United States to seriously challenge Germany.[565]

---

*As discussed in the next chapter, even with the war guarantee in effect, Chamberlain hesitated to declare war against Germany over the invasion of Poland.

**The same would, of course, have been true if Hitler had managed to get Britain to renounce the guarantee.

But why would Hitler have had to neutralize Western Europe and Britain if conquering Russia was his primary goal? An Answer: in *Mein Kampf*, Hitler explained that what happened to Germany following WWI called for revenge against France, who was Germany's "mortal enemy."[566] Another invasion of Belgium and Holland, as it was in WWI, would simply be a means to get at France. A much more powerful incentive was that Hitler knew Britain had a policy for more than four hundred years of always opposing the most powerful country on the continent.[567] So unless he could, at a minimum, force Britain into becoming a puppet of the Reich, whether before or after a German-Russian war, Germany likely would be facing British military actions endlessly.*

Following this line of reasoning, even a unilateral armistice with Britain would have simply postponed a war between Germany and Britain and its allies for a year or two while Russia and Germany fought. Although at that point Britain would almost certainly be stronger than it would be in either September 1939 or the spring of 1940, she would have had to fight Germany without the possibility of any assistance from the just-vanquished Russians.

Churchill and Others also Believed that WWII Was "Unnecessary"

In the preface to *The Gathering Storm*, Churchill recounts how Roosevelt once asked for suggestions on what to call WWII. Churchill quickly responded, "The Unnecessary War." That was not the first time Churchill had used the phrase. He had used it in private as early as the fall of 1940, but what it really connoted to him came into focus only after the war.[568]

As discussed, Buchanan as well as other authorities he respects—including Kennon and Denman—believe that World War II would have been unnecessary had Chamberlain not given a war guarantee to Poland. Of course, the war would also likely have been unnecessary if the Polish war guarantee had been backed by the Grand Alliance or some other significantly powerful coalition to oppose Hitler. Such a coalition would have to have included Russia, because any group of countries without Russia would not have posed an adequate military threat to Germany. Shirer, Manchester, and Churchill, among others, point out that the formation of the Grand Alliance, which would have encircled Germany, would have made it nearly impossible for Hitler to have started a world war.[569] Professor Reynolds asserts that this position is "open to question in light of what we know now: Hitler was determined to gobble up Poland, and after Munich, he was sure the British leaders—who he called "worms"—would not resist him."[570] But what may be more determinative than the strength of Hitler's desire to gobble up Poland,

---

Hitler's desire to neutralize, but not destroy Britain in part reflects the fact that he did have some positive feelings for the British and the Empire they had created.

was the unwillingness and inability of Britain and France to come to the Poles' assistance without Russia's help when Poland was attacked.

Halifax, on the other hand, writes that "I have little doubt that [upon Hitler's reoccupation of the Rhineland in March 1936] if we had then told [him] bluntly to go back, his power for future mischief would have been broken."[571] Hitler seemed to have had a similar thought when he told Austrian Chancellor Schuschnigg at that their February 1938 meeting in Berchtesgaden that when "we marched on the Rhineland with a handful of battalions, *that was the time I risked everything. If France had stopped us then we would have had to retreat perhaps sixty kilometers or so."*[572] [emphasis added] Halifax agreed; but he correctly notes, the British public in 1936 would almost unanimously have opposed any such action.

Others share Halifax's belief that a showing of minimal strength in 1936 would have rendered WWII "unnecessary." As Churchill told Parliament on February 22, 1938:

> Now we know that a firm stand by France and Britain with the other Powers associated with them at [the] time [the reoc-cupation of the Rhineland took place in 1936] and with the authority of the League of Nations, would have been followed by the immediate evacuation of the Rhineland without the shedding of a drop of blood, and the effects of that might have been blessed beyond all compare, because it would have enabled the more prudent elements in the German Army to regain their proper position and would not have given to the political head of Germany that enormous ascendency which has enabled him to move forward.[573]

Likewise, even Buchanan recognizes that by failing to object to Hitler's reoccupation of the Rhineland, "[t]he Allies ... lost the last chance to stop Hitler without war."[574]

Churchill felt that war could have also been avoided if, at several other places along the way, Britain had not cast away its advantage or had stood up to Hitler.[575] Churchill's list of shameful events stemming from British ineptitude includes:

- Germany rearming in violation of a solemn treaty;

- Germany achieving air superiority or at least air parity; and

- Austria being devoured by the Reich.[576]*

N.B., Churchill, only mentions actions and inactions during the time (1929 to 1939) when he was not in Government. For example, he does not discuss his time as

Churchill also saw Chamberlain's rejection of a conference of European leaders, as proposed by Roosevelt before the Anschluss, as "the loss of ... [a] chance to save the world from tyranny otherwise than by war."[577]

One other opportunity to avoid a war was, of course, at Munich. In comparison to how Chamberlain's desire to do the "proper" thing—i.e., help undo the mistakes of Versailles—led him to appease Hitler, Churchill thought that the Allies held a stronger hand and thus need not have caved in to Hitler.[578] (As noted, the evidence suggests that Churchill's assessments of the cards held by the Allies was a bit optimistic—Russia's contributing to the fight in 1938 was by no means assured.) Churchill was, however, certainly not of the view that Britain should have simply folded her cards and let Hitler walk off with the pot.

But, Shirer writes that, if at the time of Munich, Germany had gone to war against "Czechoslovakia ..., France, and Britain, not to mention Russia," "she would have been quickly and easily defeated."[579] As noted in the previous chapter, this was a view also held by the German generals who survived the war. Shirer also believes that if in the spring of 1938 Chamberlain had simply said that Britain (and France) would do whatever was required to defend the territorial integrity of Czechoslovakia, "the Fuehrer would never have embarked on the adventures which brought on the Second War."[580]

In sum, WWII might have been unnecessary if Britain and France had not given Poland a war guarantee. But the likelihood of war also would have lessened had any one of many other actions been taken earlier to restrain Hitler, not the least of which is the formation of the Grand Alliance.

On the other hand, after Germany fully rearmed, a grand-scale war against the madman Hitler was not only almost inevitable but "necessary," unless the countries of Europe (and the United States) were prepared to give Hitler all the land he wanted and allow him to complete his genocidal goals.* After Germany had been allowed to grow strong, it was unlikely that stopping Hitler could have been achieved by peaceful means or through localized skirmishes.** Moreover, as horrible as it is to say aloud, the evil and horrors that were successfully routed by full-scale war more than likely justified the evils and horrors that the war itself would inflict. Here the ends truly justified the means.

Chancellor of the Exchequer in the late 20s and his efforts to starve the Royal Navy.

As discussed, given Britain's historical opposition to the most powerful country in Europe, its peaceful coexistence with a fully armed Nazi Germany led by Hitler was likely impossible.

**In all likelihood, the best hope for peacefully stopping Hitler, would have been to form a strong Grand Alliance to tightly and permanently encircled Nazi Germany.*

The American Civil War was another war that was probably "necessary." Slavery needed to end, and the Union needed to be preserved. Neither objective would likely have ever been achieved through peaceful means. To eradicate the evil of slavery and save the Union required the horrors of the Civil War. Unfortunately, in the Civil War the scope of death and destruction quickly exceeded all expectations. The same would also be true of WWII.

Hitler's Speech of April 28, 1939—A Reply to Roosevelt and More

On April 15, 1939, Franklin Roosevelt sent Hitler a personal message asking him to pledge not to invade a list of thirty-one countries, including Poland. Hitler responded to that message in his speech to the Reichstag on April 28.[581] The speech, which lasted for over two hours, has been called one of the best Hitler ever gave.[582] Among the highlights, Hitler:

- included the usual diatribe against the Versailles Treaty and all the harm it inflicted upon the German populace;

- reiterated his positive feelings for Britain and its people;

- excoriated the Chamberlain Government for the Polish war guarantee and its adoption of a policy of encircling Germany;

- denounced and repudiated the Anglo-German naval treaty of 1935;

- expressed, nonetheless, his willingness to enter arms reduction negotiations with Britain;

- mocked Roosevelt's non-invasion request (the Reichstag laughed when he read each of the countries on Roosevelt's list);

- mentioned the additional territory that he coveted (Danzig and the Polish Corridor); and

- provided a bizarre new reason for having taken over Czechoslovakia: to avoid the possibility that *some madman* might get control of the vast stores of munitions there. [emphasis added]

While the speech is an outstanding example of demagoguery—being filled with lies, half-truths and nearly incomprehensible rhetoric—Hitler discussed several of his topics in a moderately coherent manner. Surprisingly, he occasionally even touched upon a valid point; and on more than a few occasions he comes across as a proud German sincerely looking to right the wrongs imposed by the Versailles treaty. Hitler spoke pointedly and profoundly about how the "rich" countries arrayed against him had achieved their wealth in a manner far worse and more warlike than the way Germany annexed the

Rhineland, Austria, and Czechoslovakia. But, overall, reviewing the speech requires a strong stomach and a huge dose of skepticism. The speech put two of Hitler's most defining traits into the spotlight: his malignant narcissism and his virulent nationalism.

Other topics of note in Hitler's speech included:

The Polish War Guarantee

Hitler took umbrage at the British guarantee and the ensuing temporary agreement between Poland and England to come to each other's assistance should the need arise. Hitler thought these developments conflicted with the terms of the German-Polish nonaggression pact of 1934, which he now stated, "having been unilaterally infringed by Poland, [was] therefore voided." This interpretation of the consequence of the war guarantee "allowed" Hitler to attack Poland without violating the nonaggression pact.

Hitler then said that "[s]hould the Polish Government wish to make a fresh contractual arrangement, determining its relations with Germany, I can only welcome such an idea, provided, of course, that these arrangements are based on absolutely clear obligation binding both parties equally. Germany is perfectly willing at any time to undertake such obligations and also to fulfill them."

Munich

Hitler said that the Munich conference had really never been necessary. In his opinion, it had been instigated by countries wanting Czechoslovakia to resist his demands at all costs. And when the "situation" required a solution, these countries were left seeking a more or less respectable retreat. Put differently, Hitler asserted that, without the interference of countries in Western Europe, the seemingly complex Czech "problem" would very likely have been "the easiest thing in the world to solve."

Affection for Britain

During the speech, Hitler spoke effusively of the affection he had for Britain:

> During the whole of my political activity I have always pro-
> pounded the idea of a close friendship and collaboration
> between Germany and England. ... This desire for Anglo-
> German friendship and cooperation conforms not merely to
> sentiments based on the racial origins of our two peoples but
> also to my realization of the importance of the existence of the
> British Empire for the whole of mankind. ... [T]he existence

of this empire is an inestimable factor of value for the whole of human culture and economic life.

How Allied Nations Had Achieved Their Current Prosperous Positions

Not all of Hitler's remarks about Britain, however, were laudable. At one point he casually referenced the fact that Britain had acquired its colonial territories by force, often applied quite brutally. But he then promptly acknowledged that all empires come into being this same way. In Hitler's thinking the methods used to establish an empire are of less importance than "the general good which those methods produced." As a man determined to create his own empire, Hitler praised what the British had achieved: "Now, there is no doubt that the Anglo-Saxon people have accomplished immense colonizing work in the world. For this work, I have sincere admiration."

Pointing out the way Allied nations had achieved their current level of prosperity was a theme repeated throughout the speech. Clearly Hitler was implying that it was hypocritical of the Allies to criticize Germany for using whatever means it found fit to achieve a similar degree of hegemony and wealth. At one point, responding to Roosevelt's belief that all international problems could be solved around a conference table, he said, "... no statesmen, including those of the United States and especially her greatest, made the outstanding part of their countries' history at the conference table, but by reason of the strength of their people" and that he would "not mention the innumerable struggles which finally led to the subjugation of the North American Continent as a whole." Hitler wanted the world to equate what he was doing in the name of Lebensraum with, for instance, how European settlers and then citizens of newly created America displaced the indigenous population, often by brutal means, in the pursuit of expansion.

Hitler said he regarded it "impossible to achieve a lasting friendship between the German and Anglo-Saxon peoples if the other side did not recognize that ... [j]ust as the preservation of the British Empire is the object and like purpose of Britons, so also the freedom and preservation of the German Reich is the like purpose of Germans. ... If England cannot understand our point of view, thinking perchance she may regard Germany as a vassal state, then our love and affection have indeed been wasted on England."

Disavowal of the Anglo-German Naval Agreement of 1935

Hitler told his audience that he had heard the British Prime Minister claim he was no longer able to put any trust in German assurances. Under the circumstances, Hitler said, "... we should no longer expect [Chamberlain] or the British people to bear the burden of a situation which has become onerous for them and which is only to be borne in an atmosphere of mutual confidence." Continuing, he said that when Germany became a National Socialist state, paving the way for its national resurrection, he pursued an unswerving policy of friendship with England, even proposing a voluntary restriction of German naval armaments.* That restriction was, however, "based on one condition ... that a war between England and Germany would never again be possible. This wish and this conviction are alive in me today."

Hitler said the policy of England, both unofficially and officially, left no doubt in his mind that no matter what conflict Germany might someday be forced to address, Great Britain would always oppose her—a war against Germany is taken for granted in Britain. This conclusion, he said, filled him with profound regret, because the only claim he had ever made and would continue to make on England was for the return of Germany's colonies lost after the last war. Apart from this, he asserted he never advanced a claim that could in any way have interfered with British interests or become a danger to the Empire. He had made sure that his demands were scrupulously limited to Germany's rightful territorial integrity and concerned the internal property of the German nation.**

Believing that England, both in the press and officially, now held the view that Germany should be opposed under all circumstances and has actualized this view by its policy of encirclement, Hitler declared that the grounds for the naval treaty had been removed. So as he told the members of the Reichstag, he had resolved to send on that very day a communication to the British government saying:

- "I still hope that we shall be able to avoid an armaments race with England. Should the British government ... wish to enter once more into negotiations with Germany on this problem, no one would be happier than I at the prospect of still being able to come to a clear and straightforward understanding."

- "My people and I ... do not want anything that did not formally belong to us and no State will ever be robbed by us of its property; but whoever believes that he is able to attack Germany will find himself confronted with the measure of power and resistance compared to which that of 1914 was negligible."

---

*The statement is not true. As discussed, the Anglo-German Naval Agreement of 1935 allowed Germany to construct surface ships to achieve a total tonnage equal to 35 percent of that of the Royal Navy. Rather than being a restriction on German naval armament, it actually allowed Germany to increase her navy beyond the limits set forth in the Treaty of Versailles. Roberts p. 391.

**This is hardly a statement that would ring true to most Czechoslovaks.

Response to Roosevelt's Telegram

As noted, on April 15, 1939, Roosevelt had sent Hitler a telegram asking him not to invade a host of countries. Hitler opened his April 28 speech with a sarcastic reference to Roosevelt's message and asserted that because it had been published all over the world before he had even seen it, it was appropriate for him to answer Roosevelt in a similarly public fashion.

Hitler turned his attention to the Roosevelt telegram a little more than halfway through his speech. Shirer, who was in the audience, writes that, at that point, Hitler "reached the summit of oratory" and put on quite a show.[583] He took up the points in Roosevelt's telegram. As he finished laying each point out, he would, in slightly more than a whisper, ask *"Antwort?"* (the German word for "answer"). Hitler was in full stride: each call for the *"Antwort"* would result in ever increasing laughter, to the point of raucousness, from the members of the Reichstag.

Here is one example: Hitler recited from the telegram that "Mr. Roosevelt says ... that he does not speak from selfishness, fear, or weakness, but with the voice of strength and friendship for mankind." He paused, smiled slightly, and asked *"Antwort?"*[584] Hitler then provided the answer: "If this voice of strength and friendship for mankind had been raised by America at the proper time, and particularly if it had had any practical value, then at least that treaty which was to become the source of the direst derangement of humanity and history, the Dictate of Versailles, could have been prevented."

After ticking through a number of these points and "answers," Hitler reached the most famous section of the speech. "Finally, Mr. Roosevelt requests that assurances be given him that the German armed forces will not attack, and above all, not invade, the territory or possessions of the following independent nations." He then started reading the list, pausing ever so slightly, and emphasizing each name so that the laughter in the Reichstag grew after each country's name was read. The level of rollicking joviality in the Reichstag would have made the patrons of any Bavarian beer hall proud. More importantly, in this, the last major peacetime speech he would give, Hitler never even got close to assuring Roosevelt and the world that Germany would refrain from invading other countries. He already had plans to invade Poland.

While Hitler cruelly mocked Roosevelt before the Reichstag, Chamberlain's own reaction to the President's telegram was far from sympathetic. He denounced Roosevelt's message to Hitler as "Yankee Meddling." Manchester describes Chamberlain's response as "sympathetic toward Berlin, indifferent or hostile to Washington. ..."[585]

After studying Hitler's Reichstag speech, Churchill wrote in a May 4, 1939, article for *The Daily Telegraph* that Hitler did not seem to be "conscious of the immense change which has been wrought in British public opinion by his treacherous breach of the Munich Agreement and of the complete reversal of policy which this outrage brought about in the British Government, and especially in the Prime Minister."[586] Churchill may have been trying to convince himself that Chamberlain had changed, or perhaps he was simply supplying words to fulfill his commitment for a biweekly column. In any event, though there had been a change in Chamberlain's policy since Prague, the change in Chamberlain was not as profound as Churchill suggested. By May 4, Churchill knew that. Yes, Chamberlain had issued a war guarantee to Poland in the wake of Hitler's betrayal of Czechoslovakia. And, yes, this attempt to stand up to Hitler was an important first step in creating a coalition of countries that could resist German aggression. But no meaningful second step was ever taken. As Manchester puts it, "appeasement [still] remained [Chamberlain's] faith."[587] Stated differently, "... [U]ntil it was absolutely certain that Hitler could not be appeased or deterred, Chamberlain was driven by an overwhelming compulsion to pursue the possibility of peace to the end—because to accept the inevitability of war was an important repudiation of statesmanship."[588] As we will see in the next chapter, Chamberlain's compulsion would not dissipate until the absolute last minute before Britain officially declared war at 11:15 AM, September 3, 1939—more than two full days after the Nazis invaded Poland.

Hitler speaking to the Reichstag, April 28, 1939

13

SEPTEMBER 1, 1939–MAY 9, 1940
POLAND, THE PHONEY WAR, AND NORWAY

Friday, September 1, 1939: The Invasion of Poland
Britain's "Response"—Churchill Joins the War Cabinet
September 3, 1939: Chamberlain Gives Hitler a Two-Hour Ultimatum to
Stop All Hostilities in Poland
The Fighting in Poland
October 6, 1939: Hitler Makes a Peace Offer to England and France
Chamberlain's Response and His Plan to Take No Offensive Action
Unless Provoked
Hitler's Secret Directive No. 6
Why Turn to the West? What Was Hitler's Plan for Britain?
The Phoney War; the "Bore War"
 • Its Effect on Chamberlain and His Thinking
 • Things That Occurred During the "Bore" War
Norway
 • Humiliating Errors
Interesting Glimpses of Churchill as He Emerged From the "Wilderness
Years"
 • Churchill's Off-Again On-Again Attitude Toward the Soviets
 • The Important Evolution of the Relationship Between Churchill and
Chamberlain
The Debate in the House Over Norway

Friday, September 1, 1939: The Invasion of Poland

Early in the morning after the Gleiwitz radio station incident, fifty-six German divisions (nine of them the armored panzer divisions) invaded Poland from the north, south, and west. Simultaneously the Luftwaffe unleashed sixteen hundred planes on Polish cities.[1]

Although details reaching London about the invasion were sketchy, the Cabinet was asked to gather at 11:30 AM. Chamberlain said that the Cabinet was meeting "under the gravest possible conditions. The event against which we had fought so long and so earnestly had come upon us. But our consciences are clear, and there should be no possible question now where our duty lay."[2]

Halifax advised the group that the Polish Ambassador had already come by the Foreign Office to talk with him about the German invasion and to say that circumstances called for implementing the British Guarantee to Poland. Halifax replied that, if the reports received were accurate, he did not disagree.[3]* Unfortunately, as of September 1939, Britain had only four or five divisions ready for action, compared to the French and German armies, which each had about one hundred.[4] Britain not only lacked the power to come to Poland's aid, but she had made no plans to do so.[5]

Britain's military would take months—if not longer—to get ready for combat. Even by the following spring its ability to engage in aerial warfare was suspect. An April 2, 1940, memorandum prepared by Sir Kingsley Wood, the Secretary of State for Air, put the estimated number of planes of the combatants as of March 31, 1940, were:

Germany	5,000
UK	1,840
France	1,845[6]

Moreover, not all of the RAF aircraft were modern. The French Air Force, however, was in even worse shape, with most of its planes obsolete.[7] At the start of the war, Churchill was worried about the Allies' "weakness in the air."[8]

Shirer describes the general mood in Berlin on September 1, 1939 as "gray apathy."[9] Hitler gave a speech to unenthusiastic members of the Reichstag and issued a proclamation to the German army.[10] He, of course, blamed the Polish government for failing to send a plenipotentiary to negotiate peace and recited the usual litany of false allegations of Polish aggression, not the least of which was the fake attack on the German radio station at Gleiwitz. He said he had "no other choice than to meet force with force...."[11]

Later, back at the Chancellery, Hitler was agitated, ranting that the British had wanted war all along and now he would fight them to the bitter end no matter how long it took.[12] Shirer writes that Hitler was, however, "by no means convinced that he would have to fight Great Britain at all."[13] While the German armored columns were busily advancing on the Poles and most Polish cities were being bombed, neither Britain nor France seemed intent on honoring their war guarantees.

As noted in the preceding chapter, Halifax also claimed that Poland knew that Britain intended to do nothing under the "guarantee."

The discussion in the British Cabinet was not about declaring war immediately or joining with the French to attack the Germans, even though at the
time Hitler only had ten divisions defending Germany's Western border.[14]
Rather, Cabinet members were simply contemplating sending an ultimatum
to Germany, and even then they were not in any great rush. They believed
that holding off on declaring war would give time for the evacuation of the
civilian population from London to the countryside.[15] (British Ambassador
to Germany Nevile Henderson had warned that German air attacks on
Britain would likely immediately follow any declaration of war.[16]) The Chiefs
of Staff urged a more robust response: they felt that if the Polish guarantee
were going to be implemented, then the right course was to dispatch an
ultimatum without delay.[17] At that point, the Cabinet suspended discussion
on the nature of the communication to be sent to the German Government
and instead considered various defense measures.[18]

Britain's "Response"—Churchill Joins the War Cabinet

When discussion resumed, the Cabinet agreed on a draft communica-
tion, subject to consultation with the French. Chamberlain and Halifax
were given that task; "[no] further reference to the Cabinet" was required.[19]
The key point of the proposed telegram was simply to tell Hitler that unless
Germany suspended all aggressive action against Poland and withdrew from
Polish territory, Britain would, without hesitation, fulfill her obligations to
Poland.[20] Chamberlain, anticipating agreement from the French, proposed
that the telegram be dispatched around 5:00 PM; the Cabinet agreed.[21] This
way, Chamberlain could announce the British response to the House at the
6:00 PM session he had called.

Halifax added that he had received a communication from the French
Government explaining that they wanted to declare war before Britain did.
They did not want to appear to have been dragged into the war by the British.[22]

Halifax next read Cabinet members a message received from the peripatetic
Mr. "D", the amateur Swedish diplomat who was serving as a go-between
in German-British talks. "D" said that, according to information in Berlin,
warfare had been triggered by the Poles having blown up a bridge. Hitler, he
said, declared he did not want to start a world war and wanted to negotiate
directly with Great Britain.

Almost as if he would earn frequent flyer miles for his efforts, "D"
suggested that he fly back to London in a last-minute attempt to avert a
catastrophe.[23] Likely tired of the obvious way "D" was being manipulated
by Hitler, the Cabinet wanted a stiff reply sent to the Swede, stressing that
the only way a world war could be averted was for German troops to leave
Polish territory.[24]

After the Cabinet meeting ended, Chamberlain, telephoned Churchill and asked if, prior to the 6 o'clock session in the House, he "would stop at No. 10 Downing for a few minutes."[25] Given the outbreak of war earlier that morning, Churchill thought that meeting might be about his being asked to join the Chamberlain Government.[26]

Since early July the press and others had been demanding that Chamberlain bring Churchill back into the Government. Churchill was viewed by many as a highly experienced leader who would: scare Hitler,[27] show that Britain was united,[28] and increase Britons' confidence in the Chamberlain Government.[29] His return was also seen as something that would cause Hitler to pause before taking Danzig by force.[30]

While there were mixed feelings in the Cabinet about adding Churchill, throughout the summer Chamberlain had remained opposed.[31] Winston was viewed as a pariah by a majority of Conservatives and had for some time been Chamberlain's most fervent critic. Chamberlain did not believe that the wisdom Churchill might bring to the Government outweighed "the irritation and disturbance" he would cause. The P.M. also knew that Churchill did not embrace his strategy of putting off any war for as long as possible to give Britain more time to improve its military.[32] Also, Chamberlain's enmity toward Churchill certainly did not decrease when, in early August, Winston showed his distrust of the P.M. by supporting Labour's motion to limit the length of the Parliamentary recess for fear that Chamberlain might try to pull off "another Munich."[33]* Other assertions were that Chamberlain feared that Churchill would eclipse him and the rest of the Cabinet.[34] Chamberlain's strong resolve to exclude Churchill was, however, matched by the growing determination elsewhere to see Churchill returned to Government.[35]** During the summer of 1939, Churchill's popularity among Britons grew daily.[36]

Given that on September 1, the war could not be put off any longer, despite his personal feelings, as biographer Keith Feiling writes, Chamberlain did what "he had always contemplated" doing "if war should come"[37] and called Churchill to set up a meeting at which Winston would be asked to join the Government.[38] Even so, despite the real prospect that he would shortly become a member of Chamberlain's cabinet, Churchill was still not quite ready to pull all of his punches. That is, when Churchill learned that the Cabinet was drafting a communiqué to Germany rather than a declaration

---

*Chamberlain was not the only one with negative feelings; Churchill was upset by the P.M's criticisms and attitude toward him. Gilbert, Prophet p. 1097.

**Others, like The Times, simply did not believe that Churchill was needed in the Cabinet to either frighten Hitler or show him that Britain meant business. Ibid. p. 1087.

of war, he was outraged and commenced "writing a blistering attack on the Chamberlain Government."[39] But that document would never be sent.

Churchill met with the Prime Minister late that afternoon. Chamberlain told Churchill that he saw "no hope of averting war,"[40]* and he thought it time to form a small War Cabinet made up of ministers who did not supervise any department. He then invited Churchill to join the War Cabinet as a minister without portfolio. Churchill accepted immediately.[41] The understandable bitterness that Chamberlain felt toward Churchill for his years of constant criticism was in the end simply outweighed by the political need to add Winston to the Government. Professor David Reynolds asserts that "... a top job for Churchill was essential if Chamberlain was to seem serious about the war."[42] Moreover, by Churchill being in the Government, it was thought that he would be loath to attack it or the Prime Minister.

The second sentence of Chamberlain's 6:00 PM address to the House was, "The time has come when action rather than speech is required."[43] Unfortunately, the action the House had in mind—a declaration of war—was not what the Government was prepared to deliver. Chamberlain then told the House that relevant documents describing his attempts to keep the way open for an honorable and equitable settlement of the dispute between Germany and Poland had been put in the form of a White Paper. (Manchester pointedly states the obvious: "... the last thing that the Poles needed in this hour of desperation was a White Paper exonerating the Chamberlain Government."[44]) Chamberlain then ticked through a list of some of what had taken place in the last few days of August, including Germany's demand that a Polish plenipotentiary instantly appear in Berlin, and Ribbentrop's last-minute sixteen-point proposal. He also reported that "This morning we ordered complete mobilisation of the whole of the Royal Navy, Army and Royal Air Force."[45]

Finally, he described the telegram that had just been sent to Ambassador Henderson for him to give to Foreign Minister Ribbentrop. In it, the Government sought assurances that Germany would suspend all aggressive action against Poland and be prepared to withdraw. It also stated that if she failed to so, Britain would fulfill its war guarantee. (Chamberlain did not make it known to the House that French Foreign Minister Bonnet was urging the delay of any hard and fast deadline,[46] and that, to act in concert with the French and give time to complete evacuation and mobilization, Halifax had advised Ambassador Henderson to frame the message to

---

*Manchester describes Chamberlain as being "considerably less than candid," because he was still willing to negotiate with Hitler and, despite the terms of the Agreement of Mutual Assistance with Poland, was "prepared to hesitate indefinity before fulfilling HMG's obligations to the Poles." Manchester, Alone p. 517.

Germany "in the nature of a *warning and ... not ... as an ultimatum.*"[47]) [emphasis added]

The telegram was somewhat disingenuous in that Britain had already failed to fulfill her obligations to Poland "without hesitation." The Treaty of Mutual Assistance with Poland, which had been signed just days earlier, obligated Britain to act immediately, with "all the support and assistance in its power."[48] Over the next few days, hesitation in fulfilling the war guarantee to Poland would be the Chamberlain Government's modus operandi. Their waffling would reach the point where questions started to be raised in the House as to whether the Government should even be allowed to continue.[49]

The Foreign Office contacted Mr. "D" to see if he could do something to limit the hostilities. Assured by "D" that he could, London was once again prepared to negotiate with the Nazis.[50] As Yogi Berra would have said, "It [was] like deja vu all over again."[51] Though Churchill was again concerned about Chamberlain's failure to move quickly on something as important as declaring war, as member of a War Cabinet (even one that did not yet exist), he could not (or at least felt he could not) publicly criticize the Government for failing to act.[52] Just after midnight, however, Churchill did write the Prime Minister. His letter opened on a minor issue—the fact that the average age of the members of the War Cabinet was sixty-four.[53] He then got to his real point: "The Poles have now been under heavy attack for thirty hours and I am much concerned to hear that there is talk in Paris of a further note [to Hitler]. I trust you will be able to announce our Joint Declaration of War at *latest* when Parliament meets this afternoon."[54] By the second day of the war, September 2, the Germans had broken through the Polish border defenses. The Poles were publicly calling on their British and French allies to declare war and attack Germany from the west. But no attack came. As Churchill waited to hear from the Prime Minister, he paced back and forth like a caged lion.[55] No call came.

There was a hastily arranged meeting of the existing Cabinet at 4:15 PM. Chamberlain biographer Robert Self describes the Cabinet as being "in an extremely difficult mood."[56] As soon as the session began, Halifax read his notes of a lengthy conference call he had had with the British Ambassador to Italy and Mussolini's son-in-law Count Ciano two hours earlier. During the call, Ciano mentioned that the Italian Government was feeling out the Germans about the possibility of a conference with France, Britain, Germany, and Poland provided Herr Hitler would agree to suspend hostilities.[57] Apparently, Hitler was not against considering the idea, but would not do so if the telegrams he had received the day before from Britain and

France were ultimatums. In this regard, Ambassador Henderson thereafter confirmed to the Germans that they were not ultimatums.[58]*

Halifax then told the Cabinet that based on Ciano's call, he and the Prime Minister had tentatively concluded that these points would be made in the P.M.'s speech to the House scheduled after the conclusion of the Cabinet meeting.

1. The telegram sent to the German Government the previous day had only been a final warning, not an ultimatum.
2. If the German Government asked for further time to review the telegram, we should be prepared to allow them until 12 noon tomorrow (September 3) for this purpose, subject to their agreeing to an armistice.
3. The primary condition for any conference would be that German troops should first withdraw from Poland.
4. He and the Prime Minister believed that direct negotiations between Germany and Poland would be the best course, but they were willing to see other countries participate if that was what Germany and Poland wanted.[59]

The Foreign Secretary added that, because Germany now had to also think about participating in a multi-lateral conference, the Cabinet should consider giving Germany even more time to respond to Britain's telegram—until midnight on September 3/4.[60] He noted that this was far less additional time than French Foreign Minister Bonnet wanted to give the Germans.

As Self writes, "When it became clear that Halifax and Chamberlain were still prevaricating ..." they faced a Cabinet revolt led by Home Secretary Sir Samuel Hoare. Hoare came out of the chute hard, saying that the telegram sent to Germany the previous evening "had been generally regarded [by the Cabinet] as in the nature of an ultimatum." He quickly added that he also thought there were tremendous risks in accepting any delay in Hitler's response.[61] With few exceptions, the Cabinet members opposed giving Germany more time within which to indicate its willingness to withdraw all troops from Polish territory.

Chamberlain then read out a telegram he had just received from the Polish Ambassador to Britain, Edward Raczyński. In it, the Ambassador revealed that the fighting in Poland had increased in intensity across the whole front, that Poland was being attacked by the entire German air force, and that engagement of German aircraft by Allied forces was a matter of the greatest

---

Halifax then admitted that Henderson had been authorized to tell the Germans that the telegram did not constitute an ultimatum. CAB 23 /1 48 (39) p. 2 462.

urgency. Raczyński said he had been instructed by his Government to request once again the immediate fulfillment of British obligations to Poland.[62]

After the members of the Cabinet had completed expressing their views, Chamberlain said he thought there was general agreement in the Cabinet on two main points:

1. That there should be no negotiation with Germany unless it was prepared to withdraw its troops from Poland; and
2. That it was undesirable to allow Germany longer than until tonight at midnight to make up its mind.

It was also evident that the precise terms of the communication to Germany and the statement to be made in Parliament later that afternoon would have to be settled in consultation with the French.[63] The Cabinet assigned these tasks to Halifax.[64] As Manchester writes, "Halifax ... [was to] tell the Germans that what had been a warning was now in fact an ultimatum, and that it would end [that night] at the stroke of twelve."[65] But the Foreign Secretary never told the Germans anything.

As the time for the 7:45 PM session of the House approached, the benches were packed. Churchill would later write, "There was no doubt that the temper of the House was for war."[66] The British press and public were also so inclined. Conservative MP Sir Edward Spears wrote that he had never seen Parliament "so stirred ... one and all were keyed up for the announcement that war had been declared."[67] However, in his three-minute address, Chamberlain made no such announcement. Nor did he discuss the position, unanimously approved at the Cabinet meeting just that afternoon, that Germany would only to have until midnight to agree to remove her troops from Poland. Rather, he merely revealed that he had received no reply to the message delivered to Foreign Minister Ribbentrop the previous day. He said he hoped the delay signified that Germany was considering the proposal by Italy of a ceasefire followed immediately by a conference among Germany, France, Britain, Poland, and Italy. Chamberlain quickly added, however, that Britain would not take part in any such conference while Poland was still subject to invasion, and reiterated that unless German forces were withdrawn from Poland, His Majesty's Government "will, as stated yesterday, be bound to take action. ..."[68]

Spears wrote: "...as we listened, amazement turned to stupefaction, and stupefaction into exasperation." Chamberlain did not speak of action but only of further negotiations.[69] From the benches rose murmurs of "Appeasement."[70]

Following Chamberlain's report, Arthur Greenwood, Deputy Leader of the Labour Party, took the floor and gave voice to the hostility that many House members were feeling over the Government's hesitancy to act. Greenwood said that "... there are many of us *on all sides of this House* who view with the gravest concern the fact that hours went by and news came in of bombing operations, and news today of an intensification of it, and I wonder how long we are prepared to vacillate at a time when Britain and all that Britain stands for, and human civilisation, are in peril."[71] [emphasis added] Had Churchill not been headed for the War Cabinet, he likely would have delivered a similar speech.

The House was scheduled to meet again at noon the next day (September 3). Both Greenwood and Liberal Party leader Archibald Sinclair demanded that Chamberlain tell the House by that time how his Government intended to proceed. Chamberlain later said that the Commons was becoming "out of hand with suspicions, and [was] ready ... to believe the Government guilty of any cowardice and treachery."[72]

When the House adjourned, ten Cabinet ministers assembled in the private parliamentary office of Chancellor of the Exchequer Sir John Simon to express their great displeasure that the views of the Cabinet, which had been articulated with vehemence earlier that afternoon, had been ignored by the Prime Minister.[73] They felt betrayed.[74] Simon, who shared their anger, was chosen to lead the rebels. To no avail he tried to reach the Prime Minister by telephone. At 9:00 PM, Simon and three other ministers messengered a letter to Chamberlain outlining their complaints.[75] That did the trick; Simon was finally able to get through to Chamberlain, who invited the entire group to meet with him immediately at Number 10.[76]

Elsewhere in London, a number of younger Conservatives including Anthony Eden and Alfred Duff Cooper, both of whom had previously resigned from the Chamberlain Government, were visiting with Churchill.[77] In his diary, Duff Cooper described the group as in a "bewildered rage" over the failure of the Prime Minister to take any action in response to the German invasion of Poland.[78] Some were convinced that Chamberlain "had lost the Conservative Party forever" and that it was "in Winston's power to go to the House of Commons tomorrow ... break him and take his place."[79] During the meeting, members of the group, unaware of the ongoing revolt in the Cabinet, urged Churchill to attack the Government's inaction. They believed such a declaration would lead to a vote of no confidence and then to Churchill's replacing Chamberlain. Churchill refused.[80]

Instead, Churchill wrote Chamberlain another letter in which he said:

> I have not heard anything from you since our talks [yesterday], when I understood that I was to serve as your colleague, and when you told me that this would be announced speedily. ... I really do not know what has happened during the course of this agitated day; though it seems to me that entirely different ideas have ruled from those which you expressed to me when

you said, 'the die was cast.' ... [I feel] entitled to ask you to let
me know how we stand, both publicly and privately, before
the debate opens at noon.

... [There was a] feeling tonight in the House that injury
had been done to the spirit of national unity by the apparent
weakening of our resolve. ... I therefore ask that there should
be no announcement of the composition of the War Cabinet
until we have had a talk."[81]

Manchester contends that had "Churchill turned against the prime minister," as Duff Cooper and the others wanted, "Chamberlain's government
would [have] fall[en].[82]" In contrast, Roberts describes Churchill's rejection
of the idea of trying to topple the Chamberlain Government as "sensible,"
because the majority of Conservatives "still supported Chamberlain."[83] Though
the latter statement is likely correct, whether the Chamberlain Government
would survive was a very serious issue at Number 10 that night.

Shortly after giving his ill-received speech, the Prime Minister called
Halifax, who had been in the House of Lords and not heard the proceedings
in the Commons.[84] Chamberlain told Halifax that things had gone very badly.
He said that "people [are] misinterpreting [our] inability to give a time limit
as ... half-heartedness and hesitation on our part ..." Chamberlain, who
found the experience very unpleasant, was disturbed to a degree Halifax
had never seen before. The Prime Minister asked Halifax to come down to
Downing Street immediately.[85]

When the Foreign Secretary got there, Chamberlain told him that his
speech had infuriated the House, and "unless we could clear the position,"
he did not believe the Government could maintain itself when Parliament
met the next day.[86]

Chamberlain's evening would not get any better. On the phone with
Rome, trying to turn Mussolini's proposal for a five-power conference into
reality, Chamberlain learned it would be virtually impossible for Britain's
all-important precondition—getting German forces to withdraw from
Poland—to be achieved. Italy's Foreign Minister Count Ciano said that
British insistence on German withdrawal would bring down such wrath
from Hitler that Mussolini would not risk the confrontation.[87]

Meanwhile, the group of House rebels led by John Simon had braved a
thunderstorm and arrived at Downing Street disheveled and wet. They were
shocked to see Halifax and Alexander Cadogan, the permanent Under-
Secretary for Foreign Affairs, already in the room.[88]

Simon told the Prime Minister "'very forcibly' that the ultimatum must be issued immediately."[89] Chamberlain was rattled by the revolt;[90] but he, Halifax, and Cadogan still had much work to do with the French before another Cabinet meeting was to be held that night. Chamberlain needed to impress on the French Government the precariousness of his Government's situation and "the need for an immediate synchronized ultimatum."[91]

A second Cabinet meeting was called on very short notice for 11:30 PM. At the meeting Chamberlain said he recognized the strength of feeling shown in the House (even among those who had been the most loyal supporters of his Government), and it was imperative for the Government to act.[92] He related that he, Halifax, and John Simon had had further discussions with the French Government. It appeared the French General Staff had advised the French Government that an early declaration of war would risk attacks on their communications that they were unable to resist and that might seriously endanger their forces. Telling Premier Daladier about the painful scene in the House earlier that evening, Chamberlain advised that it would be impossible for his Government to adhere to the timeline that Foreign Minister Bonnet had said the French Government wanted—

a. the French and British ambassadors should meet with German Foreign Minister Ribbentrop at noon tomorrow (Sunday, September 3) and inform him that Count Ciano's proposals for a conference could be accepted only if all German troops were removed from Polish soil; and

b. if the German Government did not signify acceptance of this proposal, the ambassadors would then deliver an ultimatum due to expire at 8:00 or 9:00 PM that night.[93]

Chamberlain then suggested the delivery of an ultimatum at 8:00 o'clock the following morning, to expire at noon; but French Foreign Minister Bonnet did not agree.[94] The P.M. told the Cabinet members that the Chiefs of Staff had suggested that the British and French ambassadors should see Ribbentrop at, say, 2:00 AM with an ultimatum to expire four hours later.

A debate then ensued among the Cabinet members on the questions of when to present the ultimatum to Germany and when the ultimatum should expire. During the debate Halifax said that the Cabinet should not feel precluded from acting before the French did.[95]

About midnight, it was unanimously agreed: the ultimatum would be delivered by Ambassador Henderson at 9:00 AM and it would expire at 11:00 AM.[96] This way, Chamberlain would know exactly what the situation was when he addressed the House at noon. It was also agreed that the Cabinet's decision would be communicated to the French Government, which was advised of the decision at 12:15 AM.[97]

When Churchill learned of the decision, the fact an ultimatum would be issued at 9:00 AM significantly changed things—the Government would act; nonetheless he sent his letter to Chamberlain anyway.[98]

September 3, 1939: Chamberlain Gives Hitler a Two-Hour Ultimatum to Stop All Hostilities in Poland

Overnight it had also been decided that Chamberlain would advise the country of Hitler's response to the ultimatum. The Prime Minister would make a radio broadcast at 11:15 AM, fifteen minutes after the deadline. At 9:00 AM Ambassador Henderson dutifully delivered the ultimatum to the Chancellery in Berlin. While doing so, he ran into Mr. "D," with whom he exchanged farewells. "D" would later note that the British Ambassador showed "profound grief and disappointment" about the situation.[99]

The time before the ultimatum expired moved slowly. It was a period when there just was not much to be said. Yet, all too soon, it was 11:00 o'clock and nothing had been heard from Germany. Just like a planned execution where no reprieve has been received from the governor, there was nothing else to do but follow through with the unpleasant task of announcing the start of World War II at 11:15 AM.

It would emerge years later that Chamberlain had actually vacillated on whether to declare war at 11:15. The September 4, 1967, edition of the London *Daily Express* contained a story in which Alvar Lidell of the BBC revealed that Chamberlain had received last-minute news that Hermann Goering was ready to fly to England to discuss the Polish situation. As late as 11:13 AM, or thirteen minutes after the British ultimatum had expired, Chamberlain was contemplating postponing the broadcast. However, "[a]t 11:14 the P.M. changed his mind again. With a sigh, he rose to his feet. The broadcast was on again."[100]

Chamberlain told the country that no response had been received from Germany by the 11:00 AM deadline, "and that consequently this country is at war with Germany."[101] He then explained his disappointment and dispelled the propaganda that Hitler had put out blaming Poland and Britain for having caused the war:

> You can imagine what a bitter blow it is to me that all my long struggle to win peace has failed. Yet I cannot believe that there is anything more or anything different that I could have done and that would have been more successful.

Up to the very last it would have been quite possible to have arranged a peaceful and honourable settlement between Germany and Poland. But Hitler would not have it. He had evidently made up his mind to attack Poland whatever happened, and although he now says he put forward reasonable proposals which were rejected by the Poles, that is not a true statement.

The proposals were never shown to the Poles, nor to us, and, though they were announced in a German broadcast on Thursday night, Hitler did not wait to hear comments on them, but ordered his troops to cross the Polish frontier. His action shows convincingly that there is no chance of expecting that this man will ever give up his practice of using force to gain his will. He can only be stopped by force.

We and France are to-day, in fulfillment of our obligations, going to the aid of Poland, who is so bravely resisting this wicked and unprovoked attack upon her people. We have a clear conscience. We have done all that any country could do to establish peace, but a situation in which no word given by Germany's ruler could be trusted and no people or country could feel themselves safe had become intolerable. And now that we have resolved to finish it, I know that you will all play your part with calmness and courage.

As such a moment as this the assurances of support that we have received from the Empire are a source of profound encouragement to us.

... Now may God bless you all and may He defend the right. For it is evil things that we shall be fighting against, brute force, bad faith, injustice, oppression, and persecution. And against them I am certain that the right will prevail.[102]

At noon Chamberlain addressed the House. (It was only the fourth time in history that Parliament had met on a Sunday.[103]) The Prime Minister addressed members' concerns from the previous evening that there had been weakening, hesitation or vacillation on the part of His Majesty's Government. He acknowledged that if he had been a member in possession of the limited information the House had, he too would very likely have felt the same way.[104] After recounting the steps surrounding the ultimatum, Chamberlain said that Britain was now at war with Germany:

This is a sad day for all of us, and to none is it sadder than to me. Everything that I have worked for, everything that I have hoped for, everything that I have believed in during my public life, has crashed into ruins. There is only one thing left for me to do; that is, to devote what strength and powers I have to forwarding the victory of the cause for which we have to sacrifice so much. I cannot tell what part I may be allowed to play myself; I trust I may live to see the day when Hitlerism has been destroyed and a liberated Europe has been re-established.[105]

France, after the substantial poking she had received from the British the previous evening, set the hour of its ultimatum to Germany at 5:00 PM September 3.[106]

The speeches that followed Chamberlain's reflected a change of atmosphere in the House from the night before. Churchill spoke in praise of Chamberlain's faithful and sincere efforts for peace and reiterated the importance of the cause for which Britain would fight: "to save the whole world from the pestilence of Nazi tyranny and to ... revive the stature of man."[107] "There was no standing ovation," but after the speeches, "MPs of all parties" surrounded Churchill and "extended congratulations to him."[108] Thereupon, as Chamberlain had requested in a note handed to Churchill when he walked into the House, Churchill again met with the Prime Minister.[109]

Chamberlain cordially welcomed him, said that he had read Churchill's letters, and then offered him the position of First Lord of the Admiralty.[110] Why Churchill received this seeming promotion from Minister without Portfolio to First Lord is a matter of speculation. Perhaps Chamberlain concluded that Churchill as a Cabinet minister with no administrative obligations would have been too disruptive if left to pick and choose what he wished to do.[111] Or perhaps Chamberlain just wanted to reshuffle his original line up of wartime ministers.[112] In any event, Churchill again accepted on the spot. He was back in the Cabinet, reprising the position he held from 1911 to 1915.

At 5:00 PM on September 3, the War Cabinet met for the first time. Much of the meeting dealt with procedure and logistics. One of the few substantive items dealt with was air action. As previously noted, the Poles had said that engagement of German aircraft by Allied forces was a matter of the greatest urgency. General Edmund Ironside, who would become Chief of the Imperial General Staff, had told the Poles months earlier that German bombing raids on Poland would be answered by British bombing raids on Germany.[113] And just that afternoon a telegram had been received from the Commander-in-Chief of the French Armed Forces, General Maurice Gamelin, suggesting that the Royal Air Force take such action that night.[114] But, rather than jumping into the fray with both feet, the War Cabinet merely authorized the Royal Air Force to drop propaganda leaflets that night in three areas of Germany,[115] it also cautioned the French not to proceed with their planned bombing.[116] The War Cabinet did authorize the immediate dispatch of a bomber force to attack the German fleet, which was suspected to have sailed into the North Sea that afternoon.[117]

The Fighting in Poland

When Hitler invaded Poland, he knew that the British and French declarations of war would merely be formalities and believed that neither country would attack Germany. Ambassador Henderson some months earlier had, in fact, told the German State Secretary Ernst von Weizsacker that if there was a war it "would be conducted defensively by the Western Powers."[118] Accordingly, on September 4, Hitler ordered that there be no German attacks on French and British passenger steamers. Five days later Hitler issued Directive 3, which required his personal consent before any other attack was made on the British or the French. As revealed in a speech to the Reichstag on September 6, he hoped that the British would be inclined to make peace even after Poland was defeated.[119]

For the first two weeks of September the Poles battled the Wehrmacht about as well as, or perhaps even a bit better than, could have been expected, especially since the Luftwaffe had quickly gained total control of the sky against the antiquated Polish Air Force. Warsaw itself was the subject of heavy aerial bombardment right from the start. Though the air defense of Warsaw initially performed well, within a week it had become substantially worn down. (Why the British Royal Air Force—the RAF—was scattering pamphlets rather than bombing Germany was a question widely being asked in London.[120]) The same was true with the ground assault of Warsaw. After the initial German attack on the city had been repelled the city was soon placed under siege. The siege lasted until September 27, when the Polish garrison officially capitulated; approximately 140,000 Polish troops were taken prisoner. (Notably, that night John ["Jock"] Colville, who at that time worked for the Foreign Office, wrote in his diary that now Hitler was "free to turn his attention westward."[121*])

The Germans took command of the war in mid-September when they defeated the Poles at the Battle of the Bzura River, which took place just west of Warsaw. Polish forces then withdrew to the southeast where they planned to defend an area (now part of Ukraine) in the hills along the borders with Romania and the Soviet Union while they awaited the support and relief from Britain and France. The French had promised an offensive on the Western

---

Colville would soon be promoted to Chamberlain's assistant personal secretary, after which he would serve in the same capacity for Prime Minister Churchill.

Front; before the war, "General Gamelin had assured the Poles that within 15 days of the German attack, forty divisions, the 'bulk of the French army' would be hurled against the Reich."[122]

No such French offensive ever took place. The historian John Lukacs writes that an Allied ground attack against Germany, while the German armies were fighting in Poland, was simply not possible "because it was not planned, and it was not planned because it was not possible."[123] Moreover, Gamelin (and the French) were defensive-minded, not offensive-minded[124]* Gamelin was also not willing to engage in any offensive operation until the French and British had built up their forces sufficiently.

While neither France nor Britain made an appearance in the war, the Soviet Union did.** On September 17, the Red Army invaded eastern Poland, the territory that fell into the Soviet "sphere of influence" according to the secret protocol of the Molotov-Ribbentrop Pact. Facing a second front, the Polish Government concluded the defense of the Romanian bridgehead was no longer feasible and ordered an emergency evacuation of all troops to neutral Romania. The Polish war ended on October 6, 1939.

Interestingly, on September 22 the British Government sent out a telegram to its diplomatic personnel abroad explaining why Britain had not lifted a finger to help Poland. As Colville wrote in his diary that night, the telegram said that "the Poles knew we could give them no effective help and realized that we could only save them in the long run—when Germany has been defeated.[***] 'To have devoted hundreds of British planes to bombing raids in Germany would have meant spectacular successes, but [also] the inevitable loss of machines which will be used more effectively on the Western front.'"[125] In his diary entry of September 28, Colville also noted that "it would probably be a good thing if Chamberlain resigned soon and left the conduct of the war to some younger and forceful successor." But who? Colville thought Churchill was too old and unstable; Halifax, though

---

*French troops were only trained and equipped for defensive actions. Taylor, Origins p. 59.

**Although Britain sent no troops to assist Poland, the British Expeditionary Force, commanded by General Lord John Gort, did begin to arrive in France starting on September 9, 1939. The BEF spent the next seven months training for action. By May 1940, the BEF had been built up to over 300,000 men. Because it was believed that the rugged terrain of the Ardennes region, which included territory in France, Germany, Belgium, and Luxembourg, would preclude a German attack through Luxembourg, and that the man-made fortifications of the venerable Maginot Line would do likewise further east, the BEF would be deployed along the border of France and Belgium where the main German attack was anticipated. Grenhan and Nicoll, Dunkirk Evacuation-Operation Dynamo pp. vii–viii.

***As discussed in the previous chapter, this also was the view of His Majesty's Government and is, on balance, probably correct.

respected, did not, he felt, have the drive needed to keep the country united and enthusiastic; and there were no outstanding personalities among younger politicians.[126]

October 6, 1939: Hitler Makes a Peace Offer to England and France

Just before Warsaw fell, German radio and newspapers started to discuss the prospects for peace.[127] At about the same time, Mr. "D" ran into an old friend, George Ogilvie-Forbes, former counselor at the British Embassy in Berlin but now serving in the same role at the embassy in Oslo.[128] "D" advised Hitler on September 26 that Ogilvie-Forbes had told him that the British Government was looking for peace but needed a way to "save face."[129] Hitler responded that the problem was easy to solve: all Britain had to do was acknowledge that Poland was gone, in which case he would guarantee the rest of Europe. Hitler then agreed with "D"'s offer to go to England and "send out feelers."[130]

That same evening, the British War Cabinet met at 6:00 o'clock to discuss a report from "D" that Goering wanted to negotiate a peace.[131] No record of the meeting was made. Biographer Robert Self reports that Chamberlain was dubious and believed that Hitler would insist on the acceptance of German territorial gains and consent to give Hitler a free hand in the East; only then might there be negotiations with Britain to settle outstanding issues.[132] The very next day, September 27, with Goering's offer still fresh in British minds, Hitler met with the heads of the Wehrmacht to tell them he had decided to attack the West on November 12.[133] Hitler and his cronies had no issue with being duplicitous.

Sometime during the following week, news leaked out that Hitler was planning to include a long-awaited peace proposal in his speech to the Reichstag on October 6.[134] On October 3, Chamberlain addressed the House about the anticipated German proposal. He refused to speculate as to how his Government would respond to a proposal that had yet to be presented, but he did say that "no man would welcome more wholeheartedly than I, any proposal which I could really feel had achieved the aims which I have described as the aims of this Government and of this country in entering into this war."[135]

In Hitler's October 6 speech, he declared that Germany had no quarrels with France, that it was one of his life's aims to reconcile the German and British peoples, and that a peace deal could be possible if Germany were allowed to retain Poland and Czechoslovakia, and if the colonies that the Versailles treaty had stripped from it were returned. In exchange, Britain could maintain her Empire.[136] Of course, he also laid out a list of "problems" yet to be solved, which included the following: "the creation of a Reich frontier ... in accordance with historical, ethnographical, and economic conditions"; "disposition of the entire living space according to the various nationalities..."; and "settlement of the Jewish problem."[137] To solve these "problems" he proposed a conference of leading nations.[138] Hitler's proposal was almost exactly as Chamberlain had predicted. The German Chancellor added that "If, however, the opinions of Messrs. Churchill and followers should prevail, the statement will have been my last. Then we shall fight. ..."[139]

Commenting on Hitler's terms, Churchill stated:

> Personally, I find them absolutely unacceptable. They are the terms of a conqueror! But we are not yet conquered! No, no, we are not yet conquered! ... Some of my Conservative friends advised peace. They feared that Germany will turn Bolshevik during the war. *But I am all for war to the end. Hitler must be destroyed. Nazism must be crushed once and for all.* Let Germany become Bolshevik. That doesn't scare me. Better Communism than Nazism.[140] [emphasis added]

At the October 7 War Cabinet meeting, Halifax agreed that Hitler's speech was unsatisfactory, containing "obscurities, contradictions and difficulties."[141] The Foreign Secretary added that he was coming increasingly to the view that his chief war aim was to eliminate Hitler.[142] After further discussion, the War Cabinet agreed that a statement in reply should be made by the Prime Minister to the House. Chamberlain and the War Cabinet recognized that Hitler's offer had to be rejected. Much as Chamberlain feared, just the prospect of Hitler's proposal had encouraged those in Britain who believed in peace-at-any-price; in fact, 75 percent of the letters Chamberlain was receiving at the time advocated stopping the war.[143]

On October 8, Mr. "D" was sent back to Germany with a stern reply from the British, who "demand[ed] the restoration of Polish statehood, immediate destruction of all aggressive weapons, and a plebiscite within Germany on Hitler's foreign policy."[144] It takes very little imagination to appreciate just how well Hitler received this reply. Chamberlain's proposed official reply to Hitler was discussed at the next day's War Cabinet meeting. It was agreed that the tone of the official reply should also be very firm, but it should definitely not shut the door—that is, the proposal should make clear that the ball was in Hitler's court.[145] At the War Cabinet meeting on October 11, a message from Australia urged that the statement stress that the countries of the British Commonwealth, along with all other free countries, were endangered by German aggression and that they would fight for the principle of the rule of law and not merely to restore the status quo of the conditions of the Versailles treaty.[146]

Chamberlain's Response and His Plan to Take No Offensive Action Unless Provoked

In his speech to the House on October 12, Chamberlain said that "the proposals which the German Chancellor puts forward for the establishment of what he calls 'the certainty of European security' are based on recognition of his conquests and of his right to do what he pleases with the conquered. It would be impossible for Great Britain to accept any such basis without forfeiting her honour and abandoning her claim that international disputes should be settled by discussion and not by force."[147] The Prime Minister then outlined many of Hitler's broken promises over the years, culminating with the reiteration that "The plain truth is that, after our past experience, it is no longer possible to rely upon the unsupported word of the present German government." Chamberlain added that "It was not ... with any vindictive purpose that we embarked on war but simply in defence of freedom. ... [S]urrender to wrongdoing would spell the extinction of all hope, and the annihilation of all those values of life which have through centuries been at once the mark and the inspiration of human progress."[148]

Hitler's proposals were labeled "vague and uncertain and contain no suggestion for righting the wrongs done to Czecho-Slovakia and to Poland." Even if that were not the case, the P.M. noted, "it would still be necessary to ask by what practical means the German Government intend to convince the world that aggression will cease and that pledges will be kept."[149] He concluded: "[A]cts—not words alone—must be forthcoming before we ... would be justified in ceasing to wage war to the utmost of our strength."[150]

The subsequent speech by Clement Attlee, the leader of the Labour Party, put frosting on the cake when, in talking about the essential difficulties of dealing with Hitler's peace proposals he said, "The first thing is that they are made by a man whose word is utterly worthless."[151]

Between October 1939 and April 1940, when the Norway campaign was started, the ball had been passed back to Hitler, as Britain waited to see if the German leader was in any way capable of rational and honorable discourse. Jock Colville, Chamberlain's assistant personal secretary, observed that while Chamberlain "would have gone further than Churchill in making concessions to a new German government even if it included some of the Nazi leaders," the Prime Minister was adamant that "nothing would ever induce him to deal with Hitler, whose supersession would be an essential prerequisite of any settlement."[152] The P.M. maintained the "utterly implacable conviction that it was 'essential to get rid of Hitler.'"[153] According to Colville, "Chamberlain realized that Hitler's brutality was matched by his unreliability," but the P.M.'s feelings also involved "an element of damaged vanity."[154] Hitler had made a fool of Chamberlain.[155]

Chamberlain's October 12 speech received a favorable reception in Britain, but not in Germany.[156] The Germans responded that, by rejecting Hitler's peace offer, Chamberlain had "chosen war."[157] Colville described the Germans as being furious.[158]

Chamberlain believed that it was too early for any successful peace negotiation—the Germans did not yet believe that they could fail to win the war. That said, he was confident that Hitler would eventually come to that conclusion. Thus, Chamberlain intended to wait and "take no offensive [action] unless Hitler beg[an] it."[159] He predicted that following this strategy Britain would win the war by spring.[160] The P.M. said that "however much the Nazis may brag and threaten, I don't believe they feel sufficient confidence to venture into a great war unless they are forced into it by action on our part."[161] Mr. Chamberlain had at last become a full-fledged player at the table. But he still did not fully appreciate that Hitler's capacity to become "extremely irrational" was a potent wild card.

Hitler's Secret Directive No. 6

Talk of peace notwithstanding, on October 10, two days before Chamberlain had given his speech in Parliament, Hitler met with his generals and presented them with Directive No. 6.* The Directive called for preparations to begin immediately for the discussed attack on the West at the earliest date possible. Hitler said that destroying the Western democracies would increase international respect for greater Germany.[162]

As explained in the Directive, the purposes of the offensive was to

1. "defeat as much as possible of the French Army and of the forces of the Allies fighting on their side," and

2. "win as much territory as possible in Holland, Belgium and Northern France, which would serve as a base for the successful prosecution of the air and sea war against England and as a wide protective area for the economically vital Ruhr Basin."[163]

October 10 was also the day on which the Soviet Union muscled Estonia, Latvia, and Lithuania into permitting the establishment of Russian garrisons on their territory. Even though the Russians offered territorial compensation, Finland adamantly opposed allowing the Soviets into their country. Over the next five weeks the Russians would push their demands, ultimately leading to an attack on Finland.

Stalin's territorial ambitions troubled Hitler.

The idea of another major offensive on the heels of the Polish war did not, however, sit well with the German High Command. Several of Germany's leading generals tried to convince Hitler that such an offensive was impossible—for example, a substantial amount of time was needed to do maintenance on the tanks used in Poland.[164] Still, Hitler continued to press the idea that an attack on the West should happen by November 12. As Shirer puts it, by early to mid-October, Hitler "was fed up with what he thought to be the unpardonable timidity of his generals."[165] But, this time, the German military commanders who opposed him would prevail. On November 5 Hitler reluctantly agreed to postpone the attack on the West until the spring of 1941.[166]*

Why Turn to the West? What Was Hitler's Plan for Britain?

Neither the British nor the French had not fought over Poland. In fact, they had taken virtually no military action against Germany since declaring war. In fact, Chamberlain had no plans to do so. Such being the case two questions arise:

- Why did Hitler feel the need to turn against the West?**

- Why couldn't he have taken the passivity of Britain and France as a de facto agreement to his having a free hand in the East?

One reason explaining Hitler's attack on the West was his alleged fear of an attack against the Ruhr Valley, Germany's prime industrial and coal-mining area.[167] As noted, however, France, which borders the Ruhr, had not shown that kind of military aggressiveness in decades. Likewise, Chamberlain planned to do nothing. Thus, it is simply unlikely that, in October 1939, Hitler suddenly became scared of the French army—although he might have had concerns about Britain's ability to bomb the Ruhr. Another possible reason for Hitler's turning against the West is suggested in *Mein Kampf*, in which he decried the results and aftermath of WWI and called for revenge against France (Germany's "mortal enemy").[168] An invasion of Belgium and

---

As coincidence would have it, on November 5 Colville wrote in his diary how incredible it was, if Germany really meant to wage war in earnest, that "she should have allowed these valuable months to slip by." Colville p. 48.

**As Hitler said in a speech to his commanders on August 22, 1939, his original plan was to establish a tolerable relationship with Poland and then go to war against the West. DGFP series D, "Memorandum of the speech by Hitler to Commanders in Chief 22 August 1939," vii. No. 192, pp. 203.*

Holland would simply be a means to get at France. Moreover, defeating France (better yet humiliating her) would abrogate the loss attributed to Germany in World War I and the debasing culmination of WWI would be eliminated from the German psyche.

Hitler did not have the same animus toward Britain. In fact, as discussed below, until mid-summer 1940 Hitler had no plan or intention to invade Britain. Notably, Directive No. 6 did not talk about an invasion of the British Isles. It only discussed using the land gained in Holland, Belgium, and Northern France "as a base for conducting a promising air and sea war against England. ..."[169] Such an air and sea war would be conducted to force Britain to enter into a peace agreement, if the subjugation of all of Western Europe proved not to be enough of an inducement.

Ostensibly, all Hitler wanted from Britain was its agreement to give him a free hand in the East. But as Air Commodore Andrew Lambert writes, "[After the fall of France,] Hitler could have consolidated his position on the continent, ignored the British, and begun his planning for [the invasion of the Soviet Union]."[170] He could have given Britain a unilateral armistice. But Hitler knew that if simply left alone, Britain might at some point become more than just a minor annoyance to him.* To ensure that this never occurred, Hitler would not be happy until he had forced Britain to agree to become a vassal state just, as France ultimately did.[171] Hitler had already picked out the individuals who would play key roles in a puppet British Government. King George would be replaced by his Hitler-sycophant brother Edward,[172] and David Lloyd George, an unabashed defeatist and Hitler sympathizer, would return to the Prime Ministership and become Britain's Pétain.[173]** There were even discussions between Hitler and the German High Command about Chamberlain and Halifax being in the new cabinet.[174]

The Phoney War; The "Bore War"

Its Effect on Chamberlain and His Thinking

The fighting in Poland lasted about five weeks. For the five months thereafter, little happened militarily. American journalists dubbed the period until the Spring of 1940 as the "Phoney War."*** Lukacs says that a better

---

*Britain's attempt to reduce the supply of iron ore flowing into Germany by attacking the Norwegian port of Narvik (discussed below) is an example of the problems Britain could pose for the Reich.

**Marshal Philippe Pétain, a war hero in France during WWI, became the disgraced head of state in collaborationist Vichy France.

***"Phoney" is the British spelling of "phony."

name for it may have been the "Reluctant War,"[175] and still others just call it the "Bore War."[176] As the Italian Ambassador to France succinctly put it, "I have seen several wars waged without being declared, but this is the first I have seen declared without being waged."[177]

At first, the advent of war had a seemingly profound effect on Chamberlain. As he wrote in his diary in early September, before war was declared, he "felt indispensable" while working for peace, because "no one else could carry out [his] policy." But since the war began, he felt that "half a dozen people" could lead the country.[178] Interestingly, he regained his sense of worth rather quickly. As reflected in his diary entry of September 10, 1939, Chamberlain believed there was a deeply rooted, widespread desire in Germany to avoid war and that it would not be long before that view would somehow find expression.[179] According to Self, Chamberlain believed that this widespread demand for peace from all across Europe would soon result in his being "called upon once more to assume the mantle of the peacemaker."[180] This view was premised on two alternative assumptions. The first was that, even though Hitler was a madman, he surely had to recognize that aggression against the West, whether or not successful, could result in frightful losses that would endanger the whole Nazi system.[181] Chamberlain's alternate assumption was that even if the German people followed Hitler down the path toward collective catastrophe, "the German economy would never stand the strain." Accordingly, Chamberlain was simply willing to do nothing but wait.[182] The P.M. planned it to be a "reluctant" war.[183]

Self notes three flaws with Chamberlain's thinking: (1) he still did not appreciate the irrationality that drove Hitler—this was a man who had written in *Mein Kampf* that "Germany will either be a world power or there will be no Germany"; (2) the political community in Britain was quickly becoming tired of the "Bore War," and a significant majority of the public was not eager to see British troops engaged in action anywhere—in polls taken between December 1939 and February 1940, by a margin of 3 to 1, Britons favored the Government's policy of waiting for the Germans to take some action[184]; and (3) he put undue faith in Britain's ability to blockade Germany successfully.[185]*

Self writes that after the declaration of war, Chamberlain privately confessed that his greatest fear was not military defeat but mounting pressure

---

*The Molotov-Ribbentrop Pact, which led to Russia supplying foodstuffs to Germany, and German air superiority at the gateway to the North Sea, would undercut the efficacy of a blockade. Self pp. 396–97. The belief that the German economy could not sustain the war was ultimately proven to be fallacious. See, Philpott, The Royal Air Force: Rearmament 1930–1939 p. 30.

from peace-at-any-price Britons.[186] While he felt that "in a waiting war ... [Britain] could outlast the Germans,"[187] he feared that down the road, pressure on the home front might make rejecting future proposals much harder. Of course, negotiating any new arrangement with the Nazis, something to which he (unlike Churchill) was not opposed,[188] would run squarely against his steadfast but painfully achieved conviction never to negotiate with Hitler again.

Things That Occurred During the "Bore War"

What happened during the so-called "Bore War"?

- Skirmishes between French and German forces along their common border and in the Saar District of southwestern Germany. But these encounters never amounted to much.

- Occasional air battles between the RAF and the Luftwaffe over the English Channel, with the first actual bombing of Britain taking place on October 16, 1939.

- Occasional Luftwaffe bombing runs on the Royal Navy's huge naval base at Scapa Flow in Northern Scotland.

- Russia's invasion of Finland in late November 1939. The Finns proved to be a much tougher opponent that Russia anticipated. This war ended in March 1940 with Finland ceding about 10 percent of the country (representing some 30 percent of its economy) to the Soviets.

- Churchill's issuing a memorandum on December 16 about German iron-ore supplies. "He consider[ed] it essential to use drastic and even illegal methods to prevent ore being shipped from Norwegian ports; he want[ed] Cabinet authority to lay minefields in Norwegian territorial waters (with the justification that German U-boats were sinking ships in those waters) in order to drive ships carrying iron ore out of territorial waters into the hands of [British] contraband control."[189]

- The selection in March 1940 of Paul Renaud as Premier, by the French Chamber of Deputies. Renaud's ascent was followed by the signing of a declaration by Britain and France saying that neither would sign a separate peace with Germany.

Norway

On January 2, 1940, at Churchill's instigation, the War Cabinet debated a daring offensive scheme involving the neutral countries of Norway and Sweden. As laid out in a report prepared by the Chiefs of Staff in late December 1939,[190] Germany's principal interest in Scandinavia was iron: the flow of iron ore from deposits in Northern Sweden—transport of the ore in the summer by train to the Baltic port of Luleå, Sweden and in the winter, when Luleå was normally ice-bound, by rail to the Norwegian port of Narvik.

Narvik, which is in the far north of Norway, is situated near the inland end of Vest Fjord, a stretch of water that is 50 miles wide at its mouth and about 100 miles long. The fjord opens to the Norwegian Sea.[191] At Narvik, iron ore was loaded onto German ore vessels, which traversed the fjord to the sea, then turned southward (staying within Norwegian territorial waters along the Norwegian coast), crossed through the Skagerrak strait between Denmark and Norway, and landed in various Baltic ports in northern Germany.

The British contemplated three options to stop the flow of iron in winter: (1) blockading Narvik with destroyers and minefields; (2) landing a force in northern Norway to occupy Narvik and possibly take possession of the Swedish ore deposits themselves;* or (3) doing both. It was suggested that these interventions might bring the Reich to its knees.[192]

---

*This idea had first been floated in the War Cabinet in September 1939; no action was taken on it then.

Churchill had been an advocate for this plan since shortly after joining the War Cabinet.[193] Implementation was delayed by Chamberlain, the French, and the cautious sea lords of the Royal Navy.[194]

The idea of the Allies' occupying a few key portions of Norway gained some momentum with the Soviet invasion of Finland in late November, 1939, and the advent of winter. Responding to that invasion, Britain and France started organizing an expeditionary force to aid the Finns. To reach Finnish territory the Allies would have to traverse the northern portions of Norway and Sweden and thus approach both the source of the iron ore mined for Germany and the route by which that ore is shipped during the winter.[195] At the Supreme War Council* meeting in Paris on February 5, 1940, the Allies agreed that any expeditionary force being sent to Finland

---

Headquartered in Paris, the Supreme War Council oversaw Allied military strategy in the early portion of WWII.

should also seize the Swedish iron mines located around Gällivare and the Norwegian transit port of Narvik.[196] But the end of the Russo-Finish war in March curtailed the Allies' plan.

Concerned both about maintaining the flow of iron ore through Narvik and having access to the North Sea, in mid-December 1939, Hitler ordered the High Command of the Wehrmacht (the Oberkommando der Wehrmacht, or OKW) to come up with a plan to invade Norway.[197] In January, a small working group made up of representatives from the German army, navy, and air force was set up within the OKW to work on the plan. On March 1, Hitler issued a formal directive calling for Germany to occupy both Denmark and Norway. Under the directive, the Germans were to do their "utmost to make the operation appear as a *peaceful* occupation, the object of which is the military protection of the neutrality of the Scandinavian States."[198] [emphasis in original] Though it was hoped that Denmark and Norway, as well as Britain and France, would be "taken by surprise,"[199] news of these German plans began making its way to London almost immediately.

On March 21, 1940, the War Cabinet was advised that fifteen ore ships with a total tonnage of eighty thousand tons had arrived in Narvik during the preceding ten days and either had sailed or were about to sail back to Germany.[200] But it was not until April 1 that the War Cabinet authorized laying mines in Norwegian territorial waters.[201] April 5 was set as the date for doing so.[202] Anglo-French troops were scheduled to land in Narvik three days later, while other troops would land at the Norwegian ports of Bergen, Trondheim, and Stavanger "to deny these bases to the enemy."[203] The operation was named "Wilfred."[204]

Manchester writes that "[h]ad this schedule been followed, the Allies would almost certainly have scored a resounding triumph."[205] However, on Saturday April 6, as Colville recounts in his diary, "from Denmark comes a rumor that [just like the British and French] the Germans are proposing to invade Norway on Monday [April 8] and to land troops at Narvik."[206] (Germany did not in fact invade Norway until April 9.)

From the very outset of the war, if not before, the German Navy believed that Norway was strategically important. Occupying the Norwegian coast would not only assure Germany's ability to maintain the flow of iron ore from Sweden during the winter but would allow the German navy to break the British blockade line across the North Sea and permit German surface ships access to the Atlantic Ocean, access Germany did not have during the whole of WWI.[207]

The first German vessels in the operation set sail in the early hours of April 3rd.[208] On Saturday, April 6, Britain also began sending troops to Norway, for the express purpose of occupying Norwegian ports and closing them to Germany.[209] As laid out in draft instructions (dated April 5, 1940) for the French troops that were to join in the attack at Narvik: "The object will be to secure the port of Narvik and the line of communications inland, as far as the Norwegian-Swedish frontier. Subsequently, an opportunity *may* arise to go on to Galivare [*sic*], and the role of the force would then become the denial of the Galivare [*sic*], ore fields to Germany"[210] The object for other forces was "to forestall the Germans and deny to them the use of the port and air facilities at Stavanger, Bergen, and Trondheim."[211] It seems like the Allies were not expecting serious trouble: "It is considered unlikely that [the Germans] could occupy Bergen or Trondheim before the arrival of our detachments."[212]

Because of squabbling between the British and the French over a wholly unrelated matter—the laying of fluvial mines in the Rhine—Churchill flew to Paris on April 5.[213] His trip set the start of "Operation Wilfred" back to April 8. "The delay proved fatal."[214]

News from RAF air reconnaissance on Sunday night April 7 revealed that German battle cruisers, with several destroyers and other vessels, were out at sea and moving very swiftly northward.[215] Analysts concluded that the German warships were heading toward Narvik.[216] As it turns out, the battle group was part of a daring German maneuver. While these ships attracted the Royal Navy's attention, a German convoy of troopships and accompanying destroyers would sneak, hopefully unnoticed, through the Skagerrak and slip along the Norwegian coast to various Norwegian ports, including Narvik.[217] The plan was to land 2,000 men at Narvik, 1,700 at Trondheim and 1,300 at Bergen.[218]

Once the German warships were discovered, the Royal Navy's Home Fleet immediately put to sea to intercept them,[219] not knowing, of course, the German ships were merely decoys.[220] At the same time, another British naval force was approaching Narvik to lay mines off the Norwegian coast, which it did between 4:30 and 5:50 AM on Monday morning, April 8.[221] But the important German convoy to Norway proceeded with no interference from the Royal Navy, except for some harassment by British submarines.[222] As Churchill described the situation to the House a month later, "it looked as though the ... German battle cruisers and other enemy warships, would be caught between our forces in the North and the main Home Fleet, both of which were superior. However, German warships got away owing to the weather conditions."[223] On the other hand, German transports had moved surreptitiously through Norwegian territorial waters, over which the Royal Navy had no control.[224]

Churchill also told the House that:

- On Tuesday morning (April 9) during a snowstorm off Narvik, the British battle cruiser *Renown* engaged the Germans' prize battleship

Scharnhorst and observed hits on her forward structure before the German ship retired at high speed.[225]

- On Tuesday afternoon the fleet was cruising south about the level of Bergen when it was attacked continually by German aircraft. One ship was sunk, and several others were damaged.

- That night, British destroyers were ordered to blockade the Vest Fjord leading to Narvik.

- Five destroyers were also ordered to attack the German destroyers which accompanied the troopships and supply ships that by then had safely reached Narvik harbor.[226]

On April 9, an hour before dawn, German ambassadors in Denmark and Norway presented their counterparts with an ultimatum: accept the protection of the Reich instantly and without resistance or Germany would seize the country by force.[227] Almost immediately, German motorized and armed forces crossed the Danish frontier, and a small naval expedition entered Copenhagen harbor. It quickly became clear that further resistance was pointless, and the Danish Government was forced to agree to the German ultimatum, although they did so under protest.[228] Norway did not, saying, "We will not submit voluntarily: the struggle is already under way."[229]

At a special meeting of the War Cabinet held at 8:30 AM, there were reports from Norway that two German warships were at Trondheim, five ships had sailed to Bergen (and the port was being occupied by German soldiers), and one ship was approaching Stavanger, where the Norwegians had a large, strategically located, air base. Reports also said that four other ships had sailed into the Oslo fjord and reached Tønsberg, a city near the mouth of the 50-mile-long fjord leading up to Oslo. The War Cabinet did not yet know that German ships had, in fact, reached Narvik.[230] According to Colville, "[T]he question everyone was asking was why did our fleet allow the Germans to establish themselves at Bergen and Trondheim."[231] The same question would have also applied to Narvik.

General Sir Edmund Ironside, the Chief of the Imperial General Staff, told the Cabinet that Britain should go ahead with its plan for seizing Narvik. Ironside said that one battalion could sail at midday and be at Narvik in three days' time. The information he had received showed that the Germans had not yet arrived, but, in fact, by 8:00 AM on April 9, the Germans held Narvik.[232] Two thousand German troops, carried on ten destroyers, had landed there.[233]

The British also thought it vitally important to prevent the Germans from establishing themselves at Trondheim and Bergen, in part because if the Norwegians were driven out of Oslo, they would retire to these other cities. Britain believed the German forces at these ports could not be very strong, probably no more than 2,000 men, and these troops had probably accomplished little more than taking the docks. Now was the critical moment: Ironside said that British forces would do everything possible to prevent the Germans from sending reinforcements, and thus would leave Bergen and Trondheim open for the Norwegians to retreat to and for the British to access as ports of entry for themselves. If necessary, the railway lines could also be torn up to prevent any German advance from Oslo.[234] First Lord of the Admiralty Churchill agreed, but he strongly advocated proceeding with the operation against Narvik as well.[235]

The following declaration, put out by wireless from the German Government, was read to the War Cabinet:

> The High Command of the German Army announces that, in order to counteract the actions against Denmark and Norway and to prevent a possible hostile attack against these countries, the German Army has taken these two countries under its protection.[236]

In response, the War Cabinet agreed that:

- the Royal Navy should take all possible steps to clear Bergen and Trondheim of enemy forces;

- preparations should be made for military expeditions to recapture Bergen and Trondheim and to occupy Narvik; and

- Halifax should inform the Norwegian Government that Britain would take all possible steps to support them against the Germans.[237]

A second War Cabinet meeting on April 9 was held at noon. By the time that meeting started, five Norwegian port cities along the south and west coasts, from Skagerrak to Narvik, had been captured by the Germans.[238] Bergen and Trondheim had fallen, and German garrisons were soon established there.[239] As historian John Lukacs puts it, the Germans simply beat the British to these ports: "The British, including Churchill, did not believe that the Germans would venture that far."[240]

Only Oslo had yet to be taken by the Nazis.[241] The Norwegian Navy and land fortresses had repelled the Germans as they sailed up the Oslo Fjord toward the capital; Norwegian forces sank several ships and substantially damaged several others.[242] Crucially, the Norwegian Royal Family, the Government, and the Parliament all had time to board a special train that took them to Hamar, a city 80 miles to the north of Oslo on Norway's largest lake. Also escaping Oslo was a convoy of trucks loaded with all the gold in the Bank of Norway, and a cache of secret papers from the foreign office.[243]

Several days earlier, on April 5, Chamberlain had delivered a major address to the Conservative National Union in which he said that, at the outset of the war, Germany's preparations for war were far ahead of what Britain had been able to accomplish. The P.M. thought it extraordinary that Hitler had not attempted to take advantage of that.[244] Telling the group that Britain had now closed the gap and using words he had used before but would come to regret, the Prime Minister said that Hitler "missed the bus."[245] Chamberlain's assessment was not accurate. As Manchester aptly puts it, "Hitler had already boarded another bus which followed its timetable with Teutonic precision and on Tuesday, April 9 at 4:10 AM began dropping off its passengers—elements from three Wehrmacht divisions—at their destinations..., the chief ports of Norway, from Oslo right up to Narvik. ..."[246] Put more acidly, "it was the British who missed the bus. ..."[247]

On the afternoon of April 9, Chamberlain advised the House that his Government, after giving notice to its Norwegian counterpart, had on the previous day laid minefields in Norwegian waters, to hinder the passage of German ships. He also announced that "Germany has today invaded Denmark and Norway."[248] Chamberlain was quick to dispose of the German assertion that the invasion of Norway was a reprisal for Britain's actions in Norwegian territorial waters. He pointed out that an operation like the one the Germans had just carried out required much planning and coordination to land troops simultaneously at several ports, to assemble the necessary naval forces, and to lay mines in Norwegian harbors.[249] Chamberlain also said the Allies did not contemplate occupying any Scandinavian territory not attacked by Germany.[250] Lastly, he disclosed that His Majesty's Government had decided to extend full aid to Norway and that Britain would fight the war shoulder to shoulder with the Norwegians. In fact, he said, powerful units of the Royal Navy were already at sea.[251]

As for Denmark, Chamberlain said that German motorized and armed forces crossed the Danish frontier at daybreak, and a considerable area of Danish territory was already occupied by German forces.[252]

That night, Colville wrote in his diary:

> The situation is becoming clearer. The Germans have scored a considerable success by seizing the Norwegian ports despite our command of the sea, and we, who started the whole business, seemed to have lost the initiative. Nevertheless, the Germans' hold on the northern ports must be precarious, we may be able to dislodge them without much difficulty and the operation may give us a chance of putting into action the

original project of denying the Gallvare [*sic*] iron-ore fields to Germany."[253]

He also noted the prescient opinion of Chamberlain's principal private secretary, Arthur Rucker, who "is convinced that, if this affair goes seriously wrong, the Government will fall or be reformed." And fall it would, thirty days later.

As April 10 began, Chamberlain seemed "depressed by the situation" in Norway and admitted that the Germans "had reason to be elated by their success."[254] By the noon War Cabinet meeting, broadcasts from Oslo were finally saying that a small German force had landed at Narvik. Churchill told the War Cabinet that the German transports that had reached Narvik the day before must have slipped by British patrols during the day's heavy weather, although it would seem hard for a flotilla of ten destroyers to just "slip by."[255] Churchill then said that orders had been given to the Royal Navy to force their way into Narvik and Bergen. Churchill, who saw the German forces that had landed as potential prizes for Britain, added that the German incursion would be liquidated within a week or two. He also was heartened to know that the Norwegians were resisting.[256]

By noon on April 10 the Germans had flown about five companies of lightly armed airborne infantry troops to the airport just outside Oslo. Norwegian troops could have easily destroyed them; but in the confusion engulfing the Norwegian capital, those troops were never deployed. Accordingly, the German infantry took the city, and the Norwegians never fired a shot.[257]

As directed, five British destroyers sailed into Narvik harbor on April 10. There they sank two German destroyers and damaged three others.[258] However, when departing the harbor, they ran into the five more German destroyers that were lying in adjacent fjords. The heavier-gunned Germans sank one British destroyer and caused the grounding of another; the three surviving British ships escaped to sea.[259] On the way out of the Vest Fjord, they managed to sink the German supply ship *Rauenfels,* which was full of reserve ammunition.[260]*

At the War Cabinet meeting on April 11, Lord Halifax related that the Norwegian Government had appointed a committee to negotiate with the Germans. He emphasized the importance of Britain getting a foothold somewhere in Norway.[261] Chamberlain pointed out that the prospect had to be faced that the Norwegian government might capitulate at any minute.[262] The

---

Churchill was later asked why a big ship was not sent in along with the destroyers days earlier. Churchill responded that the only big ship available at that time was a battle cruiser, and since "we have only three ... we felt that it would be a very great damage to the balance of the Fleet if we lost a battle-cruiser." HC Deb 08 May 1940 vol 360 cc1352–3.

meeting produced the first hint of criticism of Britain's Norway adventure. Sir Kingsley Wood, the Lord Privy Seal, said that the British public and neutral countries both were asking how the Germans had managed to successfully invade Norway in the face of the Royal Navy?[263] Among the many points raised in the ensuing discussion were:

(i) There had been a wholesale abuse of Norwegian territorial waters, which had been entirely to the advantage of the Germans.

(ii) Bad weather (a snowstorm) had acted in favor of the Germans.

(iii) A completely unscrupulous enemy enjoyed the advantage of being able to prepare and execute plans without regard to international law or the decencies of civilization.

(iv) The popular notion was that the Germans must have sent expeditions comprising transports and battleships to each of their landing sites. In fact, just in the case of Oslo the transports and warships traveled together. In all other cases, only the men-of-war had been seen in the open sea, meaning the transports must have moved surreptitiously through territorial waters, over which Britain had no control.

(v) It should be made clear that the blame attached not to Britain but to the neutrals, and we should take every opportunity to bring this point home.[264]

Chamberlain told the Cabinet that dislodging the Germans from Stavanger, Bergen, and Trondheim would be difficult because each could be reinforced fairly easily from Oslo.[265] The Prime Minister thus concluded that Narvik, which would remain relatively isolated for at least another month, offered the only possible objective of an Allied attack.[266] He added that the French were willing to participate.[267] Churchill agreed wholeheartedly with the goal of recapturing Narvik.[268] Both he and Sir Dudley Pound, the First Sea Lord, believed that besides shutting down the flow of iron ore, retaking Narvik would, more importantly, allow the British to set up a naval base where it could refuel its ships.[269] The War Cabinet agreed that Britain's first aim should be the recapture of Narvik.[270] That evening, the Military Coordination Committee concurred.[271] It was also proposed that the Royal Navy use the small Norwegian naval base located at Harstad, 15 miles north of Narvik. Finally, on April 11, three British infantry battalions neared Narvik; but out of extreme caution, their commander decided not to risk a landing there. Instead, he chose to land 35 miles to the north, where there was a contingent of Norwegian troops.[272]

That morning the London papers triumphantly reported in large headlines the recapture by British forces of both Bergen and Trondheim. Unfortunately, the stories were not true.[273] By April 10, British troops had been put ashore, but at small ports in the general vicinity rather than at Trondheim or Bergen.[274] Moreover, British troops encountering the Germans proved not to be much of a match.[275] As Churchill would tell the House on the afternoon of April 11, through the Royal Navy "we can make our will prevail ultimately in any part of the seas which may be selected for operations." But as he described after the war in *The Gathering Storm,* land operations in Norway were an entirely different story: "[We] were out-paced by the enemy moving by land across very large distances in the face of every obstacle. In this Norwegian encounter some of our finest troops, the Scots and Irish Guards, were baffled by the vigour, enterprise, and training of Hitler's young men."[276]

In a clear attempt to deflect criticism from the Royal Navy for letting the Germans successfully invade Norway, Churchill also pointed out that:

- The Royal Navy had been heavily engaged in bringing merchant shipping past extreme U-boats activity and safely into British ports;

- It was foolish to think that the strength of the Royal Navy should have been expended ceaselessly patrolling up and down the Norwegian coast, serving as targets for U-boats and wearing out their crews and machinery, on the chance that Hitler would launch a blow (like the one he did).[277]

Roberts describes Churchill's arguments as "rather lame."[278]

Churchill then told the House that in the end everything would work out well, because "Herr Hitler has committed a grave strategic error in spreading the war so far to the North." He continued: "that cursed corridor [by which the Germans ship Swedish iron ore] is now closed forever," and "[Hitler] has made a whole series of commitments upon the Norwegian coast for which he will now have to fight ... against Powers possessing vastly superior naval forces and able to transport them to the scenes of action more easily than he can."[279] All that was required now was for Britain to "act with unceasing and increasing vigour to turn to the utmost profit the strategic blunder into which our mortal enemy has been provoked."[280] Easier said than done; these prognostications would not prove correct.

There was no question that in 1940 the Royal Navy was the strongest navy in the world. In virtually every head-to-head surface naval engagement with the Germans, the Royal Navy prevailed. But as Churchill knew,[281] and as mirrored in the views of influential military theorist B.H. Liddell Hart: "...victory at sea was no longer determined solely by surface engagements." An attack from the air could render even the most invincible ship vulnerable.

Churchill owned up to fear of aerial assault, in his May 8 speech to the House about the Norway Campaign, that was why no British vessels, except for submarines, were sent into the Skagerrak strait.[282] The rationale which he advanced in his April 11 speech—that his fleet was too heavily engaged in escorting merchant shipping to British ports—was disingenuous at best. While in an earlier era the Royal Navy's surface fleet could easily have stopped all ship traffic through the Skagerrak and cut off Germany's ability to send supplies and reinforcements to its troops by sea, in 1940 overwhelming German air superiority caused the Admiralty to keep British surface ships out of the area.[283] Churchill, almost grudgingly, had to admit that "[t]he power of the air has greatly affected ... the movement of fleets and armies.[284]

To carry out the plan to retake Narvik, now dubbed Operation Rupert, two hundred and fifty men would arrive on April 13, four battalions would leave almost immediately and would arrive on the 15th, and the rest of British and French forces would follow.[285] At the April 12 War Cabinet meeting, Churchill reported that Operation Rupert was proceeding largely as planned,[286] and General Ismay Secretary of the Committee of Imperial Defence stated that there remained general agreement on the importance of securing Narvik as quickly as possible.[287]

Chamberlain revealed that the Swedes were emphasizing the vital importance of recapturing Trondheim. As a result, he had suggested putting a force ashore at Namsos a town 100 miles north of Trondheim which might be a useful jumping off place.[288] Churchill then advised the group that the recapture of Trondheim was an operation "the difficulty of which should not be underrated," because the Germans would soon be able to send reinforcements from Oslo.[289] He added that "it was not thought right to interrupt in any way the progress of operations against Narvik."[290] After hearing from both Chamberland and Churchill, the War Cabinet "[a]greed that it was important to secure a footing at Namsos as soon as possible and took note that this possibility was being studied urgently by the Staffs."[291]

Later that day, permanent Under-Secretary of State for War P.J. Grigg advised that the Norwegian Government and many people at the War Office wanted Britain to concentrate on retaking Trondheim rather than focus on Narvik. Grigg believed that both Chief of the Imperial General Staff, General Ironside, and Secretary of State for War Oliver Stanley were not acting sensibly and that "[w]e must get the P.M. to take a hand in this before [Churchill] and Tiny [Ironside] go and bugger up the whole war."[292]

A second War Cabinet meeting took place at 4:00 PM on April 12. Halifax spoke about a telegram he had received from the British Ambassador to Sweden which stressed the desirability of early military operations in southern Norway. The Ambassador added that the Norwegian Government was eager to install itself in Trondheim as quickly as possible.[293]

Halifax felt that while the operation at Narvik, the importance of which the Cabinet had reaffirmed that morning, was sound from the military point of view, it would have much less political effect than an attempt to clear the Germans out of southern Norway.[294] (As Manchester writes, "Implicit in the decision to take Trondheim was a decision to retake all Norway," even though the country's "strategic value was small."[295]) Churchill reiterated that, in the face of active German opposition, a landing at Trondheim would be very difficult and, if not properly prepared, could lead to "a bloody repulse."[296]* He also reminded the Cabinet that preparations for the expedition to Narvik had been accomplished long before the landing, which would occur within a few days.[297] He added that "we could be reasonably sure of a success," which would show that Britain could ultimately clear the Germans out of all the ports in which they had gained a foothold.[298] Stanley, the Secretary of State for War, pointed out that help from French troops would be required for a landing at Trondheim, and the French had insisted that the Narvik operation should be carried out first.[299]

Churchill, sensing that Cabinet members wanted to shift operations from Narvik to Trondheim, suggested that at the next War Cabinet meeting (to be held on Saturday, April 13), the ministers should consider landings at several points on the Norwegian coast "in order to confuse the Germans as to our intentions."[300] Halifax, realizing that momentum was shifting away from the Narvik operation, responded that he thought the most important objective now was to secure Trondheim and the railway leading from the port across the peninsula.[301] General Ismay asserted that operations in Norway were growing so big that Britain might need to withdraw some of its troops from France.[302]

Chamberlain then directed attention to a telegram from the French Mission in Sweden also emphasizing the essential importance of Trondheim. The Prime Minister then said he had become impressed with the urgency of obtaining a firm foothold at Trondheim, particularly from the political point of view, and set out the following weak rationale: "If at the moment we merely concentrated on Narvik, there was a danger lest the Norwegians and Swedes feel that our only interest was the iron ore. In that event, they might become disheartened and give up the struggle."[303] (Sweden was neutral and hardly in the "struggle," while Norway was only slightly more committed. Chamberlain was critical of both the Swedes and the Norwegians for their unwillingness to take affirmative action against the Germans.[304]) Chamberlain also opined that the division of elite French mountain infantry troops, the Chasseurs Alpins, that France was providing might be more usefully employed in operations at Trondheim than at Narvik.[305]

---

*In a letter to his sister Ida dated May 4, 1940, Chamberlain agreed, saying that "We knew it was a dangerous operation but there was the chance that we might pull it off before the Germans establish themselves." ed. Self, Vol 4 p. 525.

With Chamberlain now endorsing the shift of focus to Trondheim, Halifax said that "early action against Trondheim was imperative from the political point of view, while it seemed that if necessary, the operation at Narvik could wait.[306] Churchill, however, once again urged no alteration of the present plan for the recapture of Narvik, which he reminded the group was already in the process of being carried out.[307] Chamberlain rejected Churchill's appeal, saying that though he appreciated the importance of the Narvik project, he was "profoundly impressed" with the arguments in favor of securing Trondheim.[308] Never one to go quietly, Churchill replied that "[o]ur plans against Narvik had been carefully laid, and there seemed every chance that they would be successful if they were allowed to proceed without being tampered with. Trondheim was, on the other hand, a much more speculative affair. ..."[309] His warning to Chamberlain would go unheeded, and his words would prove prophetic.*

Following orders issued days earlier, at noon on April 13, the British battleship *Warspite* and a flotilla of nine destroyers plus supply ships arrived at Narvik. The British taskforce quickly destroyed the remaining German warships anchored there.[310] And the German troops on shore literally headed for the hills.[311] Narvik, however, could only be held long enough to destroy some of the port installations; British supply ships had been loaded in such a haphazard fashion that gathering interrelated items such as guns and ammunition could not be done quickly, and some necessary armaments had simply never been loaded.[312] As Chamberlain would disingenuously tell the House several weeks later, the very success of the naval attack by the *Warspite* made it unnecessary to use all the forces originally earmarked for the Narvik operation.[313] What Chamberlain didn't say was that he, as well as most members of the War Cabinet, wanted to shift the principal objective of the Norway campaign away from Narvik.

At the April 13 meeting of the War Cabinet, Chamberlain and virtually every member of the Cabinet officially changed the objectives of the Norway Campaign. No longer would the sole objectives of the campaign be capturing Narvik and cutting iron ore supplies to Germany during the winter. Rather, the objectives would now also include (1) giving all the support and assistance possible to the Norwegians; (2) resisting or delaying the German advance from the south; and (3) facilitating the rescue and protection of the Norwegian King and government, who had fled Oslo and were on the run

---

*As somewhat of a defense, Chamberlain later wrote his sister that Churchill had "changed his mind four times" over Trondheim. ed. Self Vol 4 p. 527 Chamberlain to his sister Ida, May 4, 1940. [emphasis in original] But the Confidential Annexes are clear on both Churchill's and Chamberlain's position about attacking Trondheim.

from German troops. It was obvious that these new objectives could be most speedily attained by capturing Trondheim.[314]

The War Cabinet decided to proceed against Trondheim despite knowing how hazardous that operation would be—it would be conducted without air cover because the Germans occupied the aerodrome at Stavanger, the only efficient air base in southwest Norway.[315] As Chamberlain later admitted before the House, the Cabinet also felt that "there was a strong probability that [German] reinforcements would be sent up the valleys which lead up from the direction of Oslo."[316] In fact, at least as early as April 15 the War Cabinet knew that a considerable number of German reinforcements were arriving in Norway by air.[317] Nonetheless, a plan to take Trondheim continued to be prepared by the joint staffs. The plan provided for two diversionary landings—at Namsos (100 miles north of Trondheim) and at Åndalsnes (a town 150 miles southwest of Trondheim)—and for a direct landing in Trondheim Fjord by a force superior in number to that of the enemy.[318] The plan was set to be carried out on April 25.[319]

Naval forces landed at Namsos on April 14[320] and were followed by three days of troop landings starting April 16.[321] A few days later, elite French mountain-infantry troops (the Chasseurs Alpins) landed there as well. A naval party landed at Åndalsnes on April 17, followed by troops on April 18 and 19.[322] Though the diversionary landings had made good progress, on April 18 the Chiefs of Staff unanimously concluded that the risk of making an opposed landing directly at Trondheim, under heavy hostile air fire, was too great.[323] They did not wish to put the Fleet at risk.[324] On April 19 the Military Coordination Committee advised the War Cabinet that it would be less costly and likely more successful to convert the diversionary landings into the main attack. Chamberlain had already approved this change, and appropriate orders were issued.[325]

At the meetings of the Supreme War Council held in Paris on April 22 and 23, it was agreed that the Allies would stand fast in Norway and that Trondheim and Narvik would remain the main objectives.[326] From that point on, however, the situation in and around Trondheim rapidly deteriorated. By April 25, it was feared that a large, well-equipped, German force would be sent to the region south of Trondheim. At the same time, intense aerial bombardment of both Namsos and Åndalsnes by the Luftwaffe had precluded the Allies from landing reinforcements, artillery, or supplies for the troops already there.

On April 27, Chamberlain explained to the War Cabinet that changes on the ground in Norway seemed likely to require modification of the decisions reached at the Supreme War Council earlier in the week.[327] It had become necessary to withdraw the troops from both Namsos and Åndalsnes, otherwise they would be destroyed by the Germans' overwhelming force.[328] When the Supreme War Council met later that day, the French hoped that Britain would postpone the evacuation. French Premier Paul Reynaud was furious, deploring "the old men [in London] who do not know how to 'take a risk." There was acrimony on both sides; the French were convinced that Britain was "perfidious" and the British branded their ally as "temperamental."[329]

Namsos and Åndalsnes were evacuated in the first few days of May.[330] Narvik, on the other hand, was successfully taken by the Allies on April 28, but was abandoned five weeks later.[331] The British simply could not provide the additional men, fighter aircraft, anti-aircraft guns, and naval support necessary to maintain control of the town.[332]

All told, Britain's Norway campaign did little to throttle German occupation of the country and led to the loss of about four thousand British lives, 1,500 of whom died when the aircraft carrier *HMS Glorious* was sunk evacuating troops from Norway.[333]

As Chamberlain acknowledged in his speech to the House on May 7, and just as had been feared, the failure of the plan to recapture Trondheim was principally due to (1) the lack of air cover—Britain never did secure airfields in Norway from which to conduct fighter operations (nor did she possess substantial aircraft carrier capacity*); and (2) the rapid arrival of German reinforcements[334] (which in letters he attributed to the Norwegian's failure to destroy railroad bridges and barricade highways).[335] The British also lacked artillery.[336]

Humiliating Errors

About the Norwegian campaign, historians have said, "almost everything that could go wrong ... did."[337] In sum, "[t]he Navy missed the Germans; it was unable to prevent German landings along the long coast of Norway; where British troops were landed, here and there, they soon retreated rather abjectly; they were out marched, outfought by the Germans nearly everywhere."[338] Lukacs asserts that Churchill was personally responsible for much of the debacle.[339] Roberts similarly believes that since Norway was a naval operations, Churchill, as the First Lord of the Admiralty, should bear much of the blame.[340] Some even have asserted, unjustifiably, that Churchill pushed Britain into pursuing an unwinnable operation.[341] All agree that there was a lack of coordination among the services, because of a lack of direction from either Chamberlain or a representative with command authority.[342] There

---

*At the time of the Norway campaign, Britain had seven operational aircraft carriers. However, only one, the Ark Royal, was modern. Two were sixteen years old, and the remaining four were WWI vintage. One in the latter group, the HMS Glorious, was completed as a battle cruiser in 1916 and converted into an aircraft carrier during the 1920s; it was sunk on the afternoon of June 8, 1940, by the German battle cruisers Scharnhorst and Gneisenau. Manchester and Reid p. 57.

also was an abundance of humiliating errors: for example, how the German flotilla was allowed to slip past the Royal Navy and seize Narvik; how British intelligence was stodgy and unreliable; how the navy and the army did not coordinate orders in the attempt to retake Narvik and Trondheim;[343] how British troops were sent to Norway with neither skis[344] nor snowshoes,[345] even though meteorologists had forecast heavy snow;[346] how two battalions were issued tourist maps that did not even contain their objective;[347] how "troops had mistakenly been left with only two days' supplies"[348] (they also lacked "artillery, anti-aircraft weapons, [and] fighter cover"[349]); and how eighteen British bi-plane fighters that landed on Lake Lesgeskogen were stranded for lack of petrol, and sixteen of them were easily destroyed by German aircraft.[350]

Roberts writes that "[h]ad the Military Coordination Committee been given teeth to do what its title implied, Churchill might have been able to get a grip on the campaign. ..."[351] For instance, Churchill may have been able to halt the War Cabinet's on-the-fly switch of the primary objective of the campaign from Narvik to Trondheim. Hitler, in turn, described the British campaign in Norway as "frivolous dilettantism,"[352] asserting that Britain's operations were pursued in an aimless and superficial manner. According to Lukacs:

> Churchill was responsible for much of the "dilettantism" of the Norway campaign. For once his intuitive grasp of the events failed him: He did not perceive what the Germans were about to do, whereas the Germans assessed the British plans far better. ... Churchill's plans for mining the [territorial waters near Narvik] started slow and late and petered out in foggy confusion at sea."[353]

In his diary entry of April 27, Colville succinctly assessed the Norway campaign and its consequences, writing that:

> The plain truth of the matter is that we have unadvisedly landed an insufficient number of troops without adequate equipment or support from the air and we have met or are meeting with a serious reverse. ... If Norway goes seriously wrong, then I suppose the popular outcry may force a reconstitution of the Government and Winston, to whom as much blame should attach as any other single individual, will ride triumphantly forward on the wave of undeserving national popularity.[354]

Two days later Colville added to the list of causes for the poor showing in Norway—the fact that most of the British troops in Norway were inexperienced and untrained territorials* or reservists.[355] As noted earlier, all of Britain's trained troops had been sent to France months before.[356]

Trying to put the best spin possible on the Norway Campaign, Chamberlain told the House on May 2 that if Britain has not achieved its objective, "neither have the Germans achieved theirs, while their losses are far greater than ours."[357] As Labour MP Sir Harold Nicolson wrote in his diary, "... if Chamberlain believed [this]..., then he was stupid. If he did not believe it, then he was trying to deceive. In either case he loses confidence."[358] Everyone knew that Norway had been a major defeat.[359] "[F]or something as serious as that, the Prime Minister must take the ultimate responsibility."[360]

One saving grace of the Norway campaign would not be known until years later: "...more than 160,000 of Hitler's best troops remained in Norway for more than four years waiting to defend against a return" of the British.[361] But British soldiers would never return.

Interesting Glimpses of Churchill as He Emerged From the "Wilderness Years"

The period from Hitler's invasion of Poland through the Norway adventure, about eight months, offers some interesting glimpses of Churchill as he emerged from his "wilderness years," the ten years when he was without a Cabinet post in any administration. What principles did Churchill purport to hold near and dear? Had he tamed his impulse to engage in acts of questionable judgment? Had he developed a capacity for loyalty, something which was never one of his long suits?

His loyalty and what it engendered would be critical in the ultimate determination of whether to enter into peace negotiations with Hitler in 1940.

Churchill's Off-Again On-Again Attitude Toward the Soviets

In a broadcast in January 1940, Churchill, a lifetime anti-communist, hailed Finland's resistance to Russian aggression and reiterated his contempt for Soviet ideology. Yet as recently as the summer of 1939, Churchill was willing to accept the Soviet Union as a coalition partner and urged the previously independent states of Lithuania, Latvia, Estonia—and Poland—to accept Red Army bases on their soil. His rationale was that those actions corresponded with British interests by diminishing Hitler's potential for Lebensraum. He believed that if "the Baltic countries have to lose their independence, it [was at least] better for them to be brought into the Soviet state system rather than the German one."[362] This reasoning, of course, bears a chilling resemblance to Chamberlain's pressure on Czechoslovakia to accept Hitler's terms at

---

Territorials were part-time volunteers in the Territorial Force component of the British Army.

Munich, for the good of world peace. Roberts calls Churchill's willingness to embrace the Soviets "a temporary expedient born of war."[363]

Churchill signaled his adoption of a pragmatic approach toward Russia years earlier when he announced in July 1934 that he favored befriending the USSR at least enough to support its admission into the League of Nations.[364] When in 1938 he told the Soviet Ambassador to Britain that as long as Nazi Germany existed, he would spare no effort against Hitler, he was confirming that partnering with Russia was no longer beyond the pale for him.[365] For a strong anti-communist like Churchill, these statements were very significant and gave some indication of just how important he believed it was to establish effective collective security against Hitler.[366]*

Even though in many respects he disliked Stalin almost as much as he loathed Hitler, and even though he despised Communism, by 1941, when Russia joined the Allies, Churchill was willing to accept a postwar world in which Stalin would likely play a major role.

In contrast, in 1940 Churchill vehemently opposed doing anything similar with Hitler. As we will see later in this book, by late May 1940 Churchill would refuse to forsake principle when Britain stood alone and refused to enter peace negotiations with Hitler. Understanding why he made such a different choice with Hitler than he had with Stalin will come under scrutiny in the chapters ahead.

Churchill's willingness to abandon principle for the sake of pragmatism (at least when it came to the Soviet Union) would appear a few years later when, in 1943, the Polish government in exile asked him to look into the 1940 mass murder of fifteen thousand Polish officers held by the Soviets. Churchill was quite dismissive, saying "There is no use prowling round the 3-year-old graves of Smolensk."[367]

The Important Evolution of the Relationship Between Churchill and Chamberlain

Chamberlain did not bring Churchill into the Government in September 1939 because he liked or even trusted him. Indeed, before Churchill joined the Cabinet, the Prime Minister had made a particularly nasty comment in the House about Churchill's judgment and fitness for office,[368] and he generally looked on Churchill as something of a leper.[369] But Chamberlain needed to bring Churchill into the Cabinet to bolster his Government; a side benefit would be that bringing Winston on board would likely shut him up.

In 1938, Churchill also told the Russian Ambassador to Britain that if the German Fascist threat disappeared and the Communist menace reared its ugly head, he would have no problem expending similar efforts against Russia. ed. Gorodetsky, Maisky Diaries p. 110.

However, quite remarkably, during the "Phoney War" there was a slow but discernable evolution of the relationship between Churchill and Chamberlain.* From the moment he joined the Government, Churchill, who had vilified Chamberlain for years, played the role of "Chamberlain's loyal, if impulsive lieutenant."[370] As Chamberlain biographer Keith Feiling writes, after Churchill joined the Cabinet "[w]e see [him] associated more nearly with the Prime Minister as the strain grew greater, proceeding with him to the Supreme Council, his persuasive vehemence brought to bear on the French and, with that, a tightening of the bonds between them."[371] Old friends and supporters even complained that Churchill had neglected them "while carrying loyalty to his governmental colleagues to absurd lengths."[372] In a letter to his sister in March 1940, Chamberlain described Churchill as being "absolutely loyal."[373]

Churchill demonstrated loyalty to the Chamberlain Government from day one. On September 2, 1939, Churchill resisted the suggestion of Alfred Duff Cooper and others to attack the Government's inaction after the German invasion of Poland. What made Churchill's act of loyalty even more noteworthy was that he potentially stood to gain politically by joining in the critical chorus: Duff Cooper and his colleagues believed a vote of no confidence might have resulted with Churchill replacing Chamberlain as Prime Minister. There were numerous other instances during the "Phoney War" and thereafter when Churchill showed that he was a loyal member of the Chamberlain Government. These included:

- The banning of any jokes or offensive remarks about Chamberlain in Churchill's household. (These had previously been common.[374])

- At a jocular luncheon in his honor in February 1940, Churchill, after talking about himself in a self-deprecating way, "pledged loyally to serve the 'Captain' for the duration of the voyage." Chamberlain, who attended, bowed in acknowledgment.[375]

- In late March 1940, Churchill told the editor of *The Manchester Guardian* that he no longer looked to become Prime Minister, and

---

Professor David Reynolds relates that although Churchill and Chamberlain had spent more than two decades engaging in political business, they and their wives had never gotten together for dinner or engaged in any "intimate social conversation." This all changed on November 13, 1939, when the Churchills had the Chamberlains over for dinner. Among other things, Chamberlain was forthcoming about a major failure in his life. He spoke at length about the six years in the 1890s he spent on a barren island in the West Indies on a family venture trying unsuccessfully to grow sisal. Reynolds suggests this get-together was another factor catalyzing a change in the relationship between these two formerly bitter rivals. Reynolds, In Command of History p. 111.

he said that Chamberlain's related fears and distrust had vanished. Churchill had also determined "that I must work well with [the P.M.] and I do, and I believe that he now likes me."[376]

- As noted above, during the Norway campaign, Churchill was willing to throw his support behind the hazardous assault on Trondheim even after the War Cabinet had, in midstream, scuttled his long-held plan to capture Narvik.[377] As Churchill explained to the House on May 8, "My eye has always been fixed on Narvik; there, it seemed to me, is a port which may lead to some decisive achievement in the war. But when the German outrage occurred, there is no dispute that we were bound to go to the aid of the Norwegians and that Trondheim was the place."[378]

- As will be discussed in more detail, Churchill accepted much of the blame for the Norway defeat during the House debates on the conduct of the Norway campaign, thus shielding Chamberlain and his colleagues in the War Cabinet.

Churchill's loyalty to Chamberlain was both appreciated and reciprocated. One example involved the Military Coordination Committee. After a War Cabinet reshuffle on April 3, 1940, Chamberlain asked Churchill, who remained First Lord of the Admiralty, to also take on the chairmanship of the MCC. That position gave Churchill no authority over the Chiefs of Staff or the ministers, over whom he had no seniority. Moreover, for some time there had been no love lost between Churchill and two of the MCC members: Samuel Hoare, the newly named Secretary of State for Air, and Oliver Stanley, the newly named Secretary of State for War. Hoare's antipathy ran deep. Back in 1934 Churchill had publicly accused Hoare, who was then Minister for India, of suborning perjury by pressuring members of the Manchester Chamber of Commerce to change the presentations they were going to provide to the Commons Select Committee on India about the effects of Indian self-government on British trade.[379]

For his part, Churchill not infrequently behaved in ways that made him a target for criticism. For example, he complained to the King that he hardly had time to do his work at the Admiralty because of his new duties at the MCC, attending House debates and War Cabinet meetings, and keeping in communication with the fleet. In actuality, he still found time to work on his multi-volume treatise, The History of the English-Speaking Peoples,[380] despite having promised not to do any writing after September 3, 1939, the day he rejoined the Admiralty.[381]*

---

*Using intermediaries to preserve his tax status, "Churchill's literary career not only continued in 1940 to 1945 but soared to quite dizzy heights." Reynolds, In

By the third week in April, the situation at the MCC had deteriorated to the point that the committee was reported to be in "an almost mutinous condition."[382] The Chiefs of Staff complained that Churchill had prevented them from meeting to discuss proposed actions while Cabinet ministers complained that he had denied them access to information from the Chiefs about potentially hazardous operations.[383] To avoid an insurrection, Churchill asked Chamberlain to take over chairing the group.[384] Once Chamberlain did, order magically returned and subsequent decisions from the committee were always unanimous.[385] Churchill thanked Chamberlain for "having got him out of a hole."[386] In his diary, Chamberlain wrote, "Winston's attitude was most difficult, challenging everything the Chiefs of Staff suggested and generally behaving like a spoiled and sulky child."[387] The subject even came up in Chamberlain's weekly audience with the King.

Self reports that during a meeting with Chamberlain on the subject of the MCC, Churchill made "seemingly genuine protestations of loyalty" while reiterating a request that Chamberlain officially create the position of Minister of Defence and name him to fill it.[388] Chamberlain said he needed time to think it over and to consult with the service ministers.[389] Colville that night wrote in his diary something most serious—that if Chamberlain refused Churchill's request, "Winston threatens to go down to the House and say he can take no responsibility for what is happening."[390] Colville continued: "To let this happen in wartime would be unthinkable: there would then be a first-class political crisis. ... On the other hand, if the P.M. gives in, Winston will have won his point by blackmail. ..."[391] Importantly, Self points out that Chamberlain made no note of any such threat having been suggested during what was "an otherwise friendly conversation," and that in any event "Churchill was not in a sufficiently strong position to risk such a dangerous gamble in the wake of the MCC fiasco and the Norwegian campaign."[392] The MCC crisis did, however, cause doubts to resurface about Churchill's judgment and leadership capabilities, including a rekindling of how those shortcomings defined Churchill during the Gallipoli crisis in 1915.[393]

Around the time of the MCC brouhaha, Chamberlain found himself debating whether to make Churchill the scapegoat for the way the Norway campaign had clearly veered off in the wrong direction.[394] Many shared the conflicting views of Conservative MP Henry "Chips" Channon, who believed on the one hand that Churchill should be dismissed from the Cabinet for his mishandling of the Norway campaign, but, on the other hand, was at a loss as to who could replace him.[395] Chamberlain felt the public would probably object to Churchill's removal from the Cabinet.[396]

Command of History *p. 17. For example, in each year of the war his speeches were compiled, published, and sold well both in Britain and the U.S. See, Ibid. p. 18.*

Also, Chamberlain certainly remembered that Churchill knew that it was the Prime Minister who had championed changing the objectives of the Norway campaign and embraced the disastrous attempt to capture Trondheim. Not only did Chamberlain refrain from making Churchill the scapegoat for Norway, he, in fact, promoted him, handing him responsibility "on behalf of the Military Coordination Committee for giving guidance and directions to the Chiefs of Staff Committee."[397] By doing so, Chamberlain broke the stalemate at the MCC in Churchill's favor and, on the eve of the Norway debates in the House, effectively gave Winston a position he had urged be created since the 1920s: Minister of Defence.[398]*

When other Cabinet members (Hoare, Simon, Hankey, and Halifax) threatened to resign rather than accept the new arrangement, Chamberlain threatened to resign himself, which, as he told them, would make Churchill Prime Minister and Defense Minister anyway. The dissidents promptly retreated.[399]

The Debate in the House Over Norway

The debate in the House of Commons over the Norway campaign started on Tuesday, May 7. Public opinion polls showed that less than a third of British voters believed that the Allies had not done everything possible during the Norway campaign, and Chamberlain's approval rating had declined to 33 percent.[400] In fact, over the preceding weekend some leaders of the Labour Party had begun to call for the resignation of the Prime Minister and several members of the War Cabinet.[401] Even Chamberlain loyalists were "beginning reluctantly to realize that Neville's days [were] ... numbered."[402] However, as Self writes, "Chamberlain had absolutely no intention of giving up without a fight and he remained confident of victory until the very end."[403]

Churchill certainly knew there was a possibility that the Chamberlain Government could fall. Since it would be reasonable to imagine he would be in line for the Prime Ministership, it would not have been surprising if Churchill had tried to distance himself from "a prime minister who might be on his way out."[404] (Of course, that could backfire and open him up for blame for

---

There is no evidence that Churchill got anything he wanted by threatening to turn on Chamberlain. But Chamberlain's actions, described above, as well as his, perhaps surprising concurrence in Churchill's position in late May not to enter into peace talks with Hitler, did not totally disabuse the notion that Churchill held something over Chamberlain's head.

While in his May 7 speech before the House, Chamberlain did not blame Churchill for any of the misadventures in the Norway campaign. There is evidence that in the previous week or so, Chamberlain had not deterred private efforts by senior officials to undermine Churchill—ed. James, Chips Vol. 4 pp. 242–246, April 26 and May 1, 1940; ed. Stuart, Reith Diaries p. 255 May 1 and 3, 1940.

the Norway fiasco.) Nevertheless, Churchill did not try to dissociate himself from Chamberlain. As Manchester writes, "He couldn't do it."[405] Instead, he accepted the important role as wrap-up speaker for the Government in the Norway debate and was vigorous in his defense of the Government's actions.

The debate started at 3:45 PM on May 7 and would not end until after 11:00 PM on May 8. What began as a parliamentary inquiry into the facts and circumstances of the Norwegian campaign turned into a "runaway grand jury"[406] that ultimately voted on whether the Chamberlain Government should be allowed to continue. When Chamberlain entered the House at the start of the debate he received a warm welcome,[407] although he also was taunted by cries of "Missed the bus."[408] In his speech, he talked primarily of what had occurred during the Norway campaign, although he did go out of his way to defend Churchill by saying that Norway was no Gallipoli.[409] On the whole, despite the speech being described as "very feeble,"[410] Chamberlain's staff believed it had been enough to save the Government.[411]

Arguably the most pointedly anti-government speech on the first day of the debate was delivered by Conservative MP and Retired Admiral of the Fleet Sir Roger Keyes. Keyes was a genuine naval hero, having served in the Dardanelles campaign in 1915. He appeared before the House in full uniform, because he wished "to speak for some officers and men of the fighting, sea-going Navy who [were] very unhappy."[412] He declared that "it is not their fault that the German warships and transports which forced their way into Norwegian ports by treachery were not followed in and destroyed as they were at Narvik." Keyes lamented that the Germans had now been given more than a month to "pour in reinforcements by sea and air, to land tanks, heavy artillery, and mechanised transport," and to develop air superiority.[413] As to Trondheim, he pulled no punches: "if a few ships had entered Trondheim Fiord as soon as the Army was ready to co-operate, the capture of Trondheim Fiord with its vital aerodrome for our fighters, and quays for landing heavy artillery, tanks, and our mechanised transport, could have been speedily effected."[414]

Keyes revealed that when he made all these same points to the Admiralty, he was told that "there was no difficulty in going into the Trondheim Fiord but that it was not considered necessary, as the Army was making good progress and [that] it [was] undesirable to risk ships."[415] What Keyes asserted was that the Admiralty staff had failed to appreciate that any attack from Namsos "was doomed" unless the German Navy's control of the Trondheim Fjord were eliminated. From Namsos, the only way British troops could approach Trondheim would be along the shore of the fjord, where they would be sitting ducks for the guns of the two German destroyers located in the fjord.[416] Failing to eliminate those German vessels was, in Keyes opinion, "a shocking story of ineptitude."[417]

Keyes called the Norway campaign another Gallipoli[418]—i.e., a brilliant plan by the First Lord of the Admiralty (Mr. Churchill in both instances) that was defeated "by the exaggerated fears in Whitehall of dangers which the men on the spot were ready to face and overcome."[419] Continuing to point the finger of blame at nameless officials in the Government, and not at Churchill,[420] Keyes added, "I have great admiration and affection for my right Hon. Friend the First Lord of the Admiralty. I am longing to see proper use made of his great abilities. I cannot believe it will be done under the existing system. The war cannot be won by committees, and those responsible for its prosecution must have full power to act, without the delays of conferences."[421]

At the end of his speech, Keyes received a standing ovation. By the time Keyes sat down, "Chamberlain knew he was in real trouble."[422] It was about 8:00 PM. The House began to empty for the dinner hour as the Speaker called on Leo Amery, a Liberal MP from Birmingham, and a friend of Churchill's. During Amery's speech, the Liberal MPs scoured the anterooms of the House "drumming up an audience." Amery delivered a strong speech. He was able to move the criticism away from the Navy (and Churchill) "toward Chamberlain and his conduct of the war."[423] He also said, "The whole of Parliament has a grave responsibility at this moment; for, after all, it is Parliament itself that is on trial in this war. If we lose this war, it is not this or that ephemeral Government, but Parliament as an institution, that will be condemned, for good and all."[424]

Amery then shifted focus to the observation that the Chamberlain Government knew for months that the Germans had been amassing troops and transports and practicing embarkation and disembarkation maneuvers, yet it had been unable to conclude that Norway was among the proposed German targets. He pointed out that "what really happened was that, while we thought we were taking the initiative, our initiative, such as it was, only coincided with a far more formidable and far better planned initiative of the enemy."[425] He went on to ask, "[E]ven if we did not realise that the Germans were acting at the same time, why were we not prepared to meet their inevitable counter-stroke?"[426]

After pointing out several other deficiencies in the way the Government had handled the Norway campaign, Amery then attacked the bureaucratic structure of the current Government and said, "We cannot go on as we are. There must be a change. First and foremost, it must be a change in the system and structure of our governmental machine."[427] He went on: "Somehow or other we must get into the Government men who can match our enemies in fighting spirit, in daring, in resolution and in thirst for victory."[428]

Amery then turned his attack to Chamberlain and the ministers close to him, albeit "with great reluctance because [they are] old friends and associates of mine." In a dramatic closing statement, Amery declared, "This is what Cromwell had said to the Long Parliament when he thought it was no longer fit to conduct the affairs of the nation: 'You have sat too long here for any good you have been doing. Depart, I say, and let us have done with you. In the name of God, go.'"[429]*

Amery's speech was merciless and is said to have shattered Chamberlain.[430] Many regarded it as "the critical moment of the entire debate."[431] In *The Gathering Storm*, Churchill writes that "These were terrible words, coming from a friend and colleague of many years, a fellow Birmingham Member, and Privy Counselor of distinction and experience."[432]

The opinion of Chamberlain's supporters on how day one had gone was mixed at best.[433] Much would be on the line when the speeches resumed the following day.

The session on May 8 started at 4:30 PM. It did not take long to see where things were headed. The first speaker of the day, Labour MP Herbert Morrison, not only delivered a vituperative speech in which he declared that Chamberlain, Hoare, and Simon must go, but he also announced that Labour believed "we must divide the House at the end of our debate today": i.e., take a vote on whether to censure or dismiss the Government.[434] This suggestion caused Chamberlain to rise in response to a "grave" situation. Chamberlain said that "this is a time of national danger, and we are facing a relentless enemy who must be fought by the united action of this country. It may well be that it is a duty to criticise the Government. I do not seek to evade criticism,"[435] he continued, "but I say this to my friends in the House—and I have friends in the House. No Government can prosecute a war efficiently unless it has public and Parliamentary support. I accept the challenge. I welcome it indeed. At least we shall see who is with us and who is against us, and I call on my friends to support us in the Lobby tonight."[436]

Although Chamberlain was not doing so, many in the House were taken aback that, during a war, the Prime Minister would seem to be turning a legitimate inquiry into the functioning of the Government into a question of member loyalty to him—a question of who were and who were not his friends.[437]

Former Liberal Party Prime Minister David Lloyd George rose to speak:

> It is not a question of who are the Prime Minister's friends. It
> is a far bigger issue. The Prime Minister must remember that

---

The Long Parliament was in session from 1640 to 1660 because, by law, it could only be dissolved by agreement of its members. In session during the English Civil War (1642–1651), its impact was wide-ranging: the trial and execution of Charles I (1649); the exile of his son Charles II (1651); the replacement of English monarchy with, first, the Commonwealth of England (1649–1653), then the Protectorate under the personal rule of Oliver Cromwell (1653–1658); and, finally and briefly, Cromwell's son Richard (1658–1659).

he has met this formidable foe of ours in peace and in war. He has always been worsted. He is not in a position to appeal on the ground of friendship. He has appealed for sacrifice. ... I say solemnly that the Prime Minister should give an example of sacrifice, because there is nothing which can contribute more to victory in this war than that he should sacrifice the seals of office.[438]

Lloyd George's intent was not only to attack the Chamberlain Government's handling of the Norway campaign and give vent to his twenty years of accumulated hatred of Chamberlain,[439] but also to shield Churchill from criticism. Like Keyes, Lloyd George didn't lay the blame at Churchill's feet for the Government's failure to fully utilize the strength of the Royal Navy. "I do not think that the First Lord (i.e., Churchill) was entirely responsible for all the things that happened there."[440] But, Churchill immediately spoke up and said, "I take complete responsibility for everything that has been done by the Admiralty and I take my full share of the burden."[441] To this Lloyd George quickly gave some avuncular advice: "The right Hon. Gentleman must not allow himself to be converted into an air-raid shelter to keep the splinters from hitting his colleagues."[442]

Four hours elapsed between the end of Lloyd George's speech and the call for Churchill to begin his. During this time Churchill went into the smoking room where he ran into his friend Harold Macmillan, then a forty-six-year-old Conservative MP. Macmillan wished Churchill good luck on his forthcoming speech but added that he hoped the speech would not be too convincing. Britain needed a new Prime Minister and he hoped that it would be Churchill. In response Churchill mildly rebuked Macmillan, saying that he had "signed on for the voyage and would stick to the ship."[443]

When Churchill finally was called on to speak, shortly after 10:00 PM, there was still a question, recorded Chips Channon, on everyone's mind: "would Winston be loyal?"[444] Every member knew that the speeches over the past two days denouncing the Government echoed the speeches that Churchill himself had been delivering for years. "It was savage irony that [Churchill] now found himself among the crew of a ship being sunk by torpedoes he had designed."[445] Channon continued: "... one saw at once that [Churchill] was in a bellicose mood, alive and enjoying himself, relishing the ironical position in which he found himself,"[446] that of defending the Prime Minister who, over Churchill's strong objection, had decided to turn away from Narvik in favor of the debacle that would be Trondheim. Nonetheless, like a great lawyer defending a client he knows to have committed the alleged crime, Churchill rose to the occasion.

When asked about Trondheim, Churchill admitted that he was a believer in focusing on Narvik; but once the decision was made to attack Trondheim instead he carried it out to the best of his ability.[447] He also explained that though it was the Chiefs of Staff who ultimately advised against proceeding with the planned frontal attack at Trondheim, he took "the fullest responsibility—and so [did] the Prime Minister and the other Ministers concerned—for having accepted the unanimous view of our expert advisers."[448] He did not accept Admiral Keyes's offer to blame the failed operation at Trondheim on the timidity of other persons or elements in the Government. Instead, he said that he personally believed that the Navy could have successfully carried troops into Trondheim Fjord and then made the frontal attack, adding that he "would have been very glad to take all possible responsibility for the step, provided that it was properly supported by expert opinion."[449] Significantly, he noted that if the attack on Trondheim had been successful, the question would, however, have arisen immediately of whether the city could be held against the German forces coming up from the south.[450] He did not think it could.[451]

Fully immunizing Chamberlain and the War Cabinet from the fallout from any wrongful decisions about the attack on Trondheim, Churchill stated, "Therefore, whatever view we may take of the chances of the attack on Trondheim, the decision to abandon it, although it was taken for different reasons from those I have just mentioned, was not only reasonable at the time, but has, I believe, saved us in the upshot from a most disastrous entanglement."[452]

Notably, no one pressed the point, and Churchill did not discuss the fact that while the Germans had planned their Norwegian operation for months, the decision to switch objectives and send troops to Trondheim rather than Narvik was almost an afterthought, taken at the urgent request of the Norwegians and implemented after only a few days of planning.[453]

Churchill had yet one more opportunity to defend the Chamberlain Government during the debate, when Arthur Greenwood, Deputy Leader of the Labour Party, asked him if the War Cabinet had been dilatory about deciding to attack Trondheim. Churchill shot back, "Not for a moment."[454] It would have been so easy for Churchill, rather than having given Greenwood such a sharp response, to have said something vague, perhaps how in retrospect and, like with most decisions, this choice could have been made sooner than it was. But Churchill refused to throw the Prime Minister and his Government under the bus, even though Chamberlain's diversion of efforts from Narvik to Trondheim was something that Churchill had strongly opposed.

Churchill batting last on the Government's team accomplished exactly what Chamberlain was expecting of him: rebut or deflect the arguments of the anti-government members.[455] As Manchester correctly points out, in his speech Churchill "did not lie, he did not distort. But it was sophistry all the same. He omitted certain facts since they reflected well upon him ... [particularly] that he had spent 7 months trying to persuade the War Cabinet that they must move on Narvik. ..."[456]

On the subject of dividing the House, Churchill said that "if the Government are to be dismissed from office, and that is a claim which has been made without scruple, then I think that in time of war at least there should be a solemn Resolution put down on the paper and full notice given of the Debate."[457]

Turning from procedure back to the complaint against the Government, he urged the members of the House to let:

- prewar feuds die;

- personal quarrels be forgotten;

- hatreds for the common enemy stay uppermost;

- party interest be ignored;[458] and

- the entire might of the nation be hurled into the struggle.[459]

In conclusion, he strongly urged the House "to deal with these matters not in a precipitate vote, ill-debated and on a widely discursive field, but in grave time and due time in accordance with the dignity of Parliament."[460]

Chamberlain was "pleased and grateful."[461] He had every reason to be. Churchill had done an outstanding job on his behalf.

Some have suggested that Churchill's loyalty was merely a thin veneer. In fact, they claim he really was out to do Chamberlain in.[462] But the weight of evidence establishes that Churchill was "startlingly loyal" to the Prime Minister.[463] As Lukacs puts it, "Churchill stood by [Chamberlain] unreservedly loyal, though knowing that his power might have come."[464] Minister of Information John Reith, on the other hand, wrote that Churchill "was loving the criticisms against the Government knowing that it was all helping to put him in power."[465]

Discussing his speech with Jock Colville months later, Churchill described it as "a wonderful opportunity" for him because "[h]e had been able to defend his chief to the utmost and ... win esteem and support in doing so. No one could say he had been disloyal or had intrigued against Chamberlain. ..."[466] As Roberts writes, Churchill "had won the allegiance of someone [Chamberlain] who had hitherto been somewhat aloof but who now rallied to him."[467]*

As we will see in future chapters, the mutual allegiance between Churchill and Chamberlain, which was substantially enhanced on May 8, would in fact grow over

Almost immediately after Churchill spoke, at approximately 11:00 PM, whether the Chamberlain Government should be allowed to continue was put to a vote. The Government prevailed, 281 to 200. However, because the Conservatives held a 213-vote majority in the House, winning by a mere eighty-one votes was hardly a ringing endorsement of Chamberlain by his own party. Rather, it was "a wholly unforeseen ... stinging rebuke."[468] As it turns out, forty-one Conservatives had voted with the opposition to oust the Government, and another sixty had abstained.[469] Chamberlain historian Keith Feiling writes that it was not just Norway that led to this result; there were "accumulated causes" "running back to earlier years."[470]

When the results of the vote were made known there was a terrific anti-Chamberlain demonstration in the House. Many members derided the P.M. by shouting "You've missed the bus" and "Go, go, go, go!"[471] Observing the bedlam from the gallery, Soviet Ambassador to Britain Ivan Maisky wrote, "Chamberlain sat in his place, white as chalk."[472] His own party had in substantial measure turned on him—the Prime Minister was gripped by indescribable disappointment and humiliation.

As Churchill started to leave, Chamberlain motioned for him to join him in his private room. That Winston would be the person whom Chamberlain chose to be with at one of the lowest points of his life may seem surprising—but was not. This was the moment when all of Churchill's efforts to show that he could be an extremely loyal member of the team, ending in that night's speech, were recognized.

Churchill would later write that Chamberlain took the vote of the House very hard. "He felt he could not go on. There ought to be a National Government. One party alone could not carry the burden. Someone must form a government in which all the parties would serve, or [Britain] could not get through."[473]

"Here, writing on the rack of humiliation, was a man who had been [Churchill's] chief adversary during the three crucial years before the outbreak of the war,"[474] the person who held the job that Churchill had coveted for forty years, the person most responsible for the Norway debacle. Yet Churchill, as Chamberlain now knew, refused to take advantage. Chamberlain had learned what Colville would come to learn and record: that, at his core, despite the distrust he had engendered over the years, Churchill had an unusual capacity for "intense loyalty" and "great compassion which he combined with personal generosity...."[475]* That night, Churchill did not suggest that Chamberlain

---

the next few weeks and become a critical factor in determining the fate of Britain and Western Democracy.

*This capacity had been on display when his loyalty to Edward VIII during the abdication came at great expense to his reputation.

take any action that might benefit Churchill, nor would he choose to simply remain silent.[476] Rather, Churchill yielded to something other than base human ambition. He chose to stand with Chamberlain.

Despite his breathtaking acts of loyalty, Churchill believed that Chamberlain's run as Prime Minister was over. He did not think it was possible for Chamberlain to reconstitute a National Government—the Labour party would almost certainly not participate in any new Chamberlain-led government.[477] Winston showed Chamberlain compassion as the two sat in the P.M.'s private office. With true sincerity, Churchill urged Chamberlain not to "take the matter grievously to heart" but rather to fight on and recognize that the Government still had a good majority in the House.[478] When Churchill left the P.M. at midnight, however, Chamberlain appeared unconvinced and seemingly uncomforted.[479]

But the P.M. would quickly bounce back. That was the nature of the man: like the Japanese proverb he was "knocked down nine times, got up ten." Within minutes of Churchill's departure, Chamberlain called the King and asked for an immediate audience; his Majesty graciously agreed. At the palace, Chamberlain told King George that he was not there to resign but to advise that it was his hope to restructure his Government as a coalition with participation of the Labour Party. He wanted to carry on.[480]

Marshal Phillipe Pétain

14

May 9–May 24, 1940 Churchill's first two weeks as Prime Minister

Thursday, May 9, 1940
- How Churchill Became the Choice to Succeed Chamberlain

Friday, May 10, 1940
- The German Invasion of Western Europe/How Churchill Became Prime Minister
- The Germans' Plan for the Invasion of Western Europe

Saturday, May 11, 1940
Sunday, May 12, 1940
Monday, May 13, 1940
Tuesday, May 14, 1940
Wednesday, May 15, 1940
Thursday, May 16, 1940
Friday, May 17, 1940
Saturday, May 18, 1940
Sunday, May 19, 1940
Monday, May 20, 1940
Tuesday, May 21, 1940
Wednesday, May 22, 1940
Thursday, May 23, 1940
Friday, May 24, 1940

Thursday, May 9, 1940

How Churchill Became the Choice to Succeed Chamberlain

During a morning meeting with Anthony Eden, Churchill said what he had been thinking late the previous evening: Labour would never join a government headed by Neville Chamberlain.[1] As a consequence, Chamberlain's run as Prime Minister would be over in a matter of days. A national-unity coalition government—a National Government—made up of all parties must be formed.[2]

With rumors of resignation in the air, Chamberlain spent much of May 9, the 250th day of the war, in meetings with Halifax, Churchill, and the leaders of the Labour Party.[3] Perhaps his most important meeting was with Halifax at 10:15 AM. The two men agreed that both Labour and the Liberals must be brought into the Government.[4] Halifax believed such a coalition was necessary and had mentioned it as long ago as September 1938, when they were riding back from the airport after returning from Munich.

Chamberlain was now coming to grips with the fact that Labour was unlikely to serve in a National Government led by him. Despite how loyally Churchill had stood up for him the night before and despite the growing bond between them, Chamberlain chose Lord Halifax, not Churchill, as the man he wanted to succeed him. Chamberlain asked Halifax if he would form a government in which Labour would hopefully join.[5] Chamberlain knew Halifax would be the choice of most Conservatives,[6] that Labour favored Halifax over Churchill,[7] and that King George himself was similarly inclined.[8] (So, too, was the Queen, who disliked Churchill.[9]) The P.M. even offered to serve under Halifax in a new government.[10] One potential, but surmountable, bar to Halifax taking over was a provision of the British Constitution prohibiting anyone with a seat in the House of Lords (such as Halifax) from sitting in the House of Commons, from where the Prime Minister must come.[11]

Halifax did not immediately agree to form a new government. In fact, the opportunity gave him a stomachache.[12] Halifax returned to the Foreign Office to ponder Chamberlain's offer. Even though he knew that he lacked the military expertise needed in a wartime P.M., Halifax still felt he could do the job. But there were other factors to consider. For one, Churchill would have to be in the Cabinet; and given Churchill's persona, as well as his experience, Halifax feared that in no time Churchill would be "running the war" and that he, himself, would quickly become Prime Minister in name only.[13]

While Chamberlain was talking with Halifax, a crisis was occurring in the French Government. Premier Paul Renaud was so intent on firing General Maurice Gamelin, who was not only the Chief of the French Army but also the Supreme Commander of the Allied forces, that he proposed to resign if his cabinet did not concur. Gamelin had been France's senior soldier for the past five years but had proven to be a most reluctant leader—some years, he left as much as 40 percent of his defense budget unspent. Gamelin was seemingly willing to go to great lengths to avoid any sort of a fight.[14]

Former Premier Édouard Daladier, now the Minister of Defense in the Reynaud Government, was a staunch defender of Gamelin, calling him a soldier with tremendous prestige and a fine military record. The French Cabinet agreed with Daladier's assessment and refused to remove the General. Renaud promptly resigned. Thus, as Hitler was poised to attack the West, France ostensibly had no government, and the head of the Allied forces was a general known for his timidity.[15]

Back on Downing Street, the Prime Minister met late in the afternoon with Halifax, Churchill, and Conservative Party Whip David Margesson.[16] The meeting concerned what to do if, as expected, Labour would not participate in a reconstituted government led by Chamberlain.[17]

Despite the importance of this meeting, no minutes were taken. As a result, there are several versions of what took place. Of these various descriptions, Roberts suggests that the most plausible is to be found in the diary of Alexander Cadogan, who was the permanent Under-Secretary of State for Foreign Affairs and someone to whom Halifax had spoken immediately after the meeting with Churchill and Chamberlain.[18] In the Halifax/Cadogan version of the meeting, Churchill made it clear he thought he was the man for the job of prime minister. Roberts has no trouble believing that Churchill made such a statement, because it would be in complete accord with the way Churchill had behaved throughout his life. "He had always thrust himself into the arena and felt no guilt or embarrassment about demanding what he saw as his due."[19]

Cadogan wrote in his diary on May 9 what Halifax had told him:

> P.M., Winston, and I discussed possibilities. P.M. said I was the man mentioned as the most acceptable. I said it would be a hopeless position. If I was not in charge of the war (operations) and if I didn't lead in the House, I should be a cypher. I thought Winston was a better choice. Winston did *not demur.* Was very kind and polite but showed he thought this [the] right solution. Chief Whip and others think feeling in the House has been veering towards him. If N.C. remains—as he is ready to do—his advice and judgments would steady Winston.[20] [emphasis in original]

As Halifax would later write in his 1954 autobiography: "I [had] no doubt ... that for me to succeed [Chamberlain] would create a quite impossible situation .... [W]hat would in fact be my position? Churchill would be running Defence ... and I should have no access to the House of Commons. The inevitable result would be that ... I should speedily become a more or less honorary Prime Minister, living in a kind of twilight just outside the things that really mattered."[21] As Lukacs puts it, the Foreign Secretary felt that "within a Halifax Cabinet, Churchill ... would be unimaginable."[22]

Churchill's version of the meeting is much more dramatic. He claims that the premiership was presented to him and that he did not lobby for it. The "Churchill version" is succinctly laid out in Colville's diary:

> Winston told me several times that when Chamberlain had summoned Lord Halifax and himself to the Cabinet Room he looked at [Churchill] sharply and said, 'Can you see any reason, Winston, why in these days a Peer should not be Prime Minister?' Winston saw a trap in this question. It would be difficult to say yes without saying frankly that he thought he himself should be the choice. If he said no, or hedged, he felt sure that Mr. Chamberlain would turn to Lord Halifax and say, 'Well since Winston agrees, I'm sure that if the King asks me, I should suggest sending for you.' Therefore, Winston turned his back and gazed out on the Horse Guards Parade without giving any reply. There was an awkward pause, after which Halifax himself volunteered the suggestion that if the King were to ask Mr. Chamberlain's opinion about his successor, he should propose Mr. Churchill.[23]

Colville also wrote that "Chamberlain told Winston and Halifax he would gladly serve under either of them. [However] Halifax categorically refused to lead a Government; Winston licked his lips ... [S]o, if [Chamberlain] does go I am afraid it *must* be Winston."[24] [emphasis in original] As Colville had previously indicated, candidates to replace Chamberlain were very few.[25]

When the meeting ended it was understood that if, as all expected, Labour would not serve under Chamberlain, then the Prime Minister. "would advise the King to send for Churchill."[26] This conclusion, of course, presumed that Labour would serve under Churchill. While the Labour ministers who spoke in the House the previous evening had, like their Liberal colleagues, carefully cast no aspersions on Churchill for the handling of the Norwegian campaign, some Labourites had never forgiven Churchill for Tonypandy.*

The all-important meeting with the leaders of the Labour Party took place at 6:15 PM.[27] Besides Clement Attlee and Arthur Greenwood, the Leader and Deputy Leader of the Labourites, respectively, Halifax, Churchill, and, of course, Chamberlain also were there. The three Conservatives sat on one side of the table while Attlee and Greenwood sat on the other.[28] At the meeting, Chamberlain pressed the two Labour leaders to join his government.[29] Just as Churchill started to add his support for Chamberlain's

---

As discussed in Chapter 4, Tonypandy was a coal miner strike in Wales in 1910 that turned violent. Churchill was wrongly considered to have broken his promise not to use troops to deal with the strikers.

position, Greenwood stopped him, saying: "We haven't come here to listen to you orating, Winston."[30]

The two questions for Atlee and Greenwood were: (1) would Labour serve in a new coalition government led by Chamberlain? and (2) if not, would Labour serve in a new coalition government led by someone else? The two told Chamberlain it was unlikely Labour would be willing to serve under him but serving under some other Conservative was possible.[31] They would put the questions to Labour's National Executive Committee, which was starting a retreat at the seaside town of Bournemouth that evening.[32] They would call the next day as soon as they had answers.[33] The two then hurried off to the train station and headed for Bournemouth.

When Churchill's son Randolph called that evening to ask if there was any news, Winston replied, in words he had come to imagine he might never get to say: "I think I shall be Prime Minister tomorrow."[34]

Friday, May 10, 1940

The German Invasion of Western Europe/How Churchill Became Prime Minister

On May 10, Britain awoke to the shattering, but perhaps not unexpected, news that Germany had invaded neutral Holland. Soon it became clear that neutral Belgium had been invaded too. This incursion was something the French and British had considered imminent since at least April 11.[35] Several French towns, among them the open towns of Nancy, Lille, Lyon, Colmar, Pontoise, and Luxeuil, had also been bombed by German airplanes, killing civilians in the process.[36]* German troops had parachuted into numerous locations throughout Holland. At the Hague, troops were brought in by seaplane.[37] It also appeared that the Germans were advancing through Luxembourg and the Ardennes toward the Meuse River in France.[38]** What would become the Battle of France had begun.

The Nazi offensive immediately caused Reynaud to withdraw his resignation and, at least temporarily, end his feud with General Gamelin.[39] After Belgium had been invaded, King Leopold lifted his prohibition of British and French soldiers being on Belgian soil and begged France and Britain to come to Belgium's aid.[40]

---

*An open town or city is one that has declared itself to be unfortified and undefended and so, by international law, exempt from enemy attack.

**The Meuse is in the northeast corner of France and runs northwesterly, roughly paralleling France's border with Luxembourg. It then turns north and heads into Belgium and Holland. For millennia, the Meuse has served as a barrier protecting France, Belgium, and Holland against invasion from the east.

In response to the Nazi invasion, Gamelin ordered the armies under his command—the French First and Seventh and the British Expeditionary Force (BEF)—into Belgium intending to engage the Germans in the Netherlands. But German forces had already crossed through most of the Netherlands. As a result, Gamelin instead committed his troops to positions along the River Dyle in central Belgium, approximately 100 miles east of Dunkirk.[41*] There they were to join up with Belgian and Dutch forces.[42] If this line could be held, a large portion of Belgium, including its principal industrial area, would be spared.[43] Hitler had repeatedly said he would never violate the neutrality of the Low countries, but because he wanted to conquer France, he decided to go through the Low Countries and follow the route the Kaiser had taken to attack France in WWI.

The British immediately ordered two squadrons of Hurricane fighters, each made up of twelve planes, to France. Another squadron, which had been packed up for duty at Narvik in Norway, would be diverted to France.[44]

The invasion had revitalized Chamberlain. He felt like a new man.[45] He had even convinced himself that under the circumstances, the country would be much better off if he postponed his resignation.[46] Privately, he told Halifax that he "had a feeling that Winston did not approve of the delay."[47]

Before and between the three War Cabinet meetings held on May 10, Chamberlain and his supporters jockeyed with those who wanted a new government without delay. The latter group was led, surprisingly, by longtime Chamberlain supporter Sir Kingsley Wood, who was the Lord Privy Seal in Chamberlain's War Cabinet.[48] Sir Kingsley told Chamberlain and the members of the War Cabinet that in his view, Hitler's attack made it even more necessary for the Prime Minister to step down so that a National Government could be formed.[49**] Although Wood's words affected Chamberlain,[50] the back and forth led to no firm resolution by the time the War Cabinet met for the third and last time that day, at 4:30 PM.

Atlee and Greenwood called Downing Street at 4:45 PM from their party's Bournemouth retreat.[51] Shortly thereafter, a private secretary entered the Cabinet room and handed a typewritten transcript of the phone call to Horace Wilson, who read the verdict:[52] Labour would not serve in any

---

Dunkirk is located on the English Channel in the far northwest of France. It is only 8 miles west of the Belgian border. Since Belgium is a small country, Dunkirk is only 180 miles west of the German border.

Dunkirk will soon take on legendary significance as the war begins to heat up.

**Even though Wood had never really shared Churchill's positions on foreign policy and, in fact, was critical of how the Royal Navy had performed in Norway, Sir Kingsley's efforts did not go unnoticed or unappreciated. He was ultimately chosen to be the Chancellor of the Exchequer in the new Churchill Government.*

government headed by Chamberlain.[53] Would they serve under a someone else? The answer:

> The Labour Party are prepared to take their share of responsibility as a full partner in a new government, under a new Prime Minister, which would command the confidence of the nation.[54]

Chamberlain glanced at the document then continued with the Cabinet's agenda as if nothing had happened.[55] The Cabinet members received a briefing on the fighting on the Continent: The Allied troop vanguard should have reached the River Dyle in Belgium;[56] German mass air attacks had begun on Belgian aerodromes in the early hours of the morning; and German parachutists had landed at various points behind the Belgian defenses.[57]

When Chamberlain got to the last item on the agenda—the current political situation—he said that, given Labour's response, he had concluded that the right course was for him to tender his resignation to the King, which he proposed to do immediately.[58] He did not disclose that he had met with Churchill and Halifax the previous day, nor did he share the outcome of those meetings. Chamberlain did say that the new Prime Minister should be authorized to assume that all members of the War Cabinet would place their resignations at his disposal; but that in the meantime, of course, they would remain in office and continue to discharge their functions until a new administration had been formed.[59]

In less than half an hour, Chamberlain was on his way to see the King.[60] As His Majesty wrote in his diary that night, Chamberlain wanted to resign; and though they both wanted Halifax to be the new P.M., Chamberlain said Halifax was ostensibly disinclined because he was a member of the House of Lords. The King thought the peerage issue could be overcome. But if Halifax would not serve, both men knew there was only one man to send for to form a government in whom Britons could feel confident.[61] The King immediately sent for Churchill, the man, the King had told confidantes, "[h]e would never wish to appoint ... to any office unless it was absolutely necessary in time of war."[62]

Writing about his meeting with King George in *The Gathering Storm,* Churchill said,

> His Majesty received me most graciously and bade me sit down. He looked at me searchingly and quizzically for some moments and then said, 'I suppose you don't know why I have sent for you?' Adopting his mood, I replied: 'Sir, I simply couldn't imagine why.' He laughed and said, 'I want to ask you to form a Government.' I said, 'I would certainly do so."[63]

While the King would later become "one of Churchill's most ardent admirers," Manchester and Reid write that, on May 10, 1940, King George's "feelings were mixed."[64]

Churchill left Buckingham Palace and returned to the Admiralty. Ignoring Chamberlain's thoughts from earlier in the day about postponing his resignation, Churchill immediately wrote the outgoing Prime Minister the following heartfelt note:

My dear Neville,

My first act on coming back from the Palace is to write and tell you how grateful I am to you for promising to stand by me and to aid the country in this extremely grievous and formidable moment. I am under no illusions about what lies ahead, and of the long dangerous defile through which we must March for many months. With your help and counsel and with the support of the great party of which you are Leader, I trust I shall succeed. The example which you have set of self-forgetting dignity and public spirit will govern the action of many and has been an inspiration to all.

In these 8 months we have worked together I am proud to have won your friendship and your confidence in an increasing measure. To a very large extent I am in your—hands—and I feel no fear of that. For the rest I have faith in our cause which I feel sure will not be suffered to fail among men.

I will write you again tonight after I have seen the Labour Leaders. I am so glad you will broadcast to our anxious people.

Believe me,

Yours ever,

Winston S. Churchill[65]*

Chamberlain was touched by this "most handsome acknowledgment."[66] He knew that "he and Churchill worked well together" and that Winston had "showed him regard and even affection at every opportunity."[67] The level of respect Churchill had for Chamberlain had grown almost constantly from

---

At the end of July, Churchill would add to his expression of gratitude to Chamberlain when he told W.P. Crozier, the editor of The Manchester Guardian, *that "I owe something to Chamberlain, you know. When he resigned, he could have advised the King to send for Halifax and he didn't." ed. Taylor,* Crozier *p. 175.*

the moment Winston was appointed to the War Cabinet until the moment he became Prime Minister and even thereafter.

Halifax received a note from Churchill similar to the one sent to Chamberlain, and he chose to reproduce it in its entirety in his autobiography.[68] Churchill also invited Halifax to continue as Foreign Secretary and to serve in the War Cabinet.[69] The note to Halifax read: "It gives me so much pleasure to feel that *we shall be fighting this business through together to the end*. I feel sure your conduct of Foreign Affairs is an essential element to our work strength. I am so grateful to you for being willing to continue your work in this great office of which you are at once the slave and the master, and that you will of course lead the [House of Lords]."* [emphasis added]

As alluded to in the note to Chamberlain, Churchill had offered Neville the Leadership of the House of Commons, the Lord Presidency of the Privy Council, and a seat in the War Cabinet.[70] However, Attlee warned that Labour would not work easily under that arrangement. After discussions with Chamberlain and then again with Attlee, it was decided that Churchill would take on the leadership of the House of Commons; Attlee would act as his deputy and do all the daily work.[71] (Churchill would come down to deal with such parliamentary matters on only "the most serious of occasions."[72])

At 9:00 PM Chamberlain broadcast his resignation on the BBC:

> In the afternoon of today it was apparent that the essential unity [needed to carry on the war successfully] could be secured under another Prime Minister, not myself. ... In these circumstances my duty was plain. I sought an audience of the King this evening and tendered to him my resignation, which his Majesty has been pleased to accept. His Majesty has now entrusted to my right hon. colleague, Mr. Winston Churchill, the task of forming a new Administration on a national basis. ... I should, perhaps, say to you that Mr. Churchill has expressed to me his strong desire that I should be a member of the War Cabinet, and I have told him that I will gladly give him any assistance that I can. ... You and I must rally behind our new leader, and with our united strength and with unshakable courage to fight and work until this wild beast, that has sprung out of his lair upon us, has been finally disarmed and overthrown.[73]

Immediately after Chamberlain's speech, Churchill went about the task of picking his War Cabinet and filling the other ministries. Members of Churchill's War Cabinet would be:

Two weeks after Churchill sent his laudatory note to Halifax, the two men would clash over whether to make overtures to Hitler about peace.

Himself in the recently created position of Minister of Defence

Neville Chamberlain (Conservative), Lord President of the Council

Clement Atlee (Labour Party Leader), Lord Privy Seal

Arthur Greenwood (Labour Party Deputy Leader), Minister without Portfolio

Lord Halifax (Conservative), Foreign Secretary

The service ministers would be:

Sir John Anderson (Independent), Home Secretary

Sir Kingsley Wood (Conservative), Chancellor of the Exchequer

Anthony Eden (Conservative), Secretary for War

A.V. Alexander (Labour), First Lord of the Admiralty

Sir Archibald Sinclair (Liberal Party Leader), Air Minister*

Churchill knew that, as important as it was to bring Labour and the Liberals into the new government, he also needed to recognize that many Conservatives were angry with him for superseding Chamberlain. Churchill knew that his ascension was "very unpleasant to many of them, after [his] long years of criticism and often fierce reproach."[74] (The loyalty of Conservatives to Chamberlain was demonstrated when, after the Norway debate, 281 Conservative MPs voted to see the Chamberlain Government continue.) For this reason, Churchill believed that adding Chamberlain to his Government and retaining Halifax were critical. As Manchester and Reid write, Churchill would have been quite "happy to see the last of Lord Halifax."[75] Elements of the Labour Party as well as others who had backed Churchill during "the lean years" wanted all "the old crowd" thrown out.[76] By that criterion, Halifax certainly would not have been included in Churchill's War Cabinet,[77] but Churchill felt obliged to keep him on at least for the present. Kingsley Wood, a longtime appeaser, was also spared the ax—having earned his spot

---

*Sinclair found it hard to accept this position. As Leader of the Liberal Party, he and his followers believed that he should instead have a seat in the War Cabinet. But Churchill was determined to keep the War Cabinet very small. Instead, he proposed that his friend Archie Sinclair join the War Cabinet "when any matter affecting fundamental political issues or party union was involved." Churchill, Their Finest Hour p.12. Most notably Archie would be in the room during key discussions just several weeks later.

as the new Chancellor of the Exchequer because of how hard he worked convincing Chamberlain not to let the German invasion of Western Europe postpone his resignation.

Churchill was trying to avoid laying blame on any individual for past misdeeds, recognizing that "official responsibility rested upon the Government of the time."[78] As he aptly writes, "No one had more right than I to pass a sponge across the past. [So] I ... resisted these disruptive tendencies" and did not remove all members of the previous Government from his administration.[79]

Chamberlain and Halifax were included in the new War Cabinet so Churchill could mend fences. More importantly, the appointments made by Churchill gave him a majority in the War Cabinet. That is, even if Chamberlain and Halifax opposed Churchill on a question, Winston could count on the support of the two Labour ministers, which would result in a vote of 3 to 2 in his favor. However, as Lukacs points out, the strict counting of votes in the War Cabinet went only so far.[80] Newcomers to the Cabinet, Attlee and Greenwood were inexperienced in military and world affairs and were members of a party very much a minority in Parliament. Thus, in the War Cabinet, they listened rather than spoke.[81] In reality, then, Churchill needed his Conservative Cabinet members to support him. Historian John Lukacs writes that "A real break between Churchill and the two eminent Conservatives would have been disastrous."[82] "Had Halifax or Chamberlain or both resigned...," the Churchill Government would have been "gravely damaged" and perhaps even become "untenable."[83]

Even the Conservative MPs who had "temporarily deserted Chamberlain" in the Norway vote did so "without really conferring their full allegiance on Churchill."[84] Chamberlain's exhortation to rally behind Churchill was not followed by many of his supporters, who remained deeply angry, as well as by other party members who remained unsure of Churchill. Here is a sampling of anti-Churchill invective:

- He was "widely distrusted as a man of unstable temperament, unsound judgment, and rhetorical (and also alcoholic) excess. ... For most of his career there hung around him an unsavory air of disreputability and unseemliness, as a particularly wayward, root less and an anachronistic product of a decaying and increasingly discredited aristocratic order."[85]

"[Churchill] may ... be the man of drive and energy the country believes him to be and he may be able to speed up our creaking military and industrial machine; but it is a terrible risk, it involves the danger of rash and spectacular exploits, and I cannot help feeling that this country may be maneuvered into the most dangerous position it has ever been in." —Jock Colville[86]*

- "[T]he gangsters will shortly be in complete control." —Lord Halifax[87]

- "...[T]his sudden coup of Winston and his rabble was a serious disaster and an unnecessary one. ... [Chamberlain,] Halifax and Oliver Stanley ... had weakly surrendered to a half-breed American..." —Rab Butler, Chamberlain's Under-Secretary of State for Foreign Affairs[88]

- Churchill is part of "the flotsam and jetsam of political drift thrown up on the beach." —former Prime Minister Stanley Baldwin[89]

Over the ensuing days and weeks, in referring to Churchill's new Government, the words "crooks," "gangsters," and "wild men" often appeared in diaries and letters.[90] "Although he was an aristocrat by birth, Churchill was widely believed to be not really a gentleman at all. On the contrary he was often described as a highly gifted but, an undeniable 'cad.'"[91]

Colville was entirely correct when he said, "Seldom can a Prime Minister have taken office with the Establishment ... so dubious of the choice and so prepared to have its doubts justified."[92]

Churchill was such a complex man that it can be hard at times to distinguish praise from censure:

- Sir Edmund Ironside, Chief of the Imperial General Staff, said, "Naturally, the only man who can succeed [Chamberlain] is Winston but he is too unstable, though he has the genius to bring the war to an end.[93]

- In February 1940, Lord Crawford, a longtime and vicious critic of Churchill, wrote:

  "People say that Churchill is tactless, that his judgements are erratic, that he flies off at a tangent, that he has a burning desire to trespass upon the domain of the naval strategist—all

---

In subsequent years Colville would come to view the events surrounding May 10 completely differently, calling it a "... point in history [when] one of the greatest administrations which has ever governed the United Kingdom was in the process of formation." Colville p. 124.

of this may be more or less true but he remains the only figure in the Cabinet with the virtue of constant uncompromising aggressive quest of victory ... [T]he more I see and hear of him the more confident I am that he represents the party of complete ... victory."[94]

A more dispassionate view of Churchill in 1940 was written by a young John F. Kennedy, who said:

> In the light of the present-day war, we are amazed at the blindness of British leaders, and the country as a whole, that they could fail to see the correctness of Churchill's arguments ...

> In studying Churchill's warnings, which have proved to be so accurate, it is necessary to realize the somewhat peculiar position he has always occupied in British politics. No one has ever questioned his ability or his dynamic energy. But these very qualities, which now cause Britain to consider him the only man who can carry through a successful war policy, have in times of peace caused him to be considered "dangerous," and a little uncomfortable to have around. Then too, Churchill has always represented the extreme viewpoint. He has never stood on middle ground—he went "all out" for anything he advocated, with the result that his opinions have always been taken advisedly by most British leaders."[95]

Nevertheless, the fact was that "[m]any ... Conservative MPs distrusted Churchill."[96] The classic Tory was orthodox, conventional, and loyal to his party. Churchill was none of these.[97] Many shared Colville's view that "[p]rovided Chamberlain and Halifax remain in the War Cabinet there will at least be some restraint on our new *War Lord*."[98] [emphasis added]

It is ironic, almost beyond measure, that the one Conservative Party member who most wholeheartedly stood behind Churchill at this time was his old adversary, Neville Chamberlain—a man who only nine months earlier begrudgingly invited Churchill into the Cabinet. Chamberlain recognized that his relationship with Churchill may not have completely healed but it had deepened. In a letter to his sister Ida on May 11, he wrote, "I must say that Winston has been most handsome in his appreciation of my willingness to help and my ability to do so. ... I know that he relies on Halifax and me."[99]

In fact, Churchill said that Chamberlain was "the best man he had" and he did not know what to do without him.[100] As Chamberlain's biographer Robert Self writes, Churchill also "demonstrated a touching and tenacious loyalty in defending Chamberlain from opponents seeking to expel him from the Government."[101]

Manchester and Reid contend that the source of Churchill's immediate problem with Conservative MPs generally stemmed from the results of the 1935 Parliamentary election.[102] In 1935, "[m]isled by Prime Minister Stanley Baldwin, who had assured ... that England's defenses were more than adequate, Britain had elected a Conservative majority that was top-heavy with irreconcilable pacifists and die-heart appeasers."[103] Churchill, although a Conservative himself, "had been their [party's] gadfly throughout the 1930s" and a vocal opponent of both pacifism and appeasement (both of which, by 1940, had been discredited).[104] Many Tory MPs also felt that the wrong man (Chamberlain) had suffered for the disastrous Norway campaign and would continue to hold that view for some time. Unlike Chamberlain, these members had not yet come to embrace Churchill and his non-traditional ways.

Many of Churchill's critics were elected in 1935, and likely would not have been re-elected had there been a required election in 1940. (Under normal conditions the time between national elections cannot exceed five years.) But the election that should have taken place in 1940 had been postponed because of the war by the Local Elections and Registration of Electors (Temporary Provisions) Act of 1939. As a result of the anger of these members and other Conservatives, whenever Churchill entered the House as Prime Minister he was greeted almost exclusively by Liberal MPs, though "Mr. Chamberlain's loyalty and support was steadfast. ..."[105] In the next few weeks, Churchill would need every bit of his former boss's loyalty and support to deal with the battles to be waged in the War Cabinet as well as those to be waged on the battlefields of Belgium and France.

The Germans' Plan for the Invasion of Western Europe

The German invasion of Western Europe, which began on May 10, 1940, consisted of three major parts (see map on p. 393):

1. In the North, the thirty divisions of Army Group B, including three panzer divisions, initiated a four-pronged assault against Holland and Belgium. The Germans properly predicted that, upon learning of this assault, British and French troops would rush into Belgium and take a stand along the River Dyle.

2. In the South, Army Group C, with nineteen divisions, feigned an attack against the eastern portion of the Maginot Line near the Swiss border. The sole purpose of this maneuver was to tie up the French forces stationed there.

3. Army Group A, commanded by General Gerd von Rundstedt, advanced its forty-five divisions, including seven panzer divisions, through Luxembourg and the Ardennes Forest, which the French believed was "impassable to strong forces."[106] Army Group A was the Germans' main attack force.

The plan was much like a football play where there is a fake toss and sweep right to the tailback (Group B), to which the defense would react, but the ball is instead handed to the fullback (the panzer divisions of Group A) to run up the largely vacated middle of the field.

In addition to the units committed to the assault, the Germans also had forty-seven divisions in reserve ("twenty in immediate reserve behind the various Army Groups and twenty-seven in general reserve"[107]).

The Allies, on paper, could match the German forces. "The grand total of Allied divisions of all qualities nominally available on May 10 was ... 135 ... practically the same number" as the Germans had.[108] Of these, 104 divisions were French and ten were British.[109] There were also 648 Allied fighter planes in France with provision for Britain to dispatch another four squadrons (sixty-four planes).[110]* General Gort, the commander of the BEF, believed that the Allied planes and crews were superior to the Germans', but that the Germans had a considerable superiority in the number of planes available.[111]

Just as in Poland, the Nazi strategy was to penetrate deep into enemy territory with mobile armored units followed by infantry.[112] More specifically, as planned by Rundstedt's staff and Hitler himself,[113] armored units from Army Group A would surprise the Allies and pour into France through the Ardennes and the gap between the Maginot Line and the Allied forces spread out along the Dyle. (This gap was the place where the Allies least expected

---

*Without making any comment on the age or quality of the Allied aircraft, the Chiefs of Staff, in their May 4, 1940, report to the War Cabinet (titled "Review of the Strategical Situation on the Assumption that Germany Has Decided to Seek a Decision in 1940") could not be sure that this number would be adequate to cover both the army front and French vital centers. CAB 66/7 WP 150 (40) Attachment p. 3 209.

the Germans to strike.[114*]) Then German forces would vault over the Meuse River at Sedan, a French city on the border with Belgium.[115]

At that point the German Army would pivot westward and race 175 miles along the north bank of the River Somme until they neared the English Channel when they would turn north.[116] This was the Nazi's sickle maneuver.[117] The Germans believed that Army Group B would have caused the Allied forces, initially positioned along the River Dyle in Belgium, to have retreated westward by then toward the English Channel. Once Group B hooked up with Group A, the Allied troops would be trapped.[118]

Hitler believed these maneuvers could isolate Britain.[119] Moreover, with naval bases and airfields close to the Channel in France, Belgium, and Holland, he could torment and blockade the UK.[120] Ultimately, his plan was to force Britain and France to sue for peace and grant him the freedom he wanted in the East.[121]

At 3:00 AM, Churchill ended what had to have been both an exhausting and exhilarating day. Recalling his emotions in *The Gathering Storm*, Churchill wrote: "At last I had the authority to give directions over the whole scene. I felt as if I were walking with destiny, and that all my past life had been but a preparation for this hour and for this trial. ... I was sure I should not fail."[122]

The Germans would get to the Meuse River by circumventing the "impenetrable" Maginot Line, instead going west across Luxembourg into Belgium and through the hilly and forested portion of the Ardennes. The Maginot Line was an eighty-five-mile long series of fortresses, obstacles, and weapon installations constructed on the French side of its borders with Italy, Switzerland, Germany, and Luxembourg. It was completed in 1935 at the then-staggering cost of Fr 7,000 million. Strong as it was, the Maginot Line did not extend across all of France's northern border: notably, it did not protect a vast 250-mile stretch of frontier along France's borders with Belgium and Luxembourg, including that portion south of the Ardennes Forest. The French believed that the terrain in and around the forest was simply too difficult for German tanks to cross. The British General Staff had, however, "long been anxious about this gap." Churchill, Their Finest Hour p. 30.

When Churchill visited the Maginot Line just before the start of the war, he spotted the great weakness in the French defense system, the fact that it ended opposite the Ardennes Forest. In his discussions with General Alphonse Georges he said, "Remember that we are faced with a new weapon, armor in great strength, on which the Germans are no doubt concentrating, and that forests will be particularly tempting to such forces since they will offer concealment from the air." Gilbert, Churchill: A Life p.128. Edward Spears, who was Churchill's representative to the French prime minister, could not remember General Georges' reply, but neither Georges nor his superior, General Gamelin, acted on, or even made note of, Churchill's advice. Manchester, Alone p. 497.

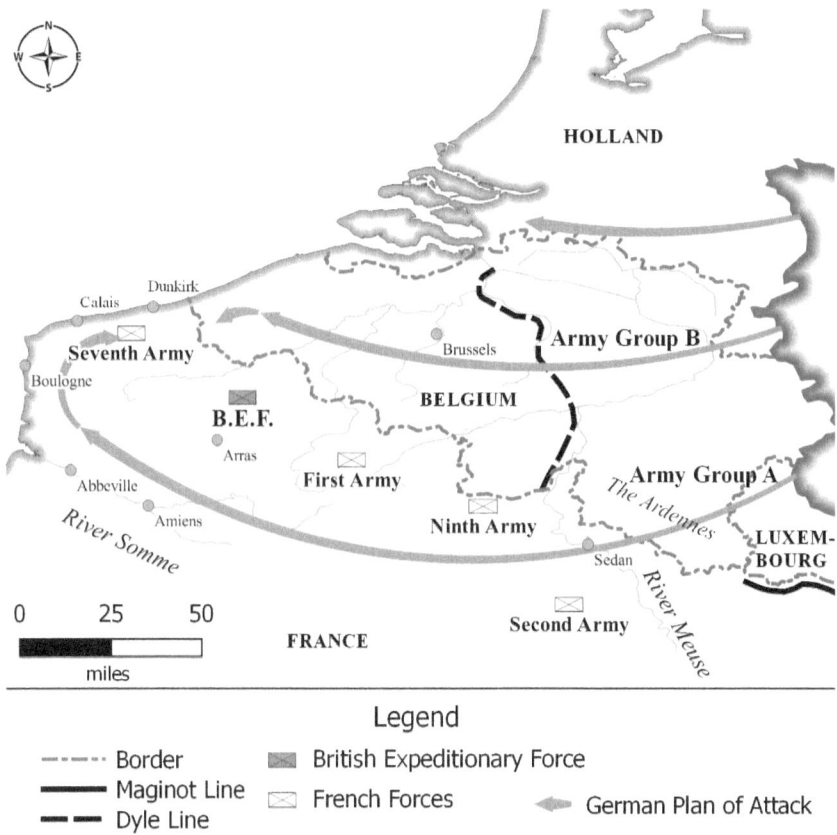

HOLLAND

Army Group B

Dunkirk

Calais

Seventh Army

Boulogne

Brussels

BELGIUM

B.E.F.

Arras

Abbeville

Amiens

First Army

Ninth Army

Sedan

Army Group A

The Ardennes

LUXEM-BOURG

River Somme

River Meuse

Second Army

FRANCE

0   25   50

miles

Legend

----- Border

——— Maginot Line

— — Dyle Line

British Expeditionary Force

French Forces

German Plan of Attack

Saturday, May 11, 1940

Upon awakening, Churchill set up a 12:30 PM meeting with Chamberlain and Halifax in the war room at the Admiralty.[123] Churchill wanted to look at the maps and talk things over. At the meeting, it was agreed that until Churchill got the War Cabinet fully assembled, the three of them would take responsibility for directing the war.[124]

In another gesture of kindness toward Chamberlain, Churchill later sent the former P.M. a note telling him that he and his wife need not rush in moving out of 10 Downing Street.[125] The Churchills stayed in their apartment at the Admiralty for another month, giving the Chamberlains the opportunity to move out at their own pace.[126]

Sunday, May 12, 1940

Much to the surprise of the French generals, armored columns from German Army Group A suddenly poured out of the Ardennes.[127] Some French military authorities had believed that the Ardennes was "impassible,"[128] and others in the French High Command had estimated that it would take a strong enemy force at least fifteen days to negotiate the heavily forested and mountainous region.[129] The Germans "did it in two."[130]

The spearhead of Army Group A had arrived: some "1,800 tanks, 17,000 other vehicles, and 98,000 men appeared on the east bank of the Meuse" across the river from the French city of Sedan.[131] (See map on p. 393.) The river "was narrow and swift" at that point and, on the steep west bank, the French had considerable heavy artillery.[132]

Monday, May 13, 1940

This was the day for Churchill's first speech to Parliament as Prime Minister. The House had not sat since May 9, the day before the invasion of the Low Countries. "[M]any members seemed to have an emotional hangover, and were slightly ashamed of the burst of emotion that helped bring Chamberlain down."[133] Some Tories were even predicting the demise of the new Churchill Government. For example, Lord J.C.C. Davidson, a former civil servant who became a Conservative Party politician and a nobleman, wrote: "the Tories don't trust Winston. ... After the first clash of war is over it may well be that a sounder Government may emerge."[134] This view was not all that dissimilar from Hitler's. He, too, thought Churchill would not last long; that Churchill's belligerent manner and warlike instincts were not compatible with most people in the British establishment.[135]

In contrast, Jock Colville grudgingly admitted that "Winston's administration, with all its faults, has drive. ... Moreover, the government has the complete confidence of the country."[136]

In his now famous *"blood, toil, tears, and sweat"* speech of May 13, which was all of seven minutes long, Churchill said:

> I beg to move, "That this House welcomes the formation of a government representing the united and inflexible resolve of the nation to prosecute the war with Germany to a victorious conclusion. ...
>
> A War Cabinet has been formed of five Members, representing, with the Opposition Liberals, the unity of the nation. The three party Leaders have agreed to serve, either in the War Cabinet or in high executive office. ...

I would say to the House, as I said to those who have joined this Government: I have nothing to offer but blood, toil, tears and sweat. We have before us an ordeal of the most grievous kind. We have before us many, many long months of struggle and of suffering.

You ask, what is our policy? I will say: It is to wage war, by sea, land and air, with all our might and with all the strength that God can give us; to wage war against a monstrous tyranny never surpassed in the dark, lamentable catalogue of human crime. That is our policy.

You ask, what is our aim? I can answer in one word: It is victory, victory at all costs, victory in spite of all terror, victory, however long and hard the road may be; for without victory, there is no survival.

I take up my task with buoyancy and hope. I feel sure that our cause will not be suffered to fail among men. At this time, I feel entitled to claim the aid of all, and I say, Come then, let us go forward together with our united strength.[137] [emphasis added]

Writer Anthony McCarten recounts: "... [Conservative MP Henry] Channon noted in his diary that the speech—widely regarded now as one of the greatest ever given by a politician—'was not well received.'"[138] At the time, no one was "confident enough to acknowledge the real power of what is now considered as masterful a display of political rhetoric as the Gettysburg Address."[139]

Former P.M. David Lloyd George addressed Parliament thirty minutes after Churchill had finished and offered this tribute:

I congratulate the country upon [Mr. Churchill's] elevation to the Premiership at this very, very critical and terrible moment. If I may venture to say so, I think the Sovereign exercises a wise choice. We know the right hon. Gentlemen's glittering intellectual gifts, his dauntless courage, his profound study of war, and his experience in its operation and direction. ... He is exercising his supreme responsibility at a graver moment and in times of greater jeopardy than have ever confronted a British Minister for all time.[140]

Lloyd George's speech "caused Churchill to weep."[141]

At the meeting of the War Cabinet held at 6:30 that evening, the members were given news about the war:

- Strong German mechanized forces were advancing in several directions along the entire front, but there were no signs of infantry columns.

- The Belgian Army did not appear to be putting up a strong resistance; and Liege, a city in east-central Belgium along the Meuse River, was probably now isolated.

- The French were not yet certain whether the main German effort would be directed through Luxemburg, just to the west of the Maginot Line, or further west through central Belgium.[142]

Though the French may not have known that the attack by Army Group A through Luxemburg was the main German effort, they should have known that Army Group A had made substantial progress. Not only had it reached the Meuse across from Sedan, but, using dive bombers, the Germans had silenced every French field-artillery peace located on the west bank. Worse still, Nazi rubber boats had reached the steeply banked west shore of the Meuse "unmolested," and "beachheads were established both north and south of Sedan."[143] Temporary bridges were going up.[144]

Tuesday, May 14, 1940

When the War Cabinet assembled again at 11:30 AM, they immediately learned the bad news that the Germans had breached the forward defenses of Sedan.[145] In an attempt to soften that blow, the members were told "the French defenses in this area were very strong and a great deal of work had been done on them recently."[146] What they were not told was that, in the Sedan sector, the French line was very thin and that the Ninth French Army stationed there "was mainly composed of troops who were definitely below the French standards."[147] Upon hearing that Hitler's forces had crossed the Meuse at Sedan, the War Cabinet had every right to be alarmed. Once the Germans broke through at Sedan, there was little to stop them.[148]

Some weeks later Churchill would tell the House that the French High Command's failure to withdraw armies from Belgium and move them to the area near Sedan, only 70 miles to the south, was a "colossal military disaster."[149] France should have repositioned its forces to stop the German offensive the moment they knew that the French lines were decisively broken.

Worse yet, Halifax informed the group that Holland could not resist the Germans much longer and was considering peace negotiations.[150] By evening, Holland was lost.[151]

Back at Sedan, the French launched a counterattack late in the afternoon with approximately seventy-five well-armored tanks, backed by infantry.[152] Not only was "the German flank ... exposed" but not all the German panzers, artillery, and infantry had yet to cross the Meuse.[153] Unfortunately, believing that the function of armor was only to support the infantry, the French had not installed radios in their tanks. Thus, they were unable to coordinate an assault, and within two hours, fifty of the French tanks were destroyed, with the rest fleeing the battlefield.[154]

While the tank battle was going on, Premier Reynaud learned at least some of what was happening at Sedan and wired Churchill.

At both the Chiefs of Staff Committee meeting held at 6:00 PM and the War Cabinet meeting at 7:00 PM, Churchill revealed he had received a wire from French Premier Reynaud. In the message, which he composed during the tank battle at Sedan, Reynaud said that the situation was very serious, and the Germans had broken through the French lines south of Sedan.[155] Churchill told the group that a similar telegram had been received by Cyril Newall, the Chief of the Air Staff, from the RAF Commander-in-Chief in France. General Ironside, the Chief of the Imperial General Staff, added that he had spoken with Supreme Allied Commander General Gamelin who, like the British, was shocked at how easily the Germans crossed the Meuse and broke through the main French positions.[156]

Reynaud thought the Germans now intended to deliver a mortal blow to Paris, a mere 125 miles away.[157] In his message, Reynaud thanked the British for sending four squadrons of fighters to France but advised that for it to halt the German advance Britain needed to send ten more squadrons at once—that day if possible.[158] Reynaud believed this intervention might be a decisive turning point in the war.

Chief of the Air Staff Newall told the Cabinet he was convinced that squadrons sent in response to Reynaud's plea would never return to Britain once they were established on the other side of the Channel; he suspected a majority of them would be lost.[159] In the discussion that ensued, it was agreed that the situation was too indistinct to permit the Cabinet to decide. Quickly obtaining clarifying information would be essential, not only to determine precisely what had happened but also to better define the future intentions of the French.[160] Out of concern though, for the picture Reynaud had painted, the Cabinet directed Newall to take all necessary preparatory steps for the early dispatch of another ten fighter squadrons once the Cabinet's questions had been answered.[161]

If the circumstances described in Premier Reynaud's wire were not bad enough, in the hour or two after he sent the telegram the situation outside Sedan deteriorated further. Thousands of French soldiers simply "threw down their rifles and ran."[162] French field commanders were "ashamed to report" what they had witnessed from their troops and the fact that there now was a huge gap in the French defensive line through which German armor, followed by infantry, was streaming.[163]

After their victory at Sedan, the Germans did not continue south toward Paris as Reynaud had feared. Rather, following plan, tanks from Army Group A headed west, paralleling the Somme, toward the Channel. The intent was to set up a pincer movement in combination with Army Group B, which was then fighting along the River Dyle in Belgium. (See map on p. 393.) The two army groups planned to act like the jaws of a giant crocodile and crush the British Expeditionary Force, much of the French Army, and twenty-two divisions of Belgians.[164]

Wednesday, May 15, 1940

In an early-morning call, Premier Reynaud had terrible news for Churchill.[165] The French counterattack at Sedan the previous evening had failed, and now the road to Paris was open.[166] Manchester and Reid paint a picture of Reynaud as hysterical and convinced that all was lost.[167] Churchill, "dumbfounded" at the speed with which horrible things were happening,[168] nevertheless refused to join Reynaud in his hopelessness.[169] The clearly frightened Reynaud now made an urgent appeal for more British ground forces.[170] Churchill responded that it was impossible for Britain to send any more troops to France at the present moment; and even if that were not the case, it would be quite impossible to get them to the scene of action quickly enough.[171]

In a subsequent conversation with France's Commander-in-Chief of the Northeast Front, General Georges, Churchill was advised that though the situation was "undoubtedly serious," the German breakthrough had been "plugged."[172] Georges made no further request for help. Churchill conveyed this relatively good news to the War Cabinet later that morning.[173] He also relayed the contents of a telegram in which Supreme Allied Commander General Gamelin asked for all possible air assistance. Gamelin said that while, between the fighting going on in the south of Belgium and the fighting around Sedan, things were serious, he viewed the situation with calm.[174]

General Hastings "Pug" Ismay, Churchill's chief military assistant, was not too happy about what was happening. General Ismay, like many others, believed the French were not fighting properly. He mused that they are a volatile race, and it may take them time to get into a warlike mood.[175]*

Lukacs's explanation for the lackluster performance of the vaunted French Army revolves around the fact that "France lost nearly a million and a half men in WWI." Lukacs, Five Days p. 84. The significant unwillingness of the French to take the

In a 10:15 AM meeting of the Defence Committee,* Air Chief Marshal Sir Hugh "Stuffy" Dowding, the head of Fighter Command, read a letter he had sent to the Under-Secretary of State for Air. The letter contained sobering facts about the losses that his fighter squadrons had suffered in the fighting.[176] He now had only thirty-six squadrons instead of the fifty-six he had been promised when the war broke out or the fifty-eight that the Air Council had estimated was the minimum necessary to defend Britain.[177] (That number—fifty-eight—had also been calculated on the assumption that Britain would be attacked from bases in Germany, not from aerodromes in France, Belgium, or Holland.[178]) Moreover, within the last few days, ten squadrons had been sent to France. Thus, in his letter he pleaded with the Under-Secretary to focus on ensuring the safety of Britain, saying:

> I must therefore request that as a matter of paramount urgency the air ministry will consider and decide what level of strength to be left to the Fighter Command for the defence of this country and will assure me that when this level is reached, no fighter will be sent across the Channel however urgent and insistent the appeals for help may be. ... If the Home Defence Force is drained away in desperate attempts to remedy the situation in France, defeat in France will involve the final, complete, and *irremediable* defeat of this country.[179] [emphasis in original]

When the War Cabinet met at 11:00 AM, Air Chief Marshal Hugh Dowding explained that "additional fighters for France could only be found by withdrawing them from the actual defences of this country."[180] In reply to a specific question from Churchill he said that "he would *not*, at this moment, advise the despatch of any additional fighters to France."[181] [emphasis in original]

The War Cabinet agreed.[182] At the meeting, the War Cabinet was told that British troops had been safely removed from Holland the previous night and that additional warships and fast merchant ships had been sent to evacuate the Dutch Army.[183] Halifax also shared the Dutch proclamation announcing the

---

offensive in this new war was thus at least somewhat understandable. France's reluctance was, compounded because in the years after World War I, its entire philosophy was to defend itself against any future German attacks. For this reason, it spent millions of dollars building the Maginot Line, behind which it believed it would be totally safe, and eschewed putting much of its budget into offensive weapons. See, Manchester, Alone p. 494.

*The Defence Committee consisted of Chamberlain, Attlee, and the minister for each of the three services. The Chiefs of Staff attended all committee meetings. Churchill, Their Finest Hour pp. 18–19.

surrender of Rotterdam and Utrecht. He added that he hoped the Netherlands would refuse to enter peace negotiations with the Germans.[184] He prayed that the Dutch had merely stopped military operations in certain areas and would remain passive but under protest.[185] In little more than a week, when the shoe was on Britain's foot and it had to decide whether to enter peace negotiations, Halifax would be an outspoken advocate for Britain seeking peace negotiations with Hitler.

Halifax increasingly looked to Italy for hope. He suggested that "it might be of some value if the prime minister ... were to send a communication to Mussolini."[186] He also proposed that the general topics of the message be cabled to the British Ambassador to Italy, Sir Percy Loraine, along with authority for him to cast the message into the most appropriate form in consideration of the situation in Rome.[187]

Churchill responded that he had already thought of sending a message to Mussolini.[188] But he had no intention of allowing anyone who reported to Halifax, such as the Ambassador to Italy, to write it. Rather, he told the War Cabinet, he would draft the message himself and then consult with Halifax. The message would tell Mussolini that: Churchill wished to assure him of the hope that Britain and Italy should not be divided by bloodshed; Britain was finding the war hard, but was confident of ultimate victory; it would be a disaster of the first magnitude if any irrevocable steps were taken; but if this were to happen, Britain would have no choice but to pursue the matter to the end, and rest assured it would.[189]

Near the end of the meeting, Churchill discussed particulars of the personal message that, at the War Cabinet's urging, he had sent to President Roosevelt describing the seriousness of the current situation.[190] In the telegram, Churchill talked about how the scene in Western Europe had "darkened swiftly" and that he thoroughly expected Britain to soon be attacked both by aerial bombing and airborne troops.[191] (Indeed, the US had just issued an announcement urging American citizens to leave both Britain and France).[192] Recognizing the precarious situation in which the French found themselves, Churchill also stated that "*if necessary, we shall continue the war alone.*" Whether true or not, he said, "we are not afraid of that." Churchill quickly added: "But I trust you realize, Mr. President, that *the voice and force of the United States may account for nothing if they are withheld too long. You may have a completely subjugated Nazified Europe established with astonishing swiftness, and the weight may be more than we can bear.*"[193] [emphasis added]

Churchill also asked Roosevelt to have the United States declare itself a nonbelligerent, which would permit America to provide Britain with all manner of supplies and assistance except troops. He listed some of Britain's immediate needs:

- a loan of forty or fifty old American destroyers; and
- the sale to Britain of
  o several hundred aircraft of the latest type,
  o anti-aircraft equipment, and
  o steel and other raw materials.[194]

The P.M. also explained that though England would pay for these goods in dollars for as long as possible, "... I should like to feel reasonably sure that when we can pay no more, you will give us that stuff all the same."[195]

Churchill knew that, given the Neutrality Act,* the strong nonintervention movement in the US, and an upcoming presidential election, coaxing America into the war would be difficult. Unbeknownst to Churchill, on the same day American Ambassador to Britain Joseph P. Kennedy had told Roosevelt that "Britain was finished and that the end would come soon" and that "he expected the Germans in London within a month."[196]** Roosevelt responded to Churchill within twelve hours. "His tone was friendly, but he did not promise much."[197]

Later that afternoon Reynaud sent another hysterical message to Churchill, again asserting that all had been lost and begging the P.M. to "[s]end all the troops and planes you can."[198] In response, Churchill decided, against Air Marshal Dowding's stern warning just that morning, that he would send four more fighter squadrons to France. He would also fly there himself the next day.[199]

Thursday May 16, 1940

On this morning Churchill sent a letter to Mussolini, who the P.M. expected to imminently enter the war on the Axis side. Despite this expectation, in the letter he asked Mussolini if it was "too late to stop a river of blood from flowing between British and Italian peoples?" Churchill then declared that "I have never been an enemy of Italian greatness nor ever at heart [your] foe...."[200] Further on in the letter, he wanted Hitler, even more than Mussolini, to know that "whatever may happen on the Continent, England will go on to the end, even quite alone, as we have done before, and I believe with some assurance that we shall be aided in increasing measure by the United States, and indeed all the Americas."[201] It is quite likely that Churchill took comfort in seeing these words put down in print—they may

---

*Congress passed the Neutrality Act in November 1939—just after the start of WWII. Among other things, the new law required the sale of arms to any belligerent to be on a cash-and-carry basis.
**As Roosevelt knew, Ambassador Kennedy was an avowed defeatist.

have even helped him overcome the real fear of Britain's having to go on alone, without much assistance from America.*

Churchill closed the letter by assuring Mussolini that his wish to avoid war with Italy was not made out of weakness or fear, but rather because "... the joint heirs of Latin and Christian civilization must not be ranged against one another in mortal strife."[202]

Forty-eight hours later, Mussolini rejected Churchill's plea, reminding him that in 1935 it was England that had proposed sanctions at the League of Nations against Italy for aggression in Abyssinia, which Mussolini described as Italy simply "securing for herself a small space in the African sun without causing the slightest injury to your interests in territories or those of others." Mussolini closed by stating sharply that "the Italian-German treaty guides Italian policy today and tomorrow in the face of any event whatsoever."[203]

Addressing the War Cabinet later in the day, Churchill said that another urgent appeal had been received from France for the dispatch of still more fighter aircraft. Apparently, German armored vehicles had broken through French defenses about 60 miles west of Sedan.[204] (See map on p. 393.)

In the ensuing discussion, the ministers expressed a range of views. Secretary of State for Air Archie Sinclair opposed sending any more fighters to France.[205] Churchill, on the other hand, said that Britain should send six squadrons, not just the four he had suggested the afternoon before. "[I]t seemed essential to do something to bolster up the French," he remarked.[206] In the end, the Cabinet agreed that arrangements should be made for the immediate dispatch of four fighter squadrons and that preparations should begin to dispatch two more fighter squadrons on very short notice.[207] (The French were not to be informed of that).[208]

General Sir John Dill, Vice-Chief of the Imperial General Staff, also updated the Cabinet about the status of the war. In Belgium, the British Expeditionary Force was largely holding its own, although the Luftwaffe's domination of the sky made the BEF's job difficult. To its right, a small contingent of German armored forces had crossed the Dyle, which prompted a pullback by the French and a consequent backward readjustment of the entire Allied line.[209]

Churchill took an extremely grave view of the news, although General Headquarters seemed not particularly disturbed. He considered that an Allied withdrawal was a quite unjustifiable reaction to penetration of the French line by a force of 120 German armored vehicles. Moreover, such a

---

*Most, including Hitler, believed that Churchill's declaration to fight on alone applied only to the defense of England. However, as Manchester and Reid note, "Churchill [also] intended ... to take the fight to Hitler." Manchester and Reid pp. 110–11.

retreat would expose the BEF to far more serious risks than if the French had remained in their present position and fought.[210]

General Dill finished by revealing that German armored forces were now believed to be more than 50 miles west of Sedan, and that orders had been issued for the French to fall back to the nearby town of Vervins.[211]

Churchill traveled to France that afternoon for an emergency meeting of the Supreme War Council. This was the first of an amazing five trips Churchill would make to France between May 16 and June 13, 1940, when the fighting was ongoing.[212] During the meeting, Supreme Commander General Gamelin told the assembled group that German armor had broken through a 40-mile-wide front only 110 miles from Paris and had scattered the French armies.[213] When Churchill asked about the location of the French Army's strategic reserve, Gamelin replied "there is none."[214]* When Churchill asked about French plans for a counterattack, Gamelin simply shrugged his shoulders.[215] Gamelin said that the Germans held superiority "in numbers," "equipment," and tactics.[216] (This statement was untrue: the Germans had fewer numbers and armaments than did the French but "they were far superior in terms of strategy and tactics."[217]) Nonetheless, Gamelin promised a counterattack from south of the Somme.[218] As Churchill would later tell Colville, "Gamelin was occupied in saving not France but his own position."[219]

At 9:00 PM Churchill wired the War Cabinet about how bad things were in France. He must have believed that France's position was extremely perilous. Amazingly, given the warning he had gotten from Hugh Dowding about sending more fighters to France, he still suggested that besides the four fighter squadrons Britain had just agreed to send to France, six more might need to be readied immediately.[220]

Churchill's terrifying telegram caused the War Cabinet to meet two hours later. After some discussion, the Cabinet surprisingly agreed to send the additional six squadrons,[221] but it would not allow them to be stationed in France.[222] By sending these ten new squadrons, Britain was doubling the number of its fighters in France and would only have twenty-nine squadrons left in all of the UK.[223]

It was becoming clearer by the hour that the French felt Britain should throw its entire military resources into the fight for France, otherwise the Germans would not be stopped, and the two allies would "go down together."[224] Britain did not share this view of how to proceed. The British

---

As Shirer points out, after the war, Gamelin would say that he had been misquoted. What he'd supposedly said was that "there are no longer any" strategic reserves. L'Aurore, Paris, November 21, 1949.

believed that if France were to fall, Britain "should go on alone."[225] Consequently, Britain resisted any further depletion of the fighter squadrons it would need to defend its own territory.

That night Allied forces in Belgium withdrew to the line: Halle—River Senne—Vilvoorde near Brussels.[226]

Friday, May 17, 1940

Churchill returned from Paris in time for the War Cabinet's 10:00 AM meeting. Chamberlain informed Churchill that his telegram from France the previous evening had greatly disturbed the members of the War Cabinet. But they realized that the battle for France might be decisive and felt that they must embrace the Prime Minister's courageous leadership.* Thus they decided that everything possible must be done to give the French a chance to rally.[227]

Churchill then gave the War Cabinet the details of his trip to France:

- When he got to France, Churchill found former Foreign Minister Daladier and General Gamelin depressed, but Premier Reynaud was in better spirits.[228]

- He learned that German Army Group A's advance to the west had slowed down, probably to re-form and re-fuel.[229]

- He showed Premier Reynaud and General Gamelin the War Cabinet's telegram agreeing to send the requested additional six fighters squadrons to France; and the news "had heartened them to a very considerable degree."[230]

- He heard that the French had sustained very heavy losses of fighter aircraft. Only one-quarter of the force with which they started the campaign remained serviceable.[231]

- Despite the French losses, Churchill made it clear that unless they made a supreme effort, Britain would not accept the grave risk to its safety by dispatching more fighters to France. But if the French would fight to their utmost, Britain would do everything possible to help them.[232]

- Finally, while the situation on much of the front facing the BEF seemed fairly satisfactory for the moment, a plan had been prepared for the withdrawal, of the British Army—in stages, if necessary. But

---

*This statement provides more evidence of the growing fondness that Chamberlain felt for Churchill. Moreover, it slightly portended what Chamberlain's position would be on other critical matters in the next ten days.

Churchill felt strongly that the Allies ought not to yield an inch of ground without fighting.[233]

General Dill, the Vice-Chief of the Imperial General Staff, then stepped forward to give the group a frank summary of the Battle of France. He explained that the French had been surprised by the direction and weight of the German attack, by the strength of the new German tanks, and by the devastating combination of the ferocity of the German air attack and the power of their armored vehicles. Compounding the troubles was the undisputed fact that some of the French troops had not fought well. Dill noted that the French also were depressed at the lack of success of their light tanks, whose number had shrunk by two-thirds. Although French heavy tanks had great initial success, half were now gone; France now faced the possibility of mustering only three armored divisions to meet an assault by three times that number on the German side. Moreover, the German armored divisions were stronger than their French equivalents.[234]

The latest information was that the Germans were now 75 miles west of Sedan, and 25 miles southwest of where German tanks were reported on the previous day.[235]

Dill looked for a ray of hope in the fact that the flower of the French Army was still in central Belgium with the BEF and had thus not been involved in the failures he had just recounted.[236] Finally, Dill said that Allied forces had withdrawn westward by about 20 miles to the line of the canal running through Brussels. But, this line was only 90 miles east of Dunkirk.[237] (See map on p. 393.)

As the meeting was winding down, Churchill announced he had received a reply from Roosevelt. Though the American President said he was considering the suggestions made in the telegram Churchill sent earlier in the week, "any efforts to aid the Allies would 'take time.'"[238] In the short term, Roosevelt would only agree to provide anti-aircraft guns and steel.[239]

Later on the 17th, Churchill admitted to Jock Colville that "our forces in Belgium will inevitably have to withdraw in order to maintain contact with the French" and that "[t]here is, of course, the risk that the BEF may be cut off if the French do not rally in time."[240] Accordingly, "[Churchill] ordered the Admiralty and Shipping Ministry to start planning a rescue fleet should the BEF need to be evacuated from Boulogne, Calais, or Dunkirk," all located in the Pas-de-Calais in northeastern France.[241] He also asked the Chiefs of Staff to report on how they would plan to continue the war if France fell.[242]

The panzers of Army Group A were about one-third of the way to the Channel. But as Churchill had advised, they had received an order to halt.

Hitler feared that the French were preparing a huge counterattack from the south against the long thin German supply line.[243]

Saturday, May 18, 1940

Things finally started to look a bit better for the Allies. The French were bringing up troops, and French artillery had had some success in destroying German tanks. The Royal Air Force was performing heroically. A French counterattack near the French city of Laon (located about 75 miles west of Sedan) met with little opposition. But the German advance was only slowed. The spearhead of Army Group A resumed heading westward, though the panzers were ordered to proceed with "a reconnaissance in force"—i.e., an advance designed to discover the position and strength of the enemy. The slowdown gave the German infantry a chance to catch up to the tanks.

Meanwhile, in Paris, on what was only the ninth day of fighting, General Gamelin had all but given up.[244]

That night the BEF's westward retreat in Belgium continued, this time to the line of the River Scheldt (the *Escaut* in French).[245] The new line was 40 miles west of the line defended just three days earlier, and only 50 miles east of Dunkirk. Moreover, the BEF's General Headquarters at Arras in France had to be abandoned because of the advance of lead elements of German Army Group A.[246]

Sunday, May 19, 1940

Advanced elements of German Army Group A were now also reported at Albert, a small city [247]105 miles west of Sedan and about 95 miles southeast of Calais. German troops were heading west, toward the city of Abbeville,[248] located near the coast about 70 miles due south of Calais. (See map on p. 393.) The Germans were now getting between the BEF and the bulk of the French Army, which was located south of the Somme.[249] The French Army was still not fighting.[250]

The immediate danger was that German Army Group A might cut the British supply and communications lines located to the west of Arras (between Amiens and Abbeville).[251] If that happened, supplies would only be able to reach the BEF through the ports of Boulogne, Calais, and Dunkirk, each of which was being attacked by the Luftwaffe. It was critical to prevent the BEF and the Belgian Army on its left from being cut off from the main French armies located to the south. Otherwise, they risked being caught in the vise being formed by German Army Groups A and B.[252]

As a part of General Gamelin's promised counterattack, orders were issued for the BEF, which was situated both in France and in nearby Belgium, along with the Belgians and the First French Army to fight their way southward along the coast.[253] They were to move along the Allied supply line to Amiens, a large city bisected by the Somme and located about 90 miles south of Dunkirk.[254] Shirer writes that these forty battle-tested divisions "might have succeeded in breaking through" the German lines,[255] if Lord Gort, the commander of the BEF, hadn't refused to follow the order given by the Chief of the General Staff General Ironside.[256] Gort's failure to follow orders was precipitated by the French First Army, which had been on his right (south), fading away. Gort told the War Office that if the gap on the BEF's right widened, he had it in mind to withdraw toward Dunkirk and fight it out there.[257] Part of the BEF's plan would be to flood the area west of Dunkirk by opening up the sluices to the River Aa.[258]

The continued disintegration of the military situation led General Ironside to tell Secretary for War Anthony Eden that "This is the end of the British Empire."[259] He did not think England "could hold out alone for more than a few months."[260]

At the morning War Cabinet meeting, Halifax read a telegram he had just received from the British Ambassador to the US, Lord Lothian, in which the Ambassador reported on a conversation he had with President Roosevelt the previous evening. Lord Lothian said that Roosevelt was very friendly and had emphasized the efforts he was making to keep Italy from entering the war. However, the President said nothing that showed he recognized Britain's pressing need for aircraft; nor had he mentioned the suggestion that the US Government should let England have aircraft at once from its own supplies, to be replaced later from orders already placed by Britain. Hearing this, Churchill, at once proposed to send another telegram to Roosevelt making Britain's *immediate* needs clear to the President.[261] He sent this telegram two days later.

Because of the continuing poor performance of the French Army, Premier Reynaud dismissed General Gamelin, the Supreme Commander, and replaced him with General Maxine Weygand.[262] Weygand immediately canceled Gamelin's counteroffensive against the German armored columns that five days earlier had punched through the French lines, taken Sedan, then turned westward. Weygand wanted to talk with the Allied commanders in Belgium before doing anything.[263]

The War Cabinet learned at its late-afternoon meeting that as a part of General Gamelin's promised counterattack, the BEF had been ordered fight its way southward along the coast,[264] but that General Gort had not carried out the order.[265] Ironside advised the group that he had told Gort that his alternative proposal—to withdraw northwestward toward Dunkirk and to fight it out there—was unacceptable. Ironside added that "[w]e might at a pinch be able to supply the BEF in a bridgehead resting on the Channel ports for a limited time, *but we could certainly never evacuate the force complete.*"[266] [emphasis added] Ironside had already suggested on the previous evening that "the BEF should advance south-west through the Bethune-Arras area ... in order to get back on to its lines of communication, [between Amiens and Abbeville] and fight its way through to join up with the French located south of the Somme."[267]

Churchill fully concurred with Ironside's objection to Gort's proposal to fall back to Dunkirk. He felt that doing so would result in the total loss of the BEF. He believed that "[o]ur forces must ... at all costs move back to Amiens."[268] The War Cabinet expressed general agreement,[269] and both the French and General Gort would be apprised of the Cabinet's position.[270]

In a speech broadcast over the BBC that evening, his first broadcast as P.M., Churchill talked about the German gains in France, but he also spoke, somewhat fancifully, of how the French armies had been regrouping over the last several days and how they had been magnificently assisted by the Royal Air Force. While saying that "it would be foolish to disguise the gravity of the hour ...," Churchill declared, "I have invincible confidence in the French Army and its leaders."[271] This statement was not true.[272] Churchill's confidence in the French was far from "invincible"; in fact, it was running out. As someone who in prewar years had deep faith in the fighting prowess of the French Army, Churchill was shocked at its abysmal performance in May and June of 1940. In the broadcast, Churchill told Britons that he had received a "sacred pledge" from Premier Reynaud that "whatever happens [France] will fight to the end, bitter or be it glorious."[273] That pledge would stay in effect for twenty-nine more days, until French sued for peace.

In his inimitable oratorical style, Churchill did a splendid job rallying the people in a time of crisis and preparing them for what was to come. Anticipating both the fall of France and a German invasion of Britain, he said, "We must expect that as soon as stability is reached on the Western Front, the bulk of that hideous apparatus of aggression which gashed Holland into ruin and slavery in a few days will be turned upon us."[274]

He also talked about how the administration that he had just assembled was made up of people from every party and every point of view; and, in splendid Churchillian fashion, he told a frightened populous that "We have differed and quarreled in the past; but now one bond unites as all—to wage war until victory is won, and never to surrender ourselves to servitude and shame, whatever the cost and the agony may be."[275] Unlike the mixed reaction to Churchill's first speech to Parliament as Prime Minister, the response from fellow politicians to his May 19 speech was very positive. Colville wrote in his diary that evening of Churchill's unbelievable doggedness:

> Our fortunes are at low ebb, but I am still confident we shall
> win in the end and perhaps a shock to our self-esteem and

feeling of security is not unwholesome. In any case, whatever Winston's shortcomings, he seems to be the man for the occasion. His spirit is indomitable and even if France and England should be lost, I feel he would carry on the crusade himself with a band of privateers.[276]

Interestingly, at the same time Churchill was reaffirming his promise to fight to the bitter end, Hitler more and more was coming to believe that the British were recognizing the futility of a war against Germany, would soon dump Churchill, and would respond favorably to a German peace offer.[277]

Meanwhile, in Dover, only 45 miles across the English Channel from Dunkirk, Vice Admiral Bertram Ramsey, Dover's naval commander, had been directed to start planning for the evacuation of the BEF from the continent.[278]

Monday, May 20, 1940

German mechanized units were advancing on the French city of Arras, which was being defended by the partially trained, 23rd Division of the BEF. General Gort was moving three divisions down to the town of Lens, just 15 miles north of Arras and only 43 miles from Amiens.[279] (See map on p. 393.)

By the close of the day, the German's 2nd Panzer Division had reached the city of Abbeville.[280] German armor, by creating "a corridor almost 200 miles long and 20 miles wide from the Ardennes to the Channel,"[281] had isolated the BEF, the Belgians, and the 1st and 7th French armies.[282] Lukacs contends that "[t]he time was now to counterattack, to cut the long German crocodile's nose...."[283] Shirer agrees that the only hope for the Allied armies fighting in Belgium was to disengage from Army Group B, turn south, fight their way across the east-west line established by the panzers of Army Group A, and join up with fresh French forces that would push northward from the Somme.[284] This was largely what General Gamelin had ordered just before he was removed.[285]

As for the Germans, as planned, after taking Abbeville, they swung north along the coast, threatening to capture the ports of Ètaples, Boulogne, Calais, and Dunkirk, all of which lay within 95 miles of each other.[286] The fall of northern France was becoming a reality.[287]

At the morning's War Cabinet meeting, Halifax introduced several telegrams that had been received. The first, dated May 18, was from the Ambassador to Portugal, who said an anonymous source had reported that the Germans contemplated extensive parachute operations in Ireland, in preparation for turning the island into their base for the invasion of Britain.[288] The second, from the British Ambassador in Rome, disclosed a rumor that if the Germans took Paris, Hitler would announce the unconditional terms on which he would conclude peace.[289] The last telegram was from the British Ambassador in Belgrade. It said that a reliable source reported the belief in diplomatic circles in Berlin that a peace offer would be forthcoming after German military successes in the Low Countries and before the "decisive attack" on England.[290]

The War Cabinet also reviewed a report prepared by the Chiefs of Staff about Britain's air defenses.[291] Halifax asked whether it would be possible for Britain to temporarily send more fighter support to France at a time of crisis in battle. Sir Cyril Newall, Chief of the Air Staff, replied that such an arrangement could be worked out, but only for a very limited period and provided the planes remained based in Britain.[292] Churchill agreed, saying that "we had reached the limit of the air assistance which we can send to France, and that we could not consider despatching further resources permanently to France. ..."[293]

The War Cabinet concurred.[294]

In the week following his May 19 broadcast, Churchill had three not necessarily consistent goals: (1) urge a French-British counteroffensive; (2) continue his efforts to get as much help as possible from America; and (3) ultimately withdraw the entire BEF from the continent.

The last objective required sending troops to Boulogne and Calais on what would amount to a suicide mission, just to slow down the German advance toward the last remaining evacuation port—Dunkirk.[295]

Looking for any argument that would persuade America to provide Britain with the war matériel it so desperately needed, Churchill sent Roosevelt an incredible telegram. In it, Churchill leaned on both guilt and fear to get the US to supply England. He started by reiterating that "our intension is, whatever happens, to fight on to the end ... and provided we can get the help we ask, we hope to run them very close in the air battles." He added, "In no conceivable circumstances will we consent to surrender."* This seemingly unambiguous declaration, however, was quickly followed by a giant "but"—Churchill suggested that if the US did not provide Britain with enough support to fend off the Germans, some future British Government might have to offer the Royal Navy to the Nazis in order to save the country. The precise wording of the telegram was this:

> If members of the present administration were finished and others came in to parlay amid the ruins, you must not be blind to the fact that the sole remaining bargaining counter with Germany would be the Fleet, and if this country was left by the United States to its fate no one could have the right to blame

---

*This is further evidence that Churchill's mind was made up—Britain would continue fighting the Nazis.

those responsible if they made the best terms they could for the surviving inhabitants.

The message went on to say:

> Excuse me, Mr. President, putting this nightmare bluntly. Evidently, I could not answer for my successors, who in utter despair and helplessness might well have to accommodate themselves to the German will.[296]

Colville was "taken aback" when Churchill said to go ahead and send the telegram.[297]

While Churchill's words can be viewed as just part of his pitch to get the arms for which Britain was desperate, Roosevelt could have hardly been pleased with Churchill's suggestion that the United States, by inaction, could become the cause of England's demise. The President also had to at least consider the possibility that Britain could soon be in a position where it had to negotiate away its Navy. The Royal Navy was the largest in the world. Were Germany to gain possession of it, overnight, Hitler's Nazi regime would become a naval power with which the United States would have to reckon. Cities along the eastern seaboard would, in short order, become vulnerable to naval bombardment. The United States had always viewed the Atlantic as a barrier far more significant and effective than the Maginot Line. Transferring the British fleet to Germany in a peace deal would weaken that barrier instantly. The situation would become even worse if Germany defeated France and also obtained the French Navy, which at the time was the fourth largest in the world, behind Britain, the United States, and Japan. The French Navy was made up of "three modern and five older battleships, eighteen heavy cruisers, twenty-seven light cruisers, sixty submarines (twenty-four had been sunk) and more than fifty destroyers."[298] Obtaining just one-third of the French fleet would almost double the size of the German Navy.[299]

Despite the gravity of events and scenarios Churchill laid out in his message, Roosevelt's response only acknowledged receipt of Churchill's telegram and said nothing about its content.[300]

Tuesday, May 21, 1940

Upon reaching Abbeville, German forces had swung north along the coast, and, as noted, now threatened to capture the ports of Ètaples, Boulogne, Calais, and Dunkirk. At the morning's War Cabinet meeting, Churchill seemed to contradict the weight of the evidence and instead conveyed his belief that there was no immediate risk of the Germans occupying those

French ports.[301] The War Cabinet seemed unconvinced by the P.M.'s optimism and decided that:

1. naval demolition parties, which had been organized and were ready to sail, should proceed to Calais and Boulogne immediately; and

2. the officer in command of the parties should have the authority to destroy any stores of petrol in these two ports, if doing so was necessary to deny them to the Germans.[302]

Meanwhile, in France, General Gort had launched an attack on the German flank with two divisions of BEF troops and sixty light French tanks. His hope was to make a successful counterattack at Arras.[303]

But dismal reports kept arriving from France. The German thrust to the coast had cut off British, French, and Belgian troops in the north of France and south of Belgium, both from the bases holding all their supplies and from the rest of the French Army farther south. Churchill decided there was nothing to do but return to the Paris next morning (May 22) and, as McCarten puts it, "attempt to shake [the French] into some form of order."[304] Churchill was both appalled at the French mismanagement and "depressed."[305] And concerns were growing about Britain's ability to extricate the BEF from the continent.[306]

In Berlin, Hitler was still optimistic about reaching an agreement with Britain. He told General Franz Halder, Chief of Staff of the Army High Command, that "[w]e are seeking contact with England on the basis of a division of the world."[307]

Wednesday, May 22, 1940

Chamberlain took the chair of the morning meeting of the War Cabinet, while Churchill had again traveled to Paris. He relayed information that stressed the seriousness of the situation in France and speculated that the German drive toward the Channel ports presaged that an attack on Britain could occur very shortly.[308] General Ironside then made his report:

• The German armored column that had been advancing on the French fishing port of Boulogne the previous day had penetrated no farther than the River Canche, located about 30 miles south of the city, where it had been heavily attacked by the RAF.

• It had been a comparatively quiet night in Boulogne. All roads leading to it had been blocked and the influx of refugees from the nearby fighting had stopped.

- The officer in command at Calais had reported that all was well and the coast road to Dunkirk was open.

- Reinforcements had been, or were being, sent to the Boulogne-Calais area to secure the ports. When these troops arrive in the Boulogne area, Britain should have a force there substantial enough to take effective action against Germany's armored columns.

- In Belgium, the BEF was holding its position on the Scheldt River.[309]

Allied counterattacks, such as one at Arras, had, however, failed to sever the Germans' long narrow supply line.[310] Neither the British nor the French tanks were up to the task. General Gort's forces at Arras had to withdraw.

At the War Cabinet meeting, Chamberlain also read a report about German invasion of the UK prepared by General Ismay for the P.M.[311] The report showed that:

- Recent events required a modification of the view that Germany could not hope to launch a successful seaborne invasion for some time.

- In light of recent experience in Norway, Holland, and France, it had to be assumed that the Germans had a plan for the invasion of Britain worked out to the last detail and that they had stockpiled all necessary special equipment such as motorized landing craft.*

- Hitler would be prepared to sacrifice 90 percent of the whole expedition if he could gain a firm bridgehead on British soil.[312]

General Ismay was also worried that the Germans would offer the French peace terms they could not refuse, which would leave Britain alone.[313] Colville dismissed this fear because Ismay was "unduly alarmist." Nor could Colville "see the French shaming themselves quite to that extent."[314]

In Paris, Churchill, Ironside, Reynaud, and Weygand worked out what came to be known as the "Weygand Plan," which really was just a reworked version of General Gamelin's recently canceled counteroffensive.[315] Under the plan:

- As soon as possible, but no later than the following day, eight divisions of the BEF and the French 1st Army would attack southward in the general direction of Bapaume, a town 18 miles due south of Arras, and

---

General Ismay's assertion, which on its face seemed entirely reasonable, turned out to be incorrect.

- Simultaneously, between eight and twenty divisions of the French Army would form a line at the Somme, about 15 miles south of Bapaume, and attack northward.

Churchill returned to London in time for the evening's War Cabinet meeting. The Prime Minister said that Weygand had "made a favourable impression by virtue of his vigour and confidence."[316] Equally important, he said that the planned attacks by the BEF and French to the southwest and by the French Army Group moving north in the direction of Amiens "should take place on the following day, 23rd May."[317] General Ironside, however, told the group that, as far as he knew, no preparations had been made for these attacks as of that noon, even though he thought Allied forces would need some time to mount its attack.[318]

Back in France, Premier Reynaud appointed eighty-four-year-old Marshal Philippe Pétain as Vice Premier.[319] Reynaud hoped that appointing the WWI hero of Verdun might instill a renewed spirit of resistance and patriotism in the French Army and increase the public's confidence in the Government.[320] Little did Reynaud know that, in less than a month, Petain would replace him, sue for peace with Hitler, then go on to lead a puppet government that collaborated with the Nazis. Reynaud felt guilty the rest of his life for having brought Petain into power.

Thursday, May 23, 1940

When General Weygand learned that General Gort had withdrawn his troops at Arras, he was furious and demanded that Reynaud protest to Churchill, who knew nothing about what had been done. Weygand asserted that "'as a result of the British retreat' the drive southward had to be abandoned."[321] But the BEF could not have moved southward even if they wanted to, because they were already "heavily engaged with the enemy."[322]

In the morning meeting, Churchill advised the War Cabinet that the promised French counterattack, on which almost everything depended, had yet to occur.[323] He then reported that Boulogne had been heavily attacked that morning by German tanks and five 9-inch batteries.[324] British forces there were in danger of being surrounded and cut off.[325] Lastly, he revealed that German armor had been reported on the Channel coast around Calais, Boulogne, and Dunkirk,[326] while German infantry columns had nearly reached Amiens.[327] Hitler's ground troops were now only 90 miles south of Dunkirk, where the Germans would shortly corner more than three hundred thousand Allied troops.

Churchill said that because the situation around the Channel ports had become critical,[328] he had sent the following telegram to Premier Reynaud:

Strong enemy armoured forces have cut communications of northern armies. [*] Salvation of these armies can only be obtained by immediate execution of Weygand's plan. *I demand that French Commanders in North and South and Belgian General Headquarters be given most stringent orders to carry this out and turn defeat into victory.* Time is vital as supplies are short.[329] [emphasis added]

Stressing the importance of the Weygand plan, Churchill told the Cabinet that "if it failed it would be necessary to make a fresh plan with the object of saving and bring back to this country as many of our best troops and weapons with as little loss as possible."[330]

Clearly concerned about the Weygand Plan and the entire situation in France, Lord Privy Seal Clement Atlee asked if Britain risked falling between two stools: i.e., that neither the plan agreed to with General Weygand would be effectively carried out, nor would Britain use her forces to the best advantage in retaining her hold on the Channel ports.[331] Vice Chief of the Imperial General Staff, General Sir John Dill responded that "the best hope still lay in carrying out the plan agreed to with General Weygand."[332] Churchill said nothing, but he would ruminate on Atlee's point.

At three that afternoon, Churchill briefed the House about the increasingly dire military situation on the continent.[333] It was only eleven days earlier that Churchill had told the House that Britain's aim was "victory, victory at all costs. ..." Fellow Conservative MP Gurney Braithwaite asked the P.M. "whether His Majesty's Government renews and reiterates the pledge of its predecessor that no peace will be concluded with the enemy except in agreement and co-operation with the Government of the French Republic?" Churchill replied "Yes, sir."[334]**

Churchill would learn two hours later that General Gort never received orders to implement the "Weygand Plan."[335] This revelation prompted Churchill to call Reynaud, but he could not get through. A second call was answered by General Weygand,[336] who had great news: he told Churchill and General Ironside that the French had begun their northward assault and just recaptured Amiens and two much smaller cities,[337] each of which had been taken over by Army Group A as it rushed toward the Channel. If

---

*With no sign of a French counterattack from the south, the BEF was cut off, and was simply unable to break through as Weygand wanted. Roberts p. 539.

**Anthony McCarten, the author of The Darkest Hours, characterizes this exchange as the first suggestion of Churchill's willingness to consider a peace deal with Nazi Germany. McCarten p. 172.

Weygand's report were true, the news would have been "stupendous, although the position of the BEF [would] remain ... critical." British forces would still have to fight their way southward against formidable German opposition to reconnect with the main body of the French Army.[338]

All the victories claimed by Weygand would, however, later prove to be false.[339] No French troops had moved up from the Somme. As Shirer puts it, "the Weygand plan existed only in the General's mind."[340]

At the 7:00 PM War Cabinet meeting, Churchill advised that he had been considering the observations made by Minister Attlee that morning about the danger of falling between two stools. He said that it might be best for the BEF to fall back to the Channel Ports.[341] General Ironside then apprised the group of the "successes" in northern France that Weygand had just trumpeted.[342] Buoyed by Weygand's report, both Ironside and his Vice-Chairman, General Dill, said they believed the Weygand plan should proceed. They also felt that "[i]f the BEF were to retire to the Channel ports, *it was unlikely that more than a small part of the force could be got away.*"[343] [emphasis added]

Summing up the situation Churchill said that "even regarding the latest news in its most favorable light, there was as yet little ground for confidence." At that moment he felt that Britain had "no choice" but to follow General Weygand's plan: "Any other course would wreck the chance of Gen. Weygand's plan succeeding."[344]

At a meeting of the Defence Committee later that evening, Churchill, announced a change of heart and that the time had come to evacuate British troops from France. "We cannot leave our army to be slaughtered or to surrender. No, never that! We must get them out."[345] He noted that any equipment they left behind could be replaced "but *if we lose the men then we lose the war.*"[346] [emphasis added] "Our men must battle through to Dunkirk. When they get there, the Navy will get them out."[347]

The BEF was retreating.[348] A brigade under the command of Brigadier General Claude Nicholson was ordered to move to Boulogne in hopes of slowing down the advancing Germans; but Boulogne had fallen , and Calais was surrounded.[349] Britons did not know how bad a spot the BEF was in.[350] That night Chamberlain wrote in his diary that the French had "done nothing"; he condemned both its generals and soldiers, who "with some exceptions ... would not fight and not even march."[351] At the King's request, Churchill went to Buckingham Palace at 10:00 PM. The King wanted to know what would happen if the Weygand Plan failed. Churchill responded that an attempt would be made to evacuate the BEF soldiers back to England; all of their guns, tanks, and other equipment would have to be left behind,[352] and the loss of life during the operation would "probably be immense."[353]

Friday, May 24, 1940

At 5:00 AM, distressed that General Gort had been accused of not carrying out his orders even though he had never received any orders to implement the "Weygand Plan," Churchill sent a telegram to Reynaud saying that there was "[no] coordination between the French, Belgian and British armies on the northern front" (The Belgians, like the BEF, had not been given any orders.[354]) He assured Reynaud that General Gort had been told to carry out the plan.[355]

Several hours later Reynaud angrily responded. Among other things, he accused the BEF of having abandoned Arras without first notifying the French. His telegram concluded with the acerbic statement that "General Weygand's orders should be obeyed."[356]

As a result of Weygand's complaint against Gort, and Churchill's own irritation over what he now felt was a failure of the French to initiate the Weygand Plan, the P.M. decided to assign Conservative MP Edward Spears the thankless task of finding out what really was happening in France, and what could be done to improve relations between the two countries.[357]

The brigade commanded by General Nicholson, which had been sent to reinforce the defense of Boulogne, were only able to make it as far as Calais, which itself was under siege. They were ordered to fight it out with the Germans there.[358]* The Germans moving up from Abbeville had already captured Boulogne, and passed Gravelines, a small city on the mouth of the Aa River. Hitler's troops were now located at "the Aa Canal between Gravelines and St. Omer" to the south, "twenty miles from Dunkirk."[359] From this position, the panzer corps was prepared to move north, even though the countryside, "full of canals, ditches and flooded areas," was considered "bad tank country." The 6th and 18th armies of German Army Group B, which were in Belgium, were ordered to move south west toward Dunkirk.[360] The intent was to close the crocodile's upper jaw, crushing the BEF, the Belgian Army, and the 1st French Army in the process. In Berlin, the press was being advised that much of the French Army was about to be obliterated, and that the BEF would be captured.

Suddenly, in what would come to be one of the most debated decisions of the war, the Germans halted the armored advance of Army Group A toward Dunkirk. This pause gave General Gort time to throw up a defense around the town and organize a full-scale evacuation of the BEF.[361]

---

*The British would shortly be forced to order the evacuation of Calais. It was expected Nicholson's brigade would abandon the city at that time.

Some authorities believe the German action, generally known as the "Halt Order," was a compassionate gesture consistent with Hitler's professed positive feelings toward Britain and an indication of the fair terms that Britain could have negotiated in a separate peace treaty with Germany.[362] It is of interest, however, that just three days before the Halt Order, Hitler had been "convinced" by Goering that the Luftwaffe could destroy "the retreating BEF."[363]

Hitler's purported regard for Britain was on display in his April 28, 1939, speech to the Reichstag. He spoke effusively of friendship and cooperation between Germany and England:

> During the whole of my political activity I have always propounded the idea of a close friendship and collaboration between Germany and England ... This desire for Anglo-German friendship and cooperation conforms not merely to sentiments based on the racial origins of our two peoples but also to my realization of the importance of the existence of the British Empire for the whole of mankind ... [T]he existence of this empire is an inestimable factor of value for the whole of human culture and economic life.[364]*

Lukacs's position about the "Halt Order" is that Hitler may not have wanted "to annihilate the entire BEF."[365] He quotes one of the members of Hitler's inner circle, General of the Luftwaffe Hans Jeschonnek, as saying that Hitler did not want Britain to suffer "a humiliating defeat."[366] Likewise, Pulitzer-Prize-winning historian John Toland writes that Hitler told Nazi Party stalwart Martin Bormann that the Halt Order was purposely intended to spare the British Army and avert an "irreparable breach between the British and ourselves."[367] Roberts writes only that the order was issued "for various [unexplained] operational reasons."[368]

Roberts also takes the position that the order originated with Hitler personally. But that conclusion is a matter of some dispute. Group A Commander General Gerd von Rundstedt and 4th Army Commander Günther von Kluge suggested that the German forces around Dunkirk should cease their advance on the port and consolidate to avoid an Allied breakout.[369] After the war, writing in *Their Finest Hour*, Churchill attributes the Halt Order to von Rundstedt's hesitance and not to any feelings of Hitler's.[370] In any event,

---

On other occasions Hitler would say it was one of his life's aims to reconcile the German and British peoples, since they had a common origin. See speech of October 6, 1940. At Munich, he even told Chamberlain they were "cousins."

Hitler certainly sanctioned the order, with the support of the Oberkommando der Wehrmacht.[371]

Shirer adds that "Rundstedt proposed that the panzer divisions ..." halt for a little while just outside Dunkirk to allow the infantry to catch up with the tanks, and that Hitler agreed.[372] As Churchill writes in *Their Finest Hour,* the BEF had intercepted a German radio message to this same effect.[373] "Hitler issued the formal order" that evening.[374]

Relying on diary entries from General Alfred Jodl, Chief of the Operations Staff of the German Army, and General Franz Halder, Chief of the Army's General Staff, along with a July 19, 1957, letter Halder had written to him, Shirer also makes a good case that the Halt Order had an altogether different purpose.[375] As Shirer explains, Goering had convinced Hitler that if the Army routed the Allied forces, then the generals would claim exclusive credit for the entire campaign, and Hitler would be pushed into the shadows. "This," Goering told Hitler, "could be prevented only if the Luftwaffe and not the Army carried out the decisive battle."[376]

Another version of the story has the Halt Order being issued on May 23 by Panzer Group Commander General Paul von Kleist,[377] out of fear that his armored divisions were getting too far ahead of the infantry. When General von Rundstedt learned about the Halt Order, which was to be in place for twenty-four hours, he approved it. But when word got to General Halder, he immediately rescinded it and ordered all panzer divisions to close in on Dunkirk as soon as possible. Von Rundstedt, humiliated by Halder's overturning his approval of a short pause in active operations, was angry and complained to Hitler. As the story goes, having been told nothing of these developments beforehand, the German leader is said to have exploded with anger. He hated the Prussian military elites and was deeply suspicious of the Army leadership. He immediately countermanded all of Halder's decisions and gave the authority over the Halt Order back to von Rundstedt.

There is probably some truth in almost all versions of the story about the Halt Order. The theory that Hitler desired to be nice to the British seems the least plausible for the simple reason that once the order was lifted, the Germans tried mightily to obliterate the BEF and prevent its evacuation from Dunkirk. On May 24, the German Supreme Headquarters issued Directive 13, which specifically called for the annihilation of the British, French, and Belgian forces in and around Dunkirk, while the Luftwaffe was ordered to prevent the escape of English forces across the Channel.[378] It seems clear that Hitler admired the British Empire, and he may even have believed that the British Empire should continue to exist. That said, the evidence does not support the contention that admiration of Britain or any desire to show mercy toward its troops was the reason for issuing the Halt Order.

Rather, as discussed in Chapter 21, unbeknownst to London at the time, Hitler was so confident that Britain would rush to make peace when France fell, he'd prepared no plan for the invasion of England.[379] What Hitler sought was Britain's agreement to his having all the freedom he wanted in the East.[380] Annihilating the BEF at Dunkirk would likely have facilitated such an agreement without necessitating the destruction of Britain.

Set forth below is a list of other theories for issuing the three-day Halt Order and corresponding rejoinder

Putative reason for the three-day Halt Order	Why this reason is unlikely to be the principal rationale for the Halt Order
The tanks needed maintenance.*	Unlikely, because (1) during the Battle of France, Germany experienced few maintenance problems with its tanks;[381] and (2) during the Halt, only routine maintenance, at best, could have been performed. Repairs would have been done at a central collection point. (The Germans did not decentralize its maintenance system until after the Russian Campaign got underway in 1941.[382]) Three days would not have been much time to transport a tank to and from a repair facility (if one existed) or to effect repairs.
The infantry needed time catch up with the tanks.	On the morning of May 23, the German infantry was near Amiens, some 90 miles south of Dunkirk. They probably would not have needed until the afternoon of May 26 (when the Halt Order was lifted) to catch up with the panzers situated outside Dunkirk.
The Germans needed time to consolidate to avoid an Allied breakout.	Maybe, but did they need three days to do so?
The troops were tired.	Something just does not ring true about giving panzer crews three days off when elimination of the enemy was seemingly so close.

Given that Goering had, just days before the Halt Order was issued, convinced Hitler that the Allied troops at Dunkirk could be wiped out by the Luftwaffe, the principal reason that Shirer lays out for the Halt Order—to let the Luftwaffe destroy the Allies so that Hitler could get all the credit for doing so—makes the most sense. A short halt of 24 hours could have been suggested for most, if not all, of the reasons discussed above. Extending the Halt to three days would have been excessive for accomplishing all reasons other than giving the Luftwaffe the chance to do what Goering said it could do: annihilate the BEF.

Put differently, logic suggests that a highly successful campaign, which likely was just days from being completed, would be halted only for the most significant of reasons. Given Hitler's profound narcissism, the only incentive significant enough for him to pause his troops for three days in the middle of a momentous campaign would more than likely be to ensure that all the credit for a glorious victory would go to him, not the Prussian generals who worked for him.**

On May 25 and 26 the Luftwaffe was thrown into the battle that now focused upon Dunkirk and the surrounding beaches.[383] But the BEF was still two or three days away from arriving there in force.[384] As a result, the Luftwaffe could not yet smash the BEF, obliging Hitler to let the army try to do the job.

———

The War Cabinet meeting of May 24 started shortly before noon. When it did, Churchill discussed the situation in France. The port of Dunkirk was still functioning satisfactorily and a considerable number of French troops, but only a few English troops, had started to arrive there.[385] Air reports revealed that there had been a definite halt that morning in the movement of German armored divisions.[386] At the time, the War Office, Churchill, and General Gort all failed to recognize the importance of the Halt.[387]

Halifax revealed a telegram from the British Ambassador in Rome, reporting that talk in German circles was that Hitler was determined to invade the United Kingdom and that British authorities were "asleep and unduly confident in the British command of the sea." Various dates and places for an invasion were being floated.[388]

With the previous evening's decision to evacuate British troops from France, Halifax was now ready to discuss the matter of getting Mussolini to broker a peace deal between Britain and Germany.[389] Thus, he chose to disclose receipt of another telegram, this one dated May 23 from the British Ambassador to France. The message relayed a suggestion by the French

---

The need for repairs or running out of petrol were cited in the War Cabinet conclusions of May 24 as possible reasons for the Halt. CAB 65/1 137 (40) p. 240 153 May 24, 1940.

**Hitler perhaps might share the glory with Goering. Unlike the generals, Goering would never try to claim glory at the expense of his Fuhrer.*

Government that President Roosevelt should be asked to make another approach to Mussolini.[390]

In typical Halifax fashion* he opened the discussion by saying he did not think much would come of such a request. Then he immediately urged the War Cabinet to fully endorse the idea.[391] He returned to the statement Churchill had proposed to make but then canceled four days earlier, and retrieved two things for the Cabinet to ask President Roosevelt to convey to Mussolini:

1. That the Allies were ready to consider reasonable Italian claims at the end of the war and would welcome Italy at a peace conference on equal terms with the belligerents, and

2. That the United States was willing to guarantee that the Allies would follow through unless Italy and the United States became engaged in a war on opposite sides.[392]

The War Cabinet agreed.[393]

The increasingly dismal situation in France had started to take a physical toll on the sixty-five-year-old Churchill. He returned to bed as soon as the Cabinet meeting ended.[394] While first telling the doctor that he was fine, he finally admitted he was suffering from an attack of dyspepsia (indigestion), something that had afflicted him for nearly a decade.[395] Ill as he was, that afternoon, Churchill nonetheless sketched out a plan that would require the garrison at Calais to fight to the death to slow the German advance along the coast toward Dunkirk.[396]

---

*Whenever Halifax wanted the War Cabinet to take some action, he had the curious habit of setting forth what he wanted, then quickly following it with some indication that he believed what he was proposing had very little chance of happening or succeeding. Here, Halifax was trying to influence the War Cabinet by implying (whether or not true) that Cabinet agreement with his proposal was expected to have very little impact. It is unlikely that Halifax's approach fooled anyone, except perhaps himself.

PART II

Hitler and Mussolini

15

Saturday, May 25, 1940

The Chiefs of Staff's Briefing Paper and Subsequent Revisions
Withdrawal to the Channel
Halifax's Desire to Involve Mussolini in Peace Discussions

The Chiefs of Staff's Briefing Paper and Subsequent Revisions

On May 25, the Chiefs of Staff (COS) produced a top-secret briefing paper titled "British Strategy in a Certain Eventuality"—i.e., the fall of France.[1] The report was not immediately widely circulated, having been initially provided only to the Prime Minister. The stated object of the report was to investigate the means (if any) by which Britain could continue to fight single-handedly should France collapse and make a peace agreement with Germany—and Britain suffer the loss of most of the British Expeditionary Force.[2]

In the first paragraph of the report, the COS noted several additional assumptions they made in preparing their report, which were supposedly "contained in Appendix A of the Annex." The first of these was that Italy would enter the war on the Axis side. The second was that the "United States of America is willing to give [Britain] full economic and financial support, *without which we do not think we could continue this war with any chance of success.*"[3] [emphasis in original]

The highlighted bombshell point, in which the COS suggested that full US support was required for Britain to even have a chance of winning the war, was, however, neither dealt with in the report nor set out in the list of assumptions laid out in the report's Appendix. In fact, the assumption set out in the Appendix was quite matter-of-fact, merely stating: "We could count on the full economic and financial support of the United States of America, possibly extending to active participation on our side."

Aside from the conclusory statement being (oddly) included in the recitation of assumptions, the only reference to Britain's ability to continue the war without substantial financial support from America is one sentence in the Annex where the same phrase is simply repeated verbatim.[4] The report contained no discussion, let alone any analysis, of what would happen if the United States did not provide "full economic and financial support."

The subject of conclusory phrase—that Britain was doomed without the full support of the United States—was also much broader than the question dealt with in the report, which was: could the United Kingdom hold out until assistance from the Empire and America made itself felt?[5]

The above notwithstanding, when the report was given to the entire War Cabinet, the phrase was almost immediately taken by the members as an "important assumption. ...."[6] Thus, the questions:

> Who inserted the conclusory phrase in the COS's report?
>
> Why was it inserted?
>
> Was it to give the casual reader of the report the feeling that the Chiefs of Staff likely did not believe that Britain could or should continue in the war alone? Or to push the War Council toward negotiating a peace agreement with Hitler?

Substantively, the report outlined and analyzed the three ways in which the COS believed "Germany might break down the resistance of the United Kingdom: (1) unrestricted air attack aimed at breaking public morale; (2) starvation of the country by attack on shipping and ports; and (3) occupation by invasion."[7]

After many pages of analysis, the report concluded that:

> These factors cannot be assessed with certainty in that it is impossible to say whether or not the United Kingdom could hold out in all circumstances. *We think there are good grounds for the belief that the British people will endure the greatest strain, if they realize—as they are beginning to do—that the existence of the Empire is at stake.*[8] [emphasis added]

Notably, despite putting the point up front, the conclusions of the report did not discuss financial assistance from the United States.

A few weeks later, in a June 11 memo to the War Cabinet, the Chiefs of Staff recharacterized the provocative point included in their May 25 report, saying: "We concluded that we should still have a good chance of winning the war single-handed *if we receive full Pan-American economic and financial cooperation, but not otherwise.*"[9] [emphasis added]

The COS reiterated this thought in a June 13 summary prepared for His Majesty's Ambassador to the United States. That message, titled "PLANS TO MEET A CERTAIN EVENTUALITY," read:

Without the full, economic, and financial co-operation of the whole of the American Continent, the task might in the event prove too great for the British Empire single-handed. Nevertheless, even if the hope of victory in these circumstances appeared remote, we should continue to fight as long as it was humanly possible to do so.[10]

The May 25 report also compared the strength of Allied and German air forces. Germany, it reported, had slightly more than 5,000 airplanes, about half of them bombers,[11] and the RAF had 1,500 airplanes, including 221 deployed to France and Norway or just returned to the UK. Of the undeployed aircraft, 860 were fighters and 400 were bombers.[12]

Churchill clearly thought the COS's report had somehow missed the mark. Thus, almost immediately, he asked the Chiefs to review the report in light of the following "Terms of Reference" that he provided:

In the event of France being unable to continue in the war and becoming neutral with the Germans holding their present position and the Belgian army being forced to capitulate after assisting the British Expeditionary Force to reach the coast; in the event the terms being offered to Britain which would place her entirely at the mercy of Germany through disarmament, cession of naval bases in the Orkneys etc.:

- What are the prospects of our continuing the war alone against Germany and probably Italy?

- Can the Navy and the Air Force hold out reasonable hopes or preventing serious invasion? And

- Could the forces gathered in this Island cope with raids from the air involving detachments not greater than 10,000 men? It being observed that a prolongation of British resistance might be very dangerous for Germany engaged in holding down the greater part of Europe.[13]

The Chiefs obliged, and as discussed below, presented their resulting conclusions to the War Cabinet on May 27.[14]

————

When the War Cabinet convened shortly before noon on Saturday May 25, Churchill told his ministers about the telegram he had received the previous night from French Premier Reynaud saying that the BEF was no longer conforming to General Weygand's plan and had withdrawn toward the Channel ports.[15] Weygand complained bitterly that, on its own, the BEF had retreated 25 miles toward the Channel ports, while, French troops moving up from the south were gaining ground.[16] Churchill said that "At that time we had had no information of any such move on Lord Gort's part,"[17] especially since Gort had been specifically forbidden to withdraw to the sea, but rather to attack southward. Churchill sent a reply to Reynaud. In it, the Prime Minister shared his belief that General Gort was still pressing southward, but if the P.M. became aware that extreme pressure had compelled Gort to deviate from the agreed plan, he would inform Reynaud at once.[18]

Later, a Staff Officer reported to the War Office that two BEF Divisions had in fact stopped moving south and had withdrawn from the area near Arras.[19] What had also come to light was that, contrary to plan, "only a very small number of French troops ... had yet crossed the Somme" and even they were not proceeding northward.[20] They were holding the southern portion of two cities located on the Somme—Amiens and parts of Perrone (about 30 miles to the east of Amiens).

Churchill told the War Cabinet he had no doubt that circumstances had forced General Gort to halt his moving southward. But Gort "should have informed us of what he was doing." Though Churchill now thought that "the French had grounds for complaint," he added that "this was no time for recriminations."[21] Chief of the Imperial General Staff General Dill had been instructed to have a staff officer fly back from France with a report on the situation at the earliest possible moment.[22] "In the meantime," the Prime Minister said, "we must tell the French that the reported withdrawal has now been confirmed."[23]

Chamberlain urged his colleagues not to make a hasty judgment about Gort's failure to keep the Government informed of what he was doing—he felt there had to be an explanation.[24] General Ironside theorized that almost certainly Gort's communications line had been cut.[25] Gort's actions had been dictated by the dire events on the ground. While having been ordered to attack southward, Gort "knew that only annihilation awaited him there."[26] Moreover, the BEF was in fact in "mortal danger," "nearly encircled [and] trapped ... 70 miles from the sea."[27] "Panzers were in Gravelines, barely 10 miles from Dunkirk," which was probably the only "remaining port of escape."[28]

Commenting on the situation, General Alan Brooke, who commanded II Corps and reported to Gort, wrote in his diary that "nothing but a miracle can save the BEF now; the end cannot be far off."[29] Worse yet, on the afternoon of May 25, Gort received a disturbing dispatch from Brooke, who said he was "convinced that the Belgian Army is closing down and will have stopped fighting by this time tomorrow," an action that would have exposed the BEF's entire "left flank."[30] That evening, Gort ordered his 5th Division, to move into whatever gap would be left by the Belgians.[31] There, between the western Belgian cities of Warneton and Ypres, each located about 25 miles southeast of Dunkirk, the division would start a battle with the Germans that would last "throughout the withdrawal [to Dunkirk], with very heavy losses."[32]

From his command post in Prémesques, a French town only eight miles south of Warneton, General Gort wired Secretary of War Anthony Eden early in the evening of May 25, explaining "what he had done and why he had done it." Even before the telegram arrived (it was delayed getting to Eden[33]), Churchill had realized that withdrawal to the Channel was necessary.[34] After consulting with Reynaud, Churchill directed Eden to send a telegram to General Gort saying, "It is clear ... that it will not be possible for the French to deliver an attack from the South. You are now authorized to operate towards coast forthwith in conjunction with the French and Belgian armies."[35]

That night, General Ironside, writing in his diary about the chances of evacuating the BEF back to Britain, grimly predicted that "We shall have lost all our trained soldiers by the next few days unless a miracle appears to help us."[36]

Withdrawal to the Channel

As soon as General Gort received Eden's telegram, the withdrawal of the BEF to the coast was on. But the more than 200,000 men of the BEF and the remnants of the First French Army would have to fight their way to the Channel[37]—and they would have to do so against German forces outnumbering them "three or four to one."[38] Over the next several days the BEF would fight by day and retreat by night.[39] Many obstacles stood in the way of the withdrawal's succeeding.

Halifax's Desire to Involve Mussolini in Peace Discussions

Given what was happening in France and how the Chiefs of Staff assessed Britain's ability to fight single-handedly if France collapsed, Halifax concluded that it made much more sense to ask Mussolini to name his terms for Italy's staying out of the war and brokering peace negotiations with Hitler than to see Britain continuing a war it could not win. Halifax was also confident that other members of the War Cabinet agreed with him.* For these reasons, he felt the time was now right to inform the members of the War Cabinet

---

*There was also no doubt that Churchill was staunchly supportive of preserving British democracy and the British Empire. A negotiated peace agreement seemed like it could provide both.

that, around May 20, an Italian press attaché named Gabriele Paresci had contacted the Foreign Office wanting to talk about Italy's remaining neutral.[40]

Halifax reported that a third party had set up a meeting at the Italian embassy between Paresci and Sir Robert Vansittart, a senior British diplomat who had formerly been permanent Under-Secretary for Foreign Affairs.[41] At the meeting, Paresci:

> ... alleging that he was speaking without instructions, had said that there are still a great many influential people in Italy who desire to see a peaceful solution of the Mediterranean problem. If His Majesty's Government saw their way to make an approach to the Italian government, with a view to exploring the possibilities of a friendly settlement, there need be no fear of their meeting with a rebuff.[42]

Halifax had then consulted with Churchill, who authorized him to pursue the matter further.[43]

Mussolini had chosen not to enter the war yet. In recent months, however, he had more often supported Hitler's positions,[44] and many suspected that in short order he would join the war on the side of Germany. Indeed, only a week earlier, in his reply to Churchill's May 16 letter, Mussolini told the P.M. he had no interest in a negotiated peace. Nonetheless, Halifax urged further pursuit of what had been discussed in the Vansittart–Paresci meeting. He noted that "very likely nothing might come of all this. Nevertheless, even if the result were merely to gain time, it would be valuable."[45] Churchill said he saw no objection to the approach suggested by Halifax: "It must not, of course, be accompanied by any publicity, since that would amount to a confession of weakness ... It was [also] very probable that at any moment Mussolini might put very strong pressure on the French, with a view to obtaining concessions from them."[46]

Halifax also drew attention to a May 24 telegram from the British Ambassador in Madrid, reporting on a conversation between Queen Ena of Spain's senior attendant and a member of the staff at the British embassy. The attendant had learned from a highly placed Spanish Fascist, with whom the Germans had talked, that the Germans wanted Italy to immediately offer a separate peace to France. The terms would be as follows: France would keep her present European frontiers; Italy would receive Tunisia; and Spain would receive Gibraltar and French Morocco. France was also to stand aside while Germany proceeded to blockade and invade England, which the Germans were convinced they could do. The offer to France would include an ultimatum that Italy would attack if these terms were not accepted.[47]

With Churchill's authorization, that afternoon Halifax again met with Italian Ambassador Bastianini at the Foreign Office.[48] Halifax would report on the meeting in some detail in a memo titled "Suggested Approach to Signor Mussolini,"[49] which he distributed to the War Cabinet late the next day (May 26). Halifax and Bastianini first discussed how Italian neutrality could be maintained but they quickly moved toward the more significant question of whether Mussolini might be willing to mediate a peace agreement between England and Germany.[50] Pursuing this question was something quite different from "what Churchill and the War Cabinet had authorized"[51]—that is, Halifax's seeking a "peaceful solution of the Mediterranean problem."

Halifax may very well have written and spoken more labyrinthinely than anyone else on the planet. More charitably, Lukacs describes Halifax's phraseology as "often convoluted and cautious."[52] Regardless of how best to characterize Halifax's communication style, at the meeting he advised Bastianini that:

> It was quite true that we intended to make an approach, in appropriate form to certain political questions. ... And in any such approach we should have which to make plain our desire that Italy should naturally take her proper place at the peace conference by the side of the belligerents. ... If and when we should receive an inclination that our approach might be received with due consideration, we should be prepared to carry the matter further and deal with it in greater detail. ... [It] might serve to open the way to the treatment of other questions, always provided that we could approach these questions on the basis of the frankest recognition of the rights and necessities of both parties.[53]

Bastianini, no slouch himself when it came to murky communication, then asked Halifax "whether he might inform his government that His Majesty's Government considered it opportune now to examine the question at issue between our two countries within the larger framework of a European settlement." After Halifax effectively said "yes," Bastianini said that he would also "like to know whether His Majesty's Government would consider it possible to discuss general questions involving not only Great Britain and Italy but other countries."[54] By this "he meant Germany, of course."[55]

Bastianini added that Mussolini wanted to achieve a settlement "that would not merely be an armistice but would protect a European peace for a century." Halifax replied that England had the same goal.[56] With the idea of a negotiated settlement with Germany in mind, on May 25 Halifax drafted a telegram to be sent to Roosevelt. Suggesting that the US President speak directly with Hitler about the terms of a peace treaty with Britain, the draft said:

> If you say to Hitler that, while you recognize his right to obtain terms that must necessarily be difficult and distasteful to those whom he defeated, nevertheless terms which intended to destroy the independence of Great Britain and France would at once touch the vital interests of the U.S., and that if such were insisted upon, you thought it inevitable that the attempt would encounter U.S. resistance, the effort might well be to make him think again. If you felt it in the event contemplated to go no further and say that, if he insisted on terms destructive of British independence and therefore prejudicial to the U.S., USA would at once give full support to G.B., the effect would of course be more valuable.[57]

Churchill did not send Halifax's telegram. According to Lukacs, "presumably" Churchill "thought it both futile and not strong enough."[58] (Only a few days earlier, Roosevelt had made his position on immediate aid to Britain quite clear.) Churchill also would have been doubtful whether anything expressed in the telegram would have had any impact on Hitler.

––––

The military situation in France continued to deteriorate. At about 2:00 PM, a message was sent from London to BEF Brigadier General Nicholson countermanding previous plans for him and his brigade to evacuate Calais and ordering him, instead, to stay and hold that city at all costs.[59] Churchill drafted the message that ordered Nicholson to fight to the death. "Every hour you continue to exist," the wire read, "is of the greatest help to the BEF. Government has therefore decided you must continue to fight. ... Evacuation will not (repeat not) take place ..."[60] In *Their Finest Hour,* Churchill talks about feeling sick when he sent that wire.[61]

After Nicholson received it, his troops engaged in street fighting while he "refused repeated German invitations to surrender."[62] The men in Calais fought until May 27th.[63] Ultimately, Nicholson and what was left of his command were captured.[64]* His efforts and those of the men who served under him helped set the stage for the evacuation of the BEF from Dunkirk. As Churchill writes, without Nicholson's valiant stand against the Germans at Calais, "all would have been cut off and lost."[65]

––––––––––

Nicholson died in captivity three years later. According to his death certificate, he threw himself out of a window due to a depressive illness.

That evening, French leaders met in Paris. General Weygand explained that the military situation was hopeless. President of the French Republic Albert Lebrun reminded the group of the agreement France had made with England in March 1940 not to enter into a separate peace. Then he added: "Still, if Germany offers such conditions that are relatively advantageous, we must examine them closely and with calm heads."[66]

Reynaud responded that if such an offer were presented, France was bound to inform the British. Deputy Prime Minister Marshal Pétain replied, "I question whether there is a complete reciprocity with the British. ... Actually, they have given only two divisions while many French divisions are still fighting."[67] French Minister of the Navy César Campinchi challenged Pétain's assessment of the military contribution of the two nations. Campinghi added that the French Government had given its word to England, and the loyalty of France must not be risked. France, he declared, must never sign a peace treaty with Germany without British concurrence.[68]

Reynaud decided he would go to London the next day to explain the situation to the British. He intended to ask them "what would happen if Paris were to fall?" He knew that their response might be "You are bound by your signature, you must fight even when hopeless."[69]

Churchill knew nothing about theses deliberations.[70] But at the 10:00 PM meeting of Britain's Defence Committee Churchill said "he would not be at all surprised if a peace offer were made to the French, having regard to their weak position and to the likelihood of an attack on France by Italy. If France went out of the War, she must, however, make it a condition that our Army was allowed to leave France intact, and to take away its munitions, and that the soil of France was not used for an attack on England. Further, France must retain her fleet. If an offer were made on these terms, he [Churchill] would accept it, and he thought that we could hold out in this country once we got our Army back from France."[71]

Churchill's statement is a further indication that he was thinking about defending Britain against a German invasion—he intended to continue fighting and not to negotiate with Hitler.

It's important to remember that when Churchill addressed the Defence Committee that evening, not a single British soldier had yet been evacuated from France.

Dunkirk. Troops waiting to be evacuated

16

Sunday, May 26, 1940

An Armada of Small Vessels Is Assembled
The 9:00 AM War Cabinet Meeting
- Chiefs of Staff Are Asked to Reassess Britain's Prospects If It Had to Continue the War Against Germany Alone

Whether to Enter a Negotiated Peace with Hitler
Reynaud Comes to London for a Lunch Meeting with Churchill and a Meeting with Halifax, Churchill, Chamberlain, and Attlee
Halifax Continues to Press About Peace Negotiations
Getting the Evacuation of the BEF Rolling
The 4:30 PM Session of the War Cabinet
The Evacuation Order

An Armada of Small Vessels Is Assembled

By the morning of May 26, the Royal Navy, in anticipation of having to rescue BEF forces from northern France, had assembled "a ragtag armada"[1] of 860 private vessels at Ramsgate, a seaside town just north of Dover that was the site of a Coastal Forces naval base. The Navy had sent the word out to yacht clubs and commandeered boats wherever it could.[2] Boats of every shape and size—everything from trawlers, paddle wheelers, and fireboats to pleasure craft—were amassed.[3] Most were shallow-draft vessels that, unlike warships, could navigate waters only a few feet deep and thus get close to the beach. This armada was now anchored three-abreast everywhere possible in Dover harbor.[4]

May 26 was a busy day for other reasons too: Hitler lifted the Halt Order; Premier Reynaud was on his way to London for crisis talks with Churchill; and, in the afternoon, German units again were advancing northward toward Dunkirk.[5]

The 9:00 AM War Cabinet Meeting

At the 9:00 AM meeting of the War Cabinet, Churchill presented a letter he received from General Edward Spears, his new personal representative, to French Prime Minister Paul Reynaud. In a meeting with several French officials,* Spears learned that:[6]

1. The French now understood that BEF commander General Gort had not in fact retreated from combat without warning or orders. That assumption had been based on old information,[7] and French Army Commander General Weygand apologized.

2. The French had concluded that further attacks to the south by the BEF and the French 1st Army would serve no purpose, and

3. General Weygand had decided to allow General Blanchard, the commander of the French First Army, to use his discretion about falling back to the Channel.[8]

After the Spears update, Churchill spoke the specific words that the Cabinet had been expecting for days: "It seems from all evidence available that we might have to face the situation in which the French were going to collapse, and that we must do our best to extricate the British Expeditionary Force from Northern France."[9]

Churchill then read a draft of the conclusions reached by the Ministers and the Chiefs of Staff on the subject the previous evening. The draft called for General Gort to withdraw his troops northward to the coast and assume that the march would start that evening (though Gort was advised not to proceed without a specific order to do so). Any order to carry out the evacuation plan must await Reynaud's concurrence at the afternoon's scheduled meeting.[10]

Admiral Dudley Pound, First Sea Lord and Chief of the Naval Staff, assured the Cabinet that the Admiralty was "putting in hand all preparations for the dispatch of a fleet of ships and small boats to evacuate the BEF."[11] Churchill said that although he would try to induce Reynaud to keep fighting—by pointing out that the French were at least honor-bound

---

At the session, Spears also reunited with eighty-four-year-old WWI hero Marshal Philippe Pétain. Pétain had only recently been brought out of retirement to join the Reynaud government in an effort to boost the county's morale. The old man reminisced about their time together during the First World War and "treated Spears like a son." It seemed to Spears that Pétain "in his great age, epitomized the paralysis of the French people." During the meeting, Pétain was calm but ineffective. See, Attachment to Confidential Annex to 65/1 145 (40) p. 1 191.

to provide, if possible, for the safe withdrawal of the BEF[12]—he warned the Cabinet to be prepared for Reynaud to say that the French could no longer carry on the fight.

Chiefs of Staff Are Asked to Reassess Britain's Prospects If It Had to Continue the War Against Germany Alone

Churchill then repeated the request he had made to the Chiefs of Staff the previous evening to consider Britain's ability to carry on in the following scenario:

- the French drop out;

- so, too, do the Belgians (after helping the BEF reach the coast);

- Hitler offers Britain peace terms insisting on unilateral disarmament, which would place the UK at the mercy of Germany; and

- Britain is forced to cede naval bases in the Orkneys (a group of islands just north of Scotland).

Ultimately, Churchill wanted to know:

> What are the prospects of continuing the war alone against Germany—and probably Italy?

> Can the Navy and the Air Force reasonably assure that a significant invasion of Britain can be thwarted, and can the forces gathered in the British Isles cope with raids from the air involving detachments of not more than ten thousand men?[13]

Chief of the Air Staff Sir Cyril Newall replied that the Chiefs had prepared such a paper, although their conclusions now needed to be reviewed, given the new parameters Churchill had added to the scenario.[14] Updating the Cabinet on the situation in France, General Dill, the new Chief of the General Imperial Staff, said that British forces were still holding out in Calais and the situation there that morning was quieter than it had been during the night.[15]

Whether to Enter a Negotiated Peace with Hitler

Believing that now was the time to negotiate peace with Hitler, Halifax could no longer stay silent. Ever more sure of his position, he told the War Cabinet in no uncertain terms that "we had to face the fact that it was not so much now a question of imposing a complete defeat upon Germany but of safeguarding the independence of our own Empire and if possible that of France."[16] Writer Anthony McCarten says that "continu[ing] with Churchill's crusade of 'victory at all costs' now seemed ludicrous."[17] "To millions, resistance seemed futile, even suicidal."[18]

In making his pitch for peace, Halifax informed the War Cabinet that in a meeting the previous evening with Italian Ambassador Bastianini,[19] the Ambassador "had clearly made soundings as to the prospect of our agreeing to a conference."[20] Bastianini reiterated that "Mussolini's principal wish was to secure peace in Europe."[21] Halifax told Bastianini that this was Britain's objective as well and that "[Britain] should naturally be prepared to consider any proposals which might lead to this, provided our liberty and independence were assured."[22] Halifax told the War Cabinet that the Ambassador had informed the French of these feelers and asked for another meeting with him this morning because "he might have fresh proposals to put forward."[23]

Churchill replied "[P]eace and security might be achieved [but] under a German domination of Europe. That we could never accept. We must ensure our complete liberty and independence. [I am] opposed to any negotiations which might lead to a derogation of our rights and power."[24]

Halifax responded that if the French were planning to negotiate for peace—and if Hitler truly wanted peace—then the Allies had a strong card to play. France, however, should make it clear to Hitler that they are treaty-bound not to make any peace settlement without Britain. "They might use this as a powerful lever to obtain favorable terms. ..."

At that point in the meeting, the May 25 report prepared by the Chiefs of Staff about Britain's ability to carry on the war single-handedly was distributed to the War Cabinet.[25] The Cabinet ministers did not, however, have time to digest the document in any detail.[26] Halifax said he gleaned from a quick read of it that Britain's ability to carry on the war alone against Germany depended in the main on its ability to establish and maintain air superiority.[27] Secretary for Air Archie Sinclair interjected that air superiority per se was not the question; instead, Britain had to prevent the Germans from achieving the level of air superiority that would allow them to invade the country.[28]

Accepting Sinclair's analysis, Halifax pointed out that if France collapsed, the Germans would no longer need large land forces and could shift their efforts to aircraft production. He added that, after their Norway successes, "Germany would [also] not now be hampered by lack of iron."[29] Sinclair responded that Germany's ability to continue an air war also would depend ultimately on its ability to maintain an adequate oil supply.[30]

Cyril Newall, the Chief of the Air Staff, felt it important to remind the Ministers that the report did not cover what was now being discussed. Its purpose, he said, was merely to provide arguments to deter the French from capitulating and to strengthen their will to keep fighting.[31] Halifax then suggested that as a "last resort we should ask the French to put their [aircraft] factories out of gear,"[32] to which Chamberlain responded, "whatever undertakings of this character we might extract from the French would be worthless, the terms of peace which the Germans would propose would inevitably prevent their fulfillment."[33] Churchill agreed, adding that "the Germans [will] make the terms of any peace offer as attractive as possible to the French, and lay emphasis on the fact that their quarrel was not with France but with England."[34]At the end of the morning meeting, the War Cabinet approved the instructions given to General Gort to prepare the BEF for evacuation from the continent through Dunkirk; instructions to the BEF forces in Calais to hold out; and, if necessary, the dispatching of troops to Dunkirk to secure the port.[35]

Reynaud Comes to London for a Lunch Meeting with Churchill and a Meeting with Halifax, Churchill, Chamberlain, and Attlee

When the War Cabinet session ended, Churchill asked the group to convene again at 2:00 PM at Admiralty House after his lunch there with Premier Reynaud.[36] Halifax returned to the Foreign Office, where he again met with the Italian Ambassador.[37] At the afternoon meeting, Churchill reported to the War Cabinet that, based on his discussion at lunch, he did not think Reynaud would object to the BEF marching to the coast, as the Cabinet had approved that morning. Reynaud, though, had not yet reached a firm decision.[38] At lunch, Reynaud followed through on the promise he had made to his colleagues the previous evening in Paris and informed Churchill of "the near hopelessness of the French military situation."[39] He revealed to Churchill what General Weygand had told him: that the Germans, with their superiority of numbers and tanks, could pierce any line the French threw up.[40] While Weygand would obey orders to fight it out as long as he could and would be prepared to go down for the honor of the flag, the General did not think that France's resistance was likely to last long against a determined German onslaught.[41]

Reynaud covered several other topics in his conversation with his British counterpart:

- He speculated that Italy would extract, as the price for peace, "the neutralization of Gibraltar and the Suez Canal, the demilitarization of Malta, and the limitation of Allied naval forces in the Mediterranean," which the French believed should be offered if it would keep Italy out of the war.[42]

- He realized that the Germans would renege on any peace terms to which they agreed.[43]

- He hinted that his intended refusal to any sign peace terms imposed on France might force him to resign.*

If the BEF were to escape the approaching German army, the French would need to continue to fight. Churchill told Reynaud that Britain was "not prepared to give in on any account. We would rather go down fighting than be enslaved to Germany. But in any case, we [are] confident that we [have] a good chance of surviving the German onslaught.[**] France, however, must stay in the war."[44] Churchill added that "if only we could stick things out for another 3 months, the position would be entirely different."[45] Reynaud repeated that though Weygand was prepared to fight on, the general believed France had insufficient power to resist the Germans.[46]

Halifax Continues to Press About Peace Negotiations

As the 2:00 PM session was closing, Churchill suggested that Halifax see the French Premier, who was still in the building. Churchill, Chamberlain, and Attlee would follow in a few minutes.[47] Before Halifax left, a discussion ensued about whether to make the approach to Italy.[48] Because Halifax agreed with Attlee that the last thing Mussolini wanted was to see Hitler dominate Europe, he thought Mussolini would be eager to try persuading Hitler to be reasonable.[49]

Churchill doubted that anything would come of an approach to Italy but said that the matter was one which the War Cabinet should consider.[50***] He also said that what was pressing now was to make sure that the French did not equate the BEF's cutting its way to the coast with Britain letting France down militarily.[51] To this end, he had Secretary of War Anthony Eden draft a telegram for Reynaud to send to Weygand.[52] The wire would have Weygand order a withdrawal of the BEF, the Belgians, and the France's 1st Army to the Channel ports.

Reynaud, in fact, resigned three weeks later.

**Another indication that Churchill had already decided to fight rather than negotiate.*

***McCarten, calls this "the first of what would become a stunning series of concessions that challenge our image of [Churchill]." McCarten p. 187. He goes on to say, "How very far Winston had come, in just a few days, from the man who would brook no thought, nor allow anyone else to think, of parley or surrender." Ibid. The correctness of McCarten's ultimate thesis—that Churchill actually did consider entering into peace negotiations with Hitler—has, however, been questioned by many (but supported by others). It will be examined more thoroughly later in this chapter as well as in later chapters.*

Getting the Evacuation of the BEF Rolling

The draft telegram for Reynaud to send to General Weygand read:

> The reports received here from the Front indicate that the offensive from the North cannot succeed in closing the gap in view of the fact that the offensive from the South cannot be launched in sufficient strength to join up with it.
>
> I have told the British Government that you have given General Blanchard full freedom of decision.
>
> I think that it would be very desirable that you should inform General Blanchard at once, that you authorize him formally to order a withdrawal towards the ports. Please inform Sir Edmund Ironside of your decision.
>
> Paul Reynaud[53]

Reynaud read the draft telegram over the phone to General Weygand at 4:05 PM.[54]

The 4:30 PM Session of the War Cabinet

Just after Reynaud left to return to France, Churchill asked the War Cabinet members to stay on at Admiralty House for an "informal" meeting.[55] The first fifteen minutes of that meeting were not included in the War Cabinet records because Cabinet Secretary Sir Edmund Bridges was not present to take minutes.[56]

Some of what took place during that quarter hour are "known" by what Chamberlain wrote in his diary that night and through Halifax's recollections, which were memorialized in the minutes of the War Cabinet's meeting at 4:30 PM the next day, May 27. At that time, Halifax told the War Cabinet that he had asked Churchill if he would he be prepared to discuss peace terms with Germany if he were satisfied that matters vital to the independence of this country were unaffected.[57]

As Roberts puts it, when Halifax posed that question, Churchill did not wish to seem "unpersuadable and obdurate to his colleagues."[58] Lukacs is more pointed: "Churchill knew that he could not answer Halifax with a categorical 'no.'"[59] Were the P.M. to have done anything to push Chamberlain over to Halifax's side on the issue, Lukacs reasons, then Churchill's position against negotiating a peace agreement would have become "difficult if not untenable."[60] Remember, even if the two Labour members of the War Cabinet agreed with Churchill, it was unlikely that Churchill's position would have prevailed on a simple three-to-two vote. (As previously discussed, matters in the War Cabinet, particularly important ones, were not approved or disapproved on a strictly numerical vote basis. Attlee and Greenwood were newcomers to the Cabinet and members of a party that was very much a minority in Parliament. So in May 1940 they mostly listened rather than spoke in the War Cabinet.[61]) For Churchill to get what he wanted he needed Chamberlain's support. As also discussed previously, the Churchill Government "could [also] not afford" Halifax's resignation.[62] Accordingly, Churchill did not, or could not, respond to Halifax's peace question with a sharp "no" ... "he felt it necessary to reassure Halifax that he was open to reason."[63]

In Halifax's account, the Prime Minister responded that "he would be thankful to get out of our present difficulties on such terms, provided we retained the essentials and the elements of our vital strength, even at the cost of some cession of territory."[64] This rather tepid response, if it were said, would appear to have shown that Churchill was not yet certain that Chamberlain (like Attlee and Greenwood) agreed with his no-peace-negotiation position.[65]

However, in his diary that night, Chamberlain recalled the interchange between the Prime Minister and Halifax, particularly Churchill's response, a bit differently than did Halifax, and that he supported what Churchill had said. The diary read:

> Halifax said why not suggest that [Mussolini's] own indepen-
> dence would be threatened if France and G.B. collapsed but
> if he would use his influence to discuss terms which did not
> menace our independence and offered a prospect of a just and
> durable settlement of Europe, we would try to meet his own
> claims .... The P.M. disliked any move toward Musso. It was
> incredible that Hitler would consent to any terms that we could
> accept—though if we could get out of this jam by giving up
> Malta & Gibraltar & some African colonies, he would jump
> at it.[*] But the only safe way to was to convince Hitler that
> he couldn't beat us ... *I supported this view.* Attlee hardly said
> anything but seems to be with Winston. ...[66] [emphasis added]**

---

*As early as 1936 Chamberlain himself had given thought to "purchasing peace" by giving Germany back her African colonies, but had concluded then that it would not achieve a lasting solution. Self p. 280.

**Notably while supporting the continuation of full-fledged war against the Nazis, Chamberlain had these doubts and thoughts about Britain's preparedness to take on Hitler—

McCarten asserts that both Chamberlain's diary and Halifax's recollection support the notion that during the Cabinet meeting on the afternoon of May 26, "Churchill reached a major turning point" and was considering peace talks with Germany.[67]* McCarten reminds us that the most critical challenge Churchill was facing at that moment was the impending BEF evacuation from Dunkirk, and there certainly were grave doubts about its success.[68] Thus, McCarten quite reasonably asks: under such circumstances, "what sane person would *not* seriously consider peace talks in preference to almost certain annihilation?"[69]** [emphasis in original]

Roberts, however, challenges the use of the Chamberlain diary entry to prove that Churchill did not wish to fight on.[70] He correctly points out that in the diary, Chamberlain not only had Churchill "put ... things [quite] colloquially" but Chamberlain also conflated two ideas: (1) buying off Mussolini to keep Italy from entering the war, and (2) giving up territory to achieve an overall peace agreement with Hitler.[71] This conflation can be seen simply by re-reading the diary entry. That is, it is not logical to believe (as the diary appears to suggest) that giving up "Malta and Gibraltar and some African colonies" would have convinced Hitler that he couldn't beat Britain.

Rather than "jump[ing] at the chance to get out of this jam" by giving up territory, as the Chamberlain diary reveals, Churchill was seeking to denigrate the idea of buying peace through ceding territory by treating it as a fanciful notion.*** Churchill sarcastically said that he'd love it if a lasting overall peace could be achieved by doing something as simple as agreeing to

---

...if only we had another year of preparation we should have been in a far stronger position and so with the French but anyway and whatever the outcome it is clear as daylight that if we had to fight in 1938 the results would have been far worse it would be rash to prophecy the verdict of history, but if full access is obtained to all the records it will be seen that I realized from the beginning of our military weakness and did my best to postpone if I could not avert the war. ed. Self Vol 4 p. 533 Chamberlain to his sister Ida, May 25, 1940.

*McCarten is not the only one who believes Churchill considered entering into peace negotiations. Pat Buchanan is another. See, Buchanan, pp.359–360. Buchanan adds that "Lukacs contends that even had Churchill entertained the idea of a negotiated peace, he resisted the temptation and became the indispensable man who made the decision to fight on." Ibid. p. 360. The latter is, however, an overstatement.

**Churchill's doctor, Lord Moran, writes that, given "the seemingly hopeless inequality ... [between] Germany and Britain" in May 1940, Britain "needed a very unreasonable man at the top"—Churchill. If he had been reasonable and "of sound judgment" he may have acted differently. Instead of getting a sage who "would have been out of his element," Britain "got instead another Joan of Arc." Moran, The Struggle for Survival p. 833.

***As historian Graham Stewart puts it, "Churchill was maintaining that [Halifax] was pursuing a pipe dream if he believed that making concessions to Italy would spare Britain the humiliation of crippling terms from Hitler." Stewart, p. 431.

give away some territory, "[b]ut the only safe way [to get out of our present difficulties] was to convince Hitler he couldn't beat us." And, as Roberts writes, the only logical way to persuade Hitler of that was "to fight on."[72]

McCarten's thesis—that on May 26 Churchill was seriously considering entering into peace talks—also ignores the fact that later in that day's meeting of the War Cabinet, Churchill requested and received permission from the group to have Minister for Air, Archie Sinclair, present "whenever this matter was discussed."[73] Sinclair, a long-time critic of appeasement, was an old friend of Churchill; he had in fact been second-in-command to Churchill in 1916 when Winston commanded the 6th Royal Scot Fusiliers at the Belgian village of Ploegstreet. More importantly, Sinclair supported Churchill's opposition to peace talks.[74] By wanting Sinclair added to the group that would deliberate the question of war versus a negotiated peace, Churchill was not moving toward peace talks with Germany, as McCarten suggests, but, rather, was stacking the deck in the War Cabinet to be sure it did not vote in favor of entering peace negotiations.

McCarten writes that including Sinclair in the deliberations was "in defiance of protocol and an attempt to strengthen a hand weakened by the facts on the battlefield."[75] Both statements are likely correct. The fact that Churchill wanted Sinclair to participate in the deliberation says much about what the P.M. was thinking. Likewise, the fact that the War Cabinet allowed Sinclair into the deliberations is quite telling as to the mindset of its ministers.

That Sinclair was Churchill's longtime friend and sympathetic to Churchill's views about peace would not have been a secret to the War Cabinet.[76] For these reasons, no member of the War Cabinet who supported Halifax's position (and opposed Churchill's) would have agreed to adding another pro-Churchill member to the group deciding whether Britain should or should not negotiate a peace agreement with Hitler. The four Cabinet members other than Churchill, who had to pass on the P.M.'s request to allow Sinclair to participate in the deliberations were Halifax (who would not have favored Sinclair's participation), Attlee, Greenwood, and Chamberlain (who, as his diary would reveal, privately supported Churchill's position). Even with both Attlee and Greenwood supporting Churchill's position, it is hard to believe that Sinclair would have been granted the extraordinary privilege of participating in the deliberation on this critical issue had Chamberlain supported Halifax's position. In the hypothetical situation of Chamberlain siding with Halifax about allowing Sinclair to participate, the Cabinet ministers would have been split two to two, meaning Churchill's opinion would have ostensibly carried the question three to two. But as discussed above, important questions in the War Cabinet were not approved or disapproved on a strictly numerical vote basis.[77]

The logical conclusion to be drawn from the fact that Churchill's request to include Sinclair was granted is that Chamberlain favored Sinclair's admission. More importantly, by favoring Sinclair's inclusion, Chamberlain showed that he, like Attlee and Greenwood, supported Churchill's position against peace negotiations, not Halifax's. Stewart is correct when he writes that whether Churchill's plan to keep fighting would prevail in the War Cabinet was "in the hands of the Prime Minister he had displaced."[78] But as demonstrated above in the vote over Sinclair, Chamberlain showed exactly where he stood. If that were not clear, he certainly made his support for Churchill's position evident to the War Cabinet at the session held the next morning. There, he told the Cabinet about a meeting he'd had with the High Commissioners from around the Empire. Chamberlain said that he had told the commissioners that even if France were to fall, he believed Britain should fight rather than negotiate with Germany.[79]

Contrary to the view espoused by Buchanan[80] and others, Churchill was not the only person refusing to consider negotiations to end the war. Chamberlain, Sinclair, Attlee, and Greenwood all held that view as well. Churchill's no-negotiations-with-Hitler position was called irrational, foolhardy, mad, and a hundred other things. Still, Churchill was not the only member of the War Cabinet to support it.

Buchanan not only calls Churchill's refusal to enter peace negotiations "heroic" but then says that had Churchill not taken that stance "Hitler would have won the war and the world."[81] Along these lines, Manchester and Reid report that political skeptics such as George Bernard Shaw and Malcolm Muggeridge felt that "had anyone but Churchill been Prime Minister in the summer of 1940, Britain would have negotiated an armistice with Hitler."[82]

Yes, absent Churchill doing as he did, history would have been different; but the favorable outcome that came about would also not have been achieved if Neville Chamberlain had not stood with Churchill in opposition to a negotiated peace in May 1940.

The natural question arises: Why would Chamberlain, a man who at almost every opportunity over the preceding few years had consistently chosen to capitulate rather than risk armed conflict with Nazi Germany, now choose fighting over negotiating. And, relatedly, what had caused the complete reversal of position between Chamberlain and Halifax since Munich? In September 1938, Chamberlain was much more willing than Halifax to give Hitler the benefit of the doubt; but now, twenty months later, in late May 1940, the converse was true.

The answers to both questions are that (1) as noted, Chamberlain felt that by taking the "soft" approach in 1938 and 1939 he had been played for a fool by Hitler, and he vowed never to let that happen again; (2) he had belatedly come to realize what could and could not be expected from Hitler[83] and that Hitler could not be trusted;* and (3) perhaps even more importantly, he had come to see Churchill as a shrewd colleague whose longstanding distrust of Hitler had proven justified.

Throughout Chamberlain's acquaintance with Churchill there had been tension between the two. For example, in 1925, when both were ministers in Baldwin's Cabinet, Chamberlain wrote that he liked Churchill—his humor, vitality and courage—"[b]ut there is somehow a great gulf between him and me which I don't think I shall ever cross."[84] Later, in 1933, when Churchill was among the first to use the term "appeasement" pejoratively to stigmatize its proponents as weak and myopic, Chamberlain deplored Churchill's actions, calling them an "abuse of his talent."[85] Moreover, during Chamberlain's tenure as P.M., there were countless times when he had been viciously attacked by Churchill. Chamberlain clearly resented these attacks and would have been justified despising Churchill to his dying day. Take what happened in August 1939. Parliament was to break for a two-month vacation. Churchill was the co-sponsor of a Labour amendment to the vacation bill calling for Parliament to reassemble in three weeks. The reason, which was known to everyone in London—including Chamberlain—was that Churchill and others feared that with Parliament adjourned, the P.M. could not be trusted and might try to make another Munich-like deal with Hitler. This and similar actions demonstrated Churchill's out-and-out disrespect for Chamberlain. And Chamberlain was a man who could really hold a grudge.**

Nonetheless, both the substantial animosity Chamberlain felt toward Churchill, and the disdain Churchill felt about Chamberlain's past actions, dissipated substantially between September 1939 and May 26, 1940. The two had created a "new relationship."[86] The transformation by which they wound up being respectful of, and incredibly loyal to, each other started on September 2, 1939, with Chamberlain's appointment of Churchill as First Lord of the Admiralty and a member of the War Cabinet.[87] Chamberlain's motive in appointing Churchill was purely practical—he needed to augment

---

*After Hitler invaded Czechoslovakia in March 1939, Chamberlain said, "No reliance [can] be placed on any of the assurances given by the Nazi leaders." CAB 23/1 12 (39) p. 8 50. He reiterated this position in October 1939 when he told the House that "The plain truth is that, after our past experience, it is no longer possible to rely upon the unsupported word of the present German Government." HC Deb 12 October 1939 vol 352 cc565–6. This was a perspective immediately seconded by Clement Attlee, whose comment about Hitler's promises was: "The first thing is that they are made by a man whose word is utterly worthless." Ibid.

**As discussed, he had held one against former P.M. Lloyd George for some twenty-three years. Chamberlain believed that Lloyd George had undercut his work as the Director of National Service in 1917, something which held him up to public reprobation for the next decade. See, Rock, Chamberlain pp. 46–48.

his War Cabinet with Britain's fiercest advocate for rearmament and wanted to keep his "enemy" close at hand—the appointment nonetheless put Churchill back in the Government for the first time in ten years, and he was extremely appreciative.

Ever the gadfly, as a member of the Chamberlain administration Churchill could more than occasionally still be annoying. Churchill and the P.M. did not agree on everything. But during Churchill's time in the Chamberlain administration, a bond was building between the two men. In fact, Chamberlain's records in 1939–40 abound with comments of admiration for Churchill.[88] They had given each other their word that they would stand or fall together in the storm.[89] Chamberlain had written Churchill that "your attitude to me is as loyal as mine is to you and I can't say more."[90] He also said that "Winston has behaved with the most unimpeachable loyalty."[91]

Even before that, during the debate on Norway in the Commons, members of the Labour Party had tried to insulate Churchill and allow the full blame for the debacle to fall on Chamberlain. But while these Labour attacks were warranted, Churchill refused to throw Chamberlain (or anyone in his Government) under the bus.[92] Rather, in his May 8, 1940 speech he not only defended the Government's actions in Norway, but urged the members of the House to "let pre-war feuds die. ... and that all the strong horses be pulling on the collar."[93]

That the loyalty flowed both ways is also evident not just in Chamberlain's May 1940 concurrence with Churchill against entering into any peace negotiations with Hitler. For example, on June 6, Churchill would write Chamberlain that he was considering inviting Lloyd George to join the Cabinet. Churchill was asking Chamberlain to sit with a man that Chamberlain loathed and whose motives he confessed he did not trust. That said, Chamberlain nonetheless agreed and added that the two-decade-long feud between him and Lloyd George should be buried. His private comment was that "one cannot refuse anything in times like these to the Prime Minister who is carrying the main burden of responsibility."[94]

Not only had Churchill been a loyal member of Chamberlain's Cabinet but he was genuinely gracious to his former boss when he himself became Prime Minister. Among other things, Churchill had made Chamberlain Lord President of the Privy Council, and he depended on him.[95] Lukacs writes that Chamberlain was not only unaccustomed to the magnanimity which Churchill had shown him but he appreciated and responded to it.[96] As a result of what truly were acts of friendship and respect, Churchill had no opposition from Chamberlain during the greatest crisis Britain had faced in centuries.[97] More importantly, "[w]hat [Churchill and Chamberlain] had come to agree on was that Hitler could not be trusted; indeed, that he must be rejected; ... that was enough."[98]

———

When the Cabinet Secretary Edward Bridges joined the 4:30 PM War Cabinet meeting on May 26, Churchill promptly directed these remarks to Halifax:

> We [are] in a different position from France. In the first place we still [have] powers of resistance and attack which they [do] not. In the second place, they [are] likely to be offered peace terms by Germany, which we would not. If France [can] not defend herself, it [is] better that she should get out of the war rather than that she should drag us into a settlement which involve[s] intolerable terms. There [is] no limit to the terms which Germany would impose upon us if she had her way. ... [I] would rather France was out of the war before she was broken up and retained the position of a strong neutral whose factories could not be used against us.[99]

Churchill added that he hoped "France would hang on":

> ... At the same time we must take care not to be forced into a weak position in which we [go] to Signor Mussolini and invite ... him to go to Herr Hitler and ask them to treat us nicely. We must not get entangled in a position of that kind before we [have] been involved in serious fighting.[100]

Halifax responded that he did not disagree with Churchill's view, but:

> ... he attached perhaps rather more importance than the Prime Minister to the desirability of allowing France to try out the possibilities of European equilibrium. He was not quite convinced that the Prime Minister's diagnosis was correct and that it was Herr Hitler's interest to insist on outrageous terms. ... On this lay-out it might be possible to save France from the wreck.[101]

To no one's surprise, Churchill disagreed.[102] Halifax tried to conclude the discussion by saying he could "see no harm in trying this line of approach."[103] Greenwood, the Labour Minister Without Portfolio, agreed but doubted Mussolini's power to take a line independent of Hitler.[104] Churchill then sought to table the discussion by saying "he thought that it was best to decide nothing until we [see] how much of the Army we [can] re-embark from France. The operation may be a great failure. ... It would also afford a real test of air superiority, since the Germans would attempt to bomb the ships and boats."[105]

Churchill thought the fatal flaw in the idea of approaching Mussolini was that it implied that if the Allies were prepared to give Germany back her colonies and to make certain concessions in the Mediterranean, then it was possible Britain could extricate itself from its present difficulties. The Prime Minister believed that, in fact, no such option was open. For example, he felt that the terms offered would prevent Britain from completing its rearmament.[106]* Halifax responded that if the terms proposed by Hitler were unacceptable, they could simply be rejected.[107]

The minutes of the War Cabinet session read as follows:

> THE PRIME MINISTER said that Hitler thought that he had the whip hand. The only thing to do was to show him that he could not conquer this country. If, on M. Reynaud's showing, France could not continue, we must part company. *At the same time, Churchill did not raise objection to some approach being made to Signor Mussolini.*"[108] [emphasis added]**

This certainly did not sound like Churchill "was considering peace talks with Germany."

**McCarten quotes Churchill as saying that "At the same time ... [I do] not raise objection to some approach being made to Signor Mussolini." McCarten p. 192. [bracketed words in McCarten's book; emphasis added] This, McCarten asserts, shows how Churchill's language and heart were changing from words like "never" to words like "consider" and agreeing to "not raise objection" to a first step taken in the peace process. Ibid. McCarten also says that Churchill made the statement to secure the support of "Halifax and Chamberlain whose support he desperately needed." Ibid. [emphasis added]*

As can be seen, the War Cabinet minutes do not, however, show that Churchill made as definitive a statement as McCarten attributes to him or, for that matter, that Churchill made any statement at all about approaching Mussolini. That is, they do not show that Churchill said or did anything to approve of Halifax's approach; they simply say that Churchill did not raise an objection. Indeed, if he had stayed silent on the point, that would fit within the ambit of "not rais[ing] an objection."

Put simply, the minutes, by their inexactness, do an extremely poor job of reflecting Churchill's position on the question. As of the date on which this book was written, the Cabinet Secretary's notebooks for the early years of the war have not been released for public view. Thus, the minutes of the session are the best evidence presently available.

John Lukacs writes that the minutes of the session were the first indication of what was to happen. The men stranded at Dunkirk were predominant in Churchill's mind. Halifax came back to the Italian matter and read out the account of his talk with Bastianini. Churchill, in turn, reiterated his position that the only thing to do was to show Hitler that he could not conquer his country. As Lukacs points out, when Churchill "did not raise objection to some approach being made to Signor Mussolini," all it "meant was that Churchill, at least momentarily, thought that he had to make some kind of concession to Halifax." Lukacs, Five Days p. 116. [emphasis in original]

A discussion ensued of what might comprise an offer to Mussolini. Suggesting that the Cabinet was quibbling about details, Halifax said he "thought that if we got to the point of discussing the terms of a general settlement and found that we could obtain terms which did not postulate the destruction of our independence, we should be foolish if we did not accept them."[109]

The War Cabinet then invited Halifax to circulate, for discussion among the group the next day, his draft of a communication to Italy, together with a record of his recent discussions with Ambassador Bastianini.[110] Toward the end of the meeting Halifax produced his "Suggested Approach to Signor Mussolini," which had been prepared after his meeting with Reynaud. The essence of it was:

> If Signor Mussolini will cooperate with us in securing a
> settlement of all European questions which safeguards the
> independence and the security of the Allies, and could be the
> basis of a just endurable peace for Europe, we will undertake
> at once to discuss, with the desire to find solutions, the matters
> in which Signor Mussolini is primarily interested.[111]

The Evacuation Order

After the meeting adjourned, a few minutes before 7:00 PM the order was given to start Operation Dynamo, the evacuation from Dunkirk. "... [N]o one thought that anything beyond a fraction of the British and French Troops, now surrounded and squeezed by the Germans, could escape to England."[112]

---

*As is revealed earlier by Chamberlain's agreement to permit Archie Sinclair,
Minister for Air and a proponent of Churchill's position, into future deliberations
on the subject of peace, the former P.M. had made his position clear. Contrary to
McCarten's assertion, after May 26, 1940, Churchill did not have to do anything
more to obtain the critical support of Neville Chamberlain. He already had it.*

17

Monday, May 27, 1940

The Germans Are North of Calais
Operation Dynamo, the Evacuations from Dunkirk, Begins; 7,700 Troops
  Are Evacuated; The Forecast for Removing Additional Troops Is Not
  Optimistic
Conversation with the French
Chamberlain Makes His Position on Peace Negotiations Clear
The War Cabinet Dissects the Reports by the Chiefs of Staff on Britain's
  Ability to Carry on the War Alone
The War Cabinet Continues to Discuss the Possibility of Peace
  Negotiations
Belgium Capitulates/Calais Had Fallen

The Germans Are North of Calais

At 7:15 AM Vice Admiral Sir James Somerville called from the Admiralty and woke Churchill. The Germans had advanced their guns to the north of Calais and were firing on ships as they approached Dunkirk.[1] The Luftwaffe was also bombing Dunkirk.[2] Because the British had decided it could not commit any more of the RAF to the battle in France, the Luftwaffe controlled the skies over Dunkirk.[3]

Operation Dynamo, the Evacuations from Dunkirk, Begins; 7,700 Troops Are Evacuated; The Forecast for Removing Additional Troops Is Not Optimistic

It had been no easy task to assemble the armada intended to evacuate the BEF from the continent. Just crossing the Channel from Ramsgate, a naval facility located just north of Dover, to Dunkirk was difficult, particularly for smaller craft. Here, the Channel was 40 miles wide and choppy. Lighted buoys and lightships had been blacked out. The British had also mined the Channel, forcing vessels to stay in narrow lanes. Worse yet, as the vessels neared the French coast, they became targets for strafing by the Luftwaffe.[4]

As bad as condition were, there was a small consolation in that things could have been worse. During the Norway campaign, Britain had sunk three German cruisers and ten or eleven of its twenty-two destroyers.[5] Moreover, Germany's only two operational battleships, the *Scharnhorst* and the *Gneisenau*—and the pocket battleship (heavy cruiser) *Luetzow*— were all put out of service for several months.[6] Proportional to the size of its navy, those losses were substantial, so much so that the German Navy, which could have significantly disrupted the Dunkirk evacuation, did not even leave port.[7] Those ships would also not be available to participate in any possible German invasion of Britain in the summer of 1940.

On May 27, the first day of the evacuation at Dunkirk, small craft made the run in toward the beach, picked up as many men as they could, and shuttled them out to the destroyers and channel ferries that lay offshore.[8] Others small vessels carried soldiers all the way back to England. Despite these heroic efforts, by the end of the day only 7,669 men had been evacuated.[9] "… [T]he little craft could not do the job alone"—a new strategy was needed if the BEF and French troops were to be saved.[10]

Conversation with the French

The 11:30 AM meeting of the War Cabinet commenced with Churchill and Chamberlain summarizing their conversation the previous afternoon with French Premier Reynaud. Although Reynaud had sought to portray the BEF's withdrawal from Arras as having made it impossible for the French to counterattack from the south, the Premier eventually accepted Britain's contrary point of view and agreed, without recrimination, that the BEF must be withdrawn to the coast.[11] General John Dill's staff pointed out to the Cabinet that just getting the entire BEF to Dunkirk would take two or three more days. The gap through which they could withdraw was very narrow, and only two roads were available.[12]

Chamberlain Makes His Position on Peace Negotiations Clear

Chamberlain then informed the Cabinet, through his discussion of a meeting he'd had with the High Commissioners for Australia, New Zealand, and South Africa the previous evening, that he supported Churchill's position; even if France were to fall, he believed Britain should fight rather than negotiate with the Germans.[13] The Commissioners had taken a most gloomy view of Britain's prospects if France went out of the war. In Chamberlain's notable response to them he pointed out that "it was too soon to give any definite opinion in the matter. Our dangers were clear, but Germany would have her difficulties also, and even fighting single-handed we might well outlast her."[14] Chamberlain then told the Commissioners that "even if France went out of the war, *there was no prospect of our giving in.* We had good reason to believe that we could withstand attack by Germany and *we will resolve to fight on.*"[15] [emphasis added]

Interestingly, there is a note in the Confidential Annex where Chamberlain's statement was recorded which reads: "(This statement would apply of course to the immediate situation arising out of the hypothetical collapse of France. It would not mean that if at any time terms were offered, they would *not* be considered on their merits)."[16] [emphasis added]

Halifax must have been disappointed to hear that his old friend, Neville Chamberlain, a man whom he had supported throughout his premiership, had (in a phrase associated with Churchill) "crossed the floor" and was now a member of the Churchill team. Halifax probably also knew at this point that getting the War Cabinet to support his position that Britain should negotiate with Hitler was highly unlikely. Nevertheless, though the odds were long, he was still going to try hard to persuade Cabinet members that his position was the correct one.

Biographer Robert Self points out how ironic it was that Chamberlain, "the high priest of appeasement," played such a pivotal role in the triumph of "Churchill's strategy of blind resistance over Halifax's pleas for a negotiated settlement."[17] As discussed, without Chamberlain's support, Churchill's position "would have been dangerously compromised, even undermined."[18] The consequences would have been profound "for the history of Churchill's wartime Government, Britain and the entire free world."[19] Chamberlain's critical support was fostered by the genuine loyalty shown to him by Churchill. Without that support, Churchill may have been forced into peace negotiations or forced to resign so that a new Prime Minister could take Britain into peace negotiations.

Churchill had been able to cast off his lifelong role as a fiercely independent critic not only of the opposition but also the leadership of whichever party he belonged.* Likewise, Chamberlain had been able to jettison his anger at Churchill and become a valuable and loyal colleague.

The War Cabinet Dissects the Reports by the Chiefs of Staff on Britain's Ability to Carry on the War Alone

At that point in the session, the Chiefs of Staff (COS) presented their review of the May 25 "Main Report" on Britain's ability to carry on the war alone, in light of the "Terms of Reference" (the hypothetical conditions) that Churchill had provided them.[20]

Churchill immediately took issue with the "Main Report," saying that it "did not give a true picture of the position." In particular, he challenged

---

*A role he had picked up from his late father.

the tables in the report purporting to show the relative strength of the RAF and the Luftwaffe.[21] In response, R.E.C. Peirce (Vice Chief of the Air Staff) conceded that the figures in the table were not completely comparable. The figures for the RAF referred to operational strength (number of aircraft ready for use), while the figures for Germany referred to first-line strength.* Peirce then handed the War Cabinet a new table attempting to show a somewhat more favorable difference when the figures were calculated more comparably.[22] The Prime Minister observed that based on the new table "... it appeared that the odds against us were only 2½ to 1," but "If our airmen were shooting down 3 to 1, the balance was on our side."[23]

Churchill next challenged the COS's assumption that the collapse of France would automatically result in German control of all French ports and airfields.[24] Chamberlain followed by reiterating a point made by Secretary for Air Sinclair, that air superiority should not be measured only by numbers of planes but by their quality and the morale of the pilots as well.[25] He did, however, express concern over the warning in the Main Report that German night bombing of aircraft factories could bring British aircraft production to a halt.[26]

In contrast to the pessimistic tone of the Main Report, in light of the "Terms of Reference" that Churchill had provided them, the supplemental review was far more optimistic. The Chiefs' "new" principal conclusion was much like the one set out in the Chiefs' May 10 report: "While our air force is in being, our Navy and Air Force together should be able to prevent Germany carrying out a serious seaborne invasion of this country."[27]**

This principal conclusion of the supplemental review was followed by two simple explanatory statements:

> Supposing Germany gained complete air superiority, we consider that the Navy could hold up an invasion for a time, *but not for an indefinite period.* [and]

> If, with our Navy unable to prevent it and our air force gone, Germany attempted an invasion, our coast and beach defences could not prevent German tanks and infantry getting a firm footing on our shores. In the circumstances envisaged above our land forces would be insufficient to deal with a serious invasion.[28] [emphasis added]

Those for which full support existed, including pilots, maintenance, etc.

**In the May 10, 1940, report the COS had concluded that "Under existing conditions, when fighter protection can be provided at any point on our coast likely to be threatened, there is no reason to revise our previous conclusion that 'so long as our naval and air forces remain in being and, provided the necessary precautions are maintained, effectively invasion is not a serious danger.'" CAB 66/7 WP (40) 153 Annex I p. 5 228 Para 6. [emphasis added]*

Despite all the cross examination and debate that took place, in the end the War Cabinet gave general approval to the bland recommendations contained in the COS's "Main Report."[29] Among those recommendations were: persuade the US to provide fighter aircraft; be economical with anti-aircraft ammunition; and strengthen Britain's intelligence system to get early warning of German preparations for an invasion.[30]

Permanent Under-Secretary of State for Foreign Affairs Alexander Cadogan wrote in his diary that "Cabinet at 11:30—as gloomy as ever. See very little light anywhere."[31] Similarly, Jock Colville's diary contained the following entry:

> ... The situation [is] much blacker than when I left on Friday. It appears that a grave deterioration has taken place in the last 48 hours: the BEF, unable to force their way southwards, have got to retreat to the coast as best they can and re-embark for England from whatever Channel ports remain open to them. The French seem to be demoralized and there is now a serious fear that they may collapse. The Cabinet are feverishly considering our ability to carry on the war alone in such circumstances, and there are signs that Halifax is being defeatist. He says that our aim can no longer be to crush Germany but rather to preserve our integrity and independence.[32]

The War Cabinet Continues to Discuss the Possibility of Peace Negotiations

The War Cabinet reconvened at 4:30 PM for what Lukacs calls "the most critical of the nine War Cabinet sessions held" in the three days from May 26 to 28.[33]*

Unlike most War Cabinet meetings, which were attended by twenty people or more and typically covered a wide variety of subjects, the 4:30 session on May 27th concerned only one topic: the suggested approach to Mussolini about peace negotiations. It was also attended by only eight: Churchill; his War Cabinet (Halifax, Chamberlain, Clement Attlee, and Arthur Greenwood); and Secretary of State for Air Archibald Sinclair, who, as discussed earlier, was participating in the deliberations by special permission. Also in the room were Alexander Cadogan and Secretary of the Cabinet Sir Edward Bridges.[34]

The War Cabinet had before it a memorandum prepared by Halifax[35] revealing that at a meeting the previous day, French Premier Reynaud had "enquired whether His Majesty's Government would join with the French

---

Interestingly, neither Churchill nor Halifax mentions this session in their postwar books.

Government in making a direct approach to Signor Mussolini." But that "Monsieur Reynaud was not given any definite reply."[36] Halifax reiterated that, since this memorandum had been circulated, President Roosevelt had approached Mussolini along the lines suggested in the memorandum.[37] Churchill had, however, already pointed out to the War Cabinet that there was much difference between a British approach to Mussolini and one coming from Roosevelt, who would be doing so ostensibly on his own initiative.[38]*

Chamberlain then referred back to Halifax's talk with Italian Ambassador Bastianini a few days earlier and said that this conversation had strongly confirmed the view he had had for some time that Mussolini saw himself coming in as a peacemaker and disposer of benefits to the various countries that were the principal players in the war. Chamberlain also thought Mussolini still had the idea that, when the vital moment came to pursue peace, he could play an important role and get a share of the spoils for Italy.[39] Chamberlain did not, however, believe that Hitler saw Mussolini as playing a part in any resolution. Essentially, Chamberlain believed that the proposed approach to Mussolini, which in part was intended to keep Italy out of the war, would serve no useful purpose.[40] The former Prime Minister was also concerned that the French might intend to tell Mussolini that they had had a magnificent scheme to repel the German invasion of France, but the BEF chose to withdraw and thus let down by her British ally, all France could do was take the best means available to extricate herself from the war. The French might add that Britain had even been unwilling to allow them the opportunity to negotiate with Italy.[41]

Once Chamberlain had made known his opposition to approaching Mussolini, the other members of the Churchill team also started attacking the proposal. Archie Sinclair agreed that the approach was useless, adding that Britain was in a tight corner and showing any weakness would both encourage the Germans and the Italians and undermine British morale. He added that the suggestion that Britain was prepared to barter away pieces of territory would also have a deplorable effect and make it difficult to continue the desperate struggle.[42] Clement Attlee and Arthur Greenwood were of a similar mind, thinking that "it would be heading for disaster to go any further with an approach to Mussolini.[43]

At that point in the debate, Churchill tried to put a stake through the heart of the idea of approaching Mussolini once and for all by listing most, if not all, of the negatives associated with doing so. The meeting minutes read as follows:

Roosevelt, Reynaud, and Halifax all believed that if peace negotiations with Germany were to have any chance of success there had to be an intermediary to whom Hitler might listen involved in the process and that there was no one other than Mussolini to fill that role.

The PRIME MINISTER said that he was increasingly oppressed with the futility of the suggested approach to Signor Mussolini, which the latter would certainly regard with contempt. Such an approach would do M. Reynaud far less good than if he made a firm stand. Further *the approach would ruin the integrity of our fighting position in this country.* ... Personally, he doubted whether France was so willing to give up the struggle as M. Reynaud had represented. ... Anyway let us not be dragged down with France. ...

At the moment our prestige in Europe was very low. The only way we can get it back was by showing the world that Germany had not beaten us. If after two or three months, we can show that we were still unbeaten, our prestige would return. Even if we were beaten, we should be no worse off than we should be if we were now to abandon the struggle. Let us therefore avoid being dragged down the slippery slope with France. The whole of this manoeuver was intended to get us so deeply involved in negotiations that we should be unable to turn back. We had gone a long way already in our approach to Italy but let us not allow M. Reynaud to get us involved in a confused situation. *The approach proposed was not only futile but involved us in a* deadly danger.[44] [emphasis added]*

Halifax clearly wanted peace negotiations immediately to avoid what loomed as a fight to the death between England and Germany over control of the British Isles. But when he suggested that Britain should get no worse terms than she would get that day, May 27, 1940, Churchill showed only a willingness to negotiate later— once Britain had lost potentially hundreds of thousands of its citizens in defending their island and had either resisted a German invasion, Confidential Annex to CAB 65/ 1 140 (40) p. 6 151, or were beaten. Ibid. p. 1 184.

McCarten thus asserts that at that point the essential disagreement became "not if [peace negotiations] should be sought, but when." McCarten p.264. [emphasis in original] Technically, McCarten is correct. What Halifax wanted was to pursue peace negotiations before Britain had suffered huge losses as it continued to fight the Germans. An analogy would have been if the Japanese had sought to end the war before Hiroshima and Nagasaki were destroyed, rather than after the US had dropped two atomic bombs and firebombed Tokyo.

The stark contrast of Churchill's position (fight first and negotiate later, if at all) makes it hard to say that Churchill "seriously entertained the prospect of a peace deal with Hitler in May 1940." Ibid. p. 259. Stated differently, if Churchill had entertained any thought of a peace deal, it was not one that would have tried to avert the looming life-and-death battle with Germany. It certainly was quite different from what Halifax wanted.

Though Chamberlain agreed with Churchill that the approach proposed by Halifax would not serve any useful purpose, he thought the Cabinet still ought to go a little further with it in order to keep the French in good temper. That is, rather than refusing to submit the letter to Mussolini as France wanted, Britain should tell France that because Roosevelt had now made an approach to Italy along the same lines as France proposed to do, it would only confuse the issue if Britain were now to barge in on its own.[45]

Even though Halifax's cause appeared to be lost, as Lukacs writes, Halifax still "felt compelled to confront Churchill directly" and more forcefully than he had on the 26th. "... [I]f their differences were irreconcilable, [Halifax] was thinking of resigning."[46] In McCarten's view, "The ensuing discussion would finally pitch Halifax and those who supported him—a large proportion of the ruling Conservative Party—full force against one of their own: Winston's stubborn will to fight on alone seemed, to Halifax, impervious to reason and against the country's best interests."[47]

Knowing that he had virtually no chance of getting the War Cabinet to approve approaching Mussolini about a negotiated peace, Halifax said he saw no particular difficulty following Chamberlain's suggestion to be gentle when telling the French that Britain did not support the idea of a letter to Mussolini. But he also wanted to address the profoundly differing points of view among the Cabinet members. He angrily added that he could not recognize any resemblance between the action he had proposed and the assertion made by both Churchill and Greenwood that, pursuant to it, Britain would be suing for terms and following a line which would lead it to disaster.[48]

Halifax then reviewed the twists and turns in his disagreement with Churchill over the past few days. According to Halifax, he had asked Churchill in the War Cabinet meeting held the previous afternoon if the Prime Minister would be prepared to discuss peace terms if he were satisfied that matters vital to the independence of the country were unaffected. Churchill, he said, responded that he would be thankful to get out of the present difficulties, provided Britain retained the essentials and the elements of its vital strength, even at the cost of some cession of territory.[49]

Halifax then asserted that Churchill had since changed his position, when declaring that two or three months would show whether Britain could stand up against the expected air assault.[50] As Halifax put it rather sarcastically, Churchill's proposal meant that the future of Britain would turn on whether the enemy's bombs happened to hit English aircraft factories. Pressing ahead, Halifax said that though Churchill was prepared to take that risk if British independence were at stake, it appeared he was prepared to take the same risk if independence was assured but the country faced avoidable disaster.[51] Halifax thought that Churchill's position was at best illogical, at worst insane. (Churchill's position that Britain would persevere irrespective of the cost, was not, however, a new one. In 1925, talking about what Britain would do if Germany controlled all the Channel ports in Europe, Churchill said, "If in addition to sea superiority we had air supremacy, ... if the worst comes to worst, [Britain could] stand alone."[52]) Churchill, not wanting to get tied up in unlikely hypotheticals, responded that "If Herr Hitler was prepared to make peace on the terms of the restoration of German colonies and the overlordship of Central Europe that was one thing. But it was quite unlikely that he would make such an offer."[53]

McCarten writes, "This was *some* admission."[54] [emphasis in original] Seemingly, it was a significant reversal of position. McCarten notes that just the day before Churchill had told the War Cabinet that German domination of Europe was something that "we could never accept."[55] McCarten asks, "What was Churchill playing at?"[56] Roberts has an answer: "... this was in fact always Churchill's [position]."[57]

Churchill may not have considered his statement to have been a change in thinking because (a) he didn't believe that Hitler would agree to a lasting peace in exchange for the restoration of former German colonies; (b) for years he had believed that if worst came to worst Britain could stand alone against Germany; (c) he had long since made up his mind not to enter into peace negotiations;* (d) Churchill believed that "[a]n accepted leader has only to be sure of what it is best to do, or at least had made up his mind about it."[58]** and (e) as Lukacs writes, "Churchill did not for a moment believe that Britain and the Empire could continue to exist across from a Europe entirely dominated by Germany."[59] Indeed, he fervently believed that "German domination of Europe was intolerable."[60] After all it had been British policy for four hundred years to oppose the strongest power in Europe, whether it was Spain, France, or Germany.[61]

Chamberlain quickly interjected that if concrete proposals were put before the War Cabinet it would be easy to settle what were and were not essential items that must be retained to assure Britain's independence.[62] Believing that Churchill had been evasive, Halifax then posed the following question:

> Suppose the French army collapsed and Herr Hitler made an
> offer of peace terms and suppose the French Government said,
> "We are unable to deal with an offer made to France alone and

---

*Churchill's viewpoint was made clear many times, including in the following: his speech to Parliament on May 13, 1940; his comments to the War Cabinet on May 15; the telegram he sent to Roosevelt that same day; his telegram to Mussolini of May 16; his speech over the BBC on May 19; his telegram to Roosevelt of May 20; his statement at the Defence Committee meeting on May 25; and his statement to Reynaud at lunch on May 26.

**As such, Churchill likely felt that nothing he said should have been construed as a change in his thinking.

you must deal with the Allies together." Suppose Herr Hitler, being anxious to end the war through knowledge of his own internal weaknesses, offered terms to the French and England, would the Prime Minister be prepared to discuss them?[63]

Churchill responded that he would not join France in asking for terms but if he were informed of the terms offered, he would be prepared to consider them.[64]

Seeing that Halifax was backing Churchill into an uncomfortable corner, Chamberlain quickly interceded again and reset the scenario. He said that, in his view, Hitler's tactics would likely be to make a definite offer to France, and when the French responded that they had Allies, Hitler would say, "I am here, let them send a delegation to Paris."[65] Posed in that fashion, the Churchill team had no problem saying that the answer to such an offer could only be "No."[66]*

As the meeting neared its end, Halifax threatened to resign if Britain refused to enter peace negotiations.[67] He told Cadogan that "I can't work with Winston anymore." Cadogan replied, "Nonsense, his rodomontades[**] probably bore you as much as they do me, but don't do anything silly under the stress of that."[68]

Halifax requested a private meeting with Churchill out in the garden of 10 Downing St.[69] What exactly they discussed is not known.[70] It is likely that Halifax threatened to resign. It is doubtful that during the brief stroll Churchill convinced Halifax of the correctness of carrying on with the war. However, Lukacs feels that Churchill was likely "able to charm and sooth

---

In his biography of Halifax, Roberts writes that when Halifax tried to pin Churchill down he was "angry at the way Churchill had twisted and misrepresented his arguments." He also was trying to "[take] advantage of Churchill's attempt to be as moderate as possible—the better to sell his policy to the War Cabinet and in particular to carry Chamberlain with him." Roberts, The Holy Fox pp. 295.

By the time Halifax pressed his case, Churchill already knew he had the support needed to reject the French proposal to approach Mussolini about peace terms. Thus, if Churchill had adopted a moderate tone, it likely was because he was sure his viewpoint would prevail. He did not want to lose any of the "votes" he had already lined up. Most particularly, although unlikely, he did not want to lose Chamberlain's support.

McCarten writes that Halifax was also angry at being hung out to dry for all in the room to see. McCarten p. 208. It is likely that Halifax was incredulous and frustrated at the fact that no one else in the War Cabinet was willing to embrace the logic of a negotiated peace, especially since, on its face, it could potentially save hundreds of thousands of lives and the existence of an independent Britain.

**Boastful statements.

Halifax somewhat," and more importantly remind the Foreign Secretary that his resignation at that moment would likely create a "national crisis."[71]

Halifax wrote this in his diary that night: "I thought Winston talked about the most frightful rot, also Greenwood, and after bearing it for some time I said exactly what I thought of them, adding that, if that was really their view, and if it came to the point, our ways must separate."[72] Amazingly, he also wrote that Churchill had surprised him when he said he would not join France in asking for terms but if he were told what the terms offered were, he would be prepared to consider them.[73]

McCarten asserts that the May 27 War Cabinet session was a victory for Halifax, that this was "the zenith of Halifax's power, and influence, for he had steered a reluctant leader from almost histrionic talk of victory at all costs to a serious embrace of the notion of peace talks, to a consideration of when, not if, such talk should take place."[74] But is this true? It seems that all Churchill did was table the question.*

Later that afternoon, after the stroll in the garden, a telegram came in from Lord Lothian, the Ambassador to the US, describing a conversation he had had with Roosevelt. Lord Lothian was left with the impression that if England were really in extremis the US would come to its aid.

At 7:00 PM the Defence Committee met to discuss the situation in France.[75] There, Churchill explained that the situation there was worsening and that the BEF's only choice was to fight their way back to the coast and be evacuated.[76] After the meeting, Churchill received the message that Belgium was trying to arrange an armistice with Germany and was suggesting a ceasefire at midnight.[77] In light of these, Churchill summoned the War Cabinet back into session at 10:00 PM.

Belgium Capitulates/Calais Had Fallen

At the meeting, the P.M. transmitted the message about Belgium. General Dill said that the collapse of the Belgians would place the BEF in serious peril. The absence of Belgian forces would create a gap on the BEF's left. General Gort had no troops with which to close that gap and prevent the Germans from breaking through it and proceeding to Dunkirk.[78] Nonetheless, Churchill advised the Belgians that Britain would do its best to evacuate as much of the Belgian Army as could make its way to Dunkirk.[79] Secretary of

---

*As it turned out, the situation three months later was that the Blitz had not yet started and Britain was hanging on in the Battle of Britain. This was at least a partial vindication of Churchill's hope that Britain could stand up against the air risk. Britain had also conducted a very successful naval operation that destroyed French ships anchored at Mers-el-Kébir in Algeria. That operation, in fact, "ended talk of a British surrender." Manchester and Reid p. 110.

State for War Anthony Eden added to the bad news by announcing it was now clear that Calais had fallen.[80]

That evening in Paris, General Spears, Churchill's personal representative to the French Government, and British Ambassador Hugh Campbell were summoned to the Ministry of War. News of the sudden Belgian surrender had infuriated Reynaud, Marshal Pétain, and General Weygand. Spears, briefly encouraged by this show of emotion, became irritated by Weygand's criticism of General Gort. In the end, Spears noted that he "sensed a break in the relationship between [France and Britain]. ..."[81]

Troops evacuating from Dunkirk back to Britain

18

TUESDAY, MAY 28, 1940

The Evacuation from Dunkirk Continues, Although Many Ships Are Lost
Mussolini Rejects Roosevelt's Most Recent Approach
Belgium Formally Surrenders
Continuing Discussion in the House and the War Cabinet
Churchill Meets with the Outer Cabinet; Tells Them That There Is No
   Chance of Britain Giving Up the Struggle, and They Approve
The Idea of Britain's Entering Any Peace Negotiations Is Closed
Low Expectations for the Dunkirk Evacuation

At the 11:30 AM War Cabinet meeting, Churchill announced that the Belgian Army had ceased firing at 0400 hours that morning.[1] The King of Belgium would now presumably become a puppet of Hitler and might obtain better treatment for his people than if he had left the country and continued to resist from foreign soil. Churchill had no doubt that history would criticize the King for having involved Britain and France in Belgium's ruin. But he himself refused to pass judgment on him.[2]

Churchill then read the ministers the terms of the armistice just agreed to by the Belgians:

1. All Belgian troop movements forbidden. Belgian troops must line up on the side of the road to await orders. They must make known their presence by means of white signs, flags, etc.

2. Orders must be given forbidding destruction of war material and stores.

3. German troops must be allowed to proceed to the coast.

4. Free passage to Ostend is demanded and no destruction permitted.

5. All resistance will be overcome.[3]

A telegram from General Gort described the situation at Dunkirk in bleak terms:

- impossible to use Dunkirk docks;

- only a few wounded can be evacuated owing to damage to the town;

- water in the Dunkirk area and elsewhere is very limited;

- 20,000 men, huddled in the dunes on the beach, now await embarkation;

- food must be landed on beaches;

- many refugees, French troops and Belgian troops are in the area;

- no doubt that if air attacks continue at present intensity, the area will become a shambles; and

- such a situation might easily arise in the next 48 hours.[4]

The Evacuation from Dunkirk Continues, Although Many Ships Are Lost

First Sea Lord Admiral Dudley Pound reported that 11,400 men had arrived in England from Dunkirk the previous night, and 2,500 more were presently in passage across the Channel. He said there were now five destroyers at Dunkirk, each of which was taking on about a thousand men; but a considerable number of troops continued to pour into the seaside town.[5] On May 28, 17,804 men would be evacuated.[6] Some three hundred thousand remained.

Whatever comfort the ministers may have felt hearing the evacuation numbers was soon dashed by the rest of Pound's report. The SS *Abukir*, a British coastal steamship that had left the nearby Belgian port of Ostend the previous night with about a thousand men on board had been torpedoed; only thirty-three survivors had been picked up.[7] The *Queen of the Channel*, a large cross-channel excursion ferry, had also been bombed and was sinking; but it was believed the survivors had been taken off.[8] The men on the bombed paddle wheel steamer SS *Fenella*, however, were not as fortunate: six hundred were reported lost. Overloaded evacuation boats often capsized, drowning the soldiers who had been aboard.[9] Based on a later dispatch, Pound reassured the War Cabinet that destroyers would be taking men off the quays throughout the day. Also, a maximum effort would be made that night to send in flat-bottomed boats to take men off the beaches; embarkation by this means being impossible during the day because of German machine-gun fire.[10]

Using destroyers was an important revision to the original evacuation plan, which had depended on small shuttle vessels; and a hunch by an ingenious senior naval officer in Dunkirk would greatly expand the role British destroyers would take in the evacuation. The officer, Captain Bill Tennant, observed that of the two long wooden breakwaters (called "moles"), which each extended nearly a mile into Dunkirk harbor, the eastern one had yet to be damaged by German air strikes.[11] Though the moles were not built for docking boats, even small ones,[12] Tennant surmised that large ships might be able to sidle up to the eastern mole and evacuate more troops than the small craft could from the beaches. The mole was less than ideal as an embarkation point because at low tide it was much higher than any ship being loaded. Evacuating soldiers therefore had to make a hazardous leap to get on board.[13] As luck would have it, the eastern mole held. With help from some ships' carpenters, it remained operational even after sustaining a direct hit from a Luftwaffe bomb. That it survived the next six days was miraculous.[14] A week later Churchill would tell the House that the entire Dunkirk evacuation had been "a miracle of deliverance."[15] More than 70 percent of the men successfully evaluated from Dunkirk left the embattled port by way of the eastern mole.

After discussing the status of the evacuation, Minister of Information Alfred Duff Cooper read a message he had just received from the Ministry, which wanted a frank statement from the War Cabinet about the situation of the BEF. It feared the absence of such a statement would badly shake public confidence, and the population would not be ready to accept the Government's assurances of ultimate victory. Duff Cooper suggested that Churchill make a short statement for the BBC's one o'clock news.[16]

Churchill said he would also make a statement in the House of Commons that afternoon. In it, he would explain that the BEF was fighting its way back to the coast under the protection of the Royal Air Force, and that the Royal Navy was continuing to evacuate troops back to Britain. He pointed out, however, that it would be foolish for him to try to forecast the success of this operation in either speech.[17] Air Marshal Sir Cyril Newall, Chief of the Air Staff, wanted the Cabinet to know that on the previous day he had issued a special order to all his Commanders-in-Chief emphasizing the need for exceptional efforts to support the BEF and the naval forces carrying out the evacuation. He had also ordered Air Officer Commanding-in-Chief, Fighter Command, Hugh Dowding to maintain continuous patrols over Dunkirk and the beaches three miles east of it, to provide escorts for bomber sorties, and to support the BEF itself.[18] Newall added that Dowding was deeply concerned how those orders might affect the air defense of Great Britain. Dowding said, "Our fighter defences are almost at cracking point. If this exceptional effort has to be repeated over Dunkirk tomorrow, the situation will be serious."[19] Newall did not accept the statement that Britain's fighter defenses were "at cracking point," but he thought it only right to bring Dowding's concern to the attention of the War Cabinet.[20] Churchill speculated that the enemy might perhaps capitalize on the situation and launch a heavy attack against the United Kingdom. "Our fighter defences," he said, "might have to be redeployed to meet it, but no doubt the enemy was fully extended like ourselves."[21]

Mussolini Rejects Roosevelt's Most Recent Approach

The group was then advised that a telegram from the Ambassador to Washington, Lord Lothian, said, "the response of Signor Mussolini to [President Roosevelt's] communication had been entirely negative."[22]

Belgium Formally Surrenders

In other bad news, Belgian King Leopold, as expected, had surrendered his entire 274,000-man army.[23] This capitulation created a twenty-mile gap between the BEF's II Corps and the coast.[24] General Gort promptly moved his 5th Division, which had been scheduled for the impossible southern adventure, into the gap left by the Belgians. There, the BEF trying to withdraw to Dunkirk felt the full fury of the Nazi attack in continual battles between the Belgian cities of Warneton and Ypres, each located about 25 miles southeast of Dunkirk.[25]

Continuing Discussion in the House and in the War Cabinet

In his speech to the House that afternoon, Churchill said that the situation facing the BEF and the French 1st Army, who were engaged with the Germans on three sides as well as in the air, was extremely grave. The Belgian surrender had made things even worse. He stated he would report back to the House when the outcome of the struggle was known, but in the meantime, the House "should prepare itself for hard and heavy tidings."[26] Lastly, he declared that "I have only to add that nothing which may happen in this battle can in any way relieve us of our duty to defend the world cause to which we have vowed ourselves; nor should it destroy our confidence in our power to make our way ... to the ultimate defeat of our enemies."[27] The House responded positively to Churchill's note of defiance.[28]

The War Cabinet met again at 4:00 PM in the Prime Minister's Room at the House of Commons to consider a message received from the French

Government reiterating its position that Britain and France should directly approach Mussolini. The meeting produced fascinating interchanges among Cabinet members and served as the prelude to Churchill's ending the discussion of the idea that Britain should seek peace negotiations. Halifax opened the session by stating, in his excruciatingly convoluted way, that senior diplomat Lord Vansittart had advised that the Italian Embassy felt Britain should clarify its desire to have mediation by Italy.[29] Churchill knew that the French wanted to see Mussolini act as intermediary between Britain and Hitler, but he was "determined not to get into that position."[30] Halifax's retort was to remind Churchill that the proposal discussed with French Premier Reynaud just two days earlier stated that, while Britain was prepared to fight to the death for its independence, it was also prepared, provided its independence could be secured, to make concessions to Italy[31]—i.e., ceding them Malta and Gibraltar.[32]

Churchill did not directly respond to Halifax. Instead, he said, "the French were trying to get us on to the slippery slope."[33] He added: "the position would be entirely different when Germany had made an unsuccessful attempt to invade this country."[34] Chamberlain interjected that making concessions to Italy would have to be part of a general settlement with Germany. No settlement with Italy that left Germany still at war would be of any value.[35] He continued, agreeing with Churchill that Premier Reynaud wanted to get Mussolini engaged in conversations and that Reynaud would then try and turn those conversations into a conference.[36] If England rejected the terms offered at that conference, Reynaud would "abuse us [just] as he had abused the Belgians [this] morning."[37]

Arthur Greenwood, Minister without Portfolio, then added: "If we agreed to the French taking an approach along the lines proposed, the integrity of our position would be seriously jeopardized."[38] At this point the discussion broadened. Halifax acknowledged there was little prospect that anything would result from an approach along the lines suggested by the French. But he quickly added that, assuming Mussolini wished to play the part of mediator and could produce terms that would not affect British independence, he believed Britain ought to consider them. To avoid appearing too pushy on the point, Halifax admitted that "this hypothesis was a most unlikely one."[39]

After Secretary of State for Air Archie Sinclair agreed there was no possibility of acceptable terms being offered at the present moment,[40] Halifax countered by saying London must not ignore the fact that it might get better terms now—before France went out of the war and British aircraft factories were bombed—than it might in three months' time.[41] Halifax's view, of course, conflicted with Churchill's belief that Britain should make no peace overture until after the fight for Britain had been concluded, either from an unsuccessful invasion attempt by Germany or from a British defeat.[42] As

Churchill reiterated, "We should get no worse terms if we went on fighting, even if we were beaten, than were open to us now."[43]

Reading a draft statement expressing his views, Churchill said that, to him, the essential point was that French Premier Reynaud wanted to get Britain to the conference table with Hitler. "If once we got to the table, we should then find that the terms offered us touched our independence and integrity. When, at this point, we got up to leave the Conference table, we should find that all the forces of resolution which were now at our disposal would have vanished. M. Reynaud had said that if he could save the independence of France, he would continue the fight. It was clear, therefore that M. Reynaud's aim was to end the war."[44]

Chamberlain generally agreed, but said it was important to understand the French position and to frame the answer to the French in a way which would be convincing to them.[45] He thought that the elements in a reply to Premier Reynaud should be along these lines:

> ...[W]e regarded the suggested offer contained in his letter as a not very substantial one, which opened up no real prospect of influencing Signor Mussolini's attitude. The only object likely to be achieved by offering these concessions was to induce Signor Mussolini to adopt the position of a mediator.
>
> In our view, mediation at this stage, in the presence of a great disaster, and at a time when many people might think that we had no more resources left, could only have the most unfortunate results. We in this country feel that we have resources left to us of which we can make good use. If, as we believe, we can hold out, we should be able to obtain terms which would not affect our independence.
>
> We concluded, therefore, that, without prejudice to the future, the present was not the time at which advances should be made to Signor Mussolini. If, however, both France and Great Britain continued to play their part in the struggle, we were likely to fare better than if we now allowed ourselves to become involved in negotiations with Signor Mussolini.[46]

The War Cabinet discussed and ultimately adopted Reynaud's suggestion that an appeal be made for Roosevelt to take part in the mediation. Seeming like an attempt to pour a bit of salt on Halifax's wound, Churchill returned to the topic of why mediation now was a bad idea,[47] saying:

> ...[T]he French wanted to get out of the war but did not want to break their Treaty obligations to us. Signor Mussolini, if he

came in as mediator, would take his whack out of us. It was impossible to imagine that Herr Hitler would be so foolish as to let us continue our re-armament. In effect, his terms would put us completely at his mercy. We should get no worse terms if we went on fighting, even if we were beaten, than were open to us now. If, however, we continued the war and Germany attacked us, no doubt we should suffer some damage, but they also would suffer severe losses. Their oil supplies might be reduced. A time might come when we felt that we had to put an end to the struggle, but the terms would not then be more mortal than those offered to us now.[48]

Roberts describes this as "an attempt [by Churchill] to seem reasonable but yet to outmaneuver Halifax."[49]

Perhaps a bit staggered, but certainly not down, Halifax responded that he still did not see what was so wrong with the French suggestion of trying out the possibilities of mediation.[50] Chamberlain, as he had done the previous day, again stepped in and sought to move on the conversation past this two-man argument. As the meeting minutes reflect he said, "it was clear to the world that we are in a tight corner," and he did not see "what we should lose if we said openly that, while we would fight to the end to preserve our independence, we were ready to consider decent terms if such were offered to us."[51] To temper this somewhat pro-mediation statement, Chamberlain promptly added, "it was right to remember that the alternative to fighting on still involved a considerable gamble."[52]

The War Cabinet agreed that Chamberlain had presented a true statement of the case.[53] As Roberts correctly notes, "[n]o official vote was taken, but [once again] Chamberlain and the two Labour members supported Churchill's stance."[54] Churchill, unable to resist one more jab at Halifax, commented that "... nations that went down fighting rose again, but those which surrendered tamely, were finished."[55] But, that statement was nothing compared to what would follow. Arthur Greenwood, whether or not intended, proceeded to pour gasoline on the fire by saying, "any course which we take is attended by great danger. The line of resistance is certainly a gamble, but [he did] not feel that this was a time for *ultimate capitulation*."[56] [emphasis added]

Halifax angrily responded that nothing in his suggestion could even remotely be described as "ultimate capitulation."[57] The Prime Minister ignored the bickering and said only that he thought "the chances of decent terms being offered to us at the present time were a thousand to one against."[58]

Chamberlain, much more the conciliator than Churchill, added that it was the War Cabinet's duty to look at the situation realistically. He also felt obliged to say he agreed with Halifax that if it were possible to get terms which, although grievous, would not threaten our independence, we should consider them.[59] That said, he added, looking at the matter realistically, he did not believe that a present approach to Signor Mussolini along the lines proposed by the French would likely produce an offer of decent terms, certainly not with Paris in Hitler's grasp, but yet uncaptured.[60] He therefore reiterated that it was no good making an approach along the lines proposed by Premier Reynaud.[61]

On the other hand, Chamberlain feared that if the Cabinet were not careful about the wording of its answer to the Premier, France might give up the struggle at once; and he did not want to give the French any pretext for capitulating immediately.[62] The War Cabinet agreed.[63]

While Chamberlain thought that an approach to Italy was useless at this point, he carefully added "it might be that we should take a different view in a short time, possibly even in a week."[64] This was a middle ground between Halifax's position (let's negotiate now) and Churchill's (let's negotiate when the battle for Britain is concluded). According to Chamberlain, the question before the Cabinet was simply how to frame a reply to the French that, without rejecting their idea altogether, would persuade them that this was the wrong time to bring in Mussolini.[65]

Churchill Meets with the Outer Cabinet; Tells Them That There Is No Chance of Britain Giving Up the Struggle, and They Approve

After a forty-five-minute break, the War Cabinet reconvened at 7:00 PM. Churchill immediately made it known he had just met with the Outer Cabinet, the twenty-five ministers who were not members of the much smaller War Cabinet.[66] No official record was kept of what Churchill said to the Outer Cabinet. Hugh Dalton, a Labour MP who attended the meeting, did, however, make extensive notes in his diary. His notes were a thoroughly interesting outpouring of what Churchill had been thinking:

> In the afternoon, all ministers are asked to meet the P.M. He is quite magnificent. The man is the only man we have for this hour. He gives a full, frank and completely calm account of the events in France. ...

> He was determined to prepare public opinion for bad tidings, and it would, of course, be said, and with some truth, that what was now happening in Northern France would be the greatest British military defeat for many centuries. We must now be prepared for the sudden turning of the war against this Island and prepared also for other events of great

gravity in Europe. No countenance should be given publicly to the view that France might soon collapse, but we must not allow ourselves to be taken by surprise by any events. It might indeed be said that it would be easier to defend this island alone than to defend this island plus France, and if it was seen throughout the world that it was the former, there would be an immense wave of feeling, not least in the USA, which, having done nothing much to help us so far, might even enter the war. But all this was speculation. Attempts to invade us would no doubt be made, but they would be beset with immense difficulty. We should mine all round our coast; our Navy was immensely strong; our air defenses were much more easily organized from this island than across the Channel, our supplies of food, oil, etc., were ample; we had good troops in this island [*], others were on the way by sea, both British army units coming from remote garrisons and excellent Dominion troops, and, as to aircraft, we were now more than making good our current losses, and the Germans were not. *I have thought carefully in these last days whether it was part of my duty to consider entering into negotiations with That Man [Hitler].*[**] But it was idle to think that if we tried to make peace now we should get better terms from Germany than if we went on and fought it out. The Germans would demand our—fleet—that would be called "disarmament"—our naval

---

The fact is, just a few weeks earlier, at the War Cabinet meeting of April 30, 1940, there had been a discussion in which Churchill had participated about the shortage of trained troops in the country (the trained troops had all been sent to France). CAB 65/4 108 (40) p. 465 297.

**At first blush, this statement would seem to say that for the preceding few days Churchill had been keeping at least somewhat of an open mind about participating in peace negotiations. As such, it appears to buttress McCarten's thesis that Churchill was considering entering into peace negotiations with Hitler. But upon closer examination it does not. As noted in the previous chapter, Churchill's carefully chosen words are not inconsistent with evidence that he had made up his mind not to engage in peace negotiations at least two weeks earlier, if not before.*

That is, he did not tell the members of the Outer Cabinet he had been thinking about whether Britain should or should not negotiate with Hitler. Rather, all he said was that he was turning over in his mind whether, as P.M., he had a duty to be open to the possibility of negotiations. The question was whether as Prime Minister he was obliged not to believe that negotiations were simply foreclosed. The seeming ease by which, what Churchill imagined Hitler's peace terms would truncate the examination of his duty merely to "consider negotiations" provides evidence, contrary to McCarten's thesis, that Churchill thought about a negotiated peace. [emphasis added]

bases, and much else. We should become a slave state, though a British Government which would be Hitler's puppet would be set up—"under Mosley [*] or some other person." And where should we be at the end of all that? On the other side, we had immense reserves and advantages. And I am convinced that every one of you would rise up and tear me down from my place if I were for one moment to contemplate parlay or surrender. *Therefore, we shall go on and we shall fight it out, here or elsewhere, and if this long island story of ours is to end at last, let it end only when each one of us lies choking in his own blood upon the ground.*[67] [**] [emphasis added]

Dalton added that when Churchill announced that Britain would fight on, there were "loud cries of approval,"[68] and "It was quite clear that, whereas the Old Umbrella [i.e., Chamberlain] ... wanted to run ... Winston's bias is all the other way."[69] This last comment by Dalton is, of course, incorrect. As we've seen, it was Halifax, not Chamberlain, who wanted peace negotiations with Hitler. Chamberlain's resolve to keep fighting had remained stout.

Churchill told the War Cabinet that the Outer Cabinet had not seemed alarmed at the precarious posture of the BEF in France, and, more importantly, had expressed the greatest satisfaction when he had told them there was no chance of Britain giving up the struggle.[70] In fact, he said he "did not remember having ever before heard a gathering of persons occupying high places in political life express themselves so emphatically."[71***]

When writing after the war about his meeting with the Outer Cabinet, Churchill added several embellishments. "I said quite casually, and not treating it as a point of special significance: 'Of course, whatever happens at Dunkirk, we shall fight on.'"[72] Churchill also writes that "at the end of the meeting [q]uite a number [of the MPs] seemed to jump up from the table and came running to my chair, shouting, and patting me on the back."[73] Lastly, "I was sure that every Minister was ready to be killed quite soon, and have all his family and possessions destroyed, rather than give in."[74] As Lukacs

---

Oswald Mosley was the leader of the British Union of Fascists.

**McCarten writes that Churchill "[d]ecided no longer to sit on the fence," and had "return[ed] to his original position," McCarten p. 229. Churchill, however, was never on the fence or in any way unsure; he always believed that Britain should fight to the death and had made the decision not to enter negotiations long before May 28.*

***McCarten writes that "Halifax and Chamberlain could see [that] ... [n]ot even their combined resignation could now shake the Churchill leadership, not after this victory with ministers. ..." McCarten p. 231. The statement is misleading about Chamberlain, who several days earlier had signaled he agreed with Churchill that Britain should not seek peace negotiations at that time.*

points out, these statements may not be one hundred percent accurate but they do contain some truthfulness.[75]

In any event, the meeting held with the Outer Cabinet stands out as an excellent example of Churchill's unquestioned ability to rally people to fight on for king, country, and the preservation of western democracy. Indeed, it is likely that the Winston Churchill who led Britain through the tribulations of World War II was born at the 6:15 PM meeting with the Outer Cabinet on May 28, 1940.

The Idea of Britain's Entering Any Peace Negotiations Is Closed

After Churchill told the War Cabinet what had occurred at his meeting with the Outer Cabinet, there was silence from all, including Halifax. The matter of peace negotiations was closed, at least for now. Three weeks later, Halifax and his minions would seek to revive the idea. At that point, they let it be known in diplomatic circles that "No opportunity for reaching compromise would be neglected if the possibility were offered on reasonable conditions, and that no 'diehards' would be allowed to stand in the way. ..."[76] But those efforts to undermine Churchill would lead nowhere.

Once Churchill had finished his report of his Outer Cabinet meeting, Chamberlain read the War Cabinet the draft reply that he and Halifax had prepared for French Premier Reynaud. Chamberlain explained it was intended to persuade Reynaud that it was worth his while to go on fighting and that Britain was not merely looking at the matter from its point of view. Churchill was extremely satisfied with the draft.[77]

As the conclusions of the session reveal, the War Cabinet agreed:

1. That a plan along the lines proposed by the French (to approach Mussolini) was unlikely to serve a useful purpose. The reply to Premier Reynaud should make it clear that Britain was looking at the matter from the point of view of France as well as itself, and with regard to Reynaud's suggestion that France and Britain ask the United States for help.[78]

2. That an appeal to Mussolini along the lines contemplated by Reynaud would tend to confirm American fears of British weakness and thus would not produce the desired effect; and that, if any appeal were to be made, it should be along these lines: Would the United States help in the defense of world liberty against the might of Nazi power, or would it stand aside and take no action in defense of the rights of man?[79]

At the time no one fully anticipated the phenomenal job Churchill would do as Prime Minister, particularly until the United States joined the war effort in earnest in late 1942. As historian Paul Addison writes in *Churchill: The Unexpected Hero,* no one foresaw that

> The politics of class and party, the barbed wire on which [Churchill] had entangled himself so often in the past were quickly cleared out of the way. In their place a vacancy arose for which sublime egotism, magnificent oratory, and a passion for warfare were outstanding qualifications. Seizing an opportunity for which he had been rehearsing all his life Churchill [would] put on a matchless performance ...[80]

Low Expectations for the Dunkirk Evacuation

The number of Allied troops in Dunkirk was about to reach nearly 375,000 men, about 225,000 of whom were British. On the night of May 28, General Ismay, Churchill's liaison with the Chiefs of Staff, wrote the following entry in his diary: "The Prime Minister asked me how I would feel if I were told that a total of 50,000 could be saved. I replied without hesitation that I would be delighted, and Churchill did not upbraid me for my pessimism."[81] This statement supports Lukacs's position that on May 28, 1940, when the idea of entering into peace negotiations with Hitler was finally rejected, Churchill believed that at best only 50,000 men would ever be evacuated from Dunkirk.[82] Yet, at the same time, he had just shut the door on peace negotiations and put England on the path of having to repel a likely German invasion all by itself.

Where was Churchill leading Britain?

PART III

19

WHAT COULD CHURCHILL HAVE POSSIBLY BEEN THINKING?

What Did Churchill Ignore or Minimize?
What Things Were or Could Have Been Influential in Churchill's Decision Not to Enter Into Peace Talks with Hitler?

As discussed in the previous two chapters, by the time that May 28 came around Churchill had likely long since made up his mind that there would be no peace negotiations with Hitler. Even though Churchill authored many books about World War II, nowhere does he talk about what facts influenced his thinking. This chapter will discuss factors he likely considered in reaching his conclusion and those he likely ignored or minimized.

———

Churchill's speech to the Outer Cabinet on the evening of May 28, 1940, was another chance for him to show off his superb rhetorical abilities. Among the points he made, he reiterated his belief that, as part of any peace negotiations, the Germans would demand the British fleet and would make Britain a slave state.

The American writer and conservative political icon Pat Buchanan wonders, "Where is the evidence that Hitler intended to demand the British fleet?"[1] And, "Where is the evidence [that Hitler] sought to make Britain a "slave state?"[2] Buchanan asserts that "in June 1940, at the apex of his power after France's surrender and the British evacuation [from Dunkirk], Hitler [said he still] wanted the British Empire to survive and endure. He wanted to end the war."[3]*

———

*Hitler had an ambiguous love-hate, or perhaps a respect-contempt, feeling, toward the British. See, e.g. Lukacs, Five Days pp. 46–47.

Roberts generally concurs with Buchanan: "Churchill was probably wrong to assume that Hitler's terms would have been overly harsh; they would probably have been quite reasonable, judging by those he offered in October 1939 and again in [July] 1940."[4] As Roberts points out, and as the preceding chapters show:

- Hitler wanted to "destroy ... Communism, Judaism and the Slavs and establish ... *Liebensraum* ... in the East."[5]

- To do all of this he had to conquer Eastern Europe and fight the USSR.[6] And,

- As long as they didn't interfere with these desires, he really had no quarrel with Britain or the British Empire.[7]

But Hitler did not want to take any chances that Britain would interfere with his freedom to do as he pleased in the East. For this reason and others noted earlier in this book, he wanted to make Britain a vassal state of the Reich, just as he would do with Vichy France.* As Lukacs writes, Hitler's plan "called for ... a partial occupation of the British island, with a new Germanophile British government established. ..."[8]

The weight of evidence supports the view that Hitler did not want a world war. Moreover, as Buchanan and Roberts agree, the reasons Churchill gave to Halifax to justify his decision not to engage in peace talks do not stand up upon thorough scrutiny. Alan Clark, a former defense aide to Prime Minister Margaret Thatcher, goes further, writing that it was Churchill's "single-minded determination to keep the war going," and it was his "obsession" with Hitler that blocked Britain from entering peace negotiations with Nazi Germany.[9]

If Clark is correct, there were several factors Churchill would have had to ignore or substantially minimize to reach his "no-negotiations" position. Conversely, for Churchill to have concluded not to seek peace negotiations, there almost certainly were factors—some small, others large; some explicit, others obscured; some practicable, others fanciful—that Churchill likely leaned on in coming to his decision. Revisionist historians mistakenly reject this idea and assert that all Churchill did was to continue plodding on the path of continuing the war.[10]

The question then becomes what was there about Churchill that caused him to accept and emphasize certain parameters and minimize or ignore others en route to reaching the conclusion to reject a search for peace.

See additional discussion in Chapter 21.

What Did Churchill Ignore or Minimize?

Churchill disregarded the view of many that continuing a crusade of "victory at all costs" seemed "ludicrous,"[11] "futile," and even "suicidal."[12] These people generally believed that proceeding with the war was almost certainly going to lead to the deaths of hundreds of thousands of Britons, the devastation of the UK by a heavy German bombing campaign, and, ultimately, a German invasion of the British homeland. The first two of these three gripping fears did come to pass.

Churchill knew from the Chiefs' Report of May 25, 1940 that maintaining air superiority was the key to Britain's ability to carry on by itself.[13] Yet he discounted both the fact that Germany had more planes than Britain[14] as well as the concerns expressed by Hugh Dowding, the head of Fighter Command, that Britain's fighter defenses were almost at a cracking point.[15]

Churchill also appeared to have given no weight whatsoever to the significant fact that, having overrun Norway, Denmark, Holland, Belgium, and France, Hitler had acquired many airfields located close to Britain. In 1940, fighter planes had a maximum round-trip range of about 300 miles; they lacked the capacity to escort bombers on the thousand-mile round-trip journey from Germany to Britain and back. However, with his conquests in Western Europe, Hitler now had airfields as close as 100 miles from London. This meant that German fighters could both escort bombers on raids over much of the UK and also fly sorties over wide portions of the country on their own.

The British Chiefs of Staff's warning that Germany, through night bombing, might be able to wipe out British aircraft production[16] is yet another factor Churchill seemed to have ignored. Britain's production capacity was alarmingly vulnerable: all fighter engine production in England took place in only two factories,[17] which the Chiefs of Staff described as a "dangerous weakness."[18] More specifically, they said:

> Under a sustained rate of attack it is extremely doubtful if we could expect to receive more than a fraction of our present production figure. Our first-line strength may, therefore, diminish rapidly both because of a high rate of wastage and a low rate of replacement. ...[19]

> Whether the attacks succeed in eliminating the aircraft industry depends not only on the material damage by bombs but on the moral effect on the workpeople and their determination to carry on in the face of wholesale havoc and destruction.[20]

Churchill also appears to have paid no attention to the concerns of the Chiefs of Staff about a shortage of anti-aircraft guns and ammunition.[21]

Just as important as the porousness of its air defenses, in the short run Britain seemed certain to lack the manpower necessary to fight a full-scale war. Yet Churchill pressed ahead. On May 28 predictions were that only fifty thousand members of the BEF would be successfully evacuated from Dunkirk.[22] Moreover, on May 25, the Chiefs of Staff projected that "during the next two or three months" the number of trained British troops available to resist an anticipated invasion was likely to be only three-and-a-half divisions (35,000 to 52,000 men).[23] Even adding the final number of actual evacuees from Dunkirk, the total was but a small fraction of the estimated seventy divisions or more Germany had available.[24]* Churchill realized—but seemed to give little to no consideration to—the fact that the Army and the Home Guard (the UK's citizen militia) were unprepared[25] and ill-equipped (there were not even enough rifles available).[26] Historian Professor A.J.P. Taylor, who served in the Home Guard, concludes that if an invasion occurred and members of the Home Guard somehow managed to assemble at their appointed rendezvous points, they would have been massacred.[27]

Likewise, there is no evidence that Churchill considered the point laid out in a subsequent report by the Chiefs that "The Germans have accepted prodigious losses in France, ... [and] are likely to be prepared to face even higher losses, and to take even greater risks than they took in Norway to achieve decisive results against this country."[28]

Then, of course, there was the matter of money. Waging war is a frightfully expensive proposition, as Britain knew full well from World War I. Britain was nearly bankrupted by that conflict and in 1940 simply could not afford another large-scale war. Thus, it was not unlikely that continuing with the war would result in a national bankruptcy and the loss of Britain's place as a world power.[29] Churchill correctly identified the crucial role the United States could have in funding a war, and from the start he heavily lobbied Roosevelt. But he seemed blind to the fact that obtaining the needed influx of huge amounts of financial and other support from the US was not at all assured. Unless the United States repealed or ignored laws requiring the payment for planes and other munitions to be in cash, British bankruptcy appeared inevitable.[30]

Besides the three-and-a-half divisions of trained and equipped troops, Britain also had three divisions of men who were partly trained and equipped, five divisions of untrained troops with little equipment, and two armored divisions. CAB 66/7 WP 168 (40) Annex p. 8 322. Some additional troops would have been available from remote garrisons and the Commonwealth countries. Training and equipping draftees would also add to the total, but not immediately.

In deciding not to enter a peace agreement with Germany, Churchill hoped that Hitler would not make good on his "threat" to make things worse for the Jews if the Western democracies forced him into a world war. In a speech before the Reichstag in January 1939, Hitler had said, "If the international Jewish financiers in and outside Europe should succeed in plunging the nations once more into a world war, then the result will not be the Bolshevization of the earth, and thus the victory of Jewry, but the annihilation of the Jewish race in Europe."[31] Churchill was not an anti-Semite like Chamberlain, Halifax, and many others in the British upper class, and it is more than likely that Hitler would have followed through on his annihilation plans even if there were a negotiated peace. But Churchill acted as if Hitler had never made the threat.

What Things Were or Could Have Been Influential in Churchill's Decision Not to Enter Into Peace Talks with Hitler?

Let's now examine the parameters Churchill almost certainly considered in reaching the conclusion not to negotiate a peace agreement with Hitler. These factors are listed, and will be discussed, according to a subjective assessment of their increasing likelihood of contributing to his ultimate decision.*

1. There were rumors that Hitler would be deposed.

2. There was a good chance Hitler would be assassinated.

3. Germany might run low on oil.

4. Continuing on would lead the US to enter the war.

5. There were reports of tremendous problems in Germany relating to apathy, heavy casualties, food shortages, and depletion of raw materials.

6. Britain had enough troops and aircraft and a good supply of food and other staples.

7. Continuing on would keep France in the war.

---

*Items 10 to 18 interrelate and the difference in importance between them is so small that they could easily be reordered without changing their importance to Churchill's decision.

482 No Peace With Hitler

8. It was unwise for Britain to enter peace negotiations while in a weak position. If Britain could survive the coming months, it could consider how to win the war afterward.

9. Hitler would turn Britain into a vassal state.

10. Churchill couldn't abide Hitler gaining control of all of Europe. Moreover, peaceful coexistence would have contravened four hundred years of British policy.

11. Hitler did not believe in either negotiations or nonviolence.

12. Churchill did not feel that entering into a peace agreement of the kind proposed by Hitler was compatible with his conscience and sense of honor.

13. Churchill hated Hitler and Nazism.

14. Churchill was a man who was ready to sacrifice everything for a principle.

15. Churchill didn't trust Hitler.

16. Churchill had long believed that Britain could stand alone against Germany.

17. Churchill had concluded that Hitler could not successfully invade Britain.

18. Britain had a duty to defend the world cause to which she had pledged itself.

1. There were rumors that Hitler would be deposed

As discussed earlier in the book, there were thoughts and plans within the German General staff to remove Hitler and his associates, both at the time of Munich* and before. In September 1938, Churchill knew of a scheme to depose Hitler as soon as he ordered German troops into the Sudetenland, but the Munich agreement removed the need for the invasion. Munich did not, however, put a permanent end to plots to depose Hitler.

Shortly after the Polish invasion, the retired Commander-in-Chief of the German Army, General Kurt von Hammerstein-Equord, who was an

---

*This was known as the Halder Plot or the Oster Conspiracy.

unabashed opponent of Hitler, had been recalled into service and given a command along the Siegfried Line in Western Germany.[32]* He devised a simple plan to get rid of Hitler: Hammerstein-Equord would urge Hitler to visit his headquarters on the Western Front and arrest the German Chancellor when he arrived.[33] Unfortunately, Hitler was suspicious and declined the invitation. Shortly thereafter, General Hammerstein-Equord was dismissed.[34]

Another plot appears in Colville's diary entry for November 28, 1939. In a lunch meeting he had with Captain Thomas Troubridge, a Naval Attaché in the British Embassy in Berlin, Troubridge said he believed Goering was so anxious for peace that he and others would soon overthrow Hitler and offer very acceptable peace terms.[35]

Two weeks later, Colville would write about an interesting paper he had read containing an account of the conversation between Alex Cadogan, the permanent Under-Secretary for Foreign Affairs, and the Duke of Württemberg, before the Duke's death in late October 1939. During the conversation, the Duke talked about a military uprising led by two anti-Nazi generals that would result in German disintegration back into the thirty-nine little states from which Bismarck formed the country in 1871.[36]

Another scheme, called the "Zossen Conspiracy,"** involved some of the same players who were involved in the "Halder Plot" of August–September 1938: General Franz Halder, Chief of Staff to the Army High Command; General Ludwig Beck, whose resignation in late August led to Halder's promotion to Chief of Staff; and Colonel Hans Oster of German Military Intelligence.[37] Once again, the impetus for the coup was an invasion that Hitler had scheduled: This time, his planned attack on Western Europe set for November 12, 1939.

Seeking assurances that Britain would not use the coup to dictate a harsh peace to Germany, Oster arranged for Dr. Josef Mueller, a Munich lawyer, to journey to Rome where the Vatican had arranged for him to meet the British Minister to the Holy See.[38] German sources report that Mueller not only obtained the assurances but also a commitment from the Pope to act as an intermediary between Britain and any new anti-Nazi regime.[39] On November 5, General Walther von Brauchitsch, the Commander-in-Chief of the German Army, met with Hitler to talk him out of proceeding with his planned November offensive. General von Brauchitsch, not known for having much backbone, nonetheless told the conspirators that if he failed to dissuade Hitler he would "join in the conspiracy to remove [him]."[40] Brauchitsch's arguments were not having any success with Hitler.

---

*This German line of defense ran opposite France's Maginot Line.
**Zossen was a town in Germany, twenty miles south of Berlin, and the site of the underground headquarters of the German Army.

At that point, Brauchitsch said that the morale of the troops was low, much like it had been in 1917–18 when "defeatism, insubordination, and even mutiny" existed within the army.[41] Hitler broke into a rage and demanded to know what the Army had done to address this unacceptable situation. Further conversation became impossible and Brauchitsch returned to his headquarters at Zossen.[42] The browbeating Brauchitsch took not only immobilized him but was enough to panic the other conspirators.[43] The "Zossen Conspiracy" was dead.

As 1939 turned into 1940, other plots began to pop up. The plotters again wanted to remove Hitler before he could launch a next military adventure, this time in Norway. They, too, sought an authoritative statement from Britain on how a new anti-Nazi regime would be treated; they did not want a repeat of what had happened after the Kaiser was removed.[44]* Key actors in this plot were the German diplomat Ulrich von Hassell, General Georg Thomas, and economist Carl Goerdeler.[45]**

Also then floating around in conspiratorial circles was the so-called "X Report" drawn up by members of the Abwehr (German military intelligence) based on Dr. Mueller's earlier contact with the Vatican. The "X Report" said, "the Pope was ready to intervene" with Britain to bring about "a new, anti-Nazi German government" and propose "reasonable peace terms."[46] General Thomas took the "X Report" to General Halder in early April, hoping to get him to act on it; but Halder, the leader of the 1938 plot, refused. By then, heavily involved in planning the invasion of Western Europe, Halder was no longer willing to "break his oath as a soldier to the Fuhrer." As Shirer writes, at that point Halder (and Brauchitsch) were thinking that Germany would win the war.[47] Only when Germany's prospects looked poor "did they seriously return to their old and treasonable thoughts, which had been so strong at Munich and at Zossen."[48]

In May 1940, not all the details of these various schemes would likely have been available to Churchill. But he certainly would have known of

---

Article 227 of the Treaty of Versailles provided for the prosecution of the Kaiser "for a supreme offence against international morality and the sanctity of treaties." But Holland, where the Kaiser lived in exile, refused to extradite him, despite appeals from the Allies.

**Goerdeler opposed some of Hitler's anti-Jewish policies and opposed the Holocaust. He would be hanged for his role in the infamous July 20, 1944, attempted assassination of Hitler. Had this assassination attempt succeeded, Goerdeler was scheduled to become the new Chancellor of Germany.*

evidence that individuals within the German military hierarchy still desired to overthrow Hitler and install an anti-Nazi regime.*

2. There was a good chance Hitler would be assassinated

By May 1940 Churchill would almost have certainly known that there had been several attempts to kill Hitler, one or two of which, while not thwarted, failed for other reasons.

Helmut Hirsch

One scheme that never got off the ground involved Helmut Hirsch. Hirsch was born in Stuttgart, Germany; he was technically an American citizen but had never visited the United States. As a Jewish man with doubtful legal status in Hitler's Germany, he had good reason to hate Nazism. As a result, he joined the Black Front, a Czechoslovakian anti-Nazi group that had been thoroughly penetrated by German intelligence.

In 1938, someone in the group, possibly the Nazi agent who later gave evidence at Hirsch's trial, sent him across the border into Germany with instructions to pick up a couple of bombs and kill Hitler. Hirsch was apprehended at the border, interrogated by the Gestapo, and beheaded in 1939.

The Halder Plot et al.

Other, more sophisticated plots from within the German military have already been expounded on in Chapter 11. Though the aim of the "Halder Plot" in August–September 1938, the "Zossen Conspiracy" of 1939, as well as von Hammerstein-Equord's plan all were to have Hitler arrested, each also considered killing Hitler if the need arose.

Maurice Bavaud's Failed Attempts

In 1938, a Swiss theology student named Maurice Bavaud bought a pistol and began stalking Hitler across Germany. The bumbling would-be assassin was convinced that the German leader was the "incarnation of Satan,"

An argument can be made that the existence of all these plots to do away with Hitler would have supported entering into a peace agreement with him as his tenure as Chancellor likely would be short. That argument, however, loses sight of the fact that for as long as the peace agreement was in effect, much like what occurred in France, Britain would be Nazified: among other things, food production and distribution would be controlled by the Nazis, the country would be policed by the Gestapo, some Britons would be sent to Germany as slave laborers, the free press would be abolished, Jews and others would be discriminated against (or worse), art treasures would be stolen, school curriculums would be drastically changed, and the King would have been removed.

and thus a threat to the Catholic Church. Bavaud considered it his duty to gun Hitler down.

At the annual Nazi Nuremberg rally in September 1938, Bavaud positioned himself on an overpass under which Hitler was scheduled to travel. As Hitler's open Mercedes staff car approached, Bavaud lost sight of his target when scores of people in front of him stood up, gave the Nazi salute, and blocked his view.

Bavaud got another chance on November 9, 1938, when Hitler and other Nazi leaders marched through Munich to celebrate the fifteenth anniversary of the Beer Hall Putsch. Bavaud took a seat in a grandstand along the parade route and waited until Hitler approached. He had his pistol tucked into his pocket; but before he could draw and take aim, once again his view was blocked by the swooning, swastika-waving crowd raising their arms in a Nazi salute. Bavaud reluctantly gave up his hunt. He was later arrested as he tried to stow away on a train leaving Germany. When the Gestapo found his gun and maps, he confessed, under interrogation, to plotting to kill Hitler. In May 1941, he was executed by guillotine in Berlin's Plötzensee Prison.

The Polish Victory Parade Plot

General Michał Karaszewicz-Tokarzewski and other members of the Polish Army planned to assassinate Hitler by detonating hidden explosives during Hitler's victory parade in Warsaw in early October 1939. They had concealed 500 kilograms of TNT in a ditch, ready to be detonated by Polish combat engineers when Hitler's car passed by. But at the last moment the parade route was changed. Abrupt changes in schedule would become a typical security measure Hitler employed.

Georg Elser's Nearly Perfect Plan

About a month later, fate, it seems, again favored Hitler. German factory worker Georg Elser, a communist vehemently opposed to Nazism, believed Hitler's regime would lead Germany into a major war and financial ruin. Like Bavaud, Elser knew that Hitler always came to Munich to celebrate the anniversary of the Beer Hall Putsch and, more specifically, to give a speech at Munich's Bürgerbräukeller brewery. Elser spent several months building a time bomb. When it was complete, he moved from his home in southern Germany to Munich and began sneaking into the Bürgerbräukeller each night to hollow out a cavity in a stone pillar behind the speaker's platform. After several weeks of such clandestine labor, Elser successfully sequestered his bomb in the pillar. Then he set it to explode precisely at 9:20 PM on November 8, 1939, at what he thought would be midway through Hitler's speech.

Elser had planned his bombing to perfection, but luck was not on his side. With the war having started a few months earlier, Hitler had moved the start time of his speech to 8:00 PM so he could be back in Berlin as soon as possible. Unbelievably, he even gave "a shorter speech than usual" and finished his remarks by 9:07. He and his entourage also did not stay around as they usually did to "reminisce with old party comrades."[49] By 9:12, Hitler had left the building.[50] Eight minutes later, Elder's bomb went off, leveling the pillar and sending a section of the roof crashing down on the speaker's podium. Seven people were killed and dozens more were injured,[51] but Hitler was not among them.

Elser was captured that same night while trying to steal across the Swiss border. After the authorities found his bomb plans, Elser spent the next several years confined to Nazi concentration camps. In April 1945, as the Third Reich crumbled, the SS dragged Elser from his cell in the Dachau camp and executed him.

Erich Kordt's Effort

At about the same time Elser was getting ready to carry out his plot, German diplomat and resistance fighter Erich Kordt was hatching an assassination plot with fellow diplomat Hasso von Etzdorf. The plan, which also involved planting explosives, had to be abandoned after the security restrictions imposed after Elser's assassination attempt made the acquisition of the necessary explosives nearly impossible.*

3. Germany might run low on oil

At its late-afternoon meeting on May 28, the War Cabinet discussed how the quality of peace terms that could then be obtained might compare with those available after further fighting between Britain and Germany. Churchill, believing better terms would be available later, noted, "If ... we continued the war and Germany attacked us, no doubt we should suffer some damage, but they also would suffer severe losses. Their oil supplies might be reduced.[52]

Plots to assassinate Hitler did not cease in May 1940. They continued through most of World War II. The most famous of these was the attempt led by Colonel Claus von Stauffenberg in July 1944, where he and his co-conspirators planted a bomb that exploded during a military briefing at Hitler's Bavarian retreat. (Hitler was not severely injured.) Other significant attempts occurred in 1943. In March, General Henning von Tresckow placed a live bomb disguised as two bottles of brandy on Hitler's plane. (The bomb failed to explode due to a defective fuse.) A week later, Colonel Rudolf von Gersdorff, who was guiding Hitler around an exhibition of captured Soviet flags and weaponry, intended a suicide bombing in which Hitler would also be killed. (Hitler departed the exhibit before the bomb was set to explode.) And on December 26, 1943, Colonel von Stauffenberg made his first attempt to explode a bomb at one of Hitler's noon briefings. But Hitler did not attend the session, deciding instead to spend Christmas in Bavaria.

Churchill was not the only member of the War Cabinet to focus on oil. Just a few days earlier, Minister without Portfolio Arthur Greenwood had noted that Germany's oil stocks were "very depleted."[53] Likewise, on May 27, Clement Attlee, the Lord Privy Seal, said the Ministry of Economic Warfare estimated that even if Britain did not bomb German production facilities, Germany's oil stocks would be causing Hitler grave anxiety by autumn, and would be critical by spring.[54]

Before the war, Britain had identified the German war machine's reliance on oil and oil products as an area of potential vulnerability. Despite being one of the most powerful industrial nations on Earth, Germany produced a negligible amount of crude oil. Furthermore, unlike Britain, it lacked an empire to give it access to crude oil from overseas.[55] Germany's need for oil was exacerbated by the fact that its blitzkrieg style of war required huge amounts of petroleum.[56] Not only could Germany not produce any domestic crude, but it struggled to import oil. During World War II, the United States was responsible for over 59 percent of the world's production; and none of this went to the Nazis.[57] Nor could Germany fill its needs with oil from the Soviet Union, even under the trade provisions of the Molotov-Ribbentrop Pact. Hence, an important reason for Hitler to invade Russia in 1941 was to take control of the Russian oil fields in the Caucasus.[58]

In 1940, Germany's principal sources of petroleum were its domestic production of synthetic oil and some crude oil imported from Romania.[59] Small amounts of oil were also imported from the Soviet Union, Estonia,[60] and other countries. (Because of the British blockade, it was difficult for Germany to import oil by sea.[61]) The Chiefs of Staff's May 25, 1940, report on how Britain could continue to fight alone after the fall of France noted that "the whole oil output of Roumania, Poland, and Germany together with such supplies as are likely to be available from Russia will not suffice to maintain German and Italian stocks."[62]

Worse yet for the Nazis, at the start of June 1940 Britain made it a priority in its night-bombing campaign to target refineries, synthetic-fuel factories, plants that produced lubricating oil (an especially vulnerable item[63]), and receiving and storage depots. Attacks on other targets of the war industry were made on dark nights, when oil targets could not be easily located from the air.[64]

Synfuel plants, besides being the largest producer of German oil, were also the most vulnerable to Allied bombing.[65] Though these plants could produce only a low-octane fuel that required complex, expensive, and time-consuming further refinement to be suitable for use in aircraft,[66] the Chiefs of Staff believed that "if synthetic plants can be destroyed, the German garrisons would be largely immobilised and her striking power cumulatively decreased."[67] The Chiefs thus concluded that "[a]ir attacks on Germany's oil centres will be an important contribution to the enemy's defeat and to the reduction of the intensity of his air offensive."[68] They predicted that through continued denial of overseas supplies to Germany, "[b]y the winter of 1940–41, a shortage of oil will force Germany to weaken her military control in Europe."[69]

Thus, Germany's oil supply, both in the short- and long-term, would have been a valid consideration in Churchill's decision to refuse to advocate for peace negotiations. Unsurprisingly, preventing oil from reaching Germany would be a subject of constant interest to London.[70]

4. Continuing on would lead the US to enter the war*

The notion that Britain could not successfully continue a war against Germany without the full economic and financial support of the United States was interjected into the very first paragraph of the Chiefs of Staff's May 25, 1940, report titled "British Strategy in a Certain Eventuality" (the Fall of France).[71] Though the War Cabinet in its discussion and decisions ultimately sidestepped the issue, the question of US support for the war did not go away.

Churchill, of course, would have loved for the United States to have joined the war effort; and given what was happening in the spring and summer of 1940, few Britons would have had a differing opinion. That said, by his statement to the Outer Cabinet, Churchill appeared to be suggesting that the mere thought, let alone actual images, of destruction and death in England** would so pull at the heartstrings of Britain's American cousins that they would clamor to join in the fight against Hitler. Was Churchill so indifferent to life that he was thinking about deliberately subjecting his people to catastrophic bombardment and worse to entice the United States into the fray? (In a 2008 article titled "Questioning the Good War," Jack Fischel suggests that the answer could be "yes" when he writes that readers of Churchill's statements are first "led to conclude that the British Prime Minister was indifferent to human life."[72])

At the Supreme War Council meeting on May 31, Churchill said that an invasion of England would have a profound effect "especially in those many

---

*Professor David Reynolds asserts that only Churchill's belief in German military weakness was a stronger justification for fighting on. Reynolds, In Command of History p. 177. In his May 28, 1940, speech to the Outer Cabinet, Churchill took the question of American assistance one step further when he said that if England had to fight the Germans alone, "there would be an immense wave of feeling, not least in the USA, which, having done nothing much to help us so far, might even enter the war." But all this was speculation. Dalton, The Fateful Years p. 335.

**Images of the havoc wreaked by German planes during the Blitz would, increase the American public's willingness to come to Britain's aid. The Blitz was a sustained bombing campaign against the UK; it lasted from September 1940 into May 1941.

towns in the New World bearing the same names as towns in the British Isles."[73] But a few days later he told Parliament, in a much more measured manner, that "in God's good time" America would enter the war and would not let Britain go down to defeat.

> [E]ven if, which I do not for a moment believe, this island or a large part of it were subjugated and starving, then our Empire beyond the seas, armed and guarded by the British Fleet, would carry on the struggle, *until, in God's good time, the new world, with all its power and might, steps forth to the rescue and the liberation of the old.*[74] [emphasis added]

By this, he appeared to have moved away from the horrible thought that he might be willing to deliberately subject his people to attack to lure the United States into the war. Instead, Churchill was likely stating something he no doubt believed: that the United States would never let Britain drown. When she was ready, the US would dive in and, with all her might, rescue her older cousin. Churchill knew that by not negotiating a peace agreement with Hitler things in England could get bad, very bad. But he also was confident that, at the end of the day (and it might take until the figurative end of the day) the United States would have Britain's back.

Later comments, however, would show Churchill in a less favorable light. In *Their Finest Hour* Churchill describes deciding, after the fall of France, to launch an attack against a flotilla of French warships, to ensure that Germany did not get control of the French fleet. This, he writes, was "a hateful decision, the most unnatural and painful in which I have ever been concerned."[75] There is a substantial difference between Churchill's ordering an attack in which Britain might kill a few thousand sailors of an erstwhile ally and subjecting hundreds of thousands of his own constituents to death from German bombardment and invasion. Accordingly, labeling his decision to attack French warships as his most painful ever seems strange, and can be viewed as indifference to the looming loss of British lives at the hands of the Nazis if there were no negotiated peace agreement. Churchill knew well that war means death—a view that could seem callous. But that callousness seems to have curiously softened with regard to the possible death of French sailors.

Other comments Churchill made in the summer of 1940 also appear to strengthen the cynical view that he was cold, calculating and may have believed that carnage in Britain was necessary to draw America into the war. For example, as Reynolds writes, he insisted "on several occasions that a Luftwaffe blitz on Britain would inflame American opinion and provoke a declaration of war."[76] Churchill made similar comments in a June 16, 1940, telegram to the Dominion Prime Ministers in which he said, "I personally believe that the spectacle of the fierce struggle and carnage in our island will draw the United States into the war," and that "the horrors [of 200,000 German stormtroopers landing on our shores] would in the last resort turn the scales in the United States."[77] Multiple historians also report that "[a]t Chequers* in August 1940, [Churchill] told de Gaulle and that 'the bombing of Oxford, Coventry, Canterbury, will cause such a wave of indignation that [the US will] come into the war!'"[78]

These statements all sit atop Churchill's response to a question on May 18 on how Britain might win the war, to which he answered, "I shall drag the United States in."[79] Thus the horrible question: when Churchill was saying that carnage in England would bring the US into the war, was he thinking about deliberately risking the lives thousands of Britons and the way of life of millions of others to do so?** Put more bluntly, was a desperate Churchill, for the greater good, willing to deliberately use British lives as bait to lure America into the fight? Thankfully, the evidence does not support a conclusion that he did.

As Fischel points out, while Churchill's statements could suggest that he was indifferent to human life, "Churchill may simply [have] recognized that the Nazis, by bombing British cities and invading, would be committing a tactical error—rousing American public opinion against Germany, thus expediting the process by which the US would enter (and, Churchill believed, end) the war."[80] This view is supported—and the opposing view (that Churchill was willing to sacrifice thousands upon thousands of his countrymen just to get America into the war) is undermined—by many things. Among them is Churchill's steadfast belief, analyzed below, that the Germans could not successfully invade the UK and that he would, if necessary, take extraordinary means to prevent it with as few losses as possible. Second, the indifference to death and destruction that some people have ascribed to Churchill might have merely been a function of his supreme confidence in the correctness of his decision. As he had shown many times throughout his life, when his confidence was in full force, potentially negative consequences of a decision he'd made simply no longer crossed his mind, like when he jumped off a 30-foot bridge as a teenager, and when he tagged along on a dangerous armored train reconnaissance mission during the Boer War. Third, Lukacs writes that in late May 1940 Churchill "knew ... Hitler was hesitant to attack the island immediately."[81]*** Assuming that Lukacs

---

*The official country residence of British Prime Ministers.

**During the Blitz alone, 32,000 civilians were killed and 87,000 were seriously injured. Two million houses (60 percent of which were in London) were destroyed, leaving 800,000 Londoners without their homes.

***There is, however, evidence to the contrary, including a statement by Churchill before the House. HC Deb 04 June 1940 vol 361 cc793.

is correct about how much Churchill knew at the time, he would have also believed that the risk to Britons of either a heavy bombing campaign or an immediate invasion would have been fairly low.

Churchill may have also seen any risk as manageable because in the late spring of 1940, as discussed below, he, and many in the War Cabinet, had the self-delusion that the United States was about to enter the war. Thus, it would have made sense to them that it would take very little (such as mere images of death and destruction in Britain) to trigger America's officially joining the war. This self-delusion can be seen by Churchill's overreaction to a simple interchange between French Premier Reynaud and President Roosevelt in mid-June 1940.

On June 10, in the throes of despair, French Premier Reynaud sent a message to Roosevelt in which he said that France would fight on even if it meant continuing the struggle from French possessions overseas.[82] On June 13, the President responded:

> Your message of 10th June has moved me very deeply. As I have already stated to you and to Mr. Churchill this Government is doing everything in its power to make available to the Allied Governments the material they so urgently require and our efforts to do still more are being redoubled. This is so because of our faith in and our support of the ideals for which the Allies are fighting.
>
> The magnificent resistance of the French and British armies has profoundly impressed the American people.
>
> I am personally particularly impressed by your declaration that France will continue to fight on behalf of Democracy even if it means slow withdrawal, even to North Africa and the Atlantic. It is most important to remember that the French and British fleets continue mastery of the Atlantic and other oceans; also to remember that vital materials from the outside world are necessary to maintain all armies.
>
> I am also greatly heartened by what Prime Minister Churchill said a few days ago about the continued resistance of the British Empire and that determination would seem to apply equally to the great French Empire all over the world. Naval power in world affairs still carries the lessons of history, as Admiral Darlan [Chief of Staff of the French Navy and Admiral of the Fleet] well knows.[83]

At the late-evening War Cabinet meeting on June 13, 1940, Churchill told his colleagues:

- "This message ... came as near as possible to a declaration of war and was probably as much as the President could do without Congress. The President could hardly urge the French to continue the struggle, and to undergo further torture, if he did not intend to enter the war to support them."[84] And,

- "If the President were not disavowed by his country, then it was clear that he would bring them in on our side in the near future."[85]

In the ensuing discussion, "[i]t was pointed out that [Roosevelt] had not stated ... that the United States would declare war" but "[o]n the other hand it was [also noted] that no head of a State could send such a message to France, urging her to continue her agony, unless he was certain that his country was *coming to her aid.*"[86] [emphasis added] Minister of Aircraft Production Lord Beaverbrook put it more forcefully when he told assembled ministers that "[i]t was now inevitable that the United States of America would declare war."[87] The Cabinet generally felt that "although the implications of [Roosevelt's] message might be clear to the Anglo-Saxon mind, they might appear in a rather a different light to the French, who would be looking for something more definite."[88] As a result, they thought it would be necessary to point out to Reynaud that

> ... *the message contained two points which were tantamount to a declaration of war*—first, a promise of all material aid, which implied active assistance; and second, a call to go on fighting even if the Government was driven right out of France.[89] [emphasis added]

Viewed objectively, Roosevelt's response says only that the United States would continue to make urgently needed war materials available to Britain and France, and nothing more. Premier Reynaud recognized this limitation; but, believing that the defeat of both Britain and France was "probable," at Churchill's insistence he sent Roosevelt a telegram on June 15 specifically asking for the United States to declare war.[90] Unsurprisingly, Roosevelt immediately declined.[91] Clearly the British were not thinking dispassionately about what it would take to get the United States to enter the war.

In any event, Britain's decision not to seek peace negotiations with Hitler in the spring of 1940 did not cause the United States to enter the war. In fact, according to Churchill, for six weeks after the collapse of France "Americans treated us in that rather distant and sympathetic manner one adopts toward a friend we know is suffering from cancer."[92] Sympathetic, but still aloof.

5. There were reports of tremendous problems in Germany relating to apathy, heavy casualties, food shortages, and depletion of raw materials

In their May 25 report, the Chiefs of Staff pointed out that "[i]n spite of immediate economic gains obtained from her conquests, Germany will still be very short of food, natural fibres, tin, rubber, nickel, and cobalt."[93]

As for food supply, the Chiefs reported that it was already a serious problem in Germany and that her acquisition of the occupied territories of Western Europe would aggravate the shortage.[94] More specifically, they explained that harvest yields in 1940 were expected to be low, and German-controlled Europe would therefore be somewhat short of breadstuffs.[95] The Chiefs also expected that "[l]ife will be sustained for a period by the heavy slaughtering of immature animals. This will be necessary because, after the end of the grazing season there will be a dearth of feeding-stuffs. It would also probably be just a matter of months before hoarding by the peasant population created a really acute shortage of food in industrial areas, including parts of Germany herself."[96]

In his notes related to the Chiefs' report, Minister without Portfolio Arthur Greenwood said that Germany, with no sources at hand, would need to import rubber, oil, materials for clothing and footwear, and, of course, food supplies for the effective prosecution of the war.[97] Additionally, "[t]hough she may have obtained new resources, for example, iron ore, her ability to use them effectively for war purposes also depends upon the possession of nonferrous metals, which she must obtain from abroad."[98]

The Chiefs' report concluded: "Given full Pan-American co-operation, we should be able to control all deficiency commodities at their source. There will be no neutrals except Japan and Russia."[99] It continued, "...provided that we can maintain control over the Allied Overseas Empires and naval control of the wider oceans and focal points leading to the blockaded area, the trickle of supplies reaching Germany by blockade running will be negligible."[100] The effect of a continued denial of overseas supplies to Germany would be widespread food shortages by the winter of 1940–41 in many European industrial areas, including parts of Germany. Moreover, by the middle of 1941, the Chiefs felt that Germany would have trouble replacing military equipment, because a large part of the industrial output of Europe would be at a standstill, handing the German administration an immense unemployment problem to manage.[101]

Greenwood concurred with the report's findings. He said, "... given a tight economic blockade, Germany can be strangled, her war effort seriously reduced, and her industrial manpower made impotent. In this connection, it is vital, as the memorandum under consideration points out, that we must take the necessary steps to secure allies to assist us in this direction."[102]

Two problems exist with the above analyses. First, if France fell and the French fleet thus became unavailable, Britain would no longer be able to effectively blockade Germany.[103] Second, the Chiefs did not discuss the volume of foodstuffs and other goods being imported from the Soviet Union. Nonetheless, as Professor Reynolds points out, in May 1940 British intelligence had persuaded itself (and most policy makers) that the German war economy was already overstretched and that Hitler had a deadline within which to win the war.[104] This view was shared by Chamberlain,[105] Attlee,[106] and Greenwood.[107] Churchill seems to have held it to some extent as well.[108] Indeed, in early June, Halifax told the War Cabinet that "The people of Germany were apathetic at the victories of the German Army and were alarmed at the prospect of a long war."[109]

Reports coming in from Germany said that the Nazis were terrified of not winning the war by the end of summer 1940, there were shortages of food and raw materials, and war production had fallen off.

These reports also declared that the Germans feared the war might well be over by Christmas.[110] To say the least, this prediction proved overly optimistic.

6. Britain had enough troops and aircraft and a good supply of food and other staples

Despite the contrary facts noted earlier, in his speech to the Outer Cabinet on May 28, Churchill shared his belief that Britain had good troops protecting the island, and they would be bolstered both by British Army units coming from remote garrisons and by excellent Dominion forces. As for aircraft, he added that, unlike the Germans, losses were being more than recouped.[111] Churchill also declared that supplies of food, oil, and other essentials were ample.

Regarding food, Churchill was basically correct. In their May 25 report on Britain's ability to carry on should France fall, the Chiefs of Staff wrote that maintaining a minimum level of essential imports was key. The report advocated "reducing now the unimportant imports (such as bananas and children's toys), so that the maximum import of important raw materials may be available to increase our stocks of ... essentials."[112]

7. Continuing on would keep France in the war

On May 26, Churchill met over lunch with French Premier Reynaud. The P.M. concluded that, just as the French had been saying for some time, France's resistance to the Germans was unlikely to continue for much longer.[113] As we have seen, the British Chiefs of Staff had put together a report about Britain's ability to fight on should France capitulate. Churchill told Reynaud, as he had done before, that Britain was not prepared to give in and, in fact, "had a good chance of surviving the German onslaught."[114] He added, "If only we [Britain and France] could stick things out for another 3 months, the position would be entirely different."[115] But of course that meant that "France … must stay in the war."[116]

That Britain did not want to see France give up (despite the occasional gripe that Britain would be better off without her[117]) was reiterated on May 28 when Churchill expressed his satisfaction with the letter Chamberlain and Halifax had drafted to send to Reynaud rejecting France's idea for mediation through Mussolini. As Chamberlain explained, the draft letter was intended to paint a picture that would persuade Reynaud it was worth France's while to go on fighting, and that Britain was not merely looking at the matter from its point of view. The Cabinet did not want to give France any pretext for giving up the struggle.[118]

By late May 1940, the question was not how Britain could keep France in the war, but rather how it could avoid hastening France's departure from the war. Put simply, if Britain had decided not to carry on with the war and showed interest in a negotiated peace with Hitler, France almost certainly would have stopped fighting immediately.

8. It was not wise for Britain to enter into peace negotiations when it was in a weak position. If Britain could survive the coming months, it could consider how to win the war afterward

At the informal War Cabinet meeting held at Admiralty House on May 26 at 4:30 PM Churchill said, "…we must take care not to be forced into a weak position in which we [go] to Signor Mussolini and invite … him to go to Herr Hitler and ask them to treat us nicely."[119] The next morning, he told the War Cabinet that if, after two or three months, Britain were still unbeaten, its prestige in Europe would have been restored and Britain would be in a stronger position from which to negotiate.[120] Minister without Portfolio Arthur Greenwood also saw benefit in Britain trying to survive for several more months. At the informal War Cabinet meeting held at Admiralty House on May 26, Greenwood said that "if we could maintain the struggle for some further weeks, we could make use of our economic power in regard to raw materials, textiles, and oil. Stocks in Germany were very depleted."[121]

The Chiefs of Staff felt similarly. In a report dated June 19, 1940, they said, "The issue of the war will almost certainly turn upon our ability to hold out during the next three months. Our efforts must therefore be concentrated on taking all steps necessary to meet the imminent threat of attack with which we are now confronted."[122] The comment was prescient. While air skirmishes had begun, the anticipated Battle of Britain would not start for another three weeks. More importantly, once the air war over Britain commenced in earnest, the outcome would be a victory for Britain by a razor thin margin. Germany did not gain air superiority over England. Britain was viewed both internally and externally in a totally different light than it had been in late May when it didn't even know if it would get the BEF safely out of Europe.*

Revisionist historians argue that in 1940 "Churchill had no plan ... except to keep fighting, hoping that something might turn up" and that "his obsessive hatred of Hitler may have blinded him, for had he accepted an accommodation with Hitler by 1941 the Empire may have been saved."[123] When they say that Churchill had no plan, they overlook the direction in his July 8 letter to Lord Beaverbrook to execute "an absolutely devastating, exterminating attack by very heavy bombers from this country upon the Nazi homeland."[124]

There may or may not be truth in the statement that a negotiated peace with Hitler would have preserved the Empire.** However, some authorities argue that the British Empire was lost even before the start of the war. What is true, is that as of May 28, 1940, despite Churchill's statement that "[e]ven if we were beaten, we should be no worse off than we should be if we were now to abandon the struggle," the fortunes of Great Britain were low, and they could have gotten worse. There would be no assurances that the inhabitants of a defeated and devastated Nazi-occupied Britain would have averted the fate that befell the Czechs and the Poles.

All reports were saying Britain could at least maintain the status quo for as long as it maintained its air force and denied the Germans air superiority over the UK. Churchill displayed both unqualified optimism and dogged determination in reaching his conclusion not to enter peace negotiations with Hitler. Still, he had to overcome the periodic doubts he had about continuing the war. One example of those doubts can be seen in the following exchange between him and General Ismay. During the flight back from Paris on June 10, Ismay told Churchill he was pleased that Britain would be fighting on alone and that "we will win the Battle of Britain," to which Churchill replied drolly, "you and I will be dead in three months' time."[125] Despite all the confidence he publicly exuded that Britain would prevail, Churchill "could sometimes admit to his colleagues that it might not turn

---

*Winning the Battle of Britain was crucial for Britain. Losing it was also the first setback for the Germans in World War II and is viewed by many as a turning point in the conflict. Bungay, The Most Dangerous Enemy p. 388.

**This will be discussed below in the context of the likely unreliability of any negotiated peace agreement with Hitler.

out that way."[126] Those doubts, however, did not deter him from doing what needed to be done.

9. Hitler would turn Britain into a vassal state

On June 15, 1940, Churchill sent Roosevelt a telegram once again laying out a picture of how a defeated Britain could become a mirror image of what was about to happen to France. The telegram read:

> [I]f resistance was beaten down here, a point may be reached in the struggle where the present Ministers no longer have control of affairs and when very easy terms could be obtained for the British island by their *becoming a vassal state of the Hitler Empire*. A pro German Government would certainly be called into being to make peace and might present to a shattered or starving nation an almost irresistible case for entire submission to the Nazi will.[127]* [emphasis added]

Historian John Lukacs would later contend that making Britain a vassal state of the Reich, just as the Fuhrer would do with Vichy France, "was exactly what Hitler had in mind" for England. A subjugated Britain would ensure that she did not interfere with the German Chancellor's intentions in the East. "As in the case of France, his plan [...would have] called for a partial occupation of the British island, with a new Germanophile British government established. ..."[128]** Hitler, who had detested Churchill for years,[129] began picking out the individuals who could play key roles in a collaborationist government. The foremost contender to replace King George was his Nazi-leaning brother Edward;[130] while David Lloyd George, an unabashed Hitler sympathizer, was a leading candidate to be appointed the new Prime Minister.[131] Chamberlain and Halifax were being considered for

---

*The telegram described a situation that Churchill knew Roosevelt did not want to occur; and it seems the P.M. was using this prospect as part of his efforts to get what he wanted from America rather than to reflect doubts about Britain's ability to stave off the Nazis. Remember that Churchill had already used this technique in a telegram sent on May 20.

**As discussed earlier in this book, evidence emerged (Directive 21, dated December 18, 1940) that once Germany had defeated Russia, Hitler would have attacked Britain with the goal of conquering or neutralizing (but not destroying) her, much as he had done with France. Lukacs, The Last European War p. 101.

If Britain could simply be ignored or be made irrelevant through a ceasefire agreement, there would have been no need to defeat Russia quickly. But Hitler believed that conquering or neutralizing Britain was essential before she grew strong enough (with or without the intervention of the United States) to impede any future plans that he may have had.

the Cabinet.[132] To accomplish this, Hitler believed that after Poland he had to turn West before he could turn East.

The subjugation of Britain was important to Hitler—whether it occurred as the result of peace negotiations in the spring or summer of 1940, or after a war with Russia. Just as he would shortly do with France, Hitler would have pressured Britain until she installed a sycophantic government and signed an armistice making her a vassal state.

10. Churchill couldn't abide Hitler gaining control of all of Europe; Moreover, peaceful coexistence would have contravened four hundred years of British policy.

Pat Buchanan strongly suggests that Britain (and France) should have taken Hitler up on his offer, iterated in varying forms on more than a few occasions, to give him freedom to do as he wanted in the East in exchange for his promise to leave them alone. But as Professor David Reynolds points out, in 1941 and 1942 when Britain was taking no offensive actions against Germany and Hitler thus thought had his free hand in the East, he was also taking actions against Britain—expanding his naval forces in an effort to control the Atlantic.[133]* Moreover, as historian John Lukacs writes, "Churchill did not for a moment believe that Britain and the Empire could continue to exist across from a Europe entirely dominated by Germany,"[134] so he refused to accept any such idea.[135]

It had been British policy for four hundred years to oppose the strongest power in Europe, whether it was Spain, France, or Germany.[136] (Even Hitler recognized this in *Mein Kampf*.[137]) This policy had last been fully evident in 1912 when Churchill was First Lord of the Admiralty. At that time Britain, which was greatly concerned about Germany building a navy to rival the Royal Navy, would not accept Germany's offer to limit the size of its growing fleet in exchange for a pledge of neutrality in any Franco-German War.[138] Commenting on Britain's historical need to challenge the continent's strongest power, Churchill said, "It is thus through the centuries we keep our liberties and maintained our life and power."[139] Churchill reiterated these sentiments to newspaper magnate Lord Rothermere in 1935 when Hitler had suggested an Anglo-German alliance. At that time, he also reminded Rothermere of the fable about the jackal and the tiger whose hunting trip together ended when the tiger ate the jackal. Commenting on Hitler's proposal, Churchill added:

As Professor David Reynolds puts it: "… when Hitler thought he had a free hand on the Continent, he started flexing his muscles on the world stage." Reynolds, "Churchill The Appeaser?" p. 203.

> If his proposal means that we should come to an understanding
> with Germany to dominate Europe, I think this would be con-
> trary to the whole of our history. We have on all occasions been
> the friend of the second strongest power in Europe and have
> never yielded ourselves to the strongest power. Thus Elizabeth
> resisted Philip II of Spain. Thus William III and Marlborough
> resisted Louis XVI. Thus Pitt resisted Napoleon, and thus we
> all resisted Wilhelm II of Germany. Only by taking this path
> and effort have we preserved ourselves and our liberties and
> reached our present position. I see no reason myself to change
> from the traditional view.[140]

These words and the fable about the tiger and jackal would still ring true
for Churchill in the spring of 1940.

As Roberts succinctly says, "Churchill saw British history as a continuum,
in which Britain's duty was to keep the balance of power in Europe."[141]
Chamberlain, perhaps surprisingly, revealed in a 1938 speech before the
House that even he believed the British Government had, and always would
have, a duty to be interested in developments in Central Europe.[142] By giving
Hitler a free rein in the East, which in late May 1940 some Britons (but not
Churchill) believed could avert their potential annihilation, Britain would
have had to forsake this duty. Moreover, appeasing a National Socialist
country would have contradicted Churchill's staunch belief that National
Socialism represented a grave threat to Western civilization—a threat even
greater than that of communism.[143]

At least as early as 1936, Churchill is on record as having opposed allowing
Hitler to have free rein in the East. At that time he told the Foreign Affairs
Committee of the Commons that if Hitler were allowed to do what he liked
in the East, Germany would, overnight, become dominant from Hamburg
to the Black Sea, and Britain would be faced by a confederacy the likes of
which had not been seen since the days of Napoleon.[144] Hitler, on the other
hand, never understood why the British, particularly Churchill, would not
accept German domination of Europe.[145] Revisionist historians are similarly
mystified. But to historians like David Reynolds, the revisionists' belief that
Britain could have maintained any true independence in an arrangement with
a dominant Germany is ridiculous.[146] Simply, even if the UK were allowed
to keep its own government, with Germany in possession of bases along the
northern and western coasts of France, the British would be acutely vulnerable to blockade and air attack and would therefore be largely dependent
on the continuing goodwill of their overlords in Berlin.[147]

11. Hitler did not believe in negotiations or nonviolence

In his biography of Lord Halifax, *The Holy Fox,* Andrew Roberts writes that Halifax failed to appreciate the fact that Hitler believed in neither negotiation nor nonviolence.[148]* Churchill did not suffer the same misapprehension. He agreed with King George that "[u]ntil Germany is prepared to live peaceably with her neighbors in Europe, she will always be a menace. We have to get rid of her aggressive spirit, her engines of war & the people who have been taught to use them."[149]

12. Churchill did not feel that entering into a peace agreement of the kind proposed by Hitler was compatible with his conscience and sense of honor

After conquering Poland, Hitler made a speech on October 6, 1939, in which he offered peace to Britain and France. Chamberlain responded in an address to the House on October 12, 1939, by saying:

> ... the proposals which the German Chancellor puts forward for the establishment of what he calls "the certainty of European security" are based on recognition of his conquests and of his right to do what he pleases with the conquered. It would be impossible for Great Britain to accept any such basis without forfeiting her honour and abandoning her claim that international disputes should be settled by discussion and not by force.[150]

Chamberlain was calling on Hitler to surrender Poland.

Churchill used similar language during the meeting of the Outer Cabinet on May 28, 1940. According to an account supplied to Lord Halifax: "...he had no doubt that we could make peace with Hitler on some terms or other provided we made no attempt to interfere with the enslavement of Europe, but this he thought would be short-lived and *he did not feel it compatible with his own conscience and honour to do so.*[151]** [emphasis added]

It can be argued that the Anglo-German Naval Treaty of 1935 is evidence to the contrary. But that treaty was the child of appeasement and was renounced by Hitler less than four years after it was signed. Moreover, during the time it was in force, Hitler submitted false information about the tonnage of ships the Reich had constructed. Shirer p. 288.

**In his autobiography, Halifax writes that in 1945, Malcom MacDonald (the son of Ramsey MacDonald, Labour Prime Minister in the 1920s and 1930s) had attended the meeting of the Outer Cabinet and related this statement to him. Halifax, p. 227.*

In the nearly eight months between Chamberlain's speech in October 1939 and Churchill's talk before the Outer Cabinet on May 28, not only had Hitler not given back Poland but, he had also gobbled up neutral Denmark, Norway, Holland, Belgium, and Luxembourg. And he was about to add France to that list. If "honour" precluded Britain from entering a peace agreement that allowed Hitler to retain the one country he had conquered by force in September 1939, London would certainly have been even more honor-bound the following spring, after Hitler had wrested dominion from five additional neutral countries.

13. Churchill hated Hitler and Nazism

Since the Russian Revolution in 1917, if not before, Churchill was a rabid anti-Communist. But he hated the Nazis even more. In early 1938, Churchill told Ivan Maisky, the Soviet Ambassador to Britain, that "Today, the greatest menace to the British Empire is German Nazism with its idea of Berlin's global hegemony. That is why, at the present time, I spare no effort in the struggle against Hitler." He added that "[i]f one fine day the German Fascist threat to the Empire disappears and the Communist menace rears its head again, then—I tell you frankly—I would raise the banner of the struggle against you once more. However, I don't anticipate the possibility of this happening in the near future, or at least within my lifetime."[152]

Just after Hitler made his peace proposal on Oct 6, 1939, Churchill said,

> Personally, I find [the provisions] absolutely unacceptable. They are the terms of a conqueror! But we are not yet conquered! No, no, we are not yet conquered! ... Some of my Conservative friends advised peace. They fear that Germany will turn Bolshevik during the war. *But I am all for war to the end. Hitler must be destroyed. Nazism must be crushed once and for all.* Let Germany become Bolshevik. That doesn't scare me. Better Communism than Nazism."[153]*

Even though Churchill despised Communism and disliked Stalin almost as much as he disliked Hitler:

- in 1936 he favored a conference on how mutual assistance furnished under the Franco-Soviet pact of 1935 could be folded into the collective security action the League of Nations would be taking;[154]

In the fall of 1939, even Chamberlain realized that it was "essential to get rid of Hitler." Self p. 399.

- in 1939 he strongly urged the formation of a Grand Alliance that included Russia; and

- in 1941, when Russia joined the Allies, Churchill showed a willingness to accept a postwar world in which Stalin would likely play a major role.

In 1940, in stark contrast, Churchill vehemently opposed doing anything similar with Hitler.

14. Churchill was a man who would sacrifice everything for a principle*

Churchill tried to operate based on principle rather than passion or politics. Examples in which he put principle ahead of all else were many and include the following:

- his introduction and support of social welfare reforms despite his aristocratic roots;

- his desire to help the White Russians against the Bolsheviks in 1919 over the objections of the Cabinet;

- his willingness to accept ostracism over his position about Dominion status for India; and

- his keenness in the early 1930s to be a voice from the wilderness on rearmament and the threat he saw in Hitler.

Of course, there were other significant instances when he would put principle aside (for good reasons and bad). These included his endorsement of continuing the inhumane post-WWI blockade of Germany until it signed the Versailles Peace treaty; his acquiescence to tariffs, which he detested, when economic circumstances demanded; and his ultimate willingness to embrace the despised Soviets as an ally to defeat Hitler.** But Churchill's belief that the evil of Nazism had to be eradicated for the sake of mankind was immutable. While other principles could be compromised, this one never could.

---

*He was so described by Manchester. Manchester, Visions p. 723.

**To maintain his essential wartime relationship with Stalin, Churchill remained silent in 1943 when he learned about the Soviets' mass murder of fourteen thousand Polish officers in 1939. Roberts p. 775.

15. Churchill didn't trust Hitler

On October 5, 1938, at a time just after Munich, Churchill spoke to the House of Commons:

> *[Nazi Germany] cannot ever be the trusted friend of the British democracy.*
>
> ...[T]here can never be friendship between the British democracy and the Nazi Power, that Power which spurns Christian ethics, which cheers its onward course by a barbarous paganism, which vaunts the spirit of aggression and conquest, which derives strength and perverted pleasure from persecution, and uses, as we have seen, with pitiless brutality the threat of murderous force."[155] [emphasis added]

Hitler provided no shortage of examples of his megalomania and treachery:

- Hitler's ravings in *Mein Kampf;*

- his attempt to violently overthrow the existing German Government in 1923;

- his willingness in 1934 to murder his rivals, including his close friend and the leader of the SA, Ernst Roehm;

- his numerous violations of the Treaty of Versailles, including
    - the restrictions on the size of the Germany Army;
    - the demilitarization of the Rhineland;
    - the preclusion of a German Air Force;
    - the limits on German shipbuilding; and
    - his violation of pledges made after Germany marched into the Rhineland, Austria and the Sudetenland that he had no further territorial demands;

- his declaration that Germany would not annex Austria;

- his duplicitous negotiations over the Sudetenland;

- his violation of the non-aggression pact he had with Stalin; and

- his breach of his pledge never to violate the neutrality of the Low Countries.

How could anyone trust Hitler?

Chamberlain told the War Cabinet on March 18, 1939, just after Hitler had invaded the remnants of Czechoslovakia, that "No reliance [can] be placed on any of the assurances given by the Nazi leaders."[156] Chamberlain reiterated this belief to the House in an October 12, 1939, response to the peace proposal Hitler made after the invasion of Poland: "The plain truth is that, after our past experience, it is no longer possible to rely upon the unsupported word of the present German Government."[157] This pronouncement was quickly seconded by Labour Party leader Clement Attlee, who added, "The first thing is that they are made by a man whose word is utterly worthless."[158]

Although Buchanan and others suggest that Britain and Nazi Germany could have peacefully coexisted, Churchill believed no such arrangement could endure.[159] Seeing no evidence to the contrary, Churchill agreed with French Premier Reynaud's assessment "that the Germans would probably not keep any terms to which they agreed."[160]

As will be discussed in Chapter 20, Churchill's wariness of Hitler commenced early and never wavered. He knew evil when he saw it. But it took many years for others to feel the same way about the German Chancellor.

A good example of Churchill's thorough distrust of Hitler can be seen with regard to the disposition of the French fleet after the capitulation of France. The armistice agreement between Germany and France called for the demobilization and disarmament of the ships of the French Navy under German supervision in their home ports, which were located mostly in the German-occupied zone. This meant that French warships would be fully armed when they came under German control. Under the armistice, the French fleet would not, however, be surrendered to Germany if those ships remained immobilized in French harbors and under the watch of the Germans.[161] Churchill did not trust Hitler to live up to these provisions; he believed that if a French warship were in a port not governed by the armistice, it should be destroyed. As a result, in late June 1940 he directed that French warships tied up in the English city of Portsmouth be seized and ordered an attack against a large flotilla of French ships berthed at the major port city of Oran in the French province of Algeria.*

The terms of German Directive 21 provide further evidence of Hitler's deceit. He and his staff had spread the word that if he were granted freedom to operate unfettered in the East, he would leave Britain alone. But even if Germany had defeated Russia, and thus had achieved his goals for the East, Directive 21 revealed that Hitler then planned to turn back to the West and complete the war against England,[162] to conquer or neutralize Britain.

---

*Unsurprisingly, Hitler would violate the terms of the armistice. When the Allies invaded North Africa in November 1942, Germany advanced into the unoccupied portion of France to seize the French warships tied up in Toulon. Rather than allow the seizure to occur, the Vichy government scuttled and blew up the portion of the French fleet anchored in Toulon.

16. Churchill had long believed that Britain could stand alone against Germany

In February 1925, Churchill wrote to former P.M. and Foreign Secretary Arthur Balfour about the ages-old antagonism between Germany and France. Churchill pointed out that at the moment Germany was prostrate, but sooner or later it would rearm. The note then discussed a hypothetical war between France and Germany and what Britain would do if Germany controlled all the Channel ports in Europe. Churchill said, "The answer depends on who has the best and most powerful weapons. If, in addition to sea superiority, we had air supremacy, we might maintain ourselves as we did in the days of Napoleon for indefinite periods, even when all the Channel ports and all the low countries were in the hands of a vast hostile military power." Churchill added: "It should never be admitted in this argument that England cannot, if the worse comes to worst, stand alone."[163]

No matter how eager Britain may have been for peace in 1940, Churchill knew she "would never give in" once the battle was joined.[164] In fact, once France fell and Britain was formally on her own, British morale actually improved.[165] Churchill's "defiant spirit" bolstered Britons then, much as it would for the next five years.[166]

In 1940, Churchill would not relent on his long-held view that England could stand alone against Germany, even if Germany held all of Western Europe. And he certainly was not about to think that England would do any less when he and its people knew that the fate of Western Civilization was at stake.

17. Churchill had concluded that Hitler could not successfully invade Britain

In *Their Finest Hour* Churchill writes, "The foundations of my thought about invasion in 1940"[167] were that a successful invasion of Britain would require Germany to have "local naval superiority and air superiority and immense special fleets and landing craft."[168] His conclusion was that Germany did not have and would not achieve any of these.[169]

A. Local Naval Superiority

As Churchill told Parliament in a speech on June 18, an effective invading force would have to be extremely large and would require a huge armada. Even a small force of only five divisions, comprising fifty to seventy-five thousand lightly equipped men, would require two hundred to two hundred and fifty ships and powerful naval forces to escort it.[170]* Germany fell short on both scores. Churchill "estimated that to put the first wave of sixty to

---

In comparison, the D-Day invasion involved 156,000 men and 6,900 ships and landing vessels.

eighty thousand German troops ashore would require almost 60 percent of all German merchant shipping."[171] This would not have included landing ammunition, tanks, and heavy artillery.[172] Buchanan echoes this thought when he writes, "Had [Hitler] ever planned to invade England he would have built troopships [and] landing barges. ..."[173]*

As for escort vessels, the German Navy was heavily depleted after the Norway campaign.[174] At the beginning of summer 1940, it had only one heavy cruiser and four destroyers readily available to protect an invasion fleet crossing the Channel and landing on British beaches.[175] (Two new super battleships, the *Tirpitz* and the *Bismarck*, were scheduled to be brought into service at the end of August.) Supporting his opinion that Hitler had no intention of invading Britain, Buchanan notes that Hitler failed to build "warships to escort his landing craft, provide fire support for the invasion, and to keep the Royal Navy out of the Channel while his invasion force was crossing."[176] By comparison, the Royal Navy had five battleships, eleven cruisers and forty-three destroyers positioned at the ends of the Channel.[177] On July 10 Churchill wrote a note to the Commander-in-Chief of Home Forces, the Chief of the General Staff, and his Chief Staff Officer, General Hastings Ismay, detailing that the Admiralty had "over a thousand armed patrolling vessels, of which two or three hundred are always at sea" looking for signs of an invasion. He thus believed that "it would be a most hazardous and even suicidal operation [for the Nazis] to commit a large Army to the accidents of the sea in the teeth of our very numerous armed patrolling forces."[178]

While the Chiefs' pessimistic report of May 25 stated that, in an invasion, "Germany would probably employ the whole of her naval forces,"[179] Shirer writes, "Hitler had no fleet worthy of mention for the coming events of the summer. When the time to invade Britain came, as it did so shortly, this proved to be an insurmountable handicap."[180] Two things highlight the plight of the German Navy in the spring of 1940. First, it had lost ten of its twenty-one destroyers during the Norway campaign.[181] Second, based on the overwhelming superiority of the British Royal Navy, the German fleet stayed in port during the Dunkirk evacuation (and for some time after that as well).[182]

Given the depleted state of the German Navy, Churchill, writing in *Their Finest Hour*, contends that only "air power could destroy" the Royal

---

Germany's plan for the invasion of Britain (issued in mid-July) called for the landing of 260,000 infantry plus another nine divisions of tanks and other motorized vehicles. Shirer p. 762. It estimated that landing just the first wave would require 3,500 ships and landing vessels. Manchester and Reid p. 133.

It should be noted, however, that the Chiefs of Staff report dated May 10, 1940, painted a different picture: "Ample shipping is at the enemy's disposal." CAB 66/7 WP (40) 153 Annex I p. 7 229. This presumably included vessels that could deliver vehicles to the landing beaches. See, Ibid.

Navy ships defending the Channel.[183]* That is, for Germany to successfully counter Britain's local naval superiority, the Luftwaffe would first have to best Britain's Fighter Command.[184]**

Air Superiority

At the 11:30 AM War Cabinet meeting on May 27, Churchill explained that corrected figures from the Chiefs of Staff showed the Luftwaffe enjoying an advantage of two-and-a-half to one over the RAF in both bombers and fighters.[185] Even so, Churchill later wrote that, in 1940, he believed that "in our own air, in our own country, and its waters, we could beat the German Air Force, [in which case] our naval power would continue to rule of the seas ... and we would destroy all enemies who set their course towards us."[186] Churchill pointed out to Parliament that, when fighting over "friendly soil," British pilots who were shot down, unlike their German counterparts, would not be captured and thus could quickly return to the fight if able.[187] On June 18, three weeks before the Germans unleashed its sixteen-week aerial assault known as the "Battle of Britain," he also declared that "our

---

*In their May 25 report, the Chiefs of Staff put the issue of Britain's ability to control the sea along its eastern and southern coasts in a somewhat different, more pessimistic, light, saying:

> Our ability to exercise command of the North Sea and Channel will depend on our ability to operate surface forces within close range of enemy air bases. Whether we shall be able to maintain effective naval forces in bases on the East and South Coasts in the face of a very heavy scale of air attack is uncertain; if we cannot do so, the chance of intercepting enemy forces before they reach our shores will clearly be less. Finally, whether we shall be able to operate surface forces in strength in the southern part of the North Sea and the Channel at all is also uncertain. At the best, we may be able to continue using our present bases and to operate surface forces in adequate strength off our South and East Coasts without prohibitive loss or damage; at the worst, we may have to face the fact that we cannot do so. All that we can say at the moment is that it would be imprudent to count upon being able to do so. ... CAB 66/7 WP (40) 168 Annex p. 8 322.
>
> Our ability to control the North Sea and Channel depends on the number of light forces that we can dispose in these waters and operate there in the face of air attack. Ibid. Annex p. 9 323.

Despite the pessimism of the Chiefs of Staff, after the German Army came up with a detailed invasion plan in mid-July 1940, even the German Navy did not believe it had the necessary ships to support the proposed landing. It felt this to be true particularly in the face of the resistance anticipated from the Royal Navy and the RAF, and thus urged Hitler to postpone the invasion until no earlier than May 1941. Shirer p. 764.

**Of course, Churchill knew and greatly feared that if France fell (as was likely), the Germans would get the French fleet, the fourth largest in the world. How Britain addressed this fear is discussed in detail in a later chapter.

fighter air strength is stronger at the present time, relatively to the Germans, who have suffered terrible losses, than it has ever been, and consequently we believe ourselves to possess the capacity to continue the war in the air under better conditions than we have ever experienced before."[188]*

In a supplemental report by the Chiefs dated May 26, 1940, they concluded that, *"While our air force is in being, our Navy and air force together should be able to prevent Germany carrying out a serious seaborne invasion of this country."*[189] [emphasis added] The supplemental report reiterated a point made in an earlier document that "if the Germans succeeded in neutralizing our air forces, it might be impossible for our naval forces to prevent the establishment and maintenance of considerable German forces in this country."[190] This hypothesis reflected the lesson learned in the Norway campaign, that airpower could undercut the effectiveness of naval power. Another report went a step further by speculating that if the Germans achieved a sufficient measure of success in the early phases of the air war over England, they might be encouraged to take the risk and invade the UK.[191]

As for Britain's Fighter Command, the Chiefs noted that the current deficiency in the number of fighters it had would make it difficult to defend the wide front they foresaw. But they believed this forecast would improve in a few months, given increases in new aircraft production.** On another optimistic note, the Chiefs commented on the marked superiority that British fighters had shown over German bombers.[192] Furthermore, in the face of the growing strength of the Luftwaffe in recent years, the British had developed capable monoplane fighters like the Hurricane and the Spitfire. But the Chiefs' report of May 25 also stated: "We cannot resist invasion by fighter aircraft alone. An air striking force is necessary not only to meet the seaborne expedition, but also to bring direct pressure to bear upon Germany by attacking objectives in that country."[193] Unfortunately, in 1940 Britain was deficient in the number of bombers she had.[194]

The Chiefs mentioned the significant strides Britain had made in developing radar.[195] Under the leadership of Hugh Dowding, the Commander of Fighter Command, Britain had developed to great advantage the world's first fully integrated air defense system.[196] The system used a network of radar stations, called Radio Direction Finding (RDF) stations, to track German aircraft from the moment they took off in Western Europe; with the added

---

Both Churchill and the Chiefs, however, ignored the fact that Germany had a significant advantage when it came to pilots, both in numbers and in experience.

**British fighter production had improved significantly. It had overtaken German production. Under the direction of Lord Beaverbrook, Churchill's Minister for Aircraft Production, by late summer 1940 Britain's monthly fighter production would be twice that of Germany. Murray, 'The Battle of Britain,' The Quarterly Journal of Military History Vol 2 No. 4 p. 13.*

assistance of ground-based spotters it could plot their course accurately enough to know when best to attack them. Each RDF station passed its information to a central Filter Room at Fighter Command headquarters, located in the Greater London municipality of Stanmore. There, a specialized team turned this data, plus information from pilots and ground observations, into a clear picture of the incoming raids; this picture, in turn, was relayed to the Operations Room for the appropriate geographic sector.* At the sector facility a controller would review the information and decide when and where to scramble his squadrons to defend against the incoming raid. The controller would then provide a stream of information to the fighter pilots to guide them to intercept the German planes.[197] The "Dowding System" would prove the vital secret weapon as the British struggled to beat back the German air assault during the Battle of Britain.

The Chiefs expected the Germans would bomb not only the British aircraft industry but also RAF airfields, trying to destroy first-line air capacity, reserves, and maintenance facilities.[198] (In their May 25 report, they noted that "we have a well dispersed system of aerodrome's and satellite landing grounds. The enemy will certainly have to employ a large force with determination before he begins to inflict serious losses to our first line strength by attack on aerodromes."[199]) This anticipated German offensive would, the Chiefs assumed, be combined with or followed by air operations against British ports and ships on the south and east coasts.[200] These assumptions were, however, made before Western Europe was invaded and without the knowledge that in the battle for France the Luftwaffe would lose 30 percent of its bombers, 30 percent of its twin-engine fighters, and 15 percent of its single-engine fighters and thus needed time to recuperate.[201]

B. Special vessels, including landing craft

As noted, Churchill "estimated that to put the first wave of 60,000 to 80,000 German troops ashore would require almost 60 percent of all German merchant shipping ... [A] second wave of 160,000 ... along with ammunition, tanks, and heavy artillery would require far more shipping than Germany had at its disposal."[202] As Buchanan explains, to accomplish such a massive undertaking Hitler would have also had to build landing craft.[203] But he did not.

During Germany's successful campaigns in Norway and Western Europe, it had not engaged in any amphibious landings. Such tactics neither were part of German Army training nor did Germany have equipment suitable for such operations—i.e., it had no dedicated landing craft.[204] The German Army

---

Nationwide, there were twenty-one such sectors, seven of which surrounded London. See map, Manchester and Reid p. 134.

simply was not designed, trained, or eager for amphibious operations.[205] In *Their Finest Hour*, first published in 1949, Churchill reveals that the question being asked in the late spring of 1940 was: "Had the Germans ... secretly prepared a vast armada of special landing-craft which needed no harbors or quays, but could land tanks, cannon, and motor vehicles anywhere on the beaches...?" Noting in passing, that it took the Allies years to develop and produce such equipment for the D-Day invasion, he answers, with a bit of hindsight, that "We had ... no reason to believe that anything of this kind existed in Germany. ..."[206]

Manchester and Reid concur: "... Nazi Germany had no landing craft and no plans to build any. ..." As a result, "German troops, if they went to England, would do so aboard river barges," which were flat-bottomed vessels, ninety by twenty feet, with a top speed of 7 mph. These boats, however, were definitely not seagoing.[207] Additionally, the Germans would have needed to build "transports to ferry tanks and artillery across the channel."[208] With all port facilities destroyed and unavailable, such transport craft would have to be specialized for unloading on beaches, where they would find themselves under withering artillery fire from the British.[209]*

The conclusion that an invasion would not be possible because Germany did not have landing craft discounts, however, another report by the Chiefs of Staff dated May 29, 1940, about a "new form of attack" which they did not believe that British naval and air forces could interdict. CAB 66/8 WP (40) 178 pp. 2, 3 29, 30. In that report the Chiefs said, "it is possible that the Germans may employ a large fleet of fast motor boats (possibly up to 200 vessels carrying 100 men apiece) to carry out a seaborne raid on a large scale." These speedboats could be assembled surreptitiously at various ports in Germany—and possibly in Holland as well, and they could traverse the North Sea during the night. Ibid. p. 2 29. "These boats would [also] be handled with the utmost boldness and would probably be run up on the beaches without regard to loss of the craft or casualties to personnel. By this means we consider that a considerable force of the enemy could be landed at many points on the coast simultaneously with air-borne raids inland. We do not consider that by naval or air action we could prevent such a landing." Ibid. p. 3 30.

When this report was discussed in the War Cabinet, Admiral Sir Dudley Pound, the Chief of the Naval Staff, revealed that motor boats may have been gathering at the German ports of Bremen and Hamburg. CAB 65/10 148 (40) p. 314 203. He also said that the Germans were known to have an organized force of ships at the Spanish port of Vigo. Ibid. Both Chamberlain and Chief of the Air Staff Sir Cyril Newall showed significant concern. See, Ibid. Churchill, however, dismissed the Chiefs' report, doubting that a raid on a large scale could be carried out by motorboats. He said that these craft would have to come over in flotillas if they were to put ashore any useful number of men at any one point. Ibid. p. 315 204. He added that the Royal Navy would simply have to "make every endeavor to intercept such raids on the high seas." Ibid. While the comment seems rather cavalier, Churchill knew that any large invasion flotilla, whether traveling by motorboat or, more likely, by much slower river barges, would have to travel at night in order to hit the beaches at

On July 9, Churchill reiterated how hazardous it would be for Hitler to launch an invasion force into the teeth of Britain's formidable armed patrolling forces. He told the War Cabinet:

> ... the Fleet as disposed should be able to deal with what remained of the German Fleet if it endeavoured to escort an invading force. If any unescorted convoys endeavoured to make landings in this country, we should, have sufficient small craft to deal with them. All round the coasts were some hundreds of armed trawlers, motor-torpedo boats and mine-sweepers which could take part in the melee, if invasion were attempted.[210]

Churchill also did not think that in the immediate future, at any rate, there was much possibility of an attack being launched from the French coast. According to the First Sea Lord's information, there was little shipping now in the Northern French ports and only one old battleship and two destroyers at Calais.[211]

Because Germany did not have local naval superiority, air superiority, or enough landing craft, Churchill believed that the probability of a successful invasion was low. However, his ultimate conclusion was not based solely on those criteria. There was another significant reason why Churchill believed a massive landing by the Nazis would be impossible: he was willing to use poison gas to repel the invaders. This is hardly surprising. As discussed earlier, during his tenure as Minister of Munitions in 1917–1918, Churchill championed the use of poison gas. In 1940, he would tell the War Cabinet, "We [have] the right to do what we like ... with our own territory."[212] As Colville reports in his diary entry of July 1, 1940, "The Prime Minister has instructed [Major General] Ismay to investigate the question of 'drenching' beaches with mustard gas if the Germans land. He considers that gas warfare would be justified in such an event."[213] Churchill felt that "the Germans would make short work of him if they caught him, and so he didn't see why he should have any mercy on them."[214]

In his marvelous treatise *The Rise and Fall of the Third Reich,* William Shirer makes the astute observation that the German military was, and historically had always been, "land-minded" and that to them, the English Channel was "an obstacle they knew not how to overcome."[215] A careful reading of Hitler's top-secret Directive No. 6, outlining his plan for attacking western Europe, dated October 9, 1939, supports Shirer's observation. That directive does not mention an invasion of Britain. Under Directive 6, preparations were being made for an attack on the West at the earliest

---

dawn. But once night fell, Luftwaffe fighters would be grounded—the Royal Navy, with its largest ships having radar, owned the night. Manchester and Reid p. 120.

date possible. "The purpose will be to defeat as strong a part of the French operational army as possible, as well as allies fighting by its side, and at the same time to gain as large an area as possible in Holland and Belgium and Northern France. ..."[216] The Directive did not, however, talk about gaining any land in Britain nor did it talk about an invasion of the British Isles. Instead, it discussed only using the land gained in Holland, Belgium, and Northern France "as a base for conducting a promising air and sea war against England. ..."[217]

From the Directive, a reasonable conclusion can be drawn that, at least initially, Hitler had no plans to invade Britain.[218] Several additional observations support this premise:

- Shirer writes that there is no mention of a possible invasion of Britain in the German records until May 21, 1940.[219]

- Hitler admitted that "[c]rossing the Channel appear[ed] very hazardous."[220]

- Once France toppled, Hitler believed the war was over. He staged a victory parade, demobilized 40 divisions (25 percent of the army),[221] and even drafted a peace treaty he was sure the British would sign.[222]

- After the armistice with France was signed, both Hitler and Goering took a respite from strategic decision-making.[223] And,

- It was not until July 2, 1940, that Hitler asked that preliminary invasion plans be prepared for use when German air superiority over the UK had been achieved.[224]

According to Roberts, even as late as mid-July 1940, Hitler did not have "enough [aircraft] for a full-scale invasion of Britain unless he could win air superiority quickly and decisively and then attack the Royal Navy from the air. ..."[225] If Britain wouldn't sign a favorable peace agreement, Hitler would unleash an air war, not to occupy British territory, but rather to force London to capitulate.*

---

*It is doubtful, of course, that Churchill knew any of this, including the paragraph of Directive No. 6 just discussed. See, Manchester and Reid p. 120. Thus, it is no surprise that the notion in the cited portion of the Directive was not discussed in Britain in 1940. However, even though Shirer says that "it was not clear to us at the time," Roberts p. 575, given Churchill's knowledge of history, it is surprising that nowhere in the records of 1940 and nowhere in his post-war writings did Churchill apparently discuss what Shirer insightfully recognized—that the German military historically detested getting its feet wet.

18. Britain had a duty to defend the world cause to which she had vowed herself

Churchill clearly believed that Britain had a duty to defend and preserve Western civilization. He spoke of this often. For example, on September 3, 1939, Churchill described the cause for which Britain chose to fight as "sav[ing] the whole world from the pestilence of Nazi tyranny and ... reviv[ing] the stature of man."[226] On May 28, 1940, when updating the House about the battle that was going on in and around Dunkirk, he said, "nothing which may happen in this battle can in any way relieve us of our duty to defend the world cause to which we have vowed ourselves."[227] Churchill would return to the subject a few weeks later. Talking starkly about what was at stake for the world, he told Parliament:

> If we can stand up to [Hitler], all Europe may be free, and the life of the world may move forward into broad, sunlit uplands; but if we fail then the whole world, including the United States, and all that we have known and cared for, will sink into the abyss of a new dark age made more sinister, and perhaps more prolonged, by the lights of a perverted science."[228]

Churchill reiterated this theme throughout the summer of 1940. He told a nationwide BBC audience on July 14 that "we are fighting *by* ourselves alone; but we are not fighting *for* ourselves alone."[229] On August 20, 1940, he addressed the House of Commons:

- "[We] have the honour to be the sole champion of the liberties of all Europe...." And,

- "We have to think not only for ourselves but for the lasting security of the cause and principles for which we are fighting and of the long future of the British Commonwealth of Nations."[230]

Among the others who supported Churchill's viewpoint was Arthur Greenwood, Minister without Portfolio in the War Cabinet. Even before Britain had declared war, Greenwood said that "Britain, ... all that Britain stands for, and human civilization are in peril" because of the Nazis.[231]

As Churchill told the House of Commons just after the war started:

> We are fighting to save the whole world from the pestilence of Nazi tyranny and in defence of all that is most sacred to man.[232]

PART IV

Author's Note: Mark Schultz, M.D., a University of Vermont Clinical Associate Professor in Psychiatry, has written an unpublished essay examining a variety of psychohistorical factors that may have influenced Churchill to choose to go to war with Hitler, despite the clear dangers inherent in that decision. Dr. Schultz has kindly adapted that essay to appear, with his permission, as Chapter 20.

Churchill as Prime Minister holding submachine gun

20

Using Personal History and Psychodynamics to Examine and Understand Churchill's Decision to Commit to War

Introduction
Winston Churchill, Warrior
Winston Churchill, from Broken Child to Nation's Father
Winston Churchill, Seeker of Redemption
Winston Churchill, Lone Wolf
Winston Churchill, Daredevil
Winston Churchill, Hitler's Nemesis

Introduction

In late May 1940, Winston Churchill had been the Prime Minister of Britain for less than three weeks. His country faced two choices: continue to fight on in what would become its own a full-fledged war with Hitler, or to beg Hitler for tolerable terms in an uncertain armistice. Germany had easily overrun Poland, Norway, Denmark, Holland, Belgium, and Luxembourg, and would conquer France in a few weeks. Italy, an alliance partner with Nazi Germany, was poised to enter the war; and Turkey was content to look the other way concerning German advances. Stalin had agreed to a nonaggression pact with Hitler that had secretly entitled the Soviet Union to gobble up the eastern portion of Poland. If that picture were not grim enough, it looked likely that some two hundred thousand British troops, nearly its entire professional army, would be captured or killed at Dunkirk in northwest France before they could be evacuated across the Channel back to England. Moreover, the Royal Air Force appeared greatly outnumbered, and English shipping was sustaining increasingly heavy losses to marauding German U-boats. The United States, though openly sympathetic to Britain's plight, seemed content to limit its tangible help.

Britain itself was still relatively unscathed by the war on the continent—Hitler had not yet unleashed his assault against the British homeland—so, if it pressed for peace, Britain might have emerged intact even though the war was raging a scant 20 miles across the English Channel. Thus, many powerful political leaders favored a negotiated peace with Hitler. Though some of them knew Hitler could not be trusted to negotiate in good faith, they abhorred the thought of another war. A goal of a brokered peace with honor and true security, though certainly preferable to war, may, however, have been more wishful thinking than an attainable outcome; and the remaining choices were odious: a peace brought about by capitulation, or an all-out war that likely would include invasion of the UK.

On May 28, Churchill announced that Britain would continue to fight against Adolf Hitler and not seek peace with the German dictator. This decision would likely cost the lives of hundreds of thousands of his country-men. When he told his Outer Cabinet that evening that "… we shall fight it out," hindsight tells us that this decision was the correct one, both because of what we came to learn of Hitler's barbarism and because we know that England managed to survive the brutal beating soon to be inflicted on it by the Luftwaffe. In hindsight, it also seems to be the only decision that would have fit Churchill's pugnacious and determined character.

What was it about Churchill, an eccentric figure with a history of ques-tionable judgments and mixed reviews within his own party, that led him to reject what may have been a more palatable pursuit of peace and instead lead his frightened, anxious country directly into the path of certain peril? What existed within Churchill's psyche that might have helped steer him away from an expedient peace and toward all-out war? And how did he come to develop the grit, strength, and confidence he would need to put his country on his shoulders and trade blow for blow with an intractably evil foe?

Winston Churchill was able to look at the decision of war versus peace not just based on the complexities and urgencies of the political and military moment, but also based on a variety of transformative personal experiences and insights from the arc of his own life:

- From his time in the service and on fields of battle, he experienced and understood war.

- From enduring an emotionally traumatic childhood, he understood suffering and developed empathy for the struggles and travails of the oppressed and endangered.

- From his days wandering in a professional or personal "wilderness" of ridicule or isolation, he understood the importance of identifying and trusting one's own instincts, of becoming self-reliant, and of seizing the reins and mastering one's own fate.

- From times of failure and ridicule, he learned perseverance and valued opportunities for redemption.

- From his inherently fearless nature, he did not shy away from danger.

- From his childhood days of being bullied and his military days of witnessing brutality, he instinctively understood that the only way to deal with Hitler was to seek his utter defeat. Bullies do not cease being bullies once they get their way.

Winston Churchill, Warrior

Thesis: Churchill's life-long immersion in military-related activities gave him an unusually nuanced view of the perils of and opportunities inherent in war, and it made him an ideal leader to shepherd Britain into and through World War II.

Churchill's life through May 1940 was as much a soldier's life—or, perhaps more accurately, a warrior's life—as it was the life of an aristocratic politician. This martial experience was a significant part of the unique skill set he brought into office when he became Prime Minister. Serving in the military was not a typical path to the British Prime Ministership in the first half of the twentieth century; in fact, seven of nine Prime Ministers preceding Churchill had spent no time in the service.

The Churchill family's military (and noble) lineage traces back to John Churchill, whom Queen Anne made the first Duke of Marlborough in 1702, in recognition of his distinguished career as soldier and statesman. Nearly two centuries later, Winston's father, Lord Randolph Churchill, pushed his son to pursue a military career, though he did so because he feared his son would not succeed in any other profession. Fortunately, military service was appealing to the boy, given, among other things, his veneration of his family's heritage, his love of history, and his physical fearlessness. "Churchill was interested in things military from a young age," writes Churchill scholar Douglas Russell. "His earliest surviving letter, written at age seven, is about toy soldiers, flags, and castles."[1] As a child, Winston engaged in elaborate and obsessional play with his set of toy soldiers. "These battles were played with an interest that was no ordinary child game."[2]

Winston pursued military studies while at Harrow, the prestigious English preparatory school he entered at thirteen. In his admittedly unhappy school days there, Churchill derived great pleasure from the School Rifle Corps, became accomplished in fencing, relished learning about famous battles, and is said to have admired Napoleon. He also wrote a strategically precocious essay about an imagined future British invasion of Russia.

As he was finishing up at Harrow, Winston remarked that he wished to enter the army, "so long as there's fighting to be had."[3] He hoped that choosing a career in the army would finally make his father proud of him. Years later, however, Winston would learn a bitter truth: that Lord Randolph's approval of his son's entering the military sprang not from "the qualities of military genius" Winston had hoped his father perceived within him, but as stated earlier, from his father's skepticism that Winston would not succeed in any other line of work.

After Harrow, Winston enrolled in the elite Royal Military Academy at Sandhurst. The pedestrian score he achieved on his third crack at the entrance exam slotted him for the less prestigious cavalry training; but he took to horsemanship with relish and became an accomplished equestrian. He began to love military life and enjoyed studying tactics, military law and other disciplines. Happy and intellectually stimulated, Winston saw his class ranking soar from ninety-second out of 102 students in September 1893 to twentieth in his class only fourteen months later. Winston graduated in December 1894.

In the spring of 1895, Winston joined the 4th Queen's Own Hussars, a regiment that, in 1854, had participated in the immortal but ill-fated Charge of the Light Brigade during the Crimean War. According to biographer Andrew Roberts, Churchill loved every aspect of being an officer in the cavalry, including the horses, the distinctive uniforms, and even the drilling. But what he consciously sought was a war he could join. "To the younger Winston, as to many British of his class and military rank, war was an adventure."[4]

Though his aristocratic lineage gave him a huge leg up in setting his military career into motion and though there was a distinct quality of dilettantism to some of his exploits, Winston was no gentleman soldier. He gravitated to, rather than avoided, armed conflicts; and his frequent demonstrations of true bravery earned him a host of military honors over the course of three decades.[5]

Churchill certainly did not let his privileged status keep him out of harm's way. Warfare was so appealing to him that even when not serving actively in the military, he sought out combat as a war correspondent. Wartime exploits also sparked and fueled his frenetic passion for writing; and each of his first six books, which included his only novel, were about war.

Churchill found himself, as both soldier and journalist, engaged in many theaters of military conflict in the late 1890s. In the three-year period from 1895 through 1898, Churchill had witnessed the Cuban armed struggle for independence from Spain, immersed himself in skirmishes on the Indian subcontinent, and twisted arms so he could fight in Lord Kitchener's army against the infamous Dervishes in the Sudan. In fact, Churchill served in the British army and Territorial army from 1893 to 1924, though not continuously;

he was a commissioned officer in five separate units, and his rank rose from Cornet to Lieutenant Colonel. With the approach and advent of the Second World War, he was made an Honorary RAF Air Commodore as well as an Honorary Colonel in three different army units.

After the Boer War, Churchill's focus turned to a different kind of battle—politics—where it remained for more than half a century. (He did resume military service for a half year in World War I, during which he commanded a battalion in Belgium and France. For weeks his position was continually shelled by German artillery; and at one point he was nearly killed by a piece of flying shrapnel.)

Even after his career path took him into politics, Churchill remained intimately connected with military matters. In 1906 he was appointed Under-Secretary of State for Colonial Affairs, during a time of a bloody Zulu rebellion in South Africa. From 1907 through 1910, he regularly attended military maneuvers in England, France and Germany.

In October 1911 Churchill became First Lord of the Admiralty, the position he held during the disastrous Gallipoli campaign in Turkey four years later; a debacle for which he received considerable blame, much of it unwarranted. During the twelve-year period starting in 1917, he would serve in several positions that affected the military and military spending: Minister of Munitions, Secretary of State for War and Air, and Chancellor of the Exchequer. On September 3, 1939, two days after Germany invaded Poland, Prime Minister Chamberlain asked him to again serve as First Lord of the Admiralty and be a member of the War Cabinet.

In sum, ever since his childhood days playing hours on end with his lead soldiers, Churchill had jumped at every chance to study and participate in war-related activities. It's not that he saw war through rose-colored glasses: indeed, his time in India and the Sudan, for instance, would have reinforced for him the reality of war's brutality. Moreover, it was also not the case that Churchill had a blood-thirsty preference for war. During a November 1934 BBC radio broadcast he said that "no one 'outside a madhouse' would want to start another war. ..."

In the course of human interaction, however, war is perhaps the most outsized of endeavors, and a fitting arena for a man like Winston Churchill, with outsized ambition, boundless self-confidence, and a powerful attraction to the dramatic. Though Winston's notoriety in combat came as much from his journalistic pursuits as from any battlefield exploits, he experienced battle and loss firsthand and demonstrated true bravery. Decades of experiencing and even embracing combat did not create the Winston Churchill who would become Britain's revered Warrior-in-Chief. Instead, war allowed him to become his truest and most successful self. It's as if the young Winston who was "eager for trouble" during the Boer War intuitively understood that "trouble" was the ingredient that brought out his best traits and would separate him from other men.

Without World War II, it is possible Churchill would be remembered more for his writings and flamboyance than for his political accomplishments. By temperament and interest, Churchill was more prepared for a life of war than a life of peace. War—which "for him," according to novelist and poet Siegfried Sassoon, "was the finest activity on earth"[6]—seemed easier for him to comprehend. War, much more than life, was the chess game in which he could see several moves ahead. On the stage that war created for him, Churchill strode as a giant, beloved by the people he served. However, on the stage that everyday life set for him, he was often seen as a loose cannon, a rogue, a spendthrift, and even at times, a buffoon. War allowed Winston Churchill to be what very well can be considered his best self.

Though he found personal acclaim in battle, and even though he spent much of the latter half of the 1930s publicly lampooning the British Government's reluctance to prepare for what he saw as a likely "Armageddon,"[7] there is no reason to believe Churchill would have kept Britain in a war merely as a selfish means of self-aggrandizement. In a speech in July 1936, Churchill said, "Nothing would give me greater pleasure than to be ... proved to be an alarmist. I would endure with patience the roar of exultation that would go up when I was proved wrong, because it would lift a load off my heart .... What does it matter who gets exposed or discomfited? If the country is safe, who cares for individual politicians ...?"[8] When Churchill, as the newly named Prime Minister, had to make the decision between continuing the war or pursuing peace, he would not recoil from war's attendant traumas and thus could coolly decide there no longer was, in fact, any rational alternative. "A country like ours ...," Churchill stated, "cannot avoid war by dilating upon its horrors. ..."[9]

Winston Churchill, from Broken Child to Nation's Father

Thesis: Churchill adapted to the hurt of parental neglect and emotional abandonment by seeking love and recognition wherever he could. The extent to which he succeeded in this search allowed Churchill to believe his countrymen could similarly overcome big obstacles, and he would ask them to do so when Britain faced Hitler without any meaningful Allied help in the early months of World War II. Being a wartime leader would both heighten his visibility and importance and create an opportunity for him to be Britain's heroic protector, which, in the process, would further distinguish him from his negligent parents.

Andrew Roberts writes that "Churchill's sublime self-confidence and self-reliance stemmed directly from the assurance he instinctively felt in who he was and where he came from."[10] If only it had been that easy. For him to become the robust, flamboyant, spellbinding, cocksure "Winston Churchill" we see in our mind's eye, Winston had to navigate the shoals of an emotionally deprived and damaging childhood.

Churchill's parents were the charming but uninterested, immature, emotionally cruel Jennie and the demanding, critical, scornful, unsympathetic Randolph. Neither parent put much effort into participating constructively, either emotionally or behaviorally, in Winston's life. "His parents paid him little attention, not even bothering to make the customary daily inspection of their infant son."[11] Though upper-class parents in Victorian England were more like "popes granting audiences" to their young children,[12] rather than engaged caretakers and nurturers, Winston's parents' "neglect and lack of interest ... were remarkable, even judged by the standards of the day." Winston was sent off to boarding school in Ascot, a town 30 miles west of London; and one academic has speculated that Winston "understood perhaps better than some of his less sensitive peers that he had been sent away to school to get rid of him. ..."[13] His parents rarely deigned to visit their son at school. During his years at the Brunswick School, young Winston constantly begged his mother to "come and see [him]," sometimes promising her "billions of kisses" if she would; "[s]he never found the time."[14] During his days at Harrow, he continually begged them to visit.

Anecdote after anecdote describe Lady Randolph's appalling lack of engagement with her young son. Winston's nanny, Elizabeth Everest, felt compelled to break Victorian protocol and complain to Lady Randolph about the disgraceful state of the two-year-old boy's "shabby" clothes.[15] When Winston was sent off to school, Lady Randolph had the seven-year-old dropped off at London's Paddington Station, forcing the young boy to catch the train on his own.[16] Despite his earnest efforts, Winston never succeeded in figuring out how to engage his socially and sexually distractible mother in a consistent and healthy relationship.

If Churchill's relationship with his mother was poor, his relationship with his father was worse. Young Winston strove throughout his life to meet his father's uncompromising and dauntingly unattainable standards. That so many examples survive of Lord Randolph's disdain for his son reveals how commonplace those castigating assessments were. "His father did not know how old [Winston] was, or which public school he attended"; and he made it clear that he favored Winston's unobtrusive younger brother Jack, chiding Winston saying that "in never doing stupid things, Jack is vastly your superior."[17] His father was uniformly harsh in his assessment of his older son's early capabilities and pessimistic about how successful his son might become as an adult; and he did not shield his sensitive son from these disdainful evaluations. When, in a letter, Winston shared his excitement about his admission to Sandhurst, his father, in a remarkably merciless reply, rebuked him first for failing to qualify for the infantry course of study and then, it seems, for generally being nothing but a profound disappointment. The reply concluded with this unambiguous verbal caning:

> *Because I am certain that if you cannot prevent yourself from leading the idle useless unprofitable life that you have had during your schooldays and latter months, you will become a mere social wastrel, one of the hundreds of the public school failures, and you will degenerate into a shabby, unhappy, and futile existence. If that is so you will have to bear all the blame for such misfortunes yourself.*[18]

No doubt emotional abandonment contributed greatly to Winston's poor social and academic adjustment: he talked back to headmasters; he was regarded as selfish; other boys disliked him; he was frequently bullied; and his school performance was so bad his mother informed him that "Your father and I are both more disappointed than we can say. ... Your work is an insult to your intelligence. ..."[19] It is not hard to imagine young Winston internalizing his parents' disdain and, as a result, struggling to feel adept and self-confident.

When he was seven, Winston was sent off to St. George's School in Ascot. There, corporal punishment was the norm, and Winston was miserable. "How I hated this school, and what a life of anxiety I lived there. ..."[20] Winston found himself in an escalating cycle of physical frailty worsened by corporal abuse by school authorities and bullying by classmates.

Ill health, presumed by later authorities to have been exacerbated by the physical abuse he received in Ascot,[21] precipitated a change in schools, to the Brunswick School in Brighton. Soon after he arrived, Winston was stabbed in the chest with a penknife after tugging at the ear of a fellow student. (In recounting the incident in a letter to her husband, Winston's mother branded her immature son the instigator, writing "I have no doubt Winston teased the boy dreadfully—& it ought to be a lesson to him."[22])

Because of his parents' emotional neglect, young Winston had to develop self-soothing and self-motivating skills at an early age. As would be expected, strategies stumbled upon in childhood were immature and often counterproductive. One adaptation, already discussed, led him to immerse himself in fantasy play with his toy soldiers; and another was to develop a penchant for risk-taking behavior. Young Winston was continually attracted to physically risky behavior. At eighteen, he purposefully jumped off a thirty-foot-high footbridge, a stunt that led to a concussion, a ruptured kidney, and a broken bone in his back.[23] Churchill's penchant for injury and close calls continued throughout his life: "[He] fell several times from horses, dislocated his shoulder while disembarking from a ship in India, crashed a plane while learning to fly and was hit by a car when he looked the wrong way to cross New York's Fifth Avenue."[24] He even was nearly killed by a charging rhinoceros during a 1907 trip to Africa.[25]

During Winston's teenage years, the quality of his adaptive and self-soothing skills improved considerably. This outcome would not at all have been anticipated: indeed, early emotional trauma can permanently retard psychological and even cognitive development in affected children. In Winston's case, there likely were a number of reasons for his successful transformation, including the lessons learned from all the early hurdles he had to overcome; getting out from under the dismissive shadow cast by his parents; finding more supportive mentors and teachers; and becoming engaged in academic and avocational pursuits in which he could excel, with success breeding more success. Winston finally found himself in environments in which his own expansive and innovative self could begin to emerge, fueled by the dogged determination that would become his hallmark. He became a voracious reader of newspapers—initially to keep up with accounts of his father's political career—and he developed hobbies like stamp-collecting and caring for goldfish.[26]

At some point in his youth Winston also would have understood that seeking his parents' recognition and love was a fruitless endeavor. So as he moved into manhood, he began to seek recognition from parental substitutes such as senior officers, newspaper editors, political mentors and even the public in general. Winston also started to tap into an innate self-assuredness that foreshadowed the energy and swagger that came to characterize his writing, his politics, his oratory and, finally, his international persona. He began to lean on a self-confidence that grew to be so sturdy it often came across as arrogance; and he discovered that he possessed the power to sway people through his spellbinding oratory. Winston had constructed a personality that melded intelligence, humor, arrogance, a budding gift for the written as well as the spoken word, latent artistic talent (he would go on to produce more than 540 paintings in his lifetime), and a shameless tendency for self-promotion. He also found a succession of perfect vehicles for exhibiting this persona: the military, journalism, and his father's vocation—politics.

Significant to the decision that he would have to make about negotiating with the Nazis, Churchill did not just grow out of his childhood psychological deprivations to become a man of high achievement—he also, perhaps surprisingly, became a moral and loving man. Much of the credit for his emotional transformation goes to his cherished nanny Elizabeth Everest. "One of her greatest gifts to Churchill," writes scholar Marvin Rintala, "was the rigorous guidance she provided him in moral principles. Otherwise, Churchill was raised in an atmosphere that was far from morally strict."[27] He learned his moral code not from his parents or at his prestigious boarding schools but at the knee of this unprepossessing spinster from Kent.

Described as "a woman of deep faith,"[28] Everest came to the Churchills as baby Winston's caretaker following twelve years tending to the daughter of a clergyman in Cumberland. She had much to do because of the neglectful attitudes of young Winston's parents. The sensitive boy loved the woman he called "Woomy." In his autobiography, Churchill said, "My nurse was my confidante. Mrs. Everest it was who looked after me and tended all my wants. It was to her I poured out my many troubles ...."[29] Everest provided emotional succor to Winston, even after he left for school. She, not his parents, visited him at school; and reportedly it was at her insistence that Winston was pulled out of St. George's School, after seeing the scars inflicted by the repeated whippings Winston received at the hands of the school's headmaster.

Examples abound throughout Churchill's long career that show how much he internalized Everest's moral teaching and modeling. If his own countrymen were acting immorally or unethically, he would call them out. For instance, he publicly decried the brutality and disrespect that famed British commander Lord Kitchener demonstrated against Sudanese combatants ("wounded [Sudanese] were left to die or shot and bayoneted where they lay").[30] During the Boer War, despite his capture, Churchill spoke out against knee-jerk anti-Boer prejudice and urged that they be treated with "generosity and tolerance."[31]

In the realm of politics, in the early years of the twentieth century Churchill became a leader in introducing social welfare legislation, including bills that provided for old-age pensions, expanded national healthcare, and established compulsory unemployment insurance. The more Churchill tried to help the wage-earning class, the more he began attacking the upper class and the Conservatives. In early 1909, he described Conservatives as "the party of the rich against the poor, ... of the lucky, the wealthy, the happy, and the strong against the left-out and the shut-out millions of the weak and poor."[32] In other words, the Tories were bullies; and Winston had learned through experience to recognize bullies and stand up to them.

Moreover, deviating from the stereotypes of his social class, he also developed true empathy for those whom society always seemed to hand the short end of the stick. As Home Secretary, a post he assumed early in 1910, Churchill championed prison reform. He ended the practice of flogging and created prison libraries. He released prisoners whose real "crime" was being poor, and reduced the penalty for minor offenses, particularly if committed by children. Under Churchill's reforms, the number of Britons incarcerated plummeted.

As Chancellor of the Exchequer, Churchill's 1925 budget was "an abrupt departure from the traditional Tory approach to ways and means." Churchill proposed to lower taxes on the poor and raise them on unearned income; have the Treasury assume responsibility for the victims of industrial distress; provide benefits to widows and orphans; reduce the age for retirement pensions from seventy to sixty-five; and provide health insurance, partially paid for by employers, to thirty million Britons.[33] Churchill had become a believer in the power of "moral forces." "Do not mock at them, for these may be years, strange as it may seem, when Right will walk hand in hand with Might."[34]

Another outcome of Elizabeth Everest's nurturance of Winston was his development of the capacity to love and his acceptance of the possibility that he could be loved in return. (This remarkable transformation was on full display as Churchill strove to comfort his battered and frightened country-men during the horrific German air assault on Britain from September 1940 to May 1941.) "Elizabeth Everest's most direct monument," wrote scholar Marvin Rintala, "... may have been Winston Churchill. That the adult Churchill was able to function was probably the consequence of Everest's love for him, which showed Churchill that he was worthy of being loved, and of his love for Everest, which showed to Churchill that he could love ..."[35]

The family Churchill established with his wife, Clementine, was the main laboratory in which he practiced and refined his skills as a loving man. Clementine and Winston had five children—one, Marigold, died of septicemia before her third birthday—and by all accounts he was a devoted father. "Is it joyous," Churchill wrote to Clementine in 1935, "to see how great and growing is the treasure we have gathered together."[36] Though at times he clashed with his son Randolph, Churchill by and large succeeded in his determination not to repeat Lord and Lady Randolph's parenting mistakes with his own children. "He vowed that, unlike his father, he would spend time with them and was an affectionate and devoted parent, building a tree house at Chartwell for the older three and, utilising his bricklaying skills, a little summer house for the youngest, Mary."[37] Later in life, daughter Mary recounted that "Both my parents were enormously affectionate, visibly so, and he was a great hugger, my father, and loved having us around." She recalled how when the family was in Chartwell, their country home in Kent, she and her siblings had the run of the home and she "never felt excluded" from her parents' life.[38]

At Chartwell, Churchill was able to find compassion and contentment. John Mather, a physician and Churchill scholar, believes that being part of "a loving and supportive family" rid Churchill of the worst of his depressive inclinations. "His daughters Sarah and Mary were joys to him; his wife

Clementine was his rock."[39] Churchill, he went on, learned to take "life in stride, finding equanimity in laughter and good fun. ... He did not take himself too seriously, often poking fun at both friends and enemies. His daughter Mary, Lady Soames, who spent a lot of time with him during the war, said of his tenacity and endurance: 'Papa had this enormous quality of never despairing.'"[40] A contented Churchill was "just Winston" to his rural neighbors, and he demonstrated an unpretentious sense of noblesse oblige.

When Churchill took the nation's helm in May 1940, England was still recovering from the wounds of WWI and the suffering brought on by economic depression, and he had to prepare his frightened and resource-strapped countrymen for another war, one that seemed unwinnable. The 1930s had been a difficult time. Though the UK escaped the worst of the Great Depression, it entered the 1930s "... in a prolonged economic stagnation of low growth. ... [t]he decline in global demand hit the UK economy," and the economy went into recession. "[There were] record levels of unemployment and growing social unrest at the extent of the recession." The 1932 unemployment rate was between 15 and 22 percent. Housing was "a seemingly intractable problem in the 30s ...," and "thousands of overcrowded, vermin-infested slums" required demolition.[41] Britain's famed National Health Service "was still a distant dream...."[42] Over thirty thousand people died of tuberculosis in England and Wales in 1934. In 1936 malnutrition led two hundred unemployed workers on a riveting twenty-six-day, 300-mile hunger march to London.[43]

Bottom line: when the time came in May 1940, Churchill's bumpy journey of healing and transformation allowed him to embrace, parent, and protect Britain in its time of extreme peril. Before he could enter productive adult life, Winston had had to emerge from a childhood of emotional pain and sustained illness and injury.* If he were to avoid crumbling under the weight of his parents' disregard and emotional renunciation—and perhaps avoid emerging in the process as a spoiled, purposeless, melancholy, alcoholic aristocrat of no redeeming social value—he would have to tap into inherent hidden resources to nurture himself and maneuver toward success. Spurred on by the never-wavering support of Mrs. Everest, leaning on the unfolding plethora of his many natural gifts, quite literally finding a unique moral voice, and soaking in the love of the family he shared with Clementine, Churchill was able to lead Britain through its most challenging hours.

It's been widely speculated that Churchill suffered from a life-long depressive or manic-depressive illness. Life reversals in an emotionally sensitive and prideful individual could easily trigger understandable depressive reactions; inherent mental illness need not be invoked as a cause.

The suffering of the British working class and the grave external traumas that seemed poised to strike the nation would likely have provoked an unconscious but powerful evocation of the arc of Winston's own formative psychological and physical battles. Churchill could now take on the role of Father to his nation naturally and sincerely, and with much less of the internal angst and psychological conflict that characterized him earlier in his life. And, given the stakes in May 1940, he would have needed all the internal strength and stability he could muster. "The neglect and emotional cruelty at the hands of his parents that could have crushed a lesser person," noted biographer Andrew Roberts, "instead gave Churchill an unquestionable desire to succeed in life ..."[44] He bulled his way through frailties and injuries to become a robust "man's man." London writer Daniel Smith speculates that it was the bullying and corporal abuse during his time at St. George's School "that made him so determined to stand up to apparently mighty foes in later life."[45] From the teenage boy who needed three tries to barely make it into Sandhurst, he twice became First Lord of the Admiralty. From his early years as a poor student he became a Nobel-Prize-winning author of dozens of works of history and fiction. Despite a lisp and perhaps a stammer, he developed into one of the twentieth century's greatest orators.

So let's ask the question: How did Churchill's triumph over the many obstacles of his youth manifest in his resistance to entering peace negotiations with Hitler?

If Churchill could conquer abandonment, isolation, and infirmity in a triumphantly sustained personal transformation, then so, he wholeheartedly believed, could Britain. Churchill's optimism about the enduring triumphant spirit of his countrymen was boundless. Britons could do anything they were determined to do. "We are an undefeated people," he proclaimed in a March 1937 speech to Parliament. "Nearly a thousand years have passed since we were conquered or subjugated by external force."[46]

As Winston had bested his tormentors, so too could Britain. Churchill did not cower at the possibility of continuing an all-out war with no allied help, because he was convinced Britain would rise to the challenge. In March 1938, Churchill told the House of Commons: "We should lay aside every hindrance and endeavor by uniting the whole force and spirit of our people to raise again a great British nation standing up before all the world; for such a nation, rising in its ancient vigor, can even at this hour save civilization."[47]

From the day he became Prime Minister, Winston would instinctively chart Britain's direction and be its caretaker, not just as the nation's Warrior Protector but also as its surrogate parent. He developed instinctual bonds with the people, perhaps as a consequence of, and as an act of indebtedness to, how dependent he was on the love and loyalty of Elizabeth Everest. He would love the people of Britain as his parents could have loved him but did not. He would express his love as a belief that Britain could find the same conquering strength and resilience he had discovered within himself. In return, he would receive the love of his people.

In his first speech as Prime Minister to the House of Commons, on May 13, 1940, Winston Churchill said that the goal is: "Victory at all costs, victory in spite of all terror, victory however long and hard the road may be; for without victory there is no survival." These were far from idle patriotic words from a skillful politician. This heart-rending sentiment could have been his own personal mantra. Throughout his childhood Churchill had to conquer the punishing effects of isolation, abandonment, emotional cruelty, bullying, illness, and injury; and conquer them he did. Churchill survived an emotionally barren childhood to emerge as a beloved father figure to his beleaguered nation, and he was ready to lead his country through whatever torments and tragedies were just over the horizon. He would be Britain's "Woomy."

Winston Churchill, Seeker of Redemption

Thesis: Before World War II, the most notable item on Churchill's military-related resume was the colossal debacle of the Gallipoli campaign in 1915. Politically, he suffered a surprising number of electoral defeats and spent most of the decade of the 1930s in a leadership "wilderness." For these failures not to define Churchill in the eyes of history—and not to confirm his father's pitiless opinion of him—successfully prosecuting a seemingly unwinnable war might offer just the right opportunity for redemption.

Churchill understood the abiding value in looking one's demons, internal and external, in the eye and not backing down. "When the first beginnings of evil which may subsequently challenge peace and freedom and even the life of the State make their appearance on the horizon," Churchill told the House of Commons on March 4, 1937, "it is right then to sound the alarm and to try, even by frantic exertions, to arouse somnolent authority to ... see that we are marching through that long, dark valley. ..."[48]

Among the influences that can be postulated as unconsciously motivating Churchill to choose to fight Hitler rather than to negotiate a peace agreement could be included a quest for redemption.

Churchill had created or seized opportunities to redeem himself since childhood. For example, he went from being a poor student at the lower reaches of his class to a young man recognized for his intellectual prowess. By the age of twenty-five he had engaged in feats of heroism in battle, achieved great popular acclaim as a writer, and followed in his father's footsteps by ascending into Parliament. By any objective measure, these accomplishments should have erased the stain of ridicule heaped upon him by his harsh father.

Another example of overcoming a hurdle in his life was how young Winston, who had a noticeable lateral lisp (he had difficulty enunciating "s" and "z" sounds) and may also have struggled with a stammer, went on to become one of the great orators of the twentieth century.

But the fascinating subplot of failure throughout Churchill's long courtship with war brings a quest for redemption into sharpest focus. As stated earlier, it took him three tries to gain acceptance to the Royal Military Academy at Sandhurst, and when he did it was to a course of study lesser in prestige: the cavalry rather than the infantry. Churchill achieved some notoriety for heroics in the Sudan; but by far, his most notable success came as the result of being captured and then escaping from a Boer prison. This exploit, both improbable and harrowing, received national attention through his own breathless written accounts, in which he turned what could rightly have been viewed as a reckless escapade into the stuff of legend.

In the fall of 1911 Churchill ascended to the position of First Lord of the Admiralty. Over the next three years he bolstered the preparedness of the British navy, advocated for a more robust Royal Naval Air Service, and pushed plans for the development of such novel armaments as the seaplane and the tank. Once World War I had begun, he was a staunch ally of countries, including France, Belgium, and Russia, which faced the brunt of German assaults. But Churchill's tenure as First Lord of the Admiralty is not remembered as a time of foresight and fortitude, but as a time of abject failure and personal humiliation.

Churchill's most enduring personal military legacy, until the advent of World War II, was the disaster at Gallipoli during the early part of World War I. In November 1914 Churchill began to raise the idea of assisting Russia by confronting Turkey and wresting control of the strategic Dardanelles Straits from the Turks. After a failed attempt by the Royal Navy to force the straits open in mid-March 1915, the Mediterranean Expeditionary Force (MEF), comprising units from Britain, Australia, and New Zealand, made an amphibious assault a month later on Turkish positions on the Gallipoli peninsula. After eight months and a half million casualties, the MEF was withdrawn. Turkey, by then a German ally, proclaimed a glorious victory, while in Britain, Churchill was excoriated for what was called a debacle. In May 1915 Churchill was relieved as First Lord of the Admiralty. Though he was retained in the Cabinet, it was in a position of humiliatingly little importance or authority.

As much as Churchill has been justifiably feted for his dogged capacity to move on from personal and professional reversals, Gallipoli stung him severely. Clementine told Churchill biographer Martin Gilbert, "The Dardanelles haunted him for the rest of his life. ... When he left the Admiralty he thought he was finished. ... I thought he would never get over the Dardanelles. I thought he would die of grief."[49] It is easy to imagine that the calumny heaped upon Churchill tapped into the deep well of pain caused by his father's scornful opinion of his "third rate" son.[50] Moreover, although Churchill was largely vindicated by the fact-finding Dardanelles Commission, its 1917 report did not deal with all the charges leveled against him nor did it prevent the public from continuing to think him responsible for the fiasco.

The searing emotional pain must have been amplified by how psychologically resonant the phenomenon of "Gallipoli" quickly became world-wide. Even now, over a century later, "Gallipoli" carries an intense emotional valance in many places around the globe. In Turkey, for example, the iconic battle is credited with hastening the Turkish War of Independence and ultimately, the Turkish Republic six years later. Today, the array of options for touring Gallipoli battle sites rivals that for viewing the American Civil War battlefields at Gettysburg. In 2015 thousands of Turks flooded Gallipoli for the heralded centennial of the revered campaign.

The debacle resounded politically—not just militarily—for Churchill. The hit to his reputation seemed to catch up with him in 1922, when he lost re-election to Parliament. During a subsequent Parliamentary election campaign in 1923, hecklers taunted Churchill with cries of "What about the Dardanelles?"[51]

Churchill also lost the March 1924 Westminster by-election—his third election loss in sixteen months. All told, of the twelve elections in which Churchill participated up to the middle of 1924, he won only six. And even though Churchill was returned to Parliament in October 1924 and served as Chancellor of the Exchequer in the Cabinet of Conservative Prime Minister Stanley Baldwin until The Conservatives' defeat in the spring of 1929, he was not asked back into the Cabinet when his Conservatives regained the majority in a resounding victory in October 1931.

One prevailing sentiment at the time: "What sensible man is going to place confidence in Mr. Churchill in any situation which needs cool headedness, moderation, or tact?" Churchill was "regarded as an anachronism"—or, worded differently, "as wine which passed its point."[52] The 1930s has been dubbed Churchill's "Wilderness Years." Though he remained active politically and wrote major works of nonfiction, his influence had ebbed, and many of his speeches were to empty seats.[53]

When Neville Chamberlain became Prime Minister in May 1937, Churchill was seen as a scaremonger—by Chamberlain, the Conservatives, and many in the general public.[54] Only after Hitler had invaded Poland in September 1939, making Churchill's many warnings about German aggression finally seem more prescient than hysterical, was Winston brought back into the Cabinet and the inner circle of British political power.

In 1931, a political insider had speculated that "the ghosts of Gallipoli will always rise up to damn him anew. ..."[55] These "ghosts" would materialize for Churchill one more time after his return to Cabinet-level power. In late autumn 1939 Churchill foresaw that Germany would want to invade Norway to maintain the flow of iron ore from Sweden and to commandeer ports closer to Britain. Churchill advocated mining the Norwegian coastal waters Germany used to transport iron ore, but his idea was rebuffed. Just as Britain was finally preparing to send troops to Norway, Hitler invaded, in early April 1940. The Germans simply beat the British to the Norwegian ports.

Despite his early advocacy of military action in Norway, Churchill nonetheless received an undue amount of criticism for a poor campaign that resulted in the loss of about four thousand British lives and in German occupation of the country.[56] The visibility that Churchill craved made him an easy target, in both the Gallipoli and Norway incidents, when blame was being meted out.

When he became Prime Minister, Churchill was still "widely distrusted as a man of unstable temperament ... [and] unsound judgment. ..."[57] John Colville, a man who would eventually become a trusted Churchill aide, wrote that Churchill:

> ... may ... be the man of drive and energy the country believes him to be and he may be able to speed up our creaking military and industrial machine; but it is a terrible risk, it involves the danger of rash and spectacular exploits, and I cannot help feeling that this country may be maneuvered into the most dangerous position it has ever been in. ...[58]

Colville also believed that "Seldom can a prime minister have taken office ... with the establishment so dubious of the choice and so prepared to have its doubts justified."[59]

Criticism and skepticism followed Churchill up to the moment of his decision that a peace settlement with Hitler was not in Britain's best interest. A peace deal that Churchill could have chosen to pursue in May 1940 may have relieved his anxious countrymen; but because it was likely to unravel, it would have been a shaky foundation on which both to protect his nation and to rebuild his reputation and stature. War would have offered the greatest opportunity for Churchill's redemption, especially on the scale he likely would have required. Moreover, Churchill saw himself as having the skills to wage a successful war, and he believed that suing for peace would be disastrous. He believed that even a failed war, if conducted bravely, would not be the albatross that a failed peace would have been. In his first broadcast as Prime

Minister, Churchill put out the call to "wage war until victory is won, and never to surrender ourselves to servitude and shame, whatever the cost and the agony may be."[60] In this one best shot at redemption, Churchill would let nothing stand in his way.

By the time he took office Churchill had concluded that a war to destroy Nazism was both inevitable and necessary. If redemption might be a byproduct of such a war, there is no evidence to suggest that Churchill consciously chose to continue all-out war with Germany in order to achieve personal vindication. Ironically, the inevitability of war in May 1940 would have had a redemptive quality all its own. For several years Churchill had inveighed against the growing Nazi menace and warned repeatedly of the price he feared Britain would have to pay for downplaying the dangers. For example, three and a half years before becoming Prime Minister, Churchill issued this warning:

> What would have been said, I wonder, if I could two years ago have forecast to the House the actual course of events? Suppose we had then been told that Germany would spend for two years £800,000,000 a year upon warlike preparations; that her industries would be organized for war, as the industries of no country have ever been; that by breaking all Treaty engagements she would create a gigantic air force and an army based on universal compulsory service, which by the present time, in 1936, amounts to upwards of thirty-nine divisions of highly equipped troops, including mechanized divisions of almost unmeasured strength, and that behind all this there lay millions of armed and trained men, for whom the formation and equipment are rapidly being prepared to form another eighty divisions addition to those already perfected. Suppose we had then known that by now two years of compulsory military service would be the rule ...; that the Rhineland would be occupied by powerful forces and fortified with great skill, and that Germany would be building with our approval, signified by treaty, a large submarine fleet. ... Yet just two years have gone by and we see it all in broad daylight. Where shall we be this time two years? I hesitate now to predict.[61]

Churchill also fretted that his beloved Britain itself, the ruler of a once-great Empire, had come to be thought of as weak during the days of appeasement. In 1933 he decried the tendency of some important leaders toward "unwarrantable self-abasement."[62] In a November 1936 speech, he declared:

[Britain's behavior] baffles friends; it fans the wrath of foes. It makes the remaining authority and influence of Britain a positive embarrassment to Europe instead of being the main anchor, as it should be, of honesty, courage, and stability. With a plan, with a theme and with a cause to which we adhere, even though circumstances run counter to it for a time, you will bring other people to conform to your movement. You have no chance of doing it while you are drifting this way and that."[63]

As with Churchill himself, war would offer the nation a chance to reclaim its honor. But just as Churchill never labored passively when in the spotlight, as he said, Britain would also have to actively seize its opportunities for redemption:

Nothing will save England if she will not save herself. If we lose faith in ourselves, in our capacity to guide and govern, if we lose our will to live, then indeed our story is told. ... [O]ur ruin will be swift and final. ... England would sink to the level of a fifth-rate Power, and nothing would remain of all her glories.[64]

Unlike the situation at the time of Gallipoli, the conduct and character of the British response to Hitler's aggression in the spring of 1940 would be in Churchill's hands to define and mold. The vacillating and failed strategy of how Britain responded to the German invasion of Norway in April 1940—a failure, like Gallipoli, caused by running a war by committee—would also have been fresh in the mind of the new Prime Minister. The lesson learned by Churchill was this: If his instincts and strategic intuitions were allowed to prevail, success would follow.

Political and press adversaries, who railed against Churchill since 1916 for Gallipoli and the 1930s for what they perceived as his reckless and hysterical warnings about Hitler, had started to come around to the belief that, maybe, this brilliant and pugnacious man was the perfect choice to lead Britain through the trials to come. Moreover, the citizenry had begun to adore him.

War was happening, Churchill was in charge, and he was intent on letting nothing stand in the way of securing victory. Writing in *The Gathering Storm,* Churchill describes how "at last I had the authority to give directions over the whole scene ...," and he "felt as if I were walking with destiny, and that all my past life had been but a preparation for this hour and for this trial. ... I was sure I would not fail."[65]

Victory against Hitler, if achieved, would be all the sweeter for Churchill if it relegated "Gallipoli" to a merely unpleasant footnote in his career instead of the undeservedly defining moment it had become. On a deeper emotional level, a victory would also show that his father's older son was "first rate" after all. Given his outsized ego, Churchill needed a victory greater in magnitude than his perceived failure at Gallipoli to finally balance the books. Political, administrative, or rhetorical successes, though welcomed, would not suffice. Shepherding Britain through a shaky, unstable, and likely ill-fated peace with Hitler likewise would not be enough. Only victory in a war for survival might provide adequate redemption.

Winston Churchill, Lone Wolf

Thesis: Churchill grew up to be an emotionally sensitive and character-ologically eccentric man who very much danced to his own tune. That, and his supreme self-assuredness, led him to forge ahead, unafraid, and often inadequately supported, where his instincts told him to go.

Much of why Britain's prospects appeared bleak in May 1940 was because of the isolated position it held in Europe. Its traditional ally, France, was about to be overrun by the German army. Former allies Italy and Russia were cooperating with Germany; Poland and Belgium had been conquered; Turkey was playing both sides against the other. The Commonwealth countries of Australia, New Zealand, and India could be counted upon; but how aggressively they might need to mobilize to react to future Japanese adventurism in their own backyards remained a dark cloud on the horizon. Lastly, though entry of the United States as an active combatant would have had a dramatic and immediately salutary effect on Britain's war efforts, 1940 was an election year in America and Roosevelt, responding to strong isolationist and noninterventionist sentiment within the country, promised that, if he were re-elected, there would be no American involvement in any foreign war. Undoubtedly, Churchill would have welcomed additional active partners in the struggle; but their absence did not dissuade him from marching, chest thrust out, into the fray. In a 1925 reflection on war on the continent, Churchill said, "It should never be admitted ... that England cannot, if the worse comes to worse, stand alone."[66]

With one important exception, his relationship with his nanny Elizabeth Everest, there are few instances where Churchill's personal and professional fortunes were notably nurtured by the encouragement of a compassionate teacher, a wise senior officer, or an inspiring political guru. Instead, he characteristically forged his own paths forward.

Starting in boyhood, Winston learned the ability to subdue his disappointments and tribulations by keeping himself busy, seeking new challenges, and pushing his personal envelope. As a teen he became an accomplished horseman; then later in life he trained to be a pilot during a time when that was a very risky endeavor. He became a talented artist, a greatly admired orator, and a writer, not only prolific but also worthy of a Nobel Prize. He immersed himself in the minutiae of the mechanics of governing and military preparedness.

When he first began to find his voice at Harrow, after emotionally downtrodden experiences at the St. George's School and Brunswick, he "consistently broke almost every rule made by the Masters or boys, was quite incorrigible, and had an unlimited vocabulary of backchat."[67] Another account describes Winston's time at St. George's School as "one long feud with ... authority."[68] Rebelliousness followed him to his next school, Harrow, where biographer William Manchester postulates that Winston's obstreperousness with school authorities stemmed from latent resentment against his emotionally depriving parents.[69]

Churchill never seemed to have gotten the memo that the road to success in a political career is typically paved with accommodation and self-effacement. Upon Churchill's first successful foray into politics—his election to Parliament in October 1900—he reprised the role of attention-seeking brat that he first displayed as a schoolboy. He became a member of a small group of aristocratic rebels nicknamed the "Hughligans"—"bright young men who were being rebellious to draw attention to themselves in the hopes of gaining office."[70] Soon, Winston would be their undisputed leader. David Lloyd George, leader of the Liberal Party, wrote that "the applause of the House is the breath of [Churchill's] nostrils. ..."[71] Day after day, Churchill savaged the leaders of his own party; and as a result he was called "a most infernal nuisance" and the most "hated man in the House of Commons."[72] In May 1904, Churchill's rebelliousness took a more unusual turn: after being in Parliament for slightly more than three years, he "crossed the floor," that is, he left his Conservative Party comrades to sit with the Liberals.

Shortly after World War I started, Churchill left his desk as First Lord of the Admiralty to personally lead troops in the defense of Antwerp in Belgium. This was the act of someone with "an entirely unbalanced mind," according to future Prime Minister Andrew Bonar Law.[73] During the Gallipoli campaign of World War I, Churchill pressed on with planned operations even after his superior had at the last minute denied the campaign the tens of thousands of troops that had already been promised. In 1925, Churchill's first budget as Chancellor of the Exchequer in Baldwin's Conservative Government proposed a dramatic strengthening of the social safety net; this proposal was described as "an abrupt departure from the traditional Tory approach. ..." In 1931 his opposition to the Government's plans for India was so vehement that he was ostracized from cabinet-level service in two successive administrations.

Much of the 1930s has been dubbed Churchill's "Wilderness Years," because though he retained his seat in Parliament, he was not asked back into the Cabinet until September 1939. For almost the entire decade, he devoted speech after speech to warning of the increasing German menace and decrying what he felt to be dangerous government inaction. These lone-wolf cries from his "Wilderness" became more strident as he failed to rouse enough of his colleagues to accept the peril he so clearly foresaw. As a result, Churchill's political isolation increased as the decade proceeded; but, unsurprisingly, he was not dissuaded from pressing on with his dire forecasts and scathing criticisms.

He also risked running afoul of the common citizen: when Prime Minister Chamberlain made a September 1938 peace-seeking trip to Germany, Churchill called it "the stupidest thing that has ever been done,"[74] despite nearly three-quarters of the British public approving the Chamberlain initiative.[75]

In the 1930s Britain was "just not ready for Churchill."[76] A 1940 analysis of Churchill by future US President John F. Kennedy expounded on the "somewhat peculiar position [Churchill] has always occupied in British politics":

> No one has ever questioned his ability or his dynamic energy.
> But these very qualities ... have in times of peace caused him
> to be considered "dangerous" and a little uncomfortable to
> have around. Then, too, Churchill has always represented the
> extreme viewpoint. He has never stood on middle ground—
> he went "all out" for anything he advocated, with the result
> that his opinions have always been taken advisedly by most
> British leaders.[77]

It is inarguable that, in his lifetime endeavor to be "seen and heard," Winston succeeded grandly, though often at the cost of being thought of as an outsider. Starting with his standing up to schoolmasters as a boy and culminating in confronting Adolf Hitler six decades later, Churchill evolved into one of the most prominent figures on the world stage, in large measure due to his pugnaciousness, tenacity, rebelliousness, and convenient disregard of propriety. The irony is that these "lone-wolf" traits ended up endearing him to his countrymen, who embraced him and his "We shall never surrender" message.[78]

Many of the speeches Churchill made to the House of Commons from 1932 to 1938 assailed the Government for its laxness in responding to the German threat and detailed in great length how dire Churchill felt that threat to be. An interesting subtext to several of these speeches is how often he reminded his audience of Britain's island nature. Though Britain over the centuries had its share of invaders, marauders, and migrants—from the Romans to the Anglo-Saxons to the Vikings and the Norman—by and large the sea spared Britain from the ravages of the continual warfare sustained by its Continental neighbors. In 1937 Churchill reminded the House that "[n]early a thousand years have passed since we were conquered or subjugated by external force."[79]

But throughout the 1930s, Churchill warned of two factors that were stripping Britain of its geographically protected status. The first was the tightening grip of geopolitical alliances. "We must remember," he declared in that same 1937 speech, that

> ... we are for the time being not any longer the masters of our own fate. That [fate] no longer depends altogether on what we decide here or what the Cabinet settle in Downing Street. It depends on what may happen in the world, on what other countries do, for good or for ill. It may be hard for our island people, with their long immunity, to realize this ugly, unpleasant alteration in our position."[80]

The second and more ominous factor was the ascension of the airplane as an instrument of war. In 1935 Churchill warned: "From being the least vulnerable of all nations we have, through developments in the air, become the most vulnerable. ..." Churchill starkly foresaw the dangers ahead. On February 7, 1934, Churchill predicted that "... we may, within a measurable period of time, in the lifetime of those who are here, if we are not in a proper state of security, be confronted on some occasion with ... the crash of bombs exploding in London and cataracts of masonry and fire and smoke. ..."[81]

Clearly, Churchill saw Britain at a dangerous crossroads where it could no longer trust in its impregnability and must instead bravely seek other options to secure its defense. Put in more colorful language:

> We are a rich and easy prey. No country is so vulnerable and no country would better repay pillage than our own. With our enormous Metropolis here, the greatest target in the world, a kind of tremendous, fat, valuable cow tied up to attract the beast of prey, we are in a position in which we have never been before, and in which no other country in the world is at the present time.[82]

It is tempting to imagine that Churchill so appreciated the vulnerabilities of Britain's island status because, emotionally and socially, he himself had been an island and "easy prey." We have seen both how alone young Winston was, and how alone he felt, as the sensitive son of psychologically neglectful parents. He was sent off to boarding schools where he often was miserable and lonely and bullied, whipped, and discounted. There are few references to Churchill developing and fostering close personal friendships during his formative years.

Hugely influential in the life and development of this lonely little island of a boy, as described earlier, was the loving role of his nanny Elizabeth Everest, "the only real friend of his childhood."[83] With Everest and then his wife, Clementine, providing consistent nurturing, support, and acceptance, Churchill:

- had developed deep intimacy with his children;

- had become able to have a few true adult friendships;

- had four decades of notoriety and (at times) acclaim in his political life; and

- had become an accomplished author, journalist, orator, and painter.

Just as Mrs. Everest could be the staunch protector of an isolated and bullied little boy, Churchill could play the same role with his vulnerable and threatened island nation. Beginning in May 1940, when Churchill became Prime Minister, the people of Britain would look to him—as children would look to a parent—for protection, wisdom, courage, and consistency under grim circumstances. With the empathy borne from his years of emotional isolation, Churchill could empower the nation's people with his fervent belief that they would prevail, even if they had to be a lone wolf without anyone coming to their aid: "We shall prove ourselves ... able to defend our island home, ride out the storm and to outlive the menace of tyranny, if necessary, for years, if necessary, alone. ..."[84]

Winston Churchill, Daredevil

Thesis: Throughout the course of his life Churchill was a risk-taker, particularly physically, and he often would opt for risk over safety whenever he had the choice. For many of his political colleagues, war was a line they could not imagine crossing, regardless of how reckless and ruthless Hitler was becoming. Not so Churchill, a man who rarely played it safe. And there would be nothing safe about Britain's going toe-to-toe with Nazi Germany all by itself.

Despite, or perhaps because of, the childhood disappointments, loneliness and ill health, Churchill's psychological development led him toward a projection of invincibility, not just driving his physical pursuits but also informing his decision-making with a kind of "odds be damned" essence.

It is far from an exaggeration to say that Churchill was attracted to reckless pursuits, starting at a young age. Certainly, he was put in harm's way by accidents, such as his fall from a donkey at age four and a near-drowning in a boating accident as a late teen, and being hit by a car while crossing New York's Fifth Avenue in December 1931. But many of his most colorful brushes with physical harm were purposeful acts of reckless abandon, to "put his head into the lion's mouth."[85] There may have been a neurologic component to his aggressive disregard for his own welfare. Indeed, a description of four-year-old Winston as a boy with "no sense of personal safety," who was "in constant motion, jumping up and down, leaping from chair to chair, rushing about and falling and hurting himself,"[86] is a suggestive picture of what would now be called Attention Deficit Hyperactivity Disorder (ADHD). Winston's schoolmaster at Harrow felt moved to write Winston's mother about the boy's "forgetfulness, carelessness, unpunctuality and irregularity in every way,"[87] which can also be characteristics of an attentional disorder. A description of Churchill in mid-adulthood—"(b)y nature flamboyant, insolent in his bearing, impatient in his mind"[88]—suggests he had not outgrown his ADHD-like qualities even then.

But whether or not Winston had ADHD—and, if he did, it certainly did not inhibit him from becoming enormously successful later in life—he indisputably was willful and callous about pushing the envelope when personal danger was involved. Earlier we learned how Winston, at eighteen, thrust himself off a 30-foot-high footbridge, thinking he could elude capture by his two companions and land unscathed in a game of "Follow My Leader."[89] Here's how Churchill later recalled the event:

> After I had been hunted for twenty minutes and was rather short of breath, I decided to cross the bridge. Arrived at its centre I saw to my consternation that the pursuers had divided their forces. One stood at each end of the bridge; capture seemed certain. ... 'Would it not,' I asked myself, 'be possible to leap on to one of [the young fir trees] and slip down the pole-like stem, breaking off each tier of branches as one descended, until the fall was broken?' I looked at it. I computed it. I meditated. ... To plunge or not to plunge, that was the question! In a second I had plunged. ...[90]

Remember that this escapade happened not when Winston was the "rushing about" four-year-old, but when he was eighteen and a graduate of Harrow. Moreover, the account just cited, in prose that hardly disguises

Churchill's joy in the escapade, was written when he was in a seemingly more sober time of life, his mid-fifties. There are no words of second-guessing (he sustained a concussion, loss of consciousness, kidney damage, and a vertebral fracture), and no sympathies for his potentially worried parents. In fact, the takeaway for Churchill about this episode is that it highlighted "my own pronounced will-to-live."[91]

As a schoolboy, Winston began to channel some of his aggressive instincts into sport. "In 1889, Churchill wrote to his 'Darling Mummy' asking her to allow him to take up fencing. Churchill went on to become an accomplished fencer and even became Public Schools Fencing Champion in 1892."[92] A couple of years later, while a student at Sandhurst, he learned to play polo.

Churchill's penchant for physical risk-taking continued into his adult life. "He only gave up playing polo when he was fifty-two—and was riding [horses] into his sixties and seventies."[93] He became an accomplished horseman, starting with his days at Sandhurst, but his descriptions seem to emphasize daring as much as they describe skillfulness. Here's how Churchill experienced being a young cavalry officer in the 4th Hussars in 1895:

> Mounting and dismounting from a bare-backed horse at the trot or canter; jumping a high bar without stirrups or even saddle, sometimes with hands clasped behind one's back; jogging at a fast trot with nothing but the horse's hide between your knees, brought their inevitable share of mishaps. ... In consequence I suffered tortures. ... [O]ne simply had to go on tearing at a lacerated muscle with the awful penalty of being thought a booby, if one begged off even for a day.[94]

Churchill not only rushed into dangerous situations in Cuba, India, and South Africa, but eagerly sought them out, both as a soldier and as a journalist. Churchill's horse was shot out from under him in Cuba; he galloped ostentatiously along a skirmish line in India; he charged into a volley of Dervish rifle fire in the Sudan; he was shot at while aboard an army train in South Africa; and he witnessed "one [deadly] skirmish after another" during the siege of Ladysmith in the Boer War.

From the Sudan, Churchill described a battle scene to his mother: "There is no doubt the charge was an awful gamble and that no formal precautions were possible. The issue as far as I was concerned had to be left to Fortune or to God—or to whatever may decide these things."[95] His daughter Mary told an interviewer in 1996: "... when [my father] was a young soldier of fortune and seeking 'reputation in the cannon's mouth,' he could have lost his life on about five or six different occasions."[96]

While Home Secretary in 1911, Churchill, who was then approaching forty, could not resist the temptation to see for himself how police were attempting to battle Latvian anarchists who had already killed three officers. He was on scene in London's East End when the bloody siege ended in a deadly fire in the house where the anarchists were hunkered down. Though the incident excited Churchill, his unnecessary risk-taking once again raised questions about his judgment. People were sure that he simply could not "resist the limelight ..." and the opportunity to appear heroic.[97]

Three years later, in the initial days of World War I, Churchill offered up yet another head-scratching reason for his countrymen to doubt the quality of his decision-making. While First Lord of the Admiralty, he traveled to the front in early October 1914 to personally oversee the defense of Antwerp from the German forces invading Belgium. Churchill thought "it was going to be my great opportunity," and in his formal petition to the Cabinet he wrote: "I feel it is my duty to offer my services because I am sure this arrangement will afford the best prospects of a victorious result." However, as recounted by renowned Churchill biographer Martin Gilbert, "when this was read to the Cabinet it gave rise to ... loud and unrestrained laughter. ..."[98] Though Churchill received some praise for his efforts in Belgium, the prevailing sentiments were those penned in the October 19 edition of *The Morning Post:* "To be photographed and cinematographed under fire in Antwerp is an entirely unnecessary addition to the risks and horrors of war."[99]

This criticism notwithstanding, Churchill ventured again into the war a year later, resigning from the Cabinet under the cloud of the Gallipoli disaster to take field command of a battalion fighting in France. For several weeks, his unit withstood German shelling, and a piece of shrapnel barely missed hitting him. He also came under machine-gun fire, and while in the bombed-out farmhouse he used as headquarters another shard of shrapnel hit a piece of equipment he was holding.[100] Perhaps hoping to erase negative public perceptions stemming from the debacle of Gallipoli, Churchill's brief time at the front instead nearly cost him his life.

From the fall of 1913 to the spring of 1914, while he was a major Cabinet official in a time of escalating world crisis, Churchill took flying lessons. Aviation was still in its infancy—the Wright Brothers' flight at Kitty Hawk had occurred less than ten years before Churchill started his lessons—and was an exceedingly dangerous avocation. Among other incidents, a monoplane in which he was due to fly side-slipped and was wrecked; his instructor was killed in another flying accident, and a lieutenant who had taken Churchill up only a week before died in the same plane they had used on that previous flight.[101] Worried, his wife asked him to stop flying altogether, but he refused, even though they had two children under the age of five. "Although clearly not a natural pilot, Churchill was foolishly fearless in his determination to

obtain his licence and only abandoned the attempt after further considerable pressure."[102] When, in the spring of 1914, Churchill finally honored his
promise to Clementine to give up flying, he had flown nearly one hundred
and forty times in seven months, or a rate of about five times per week.[103]*

Fast forward to 1940, when even the full weight of running wartime
Britain was not enough to restrain Churchill from endangering himself. On
the morning of June 11, 1940, he was flown to Briare, a town 80 miles south
of Paris, to confer with remnants of the French Government. If this trip were
not risky enough, Churchill's pilot had to dissuade him from wanting to fly
over the battlefields.[104] When the Luftwaffe began actively bombing British
cities, starting in the fall of 1940, Churchill, a man in his mid-sixties, could
frequently be seen touring the devastation, poking at the edge of unstable
bomb craters with his walking stick or clambering up a pile of rubble to get
a better look at things.[105]

On October 14, 1940, a German bomb landed next to Churchill's own
residence, No. 10 Downing Street, causing considerable damage. Even then,
Winston's impulse was not to seek shelter.

> 'The mess in the house was indescribable,' John Martin [one
> of Churchill's private secretaries], told his parents: 'windows
> smashed in all directions, everything covered with grime,
> doors off hinges and curtains and furniture tossed about in a
> confused mess. ... The hut of the soldiers who guard Downing
> Street was completely demolished. ...'[106]

Undeterred, Churchill coaxed his colleagues into resuming their dinner, after which he suggested they watch the raid from the roof of the Air
Ministry.[107] When the King was informed of what Churchill had done he
pleaded with him to take better precautions to stay safe. The King wrote
in his diary that neither he nor the country could bear to lose Churchill.[108]

Did Churchill's life as a physical risk taker influence his May 1940 decision to eschew a search for peace and instead plunge his country headlong
into an all-out war? When the moment came for Churchill to choose to
seek peace or to advocate Britain continue the war alone, his penchant for
fearlessness and episodes of recklessness would have allowed him to contemplate war as another bridge to jump off of—and survive. Other people likely
would have learned, by the age of sixty-five, to moderate their risk-taking
when contemplating how many of their nine lives they may already have
forfeited; but moderation never seems to have been one of Churchill's strong

---

*Churchill later broke his promise and got his pilot's license. In 1916, when he
was at the front, Churchill would fly himself back to England for leave, much to
Clementine's consternation. Hunt, "World War I History".*

suits. Moreover, a number of his more hare-brained escapades, particularly those he immortalized in his own eagerly awaited public prose, convinced many of his countrymen to think of Winston as a hero. His escape from a Pretoria prison is the apotheosis of this phenomenon: he was feted, cheered, and admired for an event that never should have happened in the first place.

A much more consequential example of Churchill channeling his daredevil spirit, this time with the undying gratitude of his country, was the magical rescue of British Expeditionary Force from Dunkirk. In late May 1940, German forces encircled the BEF, as well as Belgian and French troops at Dunkirk, a small town on the channel coast in northwest France. If the BEF was to be saved, Churchill had two choices: sue for peace, or trust that an unimagined solution would appear allowing the troops to be evacuated. Knowing the troops were facing strong German air and ground fire, the evacuation seemed like it would have to depend on an armada of small private boats, Churchill anticipated that only a small percentage of the trapped men would be saved. But in the end, 338,000 British, French, and Belgian troops (out of a total of some 375,000) were evacuated.

It was called a miracle. But Churchill's entire life was spent surviving one Dunkirk after another: from bad parenting, to schoolboy bullying, to leaping off the bridge, to the battle in the Sudan, to his escape in South Africa. Even his emergence from a decade of political "Wilderness" was Dunkirk-like. It's not that Churchill saw the British forces carrying out the Dunkirk evacuation as invincible or that he had an irrational belief that the evacuation plan was guaranteed to succeed. Rather, in many respects he acted as if he never doubted that his run of luck would hold. Somehow, it did.

The premise here is not that Churchill thrust his isolated nation into the next phase of a no-holds-barred shooting war because of his love of adventure or the adrenaline rush of fearlessness. Rather, what motivated Churchill was a combination of two factors: he was legitimately brave, and he would not have had an aversion to choosing a physically risky path if he were convinced that was the only logical path open to him and his country.

Churchill did not want war. Throughout the 1930s, as he was warning of the looming Nazi threat and inveighing against what he saw as government inaction, Churchill also repeatedly stressed his wish that localized conflict then stirring in central Europe could stop short of escalating into a wider war. In 1933 he said, "Our first supreme object is not to go to war."[109] And in the summer of 1934 he declared, "The object that we all seek is peace. We all wish to prevent war. We all wish that the horrors into which we were plunged twenty years ago may never be repeated in our time. ..."[110]

However fervently Churchill wished war to be averted, he was not constructed to run from conflict if, indeed, war became inevitable or an option to an unsustainable peace. "I hope we shall not indulge in panic," he told the

House in May 1935. "But I wish to say this: It is very much better sometimes to have a panic feeling beforehand, and then to be quite calm when things happen, than to be extremely calm beforehand and to get in a panic when things happen."[111] Churchill understood that inaction can be more dangerous than action, and that a good offense can indeed become the best defense.

The roots of Churchill's daredevil nature may have, in part at least, been a reaction to the intense sense of vulnerability he felt being unable to protect himself against the emotional abuse from his parents and then from the bullying at the hands of classmates and headmasters. Why wait for danger to strike? Isn't it better to take the initiative and charge headlong into it?

To his core, Churchill understood that peace did not automatically mean safety or security. After all, home life with Lord and Lady Randolph was, on its surface, uneventful. War could very well be the lesser of two evils when compared with a peace controlled and managed by an implacable and ruthless enemy. Churchill's utter fearlessness undoubtedly was part of what made him so beloved by his countrymen; and it served as a model to the frightened citizenry on how to face and survive the horrors of the war. Further, it would have been hugely empowering and inspiring for the people to believe that Churchill had the same faith in their invincibility he so evidently had in his own.

It is ironic that the cumulative result of Churchill's repeated acts of recklessness was to hone a boldness that would define him for the ages. In Churchill's life, the importance of acting, doing, challenging, risking, moving, was paramount. It provided both solace and distraction for the lonely boy, and then identity and recognition in adulthood. Throughout the 1930s, Churchill continuously goaded the Government to take action against the ever-emerging Nazi menace. Now that he was Prime Minister, he could demand action, including from his countrymen. Churchill would tell his countrymen that he and they would seize the initiative and jump off the bridge together—in a viscerally powerful act, consequences be damned.

Winston Churchill, Hitler's Nemesis

Thesis: In a deep and painful way, Churchill knew a bully when he encountered one. As a result, he was years ahead of his many colleagues in recognizing Hitler's menace; and he knew to his bones that the only way to deal with bullies definitively is to confront them.

Seemingly from the moment Adolf Hitler stepped onto the world stage, Winston Churchill had him pegged as a menace and a bully. From his painful schoolboy days, Winston would have known how to spot a bully. In a February 1938 speech, Churchill described "the great Dictators" who were then threatening European security in words that would comprise an apt definition of bullies in general: "They pursue their path towards somber and impressive objectives with ruthless consistency and purpose. They know what they want, and no one can deny that up to the present at every step they are getting what they want."[112] Roberts writes that Churchill "was the first, most eloquent, best informed and for a very long time the only senior British politician to warn of the threat that Hitler was increasingly posing to peace, civilization and the British Empire."[113]

It's not that Churchill had a "one strike, you're out" mentality regarding perceived real or potential adversaries. He was, in fact, quite capable of moderating previously held antipathies, such as towards Gandhi, Stalin and even Neville Chamberlain. However, Churchill's view of Hitler, formed early, never wavered. A classified memorandum prepared on October 18, 1930, which was seized after the end of World War II, contained the revealing report of a German counselor who encountered Churchill at a weekend house party. The memorandum indicated that Churchill believed Hitler to be a congenital liar and that "although Hitler had 'declared that he has no intention of waging a war of aggression, he, Churchill is convinced that Hitler or his followers would seize the first available opportunity to resort to armed force.'"[114] In a March 1931 newspaper article, Churchill issued a public warning of what he feared would be an approaching second twentieth-century war with Germany. Only fourteen years after the conclusion of the first world war, Churchill warned the House in November 1932:

> All these bands of sturdy Teutonic youths, marching along the streets and roads of Germany, with the light of desire in their eyes to suffer for their Fatherland, are not looking for status. They are looking for weapons ..., and when that demand is made it cannot fail to shake and possibly shatter to their foundations [all the countries of Europe]. Do not delude yourselves.[115]

In an important speech to the House of Commons in February 1934, Churchill declared that Britain was "vulnerable as we have never been before"; he strongly advocated for rearming Britain and creating "an Air Force at least as strong as that of any power that can get at us." Few agreed with him.[116] In the summer of 1934 Churchill, a staunch anti-Communist, and a long-time and vocal detractor of Stalin, proposed admission of the Soviet Union into the League of Nations in order to strengthen a continental alliance against Hitler.[117] Several years later Churchill acknowledged that he "had only one single purpose" in aligning with Stalin, and that was "the destruction of Hitler."[118]

In a series of speeches before the House of Commons in 1936, he kept up a steady, intensifying drumbeat warning of the dangers Hitler posed. In

September 1938, Churchill suggested to Lord Halifax that Britain should go to war with Hitler if Germany invaded Czechoslovakia.[119] In a press statement issued a few days later, Churchill decried "the complete surrender of the Western democracies to the Nazi threat of force" and warned, "It is not Czechoslovakia alone which is menaced, but also the freedom and the democracy of all nations."[120] On October 5, 1938, Churchill, in a speech for which he was criticized as a blackguard, railed against Chamberlain's "Munich Agreement" with Hitler:

> The whole equilibrium of Europe has been deranged. ... In a very few years, perhaps in a very few months, we shall be confronted with demands with which we shall no doubt be invited to comply. Those demands may affect the surrender of territory or the surrender of the liberty. ...[121]

> This is only the first sip, the first foretaste of a bitter cup. ...[122]

One of the reasons Churchill so frequently addressed the House to inveigh against German aggression and British dithering was that his warnings were not being heeded. Throughout the decade of the 1930s, many of Churchill's contemporaries ridiculed his increasingly strident polemics as needless alarmism. His unwillingness to mince words, especially about his scorn for the Government's pursuit of appeasement on the one hand and ineffectual half-measures for rearmament on the other, undoubtedly ruffled the feathers of the Government leaders in Churchill's rhetorical crosshairs. Churchill's uncompromising position also grated on many of Britain's upper-class elite, who were not put off by Hitler's avowed anti-Semitism and who even saw Winston's fierce opposition to the anti-Communist German Chancellor as being "disloyal to His Majesty's Government."[123]

Finally, as war moved ever closer, Churchill and his warnings could no longer be discounted. The public and the press began to clamor for Chamberlain to end Churchill's "Wandering Years" and bring him back into the Cabinet. On September 1, 1939, Prime Minister Chamberlain invited Churchill to become a member of the War Cabinet. Churchill accepted without comment. When Hitler made a hollow peace overture in an October 6, 1939, speech, he cited Churchill by name as the person who could doom Europe to all-out war. Churchill unequivocally rejected Hitler's proposed peace terms:

> I find them absolutely unacceptable. They are the terms of a conqueror! But we are not yet conquered! No, no, we are not yet conquered! ... I am all for war to the end. Hitler must be destroyed. Nazism must be crushed once and for all.[124]

John Simpson, world affairs editor of the BBC, wrote in 2015, "During the 1930s [Churchill] had visited Hitler's Germany and seen for himself the potential for evil there. Few people, either in the UK or the US, wanted to know. ..."[125] John F. Kennedy, in his spring 1940 analysis of Churchill, commented that:

> In light of the present-day war, we are amazed at the blindness of British leaders, in the country as a whole, that they could fail to see the correctness of Churchill's arguments. ... Churchill's warnings ... have proved to be so accurate.[126]

Unlike most of his British political contemporaries, Churchill looked at the threat Hitler posed through an experienced military lens and not just through a political lens. While other accomplished politicians were acting as if Hitler could be contained by the usual thrusts and parries of diplomacy, Churchill, whom many had labeled a "scaremonger,"[127] intuitively understood that Hitler was not just a worthy geopolitical adversary but, more ominously, a ruthless enemy capable, and likely eager, to inflict wanton death and destruction to attain his aims. For too long a significant number of Churchill's colleagues, many of whom were trained as barristers, treated Hitler as they might treat opposing counsel: someone to spar strenuously with in court during the day but then share a pint with after work was finished. Churchill, on the other hand, saw Hitler not merely as a wartime antagonist but as an existential threat to the treasured tenets of Western civilization. In an October 1938 speech to the House of Commons, Churchill railed against "the Nazi Power, ... which spurns Christian ethics, [and] which cheers its onward course by a barbarous paganism. ..."[128] And in his June 18, 1940, speech to the House, Churchill proclaimed:

> If we can stand up to [Hitler], all Europe may be free, and the life of the world may move forward into broad, sunlit uplands; but if we fail then the whole world, including the United States, and all that we have known and cared for, will sink into the abyss of a new dark age made more sinister, and perhaps more prolonged, by the lights of a perverted science.[129]

By May 1940 Churchill "had only one single purpose—the destruction of Hitler—and his life was much simplified thereby."[130] By May 1940, Churchill was convinced that the British public would soon come to understand the enormity of Hitler's evil, which Churchill came to call "a monstrous tyranny, never surpassed in the dark, lamentable catalogue of human crime." He didn't have to wait long: with poignant and tragic consequences, his decision to eschew peace negotiations with Germany led to Hitler ordering brutalizing German air assaults on Britain; these raids, which killed tens of thousands, commenced in July 1940 and lasted nearly a year.

Peace is not achieved by avoiding a bully; peace is achieved by confronting a bully. As oxymoronic as it might sound, by choosing to go to war, Churchill, known for his bellicosity and bluster, believed he was in fact picking the only path that could lead to real peace. "... [T]he only safe way," he said, to find peaceful resolution, "was to convince Hitler he couldn't beat us."[131] In other words, Churchill saw war as a means to an ultimate peace with Germany. He would become an immovable force, absorbing whatever Hitler threw at him, instead of accepting a dishonorable and intolerable capitulation. Moreover, even if Britain should be defeated, the struggle would have been just and honorable and would, he was convinced, sow the seeds of future success. "Nations that went down fighting," Churchill fervently believed, "rose again, but those which surrendered tamely, were finished."[132] So Churchill was certain that, one way or the other, Britain would come out on top.

Departing from the appeasement sentiment rife in Britain before he took office, Churchill believed that war was not to be avoided at all costs; rather, war was a tool to create peace if no other tool were available or appropriate. War could be the ultimate and logical solution if peace were being threatened by a foe refusing to negotiate reasonably or threatening to unleash unthinkable terror. Churchill knew that Hitler checked both boxes. Churchill had trained all his life to fight; and, as a result, he proved to be a formidable foe indeed to the German corporal now running his country.

Churchill knew there was evil in the world. By having the capacity to identify evil, by having had personal experiences witnessing and being accosted by bullies and brutes, and through intuition and experience having the wisdom to declare Hitler early on as being irredeemably treacherous, Churchill would have had no compunction about fighting him in war. How to fight that war might be complex, but the "why" was clear. Churchill was 100 percent right about Hitler. Writing after the war, Churchill reminds us of the clarity of his thinking:

> [W]herever men are fighting against barbarism, tyranny, and massacre, for freedom, law, and honour, let them remember that the fame of their deeds, even though they themselves be exterminated, may perhaps be celebrated as long as the world rolls round.[133]

PART V

Drawing by Rick Young

21

May 29, 1940 to June 22, 1941
The Evacuation from Dunkirk,
The Battle of Britain, The Blitz, and the
Invasion of the Soviet Union

The Evacuation from Dunkirk/The Fall of France
- May 29, 1940
- May 31, 1940
- June 3, 1940
- June 4, 1940
- June 5, 1940
- The War in France Intensifies

Stalin Moves on Lithuania, Latvia, Estonia, and Romania
Churchill's Attempt to Warn Stalin about Hitler
Keeping the French Fleet from Falling into Nazi Hands
- June 16, 1940
- June 17, 1940

Halifax's Surreptitious Efforts Toward a Peace Agreement with Hitler
Their Finest Hour
Dealing with the Pétain Government: France's Armistice with Germany
- The British Plan to Destroy the French Warships Anchored in Algeria
- June 28, 1940
- June 29, 1940

July 2, 1940—Hitler at Last Asks For Plans to Be Drawn Up For an
    Invasion of Britain
July 3, 1940—The Royal Navy's Seizure of French Ships Anchored in
    Britain and Its Attack on the French Flotilla at Mers-el-Kébir
July 4, 1940—Effects of the Attack at Mers-el-Kébir
July 8, 1940—A Similar Attack on French Ships Anchored in Dakar
    Senegal
July 10, 1940
- The Battle of Britain Commences

July 16, 1940—Plans for Operation Sea Lion
July 19, 1940—Another German Peace Offer
July 30, 1940
  • Hitler Advised to Postpone the Invasion of Britain
  • Planning Begins for the Invasion of the Soviet Union
The Air War over Britain Intensifies
The Blitz
England Winds Up Not Losing the Battle of Britain
Impact of the Blitz
    – on German Plans to Invade Britain
    – on Britons
Chamberlain's Final Days
Italy's Invasion of Greece; Her Adventure in North Africa
Growing Tension Between Germany and the Soviet Union
Germany Delays the Invasion of Russia to Deal with Greece and
    Yugoslavia
Another Attempt at Peace with Britain? Rudolph Hess's Mission
Germany Invades the Soviet Union

I n his 2004 book *Churchill: The Unexpected Hero*, British historian Paul Addison writes that "It is scarcely an exaggeration to say that between June 1940 in December 1941, Churchill carried the world on his shoulders. The burdens he bore, and anxieties he endured would have crushed many a lesser mortal."[1] As we have seen, on May 28, 1940, he had just relieved himself of one burden—whether not to negotiate a peace agreement with Hitler. With no respite, the immediate question facing Churchill was how many soldiers would, in fact, be rescued from the beaches at Dunkirk.

The Evacuation from Dunkirk/The Fall of France

May 29, 1940

At the 11:30 AM War Cabinet meeting on May 29, Churchill reported that forty thousand members of the BEF had been rescued from France so far, and with twenty-seven destroyers on scene, the evacuation from Dunkirk was proceeding at the rate of two thousand men per hour.[2] Sadly, the Chief of Naval Staff had to tell the group that the HMS *Wakeful* was torpedoed and sunk as it was pulling away from Dunkirk; 639 of the 640 Allied troops aboard were killed.[3]

Churchill was still "not confident about the survival of most of the [BEF]."[4] So while he had told the French that their troops would also be evacuated, he made it clear that British troops should not delay their evacuation to wait for the French to arrive in Dunkirk. Any delay was likely to compromise the already shaky status of the rescue operations. Churchill was quick to reiterate that any French troops that arrived at the coast should be evacuated with the BEF.[5]

Secretary of War Anthony Eden reported that the Royal Navy had been able to use flat-bottomed barges to deliver a supply of water and food to Dunkirk; these boats, called lighters, would, if necessary, be run aground on the beaches to make sure the provisions made it to the desperate troops. Eden told the Cabinet members that troops reaching the beaches east of Dunkirk were moving westward, because chances of evacuation were better the nearer the men were to Dunkirk.[6]

At the 5:30 PM meeting of the War Cabinet on May 30, First Lord of the Admiralty A.V. Alexander announced that by noon that day, a total of 101,154 men had been evacuated from France.[7]* As mentioned, the War Cabinet also discussed a report by the Chiefs of Staff that the Germans might employ a large fleet of fast motorboats (each holding up to two hundred men) to invade Britain.[8] The Chiefs believed that such an invasion could not be prevented.[9] Chief of the Air Staff Sir Cyril Newall felt that the Government should warn the country of the imminent danger. He warned that additional labor to build beach defenses would be required on a large scale.[10] Chamberlain said the Commander-in-Chief of the Home Forces fully concurred with the concerns and recommendations of the Chiefs of Staff and had ordered immediate construction of defense works on the beaches.[11]

As also noted earlier, Chief of Naval Staff Admiral Dudley Pound reported there had been definite signs of German activity along the Norwegian coast, and there were also indications that motorboats were assembling at Bremen and Hamburg.[12] He also said the Germans were known to have an organized force of ships at the port of Vigo, Spain.[13] He wondered about the possible significance of the fact that the Germans had left one particular stretch of sea, opposite the British coast, clear of mines.[14] Pound hoped the production of anti-tank mines to be laid on the beaches would start in a week. Lastly, he shared his fear that, because of the speed of the motorboats and the fact that they might be able to cross the Channel in darkness, the Royal Navy could not guarantee that destroyer patrols could intercept them before they reached English beaches.[15]

The ensuing discussion touched upon these principal points:

1. Though there was some doubt about the precise number of motor-boats the Germans possessed, the assumption was that they could be constructed quickly.

During the day and night of the 29th, more than forty-seven thousand men were evacuated from Dunkirk's beaches and the long wooden breakwater known as the eastern mole. CAB 65/10 149 (40) p. 314 203.

2. While the wake such boats would leave should be visible to air reconnaissance, experience had shown that it was by no means easy to keep track of the German motor torpedo boats that had been operating recently off the Channel ports.

3. These craft could be readily disguised as barges and thus evade air reconnaissance. Even if suspicious numbers of the boats were observed in German or Dutch harbors, it would be difficult to take effective action against them by night bombing.

4. Coast-watching service had been greatly strengthened, and a constant watch was being maintained. Small-boat patrols along the coast had also begun.[16]

Churchill's contribution to the discussion was significant. First, he doubted whether a raid on a large scale could be carried out by fast motorboats.* Such craft would have to come over in flotillas if they were to put ashore a useful number of men at any one point; and the Navy would be actively hunting for them on the high seas.[17] Second, the P.M. reiterated his view that Britain should not hesitate to contaminate her beaches with poison gas if this course would be to her advantage. He added, "We [have] the right to do what we like ... with our own territory."[18]

In the end, the War Cabinet approved the report of the Chiefs of Staff without endorsing any specific actions to be taken against the threat of German fast motorboats.

A telegram was sent from General Edmund Ironside, Chief of the Imperial General Staff, to French Military Commander General Maxime Weygand, informing him that Lord Gort had been ordered to hold his present position at Dunkirk as long as possible, to allow for the maximum evacuation of Allied troops. The telegram recognized that the position at Dunkirk could not be held indefinitely and that Gort had been given orders to evacuate. It also requested that Weygand give similar orders to the senior French commander in the Dunkirk region so that he and General Gort could act in concert.

May 31, 1940

Everybody was elated by the surprisingly successful evacuation of troops from Dunkirk. What looked poised to be one of modern history's worst military disasters was itself being rescued by an outstanding combination

---

Believers in the fast motorboat threat included Chief of Fighter Command Hugh Dowding and Lord Gort, the leader of the BEF. Colville p. 246.

of organization—the evacuation was being carried out by 222 war ships and 665 other vessels.

At the Supreme War Council in Paris, Churchill informed the group that "up to noon that day, 165,000 men had been evacuated."[19] General Weygand responded aggressively to the news, asserting that the French were being left behind.[20] He knew better though: Weygand had been aware of Operation Dynamo for six days but had never authorized French participation in the evacuation.[21] The French translator at the War Council meeting misunderstood Churchill's reply to Weygand as being that the British soldiers at Dunkirk would embark before the French, but Churchill interrupted him and, in his best French, said that the soldiers from both countries would leave together, "arm in arm."[22]

The meeting then followed what had become a familiar script for these gatherings: France asked for more RAF fighter squadrons, and Britain said it could not provide them without seriously jeopardizing the defense of the UK.[23] What concerned Churchill most was the readily apparent despondency of the French, with the notable exception of Premier Reynaud.[24] Churchill's trusted military aide General Hastings "Pug" Ismay thought that Marshal Philippe Pétain, France's Deputy Prime Minister, "looked senile, uninspiring, and defeatist."[25] Despite the gloom, Churchill felt obliged to say "we have only to fight on to conquer. ... Even if one of us is struck down the other must not abandon the struggle—should one comrade fall in battle, the other must not put down his arms until his wounded friend is on his feet again."[26]

Near the end of the meeting, one of the Frenchmen said that if the events continued on the present course, France might have to reappraise its foreign policy, including its ties to Britain. Pétain agreed. General Edward Spears, Britain's military liaison to the French Army, looked directly at Pétain and said, "That would not only mean blockade but bombardment of all French ports in German hands."[27] Not discussed was the Anglo-French pact signed by both governments in March, where each agreed to "neither negotiate nor conclude an armistice or treaty of peace except by mutual agreement."[28] After the meeting, Churchill told Spears that the French leadership thought themselves already defeated.[29]

Throughout June, the Channel was calm and skies were clear. Both the military and the general populous felt a Nazi invasion was imminent.[30] Signposts had been removed from the countryside, to confuse invading troops. The government also mailed out pamphlets that told householders what to do when the invasion began. People started turning everyday items like garden rakes into crude weapons.[31] Understandably, most Britons were scared. Years later, Churchill would note that "... those that knew the most were the least scared."[32] Manchester and Reid write that "[t]hose words were written long after the fact, but they reflect[ed] his belief during 1940."[33]

Churchill was not the only one outwardly confident. During the French campaign and for weeks thereafter, Hitler had little doubt that, after France was defeated and Britain thus was forced to fight on alone, London would be anxious to negotiate a peace agreement.[34] His belief was buttressed by (a) the licking the British had taken both in Norway and in France, and (b) the "reasonableness" of his peace terms—all he wanted was "a free hand" in the East.[35]

Why Britain would continue to fight on against hopeless odds when it could negotiate a peace agreement and end the war "unscathed, intact, and free" was a question not only in Hitler's mind but in the minds of millions of Britons. Perhaps the only place the question was not being entertained was on Downing Street.[36] In *Their Finest Hour* Churchill would write that everyone there knew the answer.[37] Nevertheless, so confident was Hitler about British capitulation that, despite Churchill's speeches about fighting to the bitter end (and contrary to German meticulous attention to detail), the Nazis had not even drawn up plans for an invasion of England.[38] As famed Hitler chronicler William Shirer writes, not only did the Germans have no plans but they "scarcely [had] any will for exploiting the greatest military victories in the history of their soldering nation."[39] As noted earlier, Hitler's top-secret Directive No. 6, dated October 9, 1939, did not mention any invasion of Britain. Instead, it only discussed using the land gained in Holland, Belgium, and Northern France "as a base for conducting a promising air and sea war against England. ...."[40] After the war, German General von Rundstedt said, "... The Fuehrer never really wanted to invade England. He never had sufficient courage. ... He definitely hoped that the English would make peace. ..."[41]* Historian John Lukacs makes the following observation: "[Hitler] may not have had his heart in attacking England. ... [H]ad he known that he could invade or destroy England he would have done so. [And i]t is a mistake to pay too much attention to his repeated statements of admiration for the English race."[42]

Hitler believed that the defeat of France would cause Britain to come begging for peace.[43] Once France started toppling, everyone in Berlin, including the military, felt that "the war was as good as over."[44] But should Britain need more "encouragement," Hitler's initial idea was to unleash an air and sea campaign,[45] which he did on July 10 as the opening act of the Battle of Britain. Just in case that campaign failed to discourage the British, on July 2, 1940, Hitler asked that preliminary planning commence for an invasion to

---

With the fall of France, the Germans demobilized forty army divisions. Shirer writes that Hitler wanted to demobilize between 75 percent and 100 percent of the army because its task had been fulfilled. Shirer p. 758.

occur if and when daylight air superiority was achieved.[46]* As Lukacs puts it, "[Hitler] wanted to make the English quit the war either through persuasion or through force."[47]

But not only did Churchill have no intention of quitting the war, in early June he formed a small new expeditionary force to send to Brittany in western France. This was done not for its military value but as a last-ditch attempt to keep France in the war.[48] A brigade from the 52nd Lowland Division landed in Normandy on June 7.[49]

June 3, 1940

At the War Cabinet meeting of June 3, Chief of British Fighter Command Hugh Dowding told the Cabinet that recent operations at Dunkirk had taken a substantial toll on Britain's overall fighter strength and he faced a formidable task in reconstituting the Home Defence squadrons.[50] The War Cabinet concluded that "the very serious losses of the past three weeks made it quite impossible for [Britain] to send any further fighter squadrons to France at the present time."[51]

June 4, 1940

The last soldiers came off the beaches of Dunkirk on June 4. A total of 338,225 British, French, and Belgians troops had been evacuated.[52] This remarkable rescue was achieved in no small measure by the valiant efforts of 40,000 French troops to hold off German advances toward Dunkirk. Unfortunately, those troops never got to evacuate and were all taken prisoner by the Germans when Dunkirk fell.[53]

That same day, Churchill delivered his famous "we shall fight on the beaches" speech to the House. In it, he laid out the events leading up to the Dunkirk evacuation, including how holding out at Calais had created time for the rescue, and how the evacuation was carried out under an almost ceaseless hail of bombs and artillery fire. He spoke of the loss of both men and materiel and how, with all of the Channel ports in France and Belgium now in German hands, Hitler had a plan for invading the British Isles.** In true Churchillian form he proclaimed:

> We shall prove ourselves once more able to defend our island
> home, ride out the storm of war and to outlive the menace of

---

*British fighters flew only on nights when the moon was full. Lukacs, The Last European War p. 93. At night, German bombers flew without fear of the RAF or anti-aircraft fire but were far less accurate than in daylight. Manchester and Reid p. 120.

**As was learned later, at the time Hitler had no plans to invade Britain.

tyranny, if necessary, for years, if necessary, alone. ...[*] We
shall defend our island whatever the cost may be. ... *We shall*
fight on beaches, we shall fight on the landing grounds, we
shall fight in fields and in the streets, we shall fight in the hills.
We shall never surrender.[54] [emphasis added]

In this speech Churchill made a small but significant change from his
first, where he had said Britain would fight for as long as it took "to achieve
victory, victory at all costs, victory in spite of all terror, victory, however long
and hard the road may be." In contrast, his June 4 speech implied that, on
top of British determination, "victory" would rest on one other crucial factor:

> [T]his island or ... our empire beyond the seas, armed and
> guarded by the British Fleet, *will carry on the struggle until*
> *in God's good time the New World, with all its power and*
> *might, steps forth to the rescue and liberation of the Old.*[55]
> [emphasis added]

Henry (Chips) Channon, a Conservative MP, wrote that "[Churchill]
was eloquent and oratorical and used magnificent English; several Labour
members cried."[56] Historian Brian Gardner said that the address had "elec-
trified not only his own country, but the world. With that, Churchill won
the complete confidence of the British people, which he had never before
enjoyed. Whatever was to happen, Churchill's place in the national life was
assured; he would never be in the wilderness again."[57] In America, only one-
third of people polled believed that Britain would win the war. Roosevelt
himself was skeptical.[58]

June 5, 1940

At about this time, despite his valuable contributions both as Lord
President of the Council and as a member of Churchill's War Cabinet, Neville
Chamberlain was coming under attack as news of the war worsened.[59] The
Anti-Chamberlainites, looking for scapegoats, decided the blame should fall
on the prewar leaders who would be dubbed the "Guilty Men" in a soon-to-
be-published book of the same name.** Besides Chamberlain, the "Guilty
Men" in Churchill's Government were: Lord Halifax, Chancellor of the
Exchequer Sir Kingsley Wood, and Secretary of State for Dominion Affairs

---

"...if [Churchill] knew he could defy Hitler, he also knew that he couldn't defeat
him, not without allies." Wheatcroft p. 227.

**When Guilty Men *was published, a Gallup poll showed that 77 percent of voters*
wanted Chamberlain dismissed from the Government. Britons also "scorn[ed] any
suggestion of negotiations [with Hitler]." Manchester and Reid p. 116.

Sir Thomas Inski.* Chamberlain expected additional smears to come from Labour MPs, whose party was one of the key components of Churchill's coalition government.[60] Chamberlain went to Churchill fully intending to resign. Churchill would not hear of it and reassured Chamberlain that he was a valuable member of the Government.[61] Once again, Chamberlain was "deeply gratified by Churchill's touching declaration of loyalty."[62]

Not wanting to directly attack the Labourites, Chamberlain asked Churchill to defend him against further press and Parliamentary attacks by calling for national unity.[63] Churchill agreed, and he issued a ferocious warning that "ministers who were not prepared to work within the existing government should resign."[64]

The War in France Intensifies

Meanwhile, the war in France was intensifying. On June 5, the Germans launched the second part of their invasion of France, going on the offensive against French forces amassed along the Somme and Aisne rivers located between Dunkirk and Paris. The French line held for two days. On June 9, the Germans crossed the Seine, and the following day the French Government fled Paris.

On June 10 Italy declared war on France and Britain. Continuing his efforts to convince Roosevelt that Britain must not be allowed to fall, Churchill wired Roosevelt: "If we go down, Hitler has a very good chance of conquering the world."[65]

That night, as the German armies advanced toward Paris, Churchill decided to fly there, "hoping to persuade the French to defend [Paris]."[66] Before he left England, he learned the French Government had abandoned Paris; so the scheduled meeting would be held at Briare, a town 80 miles to the south.[67] On the morning of June 11, en route to Briare, Churchill recklessly wanted to fly over the battlefields; but the pilot, informing the P.M. that he and the fighter escorts had to follow "precise instructions from the Air Ministry," told Churchill no.[68]

At the meeting in Briare, the French all appeared dejected, with the notable exception of Charles de Gaulle, whom Reynaud had made a General and Under Secretary of State for Defense and War. It was clear that France was nearing the end of organized resistance.[69] Hoping to cheer the group up a bit, Churchill revealed that a Canadian division would land in France that night, joining the three British divisions of the Second BEF already in Brittany.[70] That news had no effect on French morale.[71]

Still other "Guilty Men" were former Prime Ministers Ramsay MacDonald and Stanley Baldwin, Lord High Chancellor Sir John Simon, former Secretary of State for Air Sir Samuel Hoare, and trusted Chamberlain advisor Sir Horace Wilson.

Churchill continued his efforts to rekindle the French fighting spirit, suggesting that France fight the Germans in the streets of Paris[72] and, if all else failed, resort to guerrilla warfare.[73] The French leaders responded tepidly:

- General Weygand said he had already informed the Paris deputies that the city would be declared 'open.' No attempt at resistance would be made there, because it was full of defenseless people and he could not bear to see it destroyed by German bombardment.[74]

- In an angry tirade, Pétain dismissed Churchill's suggestions out of hand and railed that Churchill's pledge that Britain "would fight on alone [was] absurd."[75]

- Weygand, Pétain, Reynaud, and General Alphonse Georges demanded that every plane left in the RAF must be committed to the battle, which was now raging only 60 miles away.[76] Reynaud said that if the aircraft were withheld, "without doubt history will say that the Battle of France was lost for lack of planes."[77]

Apparently remembering the warning of Air Chief Marshal Dowding, that sending more fighter squadrons to France would jeopardize the defense of the UK, Churchill reluctantly refused to send more planes. Instead, he told the French it was critical that Britain be able to command the sky over England when Germany hurls the Luftwaffe against her. And if the British prevailed, "we will win it all back for you."[78] Churchill biographer Andrew Roberts calls the decision not to send more planes to France "one of the most critical judgments [Churchill] ever made."[79] It may have also been the sanest.

After the group finished dinner, Churchill and Reynaud had coffee and brandy together. Reynaud confided that General Weygand believed that "in three weeks Britain would have her neck wrung like a chicken." He also said Pétain had advised that it would "be necessary to seek an armistice."[80] Churchill returned to England the next day, in time to attend the 5:00 PM War Cabinet meeting. As reported in the conclusions of that meeting, Churchill had a two-part response to Reynaud's and Weygand's view that an all-out attack by the entire Allied air forces might even now turn the tide of the war. First, Churchill said he did not believe that such a massive showing of air power would prove decisive. But second, he promised the French that the War Cabinet would earnestly consider whatever air support Britain could give.[81]

Just after midnight Reynaud phoned Churchill. He and his advisors had moved again, this time from Briere to the city of Tours, about 145 miles southwest of Paris. He asked Churchill to meet him there that afternoon. Taking off at 11:00 AM on June 13 were Churchill, his bodyguard, Lord

Halifax, General Ismay, Minister of Aircraft Production Lord Beaverbrook, and permanent Under-Secretary of State for Foreign Affairs Alexander Cadogan. Churchill's plane, escorted by twelve Spitfires and detouring around the Channel Islands, landed on a pockmarked landing strip in Tours.[82] But no one was there to meet the British. Two French Air Force officers, who just happened to be at the aerodrome having their lunch, volunteered to drive the group into town in their small cars.[83]

The group caught up with Reynaud at the Prefecture. Weygand and Pétain did not attend the meeting. They believed that further opposition to the Germans was useless.[84] Reynaud announced that France had come to the end of the line and again brought up the pledge which had been made at France's insistence and signed by Reynaud, that neither ally would make a separate peace. The French wanted to be let off that hook,[85] but Churchill refused.[86] Churchill said that "England will fight on. She has not and will not alter her resolve: no terms, no surrender." He hoped France "would carry on fighting south of Paris and, if it came to that, in North Africa."[87] Churchill reminded Reynaud of America's firm promise to help, but he knew that Roosevelt, who was seeking re-election for a third term, could not do much at the time. Both men realized "Roosevelt's hands were tied."[88]

Reynaud reiterated his plea that Britain allow France to enter into a separate peace. Churchill refused for a second time, adding that "the French could not withdraw from the war and remain on good terms with the British."[89] Reynaud warned, "This might result in a new and very grave situation in Europe."[90] Churchill had tears in his eyes when the meeting was over and he said goodbye to Reynaud.[91] The Germans entered Paris unopposed on June 14, 1940. Weygand informed the commander of the 2nd BEF in Brittany that all organized resistance would soon be over. Shortly thereafter, Churchill ordered the 2nd BEF back to Britain.[92]

Stalin Moves on Lithuania, Latvia, Estonia, and Romania

On June 14 Stalin delivered an ultimatum to Lithuania, demanding that its Government resign. The Lithuanians quickly issued a conditional acceptance. But the Russians, who found that unacceptable, invaded the country the next day. Similar ultimatums were sent to Latvia and Estonia before they too were overrun by the Soviets.[93] Stalin's desires did not end with the seizure of the Baltic countries. A few days later he claimed part of Romania, a country on whose oil Germany dearly depended. (Because of the British blockade, Germany "could no longer import oil by sea."[94]) On June 27, Soviet troops marched into Romania; and though they avoided regions of oil and food production,[95] the relationship between Germany and Russia was starting to show some strain.

Churchill's Attempt to Warn Stalin about Hitler

Two days before the Romanian incursion, Churchill wrote a personal letter to Stalin outlining his belief that the German hegemony in Europe would have substantially negative implications for both England and Russia.[96] Stalin did not respond, but rather handed the letter over to the Germans.[97] The notion that Germany would turn on Russia was nothing new: it had been laid out in *Mein Kampf*, where Hitler wrote, "[We] turn our gaze toward the lands of the East. ... If we speak of soil in Europe today we must think principally of Russia and her boarder vassal states. ... [T]he [giant] empire in the east is ripe for collapse. And the end of the Jewish rule in Russia will also be the end of Russia as a state."[98] Nothing in Germany's pact with Stalin had changed Hitler's intentions. It merely delayed them.[99] American author and conservative pundit Pat Buchanan asserts that "... by his refusal even to consider a negotiated peace, or armistice, Churchill caused Hitler to commit his fatal blunder: invading Russia," and in doing so Churchill both brought about "the destruction of Hitler's Reich and ... the continuation of the war from 1940 to 1945."[100]

Buchanan attributes much too much to Churchill. He cites the opinion of British diplomat Roy Denman discussing what he believed was Britain's unwarranted fear that after Poland Hitler would attack the UK—hence the reason for the British guarantee of Poland. Denman suggests that but for the guarantee given by Chamberlain, immediately after conquering Poland, Russia would have been Hitler's next target. Just as "he had made clear in *Mein Kampf*, ... [he] would have marched against Russia."[101] Buchanan also cites the following quote from British historian Ian Kershaw: "By the late autumn it was clear that [Hitler] had returned to the chosen path *from which he had never seriously wandered*: attacking the Soviet Union at the earliest opportunity with the strategic aim of attaining final victory in the war by conquering London via Moscow."[102] [emphasis added] Considering Hitler's hatred for Communist Russia, his mission in life to destroy the Jewish-Bolshevik state, and his desire for Lebensraum, it is clear that Hitler's own compulsions, and not anything Churchill did, brought about the bloodbath that was the German attack on the Soviet Union.*

While Hitler may, under the circumstances that existed in 1940, have decided to invade Russia in part to shatter any British hope of prevailing in the war, that was a secondary consideration. Germany was totally content, or so it said, with leaving Britain alone as long as Britain let Germany do whatever it wanted in the East. Simply by turning East after having substantially

---

Upward of 26 million people, civilians, and military, are said to have been killed as a result of the invasion. Seven out of ten German soldiers who died in WWII were killed on the Russian front.

weakened Britain by the fighting in France and the air war over England, Germany may very well have gotten most everything it said that it wanted without having engaged in the Battle of Britain or the Blitz.

What Churchill's actions did was to keep Britain involved in WWII. But how active would Britain have remained after May 28, 1940 if Hitler and Mussolini had just ignored her? Would she ever have been able to mount anything like the second front that Hitler feared? Or would she have been little more than an annoyance to the Reich?

Keeping the French Fleet from Falling into Nazi Hands

One of the great concerns Churchill had about the fall of France was that the French Navy would fall into Nazi hands. At the time France had "the fourth largest [navy] in the world behind Britain, the United States and Japan." It included "three modern and five older battleships, eighteen heavy cruisers, twenty-seven light cruisers, sixty submarines (twenty-four of which had already been sunk), and more than fifty destroyers."[103] Were Hitler to have grabbed just one-third of the French fleet, the German Navy would have doubled in size overnight.[104] Moreover, with a French surrender and resulting unavailability of French war ships, Britain could not maintain the naval blockade of the Baltic by herself.[105]

First Sea Lord Admiral Dudley Pound had been telling the War Cabinet that Admiral François Darlan, Chief of Staff of the French Navy and Admiral of the Fleet, was taking "'all possible steps' to prevent his ships from falling into Nazi hands."[106] On June 3, Darlan swore that if an armistice occured he would mutiny and lead the fleet to fight under the British flag. Darlan also promised Churchill at the meeting of June 11–12 that he would never surrender the French Navy to the enemy;[107] if need be, the fleet would sail to Canada instead.[108] That said, Darlan's indignation over the rumored armistice between France and Germany[109] softened when, on June 15, France asked the British War Cabinet for authorization to inquire through the United States about possible terms of a separate peace with Germany.[110] At that point Darlan was willing to accept an armistice, provided the French fleet was kept out of German hands.* Despite Darlan's continued assurance that the French fleet would not be surrendered to Germany, Churchill was concerned that Darlan might be overruled by the politicians.

Darlan was a complex character. He had a deep hatred of the British and believed there was no real difference between England and Germany,

---

*Darlan's change of position about the general acceptability of an armistice may have been influenced by advanced knowledge that when Reynaud was replaced, Darlan would immediately be appointed Minister of the Navy by Reynaud's successor, Philippe Pétain.

which he had assumed would win the war. In fact, he had already told the British ambassador to France that he was "certain that Great Britain would be conquered by Germany within less than five weeks. ..."[111] Darlan had also repeatedly rejected British requests to place the whole French fleet in British custody or, at the very least, park it in the French West Indies.

On June 15 Reynaud stated that France would continue to fight, even if the French Government had to withdraw to North Africa.[112] Unfortunately, Reynaud may have been the only person in France who felt that way.

Also on the 15th, Churchill sent Roosevelt a telegram that included the specter of a defeated Britain becoming a mirror image of Vichy France.* This wire, like the one he had sent the President on May 20, again suggested that there could be circumstances under which a future British Government might have to turn the Royal Navy over to the Nazis as part of a deal to save some semblance of the UK. The telegram read in part:

> Although the present Government and I personally would never fail to send the [British] fleet across the Atlantic if resistance was beaten down here, a point may be reached in the struggle where the present Ministers no longer have control of affairs and when very easy terms could be obtained for the British islands by their becoming a vassal state of the Hitler empire. A pro-German government would certainly be called into being to make peace and might present to a shattered or starving nation an almost irresistible case for entire submission to the Nazi will. The fate of the British Fleet as I have already mentioned to you would be decisive on the future of the United States. ... If we go [down] you may have the United States of Europe under the Nazi command far more numerous, far stronger, far better armed than the New [World].[113]

June 16, 1940

As an indication of just how despondent the British were about the possibility of the French fleet coming under Nazi control, on June 16 the War Cabinet held sessions at 10:15 AM and 3:00 PM to talk about France.** At

---

In response to Churchill's implicit threat, exactly one month later Roosevelt told the P.M. that he could persuade Congress to send fifty old destroyers to Britain on two conditions: (1) Britain would secretly agree never to allow the Royal Navy to be scuttled or surrendered, and (2) Britain would sell or lease its naval bases in North America to the US. Colville p. 223.

**June 16 would also be the first time that Chamberlain made a reference in his diary to the "considerable pain" he was suffering in his abdomen. Despite the pain*

the morning session, the Cabinet considered France's request that the British Government initiate an inquiry through the United States Government on what armistice terms Germany would offer France.[114] However, most of the discussion centered on the disposition of the French fleet in the event of such an armistice.

At 12:35 PM, London sent a telegram to Premier Renaud following up on the War Cabinet's morning discussion:

> ... [P]rovided, but only *provided, that the French Fleet is sailed forthwith for British harbours pending negotiations, His Majesty's Government give their full consent to enquiry by the French Government to ascertain the terms of an armistice for France.* His Majesty's Government being resolved to continue the war wholly exclude themselves from all part in the above mentioned enquiry concerning an armistice.[115] [emphasis added]

At the 3:00 PM session the War Cabinet discussed a planned Declaration of Union under which Britain and France would fuse together into one country.[116] Roberts describes the desperate plan as "an outlandish proposal."[117]

June 17, 1940

That evening Reynaud resigned as the Premier of France. Eighty-four-year-old Marshal Philippe Pétain formed a new government with a view to seeking an armistice with Germany. As the preliminary step, Pétain ordered the French Army to lay down its arms.[118] He also appointed General Weygand as Minister of Defense and Admiral Darlan as the Minister of the Navy in the new government.[119] At the June 17 meeting of the British War Cabinet, Halifax read a telegram from the British Ambassador to France Sir Ronald Campbell, reporting on a conversation he'd had with Admiral Darlan about the French fleet. Darlan said, "So long as I can issue orders to it you have nothing to fear."[120] That statement did not ease Churchill's concern about the disposition of the French fleet. As a result, Ambassador Campbell was

---

Chamberlain maintained a full schedule. X-rays would reveal a partial obstruction of his lower bowel, which required a colostomy. He entered the hospital on July 29, 1940. His doctors discovered that he was suffering from terminal bowel cancer, but they kept the news from him. During Chamberlain's extensive convalescence, Churchill would keep him abreast of war developments and regularly urged him not to return until he was fully fit. "Churchill had been deeply moved [not only] by Chamberlain's distress" but also by "the loyalty [Neville] had showed him since May." Self p. 444. [emphasis added] Chamberlain was once more "deeply touched by the kindness." Ibid. p. 443. Although not at full speed, Chamberlain returned to work on September 12.

instructed to give Marshal Pétain the telegram that had been sent to Reynaud the previous day concerning France's exploration of armistice terms.[121] Churchill also suggested that Halifax send a new telegram directly to Pétain, pointing out that, if the French Government sought an armistice without the fleet having sailed to British ports, Britain's consent with regard to that agreement would not be forthcoming.[122]

In the telegram Halifax sent to Pétain he added that turning the French fleet over to the Germans "would scarify [the names Pétain and Weygand] for a thousand years."[123] Shortly thereafter, Paul Baudouin, the new French Foreign Minister, announced that the French fleet would sail to Algeria to prevent it from falling into German hands.[124] Most of it never did. Similarly, on June 18 Darlan told the First Lord of The Admiralty during a meeting in Bordeaux that, if the terms of the armistice were "dishonourable," the French fleet "would continue to fight to the end and anything that escaped would go to a friendly Country or be destroyed."[125] Churchill remained unconvinced.

Halifax's Surreptitious Efforts Toward a Peace Agreement with Hitler

Amid the crisis over the disposition of the French fleet, the dispute between Churchill and Halifax over entering a peace agreement with Hitler resurfaced just three weeks after it had ostensibly been put to bed at the War Cabinet meeting of May 28. Richard (Rab) Butler, Under-Secretary of State for Foreign Affairs and a longtime Churchill detractor, reopened the subject of peace negotiations by telling Sweden's Ambassador to Britain that "[n]o opportunity would be neglected for concluding a compromise peace if the chance were offered on reasonable conditions. ... The so-called diehards would not be allowed to stand in the way of negotiations."[126] Through Butler, Halifax also let the Swedish Ambassador know that "[c]ommon sense and not bravado would dictate the British Government's policy."[127] The Swedish Ambassador informed his Foreign Minister, that members of the British Parliament were telling him similar things—there was hope that negotiations would begin soon and that Halifax would replace Churchill.[128]

On June 18, the Italian Ambassador to Sweden sent a report back to Rome saying that the British had asked for an audience with Sweden's Foreign Minister and said that "the London Government was ready ... 'to discuss peace.'"[129] According to Churchill biographers William Manchester and Paul Reid, British ambassadors to two neutral counties were also trying to set up diplomatic conversations with their Nazi counterparts.[130]

When British intelligence brought news of all this activity to Churchill's attention about a week later, Churchill "asked Halifax for an explanation."[131] The Foreign Secretary claimed that Butler's message had been badly misconstrued by the Swedish Ambassador. But this was implausible, given that the Swedish Ambassador had been educated in Britain and was fluent in English.[132] A more likely explanation was that Butler and Halifax both were caught up in an exercise of poor judgment. Despite Butler's history of antagonism toward Churchill, the P.M. chose not to end the man's career over what Churchill termed "odd language." Butler was allowed to remain in the Foreign Office for another year.[133] Halifax, on the other hand, who in August was again quoted in the press as inviting Hitler "to make a new and more generous peace offer,"[134] was named Ambassador to the United States a few months later and was gone from the War Cabinet.

Their Finest Hour

On June 18, with France's surrender certain, Churchill addressed the House for thirty-six minutes, giving what has come to be known as his "This Was Their Finest Hour" speech. The speech has been described as Churchill's "most eloquent challenge to the Nazis."[135] The defiant words were heard by millions of Britons when they were broadcast four hours later. It is probably the best-remembered Churchill speech of the war, particularly for the magnificent peroration:

> *Hitler knows that he will have to break us in this Island or lose the war.* If we can stand up to him, all Europe may be free and the life of the world may move forward into broad, sunlit uplands. But if we fail, then the whole world, including the United States, including all that we have known and cared for, will sink into the abyss of a new Dark Age made more sinister, and perhaps more protracted, by the lights of perverted science. *Let us therefore brace ourselves to our duties, and so bear ourselves that if the British Empire and its Commonwealth last for a thousand years, men will still say, 'This was their finest hour.'* HC Deb 18 June 1940 vol 362 cc60. [emphasis added]

Dealing with the Pétain Government: France's Armistice with Germany

At the War Cabinet session on June 20, First Lord of the Admiralty Alexander revealed that at a meeting in Bordeaux the previous day with Marshal Pétain,[136] he had told Pétain about Britain's heavy destroyer losses. Pétain responded that he appreciated England's position but that Britain would still have no difficulty resisting a German invasion. Pétain added that it was unlikely the French Government would agree to turn their destroyers over to Britain; but Pétain did reiterate that he also would never allow the French fleet to fall into German hands.[137] Churchill, responding to what seemed like a serious risk that the French might scuttle a considerable part of their fleet rather than bring it to British ports, suggested the French might be persuaded to make greater efforts to safeguard the vessels if the United States offered to buy them.[138]

In a related development, the Admiralty had just learned that the French Government was moving from Bordeaux to the southern city of Perpignan preparatory to evacuating to North Africa.[139] As a result, Britain promptly diverted several merchant ships to Port-Vendres, a French harbor on the Mediterranean coast 20 miles south of Perpignan. There, the British ships would remain in readiness to transport the French Government to Algeria. Two British destroyers had also been ordered to Port-Vendres to act as escorts; however, later in the day the Admiralty learned that the move to North Africa had been canceled. Something seemed afoot: Ambassador Campbell feared that the idea of sending the nucleus of the French Government to North Africa might have been abandoned.[140]

On June 22 the First Lord of the Admiralty told the War Cabinet that the French commander at Portsmouth had received orders from Admiral Darlan that the French warships currently in British ports were to leave for Dakar, Senegal, an Atlantic port on the west coast of Africa. The War Cabinet agreed not to risk upsetting Darlan by protesting this move, particularly when French warships elsewhere in the world were still sharing harbors with Royal Navy vessels.[141]

Churchill was eager to send a further message to the French Government reminding them to keep His Majesty's Government in their confidence at this critical juncture, and, in keeping true to the solemn obligations which Paris had agreed to honor, to refuse to permit its resources to be used by Germany against Britain.[142] Near the end of the War Cabinet meeting, Halifax read a telegram from the French disclosing that the German conditions for an armistice had just been received in Bordeaux. These conditions filled nine pages, and the French said it was impossible to telegraph the text verbatim. The document, including the conditions about the French fleet, would be telegraphed separately.[143] Later that day, without consulting Britain or even having sent London the proposed terms, Pétain's Government signed the armistice. Britain viewed this act as a significant betrayal.[144]

Under the agreement, the Pétain Government was allowed to retain limited control of 40 percent of France, an area that contained about a third of the country's population,[145]* but, significantly, excluded Paris. The Germans

---

In early July, the French Government moved to the spa resort town of Vichy in central France. The section of the country not occupied by the Germans under the

would occupy the other 60 percent of the country. Lukacs views Hitler's choosing not to occupy all of France and her colonies in North Africa as a sign that he saw the war in the West as being over. Though not crushed, France had been defeated. Hitler now waited for a signal from London that a similar agreement could be reached, quickly confirming an actual end of the war.[146] While Hitler waited, Lukacs says, "he canceled the plan for a mass attack by 220 German bombers on [the British port city of] Southampton,"[147] and let it be known to the Italians that what he wanted now was "Peace."[148] The awaited signal from England never came.

Churchill learned the terms of the armistice on the evening of June 19.[149] Article VIII provided that:

> The French war fleet is to collect in ports to be designated more particularly, and under German and/or Italian control to demobilize and lay up—with the exception of those units released to the French Government for protection of French interests in its colonial empire.

> *The German Government solemnly declares to the French Government that it does not intend to use the French War Fleet which is in harbors under German control for its purposes in war, with the exception of units necessary for the purposes of guarding the coast and sweeping mines.*[150] [emphasis added]

In the discussion that took place in War Cabinet on June 24, Clement Attlee, the Lord Privy Seal, pointed out the illusory nature of the Germans' pledge not to use the French fleet for their own purposes. The German Government could denounce the armistice at any time, just by claiming one of its terms had been infringed.[151] Britain's Minister of Information Alfred

---

armistice agreement thus became known as "Vichy France." In the months and years after the armistice, Marshal Pétain and his government collaborated with Germany. Pétain and his underlings, including Admiral Darlan, never resisted requests by the Germans to provide aid to the Axis Powers. Among other things Pétain had Reynaud arrested and handed over to the Nazis who sent him to a concentration camp, where he remained for the rest of the war.

Pétain's puppet government was nevertheless internationally recognized, notably by the US, at least until the German breached the armistice and occupied all of France in late 1942.

After the war, Pétain was tried and convicted of treason. He was originally sentenced to death; but because of his age and World War I service, his sentence was commuted to life in prison. A few other Vichy officials, including Pétain's successor, Pierre Laval, were tried, convicted, and executed shortly after the war. Others were ultimately granted amnesty. Darlan, who at various time cozied up to the Nazis and the Allies, was assassinated in 1942.

Duff Cooper revealed a message, reportedly received by the commander at Gibraltar, which stated that Admiral Darlan had reaffirmed his explicit assurances that under no circumstances would the French Government hand over their fleet intact to the Germans. Such an assurance would, however, amount to an admission that the French Government had decided to "break the terms of the Armistice as soon as they had signed them."[152] Churchill, in turn, warned not to place too much weight on "these private messages." The situation had to "be faced in the light of public documents and in view of the terms of the Armistice to which the Bordeaux Government had agreed."[153] He added that the covert suggestion that French authorities might scuttle their ships also could not "be relied on."[154] "Once the German occupation of French territory was complete, and the French Government was entirely at the mercy of the Germans, there was nothing to prevent Germany from imposing peace terms on France even more onerous than those to which the French had agreed in the Armistice."[155]

The British Plan to Destroy the French Warships Anchored in Algeria

Admiral Pound, the First Sea Lord, told the War Cabinet that the most important French ships to eliminate from action were the battle cruisers *Dunkerque* and *Strasbourg*, which, along with two other capital ships, twenty-one destroyers and an unknown number of submarines were reported to be based at Mers-el-Kébir, an Algerian port not far from the city of Oran.[156] Pound said there were Royal Navy ships available to deal with the French flotilla, including the battleships HMS *Hood* and HMS *Resolution* and the aircraft carrier HMS *Ark Royal*.[157] He noted, however, that an operation against the French might well result in the loss or partial disablement of both British battleships, which seemed a heavy price to pay even for the elimination of the French task force.[158] Admiral Pound believed that Britain would be more likely to achieve the objective of neutralizing the French fleet by trusting in the assurances given by Admiral Darlan.

Churchill's opinion was that the ships that mattered most were the battleships *Jean Bart* and *Richelieu*, which were presently unarmed and should prove easy to secure once they left the shelter of French ports.[159] He agreed that an operation to destroy the task force anchored at Mers-el-Kébir could be very costly and might not succeed.[160] The next day, June 25, the War Cabinet authorized the Admiralty to capture the *Jean Bart* and the *Richelieu* should they put out to sea.[161] The Cabinet directed that in doing so every effort should be made to avoid bloodshed. No communication was to be made to the French Government until the operation had been completed.[162]

That same day Churchill spoke to the House. Referring to Article VIII of the armistice and Hitler's statement that Germany did not intend to use the French fleet, Churchill reiterated what Attlee had said to the War Cabinet and asked, "What is the value of that? Ask half a dozen countries, what is the value of such a solemn assurance? Furthermore, [the armistice] ... can at any time be voided on any pretext of non-observance. ..."[163]*

What to do? British playwright and political activist George Bernard Shaw suggested Britain declare war on France and capture the fleet, which he believed would gladly switch over to the British side.[164] Churchill thought that using force to cripple the Vichy Government would enrage it. Of course, he also understood that, as the blockade of France tightened, Vichy's "hostility would become inevitable."[165]

On June 26, Admiral Pound told the War Cabinet that, in view of the terms of the armistice between France and Italy, a grave risk existed that the *Dunkerque* and *Strasbourg* would soon proceed from Algeria to a French or Italian port on the north coast of the Mediterranean.[166] He expanded the point a day later when he confirmed to the War Cabinet that an operation against the French vessels anchored at Mers-el-Kébir could be carried out on or before July 3 by a task force far stronger than the French ships anchored there.[167] Churchill summed up the discussion:

> He thought that the War Cabinet had approved in principle that the operation proposed against the ships in Oran should take place on the 3rd of July. It might be combined with further operations in the Mediterranean, or with operations designed to secure the *Richelieu* and the *Jean Bart*.
>
> The possibility that we might offer the French to agree to the ships being interned in American ports was also mentioned. This would require consideration from the political point of view. Meanwhile, plans for the operation should be drawn up, and should be considered later.[168]

The P.M. also did not believe it likely that the French ships would be leaving Algeria any time soon.[169]

Churchill's skepticism proved well-founded. Much of the French fleet sat quietly at anchor in the harbor of Vichy-controlled Toulon for two and a half years. But when the Allies landed in North Africa in November 1942, Germany invaded the unoccupied portion of France to seize the French warships tied up in Toulon. The Vichy Government did not allow the seizure to occur. Rather, it scuttled the ships. Shirer pp. 924–25.

June 28, 1940

Halifax revealed that a communication had been received from the French Government in Bordeaux imploring Britain to revoke the instructions issued to her Commander-in-Chief of the Mediterranean and permit French ships moored at Alexandria, Egypt, to leave the harbor for French ports.[170] Admiral Pound then reported having received a similar message from Admiral Darlan about holding up the French ships anchored at Alexandria and in the United Kingdom.[171] Pound told the Cabinet that he had responded quite bluntly to the message "... If the French ships under our control tried to get away, we should fire on them."[172]

June 29, 1940

Darlan issued an order to the commanders of all French overseas ports saying, "As a result of the restraints placed by the British on certain French warships," British warships were to be prevented from communicating with or obtaining supplies at those ports.[173] Moreover, French ships should be prepared to resist attack by the British Navy.[174] Halifax informed the War Cabinet that the US Under Secretary of State had just told him the surrender of the French fleet was the most degrading surrender in history. The American official also reiterated that the United States had been given an explicit promise that the French fleet would not be surrendered to the Germans, and said that any military action Britain might take in respect to the French fleet would be applauded in the United States.[175]

At that day's War Cabinet meeting, First Lord of the Admiralty Admiral Alexander also reported that approximately forty barges, each about three hundred feet long, had been sighted moving toward the Dutch harbor city of Enkhuizen in the Zuyder Zee, a mostly closed-off inlet of the North Sea in the northwest of the Netherlands. That activity most likely was part of practice landings by German forces.[176] Suspicions of an imminent German invasion were also aroused two weeks later when the Cabinet reviewed an intelligence report revealing that the Nazis were assembling an array of small craft in Norway.[177] But as Shirer writes, "... we know now that the Germans did not begin to assemble the invasion fleet until September 1."[178]

July 2, 1940—Hitler at Last Asks For Plans to Be Drawn Up For an Invasion of Britain

Despite the reports of German coastal activities, Berlin continued to believe the war was over.[179] But because Hitler had not yet heard from Britain about negotiating a peace agreement, and because he believed Churchill was not acting like a sane person,[180] on July 2, he at last asked for plans to be drawn up to invade Britain if and when German air superiority could be achieved.[181] This order led to Directive No. 16, which was issued two weeks later—a week after the start of the Battle of Britain. As American author Erik Larson writes:

> Until now [Hitler] had shown little interest in invasion. With the fall of France and the disarray of Britain's army after Dunkirk, Hitler had assumed that England, in one way or another, would withdraw from the war. It was crucial that this happen, and soon. England was the last obstacle in the west, one Hitler needed to eliminate so that he could concentrate on his long-dreamed-of invasion of Soviet Russia and avoid a two-front war. ...[182]

Before the ink was dry on Directive No. 16, the German Navy started ticking off the obstacles it expected to face carrying out an invasion.[183] The Army saw dangers as well.[184] In his July 22 diary entry, General Franz Halder, Chief of Staff of the German High Command (OKW), revealed that during Hitler's conference with the OKW the previous day, the view remained that Germany had won the war with Britain and that "[a] reversal in the prospects of success [was] impossible." As noted, Hitler also admitted that because "[c]rossing the Channel appear[ed] very hazardous,"[185] it was crucial that an "invasion [was] to be undertaken only if no other means [were] left to come to terms with Britain."[186] Halder's diary entry read: "Hitler [was to] decide by the middle of next week [after the submission of a report from Admiral Erich Raeder, leader of the German Navy] whether invasion will be carried out through this fall. If not now, not before May next."[187]

Both Lukacs and Shirer point out that Hitler eventually stopped hesitating and became serious about plans to invade Britain in the early fall.[188] Hitler, however, still could not understand what was going on in Britain; he soon came to believe that Britain had not yet sought him out for a peace agreement because London was still pinning its hopes on Russia[189]—and that as the result of war between Germany and Russia, either Russia would emerge victorious or Germany would be too spent to constitute a threat to Britain. He felt that, given such "aberrant thinking" in Britain, London may have to be compelled to make peace. In contrast, General Halder believed destroying the Britain Empire would not benefit Germany, and it would be "something from which only Japan, the United States, and others would profit."[190]

July 3, 1940—The Royal Navy's Seizure of French Ships Anchored in Britain and Its Attack on the French Flotilla at Mers-el-Kébir

Britain's plan to secure the French fleet resulted in a series of actions conducted on July 3, 1940. In Phase 1—Operation Grasp—armed boarding parties carried out surprise raids in the wee hours of the morning and took over all the French warships anchored at Portsmouth, Plymouth, Falmouth, Southampton, and Sheerness. There was virtually no resistance.[191] Churchill pointed out that this showed just "how easily the Germans could have taken possession of any French ships lying in ports which they controlled."[192] In Phase 2—Operation Catapult—also carried out that day, the Royal Navy destroyed French ships at Mers-el-Kébir.[193] Much of the French Atlantic squadron was anchored there, including two battleships, the *Provence,* and the *Bretagne;*[194] two modern battlecruisers, the *Dunkerque* and the *Strasbourg,*[195] as well as several light cruisers, destroyers, and submarines.[196]

A substantial British task force, including the HMS *Hood, Valiant, Resolution,* and *Ark Royal,* arrived off Mers-el-Kébir.[197] The British, led by Vice Admiral Sir James Somerville, gave the French commander, Admiral Marcel-Bruno Gensoul,[198] four choices:

- sail with the Royal Navy against Nazi Germany and Italy;
- sail with a reduced crew to a British port;*
- sail with a reduced crew to a French colonial port or to the United States, where the ships would be disarmed for the duration;** or
- sink his vessels within six hours.[199]

After hours of discussion, Gensoul said that he would never permit any vessel to be taken intact by the Nazis.[200] But he would also defend himself by force against the British.[201] Speaking through the Admiralty, Churchill directed Somerville to begin operations, distasteful as they were.[202] Realizing that the French were stalling—buying time for its vessels to get ready to put out to sea, at 6:00 PM the British task force opened fire. Within ten minutes, one French battleship had been blown up and another had been beached. The *Dunkerque* ran aground, only to be destroyed a few minutes later by torpedo bombers from the *Arc Royal;* 1,250 French sailors were killed. Only the *Strasbourg* escaped.[203]

---

*If either of the first two options were chosen, Britain would return the ships to France after the war or pay full compensation if they were destroyed.
**The crews would be repatriated at the earliest possible moment.

Upon hearing of the attack, Pétain's government "was apoplectic. Darlan vowed revenge." Paul Laval, the new Minister of Foreign Affairs for the Vichy Government, wanted to declare war on England. "Pétain broke off diplomatic relations with Britain"[204] and reversed a pledge by former Premier Reynaud to turn four hundred captured Luftwaffe pilots over to the British. Those pilots were instead sent back to Germany.[205]

July 4, 1940—Effects of the Attack at Mers-el-Kébir

Churchill recounted the entire story of Mers-el-Kébir to the House. At the end of the speech, Churchill received a grand ovation, and he was touched by it.[206] Later Churchill got the opportunity to discuss the Mers-el-Kébir attack with the American Secretary of State, Cordell Hull, who neither approved of the attack nor trusted Churchill's motives. Tellingly, Churchill advised Secretary Hull there was another reason for the attack beyond destroying the French Navy. He said that "since many people throughout the world believed that Britain was about to surrender, he had wanted by this action to show that she still meant to fight."[207]

Mers-el-Kébir ended all talk in the UK of a British surrender.[208] Months later, Harry Hopkins, President Roosevelt's top advisor, told Jock Colville "that it was [Mers-el-Kébir] which convinced Roosevelt, in spite of opinions to the contrary, that the British would go on fighting, as Churchill had promised, if necessary for years, if necessary, alone."[209]

July 8, 1940—A Similar Attack on French Ships Anchored in Dakar Senegal

A small flotilla of Royal Navy ships—the aircraft carrier HMS *Hermes,* the heavy cruiser HMS *Dorsetshire* and the sloop HMS *Milford*—unleashed a Mers-el-Kébir-style attack on the French naval base at Dakar in Senegal.[210] The British were intent on rendering the battleship *Richelieu,* anchored there, unserviceable to the enemy. Using motorboats to launch depth charges and aircraft to fire torpedoes, they managed to disable the *Richelieu.*[211] But the ship would be repaired, and in September it was used by the Vichy Government against the Allies in another battle at Dakar. Several days after the July 8 attack, Britain informed French naval authorities that it would take no further action against French ships in French colonial or North African ports.[212]

July 10, 1940

At the War Cabinet meeting on July 10, Halifax recounted a recent conversation that the British Ambassador to Switzerland, David Kelly, had with Carl Burckhardt, the acting President of the International Red Cross. Burckhardt had just returned from Berlin where he engaged in one-on-one discussions with several top Nazi officials, including State Secretary Ernst von Weizsäcker. Each of the Germans told Burckhardt that Hitler was hesitating before attacking England because he was still hoping to work out an arrangement with London[213] (a view with which Shirer concurs).[214] Ambassador Kelly told Burckhardt that Britain's distrust of Hitler, apart from anything else, was a fatal obstacle to peace.[215]

The Battle of Britain Commences

July 10 turned out to be a tragically historic day. On that day Germany launched the Battle of Britain, which featured massive German airstrikes against British targets over the ensuing sixteen weeks.[216] The Luftwaffe at first targeted ports and coastal-shipping convoys.[217] These attacks gradually intensified throughout the month.[218] With no sign of British capitulation, the Luftwaffe, starting August 1, shifted its attacks to RAF airfields and infrastructure.[219] Later, the Luftwaffe also began targeting factories involved in aircraft production and other strategic infrastructure.[220]

Once the German aerial onslaught had begun, many government officials— including Harold Nicolson, then Parliamentary Secretary at the Ministry of Information; Sir Alan Brooke, who had served under General Gort in France; and Jock Colville—all felt that an invasion was imminent.[221] On July 14 Colville even noted that Churchill himself "thinks it highly probable."[222]

July 16, 1940—Plans for Operation Sea Lion

As mentioned earlier, on July 16 Hitler issued Directive No. 16 about preparations for what came to be known as "Operation Sea Lion": the invasion of England.[223] The first sentence of the directive read: "Since England, in spite of her hopeless military situation, shows no signs of being ready to come to an understanding, I have decided to prepare a landing operation against England, and, *if necessary, to carry it out.*"[224] [emphasis added] Clearly, Hitler was still hoping that he would not have to implement Operation Sea Lion. As American historian Williamson Murray writes, "'Sea Lion' would have represented a desperate risk with a small chance of success. It is clear that Hitler had serious doubts about this operation from the beginning."[225]

The next day, July 17, the German Army High Command ordered "thirteen [hand-picked] divisions to the jumping off place on the Channel coast." These ninety thousand troops were to serve as the "first wave of the invasion" of Britain.[226] That was also the day a detailed invasion plan was completed.[227] The ambitious plan called for landings to be made along some 200 miles of England's southern coast.[228] By the end of the third day of the invasion, the High Command wanted to have landed a total of two hundred and sixty thousand infantry men plus six panzer divisions reinforced by three motorized divisions.[229] As noted, the German Navy doubted it could accomplish such a broad landing. It calculated that "[j]ust putting the first wave ashore ... would require 1,722 barges, 1,161 motor boats, 471 tugs, and 155 transports."[230] This force included no naval escorts for the armada. While Hitler recognized the Navy's concern, he also stressed the need to bring the war to an end and said that the landing "would have to be completed by September 15."[231] Though outwardly Hitler was finally exhibiting an interest in invading Britain, it was still something he did not really want to do.

July 19, 1940—Another German Peace Offer

On Friday July 19, 1940, Hitler delivered a speech to the Reichstag that contained a direct plea for peace he hoped would finally appeal to Great Britain. Of course, he also couldn't refrain from hurling insults at Churchill, such as: "I feel a deep disgust for this type of unscrupulous politician who wrecks whole nations."[232] The United Press wire story "Hitler offers Britain 'peace or destruction'" read in pertinent part:

BERLIN, July 19, 1940 (UP)—Adolf Hitler today addressed an "appeal to reason" to Great Britain to avert "destruction of a great world empire," but he made it clear that rejection would mean an attack with all of the forces at the command of the Axis powers. ...

"I feel myself obliged to make one more appeal to reason to England."

"I do this not as a victor, but for the triumph of common sense."

Without delivering any ultimatum, Hitler said that it had never been his desire or his aim to destroy the British Empire.

The Fuehrer warned against interpreting his appeal as weakness. ...

The Fuehrer said that his cardinal aims in foreign policy had been friendship with Britain and with Italy. ...

As he spoke, German airplanes ranged over the British Isles again and dive bombers slashed at British shipping in what Nazi [sic] had said was a mere preliminary to the long threatened "blitzkrieg" offensive by Germany and Italy in an attempt to invade England for the first time in nine centuries. ...[233]

In his speech, Hitler specifically threatened Londoners, saying that without agreement an "awful vengeance will be brought on them. Not, of course on Churchill who will run away to Canada, but on the people themselves."[234]

As Shirer writes, waging war against England was "easier said than done." Hitler and his military had never "seriously considered how to wage war against Britain."[235] Shirer also reveals what should have been obvious, but wasn't: that the German military were, and historically had always been, "land-minded,"[236]* as the British were, and had for centuries been, sea-minded. Thus, the English Channel "loomed in [German] minds ... as an obstacle they knew not how to overcome."[237] German planners simply didn't know how to invade Britain. After all, this was "the first time in history that any German military staff had been asked ... to consider" the question.[238]

Some German leaders, including Propaganda Minister Joseph Goebbels, speculated that Churchill, like Reynaud, would resign so that his country could establish a more reasonable government and enter into a peace agreement.[239] As soon as Hitler's speech was heard over the radio, however, both the British press and the BBC rejected it, with no prompting from the Government.[240] At the July 20 War Cabinet meeting, Hitler's speech generated little discussion. A suggestion was made that resolutions should be debated in both Houses on July 25, expressing Britain's resolve to fight on until Nazism had been defeated. The ministers envisioned that these resolutions could be proposed and seconded by Members in the Commons and by Peers in the House of Lords; and after a short and rather formal debate, a free vote be allowed.[241] In the meantime, the press would be informed that because the Prime Minister was not proposing to make a statement, they should refrain from suggesting that there was anything in Hitler's speech that called for an official reply.[242]

The official rejection of Hitler's peace proposal took place on Monday, July 22, in a radio speech by Lord Halifax.[243] That Halifax delivered the address was happenstance. As Halifax explains, at that time, one member of the War Cabinet made a broadcast to the nation every fortnight. "[It just] happened to fall to my turn" to do that day's broadcast.[244]

Britain's rejection of Hitler's peace proposal notwithstanding, the Vatican proposed a settlement, and on August 1, King Gustav of Sweden proposed a conference "to examine the possibility of making peace."[245] Some members of the English establishment thought these suggestions merited discussion.[246]**

---

*Germany's invasion of Norway had involved transporting troops by ship. That campaign, however, was of a much smaller scale than an invasion of Britain, and it was against an unsuspecting country with little in the way of shore defenses. No D-Day type amphibious assaults under withering fire were involved.

**As noted, Halifax was being quoted in the press as "inviting" Hitler "to make a new and more generous peace offer." Manchester and Reid p. 115.

July 30, 1940

Hitler Advised to Postpone the Invasion of Britain

Back in Berlin, still concerned about its ability to carry out the grandiose plan proposed for the invasion of Britain, on July 30 the German Naval War Staff advised Hitler to postpone the invasion until May 1941 or later.[247] The German Navy simply did not believe it had the necessary ships to support the broad landing desired by the Army, particularly in the face of the resistance anticipated from the Royal Navy and the RAF.[248] The feud between the German Navy and Army was on.[249]

Planning Begins for the Invasion of the Soviet Union

At about this time, Hitler was again telling his military chiefs that "Britain's hope lies in Russia and America" and that, as Manchester and Reid write, London was "'back on her feet' sustained in part by her Russian hopes."[250] As Lukacs puts it, Hitler felt that "if Russia were eliminated, England's last hope for a possible ally in Europe would vanish, and the Americans would have their hands full with Japan."[251] Partly to dash Britain's Russian hopes once and for all, on July 31, Hitler told his generals to start preparing immediately for "Operation Barbarosa," the invasion of Russia.[252] Hitler had wanted the invasion of the Soviet Union to take place in the fall of 1940.[253] But General Wilhelm Keitel, Chief of the German Armed Forces High Command, was concerned about weather and the logistics of moving the army, then situated in the West, to Eastern Europe, particularly in a way not to arouse Stalin's suspicions. Keitel managed to talk Hitler into sliding the date for the invasion to the spring of 1941.[254] The idea of invading Britain was also dissipating.[255]

Roosevelt, no longer sure that Britain could hold out, prepared to circumvent Congress and offer Britain the fifty old destroyers that London had begged him for.*

The Air War over Britain Intensifies

"During the month of July, the RAF lost 70 aircraft and the Luftwaffe lost more than 180," the majority of which were bombers.[256] On August 1, Hitler issued Directive No. 17, which expressed his intention "to intensify the

---

*This decision was announced publicly the beginning of September. Lukacs, Five Days pp. 206–07.

As noted earlier in this chapter, Roosevelt was also responding to Churchill's implicit threat that, without adequate assistance from America, at some point, transfer of the Royal Navy to the Nazis could be part of a deal Britain might have to strike with Hitler.

air and sea warfare against the English Homeland."[257] It ordered Luftwaffe attacks against RAF units, their ground installations, and supplier organizations, as well as factories producing aircraft and anti-aircraft equipment.[258] The Directive also ordered attacks against stores of food located at ports and elsewhere. Notably, the Directive continued the order that terror attacks as measures of reprisal were not to be undertaken without Hitler's permission.[259] Larson points out that this provision was included "[t]o help avoid scuttling any opportunity for a peace deal. ..."[260]

In response to the Directive, Goring gave orders on August 12 to launch *der Alderangriff* (the "Eagle Attack") three days later; the objective was to achieve air superiority over Britain.[261] In preparation, on August 13 and 14 the Luftwaffe launched massive raids, mostly against RAF fighter bases. As military historian and retired RAF Air Commodore Andrew Lambert writes:

> The aims of Göring's "great battle" were for the Luftwaffe to grasp air superiority, destroy the rest of the RAF, prepare the ground for invasion (while protecting its own bases and ports), and perhaps even coerce the British into surrender. If invasion were ordered, the Luftwaffe would [then be in a position to] defeat the Royal Navy's task forces, protect the invasion fleet, and provide support for the offensive on London—quite a tall order!

> For the RAF, in contrast, the task was simple: survive.[262]

Luftwaffe attacks continued to intensify. The German air assault on August 15 involved 30 percent more aircraft than normal. Despite Germany's superior numbers, the battle, however, was "going against the Luftwaffe."[263] The reason in large part was the combination of poor leadership,[264] "appalling intelligence,"[265] and Britain's Fighter Command use of "the Dowding System," which the head of Fighter Command, Hugh Dowding, had developed years earlier.[266]

As explained in Chapter 19, the Dowding System used a network of radar installations, called Radio Direction Finding (RDF) stations, to track German aircraft from the moment they took off in Western Europe. Their course could be plotted so accurately that the RAF would know when best to attack them. Each RDF station passed its information to a central Filter Room at Fighter Command Headquarters. There, a specialized team added this data to information from pilot and ground observations to create a clear picture of the incoming raids; this analysis was then sent to the Operations

Room for the appropriate geographic sector being alerted.* A sector controller would review the information and decide when and where to scramble
his local squadrons to best defend against the incoming raid. A stream of
information would be provided to the fighters to guide them in intercept-
ing the German bombers.[267] There was a "constant chatter between sector
stations and pilots."[268] The progress of both RAF and German aircraft was
plotted on a huge table map by members of the Women's Auxiliary Air Force
"using croupier rakes to move colored counters representing ..." the various
planes.[269] More importantly, using this system, British fighters were being
accurately directed to where and when to best attack German bombers.[270]

On August 24, the Germans started attacking Fighter Command sector
stations themselves. Over the next few weeks the Germans "made more
than a thousand sorties" a day over Britain to destroy these facilities.[271] The
Germans also incorporated more fearsome Messerschmitt Bf 110 fighters
into their bombing groups.[272] The numerical advantage of the Luftwaffe
was beginning to show.** Many fighter fields in the south of England were
extensively damaged, and six of the nine sector stations around London
had been severely bombed,*** threatening the entire Dowding System.[273]
In addition, RAF aircraft losses were now exceeding those of the Luftwaffe,
and Britain had lost about a quarter of its available fighter pilots.[274] What's
more, "[u]nlike the Luftwaffe, the RAF did not have a bottomless reserve
of trained pilots."[275] Simply put—Fighter Command had been staggered.

The Blitz

Despite nearly dealing Fighter Command a knockout blow, on September 7,
1940, Germany changed its air offensive strategy against Britain to bombing London itself.[276] The Battle of Britain was entering a final but deadlier
phase: the Blitz had just begun. Except for the evening of November 4,[277]
London was bombed on seventy-six straight nights.[278] Roberts explains that

---

*Nationwide, there were twenty-one such sectors, nine of which surrounded
London. See, Manchester and Reid pp. 134, 138.

**It bears noting that after years of only modest airplane production, in July 1940
Britain produced 496 fighters, or four times more than it had manufactured before
Dunkirk. In August it produced an astounding 1,081. Manchester and Reid p. 143.

The War Cabinet invited the Prime Minister to consider recommending that the King
grant honors and declarations in connection with civilian war work, including the
management staffs of munitions and aircraft factories. CAB 65/2 244 (40) p. 33 24.

***Dowding always believed that much of the aerial fighting would take place over
London. Manchester and Reid p. 139.

Hitler's "switching the Luftwaffe from carrying out daylight raids on RAF installations in southern England to undertaking night raids on London was a major strategic blunder, because it allowed Fighter Command to repair its runways, hangars and command and control stations."[279] Shirer says this tactical shift was "comparable in its consequences to Hitler's calling off the armored attack on Dunkirk [his "Halt Order"] on May 24."[280]

There were two principal reasons for the shift in strategy. First, the Germans felt that their attempt during July and August to achieve air superiority and to get Britain to quit the war was not succeeding. Because of poor intelligence, they were mistaken. Second, Hitler believed that Britain had opened the door to the bombing of cities by bombing Berlin, and he was angry. The fact is that the first step down this road was neither intentional nor was it taken by the British. On the night of August 23 a few German planes had mistakenly dropped bombs on the center of London.[281] In the process they destroyed several homes and killed a few civilians.[282] Churchill assumed the bombing was deliberate and chose to respond over the next few nights by sending planes to bomb Berlin.[283] While the air attack on Berlin was generally ineffectual and only killed a few German civilians,[284] it had a very negative effect on German morale; [285] after all, Hitler and Goering had repeatedly assured Germans citizens that it was militarily impossible for the Reich to be bombed.[286] Angry and frustrated, on August 30, Hitler "lifted the ban on bombing London."[287]

England Winds Up Not Losing the Battle of Britain

As Manchester and Reid put it, as a result of poor intelligence "… the German high command did not grasp the implications of the Luftwaffe successes [in the latter stages of the Eagle Attack]."[288] As a result, the RAF, which may not have been able to carry on for more than a few more weeks,[289] wound up "winning" or, more precisely, not losing, the Battle of Britain. Hitler "had conquered France in six weeks. Now, almost twelve weeks after the French surrender, the English—their army weak but rebuilding, their navy spread thin, their air force down on one knee—had fought him to a standstill."[290] In Churchill's famous speech to the House on August 20, he heaped well-deserved praise, though perhaps a few weeks prematurely, on the pilots of the RAF's Fighter Command:

> The gratitude of every home in our Island, in our Empire, and indeed throughout the world, except in the abodes of the guilty, goes out to the British airmen who, undaunted by odds, unwearied in their constant challenge and mortal danger, are turning the tide of world war by their prowess and by their

devotion. *Never in the field of human conflict was so much owed by so many to so few.*[291] [emphasis added]

Hitler hoped that the bombing of London every night would create mass hysteria and lead to England's capitulation without Germany having to invade the country. On its face, the plan was plausible. Though the buildings in London had exteriors of brick and stone, their internal structures—rafters, beams, flooring—were all wood, dry, old, and highly flammable.[292] As a result, the Blitz caused massive destruction and huge fires. It did not, however, undercut the determination of the British people. They withstood the Blitz unflinchingly.

There is an argument that neither the Battle of Britain nor the Blitz was necessary. The argument goes like this: In June 1940, Hitler was in a situation similar to the one that existed immediately after the defeat of Poland, where he could have chosen to turn and attack the West or turn east and attack Russia. As Commodore Lambert writes, "Hitler could have consolidated his position on the continent, ignored the British, and begun his planning for [Operation] Barbarossa."[293]* He could have given Britain a unilateral armistice if all he wanted was freedom in the East without fear of Britain's starting a second front, or at least not starting one immediately. Indeed, after the Battle of Britain concluded in the early Fall of 1940 the only significant actions in which Britain was involved for some time were: a bombing campaign focused primarily on attacking aerodromes, invasion ports, oil and industrial targets, and German U-boat facilities;[294] flying sorties against enemy shipping;[295] rebuffing an Italian attack into Egypt that Fall;[296] continuing to pursue those Italian forces through Libya in the winter of 1941;[297] and sending sixty-thousand troops to northern Greece to help shore up the Balkans in March 1941.[298]** British bombing did get more active in the spring of 1942 after the Air Ministry issued a directive to the RAF Bomber Command to strike Germany's workforce by bombing population centers. Britain became more aggressive after the US managed to mobilize and join the war effort in 1942.***

---

*As discussed earlier in this book, it is however unlikely that Britain would have been permanently spared had Hitler turned east. Directive 21, dated December 18, 1940, shows that once Germany had defeated Russia, Hitler would have attacked Britain with the goal of conquering or neutralizing (but not destroying) the country, much as he had done with France. Lukacs, The Last European War p. 101.

**This is not to say that after Germany invaded the Soviet Union in June 1941 Britain did not supply planes and other armaments to Russia. See, e.g., CAB 65/1 25 (42) p. 128 101 February 25, 1942.

***Notably, the United States joined the war in Europe only after the Japanese attack on Pearl Harbor on December 7, 1941. She immediately declared war on Japan. Then, on December 11, Hitler declared war on the US. Hitler had been

In any event, while the fighting in the skies over England continued in 1940, tensions grew between Russia and Germany, stemming from the Soviet takeover of Latvia, Estonia, and Lithuania. Hitler also feared that a war would break out between Hungary and Romania over Transylvania, which Romania had grabbed after WWI, and that Russia might get involved and occupy all of Romania. Such an outcome would have cut Germany off from her main source of crude oil.[299] For that reason, on August 28, Hitler ordered several of his panzer and related divisions to get ready to seize the Romanian oil fields.[300] The crisis was averted when Hungary and Romania agreed to arbitrate the issue.[301]

Impact of the Blitz

—on German Plans to Invade Britain

On September 1, 1940, ships began to head from German ports on the North Sea to embarkation sites along the Channel. Two days later, the date for the invasion of Britain was pushed back from September 15 to September 21.[302] Orders to carry out the landing were to be given on September 11.[303] However, Hitler continued to vacillate about whether to invade Britain at all. He was still firmly convinced that Britain could be defeated *without* an invasion.[304]

As noted, on Saturday, September 7, the Germans had begun the Blitz. The raid against London that evening was carried out in two waves by a total of six hundred and twenty-five bombers. It was the most devastating air attack on a city that the world had ever seen.[305] Three hundred Londoners were killed.[306] The German High Command quickly came to believe that the bombing of London would be so successful that an invasion might not be necessary.[307]

As a result, on September 10, Hitler once again postponed the date for issuing the order to launch the invasion, this time until the 14th. The good news for the Germans—an apparently significant initial success for the night-time Blitz—was tempered by poor weather and the ongoing interference by the RAF and Royal Navy, both of which adversely affected German Navy's plans to assemble its invasion fleet.[308] Through a German Supreme Command directive released on September 14, the date for issuing the invasion order was postponed again—this time by three days.[309]

---

advised that under its agreement with Japan and Italy, Germany did not have to declare war on America. Shirer p. 894.

    But he could no longer control his pent up anger over Roosevelt's verbal attacks against him, and the US's supplying war materiel to Britain. Ibid. pp. 895, 897–98. In his blind rage, Hitler would ignore America's great industrial strength and the relative ease in which she would turn that into military strength. This would be a fatal mistake.

Emboldened by its new strategy of bombing London, on September 15, the Germans decided to try something even bolder: daylight bombing of the British capital. The September 15 raid was carried out by several hundred bombers escorted by approximately six hundred fighters.[310] But, the armada was detected and intercepted successfully by the rejuvenated Fighter Command long before it neared London.[311] Several hours later, still during daylight, an even larger bomber grouping tried to get through, but it too was decimated.[312] Daylight bombing of London proved far too costly to the Germans, and it was halted.

Germany also recognized that the RAF was still able to successfully attack German-held French ports and destroy or damage the barges to be used for the invasion. Thus, on September 17, Hitler decided to postpone Operation Sea Lion indefinitely.[313] Two days later, he ordered the invasion fleet to be dispersed.[314] Of course, no one in London knew any of this. In fact, at the War Cabinet meeting on Monday, September 23, Churchill told the Cabinet members that a number of indications pointed to the possibility of a German invasion attempt over the upcoming weekend.[315] But, no invasion took place that weekend, or ever. The formal directive calling off Operation Sea Lion was issued in Berlin on October 12.[316]

What a moment! The RAF's Fighter Command had just staved off an invasion, even if just barely, by denying the Luftwaffe air superiority over England. In the process it had handed Nazi Germany its first military setback. Unlike the evacuation of 330,000 men from Dunkirk, it was not a miracle. Rather, it was based in large part on the integrated radar and communication system developed by Fighter Command head Hugh Dowding, the "true hero of the Battle of Britain."[317] For the badly outnumbered RAF, thwarting the Luftwaffe was a monumental achievement. This stunning success, along with the marked transformation of the Army since the summer began,[318] in many people's eyes vindicated Churchill's position, stated back in May, that Britain should wait ninety days and then reassess its situation rather than rush into peace negotiations with Hitler. It actually took some one hundred and fifty days for the situation to become clear, but, at least for the moment, it appeared that Churchill had been correct.

—on Britons

Despite calling off the invasion, the Germans continued the Blitz, still hoping to break civilian morale, perhaps create another opportunity for an invasion or capitulation, and deliver retribution for the British bombing of German cities.[319] Conceivably, the Nazis also intended to plant the seeds of civil disorder, even rebellion among the English. Working-class residents of London's East End always resented the fact that they suffered disproportionately from the bombing. At the depth of their bitterness, on September 17,

Harold Nicolson wrote in his diary that "it is said even the King and Queen were booed the other day when they visited the destroyed areas." Nicholson noted a Liberal Party MP's observation that "if only that the Germans had sense not to bomb west of London Bridge there might have been a revolution in the country."[320] However, if there were ever a chance of an East Ender uprising, it ended several weeks later when, with the Royal Family in residence, Buckingham Palace was bombed during a midday raid. Government censors wanted to suppress the story, but Churchill told them to "[s]pread the news at once. Let the humble people of London know that they are not alone, and that the King and Queen are sharing their perils with them."[321] Once again, Churchill's instincts were spot on.

Churchill would frequent sites of recent bombings. He would "poke at the edge of bombing craters with his walking stick" or "scramble up a pile of rubble to get a better look at things. In each case he always sought out the people.[322] As Mollie Panter-Downes, a well-known British novelist and columnist for *The New Yorker,* wrote: "Churchill possessed a great gift for making them forget discomfort, danger, and loss and remember that they were living history."[323] On September 21, Edward R. Murrow, doing his nightly CBS broadcast from London to America from the rooftop of the BBC, spoke about the character of the people of London:

> I'm standing on a rooftop looking out over London. At the moment, everything is quiet. For reasons of national as well as personal security, I am unable to tell you the exact location from which I am speaking.
>
> Off to my left, far away in the distance, I can see just that faint red, angry snap of anti-aircraft bursts against the steel-blue sky. But the guns are so far away that it's impossible to hear them from this location. About five minutes ago the guns in the immediate vicinity were working.
>
> I can look across just at the building not far away and see something that looks like a splash of white paint down the side. And I know from daylight observation that about a quarter of that building has disappeared, hit by a bomb the other night.
>
> Streets fan out in all directions from here, and down on one street I can see a single red light, and just faintly the outline of a sign standing in the middle of the street. And again I know what that sign says, because I saw it this afternoon. It says:

"Danger: Unexploded Bomb." Off to my left still, I can see just that red snap of the anti-aircraft fire.

I was up here earlier this afternoon, and looking out over these housetops, looking all the way to the dome of St. Paul's, I saw many flags flying from staffs. No one ordered these people to put out the flags. They simply feel like flying the Union Jack above their roofs. No one told them to do it, and *no flag up there was white*.[324] [emphasis added]

In time, Britain's defenses against the Blitz improved, anti-aircraft guns were more successful, and the unescorted Luftwaffe bombers had to bomb from higher altitudes, which decreased their accuracy.[325]

Chamberlain's Final Days

With his health on the decline due to bowel cancer, Chamberlain attended his last War Cabinet meeting on September 18, 1940. When he left London for the last time on September 19, he took comfort in the fact that England had survived the Battle of Britain and that the German invasion threat seemed to be dissipating.[326] On September 22, he resigned. Churchill initially declined to accept the resignation and pleaded with Chamberlain to give himself a fair chance to recover. The former Prime Minister "was deeply touched and grateful for Churchill's 'generous attitude'" but recognized that this was only "an interim expression of courtesy."[327] Churchill then offered to make him a knight in the prestigious Order of the Garter, but Chamberlain refused, saying that he would "prefer to die plain 'Mr. Chamberlain' like my father before me, unadorned by any title."[328] Facing the inevitable, Chamberlain drafted his own obituary, which has been described by many as being "unrepentant." Chamberlain wrote:

> [I]t was in the hope of doing something to improve the conditions of life for the poor people that brought me at past middle life into politics, and it is some satisfaction to me that I was able to carry out some part of my ambition, even though its permanency may be challenged by the destruction of war. *For the rest I regret nothing that I have done and I see nothing undone that I ought to have done*. I am therefore content to accept the State that has so suddenly overtaken me and I only trust that I may not have to bear my disabilities too long.[329] [emphasis added]

Chamberlain died on the morning of November 9, 1940, at the age of 71. Churchill sent the following note to Chamberlain's widow, Anne:

During the long violent months of war we had come closer together than at any time in our 20 years of friendly relationship amid the ups & downs of politics. I greatly admired his fortitude and firmness of spirit. I felt when I served under him that he [would] never give in & I knew when our positions were reversed that I [could] count upon the aid of a loyal and unflinching comrade.[330]

On November 12, Churchill gave a eulogy for Chamberlain in Parliament; he reprised it at the late P.M.'s funeral in Westminster Abbey two days later.

It fell to Neville Chamberlain in one of the supreme crises of the world to be contradicted by events, to be disappointed in his hopes, and to be deceived and cheated by a wicked man.

Whatever else history may or may not say about these terrible, tremendous years, we can be sure that Neville Chamberlain acted with perfect sincerity according to his lights and strove to the utmost of his capacity and authority, which were powerful, to save the world from the awful, devastating struggle in which we are now engaged.

... [T]here were certain qualities, always admired in these Islands, which he possessed in an altogether exceptional degree. He had a physical and moral toughness of fibre which enabled him all through his varied career to endure misfortune and disappointment without being unduly discouraged or wearied.

When, contrary to all his hopes, beliefs and exertions, the war came upon him, and when, as he himself said, all that he had worked for was shattered, there was no man more resolved to pursue the unsought quarrel to the death. The same qualities which made him one of the last to enter the war, made him one of the last who would quit it until the full victory of a righteous cause was won.

I had the singular experience of passing in a day from being one of his most prominent opponents and critics to being one of his principal lieutenants, and on another day of passing from serving under him to become the head of a Government of which, with perfect loyalty, he was content to be a member.

Members of all parties, without a single exception, feel that we do ourselves and our country honour in saluting the memory of one whom Disraeli would have called an "English worthy."[331]

In the end, Churchill did not blame Chamberlain for Britain's failure to rearm soon enough and keep ahead of the expansion of the German army and air force.

―――

Italy's Invasion of Greece; Her Adventure in North Africa

On September 27, 1940, the Three-Power Pact (also known as the Tripartite Pact) was signed in Berlin by the three Axis powers: Italy, Japan, and Germany.[332] A week later, on October 4, Hitler and Mussolini met at the Brenner Pass on the border of Italy and Austria to discuss the possibility of Spain entering the war on the side of the Axis. When Mussolini learned, a few days after the meeting, that Germany was sending troops into Romania (a country Italy had long coveted), he "was indignant" that Hitler had said nothing to him about it when they met.[333] Mussolini decided that when he carried out his plan to invade Greece—something the Germans had told him not to do—Hitler would also find out about it for the first time in the newspapers.[334]

Mussolini set Monday, October 28, as the date for his secret invasion of Greece.[335] However, before that time, Hitler caught wind of the Italian dictator's planned invasion and immediately demanded to meet with Mussolini. The date Mussolini suggested for the meeting—October 28 in Florence[336]— was the same day the Italian Army moved south from occupied Albania and crossed the border into Greece. Not to be outdone by his German partner in his desire to deceive, Mussolini wrote a letter to Hitler backdated to October 19 informing him of the operation Italy was "planning."[337] When Hitler got off the train in Florence, Mussolini promptly announced, "Fuehrer, we are on the march! Victorious Italian troops crossed the Greco-Albanian frontier at dawn today!"[338] Hitler, too late to stop the incursion, was furious. Mussolini enjoyed his revenge—briefly.[339]

Once the invasion started, the Greek Prime Minister immediately contacted Churchill, seeking help.[340] On Friday, November 1, the War Cabinet generally believed that Britain should do everything she could do to help Greece.[341] Fifteen planes were sent.[342] During the next meeting three days later, Halifax reported that the Greeks had asked Britain for still more aircraft, as well as anti-aircraft guns, anti-tank guns and rifles.[343] Churchill declared it was essential to help Greece resist the Italian attack, and he said that public opinion favored British intervention in Greece.[344] The War Cabinet agreed to send five RAF squadrons (two squadrons of fighters and three squadrons of medium bombers) to Greece.[345]

Two weeks later it agreed to also send twelve Gladiators (a remarkably fast biplane fighter) for use by the Greek Air Force.[346] With Britain's assistance, the Greeks quickly pushed the Italians back into Albania.[347]

The Italian misadventure in Greece came at a time when the Axis had other desires and concerns. Back in September, with a force of three hundred thousand men[348] Italy had crossed into Egypt from its African colony of Libya to take over Egypt and the Suez Canal.[349] By treaty, both were under the protection of the British Crown. Italy's campaign was part of a fairly farfetched plan to eliminate Britain's position in the Mediterranean[350] and cut off its supply of oil from Iran.[351] To accomplish this would also require destroying the Royal Navy bases at Alexandria and Port Said, capturing Gibraltar, and the closure of its straits.[352] For his part, Hitler was more concerned that the British might occupy Crete, from which she could easily bomb the oil fields he coveted. What's more, should the British gain a foothold in Greece, they could threaten Germany's position in the Balkans.[353] Unfortunately for the Axis, after an initial retreat, the British Army was able to rebuff Italy's attack into Egypt, forcing the Italians to withdraw back into Libya. In the process the British eventually captured one hundred and thirty thousand Italian soldiers and confiscated nearly five hundred tanks.[354]

In February 1941, although he did not want to deplete his resources for the upcoming invasion of Russia, Hitler dispatched General Rommel and two armored divisions to Libya. He could not let Italy, his Axis ally, be humiliated.[355] In a month Rommel went on the offensive and forced the British to retreat all the way back into Egypt.[356] Later, Hitler would also make up for an Italian misadventure in Greece.

Growing Tension Between Germany and the Soviet Union

In mid-November 1940, Hitler and German Foreign Minister Joachim von Ribbentrop met with Soviet Foreign Minister Vyacheslav Molotov to discuss possible inclusion of Russia as the fourth member of the Axis and to explore the overlapping spheres of the interest of Russia, Germany, Italy, and Japan.[357] Molotov demanded specifics, but Hitler remained vague. Whenever the conversation turned to Finland and Romania, the discussion became heated.[358] Back in September the German Ambassador to the USSR, Friedrich-Werner Graf von der Schulenburg, had casually informed Molotov that German reinforcements for northern Norway would be sent by way of Finland.[359] Molotov asked about Germany's agreement with Finland.[360] Much of what he knew, including reports of German troops having landed at three different Finnish ports, had come to him through the press rather than through Berlin.[361] On October 2, Berlin wired Molotov what purported to be the text of its agreement with Finland.[362] A few days later, Molotov was informed that Germany was also sending a military mission to Romania.[363] Molotov demanded to know how many troops were being sent to Romania. His inquiry led to a long letter from Ribbentrop to Stalin filled with nonsense, lies, and subterfuge. Among other things, it explained that Germany's moves in Finland and Romania should really be looked upon as a boon to Russia.[364]

Mutual distrust hung in the air during the Ribbentrop-Molotov meetings. Molotov was disinclined to talk about carving up the British Empire, which was a key discussion topic,[365] and handing out pieces in distant places. He wanted to discuss lands closer to Europe, such as Turkey, Bulgaria, and Romania.[366] He also said bluntly that the Soviet Union believed a German guarantee of Romania's sovereignty was against the interests of Soviet Russia.[367] As for "territorial ambitions," Hitler encouraged Russia to look south, in the direction of the Indian Ocean, while Germany planned to preserve its access to Finland's resources and remove Soviet influence from the Balkans.[368]

The meeting was interrupted by an air raid. Ribbentrop and Molotov headed to a small, sumptuously furnished bomb shelter and continued their discussions. Molotov said the Germans were assuming that the war against England had already been won to which Ribbentrop reiterated that, yes, Britain was finished. Molotov replied drolly, "If that is so, why are we in this bomb shelter and whose are these bombs which fall?"[369]*

On November 26, 1940, Molotov told the German Ambassador to Moscow that Russia was prepared to join the Axis, with several conditions, the most significant of which were:

- the withdrawal of German troops from Finland, which would be in the Soviet's sphere of influence;

- the establishment of Russian land and naval bases in Bulgaria within range of the Bosporus and the Dardanelles; and

- an agreement that if Turkey objected to Russia's controlling its straits, then the four Axis members would jointly take military action against it.[370]

Hitler, recognizing that in Stalin he had met his match, decided he'd had enough. "Russia must be smashed as soon as possible."[371] On December 18, 1940, Hitler issued Directive No. 21, which ordered the German Army to

---

*This story was told to Churchill by Stalin in August 1942, but only after Stalin asked Winston if he had gotten wind of Molotov's meeting with Ribbentrop and sent bombers specifically to disrupt it. When Churchill nodded, Uncle Joe told the tale. Churchill, Their Finest Hour pp. 517–18.

be prepared to attack Russia *"even before the conclusion of the war against England."*[372] [emphasis added]

Germany Delays the Invasion of Russia to Deal with Greece and Yugoslavia

Hitler called a meeting for January 19–22, 1941 to talk with Mussolini about Italy's poor performance both in Greece and in Egypt. At the meeting Hitler said he would like to be helpful to the Italians. At the time, however, his principal thoughts were on attacking the Soviets.[373] But before Operation Barbarossa could get under way, Hitler had some tidying up to do on his southern flank in the Balkans. On January 31, Hitler issued a directive stating that in April the Wehrmacht would join the Italian Army in attacking Greece through Bulgaria.[374] Not only did Hitler fear that British troops in

Africa would soon be sent to Greece, but, more specifically, he worried that if a British base were established in Greece, the RAF could more easily bomb Romanian oil fields than it could from Crete.[375]

By late February 1941, in advance of an invasion of Russia, Germany had some six hundred and eighty thousand troops in Romania.[376] On February 28, rather than have those units turn north and east and march into the Soviet Union, they moved south across the Danube into Bulgaria, which on March 1 joined Germany, Italy, and Japan in the Tripartite Pact.[377] Hitler's short-term goal also included bringing Yugoslavia and Greece within Germany's orbit.[378] But the Yugoslavs were not as accommodating as the Bulgarians. As a result, on March 4, Yugoslav Regent Prince Paul was called to a meeting with Hitler, who not only made his usual threats but offered a bribe to the Prince: the Greek port city of Salonika (Thessaloniki).[379]

On March 7, 1941, with the war in North Africa against the Italians going well, the British War Cabinet, over objections by the Chiefs of Staff,[380] agreed to send sixty thousand troops to northern Greece to shore up the Balkans.[381] A majority of the troops would come from Australia and New Zealand; the rest would be diverted from North Africa.[382]

Before March had ended, Prince Paul of Yugoslavia signed the Tripartite Pact and agreed that his country would become a virtual puppet state.[383] The next day Prince Paul was deposed in a coup "partially engineered" by Britain.[384] Paul's nephew, Prince Peter, the seventeen-year-old heir to the throne, was named King.[385]

In a rage and believing that the Yugoslavian coup would interfere with his plans both for the invasion of Greece and Operation Barbarossa, Hitler issued Directive No. 25.[386] It called for the immediate invasion of Yugoslavia by Germany, Hungary, and Bulgaria; the total destruction of the Yugoslavian capital Belgrade; and, "if possible," the simultaneous invasion of Greece.[387]

Hitler also told the German High Command that "the beginning of the Barbarossa operation, will have to be postponed up to 4 weeks [i.e., to approximately June 12]."[388] He would later lay the blame for this delay on Mussolini.[389]

Hitler invaded Yugoslavia and Greece on April 6, 1941.[390] As promised in Directive No. 25, Belgrade was destroyed.[391] Yugoslav resistance to the Nazis ended on April 18.[392] Meanwhile, in Greece, the British and the Greeks could not stave off attacks by the German panzers, which were well supported by the Luftwaffe.[393] "The RAF ... were outmatched in numbers."[394] On April 17 the British decided to evacuate Greece.[395] One week later the Greeks capitulated.[396] The British made another Dunkirk-like exit.[397] In late May, the Germans launched an airborne assault against Crete and successfully took the island from the British.[398]

Another Attempt at Peace with Britain? Rudolph Hess's Mission

In the early evening of May 10, 1941, Rudolph Hess, the Deputy Fuhrer of Nazi Germany, got in a small Messerschmidt fighter-bomber and flew west. He was trying to reach Scotland, where he hoped to arrange peace talks with the Duke of Hamilton. Hess had met the Duke at the 1936 Olympic games[399] and erroneously believed him to be a prominent opponent of Churchill's war policy. Hess displayed considerable navigational skill. On a dark, foggy night, flying over largely unfamiliar terrain using only charts and maps while trying to evade British air defense, he made it to within twelve miles of his planned destination. There he ran out of gas and was forced to bail out.[400]

Some historians say that Hitler knew about Hess's plan, while others claim Hitler was furious when he learned about it. Lukacs writes, "Hitler and Hess were of the same mind. To make peace with Britain"—sooner than later.[401] On May 29, 1941, Hitler told his friend, German diplomat Walther Hewell, that the defeat of Russia "… will force England to make peace. Hope this year."[402] As Lukacs insightfully notes, Hitler believed that time was of the essence, because "Britain was still not strong enough to cause serious trouble in Germany's rear."[403] Putting it in different words, Hitler repeated this sentiment when he said, "Now we have the possibility to smash Russia while all our backs are free. This opportunity will not recur."[404]

Whether he knew what Hess had planned or not, Hitler disavowed Hess's mission and called him delusional.[405] Churchill writes that he too assigned no substance to Hess' mission.[406] Hess would spend the rest of the war in prison in Britain, where he was often visited by British intelligence officers.[407] Over time he showed signs of serious mental illness. When the war ended, he was tried as a war criminal at Nuremberg and sentenced to life imprisonment. He spent the rest of his life, forty-six years, in Spandau Prison in Berlin. In 1987, at the age of ninety-three, he was found hanging from a lamp cord in a garden building.[408]

At the time of Hess's bizarre flight, the likelihood of Hitler attacking the Soviets was becoming obvious. For example, on May 16, Churchill wrote that "it looked as if Hitler is massing against Russia."[409] By mid-June even Mr. "D"—the ersatz Swedish peacemaker Birger Dahlerus—was transmitting messages from Goring to the British embassy in Stockholm saying that Germany would soon attack the Soviet Union.[410]

Germany Invades the Soviet Union

At 3:15 AM on June 22, 1941, the German invasion of Russia commenced, a critical five weeks later than Hitler had planned.* Artillery blasted, and

---

Hitler later said, "If the Italians hadn't attacked Greece and needed our help, the war would have taken a different course. We could have anticipated the Russian

swarms of German planes set out to destroy the Soviet Air Force as it sat on the ground.[411] Three million men in 159 divisions with three thousand tanks poured into Russia. Hitler predicted the war would be over in six weeks.[412] British and American intelligence agreed; their predictions said it would be over in three months at the most.[413] Goebbels felt it might take four.[414] All were grossly optimistic: the German fight against Russia went on for almost four years, until the war in Europe ended in May 1945.

Unsurprisingly, the German invasion "brought about a de facto alliance between Britain and Russia."[415] As Churchill said in a BBC broadcast on the date of the invasion of the Soviet Union:

> ... We are resolved to destroy Hitler and every vestige of the Nazi regime. From this nothing will turn us—nothing. We will never parlay, we will never negotiate with Hitler or any of his gang. ... Any man or State who fights on against Nazidom will have our aid. ...

> It follows, therefore, that we shall give whatever help we can to Russia and to the Russian people.

> [Hitler's] invasion of Russia is no more than a prelude to an attempted invasion of the British Isles. He hopes, no doubt, that all this may be accomplished before the Winter comes and he can overwhelm Great Britain before the fleets and air power of the United States will intervene.[*] He hopes that he may once again repeat upon a greater scale than ever before that process of destroying his enemies one by one, that which he has so long thrived and prospered, and then the scene will be clear for the final act, which without all his conquests would be in vain, namely, the subjugation of the Western Hemisphere to his will and to his system.[416]**

The fight between Germany and the Soviet Union would not be over by winter. In fact, the two countries slugged it out over the next four years, with each side suffering horrendous casualties.

---

cold by weeks and conquered Leningrad and Moscow. There would have been no Stalingrad." Riefenstahl, A Memoir p. 295.

*N.B.: Churchill said these words six months before the Japanese attacked Pearl Harbor.

**Today we know about the unbelievable sacrifices the Soviets made during four years of resisting the Nazi invasion of their homeland and driving the Wehrmacht all the way back to Berlin. None of that could have been foreseen when Churchill embraced Russia as an ally in the war against Hitler. Reynolds, "Churchill the Appeaser?" p. 207.

Churchill on the balcony at Whitehall on V-E Day

Stalin, Roosevelt, and Churchill at Tehran 1943

22

Churchill Thereafter

The US Joins the European War
- With the Soviet Union and the United States as Allies, Churchill Got More Than He Bargained For

The War Goes Poorly
- Churchill Seeks Several Votes of Confidence From the House. Why?
- Churchill Faces An Unsolicited No-Confidence Motion

Tobruk, Libya, June 1942—One of the Low Points in the War
- Talking to Stalin. Had Churchill Learned From His Predecessor's Mistakes in Dealing With a Dictator? Was Churchill Naïve?

The End of the Beginning

After North Africa, What?
- January 1943—The Apex of Churchill's Time as Prime Minister
- The Casablanca Conference
- Sicily
- The First Quebec Conference: Was a Change in the Wind?
- The Invasion of Italy, September 1943
    - Salerno—Churchill offers to personally lead the invasion forces

Tehran Conference—November 1943
- Churchill and Britain Demoted to the Minor Leagues; The Effects on Churchill

The Cross-channel Invasion of Northwest France (Operation Overlord)
- Churchill's Petulance Over D-Day. The Reemergence of Churchill's Impulse to Throw Himself into Combat without Considering the Consequences

Another Churchill Proposal Rejected by Roosevelt; Churchill Makes a Back Room Deal with Stalin about Spheres of Influence

Poland and Russia, Again

Saving Democracy in Greece; Churchill Didn't Do It to Prove Anything to Anyone

599

January–March 1945
- Yalta
- Could Stalin be Trusted?
- Churchill's Visit to the Front. Newfound Feelings for the People of Germany. But What About the Japanese?

April–Late July 1945
- Roosevelt Dies on April 12
- Victory in Europe
- Back to Work
  - *Churchill's fear that the Soviets might subjugate all of Western Europe*

The General Election of 1945
- The Beveridge Report
- The End of the National Coalition
- The Campaign

The Potsdam Conference
- Time Out for the Election Results
- Wrapping up Potsdam

Winston Churchill, Leader of the Opposition July 27, 1945–October 25, 1951
- Churchill after "The Order of the Boot"
- The Iron Curtain Speech/Churchill the Cold Warrior
- Had Churchill Become a Sociopath and the Greatest Warmonger Ever?
- European Unity to Help Counterbalance the Soviet Union's Presence in Europe
- Independence for India / Churchill's Empathy for the Indians
- The Dream
- Life in Britain During Attlee's Government
- The General Election of 1950
- The General Election of 1951

Churchill's Second Tour as Prime Minister: October 26, 1951–April 5, 1955
- The Tired Old Cold Warrior Who Wouldn't Quit

Had Churchill Mellowed on Matters of Race?
- Did Racial or Religious Bias Affect His Actions as Prime Minister?
  - Did Churchill's actions in connection with 1943 famine in India constitute genocide based on race?
  - Did Churchill fail to speak out against the Holocaust?
  - Did Churchill want to "keep England white?"

Churchill's Last Decade: April 6, 1955–January 24, 1965
- The Final Chapter

Not long after the de facto alliance between Britain and the Soviet Union, Stalin commenced doing something that he would do continually for the next few years. He urged, and would later repeatedly demand, that Britain open a second front to take some of the pressure off Russia, which was then engaged in fierce combat with the Nazis. He wanted Britain to make a cross-channel invasion of northwestern France as well as open a front in the Arctic as soon as possible.[1]* Churchill said that he was willing to do "[a]nything sensible." But he begged Stalin "to realise limitations imposed upon us by our resources and geographical position."[2] Churchill added that such an invasion could be a bloody fiasco.[3]

Instead, Britain would supply Russia with military equipment. Indeed, the first of the Arctic convoy to Russia in August 1941 contained thirty-two Hurricane fighters, which Britain could ill afford to send.[4] Military equipment would be shipped to Russia both by Britain and the United States throughout the war.

Early on, German forces achieved significant victories against the Soviets, inflicting, but also sustaining, heavy casualties in the process.** Ultimately, the fortunes of war changed for Germany. At the end of 1941, the German offensive stalled just outside Moscow.[5] The first blizzards of the season had begun, and a subsequent Soviet winter counteroffensive pushed German troops back.[6] At that point, Hitler relieved Field Marshal Walther von Brauchitsch of his position as Commander in Chief of the German Army and assumed the role himself.[7] Because Germany's oil supply had become severely depleted, a large-scale German offensive in 1942 would seek to capture the Baku oil fields in Azerbaijan.[8]

Six weeks after the invasion of the Soviet Union, with the US still officially neutral, Churchill would have the first of nine wartime meetings with President

---

*An early cross-channel invasion was also favored by the American Chief of Staff, General George C. Marshall. Addison, Churchill: The Unexpected Hero p. 199. In April 1942, Roosevelt, who had been in the war for only four months, sent Marshall to London hoping to convince the British that an invasion of Western France (initially named Operation Roundup) should be accomplished either that year or in 1943. Churchill seemed to agree, but he was disabused of this notion by the British Chiefs of Staff led by Gen. Alan Brooke. Ibid. p.192.

Churchill, while still a proponent of a cross-channel operation, came to believe that an unsuccessful invasion of France could lead to defeat in the European war or America's shifting all her energies into fighting the Japanese. Manchester and Reid p. 604.

**Reacting to these successes against Russia, on July 25, 1941, Hitler predicted that "Great Britain will not continue to fight if she sees there is no longer a chance of winning." Hinsley, Hitler's Strategy p. 13. On October 28, 1941, Hitler said that "the fall of Moscow might even force England to make peace at once." Lukacs, June 1941 p. 137.

Roosevelt. At this one, held on warships off the coast of Newfoundland, they discussed their vision for the post-war world. These ideas became known as the Atlantic Charter.[9]* Upon his return to England, Churchill spoke about his meeting with Roosevelt in a broadcast on August 24, 1941, in which he also described the fighting going on in Eastern Europe. Not only was the fighting there fierce, but as the Wehrmacht advanced eastward, troops known as the Einsatzgruppen would move into towns that fell to the Nazis and execute the Jewish inhabitants.[10]

The US Joins the European War

With the Soviet Union and the United States as Allies, Churchill Got More Than He Bargained For

On Sunday, December 7, 1941, the Japanese launched a sneak attack on the US Naval base at Pearl Harbor, Hawaii, sinking or seriously damaging twenty ships and killing twenty-four hundred. The US declared war on Japan the next day. Churchill now worried that America would fight against the Japanese but not assist Britain and Russia in the ongoing war in Europe.[11] Hitler relieved the Prime Minister's concern on December 11, when he declared war on the United States—as he had promised the Japanese he would do.[12]

Hitler had been advised that under its agreement with Japan and Italy, Germany did not have to declare war on America.[13] Moreover, he declared war on the US even though he had urged Japan not to attack America but to go after the British and the Russians.[14] But he could no longer control his pent up anger over Roosevelt's verbal attacks against him, and the US's supplying war materiel to Britain.[15] In his blind rage, Hitler made a fateful mistake: ignoring America's great industrial strength and the relative ease with which she could turn that into military strength against Germany. Had Germany remained neutral in America's war with Japan, from a political perspective "it would have been very difficult for Roosevelt to [have] join[ed] the European war."[16]

The Atlantic Charter was a key first step toward the establishment of the United Nations.

Among the principles annunciated in the document: the United States and Britain agreed not to seek territorial gains from the war; they opposed any territorial changes made against the wishes of the people concerned; they agreed to support the restoration of self-government to any nation that had lost it during the war; they reiterated the belief that people should have the right to choose their own form of government; they also called for international cooperation to secure improved living and working conditions, freedom of the seas, and for all countries to disavow the use of force.

Much to Churchill's relief, among other things, Roosevelt understood and agreed that defeating Hitler was the top priority. Defeating the Japanese would have to wait.[17] The US had no illusion that the war would be won quickly. Roosevelt did not see victory before 1943—and if things did not go perfectly, not until 1944 or 1945.[18]

After years of trying, now Churchill had what he wanted—US involvement in the war against Hitler as well as an alliance with the Soviet Union, which at that point was actively engaged in staving off a Nazi invasion. But as the old saying goes, be careful what you wish for. Churchill was about to be tossed into a whirlpool of war politics among the Allies the likes of which he'd never experienced. He would spend much of the next three and a half years arguing with, cajoling, and submitting to his allies.* This would prove difficult and sap his strength. He said, "There is only one thing worse than fighting with allies,"—"fighting without them."[19]

His first of many such fights came when he resisted the idea (supported by Stalin) of US Chief of Staff George C. Marshal for a prompt cross-channel invasion of France. Churchill and his Chief of Staff, Alan Brooke, would, in fact, resist any attempt to invade western France until they believed British and US forces were ready to undertake such an operation—one that was critical to winning the war in Europe.

There were also times when Churchill showed his eccentricities, impatience, and obstinance while having to adapt to playing a subservient role as the power of the US and the Soviet Union increased and Britain's declined. Throughout, Churchill would exhibit his lifelong passion to be where the action was by traveling ceaselessly throughout the war for one-on-one meetings with Roosevelt and, to a lesser extent, Stalin, but also by visits to the front lines and conferences of all leaders. As his power decreased, these long, tiring, and hazardous trips increased as he strove desperately to remain relevant to the war effort and shaping the post-war world.**

---

*He would also, although with great reluctance, often defer to his Chiefs of Staff and Alan Brooke (Chief of the Imperial General Staff starting in 1941) on military matters and to the War Cabinet on political questions. Manchester and Reid p. 684.

As his doctor, Lord Moran, writes—after Pearl Harbor, "a new Winston appeared" in his dealings with Roosevelt; one who was much more willing to listen than he ever had been. Moran, Struggle p. 836.

**In 1943, well before the advent of swift and comfortable jet airliners, the sixty-eight-year-old Churchill traveled 110,000 miles. Addison p. 204. He also suffered a severe bout of pneumonia that sidelined him for a month. Ibid. As the late Paul Addison, formerly Director of the Centre for Second World War Studies at the University of Edinburgh, aptly puts it: "... he was a leader on the brink of exhaustion for the rest of the war." Ibid.

The War Goes Poorly

Churchill Seeks Several Votes of Confidence From the House. Why?

By the time America joined the war effort, Churchill had been Prime Minister for about a year and half. During that time, Britain's war effort amounted to little more than treading water. If that weren't bad enough, in early 1942 things got worse. General Erwin Rommel, whose Afrika Korps was brought in to bolster the hapless Italians in North Africa, started to show success in pushing the British forces back,[20] while the Japanese were also showing success against the British in Burma, Malaysia, and Singapore.[21] Author Geoffrey Wheatcroft describes this time as a period of "miserable defeat."[22] But 1940 and 1941, when England was alone and struggling for existence, was also the period from which most of the iconic memories we have of Churchill come. Almost all of his inspirational speeches were made during this period, as were his efforts to help Britons get through the Battle of Britain and the Blitz. His forte—charismatic leadership—was less suited for the careful war planning that took over after the Americans joined the war effort.[23]

Churchill believed that most Conservatives detested him. Fed up with criticism both from Chamberlainites in the House and the press about running the war, Churchill felt that if someone else could do the job of Prime Minister better than he could, he would yield the office to him. Churchill's Government felt the need for reaffirmation and submitted a motion in the House asking it to approve the Government's action in sending help to Greece back in March and to declare its confidence in the Government's handling of the war.[24] Lloyd George regretted that this discussion of the Government's conduct should take place on a Motion of Confidence, noting that the debates after Norway and Dunkirk were not handled in this way.[25] The Government's motion was approved, 447 to 3.[26] But this only dampened criticism for a while. Thus, in January 1942 Churchill demanded that the next debate over his conduct of the war be three days long, conducted in "the fullest and freest manner" and end in a vote of confidence about his Government.[27] At the end of January 1942, the House of Commons argued Churchill's fate for three full days.

Among other things, during the long session, Churchill's detractors pointed out the many "mistakes" the Government had made in prosecuting the war and criticized Churchill's also serving as Minister of Defence.[28]

Churchill defended his Government, saying:

> In spite of the shameful negligence, gross muddles, blatant incompetence, complacency, and lack of organising power which are daily attributed to us—and from which chidings we

endeavour to profit—we are beginning to see our way through. It looks as if we were in for a very bad time, but provided we all stand together, and *provided we throw in the last spasm of our strength, it also looks, more than it ever did before, as if we were going to win.*[29] [emphasis added]

When the vote was taken on January 29, 1942, Churchill had prevailed by a vote of 464 to 1.[30] Despite the overwhelmingly favorable results, the constant criticism was wearing on Churchill.[31] Churchill's bodyguard, Walter Thompson, saw "an increasing sense of frustration and depression [in the P.M.]. To some of those closest to him he hinted that he was seriously thinking of handing over his responsibilities."[32]

This would not, however, be the last vote of confidence Churchill's Government would seek during the war. On March 28, 1944, the Government suffered its first wartime defeat in the House of Commons, by a vote of 117 to 116. The Government was proposing equal pay for male and female teachers in Britain.[33] For some reason, the Government decided to treat the matter as a vote of confidence, a move which MP Harold Nicholson wrote, "ruffled and annoyed" everyone except Churchill "who really enjoyed it."[34] Perhaps it was because Churchill knew that the Government would prevail, which it did, 425 to 23.[35]

But why had Churchill felt so great a need for the House to publicly show its support that he would request a vote of confidence on at least three occasions in slightly more than a two-year period?

The need for validation and reassurance from time to time is only human. It is normal and healthy. A need for constant reassurance, is, however, often driven by anxiety. In those circumstances, unsurprisingly, reassurance can almost become addictive.

Reassurance-seeking is often examined through the lens of attachment theory—the premise being that a person's earliest bonds with his or her caregivers sets the precedent for how he or she deals with anxious situations. People who need a lot of reassurance have an anxious attachment style that may have been caused by their parents' being unavailable when they were growing up or being inconsistent (supportive one moment and cold and disengaged in the next moment). As we have seen, Churchill's parents fit both categories.

It should also be noted, however, that Churchill's reassurance-seeking largely came to the fore only on matters of great importance: his handling of Britain's participation in the life-and-death struggle that was World War II or after he experienced substantial criticism—much like the criticism he had received years before about Gallipoli. Criticism as hurtful as that he had received from his father when he was growing up. Such criticism would itself likely generate some anxiety in and of itself. As discussed earlier, Churchill was a man of supreme self-assurance, so much so that he would often forge ahead unafraid, often inadequately supported, where his instincts told him to go. Such displays of self-assuredness helped transform the politician Churchill into the revered, iconic "Churchill."

Such being the case, all that his requests for reaffirmation might have indicated is that, while generally self-assured, there may have been a limit to that quality within him. If anxiety exceeded his level of self-assuredness, it likely manifested itself in a need for reassurance, some way to reduce the anxiety, or both. The reassurance Churchill sought in March 1944 involved a matter (parliamentary defeat of a bill providing equal pay for male and female teachers) that would not, on its face, seem to have generated much anxiety, particularly when compared to criticism as to how he was running the war. Thus, the need for reassurance in that instance may have been a manifestation of unrelated anxiety such as over the all-important invasion of France that was set to occur in a little over two months.*

Churchill Faces An Unsolicited No-Confidence Motion

During the spring of 1942 Britain continued to suffer military setback after setback. The Japanese were having success in Burma and Malaysia.[36] In February, Britain suffered a humiliating loss at Singapore where one hundred thousand troops were taken prisoner.[37] Then, to add insult to injury, while Churchill was away in Washington conferring with Roosevelt and other American war strategists, on June 21, 1942, General Rommel and his Afrika Korps retook the "key to the British defenses"—the port city of Tobruk, Libya.[38]** In the process, Rommel captured over fifty thousand British and Dominion troops.[39] Two days later, Rommel's troops were in Egypt. By the end of the month, they were at El Alamein, Egypt (only 65 miles from the Nile) and once re-supplied, would be on their way to capturing the Suez Canal and invading the oil rich lands of the Middle East.[40]

Upon returning from Washington, Churchill faced another no-confidence motion in the House; this one was unsolicited. Once again, the issue was how Churchill was conducting the war. During the debate on July 1 and 2, stinging allegations were made: the main strategy of the war was wrong; the P.M. did not understand the weapons being used by the enemy; Britain

---

*As D-Day approached, Chief of the Imperial Staff Gen. Brooke wrote in his diary of the increasing anxiety he felt, saying that the impending invasion was "eating into [his] heart" and he never wanted to go through anything like this again. Alanbrooke and Danchev, War Diaries p. 551.

**Tobruk and its British defenders had been under siege from February until November 1941, at which time the siege was broken. Still, as noted, the Afrika Korps captured it in June 1942.

had produced the wrong weapons, those weapons were being managed by men untrained in their use; and those men had not studied the use of modern weapons.[41] Secretary of State for War Sir James Grigg was specifically attacked as incompetent.[42]

The assault on Churchill's Government was led by Aneruin Bevan, a Labour MP whose final gibe was directed at Churchill himself. Bevan told the House that "the Prime Minister has great qualities, but obviously picking men is not one of them."[43]*

Churchill labeled Bevan's attack as a "diatribe" containing "bitter animosity" filled with "carefully aimed and calculated hostility."[44] As the P.M. told the House, he doubted that anyone felt the pain of reverses such as at Tobruk any greater than members of the Government, including himself, who were responsible for the conduct of the war.[45] Churchill added that verbal attacks such as Bevan's not only weakened Government Ministers' confidence in themselves but also "undermine[d] him in his own heart."[46] Things like the debate following Tobruk were anything but the affirmation and redemption that Churchill had sought when he assumed the Prime Ministership. But, Roberts writes that Churchill's early traumas in life had made him tough enough to survive these situations.**

---

*Bevans was a great speaker whose insults annoyed Churchill. Addison p. 190.

**Churchill faced yet another unsolicited wartime confidence vote filed by Labour on December 8, 1944. This one stemmed from his having involved Britain in a Communist-led civil war in Greece. He had ordered the commander of five thousand British troops in Athens to use deadly force if necessary to reestablish order there. Manchester and Reid p. 885. This order was viewed as an undue interference in the internal affairs of an ally by both the US and the Labourites in Britain. Ibid. During the debate, Churchill argued that Britain was only defending the right of Greeks to choose the kind of government they wanted. See, HC Deb 08 December 1944 vol 406 cc908-1013. Interestingly, unlike in the debate of July 2, 1942, in his 1944 speech Churchill reflected little annoyance at his Government's having been subjected to a vote of no confidence. At one point he commented that "... personally I have found [today's debate] rather enjoyable, so far." Ibid. cc928.

To what can the difference in Churchill's attitude toward the no confidence proceeding in July 1942 and those in 1944 be attributed? Isn't the answer that in 1942, Churchill did not know if the Allies would win the war, while in late 1944 (especially before the Battle of the Bulge which would not start until December 16, 1944) victory over Germany (with all the vindication of Churchill's actions and persona that would accompany it) seemed assured.

In late 1944 Churchill managed to retain his positive outlook even though his Government only prevailed on the confidence motion by a margin of 270–30. HC Deb 08 December 1944 vol 406 cc 1029. Although substantial, this was much narrower than the vote in 1942.

Tobruk, Libya, June 1942—One of the Low Points in the War

Talking to Stalin. Had Churchill Learned From His Predecessor's Mistakes in Dealing With a Dictator? Was Churchill Naïve?

The defeat at Tobruk in June 1942 represented one of the lowest points in the war.[47] Worse yet, merchant ship losses that month were the worst experienced during the war.[48] When asked about the defeats in North Africa, Churchill said, "The Germans wage war better than we do. Especially tank wars. Also, we lack the 'Russian spirit: die but don't surrender."[49] As noted, a few days after his victory at Tobruk, Rommel reached El Alamein, Egypt,[50]* where he halted his offensive. Due to the Allies' successful efforts to curtail Axis shipping in the Mediterranean, Rommel had run out of supplies;[51] he would be unable to continue until August 31st.[52]

The seriousness of the Allies' situation in North Africa prompted a personal visit from Churchill in early August.[53] He then flew on to Moscow for a face-to-face meeting with Stalin. The Russian leader did not see Operation Torch (the invasion of North Africa by British and American troops), as opening a second front and was still demanding that the British and Americans do so.[54] Churchill told Stalin that opening a second front in Europe wasn't possible any time soon. Of course, part of the reason was that men and materiel had gone to Operation Torch instead of the buildup for the cross-channel invasion.[55] Churchill, his advisors, and Roosevelt firmly believed that, much as in a prize fight, the Allies needed to land a number of hard body blows against Germany (such as in North Africa and elsewhere) before going for a knockout blow to the jaw—the invasion of Western France.** The Afrika Korps had to be defeated in North Africa, the Mediterranean had to be cleared of German and Italian warships, Germany needed to absorb more losses on the Russian front, Italy needed to be defeated, and Germany needed to be subjected to heavy bombing before any cross-channel invasion of France could be undertaken.[56]

Stalin at first appeared to take the news of the delay in opening the second front well.[57] But things were different the next day when Stalin implied that the British were not opening the second front because they feared facing the Germans—that they were cowards. Churchill was infuriated by Stalin's

---

*El Alamein is only 65 miles west of the Nile.

**Both Roosevelt and Churchill favored a second front, not only because of its importance to the war effort, but also because they believed it would give them leverage to postpone the discussion Stalin wanted on post-war boundaries until after the war. However, an important thing boding against opening a second front in 1942 or '43 was that the Americans had yet to prove themselves in battle. Roberts pp. 605, 639, 643, 644.

insinuation but somehow did not lose his temper.[58] In doing so, Churchill showed a self-control that did not exist just a few years earlier.

At one point, much like Chamberlain had done during his 1938 meeting with Hitler at Godesberg, Churchill threatened to fly back to London without an understanding.[59] Churchill's thoroughly calculated ploy worked.[60] He had learned something from the Munich "negotiations" and his "lifetime of preparation" that would allow him to calm down the Soviet dictator.[61] Of course, at the time, the Soviets were desperate for the continued flow of planes, tanks, and trucks from the US and Britain.[62]

When their final session ended, Churchill and Stalin sat down for a long evening of eating, drinking, and swapping stories. After two decades of mutual vilification, the two men had a terrific time.[63] The next day Churchill said that Stalin was a "great man."[64] Upon his return to London, in words reminiscent of Chamberlain's report about Hitler following their pre-Munich meeting in Godesberg, Churchill told the War Cabinet that he and Stalin had "established a personal relationship which will be helpful."[65] He later told the House about Stalin's marvelous sense of humor—something that he said, "is of high importance ... particularly to great men and great nations."[66] Even as late as the Potsdam conference in 1945, Churchill was saying how much he liked Stalin.[67] and Eden wrote that "[Churchill] is again under Stalin's spell."[68] Churchill, it seems, was just as naïve as Chamberlain had been.* Far from feeling that Churchill was a friend, Stalin did not like him,[69] described him as someone who would steal a kopeck out of your pocket,[70] and believed that Churchill hoped to see the Soviets defeated so that Britain could negotiate a sweetheart deal with Germany.[71]

Author Geoffrey Wheatcroft makes the interesting observation that there were significant benefits to the British and Americans from delaying the cross-channel invasion. First, the longer the intense fighting between the Germans and the Russians went on, the more the Wehrmacht would be weakened—thus making a cross-channel invasion of France easier, with likely fewer Anglo-American casualties. Moreover, it would be the Russians

---

*As Self put it with regard Chamberlain's dealing with Hitler, Chamberlain's "tragic misapprehension stemmed directly from [his] faith in the value of the 'personal touch.'..." Self p. 314. "His mistake was ... that of the little boy who played with a wolf under the impression that it was a sheep—a pardonable zoological error, but apt to prove fatal to the player who makes it." Duff Cooper, "Chamberlain: A Candidate Portrait," n.d. [November 1939] MRGN 1/5. Unfortunately, all of the above turned out to be true of Churchill's dealings with Stalin as well. He believed that his one-on-one dinners and meetings with Stalin "would yield results." Manchester and Reid p. 649. Churchill had not learned from his predecessor's great mistake with Hitler.

(not the British or the Americans) who would be weakening the Wehrmacht* and incurring the huge number of casualties it would take to do so. The downside of delaying the invasion was that the longer the delay, the further west Stalin's troops would likely get before meeting up with Allied forces proceeding eastward after the cross-channel invasion. Put differently, the longer the delay, the farther west the Iron Curtain would fall. Of course, if the Red Army wound up doing that much more of the fighting and dying, Stalin would not be completely wrong to claim more of Europe as a reward.

The End of the Beginning

While Stalin and Churchill were meeting in Moscow in August 1942, the British forces in North Africa received reinforcements and more skilled field commanders;** they had been thoroughly resupplied; and they had received new tanks and planes (largely American-made.)[72] In the next battle, Rommel was stopped by the British at Alam el Halfa, Egypt.[73] When the two sides next clashed, in late October 1942, the British retook El Alamein.[74]

Rommel's forces had never been fully resupplied. From bases on the island of Malta, located in the Mediterranean between Italy and Libya, British bombers, surface vessels, and submarines sank many ships trying to bring supplies to the Afrika Korps.[75] Without adequate reserves of men and materiel, the defeat at El Alamein marked the beginning of the end for the Afrika Korps.[76] On November 8, 1942, some one hundred thousand British and American troops under the command of US General Dwight D. Eisenhower landed on beaches in Algeria and Morocco.[77]*** A few days later, British paratroopers landed 100 miles east of Algiers, halfway to Tunis, the capital of Tunisia.[78] The Allied landing was called Operation Torch.

The victory at El Alamein coupled with the successful landings of Operation Torch greatly brightened the military prognosis and Churchill's future.[79] Indeed, on November 10, 1942, he felt free enough to make his famous but cautious assessment of the war—"Now, this is not the end. It is not even the beginning of the end. But it is, perhaps, *the end of the beginning*."[80] [emphasis added]

Before D-Day, the Soviets caused 93 percent of Germany's battle casualties. Reynolds, Churchill the Appeaser? p. 209.

**Generals Bernard Montgomery and Sir Harold Alexander.*

***As noted earlier, the Allied invasion of North Africa caused the Germans to invade Vichy France and attempt to get control of the remnants of French fleet anchored at Toulon. In response, the French scuttled the ships anchored there. Shirer p. 925.*

After North Africa, What?

January 1943—The Apex of Churchill's Time as Prime Minister

Churchill believed that Operation Torch had to be a springboard to one or more places.[81] After Torch, he wanted to proceed with a cross-channel invasion in 1943* *and* in the Mediterranean (both he and General Brooke, liked the idea of invading Sicily and then Italy, but Churchill also wanted to attack Vienna, the Balkans, and the Aegean, most notably, the island of Rhodes).[82]** His brain was "teeming with ideas for seizing the initiative ..."[83] Although he needed little encouragement, Churchill got some from Roosevelt.[84]

But Churchill's idea of attacking everywhere reinforced ideas within the US military that Churchill was fixated on eccentric operations.[85] There was perhaps also a whiff of Gallipoli and Antwerp in the air. Manchester and Reid write that Churchill was exhibiting the "abiding" trait—"impatience ..."[86] His going off in all directions was a quality that earlier in his life had led to poor decisions—like wanting to lead an untrained group of navy men in the defense of Antwerp and rushing out to see the shootout on Sidney Street in London's East End. After everything Churchill had done to overcome his reputation for making poor decisions, would he need redemption for coming up with plans as Prime Minister which some believed bordered on the nonsensical?

More immediately, the Allies plan was to take Tunisia and expel all Axis forces from Africa. General Eisenhower was selected as the Supreme Commander for Operation Torch.[87] But in November 1942, German reinforcements had started to pour into Tunisia.[88] Accordingly, Eisenhower's forcing the Axis out of Tunisia would not be easy. It would depend not only on US resources,[89] but also daring initiative—something which had been shown by the American forces only sparingly.***

---

*This was supported by Stalin and US Chief of Staff George Marshall, but opposed by British Chief of Staff Alan Brooke, who remained opposed to any premature invasion of the continent. Manchester and Reid p. 604.

**US Chief of Naval Operations Adm. Ernest King opposed the Mediterranean approach. On the other hand, Roosevelt initially seemed encouraging. Manchester and Reid p. 603. In fact, key Roosevelt advisor Harry Hopkins very much liked Churchill's idea of a second, third, and if necessary, fourth front. Ibid. p. 604.

***A good portion of Eisenhower's troops had not even moved from where they had landed because of a lingering fear among their leadership that Hitler would unleash a paratroop attack on their rear from Spain. Manchester and Reid p. 597.

Churchill feared that if the effort in Tunisia failed, America would abandon her commitment to winning the war in Europe first and shift all her resources to the war against Japan.

Just after Eisenhower's announcement on Christmas Eve 1942, that winter rains would force a two-month shutdown of the push to take Tunisia, General Alan Brooke, was seriously critical of Eisenhower for immersing himself into politics, as well as for a lack of knowledge on military matters. Brooke believed that Eisenhower lacked the requisite technical and strategic experience.[90] American Chief of Staff General George Marshall later told Churchill that he was surprised, given Eisenhower's lackluster performance, that Britain had not asked for him be relieved of command.[91]*

The Casablanca Conference

At the Anglo-American conference held in Casablanca in January 1943 Roosevelt and Churchill agreed on many things. First, they codified the need to defeat Hitler before defeating Japan. They also agreed on the need to: gain control of the Atlantic;** get as much aid as possible to the Soviet Union; expel all Axis forces from Tunisia, then follow Churchill's Mediterranean strategy—invade Sicily no later than July and afterward invade Italy;*** and continue to build up American forces in Britain preparatory to a cross-channel invasion at some point in the future.[92]**** At the meeting, held only

---

In February 1941 Eisenhower was only a Lieutenant Colonel and had never been an active field commander. But within seventeen months (by July 1942) he had been promoted four ranks—to a three-star general—the rank he held during the invasion of North Africa. He would receive a fourth star in February 1943—the rank he held during the push for Tunisia and the invasions of Sicily, Italy, and Western France. Manchester and Reid p. 540. In late 1944, he was awarded a fifth star, as was General Douglas MacArthur, Commander of US forces in the Pacific.

**In mid-March 1943 Churchill learned that Britain had finally broken the German naval code. Manchester and Reid p. 648. This greatly helped the Allies win the Battle of the Atlantic. Before using this new tool, Atlantic convoys were sailing with little protection and paying a dear price, because escort ships normally assigned to convoy duty were needed for the run-up to the invasion of Sicily. Ibid. p. 649.*

***Churchill never forgot that the Balkans lay just across the Adriatic from Italy's east coast.*

****Churchill believed that Stalin should be advised of what he and Roosevelt had worked out for Italy, Roberts p. 769, and that they were aiming for a cross-channel invasion in August 1943. CAB 120/77. After Casablanca, Churchill tried to keep Stalin apprised of the Western Allies' efforts to build up sufficient forces in Britain to undertake the cross-channel invasion. But given the continuing demands of wrapping up the fighting in North Africa and then invading Sicily and Italy, Churchill would have little to say to Stalin that pleased him. Churchill reiterated that a premature invasion would be a failure. He also reassured Stalin that the British and Americans would maintain their extensive bombing campaign against Germany. Manchester and Reid p. 663.*

This above-referenced plan, over which Roosevelt and Churchill would argue both between themselves and with Stalin, was the general scheme the Allies would follow until the great invasion of France occurred on D-Day, June 6, 1944. It was also a

thirteen months after Pearl Harbor, the Americans, still not fully prepared for war, deferred to Churchill on matters calling for strategic judgment.* They would never do so again.[93] Casablanca was the apex of Churchill's time as Prime Minister.

During the wrap-up session of the Casablanca conference, Roosevelt said the Allies would demand an unconditional surrender from each member of the Axis. That fact had been agreed to at the conference[94] but was to be kept secret. Churchill was indignant at Roosevelt's letting it slip out.[95] But the slip turned out to be beneficial in that it let Stalin know that "the Americans and British were in for the duration"** and expected the same from him.[96]***

Shortly after the Casablanca conference word came that, after more than five months of fighting at a huge cost, the Soviets had achieved a major victory over the Nazis at Stalingrad.**** Churchill was elated at the news.[97] The victory at Stalingrad did not slow down or soften Stalin's demands that the US and Britain open a second front. In a telegram dated March 15, 1943, Stalin added that the delay in opening the second front "arouses grave anxiety in me ..."[98] Stalin also complained that the Soviets were shouldering the entire weight of the war. Both Roosevelt and Churchill knew that what Stalin

---

plan for which there were many views about each step. Churchill often battled with his advisors, Roosevelt (or various of his advisors), or Stalin. As a result, Churchill would spend much of the next few years in meetings with Roosevelt in Washington and elsewhere, meetings with Stalin in Moscow, and at conferences among the Big Three (himself, Roosevelt, and Stalin). The travel and the disagreements among the Allies took a physical and mental toll on the Prime Minister.

*Churchill was pleased to be a central figure at Casablanca and was also satisfied with the agreements reached there. Roberts p. 768.

**Based on Britain's secrecy about Rudolph Hess' May 1941 peace mission, Stalin feared that an Anglo-German peace agreement might be forthcoming. Reynolds, Churchill the Appeaser? p. 212.

***Both the British and the Americans feared that Stalin might at some point make a separate peace deal with Hitler. Reynolds, Churchill the Appeaser? p. 212.

****The battle of Stalingrad started on August 23, 1942, when the Germans attacked the city, which was on the left bank of the Volga River 1,500 miles southeast of Moscow. It was one of the bloodiest battles in the history of warfare; including Russian civilian, there were about two million total casualties. Battle of Stalingrad, Available at: https://www.history.com/topics/world-war-ii/battle-of-stalingrad. The German attack initially succeeded; the Luftwaffe had destroyed most of the city and the German 6th Army was fighting within the city limits. Manchester and Reid pp. 570, 571. The Nazi attack later stalled in the face of Soviet reinforcements brought in from across the Volga. In the final phase of the battle (November 1942–February 1943) a force of one million Soviets killed or captured three hundred thousand Romanian, Hungarian, and Italian troops, Manchester and Reid p. 599, while twenty-four Nazi generals and ninety-one thousand Germans surrendered. Shirer p. 932. In the last two months of the battle 145,000 German soldiers were killed. See, Ibid. p. 932. Stalingrad was the worst defeat ever suffered by Germany in any war. Goerlitz, History of the German General Staff p. 431.

was saying was true; at that moment there was, however, nothing that they could do about it except keep shipping military equipment to the Soviets.[99]

Sicily

In April 1943, Churchill was not at all happy when he learned that Eisenhower, whose bona fides had been questioned, had said that the recent deployment of two German divisions in Sicily might preclude the Allies from invading.[100] Thinking aloud, the Prime Minister asked, "What would Stalin think of this when he has 185 German divisions on his front, I cannot imagine."[101]

The Allies took full control of Tunisia on May 13, 1943. With help from Churchill, Eisenhower overcame any hesitancy he had about invading Sicily.[102] The invasion of Sicily commenced on July 10, 1943.[103] After thirty-eight days, not only was the island taken by the Allies, but, while that operation was being carried out, Mussolini was overthrown.[104] On the Eastern front during this time, the Russians defeated the Germans at the battle of Kursk. From then on, the Nazis would be on the defensive in the East.[*]

The First Quebec Conference: Was a Change in the Wind?

On his way to a meeting with Roosevelt in Quebec in August 1943, Churchill got his first look at the details of the cross-channel invasion, now named Operation Overlord.[105] He liked the plan but recommended that more troops be involved and that the invasion beaches be widened. His suggestions were accepted—five months later.[106] The slowness with which Churchill's ideas were reviewed suggested that there was some sort of change in the wind. Even before of the Quebec conference started, Roosevelt made it clear that despite the implied understanding that the British would command the cross-channel invasion, he wanted an American to do the job.[107] His rationale? Most casualties in the invasion would be American.[108] In a major concession, Churchill agreed, believing that Chief of Staff General George Marshall would be the American selected.[109] Churchill also believed that Eisenhower would replace Marshall as Chief of Staff, that British

---

Kursk, the last German offensive in Russia, took place in July and August 1943 about 300 miles southwest of Moscow. Approximately 700,000 German troops and 2,400 tanks confronted a Soviet force over a million strong with 3,400 tanks. Manchester and Reid p. 693. The Soviets prevailed decisively. The German assault was stopped cold, and the Nazis were forced to retreat. Shirer p. 1006.

Following the victory at Kursk, six million Soviet troops launched counter offensives along a 1,500-mile front. They drove the Germans westward. See, Ibid.

For the next two years the Soviets continually forced the Germans to retreat. The Russians recaptured Warsaw on January 17, 1945, and took control of Berlin on May 2, 1945.

General Harold Alexander, then Deputy Commander of Allied forces in the Mediterranean would replace Eisenhower as the Supreme Commander of all Allied Forces in the Mediterranean, and that the King's cousin, Louis "Dickie" Mountbatten, would be named as the Supreme Allied Commander of the South East Asia Command.[110]

As Churchill saw it, allowing an American to be in charge of Operation Overlord would not only mollify Roosevelt, it would get his man into the top job in the Mediterranean and reopen the door for his dormant Mediterranean schemes.[111]* What Churchill didn't foresee was that (1) General Marshall would not be the man Roosevelt would choose for the job of overseeing the invasion, and (2) that the actual choice, General Eisenhower, would evolve into the Supreme Allied Commander for all forces in Europe for the rest of the war.[112]** A Briton would not lead the charge to victory.

The Invasion of Italy, September 1943

With Sicily conquered, the next move was to invade Italy, which lay just across the two-mile-wide Straits of Messina. This took place on September 3, 1943, when a small Allied force landed at Calabria on the toe of southern Italy. The landing was quickly followed by Italy's surrender on September 8, 1943.[113] While the surrender meant that the Italians would switch teams and now fight on the side of the Allies, given the movement of German troops from the Eastern front to Italy,[114] much fighting would occur before Italy was conquered.[115] Bottom line: there would be no cross-channel invasion in 1943 and the "three Big Boys" as they were called, needed to confer.[116]

Salerno—Churchill offers to personally lead the invasion forces

The Allies' main invasion force, largely made up of the American 5th Army, landed at Salerno (on the west coast of Italy just south of Naples) on September 9, 1943.[117] The plan was to move north, capture Naples and its extensive port facilities, then move on to Rome (170 miles north). To ensure the element of surprise, the landing at Salerno was not preceded by naval or aerial bombardment.[118] However, surprise was not achieved, and the landing

---

*By agreeing to have an American in charge of Operation Overlord, Churchill broke a promise to General Brooke that he could lead the operation. Addison p. 201. Churchill expressed no regret to Brooke at what had happened. Alanbrooke and Danchev, War Diaries p. 442. Backing out of a promise like this was not something that Churchill often did. But had Churchill fought for Brooke, he almost certainly would have lost the fight.

**Within a few weeks of his selection as Supreme Commander of Operation Overlord, Eisenhower demanded and received complete control of all Allied air forces. Manchester and Reid p. 781.

force, which was larger than that planned for Operation Overlord,[119] faced heavy resistance and was pinned down on the beach.[120]

Day by day, the Nazis increased their manpower on the beach perimeter and improved their chances of repelling the Allied invasion force.[121] This resulted in two things: British General Alexander, Deputy Commander of Allied forces in the Mediterranean, went to Salerno, and Churchill, reminiscent of his actions in 1914 at Antwerp, proposed to fly to Salerno and personally take charge of the operation. Not only was Churchill's idea insane on its face, but it suggested that, even though he had become one of the most important men in the world, he would or could not control the impulse to throw himself into combat with no thought of the consequences.

By September 19, 1943, the 5th Army finally secured the beachhead at Salerno and started its slow advance north toward Naples.[122] By early October, the British 8th Army had moved up the Adriatic Coast to Bari at the ankle of the Italian peninsula.[123] With the Balkans lying just across the Adriatic, Churchill still wished to capture the island of Rhodes, which was southwest of Athens off the Turkish Coast, and in doing so secure the Balkans' right flank. General Brooke, Chief of the Imperial Staff, thought the P.M.'s plan to invade Rhodes at that point was madness and that Churchill was "most unbalanced." He added, "God knows how we shall finish this war if it goes on."[124] Based on Eisenhower's advice, Roosevelt rejected Churchill's proposal to invade Rhodes. Churchill was bitter at Eisenhower's action.[125] Although it did not affect their personal relationship,* Churchill, told Eisenhower he planned to put Rhodes on the agenda at the upcoming conference of the "Big 3" in Tehran.[126]

Tehran Conference—November 1943

Churchill and Britain Demoted to the Minor Leagues; The Effects on Churchill

In late November 1943, Roosevelt, Stalin, and Churchill met in Tehran.** Stalin only wanted to discuss two things—the second front and Russia's post-war western boundary.[127] Prior to the meeting, Roosevelt refused to meet with Churchill to prepare for the conference and advised the Prime Minister that he planned to deal with Stalin independently.[128]*** Roosevelt,

---

The war had not diminished Churchill's uncanny ability in most instances to compartmentalize and not let a policy or political disagreement with a colleague affect his feelings about the person.

**Tehran would be the first of three conferences held by the leaders of the Allies about the war and its aftermath.*

***For some time, Roosevelt had felt he could make substantial progress with Stalin in a one-on-one meeting. Manchester and Reid p. 657. This notion of personal*

for alleged security reasons, even moved the American delegation into the Russian embassy.[129] Then, without even discussing the subject with Churchill, Roosevelt announced that after the war Russia should be given some of Britain and America's merchant marine fleets.[130] Worse still, Roosevelt and Stalin rejected the bulk of Churchill's Mediterranean schemes to attack the Balkans and Rhodes.[131]* Churchill realized he and Britain had been demoted to minor league status.[132] He and his country had been marginalized.[133]**

In response to Stalin's dismay that no commander had yet been chosen for Operation Overlord, at a stop in Cairo on the way back home from Tehran, Roosevelt chose General Eisenhower for the job;[134] Roosevelt couldn't let George Marshall leave Washington.[135]***

Churchill's personal doctor, Lord Moran, wrote that Churchill sees "he cannot rely on the President's support ... [Stalin] will be able to do as he pleases"**** and that "The P.M. is appalled by his own impotence."[136]

"Nevertheless Churchill managed to contain his frustration and stuck to the principle that no dispute with the United States must ever be pushed to the point where it would imperil the alliance ..."[137]***** The late historian Paul Addison calls this an example of "one of [Churchill's] greatest strength as a war leader" ... "his ability to focus on the main priorities to the exclusion of all else."[138]

As Churchill's bodyguard, Walter Thompson, reveals, the P.M. left Tehran tired both physically and mentally.[139] At a stopover in Tunis he would have

---

diplomacy seems to infect many men in power. As discussed earlier in this book, Neville Chamberlain felt the same way about Hitler. So too, Churchill believed that all would be well with the world "if only I could dine with Stalin once a week ... We get on like a house on fire." Gilbert, Road to Victory p. 664.

*The Americans questioned Churchill's motives. They felt he might be trying to redress mistakes he made in WWI. Manchester and Reid p. 728. Stalin was intent on keeping the British and the Americans out of countries on which he had set his sights—such as the countries in the Balkans and much of Eastern Europe. Ibid. p. 757.

**Years later Churchill would claim that Britain had a substantial say until July 1944, after which America took command. Moran, Struggle p. 614.

***While Eisenhower got command of Operation Overlord in late 1943, in January 1944, several British generals were also appointed to a high-ranking positions. General Arthur Tedder was appointed Deputy Supreme Allied Commander for Operation Overlord; General Harold Alexander, who Churchill believed would take over the Mediterranean command, was named overall commander in Italy, while General Henry "Jumbo" Wilson became the Supreme Allied Commander in the Mediterranean. Roberts p. 809.

****Churchill even suggested that Stalin could be as big a menace to the free world as Hitler had been. Moran, Struggle p. 151.

*****While Roosevelt and Churchill would have their differences about the conduct of the war, Churchill always believed that Roosevelt was a great man. Moran, Struggle p. 837.

another severe bout of pneumonia.[140] This caused him tell Thompson what a good place Tunis, with its ruins of Carthage, would be to die.[141]

When he returned to England and spoke before the House at the end of March 1944 about the forthcoming invasion of France, his speech was described as that of "an old man."[142] Likewise, the strain on Churchill showed also as he became quite confused during a subsequent Prime Minister's Questions session in the House.[143] On some days, his advisors seriously questioned his "balance of mind"[144] and whether he could still make decisions.[145] For example, in his diary, General Brooke writes that during a Chiefs of Staff meeting in March 1944, Churchill claimed he had found a new island off the coast of Sumatra and proposed that a fleet of Royal Navy ships be sent to capture it.[146] General Brooke began to think Churchill was in "Wonderland"[147] and didn't believe the P.M. would make it until the end of the war.[148] This anecdotal information aside, Manchester and Reid caution that during the period many diarists also reported that Churchill was in "top form" as frequently as they noted fatigue or lapses in his performance.[149]

As a likely result of Churchill's having been minimalized, in the winter of 1944, he and the Chiefs of Staff began planning Britain's role against Japan once the war in Europe was over—even though the US was not anxious for the British to participate. The Americans were coming to the view that they could defeat the Japanese without Britain's assistance.[150]

The Cross-channel Invasion of Northwest France (Operation Overlord)

Early in 1944, Eisenhower and his advisors recognized that the invasion scheduled for May had to be postponed. The Allies needed more time to assemble the invasion force and destroy both the Luftwaffe and rail lines in northwestern France.[151] Because the invasion had to be accomplished just after dawn on an incoming tide with a nearly full moon, the next window was in the first week of June.[152] In the months before the invasion, the Allied armies practiced landings on British beaches while the Allied air forces worked to perfect the air strategy for D-Day which was to disable every road, bridge, rail line, and tunnel in Normandy to make Germany's reinforcement of its coastal defenses as difficult as possible.[153]

Churchill's Petulance Over D-Day. The Reemergence of Churchill's Impulse to Throw Himself into Combat without Considering the Consequences

Despite the postponement until June, Churchill was pleased that the cross-channel invasion was about to happen. Although he never said a word about it to his Chief of Staff, General Brooke, he even planned to be on a warship off the coast of Normandy to witness the invasion.[154] King George was thinking of joining him.[155] Eisenhower and the Commander of Naval Operations for the invasion, British Admiral Bertram Ramsay, were among the many who adamantly opposed both Churchill and the King being spectators.[156] While King George agreed not to go, Churchill stood firm and said that he definitely would be present.[157] The King thought that the P.M. was acting selfishly by resisting the advice of his military leaders. Once again, Churchill had to be where the action was—at the scene of combat—no matter what the risk or the consequences. Indeed, in response to a written appeal from the King, a petulant Churchill made it clear that he relied on his own judgment to determine the extent of risk that he, as Prime Minister, could run and did not want to have his freedom of movement impinged. In the end, he said he would defer to the King's wishes and commands.[158]

In many ways, this and incidents like it* show that Churchill, then in his late sixties, was, at his core, no different from the young war correspondent he had been during the Boer War when he couldn't wait to board the armored reconnaissance train everyone knew was heading out on a very dangerous mission. In fact, as King George properly concluded, in 1944, Churchill was a worse version of himself. Back in 1899, when Churchill boarded the train likely to be attacked, there was no one relying on him for anything. That was not the case in 1944. By then he had become the irreplaceable leader of Britain and millions of people for whom he had become a surrogate parent needed him to get them through the war.

When an alcoholic is presented with easy access to the liquor cabinet, as the draw of the liquor takes control, thoughts about the consequences of his imbibing, both to himself and his family, get fogged over—they slip to a remote corner of his mind. A similar pattern can be seen in persons having a problem with drugs, gambling, kleptomania, smoking, or other addictions. So too, to Churchill, the chance to be in or near combat was something, the alure of which, was so powerful as to easily overwhelm any thoughts he might have about the potential consequences of his actions on others—in this case the people of Britain and the entire free world, not to mention is own family. When that red cape of combat was figuratively waived in front of him, all he could see was the short-term gratification that being involved would bring him—and he charged ahead.

_____

*As noted, Churchill's offer to personally command the Allied invasion forces in Salerno, Italy, and, as will be discussed, his actual visits to Normandy and the Rhine are other examples in which he did not keep this impulse under control. N.B., on his way to meet with the French leadership just before France fell, Churchill had also wanted to fly over active battlefields.

As a small boy in Ireland, his parents turned their backs on him and constantly indulged themselves in a risky activity they greatly enjoyed—hunting daily on their large horses. They did not give a wit about the impact on Winston, their only child at the time, if they were killed or maimed. Now, sixty-five years later, Churchill wanted to engage in something risky that would also please him greatly. To meet his own needs,* he was willing to cast aside the role that he had so successfully created—the rock on which Britons could depend without question—and indulge himself.

Such a rock (which is what a parent is supposed to be) is on duty 24 hours a day, 365 days a year and is never allowed to ignore his/her fiduciary-like duty to refrain from any activity that has a likelihood of significantly impairing their ability to protect those in their care. Churchill knew this intellectually. And while much better at parenting than his selfishly neglectful parents, when it came to being in or near combat and running the risk of death, he still could not fully control the impulse to indulge himself, even though he knew he was risking his ability to continue as the surrogate father of the nation and perform his duties as Britain's "Woomy." At least he could not control that impulse without being commanded to do so by the King. (That he could control it when ordered shows that the lure of combat, while strong, was not an irresistible impulse. Churchill could resist it when he really wanted to or was forced to.)

While he did not ultimately go and see the D-Day invasion up close and in person, he did visit the landing site and the front in Normandy six days later. Even this action, which was far less dangerous than standing at the rail of a warship actively involved in the D-Day landing, was something for which he was criticized as self-indulgent.[159] Unfortunately, as we have already seen and will see again, that was not the only time during the war when Churchill would indulge himself in a similar way. This was not just Winston being Winston; it now was Winston putting his psychological needs well above his duty to his country.

Another Churchill Proposal Rejected by Roosevelt; Churchill Makes a Back Room Deal with Stalin about Spheres of Influence

The landing in Normandy on June 6, 1944, was a stunning success and the first of many blows by the Western Allies going for the knockout of Nazi Germany. It would come four years and two days after the last solder had

---

As Manchester suggests, Churchill's need may have been an unconscious one for attention. Manchester, Visions p. 346. Needs like this can be caused by an insecurity arising from bad life experiences such as poor parenting.

been successfully evacuated from Dunkirk. While the Normandy invasion was a costly operation (nine thousand casualties, including three thousand dead) the toll was at the low end of what was expected.[160] A string of military successes ensued over the next seven weeks.

Another Anglo-American strategy session was held in Québec in September 1944. Churchill continued to show concern about the westward advances of the Soviets and proposed stationing Allied troops at Istria (a peninsula jutting into the Adriatic south of Trieste, Italy) as a staging area for the Balkans. The Americans rejected Churchill's idea. As a result, Russia moved into the Balkans and they fell under communist domination for the next half century.[161] Not dissuaded by yet another American dismissal of one of his ideas, Churchill decided to take matters into his own hands when the next issue came up. In early October 1944 he flew to Moscow and met with Stalin at the Kremlin. When their first session neared its end, he handed Stalin a sheet of paper on which he had handwritten the degree of influence he believed Russia and the Western Allies should have in the postwar in each listed country. The so-called "Percentages Agreement" read:

> Romania: Russia 90%; the others 10%
>
> Greece: Great Britain in accord with the USA. 90%
>
> ~~The Others~~ Russia 10%
>
> Yugoslavia: 50/50%
>
> Hungary: 50/50%
>
> Bulgaria: Russia 75%; the others 25%[162]

After analyzing it, Stalin approved the document.[163] Knowing how it reeked of an earlier era when empires set up spheres of influence in foreign counties, Churchill proposed to burn the sheet and did not mention it when he wrote to Roosevelt about the meeting with Stalin.[164]*

Poland and Russia, Again

The Percentages Agreement did not refer to Poland, but Poland and its borders were and would remain a significant issue for some time to come.

There was little chance of a 50–50 influence sharing in Hungary, Yugoslavia, Romania, or Bulgaria (the latter two were already occupied by the Soviets). Greece was also likely to soon face a communist insurrection. Such being the case, it did not appear to be much of a deal for the West. Still, as Churchill knew, the Americans had no interest in Greece, and this was the last chance to keep her from slipping to the communists, something that was important for him to prevent. Addison p. 207. Stalin at least would live up to his word and didn't supply or foment an insurrection in Greece. See, Ibid. p. 209.

Churchill believed the eastern border of Poland as proposed by the Soviets—the Curzon line (the border established between Russia and Poland after WWI)—represented as good a deal as possible for the Poles as to where the final border between Poland and Russia would be established.[165] The Prime Minister of the Polish government-in-exile in London, Stanislaw Mikolajczyk, strongly disagreed. Under the Soviet proposal, many cities where most citizens were Polish would remain with Russia.[166] Churchill, in a move reminiscent of Chamberlain's pressuring the Czechs at the time of Munich, "threatened to wash his hands of [the Poles]" if they did not accept the Curzon line border.[167] He then added: "You will start another war in which twenty-five million lives will be lost but you don't care." … "You [Poles] are absolutely incapable of facing facts." He also suggested that all the Poles could do was to hate the Russians.[168]

Churchill also tried to convince Mikolajczyk that the Russians had "changed" but undercut himself, something he rarely did, when he told the Polish Prime Minister that if Poland did not accept the Curzon line as its eastern border, the Soviets would liquidate the Poles.[169]

What does all of this say about Churchill? It seems like a repetition of his pre-war belief that the Poles were incredibly obstinate on any matter involving Russia. Though in 1939, this belief had not prevented him from standing by Poland even though she had prevented the formation of the Grand Alliance, in 1945 he would not let her rejection of what he thought was a reasonable proposal dictate Britain's position on this issue.

Any frustration he may have had over Polish stubbornness also did not affect his belief that the Poles should have a free election to decide the type of government they wanted. Again, his ability to compartmentalize came to the fore—something we have already seen in his relationship with colleagues. His support for a free election in Poland did not flow from any love of the Poles but arose from his inherent democratic instincts and the fact that Stalin had agreed to this at both the Tehran and Yalta conferences. Thus, on this issue, just as he had done in the past, Churchill would not let his frustration with the Poles prevent him from doing what he believed to be the right thing.

Saving Democracy in Greece; Churchill Didn't Do It to Prove Anything to Anyone

In early October 1944, the Nazis evacuated Greece. They were desperately in need of troops to fight the Russians who were moving in on Germany from the East and the British and Americans moving in from the West. On October 18, British forces arrived in Greece to install a provisional government and prepare to restore the monarchy.[170] As discussed earlier, a Communist uprising broke out in Greece on December 3, 1944.[171] Churchill ordered the commander of five thousand British troops in Athens to use deadly force if necessary to reestablish order there.[172]

Despite the efforts of the British Army, the shooting in Athens continued for weeks. With no cease-fire in sight and without consulting the War Cabinet, at one in the morning on Christmas Day, Churchill and Foreign Secretary Eden flew to Athens hoping to talk to all the parties involved.[173] Much as he had done back in 1921 with the representatives from the Irish Republican Army, Churchill communicated well with representatives of the Greek communist guerrillas.[174] The communists even liked him.[175]

Although he left Athens with no agreement, Churchill soon got what he wanted. That is, Stalin adhered to the Percentages Agreement he had made with Churchill a few months earlier and did not fund the Greek communists.* He allowed them to be crushed,[176] and they were forced to surrender on January 11, 1945.[177] As a result, Greece managed to stay a free country.

Unlike previous madcap adventures, Churchill's jaunt to Athens was not just to be where the action was or to grab headlines. This time, he was a man on a mission, even if the mission were unlikely to bring him much glory. He was only one of a few in the world who thought it important to save democracy in Greece.

Not only did Churchill not receive much praise for what he did, he became the subject of a confidence vote and much criticism for supporting the monarchists rather than the Greek communists.[178] Yet unlike so many of his past "achievements," what he did in Greece was something on which he could *and did* look back with unabashed satisfaction. A year later, paraphrasing the prophet Zechariah, he told his wife that "All the cabinets of Central, Eastern, and Southern Europe are in Soviet control, excepting only Athens. This brand I snatched from the burning on Christmas Day."[179] He saved democracy in Greece, and perhaps for the first time in his life didn't do it to prove anything to anyone dead or alive—he did it for himself because it was the right thing to do. Now the question would be, could he add this achievement to his list of accomplishments and no longer need redemption?

January–March of 1945

By January 1945, seven months after D-Day, the Allied forces in Western Europe had survived the Battle of the Bulge** and regained their positions

---

*Stalin also restrained communist groups trying to seize power in France and Italy. Wheatcroft p. 347.

**The Battle of the Bulge (Operation Autumn Mist) was Hitler's last-ditch surprise counter-offensive. It began the night of December 15, 1944. Shirer p 1097. Much like the plan by which they had swept into and through France in 1940, under Autumn Mist, German forces would come through the Ardennes Forest. They were then to break through the Allies' lines in Belgium, split the US 1st and 3rd Armies,

near the Rhine. In the East, the Soviets, after a long fight, had finally taken Warsaw.[180] The end of the war in Europe, which had gone on for five and a half years, was in sight.

Yalta

In early February 1945, Stalin, Churchill, and Roosevelt (whose health was faltering and would be dead within two months)[181] met for eight days in Yalta, located in Russia on the Crimean coast of the Black Sea. Even before the conference, Churchill felt that Roosevelt was again distancing himself. At the conference, among other things, the three leaders discussed the post-war future of Germany and the nations of Eastern Europe. They reached agreement on independence for Poland and holding free elections in Eastern Europe.[182]*

To Churchill, "Poland had indeed been the most urgent reason for the Yalta Conference."[183] Stalin wanted Poland's western border shifted further west. As for Poland's eastern border, Russia was adamant and would accept nothing further east than the border to established between Russia and Poland after WWI—the Curzon line.[184] In exchange, Russian wanted Poland's existing western border to be moved west as far as the Oder and West Neisse rivers and encompass much historically ethnic German territory including East Prussia.[185] Doing so would bring millions of ethnic Germans into a newly defined Poland.[186] Although Churchill pushed for the annexation of less German territory, his efforts went for naught.[187] With Truman's OK and Churchill's perfunctory consent, Stalin got the Polish borders that he wanted.[188] Because Poland's western border was established at the Oder and Neisse rivers, and Stalin wanted no Germans living in the new Poland,[189] over twelve million ethnic Germans were expelled from the country.[190] This represented the largest migration in recent European history.[191]**

It was also agreed that a provisional government headed by Polish communists would be installed and would hold elections as soon as possible.[192]

---

then push all the way from Boulogne Belgium to the port of Antwerp. Ibid. p.1090. Hitler believed doing so would result in a massive defeat for the Allies—one that would seriously affect their ability to supply their troops and thus limit the Allies' ability to advance into Germany from the west. Ibid.

*For Churchill independence and free elections for Poland was very important because Britain had gone to war to assure Polish independence.

**Because of the new western border of Poland and the East-West division of Germany, most of the Germanic population east of the Elbe River (which runs from Czechoslovakia northwest past Dresden all the way to Hamburg), some fourteen million people tried to relocate to areas in the West occupied by the Allies. This included the German populations of East Prussia, Poland, and ironically, the Sudetenland in Czechoslovakia. In the process more than a million people died of starvation. Manchester and Reid p. 934.

Could Stalin be Trusted?

On February 19, 1945, Churchill told the War Cabinet that in a conversation with Stalin, the Russian Premier admitted that over the years, Russia had committed many sins against Poland but it was not the intention of the Soviet Government to repeat them. Churchill believed that Stalin had been sincere when he said that,[193] and he felt the Russians would do what they said they would.[194] As he told the House on February 27: "I feel also that their word is their bond." Churchill recognized that he sounded like Chamberlain did after his pre-Munich meeting with Hitler at Godesberg in 1938—something that led him to comment: "[p]oor Neville Chamberlain believed he could trust Hitler. He was wrong, but I don't think I am wrong about Stalin.[195]* (As noted, Foreign Secretary Eden believed that Churchill was wrong and was under Stalin's spell.) These public professions notwithstanding, when asked by the King if Stalin could be trusted, Churchill's response was a good deal more equivocal.[196]

Still, because the Russians had so strictly observed their part of the bargain over Greece,[197] Churchill was somewhat surprised when he learned that they might not carry out terms of the agreement about holding elections in Poland.[198]** He also noted with trepidation that after the war, the Soviets "would be left in a position of preponderant power and influence throughout the whole of Europe."[199] Churchill was also not unmindful of the fact that in early 1943 Stalin had threatened to continue to march westward and engulf all of Europe if by the time the Soviet Union had restored her prewar boundaries, the British, and Americans were not fighting the Nazis on the continent.[200] In February 1945 Churchill reiterated the fear he felt at Tehran fifteen months earlier: that Russia might turn into an enemy of her

---

Prof. David Reynolds suggests that while "Churchill had his blind spots about ... Stalin ... Chamberlain's vision was clouded about Hitler." Reynolds points out that there is a difference between trusting an ally and trusting an enemy. Reynolds, Churchill the Appeaser? pp. 219–20. Moran writes that even if Churchill had such a blind spot he was also among the first to recognize what Stalin was actually up to, while Franklin Roosevelt never did. Moran, Struggle p. 835.

That said, both Churchill (who, as noted, believed that he had a personal relationship with Stalin) and Roosevelt (who believed he could make progress with the Russian dictator one-on-one) had failed to take away another very fundamental thing from Chamberlain's interactions with Hitler—that diplomacy, at least with dictators, based on personal relationships can easily cloud the assessment of the dictator's motives and veracity. Unlike Churchill's distant, objective, and clear assessment of Hitler in the 1930s, close dealings with Stalin seemed to have gotten in the way of his proper assessment of Stalin's trustworthiness.

**Churchill would later write that "[Poland] was to prove the first of the great causes which led to the breakdown of the [alliance among Britain, the US, and the USSR]." Churchill, Triumph and Tragedy p. 434.*

allies.[201] Much to Churchill's dismay, there was no alliance in Europe able to deal with the danger posed by the Soviets.[202]

By late March 1945, the alleged personal relationships Churchill and Roosevelt had with Stalin notwithstanding, there was scant evidence that the election Stalin promised would be taking place in Poland or that the members of the provisional Polish government had any intentions of relinquishing their positions. Churchill told Roosevelt that therefore, Britain and the US needed to take a firm stance with Stalin on Poland. On March 29, 1945, the President sent a sharply worded telegram to Stalin saying that the continuance of the provisional government in Poland was unacceptable.*

Stalin's reply was non-responsive. It concerned itself with alleged secret negotiations between America's Office of Strategic Services (the OSS was the predecessor of the Central Intelligence Agency).[203] What followed were several denials, including one from Roosevelt on April 4[204] and one from Churchill on April 5[205]—and a scathing reply from Stalin.[206]

In the final communication Churchill would have with Roosevelt, the Prime Minister expressed his astonishment that Stalin would send such an insulting message.[207] Churchill also reiterated something that he had said about the Nazis—that the Russians (like the Nazis) would never feel that the West feared them, or could be bullied into acquiescence.[208]

At the War Cabinet meeting of April 24 Churchill stated that "it was out of the question that the governments of the United Kingdom and the United States should acquiesce in any attempt by the Soviet Government to avoid implementing the decisions reached at Yalta on Poland."[209] On April 26, Churchill sent Stalin a masterly telegram in a final effort to resolve the crisis over Poland.[210] In it, he talked about the agreement at Yalta that representatives of each ally were to have free access to areas controlled by the others and the uncomfortable evolving divide between countries dominated by the Soviets and countries in the British and American camp.[211] Churchill was correct: Poland had effectively become another Soviet republic.[212] Stalin firmly believed that his system should be imposed on any country his army could reach.[213]

---

*At about the same time, in what Churchill called a "sinister episode," he learned that, despite Soviet guarantees of safe conduct, the Russians had arrested fourteen non-communist Polish leaders. Churchill, Triumph and Tragedy p. 434. The fourteen were to be put on trial in the Soviet Union. Ibid. Stalin called the fourteen "diverginists." Manchester and Reid p. 923. Churchill also wanted to take a firm position with Stalin over these arrests, but the US would not join him in this. Eleven of the Poles were convicted and received prison sentences that ranged from four months to ten years. Roberts p. 868.

Churchill's Visit to the Front. Newfound Feelings for the People of Germany. But What About the Japanese?

On March 23, 1945, the British army began its main thrust to cross the Rhine. Much as Churchill had wanted to see the invasion of France, he also had to go to the front to see this.[214] According to the King, Churchill was very restless and was still having a hard time with having been demoted, as it were, by Roosevelt.[215] When Churchill reached the Rhine, the Germans were still actively shooting. Unconcerned, he promptly climbed up on a destroyed bridge to get a better look at the scene.[216] He loved it—he was back in the action.[217]* The next day, he had another exhilarating adventure. He and newly promoted British Field Marshal Bernard Montgomery got into a landing craft and were ferried across the Rhine where he and Montgomery walked quietly for about thirty minutes.[218] Unsurprisingly, Churchill had lost none of his willingness to put himself in harm's way. At seventy, he still had "no sense of personal safety." Moreover, he still could not control the impulse to indulge himself and do whatever he wanted even though millions of Britons now relied on him.

During his visit he also got to see some of the German citizens against whom Britain had waged all-out war for nearly six years. Churchill was "moved and upset" at what he saw of the plight of the German civilian population.[219] Some might have perceived him as being insincere, but an innate part of him had pity for those unfortunate people.[220]** He would

---

*General Brooke added: "I knew that he longed to get into the most exposed position possible. I honestly believe that he would really have liked to be killed on the front at this moment of success." eds. Danchev and Todman, War Diaries p. 678.

**The struggle within him to be either a relentless warrior or a compassionate human had shown itself earlier in his life. Throughout the war, the RAF had been accused of deviating from its stated plans to attack only military and industrial targets and actually bombing civilian areas of Germany. Addison p. 194.

Churchill, although one who often said that the enemy must be made continually to "burn and bleed," e.g., ed. James, Complete Speeches Vol. VII p. 6742, and believed that bombing was essential to an Allied victory, see, Reynolds Churchill the Appeaser? p. 217, still had occasional pangs of conscience. For example, in 1943, after Bomber Command unleashed thousand-plane fire bombings of Cologne and other cities, and had destroyed 75 percent of Hamburg, Churchill asked if the bombing had gone too far. Addison p. 194. At that time, Britain was dropping huge quantities of bombs on Germany though after the first few months of 1943, Nazi bombing attacks on Britain had all but stopped. See, Manchester and Reid pp. 615, 704–05. Churchill would reraise the question at the end of March 1944. Wheatcroft p. 333.

Of course, in the end, Churchill always supported the use of ruthless methods where he believed that "military necessity required them." Addison p. 194. In fact, when in 1943 he learned of some German successes in Russia, he told his military Chiefs that Britain would retaliate by dropping poison gas on German cities. Manchester and Reid p. 647.

also soon come to call on his long-held belief that "Magnanimity in victory made good strategic as well as humanitarian sense ..."[221] On V-E Day, he would tell an assembled crowd that "[Germany now] awaits our justice and our mercy."[222]*

While his feeling of compassion may have legitimately applied to the Germans who had had the fight knocked out of them and soon would be citizens of a defeated country, at that moment he had no similar feelings for the people of Japan. Indeed, early on he had favored firebombing Japanese cities.[223] With a seemingly substantial portion of the war in the Pacific still left to be fought, in July 1945 Churchill would actively support America's use of the atomic bomb against the Japanese.[224]** (N.B.—he also felt that the use of an atomic bomb or any device that could obliterate German cities was justified.[225]) Churchill, like many others, felt that using the bomb would greatly shorten the war and in doing so reduce the number of people killed.[226] He also believed the Japanese should be given a warning that their country stood to be destroyed in a manner never before seen on earth. Truman disagreed; he believed that Japan had forfeited any entitlement it might have to such a warning because of its sneak attack at Pearl Harbor.[227] As a middle ground, the Potsdam Declaration, which would be issued at the end of the conference on July 26, warned Japan to surrender unconditionally or face "prompt and utter destruction."[228]*** There is, however, no record of Churchill's expressing any pity for the unfortunate people of Japan who had experienced extensive fire bombing and the use of two hellish nuclear weapons.**** Churchill's silence could have been because the Japanese were not Caucasian. Of course, unlike the situation with Germany, Britain had never been involved in any military actions against the Japanese homeland. Churchill had never seen, firsthand, the toll that the war had taken on the average Japanese; he knew the Japanese

---

No one doubts that the death and destruction in Germany was horrible and that having some empathy for the war-ravaged average Germans was only human. Wheatcroft writes that, nonetheless, when Allied troops came across extermination camps like Auschwitz, Bergen-Belsen, Dachau, and Treblinka, "they were inclined to think the Germans had received their just desserts." Wheatcroft p. 334.

**Since Britain had participated in the Manhattan project, it had been agreed in 1943 that to use the atomic bomb both Britain and the US had to approve. Manchester and Reid p. 947. Churchill specifically agreed to dropping the bomb on Hiroshima and on Nagasaki. Addison p. 212. On August 1, 1946, a law was enacted that precluded any other country from accessing US nuclear data. Thus, British participation in the project ended. Roberts pp. 896–97.*

***After Hiroshima was bombed on August 6, 1945, Truman more forcefully warned Japan that the US would drop another bomb if she did not surrender immediately. When no surrender was forthcoming, on August 9, 1945, the US dropped a second atomic bomb on Nagasaki.*

****N.B. when the atomic bombs were dropped on Japan, Churchill was no longer Prime Minister.*

had been inhumane to British and American prisoners of war, and, up to the very end of the war, the Japanese leadership and citizenry had demonstrated a willingness to fight to the death to maximize Allied casualties.*

April–Late July 1945

Roosevelt Dies on April 12

Trying to regain some of his physical strength, in early April President Roosevelt traveled to the Little White House in Warm Springs Georgia. There, on the afternoon of April 12, he suffered a massive cerebral hemorrhage. Churchill learned of President Roosevelt's death at midnight London time and immediately sent off telegrams to President Truman and Eleanor Roosevelt. In his cable to Mrs. Roosevelt he said he had lost "a dear and cherished friend."[229]

Although there is some debate on the subject, Churchill wanted to attend Roosevelt's funeral.[230] But, with the war coming to an end necessitating a lot of quick decisions on important matters, King George among others finally persuaded Churchill to send Anthony Eden in his place.[231]** Churchill instead paid tribute to Roosevelt in a speech to the House of Commons on April 17 in which he spoke of the 1,700 messages between him and the President since 1940, and called Roosevelt "the greatest American friend we have ever known and the greatest champion of freedom who has ever brought help and comfort from the new world to the old."[232]

Victory in Europe

Early in the morning of May 7, 1945, just three weeks after Roosevelt's death, German General Alfred Jodl signed an unconditional surrender at the headquarters of the Supreme Commander of Allied Forces, General Dwight Eisenhower.[233] The war in Europe would officially end at midnight May 8.[234] May 8 was declared a holiday.[235] At 3:00 PM, Churchill did a radio broadcast to the nation at the end of which his voice "broke slightly with emotion."[236] He later reprised the speech before the House. When he got there, he received a raucous standing ovation.[237]

His next stop was Buckingham Palace, where, just as Chamberlain had done upon returning from Munich in 1938, Churchill went out on the balcony with the Royal family to accept the adulation of the jubilant crowd that

---

*N.B., as discussed later in this chapter, Churchill would show empathy for the non-white citizens of India during the Muslim–Hindu fighting that followed Indian independence in 1947.

**The decision was made only 45 minutes before Churchill was scheduled to fly to New York. Roberts p. 871.

had gathered.[238] When the crowd noticed Churchill, "there was a deep, full throated, almost revenant roar."[239] Later in the day he addressed another crowd from a balcony at Whitehall. He told them "this is your victory," and they yelled back "*No*, it's yours."[240] What a vindication this day had been for Churchill and the path he had chosen for Britain. It was "the greatest day of his long life."[241]

Back to Work

But Churchill had very little time to savor the well-deserved adulation. Now not only did he have to deal with what the Soviets were doing and planning on the continent and the prospects of mass starvation in post-war Germany,[242] but also an election, and another meeting with Stalin and the new American President, Harry Truman, to be held about the same time.[243] The war had sapped Churchill's strength,[244] and there was great doubt in London that the Prime Minister was up to the tasks in front of him.

At the Cabinet meeting on May 13 Churchill spoke about communications he'd had with President Truman about the need to reaffirm

> the principle that all territorial claims should be left to be determined by the peace settlement and not prejudged by the unilateral establishment of sovereignty through military occupation. He thought it especially important that the Governments of the United Kingdom and the United States take a firm stand on this issue of principle before the Anglo-American forces in Europe had been substantially reduced."[245]

In this regard, he had also suggested to Truman that the US delay the removal of its troops and planes from Europe, at least for few weeks.

Churchill's fear that the Soviets might subjugate all of Western Europe

In a radio broadcast later that same day, Churchill warned Britons of Russian efforts to install totalitarian governments in the countries she had re-taken from the Nazis. He did not, however, tell them of his greater fear: that the Soviet Army would, over time, continue westward and subjugate all of Western Europe and that a war with the Soviets might become necessary.[246] Although both Conservatives and Labourites shared his concerns about Russia, Britons did not have the will to confront the Soviets,[247] and just as the situation had been a decade earlier, in May 1945 Britain was in no shape, financially or militarily, to deter any such threat.[248]

Still, on May 22, "as instructed" by Churchill himself,[249] the Joint Planning Staff presented the P.M. with an ultra-top-secret memorandum,* about "Operation UNTHINKABLE"—a total war against Russia over her failure to give Poland a "square deal."[250] The memo noted that in Central Europe "the Russians enjoy a superiority of approximately three to one" over the Allied forces[251] and concluded that:

a. If our political objective is to be achieved with certainty and with lasting results, *the defeat of Russia will be necessary.*

b. The result of a total war with Russia is not possible to forecast, but one thing certain is that to win it would take us a very long time.[252] [emphasis added]

As noted, there was no country in Europe able to fight any such war. Churchill mused about creating an alliance that included Britain, France, and Germany and arming them with captured German weapons to fight the Soviets.[253]

Unsurprisingly, adjectives used to describe Operation UNTHINKABLE included "fantastic," "impossible," and "barely sane."[254]

The General Election of 1945

The Beveridge Report

Seeds for the election of 1945, were planted as early as the fall of 1942. At that time a government report, named for its author, economist William Beveridge, was issued. The Beveridge Report called for a great expansion of the social safety net that Churchill and Lloyd George had created thirty-five years earlier. Among other things, the report touched on improving social security, unemployment insurance, pensions, maternity care, and reforms in health insurance, housing, and education. It appeared to cover every financial circumstance that a low-income Briton might face from birth until death.[255]

On March 21, 1943, Churchill made his first broadcast about what Britons were likely to face once the war was over. In that program he responded very favorably to the Beveridge Report but did not hide the fact that taxes would have to be higher in order to pay for all the programs outlined in it.[256] Churchill sounded every bit the Tory Democrat that he had been and still was at his core. He was, however, inclined to postpone any vote on implementing any suggested legislation until after the war had been won.[257]

The memo stated that "Owing to the special need for secrecy, the normal staffs Service Ministries have not been consulted [with regard to this memo]."

In March 1943, his mind was still just about as good as it had been when he was a social reformer second to none back in 1908, but physically he was showing signs of his age.[258] In a subsequent broadcast in 1944, Churchill talked about doing away with slums and improving education. But Britons were unimpressed. Unlike most Churchill speeches, it did not rouse the public.[259] Colleagues thought that during the speech the P.M. seemed like a "worn out petulant old man."[260]

The End of the National Coalition

Shortly, Labourites were advising Attlee that the party should leave the National coalition but still swear loyalty to Churchill on matters affecting the war effort. They feared a loss of their political identity unless they were free to oppose the Tories on the domestic issues.[261] While Attlee did not withdraw Labour from the Government at that time, two years later, with victory over Germany only weeks away, Labour advised the Prime Minister that it no longer wished to remain a part of the National Government coalition.[262] There had not been a national election in Britain for ten years, but with the war ending, the moratorium on a national election would be ending, too. Although Churchill would have liked for the National Government to have remained intact until after the defeat of Japan,[263] now there would have to be an election soon after Germany was defeated.

At the further insistence of Labour, the National Government ended on May 22, 1945, with a letter from Churchill to the King.[264] Churchill also advised the King that he wished to form a Conservative-only caretaker government to serve until after the general election, which had been set for July 5th.[265] (It had been agreed that the results of the election would, however, not be announced until three weeks later to allow the votes of soldiers serving overseas to be counted.[266*]) On May 23, King George requested that Churchill form the new government.[267]

In the months before the war ended, the Conservatives had fared poorly in the several by-elections that had been held.[268] This did not bode well for Churchill and the Conservatives. Harold Nicholson, a well-known Labour MP from Leicester, believed that Churchill had become an "electoral liability" for the Tories,[269] even though near war's end his favorability rating exceeded 90 percent and remained in the 80 percent range after V-E Day.[270]

At the end of May, it was tentatively agreed that the meeting of Churchill and Truman with Stalin would take place on July 15 in the German city of Potsdam, located 20 miles southeast of Berlin. While Potsdam had been damaged during the war, it was still functional. Churchill, Triumph and Tragedy p. 578.

The Campaign

As the election drew closer, it became clearer that Britons, who had lived under wartime restrictions for nearly six years, wanted a better life in the form of eliminating poverty through better housing and better social services.[271] Churchill, who had been out of the country constantly during the war, had not personally been managing the war economy.[272]

The wartime controls that had caused all classes to share, thus making British society a bit more just, did not resonate with Churchill. Instead, the Conservatives would campaign on undoing the war restrictions imposed on Britons and beginning a four-year plan for demobilizing and reenergizing the economy.[273] Labour's platform included nationalizing the Bank of England and the railroads, as well as the steel and coal industries;[274] increasing housing; providing national insurance; and allowing Britons to vote out the Chamberlainite appeasers who had been in office for the last ten years.[275] Near the very end of the campaign, Churchill privately directed that legislation be prepared to establish both a national health service and a national insurance plan. Though this seemed surprising, the fact is, that Churchill was at heart still the Tory Democrat extraordinaire who had long been a supporter of these and other social welfare programs proposed by Labour.[276]

Years earlier, Churchill had told Colville that history showed if he led Britain to victory in the war, he would not retain his popularity.[277]* As the election approached, he felt he would lose the vote of the members of the armed services.[278] Even so, Conservative leaders were still optimistic. And despite his trepidations, Churchill persuaded himself that the Conservatives would win a majority.[279]** After all, Churchill had something to prove—he had never been the head of a party during any election, let alone a successful one. During the campaign, he gave many speeches to enthusiastic crowds throughout the UK,[280] but this electioneering came at a high price. As July

---

*Churchill referenced the Duke of Wellington, who lost an election shortly after defeating Napoleon at Waterloo in 1815, and Disraeli, who also lost the general election of 1880 after bringing home peace with honor from the Congress of Berlin in 1878. See, Colville p. 428.

**In a radio broadcast on June 4, 1945, Churchill stated that a Labour government would not allow Britons to express any discontent with its policies—that they would introduce something like a more humane Gestapo to suppress dissent. Addison p. 214; Roberts p. 881. Wheatcroft writes that "Even now it's hard to believe that [Churchill] uttered words so disgraceful and so stupid." Wheatcroft, Churchill's Shadow p. 326. By that statement, Churchill appeared to have shot himself in the foot. Many Conservatives were taken aback, Addison p. 214, although today, historians don't believe the remark had much effect on the election results. Roberts p. 881. Still, it was an extremely poor choice of words, which Labour leaders would remember, Addison p. 215, and it would be added to the many phrases Churchill uttered that would forever be held against him.

5th neared, Churchill admitted that he had never been more tired—other than the time he escaped from prison in 1899 during the Boer War.[281]

Immediately after the election, Churchill went on a week's vacation to the French coast, during which time he was to start preparation for the Potsdam Conference, something he had not done during the election campaign.[282] He would also not do it while on vacation.[283]

The Potsdam Conference

The Conference started on July 17, 1945. Knowing that the election results would be announced on July 26 and there was no guarantee that the Conservatives would prevail and he would remain Prime Minister, Churchill brought the head of the Labour Party, Clement Attlee, to the conference. Churchill particularly wanted to show Stalin that Britain was unified.[284]

Just as the conference was getting underway, Truman and Churchill learned that America's top-secret attempt to detonate an atomic bomb had been successful.[285] Churchill urged Truman to tell Stalin about the new weapon before using it on Japan.[286] During the conference, the President "casually mentioned [to Stalin] that we have a new weapon of unusual destructive force. The Russian Premier showed no special interest."[287]*

While Stalin was moderately stoic, Churchill was ecstatic over the news. Even though it was the US, not Britain, which had the bomb, Churchill believed that in one fell swoop the Soviet Union's huge military advantage in Europe had been dissipated.[288]

Items on Churchill's agenda at Potsdam included Poland, the continuation of America's Lend-Lease program, and the fact that Britain had a food shortage.[289]

Time Out for the Election Results

Churchill and Attlee returned to Britain on July 25. By noon on the 26th, it was clear that Labour would win the election in a landslide. Longtime advisor to the King, Tommy Lascelles, after running into Churchill later that day, noted that the Prime Minister was not in a down mood and simply attributed the Conservatives' defeat to the suffering the British people had experienced for the past half dozen years.[290]** At least for the moment,

---

The Soviets were at the time working to produce their own bomb, and through spying, knew much about the status of the US bomb.

**Roberts attributes Churchill's acceptance of the defeat to the fact that as a student of history, he knew of many examples in which voters had seemed ungrateful, e.g., the situations involving Wellington and Disraeli about which he spoke with Colville, Colville p. 428, as well as situations involving his hero, the Duke of Marlborough, Queen Anne's turning to the Tories, and French Prime Minister Clemenceau not winning the French presidency in 1920. Roberts p. 888.*

Churchill almost seemed to be relieved to have the burdens of office lifted from his shoulders.

Labour won 393 seats. Despite garnering almost 40 percent of the vote, the Conservatives won only 213.[291] While many Tories went down to defeat, Churchill, running from a new district made up of only part of his old one in Epping, was reelected handily.[292]

Churchill personally tendered his resignation to the King that evening. Churchill was quite calm at this sad meeting.[293] At 9:00 PM the BBC broadcast a concession speech that Churchill had written earlier in the day. In it, Churchill regretted not being permitted "to finish the work against Japan." He also expressed "profound gratitude [to the British people] ... for the unflinching, unswerving support which they gave me during my task, and for the many expressions of kindness which they have shown towards their servant."[294]

Wrapping Up Potsdam

On July 27, the new Prime Minister, Clement Attlee, returned to Potsdam for the rest of the conference, which concluded on August 2. No agreement on elections in Poland had been reached, and the Red Army remained firmly in control of Central Europe.[295] Among the things agreed to at Potsdam were the division of Germany and Berlin into four zones, and that German war criminals would be arrested and tried for war crimes.[296]

Winston Churchill, Leader of the Opposition July 27, 1945– October 25, 1951

Churchill after "The Order of the Boot"

After Churchill's defeat, the King felt that Britons had been ungrateful to their wartime leader and offered Churchill an appointment to the prestigious Order of the Garter.* It is reported that Churchill responded, "Why should I accept the Order of the Garter from His Majesty when the people had just given me the order of the boot?"[297]

Despite Churchill's outward seeming acceptance of the will of the people, Roberts reports that the defeat "stung badly."[298] At one point, Churchill admitted that he had been "ready to retire and die gracefully."[299] But over the objection of his wife, Churchill soon decided to remain as party leader and seek redemption through a Conservative victory in the next general election.[300] His decision also ignored the consternation of younger Conservatives

---

*The Order of the Garter is the most senior order of knighthood in the British honors system. This was the third time the honor had been offered to Churchill by the King. Churchill would accept the appointment the fourth time it was offered.

like Anthony Eden who coveted Winston's position as party head, and cries from his doctor to take a long rest.[301] As it turned out, the next decade did not, in fact, appreciably add to Churchill's stature.

When Churchill left 10 Downing Street after the election, he did not leave empty handed. He took with him sixty-eight volumes of war correspondence and other papers.[302] Whether these documents belonged to him or the Crown was far from clear.[303] But Prime Minister Attlee didn't seem to care. He was more than happy for Churchill to use them to write books and not interfere with the new Labour Government's agenda.[304]

In the years after the defeat of 1945, Churchill would indeed spend much of his time writing. During this time he produced *The Second World War*, his widely praised six-volume set of memoirs. Professor David Reynolds writes that Churchill's goals for *The Second World War* were to "search for vindication"[305] and to make money.* He was quite successful in the latter regard, having received the equivalent of $16 million for producing the set.[306] Moreover, several of Churchill's rich friends bought his house, Chartwell, from him for £50,000, then donated the property, along with funds for its upkeep, to the National Trust on the condition that the Churchills could live there for free for the rest of their lives.[307] As a result, Churchill's finances during the period where much better than they ever had been.[308] So much so that in 1949, never one to let the existence of risk stop him, Churchill began buying race horses,[309] ultimately owning thirty-seven.[310]

Neither writing—nor later—horse racing, interfered with Churchill's re-assuming and performing his historical role as principal critic of any British Government of which he was not a part. He constantly accused the Attlee Government of mismanagement. Churchill did not object to Labour's programs nearly as much as he quarreled with the way the Labourites implemented them.[311]** Manchester and Reid report that Churchill enjoyed being the leader of the opposition.[312] However, Churchill's personal physician, Lord Moran, reminds us that Churchill was never happy when he was out of Government and suggests that the former Prime Minister's heart was not in the job of opposition leader—he did not feel he was serving a useful purpose.[313]***

Churchill did not consider the books to be history. Addison p. 227.

Points made in the books are well supported. Thus, they seem to be "a definitive account of the events." But as historian Paul Addison reminds us, they were written by a politician who was "seeking to define his place in history." Ibid. Even at six volumes in length, the books leave out much of why Churchill took certain actions. Ibid.

**In 1949 he also chastised the Attlee Government for failing to recognize the state of Israel, which had been created the year before. Roberts p. 912.*

***According to Dr. Moran, also gone was Churchill's capacity for work and much of his self-confidence. Moran, Struggle p. 839.*

In either event, although he certainly didn't see it this way, losing the 1945 election was a positive thing for Churchill. It would not have been any easier for him to deal with the tremendous problems of post-war Britain than it was for the Atlee Government.[314]

The Iron Curtain Speech/Churchill the Cold Warrior

It would not be long before Churchill would assume another familiar role: telling the western democracies of an existential threat to their existence. He had received an invitation from the President of Westminster College in Fulton, Missouri, to speak on campus. As "the most illustrious man alive,"[315] he received many invitations of this sort. But this one was different. It contained a handwritten postscript written by President Truman inviting Churchill to Washington and to travel to Missouri with him for the speech on the presidential train.[316] The former P.M. gladly accepted. The invitation came at a most propitious time. Churchill was still bitter about by his election loss six months earlier and was a bit rudderless, much as he'd been in the wilderness back in the 1930s.[317]

In Missouri, on March 5, 1946, Churchill gave a memorable speech. In it he said, "I have a strong admiration and regard for the valiant Russian people and for my wartime comrade, Marshal Stalin. ... We welcome Russia to her rightful place among the leading nations of the world."

That said, then he added that "From Stettin in the Baltic to Trieste in the Adriatic, an iron curtain has descended across [Europe]" behind which "in many cases [there is an] increasing measure of control from Moscow." He also pointed out that there were instances in which the American and British armies had, under their agreement with the Soviets, withdrawn westward by 150 miles "to allow our Russian ally to occupy this vast expanse of territory which the Western Democracies had conquered." He then asserted the Soviets were trying to establish pro-communist governments in that area. This, he said, "is certainly not the Liberated Europe we fought to build up. Nor is it one which contains the essentials of permanent peace."*

He argued that "The safety of the world requires a new unity in Europe, from which no nation should be permanently outcast,"** as well as the

---

*Compared with the warnings he had given in the '30s about Hitler's Germany, his statements about the Soviets were quite moderate. Addison p. 222.

**He was a strong believer in the reconciliation of France and Germany, Addison p. 228, and believed that Germany should be rearmed for the looming confrontation with the Soviet Union. See, Manchester and Reid p. 936. (N.B., in Tehran, to show solidarity with Stalin, Churchill had said that Germany should not be rearmed for at least fifty years. And in 1941 he had agreed with Stalin that Germany should be dismembered and made into an agricultural society.) Ibid. p. 758. Churchill also saw Britain allying herself with a reinvigorated France. Ibid. p. 658. On the other hand, American Vice President Henry Wallace believed that Churchill's idea of maintenance and enhancement of "the fraternal association of the English-speaking peoples" and the "continuance of the intimate relationship between our military advisors." Such a united front, he stressed, must then exude strength because "there is nothing [the Soviets] admire so much as strength, and there is nothing for which they have less respect than weakness, especially military weakness." As he pointed out, his message was virtually the same one he had espoused about Germany in the early '30s, when "no one paid attention."[318]

Many disliked Churchill's speech; among them were Eleanor Roosevelt, Congressional Democrats,[319] and Labour MPs.[320] To no one's surprise, Stalin did not like the speech either and immediately called Churchill a warmonger.[321] He also characterized the speech as a call for non-English-speaking countries to acknowledge some sort of Anglo-American superiority.[322] On the other hand, Truman liked what Churchill had to say,[323] but since much of the reaction to the speech was negative,[324] Truman's official response was subdued.[325]

Had Churchill Become a Sociopath and the Greatest Warmonger Ever?

Churchill was an unabashed believer in exploiting America's being the only country to possess the atom bomb.* At a lunch with Canadian Premier Mackenzie King in late 1947 Churchill spoke of the sobering ultimatum that he suggested be given to the Soviets[326]:

> We fought for liberty and are determined to maintain it. We will give you what you want and is reasonable in the matter of boundaries. We will give you ports in the North. We will meet you in regard to conditions generally. What we will not allow you to do is to destroy Western Europe; to extend new regimes further there. If you do not agree to that here and now, within so many days, we will attack Moscow and your other cities and destroy them with atomic bombs from the air.[327]

---

rearming Germany would be double crossing the Soviets and laying the seeds for World War III. Wallace also believed, as Churchill would eventually, that it was imperative for the West and the Soviet Union to come to an overall agreement to avoid the possibility of war. Ibid.

This was made clear on numerous occasions, including in a speech at Zurich University in September 1946. See, ed. James, Complete Speeches Vol VII pp. 7380–82. The Attlee Government believed that European security would be best maintained through the processes of the United Nations. Manchester and Reid p. 964.

While Churchill loved America's monopoly on nuclear weapons, he also pushed the Labour Government to hasten the day when Britain would possess the bomb as well. Ibid. p. 1002. Britain would not explode an atomic weapon until October 1952.

He estimated that the Soviets would not have an atom bomb until 1954. Such being the case, he felt that a final battle between a unified Europe (with the US in a back-up role) and the Soviets should take place before then.[328] Shockingly, Bertrand Russell, famed left-leaning British intellectual, pacifist, and future Nobel laureate, joined Churchill, in urging a war against Russia while the US had the bomb and the Soviets did not.[329]

The Question: had Churchill become a sociopath and the greatest warmonger the world had ever seen—or was he the ultimate pragmatist? How does his logic differ from his and Truman's willingness to use the atomic bomb in Japan because doing so would ultimately result in a net saving of lives?

In the latter regard, there is a significant difference between using a weapon, even one of enormous power, during a war, and threatening its use in peacetime to bully another country into submission, even if that country were one as malevolent as Stalin's Soviet Union. It is also one thing for such a threat to come from the leader of the country that possessed the bomb and quite another for the notion to come from a politician who was no longer in power in a country that did not have nuclear weapons.

Some indication that the idea of bringing the Russians in line by threatening to drop nuclear weapons on them was mostly idle talk, albeit scary, and not a proposal to be seriously considered came at the October 1946 dinner held in New York in memory of former Governor Al Smith. There, Churchill asserted that the Soviet Union's "violently aggressive" stance was not a "prelude to war"[330]—that it was just a posture being pushed by the hardline members of the Russian Politburo.[331]* Churchill's enthusiasm for nuclear extortion diminished even further after August 1949, when the Soviets detonated their own atomic bomb.[332] Thereafter he quickly came to realize that the use of nuclear weapons would be devastating not only for the Soviet Union, but for the United States and Britain as well.[333] He would embrace the doctrine of mutually assured destruction for deterring nuclear war.[334] In time, he would, however, become concerned that the doctrine did not cover madmen like Hitler.[335]

Churchill would spend a good portion of his remaining time in politics seeking to arrange a summit meeting at which major differences between countries having the bomb could be resolved. This quest greatly tempered whatever image remained of him as a war monger.

---

*As to the Politburo, in a note President Truman sent to Churchill on September 24, 1947, discussing Stalin's heartlessness in never showing gratitude for the contributions that America and Britain had made to save Russia, Truman wrote that unlike Hitler, "Joe Stalin has [a heart] but the Polit Bureau won't let him use it." Letter dated September 24, 1947: Harry S. Truman papers.

European Unity to Help Counterbalance the Soviet Union's Presence in Europe

In ensuing years, Churchill continued to press for European unity to counter-balance the Soviet Union's presence in Europe. This included calls for amity between France and West Germany as well as Britain's having close ties with the Germans.[336] He also never relented on the thesis that the only way to deal with the Soviets was from a position of strength. Returning to his pre-1930 anti-communist roots, in early 1949 he even went to far as to say that "[the Soviet Politburo] is quite as wicked but much more formidable than Hitler ..."[337] and that "... the strangling of Bolshevism at its birth would have been an untold blessing to the human race."[338]*

As is often the case, here circumstances arose that destroyed Churchill's plan for a European alliance but replaced it with another that was better. In June 1948, escalating tensions between the West and the Soviets turned into a major crisis. The Soviets blocked all rail and road traffic into the zones of Berlin controlled by the western powers. Within days, West Berliners would be short of food, medicine, and other necessities of life. Choosing not to take military action, the Western powers immediately started the Berlin Airlift, which, during the year it lasted, flew in vast quantities of necessary goods, including coal and oil, to assure the survival of the citizens of West Berlin.

Soviet actions in the months before the blockade had already brought about an alliance of many European countries (Britain, France, Belgium, the Netherlands, and Luxembourg) under the Treaty of Brussels, signed in March 1948.** But this association was toothless without the US. As such, it was easily superseded by the creation of the North Atlantic Treaty Organization (NATO) on April 4, 1949, which not only added the US to the group but also brought in Denmark, Norway, Portugal, Canada, Italy, and Iceland.[339]*** Under the NATO treaty, the signatories agreed that "... an armed attack against one or more of them in Europe or North America shall be considered an attack against them all ..."[340] In addition, after the creation of NATO, Truman followed Churchill's urgings and soon told reporters he would not be unwilling to use the atomic bomb again if that were necessary to protect

---

*Several years later, he would, with reasonable accuracy, also predict when Communism would be defeated. See, Roberts p. 913.

**Not only did Churchill want West Germany to be a part of this alliance, but he wanted it to be rearmed. ed. Reynolds, The Origins of the Cold War in Europe p. 13. N.B., this contradicted what he argued at Tehran, where he said Germany should be dismembered and demilitarized for at least fifty years. Manchester and Reid p. 758. Of course, he said that largely to show unity with Stalin, who was his ally at the time. Ibid.

***This statement was made several months before the Soviets had the atomic bomb.

the security of a democracy anywhere in the world.[341]* Upon hearing this, Churchill was pleased.[342]

Just six weeks after the formation of NATO, the Soviets lifted the blockade of Berlin.[343] Unfortunately, the relaxation of tensions over Germany did not last long. In October 1949, the Communist Party in the sector of Germany occupied by the Soviets announced that it was turning the sector into the German Democratic Republic—a communist puppet state that came to be known as East Germany.[344]

Independence for India/Churchill's Empathy for the Indians

In August 1947, after two hundred years of British rule, majority-Hindu India became independent. At the same time, the Muslim-led country of Pakistan was created by dividing three provinces in northern India along religious lines.[345] As a result, hordes of Hindus and Sikhs left Pakistan for India, while Muslims fled India for Pakistan.[346]**

As discussed earlier, for years Churchill had opposed Indian independence, fearing that under Hindu leadership, without British troops to maintain stability, there would be an immediate resumption of the historical religious warfare between Muslims and Hindus.[347] Despite the partition of India and the creation of Muslim Pakistan, Churchill's prediction came true.[348] Blaming Attlee's Government for the huge loss of life, Churchill said that the slaughter in India "... is a horror, which should raise grief and heart-searching in all concerned."[349] He believed that had the British transferred power to the Indian authorities more gradually than they did, it would have saved 250,000 lives.[350] For reasons unknown, the British had advanced the date of the transfer.[351] The British had wanted to get out, and their successors wanted to take control.[352] The only force able to restore order, the British Indian Army, was not functioning properly, having itself been split along religious lines—with Muslim soldiers going to Pakistan and Hindu soldiers going to India.[353]

The Dream

In 1947, at age seventy-three, Churchill wrote a most interesting work titled *The Dream*,[354] which was supposedly based on a dream he had had. Unlike anything else he ever wrote, *The Dream* was not published upon its completion. Rather, because of its intensely personal subject matter, in his will he bequeathed it to his wife.[355] It was published after his death in 1965.

Despite Churchill's efforts, West Germany would not be allowed to join NATO until 1955. "West Germany joins NATO" History.com. Available at: https://www .history.com/this-day-in-history/west-germany-joins-nato.

**It is estimated that between 10 and 20 million people were displaced.*

The Dream is set in November 1947. Churchill is painting a copy of a portrait of his late father when he is visited by Lord Randolph himself. Randolph is described as in his physical prime but with no memory of anything that occurred after 1894.*

At the outset, Lord Randolph, who is "in the best of tempers" asks Winston a bit about his painting and almost immediately denigrates Winston's talent, saying he is clearly not good enough to earn a living as an artist. Winston says he paints for amusement and is a writer by profession. Randolph goes on to ask Winston a few impersonal questions including: What year it is?, followed by Who is the King?, What institutions and buildings are still in existence?, What party is in power?, What has happened to politicians he knew?, and What is the status of Ireland? He also asks whether there had been a war, and the status of the Church of England. At that point, Winston interjects a glowing complement about a speech Randolph gave on the Church of England in 1884.

They then discuss the relaxation of the formal rules of dress and Winston, unlike his father, reveals that he liked the old, more formal ways. At one point Randolph asks Winston if he still supports the House of Commons. When Winston says, "Yes, you brought me up to that," Randolph instantly and sharply reproaches his son, saying that he would never have talked politics "with a boy like you" and immediately rattles off all of Winston's failings as boy: poor grades, failure to qualify for the infantry, lack of any other prospects. Still, Lord Randolph quickly adds, "But ... you were very young, and I loved you dearly." Randolph then explains that "old people are often impatient with [the] young" and that fathers always believe their sons will inherit all their good points and none of their faults. Remembering Winston's fondness for playing soldier, Randolph adds that he hopes that Winston's military career was successful.

On a personal level, Randolph only asks Winston a few perfunctory questions such as—Is Winston married? Does he have kids? Grandkids? Winston obliges with short answers to each question, but with a modesty he did not possess in real life, never reveals anything of what he had actually accomplished. Randolph responds, "I am so glad." Then quickly says, "[b]ut tell me more about these other wars." Winston tells his father about the horrors of WWII, the Holocaust, the Soviet Union's takeover of Eastern Europe, and the Cold War. Randolph exudes both pride and surprise at Winston's depth of knowledge on these matters. Randolph then wonders aloud why Winston had not gone into politics, adding, "You might even have made a name for yourself."

---

*N.B., Randolph died in January 1895.

Despite the redemption Churchill earned by standing up to Hitler and leading Britain through the horrors of World War II, *The Dream* appears to show that Churchill still wanted and needed more.[356] The few noted sentences from the book are words Winston wanted to hear from his father but never did. While what he had accomplished in life did not remove the void that Lord Randolph had created, it at least appears to have permitted Winston to articulate exactly what he wanted to hear from his father, and more importantly, to believe that he was entitled to such praise.

But if *The Dream* was meant to finally give Winston the chance to show his father that he was wrong about his older son—why wouldn't he have told Randolph that he had become Prime Minister? Could he have been ashamed that he had been marginalized by his two allies and then lost the 1945 election? Notably, too, in the story Winston seems devoid of any resentment, or even hurt, in relation to his father. He even took pains to flatter Lord Randolph about an 1884 speech, as if he had accepted the fact that Randolph was always most interested in Randolph.

Thus, in many ways, Winston seems like a person who had resolved his father issues. But if that were the case, then why would he have written *The Dream?* One thought: it was 1947, and Winston, while still a world citizen of historical proportions,[357] was no longer one of the three most powerful men in the world.* Having been "demoted" by Roosevelt in late 1943 and tossed out of office so emphatically in July 1945, it would not have been unrealistic for him to think that he would never recapture the glory days of 1940 to 1942 and that, like his father, he had become a historical figure who mattered little to the present. Such being the case, Winston may have conjured up Randolph, another politician put out to pasture before his time, to join him.

Whether in 1947 Churchill believed he had been put out to pasture, when he wrote *The Dream*, Churchill was still the most illustrious man alive[358] and one of the world leaders in the post-WWII struggle with the Soviets that came to be known as the Cold War. Although he wouldn't have known it when he wrote *The Dream,* in the autumn of 1949, Churchill received the *New York Times* Literary prize for the first two volumes of his WWII memoirs.[359] Moreover, in January 1950, *Time* magazine would name him the *Man of the Half Century* and offer this resplendent praise: "That a free world survived in 1950, with a hope of more progress and less calamity, was due in large measure to his exertions."[360]

As discussed earlier, he had not been in the top echelon of powerful men at least since the Tehran conference in November 1943, where his power had been eclipsed by both Stalin and Roosevelt.

Life in Britain During Attlee's Government

The advent of Attlee's Labour Government did not greatly improve the life of the average Briton. In the winter of 1947, among other things, heat, electricity, clothes, work, and food were all in short supply. CARE packages the US and the Commonwealth helped sustain millions.[361] More than three million people were unemployed.[362] Throughout the term of the Attlee Government, Churchill thoroughly castigated its handling of the British economy.

By 1949, popular support for Attlee's Government had declined substantially as life in Britain had not improved nearly as much as had been expected. Among other things, food rationing was still in place.[363]

The General Election of 1950

In early January 1950, just as Churchill was being declared the Man of the Half Century, Prime Minister Attlee called for a general election, which would take place on February 23. Much as was the case in May 1940, the future would be difficult for whomever became Prime Minister.[364] Against the advice of his doctor, Churchill enthusiastically began campaigning.[365] Since the end of the war, the Labour Government had enacted many programs aimed at improving the lives of Britons, nationalized many industries,* and not only granted independence to India, but to Burma and Ceylon as well. While many of these actions were real accomplishments, they came at a cost that included continued rationing and increased taxes.[366]

Although America no longer had a monopoly on atomic weapons, Churchill was steadfast in his belief that her nuclear arsenal assured world peace. He was also adamant that there should be "a parley at the summit" "to bridge the gulf between" East and West.[367]

The turnout for the 1950 election (84 percent) was the highest since 1906 and has never been exceeded.[368] When the votes were counted, Labour had lost 78 seats and the Conservatives had picked up 85, but that was not sufficient to change the Government. Labour still held a six-seat majority: Labour 315, Liberals 9, Conservatives 298.[369] After the election, the now seventy-five-year-old Churchill was described as energetic and in high spirits. He was "[n]o extinct volcano."[370] Even though Clementine still wanted him to retire from politics,[371] he refused, fervently believing that he would be the Prime Minister again.[372] Clementine felt that Winston's stature would likely be diminished by another term as Prime Minister,[373] but Churchill still had a lifelong goal to achieve—being sent to the Prime Ministership by a vote of ordinary Britons.[374] He still had something to prove.

This nationalization encompassed 20 percent of the UK's gross domestic product. Roberts p. 925.

Shortly after the 1950 election, squabbling within the Labour Party on budget matters boiled over into an unsuccessful vote of confidence about the Attlee Government.[375] Then, in June 1950, Attlee and the rest of the Western leaders faced a major crisis—with help from the Soviet Union, North Korea had crossed the 38th parallel and invaded South Korea.[376]

The General Election of 1951

Hoping to increase Labour's slim majority in the House, in September 1951 Attlee announced a general election to be held on October 25.[377] Churchill was ready for what he knew would be the last general election campaign of his life. Once again, he resisted calls from younger Tories to step aside.[378]* An election victory by the Conservatives would prove that, despite the elections of 1945 and 1950, Churchill could get a majority of the British people behind him once again. Moreover, the vote would finally dispel some of the things that were linked to him when he was appointed P.M. in 1940, such as a distrust of his judgment and an unsavory air of disreputability that came with him into the Prime Ministership. Last, but not least, it would be one more refutation of his father's low expectations for him. In short, an election victory would provide Winston with redemption on several levels—something that, at age seventy-six, he still appeared to need.

During the election campaign Churchill promised to construct three hundred thousand new houses and impose an excess profits tax on corporations.[379] Labour portrayed Churchill as a warmonger—someone whose finger Britons did not want on the trigger.[380] Churchill responded that he did not believe there would be another world war and said that in any event, "It will not be a British finger that starts a Third World War."[381] Churchill himself was easily reelected. The Conservatives won the general election, but barely; eking out a seventeen-seat majority. The Conservatives won 321 seats, Labour 295, the Liberals 6, and others 3.[382] This was hardly a mandate or the expunging of longstanding conceptions that Churchill had hoped for.[383]

Churchill's Second Tour as Prime Minister: October 26, 1951–April 5, 1955

The Tired Old Cold Warrior Who Wouldn't Quit

Churchill became Prime Minister once again on October 26, 1951. His second term was not his finest hour. Once again, Churchill named himself as Defence Minister;[384] a move that did not go unnoticed or uncriticized.[385]

During the campaign, Churchill did allude to passing the torch to Foreign Secretary Eden, causing some to believe that he would retire about a year after the election. Roberts p. 924. But this was not to be.

Anthony Eden, still Churchill's heir apparent, wanted to be named Deputy Prime Minister (a position that formally existed in the Attlee Government[*]) but was denied that title by Churchill and again appointed Foreign Secretary.[386] Another noteworthy appointee to the Cabinet was Rab Butler, a former Churchill detractor, who in the summer of 1940 had worked for Halifax planting false rumors that Britain was open to peace negotiations. Butler was chosen for the prestigious job of Chancellor of the Exchequer.[387][**] Churchill also appointed Clement Davis, who had supported the no-confidence motion against Churchill's Government back in 1942, as Minister of Education.[388] Churchill again showed that he was magnanimous and not a man who generally held grudges.

Upon Churchill's taking office again, Attlee informed him that Britain was in fact trying to build an atomic bomb.[389][***] Churchill saw a British bomb as his ticket to the summit meeting that he envisioned would bring about world peace.[390] It fit in perfectly with his philosophy of negotiating only from strength. He also believed that it would help strengthen the Anglo-American bond.[****] Trying to bring about such a summit was something for which he would fight throughout his second term.[391] He felt that he could not leave office until he negotiated an end to the Cold War.[392][*****]

In the early part of his term he traveled to Washington, and in what would be his third time, spoke before a joint session of Congress on January 17, 1952. There he said, to much laughter and applause, that "I have not come here to ask you for money to make living more comfortable or easier for us in Britain."[******] Rather, he spoke about Britain's support for US foreign

---

*During the first Churchill Government, Clement Attlee assumed that title when he chaired War Cabinet meetings in Churchill's absence.

**When Churchill became Prime Minister in May 1940, Butler had called him a "half-breed American"—and was not alone in saying so. Wheatcroft p. 232.

***Since 1949, American bombers armed with nuclear weapons had been based in the UK at East Anglia, northeast of London.

****He also viewed restoration of the special relationship between America and Britain as a most urgent task. Manchester and Reid p. 234. Unfortunately neither President Truman nor, President Eisenhower shared Churchill's view of the relationship. In fact, Eisenhower, who admired and respected Churchill, found the P.M.'s thinking to be "sentimental" and outdated. Addison p. 235.

*****This bears all the earmarks of yet another attempt at redemption—this one for the things he did and his thoughts about waring with Russia before she became a nuclear power.

******This is not to say that things in Britain were just fine. They weren't. Churchill's Government was desperate to save money wherever they could. For example, cheap meat was being imported from Canada even though there had been an outbreak of foot-and-mouth disease there. Other things being contemplated to save money included bringing the Mediterranean fleet home. See, Day and Davies, "Records Reveal Queen's 'cut-price' Coronation" The Guardian, August 7, 2007.

policy throughout the world.[393] While those in the audience found the Prime Minister "formidable and magnificent" he also "seemed to be weakening."[394] Age and successive illnesses had definitely slowed Churchill down. Shortly, he would have more health problems: a severe case of pneumonia as well as cerebral arterial spasms.[395] His doctor warned that Churchill was under too much stress. While the P.M. refused to resign, he did step down as Defence Minister.[396]

Three months into Churchill's second term, King George VI died on February 6, 1952, at age fifty-six. His twenty-five-year-old daughter Elizabeth assumed the throne.[397] A year later, Joseph Stalin died, making Churchill the only major WWII leader still alive, even though he was the oldest of them all and in poor health.[398]

In a speech to the House on May 11, 1953, he said, "I do not believe that the immense problem of reconciling the security of Russia with the freedom and safety of Western Europe is insoluble."[399] Ironically, because this hope for a negotiated settlement of the problems between East and West was articulated before the Korean war ended, it lead to Churchill, of all people, being denounced as an appeaser by US Senator William Knowland of California.[400] Nonetheless, Churchill pressed newly elected President Eisenhower for a meeting to lay out plans for a summit conference with the Soviets. Eisenhower agreed to the meeting, which would be held in Bermuda at a yet to be determined date,[401] but Eisenhower was not enthusiastic about a summit conference. US Secretary of State John Foster Dulles, for whom Churchill would develop a deep dislike, was even less favorably inclined.[402]

Queen Elizabeth's coronation took place on June 2, 1953. Two weeks later Churchill suffered a severe stroke which paralyzed his left side.[403] News of the stroke was suppressed by the Government and the press and thus was hidden from public.[404]* Not even MPs knew the nature or extent of Churchill's affliction. Plans for the Bermuda meeting were put on hold. Churchill again refused to step down as P.M. (But, it should be noted that at the time of Churchill's stroke, Foreign Secretary Eden was hospitalized in Boston and was also incapacitated.[405]) After more than a month of convalescence, the P.M. had largely recovered from the stroke.[406]** The Korean War ended on July 27. Just a few days before that Churchill told his personal secretary, John Colville, that he would probably resign as Prime Minister in October

---

*Colville describes how difficult it was keeping a lid on such a story and expresses the belief that the press would not have done so for anyone else but Churchill. Sunday Times March 6, 1955.

While Churchill was incapacitated, his son-in-law Christopher Soames ran things at 10 Downing Street. Addison p. 232.

**Although his doctor feared he might not survive, amazingly, Churchill chaired the Cabinet meeting held the next day. Roberts p. 939.

or November.[407] But Colville was careful to note in his diary that Churchill still wanted to reach a deal with the Soviets first.[408] Of course, Churchill did not resign in 1953.

In October 1953 he was awarded the Nobel Prize for literature.* In November, he made his first speech to Parliament since the stroke. It is said that no one in the House except Cabinet members knew that he had been so ill.[409] Buoyed by this final step in the recovery process, Churchill again pressed President Eisenhower for something he believed more important than a Nobel Prize—the meeting in Bermuda preparatory to an Anglo-American-Soviet summit.[410] Eisenhower agreed to meet in Bermuda in early December. The date picked by Eisenhower for the meeting conflicted with the Nobel Prize ceremony, but that didn't matter to Churchill. Clementine was sent to Stockholm to accept the prize and the tax-free £12,500 that accompanied it.[411] Churchill had more compelling things to do.

At the Bermuda meeting, Churchill's hopes for a summit with the Russians were dashed. Given Senator Joseph McCarthy's rants about the US State Department's being filled with Communists and the general anti-Communist craze that gripped America more generally, Eisenhower did not feel that he could extend a hand of friendship to the Soviets at that moment.[412] This was particularly true if the British and Churchill were seen as having pushed him into doing so.[413]

Six months later, on June 25, 1954, President Eisenhower surprisingly OK'd Churchill's idea for Britain to have bilateral talks with Russia.[414] The President also suggested preliminary talks be held with France and Germany before Churchill's meeting with the Soviets and further agreed that Germany should be rearmed and admitted into NATO.[415] Given the green light to parley with the Russians, there was no way Churchill would step down as Prime Minister.[416] Nonetheless, on the voyage back to England, the long-suffering Eden again asked Churchill when he planned to resign. Because Churchill believed it would be after Anglo-Soviet talks about arms reduction, he set September 20, 1954, as the tentative day to step down.[417]

Also on the trip back to the UK, after consultation with the Foreign Secretary, Churchill decided to send a personal message to Soviet Minister of Foreign Affairs Molotov about holding such a meeting.[418] A draft of the message was sent to Chancellor of the Exchequer Butler for his review and comment,[419] and the final message was sent on July 4.[420] As Churchill advised the members of the Cabinet on July 7, he had received a friendly reply from Molotov revealing Soviet interest in such a meeting.[421] He said it would now be for the Cabinet to decide, once President Eisenhower's views were known, what further message, if any, should be sent to Molotov.

At that point he had written thirty-seven books.

The Cabinet was, however, disinclined to talk with the Soviets.[422] Lord Salisbury, President of the Council, even announced his intention to resign because he disliked the idea of discussions with the Soviets and objected to the Prime Minister's having approached Molotov without first consulting the Cabinet.[423] The matter was, however, concluded several weeks later when a note was received from the Russians demanding that the meeting be of thirty-two powers, not just Britain and Russia. In the face of this, "Churchill's last great foreign policy initiative ended."[424] Salisbury was pleased.[425] But now, despite his promise to resign on September 20, Churchill started to show signs that he would renege.[426] In fact, in a few weeks he did just that. In a letter to Eden, he said he would reorganize the Government and stay in office.[427] He told Eden that the job of Prime Minister would be Eden's before he turned sixty; but Eden was only fifty-seven then and not happy.[428]

At the family Christmas celebration later that year, Churchill's oldest child, his daughter Diana, mused about all the things that Winston had experienced in his life. He responded darkly that "I have achieved a great deal to achieve nothing at all."[429]

As 1954 turned into 1955, Churchill, tiring of the job, finally reached the conclusion to resign but did not make public his intention which was to step down at the start of the Easter recess.[430] Of course, as the date drew nearer and there was the possibility of Eisenhower coming to Paris on May 8, the tenth anniversary of VE-Day, Churchill thought about changing his mind.[431] When there was another rumor in late March that the new Soviet leader, Nikolai Bulganin, had shown interest in a four-power summit,[432] Churchill determined once again to postpone his resignation. In a move that was beneath him, Churchill did not tell Eden of this decision himself. Rather, Churchill asked Chancellor of the Exchequer Butler to advise Eden of this latest change in his retirement plans.[433]* Despite Churchill's change of heart, the Edens did not cancel a farewell dinner for Churchill they were hosting that very evening, March 29.[434] The dinner threatened to be extremely tense.

The next morning, when asked, Churchill told a very surprised Colville that the dinner had been congenial. The Prime Minister then said that he did not believe there would be a summit meeting and thus did not see a good reason for him to remain Prime Minister.[435] As Colville explains, Churchill thrived on "showdowns" but could not resist "amiability" of the kind that the Edens had shown him.[436]**

---

*He even asked the Queen if she had a problem with his postponing his departure. She didn't. Colville p. 708.
**In this way, he was much like Neville Chamberlain, who could not resist Churchill's amiability fifteen years earlier when Winston became Prime Minister.

A planned farewell dinner attended by Queen Elizabeth and her husband, Prince Philip, was held at 10 Downing Street on April 4. Churchill went to Buckingham Palace and resigned the next day.[437]

Given Churchill's numerous vacillations about resigning, understandably, the relationship between Eden and the P.M. had soured. It was extremely hard for Churchill to leave Government after sixty years in public service, even though he was becoming less and less able to handle the job of Prime Minister.[438] Colville likened him to a fish that expends its last bit of energy trying to evade being scooped up in the fisherman's net.[439] While that was likely true, the saga of Churchill's refusal to resign was a sorry attempt on his part to stay in the limelight. Because of Churchill's lifelong need for attention, his clinging on to power for far longer than he should have was predictable.

While he was never able to achieve a summit meeting and end the Cold War, during his second tour as Prime Minister food rationing in Britain finally ended (1954); a substantial number of houses were built (est. one million); and the British economy was put back on a road leading to prosperity.[440]

Had Churchill Mellowed on Matters of Race?

As has been pointed out earlier in this book, various comments, actions, and attitudes attributed to Churchill have been called "racist" or otherwise unacceptable by twenty-first century standards. Such instances include his making disparaging comments about Turkish soldiers during World War I: "Johnnie Turk" was not much of a soldier;[441] hearing in 1942 that upon a Japanese invasion of India, the Indian Congress Party would not advocate helping the British defend the country, he said, "I hate Indians. They are a beastly people with a beastly religion."[442]* He called the Palestinians "barbaric hordes who ate little but camel dung." And of the Sudanese, he boasted of

---

Churchill historian Richard Langworth disputes the assertion that this statement from the Diary of Secretary of State for India Leo Amery is prima facie evidence of Churchill's inherent racism. In this regard, Langworth agrees with the late American intellectual and conservative author William F. Buckley Jr., who stated at the 1995 Churchill Conference in Boston that "[Churchill was] working his way through disputatious bureaucracy from separatists in New Delhi ... I don't doubt that the famous claim came to his eyes when he said this with mischievous glee—an offense, in modern convention of genocidal magnitude." Langworth, "Churchill and India: Again & Again & Again & Again," Finest Hour, Autumn 2007; Moran, Struggle p. 140.

Historian Zareer Masani explains that Churchill had teased Leo Amery since childhood and liked to cut off Amery's long speeches about India by making an outrageously racist statement that was not to be taken seriously but was purposely designed to shock Amery and shut him up. Amery did not take kindly to this, once accusing Churchill of being like Hitler and more often writing Churchill's words down verbatim in his diary. As a result, Amery's diary contains a great many seemingly callous remarks from Churchill. Masani, "Churchill and the Genocide

killing three "savages." He also underestimated the Japanese[443] and spoke of them as "he might of little children."[444] Churchill's doctor, Lord Moran, also sets forth the following anecdote in his diary entry of April 8, 1955:

> Someone asked Winston if he had seen the film *Carmen Jones,* in which the chief character was a negress. Winston replied that he didn't like "blackamoors," and had walked out early in the proceedings. He asked, a little irrelevantly, what happened when blacks got measles. Could the rash be spotted? When he was told that there was a very high mortality among Negroes from measles he growled: "Well, there are plenty left. They've a high rate of production," and he grinned good-humouredly."[445]*

Churchill was a Victorian who thought of people based on the color of their skin,[446] and that white people were superior.[447] Moreover, particularly when angry or frustrated, or just to seem witty, Churchill would resort to the use of the racist tropes of the day whether he meant what he said or not. Historian and broadcaster Zareer Masani advises that offensive comments like those noted above "need to be seen in the context of [Churchill's] penchant for making outrageous comments that he didn't really mean in order to shock or tease."[448]** As Professor Richard Toye explains, despite all this, Churchill believed there was a "need to act humanely toward supposedly inferior races, that might in their own way be worthy of admiration."[449] Indeed, "throughout his career he often spoke up for the welfare of indigenous people."[450]***

_____

Myth: *Last word on the Bengal Famine," The Churchill Project, Hillsdale College, January 27, 2021.*

As pointed out earlier, despite the ferocity with which Churchill opposed independence and Dominion status for India and the very sharp words he had for Gandhi in the 1930s, the two had a reproachment. But things deteriorated as Gandhi turned up the pressure for independence during Churchill's premiership.

It is worth noting that Churchill not infrequently had great praise for Indian soldiers and officers. See, Roberts p. 977. Roberts writes that these words did not come from a "man who hated Indians." Ibid. Churchill also showed empathy for the non-white citizens of India during the Muslim—Hindu fighting that followed Indian independence in 1947.

**Churchill has been rebuked for statements such as this. Moran, Struggle p. 757.*

***His secretary, John Colville, writes that Churchill's anger was "like lightning" and he frequently made impulsive remarks about people and events, but those comments were often modified upon reflection. Colville p. 127.*

****Early in his life, Churchill had spoken against the mistreatment of blacks by the Boers. As mentioned earlier, he even tried to get blacks the right to vote when South Africa achieved Dominion status. He also ended the mistreatment of the Chinese there. During a 1954 discussion of the ongoing Mau Mau rebellion against colonial rule in Kenya, Churchill rejected the prevailing view that members of the*

He even believed that members of these races "might earn equal treatment if they reached an approved cultural standard."[451] Likewise, he did not feel that there should be barriers which prevented a man from reaching as high as his abilities could take him,* but on the other hand, he had little problem if the white majority in a country were slow to adopt this view.[452]

There are also examples of Churchill opposing actions which could be viewed as simply treating non-white people unfairly. One of these was his absolute abhorrence of the caste system and the way Hindus in India treated sixty million of their own people—the Untouchables.[453] Another such example was when he was advised at a Cabinet meeting in 1942 that American army officers were imposing a "Whites only" policy in some British restaurants. He and the Cabinet made it clear that British authorities would not help enforce segregation: admission to pubs, theaters, movies, and so on would not be restricted on the basis of race.[454] Thereafter, Black Americans in Britain enjoyed a freedom they did not have in large parts of their own country.**

Although not a religious man, Churchill also had a hierarchical view of people based on religion—with Protestants and Catholics at the top of that list.[455] However, as his abhorrence of the merciless treatment of Jews by the Nazis indicates, his hierarchical thinking was in no way limited his disgust at non-Christians being treated inhumanely.

His generally centered view of right and wrong, did, and still does not, preclude his being accused of proceeding with, or failing to act on, matters of consequence based on racial, cultural, or religious prejudice.

Did Racial or Religious Bias Affect His Actions as Prime Minister?

Did Churchill's actions in connection with 1943 famine in India constitute genocide based on race?

One such assertion is that Churchill's actions during the 1943 famine in Bengal constituted the genocide of an estimated three million non-whites. The assertion has been fueled largely by the racist statements attributed to him about Indians. Those statements notwithstanding, the evidence does not support the assertion that he was complicit in the tragedy that hit India

---

Kikuyu tribe were primitive and stupid, declaring instead that they were people of substance. Toye, Churchill's Empire *p. xvi.*

It is also reported that Churchill did not know or care who in his crowd was a homosexual. Manchester and Reid p. 613.

**In December 1953, upon arriving in Bermuda for a conference with President Eisenhower, when Churchill learned that no blacks had been invited to the Governor's banquet scheduled for the first night of the conference, he insisted that two be asked immediately. Colville p. 682.*

in 1943 or that racial prejudice in any way influenced his actions related to the famine.[456] To the contrary, the evidence supports the position that he did everything reasonably possible to provide food to Bengal at a very tense time amid a global war.

East Bengal (now the lower part of Bangladesh) was hit by a cyclone in October 1942 that destroyed its rice crop.[457] As a result, rice which should have been planted in the winter of 1943 was largely consumed, and the rice harvest in Bengal in the summer of 1943 was poor.[458]* The duly elected local Muslim administration did an inadequate job of handling the problem, and the British Viceroy at the time, Lord Linlithgow, did not start dealing with the resulting situation early enough.[459] The peasants of Bengal, even in good times, did not have food in abundance. In the past, food shortages had been dealt with by transporting food from northern India to Bengal by rail and importing rice from Burma and other Southeast Asian countries.[460] But the cyclone of October 1942 had not only reduced the size of the winter crop in northern India; it also washed out the rail lines there.[461] At the same time, rice from Burma and the rest of Southeast Asia was unavailable, as those countries were occupied by the Japanese.[462] Thus, the British Raj encountered "the greatest humanitarian crisis it had faced in more than half a century."[463]

During the summer of 1943, when starvation was setting in, the Government of India requested that Britain ship 500,000 tons of wheat to India during the period September 1943 to February 1944.[464] A July 30, 1943, review and analysis by the War Cabinet's Shipping Committee pointed out that:

1. for fiscal year April 1, 1943–March 31, 1944, India was likely to have a grain shortage in the order of 1.35 million tons;
2. grain producers were continuing to hold stocks in the anticipation of increased prices due to inflation. They also feared a Japanese invasion;
3. the India Office stated that famine conditions had already been reported in some parts of the country including Travancore, Cochin, and Bengal;[465]
4. out of a maximum of 30,000 tons of grain per month available in Australia, after meeting whatever requirements were determined necessary for Ceylon and the Middle East, some of this grain might be available for India; and
5. up to 100,000 tons of barley could be shipped to India from Iraq.

---

*To make an extremely bad situation even worse, in the spring of 1944 the area was hit with unseasonable rains, which again diminished the harvest. CAB 65/1 55 (44) p. 252 43 April 24, 1944.

In sum, the review showed that less than one third of the amount requested could be provided.[466]

These facts notwithstanding, in early August 1943, the War Cabinet concluded that the shortage of grain in India did not result from a physical deficiency. Rather, Cabinet members believed it stemmed from hoarding in anticipation of substantial inflation.[467] As a result, the Cabinet authorized the Minister of War transport to arrange for 100,000 tons of barley to be sent to India from Iraq[468] but took no further action on India's request, although it remained open to having the Secretary of State for India, Leo Amery, raise the matter again.[469]

On September 24, 1943, Amery asked the War Cabinet to reconsider its position in view of the continued deterioration of the food situation in India.[470] He wanted a firm assurance that another 500,000 tons of cereal would be shipped to India before March 1944.[471] At that time, the Chiefs of Staff endorsed the view of the Commander-in-Chief of India that it was of the highest strategic importance that India receive all possible aid in dealing with the food situation.[472] It was needed to help stave off a possible Japanese invasion.[473]*

Churchill said that "Something must be done."[474] The War Cabinet concurred and authorized the shipment of up to 200,000 tons of grain to India by the end of 1943. The Cabinet also agreed that the matter would be reviewed at that time in light of the Indian grain harvest.[475] But on November 10, 1943, Amery again put the matter of shipping grain to India back in front of the War Cabinet—a further review could not wait until the end of the year.[476] (Amery went one step further by submitting a Parliamentary Question to be heard in the House the following day. The answer to the question would highlight that shipping was unavailable to convey 100,000 tons of wheat which had been offered by the Canadian Government.[477]) Recognizing the general unavailability of merchant vessels,** Amery did not press the War Cabinet to commit to a long-term program. He merely said it was essential that another 50,000 tons of Australian wheat be shipped to India by the end of 1943 and that an additional 100,000 tons be shipped in January or February.[478] Minister of War Transport Lord Frederick Leathers said another shipment before the end of 1943 was impracticable, but that it should be

---

*At that time, "Japan was poised on the border of India. ..." Herman, *Without Churchill.*

**The lack of shipping had caused Roosevelt to conclude that the cross-channel invasion of France could not take place until 1944. Manchester and Reid p. 604.*

possible to ship up to 100,000 tons in the first two months of 1944.[479]* And the War Cabinet approved shipping that amount.[480]

While the War Cabinet was slow on the uptake during the summer of 1943, when Secretary Amery pressed it to act both in late September and early November, with help from the P.M., the Government stepped up and responded. By early 1944, the Churchill Government had shipped 320,000 tons of grain to India from Iraq, Australia, and Canada.[481] This was 64 percent of the 500,000 tons Amery had first requested.

When people are starving, providing only two-thirds of what was needed is far from acceptable. But it bears remembering that this modest level of accomplishment was achieved in some extreme circumstances. That is, especially earlier in the war, the Germans had exacted a terrible toll on Britain's merchant fleet and thus its cargo carrying capacity had been significantly reduced.[482]** Additionally, when the grain was sorely needed in India, Britain was using its ships both to bring in food for the citizens of the UK and war materiel for its armed forces. She was also shipping critically needed planes and other equipment to the Soviets, and starting to amass supplies, equipment, and troops that would be required for Operation Overlord, the all-important cross-channel invasion of France.***

That said, Britain's effort in 1942–'43 was not enough; India needed more grain. Churchill was willing to do all he could, but told the newly appointed Viceroy, Lord Wavell, not to "ask [for] the impossible."[483] At that point, with D-Day only a few months away, merchant ship availability was practically nil.[484] Churchill told the Viceroy a few days later that "We have given a great deal of thought to your difficulties, but we simply cannot find the shipping."[485]

By the spring of 1944 it was estimated that for the year, nearly a million tons of grain needed to be imported to sustain the civilian population of India and provide the army with what it needed.[486] The good news was that the volume of wheat could be bought in Australia. The bad news was that Britain did not have ships available to transport the grain.[487] Given the

---

*This amount would be at the expense of replenishing the stocks in the Middle East. CAB 65/2 152 (43) p.151 104.

**For example, in 1942, German submarines sank an average of 520,000 tons of Anglo-American shipping per month. This was a rate faster than could be replaced by the Allies' shipyards. CAB 65/2 152 (43) p. 151 104.

***Additionally, at this time a large fleet of Japanese was also on station in both the Bay of Bengal and the Indian Ocean. See, Campaign Summaries of World War 2, Indian Ocean & South East Asia, including Burma 1939–1945. Available at: https://www.naval-history.net/NAVAL1939-45Campaigns .htm; Roberts p. 786. This added a significant element of risk to any effort to ship grain to Bengal. Roberts p. 788.

seriousness of the situation, on April 24, Amery asked the War Cabinet to apprise the United States of the situation and request her assistance.[488] At the meeting, Churchill added that:

- He had great sympathy for the sufferings of the people of India;

- It was clear that the Government could provide more relief for the Indian situation only at the cost of incurring grave difficulties in other directions; and

- He was skeptical as to any help being forthcoming from America, save at the cost of operations for the United Kingdom import programme; nonetheless

- He agreed to urge the US to assist with transporting grain to India.[489]

Churchill did just that—but the Americans promptly responded that they could not provide the requested assistance because their ships were needed to supply the war effort in the Pacific and Operation Overlord.[490] Still, by the close of 1944 Britain had managed to provide India with the one million tons of grain from Australia.[491]

When people are starving, not getting enough food to them promptly does not exemplify stellar performance. As Allen Packwood, Director of the Churchill Archives Centre at the University of Cambridge, states, without minimizing the horror of the famine, it came about in the midst of a global war with "conflicting priorities and demands"[492] The willingness of Churchill and his Government to provide more than 1.3 million tons of grain to India in 1943 and 1944 is the absolute antithesis of a genocide, let alone one based on race. Historian Arthur Herman articulately writes: "Far from seeking to starve India, Churchill and his cabinet sought every way to alleviate the suffering without undermining the war effort."* They did so for humanitarian reasons and because, as noted, getting as much food to India as possible "was of the highest importance from the strategic point of view" as well. It was needed to help stave off any possible Japanese invasion.[493] "The war—not starving Indians ... remained the principal concern."[494]

Lastly, in determining if there were any racial implications in of any of Churchill's actions, it bears noting that his performance over the famine in India was eminently more humane than was his failure to oppose maintaining the blockade of food shipments to the Caucasian population of Germany

---

*As the title of Herman's 2010 article says, "Without Churchill, India's Famine Would Have Been Worse." Herman, "Without Churchill."

at the end of WWI.* Likewise, in 1943, as "... the citizens of Dresden, Hamburg, Berlin and a dozen other German cities were about to find out ..." "Churchill could be ruthless in pursuing his main objective. ..." "But no racist or imperialist motives can be imputed there."[495]

Did Churchill fail to speak out against the Holocaust?

Some have also accused Churchill of being a leader who knew much about the Holocaust early on yet chose not to speak out about it.[496] On balance, the evidence does not, however, support this assertion either. From the start, Churchill detested the Nazis' racial dogma and their persecution of the Jews.[497] As discussed, unlike most of his contemporaries, he was not anti-Semitic and was a Zionist.

Churchill mentioned mass killings in the East as early as August 24, 1941, just two months after the Nazis invaded the Soviet Union and the Soviets joined the Allies.[498] In a broadcast that evening he said:

> As [Hitler's] armies advance, whole districts are being exterminated. Scores of thousands, literally scores of thousands of executions in cold blood are being perpetrated by the German police troops upon the Russian patriots who defend their native soil."**

Churchill was, however, criticized, and rightly so, for not highlighting the fact that the exterminations and executions referenced were of Jews and not euphemistic "Russian patriots."[499]***

Of course, Hitler had threatened to "annihilate the Jewish race in Europe" in the event of a world war. And once the Soviet Union was attacked in June 1941, Nazi leaders and Nazi propaganda frequently referenced this threat.

As discussed in Chapter 6, Churchill advocated for shipping food into Germany immediately after the Armistice became effective on November 11, 1918.

He was overruled by Prime Minister Lloyd George. A few months later, however, he was willing to put his principles aside and stand with the Prime Minister, who was using the denial of food to the civilian population of Germany to expedite the German Government's agreement to peace terms.

In 1943, with no one above him in the hierarchy, Prime Minister Churchill was able to go with his humanitarian instincts and get as much food to India as he could, particularly where doing so was also seen as militarily imperative.

**The text of the broadcast is available at http://www.ibiblio.org/pha/policy/1941/410824a.html

***People in occupied Western Europe who listened to the speech (a crime punishable by death in Nazi-occupied counties) said in post-war interviews that the speech gave them hope. Roberts p. 678. The text of the broadcast is available at http://www.ibiblio.org/pha/policy/1941/410824a.html

Accordingly, notwithstanding Churchill's poor choice of words, it is unlikely that many people listening to Churchill's broadcast that August night doubted he was telling them that the Jews of eastern Europe were being executed by the invading Nazis.

In October 1942, Churchill also wrote a public letter to the Archbishop of Canterbury in which he called the systematic cruelties to which the Jewish people have been exposed among the most terrible events of history.[500] The Polish government-in-exile claimed that two million Polish Jews had been shipped off to Nazi extermination camps.[501] In response, Foreign Secretary Eden addressed the House on December 17, 1942, and read the Allied Declaration that Britain and eleven other countries—including the US and the Soviet Union—had just issued. The declaration spoke about the "numerous reports ... that the German authorities... Are now carrying into effect Hitler's oft repeated intention to exterminate the Jewish people in Europe." It said that Jews were being transported to Poland "which has been made the principal Nazi slaughterhouse." The declaration concluded with the vow that "those responsible for these crimes shall not escape retribution."[502] When Eden finished, members of the House stood in silence.[503] This did not do much to change the plight of European Jewry, but it was more than what Roosevelt did at the time.

Did Churchill want to "keep England white"?

Many authors, including Andrew Roberts, Geoffrey Wheatcroft, Paul Addison, Peter Hennessy, William Manchester, and Paul Reid have reported that in January 1955, during a Cabinet discussion about a bill that was being drafted to restrict immigration into the UK from the West Indies, Churchill suggested that "Keep England White" would be a good slogan for the campaign.[504]

A review of the Cabinet conclusions for January 1955 reveals that the bill was discussed briefly during the meetings of January 13, 20, 24, and 31, 1955, but that there is nothing in the minutes of those sessions showing that the P.M. or anyone else made the statement attributed to Churchill. Likewise, the notes of these meeting taken by Cabinet Secretary Sir Norman Brook and memorialized in the Cabinet Secretary's notebook[505] do not reveal that any such statement was made.

However, the private diary of future Prime Minister Harold Macmillan, then the Minister of Defence, contains the following short statement in the entry for January 20, 1955, about the Cabinet meeting he had attended that day: "More discussion about the West Indian immigrants. A Bill is being drafted—but it's not an easy problem. P.M. thinks 'Keep England White' a good slogan!"[506] The entry does not reveal whether Churchill said this in earnest or just to seem witty. But notes of a Cabinet meeting held nearly a year earlier do shed light on the question.

The matter of West Indian immigration was discussed by the Cabinet, on February 3, 1954, and the Cabinet conclusions for that day state:

> The Prime Minister said that the rapid improvement of communications was likely to lead to a continuing increase in the number of coloured people coming to this country, and their presence here would sooner or later come to be resented by large sections of the British people. It might well be true, however, that the problem had not yet assumed sufficient proportions to enable the Government to take adequate counter-measures.[507]

The notes of the meeting taken by Sir Norman Brook go into greater detail and attribute these remarks about the immigration of coloured workers to the Prime Minister:

> Problems wh. will arise if many coloured people settle here. Are we to saddle ourselves with colour problem in the U.K?
>
> Attracted by the Welfare State.
>
> Public opinion in U.K. won't tolerate it once it gets beyond certain limits.
>
> Ques. is wtr it is politically wise to allow public feeling to develop a little more—before takg. action.
>
> Wd . Like also to study possibility of "quota"—no. not to be exceeded
>
> May be wise to wait as at x/. but it wd be fatal to let a develop too far.[508]

These notes make clear that Churchill was leaning toward limiting black immigration into the UK and using racial stereotyping in the process.

Accordingly, even if his remark a year later about an appropriate slogan were said to appear witty, here we have evidence of his advocating an action which was race-based and did not treat non-white people fairly or like individuals. This was not dissimilar in character from his Government's attempt in 1942 to persuade the US to restrict the number of black troops sent to England.

Given the above, it appears that Churchill could oppose negative race-based actions when those actions were abstractions not affecting the lives of average Britons or were otherwise minor. But when the issue involved things in his own back yard, such as the number of blacks that should be allowed into the UK, his core racist beliefs would emerge and affect his decision making, even though the proposed action would objectively not be fair to non-whites. This phenomenon was not unique to Churchill, and unfortunately, is still widely exhibited today, even among people who do not otherwise show that they have any beliefs which could be considered racist.

In sum, Churchill was a racist—but. He talked the talk, even though he may have done so only out of anger, frustration, to tease, or to seem witty. His actual views on race were complex[509] and "in some ways, more sympathetic than has generally been recognized."[510] In comparison to his contemporaries, who admittedly set a low bar, he was "more informed and relatively enlightened."[511] He did not believe that race or religion should be used to treat any group inhumanly. Likewise, although with at least one glaring exception involving black immigration to the UK (when the matter fell close to home), he also did not support treating groups unfairly on the basis of race or religion. Perhaps a somewhat accurate shorthand description of Churchill might be that he was a racist—but not a fully practicing one.

Churchill's Last Decade: April 6, 1955–January 24, 1965

Immediately after Churchill's resignation, Eden was asked to form a new Government; which he did; the Churchills then set off for Sicily.[512]* One of the next things Eden did as Prime Minister was to set a general election for May 26, 1955. In that election the Conservatives increased their majority to fifty-nine seats and Churchill was again re-elected to Parliament.[513] Churchill had wanted to campaign nationally for the party, but his efforts were not wanted.[514]

Churchill returned to working on his *History of English Speaking People*, a project for which he had signed a contract in 1932 but on which he had stopped work back in 1939.[515] The first volume of the treatise was published in April 1956.[516]

In mid-May 1955, the Soviets confirmed their interest in a four-power summit conference among the United States, Britain, France, and itself. The prize Churchill had pursued for so long had fallen to his successor.[517] Eisenhower, who knew how much missing the summit hurt Churchill, wrote him a letter expressing the President's low expectations for the meeting and how much Winston's "courage and vision" would be missed.[518] The summit

---

*Upon his return from Sicily, Churchill told Dr. Moran that since he was now retired and without purpose, he expected to die soon. Moran, Struggle p. 7.

was held in Geneva in July 1955. While it was hailed as a first step to easing Cold War tensions, no agreements were reached there.

Churchill's doctor paints a dark picture of the last years of Churchill's life, e.g., Winston's being lonely and despondent and having given up reading.[519] But some historians speak of Churchill's being a voracious reader, painting, taking walks, and bricklaying for a good many of his remaining years.[520] He also traveled fairly extensively, taking many long trips as the guest of Greek shipping magnate Aristotle Onassis aboard the *Cristina*, Onassis' luxurious 325-foot yacht.[521] The last of these took place in 1961 when the *Cristina* sailed to the Caribbean and then along the east coast of the United States as far north as New York City.[522]

In 1959, Churchill was again reelected to the House, where he served until retiring in 1964.[523] Later that year he laid the cornerstone for Churchill College at Cambridge. Among other honors he received late in life, on April 9, 1963, although he did not attend the ceremony in person, President John F. Kennedy bestowed honorary United States citizenship on him.[524] Having this honor presented by President Kennedy was particularly appropriate because as shown earlier in this book, as a Harvard senior in 1940, Kennedy had written an elegant contemporaneous assessment of Churchill's efforts to alert Britain and the world of the dangers posed by Nazi Germany.

As Churchill entered his late eighties, infirmities started to pile up. His memory started to fade, he contracted pneumonia and pleurisy, and had several strokes after which he suffered a hairline spinal fracture and a broken hip.[525] During this time, several of his wartime colleagues, including his longtime science advisor Professor Lindemann, former US Chief of Staff and later Secretary of State George Marshall, and his old friend Lord Beaverbrook passed away. And in 1963, Churchill's oldest child, Diana, committed suicide.

The Final Chapter

In the early '60s, decline, albeit in fits and starts, set in and was uncompromising.[526] Churchill last visited the House of Commons in July 1964. On his ninetieth birthday, November 30, 1964, he received seventy thousand cards and telegrams.[527]

On January 12, 1965, Churchill suffered yet another stroke; one which rendered him unconscious. Though he never regained consciousness, contrary to the doctors' prognosis, he managed to live for nearly another two weeks. He had a final goal—one he had predicted years earlier[528]—to live until January 24, the seventieth anniversary of his father's passing. At ninety, he'd lived twice as long as had his father.

As a fitting tribute to all that he had done for Britain, his body lay in state in Westminster Hall for three days and nights, during which time three hundred and twenty thousand people passed by.[529]* After that he was given a state funeral; something that only two non-royals had received in more than a century—the Duke of Wellington and Prime Minister Gladstone.[530] Unlike those funerals, Churchill's was attended by the reigning monarch. Queen Elizabeth II was joined by dignitaries from more than one hundred and ten counties.[531] In words Lord Randolph might have used had he reappeared in a dream: It looked like Winston had made a name for himself. Whether Winston, who always "doubted whether his place in history was secure"[532] fully believed that may be another story.

Returning to England from visit with Roosevelt

This number would have been greater had the temperature not been below zero. Roberts p. 962.

Churchill and Stalin

Drawing by Rick Young

ENDNOTES

Chapter 1

1 Randolph Churchill, *Youth* p. 8   2 *Companion Volumes* V part 2 p. 820   3 Randolph Churchill, *Youth* pp. 15–16   4 Letter to Lord Randolph from his father, August 31, 1873, reprinted in Randolph Churchill, *Youth* p. 19   5 Birmingham University Archives, Avon papers, 20/1/24   6 Manchester, *Visions* p. 112   7 Ibid. p. 111   8 Ibid. p. 116   9 Roberts, *Churchill: Walking with Destiny* p. 8   10 Manchester, *Visions* p. 112   11 Ibid. pp. 113–14   12 Ibid. p. 114   13 Churchill, *My Early Life* pp. 1–2   14 Manchester, *Visions* pp. 115–16   15 Churchill, *My Early Life* p. 4   16 Manchester, *Visions* p. 116   17 Randolph Churchill, *Youth* p. 37   18 Manchester, *Visions* pp. 117–18   19 Randolph Churchill, *Youth* p. 37   20 Manchester, *Visions* p. 121   21 Roberts, p. 13   22 Gilbert, *A Life* p. 2   23 Sheridan, *Nuda Veritas* p. 14   24 Brendon, *Churchill* p. 8   25 Roberts, p. 14   26 Manchester, *Visions* p. 124   27 Randolph Churchill, *Youth* p. 43   28 Manchester, *Visions* p. 125   29 Baring, *Puppet Show* p. 71   30 Randolph Churchill, *Youth* p. 43   31 Baring, *Puppet Show* p. 71   32 Roberts, p. 15   33 Manchester, *Visions* p. 127   34 Roberts, p. 14   35 Randolph Churchill, *Youth* p. 63   36 Manchester, *Visions* p. 128   37 Ibid. p. 139   38 Ibid. p. 128   39 Ibid. p. 128   40 Ibid. p. 134   41 Vale and Scadding, "Pneumonia" p. 2. Available at: http://doi.org/10.1177/096772018754646   42 Manchester, *Visions* p. 133   43 James, *Failure* p. 10   44 Manchester, *Visions* p. 134   45 Ibid.   46 Ibid. p. 135   47 *Companion Volumes*, I part 1 pp. 105, 113, 127   48 Randolph Churchill, *Youth* pp. 65, 73   49 Manchester, *Visions* p. 146   50 Ibid. p. 147   51 Ibid.   52 Ibid. pp. 147–48   53 Ibid. p. 154   54 Randolph Churchill, *Youth* p. 93   55 Ibid.   56 Manchester, *Visions* p. 151   57 Randolph Churchill, *Youth* p. 94   58 Ibid. p. 95   59 *Companion Volumes*, I part 1 p. 152   60 Randolph Churchill, *Youth* p. 105   61 Colville, *The Fringes of Power* p. 444   62 Manchester, *Visions* p. 153   63 *Companion Volumes*, I/1 p. 227   64 Letter of H.O.D. Davidson, July 12, 1888. reprinted in Randolph Churchill, *Youth* p. 109   65 ed. Eades, *Contemporaries* p. 19   66 Roberts, p. 20   67 Ibid. pp. 20, 21   68 Ibid. p. 21   69 Letter from Lady Randolph to Winston, June 12, 1890, reprinted in Randolph Churchill, *Youth* p. 124   70 Ibid. p.125   71 Randolph Churchill, *Youth* p. 121   72 Gardiner, *Prophets, Priests, and Kings* p. 235   73 Churchill, *My Early Life* p.24   74 Manchester, *Visions* p. 171   75 Letter of December 9, 1891, reprinted in Randolph Churchill, *Youth* pp. 154–55   76 Letter of December 15, 1891, reprinted in Randolph Churchill, *Youth* p. 156   77 Letter of December 16, 1891, reprinted in Randolph Churchill, *Youth* p. 156–57   78 Letter of December 18, 1891, reprinted in Randolph Churchill, *Youth* p. 158   79 Letter of December 27, 1891, reprinted in Randolph Churchill, *Youth* p. 164   80 Manchester, *Visions* p. 173   81 Ibid. p. 175   82 Churchill, *My Early Life* p. 5   83 Quoted in Roberts, p. 27   84 Randolph Churchill, *Youth* p. 129   85 Manchester, *Visions* p. 176   86 Randolph Churchill, *Youth* p. 178   87 *Companion Volumes*, I part 1 p. 365   88 Randolph Churchill, *Youth* pp. 182, 184   89 Ibid. p. 186   90 Letter of August 7, 1893, reprinted in Randolph Churchill, *Youth* p. 191   91 Letter from J.D.G. Little (Winston's and Jack's companion in Switzerland) to Lord Randolph, August 19, 1893, reprinted in Randolph Churchill, *Youth* p. 192   92 Letter of August 14, 1893, reprinted in Randolph Churchill, *Youth* p. 192   93 Churchill, *My Early Life* p. 34   94 Randolph Churchill, *Youth* p. 199   95 Scott, *Churchill at the Gallop*, passim   96 Farwell, *Kipling* p. 145   97 Letter dated October 24, 1893, reprinted in Randolph Churchill, *Youth* p. 206   98 Manchester,

Visions pp. 187–88   99 Letter dated April 21, 1894, From Lord Randolph to Winston, reprinted in Randolph Churchill, *Youth* p. 211   100 Letter dated May 1, 1894, reprinted in Randolph Churchill, *Youth* p. 214   101 *Companion Volumes* I part 1 p. 419   102 Letter dated October 29, 1893, reprinted in Randolph Churchill, *Youth* pp. 207–08   103 Manchester, *Visions* p. 191   104 *Companion Volumes* I part 1 pp. 424, 425   105 Manchester, *Visions* p. 201   106 John H. Mather, M.D. "'Keeping the Memory Green and the Record Accurate' Leading Churchill Myths (6) 'Lord Randolph Churchill Died of Syphilis,'" Finest Hour No. 117 Winter 2002–03   107 Manchester, *Visions* p. 203   108 Letters from Winston to his mother dated November 2 and November 8, 1894, reprinted in Randolph Churchill, *Youth* pp. 228, 229   109 Ibid. p. 227   110 Manchester, *Visions* p. 208   111 Quoted in Manchester, *Visions* p. 216   112 Ibid. p. 210   113 Churchill, *My Early Life* p. 84   114 Churchill Archives at Churchill College Cambridge, Churchill's *Annual Register* 1874 p. 94   115 Letter of April 5, 1897, from Winston to his mother, excerpted in Randolph Churchill, *Youth*, pp. 305, 306

Chapter 2

1 Millard, p. 21   2 Ibid. p. 59   3 Ibid. p. 60   4 Randolph Churchill, *Youth* p. 446   5 Millard, p. 104   6 Atkins, *Incidents* p. 128   7 Pakenham, *Boer War* p. 178   8 Millard, p. 127   9 Pakenham, *Boer War* p. 172   10 Millard, p. 129   11 Churchill, *My Early Life* p. 249; Randolph Churchill, *Youth* p. 449   12 Millard, pp. 131, 132   13 Ibid. p. 132   14 Ibid. pp. 146–150   15 Ibid. p. 156   16 Manchester, *Visions* p. 306   17 Millard, p. 207   18 Ibid. pp. 212, 213   19 Randolph Churchill, *Youth* p. 481   20 Millard, p. 234   21 Manchester, *Visions* p. 307   22 Ibid.   23 Millard, p. 238   24 Ibid. p. 250   25 Ibid. p. 251; Manchester, *Visions* p. 307   26 Manchester, *Visions* p. 310   27 Millard, p. 294   28 Ibid.   29 Ibid. pp. 295, 296   30 Manchester, *Visions* p. 316   31 Ibid. pp. 320–21

Chapter 3

1 Roberts, p. 75   2 Randolph Churchill, *Young Statesman* p. 1   3 Ibid. p. 2   4 Ibid. p. 3   5 Roberts, p. 81   6 Randolph Churchill, *Young Statesman* p. 1   7 Manchester, *Visions* p. 341   8 Ibid. p. 346   9 Morgan, *Churchill: Young Man in a Hurry* p. 151   10 Manchester, *Visions* pp. 344–45   11 Randolph Churchill, *Young Statesman* p. 38   12 Manchester, *Visions* p. 346   13 Randolph Churchill, *Young Statesman* p. 47   14 Ibid. p. 48   15 Speech of April 14, 1902, excerpted in Randolph Churchill, *Young Statesman* p. 48   16 Quoted in Randolph Churchill, *Young Statesman* p. 49   17 Ibid. p. 50   18 Manchester, *Visions* p. 352; Ibid. pp. 50, 55   19 Manchester, *Visions* p. 354   20 Ibid. p. 352   21 Roberts, p. 87   22 Randolph Churchill, *Young Statesman* p. 271   23 Roberts, p. 88   24 Randolph Churchill, *Young Statesman* p. 55   25 Ibid. p. 61; Manchester, *Visions* p. 357   26 Manchester, *Visions* p. 353   27 Letter dated May 25, 1903 reprinted in Randolph Churchill, *Young Statesman* p. 58   28 Ibid.   29 Letter dated May 26, 1903, reprinted in Randolph Churchill, *Young Statesman* p. 58   30 Manchester, *Visions* p. 355   31 Ibid. p. 358   32 Randolph Churchill, *Young Statesman* p. 62   33 Ibid. p. 75   34 Manchester, *Visions* p. 358   35 Ibid. p. 359   36 Ibid. p. 361   37 Ibid. p. 356   38 Ibid. p. 363; Roberts, p. 92   39 Manchester, *Visions* p. 365; Roberts, p. 89   40 Randolph Churchill, *Young Statesman* p. 78   41 Manchester, *Visions* p. 364   42 Roberts, p. 94   43 Birkenhead, *Contemporary Personalities* p. 118   44 Manchester, *Alone* p. 598   45 Roberts, p. 98   46 ed. Vincent, *Crawford* p. 83   47 Quoted in Randolph Churchill, *Young Statesman* p. 267–68   48 Quoted in Randolph Churchill, *Statesman* p. 142   49 Randolph Churchill, *Young Statesman* p. 169

Chapter 4

1 Roberts, p. 111   2 Manchester, *Visions* p. 393   3 Roberts, p. 115   4 Manchester, *Visions* p. 393   5 Randolph Churchill, *Young Statesman* p. 253   6 Roberts, p. 119   7 Manchester, *Visions* p. 393   8 Roberts, p. 121   9 Randolph Churchill, *Young Statesman* p. 379   10 Enright, *The Wicked Wit of Winston Churchill* 2011. Available at: https://tinyurl.com/ysua3vbx   11 HC Deb 12 July 1910 Vol 19 cc225   12 Randolph Churchill, *Young Statesman* p. 387   13 Letter from Churchill to Sir E. Grey dated December 20, 1911, reprinted in Randolph Churchill, *Young Statesman* pp. 389–90   14 "Votes for Women! Women Finally Granted the Right to Vote in the UK." Available at: https://winstonchurchill.org/the-life-of-churchill/rising-politician/1910-1919/votes-for-women-2/   15 Randolph Churchill, *Young Statesman* p. 387   16 "Votes for Women! Women Finally Granted the Right to Vote in the UK." Available at: https://winstonchurchill.org/the-life-of-churchill/rising-politician/1910-1919/votes-for-women-2/   17 Ibid.   18 Manchester, *Visions* p. 404   19 Roberts, p. 118; Randolph Churchill, *Young Statesman* p. 269   20 Roberts, p. 129   21 Randolph Churchill, *Young Statesman* p. 271   22 Manchester, *Visions* p. 406   23 Roberts, p. 128   24 Randolph Churchill, *Young Statesman* p. 273   25 ed. James, *Complete Speeches* Vol 1 pp. 1151–52   26 Roberts, p. 130   27 Randolph *Churchill, Young Statesman* p. 314   28 Roberts, p. 133   29 Manchester, *Visions* p. 393, 410   30 Ibid. p. 411   31 Ibid. p. 410   32 ed. Soames, *Speaking* p. 32   33 Manchester, *Visions* p. 408   34 Randolph Churchill, *Young Statesman* p. 253   35 Letter of February 1, 1910, from Asquith to Churchill reprinted in Randolph Churchill, *Young Statesman* p. 310   36 Letter of February 5, 1910, from Churchill to Asquith reprinted in Randolph Churchill, *Young Statesman* p. 310   37 Ibid. pp. 310–11   38 Randolph Churchill, *Young Statesman* p. 326   39 Roberts, p. 138   40 Gilbert, *Other Club* p. 11   41 Blunt, *Diaries* Vol II p. 416   42 Addison, *Churchill on the Home Front* p. 119   43 Roberts, p. 137   44 Manchester, *Visions* p. 415   45 Randolph Churchill, *Young Statesman* p. 373   46 Roberts, p. 143; Gilbert "Churchill and Eugenics." Available at: https://winstonchurchill.org/publications/finest-hour-extras/churchill-and-eugenics-1   47 Roberts, p. 143   48 Randolph Churchill, *Young Statesman* p. 354   49 Letter from the Under-Secretary of State for War to the Mayor of Newport, May 21, 1910, reprinted in Randolph Churchill, *Young Statesman* p. 358   50 Manchester, *Visions* p. 422   51 HC Deb 22 August 1911 Vol 29 cc2327   52 Manchester, *Visions* p. 423   53 Roberts, p. 144   54 HC Deb 30 May 1911 Vol 26 cc1017   55 Randolph Churchill, *Young Statesman* p. 272   56 Manchester, *Visions* p. 419   57 Martin, *Battle* p. 88   58 *Companion Volumes* II/2 p. 1033   59 Ibid.   60 Roberts, p. 148   61 Ibid. 149   62 Manchester, *Visions* p. 419   63 Ibid. p. 420   64 Roberts, p. 150

Chapter 5

1 Manchester, *Visions* p. 426   2 Ibid. pp. 426–27   3 McCarten, pp. 42–43   4 Roberts, p. 157   5 ed. Roskill, *Hankey* I p. 104   6 McCarten, p. 44   7 Ibid.   8 Jackson, *Churchill* p. 128   9 Roberts, p. 186   10 Ibid. p. 189   11 Manchester, *Visions* p. 499   12 Gilbert, *Challenge* pp. 111–12   13 McCarten, p. 45   14 Roberts, p. 191; Best, *Greatness* p. 56   15 *Morning Post*, October 19, 1914   16 Addison, *Churchill: The Unexpected Hero* p. 74   17 ed. Wilson, *Scott* p. 112   18 Brendon, *Churchill* p. 64   19 Manchester, *Visions* p. 515   20 Ibid. p. 517; Churchill, *World Crisis* Vol II p. 91   21 Manchester, *Visions* p. 512   22 Ibid. p. 511   23 Ibid. p. 527   24 Gilbert, *Challenge* p. 547   25 Manchester, *Visions* p. 121   26 Bonham Carter, *Winston Churchill As I Knew Him* p. 361   27 *Companion Volumes* III/1 p. 236   28 Manchester, *Visions* p. 521   29 Ibid. p. 514   30 Ibid. p.515; Roberts, p. 206   31 Strachan, *First World War* p. 113   32 Ibid.   33 *Companion Volumes* III/1

p. 95   34 Roberts, p. 199   35 *Companion Volumes* III/1 pp. 279, 297
36 Manchester, *Visions* p. 515   37 Ibid.   38 Ibid. p. 516   39 Ibid. p. 519
40 *Companion Volumes* III/1 p. 367   41 Gilbert, *Challenge* p. 234   42 Manchester,
Visions pp. 519–20   43 Secretary's Notes of January 8, 1915 War Council
Meeting, CAB 41/1/12   44 Ibid.   45 Parliamentary Archives, House of Lords
LG/C/4/11/3   46 Manchester, *Visions* p. 520   47 Ibid. p. 524   48 Ibid. p. 525
49 Roberts, p. 202   50 Nicholson, *George V* p. 263   51 Roberts, p. 202   52 James,
Failure p. 75   53 Roberts, p. 204   54 Manchester, *Visions* p. 533   55 *Companion
Volumes* III /1 p. 516   56 Manchester, *Visions* p. 530   57 Quoted in Manchester,
Visions p. 531   58 *Companion Volumes* III /1 p. 554–55   59 Churchill, *World Crisis*
Vol 2 p. 85   60 Churchill, *Thoughts* p. 12   61 ed. Coates, *The Dardanelles Commission*
p. 6.   62 Manchester, *Visions* p. 534   63 Roberts, p. 205   64 Churchill, *World Crisis*
Vol 2 p. 242   65 Manchester, *Visions* p. 540   66 Ibid. p. 524   67 Roberts, p. 208   68 Lee,
Journal of Military History, Vol 64, No. 2 April 2000   69 Manchester, *Visions* p. 549
70 Ibid.   71 Ibid.   72 Ibid.   73 Moorehead, *Gallipoli* p. 143   74 Manchester, *Visions*
p. 551   75 Ibid.   76 *Companion Volumes* III/2 pp. 852, 855; Moorehead, *Gallipoli*
p. 165   77 Gilbert, *Challenges* p. 27   78 Manchester, *Visions* p. 549   79 Bell,
Dardanelles p. 157   80 Manchester, *Visions* p. 557   81 Ibid. p. 558   82 Ibid. pp. 557,
558   83 Roberts, p. 214   84 ed. Taylor, *Lloyd George* p. 50   85 *Companion Volumes*
III 2 pp. 914, 915, 920, 922, 923–24   86 Manchester, *Visions* p. 561   87 Ibid.
p. 559   88 ed. Taylor, *Lloyd George* p. 52   89 Ibid.   90 Moorehead, *Gallipoli*
p. 171   91 Manchester, *Visions* p. 561   92 Ibid. p. 564   93 Ibid. p. 565   94 Gilbert,
Never Despair p. 1154   95 *Companion Volumes* III/2 pp. 1100, 1101, 1103   96 Roskill,
Hankey I p. 232   97 See, Manchester, *Visions* p. 570   98 Roskill, *Hankey* Vol I
p. 232   99 Churchill, *World Crisis* 1 p. 252   100 Churchill, *Their Finest Hour*
p. 15   101 Gilbert, *Challenges* p. 473   102 Soames, 'Human Being' p. 3   103 ed.
Soames, *Speaking* p. 121   104 Manchester, *Visions* p. 563   105 Gilbert, *In Search of
Churchill* p. 200–213   106 Moorehead, *Gallipoli* p. 236   107 Roberts, p. 208   108 Ibid.
p. 209   109 Ibid.   110 Ibid.   111 Ibid. p. 231   112 Ibid.   113 Manchester, *Visions*
p. 573   114 ed. Smart, *Bernays* p. 124   115 Roberts, p. 232   116 ed. Soames,
Speaking pp. 114–15   117 Ibid. p. 115   118 Ibid. p. 113   119 Churchill, *Thoughts*
p. 110   120 ed. Soames, *Speaking* p. 169   121 Manchester, *Visions* p. 593   122 Gilbert,
Challenges pp. 657, 658, 672   123 Roberts, p. 239   124 *Companion Volumes* II/3
p. 1418; Roberts, p. 241   125 ed. Soames, *Speaking* p. 119   126 Roberts, p. 237
127 ed. Soames, *Speaking* pp. 137   128 Roberts, p. 237   129 Manchester, *Visions*
p. 590   130 Ibid. p. 591   131 ed. Soames, *Speaking* pp. 163–64   132 HC Deb 07
March 1916 Vol 80 cc1420–30   133 Manchester, *Visions* p. 596   134 Ibid.
135 HC Deb 07 March 1916 Vol 80 cc1430   136 Manchester, *Visions* p. 596
137 Ibid. p. 597   138 Ibid.   139 *Companion Volumes* II/3 p. 1414   140 Roberts,
p. 244   141 Manchester, *Visions* p. 601   142 Ibid.   143 Gilbert, *Challenge*
p. 800   144 Gilbert, *Torment* p. 2   145 Roberts, p. 248   146 ed. Roskill, *Hankey* I
p. 286   147 Roberts, p. 244   148 Manchester, *Visions* p. 614   149 Ibid.   150 Gilbert,
Torment p. 9   151 Manchester, *Visions* p. 614   152 ed. Coates, *The Dardanelles
Commission* p. 291   153 Manchester, *Visions* p. 614   154 Roberts, p. 228   155 Ibid.
p. 248   156 Ibid.   157 Gilbert, *Torment* p. 2   158 HC Deb 19 December 1916 Vol 88
cc1358   159 Manchester, *Visions* p. 611   160 Gilbert, *Challenge* p. 45   161 Manchester,
Visions p. 611   162 Eden, *Reckoning* p. 277   163 Gilbert, *Torment* pp. 17, 21   164 Ibid.
p. 15   165 Ibid.   166 Churchill, *The World Crisis* Vol 3 p. 255   167 Quoted in
Gilbert, *Torment* p. 22   168 *Sunday Times,* June 3, 1917   169 *The Morning Post,* July
18, 1917   170 Manchester, *Visions* p. 617   171 Gilbert, *Torment* p. 35   172 Ibid.
p. 35–36   173 Ibid. p. 37   174 Ibid. p. 53   175 Ibid. p. 42   176 Roberts, p. 254
177 Gilbert, *Torment* p. 54   178 Manchester, *Visions* p. 619   179 ed. Soames, *Speaking*
p. 214   180 Manchester, *Visions* p. 619   181 Ibid. p. 614; HC Deb 20 March 1917
Vol 91 cc1786   182 Manchester, *Visions* p. 628   183 Shirer pp. 52–53   184 Roberts,
p. 266   185 ed. James, *Complete Speeches* Vol III p. 2645

Chapter 6

1 Gilbert, *Torment* pp. 179–80   2 *Companion Volumes* IV/1 p. 479   3 Maynard, 'Torrey Splits' p. 25   4 ed. James, *Complete Speeches* in speeches delivered on 3 January 1920, 8 July 1920, 25 September 1924, 23 October 1924, 24 October 1924; 25 October 1924; 27 October 1924, 28 November 1925, 19 June 1926, and 23 July 1927; See also Roberts, p. 271   5 Roberts, p. 271   6 Ibid.   7 CAB 23/5 598 (19) p. 4 57   8 Roberts, p. 276   9 McCarten, p. 50   10 Buchanan, p. 78   11 Nicholson, *Peacemaking 1919* p. 59   12 Roberts, pp. 262–63   13 Ibid. p. 263   14 Shirer, p. 59   15 HC Deb 03 March 1919 Vol 113 cc83–84   16 Scott Manning, "Buchanan is Wrong." Churchill had No "Starvation Blockade." Available at: https://scottmanning .com/content/churchill-had-no-starvation-blockade/; Scott Manning, "Human Smoke on Churchill and the Blockade of Germany." Available at: https://scottmanning.com/ content/human-smoke-on-churchill-and-the-blockade-of-germany/   17 Nicholson, *Peacemaking 1919* p. 59; Roberts, pp. 262–63   18 Available at: https://www.britannica .com/event/Fourteen-Points   19 Nicholson, *Peacemaking* p. 101   20 Ibid. p. 88   21 Ibid. p. 52   22 Taylor, *Origins* p. 28   23 Nicholson, *Peacemaking* pp. 58, 94   24 Roberts, p. 273   25 Churchill, *World Crisis* Vol IV p. 41   26 Nicholson, *Peacemaking* p. 44   27 Shirer, p. 57   28 Buchanan, p. 85   29 Ibid. p. 107   30 Shirer, p. 59   31 Ibid.   32 Taylor, *Origins* p. 24   33 Available at: https://avalon.law.yale .edu/20th_century/leagcov.asp   34 Kennedy, *Why England Slept* p. 6   35 Ibid. p. 7   36 Ibid. p. 8   37 Available at https://avalon.law.yale.edu/imt/partv.asp 38 Available at: https://history.state.gov/historicaldocuments/frus1919Parisv13/ ch10subch1   39 Kennedy, pp. 10, 12   40 Ibid. p. 12   41 Ibid. p. 13   42 Eberhard, *The Weimar Republic* 2nd ed. p. 7   43 https://encyclopedia.ushmm.org/content/en/ article/the-weimar-republic   44 Ibid.   45 IHS: *B.R. Mitchell, International Historical Statistics* p. 160   46 Eberhard, *The Weimar Republic* 2nd ed. p. 3   47 Available at: https://www.jewishvirtuallibrary.org/background-and-overview-of-the-nazi-party- nsdap   48 Manchester, *Visions* p. 695   49 Ibid.   50 Halifax, p. 89   51 Roberts, p. 284   52 Halifax p. 90   53 Ibid.   54 Manchester, *Visions* p. 714   55 Roberts, p. 267   56 Ibid.   57 Ibid. p. 276   58 Ibid. pp. 276–77   59 Manchester, *Visions* pp. 716, 717   60 Ibid. p. 717   61 CAB 23 /1 29 (20) p. 1 141   62 Roberts, p. 277 63 Ibid.   64 Ibid. p. 278   65 Ibid. p. 287   66 Ibid. p. 288   67 Manchester, *Visions* p. 723   68 Ibid.   69 Ibid.   70 ed. Muller, *Thoughts* p. 214   71 Roberts, p. 288   72 Ibid.   73 Manchester, *Visions* p. 724   74 Roberts, p. 288   75 Churchill, *World Crisis* p. 369   76 Manchester, *Visions* p. 735   77 Roberts, p. 290   78 Ibid. p. 289   79 Roberts, p. 290   80 Gilbert, *Torment* p. 825   81 CAB 23 /1 48 (22) p. 6 7   82 Ibid.   83 Ibid. p.7 8   84 Ibid. p.2 3   85 Gilbert, *Torment* pp. 824, 827   86 CAB 23/1 49 (22) pp. 1–4, 54–58   87 James, *Failure* p. 159   88 CAB 23/1 52 (22) p. 2 108   89 Roberts, p. 290; Gilbert, *Torment* pp. 827–28   90 Gilbert, *Torment* p. 829   91 CAB 23, Draft Conclusions of a Conference of Ministers, September 29, 1922 at 11:30 AM, p. 5 133   92 Gilbert, *Torment* p. 843   93 Ibid. p. 845   94 Roberts, p. 291   95 Gilbert, *Torment* p. 857   96 Ibid. p. 846   97 Ibid. p. 851   98 Roberts, p. 291; Gilbert, *Torment* p. 859   99 Gilbert, *Torment* p. 858   100 Ibid. p. 861   101 Roberts, p. 291   102 Ibid. p. 292   103 Manchester, *Visions* p. 738   104 Roberts, p. 292 105 Manchester, *Visions* p. 745

Chapter 7

1 Manchester, *Visions* p. 746   2 Ibid. p. 747   3 Roberts, p. 303   4 Manchester, *Visions* p. 747   5 Roberts, p. 303   6 Ibid.   7 Manchester, *Visions* p. 747   8 Ibid. p. 748–49   9 Ibid. p. 749   10 Roberts, p. 304   11 Manchester, *Visions* p. 750 12 *Companion Volumes* V pp. 92–3, 96   13 Manchester, *Visions* p. 750 14 Ibid.   15 Ibid.   16 Ibid.   17 ed. Soames, *Speaking* p. 280   18 Gilbert, *Prophet* p. 32   19 Manchester, *Visions* p. 750   20 Quoted in Gilbert, *Prophet* p. 32 21 Manchester, *Visions* p. 751   22 Ibid.   23 James, *Failure* p. 169   24 Roberts, p. 305   25 Gilbert, *Prophet* p. 37   26 Manchester, *Visions* p. 782   27 Ibid. 783   28 Ibid.   29 Ibid. p. 754   30 Ibid.   31 Gilbert, *Prophet* p. 39   32 Ibid. p. 40   33 Ibid. p. 42   34 Ibid. p. 45   35 Roberts, p. 307   36 Colville, p. 345

37 Excerpted in Gilbert, *Prophet* p. 48   38 Churchill, *Nash's and Pall Mall* magazine, "Shall We All Commit Suicide" September 24, 1924   39 Gilbert, *Prophet* p. 52   40 Roberts, p. 307   41 Shirer, p. 62   42 Heiden, *Der Fueher* pp. 131–33   43 Shirer, p. 66   44 Ibid. p. 68   45 Trueman, "The Beer Hall Putsch Of 1923." Available at: https://www.historylearningsite.co.uk/modern-world-history-1918-to-1980/weimar-germany/the-beer-hall-putsch-of-1923/   46 Shirer, p. 68   47 Ibid. pp. 69–70   48 Ibid. p. 70   49 Ibid.   50 Trueman, "The Beer Hall Putsch Of 1923"   51 Ibid.   52 Ibid.   53 Shirer, p. 75   54 The Beer Hall Putsch. Available at: https://alphahistory.com/nazigermany/beer-hall-putsch/   55 Quoted in Shirer, p. 76   56 Roberts, p. 307   57 The Beer Hall Putsch. Available: at: https://alphahistory.com/nazigermany/beer-hall-putsch/

Chapter 8

1 Chartwell Papers at Churchill Archives, Cambridge 2/136/4   2 Gilbert, *Prophet* p. 57   3 Ibid. p. 59   4 Feiling, p. 117   5 Gilbert, *Prophet* p. 59   6 Self, p. 1 05   7 Gilbert, *Prophet* p. 59   8 Ibid. p. 62   9 Ibid. p. 60   10 ed. Middlemas, *Whitehall Diary* I, p. 303   11 *Manchester Guardian* 10/7/24   12 Manchester, *Visions* p. 785   13 Roberts, p. 308; Gilbert, *Prophet* p. 58   14 Feiling, p. 110   15 Roberts, p. 309   16 Manchester, *Visions* p. 787   17 HC Deb 12 November 1936 Vol 317 cc1143   18 *World Jewry* Vol 8–11 Germany: Years of Decision, p. 8   19 *Companion Volumes* V/1 p. 306   20 Roberts, p. 311   21 Manchester, *Visions* p. 790   22 BBC Broadcast "Personality and Power" November 24, 1970, Available at: https://tinyurl.com/36eu2mhf   23 Jackson, *Churchill* p. 189   24 Roberts, p. 310   25 Manchester, *Visions* p. 788   26 Ibid. p. 789   27 Ibid. p. 788; Gilbert, *Prophet* p. 119   28 Gilbert, *Prophet* p. 79   29 CAB 23/1 2 (25) p. 1 158; Roberts, p. 312   30 ed. James, *Churchill Speaks* p. 489   31 *Companion Volumes* V/1 p. 908; *Times* January 21, 1927   32 Quoted in Manchester, *Visions* p. 816   33 Roberts, p. 649   34 Gilbert, *Prophet* pp. 92–93   35 Roberts, p. 313   36 Gilbert, *Prophet* p. 97   37 HC Deb 28 April 1925 Vol 183 cc53   38 Keynes, *Economic Consequences* p. 10   39 Sayers, "The Return to Gold" in *The Gold Standard and Unemployment Policies* p. 88   40 Roberts, p. 314   41 Ibid.   42 Gilbert, *Prophet* p. 147   43 Roberts, p. 318   44 Ibid.   45 Manchester, *Visions* p. 799   46 Gilbert, *Prophet* p. 157   47 Blake, '*Conservative*' p. 8   48 Roberts, p. 320; Gilbert, *Prophet* p. 158   49 Gilbert, *Prophet* p. 162   50 Ibid. p. 159   51 Manchester, *Visions* pp. 800–01   52 Roberts, p. 321   53 Ibid.   54 Manchester, *Visions* p. 804   55 HC Deb 08 December 1926 Vol 200 cc2238   56 Gilbert, *Prophet* p. 181   57 *Companion Volumes* V/1 p. 717   58 Manchester, *Visions* p. 805   59 Ibid. p. 806   60 Ibid. p. 807   61 Gilbert, *Prophet* pp. 219–20   62 Manchester, *Visions* p. 808   63 HC Deb 08 December 1926 Vol 200 cc2243–44   64 Ibid. cc2247   65 Ibid.   66 Ibid. cc2248   67 CAB 23/5 40 (26) pp. 6–7 129–130   68 Gilbert, *Prophet* p. 124   69 Roberts, p. 310   70 Kennedy, p. 15   71 Ibid.   72 Ibid.   73 Kolb, *The Weimar Republic,* 2nd ed. p. 53   74 Ibid. p. 59   75 Clough, Moodie, and Moodie, *Economic History of Europe;* Twentieth Century, p. 135. Available at: https://link.springer.com/chapter/10.1007/978-1-349-00298-6_19   76 Ibid.   77 Kolb, pp. 59–60   78 Ibid. p. 60   79 Available at: https://encyclopedia.ushmm.org/content/en/article/adolf-hitler-1924–1930   80 Ibid.

Chapter 9

1 Article VIII of the Covenant of the League of Nations   2 Kennedy, p. 18   3 Ibid. p. 19   4 Taylor, *Origins* p. 33   5 Kennedy, p. 19   6 Buchanan, p. 123   7 James, *Failure* p. 182   8 Gilbert, *Prophet* p. 409   9 Ibid.   10 Ibid.   11 HC Deb 23 March 1933 Vol 276 cc540   12 Ibid. cc548   13 Ibid. cc540   14 Kennedy, p. 16   15 Manchester, *Visions* p. 820   16 Gilbert, *Prophet* p. 313   17 Ibid. p. 335   18 Manchester, *Visions* p. 820   19 Quoted in Manchester, *Visions* p. 820   20 Ibid. p. 821   21 Gilbert, *Prophet* pp. 314, 321   22 Manchester, *Visions* p. 821   23 Roberts, p. 335   24 Gilbert, *Prophet* pp. 321, 322   25 Manchester, *Visions* p. 822   26 Manchester, *Alone* p. 262   27 Buchanan, p. 358; Manchester, *Alone* p. 103   28 Manchester, *Alone*

p. 267   29 Ibid. p. 268   30 Ibid. p. 83   31 Gilbert, *Prophet* p. 335   32 Ibid.
pp. 335–36   33 *Companion Volumes* V/2 pp. 61–62; Roberts, p. 337; Gilbert, *Prophet*
p. 344   34 Roberts, p. 339   35 Ibid. p. 340   36 Manchester, *Visions* p. 839   37 Gilbert,
Prophet p. 352   38 Ibid.   39 Ibid. p. 353   40 Manchester, *Visions* p. 839   41 McCarten,
p. 56   42 Gilbert, *Prophet* p. 354   43 Manchester, *Visions* p. 840   44 Ibid. p. 845
45 HC Deb 07 November 1929 Vol 231 cc1317–18   46 Gilbert, *Prophet* p. 355   47 Ibid.
48 Manchester, *Visions* p. 850   49 Quoted in Gilbert, *Prophet* pp. 356–57   50 Olson,
Troublesome Young Men p. 76; *Daily Mail* November 11, 1929   51 Gilbert, *Prophet*
p. 357   52 Halifax, p. 145   53 Gilbert, *Prophet* p. 357   54 Roberts, p. 342
55 Manchester, *Visions* p. 841; Manchester, *Alone,* p. 158   56 Manchester, *Visions*
p. 842   57 Ibid. p. 841   58 James, *Failure* p. 222   59 Roberts, p. 342   60 Kennedy,
p. 16   61 Gilbert, *Prophet* p. 367   62 Roberts, p. 343   63 Gilbert, *Prophet* p. 368
64 Ibid. p. 367   65 Ibid. p. 368   66 Ibid. p. 375   67 Ibid.   68 Ibid. p. 376; Manchester,
Visions p. 848   69 ed. Ball, *Conservative Politics* p. 366   70 Shirer, p. 137   71 Quoted
in Manchester, *Alone* p. 82; Roberts, p. 345   72 Kennedy, p. 27   73 Manchester, *Visions*
p. 851   74 Ibid.   75 HC Deb 26 January 1931 Vol 247 cc689–761   76 Buchanan,
p. 355   77 Gilbert, *Prophet* p. 379   78 Halifax, p. 145   79 Ibid.   80 Gilbert, *Prophet*
p. 390; Speech in the House by Major Pole HC Deb 12 March 1931 Vol 249 cc1485
81 Olson, p. 75; Manchester, *Alone* p. 84   82 Gilbert, *Prophet* p. 413   83 Ibid.
p. 418   84 HC Deb 03 December 1931 Vol 260 cc1287   85 Gilbert, *Prophet*
p. 419   86 Ibid. p. 420   87 Tolppanen, 'Accidental' p. 12   88 *Daily Mail* January 5,
1932   89 Tolppanen, 'Accidental' p. 12   90 'European Diplomacy Astounded'
The Palestine Bulletin April 13, 1931. Available at: https://tinyurl.com/3jvyj25j
91 Manchester, *Alone* p. 85   92 Halifax, p. 181   93 War Memoirs, April 26, 1948,
Life Magazine Vol 24, No. 17 p. 48   94 Gilbert, *Prophet* p. 413   95 Ibid. p. 414   96 HC
Deb 15 September 1931 Vol 256 cc705   97 Gilbert, *Prophet* p. 414   98 Manchester,
Visions p. 859   99 Gardner, p. 2   100 Kennedy, p. 33   101 Shirer, p. 152
102 Ibid. p. 150   103 Kennedy, p. 29   104 Ibid. p. 31   105 Ibid. p. 32   106 Ibid.
p. 20   107 Ibid.   108 Ibid. pp. 20–21   109 Manchester, *Alone* p. 3   110 Ibid.
pp. 84–85   111 Ibid. p. 74   112 Ibid. p. 75   113 Ibid. p. 117   114 Shirer, p. 157
115 Taylor, Origins p. 44   116 Ibid. p. 67   117 Manchester, *Alone* p. 67   118 Ibid.
119 Shirer, p. 164   120 Ibid. p. 163   121 Manchester, *Alone* p. 62   122 Ibid.
123 Shirer, p. 167   124 Ibid.   125 Ibid. p. 168   126 Ibid. p. 176   127 Ibid.   128 Ibid.
p. 177   129 ed. James, *Complete Speeches* Vol V pp. 5197–5206   130 HC Deb 10
November 1932 Vol 270 cc633   131 Ibid.   132 Manchester, *Alone* p. 95   133 HC Deb 23
November 1932 Vol 272 cc83   134 Ibid. cc81   135 Shirer, p. 182   136 Ibid.   137 Ibid.
p. 184   138 Manchester, *Alone* p. 64   139 Shirer, p. 184   140 Ibid. p. 185   141 Ibid.
p. 189   142 CAB 23/3 9 (33) pp. 4, 5 139, 140   143 Ibid. pp. 5–6 140–41   144 Ibid. p.6
141   145 Gilbert, *Prophet* p. 457   146 Shirer, p. 192   147 Ibid.   148 Available at:
https://ghdi.ghi-dc.org/sub_document.cfm?document_id=23   149 Shirer, pp. 194–95
150 Ibid. p. 194   151 Ibid. p. 195   152 Ibid. p. 196   153 Ibid.   154 Ibid.
p. 199   155 Ibid.   156 HC Deb 23 March 1933 Vol 276 cc543   157 Ibid.   158 Ibid.
159 HC Deb 13 April 1933 Vol 276 cc2793   160 HC Deb 23 March 1933 Vol 276
cc543   161 Ibid.   162 Manchester, *Alone* p. 98   163 Ibid. p. 99   164 Roberts,
p. 367   165 HC Deb 13 April 1933 Vol 276 cc2792   166 Kennedy, p. 55   167 Ibid.
168 Ibid. p. 54   169 Ibid. pp. 51–52   170 Manchester, *Alone* p. 112   171 Kennedy,
p. 68   172 Ibid.   173 Faber, p. 189 et seq.   174 Ibid. 191   175 Ibid. 193
176 Manchester, *Alone* p. 126   177 Ibid. p. 110   178 Kennedy, p. 55   179 Todman,
Into Battle p. 67   180 Roberts, p. 376   181 Kennedy, p. 84   182 HC Deb 07 February
1934 Vol 285 cc1193   183 Ibid. cc1197   184 Ibid.   185 HC Deb 07 February 1934
Vol 285 cc1199   186 Roberts, p. 377   187 Kennedy, p. 62   188 HC Deb 08 March 1934
Vol 286 cc2028   189 Ibid. cc2030   190 Gilbert, *Prophet* p. 507   191 HC Deb 08
March 1934 Vol 286 cc2078   192 Ibid. cc2064   193 Ibid. cc2065; Gilbert, *Prophet*
p. 508   194 CAB 23/ 3 10 (34) p.15 292   195 Shirer, p. 205   196 Ibid. p. 208
197 Ibid. p. 206   198 Ibid. p. 207   199 Ibid. p. 206   200 Ibid. p. 224   201 Ibid.
p. 221   202 Ibid.   203 Ibid. p. 222   204 Ibid. pp. 223, 224   205 Ibid. p. 219   206 Law
Regarding Measures of State Self-Defence, issued on July 3, 1934   207 ed. James,
Complete Speeches Vol V p. 5377   208 Roberts, p. 379   209 Todman, *Into Battle*

p. 68   210 ed. Gorodetsky, *Maisky Diaries* p. 28   211 Roberts, p. 380   212 ed. Soames, *Speaking* p. 360   213 Gilbert, *Prophet* p. 565   214 Hitler, *Mein Kampf,* Complete and Unabridged Fully Annotated (New York: Reynal & Hitchcock, 1939) p. 3   215 Churchill, *The Gathering Storm* p. 206   216 Available at: http://der-fuehrer.org/reden/english/ 35-05-21.htm; *New York Times* May 23, 1935   217 Available at: https://avalon.law .yale.edu/wwii/ylbk001.asp   218 *New York Times,* July 12, 1936; Taylor, *Origins* p. 139   219 Taylor, *Origins* p. 139   220 HC Deb 19 July 1934 Vol 292 cc1275 221 Kennedy p. 69   222 HC Deb 19 July 1934 Vol 292 cc1273–74   223 Ibid. cc1274– 75   224 Ibid. cc2366   225 Ibid. cc2325   226 Ibid.   227 Kennedy, pp. 72–73   228 HC Deb 30 July 1934 Vol 292 cc2331   229 Ibid. cc2335   230 CAB 24/257 C.P. 265 (34) pp. 6–7 212–213; CAB 23 /2 42 (34) p. 2–3 233–34   231 CAB 23/2 42 (34) p. 6 237   232 Ibid. pp. 6–8 237–239   233 Ibid. pp. 8–9 239–40   234 HC Deb 28 November 1934 Vol 295 cc857–983   235 Manchester, *Alone* p. 266   236 Ibid. p. 265   237 HC Deb 28 November 1934 Vol 295 cc866   238 Ibid.   239 Manchester, *Alone* p. 123   240 HC Deb 28 November 1934 Vol 295 cc875   241 Ibid. cc876   242 Ibid. cc882–83   243 Ibid. cc878   244 Ibid.   245 Kennedy, p. 66   246 Manchester, *Alone* p. 124   247 Ibid. p. 140 248 Kennedy, p. 100   249 Ibid. p. 102   250 Ibid. pp. 102–03   251 Ibid. p. 95 252 Buchanan, p. 149   253 Ibid.   254 HC Deb 19 March 1935 Vol 299 cc1015 255 Ibid.; Kennedy, p. 91   256 Gilbert, *Prophet* p. 625   257 Kennedy p. 81   258 HC Deb 19 March 1935 Vol 299 cc1053   259 Ibid. cc1055   260 HC Deb 19 March 1935 Vol 299 cc1055   261 Ibid. cc1056   262 Ibid. cc1057   263 Manchester, *Alone* p. 138 264 Ibid.   265 HC Deb 22 May 1935 Vol 302 cc367   266 Brett Holman, "The Air Panic Of 1935: British Press Opinion Between Disarmament And Rearmament," *Journal of Contemporary History,* Vol 46, Issue 2, April 2011, pp. 288–307; Kennedy, p. 98 267 HC Deb 22 May 1935 Vol 367 cc360   268 Ibid. cc368   269 Kennedy, p. 103 270 HC Deb 24 October 1935 Vol 305 cc357   271 Ibid.   272 Kennedy, p. 104   273 HC Deb 12 November 1936 Vol 317 cc1104   274 Ibid. cc1145   275 CAB 23/3 51 (35) p. 4 363   276 CAB 23/3 51 (35) p. 6 365   277 Roberts, p. 390   278 Ibid.   279 *Companion Volumes* V/2 pp. 1169–70   280 Gilbert, *Prophet* p. 618   281 Ibid. p. 619   282 Ibid. p. 618   283 Olson, p. 76   284 Manchester, *Visions* p. 157   285 Gilbert, *Prophet* p. 619   286 CAB 23/2 33 (35) p. 3 5   287 Ibid. p. 2 4   288 Buchanan, p. 146 289 Manchester, *Alone* p. 143   290 ed. Soames, *Speaking* p. 347   291 Roberts, p. 391 292 Roberts, p. 391   293 Gilbert, *Prophet* p. 663   294 Churchill papers, 4/84–5 295 CAB 23/4 33 (35) p. 7 9   296 Ibid. p. 2 53   297 Ibid. p. 3 53   298 Conference Of Ministers, To Discuss Italo-Abyssinian Dispute, 21 August 1935, Conclusions of Meetings of the Cabinet Vol XLIX p. 14 163   299 CAB 23/6 45(35) p. 11 244 300 Manchester, *Alone* p. 160   301 CAB 23/2 50 (35) p. 5 337   302 Ibid. pp. 2–3 334–35   303 Ibid. p. 5 337   304 Ibid. p. 14 346   305 Ibid. p. 5 337   306 Ibid. p. 17 349   307 Ristuccia, "1935 Sanctions Against Italy: Would Coal And Crude Oil Have Made a Difference?" p. 35 Available at: https://www.nuffield.ox.ac.uk/economics/ history/paper14/14paper.pdf   308 CAB 23/2 50 (35) pp. 17–18 349–50   309 Ibid. p. 1 392   310 Ibid. p. 5 396   311 Ibid. p. 5 414   312 Roberts, p. 392   313 HC Deb 24 October 1935 Vol 305 cc368   314 Ibid. cc362   315 CAB 24/260 CP (36) 53 p. 1 314, February 22, 1936   316 CAB 23/ 5 11 (36) p. 13 132   317 Manchester, *Alone* p. 151   318 McCarten, p. 59   319 May, *Strange Victory* p. 173   320 Langworth, 'How Churchill Saw Baldwin' *Finest Hour,* No. 101 Winter 1998–99, p. 29   321 Gilbert, *Churchill a Life* p. 862   322 Langworth, 'How Churchill Saw Baldwin' *Finest Hour,* No. 101 Winter 1998–99, p. 29   323 Ibid. pp. 119–20   324 CAB 23 /2 7 (36) p. 5 107   325 Manchester, *Alone* p. 223   326 Ibid. p. 224   327 Williams, *People's King* passim   328 Manchester, *Alone* p. 222–23329 Ibid. p. 219   330 ed. Hart—Davis, *King's Counselor* p. 415   331 Freeman, "The Uncrowned King: Edward VIII" *Finest Hour* No. 184 (2nd quarter 2019) p. 21   332 Ibid.   333 Manchester, *Alone* p. 229   334 Ibid. p. 227   335 Amery, *Amery Diary,* December 7, 1936, p. 432   336 Winterton, *Orders of The Day* p. 223   337 *The Times,* December 8, 1936   338 Freeman, "The Uncrowned King" p. 21   339 Manchester, *Alone* p. 232   340 Available at: https://www.historyplace .com/speeches/edward.htm   341 Langworth, "Churchill and the Rhineland" *Finest Hour* No. 141, Winter 2008–09 p. 16   342 Kershaw, *Nemesis,* p. xxxv   343 Langworth, "Churchill in the Rhineland" p. 16; Roberts pp. 397–98   344 ed. James, *Complete*

Speeches Vol VI p. 5699   345 HC Deb 26 March 1936 Vol 310 cc1524   346 Shirer, p. 291   347 Langworth, "Churchill and the Rhineland" p. 16   348 Halifax p. 200   349 Buchanan p. 1 70   350 HC Deb 26 March 1936 Vol 310 cc1444   351 Ibid. cc1446   352 Ibid. cc1529   353 Ibid.   354 Ibid.; Gilbert, *Prophet* p. 718   355 See, discussion in the British Cabinet meeting of March 20, 1935 attached to conclusions CAB 23/1 16 (35) p. 5 243   356 HC Deb 06 April 1936 Vol 310 cc2485   357 Ibid.   358 Langworth, "Churchill and the Rhineland" pp. 20–21   359 ed. Nicholson, *Nicholson Diaries* Vol II p. 266 2   360 Roberts, p. 406   361 Ibid. pp. 420–21   362 Sir Maurice Hankey's notes of dinner with Churchill on April 19, 1936, quoted in Gilbert, *Prophet* p. 723; Roberts, p. 407   363 Churchill Archives at Churchill College Cambridge, Chartwell and at Churchill Archives Cambridge CHAR 2/260/93 Letter from WSC to Ivan Maisky, Soviet Ambassador to Britain   364 Kennedy, p. 118   365 Ibid. p. 120   366 Ibid. p. 119   367 Ibid. p. 126   368 Ibid. p. 127   369 Ibid.   370 Kennedy, p. 115

Chapter 10

1 Kennedy p. 149   2 Ibid.   3 Ibid. p. 155–6   4 Manchester, *Alone* p. 239   5 Roberts, p. 417; Ibid. p. 243   6 Manchester, *Alone* p. 243   7 Lukacs, *Five Days* p. 50   8 Buchanan, p. 225   9 Kennedy, p. 156   10 Lukacs, *Five Days* p. 50.   11 Rock, *Appeasement on Trial* p. 8   12 Kennedy, p. 157   13 Manchester, *Alone* p. 264   14 Ibid.   15 Ibid.   16 Ibid.   17 Ibid.   18 Feiling, p. 329   19 Gilbert, *A Life* p. 581   20 McCarten, p. 60; Churchill, *The Gathering Storm* p. 249   21 McCarten, p. 60   22 Ministry of Foreign Affairs of the USSR, "Documents and Materials relating to the eve of the Second World War," Vol I, November 1937–1938 p. 20   23 Taylor, *Origins* p. 137   24 Ministry of Foreign Affairs of the USSR, "Documents and Materials relating to the eve of the Second World War," Vol I, November 1937–1938 p. 19   25 McCarten, p. 94   26 Buchanan, p 187   27 Lidell Hart, *History of The Second World War* p. 8; Henderson, p. 96   28 Lukacs, *Five Days* p. 62   29 CAB 23/4 11 (38) p. 5 326   30 Summary of The Discussion Referred to in the Note at the End of Conclusion CAB 23/3 43 (37) p. 2 166   31 Ibid.   32 Ibid. p. 3 167   33 McCarten, p. 60   34 Quoted in Feiling p. 333   35 Manchester, *Alone* p. 241   36 HC Deb 24 March 1938 Vol 333 cc1410   37 Kennedy, p. 181   38 Manchester, *Alone* p. 244   39 Ibid.   40 Ibid. p. 245   41 Taylor, *Origins* p. 135   42 Kennedy, pp. 156, 167–68   43 Ibid. p. 172   44 Taylor, *Origins* p. 134   45 Roberts, *The Holy Fox*, p. 67   46 Manchester, *Alone* p. 99   47 Speech of March 17, 1939. Available at: https://avalon.law.yale.edu/wwii/blbk09 .asp   48 Manchester, *Alone* p 287   49 HC Deb 22 February 1938 Vol 332 cc246–47; HC Deb 23 March 1933 Vol 276 cc540   50 Lukacs, *Five Days* p. 57   51 Ibid.   52 Gilbert, *The Roots Of Appeasement,* p. 209   53 Manchester, *Alone* p. 255   54 Ibid.   55 Taylor, *English History* p. 511   56 John Stuart Mill, Inaugural Address Delivered to the University of St Andrews, February 1, 1867   57 Kennedy p. 167   58 Churchill, *The Gathering Storm* p. 234   59 Ibid.   60 Ball, *Post-War German-Austrian Relations* pp. 11–15   61 Stackelberg, *Hitler's Germany: Origins* pp. 161–62   62 Ball, *Post-war German-Austrian Relations* pp. 18–19; Guibernau, *The Identity of Nations,* pp. 70–75   63 Buchanan, p. 183   64 Ibid.   65 Ibid.   66 Lamb, *Mussolini As Diplomat* p. 91   67 Buchanan, p. 184   68 Secret addendum to CAB 23/1 1 (38) p. 2 7; Manchester, *Alone* p. 248   69 Secret addendum to CAB 23/1 1 (38) p. 2 7   70 Ibid.; Manchester, *Alone* p. 248   71 Secret addendum to CAB 23/1 1 (38) p. 1 6   72 Ibid. p. 3 8; Manchester, *Alone* p. 248   73 Churchill, *The Gathering Storm* p. 254–55   74 CAB 24 275 (38) 236 (CP 54 (38)); CAB 24 275 (38) 238 236 (CP 55 (38))   75 CAB 23/4 11 (38) p. 4 325   76 Ibid.; Self p. 293   77 CAB 24 275 (38) 255) (CP 58 (38))   78 CAB 23/4 11 (38) p. 4 325, March 9, 1938   79 Ibid. p. 5 326   80 Churchill, *The Gathering Storm* p. 259   81 Ibid. p. 223   82 Ibid.   83 Ibid. p. 232; CAB 23/1 7 (38) p. 3 226   84 Kennedy, p.166   85 Ibid.   86 Ibid.   87 Ibid.   88 Churchill, *The Gathering Storm* p. 262; Manchester, p. 247   89 Taylor, *Origins* p. 142   90 Shirer, p. 325; Manchester, *Alone* p. 247; Taylor, *Origins* p. 143   91 CAB 23/2 5 (38)p. 2 110   92 Ibid.   93 Schuschnigg, *Austrian Requiem* pp. 16–17   94 Lukacs, *The Last European War* p. 12.   95 Churchill, *The Gathering Storm* p. 263; Shirer, p. 331   96 Churchill, *The Gathering Storm* p. 263; Manchester, *Alone* p. 248   97 Lukacs, *The Last European War* p. 12   98 Taylor,

Origins p. 143   99 Shirer, p. 331   100 Ibid. p. 344   101 Available at: http://der-fuehrer
.org/reden/english/38-02-20.htm   102 Ibid.   103 Shirer, p. 333   104 Taylor, *Origins*
p. 144   105 Churchill, *The Gathering Storm* p. 240   106 Ibid. p.227; Rose, *The
Resignation Of Anthony Eden* p. 915   107 CAB 23/1 7 (38) p. 1 224   108 Carley,
p. 88   109 Shirer, p. 344   110 CAB 23/1 7 (38) p. 1 224   111 Kennedy, p. 167
112 Ibid.   113 HC Deb 24 March 1938 Vol 333 cc1400; Taylor, *Origins* p. 134
114 *Guardian* February 23, 1938   115 HC Deb 21 February 1938 Vol 332 cc49
116 Ibid. cc248   117 Ibid.   118 Rose, *The Resignation Of Anthony Eden* pp. 911,
930   119 Churchill, *The Gathering Storm* p. 267   120 Shirer, pp. 334–35   121 *New
York Times* February 25, 1938   122 Shirer, p. 335; Churchill, *The Gathering Storm*
p. 267; Taylor, *Origins* p. 146   123 Shirer, p. 335   124 Manchester, *Alone* p. 273;
Churchill, *The Gathering Storm* p. 267   125 Manchester, *Alone* p. 272   126 Churchill
Papers 2/328   127 Shirer p. 350   128 Ibid. p. 335   129 Taylor, *Origins* p. 147
130 Shirer, p. 337   131 Churchill, *The Gathering Storm* p. 268   132 Manchester,
Alone p. 274   133 Ibid.   134 See, Shirer, p. 338   135 Ibid.   136 Churchill, *The
Gathering Storm* p. 268   137 CAB 23/1 12 (30) p. 2 346   138 Ibid.   139 Churchill,
The Gathering Storm p. 268   140 Taylor, *Origins* p. 148   141 *Documents On German
Foreign Policy (DGFP)*, Vol I p. 578   142 *Nuremberg Documents on Nazi Conspiracy*,
Vol 1 pp. 501–2; HC Deb 14 March 1938 Vol 333 cc48   143 Taylor, *Origins* p. 148;
See, Shirer, p. 339   144 Taylor, *Origins* p. 148   145 Shirer p. 345   146 Schuschnigg,
Ein Requiem in Rot-Weis-Rot, pp 102–3; Nuremberg Documents Vol I pp. 138–39;
Shirer, pp. 335, 336, 343   147 Manchester, *Alone* p. 274   148 Buchanan p. 195
149 Taylor, *Origins* p. 148   150 Shirer, p. 347   151 Taylor, *Origins* p. 149; Churchill,
The Gathering Storm p. 271; Shirer, p. 347   152 Shirer, p. 350; Manchester, *Alone*
pp. 280–81   153 Manchester, *Alone* pp. 278–79; Taylor, *Origins* p. 149; Shirer, p. 350
154 Taylor, *Origins* p. 150   155 *DGFP* Vol I p. 263; Shirer, p. 344   156 CAB 23/1
12 (38) p. 1 345   157 Ibid. p. 5 349   158 Ibid.   159 Gilbert, *Prophet* p. 911
160 Manchester, *Alone* p. 274; Ripsman and Levy "Wishful Thinking or Buying Time?
The Logic of British Appeasement in the 1930s" 33 *MIT Journal: International Security*
pp. 148–181   161 CAB 23/12 5 (38) pp. 52, 56 160, 164   162 Ibid. p. 54 162   163 ed.
Winkler *British Labour Seeks A Foreign Policy*, Chapter 9   164 HC Deb 14 March
1938 Vol 333 cc52   165 Shirer, p. 353   166 Manchester, *Alone* pp. 280–81   167 CAB
23/1 12 (38) p. 3 347   168 Ibid. p. 6 359   169 ed. Dilks *Cadogan Diaries* p. 62
3/12/38   170 HC Deb 14 March 1938 Vol 333 cc97–98   171 Ibid. cc95   172 HC Deb
14 March 1938 Vol 333 cc97; Churchill, *The Gathering Storm* p. 273   173 CAB 23/1
12 (38) p. 7 351   174 HC Deb 14 March 1938 Vol 333 cc99   175 Reprinted in Feiling,
pp. 347–348   176 Ibid.   177 See CAB 23/1 15 (38) p. 1 32   178 CAB 23/1 15 (38) p. 1
32   179 Ibid. p. 3 34   180 Ibid. p. 7 38   181 CAB 23/1 15 (38). p. 7 38   182 Ibid.
p. 10 41   183 Ibid. p. 7 38   184 Ibid. p. 3 34   185 HC Deb 24 March 1938 Vol 333
cc1407   186 Ibid.   187 Churchill, *The Gathering Storm* p. 274   188 Ministry of Foreign
Affairs of the USSR, "Documents and Materials relating to the eve of the Second World
War," Vol I, November 1937–1938 p. 91; *DBFP* (Documents on British Foreign Policy)
Series 3, Vol I No. 107   189 Churchill, *The Gathering Storm* p. 274   190 Manchester,
Alone p. 286   191 Churchill, *The Gathering Storm* p. 276   192 HC Deb 24 March 1938
Vol 333 cc1401   193 Ibid. cc1400   194 Ibid. cc1402   195 HC Deb 24 March 1938
Vol 333 cc1405, 1406   196 Ibid. cc1406

Chapter 11

1 Manchester, *Alone* p. 289   2 Kennedy, p. 181   3 Shirer, p. 357   4 Taylor, *Origins*
p. 161   5 Ibid. p. 162   6 Faber, p. 169   7 Manchester, *Alone* p. 289   8 Shirer,
p. 358   9 Buchanan, p. 215   10 Ibid.   11 CAB 23 /1 37 (39) p.10 44   12 Ibid.;
Buchanan, p. 215   13 Adamthwaite, *The Making of the Second World War* p. 189
14 Ibid.   15 Buchanan, p. 215   16 Ibid. p. 219   17 Shirer, p. 422   18 Buchanan,
p. 210   19 Taylor, *Origins* p. 189   20 Buchanan, p. 215   21 Carlton, *Anthony Eden*,
p. 137; Taylor, *Origins* p. 168   22 Gedye, *Fallen Bastions* p. 410; Manchester, *Alone*
p. 316   23 Faber, p. 176; Shirer, p. 376; See, HC Deb 21 June 1938 Vol 337 cc955
24 Shirer, p. 376.   25 Faber, p. 257   26 *DGFP* series D, Vol II No. 436 p. 706   27 Shirer,

p. 376   28 ed. Self, Vol 4 p. 394, Chamberlain to his sister Ida, September 19, 1938; Feiling, p. 367   29 *DGFP* series D, Vol II No. 436 p. 706   30 Smith, *The Dark Summer* p. 207   31 Faber, p. 173   32 BBC Radio Broadcast September 27, 1938. Available at: https://encyc.org/wiki/Chamberlain's_Radio_Broadcast,_September_27,_1938   33 HC Deb, 24 March 1939 5s, 333, Col 1393 413   34 CAB 23 /1 15 (38) p. 2 33 March 28, 1938   35 Self, p. 295   36 CAB 23/1 15 (38) p. 5 36   37 CAB 23/1 15 (38) p. 3 34 38 Crowson, *Facing Fascism* pp. 90–92; Gallup, *Gallup International Opinion Polls,* p. 8   39 CAB 23/1 15 (38) p. 6 37   40 Ibid. p. 1 32   41 Ibid. p. 9 40   42 "Visit of French Ministers to London," meeting summary, CAB 24/276 (38) p. 303 239 CP 109 (38), May 3, 1938   43 ed. Self, Vol 4 pp. 443–44, Chamberlain to his sister Ida, March 20, April 16, 1938; Henderson, *A Failed Mission* pp. 128–29; CAB 23/1 15 (38) p. 3 34   44 Self p. 303   45 CAB 24/ 109 CP (38) p. 34 306   46 CAB 23/6 24 (38) p. 6 297 47 Kennedy, p. 186   48 Taylor, *Origins* p. 167; Buchanan, pp. 219–20   49 Buchanan, p. 216.   50 Faber, p. 181; Manchester, *Alone* p. 319; Shirer, p. 363   51 Faber, p. 180; Manchester, *Alone* p. 320; Taylor, *Origins* p. 165; Shirer, p. 361   52 Shirer, p. 361 53 Taylor, *Origins* p. 365   54 Shirer, p. 364   55 *DGFP* Series D, Vol II No. 109 pp. 322–23   56 Buchanan, p. 216   57 E.g., Ambassador Henderson's conversation with Foreign Minister Ribbentrop described in Faber p. 181; Buchanan, pp. 216–17 58 *DBFP* Series 3, Vol I No. 264 p. 341, Halifax to Henderson, May 22, 1938   59 Self p. 304   60 Buchanan, p. 217   61 Self, p. 306   62 Shirer, p. 364   63 Ibid.   64 Buchanan, p. 217   65 Tansill, *Back Door to War* p. 397   66 Faber, pp. 184–85   67 Manchester, *Alone* p. 321   68 Faber, p. 185–86   69 Kershaw, *Hitler* p. 101   70 Faber, p. 185 71 e.g., *DBFP* Series 3, Vol I No. 316 p. 380, Henderson to Halifax, May 25, 1938; Buchanan, p. 218   72 Manchester, *Alone* p. 320   73 Ibid.; Bullock, *Hitler* p. 447 74 Buchanan, p. 219   75 Turk, *The History of Germany* p. 123   76 Manchester, *Alone* p. 331   77 CAB 23/1 36 (38) pp. 4–10 289–295   78 Ibid. p. 7 292   79 Ibid. pp. 8, 10, 293, 295   80 Kershaw, *Hitler* pp. 96, 101   81 CAB 23/1 36 (38) p. 29 314   82 Faber, p. 233   83 *Daily Express,* September 1, 1938   84 ed. Self, Vol 4 p. 342, Chamberlain to his sister Ida, September 3, 1938   85 Taylor, *Origins* p. 167   86 CAB 23/1 37 (38) p. 2 4; Manchester, *Alone* p. 322   87 Manchester, *Alone* p. 322; Faber p. 243   88 Faber, p. 243   89 Wheeler–Bennett, *The Nemesis Of Power* p. 418   90 *The Times* September 7, 1938   91 Manchester, *Alone* p. 331   92 Faber, p. 192   93 *DBFP* Series 3, Vol II p. 271, n.1   94 Faber, p. 194   95 *DGFP* Series D, Vol II No. 443 pp. 722–23, Kordt to German Foreign Ministry 8 September 1938   96 *The History Of The Times* p. 934   97 Laffan, "The Crisis Over Czechoslovakia, January to September 1938" *Survey of International Affairs,* Vol II p. 302   98 *DBFP* Series 3, Vol II Appendix III, "Text of The Prime Minister's Statement to The Press," September 11, 1938 p. 681   99 Hitler and Domarus, *The Essential Hitler* p. 626   100 Ibid. p. 627   101 Ibid.   102 Ibid.   103 Ibid.   104 Ibid.   105 CAB 23/1 37 (38) p. 7 9   106 Ibid. p. 6 8   107 Ibid. p. 7 9   108 Ibid. p. 23 25   109 CAB 23/1 38 (38) p. 4 37   110 *DBFP* Series 3, Vol II No. 862, p. 314 Halifax to Henderson, September 13, 1938   111 Self, p. 310   112 Ibid.   113 CAB 23/1 38 (38) p. 8 41   114 Ibid. p. 1–2, 34–56   115 Faber p. 273   116 CAB 23/1 38 (38) p. 5 38 117 Ibid.   118 Lord Swinton, *60 Years of Power* pp. 111–14   119 ed. Norwich, *Duff Cooper Diaries,* September 14, 1938 p. 259   120 CAB 23/1 38 (38) pp. 6–9 39–42, September 14, 1938   121 Ibid. pp. 20–25 53–58   122 Ibid. p. 14 47, Statement of the Secretary for War, Leslie Hore-Belisha   123 Ibid. pp. 25, 27, 58, 60   124 Ibid. p. 25 58   125 See, CAB 23/1 39 (38) p. 23 86, September 17, 1938   126 Madge & Harrison, *Britain by Mass-Observation* p. 65   127 *DBFP* Series 3, Vol II No. 890 p. 334. Henderson to Halifax, September 15, 1938   128 ed. Harvey, *The Diplomatic Diaries of Oliver Harvey* p. 180   129 Self, p. 312   130 Faber, p. 283   131 Shirer, p. 385   132 Faber, p. 282   133 *DBFP* Series 3, Vol II No. 849 Henderson to Halifax, September 13, 1938, p. 306   134 Ibid.   135 ed. Dilks, *Cadogan Diaries* p. 108   136 Churchill College (Cambridge), *The Diary of Sir Thomas Inskip,* September 14, 1938, p. 1   137 Manchester, *Alone* p. 420   138 Self p. 312   139 Spitzy, *How We Squandered The Reich* p. 239   140 Quoted in Faber, p. 277   141 Buchanan, p. 228   142 Manchester, *Alone* p. 335   143 Taylor, *Origins* p. 170   144 Churchill, *The Gathering Storm* p. 299   145 Lukacs, *The Last European War* p. 15   146 Taylor, *Origins* p. 170   147 Manchester, *Alone* p. 322   148 Shirer, pp. 393–94   149 Churchill, *The*

Gathering Storm p. 299   150 Ibid. p. 300   151 See, *DBFP* Series D, Vol II No. 489
p. 801, Henlein to Hitler September 15, 1938   152 Churchill, *The Gathering Storm*
p. 300   153 Faber, pp. 291–92   154 Schmidt, *Hitler's Interpreter* p. 93   155 HC
Deb 28 September 1938 Vol 339 cc14; Kershaw, *Hitler* p. 111   156 Kershaw, *Hitler*
p. 111   157 Shirer, p. 385   158 HC Deb 28 September 1938 Vol 339 cc15; ed. Self, Vol 4
p. 348, Chamberlain to his sister Ida, September 19, 1938; Dalton p. 179   159 Faber
pp. 293–94   160 Ibid. p. 294   161 Weinberg, *The Foreign Policy of Hitler's Germany:*
p. 433   162 Faber, p. 294   163 Ibid. p. 300   164 CAB 24 / 279 CP (38) 202 p. 5 10
The Prime Minister's visit to Germany: Notes by Sir Horace Wilson, September 16,
1938   165 Self p. 314   166 ed. Norwich, *Duff Cooper Diaries,* September 17, 1938
p. 260   167 Faber, pp. 294–296   168 Self p. 300   169 HC Deb 28 September 1938
Vol 339 cc15   170 Faber, p. 313   171 CAB 23/1 39 (38) p. 18 81 September 17, 1938
172 Ibid. p. 22 858   173 Ibid.   174 Shirer, p. 389   175 *DBFP* Series 3, Vol II No. 928
p. 373   176 CAB 23/1 40 (38) p. 4 117   177 Ibid.   178 Feiling, p. 368; Churchill, *The
Gathering Storm* p. 302; Manchester, *Alone* p. 337   179 CAB 23/1 40 (38) p. 5 118
180 Ibid.   181 Ibid. p. 6 119   182 Ibid. p. 7 120   183 Ibid.   184 Ibid.   185 CAB 23/1 40
(38) p. 7 120; Faber p. 305   186 CAB 27 646/41–44, "The Czechoslovakian Crisis 1938,
Notes Of Informal Meetings Of Ministers" 6th meeting September 18, 1938   187 Faber
p. 306   188 Ibid. p. 307   189 CAB 23/1 40 (38) p. 8 121   190 *DBFP* Series 3, Vol II
No. 928 p. 387 "Record of an Anglo-French Conversations" held at 10 Downing St.,
September 18, 1938; Churchill, *The Gathering Storm* p. 271   191 Faber, p. 317
192 Manchester, *Alone* p. 337   193 Churchill, *The Gathering Storm* pp. 301–02
194 CAB 23/2 40 (38) p. 23 136   195 Shirer, p. 389   196 See, statement at CAB 23/1
41 (38) p. 1 142   197 CAB 23/1 40 (38) Appendix ¶7 137   198 Ibid. Appendix ¶8
199 Faber, p. 318   200 HC Deb 28 September 1938 Vol 339 cc17; Shirer, pp. 389–90;
Faber, pp. 319–20   201 Faber, p. 320   202 ed. Dilks, *The Diaries of Sir Alexander
Cadogan* p. 102   203 Manchester, *Alone* p. 338; Shirer, p. 390   204 Shirer, p. 390;
Churchill, *The Gathering Storm* p. 303   205 Wheeler-Bennett, *Munich* p. 123.
206 HC Deb 28 September 1938 Vol 339 cc17   207 Bruegel, *Czechoslovakia Before
Munich* p. 280   208 Shirer, p. 390   209 HC Deb 28 September 1938 Vol 339
cc17   210 Faber, p. 324; Shirer, p. 391, Churchill, *The Gathering Storm* p. 306
211 Faber, p. 173   212 Margach, *The Abuse of Power* p. 53   213 Manchester,
Alone p. 334   214 Self, p. 316   215 Quoted in Churchill, *The Gathering Storm*
pp. 303–04   216 CAB 23/1 41 (38) p. 4 145   217 Ibid. p. 5 146   218 Ibid. pp. 5–6
146–47   219 Ibid. p. 22 163   220 Manchester, *Alone* p. 340   221 Roberts, p. 431
222 Churchill, *The Gathering Storm* p. 306   223 Faber, p. 326   224 Corvaja, translator
Miller, *Hitler & Mussolini* p. 72   225 HC Deb 28 September 1938 Vol 339 cc20;
Faber, p. 329   226 Self, p. 316   227 Faber, p. 328   228 CAB 23/1 42 (38) p. 1
168   229 Manchester, *Alone* p. 341; Faber, pp. 330– 31   230 Faber, pp. 330–31
231 Manchester, *Alone* p. 341; Ibid. p. 331   232 *DBFP* Series 3, Vol II No. 1068
p. 495, note 4 British delegation (Godesberg) to Newton, September 24, 1938, enclosing
text of the memorandum   233 Ibid.   234 Faber, p. 331   235 Ibid. pp. 331–32
236 Manchester, *Alone* p. 341; Shirer, p. 393   237 Manchester, *Alone* p. 341; Shirer,
p. 393   238 Manchester, *Alone* p. 341; Shirer, p. 393   239 HC Deb 28 September 1938
Vol 339 cc20   240 Ibid.   241 Faber, p. 333; Manchester, *Alone* p. 341   242 *DBFP*
Series 3, Vol II No. 1027 p. 461, Halifax to Newton, September 22, 1938   243 Faber,
p. 334   244 Self, p. 317   245 Ibid.   246 *DGFP* Series D, Vol II, No. 572 p. 888
247 Faber, p. 335   248 *DBFP* Series 3, Vol II No. 1043 p. 480 telegram Sept 23, 1938
at 1:15 PM   249 Taylor, *Origins* p. 180   250 CAB 23/1 46 (38) p. 9 269   251 Taylor,
Origins p. 180   252 Faber, p. 336   253 Taylor, *Origins* p. 180   254 Faber p. 338
255 Ibid.   256 Self, p. 317; Ibid. p. 337; Shirer, p. 394   257 CAB 23/1 42 (38) p 6
173   258 Faber, p. 337   259 CAB 23/1 42 (38) p. 8 175   260 *DBFP* Series 3, Vol II
No. 1058 p. 490, Halifax to British delegation (Godesberg) September 23, 1938 10
PM   261 CAB 23 /1 42 (38) p. 8 175   262 *DBFP* Series 3, Vol II No. 1073 p. 499
263 CAB 23 /1 42 (38) p. 9 176   264 Ibid.   265 Ibid.; *DBFP* Series 3, Vol II No. 1073
p. 503   266 Manchester, *Alone* p. 342   267 *DBFP* Series 3, Vol II No. 1068 Appendix
p. 496, British delegation (Godesberg) to Newton, September 24, 1938 enclosing text
of the memorandum   268 Faber, p. 340   269 CAB 23 /1 42 (38) p. 9 176   270 Ibid.

p. 10 177   271 Ibid.   272 Ibid. p. 11 178   273 Ibid.   274 Shirer, p. 394
275 Manchester, *Alone* p. 343   276 Corvaja, *Hitler and Mussolini* p. 73   277 Faber,
p. 341   278 Ibid.   279 CAB 23/1 42 (38) p. 12 179   280 Shirer, p. 395; Manchester,
Alone p. 343   281 Shirer, p. 395   282 HC Deb 28 September 1938 Vol 339 cc22
283 Lukacs, *The Last European War* p. 19   284 Ibid. p. 15   285 Ibid.   286 ed.
Dilks, *Cadogan Diaries,* September 24, 1938 p. 103   287 Manchester, *Alone* p. 344
288 Colville, p. 15; Faber, p. 360   289 CAB 23 /1 42 (38) p. 12 179   290 Ibid.   291 Ibid.
292 CAB 23/1 42 (38) p. 13 180   293 Ibid.   294 Self, p. 314   295 Duff Cooper,
"Chamberlain: A Candidate Portrait," n.d. [November 1939] MRGN 1/5   296 CAB 23 /1
42 (38) p. 13 180   297 Ibid.   298 ed. Dilks, *Cadogan Diaries* pp. 103, 105; Faber,
p. 346   299 ed. Dilks, *Cadogan Diaries* p. 103   300 Faber, p. 348   301 ed. Dilks,
Cadogan Diaries p. 105   302 CAB 23/1 42 (38) p. 4 198   303 Ibid.   304 Ibid. p. 5
199   305 Ibid.   306 See Ibid. pp. 8–22 203–218   307 Ibid. p. 6 200   308 Self, p. 318;
Faber, p. 350   309 CAB 23/1 43 (38) p. 30 225   310 Ibid. pp. 30–31 225–26   311 Ibid.
p. 31 226   312 CAB 23/1 44 (38) p. 4 238   313 Ibid. p. 1 235   314 Ibid. p. 2 236;
CAB 23/2 45 (38) p. 3 249   315 CAB 23/1 44 (38) p. 6 240   316 Ibid. p. 6–7 240–241
317 Ibid. pp. 7 241   318 *DGFP* Series D, Vol II No. 619 pp. 944–45 Text of Chamberlain's
letter to Hitler September 26, 1938   319 Self, p. 321   320 CAB 23/2 45 (38) p. 2 248
321 Schmidt, *Hitler's Interpreter* pp. 95–102; Wilson's brief report of the meeting
to the Cabinet CAB 23/1 46 (38) p. 3 263   322 Smith, p. 98   323 Ibid.   324 Self,
p. 321   325 *DBFP* Series 3, Vol II No. 1115 p. 552, Henderson to Halifax, 26 September
1938   326 Shirer, p. 397   327 Ibid. 398   328 Bullock, *Hitler* p. 461   329 Amery,
p. 278   330 Shirer, p. 398   331 Churchill, *The Gathering Storm* p. 309   332 Ibid.
333 Ibid.   334 *DBFP* Series 3, Vol II No. 1111 p. 550, note 1   335 Gilbert, *Prophet*
p. 984   336 Faber p. 370   337 Gilbert, *Prophet* pp. 984–85   338 Churchill, *The
Gathering Storm* p. 310   339 Ibid.; Faber pp. 364–65   340 Churchill, *The Gathering
Storm* p. 309   341 Ibid.   342 Manchester, *Alone* p. 344   343 Churchill, *The Gathering
Storm* p. 309–10   344 Ibid. p. 316   345 Taylor, *Origins* p. 182; Manchester, *Alone*
p. 344   346 *The Times,* September 27, 1938, p. 12   347 Faber, p. 371   348 Ibid.
349 Shirer, p. 398   350 *DGFP* Series D, Vol II No. 634 p. 964 'Memorandum on the
conversation between the Fuhrer and Sir Horace Wilson." September 27, 1938
351 Henderson p. 160   352 *DGFP* Series D, Vol II No. 634 p. 965 "Memorandum
on the conversation between the Fuhrer and Sir Horace Wilson." September 27,
1938   353 Ibid.   354 CAB 23/ 1 46 (38), p. 6 266   355 CAB 23/1 46 (38), pp. 5–6
265–66   356 Ibid. p. 6 266   357 Lipski, *Diplomat in Berlin* p. 403   358 CAB 23/1
46 (38) p. 9 269   359 Ibid.   360 Shirer, pp. 399, 401   361 Ibid. p. 401   362 Lukacs,
The Last European War, p. 48   363 Churchill, *The Gathering Storm* p. 310   364 Ibid.
365 Ibid. p. 311   366 Faber p. 187   367 Kershaw, *Hitler* p. 101   368 Weinberg, *The
Foreign Policy of Hitler's Germany* p. 384   369 Toland, *Adolf Hitler* p. 467   370 Faber,
p. 189   371 Ibid.   372 Churchill, *The Gathering Storm* p. 311   373 Ibid. Shirer,
p. 488   374 Quoted in Toland, *Adolf Hitler* p. 472   375 The document was published
by Professor Bernard Lavergne in *L'Annee Politique Francais et Etrangere,* November
1938; Ripka, *Munich Before and After* p. 212   376 Churchill, *The Gathering Storm*
pp. 313–14   377 Ibid. p. 314   378 Quoted in Churchill, *The Gathering Storm* p. 319
379 Shirer, p. 401   380 Calleo, *The German Problem Reconsidered* p. 103   381 Taylor,
Origins p. xxi   382 Ibid. p. 171; Churchill, *The Gathering Storm* p. 311 et seq.
383 McMenamin, "Regime Change, 1938: Did Chamberlain 'Miss the Bus'?," 162 *Finest
Hour* 22   384 Office of the U.S. Chief Counsel for the Prosecution of Axis War
Criminals, *Nazi Conspiracy and Aggression Supplement B* pp. 1547–1571   385 Shirer,
p. 375   386 Churchill, *The Gathering Storm* p. 312; Parssinen, *The Oster Conspiracy of
1938* p. 108   387 McMenamin, "Regime Change"   388 Ibid. *DBFP* Series 3, Vol II
p. 686   389 Shirer, p. 380   390 McMenamin, "Regime Change"; Roberts, *The Holy Fox,*
p. 144; Meehan, *The Unnecessary War* p. 144   391 *DBFP* Series 3, Vol II p. 686
392 Shirer, p. 381   393 McMenamin, "Regime Change"   394 Faber, p. 238
395 Ibid. Meehan, pp. 152–54   396 Wheeler-Bennett, *The Nemesis of Power* p. 418
397 Henderson, pp. 165–66   398 Shirer, p. 399   399 Henderson, pp. 165–66
400 Shirer, p. 400   401 CAB 23/1 46 (38) p. 2 262   402 Ibid. p. 3 263   403 *DBFP*
Series 3, Vol II No. 1136 p. 570, Halifax to Newton, September 27, 1938 at 5:45 PM

404 Ibid. p. 571, Halifax to Newton, September 27, 1938 at 6:00 PM   405 CAB 23/1 46 (38) p. 3 263   406 Shirer, p. 401   407 Available at: https://tinyurl.com/3p8jceew; *New York Times,* September 28, 1938   408 See Roberts, p. 432   409 Shirer, p. 397   410 *DBFP* Series 3, Vol II No. 1144 pp. 576–79; Henderson to Halifax, September 27, 1938   411 Faber, p. 381   412 Ibid. p. 382   413 *DBFP* Series 3, Vol II No. 1158 p. 587, Halifax to Henderson, enclosing message from Chamberlain to Hitler, September 28, 1938   414 Corvaja p. 74   415 Faber, p. 395   416 Ibid.   417 Faber, p. 395, n. 15   418 HC Deb 28 September 1938 Vol 339 cc5–28   419 ed. Nicholson, *Nicholson Diaries* Vol I p. 370   420 HC Deb 28 September 1938 Vol 339 cc5–28   421 Buchanan, p. 235; Faber pp. 397–399   422 Kershaw, *Hitler* p. 119   423 Shirer, p. 404   424 ed. Nicholson, *Nicholson Diaries* Vol I p. 370   425 Faber, p. 402   426 Self, p. 324 427 Faber, pp. 405; Shirer, p. 417; Churchill, *The Gathering Storm* p. 317   428 Faber, p. 406   429 Self, p. 324   430 Manchester, *Alone* p. 350; Faber, p. 406   431 Faber, p. 407; Shirer, p. 416   432 Nogueres, p. 268   433 Schmidt, *Hitler's Interpreter* p. 110 434 Laffan, "The Crisis over Czechoslovakia," *Survey of International Affairs* 1938 Vol II p. 441, n.3   435 Shirer, p. 421   436 Faber, p. 423   437 Lukacs, *The Last European War* p. 17   438 Shirer, p. 422   439 Buchanan, pp. 210–11   440 Faber, p. 410; Shirer, p. 417   441 Manchester, *Alone* p. 351   442 Faber, p. 412   443 Manchester, *Alone* p. 352   444 Ibid.; Faber, p. 412   445 Manchester, *Alone* p. 354   446 Faber, p. 413   447 Statement of Czech Foreign Minister Kamil Krofta on September 30, 1938, quoted in Faber, p. 413   448 Ripka, *Munich: Before and After,* pp. 231–32 449 Churchill, *The Gathering Storm* p. 319   450 Shirer, p. 422   451 Thorpe, *Alec Douglas-Home* p. 83   452 Available at: https://sourcebooks.fordham.edu/mod/ 1938PEACE.asp   453 Self p. 325   454 Schmidt, *Hitler's Interpreter* pp. 112–13 455 BBC Written Archives, R19/21/2172, "I Was There" series, interview with Sir Alec Douglas-Home, 14 January 1968   456 Spitzy, *How We Squandered The Reich* p. 254   457 Taylor, *Origins* p. 199   458 Manchester, *Alone* p. 352   459 Self p. 325   460 Strang, *Home, The Way the Wind Blows,* pp. 64, 66   461 Smith, *The Dark Summer* p. 105   462 Faber, p. 421; Dubrov, *Isaiah Berlin: The Journey of a Jewish Liberal* p. 350   463 Kennedy, p. 186   464 Lukacs, *The Last European War* pp. 14–15   465 Buchanan, p. 236   466 ed. Self, Vol 4 pp. 441–42, Chamberlain to his sister Ida, September 19, 1938   467 Shirer, p. 387   468 Lukacs, *The Last European War* p. 15   469 Manchester, *Alone* p. 348   470 Kirkpatrick, *The Inner Circle* p. 135   471 Dutton, *Neville Chamberlain* p. 52   472 Olson, p. 144   473 Roberts, p. 434   474 Ibid.   475 London School of Economics Archive, 1/1/5, "Munich 1938" interview with Sir John Colville   476 Taylor, *Origins* p. 186; Shirer, *The Collapse of the Third Republic* p. 331   477 Manchester, *Alone* p. 356   478 Shirer, p. 426 479 Ibid.   480 Ibid. p. 427   481 Taylor, *Origins* pp. 187–88   482 Tansill, *Back Door to War* p. 430   483 *The Times,* October 1, 1938   484 Quoted in Tansill, *Back Door to War* p. 430   485 Self, p. 325   486 Olson, p. 10   487 Manchester, *Alone* p. 347 488 Ibid.   489 Dutton, *Neville Chamberlain* p. 54   490 McDonough, pp. 106–07, 124–133   491 Kennedy, p. 184   492 Ibid. pp. 184–85   493 Thomas, *Hurricane Squadron Ace* p. 14   494 CAB 23/1 47 (38) p. 1 280   495 Ibid.   496 Ibid. pp. 1–2 280–81   497 Ibid. p. 6 285   498 Ibid. p. 7–8 86–87   499 HC Deb 03 October 1938 Vol 339 cc29–40   500 Halifax, p. 199   501 HC Deb 03 October 1938 Vol 339 cc45 502 Ibid. cc151   503 Ibid. cc49   504 Ibid. cc50   505 HC Deb 05 October 1938 Vol 339 cc359–373   506 Ibid. cc360   507 Ibid.   508 Ibid. cc361   509 HC Deb 05 October 1938 Vol 339 cc365   510 Ibid. cc359–373   511 Ibid. cc362   512 Manchester, *Alone* p. 416   513 Lukacs, *The Last European War* p. 16   514 Churchill, *The Gathering Storm* p. 327   515 ed. Self, Vol 4 p. 444, Chamberlain to his sister Ida, October 9, 1938   516 Shirer, p. 421   517 Ibid.   518 Taylor, *Origins* p. 186   519 Halifax p. 202 520 Feiling, p. 381   521 Roberts, p. 434   522 Manchester, *Alone* p. 421   523 Roberts, p. 445   524 Buchanan, p. 236   525 Quoted in Feiling p. 385   526 Buchanan, p. 414 527 Churchill, *Gathering Storm* p. 302   528 Buchanan p. 229; Consiel Slovak, Geneva, *Shall Millions Die for "this Czechoslovakia"* p. 25   529 See HC Deb 14 March 1938 Vol 333 cc99; See also, *The Gathering Storm* p. 302   530 Buchanan, p. 229   531 Kennedy p. 187   532 Ibid.   533 Ibid.   534 Ibid.   535 Thomas Jones, *A Diary with Letters 1931–1950* pp. 409–411   536 Churchill College (Cambridge), *The Diary of Sir Thomas*

Inskip, September 14, 1938 p. 1   537 Chamberlain's speech of March 17, 1939, British War Bluebook No. 9   538 ed. Self, Vol 4 p. 44, Chamberlain to his sister Hilda, December 30, 1939; Self, p. 412   539 ed. Self, Vol 4 p. 534, Chamberlain to his sister Ida, May 25, 1940   540 Self, p. 435   541 Maurer, "Churchill, Air Power, and Arming For Armageddon," *Finest Hour* No. 185, Third Quarter 2019   542 Halifax, p. 200   543 Buchanan p. 223   544 Ibid.   545 Manchester, *Alone* p. 422   546 Taylor, *Origins* p. 182   547 Faber pp. 343, 344   548 Lukacs, *Five Days* p. 10   549 Buchanan p. 230   550 Ibid.   551 Ibid.   552 Ibid.   553 CAB 23/1 – (39) p. 20 305 Notes of Meeting of Ministers August 30, 1938   554 Taylor, *Origins* p. 163   555 Ibid. 556 Geoffrey Roberts, *The Czechoslovakian Crisis of 1938* pp. 4–5   557 Ibid. 558 Churchill, *The Gathering Storm* p. 305   559 Manchester, *Alone* p. 450 560 Churchill, *The Gathering Storm* p. 305   561 Taylor, *Origins* p. 163   562 Manchester, *Alone* p. 325   563 Ibid.   564 Lukacs, *The Last European War* p. 16   565 Shirer, 376   566 Churchill, *The Gathering Storm* p. 313   567 Taylor, *Origins* p. 172   568 Shirer, p. 423   569 Ibid.   570 General Manstein's testimony, August 9, 1946, Trial Of The Major War Criminals, Nuremberg Documents And Testimony, Vol XX p. 606; Gen Keitel's testimony, April 4, 1946, Trial Of The Major War Criminals, Nuremberg Documents And Testimony, Vol X p. 509   571 Shirer, p. 423   572 Taylor, *Origins* p. 167   573 Ibid.   574 General Jodl's testimony, June 4, 1945, Trial of The Major War Criminals, Nuremberg Documents And Testimony, Vol XV, p. 361; General Manstein's testimony, August 9, 1946, Trial of the Major War Criminals, Nuremberg Documents and Testimony, Vol XX p. 606   575 *DGFP* Series D, Vol II No. 192 pp. 202 Memorandum of the speech by Hitler to Commanders in Chief August 1939   576 Churchill, *The Gathering Storm* p. 325   577 Dutton, *Neville Chamberlain* p. 57   578 Faber p. 315   579 Shirer, p. 421   580 Faber, epilogue p. 430; Shirer, p. 421   581 Faber, epilogue p. 411   582 Shirer, p. 427   583 Buchanan, p. 210; Shirer, p. 427   584 Schacht on the stand at Nuremberg, May 2, 1946, Trial of the Major War Criminals, Nuremberg Documents and Testimony, Vol XII p. 531; Kershaw, *Hitler* p. 122   585 *DGFP* Series D, Vol IV No. 81 pp. 99–100 Directive by the Fuhrer for the Wehrmacht, 21 October 1938   586 Kirkpatrick, *The Inner Circle* p. 131; Manchester, *Alone* p. 389   587 Churchill, *The Gathering Storm* p. 343   588 Buchanan, pp. 228–29   589 Churchill, *The Gathering Storm* p. 332   590 Ibid.   591 Manchester, *Alone* p. 437; Feiling p. 375   592 Halifax, p. 201   593 Ibid. p. 198   594 Ibid. pp. 199–200   595 Ibid. p. 201   596 Lukacs, *The Last European War* p. 15 597 Ibid.   598 Taylor, *Origins* p. 192   599 Faber, epilogue p. 431   600 Lukacs, *Last European War* p. 32   601 *DBFP,* 3rd Series, Vol III, No. 325 p. 173 "Anglo-French Meeting," November 24, 1938   602 Tansill, *Back Door to War* p. 509   603 Buchanan, p. 242   604 Feiling p. 413   605 Shirer p. 455   606 Ibid. p. 458   607 Buchanan, p. 243   608 Ibid. p. 244   609 Shirer, p. 457   610 Tansill, *Back Door to War* p. 510 611 Feiling p. 414   612 Taylor, *Origins* p. 199   613 Roberts p. 441   614 *Manchester Guardian* November 12, 1938; *Montreal Gazette* November 12, 1938   615 Kershaw, *Making Friends,* p. 260; Shirer, p. 430, n. 5   616 Paul Johnson, *Modern Times* p. 356 617 Buchanan, p. 241   618 Crowson, *Facing Fascism* p. 31   619 Roberts, p. 442

Chapter 12

1 Manchester, *Alone* p. 421   2 Faber, p. 420   3 Taylor, *Origins* p. 200   4 Buchanan, p. 237   5 ed. Gibson, *The Ciano Diaries,* January 11, 1939 p. 10   6 Ibid.   7 Taylor, *Origins* p. 200   8 Shirer, p. 438–39   9 CAB 23/1 10 (39) p. 1 379   10 Churchill, *The Gathering Storm* p. 341   11 Shirer p. 429   12 Taylor, *Origins* p. 202   13 Churchill, *The Gathering Storm* p. 342   14 Ibid.   15 Manchester, *Alone* p. 390   16 Shirer, p. 444   17 Fest, *Hitler* pp. 570–71   18 Manchester, *Alone* p. 391   19 HC Deb 15 March 1939, Vol 345 cc436; Shirer, p. 448   20 See CAB 23/2 11 (39) p. 2 6   21 Ibid. p. 3 7   22 Ibid.   23 Churchill, *The Gathering Storm* p. 343   24 HC Deb 15 March 1939 Vol 345 cc436   25 Ibid.   26 Self, p. 351   27 HC Deb 15 March 1939 Vol 345 cc437; CAB 23/2 11 (39) p. 3 9   28 HC Deb 15 March 1939 Vol 345 cc437   29 Ibid. cc440 30 Ibid. cc440   31 Self, p. 352   32 CAB 23/2 11 (39) p. 5 9 March 15, 1939 33 Self, p. 351   34 CAB 23/2 11 (39) p. 4 8   35 *Documents on German Foreign*

Policy, (DGFP) Series D, Vol IV No. 234 pp. 274–75   36 Shirer, p. 451   37 Taylor, *Origins* p. 191   38 Ibid.   39 Kissinger, *Diplomacy* p. 316   40 Kershaw, *Hitler* p. 84   41 Buchanan, p. 250–51   42 Lukacs, *The Last European War* p. 39   43 Hitler's speech to the Reichstag, April 28, 1939. Available at: https://archive.org/details/ 1034858   44 Ibid.   45 Roberts, *The Holy Fox*, p. 195   46 Ibid. pp. 195–96; Buchanan, p. 252   47 Buchanan, p. 252   48 Lukacs, *The Last European War* pp. 35–36   49 Self, p. 352   50 Ibid.   51 Manchester, *Alone* pp. 393–94   52 Available at: https:// avalon.law.yale.edu/wwii/blbk09.asp   53 Ibid.   54 Ibid.   55 Manchester, *Alone* p. 392   56 Churchill, *The Gathering Storm* p. 344   57 Ibid.   58 Self, p. 353   59 HC Deb 03 April 1939 Vol 345 cc2484, 2486   60 CAB 23/1 12 (39) p. 8 50   61 Ibid. p. 20 62   62 Ibid.   63 CAB 23/1 13 (39) p. 3 76 March 20, 1939   64 Ibid. p. 4 77   65 Halifax, p. 203   66 Ibid.   67 Ibid.   68 Shirer, p. 460; Manchester, *Alone* p. 448   69 HC Deb 14 March 1938 Vol 333 cc99   70 Shirer, p. 460   71 Manchester, *Alone* p. 448; Shirer, p. 460   72 Manchester, *Alone* p. 448   73 CAB23/2 14 (39) p. 3 94   74 *DBFP* Series 3, Vol IV No. 484 p. 459 "Anglo French conversation" March 22, 1939, 5 PM   75 Feiling, p. 404   76 Shirer, p. 460   77 Smith, p. 164   78 ed. Self, Vol 4 p. 39, Letter of March 26, 1939   79 *DBFP* Series 3, Vol IV No. 484 p. 459 "Anglo French conversation" March 22, 1939, 5 PM   80 Manchester, *Alone* p. 451   81 Ibid. 82 Buchanan, p. 254   83 CAB 23 /2 14 (39) p. 5 95   84 Taylor, *Origins* p. 210; Shirer, p. 461   85 Shirer, p. 471   86 Available at https://avalon.law.yale.edu/wwii/blbk09 .asp_   87 Speech of Józef Beck before the Polish Parliament, May 5, 1939. Available at: https://tinyurl.com/bdessp8x.   88 *DGFP* Series D, No. 126 p. 168 Minutes By Ribbentrop Feb 1, 1939   89 Shirer, p. 462   90 Taylor, *Origins* p. 210: Buchanan, p. 254   91 Available at: https://avalon.law.yale.edu/wwii/blbk09.asp   92 Taylor, *Origins* p. 207   93 Ibid. Chamberlain's statement to the Cabinet on March 30, 1939, CAB 23/1 16 (39) p. 7 162; Ibid.   94 *DGFP* Series D, Vol VI No. 99 p. 117 "Directive by the Fuhrer" March 25, 1939   95 Ibid.   96 Shirer, p. 465   97 CAB 23/1 16 (39) p. 2 157 98 Ibid.   99 Ibid. p. 3 158   100 Ibid. p. 7 162   101 Ibid.   102 Ibid.   103 CAB23/1 16 (39) p. 20 175   104 Ibid.; Accord, HC Deb 31 March 1939 Vol 345 cc2415 105 Shirer p. 465   106 Roberts, *The Holy Fox* p. 198; Buchanan, p. 254; Taylor, *Origins* p. 209   107 Shirer, p. 465   108 Taylor, *Origins* p. 212   109 Special distribution of secured telephone conversation from British Ambassador to Poland Sir H. Kennard 7:50 PM March 30, 1939, attachment to CAB 23/17 (39) 199   110 Lukacs, *The Last European War* p. 37   111 Ibid. p. 439   112 Buchanan, p. 266   113 Halifax, p. 207–08   114 Ibid. p. 209   115 Buchanan, p. 267   116 HC Deb 31 March 1939 Vol 345 cc2415 117 Buchanan, p. 270–71   118 Taylor, *English History* p. 441   119 Buchanan, p. 255   120 Roberts, p. 451   121 Shirer, p. 466   122 Manchester, *Alone* p. 407   123 Buchanan, p. 260   124 Taylor, *English History* pp. 94–95   125 Buchanan, p. 334   126 HC Deb 19 May 1939 Vol 347 cc1833   127 Ibid. cc1834   128 Ibid. cc1833   129 Ibid. cc1834   130 Manchester, *Alone* p. 404   131 Fergusson, *The War Of The World* p. 377   132 Shirer, p. 465   133 Johnson, *Modern Times* p. 353 134 Buchanan, p. 414   135 Shirer, p. 468   136 Taylor, *Origins* p. 218   137 Feiling, pp. 416–17   138 Taylor, *Origins* p. 218   139 Manchester, *Alone* p. 405   140 Buchanan, p. 257   141 Ibid.   142 HC Deb 03 April 1939 Vol 345 cc2499   143 Taylor, *Origins* p. 225   144 Churchill, *The Gathering Storm* pp. 311–12   145 ed. James, *Complete Speeches* Vol VI p. 6095   146 HC Deb 03 April 1939 Vol 345 cc2500–01   147 Gilbert, *Prophet* p. 1053   148 ed. Nicholson, *Nicholson Diaries* Vol I p. 394   149 HC Deb 19 May 1939 Vol 347 cc1833   150 Gilbert, *Prophet* p. 1054   151 Stewart, p. 357 152 Manchester, *Alone* p. 405   153 Buchanan, p. 257   154 ed. James, *Chips* 3 and 13 April 1939   155 Taylor, *Origins* p. 215   156 Ibid. p. 212   157 HC Deb 03 April 1939 Vol 345 cc2510   158 Taylor, *Origins* p. 212   159 Ibid.   160 Shirer, p. 469 161 Available at: https://archive.org/details/1034858   162 Churchill, *The Gathering Storm* p. 346   163 ed. James, *Complete Speeches* Vol VI p. 6123; Roberts, p. 453 164 Manchester, *Alone* p. 405   165 Churchill, *The Gathering Storm* p. 347 166 Buchanan, p. 258   167 Ibid. pp. 258–59   168 Ibid. p. 415   169 Ibid. p. 285; Churchill, *Step by Step* p. 359   170 Halifax, p. 210   171 Ibid.   172 Stewart, p. 357   173 CAB 23/ 2 24 (39) p. 7 61   174 Ibid.   175 CAB 24 162 285 (39), (CP (39) 95)   176 CAB 23/ 2 24 (39) p. 7 61   177 Churchill, *The Gathering Storm* p. 344

178 HC Deb 03 September 1939 Vol 351 cc295   179 Stewart, p. 356   180 Buchanan,
p. 267   181 Roberts, *The Holy Fox* p. 194   182 Ibid. p. 198   183 Buchanan,
p. 268   184 Manchester, *Alone* p. 479   185 Halifax, p. 209   186 Taylor, *Origins*
p. 206; Self, p. 357   187 CAB 23 /1 48 (39) p. 9 469   188 See the conclusions of the
British Cabinet meeting held at 4:15 PM on September 2, 1939, CAB 23 /1 48 (39) pp. 10
470   189 CAB 23/5 2 (39) p. 12 21   190 Ibid.   191 Ibid.   192 Taylor, *Origins*
p. 221   193 *DGFP* Series D, Vol II No. 192 p. 203   194 *DBFP* Series 3, Vol V No. 692
p. 749 "Halifax to Kennard," June 1, 1939   195 Taylor, *Origins* p. 221   196 *DGFP*
Series D, Vol II No. 192 p. 203, "Memorandum of the speech by Hitler To Commanders in
Chief" August 22, 1939   197 Manchester, *Alone* p. 451   198 Ibid.   199 CAB 23/2 24
(39) p. 4 58; Manchester, *Alone,* p. 452   200 Carley, 'End of The Low Dishonest Decade:
Failure of The Anglo-Franco-Soviet alliance in 1939,' 45 *Europe-Asia Studies* 303 (1993);
Carley, 'Fiasco: The Anglo-Franco-Soviet Alliance That Never Was and the Unpublished
British White Paper, 1939–1940,' 41 701, 702 (2018); Shirer, p. 479   201 CAB 23/2 24
(39) p. 4 58; Manchester, *Alone* p. 452   202 Shirer, p. 466   203 Ibid. p. 489
204 Manchester, *Alone* p. 452   205 Manchester, *Alone* p. 453   206 Taylor, *Origins*
p. 224   207 Churchill, *The Gathering Storm* p. 362   208 Ibid.   209 ed. Borowski,
"Military Planning in the 20th Century," 11th Military History Symposium October
10–12, 1984, p. 50   210 Churchill, *The Gathering Storm* p. 362   211 Ibid.
212 Ibid. p. 365   213 Taylor, *Origins* p. 257   214 CAB 23/ 2 24 (39) p. 7 61
215 Ibid.   216 Taylor, *Origins* p. 225   217 CAB 23/ 2 26(39) p. 14 129   218 Ibid.
219 Confidential Annex to CAB 23 1 30 (39) p. 1 294 May 30, 1939   220 *Daily
Telegraph,* May 4, 1939   221 CAB23/1 12 (38) p. 5 349   222 Self p. 369   223 Churchill,
Step by Step p. 359; Buchanan, p. 285   224 *Daily Telegraph,* May 4, 1939   225 CAB
23/1 28 (39) p. 7 275, May 17, 1939   226 ed Self, Vol 4 p. 404 April 9, 1939   227 Shirer,
p. 480; Roberts, p. 452   228 Self, p. 369   229 Churchill, *The Gathering Storm*
p. 365   230 Manchester, *Alone* p. 454   231 Taylor, *Origins* p. 240; Shirer, pp. 480,
492   232 See CAB 23/1 27 (39) p. 2 156   233 Taylor, *Origins* p. 237   234 Manchester,
Alone p. 457   235 Taylor, *Origins* p.237   236 Churchill, *The Gathering Storm*
p. 364   237 Shirer, p. 479   238 CAB 23/1 27 (39) p. 2 156   239 Self, p. 369; Shirer,
pp. 480, 492; Taylor, *Origins* p. 227   240 Taylor, *Origins* p. 228   241 CAB 23/1 38 (39)
p. 2 186   242 HC Deb 19 May 1939 Vol 347 cc1848   243 HC Deb 05 October 1938 Vol
339 cc362   244 HC Deb 03 April 1939 Vol 345 cc2501   245 Buchanan, p. 285; Accord,
Churchill, *Step by Step* p. 359   246 CAB 23/1 27 (39) p. 3 157   247 HC Deb 19 May
1939 Vol 347 cc1809 et seq, 1824   248 Ibid. cc1836   249 Churchill, *The Gathering
Storm* p. 373   250 HC Deb 19 May 1939 Vol 347 cc1839   251 Taylor, *Origins*
p. 224   252 HC Deb 19 May 1939 Vol 347 cc1831, 1834   253 Ibid. cc1833   254 Ibid.
cc1834   255 Ibid. cc1833   256 HC Deb 19 May 1939 Vol 347 cc1834   257 Ibid. cc1829–
30   258 Self, p. 450   259 Overy, *1939* p. 29   260 UK Parliament, *Winston Churchill—
The Greatest Briton,* Appendix 1: Transcript of a Speech by Churchill broadcast on BBC
Radio, 10 PM, November 15, 1934   261 Self, p. 367   262 *DGFP* Series D, Vol VI No.
433 p. 576 "Schmundt's minutes" May 23, 1939   263 Ibid. pp. 574–80   264 Feiling,
p. 409   265 Shirer, p. 488   266 CAB 23/1 30 (39) pp. 5, 7, 273, 275   267 Ibid. p. 3–5
271–73   268 CAB 23/1 30 (39) pp. 7–10 275–78   269 Ibid. p. 10 278   270 Manchester,
Alone p. 468; Accord, Taylor, *Origins* p. 225   271 Taylor, *Origins* p. 226   272 Ibid.
273 Shirer, p. 489   274 CAB 23/1 30 (39) p. 1 285   275 Shirer, p. 490   276 Ibid.
p. 491   277 Buchanan, p. 285   278 Harbutt, *The Iron Curtin* p. 25   279 Churchill,
The Gathering Storm p. 327   280 Manchester, *Alone* p. 458–59   281 Lukacs, *Five
Days* p. 217   282 Buchanan, p. 344   283 Buchanan, p. 348–49   284 Taylor, *Origins*
p. 228   285 Buchanan, p. 346   286 Cameron and Stevens, translators, *Hitler's Table
Talk* p. 490   287 Buchanan, p. 346   288 Shirer, p. 804   289 Ibid. p. 805   290 Available
at: http://der-fuehrer.org/reden/english/wardirectives/21.html   291 Lukacs, *June 1941*
p. 92   292 Lukacs, *The Last European War* p. 138   293 Ibid. p. 101   294 Churchill's
June 22, 1941, speech over the BBC. Available at: https://www.jewishvirtuallibrary.org/
churchill-broadcast-on-the-soviet-german-war-june-1941   295 Self p. 368   296 Shirer,
p. 490   297 *Daily Telegraph,* June 8, 1939   298 Churchill, *The Gathering Storm*
p. 389   299 Shirer, p. 496   300 Roberts, p. 456   301 CAB 23/1 33 (39) p. 3 6
302 Ibid. p. 1 4   303 CAB 23/4 35 (39) p. 6 77   304 Ibid. p. 10 81   305 Self,

p. 370   306 Taylor, *Origins* p. 215   307 Self, p. 370   308 CAB23/1 16 (39) p. 20
176 March 31, 1939   309 CAB 23/2 40 (39) p. 2 277 August 2, 1939   310 Taylor,
Origins p. 206   311 Randolph Churchill, *Into Battle* p. 113   312 Taylor, *Origins*
p. 245   313 Ibid.   314 CAB 23/8 37 (39) p. 15 159   315 CAB 23/1 38 (39) p. 2 186 July
19, 1939   316 Ibid. pp. 2–3 186–87   317 Ibid. p. 3 187   318 Ibid.   319 Manchester,
Alone p. 476   320 Ibid.   321 Taylor, *Origins* pp. 252–53   322 CAB 23 /2 40 (39) p. 2
277   323 Feiling, p. 411   324 Ibid.   325 Manchester, *Alone* p. 485   326 Shirer,
p. 517   327 Ibid.   328 Taylor, *Origins* p. 243   329 Ibid. p. 244   330 Manchester,
Alone p. 476   331 Shirer, p. 504   332 Taylor, *Origins* p. 256   333 Manchester, *Alone*
p. 476   334 Ibid.   335 Ibid.   336 Ibid.   337 CAB 23/3 41 (39) p. 3 317; Taylor, *Origins*
pp. 256, 258; Manchester, *Alone* p. 478   338 CAB 23/3 41 (39) p. 4 318   339 *DBFP*
Series 3, Vol II No. 52 p. 53 "Kennard to Halifax" August 18, 1939   340 Taylor, *Origins*
p. 261   341 Shirer, *Collapse* pp. 447–450   342 Taylor, *Origins* p. 256   343 Feiling,
p. 412   344 Ibid.   345 Ibid. p. 411   346 Manchester, *Alone* p. 479; Taylor, p. 258
347 Taylor, *Origins* p. 226; Manchester, *Alone* p. 478   348 Manchester, *Alone*
pp. 478–79   349 HC Deb 03 April 1939 Vol 345 cc2510   350 Manchester, *Alone*
p. 479   351 Ibid.   352 HC Deb 19 April 1939 Vol 112 cc698   353 Taylor, *Origins*
p. 227   354 Ibid.   355 Ibid. p. 259   356 Ibid.   357 Ibid. p. 260   358 *DGFP* Series D,
Vol II No. 142 pp. 156–57 "Ribbentrop to Schulenberg" August 20, 1939   359 Taylor,
Origins p. 261   360 Manchester, *Alone* p. 481   361 Ibid. p. 484   362 Feiling, p. 414
363 CAB 23/3 41(39) p. 7 321   364 Ibid.   365 Ibid. p. 9 323   366 Ibid.   367 *DBFP*
Series 3, Vol I No. 659 p. 692 "Minute by Makins" August 14, 1939   368 Manchester,
Alone p. 481   369 Taylor, *Origins* p. 250   370 Ibid. p. 219   371 Ibid. p. 251   372 *DBFP*
Series 3, Vol I No. 659, pp. 693–95 Minute by Makins" August 14, 1939   373 CAB 23 /5
41 (39) p. 9 323   374 Ibid.   375 Ibid.   376 Taylor, *Origins* p. 249   377 CAB 23 /5 41
(39) p. 11 325   378 Overy, *1939* p. 19   379 Ibid.   380 CAB 23 /5 41 (39) p. 11 325
381 Ibid. p. 13 327   382 Manchester, *Alone* p. 464   383 CAB 23 /5 41 (39) p. 13
327   384 Manchester, *Alone* p. 493   385 CAB 23/5 41 (39) p. 13 327   386 Taylor,
Origins p. 266   387 Self, p. 363; Taylor, *Origins* p. 206   388 The British War Bluebook
No. 56   389 Manchester, *Alone,* p. 501   390 Shirer, p. 562   391 Manchester, *Alone*
p. 502   392 British War Bluebook No. 60   393 Churchill, *The Gathering Storm* pp. 396–
97   394 British War Bluebook No. 61; Manchester, *Alone* p. 498   395 Overy, *1939*
p. 25   396 Lukacs, *The Last European War* p. 44   397 *DGFP* Series D, Vol II No. 192
pp. 202–204 "Memorandum of the speech by Hitler To Commanders in Chief" August 22,
1939   398 Churchill, *The Gathering Storm* p. 367   399 Taylor, *Origins* p. 266
400 Manchester, *Alone* p. 498   401 Taylor, *Origins* p. 261   402 Manchester, *Alone*
p. 499   403 Ibid. p. 498   404 Ibid.   405 Ibid.   406 Self, p. 369   407 Churchill, *The
Gathering Storm* p. 395   408 *New York Times,* "Italy Holds Aloof in Danzig Dispute"
July 5, 1939   409 See Special Distribution to CAB 23/1 42 (39) 367 (August 24, 1939)
410 Overy, *1939* p. 20   411 Ibid. p. 26   412 British War Bluebook No. 60   413 CAB 23/ 2
42 (39) p. 3 354   414 Ibid. p. 4 355   415 CAB 23/1 42 (39) p. 1–2 352–353   416 Ibid.
Annex II, p. 363   417 HC Deb 24 August 1939 Vol 351 cc6   418 Ibid.   419 Ibid.
cc8   420 Overy, *1939* p. 32   421 Shirer, p. 569   422 Ibid. p. 570   423 Shirer, *Berlin
Diary* p. 183 August 24, 1939   424 British War Bluebook No. 19   425 Overy, *1939*
p. 36–37   426 Ibid. p. 37   427 Manchester, *Alone* p. 503   428 Ibid. p. 500   429 Overy,
1939 p. 34   430 Manchester, *Alone* p. 505   431 Overy, *1939* p. 33   432 Manchester,
Alone p. 512   433 Feiling, p. 414   434 Ibid.   435 The British War Bluebook No. 68
436 Overy, *1939* p. 34   437 Ibid. pp. 36–37   438 *DGFP* Series D, Vol VII pp. 285–86
Mussolini's letter to Hitler, August 25, 1939   439 Overy, *1939* p. 36   440 Ibid.; Shirer,
pp. 564, 569; Manchester, *Alone* p. 506   441 Feiling, pp. 416   442 Seib, *Broadcasts from
the Blitz* p. 1   443 Overy, *1939* p. 29   444 Kershaw, *Hitler* p. 215   445 Overy, *1939*
p. 36   446 Churchill, *The Gathering Storm* p. 397   447 Shirer p. 570   448 CAB 23/1
43 (39) p. 1 370   449 Overy, *1939* p. 38   450 Ibid. p. 40   451 CAB 23/1 43 (39) p. 1
370   452 Ibid.   453 Ibid. p. 2 371   454 Ibid.   455 Ibid.   456 Ibid. pp. 2–3 371–372
457 Shirer, p. 566   458 CAB 23/1 43 (39) p. 3 372   459 Shirer, p. 569   460 Ibid.
461 Churchill, *The Gathering Storm* p. 344   462 *Daily Telegraph,* August 26, 1939
463 Overy, *1939* p. 41   464 CAB 23/1 43 (39) p. 3 372   465 Ibid.   466 CAB 23/ – 44
(39) Annex p. 1 398 August 27, 1939   467 CAB 23/1 43 (39) p. 4 373 August 26, 1939

468 Ibid.   469 Ibid. p. 3–4 372–73 August 26, 1939   470 Ibid. p. 5 374   471 Ibid.
p. 6 375   472 Shirer, p. 549   473 CAB 23/1 43 (39) p. 7 376   474 Ibid. p. 7 378
475 Ibid.   476 Ibid. p. 8 379   477 Shirer, p. 568   478 CAB 23/2 45 (39) p. 3 409
479 *DGFP* Series D, Vol VII pp. 564–66 Halder's diary, entry of August 28, 1939
480 CAB 23/ 4 44 (39) p. 5 396   481 CAB 23/1 43 (39) p. 3 372 August 26, 1939
482 Ibid.   483 Shirer p. 570   484 Ibid. p. 571   485 Overy, *1939* p. 52; Shirer, p. 572
486 Annex to CAB 23 /1 44 (39) p. 2 399 August 27, 1939   487 Ibid.   488 Ibid.
489 Ibid. p. 4 401   490 Ibid. p. 2 399   491 Ibid. p. 4 401   492 Ibid.   493 Ibid.
494 Ibid. p. 2 399   495 Shirer, p. 573   496 Annex to CAB 23/1 44 (39) pp. 2–3
399–400 August 27, 1939   497 Shirer, p. 574   498 Manchester, *Alone* p. 509; Ibid.
p. 575   499 Annex to CAB 23/2 45 (39) p. 1 417   500 CAB 23/2 45 (39) p. 8 414
501 Ibid.   502 Manchester, *Alone* p. 509; Overy, *1939* p. 56; Shirer p. 574   503 Overy,
1939 pp. 55–56   504 Ibid. p. 56   505 Manchester, *Alone* p. 512   506 British War
Bluebook No. 74   507 Overy, *1939* p. 57   508 British War Bluebook No. 74   509 British
War Bluebook No. 75   510 Ibid.   511 Shirer, pp. 576–77   512 Ibid. p. 577; Overy, *1939*
p. 58   513 Shirer, p. 577   514 Ibid.   515 British War Bluebook No. 78   516 Feiling,
p. 415   517 British War Bluebook No. 81   518 CAB 23/1 46 (39) p. 1 421   519 Overy,
1939 p. 59   520 Shirer, p. 579   521 CAB 23/1 46 (39) p. 2 422   522 British War
Bluebook No. 78; Overy, *1939* p. 58; Shirer, pp. 577–78   523 CAB 23/1 46 (39) p. 2
422   524 British War Bluebook No. 78   525 Annex to CAB 23/3 46 (39) p. 1 439
August 29, 1939   526 Ibid.   527 Ibid. pp. 1–2 439–40 August 29, 1939   528 Shirer,
p. 579   529 Ibid. p. 583   530 Ibid. p. 584; Overy, *1939* pp. 59–60   531 British War
Bluebook No. 89   532 Ibid.   533 Overy, *1939* p. 61   534 Ibid.   535 British War
Bluebook, No. 90   536 British War Bluebook, No. 93   537 Shirer, p. 584   538 Ibid.
539 Ibid.   540 Ibid.   541 Ibid. p. 587   542 Overy, *1939* p. 62   543 Shirer, p. 587
544 Overy, *1939* p. 62   545 Secretary of State for Foreign Affairs, *Correspondence
between H.M. Government in the United Kingdom and the German Government,
August 1939* p. 16   546 British War Bluebook, No. 90   547 Shirer, p. 593   548 British
War Bluebook No. 98   549 Shirer, p. 589   550 Overy, *1939* pp. 53–54   551 Ibid.
p. 96   552 Lukacs, *The Last European War* p. 50, n. 54   553 Available at: https://
www.historyonthenet.com/how-many-people-died-in-world-war-2   554 Feiling,
p. 414   555 *The New York Times,* September 10, 1939   556 Feiling, p. 4; Overy, *1939*
pp. 113, 123   557 Taylor, *Origins* p. 252   558 William Henry Chamberlin, *America's
Second Crusade,* p. 51   559 Denman, *Missed Chances: Britain And Europe in the
Twentieth Century* p. 8   560 George Kennon letter to Pat Buchanan, November 5, 1999,
cited in Buchanan pp. 273–74   561 Buchanan, p. 414   562 Taylor, *Origins* p. 228
563 CAB 23/1 12 (39) p. 8 50   564 Available at: http://der-fuehrer.org/reden/english/
wardirectives/21.html   565 Churchill's June 22, 1941, speech over the BBC. Available at:
https://www.jewishvirtuallibrary.org/churchill-broadcast-on-the-soviet-german-war-
june-1941   566 Hitler, translator Manheim, *Mein Kampf* p. 619   567 Hitler's
proclamation September 3, 1939. Available at: https://avalon.law.yale.edu/wwii/gp4
.asp   568 Reynolds, *In Command of History* p. 90   569 Manchester, *Alone*
p. 452; Shirer, p. 489   570 Reynolds, *In Command of History* p. 108   571 Halifax,
p. 200   572 Schuschnigg, *Austrian Requiem* p. 17   573 HC Deb 22 February 1938
Vol 332 cc247   574 Buchanan, p. 181   575 HC Deb 22 February 1938 Vol 332
cc246   576 Churchill, *The Gathering Storm* pp. 310–11   577 Ibid. p. 346   578 Ibid.
pp. 254–55   579 Shirer, p. 426   580 Ibid. p. 364   581 Available at: https://tinyurl
.com/2nk6uwpb   582 Shirer, pp. 471, 474   583 Ibid. p. 472   584 Ibid.   585 Manchester,
Alone p. 421   586 *Daily Telegraph,* May 4, 1939   587 Manchester, *Alone* p. 439
588 Self, pp. 361–62

Chapter 13

1 Manchester, *Alone* p. 516   2 CAB 23 /1 47 (39) p. 1 443   3 Ibid. p. 1–2 443–44
4 Bethell, p. 90   5 Buchanan, p. 297   6 CAB 66/7 W.P. (40) 121 p. 8   7 Shirer,
p. 737   8 Gilbert, *Prophet* p. 1095   9 Shirer, p. 597   10 Ibid. pp. 598, 599   11 Ibid.
p. 599   12 Ibid. p. 600   13 Ibid. p. 600   14 Manchester, *Alone* p. 517   15 CAB 23/1
47 (39) p. 4 446   16 Roberts, p. 457   17 CAB 23 /1 47 (39) p. 5 447   18 Ibid.

19 Ibid. p. 8 450   20 Ibid. p. 6 448   21 Ibid. p. 8 450   22 Ibid. p. 6 448   23 Ibid. p. 7 449   24 Ibid.   25 Manchester, *Alone* p. 517   26 Ibid.   27 Gilbert, *Prophet* p. 1085   28 Ibid. p. 1083   29 Ibid. p.1080   30 Ibid. p. 1084   31 Ibid. p. 1081   32 Ibid. p. 1091   33 Manchester, *Alone* p. 485   34 Wheatcroft, *Churchill's Shadow* p. 366   35 Ibid. p. 1082   36 Ibid. p. 1094   37 Feiling, p. 430   38 Ibid.; Manchester, *Alone* p. 517   39 Manchester, *Alone* p. 517   40 Ibid.   41 Ibid.   42 Reynolds, *In Command of History* p. 107   43 HC Deb 01 September 1939 Vol 351 cc127   44 Manchester, *Alone* p. 518   45 HC Deb 01 September 1939 Vol 351 cc131   46 Self, p. 379   47 Manchester, *Alone* p. 520   48 Ibid.   49 Ibid. p. 517   50 Ibid. p. 520   51 Scott, "The 50 Greatest Yogi Berra Quotes" *USA Today* March 28, 2019 Available at: https://ftw.usatoday.com/2019/03/the-50-greatest-yogi-berra-quotes   52 Manchester, *Alone* p. 521   53 Gilbert, *Prophet* p. 1107   54 Churchill, *The Gathering Storm*, p. 406   55 Manchester, *Alone* p. 521   56 Self p. 379   57 CAB 23 /1 48 (39) p. 1 461   58 Ibid.   59 Ibid. p. 4 464   60 Ibid.   61 Ibid. p. 5 465   62 Ibid. pp. 9–10 469–70   63 Ibid. p. 11 471   64 Ibid.   65 Manchester, *Alone* p. 523   66 Churchill, *The Gathering Storm* p. 406   67 Spears, *Assignment* Vol I p. 18   68 HC Deb 02 September 1939 Vol 351 cc281   69 Spears, *Assignment* Vol I p. 20   70 Self, p. 380   71 HC Deb 02 September 1939 Vol 351 cc282–83   72 Self, p. 380   73 Ibid.   74 Manchester, *Alone* p. 530   75 Ibid.   76 Ibid. pp. 530–31   77 Roberts, p. 458   78 Ibid.   79 Duff Cooper, *Old Men Forget* pp. 59–60   80 *Companion Volumes* V/3 p. 1603   81 Churchill Archives, The Churchill Papers (4/96)   82 Manchester, *Alone* pp. 527–28   83 Roberts, p. 458   84 Halifax, p. 214   85 Ibid.   86 Ibid.   87 *DBFP* Series 3, Vol II No. 739 September 2, 1939, p. 523   88 Manchester, *Alone* p. 531   89 Self, p. 380   90 Ibid.   91 Ibid. p. 381   92 CAB 23/1 49 (39) p. 1 474   93 Ibid. p. 2 475   94 Ibid. pp. 2–3 475–6   95 Ibid. p. 6 479   96 Ibid. p. 10 483   97 Ibid. pp. 10–11 483–84   98 Manchester, *Alone* p. 534   99 Ibid.   100 Mosley, *On Borrowed Time* p. 461   101 Transcript of Chamberlain's broadcast. Available at: https://avalon.law.yale.edu/wwii/gb3.asp   102 Ibid.   103 Halifax, p. 215   104 HC Deb 03 September 1939 Vol 351 cc291   105 Ibid. cc292   106 Lukacs, *The Last European War* p. 50   107 HC Deb 03 September 1939 Vol 351 cc294–95   108 Manchester, *Alone* p. 537   109 Roberts, pp. 458, 459   110 Manchester, *Alone* p. 537; Roberts, p. 459   111 Addison, *Unexpected* p. 154   112 Manchester, *Alone* p. 537   113 Davies, *God's Playground* p. 432   114 CAB 65/2 1 (39) p. 3 16   115 Ibid. p. 4 16   116 Annex II to CAB 65/2 1 (39) p. 7 18   117 CAB 65/2 1 (39) p. 4 16   118 *DGFP* Series D, Vol I, No. 385 May 15, 1939 p. 503   119 Lukacs, *The Last European War* pp. 56, 59   120 Colville, p. 25   121 Ibid. p. 27   122 Davies, *Europe A History* p. 432   123 Lukacs, *Five Days* p. 12   124 Manchester, *Alone* p. 494; *New York Times Magazine* "The Imperturbable Gamelin" February 9, 1940   125 Colville, p. 25   126 Ibid. pp. 29, 50   127 Shirer, p. 639   128 Ibid.   129 Ibid.   130 Ibid. p. 640   131 Self, p. 399   132 Ibid.   133 Brauchitsch testimony at Nuremberg, Documents and Testimony Trial of the Major War Criminals Vol XX p. 573–575   134 See CAB 65/12 39 (39) p. 325 218   135 HC Deb 03 October 1939 Vol 351 cc1877   136 Available at: https://hitler.org/speeches/10-06-39.html; Roberts, p. 474   137 Available at: https://hitler.org/speeches/10-06-39.html; Roberts, p. 474   138 Available at: https://hitler.org/speeches/10-06-39.html   139 Ibid.; Roberts, p. 474   140 ed. Gorodetsky, *Maisky Diaries* p. 231   141 CAB 65/ 7 40 (39) p. 330 221   142 Ibid.   143 ed. Self, Vol 4 p. 454 Chamberlain to his sister Ida, October 8, 1939   144 Self, pp. 399–400   145 CAB 65/8 42 (39) p. 343 230   146 CAB 65/ 17 44 (39) p. 363 242   147 HC Deb 12 October 1939 Vol 352 cc565   148 Ibid. cc565–66   149 Ibid. cc567   150 Ibid.   151 Ibid. cc568   152 Colville, p. 34   153 Self, p. 399   154 Colville, p. 35; Self, p. 399   155 Colville, p. 35   156 CAB 65/16 46 (39) p. 361 253   157 Shirer, p. 643   158 Colville, p. 40   159 Self, p. 401   160 Ibid.   161 Ibid. p. 402   162 Delgado, *Second World War Diary—Part 1* p. 46   163 Available at: http://der-fuehrer.org/reden/english/wardirectives/06.html   164 Shirer, pp. 643–44   165 Ibid. p. 647   166 Lukacs, *The Last European War* p. 59   167 Shirer, p. 645; See also Directive No. 6   168 Hitler, translator Manheim, *Mein Kampf* p. 619   169 Available at: http://der-fuehrer.org/reden/english/wardirectives/06.html   170 Lambert, "Churchill, Hitler, and the Battle of Britain," 185 *Finest Hour* 19 (2019). Available at: https://winstonchurchill.org/publications/finest-hour/finest-hour-185 Churchill-hitler-and-the-battle-of-britain/   171 Lukacs, *The Last European War* p. 101   172 *DGFP* Series D,

Vol X No. 152 p. 188   173 Manchester and Reid, pp. 116–17   174 Halder, *Halder's Diary* Vol IV part 2 July 22, 1940, p. 127   175 Lukacs, *Five Days* p. 12   176 Self, p. 383   177 Colville, p. 28   178 Feiling, p. 417   179 Ibid.   180 Self, p. 394   181 Ibid. pp. 395, 397   182 Ibid. p. 395   183 Lukacs, *Last European War* p 56   184 Gallup, *Gallup International Public Opinion Polls* pp. 24–33   185 Lukacs, *Last European War* p. 61   186 Self, p. 398   187 ed. Self, Vol 4 pp. 451, 456, 460 Chamberlain to his sister Ida, September 8, 22 and 23 October 1939   188 Self, p. 398   189 Colville, p. 58   190 CAB 66/ 7 WP (39) 79; Churchill's comments at the War Cabinet meeting of September 19, 1939, CAB 65/11 20 (39) p. 159 115   191 CAB 65/2 84 (40) p. 246 163   192 Colville, p. 71   193 CAB 65/11 20 (39) p. 159 115   194 Lukacs, *Last European War*, p. 72   195 Shirer, p. 675   196 Churchill, *The Gathering Storm*, p. 561   197 Shirer, p. 678   198 *DGFP* Series D, Vol III "Directive for Fall Wesserubung" March 1, 1940, No. 644 p. 831   199 *Ibid.* p. 832   200 CAB 65/2 74 (40) p. 152 107   201 Ibid. p. 194 131; Manchester, *Alone* p. 625   202 Manchester, *Alone* p. 628   203 Churchill, *The Gathering Storm* p. 579   204 Manchester, *Alone* p. 625   205 Ibid. pp. 625–26   206 Colville, p. 97   207 Shirer, p. 673   208 Ibid. p. 697   209 Lukacs, *The Last European War* p. 73 n. 39   210 CAB 66/7 WP (40) 122 Enclosure I p. 1 15   211 Ibid. Enclosure II p. 4 18   212 Ibid. p. 5 19   213 Colville, pp. 94–95   214 Manchester, *Alone* p. 628   215 CAB 66/7 WP 127 (40) p. 3 50; HC Deb 11 April 1940 Vol 359 cc740, 741   216 Report of Sir Samuel Hoare, the Secretary of State for Air at the War Cabinet meeting of April 8, 1940, CAB 65/2 84 (40) pp. 246–7 163–64   217 HC Deb 07 May 1940 Vol 360 cc1143   218 The Norway Campaign. Available at: https://war-experience.org/events/the-1940-norway-campaign/   219 CAB 66/7 WP 127 (40) p. 3 50; HC Deb 02 May 1940 Vol 360 cc908   220 HC Deb 07 May 1940 Vol 360 cc1143   221 CAB 66/7 WP 127 (40) p. 3 50; HC Deb 11 April 1940 Vol 359 cc740, 741   222 HC Deb 07 May 1940 Vol 360 cc1143   223 HC Deb 11 April 1940 Vol 359 cc741   224 CAB 65/5 87 (40) p. 269–70 178   225 CAB 66/7 WP 127 (40) p. 4 50   226 HC Deb 11 April 1940 Vol 359 cc741–744   227 Shirer, p. 697   228 Ibid. p. 698   229 *DGFP* Series D, Vol IX, Telegram, April 9, 1940, No. 65, p. 102   230 CAB 65/1 85 (40) p. 255 169   231 Colville, p. 98   232 CAB 66/7 WP 127 (40) p. 4 50   233 *New York Times,* "By Winston Churchill: The Second World War" May 15, 1948   234 CAB 65/1 85 (40) p. 255 169   235 Ibid. pp. 255–56 169   236 Ibid. p. 257 170   237 Ibid. pp. 257–58 170–1   238 CAB 66/7 WP 127 (40) p. 4 50; Shirer, p. 701–02   239 The Norway Campaign. Available at: https://war-experience.org/events/the-1940-norway-campaign/   240 Lukacs, *The Last European War* p. 73   241 Shirer, p. 702   242 Ibid. pp. 702–03   243 Ibid. p. 703   244 Chamberlain's explanation in his speech to the House on May 7, 1940, HC Deb 07 May 1940 Vol 360 cc1082   245 *The Times* April 6, 1940   246 Manchester, *Alone* p. 629   247 Lukacs, *The Last European War*, p. 73   248 HC Deb 09 April 1940 Vol 359 cc507   249 Ibid. cc508   250 Ibid.   251 Ibid. cc509   252 Ibid. cc508   253 Colville, p. 99   254 Ibid. p. 100   255 Shirer, p. 707   256 CAB 65/1 86 (40) p. 261 173   257 Shirer, pp. 703–04   258 CAB 66/7 WP 127 (40) p. 4 50; HC Deb 11 April 1940 Vol 359 cc744   259 CAB 66/7 WP 127 (40) p. 4 50; HC Deb 11 April 1940 Vol 359 cc744   260 CAB 66/7 WP 127 (40) p. 4 50; HC Deb 11 April 1940 Vol 359 cc744   261 CAB 65/5 87 (40) p. 269 178   262 Ibid. p. 273 180   263 Ibid. p. 269 178   264 Ibid. pp. 269–70 178   265 Confidential Annex to CAB 65/5 87 (40) p. 1 158   266 Ibid.   267 Ibid.   268 Ibid.   269 Ibid. p. 2 159   270 Ibid. p. 4 161   271 Confidential Annex to CAB 65/5 88 (40) p. 1 163   272 Shirer, p. 707   273 HC Deb 11 April 1940 Vol 359 cc741   274 Lukacs, *Last European War* p. 74   275 Ibid.   276 Churchill, *The Gathering Storm* p. 649   277 HC Deb 11 April 1940 Vol 359 cc746   278 Roberts, p. 490   279 HC Deb 11 April 1940 Vol 359 cc746–7   280 Ibid. cc747   281 Manchester, *Alone* p. 632   282 HC Deb 08 May 1940 Vol 360 cc1349   283 Ibid.; Manchester, *Alone* p. 632   284 HC Deb 08 May 1940 Vol 360 cc1349   285 Confidential Annex to CAB 65/5 88 (40) p. 1 163   286 Ibid. p. 1 165   287 Ibid. p. 2 166   288 Ibid. p. 3 167   289 Ibid. pp. 3–4 167–68   290 Ibid. p. 3 167   291 Ibid. p. 4 168   292 Colville, p. 102   293 Confidential Annex to CAB 65/3 90 (40) p. 1 181   294 Ibid.   295 Manchester, *Alone* p. 638   296 Confidential Annex to CAB 65/3 90 (40) p. 1 181   297 Ibid.   298 Ibid. pp. 1–2 181–82   299 Ibid. p. 2 182   300 Confidential Annex to CAB 65/3 91 (40) p. 1 184   301 Ibid.   302 Ibid.   303 Ibid.   304 ed. Self, Vol 4

p. 525 Chamberlain to his sister Ida May 4, 1940   305 Confidential Annex to CAB 65/3 91 (40) p. 2 185   306 Ibid.   307 Ibid.   308 Ibid.   309 Ibid. p. 3 186   310 CAB 66/7 WP 131 (40) p. 4 75   311 CAB 65/2 92 (40) p. 311 204   312 Roberts, p. 489   313 HC Deb 02 May 1940 Vol 360 cc909   314 Ibid.   315 Ibid.   316 Statement of Chamberlain to the House on May 7, 1940, HC Deb 07 May 1940 Vol 360 cc1077   317 CAB 65/1 93 (40) p. 323 211   318 Statement of Churchill to the House on May 8, 1940, HC Deb 08 May 1940 Vol 360 cc1353   319 Ibid. cc1354   320 CAB 66/7 WP 131 (40) p. 4 75   321 Ibid. p. 10 78; CAB 65/3 96 (40) p. 355 230   322 HC Deb 02 May 1940 Vol 360 cc909   323 CAB 66/7 WP 133 (40) Annex I p. 1 102; CAB 66/7 WP 133 (40) Annex II pp. 1, 2 105; HC Deb 08 May 1940 Vol 360 cc1354; Manchester, *Alone* p. 638   324 CAB 66/7 WP 133 (40) Annex I p. 1 102; The Norway Campaign. Available at https://war-experience.org/events/the-1940-norway-campaign/   325 CAB 66/7 WP (40) 133 Annex I p. 1 102; HC Deb 08 May 1940 Vol 360 cc1354   326 CAB 66/7 WP (40) 135 p. 1 128   327 CAB 65/4 105 (40) p. 436 279   328 HC Deb 08 May 1940 Vol 360 cc1354   329 Jackson, *The Fall of France:* pp. 84–85   330 Roberts, p. 493   331 Manchester, *Alone* p. 646   332 CAB 66/7 WP (40) 165 pp. 2, 4 292, 294   333 Manchester and Reid, p. 57   334 HC Deb 07 May 1940 Vol 360 cc1080   335 ed. Self, Vol 4 p. 525 Chamberlain to his sister Ida, May 4, 1940   336 See, CAB 65/3 104 (40) p. 427 274   337 Roberts, p. 488   338 Lukacs, *Five Days* p. 12   339 Ibid.   340 Roberts, p. 488   341 Blake, Times Literary Supplement, April 22, 1994; Roberts, p. 488   342 Roberts, p. 488   343 Ibid. p. 489   344 Manchester, *Alone* p. 637   345 Colville, p. 107   346 Manchester, *Alone* p. 639   347 Ibid. p. 637   348 Ibid. p. 638   349 Ibid. p. 636   350 CAB 65/ 1 105 (40) p. 433 278   351 Roberts, p. 488   352 Lukacs, *The Last European War* p. 271; Manchester, *Alone* p. 640   353 Lukacs, *The Last European War* p. 271   354 Colville, p. 112   355 Ibid. pp. 113–4; Manchester, *Alone* p. 636   356 Manchester, *Alone* p. 636   357 HC Deb 02 May 1940 Vol 360 cc912   358 ed. Nicolson, *Nicolson Diaries* Vol II p. 75   359 Ibid.   360 Roberts, p. 493   361 Manchester and Reid, p. 58   362 ed. Gorodetsky, *Maisky Diaries* p. 232   363 Roberts, p. 475   364 ed. Gorodetsky, *Maisky Diaries* p. 28   365 Ibid. p. 110   366 Roberts, p. 380   367 Raico, *Rethinking Churchill and World War I* p. 324   368 HC Deb 17 November 1938 Vol 341 cc1196   369 Manchester, *Alone* pictures following p. 448   370 Self, p. 417   371 Feiling, p. 435   372 Self, p. 417   373 ed. Self, Vol 4 p. 513, Chamberlain to his sister Ida, March 30, 1940   374 Manchester, *Alone* p. 598   375 ed. James, *Chips* p. 234   376 Roberts, p. 486   377 Manchester, *Alone* p. 638   378 HC Deb 08 May 1940 Vol 360 cc1353   379 Roberts, pp. 377–79   380 Roberts, p. 490   381 Reynolds, *In Command of History* p. 9   382 ed Self, Vol 4 p. 379 Chamberlain to his sister Hilda, April 6 and to his sister Ida, April 27, 1940   383 Self, p. 418   384 Roberts, p. 490   385 ed. Self, Vol 4 p. 520; Colville, p. 104   386 Self, p. 418   387 ed. Self, Vol 4, p. 522; Self, p. 418   388 Self, p. 419   389 Ibid.   390 Colville, p. 108   391 Ibid.   392 Self, p. 419   393 Ibid. p. 418   394 Roberts, p. 491   395 ed. James, *Chips,* p. 242   396 Self, p. 419   397 Gilbert, *Churchill War Papers, at the Admiralty* p. 1169   398 Roberts, p. 492   399 Self, p. 420   400 Gallup, *Gallup International Public Opinion Polls* p. 33   401 Self, p. 421   402 ed. James, *Chips* pp. 242–244, April 26 and 30, May 2, 3, and 5, 1940; ed. Nicholson, *Nicholson Diaries,* Vol II p. 74 April 30, 1940   403 Self, p. 421   404 Manchester, *Alone* p. 644   405 Ibid.   406 Ibid. p. 647   407 Self, p. 422   408 Manchester, *Alone* p. 648   409 HC Deb 07 May 1940 Vol 360 cc1075   410 Manchester, *Alone* p. 648   411 Colville, p. 117   412 HC Deb 07 May 1940 Vol 360 cc1125   413 Ibid.   414 Ibid. cc1125–6   415 Ibid. cc1126   416 Ibid.   417 Ibid. cc1127   418 Ibid.   419 Ibid. cc1128   420 Self, p. 423   421 HC Deb 07 May 1940 Vol 360 cc1129   422 Manchester, *Alone* p. 649   423 Ibid.   424 HC Deb 07 May 1940 Vol 360 cc1140   425 Ibid. cc1143   426 Ibid.   427 Ibid. cc1146   428 Ibid. cc1150   429 Ibid.   430 Manchester, *Alone* p. 650   431 Self, p. 423   432 Churchill, *The Gathering Storm* p. 659   433 Self, p. 423   434 HC Deb 08 May 1940 Vol 360 cc1265, 1361   435 Ibid. cc1266   436 Ibid.   437 Williams, *Politics—Grave And Gay* (n.d.) p. 112   438 HC Deb 08 May 1940 Vol 360 cc1283   439 Self, p. 425   440 HC Deb 08 May 1940 Vol 360 cc1282   441 Ibid.   442 Ibid.   443 Macmillan, *The Blast of War* p. 61   444 ed. James, *Chips* p. 246   445 Manchester, *Alone* p. 659   446 ed. James, *Chips* p. 246   447 HC Deb 08 May 1940 Vol 360 cc1353   448 HC Deb 08 May 1940 Vol 360

cc1354   449 Ibid. cc1355   450 Ibid.   451 Ibid. cc1356   452 Ibid. cc1356–7
453 HC Deb 07 May 1940 Vol 360 cc1144   454 HC Deb 08 May 1940 Vol 360
cc1359   455 Manchester, *Alone* p. 648   456 Ibid. p. 656   457 HC Deb 08 May 1940
Vol 360 cc1362   458 Ibid.   459 Ibid.   460 Ibid.   461 Manchester, *Alone* p. 657
462 McCarten, p. 10   463 Ibid. p. 9   464 Lukacs, *Five Days*, p. 12   465 ed. Stuart,
Reith Diaries, p. 249   466 Colville, p. 310   467 Roberts, p. 501   468 Manchester,
Alone p. 657   469 Ibid.   470 Feiling, p. 432   471 ed. Nicholson, *Nicholson Diaries*
Vol II pp. 180, 181   472 ed. Gorodetsky, *Maisky Diaries*, p. 275   473 Churchill,
The Gathering Storm, p. 661   474 Manchester, *Alone* p. 659   475 Colville, p. 125
476 Manchester, *Alone* p. 659   477 Ibid. p. 660   478 Churchill, *The Gathering Storm*,
p. 661   479 Manchester, *Alone* p. 659   480 Ibid. p. 660

Chapter 14

1 Avon Papers at Birmingham University Archives 20/I/20, and 20/I/23   2 Eden,
Memoirs: Facing the Dictators p. 28   3 Self, p. 429   4 Roberts, pp. 501–02   5 Ibid.
p. 502   6 Ibid. p. 504   7 Self, p. 430   8 Lukacs, *Five Days* p. 12   9 Ibid. p. 22
10 Roberts, p. 502   11 Ibid. p. 507   12 Ibid. p. 502   13 Roberts, *Holy Fox* p. 266
14 Osbourn, *Operation Pike* p. 3   15 Manchester, *Alone* pp. 668–69   16 Ibid.
p. 663   17 Halifax, pp. 223–24   18 Roberts, p. 506   19 Ibid. p. 507   20 ed. Dilks,
Cadogan Diary p. 280   21 Halifax, p. 224   22 Lukacs, *Five Days* p. 3   23 Colville,
p. 123   24 Ibid. p. 121   25 Ibid. pp. 29, 50   26 Roberts, pp. 508–09   27 Halifax,
p. 224   28 Churchill, *The Gathering Storm* pp. 661–62   29 Roberts, p. 503
30 Thompson, *1940*, p. 92   31 Manchester, *Alone* p. 663   32 Ibid.   33 Ibid.
34 Gilbert, *Finest Hours* p. 305   35 CAB 66/7 WP (40) 126 p. 2 47   36 CAB 65 /2 118
(40) p. 82 52   37 Ibid. p. 83 53   38 Ibid.   39 Manchester, *Alone* p. 671   40 Churchill's
speech to the House on June 4, HC Deb 04 June 1940 Vol 361 cc789   41 Shirer, p. 716
42 Manchester, *Alone* p. 670   43 Grenhan and Nicoll, *Dunkirk Evacuation-Operation
Dynamo* p. viii   44 CAB 65/1 117 (40) p. 76 48   45 Manchester, *Alone* p. 672   46 Ibid.;
Roberts, p. 510   47 Halifax Papers, Diary 5/10/40 p. 2   48 Roberts, p. 510; Manchester,
Alone p. 672   49 Roberts, p. 510; Manchester, *Alone* p. 672   50 Manchester, *Alone*
p. 672   51 Roberts, p. 510   52 Manchester, *Alone* p. 673   53 CAB 65/5 119 (40)
p. 94 59   54 Ibid.   55 Manchester, *Alone* p. 673   56 CAB 65/1 119 (40) p. 91 58
57 Ibid. p. 94 59   58 CAB 65/5 119 (40) p. 94 59   59 Ibid.   60 Manchester, *Alone*
p. 674   61 Roberts, p. 511   62 Diary of Mackenzie King, June 10, 1939, Canadian
National Archives, Item 20426   63 Churchill, *The Gathering Storm* p. 665
64 Manchester and Reid, p. 51   65 Reproduced in its entirety in McCarten, p. 80
66 Self, p. 431   67 Roberts, p. 512   68 Halifax, pp. 225–26   69 Ibid. p. 225
70 Churchill, *Their Finest Hour*, p. 9   71 Ibid.   72 Ibid.   73 *The Times*, May 11,
1940   74 Churchill, *Their Finest Hour* p. 9   75 Manchester and Reid, p. 58   76 Ibid.;
Churchill, *Their Finest Hour*, p. 10   77 Churchill, *Their Finest Hour* p. 10   78 Ibid.
79 Ibid.   80 Lukacs, *Five Days* pp. 70–71   81 Ibid. p. 71   82 Ibid.   83 Ibid.   84 Ibid.
p. 56   85 Cannadine, *Aspects Of Aristocracy*, 132   86 Colville, p. 122   87 Howard,
Rab p. 94   88 Colville, p. 122; Manchester and Reid, p. 54   89 Quoted in Manchester
and Reid, p. 54   90 Lukacs, *Five Days* p. 23   91 Cannadine, *Aspects of Aristocracy*
p. 161   92 Personal interview William Manchester with Sir John Colville, October 8,
1980, referenced in Manchester, *Alone* p. 677   93 eds. Macleod and Kelly, *The Ironside
Diaries* p. 293   94 ed. Vincent, *Crawford* p. 614   95 Kennedy, p. 66   96 Lukacs, *Five
Days* p. 22   97 Manchester, *Alone* p. 677; Colville, p. 128   98 Colville, p. 122   99 ed.
Self, Vol 4 p. 530   100 King, *With Malice Toward None*, p. 50   101 Self, p. 436
102 Manchester and Reid, p. 54; Lukacs, *Five Days* p. 211   103 Manchester and Reid,
p. 54   104 Ibid.   105 Churchill, *Their Finest Hour* p. 10   106 Manchester, *Alone* p. 666;
Manchester and Reid, p. 61   107 Churchill, *Their Finest Hour* p. 30   108 Churchill,
Their Finest Hour p. 30; Shirer, p. 719   109 CAB 66/7 WP 145 (40) Annex p. 5 191
110 Ibid.   111 CAB 66/7 WP 150 (40) Attachment p. 2 208   112 Manchester and Reid,
p. 61   113 Lukacs, *The Last European War* p. 77   114 Ibid.   115 Ibid.; Manchester,
Alone p. 666; Manchester and Reid p. 61; 116 Manchester, *Alone* p. 666; Manchester
and Reid, p. 61; Shirer, p. 718   117 Lukacs, *The Last European War* p. 77   118 Ibid.;

Manchester, *Alone* p. 666   119 Shirer, p. 717   120 Ibid.   121 Ibid.   122 Churchill, *The Gathering Storm*, p. 667   123 McCarten, p. 105   124 Ibid.   125 Ibid. p.116 126 Ibid.   127 Roberts, p. 526   128 Ibid.   129 Manchester and Reid, pp. 62 130 Ibid.   131 Ibid.   132 Ibid.   133 Lukacs, *Five Days* p. 14   134 Gilbert, *Finest Hour* p. 327   135 Lukacs, *Five Days* p. 14   136 Colville, p. 129   137 HC Deb 13 May 1940 Vol 360 cc1501–2   138 McCarten, pp. 123–24   139 Ibid. p. 124   140 HC Deb 13 May 1940 Vol 360 cc1510   141 McCarten, p. 124   142 CAB 65/ 1 120 (40) p. 109 71   143 Manchester and Reid, p. 62; Churchill, *Their Finest Hour* p. 40   144 Manchester and Reid, p. 62; Churchill, *Their Finest Hour* p. 41   145 CAB 65/1 121 (40) p. 117 76   146 Ibid.   147 Churchill, *Their Finest Hour* p. 36; Manchester and Reid, p. 61 148 Grenhan and Nicoll, p. ix   149 HC Deb 18 June 1940 Vol 362 cc51   150 CAB 65/3 121 (40) p. 118 76   151 Colville, p. 130   152 Manchester and Reid, p. 62   153 Ibid. 154 Ibid.   155 CAB65/1 122 (40) p. 125 81   156 Ibid.; Churchill, *Their Finest Hour* p. 40   157 CAB 65/1 122 (40) p. 125 81   158 Ibid.   159 Ibid.   160 Ibid.   161 CAB 65/1 122 (40) p. 127 82   162 Manchester and Reid, p. 62   163 Ibid. p. 63   164 Shirer, p. 724   165 CAB 65/1 123 (40) p. 131 85   166 Ibid.   167 Manchester and Reid, p. 64   168 Shirer, p. 720   169 CAB 65/1 123 (40) p. 131 85   170 Ibid.   171 Ibid. 172 Ibid.   173 Ibid.   174 Ibid.   175 Colville p. 131   176 CAB 66/7 WP 159 (40) Attachment p. 3 264   177 Ibid.   178 Ibid.   179 ed. Dilks, *Cadogan Diaries* p. 311; See Lukacs, *The Last European War* p. 79   180 Confidential Annex to CAB 65/2 123 (40) p. 2 72   181 Ibid.   182 Ibid. p. 8 78   183 CAB 65/4 123 (40) p. 133 86 184 Ibid.   185 Ibid.   186 Ibid. p. 135 87   187 Ibid.   188 Ibid.   189 Ibid.   190 Ibid. p. 137 88   191 Roberts, p. 530   192 CAB/65 10 123 (40) 137 88   193 ed. Kimball *Complete Correspondence* I p. 37; Lukacs, *Five Days* pp. 70–73   194 ed. Kimball, *Complete Correspondence* I p. 37   195 Ibid.; Lukacs, *Five Days* pp. 70–73 196 Manchester and Reid, p. 110   197 Lukacs, *Five Days* p. 73   198 Manchester and Reid, p. 64   199 Ibid.   200 Churchill Archives, Correspondence between WSC and Benito Mussolini (05/16/1940-05/18/1940), CHUR 4/152 pp. 5   201 The Churchill Papers (Char 20/14), Churchill Archives Centre (Cambridge)   202 Churchill Archives Correspondence between WSC and Benito Mussolini (05/16/1940–05/18/1940), CHUR 4/152 pp. 5   203 Ibid. pp 6   204 Confidential Annex to CAB 65/1 124 (40) p.1 82   205 Ibid. p. 3 84   206 Ibid. p. 2 83   207 CAB 65/ 1 124 (40) p. 143 92   208 Confidential Annex to CAB 65/1 124 (40) p. 5 86   209 CAB 65/13 124 (40) p. 150 95   210 Ibid.   211 Ibid.   212 Roberts, p. 531   213 Grenhan and Nicoll, p. viii   214 Shirer, p. 726   215 Colville, p. 261 No. 2   216 Ibid. p. 177   217 Roberts, p. 531   218 Ibid. p. 532   219 Colville, p. 177   220 CAB 65/1 125 (40) p. 153 98; Roberts, p. 532; McCarten, p. 151   221 CAB 65/1 125 (40) p. 153 98   222 Ibid. 223 Ibid.   224 Manchester and Reid, p. 67   225 Ibid.   226 CAB 66/7 WP (40) 165 p. 7 309   227 CAB 65/1 126 (40) p. 159 101   228 Ibid. p. 157 101   229 Ibid.   230 Ibid. 231 Ibid.   232 Ibid.   233 Ibid.   234 Ibid. p. 158 101   235 Ibid. p. 159 102   236 Ibid. p. 158 101   237 Ibid.   238 McCarten, p. 154   239 Roberts, p. 530   240 Colville p. 134   241 Roberts, p. 533   242 Ibid.   243 Shirer, p. 726   244 Manchester and Reid, p. 70   245 CAB 66/7 WP (40) 167 p. 8 309   246 Ibid.; CAB 65/1 129 (40) p. 181 116   247 CAB 65/1 129 (40) p. 181 116   248 Roberts, p. 534   249 CAB 65/1 129 (40); Roberts, p. 534   250 ed. Dilks, *Cadogan Diaries* p. 283   251 CAB65/1 129 (40) p. 181 116   252 Ibid.   253 ed. Dilks, *Cadogan Diaries* p. 286; Shirer, p. 728   254 Roberts, p. 535   255 Shirer, p. 728   256 Roberts p. 535   257 Confidential Annex to CAB 65/1 130 (40) p. 2   258 Nicoll and Grenhan, p. x   259 Eden, *The Reckoning* p. 123 260 Ibid.   261 CAB 65/8 129 (40) p. 186 118   262 Shirer, p. 728   263 Ibid. 264 ed. Dilks, *Cadogan Diaries* p. 286; Shirer, p. 728   265 Roberts, pp. 535–36 266 Confidential Annex to CAB 65/1 130 (40) p. 1 95   267 Ibid.   268 Ibid. pp. 2–3 96–97   269 Ibid. p. 3 97   270 Ibid. p. 4 98   271 Quoted in Roberts, *Hitler and Churchill: Secrets of Leadership* p. 92   272 Lukacs, *Five Days* p. 26   273 Available at: https://winstonchurchill.org/resources/speeches/1940-the-finest-hour/be-ye-men-of-valour/   274 Ibid.   275 Ibid.   276 Colville, p. 136   277 Lukacs, *Five Days* p. 16 278 Nicoll and Grenhan, p. ix   279 CAB 65/1 131 (40) p. 191 123   280 Manchester and Reid p. 70   281 Ibid.   282 Ibid. pp. 70–71   283 Lukacs, *The Last European War* p. 80   284 Shirer p. 728   285 Ibid.   286 CAB 65/1 132 (40) 201 129   287 CAB 65/2 131

(40) p. 192 123   288 CAB 65/3 131 (40) p. 192 123; CAB 65/6 121 (40) p. 120
77   289 CAB 65/7 131 (40) p. 194 124   290 CAB 65/8 131 (40) p. 194 124   291 CAB
66/7 WP (40) 159 262   292 Confidential Annex to CAB 65/10 131 (40) pp. 2–3 101–
02   293 Ibid. p. 3 102   294 Ibid.   295 Lukacs, *Five Days* p. 26   296 ed. Kimball,
Churchill & Roosevelt Vol 3 p. 40   297 Colville, p. 136   298 Manchester and Reid,
pp. 105–06   299 Ibid. p. 106   300 Kimball, *Churchill & Roosevelt* Vol 1 p. 41   301 CAB
65/11 132 (40) p. 206 131   302 Ibid.   303 Manchester and Reid, pp. 72–73; CAB 65/1
132 (40) p. 201 129   304 McCarten, p. 167   305 Colville, p. 138   306 Manchester and
Reid, p. 71   307 Halder, *The Halder Diaries* Vol IV p. 24   308 CAB 65 /1 133 (40) p. 213
136   309 Ibid. pp. 215–16 137   310 Manchester and Reid, p. 73   311 CAB 65/11
133 (40) p. 221 140   312 Annex to CAB 65/11 133 (40) p. 222 140   313 Colville,
p. 138   314 Ibid.   315 Manchester and Reid, p. 72; Shirer, p. 728   316 Confidential
Annex to CAB 65/1 134 (40) p. 1 109   317 Ibid. p. 2 110   318 Ibid.   319 Lukacs,
Five Days p. 87   320 Jackson, *France: The Dark Years, 1940–1944* pp. 124–125,
133; Manchester and Reid, p. 88   321 Manchester and Reid, p. 73   322 Ibid. p. 72
323 CAB 65/1 135 (40) p. 227 145   324 Ibid.   325 Ibid.   326 Colville, p.139;
Roberts, p. 539   327 Colville, p. 139   328 CAB 65/1 135 (40) p. 227 145   329 Ibid.
330 Ibid.   331 Ibid. p. 228 145   332 Ibid.   333 HC Deb 23 May 1940 Vol 361
cc314   334 Ibid. cc330   335 Manchester and Reid, p. 72   336 CAB 65/1 136 (40)
p. 234 149   337 Ibid.   338 Colville, p. 139   339 Lukacs, *Five Days,* p. 26, n. 35;
Roberts, p. 539   340 Shirer, p. 728   341 CAB 65/1 136 (40) p. 234 149, May 23,
940   342 Ibid.   343 Ibid.   344 Ibid. p. 235 150   345 Potter, *Pim* p. 5; Roberts,
p. 539   346 Potter, *Pim* p. 5   347 Ibid.   348 Lukacs, *Five Days* p. 27   349 Ibid.
350 Lukacs, *Five Days* p. 38   351 Chamberlain Diary I/20   352 Gilbert, *Finest Hour*
p. 387   353 Roberts, 'Hidden Diaries' *The Sun,* May 5, 2020. Available at: https://www
.thesun.co.uk/news/11556640/king-george-wartime-diaries-revealed/   354 Gilbert,
Finest Hour p. 388   355 Ibid.   356 Reynaud, *In The Thick of the Fight, 1930–1935*
pp. 370–71   357 Manchester and Reid p. 73   358 *Churchill War Papers* Vol II
p. 139   359 Shirer pp. 728, 731   360 Ibid. p. 731   361 Roberts p. 541   362 Lukacs,
Five Days p. 42; Lukacs, *The Last European War* pp. 90–91   363 Lukacs, *Five Days*
p. 42   364 Available at: http://comicism.tripod.com/390428.html#:~:text=Hitler%20
Speech%3A%20April%2028%2C%201939&text=Members%20of%20the%20
German%20Reichstag%3A&text=Providence%20granted%20that%20I%20
might,alone%20has%20been%20my%20   365 Lukacs, *Five Days,* p. 41   366 Ansel,
Hitler Confronts England, p. 85   367 Toland, *Adolf Hitler* Vol 2 p. 705   368 Roberts,
p. 541   369 Krause, Döhring, and Plaim, *Living with Hitler* part 2 note 54; Phifer,
A Handbook of Military Strategy and Tactics p. 64   370 Churchill, *Their Finest Hour*
p. 78   371 Phifer, *Handbook of Military Strategy* p. 64   372 Shirer, p. 732; Accord,
Manchester and Reid, p. 74   373 Churchill, *Their Finest Hour,* p. 76   374 Shirer,
p. 732   375 Ibid. pp. 732–33   376 Shirer, p. 733   377 History Extra, 9 Things You
(Probably Didn't Know About Dunkirk). Available at: https://www.historyextra.com/
period/second-world-war/dunkirk-facts-history-east-mole-hitler-halt-order-douglas-
jardine/   378 402 Bond, *Britain, France, and Belgium 1939–1940* pp. 104–105
379 Shirer, p. 747   380 Ibid.   381 US Army, *Historical Study German Tank Maintenance
In World War II,* p. 1. Available at: https://history.army.mil/html/books/104/104-7/
cmhPub_104-7.pdf   382 Ibid.   383 Churchill's address to the House HC Deb 04 June
1940 Vol 361 cc789   384 Churchill, *Their Finest Hour* pp. 76–78   385 CAB 65 /1 137
(40) p. 239 153   386 Ibid. p. 240 153   387 Lukacs, *Five Days,* p. 43   388 CAB 65 /9 137
(40)   389 McCarten, p. 179   390 CAB 65 /7 137 (40) p. 243 155   391 Ibid.   392 Ibid.
393 Ibid.   394 McCarten, p. 177   395 Gilbert, *Prophet* p. 390   396 McCarten, p. 177

Chapter 15

1 CAB 66/7 WP (40) 168   2 Ibid. p. 1 319   3 Ibid.   4 Ibid. Annex, p. 5 321
5 Ibid. p. 1 319   6 May 26 notes of Minister without Portfolio Greenwood, CAB
66/8 WP (40) 171 p. 2 6   7 CAB 66/7 WP (40) 168 p. 1 319   8 CAB 66/7 WP (40)
168 Annex p. 10 323   9 CAB 66/8 WP (40) 201 p. 1 168; CAB 66/8 WP (40) 201
p. 4 171   10 CAB 66/8 WP (40) 203 pp. 2 182   11 Appendix B to CAB 66/7 WP (40)

168 p. 14 325   12 Appendices C1 and C2 to CAB 66/7 WP (40) 168 pp. 15, 16, 325, 326   13 CAB 66/7 WP (40) 169 p. 1 330   14 Ibid. pp. 1–4 330–34   15 CAB 65/1 138 (40) p. 251 160   16 Manchester and Reid, p. 75   17 CAB 65/1 138 (40) p. 251 160   18 Ibid.   19 Ibid.   20 Ibid.   21 Ibid.   22 Ibid.   23 Ibid.   24 Ibid.   25 Ibid. 26 Manchester and Reid, p. 76   27 Ibid. p. 75   28 Ibid.   29 Ibid.   30 Ibid. p. 76 31 Ibid. pp. 76, 79   32 Ibid. p. 79   33 Ibid. p. 76   34 Ibid.   35 Ibid.   36 Ibid. p. 81   37 Ibid. pp. 79–80   38 Ibid. p. 79   39 Ibid. p. 80   40 Roberts, p. 541; Lukacs, *Five Days* pp. 91–92   41 CAB 65/8 138 (40) p. 255 162   42 Ibid.   43 Ibid.   44 Lukacs, *Five Days* pp. 90–91   45 CAB 65/8 138 (40) p. 255 162   46 Ibid.   47 Ibid.   48 Roberts, p. 541; Lukacs, *Five Days* p. 92   49 CAB 67/7 WP (40) 170 pp. 1 et seq. 335–40 50 Roberts, p. 541   51 Ibid.   52 Lukas, *Five Days* p. 144, n. 7   53 CAB 67/7 WP (40) 170 Annex, p. 1 338   54 Annex to CAB 66/7 WP (40) 170 p. 2 339   55 Lukacs, *Five Days* p. 93   56 Annex to CAB 66/7 WP (40) 170 p. 2 339   57 Halifax Papers, A. 410.4.I   58 Lukacs, *Five Days* p. 144   59 Churchill, *Their Finest Hour* pp. 81–82 60 Ibid. p. 82   61 Ibid.   62 Roberts, p. 540   63 Ibid.   64 CAB 65/1 143 (40) p. 278 178 May 27, 1940   65 Churchill, *Their Finest Hours* p. 82   66 Lukacs, *Five Days* p. 88   67 Ibid.   68 Ibid.   69 Ibid. p. 89   70 Ibid. p. 97   71 CAB 69/1 WP (40) p. 4 58, Minutes of a Meeting of ministers and the Chiefs of Staff held at the Admiralty on 25th May 1940 at 10:00 PM

Chapter 16

1 Manchester and Reid, p. 83   2 Ibid.   3 Ibid.   4 Ibid.   5 Lukacs, *Five Days* p. 137 6 Confidential Annex to CAB 65/ 1 139 (40) p. 1 138   7 Attachment to Confidential Annex to 65/ 1 145 (40) p. 1 191   8 Confidential Annex to CAB 65/ 1 139 (40) p. 1 138 9 Confidential Annex to CAB 65/ 1 139 (40) p. 2 139   10 Ibid. at Appendix p. 1 144 11 Ibid. p. 3 140   12 Ibid. p. 2 139   13 Ibid. p. 3 140   14 Ibid.   15 Ibid. 16 Confidential Annex to CAB 65/ 1 139 (40) pp. 3–4 140–41   17 McCarten, p. 183 18 Manchester and Reid, p.110   19 Confidential Annex to CAB 65/ 1 139 (40) p. 4 141   20 Ibid.   21 Ibid.   22 Ibid.   23 Ibid.   24 Ibid.   25 Ibid.   26 Lukacs, *Five Days* p. 108   27 Confidential Annex to CAB 65/ 1 139 (40) p. 5 142   28 Ibid. 29 Ibid.   30 Ibid.   31 Ibid.   32 Ibid.   33 Ibid.   34 Ibid.   35 Ibid. p. 6 143   36 CAB 65/1 139 (40) p. 261 166   37 Lukacs, *Five Days* p. 111   38 Confidential Annex to CAB 65/1 140 (40) p. 1 146   39 Ibid.; Lukacs, *Five Days* p. 111   40 Confidential Annex to CAB 65/1 140 (40) p. 1 146   41 Ibid.   42 Ibid. p. 2 147   43 Ibid.   44 Ibid.   45 Ibid. 46 Ibid.   47 Ibid.   48 Ibid.   49 Ibid.   50 Ibid. p. 3 148   51 Ibid.   52 Ibid. 53 Attachment to Confidential Annex to CAB 65/1 140 (40)   54 Ibid.   55 Ibid. p. 3 148   56 Ibid.   57 Confidential Annex to CAB 65/ 1 142 (40) pp. 5–6 179–180 58 Roberts, p. 542   59 Lukacs, *Five Days* p. 113   60 Ibid. p. 120   61 Ibid. p. 71 62 Stewart, *Burying Caesar* p. 431   63 Ibid.   64 Confidential Annex to CAB 65/1 142 (40) pp. 5–6 179–180   65 Roberts, p. 542   66 Chamberlain Diary, NCA 24/2; Buchanan, p. 359–60   67 McCarten, p. 188   68 Ibid. p. 210   69 Ibid. p. 261   70 Roberts, p. 542   71 Ibid.   72 Ibid.   73 Confidential Annex to CAB 65/ 1 140 (40) p. 7 152 74 Roberts, p. 543; Lukacs, *Five Days* p. 117   75 McCarten, p. 203   76 Roberts, p. 543; Lukacs, *Five Days* p. 117   77 Lukacs, *Five Days* p. 71   78 Stewart, p. 431 79 Confidential Annex to CAB 65/1 141 (40) p. 2 162   80 Buchanan, p. 316   81 Ibid. p. 358   82 Ibid.; Manchester and Reid, p. 116   83 Lukacs, *Five Days* p. 121–22 84 *Companion Volumes* V/1 p. 533   85 Manchester, *Alone* p. 99   86 Lukacs, *Five Days* p. 121   87 Ibid. pp. 121–22   88 Feiling, p. 447   89 Ibid.   90 Ibid. 91 Ibid.   92 Feiling, p. 439   93 HC Deb 08 May 1940 Vol 360 cc1362   94 Feiling, p. 447   95 Lukacs, *Five Days* p. 121   96 Ibid. p. 122   97 Ibid.   98 Ibid. 99 Confidential Annex to CAB 65/ 1 140(40) p. 3 148   100 Ibid. p. 4 149   101 Ibid. 102 Ibid.   103 Ibid.   104 Ibid.   105 Ibid. p. 5 150; Lukacs, *Five Days* p. 116 106 Confidential Annex CAB 65/1 140(40) p. 6 151   107 Ibid.   108 Ibid.   109 Ibid. 110 Ibid. p. 7 152   111 CAB 66/7 WP (40) 170   112 Lukacs, *Five Days* p. 136

Chapter 17

1 Lukacs, *Five Days* p. 137   2 Ibid.   3 Ibid.   4 See Manchester and Reid, p. 84
5 Chamberlain's report to the House on May 2, 1940, HC Deb 02 May 1940 Vol 360
cc911   6 Shirer, p. 711   7 Roberts, p. 493   8 Manchester and Reid, p. 84   9 Shirer,
p. 735   10 Manchester and Reid, p. 84   11 Confidential Annex to CAB 65/1 141
(40) p. 1 161   12 Ibid. p. 2 162   13 Ibid.   14 Ibid.   15 Ibid.   16 Ibid.   17 Self,
p. 438   18 Ibid.   19 Ibid.   20 CAB 66/7 WP (40) 171   21 Confidential Annex to
CAB 65/9 141 (40) p. 1 165   22 Ibid. p. 2 166   23 Ibid.   24 Ibid. pp. 2–3 166–67
25 Ibid. p. 3 167   26 Ibid.   27 CAB 66/7 WP (40) 169 p. 2 331   28 Ibid.
29 Confidential Annex to CAB 65/9 141 (40) p. 6 170   30 CAB 66/7 WP 168 p. 4
320   31 ed. Dilks, *Cadogan, Diaries* p. 290   32 Colville, pp. 140–141   33 Lukacs,
Five Days at 146   34 Confidential Annex to CAB 65/1 142 (40) p. 1 175   35 CAB 66/7
W.P. (40) 170 p. 1 335   36 Ibid.   37 Confidential Annex to CAB 65/1 142 (40) p. 1
175   38 Ibid.   39 Ibid. p. 2 176   40 Ibid.   41 Ibid. p. 3 177   42 Ibid.
43 Ibid. p. 4 178   44 Ibid. pp. 4–5 178–79   45 Ibid. p. 5 7   46 Lukacs, *Five Days*
p. 146   47 McCarten p. 203   48 Confidential Annex to CAB 65/1 142 (40) p. 5
179   49 Ibid. pp. 5–6 179–180   50 Ibid. p. 6 180   51 Ibid.   52 Gilbert, *Prophet*
p. 124   53 Confidential Annex to CAB 65/1 142 (40) p. 6 180   54 McCarten,
p. 211   55 Confidential Annex to CAB 65/1 139 (40) p. 4 141   56 McCarten,
p. 210   57 Roberts, p. 543   58 Churchill, *Their Finest Hour* p.15   59 Lukacs,
Five Days p. 214   60 Ibid. p. 122   61 Roberts, p. 389; Buchanan, pp. 20–21
62 Confidential Annex to CAB 65/1 142 (40) p. 6 180   63 Ibid.   64 Ibid.
65 Ibid.   66 Ibid.   67 Roberts, p. 544; Lukacs, *Five Days* p. 153   68 ed. Dilks,
Cadogan Diaries p. 291   69 McCarten, p. 214; Lukacs, *Five Days* p. 153
70 Lukacs, *Five Days* p. 153   71 Ibid. p. 155   72 Lord Halifax diary, A7/8/4 p. 142
May 27 1940 (University of York digital Library). Available at: https://tinyurl.com/
29t6f5uf   73 Ibid.   74 McCarten, p. 214   75 Ibid. p. 216   76 Ibid.   77 Ibid.
78 CAB 65 /1 143 (40) p. 277 178   79 Ibid.   80 Ibid.   81 Spears, *Prelude to Dunkirk*,
pp. 237–239, 244–251

Chapter 18

1 CAB 65/1 144 (40) p. 283 182   2 Ibid.   3 Ibid.   4 Appendix A to Confidential Annex
to CAB 65/1 146 (40) 205   5 CAB 65/2 144 (40) p. 285 183   6 Shirer, p. 735   7 CAB
65/2 144 (40) p. 285 183   8 Ibid.   9 Manchester and Reid, p. 84   10 CAB 65/2
144 (40) p. 285 183   11 "9 things you (probably) didn't know about Dunkirk"
HistoryExtra. Available at: https://www.historyextra.com/period/second-world-war/
dunkirk-facts-history-east-mole-hitler-halt-order-douglas-jardine/   12 Manchester
and Reid, p. 83   13 Ibid. p. 84   14 Roberts, p. 545   15 HC Deb 04 June 1940 Vol
361 cc7906   16 CAB 65 /2 144 (40) p. 285 183   17 Ibid. pp. 285–86 183   18 Ibid.
p. 286 183   19 Ibid.   20 Ibid.   21 Ibid.   22 Ibid. p. 287 184   23 Manchester
and Reid, p. 77   24 Ibid.   25 Ibid. p. 80   26 HC Deb 28 May 1940 Vol 361
cc421   27 Ibid.   28 McCarten, p. 221   29 Confidential Annex to 65/1 145 (40) p. 1
184   30 Ibid.   31 Ibid.   32 Ibid. p. 2 185   33 Ibid. p. 1 184   34 Ibid.   35 Ibid. p. 2
185   36 Ibid.   37 Ibid.   38 Ibid.   39 Ibid.   40 Ibid.   41 Ibid.   42 Confidential
Annex to CAB 65/1 142 (40) pp. 4–5 178–79; Confidential Annex to CAB 65/1 145
(40) p. 1 184   43 Confidential Annex to 65/1 145 (40) p. 4 187   44 Ibid. p. 3 186
45 Ibid.   46 Ibid.   47 Ibid. p. 4 187   48 Ibid.   49 Roberts, p. 545   50 Confidential
Annex to 65/1 145 (40) p. 4 187   51 Ibid.   52 Ibid.   53 Ibid.   54 Roberts, p. 545
55 Confidential Annex to 65/1 145 (40) p. 4 187   56 Ibid.   57 Ibid.; McCarten,
p. 224   58 Confidential Annex to 65/1 145 (40) p. 4 187   59 Ibid. pp. 4–5 187–88
60 Ibid. p. 5 188   61 Ibid.   62 Ibid.   63 Ibid.   64 Ibid.   65 Ibid.   66 Ibid. p. 6
189   67 Dalton, *The Fateful Years*, pp. 335–36; ed. Pimlott, *Second World War
Diaries of Hugh Dalton* pp. 27–29   68 Dalton, *The Fateful Years*, p. 336   69 ed.
Pimlott, *Second World War Diaries of Hugh Dalton* p. 29; Dalton, *The Fateful Years*,
p. 335   70 Confidential Annex to 65/1 145 (40) p. 6 189   71 Ibid.   72 Churchill,
Their Finest Hour, p. 100   73 Ibid. pp. 99–100   74 Ibid.   75 Lukacs, *Five Days*
p. 4   76 Roberts, *The Holy Fox* p. 310   77 Confidential Annex to CAB 65/ 1 140 (40)

p. 6 189   78 CAB 65/1 145 (40) p. 292 187   79 Ibid.   80 Addison, *The Unexpected Hero* p. 249   81 Ismay, *The Memoirs of General Lord Ismay* p. 142   82 Lukacs, *Five Days* p. 175

Chapter 19

1 Buchanan, p. 360   2 Ibid.   3 Ibid.   4 Roberts pp. 545–46; Manchester and Reid, p. 129   5 Roberts, pp. 545–46   6 Ibid.   7 Ibid.   8 Lukacs, *The Last European War* p. 101; Manchester and Reid, p. 129   9 Clark, "A Reputation Ripe for Revision," *London Times,* January 2, 1993   10 Schwarz, "Rethinking Negotiation with Hitler," *New York Times* November 25, 2000   11 McCarten, p. 183   12 Manchester and Reid, p. 110   13 CAB 66/7 WP (40) 169   14 Confidential Annex to CAB 65/9 141 (40) p. 2 166   15 CAB 65 /3 144 (40) p. 286 183   16 CAB 66/7 WP (40) 169 p. 2 331   17 CAB 66/7 WP (40) 153 Annex I p. 6 228 Para 7   18 CAB 66/7 WP (40) 168 Annex p. 6 321   19 Ibid.   20 CAB 66/7 WP (40) 169 p. 3 332   21 Ibid. Annex p. 7–8 322   22 Lukacs, *Five Days* p. 175   23 CAB 66/7 WP 168 (40) Annex p. 8 322   24 Ibid. p. 7 322   25 Lukacs, *Five Days* p. 196; Manchester and Reid, p. 124   26 CAB 66/7 WP 168 (40)Annex p. 8 322   27 Taylor, *English History,* p. 492   28 CAB 66/8 WP (40) 213 p. 2 243   29 Schwarz, *New York Times,* Nov. 25, 2000   30 Roberts, p. 587   31 Tolland, *Adolf Hitler* p. 511   32 Shirer, p. 648   33 Ibid.   34 Ibid.   35 Colville, p. 54   36 Ibid. p. 57   37 Shirer, p. 648   38 Ibid.   39 Wheeler-Bennett, *Nemesis* p. 491   40 Shirer, p. 650   41 Ibid.   42 Ibid. pp. 650–51   43 Ibid. p. 651   44 Shirer, *Nemesis* pp. 692–93   45 Ibid.   46 Ibid. p. 693   47 Ibid. pp. 693–94   48 Ibid. p. 694   49 Shirer, p. 653   50 Ibid.   51 Ibid.   52 Confidential Annex to 65/1 145 (40) p. 4 187   53 Confidential Annex to 65/– 140 (40) p. 3 148 May 26, 1940   54 Confidential Annex to 65/– 141 (40) p. 4–5 168–69 May 27, 1940   55 Brew, "How Oil Defeated the Nazis". Available at: https://oilprice.com/Energy/Crude-Oil/How-Oil-Defeated-The Nazis.   56 Ibid.   57 Mawn, "China's Proposed Belt and Road Initiative," *Defense Info.* Available at: https://defense.info/re-thinking-strategy/2018/10/oil-and-war/   58 Mawn, "China's Proposed Belt and Road Initiative"   59 CAB 66/8 WP (40) 191 p. 3, 4 108, 109   60 CAB 66/7 WP (40) 185 p. 7 68   61 Shirer, p. 800   62 CAB 66/7 WP (40) 168 p. 11 324   63 CAB 66/8 WP (40) 191 p. 3 108   64 Brew, "How Oil Defeated the Nazis"   65 CAB 66/8 WP (40) 191 p. 3 108   66 Mawn, "China's Proposed Belt and Road Initiative"   67 CAB 66/7 WP (40) 168 p. 12 324   68 Ibid. p. 3 320   69 Ibid.   70 CAB 66/8 WP (40) 191   71 CAB 66/7 WP (40) 168   72 Fischel, "Questioning the Good War," VQR Summer 2008. Available at: https://www.vqronline.org/questioning-good-war#   73 Reynolds, *In Command of History* p. 177   74 HC Deb 04 June 1940 Vol 361 cc787   75 Churchill, *Their Finest Hour* p. 232   76 Reynolds, *In Command of History* p. 176   77 June 16 telegram quoted in Reynolds, *In Command of History* p. 177   78 Roberts, p. 582; Reynolds, *In Command of History* p. 176   79 Gilbert, *Finest Hour* p. 358   80 Fischel, "Questioning the Good War"   81 Lukacs, *The Last European War* p. 98   82 US Department of State, *Peace and War: United States Foreign Policy 1931–1941,* pp. 548–49   83 Annex I to Confidential Annex to 65/1 165 (40) p. (i) 297   84 Confidential Annex to 65/1 165 (40) p. 2 292   85 Ibid. 86 Ibid. p. 3 293   87 Ibid. p. 2 292   88 Ibid. p. 3 293   89 Ibid.   90 Available at: https://www.mtholyoke.edu/acad/intrel/WorldWar2/reynaud2.htm   91 Ibid.   92 King, p. 109   93 CAB 66/7 (40) 168 p. 3 20   94 Ibid. Annex p. 11 324   95 Ibid. Annex p. 12 324   96 Ibid.   97 CAB 66/8 WP 171 p. 1 5   98 Ibid.   99 CAB 66/7 (40) 168 p. 3 320   100 Ibid. Annex p. 12 324   101 CAB 66/7 (40) 168 p. 3 320   102 Ibid. Annex p. 12 324   103 Roberts, p. 569   104 Reynolds, *In Command of History* p. 174   105 Confidential Annex to 65/1 140 (40) p. 4 149   106 Ibid. p. 3 148   107 Confidential Annex to 65/1 140 (40) p. 3 148   108 Reynolds, *In Command of History* p. 174   109 CAB 65/ 1 161 (40) p. 417 273   110 Colville, p. 144   111 Dalton, *The Fateful Years* p. 335   112 CAB 66/7 WP 168 p.9 323   113 Confidential Annex to CAB 65/ 1 140 (40) p. 1 146   114 Ibid. p. 2 147   115 Ibid.   116 Ibid.   117 Ibid. p. 3 148   118 Confidential Annex to 65/1 145 (40) p. 5 188   119 Confidential Annex to CAB 65/ 1 140 (40) p. 4 149   120 Confidential Annex to CAB 65/1 142 (40) pp. 4–5 178–79   121 Confidential Annex to CAB 65/ 1 140 (40) p. 3 148   122 CAB 66/8 WP (40) 213 p. 2 243   123 Lukacs, *Five Days* pp. 215–16   124 Colville, p. 186   125 eds. Blake and Louis, *Churchill* p. 249

126 Roberts, p. 555   127 Reproduced in full in Churchill, *Their Finest Hour* p. 188
128 Lukacs, *The Last European War* p. 101   129 Manchester and Reid, p. 129
130 *DGFP* Series D, Vol X No. 152 p. 188   131 Manchester and Reid, pp. 116–17
132 *Halder's Diary* Vol IV part 2 July 22, 1940, p. 127   133 Reynolds, *"Churchill
The Appeaser?"* pp. 197–220   134 Lukacs, *Five Days* p. 214   135 Lukacs, *The Last
European War* p. 90   136 Buchanan, p. 20; Roberts, p. 389   137 Hitler, translator
Manheim, *Mein Kampf* pp. 613–14   138 Buchanan, p. 19   139 *Companion Volumes*
V/3 p. 143   140 Ibid. part 2 pp. 1169–70   141 Roberts, p. 390   142 HC Deb 14
March 1938 Vol 333 cc49–50   143 Lukacs, *Five Days* p. 217   144 ed. Nicholson,
Nicholson Diaries Vol I p. 269   145 Lukacs, *The Last European War* p. 90
146 Schwartz, *New York Times* November 25, 2000   147 Ibid.   148 Roberts,
The Holy Fox p. 64   149 Manchester and Reid p. 116   150 HC Deb 12 October 1939
Vol 352 cc565   151 Halifax, p. 227   152 ed. Gorodetsky, *Maisky Diaries* p. 110
153 Ibid. p. 231   154 Churchill, *The Gathering Storm* pp. 273–74   155 HC Deb 05
October 1938 Vol 339 cc370   156 CAB 23/1 12 (39) p. 8 50   157 HC Deb 12 October
1939 Vol 352 cc565–6   158 HC Deb 12 October 1939 Vol 352 cc568   159 Halifax,
p. 227   160 Confidential Annex to CAB 65/ 1 140 (40) p. 2 7   161 Lukacs, *The Last
European War* p. 85   162 Available at: http://der-fuehrer.org/reden/english/wardirectives/
21.html   163 Gilbert, *Prophet* p. 124   164 Langworth, 'How Churchill Saw Baldwin' 101
Finest Hour, Winter 1998–99, p. 29   165 Manchester and Reid, p. 117   166 Ibid.
167 Churchill, *Their Finest Hour* p. 283   168 Ibid. p. 249   169 Ibid.   170 HC Deb 18
June 1940 Vol 362 cc55   171 Manchester and Reid, p. 121   172 Ibid.   173 Buchanan,
p. 330   174 Barley, p. 391; Shirer, p. 711   175 Price, 'Myth and Legend', *Aeroplane
Monthly* p. 14   176 Buchanan, p. 331   177 Price, 'Myth and Legend', p. 14
178 Churchill, *Their Finest Hour* p. 286; Manchester and Reid, p. 131   179 CAB 66/7
WP (40) 168 Annex, p. 8 322   180 Shirer, p. 711; Lukacs, *The Last European War*
p. 248   181 Manchester and Reid, p. 132   182 Roberts, p. 493   183 Churchill, *Their
Finest Hour* p. 282   184 Barley, "Contributing to its Own Defeat": pp. 387–411, p. 401;
Manchester and Reid, p. 139   185 Confidential Annex to CAB 65/9 141 (40) p. 2 166;
Churchill, *Their Finest Hour* p. 283   186 Churchill, *Their Finest Hour* p. 283   187 HC
Deb 18 June 1940 Vol 362 cc57   188 Ibid.   189 CAB 66/7 WP (40) 169 p. 2 331
190 CAB 66/7 WP (40) 153 Annex I p. 5 228 Para 6   191 Ibid. Annex I p. 6 228 Para 8
192 Ibid. Annex I p. 6 228 Para 7   193 CAB 66/7 WP (40) 168 Annex p. 7 322
194 Ibid.   195 Barley, 'Contributing to its Own Defeat' p. 389   196 Ibid.   197 *An
Overview of the Dowding System.* Available at: http://beyourfinest.com/dowding-system-/ ;
Lambert, Churchill, Hitler, and the Battle of Britain, 185 *Finest Hour* p. 19 (2019).
Available at: https://winstonchurchill.org/publications/finest-hour/finest-hour-185/
churchill-hitler-and-the-battle-of-britain/   198 CAB 66/7 WP (40) 153 Annex I p. 6 228
Para 10   199 CAB 66/7 WP (40) 168 Annex p. 6 321   200 CAB 66/7 WP (40) 153 Annex I
p. 6 228 Para 10   201 Murray, "The Battle of Britain" p. 10   202 Manchester and Reid,
p. 121   203 Buchanan, p. 330   204 Barley, p. 391   205 Ibid.   206 Churchill, *Their
Finest Hour* p. 283; Shirer, p. 761   207 Manchester and Reid, p. 130   208 Buchanan,
p. 330   209 Manchester and Reid, p. 121   210 Confidential Annex to CAB 65/3 198 (40)
p. 1 37   211 Ibid.   212 CAB 65/10 148 (40) p. 315 204   213 Colville, p. 182   214 Ibid.
p. 219   215 Shirer, p. 757   216 Available at: http://der-fuehrer.org/reden/english/
wardirectives/06.html_quoted in Shirer, p. 644   217 Ibid.   218 Shirer, p. 747   219 Ibid.
p. 759   220 *Halder's Diary* Vol IV Part 2 July 22, 1940 p. 126   221 Larson, *The
Splendid and the Vile* p. 119   222 Ibid.; Deighton, *Fighter* p. 8; Shirer, p. 751
223 Murray, 'The Battle of Britain' p. 10   224 Shirer, pp. 751, 761   225 Roberts,
p. 575   226 HC Deb 03 September 1939 Vol 351 cc294–5   227 HC Deb 28 May 1940
Vol 361 cc421   228 HC Deb 18 June 1940 Vol 362 cc60   229 Manchester and Reid,
p. 128   230 HC Deb 20 August 1940 Vol 364 cc1132–274   231 HC Deb 02 September
1939 Vol 351 cc282–3   232 HC Deb 03 September 1939 Vol 351 cc295

Chapter 20

1 Russell, "The Military Churchill," *Finest Hour* 181, Summer 2018   2 Brendon, *Churchill*
p. 8   3 Randolph Churchill, *Youth* p. 121   4 Pettengill, "Douglas S. Russell Speaks to the

Society in Michigan," *International Churchill Society,* May 14, 2011   5 Orders, Decorations and Medals," *International Churchill Society, winstonchurchill.org*   6 "Summer 1918 (Age 43): Toward final Victory." Available at: https://winstonchurchill.org/the-life-of-churchill/rising-politician/1910-1919/summer-1918-age-43/   7 HC Deb 5 November 1936 Vol 317 cc312   8 HC Deb 20 July 1936 Vol 315 cc114   9 HC Deb 24 March 1938 Vol 333 cc1444   10 Roberts, p. 10   11 Rintala, "The Love of Power and the Power of Love: Churchill's Childhood," *Political Psychology,* 5(3) p. 382   12 Manchester, *Visions* p. 111   13 Rintala, p. 384   14 Manchester, *Visions* p. 134   15 McMenamin, "Action This Day—Spring 1877, 1902, 1927, 1952," *Finest Hour* 114, Spring 2002   16 Rintala, p. 384   17 Ibid. p. 382   18 Letter of August 7, 1893, reprinted in Randolph Churchill, *Youth* pp. 188–190   19 Letter from Lady Randolph to Winston June 12, 1890 reprinted in Randolph Churchill, *Youth* p. 125   20 Churchill, *My Early Life* p. 12   21 Capet, "Abstracts: Drs. Vale and Scadding Consider Aspects of Churchill's Health," *The Churchill Project, Hillsdale College,* March 26, 2018   22 Ricks, *Churchill and Orwell,* p. 6   23 Churchill, *My Early Life,* p. 30   24 Greenspan, "10 Things You May Not Know About Winston Churchill," History.com, June 17, 2020   25 Manchester, *Visions* p. 393   26 Ibid. p. 128   27 Rintala, p. 387   28 "Mrs. Everest," *cabbieblog .com,* July 11, 2017   29 Churchill, *My Early Life* p. 5   30 Field, "Officer Cadet to Lieutenant Colonel: Winston Churchill in the British Army," *forces.net,* July 9, 2019   31 Gilbert, *Churchill: A Life* p. 125   32 ed. James, *Complete Speeches* Vol 1 pp. 1151–52   33 Manchester, *Visions* p. 788   34 HC Deb 04 March 1937 Vol 321 cc581   35 Rintala, p. 387   36 Manchester, *Alone* p. 258   37 "Family Man: Churchill the Father," *International Churchill Society.* Available at: https://winstonchurchill.org/the-life-of-churchill/life/family-man/churchill-the-father/   38 "Life with My Parents: Winston and Clementine," *Finest Hour* Issue 91, Summer 1996   39 Mather, "Churchill's Character: Hardiness, Resilience and Personal Toughness," *The Churchill Project, winstonchurchill .hillsdale.edu,* March 11, 2019   40 Ibid.   41 Ibid.   42 Ibid.   43 Pemberton, "'Malnutrition in England' University College Hospital Magazine 1934 Some reflections in 2003 on the 1930s," *International Journal of Epidemiology,* Vol 32, issue 4, August 2003, pp. 496–98   44 Roberts, p. 30   45 Smith, "9 things you (probably) didn't know about Winston Churchill," *HistoryExtra,* January 2015   46 HC Deb 04 March 1937 Vol 321 cc574   47 HC Deb 24 March 1938 Vol 333 cc1455   48 HC Deb 04 March 1937 Vol 321 cc573   49 Gilbert, *Challenges* p. 473   50 Roberts, p. 26   51 Klein, "Winston Churchill's World War Disaster"   52 Manchester, *Alone* pp. 84–85   53 Ibid. p. 83   54 Ibid. p. 243   55 Klein, "Winston Churchill's World War Disaster"   56 Manchester and Reid, p. 57   57 Cannadine, *Aspects of Aristocracy,* 132   58 Colville, pp. 1–2   59 Personal interview William Manchester with Sir John Colville 10/8/80 referenced in Manchester *Alone* p. 677 n. 277   60 Churchill, "Be Ye Men of Valour," BBC Broadcast May 19, 1940. Available at: http//:1d4vws37vmp124vlehygoxxd-wpengine.netdna-ssl.com   61 HC Deb 12 November 1936 Vol 317 cc1099–1100   62 Churchill, *While England Slept* p. 72   63 HC Deb 05 November 1936 Vol 317 cc315   64 Churchill, *While England Slept* pp. 72–73   65 Churchill, *The Gathering Storm,* p. 667   66 Gilbert, *Prophet* p. 124   67 ed. Eades, *Contemporaries* p. 19   68 Baring, *Puppet Show* p. 71   69 Manchester, *Visions* p. 116   70 Roberts, p. 81   71 George, *My Brother and I* p. 211   72 Manchester, *Visions* p. 361   73 Addison, *Churchill* p. 74   74 ed. Harvey, *The Diplomatic Diaries of Oliver Harvey* p. 180   75 Madge & Harrison, *Britain by Mass-Observation* p. 65   76 Manchester, *Alone* p. 124   77 Kennedy p. 66   78 HC Deb 04 June 1940 Vol 361 cc796   79 HC Deb 04 March 1937 Vol 321 cc574   80 Ibid.   81 HC Deb 07 February 1934 Vol 285 cc1197   82 Churchill, *While England Slept* pp. 131–32   83 Rintala, p. 385   84 HC Deb 04 June 1940 Vol 361 cc795   85 "Man of Action," *International Churchill Society, winstonchurchill .org*   86 Manchester, *Visions* p. 121   87 Fletcher, "Spencer Churchill (p) at Harrow School 1888–1892," *International Churchill Society, Finest Hour* 133, Winter 2006–07, p. 30   88 Dangerfield, *The Strange Death of Liberal England* p. 89   89 Churchill, *My Early Life* p. 30   90 Ibid. pp. 29–30   91 Ibid. p. 30   92 "Man of Action." Available at: https://winstonchurchill.org/the-life-of-churchill/life/man-of-action/   93 Ibid.   94 Churchill, *My Early Life* p. 63   95 "Man of Action"   96 "Life with

My Parents"   97 Roberts, p. 149   98 *Companion Volumes* III/1, p. 166   99 *The Morning Post,* October 19, 1914   100 Hunt, "World War 1 History: Winston Churchill in the Trenches," *Owlcation.com, October 7, 2017*   101 ed. Soames, *Speaking* p. 78   102 "Flying," *International Churchill Society, winstonchurchill.org*   103 Roberts, p. 171   104 Manchester and Reid, p. 91   105 Ibid. p. 182   106 Churchill Archives BRG I/2   107 Roberts, p. 604   108 Ibid. p. 605   109 HC Deb 23 March 1933 Vol 276 cc539   110 HC Deb 13 July 1934 Vol 292 cc729   111 HC Deb 22 May 1935 Vol 302 cc421   112 HC Deb 22 February 1938 Vol 332 cc246   113 Roberts, p. 365   114 Quoted in Manchester, *Alone* p. 82; Roberts, p. 345   115 HC Deb 23 November 1932 Vol 272 cc81   116 HC Deb 07 February 1934 Vol 285 cc1199   117 Roberts, p. 380   118 Colville, p. 404   119 Gilbert, *Churchill: A Life* p. 595   120 Quoted in *Churchill, The Gathering Storm* p. 273   121 HC Deb 05 October 1938 Vol 339 cc371   122 Ibid. cc373   123 Manchester, *Alone* p. 255   124 ed. Gorodetsky, *Maisky Diaries* p. 231   125 Simpson, "Winston Churchill: How a flawed man became a great leader," *BBC.com,* January 23, 2015   126 Kennedy, p. 66   127 Manchester, *Alone* p. 243   128 HC Deb 05 October 1938 Vol 339 cc370   129 HC Deb 18 June 1940 Vol 362 cc60   130 Colville, p. 404   131 Roberts, p. 542   132 Confidential Annex to 65/1 145 (40) p. 4 187   133 Churchill, *A History of the English-Speaking Peoples*, Vol 1: p. 60

Chapter 21

1 Addison, *Churchill: The Unexpected Hero* p. 182   2 CAB 65/1 146 (40) p. 295 190   3 Available at: http://vandwdestroyerassociation.org.uk/HMS_Wakeful/index .html   4 Lukacs, *Five Days* pp. 196–97   5 Confidential Annex to CAB 65/1 146 (40) p. 1 202   6 Ibid.   7 CAB 65/1 148 (40) p. 311 202   8 CAB 67/– W.P. (40) 178   9 CAB 65/10 149 (40) pp. 314–316 203–04   10 Ibid. p. 314 203   11 Ibid.   12 CAB 65/10 149 (40) p. 314 203   13 Ibid.   14 Ibid. pp. 314–15 203–04   15 Ibid. p. 315 204   16 Ibid.   17 Ibid.   18 Ibid.   19 McCarten, p. 243   20 Spears, *Assignment* Vol I p. 295   21 Manchester and Reid, p. 89   22 Spears, *Assignment* Vol I p. 308   23 Spears, *Assignment* Vol I pp. 305–06   24 Ibid. p. 313   25 Ismay, *Memoirs* p. 133   26 Spears, *Assignment* Vol I pp. 313–14   27 Manchester and Reid, p. 90   28 Ibid.   29 Spears, *Assignment* Vol I pp. 318–19   30 Manchester and Reid, p. 122   31 Ibid. p. 123   32 Churchill, *Their Finest Hour* p. 299   33 Manchester and Reid, p. 123   34 Shirer, p. 747   35 Ibid.   36 Ibid.   37 Churchill, *Their Finest Hour* p. 177–78   38 Larson, pp. 119, 134; Shirer, p. 747   39 Shirer, p. 756   40 Available at: http:// der-fuehrer.org/reden/english/wardirectives/06.html   41 Shulman, *Defeat in the West* p. 59   42 Lukacs, *The Last European War* p. 111   43 Ibid. p. 90   44 Shirer, p. 751; Manchester and Reid, p. 129   45 Shirer, p. 760   46 Ibid. p. 751, 761   47 Lukacs, *The Last European War* p. 93   48 Roberts, p. 549   49 Ibid. pp. 549, 550   50 Confidential Annex to CAB 65/10 153 (40) p. 5 238   51 Ibid. p. 7 240   52 Roberts, p. 550   53 Wheatcroft, p. 227   54 HC Deb 04 June 1940 Vol 361 cc796   55 HC Deb 04 June 1940 Vol 361 cc796   56 ed. James, *Chips* p. 256   57 Brian Gardner, *Churchill In Power* p. 55   58 Wheatcroft, p. 227   59 Self, p. 439   60 Ibid. p. 440   61 Ibid.   62 Ibid.   63 ed. Self, Vol 4 p. 537 Chamberlain to his sister Ida, June 8, 1940   64 Ibid. p. 543 Chamberlain to his sister Ida June 21, 1940; Chamberlain and Amery diaries, both June 18, 1940; Self, p. 441   65 Churchill, *Their Finest Hour* p. 401   66 Manchester and Reid, p. 91   67 Ibid.   68 Ibid.   69 CAB 65/3 163 (40) p. 436 284   70 Roberts, p. 554; CAB 65/2 163 (40) p. 435 284   71 Manchester and Reid, p. 92   72 Spears, *Assignment* Vol 2 p. 150   73 Ibid. p. 155   74 CAB 65/3 163 (40) p. 437 285   75 Manchester and Reid, p. 93   76 Ismay, *Memoirs* p. 139   77 Manchester and Reid, p. 93   78 Ismay, *Memoirs* p. 140   79 Roberts, p. 555   80 Manchester and Reid, pp. 94–95   81 CAB 65/3 163 (40) p. 438 285   82 Manchester and Reid, p. 96; Roberts, p. 556   83 Roberts, p. 556   84 Ibid. p. 557   85 Confidential Annex to CAB 65/1 165 (40) p. 1 293; Manchester and Reid, p. 97   86 Confidential Annex to CAB 65/1 165 (40) p. 1 293; Roberts, p. 557   87 Manchester and Reid, p. 97   88 Ibid.   89 Ibid. p. 98   90 Spears, *Assignment* Vol 2 p. 213   91 Thompson, *Shadow* p. 56   92 Jackson, *Churchill* p. 265   93 Shirer, p. 794   94 Ibid. p. 800   95 Ibid. p. 795   96 Churchill, *Their Finest Hour* p. 120   97 Shirer, p. 795   98 Hitler, translator Manheim, *Mein*

Kampf, pp. 164–65   99 Shirer, p. 796   100 Buchanan, p. 366   101 Denman, *Missed Chances* p. 3   102 Kershaw, *Fateful Choices* p. 70   103 Manchester and Reid, pp. 105–06   104 Ibid. p. 106   105 Ibid.   106 Ibid.   107 CAB 65/3 163 (40) p. 437 285   108 Confidential Annex to CAB 65/3 163 (40) p. 3 286   109 Manchester and Reid, p. 105   110 Confidential Annex to CAB 65/1 168 (40) p. 1 313 June 16, 1940 111 Manchester and Reid, p. 106   112 Confidential Annex to CAB 65/ 6 167 (40) p. 1 308   113 Kimball, *Complete Correspondence* Vol 1 pp. 49–51   114 Confidential Annex to CAB 65/ 1 168 (40) p. 1 313   115 Confidential Annex to CAB 65/ 1 168 (40) Appendix I p. 1 320   116 The Declaration of Union can be found in Annex II to CAB 65/1 169 (40) p. 489 317   117 Roberts, p. 560   118 Colville, p. 161   119 CAB 65/4 170 (40) p. 494 320   120 Ibid. p. 495 321   121 CAB 65/4 170 (40) p. 495 321   122 Ibid.; CAB 65/10 171 (40) p. 510 328   123 Colville, p. 163   124 Roberts, p. 560   125 Gilbert, *Finest Hour* p. 568   126 Woodward, *British Foreign Policy in the Second World War* Vol I p. 204 note; Lukacs, The Last European War, p. 97, n. 52   127 Woodward, *British Foreign Policy in the Second World War* Vol I p. 204 note   128 Ibid.   129 Italian Diplomatic Documents Nineth Series Vol V, No. 47 p. 37; Lukacs, *The Last European War* p. 97 note 52   130 Manchester and Reid, p. 116   131 Roberts, p. 561   132 Ibid.   133 Ibid. 134 Manchester and Reid, p. 115   135 Ibid. p. 114   136 CAB 65/ 3 173 (40) p. 526 339   137 Ibid.   138 Ibid. p. 527 340   139 Ibid. p. 539 347   140 CAB 65/ 4 175 (40) p. 551 354   141 Ibid.   142 Ibid. p. 552 354   143 Ibid.   144 Manchester and Reid, p. 106   145 Lukacs, *The Last European War* p. 85   146 Ibid. p. 92   147 Ibid.   148 Ibid. 149 Manchester and Reid, p. 107   150 Available at: https://avalon.law.yale.edu/wwii/ frgearm.asp   151 Confidential Annex to CAB 65/2 180 (40) p. 3 344   152 Ibid. 153 Ibid.   154 Ibid.   155 Ibid.   156 Confidential Annex to CAB 65/2 180 (40) p. 1 342   157 Ibid.   158 Ibid. p. 2 343   159 Ibid.   160 Ibid.   161 Confidential Annex to CAB 65/2 182 (40) p. 1 347   162 Ibid.   163 HC Deb 25 June 1940 Vol 362 cc305–06 164 Colville, p. 171   165 Manchester and Reid, p. 107   166 Confidential Annex to CAB 65/5 183 (40) p. 2 350   167 Confidential Annex to CAB 65/5 184 (40) p. 2 353 168 Ibid.   169 Ibid.   170 Confidential Annex to CAB 65/7 185 (40) p. 1 356   171 Ibid. 172 Ibid.   173 Confidential Annex to CAB 65/8 187 (40) p. 1 358   174 Ibid.   175 Ibid. p. 2 359   176 CAB 65/9 187 (40) p. 645 417   177 Confidential Annex to CAB 65/3 198 (40) p. 1 37   178 Shirer, p. 762   179 Manchester and Reid, p. 129   180 Larson, p. 119   181 Shirer, p. 751   182 Larson, p. 119; Shirer, p. 797   183 Larson, p. 120; Shirer, p. 752; German Naval Staff War Diary, July 30, 1940 p. 240–41   184 Larson, p. 120   185 *Halder's Diary* Vol IV part 2 July 22, 1940 p. 126   186 Ibid.   187 Ibid. p. 127   188 Lukacs, *The Last European War* p. 93; Shirer, p. 762   189 Lukacs, *The Last European War* p. 93; Shirer, p. 752   190 Shirer, pp. 752–53   191 Confidential Annex to CAB 65/5 192 (40) p. 1 14   192 Tute, *Deadly Stroke,* pp. 73–87   193 Manchester and Reid, p. 108   194 Roberts, p. 573   195 Ibid.; Manchester and Reid, p. 108   196 Roberts, p. 573   197 Ibid.   198 Ibid.   199 Telegram attached to CAB 65/12 191(40) pp. 1–2 35; HC Deb 04 July 1940 Vol 362 cc1047;   200 Tute, *Deadly Strokes* pp. 95–96 201 Confidential Annex to CAB 65/5 192 (40) p. 2 15   202 Manchester and Reid, p. 109   203 Ibid.   204 Ibid.   205 Ibid.   206 Tute, *Deadly Stroke* p. 17   207 Manchester and Reid, p. 110   208 Ibid.   209 Tute, *Deadly Stroke* p. 17   210 Confidential Annex to CAB 65/2 198 (40) p. 1 35   211 Ibid.   212 CAB 65/4 200 (40) p. 82 82   213 Attachment to CAB 65/ 5 199 (40) pp. 1–2 79   214 Shirer, p. 757   215 Attachment to CAB 65/ 5 199 (40) pp. 1–2 79   216 Manchester and Reid, p. 140   217 CAB 65/1 200 (40) 81 82; Manchester and Reid, p. 140   218 Shirer, p. 775   219 See Directive 17, August 1, 1940   220 Ibid.   221 Manchester and Reid, pp. 126–27; Colville, p. 195   222 Colville, p. 195   223 Lukacs, *The Last European War* p. 93   224 Available at: http://der-fuehrer .org/reden/english/wardirectives/16.html   225 Murray, 'The Battle of Britain', *The Quarterly Journal of Military History* Vol 2 No. 4 p. 12   226 Shirer, p. 762 227 Ibid.   228 Ibid. p. 763   229 Ibid. p. 762   230 Manchester and Reid, p. 133 231 Shirer, p. 763   232 Quoted in Manchester and Reid, p. 129   233 Oechsner, "Hitler offers Britain 'peace or destruction'" United Press wire story July 19, 1940. Available at: https://www.upi.com/Archives/1940/07/19/Hitler-offers-Britain-peace- or-destruction/6824181303557/   234 ed. Eades, *Contemporaries* p. 211   235 Shirer, pp. 756–57   236 Ibid. p. 757   237 Ibid.   238 Ibid. p. 758   239 Lukacs, *The Last*

European War p. 93   240 Churchill, *Their Finest Hour* p. 230; Shirer, p. 755   241 CAB 65/ 11 209 (40) p. 137 119   242 Confidential Annex to CAB 65/2 211 (40) p. 149 127   243 Hinsley, *Hitler's Strategy* p. 82   244 Halifax, p. 229   245 Manchester and Reid, p. 115   246 Ibid.   247 German Naval Staff War Diary, July 30, 1940 p. 240– 41   248 Ibid. p. 241; Shirer, p. 764   249 Shirer, p. 766   250 Manchester and Reid, p. 119   251 Lukacs, *Five Days* p. 206   252 Ibid.   253 Shirer, p. 797   254 Ibid. 255 Ibid.   256 Manchester and Reid, p. 141   257 Available at: http://der-fuehrer.org/ reden/english/wardirectives/17.html   258 Ibid.   259 Ibid.   260 Larson, p. 120 261 Manchester and Reid, p. 145; Shirer, p. 774   262 Lambert, "Churchill, Hitler, and the Battle of Britain," 185 *Finest Hour* 19 (2019) Available at: https://winstonchurchill .org/publications/finest-hour/finest-hour-185 Churchill-hitler-and-the-battle-of-britain/ 263 Shirer p. 776   264 Manchester and Reid, p. 144   265 Ibid.   266 Ibid. pp. 144–45 267 *An Overview of the Dowding System.* Available at: http://beyourfinest.com/ dowding-system-/; Lambert, "Churchill, Hitler, and the Battle of Britain," 185 *Finest Hour* 19   268 Shirer, p. 776   269 Manchester and Reid, p. 138   270 Shirer, p. 776   271 Roberts, p. 588; Shirer, p. 777   272 Manchester and Reid, p. 146; Shirer, p. 775   273 Shirer, p. 777   274 Churchill, *Their Finest Hour* pp. 331–32 275 Manchester and Reid, p. 148   276 CAB 65/1 246 (40) p. 45 32; Lukacs, *Five Days* p. 207   277 Roberts, p. 615   278 Lukacs, *The Last European War* p. 111   279 Roberts, p. 592   280 Shirer, p. 777   281 Lukacs, *The Last European War* p. 110; Manchester and Reid, p. 150–51   282 Shirer, pp. 777–78   283 Lukacs, *The Last European War* p. 110   284 Ibid.   285 Shirer, p. 778   286 Roberts, p. 597   287 Lukacs, *The Last European War* p. 110   288 Manchester and Reid, p. 150   289 Ibid.; Shirer, p. 777   290 Manchester and Reid, p. 153   291 HC Deb 20 August 1940 Vol 364 cc1166–67   292 Manchester and Reid, p. 174   293 Lambert, "Churchill, Hitler, and the Battle of Britain"   294 CAB 66/12 WP (42) 89 pp. 7–8 42; CAB 66/13 WP (42) 46 p. 8 20   295 CAB 66/12 WP (42) 171 p.11 84   296 Lukacs, *The Last European War* p. 122; CAB 66/12 WP (42) 88 pp. 6 –7 41–42   297 Lukacs, *The Last European War* p. 125   298 Confidential Annex to CAB 65/1 26 (41) p. 4 39; HC Deb 30 April 1941 Vol 371 cc444; Roberts, pp. 635, 637   299 Shirer, p. 800   300 Ibid.   301 Ibid. 302 Ibid. p. 768   303 Ibid.   304 Ibid.   305 Ibid. pp. 768, 780   306 Roberts p. 592 307 Shirer p. 769   308 Ibid. p. 770   309 *Fuehrer Conferences On Naval Affairs,* 1940, pp. 137–38   310 Shirer, p. 781   311 Ibid.   312 Ibid.   313 *Fuehrer Conferences On Naval Affairs*, 1940, p. 138   314 Shirer, p. 773   315 CAB 65/3 256 (40) p. 96 71   316 Shirer, p. 774   317 Manchester and Reid, p. 136   318 Manchester and Reid, p. 157   319 Roberts, p. 597   320 ed. Nicholson, *Nicholson Diaries* Vol II pp. 114–15 321 Mosley, *Battle of Britain* p. 139   322 Manchester and Reid, p. 182   323 Panter-Downs, *London War Notes* pp. 136–37   324 Available at: https://www.billdownscbs. com/2015/09/1940-edward-r-murrow-from-london.html   325 Roberts, p. 592   326 Self, p. 444   327 Eden, *The Reckoning* p. 129   328 Churchill to Chamberlain, 29, 30 September and reply 1 October 1940, NC7/9/99–102 1   329 Simon to Chamberlain, October 3 and reply October 5, 1940, Simon MSS 87/3, 5.   330 Churchill to Anne Chamberlain, November 11,1940 NC7/9/107   331 HC Deb 12 November 1940 Vol 365 cc1617–23   332 CAB 65/5 260 (40) p. 121 88   333 Shirer, p. 815   334 ed. Gibson, *The Ciano Diaries* p. 300   335 Shirer, p. 816   336 Ibid.   337 Ibid.   338 Schmidt, *Hitler's Interpreter* p. 200   339 Shirer, p. 816   340 Car, *Fall Of Greece* p. 38   341 Confidential Annex to CAB 65/1 281 (40) p. 1 3   342 Confidential Annex to CAB 65/2 282 (40) p. 2 9   343 Ibid. p. 1 8   344 Ibid.   345 Ibid. p. 2 9   346 Confidential Annex to CAB 65/2 291 (40) p. 1 32   347 Shirer, p. 818   348 Wheatcroft, p. 226   349 Lukacs, *The Last European War* p. 122   350 See Directive 18. Available at: http://der-fuehrer.org/reden/ english/wardirectives/18.html   351 Shirer, p. 757   352 See Directive 18. Available at: http://der-fuehrer.org/reden/english/wardirectives/18.html   353 Shirer, p. 818 354 Lukacs, *The Last European War* p. 122   355 Wheatcroft, p. 230   356 Ibid. 357 Shirer, p. 804   358 Ibid. pp. 805–6   359 Ibid. p. 801   360 Ibid. p. 802   361 Ibid. 362 Ibid.   363 Ibid. p. 803   364 Ibid.   365 Ibid. p. 804   366 Ibid. p. 806   367 Ibid. p. 803   368 Ibid. p. 808   369 Churchill, *Their Finest Hour* p. 518   370 Shirer, p. 809   371 *Halder's Diary,* Vol V January 16, 1941 p. 84   372 Available at: http:// der-fuehrer.org/reden/english/wardirectives/21.html   373 Shirer, p. 821   374 Lukacs,

The Last European War p. 123   375 Shirer, p. 823   376 Shirer, p. 822   377 Ibid.
p. 823; Lukacs, *The Last European War* p. 123   378 Lukacs, *The Last European War*
p. 123   379 Shirer, p. 823   380 WP (41) 39 cited in Confidential Annex to CAB 65/–
24 (41)   381 Confidential Annex to CAB 65/1 26 (41) p. 4 39; HC Deb 30 April 1941
Vol 371 cc444; Roberts, pp. 635, 637   382 Telegram From Eden to Churchill Mar 7, 1941,
2:55 AM Attached to Confidential Annex to CAB 65/1 26 (41) 53   383 Shirer, pp. 823,
824   384 Lukacs, *The Last European War* p. 127   385 Ibid.; Roberts, p. 643
386 Shirer, p. 824   387 Available at: http://der-fuehrer.org/reden/english/wardirectives/
25.html   388 OKW minutes of the meeting, *Nazi Conspiracy and Aggression* (part
of the Nuremberg documents) Vol IV p. 277 (N.D. 1746-PS, Part II) 2   389 Lukacs,
The Last European War p. 122   390 Roberts, p. 645   391 Shirer, p. 826   392 Roberts,
p. 647   393 Shirer, p. 826   394 Confidential Annex to 65/ 2 42 (41) p. 2 130
395 Telegram from Churchill to Commander in Chief Middle East. Attachment
to Confidential Annex to 65/ 2 41 (41) 125; Confidential Annex to 65/ 2 42 (41)
p. 2 130   396 Roberts, p. 648   397 HC Deb 30 April 1941 Vol 371 cc445; Shirer,
p. 826   398 Shirer, p. 826   399 Churchill, *The Grand Alliance* p. 50   400 Hancock,
"Will We Ever Know Why Nazi Leader Rudolf Hess Flew to Scotland in the Middle
of World War II?" *Smithsonian Magazine,* May 10, 2016   401 Lukacs, *The Last
European War* p. 134   402 Lukacs, *June 1941* p. 92   403 Lukacs, *The Last European
War* p. 138   404 Ibid. p. 138 n 28   405 Ibid.   406 Churchill, *The Grand Alliance*
p. 49   407 Hancock, *"Will We Ever Know Why?"*   408 Ibid.   409 Churchill, *Grand
Alliance* p. 283   410 Lukacs, *The Last European War* pp. 136–37   411 Ibid. pp. 139–40
412 Ibid.   413 Ibid.   414 Ibid.   415 Lukacs, *Five Days* p. 80   416 Available at: https://
www.jewishvirtuallibrary.org/churchill-broadcast-on-the-soviet-german-war-june-1941

Chapter 22

1 Churchill, *The Grand Alliance* p. 383   2 Ibid. p. 384   3 Ibid. p. 385   4 Addison,
Churchill: The Unexpected Hero p. 186   5 Shirer, pp. 860–866   6 Ibid. p. 861–866
7 Ibid. pp. 866, 867   8 Manchester and Reid, p. 517   9 Wheatcroft, *Churchill's Shadow*
p. 237   10 Shirer, pp. 958–59   11 Wheatcroft, p. 241   12 Shirer, p. 883   13 Ibid.
p. 894   14 Ibid. p. 883   15 Ibid. pp. 895, 897–98   16 Wheatcroft, p. 242   17 Roberts,
p. 708   18 Ibid. p. 709   19 eds. Danchev and Todman, *War Diaries* p. 445   20 Roberts,
p. 709   21 Roberts, pp. 709–10   22 Wheatcroft, p. 247   23 Moran, *Struggle* p. 834
24 HC Deb 06 May 1941 Vol 371 cc727   25 HC Deb 07 May 1941 Vol 371 cc867
26 Ibid. cc946   27 HC Deb 27 January 1942 Vol 377 cc592, 593   28 Ibid. cc640
29 Ibid. cc685   30 HC Deb 29 January 1942 Vol 377 cc1019   31 Roberts, p. 716
32 Pawle, *Warden* p. 163   33 Addison, p. 214   34 ed. Nicholson, *Nicholson Diaries*
Vol II p. 358   35 HC Deb 30 March 1944 Vol 398 cc1654   36 Roberts, pp. 709–10
37 Manchester and Reid, p. 484   38 Shirer, p. 911   39 HC Deb 02 July 1942 Vol 381
cc584   40 Shirer, pp. 911, 912   41 HC Deb 02 July 1942 Vol 381 cc529   42 Ibid.
cc539   43 Ibid.   44 Ibid. cc584   45 Ibid. cc588   46 Ibid. cc583   47 Shirer,
p. 912   48 Roberts, p. 740   49 ed. Gordetsky, *Maisky Diaries* p. 440   50 Shirer,
p. 911   51 Ibid. pp. 912, 913   52 Ibid. p. 914   53 Roberts, p. 751   54 Addison,
p. 193   55 Manchester and Reid, p. 603   56 Roberts, p. 746   57 Ibid. p. 752   58 Ibid.
p. 753   59 Ibid. p. 754   60 ed. Wheeler-Bennett, *Action* p. 255   61 Roberts, p. 754
62 Ibid.   63 Ibid. p. 755   64 Manchester and Reid, p. 755   65 Quoted in Roberts
p. 756   66 Ibid.   67 Manchester and Reid, p. 947   68 Eden, *The Reckoning*
p. 634   69 Manchester and Reid, p. 770   70 Ibid.   71 Roberts, p. 757   72 Shirer,
p. 919   73 Manchester and Reid, p. 570   74 Shirer, p. 920   75 Ibid. p. 912   76 Ibid.
pp. 920–925   77 Ibid. p. 923   78 Manchester and Reid, p. 597   79 Addison, p. 193
80 ed. James, *Complete Speeches* Vol VI p. 6693   81 eds. Danchev and Todman,
War Diaries pp. 342, 346   82 Manchester and Reid, p. 603   83 Addison, p. 199
84 Manchester and Reid, pp. 603, 627   85 Ibid. p. 605   86 Ibid. p. 602   87 Ibid.
p. 627   88 Shirer, p. 925   89 Manchester and Reid, p. 597   90 Manchester and
Reid, pp. 612, 627, 639   91 Ibid. p. 638   92 Roberts, p 769; Ibid. p. 627; Addison,
p. 199   93 Manchester and Reid, p. 641   94 Wheatcroft, p. 266   95 Manchester
and Reid, p. 631   96 Ibid. p. 632   97 Ibid. p. 637   98 Churchill, *Closing The Ring*

p. 751   99 Ibid. pp. 646, 651   100 Roberts, p. 774   101 Gilbert, *Road to Victory*
pp. 338, 379   102 Addison, p. 200   103 Ibid.   104 Shirer, p. 997   105 Manchester
and Reid, p. 707   106 Ibid.   107 Gilbert, *Road to Victory* p. 397   108 Thompson,
Assignment Churchill p. 280   109 Manchester and Reid, p. 712   110 Ibid.
p. 714   111 Ibid. p. 713   112 Ibid.   113 Shirer, p. 1000   114 Ibid.   115 Roberts,
pp. 811–12   116 Manchester and Reid, p. 719   117 Ibid. p. 726   118 Ibid.   119 Ibid.
p. 733   120 Ibid.   121 Ibid.   122 Ibid. p. 735   123 Ibid.   124 eds. Danchev and
Todman, *War Diaries* p. 458–59   125 Manchester and Reid, p. 737   126 Eisenhower,
Crusade, p. 195   127 Manchester and Reid, p. 719   128 Addison, p. 201   129 Martin,
Downing Street p. 122   130 Manchester and Reid, p. 754   131 Addison, p. 201
132 Ibid. p. 202; Moran, *Struggle* p. 151   133 Reynolds, *Churchill the Appeaser?* p. 219;
See Toye, *Churchill's Empire: The World that Made Him and the World He Made,*
p. 244   134 Roberts, p. 807   135 Ibid.   136 Moran, *Struggle* p. 151   137 Addison,
p. 202   138 Ibid.   139 Thompson, *Sixty Minutes with Churchill* p. 77   140 Roberts,
p. 808   141 Thompson, *Sixty Minutes* p. 77   142 ed. Hart-Davies, *King's Counselor*
p. 209   143 Colville, p. 485   144 Alanbrooke and Danchev, *War Diaries* p. 528;
Manchester and Reid, p. 818   145 Alanbrooke and Danchev, *War Diaries* p. 530
146 Ibid. p. 532   147 Ibid.   148 eds. Danchev and Todman, *War Diaries* p. 537;
Addison p. 204   149 Manchester and Reid, p. 819   150 Alanbrooke and Danchev,
War Diaries pp. 525–26   151 Manchester and Reid, p. 797   152 Ibid.   153 Ibid.
p. 823   154 Alanbrooke and Danchev, *War Diaries* p. 553   155 Roberts, p. 819
156 Ibid.   157 Ibid.   158 Ibid. p. 820   159 Roberts, p. 825   160 Stacey,
Victory Campaign III p. 652   161 Roberts, pp. 838–39   162 PREM 3/66/7   163 Roberts,
p. 843   164 Ibid. pp. 843–44   165 Roberts, p. 844   166 Ibid.   167 Dilks, *Churchill
and Company* p. 195   168 Ibid.   169 Roberts, p. 844   170 Vulliamy and Smith,
"Athens 1944: Britain's Dirty Secret" *The Guardian* November 30, 2014. Available at:
https://www.theguardian.com/world/2014/nov/30/athens-1944-britains-dirty-
secret   171 Roberts, p. 849   172 Manchester and Reid, p. 884   173 Addison,
p. 208   174 Roberts, p. 852   175 Ibid.   176 Wheatcroft, p. 347   177 Roberts,
p. 853   178 Wheatcroft, p. 347; Addison, p. 209   179 ed. Soames, *Speaking*
p. 541   180 Shirer, p. 1097   181 Manchester and Reid, p. 890   182 Roberts,
p. 866   183 Churchill, *Triumph and Tragedy* p. 366   184 Roberts, p. 860
185 Manchester and Reid, p. 946   186 Wheatcroft, p. 330   187 Roberts, p. 860
188 Wheatcroft, p. 330   189 Manchester and Reid, p. 934   190 Roberts, p. 860;
Wheatcroft, p. 330   191 Roberts, p. 860   192 Manchester and Reid, p. 900
193 Confidential Annex to CAB 23 /1 22 (45) p.1 77   194 Confidential Annex to
CAB 23/2 23 (45) p. 1 82 February 21, 1945   195 ed. Pimlott, *Dalton Diary*
pp. 835–36   196 Roberts, p. 865–66   197 Confidential Annex to CAB 23 /5 26 (45)
p. 3 95 March 6, 1945   198 Ibid. p. 4 94   199 Confidential Annex to CAB 65/1 39
(45) p. 1 3, April 3, 1945   200 Manchester and Reid, p. 651   201 Colville, p. 562
202 Manchester and Reid, p. 957   203 Confidential Annex to 65/1 40 (45) p. 1
8   204 Roberts, p. 870   205 Confidential Annex to 65/1 40 (45) pp. 2–3, 9–10
206 Manchester and Reid, p. 911   207 Ibid.   208 Duff Cooper, *Old Men Forget*
p. 329   209 Confidential Annex to 65/1 50 (45) pp. 1–2, 22–23   210 Colville, p. 592;
Manchester and Reid, p. 917   211 Manchester and Reid, p. 917   212 ed James, *Complete
Speeches* Vol VII p. 7214   213 Djilas, *Conversations* p. 114   214 Manchester and
Reid, p. 907   215 Roberts, p. 867   216 Manchester and Reid, p. 907   217 Ibid.
218 Ibid.; Churchill, *Triumph and Tragedy* p. 867   219 Colville, p. 579   220 Roberts,
p. 867   221 Ibid.   222 ed. James, *Complete Speeches* Vol VII p. 7155   223 Manchester
and Reid, p. 945   224 Roberts, p. 883   225 Manchester and Reid preamble p. 22
226 Roberts, p. 883   227 Manchester and Reid, p. 947   228 Ibid.   229 Manchester
and Reid, p. 912   230 Roberts, p. 871; Gilbert, *Road to Victory 1941–1945* pp. 1291–93
231 Roberts p. 871   232 Available at: http://www.ibiblio.org/pha/policy/1945/1945-04-
17a.html   233 Roberts, p. 874   234 Ibid.   235 Ibid.   236 Ibid.; Manchester and Reid,
p. 925   237 Manchester and Reid, p. 927   238 Roberts, p.875   239 Panter-Downes,
p. 376   240 Ibid. p. 377–78   241 Roberts, p. 876   242 Manchester and Reid,
p. 967   243 Colville, p. 599   244 Ibid.   245 Confidential Annex to CAB 65/1 65 (45)
p. 3 36   246 Manchester and Reid, p. 935   247 Ibid. p. 921   248 ed. James, *Complete*

Speeches Vol VII p. 5694   249 Manchester and Reid, pp. 935, 938   250 CAB 120–691 p. 1   251 Ibid. p. 2   252 Ibid. p. 3   253 Manchester and Reid, p. 936   254 Wheatcroft, p. 326   255 Addison, p. 213; Manchester and Reid, p. 619   256 ed. James, *Complete Speeches* Vol VII p. 6760   257 Addison p. 214   258 Roberts, p. 773   259 Manchester and Reid, p. 819   260 ed. Nicholson, *Nicholson Diaries* Vol II pp. 356–57   261 Manchester and Reid, p. 653   262 Roberts, p. 870   263 Manchester and Reid, p. 921   264 Roberts, p. 878   265 Ibid.   266 Manchester and Reid, p. 938   267 Roberts, p. 879   268 Roberts, p. 878   269 Ibid.   270 Manchester and Reid, p. 938   271 Ibid. p. 940   272 Addison, p. 213   273 Manchester and Reid, pp. 943–44   274 Ibid. p. 954   275 Roberts, p. 882   276 Manchester and Reid, p. 944   277 Colville, p. 428   278 ed. Hart-Davies, *King's Counsellor* p. 336   279 Roberts, p. 882   280 Manchester and Reid, p. 943   281 eds. Danchev and Todman, *War Diaries* p. 702   282 Manchester and Reid, p. 944   283 Ibid.   284 Manchester and Reid, p. 945   285 Roberts, p. 883   286 Manchester and Reid, pp. 947–48   287 Truman, *1945 Year of Decisions* p. 416   288 Bryant, *Triumph in the West* pp. 363–64   289 Manchester and Reid, p. 948   290 ed. Hart-Davis, *King's Counsellor* p. 342   291 Roberts, p. 888   292 Manchester and Reid p. 949   293 Roberts, p. 885   294 ed. James, *Complete Speeches* Vol VII p. 5694   295 Manchester and Reid, p. 949   296 Office of the Historian (US) "The Potsdam Conference, 1945." Available at: https://history.state.gov/milestones/1937-1945/potsdam-conf   297 ed. Langworth, *Churchill In His Own Words* p. 41   298 Roberts, p. 887   299 Manchester and Reid, p. 955   300 Reynolds, *In Command of History* pp. 13, 222   301 Ibid.   302 Wheatcroft, p. 367   303 Ibid. 304 Ibid. p. 368   305 Reynolds, *In Command of History* p. 504   306 Roberts, p. 907   307 Wheatcroft, p. 261   308 Manchester and Reid, pp. 968, 973   309 Roberts, p. 911   310 Colville, *The Churchillians* pp. 26–27   311 Manchester and Reid, p. 976   312 Ibid. p. 980   313 Moran, *Struggle* p. 838   314 Wheatcroft, p. 342 315 Wheatcroft, p. 341   316 Manchester and Reid, p. 957   317 Wheatcroft, p. 341   318 Available at: https://www.nationalchurchillmuseum.org/sinews-of-peace-iron-curtain-speech.html   319 Roberts, p. 896   320 Addison, p. 222 321 Manchester and Reid, p. 961   322 Ibid.   323 *New York Times* March 6, 1946   324 Roberts, p. 896   325 Manchester and Reid, pp. 961–962   326 Addison, p. 224   327 Pickersgill and Forster, *The Mackensie King Record:* Vol IV p. 112 328 Manchester and Reid, p. 978   329 Ibid. pp. 982–83   330 Gilbert, *Never Despair* p. 352   331 Ibid.   332 Addison, p. 225   333 Roberts, p. 911   334 Ibid. pp. 916, 948   335 Ibid. p. 916   336 Roberts, pp. 899, 900   337 ed. James, *Complete Speeches* Vol VII p. 7797   338 Ibid. p. 7774   339 Manchester and Reid, p. 983   340 Available at: https://www.nato.int/cps/en/natohq/official_texts_17120.htm   341 Gilbert, *Never Despair* p. 467   342 Manchester and Reid p. 984   343 Ibid.   344 Ibid.   345 "How the Partition of India happened–and why its effects are still felt today," The Conversation. Available at: https://theconversation.com/how-the-partition-of-india-happened-and-why-its-effects-are-still-felt-today-81766   346 Ibid.   347 Gilbert, *Prophet* pp. 356–57   348 "How the Partition of India happened-and why its effects are still felt today,"   349 ed. James, *Complete Speeches* Vol VII p. 7549   350 Gilbert, *Never Despair* p. 375; Langworth, "Churchill and India: Again & Again & Again & Again," 136 *Finest Hour,* Autumn 2007   351 Mishra, "Exit Wounds: the legacy of Indian partition" The New Yorker, August 13 2007   352 Ibid.   353 Ibid.   354 Available at: https://winstonchurchill.hillsdale.edu/winston-churchills-dream-1947/   355 Roberts, p. 904   356 Roberts, p. 906   357 Ibid. p. 897   358 Wheatcroft, p. 341   359 Roberts, p. 914   360 *Time* January 6, 1950   361 Manchester and Reid, p. 975; Addison, p. 219   362 Addison, p. 219   363 Roberts, p. 913   364 Manchester and Reid, p. 993   365 Ibid. p. 993; Roberts, p. 915;   366 Roberts, p. 916   367 ed. James, *Complete Speeches* Vol VII p. 7943   368 Roberts, p. 916   369 Manchester and Reid, p. 996   370 ed. James, *Chips* p. 442   371 Manchester and Reid, pp. 996, 1011   372 Gilbert, *Never Despair* p. 514   373 Manchester and Reid, p. 1011   374 Ibid. p. 1012   375 Ibid. p. 996 376 Ibid. p. 1000   377 Roberts, p. 919   378 Ibid. p. 1015   379 Ibid. p. 1014   380 Ibid. p. 920; Addison, p. 231   381 ed. James, *Complete Speeches* Vol VII p. 8253 382 Roberts, p. 920   383 Manchester and Reid, p. 1016   384 Roberts p. 921

385 Manchester and Reid, p. 1017   386 Roberts, p. 921   387 Ibid.   388 Ibid. p. 922
389 Manchester and Reid, p. 1019   390 Ibid.   391 Ibid. p. 1021   392 Ibid.
393 *Congressional Record,* January 17, 1952 p. 276   394 ed. Nicholson, *Nicholson Diaries* Vol III p. 378   395 Manchester and Reid, p. 993   396 Roberts, p. 930
397 Wheatcroft, p. 382   398 Roberts, p. 936   399 HC Deb 11 May 1953 Vol 515
cc897   400 Wheatcroft, p. 385   401 Manchester and Reid, p. 1023   402 Addison,
p. 235   403 Ibid. p. 232   404 Colville, p. 669   405 Ibid.   406 Ibid. p. 672
407 Ibid.   408 Ibid.   409 Manchester and Reid, p. 1024   410 Ibid. p. 1026
411 Ibid.   412 Manchester and Reid, p. 1027   413 Ibid. p. 1028   414 Colville,
p. 692   415 Manchester and Reid, p. 1029   416 Colville, pp. 692–93   417 Roberts,
p. 945   418 Confidential Annex to CAB 128/4 47 (54) p. 1 354 July 7, 1954
419 Ibid.   420 Ibid. p. 2 354-A 4   421 Ibid.   422 Roberts, p. 945   423 Colville,
p. 701   424 Gilbert, *Never Despair* p. 1036   425 Colville, pp. 702–03   426 Ibid.
p. 703   427 Ibid. p. 705   428 Manchester and Reid, p. 1030   429 Sarah Churchill,
A Thread in the Tapestry p. 17   430 Colville, p. 705   431 Ibid. p. 706   432 Gilbert,
Never Despair p. 1113   433 Colville, p. 707   434 See, Gilbert, *Never Despair* p. 1115
435 Colville pp. 707–708   436 Ibid.   437 Ibid. p. 709   438 Ibid. pp. 706–07   439 Ibid.
p. 707   440 Roberts pp. 949–50   441 James, *Failure* p. 75   442 eds. Barnes and
Nicolson, *Leo Amery Diaries Vol 2 Empire at Bay* p. 833   443 Manchester and Reid,
pp. 405–07   444 Ibid. p. 407   445 Moran, *Struggle* p. 692   446 Ibid. p. 140   447 Toye,
Churchill's Empire p. xii; Roberts, p. 209   448 Masani, "Churchill and the Genocide
Myth"   449 Toye, *Churchill's Empire* p. xii   450 Ibid. p. 59   451 Ibid. p. xii   452 Ibid.
p. xiv   453 Gilbert, *Prophet* pp. 356–57   454 ed. Gilbert and Arnn, *The Churchill
Documents* Vol 17 p. 1278; Roberts p. 760   455 Heyden, "The 10 Greatest Controversies
of Winston Churchill's Career"   456 Accord, Langworth, *Winston Churchill, Myth and
Reality* p. 149   457 Roberts p. 786   458 Herman, "Without Churchill"   459 James,
Churchill and Empire p. 304   460 Roberts p. 786   461 Ibid. p. 786–87   462 Ibid.
p. 786   463 Herman, "Without Churchill"   464 Report of the Shipping Committee,
CAB 66/39 W.P.(43) 345 p. 2 dated July 30, 1943   465 Ibid.   466 Ibid.   467 CAB
65/1 111 (44) p. 207 74 August 4, 1944   468 Ibid. p. 208 74; CAB 65/1 131 (43) p. 49
143 September 24, 1943   469 CAB 65/1 111 (44) p. 208 74 August 4, 1944   470 CAB
65/1 131 (43) p. 49 143 September 24, 1943   471 Ibid.   472 Ibid.   473 CAB 65/1 131
(43) p. 49 143 September 24, 1943   474 eds. Barnes and Nicolson, *Leo Amery Diaries
Vol 2 Empire at Bay* pp. 933–34   475 CAB 65/1 131 (43) p. 49 143 September 24,
1943   476 CAB 65/2 152 (43) p. 151 104   477 Ibid. p. 152 104; HC Deb 11 November
1943 Vol 393 cc1278–79   478 CAB 65/2 152 (43) p. 151 104   479 Ibid.   480 Ibid.
p. 152   481 *Companion Volumes* IXX p. 1543   482 Roberts, p. 788   483 Herman,
"Without Churchill"   484 CAB 65/6 23 (44) p. 109 88 February 21, 1944   485 Masani,
"Churchill and the Genocide Myth   486 CAB 65/1 55 (44) p. 252 43 April 24, 1944
487 Roberts p. 788   488 CAB 65/1 55 (44) p. 252 43   489 Ibid. p. 253 44 April 24,
1944   490 Roberts p. 788   491 Ibid.   492 Masani, "Churchill and the Genocide
Myth"   493 CAB 65/1 131 (43) p. 49 143 September 24, 1943   494 Herman, "Without
Churchill"   495 Ibid.   496 See e.g. Wheatcroft, p. 350   497 Soames, *Speaking* p. 399;
Addison p. 252   498 Wheatcroft, p. 269   499 Ibid. p. 239   500 Available at: https://
www.jewishvirtuallibrary.org/churchill-broadcast-regarding-his-meeting-with-roosevelt-
august-1941   501 Manchester and Reid, p. 607   502 HC Deb 17 December 1942
Vol 385 cc2082   503 Ibid. cc2087   504 Roberts, p. 943–44; Manchester and
Reid, p. 573; Wheatcroft, p. 386; Addison, p. 233; Hennessy, *The Prime Minister*
p. 205   505 CAB 195/13   506 ed. Catteral, *The Macmillan Diaries* p. 382   507 CAB
123/4 7 (54) p. 54 80   508 CAB 195/11/90 p. 398–99   509 Toye, Churchill's Empire
p. xii   510 Quinault, "Churchill and Black Africa" *History Today* (June 2005)
p. 31   511 Ibid. p. 36   512 Colville, p. 709   513 Roberts, p. 951   514 Moran,
Struggle p. 694   515 Ibid. p. 953   516 Roberts, p. 954   517 Gilbert, *Never Despair*
p. 1151   518 Manchester and Reid, p. 1037   519 Moran, *Struggle* pp. 840–41;
Manchester and Reid, p. 1041   520 Ibid.; Roberts, pp. 953, 958   521 Manchester and
Reid, pp. 1042, 1045; Roberts, p. 957   522 Manchester and Reid, pp. 1045–46   523 Ibid.
p. 1051   524 Ibid. p. 1051   525 Roberts, pp. 956, 957, 958; Manchester and Reid,

pp. 1049, 1050   526 Halle, *The Irrepressible Churchill: Stories, Sayings, and Impressions of Sir Winston Churchill* p. 325   527 Manchester and Reid, p. 1051   528 Roberts, p. 961   529 Ibid. p. 962   530 Manchester and Reid, p. 1053   531 Ibid.   532 Addison, p. 243

Bibliography

Books

Adamthwaite, Anthony P., *The Making of the Second World War* 1977

Addison, Paul,
    Churchill on the Home Front 1900–1955, 1992
    Churchill: The Unexpected Hero 2006

Alanbrooke, Lord Alan and Danchev, Alex, *War Diaries, 1939–1945: Field Marshall Lord Alanbrooke* 2002

American Psychiatric Association, The Principles of Medical Ethics, With Annotations Especially Applicable to Psychiatry, 2013.

Amery, Leo, *The Empire at Bay: The Leo Amery Diaries 1929–1945*, 1987

Atkins, J.B., *Incidents and Reflections* 1947

Ball, Mary Margaret, *Post-War German-Austrian Relations: The Anschluss Movement, 1918–1936*, 1937

ed. Ball, Stuart, *Conservative Politics in National and Imperial Crisis* 2016

Baring, Maurice, Puppet Show of Memory 1922

eds. Barnes, John and Nicolson, David, *Leo Amery Diaries Vol 2: Empire at Bay* 1988

Berg, A. Scott. *Lindbergh* 1998

Best, Geoffrey, *Churchill: A Study in Greatness* 2001

Bethell, Nicholas, *The War Hitler Won: The Fall of Poland, September 1939*, 1973

Bew, John, *Citizen Clem: A Biography of Attlee* 2016

Biegánsk, Witold, *Poland Resistance Movement in Poland and Abroad, 1939–1945* 1987

Birkenhead, The Earl of
> Contemporary Personalities 1924
> Halifax; the life of Lord Halifax 1965

Bond, Brian, Britain, France, and Belgium 1939–1940, 1990

Bonham Carter, Violet. Winston Churchill As I Knew Him 1967

Bruegel, J., Czechoslovakia Before Munich: The German Minority Problem and British Appeasement Policy, 1973

Bryant, Arthur, Triumph in the West: 1943–1945, 1959

Birkenhead, 2nd Earl of, The Prof in Two Worlds: The Official Life of Professor F. A. Lindemann, Viscount Cherwell 1961

Blunt, Wilfred Scawen, My Diaries 2 volumes 1932

Boothby, Lord, Recollections of a Rebel 1978

Brendon, Piers, Winston Churchill 2001

Brett-Smith, Richard, Hitler's Generals 1977

Buchanan, Patrick J., Churchill, Hitler and "The Unnecessary War" 2008

Bullock, Alan, Hitler: A Study in Tyranny, 1962

Bungay, Stephen The Most Dangerous Enemy: A History of the Battle of Britain. 2000

Burckhardt, C.J., Meine Danzinger Mission 1937–1939, 1960

eds. Cannadine, David, Quinault, Roland, Winston Churchill in the Twenty-first Century 2004

Calleo, David, The German Problem Reconsidered: Germany and the World Order, 1870 to the Present, 1988

Carley, Michael Jabara, 1939: The Alliance That Never Was And The Coming Of World War II, 1999

Car, John, The Defence and Fall of Greece 1940–41, 2013

ed. Caterall, Peter, The Macmillan Diaries: The Cabinet Years 1950–57, 2004, 2012

eds. Danchev, Alex and Todman, Daniel, War Diaries 2001

Dangerfield, George, The Strange Death of Liberal England 1935

Carlton, David, *Anthony Eden: A Biography,* 1981

Chamberlin, William Henry, *America's Second Crusade* 1950

Charmley, John, *Churchill: The Edge of Glory* 1993

Churchill College (Cambridge), *The Diary of Sir Thomas Inskip* 1970

Churchill, Randolph S.,

    Into Battle 2006

  The Official Biography:

    Vol. I: *Winston S. Churchill: Youth 1874–1900* 1966

    Vol. II: *Winston S. Churchill: Young Statesman 1901–1914* 1967

Churchill, Sarah, *A Thread in the Tapestry* 1967

Churchill, Winston S.,

    A Grand Alliance 1950

    A History of the English-Speaking Peoples, Vol. 1: The Birth of Britain, 1956

    Closing The Ring 2010

    London to Ladysmith via Pretoria 1900

    Lord Randolph Churchill 2 vols. 1906

    Marlborough: His Life and Times 2 vols. 2002 (first published in 4 vols. 1933–8)

    My African Journey 1908

    My Early Life 1930

    The Gathering Storm 1948

    The Grand Alliance 1950

    The Dream 1966

    The War Speeches of the Rt Hon Winston S. Churchill 1951

    The World Crisis 5 Vols 1923–31

    Their Finest Hour 1949

    Thoughts and Adventures 1932

    Triumph and Tragedy 1954

    While England Slept: A Survey of World Affairs 1932–1938

Clough, Shepard B., Moodie, Thomas, Moodie, Carol. *Economic History of Europe; Twentieth Century* 1968 ed. Coates, Tim, *Defeat at Gallipoli; The Dardanelles Commission, Part II 1915–16*, 2000

Colville, John,
> *The Churchillians* 1981
>
> *The Fringes of Power, Downing Street diaries 1939–1955*, 1985

Corvaja, Santi, (translator. Miller, Robert) *Hitler and Mussolini: The Secret Meetings.* 2001

Crowson, Nick. *Facing Fascism: The Conservative Party and The European Dictators 1935–1940*, 2002

ed. Dalton, Ben, *The Political Diary of Hugh Dalton, 1918–1940, 1945–60*, 1986

Dalton, Hugh, *The Fateful Years: Memoirs, 1931–1945*, 1957

Dangerfield, George *The Strange Death of Liberal England* 1935

Davies, Norman,
> *Europe: A History* 1996
>
> *God's Playground a History Of Poland In 2 Volumes*; vol. II: 1795 to the present 1982

Delgado, Jose, *Second World War Diary—Part 1* 2020

Denman, Roy, *Missed Chances: Britain And Europe in the Twentieth Century* 1997

D'Este, Carlo, Warlord: A Life of Winston Churchill At War, 1874–1945, 2008

Dilks, David, *Churchill and Company: Allies and Rivals in War and Peace* 2012

ed. Dilks, David. *The Diaries of Sir Alexander Cadogan, O.M.: 1938–1945*, 1971

Dix, Anthony, *The Norway Campaign and the Rise of Churchill* 2014

Djilas, Milovan, Conversations with Stalin 1962

Dormarus, Max,
> *The Complete Hitler: Speeches and Proclamations 1932–1945*, 4 Vol 1962
>
> (translator Romane, Patrick) *The Essential Hitler, Speeches and Commentary* 2007

Dubrov, A., *Isaiah Berlin: The Journey of a Jewish Liberal* 2012

Duff Cooper, Alfred,
> *Old Men Forget* 1953
>
> *"Chamberlain: A Candid Portrait,"* n.d. [November 1939] MRGN 1/5

Dutton, David, *Neville Chamberlain* 2001

Eden, Anthony,
> *Memoirs: Facing the Dictators* 1962
>
> *Memoirs: The Reckoning* 1965

Enright, Dominique. *The Wicked Wit of Winston Churchill* 2011. Available at: https://tinyurl.com/ysua3vbx

Eisenhower, Crusade in Europe 1948

Erikson, Erik, Young Man Luther: A Study in Psychoanalysis and History 1993

Faber, David, *Munich, 1938 Appeasement and World War II* 2008

Feiling, Keith, *Life of Neville Chamberlain* 1946

Ferguson, Niall, *The War of the World: Twentieth-Century Conflict and the Descent of the West* 2006

Fest, Joachim, *Hitler* 1974

Gallup, George H.,
> *The Gallup International Public Opinion Polls* 1940
>
> *The Gallup International Public Opinion Polls* 1976

Gardner, Brian,
> *Churchill and his Time,* 2021
>
> *Churchill in Power As Seen by His Contemporaries* 1970

Gedye, G., *Fallen Bastions: The Central European Tragedy,* 1939

Geneva Consiel Slovak, *Shall Millions Die for "this Czechoslovakia"?* 1938

George, William, *My Brother and I* 1958

ed. Gibson, Hugh, *The Ciano Diaries, 1939–1943: The Complete, Unabridged Diaries of Count Galeazzo Ciano, Italian Minister for Foreign Affairs, 1936–1943,* 1945.

Gilbert, Martin

> *Churchill: A Life* 1991
>
> *In Search of Churchill* 1994
>
> *Churchill at War: His 'Finest Hour' in Photographs, 1940–1945,* 2003
>
> *Churchill War Papers, at the Admiralty* 1993
>
> *Road to Victory* 1986
>
> *The Roots of Appeasement* 2015
>
> *Winston Churchill and The Other Club* 2011

> **The Official Biography:**
>
> Vol. III: *Winston Churchill: The Challenge of War 1914–1916,* 1971 *Companion Volume III* (in two parts)
>
> Vol. IV: *Winston Churchill: World in Torment 1916–1922,* 1975 *Companion Volume IV* (in three parts)
>
> Vol. V: *Winston Churchill: The Coming of War 1922–1939,* 1976 *Companion Volume V* (in three parts)
>
> Vol. V: *Winston S. Churchill: The Prophet of Truth, 1922–1939,* 1976
>
> Vol. VI: *Winston Churchill: Finest Hour* 1939–1941, 1983
>
> Vol. VIII: *Winston Churchill: 'Never Despair' 1945–1965,* 1988

ed. Gilbert, Martin and Arnn, Larry P.,

> *The Churchill Documents* vol 17: *Testing Times* 2014
>
> *The Churchill Documents* vol 19: *Fateful Questions* 2017

Goerlitz, Walter, *History of the Germany General Staff* 2015

Golland, Jim, *Not Winston, Just William?: Winston Churchill at Harrow School,* 1988

ed. Gorodetsky, Gabriel, *The Maisky Diaries: Red Ambassador to the Court of St James's 1932–1943,* 2015

Grehan, John & Nicoll, Alexander, *Dunkirk Evacuation-Operation Dynamo,* 2020

Halder, Franz, *The Halder Diaries: The Private War Journals of General Franz Halder,* 1976

Halifax, Lord Edward, *Fullness of Days* 1956

Halle, Kay,

    Winston Churchill on America and Britain 1970

    The Irrepressible Churchill: Stories, Sayings and Impressions of Sir Winston Churchill 1985

    The Irrepressible Churchill 2010

Harbutt, Fraser J., *The Iron Curtin: Churchill, America and the origins of the Cold War*, 1966

ed. Harvey, John, *The Diplomatic Diaries of Oliver Harvey 1937–1940*, 1970

Henderson, Nevile, *Failure of a Mission* 1940

Hennessy, Peter, *The Prime Minister: The Office and Its Holders since 1945*, 2000

Higgins, Trumbull, *Winston Churchill and the Dardanelles* 1963

Hinsley, F. H., *Hitler's Strategy* 1951

Hitler, Adolph & Domarus, Max, *The Essential Hitler: Speeches and Commentary* 1956

Hitler, Adolph,

    Mein Kampf, translator Ralph Manheim, 1943 Houghton Mifflin

    Mein Kampf, Complete and Unabridged Fully Annotated 1939

Lord Home, *The Way the Wind Blows* 1976

Howard, Anthony, *Rab: The Life of R.A. Butler* 1987

Ismay, Hastings Lionel, *The Memoirs of General Lord Ismay* 1960

Jackson, Ashley, *Churchill* 2011

Jackson, Julian,

    A Certain Idea of France: The Life of Charles de Gaulle 2018

    The Fall of France: The Nazi Invasion of 1940, 2004

James, Lawrence, *Churchill and Empire: A Portrait of an Imperialist* 2014

James, Robert Rhodes

    ed. '*Chips': The Diaries of Sir Henry Channon* 1967

    Churchill: A study in Failure, 1900–1935, 1981

    Gallipoli 1984

    ed. *Winston S. Churchill: His Complete Speeches* 8 vols. 1974 ed. Jedrzejewicz, Waclaw, *Diplomat in Berlin: Papers and Memoirs of Jozef Lipski, Ambassador of Poland* 1968

Jenkins, Roy, *Churchill*, 2001, 2001

Johnson, Boris, *The Churchill Factor: How One Man Made History*, 2014

Johnson, Paul, *Modern Times: The World From the Twenties to the Eighties* 1983

Jones, Thomas, *A Diary with Letters 1931–1950*, 1954

Kennedy John F., *Why England Slept* 1940

Kershaw Ian,

> *Fateful Choices: Ten Decisions That Changed the World 1940–1941*, 2007
>
> *Hitler: Nemesis 1936–1945*, 2000
>
> *Making Friends with Hitler: Lord Londonderry and Britain's Road to War* 2004

Keynes, John Maynard, *The Economic Consequences of Mr. Churchill* 1925

ed. Kimball, Warren, *Churchill and Roosevelt: the Complete Correspondence, 3 vols.* 1984

King, Cecil, *With Malice Toward None* 1971

Kirkpatrick, I., *The Inner Circle*, 1959

Kissinger, Henry, *Diplomacy* 1994

Kolb, Eberhard, *The Weimar Republic*, 2nd ed. 2005

Krause, Karl Wilhelm, Döhring, Herbert, Plaim, Anna, *Living with Hitler: accounts of Hitler's household staff* 2018

Laffan, R. "The Crisis over Czechoslovakia, January to September 1938," *Survey of International Affairs 1938*, 1951

Lamb, Richard. *Mussolini As Diplomat: Il Duce's Italy On The World Stage* 1999

ed. Langworth, Richard M., *Churchill By Himself: The Definitive Collection of Quotations* 2008

Langworth, Richard M.,

> *Churchill In His Own Words* 2012

Winston Churchill, Myth and Reality: What He Actually Did and Said 2017

Larson, Erik, *The Splendid and the Vile: A Saga of Churchill, Family, and Defiance During the Blitz* 2020

Lavergne, Bernard, *L'Annee Politique Francais et Etrangere*, 1938.

ed. Lee, Bandy X. *The Dangerous Case of Donald J. Trump*, 2017

Leixner, Leo, *From Lemberg to Bordeaux: A German War Correspondent's Account of Battle in Poland, the Low Countries and France, 1939–40*, 2017

Lidell Hart, Sir Basil. H.

History Of The Second World War 1970

The Liddell Hart Memoirs, Vol. 2, 1965

Lipski, Josef , *Diplomat in Berlin 1933–1939*, 1968

ed. Lough, David, *My Darling Winston: The Letters Between Winston Churchill and His Mother* 2018

Lukacs, John,

Five Days in London May 1940, 1999

June 1941, Hitler and Stalin 2007

The Last European War, September 1939–December 1941, 1976

Macleod, Iain, *Neville Chamberlain* 1962

eds. Macleod, R. and Kelly, D, *The Ironside Diaries, 1937–1940*, 1962

Macmillan, Harold,

The Blast of War 1967

Winds of Change 1966

Madge, C. & Harrison, T. *Britain by Mass-Observation*, 1939.

Manchester, William,

The Last Lion, Winston Spencer Churchill, Visions of the Glory 1874–1932, 2013

The Last Lion, Winston Spencer Churchill, Alone, 1932–1940, 2013

Manchester, William, and Reid, Paul, *The Last Lion, Winston Spencer Churchill, Defender Of The Realm, 1940–1965*, 2013

Manheim, Ralph, translator *Mein Kampf* 1943

ed. Marder, Arthur J., *Fear God and Dreadnought: The Correspondence of Admiral Lord Fisher* 3 vols. 1952–59

Margach, J. The *Abuse of Power: The War Between Downing Street and the Media from Lloyd George to Callaghan*, 1978

Martin, Hugh, *Battle: The Life Story of the Rt Hon Winston Churchill* 1932

Martin, John, Downing Street: The War Years 1992

May, Ernest R., *Strange Victory: Hitler's Conquest Of France* 2001

McCarten, Anthony, *Darkest Hours, How Churchill Brought England Back from the Brink* 2017

McDonough, Frank. *Neville Chamberlain, Appeasement, and the British Road to War.* 1998

Meehan, Patricia, *The Unnecessary War: Whitehall and the German Resistance to Hitler* 1992

ed. Middlemas, Keith, *Thomas Jones: Whitehall Diary* 3 vols. 1969–71

Millard, Candice, *Hero of the Empire,* 2016

Mitchell, B.R., *International Historical Statistics, Europe 1750–1988,* 1992

Moorehead, Alan,
    Gallipoli, 1956
    The Russian Revolution, 1958

Moran, Charles (Lord Moran), *Churchill: Taken from the Diaries of Lord Moran: The Struggle for Survival* 1966

Morgan, Ted, *Churchill: Young Man in a Hurry, 1874–1915,* 1984

Morris, James, *Farewell the Trumpets; An Imperial Retreat* 1978

Mosley, Leonard, *On Borrowed Time: How World War II Began* 1969

ed. Muller, James W., *Winston Churchill: Thoughts and Adventures* 2009

Neilson, Frances, *The Churchill Legend,* 1905

Nicholson, Harold,
    King George V 1984
    Peacemaking 1919, 1933

ed. Nicholson, Nigel,
    Harold Nicholson: Diaries and Letters 3 vols. 1966–8

Noguères, H., *Munich, or the Phoney Peace,* 1965

ed. Norwich, John Julius, *The Duff Cooper Diaries,* 2005

Office of the U.S. Chief Counsel for the Prosecution of Axis War Criminals,
    Nazi Conspiracy and Aggression Supplement B 1948

Olson, Lynne, *Troublesome Young Men* 2007

Osbourn, Patrick, *Operation Pike: Britain Versus the Soviet Union, 1939–1941,* 2000

Overy, Richard, *1939: Countdown to War* 2009

Packwood, *How Churchill Waged War* 2018

Pakenham, Thomas, *The Boer War* 1979

Panter-Downs, Mollie, *London War Notes, 1939–1945,* 1971

Parssinen, Terry. *The Oster Conspiracy of 1938: The Unknown Story of the Military Plot to Kill Hitler.* 2012

Pawle, Gerald, *The War & Colonel Warden* 1965

Penn, Geoffrey, *Fisher, Churchill, and the Dardanelles* 1999

Petrie, Sir Charles, *The Carlton Club* 1955

Phifer. Michiko, *A Handbook of Military Strategy and Tactics* 2012

Philpott, Ian M., The *Royal Air Force: Rearmament 1930–1939,* 2005

Pickersgill and Forster, *The Mackensie King Record* in four volumes 1948

ed. Pimlott, Ben, *The Second World War Diary of Hugh Dalton* 1986

Pridham, Geoffrey. *Nazism, 1919–1945: Foreign policy, War and Racial Extermination.* 1998

Potter, John, *Pim and Churchill's Map Room* 2014

ed. Pottle, Mark, *Champion Redoubtable: The Diaries and Letters of Violet Bonham Carter 1914–1945,* 1998

Pyle, Ernie, *Brave Men* 1944

Raico, *Rethinking Churchill and World War I : The Turning Point, the Costs of War: America's* Pyrrhic Victories (second Expanded edition) 1999

Reith, J.C.W., *Into the Wind* 1940

Reynaud, Paul, *In The Thick of the Fight, 1930–1935,* 1955

Reynolds, David, *In Command of History* 2005

 ed. Reynolds, David, *The Origins of the Cold War in Europe* 1994

Ricks, Thomas E., *Churchill & Orwell: The Fight for Freedom* 2017

Riefenstahl, Leni, *A Memoir* 1995

Ripka, H., *Munich: Before and After,* 1939

Roberts, Andrew,
> *Churchill, Walking with Destiny* 2018
> *Eminent Churchillians* 1994
> *Hitler and Churchill: Secrets of Leadership* 2003
> *The Holy Fox: A Life of Lord Halifax* 1991

Roberts, Geoffrey, To the Brink of War: The Czechoslovakian Crisis of 1938, 1995

Rock, William R.
> *Appeasement on Trial; British foreign policy and its critics 1938–1939,* 1966
> *Neville Chamberlain* 1969

ed. Roskill, Stephen, *Hankey: Man of Secrets* 3 vols. 1970–74

Schmidt P., *Hitler's Interpreter,* 1951

Scott, Brough,
> *Galloper Jack* 2003
> *Churchill at the Gallop* 2017

Seib, Phillip, *Broadcasts from the Blitz: How Edward R. Murrow Helped Lead America Into War,* 2006

Self, Robert,
> *Neville Chamberlain, a Biography* 2006
> ed. *The Neville Chamberlain Diary Letters* vols. I–IV 2005

Sheridan, Clare, *Nuda Veritas* 1934

Shirer, William L.

    Berlin Diary: the Journal of a Foreign Correspondent 1941

    The Collapse of the Third Republic: An Inquiry into the Fall of France in 1940, 1969.

    The Rise and Fall of the Third Reich 1959

    20th Century Journey: The Nightmare Years 1930–1940. A Memoir of the Life and Times 1984

Shulman, Milton, *Defeat in the West* 1947

Schuschnigg, Kurt, Austrian Requiem 1946

Smart, Nick, *The Diaries and Letters of Robert Bernays,* 1996

Smith, Gene, *The Dark Summer: An Intimate History of the Events That Led to World War II,* 1987

Smith, Stan (ed.), *The Cambridge Companion to W. H. Auden,* 2004

ed. Soames, Mary, *Speaking for Themselves: The Personal Letters of Winston and Clementine Churchill* 1999

Spears, Sir Edward.,

    Assignment to Catastrophe Volume I: Prelude to Dunkirk, 1954

    Liaison, 1914: *A Narrative of the Great Retreat,* 1931

Spitzy, R., *How We Squandered the Reich,* 1997

Stacey, Colonel C.P., *The Victory Campaign. The Operations In Northwest Europe 1944–1945. Volume III* 1960

Stelzer, Cita, *Working with Winston,* 2019

Stewart, Graham, *Burying Caesar: The Churchill-Chamberlain Rivalry,* 1999

Stackelberg, Roderick. *Hitler's Germany: Origins, Interpretations, Legacies.* 1st Edition 1999

Strachan, Hew, *The First World War,* 2003

Strang, Baron William. *Home and Abroad,* 1983

Strom, Anne *Uncle, Give Us Bread,* 1936

ed. Stuart, Charles, *The Reith Diaries,* 1975

Swinton, Lord Phillip, *Sixty Years of Power, Some Memories of the Men Who Wielded It,* 1966

Tansill, Charles Callan, *Back Door to War: The Roosevelt Foreign Policy 1933–1941,* 1952

Taylor, A.J.P,
> *English History: 1914–1945,* 1965
> *Lloyd George: A Diary by Frances Stevenson,* 1971
> *The Origins of the Second World War,* 1966

Taylor, Telford, *Munich: The Price of Peace,* 1979

The History of The Times, Volume IV: The 150th Anniversary and Beyond, 1912–1948, 1952

Thomas, Nick, *Hurricane Squadron Ace: The Story of Battle of Britain, Air Commodore Peter Brothers, CBE, DSO, DFC and Bar,* 2014

Thompson, Julian; Pedersen, Peter; Oral, Haluk, *Gallipoli,* 2015

Thompson, Laurence, *1940,* 1966

Thompson, Walter,
> *Assignment: Churchill,* 2011
> *Sixty Minutes with Churchill,* 1957

Thorpe, D. R. *Alec Douglas-Home,* 1996

Todman, Daniel, *Britain's War,* vol. I: *Into Battle 1937–1941,* 2016

Toland, John, *Adolf Hitler,* 1976

Toye, Richard *Churchill's Empire: The World that Made Him and the World He Made,* 2011

Truman, Harry S., *1945 Year of Decisions,* 1999

Turk, Eleanor L., *The History of Germany,* 1999

Tute, Warren, *The Deadly Stroke,* 2007

U.S. Department of State, Publication 1983, *Peace and War: United States Foreign Policy 1931–1941,* 1943

ed. Vincent, John, *The Crawford Papers: The Journals of David Lindsay, Twenty-Seventh Earl of Crawford and tenth Earl of Balcarres during the Years 1892 to 1940,* 1984

Weinberg, G. *The Foreign Policy of Hitler's Germany: Starting World War II 1937–1939,* 1980

Wheatcroft, Geoffrey, 2021

Wheeler-Bennett, J.,

> Action This Day; Working With Churchill, 1969
>
> Munich: Prologue to Tragedy, 1948
>
> King George VI; his life and reign, 1958
>
> The Nemesis of Power, 2nd ed. 2005

Williams, Herbert, Politics—Grave and Gay, 1949

Wilson, John, CB: A Life of Sir Henry Campbell-Bannerman, 1973

ed. Wilson, Trevor, The Political Diaries of C.P. Scott, 1970

Windsor, The Duke of, A King's Story, 1953

Winkler, Henry, British Labour Seeks A Foreign Policy, 1900–1940, 2004

ed. Wolf, Michael, The Collected Essays of Sir Winston Churchill 4 vols. 1974

Woodward, Sir Llewelly and Margaret Lambert British Foreign Policy in the Second World War Vol I 1970

World Jewry Vol 8-11 Germany: Years of Decision 1965

Articles, etc

An Overview of the Dowding System Available at http://beyourfinest.com/dowding-system-/

Anderson, K.D. "Weather Services at War," The Royal Meteorological Society's History of Meteorology and Physical Oceanography Special Interest Group, January 2009. Available at: https://www.rmets.org/occasional-papers-meteorological-history

Ansel, Walter Hitler Confronts England 1960

Atkinson, Harry, "The Dardanelles, An Australian Perspective," Finest Hour 169, Summer 2015, Available at https://winstonchurchill.org/publications/finest-hour/finest-hour-169/the-dardanelles-an-australian-perspective/

Barley, M. P., 'Contributing to its Own Defeat: The Luftwaffe and the Battle of Britain,' Defence Studies, 4:3, pp. 387–411 (2004)

> Available at : https://www.tandfonline.com/doi/full/10.1080/1470 243042000344812

Barnett, Katherine, "'100,000 Kisses': The Woman Who Raised Winston Churchill," Finest Hour 175, Winter 2017, Available at https://winstonchurchill.org/publications/finest-hour/finest-hour-175/woman-who-raised-winston-churchill-elizabeth-everest/

Blake, Robert,

> 'Churchill and the Conservative Party' Crosby Kemper Lecture, Westminster College, Fulton, Mo. April 1987

> Times Literary Supplement April 22, 1994

ed. Borowski, Col. Harry R., "Military Planning in the 20th Century," 11th Military History Symposium, October 10–12, 1984

Brendon, Piers, "Leading Myths—The Castlerosse Affair," Finest Hour 180, Spring 2018, Available at https://winstonchurchill.org/publications/finest-hour/finest-hour-180/leading-myths-castlerosse-affair-churchill-archives/

Brew, Gregory, "How Oil Defeated the Nazis" 2019
Available at: https://oilprice.com/Energy/Crude-Oil/How-Oil-Defeated-The-Nazis.

Capet, Antoine, "Abstracts: Drs. Vale and Scadding Consider Aspects of Churchill's Health, *The Churchill Project, Hillsdale College*, March 26, 2018

CAMPAIGN SUMMARIES OF WORLD WAR 2, INDIAN OCEAN & SOUTH EAST ASIA, including Burma 1939–1945. Available at https://www.naval-history.net/NAVAL1939-45Campaigns.htm

Carley, Michael Jabara,

> 'End Of The Low Dishonest Decade: Failure Of The Anglo-Franco-Soviet alliance in 1939,' *45 Europe-Asia Studies 303* (1993)

> 'Fiasco: The Anglo-Franco-Soviet Alliance That Never Was and the Unpublished British White Paper, 1939–1940,' *International History Review* Vol. 41, no. 4, July 2019

Carson, James, "Lord Randolph Churchill's Astonishing Letter to His son About Being a Failure," *historyhit.com*, November 29, 2018

Cowles, Virginia, *Winston Churchill, the Era and the Man* 1953

Cundy, Alyssa, "A 'Weapon of Starvation': The Politics, Propaganda, and Morality of Britain's Hunger Blockade of Germany, 1914–1919" (2015), *Theses and Dissertations (Comprehensive)* 1763. https://scholars.wlu.ca/etd/1763

D'Amato, Anthony, "Legal and Moral Dimensions of Churchill's Failure to Warn," *Northwestern University School of Law Scholarly Commons Faculty Working Papers*, Paper 79, 2010

Daniels, Anthony M. and J. Allister Vale,
> "Did Sir Winston Churchill suffer from the 'black dog'? *Journal of the Royal Society of Medicine*, 2018, Vol. 111 (11)

Day, Peter and Davies, Caroline, "Records Reveal Queen's 'cut-price' Coronation" *The Guardian* August 7, 2007

Doward, Jamie, "Revealed: secret affair with a socialite that nearly wrecked Churchill's career," *theguardian.com*, February 24, 2018

"Elizabeth Everest's Faith," Available at http://www.emshancock.com/elizabeth-everests-faith/

Elms, Alan C., "Sigmund Freud, Psychohistorian," *Annual of Psychoanalysis*, Vol. XXXI, 2003

"Family Man: Churchill the Father," Available at https://winstonchurchill.org/the-life-of-churchill/life/family-man/churchill-the-father/

Field, Jacob F., "Officer Cadet to Lieutenant Colonel: Winston Churchill in the British Army," *forces*.net, July 9, 2019

Fischel, Jack R., " Questioning the Good War," VQR Summer 2008. Available at: https://www.vqronline.org/questioning-good-war#

Fletcher, Geoffrey J., "Spencer Churchill (p) at Harrow School 1888-1892, Finest Hour 133, Winter 2006-07. Available at https://winstonchurchill.org/publications/finest-hour/finest-hour-133/spencer-churchill-p-at-harrow-school-1888-1892-2/

"Flying," Available at https://winstonchurchill.org/the-life-of-churchill/life/man-of-action/flying/

Freeman, David, 'The Uncrowned King: Edward VIII' *Finest Hour* no. 184 Second Quarter 2019

Gardiner, Juliet, "Are the 2010s really like the 1930s? The truth about life in the Great Depression," *The Guardian*, March 4, 2017

Gardiner, A.G., *Prophets, Priests and Kings* 1917

Gardner, Brian,
> *Churchill and his Time: A Study in a Reputation 1939–1945* 1968

Gilbert, Martin, 'Churchill and Eugenics' *International Churchill Society* May 31, 2019. Available at https://winstonchurchill.org/publications/finest-hour-extras/churchill-and-eugenics-1/

Greenspan, Jesse, "10 Things You May Not Know About Winston Churchill, *History.com,* June 17, 2020

Hancock, Brian, "Will We Ever Know Why Nazi Leader Rudolf Hess Flew to Scotland in the Middle of World War II?" *Smithsonian Magazine,* May 10, 2016

ed. Hart-Davis, Duff, *King's Counselor*: Abdication and War: the Diaries of Sir Alan "Tommy" Lascelles, 2006

Hauner, Milan, "Did Hitler Want a World Dominion," *Journal of Contemporary History,* Vol. 13, No. 1, January 1978

Heyden, Tom, "The 10 greatest Controversies of Winston Churchill's career," *BBC News Magazine, bbc.com,* January 26, 2015

Herman, Arthur, "Without Churchill India's Famine Would Have Been Worse" *Finest Hour* No. 149, Winter 2010–11

Historic England, "Home From the War: What Happened to Disabled First World War Veterans," *Heritage Calling,* December 14, 2018

Hunt, David, "World War 1 History: Winston Churchill in the Trenches," *Owlcation.com*, October 7, 2017

Ives, William, 'The Dardanelles and Gallipoli' *Finest Hour* no. 126 2005

Jones, R.V. "Churchill as I knew Him' Crosby Kemper Lecture, Westminster College, Fulton Mo. March 1992

Keohane, Nigel, '"Sitting with the Enemy: The Asquith Coalition through a Conservative Lens" *Conservative History Journal* vol. II issue 4 Autumn 2015

Kimball, Warren, "'Beggar My Neighbor: America and the British Interim Finance Crisis, 1940–1941" *Journal of Economic History* vol. XXIX no. 4 December 1969

Klein, Christopher, "Winston Churchill's World War Disaster," *History Stories, history.com*, September 3, 2018

Kohut, Thomas A., "Psychohistory as History, *The American Historical Review*, Vol. 91, No. 2 (April 1986).

Langworth, Richard M,

> "Churchill and Common Folk: A Case of Misconception," *The Churchill Project, winstonchurchill, Hillsdale.edu,* January 18, 2018

> "Churchill and the Rhineland" *Finest Hour* no. 141, Winter 2008–9

> 'How Churchill Saw Baldwin' *Finest Hour* no. 101, Winter 1998–99

> "Churchill and India: Again & Again & Again & Again," *Finest Hour* no. 136, Autumn 2007

> "Myth 'Churchill Caused the 1943–1945 Bengal Famine'" *Finest Hour* no. 142, Spring 2009

Lambert, A. P. N., *Churchill, Hitler, and the Battle of Britain,* 185 Finest Hour 19 (2019) Available at https://winstonchurchill.org/publications/finest-hour/finest-hour-185/churchill-hitler-and-the-battle-of-britain/

Lee, John, 'Fisher, Churchill, and the Dardanelles by Geoffrey Penn' *Journal of Military History* vol. 64, no. 2 2000.

Levin, Aaron, "Goldwater Rule's Origins Based on Long-Ago Controversy," *Psychiatric News*, Vol. 51, Issue 17, September 2, 2016, American Psychiatric Association.

"Life with My Parents: Winston and Clementine," Finest Hour Issue 91, Summer 1996

Maurer John H., "Churchill, Air Power, and Arming For Armageddon," *Finest Hour* no. 185, Third Quarter 2019

"Man of Action," Available at https://winstonchurchill.org/the-life-of-churchill/life/man-of-action/

Masani, Zareer, "Churchill and the Genocide Myth: Last word on the Bengal Famine, the Churchill Project Hillsdale College, January 27, 2021

Mather, John H., MD

> "Churchill's Character: Hardiness, Resilience and Personal Toughness," *The Churchill Project, winstonchurchill.hillsdale .edu*, March 11, 2019

> "'Keeping the Memory Green and the Record Accurate' Leading Churchill Myths (6) ' Lord Randolph Churchill Died of Syphilis." Finest Hour No. 117 Winter 2002–03

"Lord Randolph Churchill: Maladies Et Mort," Available at https://winstonchurchill.org/resources/myths/lord-randolph-churchill-maladies-et-mort/

Maurer, John H., "'Winston Has Gone Mad": Churchill, the British Admiralty, and the Rise of Japanese Naval Power' *Journal of Strategic Studies* vol. 35 no. 6, 2012

Mawn, Captain Paul E, USN (retired), "China's Proposed Belt and Road Initiative", *Defense.Info* 2018. Available at: https://defense.info/re-thinking-strategy/2018/10/oil-and-war/

Maynard, Luke, 'Tory Splits over Revolutionary Russia 1918–20' *Conservative History journal* vol. II issue 4 Autumn 2015

McMenamin, Michael,

"Action This Day—Spring 1877, 1902, 1927, 1952," Finest Hour 114, Spring 2002, Available at https://winstonchurchill.org/publications/finest-hour/finest-hour-114/action-this-day-spring-1877-1902-1927-1952/

'Regime Change, 1938: Did Chamberlain "Miss the Bus"?', *Finest Hour No 162* Spring 2004

Mishra, Pankai, "Exit Wounds: the legacy of Indian partition," *The New Yorker*, August 13 2007

"'Mrs' Everest," *cabbieblog.com*, July 11, 2017

Murray, Williamson 'The Battle of Britain: How Did "The Few" Win?', *The Quarterly Journal of Military History* Vol 2 No, 4 1990)

"9 things you (probably) didn't know about Dunkirk" *HistoryExtra*. Available at https://www.historyextra.com/period/second-world-war/dunkirk-facts-history-east-mole-hitler-halt-order-douglas-jardine/

Overy, R.J. 'Germany and the Munich Crisis: a Mutilated Victory?' *Diplomacy and Statecraft* Vol. 10, no. 2–3, July 1999

Pemberton, John, "'Malnutrition in England' University College Hospital Magazine 1934 Some reflections in 2003 on the 1930s," *International Journal of Epidemiology*, vol. 32, issue 4, August 2003

Pettengill, Robert, "Douglas S. Russell Speaks to the Society in Michigan," May 14, 2011 Available at https://winstonchurchill.org/publications/churchill-bulletin/bulletin-036-jun-2011/douglas-s-russell-speaks-to-the-society-in-michigan/

Pettinger, Tejvan, "The UK Economy in the 1930s," *EconomicsHelp.org*, November 13, 2017

Philpott, William J., 'Kitchener and the 29th Division' *Journal of Strategic Studies* vol. 16 no. 3 September 1993

Price, Alfred, 'Myth and Legend', *Aeroplane Monthly* (Nov. 1997)

Quinault, Roland," Churchill and Black Africa" *History Today* (June 2005)

Reynolds, David, " Churchill the Appeaser? Between Hitler, Roosevelt and Stalin in World War Two," eds. Dockrill, M. & McKercher, B., *Diplomacy and World Power: Studies in British Foreign Policy, 1890–1951,* 1996

Rintala, Marvin, "The Love of Power and the Power of Love: Churchill's Childhood," *Political Psychology, 5*(3), 1984.

Ripsman, Norrin and Levy Jack S. "Wishful Thinking or Buying Time? The Logic of British Appeasement in the 1930s" MIT Journal: International Security Volume 33, No. 2 (Fall 2008)

Rose, Norman. "The Resignation Of Anthony Eden." *The Historical Journal,* 25, 1982

Royal College of Psychiatrists, "Goldwater Rule," https://www.rcpsych.ac .uk/improving-care/campaigning-for-better-mental-health-policy/other-policy-areas/goldwater-rule/.

Royde-Smith, John, and Dennis E. Showalter, "World War I." *Encyclopedia Britannica*, March 17, 2021, https://www.britannica.com/event/World-War-I

Russell, Douglas S.,

>"The Military Churchill," Finest Hour 181, Summer 2018, Available at https://winstonchurchill.org/publications/finest-hour/finest-hour-181/military-churchill/

>"Orders, Decorations and Medals," Available at https://winston churchill.org/the-life-of-churchill/young-soldier/orders-decorations-and-medals/

Safi, Michael, "Churchill's policies contributed to 1943 Bengal famine— study," *The Guardian, theguardian.com,* May 29, 2019

Sayers, R.A., "The Return to Gold" in The Gold Standard and Unemployment Policies Between the Wars 1980

Schwarz, Benjamin, *Rethinking Negotiation with Hitler*, NY Times Nov. 25, 2000

Scott, Nate, "the 50 Greatest Yogi Berra Quotes" USA Today March 28, 2019 Available at https://ftw.usatoday.com/2019/03/the-50-greatest-yogi-berra-quotes

Seerey-Lester, John, "Titan in the Bush," *Sporting Classics*, March/April 2017

Shaw, Albert. Review of Reviews, Vol. 82. 1930.
>
> Available at: https://www.google.com/books/edition/Review_of_Reviews/xvXVAAAAMAAJ?hl=en&gbpv=1&bsq=simon+commission+june+1930+2+volume+report+self-government&dq=simon+commission+june+1930+2+volume+report+self-government&printsec=frontcover

Simpson, John, "Winston Churchill: How a flawed man became a great leader," *BBC.com,* January 23, 2015.

Smith, Daniel, "9 things you (probably) didn't know about Winston Churchill," *HistoryExtra,* January 2015

Smithson, Alex, "Case Study #5: Sir Winston Churchill/The Greatest Briton," *Mother Nature Blog, https://asterisk15.wordpress.com/2015/02/28/case-study-5-sir-winston-churchill-the-greatest-briton/,* February 28, 2015

Soames, Mary, 'Winston Churchill: The Great Human Being' Crosby Kemper Lecture, Westminster College, Fulton, Mo. April 1991

"Summer 1918 (Age 43): Toward final Victory, " Available at https://winstonchurchill.org/the-life-of-churchill/rising-politician/1910-1919/summer-1918-age-43/

Taube, Michael, "The Friendships of Winston Churchill," *Claremont Review of Books, https://claremontreviewofbooks.com/the-friendships-of-winston-churchill/,* December 31, 2019

Tolppanen, Bradley P, , 'The Accidental Churchill' *Churchillian* Winter 2012

Tooze, Adam, *The Wages of Destruction: The Making And Breaking of the Nazi Economy* 2006

US Army, *Historical Study German Tank Maintenance In World War II,* Department of the Army Pamphlet No. 20-202 (1954)

Vale, Allister, and Scadding, John

'Did Winston Churchill Suffer a Myocardial Infarction in the White House at Christmas 1941?' *Journal of the Royal Society Medicine* vol. II no. 12 2017

"Winston Churchill ...Treatment for Pneumonia in March 1986" *Journal of Medical Biography.* Available at : Http://doi.org/ 10.1177/096772018754646

The War, episode 6, Directed by Ken Burns and Lynn Novick, Florentine Films, Public Broadcasting Service 2007

Vulliamy, Ed and Smith, Helena, "Athens 1944: Britain's dirty secret" *The Guardian* November 30, 2014 Available at https://www.theguardian .com/world/2014/nov/30/athens-1944-britains-dirty-secret

"Winston Churchill and Michael Collins 1919-22: their conflicting views of Ireland and its future," *History Ireland, historyireland.com*

Yackley, Ayla Jean, "Turks honor Gallipoli dead as passion for Ottoman past grows," *Reuters.com,* March 18, 2015

Yagoda, Ben, "What Drove Sigmund Freud to Write a Scandalous Biography of Woodrow Wilson?" *Smithsonian Magazine,* September 2018, https:// www.smithsonianmag.com/history/what-drove-sigmund-freud-write- scandalous-biography-woodrow-wilson-180970042/

Governmental Material from the British Archives

CAB 23 Interwar Cabinet Conclusions	e.g. CAB 23/ 1 25 (36) p. 1 300
CAB 24 WWI and Interwar memoranda	e.g CAB 24/260 CP (36) 53 p. 1 314
CAB 65 WWII Cabinet Conclusions 204	e.g CAB 65/2 51 (40) p. 311
CAB 66 WWII memoranda	e.g CAB 66/7 WP (40) 131 p.4 75
CAB 67 WWII memoranda	
Documents on British Foreign Policy	DBFP

Documents on German Foreign Policy   DGFP

House of Commons debate   e.g. HC Deb 24 March 1938
vol 333 cc 1455

INDEX

4th Queen's Own Hussars, 17, 520
7th Duke of Marlborough,
  Churchill, Randolph (Senior), 3

A

Abyssinia, Mussolini's invasion,
  145–147, 153
Afrika Korps, 610
Agreement of Mutual Assistance,
  267
    Anglo-Polish Treaty of Mutual
    Assistance, 296–297
air force, German compared to
  British, 141
Amery, Leo, 110, 159, 209,
  370–371 650n, 654–656
Anglo-German alliance, 143
Anglo-German Naval Agreement,
  144–145
Anglo-Polish Treaty of Mutual
  Assistance, 296–297
Anschluss
    British and French response,
    170–173
    move toward, 162–167
anti-Semitism, 80, 129, 130, 161,
  251, 481, 548, 657–658
    Chamberlain, Neville, 197, 252
ANZAC troops, Dardanelles/
  Gallipoli campaign, 56–57
appeasement, 156, 159–161, 167,
  170, 196, 200, 206, 251, 274,
  322, 330, 390, 446, 453, 501,
  548

Czechoslovakia takeover and,
  250
Ashton-Gwatkin, Frank, 246
Asquith, Henry, 35
    coalition government
    formation, 57–59
    resignations under, 65
    Stanley, Venetia, 57
Attlee, Clement, 121, 122, 170,
  273, 341, 380, 385, 387, 399,
  416, 439, 440, 442, 444,
  445,446, 455, 456, 488, 495,
  505, 571, 573, 632, 634, 635,
  636, 638, 641, 644, 645, 646
Austria
    annexation plans, 164
    anschluss, 162–167
    Germany-Austria, 162
    plebiscite, 168–170

B

Baden, Max von, 79
Baldwin, Stanley, 94f
    1935 general election, 147–148
    Churchill as warmonger, 148
    Prime Minister, 142
Balfour, Arthur, 29, 30–32
Balfour Declaration of 1926, 112
Battle of Britain
    air war intensification,
    581–583
    Dowding System, 582
    Göring's great battle, 582
    Hitler to Reichstag, "peace or
    destruction," 579–580

launch, 578
postpone advice to Hitler, 581
RAF pilots, praise for,
    584–585
RDF (Radio Direction Finding)
    stations, 582
Battle of Somme, 64
Bavaud, Maurice, 485–486
Beck, Józef, 246
Beck, Ludwig, 212–213
Beer Hall Putsch, 91–92
BEF (British Expeditionary Force),
    338
    Belgium, 382, 402
    evacuation, telegram, 441
    France, retreat, 416–417
    General Headquarters
        abandoned, 406
    Nicholson, Claude, 416,
        432–433
    rescue from Dunkirk, 465–
        466, 554–555
    withdrawal, 427–429
Belgium
    German invasion, 381–382
    surrender, 461–462
        formal, 466
    WWI and, 47
Beneš, Edvard, 180–183
Berchtesgaden meeting, 189–193
Bernstorff, Albrecht von, 152
Beveridge Report, 631–632
Black Dog, 59
Black Thursday, 111
the Blitz, 583–584
    Churchill visits bomb sites, 588
    East End of London, 587–588
    impact
        on Britons, 587–589
        on German plans to
            invade, 586–587
    necessity, 585

Boer republics self-government,
    32–33
Boer War, 22–26
    war correspondence, 20
Bolsheviks
    seizure of power, 68
    White Russians and, 71–72
Bonar Law, Andrew, 48
    resignation, 87
Boothby, Robert, 99
Bore War (Phoney War), 344–347
Broderick, William, 28
Bruening, Heinrich, 115–116
Burnham, Charles, 25–26

C
Cadogan, Alexander, 206
    Chamberlain resignation,
        379–380
Cairo, 19
Calais, 451
    fall, 461–462
capitalism, SA (Sturmabteilung)
    and, 133
Carden, Sackville, 52
Casablanca conference, 612–614
Case White, 259
Chamberlain, Austin, 94f
Chamberlain, Joseph, 19
    Imperial preference, 29–30
Chamberlain, Neville, 109, 111,
    174, 244f
    on aggression toward Czechs,
        248
    appeasement, 156, 159–161
    antagonism between him and
        Churchill, 98n, 109, 110n,
        111, 117, 122, 128, 134, 137,
        143n, 148n, 155, 160, 161,
        171, 189, 226, 229, 231, 236,
        244, 252, 264n, 272, 273,
        275, 280, 282–283, 316

anti-Semitism 197, 252
Berchtesgaden meeting,
    189–193
Birmingham speech, 3/17/1939,
    251–253
broadcast of war declaration,
    334–335
bullying of Czechoslovak and,
    196–197
Chancellor of the Exchequer,
    1923, 1931, 120
    declined 1924, 96
Churchill, relationship
    evolution, 364–368
conversion, 251–254
death, 589–591
double-barreled policy, 159
Germany and Treaty of
    Versailles, 156
Godesberg meeting, 198–206
handling of news of Polish
    invasion, 330–334
Hitler Munich meeting invite,
    9/28/1938, 218–219
Jewish immigration to
    Palestine, 252
move out of Downing Street,
    393
Munich Agreement Sept 1938,
    219–233
Munich Agreement versus
    Godesberg Memorandum,
    226
Mussolini, telegram tp
    9/28/1938, 218
Plan Z, 187–194
pride over Munich Agreement,
    222–223
Prime Minister starting
    5/31/1937, 155–156
radio broadcast about
    Czechoslovakia, 217

recognition of Hitler's evil, 161
relationship transformation
    with Churchill, 446–447
resignation
    BBC broadcast, 385
    lead up, 377–383
response to Hitler's peace
    proposal of 10/12/1939,
    341–342
Reynaud meeting with,
    5/26/1940, 439
statement of intent to meet
    Hitler's demands 9/27/1938,
    211
support for Churchill's
    position, in the War Cabinet
    debate 452–453
ultimatum to Germany,
    9/3/1939, 334–337
war guarantee to Poland,
    257–259
Chanak, Turkey, 83–85
Channon, Chips, 372
Charge of the Light Brigade,
    Crimean War, 17
Churchill, Clementine, 70f
    family affection, 527
Churchill, Jack, 3
    favoring by father, 523–524
Churchill, Jennie. See Jerome,
    Jennie
Churchill, John, 3, 519
Churchill, Randolph (7th Duke of
    Marlborough), 3
Churchill, Randolph (Lord), 3, 4,
    21f, 519
    Chancellor of the Exchequer, 9
    death, 16–17
    election to Parliament, 5
    move to Ireland, 5
    parenting, 4–5
    Salisbury and, 9–10

Secretary of State for India, 9
CHURCHILL, WINSTON
   LEONARD SPENCER
   BATTALION COMMANDER
   ON WESTERN FRONT
   1915–1916
      Queen's Own Oxfordshire
      Hussars, resignation
      from cabinet in
      November 1915 to serve,
      60–63
   BOARD OF TRADE—1908
      president, 35–36
   CHANCELLOR OF THE
   EXCHEQUER, 1924–1929,
   94f
      Chancellor of the
      Exchequer, 94f
         defense spending,
         97–98
         disarmament, 97–98
         father's robes, 96
         Gold Standard, return
         to, 99–100
         service, 95–97
         social programs,
         97–98
      negotiating skills, war
      debt, 98
   CHILDHOOD/SCHOOLING
      ADHD (Attention Deficit
      Hyperactivity Disorder),
      541
      beatings at school, 7, 11,
      524
      boarding school
         beatings, 7, 11, 524
         the Brunswick School,
         8–10
         Harrow, 10–13
            military studies,
            519

      lone wolf tendencies,
      537
      parents' visits, begging
      for, 7, 8–9, 523
      St. George School, 7–8
   bullying in childhood
      and recognition of
      Hitler as, 546–550
      St. George's School,
      524
      understanding of
      Hitler and, 519
   childhood
      bullying,
         understanding of
         Hitler and, 519
      Ireland years, 5
      shabby clothing, 5–6
      toy soldiers, 6–7, 524
      trauma, development
      of empathy and, 518,
      526
      Woomy, 5
   discipline problems in
   school
      the Brunswick School,
      8
      Harrow, 11
      St. George School, 7–8
   Everest, Elizabeth Anne
   (Woomy), 4–5
      emotional support,
      526
      empathy, Winston's
      development of, 518,
      526
      Winston's capacity for
      love, 527
   family lineage of military
   service, 519–522
   fencing, Harrow, 11
   Harrow, 10–13

lone wolf tendencies,
537
military studies, 519
School Rifle Corps,
519
illness, at Harrow, 11
parents. *See also* Churchill,
Randolph; Jerome,
Jennie
death of Lord
Randolph, 16–17
emotional neglect by,
5–6, 523–524
coping
mechanisms,
524–525
favoring brother,
523–524
idolization of, 13
letter to/from Jennie,
6, 11–15, 17, 18, 19,
letters to/from Lord
Randolph 14, 15
loss of pocket watch,
15
Sandhurst military,
14–15
visits to boarding
schools, Winston's
begging, 7, 8–9, 523
Sandhurst, 13–16
admissions, 13–14
cavalry admittance, 14
father's response, 524
loss of pocket watch,
15
Royal Military
Academy, 520
toy soldier, 6–7
trip while at Harrow
remedial French, 13

trauma of childhood
development of
empathy, 518, 526
personal
transformation and,
529–530
as young man, 20*f*
FIRST LORD OF THE
ADMIRALTY 1911–1915
Antwerp, WWI, 47–48
First Lord of the
Admiralty, 45–46, 531
removal as, 57–58
Gallipoli campaign
ghosts of for Churchill,
533
lifelong effects,
531–532
RND (Royal Naval
Division), 47–48
FIRST LORD OF THE
ADMIRALTY 1939–1940
Norway Campaign,
347–363
trip report to War Cabinet
5/17/40, 404–405
HOME SECRETARY—
1910–1911
Home Secretary position
eugenics and, 41–42
prison reform and, 41
Tonypandy riots,
42–43
Latvian anarchists on
Sidney Street 1910, 43,
543
LEADER OF THE
OPPOSITION 1945–1951
atomic bomb, 646
Churchill's support for,
628

ultimatum suggestion
to Soviets, 638–639,
646
US nuclear bombers stationed
in Britain, 628
MILITARY CAREER
family lineage of military
service, 519–522
military career, 17–19
4th Queen's Own
Hussars, 17
Boer War, 23–26
cavalry admittance at
Sandhurst, 14, 520
commissioned officer,
520–521
Cuba, 17–18
experience informed
opinion on Hitler,
549
family lineage and,
519–522
father's support, 12
Grenadier Guards,
61–63
India, 18–19
resignation from,
19, 23
return from France,
63–64
Sudan, 19
**MINISTER OF
MUNITIONS—1917**
66–69
**OTHER FACTS ABOUT
CHURCHILL**
air-to-air communications,
66n
belief in military
superiority of British,
506–513

British Empire as
Churchill's secular
religion, 113
Chancellor of the Dutchy
of Lancaster, 58
Chartwell, 527–528
correspondence removed
from 10 Downing, 636
daylight saving time, 66
death, 661–662
drawing by Rick Young,
552f, 663f
The Dream, 641–643
family lineage of military
service, 519–522
family with Clementine,
affection in, 527
flying lessons 1913–14,
543–544
Follow My Leader game,
541–542
health
appendectomy, 85
blood transfusion, 66
concussion, donkey
incident, 5
diphtheria, 10
doctor's warnings in
second term, 647
dyspepsia, 422
fading, 661
physical abuse in
school, 524
pneumonia, Tunis and,
617–618
stroke (1953), 647–648
stroke (1965), 661
injuries
automobile accident in
NY (1931), 118
at Harrow, 11

jump off foot bridge, 14
letters, oldest surviving, 6
Man of the Half Century, 644
Order of the Garter offered, 635
plastic surgery, 66n
tank idea, 43, 66
women's suffrage, Churchill on 36–37
PARLIAMENT/ PARLIAMENTARY ELECTIONS
Independent Anti-Socialist platform (1924), 88–89
military spending vote 1901, 28
Parliament
Asquith government collapse, 65
Churchill, Randolph, 5
Corn Tax, 29
crossing the floor (1904), 31–32
elected as a Liberal (1906), 32
elected as Conservative (1924), 95–97
father's seat, 31
first speech to as Prime Minister, 394
Fourth Party (Lord Randolf), 28
Hughligans, 28
invitation to run (1900), 19–20
Irish question, 80–82
return during Grenadier Guard service, 62–63
social reform, 38

social welfare efforts, 37–38
twins of Social Reform, 1908, 38n
West Leicester election campaign (1924), 87–88
PERSONALITY TRAITS, ETC.
ADHD (Attention Deficit Hyperactivity Disorder), 541
belief in military superiority of Britain, 506–513
bullying in childhood and recognition of Hitler as, 546–550
Churchill's loyalty to government, 364–368, 446–447
Churchill's subservient role, problems, 613
compartmentalization abilities, 618–619
coping mechanisms from emotional neglect, 524–525
daredevil traits, 540–546
The Dream, 641–643
empathy
development, 518, 526
examples, 526–527
political career and, 529–530
eugenics, 41–42
Everest, Elizabeth Anne (Woomy), 4–5
emotional support, 526
empathy, development, 518, 526

Winston's capacity for love, 527
family with Clementine, affection in, 527
fearlessness, 519
flying lessons 1913–14, 543–544
Follow My Leader game, 541–542
Gallipoli campaign *see* Dardanelles/ Gallipoli
ghosts of for Churchill, 533
lifelong effects, 531–532
lone wolf tendencies, 538–539
racial attitudes, 113n
racism, 650–652
Holocaust, 657–658
Indian famine and, 652–657
keeping England white, 658–660
recognition, seeking, 525–526
redemption seeking, 530–536
risk taking, 540–546
sociopathy *versus* pragmatism in Churchill, 638–639
sports, daredevil traits and, 542
trauma of childhood development of empathy, 518, 526
personal transformation and, 529–530
trouble, "eager for trouble," 521–522

Prime Minister, selection process 5/9/1940, 377–383
PRIME MINISTER 1940–1945
D-Day, Churchill's desire to participate, 618–620
early reactions, 385–390
first speech to Parliament as PM, 394
German invasion of Western Europe, 392–393
no-confidence motion, 606–607
papers removed from 10 Downing, 636
Percentages Agreement with Stalin, 621
resistance to peace negotiations
belief that Hitler would have harsh demands, 477–478
buying peace by ceding territory, 442–444
Churchill's refusal to enter talks, 444–445
ignored issues, 479–481
influences, possible assassination possibilities 483–487
belief that Britain could go alone, 506
Britain as vassal state, 498–499
Britain's military superiority, 506–513
Britain's resources, 495
duty to defend vow, 514

effects of peaceful
coexistence,
499–500
German oil supplies,
487–489
Germany's shortages,
494–495
Hitler, hatred of,
502–503
Hitler, lack of trust,
504–505
Hitler, negotiations or
nonviolence, 501
Hitler controlling
Europe, 499–500
incompatibility with
conscience, 501–502
keeping France
involved, 495–496
Nazism, hatred of,
502–503
principles, sacrifices
for, 503
U.S. entry, 489–493
weak position of
Britain, 496–498
return from visit with
Roosevelt, 662f
subservient to
Roosevelt after
Casablanca, 613
no-negotiations stance,
477–479
recognition, seeking,
525–526
redemption seeking,
530–536
Tehran conference,
616–618
visit to the front (1945),
627

votes of confidence,
604–606
at Whitehall on V-E Day,
598f
with Roosevelt and Stalin,
598f
with submachine gun, 516f
PRIME MINISTER
1951–1955, 645–650
Cabinet appointments,
645–646
discussions with
Soviets, 648
doctor's warnings, 647
Eisenhower proposed
meeting with
regarding summit
with USSR (1954),
647
Queen Elizabeth
coronation, 647
resignation, 649–650
PRIVY COUNSELOR—
1907, xv
SECRETARY FOR WAR AND
AIR—1919–1921, 71
SECRETARY OF STATE
FOR THE COLONIES
1921–1922, 71
appointment June 1921, 80
Settlement of Irish
question, 1921, 80–82
SPEECHES/LECTURES, 22f,
27, 29, 30, 36, 46, 62, 72, 73,
90, 96n, 109, 109n, 111, 117,
118, 125, 128, 131, 137, 142,
148n, 151, 152, 155, 171,
172, 229, 230, 261, 262, 265,
272, 273, 336, 356, 372–375
"blood, toil, tears, and
sweat" speech, 394–395

first speech to Parliament
as PM, 394
Iron Curtain speech,
637–638
lectures, South African
adventures 1900, 27
praising French Army
5/19/1940, 408, 480
"This Was Their Finest
Hour," 569
"We shall fight on the
beaches," 559
UNDER-SECRETARY
OF STATE FOR THE
COLONIES—1905, 32
AS WAR CORRESPONDENT
Boer War
eager for trouble,
521–522
escape from the Boers,
24–26
Estcourt, train wreck,
23–24
The Daily Telegraph war
correspondent, 18
war correspondent,
520–521, 22*f*
army commission and,
26
Boer War, 20, 22–26
Cuban war of
independence, 17–18
India, 18–19
newspapers competing
for, 23
WILDERNESS YEARS
1929–1939
see disarmament
see India
defense spending, 108, 114,
116, 120, 121, 127, 131,

134, 140, 142, 143, 148,
151, 153, 155, 158
Free trade, 115, 119
first public warning about
Hitler
Conservative Business
Committee, resignation,
117
Churchill not invited into
the Baldwin Government
(1935), 147–148
Churchill's warnings
about Nazi Germany,
118, 139
wilderness years, 110, 532,
538
emergence from,
363–368
lone wolf tendencies,
538–539
WRITINGS
The Dream, 641–643
*History of English
Speaking People,* 660
My Early Life, 15, 18, 31n
Nobel Prize for Literature,
18, 648
The Second World War,
636
class warfare, 39–41
Coal Mines (Eight Hours) Act, 101
Collins, Michael, 81–82
Colonial Conference, 29–30
Colville, John (Jock), 204, 234n,
337, 338, 341, 342, 343n, 349,
351, 353, 362, 367, 374, 375,
380, 388, 389, 394, 403, 405,
408, 411, 413, 455, 483, 512,
533, 556n, 566n, 577, 578, 633,
634n, 647, 648, 649, 650, 651n,
652n

Communism, Churchill's opinion, 502–503

Cooper, Duff, 227–228, 331, 332, 365, 465, 572, 609n

Corn Tax, 29

COS (Chiefs of Staff)
assessment of Britain's continuing war alone May 1940, 437
briefing paper (May 25, 1940), 425–426
Terms of Reference, 427
Main Report (May 25, 1940), 453–455

Crimean War, Charge of the Light Brigade, 17

Cuba, Churchill's military service, 17–18

Curzon line border, 622

Czechoslovakia
Anglo-French ultimatum, 194–198
appeasement and, 250
Berchtesgaden meeting, 189–193
Bohemia, Wehrmacht in, 247
claims against by Hitler, 186, 199
German invasion, 176–187
Godesberg meeting, 198–206
Goering at Nuremberg rally September 1938, 186
Hitler takeover, 246–254
Hitler's demands, 199–203
Hitler's justification for takeover, 250–251
Lebensraum plans and, 175
Moravia, Wehrmacht in, 247
Polish Government's ultimatum, 9/30/1938, 239
Russian protection discussions 1938, 173–174
Sudeten German threat, 172–173

D

"D" (Birger Dahlerus), 283

Dahlerus, Birger ("D"), 283
message in War Cabinet meeting, 325, 328
Poland invasion and, 302–307

Daladier, Èdouard, 180
on Hitler's threatened invasion of Czechoslovakia, 187
return from Munich, 224–225

Dardanelles/Gallipoli campaign, 48–50
ANZAC troops, 56–57
Carden, Sackville, 52
Dardanelles Commission, 64–65, 68
Fisher, Jackie, 50–51
Hamilton, Ian, 55–56
Kitchener, Herbert (Lord), 52
legacy with Churchill, 59
Phase 1, 50–55
Phase 2a, 55–57
Phase 2b, 59–60
War Council, 52–54

Darlan, François, 565–566

Dawes, Charles, 104–105

D-Day, Churchill's desire to participate, 618–620

death
date of Churchill's, 661
date of Churchill's father, 17

Defence Requirements Committee, 130

defense spending, 38–39

Derby, Lord, on Churchill leaving military in 1916, 63

Diana (Princess), 3

Directive No. 6, 342–343

disarmament 74, 78, 107

Geneva Disarmament
Conference, 121
Germany, 78–79
in Britain during the 1920's
and early 1930's, 78, 97,
104, 107, 108, 121, 125, 127,
131, 132
League of Nations commission
on, 107
RAF expansion after 1934,
131, 140, 148, 155, 158
Ten Year Rule and, 107–108
Disraeli, Benjamin
Tory Democracy, 5
DNVP (German National People's
Party), 126
Dollfuss, Englebert, 135
Dowding, Hugh "Duffy," 399, 582
Dowding System, 582
Duke of Marlborough, 3
Dunkirk
evacuation (Operation
Dynamo), 450–452,
464–466, 474
fall of France and, 554–563
Luftwaffe, 451

E
Ebert, Friedrich, 77, 79
economy
Keynes on Churchill and, 99
National Government and, 119
Eden, Anthony, 147
resignation as Foreign
Secretary February 1938,
166–167
Edward VIII (King)
abdication, 149–151
as Hitler's guest, 157
visit with Hitler, 154f

Eisenhower, Dwight
Churchill's bitterness toward
(1943), 616
Commander in N. Africa
(1942), 610, 611
Commander in Sicily
(1943), 614
Churchill's
questioning, 614
Commander Operation
Overlord (1944)/Supreme
Commander all Allied
Forces, 614–615, 617, 618
criticism of (1942), 612
as President of the United
States
view of special relationship
with Britain, 646n
Churchill's push for
summit meeting with
Soviets (1954–1955) 647,
648
Elizabeth (Queen), coronation, 647
Elser, Georg, 486–487
Estonia, Stalin and, 563
European alliance post WWII,
Soviet Union and, 640–641

F
Ferdinand, Franz, assassination, 46
Fisher, Jackie, Dardanelles/
Gallipoli campaign, 50–51
Flapper Election, 109
Foch, Ferdinand, 75
Fourteen Points (Wilson), 73–74
Fourth Party (Lord Randolph), 28
France
agreement with Britain (1940)
not to negotiate armistice
with Germany without
mutual consent, 557

Allied invasion of (1944), 618–620
armistice with Germany June 1940, 569–574
fall of in June 1940, 554–563
French Air Force, 153
householder preparations for invasion, 557–558
mediation suggestions, 467–470
Rhineland evacuation, 116
Sedan fighting in, May 1940, 396–399
ultimatum to Germany 9/3/1939, 336
war intensification, 561–563
Free Food League, 29
free trade, 29–31, 73, 88, 97, 111, 115, 119
French, John, 60–61
French Fleet
armistice with Germany, 569–574
British attack on Mers-el-Kebir, 576–577
British seizure of ships, 576–577
Dakar (Senegal) attack, 577
Darlan, François, 565–566
saving from Nazis, 565–568

G
Gallipoli, 45, 48–60. *See also* Dardanelles/Gallipoli campaign
Gamelin, Maurice, 378–379
Gandhi, Mahatma
arrest, 114
Dominion status for India, 113
prison release, 117
General Strike of 1926, 100–102

Geneva Disarmament Conference, 121
German withdrawal from, 130
George V (King), death, 149
George VI (King), 150
first meeting with Churchill, 383–384
German Jews, persecution, formal, 129
German Navy mutiny 1918, 79
German-Soviet Frontier Treaty 1939, 290n
Germany
Air Force, 138, 140
compared to Britain, 141
armistice with France, 569–574
Beer Hall Putsch, 91–92
British WWI blockade post armistice, 72–74
Case White, 259
dictatorship established, 128
disarmament, 78–79
early WWII protocol against attacking French and British, Sept 1939, 337
expansion goals, 156–157
Greece, attack on, 594–595
invasion of France, 47
joint declaration against, 254–256
Lebensraum plans, 156–157, 164
Czechoslovakia and WWI, 9/3/39, 175
military unrest in 1938, 212–215
motorboat assembly in 1940, 555–556
Night of the Long Knives, 132–135
offensive in the West, 68

oil supplies, 487–489
parliamentary elections,
    1932–33, 123–124, 128
presidential election 1932, 122
rearmament, 136–139
reparations post WWI, 104
    Depression and, 123
    Lausanne conference and,
    123
revenge against France, 314
Rhineland entry, 151–153
shortages, 494–495
Sudetenland occupation, 199
Treaty of Versailles, 75–77
ultimatums to withdraw from
    Poland, 334–337
unification of President and
    Chancellor 1934, 135
Germany-Austria, 162
Gladstone, William, 6
Gleiwitz radio station, 310
Godesberg meeting, 198–206
    British-French proposal, 205
    Godesberg Memorandum,
    202–203, 205, 220
        Munich Agreement and,
        226
    rejection of Hitler's proposal,
    207–209
Goering, Hermann
    Battle of Britain, 582
    Beer Hall Putsch, 92
    on Czechs, Nuremberg rally
        September 1938, 186
    hunting trip with Halifax,
    154f, 157–158
    Minister of the Interior for
        Prussia, 126
    Minister without Portfolio, 126
    Reichstag president
        appointment, 126

Gold Standard, Britain's return to,
    99–100
Gort (Lord), John
    general in charge of the BEF
        in France, 461, 1939–1940,
        338n, 407–439, 461–466,
        556
Government of India Act of 1919,
    78
Grand Alliance, 267–290
Greece
    attack by Italy, German follow
        up, 591, 594–595
    democracy maintained in,
        622–623
Grenadier Guards, 61–63

H
Hácha, Emil, 246
Halder Plot, 483
Halifax (Lord), 110, 244f
    communication style, 431
    communiqué 9/26/1938 re:
        defending Czechoslovakia,
        210–211
    on Gandhi, 117
    on German plans to annex the
        Sudetenland, 184–185
    on Goebbels, 157–158
    on Hitler in Rhineland, 151
    on Hitler's peace proposal of
        Oct 1939, 340
    hunting trip with Goering in
        1937, 154f, 157–158
    Lord Privy Seal, 147
    on madness of Hitler, 186–187
    meetings May 9, 1940 re:
        Prime Ministership, 379–380
    memoir, Munich Agreement,
        241–242

Mussolini, desire to involve in
  peace discussions May 1940,
  429–432, 440, 450
Nazism, wish for destruction
  of, 206
on negotiating peace with
  Hitler, 437–439, 440
  surreptitious efforts,
  568–569
Reynaud meeting 5/26/40, 439
Secretary of State for War
  1935, 142
telegram draft to Roosevelt
  5/25/40, 431–432
Viceroy of India, 110
War Cabinet, May 26-28,
  1940, 455–461
War Cabinet under Churchill,
  386–387
Halt Order 5/24/40, 417–421
Hamilton, Ian, Dardanelles/
  Gallipoli campaign, 55–56
Hammerstein-Equord, Kurt von,
  482–483
Hankey, Maurice, 58
Henderson, Neville, 179, 189, 201,
  208, 209, 210, 215, 216, 236,
  265, 289, 295, 296, 298, 299,
  300, 301, 302, 303, 304, 305,
  308, 309, 325, 327, 329, 333,
  334, 337
Henlein, Konrad, 176
Hess, Rudolph, Duke of Hamilton
  and, 596
Hindenburg, Paul von, 79
  Brueining financial policies,
  115–116
  death, 135
  General during WWI
    transferred power to
    Weimar Republic,
    9/1918, 79
  before Germany signed
    Versailles Treaty, advised
    that further German
    resistance impossible, 77
  President of Weimar Republic
    1925–1934, 115, 122
    Appointed Hitler
    Chancellor 2/1933, 126
    Suspended portions of
    German constitution
    guaranteeing freedom
    2/1939, 127
History of English Speaking
  People, 660
Hitler, Adolf
  on allied nations, 319
  Anglo-German Naval
    Agreement of 1935
    disavowal, 319–320
  appeasement, Chamberlain
    and, 156
  April 28, 1939, speech, 317–
    322, 322f
  assassination possibilities
    Bavaud, Maurice, 485–486
    Elser, Georg, 486–487
    Halder Plot, 483
    Hirsch, Helmut, 485
    Kordt, Erich, 487
    plots, 485–487
    Polish Victory Parade Plot,
    486
    Zossen Conspiracy, 483
  Austria interests, 135
  British Empire liquidation, 279
  on Chamberlain, 192
  Chancellor, 126–127
  Churchill's hatred of, 502–503
  Churchill's lack of trust,
    504–505
  Churchill's warnings about,
    547–548

Czechoslovakia takeover,
246–254
depose rumors, 482–485
Directive No. 6, 342–343
early take on, 161
eligibility for presidential
election in 1932, 122
Fuhrer of the Reich, 134
Godesberg Memorandum,
202–203, 220
high treason trial, 1924, 92–93
invasion of Britain, request
for plans to be drawn up,
574–575
invitation to National Socialist
German Worker's Party, 79
Landsberg prison, 93
megalomania, examples, 504
Mein Kampf, 93
military abilities, 260
military oath of obedience, 135
mistrust, broad, 504–505
murder as political strategy,
134
negotiations, opinion, 501
nonviolence, opinion, 501
"On the Jewish Question," 80
peace proposal, October 6,
1939, 339–341
plans for Britain, 343–344
public warnings by Churchill,
118
recognition as bully, 546–550
Reichstag speech, "peace or
destruction," 579–580
Roosevelt's telegram of
4/15/39, response, 321–322
SS (Schutzstaffel/Protection
Squadron), formation, 105
Treaty of Versailles violation,
130
X Report, 484

Hitler's nemesis (Churchill),
546–550
HMS Dreadnought, 38
Holocaust, Churchill on, 657–658
Home Rule. *See* Irish Home Rule
Howard, John, 25
Hughligans, 28, 537
Hungary, demands for Slovakia,
239
hydrophones, 66n

I
Imperial preference, 29–30
India
caste system, 113
civil disobedience start, 117
Dominion status, 112–114,
143–144
Round Table conference,
115
Simon Commission,
114–115
famine of 1943, 652–657
independence, 641
Inskip, Thomas, 143n, 189, 190,
240, 248
invasion of Britain. *See* Battle of
Britain
Ireland
Black and Tans, 81
Easter Rising, 80
IRA (Irish Republican Army),
81
Irish Free State, 82
Irish Home Rule, 19, 31, 40,
81
Irish Nationalist Party, 40
Irish question, 80–82
Irish Republic, 80
Sinn Féin Party, 81
Iron Curtain speech 3/5/1946,
637–638

Ironside, General Edmund
  comments
    about Churchill as possible
      PM, 388
    about German invasion of
      France, 397
    about Britain's ability to
      hold out, 407
    about ability to evacuate
      BEF from France, 407–
      408, 416, 429, 556
  Gort refusal to follow orders,
    407
  Norway campaign, 351, 352,
    357
  promise to Poles prior to
    German invasion, 336
  report on German invasion
    of France of May 22, 1940,
    412–413
  Weygand Plan, 413–416
Irwin (Lord). See Halifax (Lord)
Ismay, Hastings "Pug," 398
  report on likely German
    invasion of the UK of May
    22, 1940, 413
Italy see also Mussolini
  Allied invasion of 1943,
    615–616
  invasion of Abyssinia by, 140,
    145
  invasion of Greece by, 591–592
  performance in North Africa,
    592

J
Japan
  atomic bomb use, Churchill's
    support for, 628
  invasion of Manchuria, 120
  Pearl Harbor attack, 602–603
Jerome, Jennie, 3, 20f

background, 4
  Lady Randolph, 4
  parenting, 4–5
Jerome, Leonard, 4
Jewish immigration to Palestine,
  Chamberlain and, 252n
joint declaration proposed against
  Germany March 1939, 254–256

K
Kahr, Gustav von, 91–92
Kemal Atatürk, Mustafa, 83–85
Kennedy, John F., Why England
  Slept, 121
Keyes, Roger, 369–370
Keynes, John Maynard, 75
  on Gold Standard, 99
Kirkpatrick, Ivone, 201
Kissinger, Henry, on Hitler and
  Czechoslovakia, 250
Kitchener, Herbert (Lord), 19, 47
  Dardanelles/Gallipoli
    campaign, 52
  death, 63–64
Kleist, Ewald von, 215
Kordt, Erich, 487
Kordt, Theodor, 215
Kristallnacht, 243–244

L
Labour Government collapse
  (1931), 119
Labour Party, refusal to serve
  under Chamberlain, 5/10/1940,
  380–383
Lativa, Stalin and, 563
Lausanne conference, 123
League of Nations
  creation, 77
  disarmament commission, 107
  disillusion with, 152
  German withdrawal, 130

Manchuria events, 122
Mussolini invasion of
Abyssinia, 145–146
Treaty of Versailles and, 76
Lithuania
Memel re-annexation, 255
Stalin and, 563
Litvinov, Maxim, 254
on assistance to
Czechoslovakia, 236
Litvinov proposal, 268
Lloyd George, David, 28, 371–372
Churchill's exclusion from new
government 1916, 65–66;
appointed Churchill Minister
of Munitions July 1917, 66,
67
new government formation
Dec. 1916, 65–66
Paris Peace Conference, 74
tribute to Churchill in
Parliament 5/13/1940, 395
twins of Social Reform, 1908,
38n
Locarno Treaties, 103
Lord Halifax. See Halifax (Lord)
Ludendorff, General Erich, 79,
91–92
high treason trial, 92–93

M
MacDonald, Ramsey, 109, 119
resignation, 142
Maginot Line, 392
Maisky, Ivan, meeting with
Churchill, 261
Manchuria
Japanese invasion, 120
League of Nations and, 122
Marjoribanks, Edward, 10
Marlborough (Duke), Churchill,
John, 109, 519

MEF (Mediterranean
Expeditionary Force), 531
Mein Kampf (Hitler), 93
Mental Deficiency Act of 1913, 42
Mers-el-Kébir attack, 577
Mikolajczyk, Stanislaw, 622
Molotov, Vyacheslav, 592–593
military talks, 282
mutual assistance pact, 271
Soviet-German non-aggression
pact, 285
Molotov-Ribbentrop Pact,
290–292, 345
Munich Agreement, 219–233
aftermath, 239–243
alternate outcome hypotheses,
233–239
Chamberlain's pride, 222–223
Churchill's attack against, 226
Churchill's speech to House
about, 229–231
Cooper, Duff, 227–228
Daladier's return reception,
224–225
King welcomes Chamberlain
immediately after, 224
Munich Agreement alternate
outcome hypotheses,
233–239
Mussolini, Benito, 98–99, 244f
Abyssinia invasion, 140,
145–147
resulting economic
sanctions/oil embargo
by League of Nations,
and Italian reaction,
146–147, 153
attitudes toward Britain, 145
Churchill letter, 5/16/1940,
401–402
on Danzig's return, 292
invasion of Greece, 591–592

peace discussions and, 429–432, 440, 450, 456–458
rejection of Roosevelt approach, 5/28/1940, 466
request by French for Roosevelt to approach, 5/23/1940, 422

N
nanny, Elizabeth Anne Everest (Woomy), 4–5
Narvik, Norway, 354–356
National Government, 119
  end (May 22, 1945), 632
  Labour's refusal to participate in under Chamberlain, 377–378
  landslide win 1931, 119–120
National Socialist German Worker's Party, 79. *See also* Nazi Party
NATO (North Atlantic Treaty Organization), formation, 640–641
Nazi Party, 79
  Czech, 176
  legalization, 105
  Nuremberg rally 9/10/1938, 186
  SGP (Sudeten German Party), 176–177
Nazism, 279
  Churchill's hatred of, 502–503
Nehru, Jawaharlal, arrest, 113
Nicholson, Claude, 416, 432–433
non-aggression pact, Soviet-German Aug. 1939, 285–287
Norway
  Allied plans for occupation of portions, 347–349
  Britain's errors, 361–363
  British aid and fighting, 353
  German decoy ships, 350
  Hitler's invasion plans, 349
  House of Commons debate, 5/7–8/1940, 368–376
  Narvik, 354–356
  Operation Rupert, 357
  Royal Navy and, 356–357
  Trondheim, 358–360
NUM (National Union of Mine Workers), general strike of 1926, 100–102

O
Ogilvie-Forbes, George, 339
oil supplies, 487–489
Oldham Conservative Association, 19
Operation Barbarossa, 585, 594
Operation Catapult, 576–577
Operation Dynamo, 450, 451–452
Operation Grasp, 576–577
Operation Overlord, 614–615, 618–620
Operation Rupert, 357
Operation Sea Lion, 578–579
Operation Torch, 608–610
Operation UNTHINKABLE, 631
Operation Wilfred, 349–350
Ottoman Empire, WWI, 49–50
Outer Cabinet, May 28, 1940, meeting, 470–473
Overwhelming Encirclement, 152

P
Pact of Locarno, 103
Papen, Franz von, 123–124
Paris Peace Conference, 72, 74–75
  Fourteen Points (Wilson), 73–74
  League of Nations, 77
Parliament Bill, 40–41, 44
Peace Ballot, 139–140

peace negotiations debate in May
   1940
    approaching Mussolini, 440,
      450, 456–458
    Britain's entry closed, 473–474
    Chamberlain's position,
      452–453
    Churchill considers, 443
    German, Britain's rejection,
      340–341, 501, 579–580
    Halifax surreptitious efforts,
      568–569
    minimizations by Churchill,
      479–481
    question of entering into with
      Hitler, 437–439
    resistance to. *See* Churchill,
      Prime Minister, resistance to
      peace negotiations
    Sinclair's presence when
      discussing, 444–445, 456,
      467
    War Cabinet sessions (May
      26-28, 1940), 455–461, 467
Pearl Harbor attack, 602–603
People's Budget, 39–41
Pétain, Phillipe, 344n, 376f
    armistice with Germany,
      569–574
    Vice Premier appointment, 414
Phoney War (Bore War), 344–347
Plan Z, 187–194
Poland
    Agreement of Mutual
      Assistance, 267n
    Anglo-Polish Treaty of Mutual
      Assistance, 296–297
    assistance from Britain,
      256–258, 265–267
    Curzon line border, 622
    Danzig return, 255
    invasion of, 323–325
      British Cabinet meeting,
        9/1/1939, 323–324
      British response, 265–267,
        325–334
      Chamberlain's handling,
        330–334
      days prior to, 292–298,
        302–312
      Gleiwitz radio station, 310
      Hitler's speech 9/1/39, 324
      Raczyński telegram
        reporting on, 328
      ultimatum to Hitler
        9/3/1939, 334–337
      War Cabinet agreement to
        terms of ultimatum, 330
      White Paper 9/1/1939
        outlining British
        attempts to achieve
        settlement of dispute,
        327
    mutual assistance, Britain and,
      262
    Phoney War (Bore War),
      344–347
    Red Army of Poland, invasion
      9/17/1939, 338
    rejection of Hitler's offer in
      Nov. 1938, 243
    war inevitability, 312–314
Polish Corridor, 75
Polish Victory Parade Plot to
    assassinate Hitler, 486
Potsdam conference, 634–635
Potsdam Declaration, 628
press, British, pro-German feelings,
    129–130

Q

Quebec conference, 614–615

R

Raczyński, Edward, Polish Amb.,
   initial telegram, Polish invasion,
   329–330
RAF (Royal Air Force)
   defense spending and, 153
   expansion, 131
   Main Report on Britain's
      ability to fight on alone
      (May 25, 1940), 454
RDF (Radio Direction Finding)
   stations, 582
rearmament
   in Britain, 136–139
   German, 136–139
   German prior to war, 214
   start of, 127
Reichstag
   fire (1933), 127
   Goering president
      appointment, 126
Reynaud, Paul
   appeal to Britain for more
      troops, airplanes, 397–398,
      401, 410, 562
   Churchill lunch meeting,
      439–440
   Germans at Sedan, 397–398
   Halifax, Churchill,
      Chamberlain, Attlee meeting,
      439–440
   resignation, 378–379, 567–568
   withdrawal, 381
Rhineland
   French evacuation, 116
   German troops enter, 151–153
   reoccupation, failure to object,
      315
   Treaty of Versailles, 151
Ribbentrop, Joachim von, 156–157,
   201

Soviet-German non-aggression
   pact, 285
Ribbentrop-Molotov meetings,
   592–593
RND (Royal Naval Division),
   47–48
Roehm, Ernst, 132, 134
Romania, Stalin and, 563
Roosevelt, Franklin
   Churchill letters, 400–401,
      405
      immediate British needs,
         407
      on inaction of U.S.,
         410–411
   death, 629
   Mussolini rejection of his
      approach, 5/28/1940, 466
   request to approach Mussolini,
      5/24/1940, 422
   with Stalin and Churchill, 598f
   Tehran conference, 616–618
   telegram to regarding potential
      transfer of British Navy, 566
Royal Military Academy
   (Sandhurst), 520
Royal Navy
   armada assembly at Ramsgate,
      435
   Norway invasion and, 356–357
Royal Scots Fusiliers, 44f
Ruhr Valley, fears of attack, 343
Russia. *See* Soviet Union
Russian alliance with thought
   about (1936), 153

S

SA (Sturmabteilung)
   execution squad, 133–134
   Night of the Long Knives and,
      132–135
   Roehm, Ernst, 132–133

Schleicher, Kurt von, 120–126,
    133, 134
School Rifle Corps, Harrow, 11
Schuschnigg, Kurt Von, 135
    annexation of Austria and,
        163–165
    Mussolini and, 167
    plebiscite announcement,
        168–170
The Second World War, 636
SGP (Sudeten German Party),
    176–177
Sidney Street Latvian anarchists,
    1910, 43
Simon Commission, Dominion
    status for India, 114–115
Simpson, Wallis, 149–151
Sinclair, Archibald
    Leader of Liberal Party 331,
        386
    Secretary for Air (1940) 386
    defined "air superiority,"
        9/25/1940, 438
    demanded that Chamberlain
        tell Parliament how he
        intended to proceed
        9/2/1939, 332
    opposed sending more fighters
        to France 5/16/1940, 402
    presence in War Cabinet May
        1940 when discussing peace
        talks, 444–445, 456, 467
    reason he was added to
        discussion of peace
        negotiations, 444
Sinn Féin Party, 81
Slovak State, 246–247
Smith, F.E. (Lord Birkenhead), 13
Snowden, Philip, 119
South Africa Act of 1909, 33
Soviet Union
    attack on Finland, 342n

Berlin blockade 1947, 640
Bolsheviks, 71–72
    seizure of power, 68
Britain supplies military
    equipment, 601
Churchill's attitude changes,
    363–364
European alliance and,
    640–641
German invasion of in 1941,
    596–597
Molotov, Vyacheslav, 592–593
Operation UNTHINKABLE,
    631
plans for German invasion of,
    581
protection of Czechoslovakia
    in 1938, 173–174
Red Army invasion of Poland
    9/17/1939, 338
ultimatum suggestion from
    Churchill in 1947, 638–639
White Russians, 71
WWI involvement, 46
Spears, Edward, letter re:
happenings within the French
Army, 5/26/1940, 436
speeches
    Chamberlain's Birmingham
        speech, 251–253
    Hitler, Polish invasion speech,
        324
    Hitler on April 28, 1939,
        317–322
    Hitler to Reichstag, "peace
        or destruction," 7/19/1940
        579–580
    Munich Agreement, speeches
        to House, 229–231
SS (Schutzstaffel/Protection
Squadron)
    execution squad, 133–134

formation, 105
St. George School, 7–8
  beatings and bullying, 524
Stalin, Josef
  and Churchill, 663*f*
  Churchill's opinion, 502–503
  Churchill's warnings about
    Hitler, 564–565
  Estonia, 563
  Latvia, 563
  Lithuania, 563
  on Operation Torch, 608–610
  on Romania, 563
  Percentages Agreement with
    Churchill, 621
  requests to open a second front
    against Germany, 601, 608,
    613, 616
  with Roosevelt and Churchill,
    598*f*
  Tehran conference, 616–618
  trust in over Poland, 625–626
Stanley, Venitia, 57
stock market, Black Thursday, 111
Strasser, Gregor, 124–125
Stresa Front, 140
Stresemann, Erst, 104
Sudeten Germans, Czechoslovakia
  and, 172–173
Sudetenland, 176–178
  British and, 178–181
  Hitler's demands, 199–201
  map, 177
  SGP (Sudeten German Party),
    176–177
Supreme War Council, 348

T
Tehran conference, 616–618
Ten Year Rule, 107–108
Three-Power Pact (Tripartite Pact),
  591–592

Paul (Prince) of Yugoslavia,
  595
Tobruk, Libya, Allied defeat,
  608–610
Tonypandy riots, 42–43
Tory Democrats, 19
trade unions, Glasgow, 67
Treaty of London, 47
Treaty of Versailles, 72–73, 75–77
  Carthaginian peace (Keynes),
    75
  disapproval of, 160n
  Ebert, Friedrich, 77
  Foch, Ferdinand, 75
  Hitler's violation, 130
  League of Nations and, 76
  Rhineland as military base,
    151
  Scheidemann, Philipp, 77
  signing, 79
  Weimar Republic, 79
Tripartite Pact. *See* Three-Power
  Pact (Tripartite Pact)
  Paul (Prince) of Yugoslavia,
    595
Trondheim, Norway, 358–360
TUC (Trade Union Congress), 100
Tunisia, 611–612
  Allied control, 614

U
U.S.
  Churchill subservient to after
    Casablanca, 613
  Churchill's suggestions of
    inaction by, 410–411
  entry if Britain continued
    alone, 489–493
  joining European war,
    602–603

V

van der Lubbe, Marinus, 127
Vane, Frances, 3
V-E Day, 629–630
Viscount Halifax, 110n
von Brauchitsch, Walther, 483–484

W

War Cabinet
  agreement terms 9/2/1939, 330
  Churchill joins Chamberlain's,
    325–328
  Churchill selection of his,
    385–386
  French Fleet and, 566–567
  French suggestion to approach
    Mussolini, 467–469
  initial meeting of
    Chamberlain's, 336–337
  May 26, 1940
    air superiority, 438
    assessment of continuing
      war alone, 437
    negotiated peace with
      Hitler question, 437–439
    second session, 441–442
    second session, minutes,
      449–450
    Spears update from
      Raynaud, 436–437
  May 26–28, 1940, 455–461
    agreements, 473–474
  May 28, 1940, 466–470
    appeal to Roosevelt to
      participate in mediation,
      468–469
    Outer Cabinet, 470–473
  Mr. "D" message re: Polish
    activity, 9/1/1939, 325, 328
War Council, Dardanelles/Gallipoli
  campaign, 52–54

war guarantee 1939, Poland and,
  257–267
Weimar Republic, 69
  Bruening, Heinrich, 115–116
  German stabilization after, 104
  Schleicher, Kurt von, 120–126,
    133, 134
  Social Democrats and, 79
  Treaty of Versailles, 77, 79
Western Europe and fear of
  Soviet subjugation after WWII,
  630–631
Western Europe invasion by
  Germany in May 1940, 381–390,
  393 (map)
  Ardennes, 394
  Army Group A, 391
  Army Group B, 390
  Army Group C, 391
  BEF retreat, 416–417
  Channel ports, 414–415
  Churchill letter to Mussolini,
    401–402
  Churchill letter to Roosevelt,
    400–401
  Churchill speech praising
    French Army 5/19/1940, 408
  Churchill telegrams to
    Roosevelt, 405, 407
    on inaction of U.S.,
      410–411
  France, 396–399
  French pullback, 402–403
  French reserves, 403–404
  Halt Order, 417–421
  major parts, 390–391
  rumors of German activity and
    plans, 409–410
  strategy, 391–392
  Weygand Plan, 413–416
Westminster campaign 1924,
  88–89

Weygand, General Maxime, 407
    Weygand Plan, 413–416
White Paper, Polish invasion, 327
Wilcox, Clarissa, Native American
    roots, 4
Wilson, Henry, assassination of
    (1922), 82
Wilson, Horace, 201
Wilson, Woodrow, Fourteen
    Points, 73–74
women voters, 109
women's suffrage Churchill on,
    36–37
Wood, Edward, 80. *See also*
    Halifax (Lord)
Woomy. *See* Everest, Elizabeth
    Anne
WWI, 46–47
    Antwerp, 47–48
    armistice, 69
    Belgium and, 47
    Bolsheviks seizure of power, 68
    British blockade of Germany
        post armistice, 72–74
    British debt to U.S., 98
    Dardanelles/Gallipoli
        campaign, 48–57
    Dawes Plan, 104–105
    denying food to Germany so as
        to force signing of Versailles
        Treaty, 73
    Ferdinand assassination, 46
    German disarmament
        thereafter, 78–79
    German reparations, U.S. and,
        104
    Ottoman Empire and, 49–50
    Paris Peace Conference, 72,
        74–75
    RND (Royal Naval Division),
        47–48
    Russian involvement, 46
    Treaty of Versailles, 72–73,
        75–77
    war debt, 98
    Weimar Republic, 69

X–Y–Z
X Report, 484

Yalta Conference, 624
Yugoslavia, German invasion of,
    595

Zossen Conspiracy, 483

www.ingramcontent.com/pod-product-compliance
Lightning Source LLC
Chambersburg PA
CBHW020426130626
46549CB00001B/2